THE CAMBRIDGE HISTORY OF
LATIN AMERICA

VOLUME V

c. *1870 to 1930*

THE CAMBRIDGE HISTORY OF LATIN AMERICA

VOLUME I *Colonial Latin America*

VOLUME II *Colonial Latin America*

VOLUME III *From Independence to* c. *1870*

VOLUME IV c. *1870 to 1930*

VOLUME V c. *1870 to 1930*

THE CAMBRIDGE HISTORY OF LATIN AMERICA

VOLUME V

c. *1870 to 1930*

edited by

LESLIE BETHELL

Reader in Hispanic American and
Brazilian History at University College London

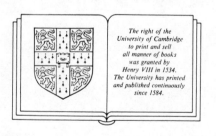

The right of the
University of Cambridge
to print and sell
all manner of books
was granted by
Henry VIII in 1534.
The University has printed
and published continuously
since 1584.

CAMBRIDGE UNIVERSITY PRESS

Cambridge

London   New York   New Rochelle

Melbourne   Sydney

Published by the Press Syndicate of the University of Cambridge
The Pitt Building, Trumpington Street, Cambridge CB2 1RP
32 East 57th Street, New York, NY 10022, USA
10 Stamford Road, Oakleigh, Melbourne 3166, Australia

First published 1986

Printed in Great Britain at the University Press, Cambridge

British Library cataloguing in publication data

The Cambridge history of Latin America.
Vol. 5, c. 1870–1930
1. Latin America – History
I. Bethell, Leslie
980   F1410

Library of Congress cataloguing in publication data

Main entry under title:
The Cambridge history of Latin America.
Includes bibliographies and indexes.
Contents: v. 1–2. Colonial Latin America
v. 5. c. 1870–1930.
1. Latin America – History – Collected works.
I. Bethell, Leslie.
F1410.C1834 1984   980   83–19036

ISBN 0 521 24517 6

CONTENTS

Contents   ix

PART FIVE. BRAZIL

     WARREN DEAN, *Professor of History, New York
     University*
     Economic policy and the creation of a national
        market   688
     The growth of export demand   693
     Factors of production   701
     Agriculture and stock raising   709
     Energy and transportation   711
     Manufacturing   714
     The crisis of export orientation   719
     Conclusion   722

20   Brazil: the age of reform, 1870–1889   725
     EMÍLIA VIOTTI DA COSTA, *Professor of History,
     Yale University*
     Economic and social change   728
     The political system of the Empire   735
     The politics of reform   750
     Conclusion   777

21   Brazil: the social and political structure of the First
     Republic, 1889–1930   779
     BORIS FAUSTO, *Universidade de São Paulo*
     Demographic and social change   779
     Political and social structures   787
     The political process   811

     Bibliographical essays   831
     Index   925

MAPS

FIGURES

GENERAL PREFACE

In the English-speaking and English-reading world the multi-volume Cambridge Histories planned and edited by historians of established reputation, with individual chapters written by leading specialists in their fields, have since the beginning of the century set the highest standards of collaborative international scholarship. *The Cambridge Modern History*, planned by Lord Acton, appeared in sixteen volumes between 1902 and 1912. It was followed by *The Cambridge Ancient History*, *The Cambridge Medieval History* and others. The *Modern History* has now been replaced by *The New Cambridge Modern History* in fourteen volumes, and *The Cambridge Economic History of Europe* has recently been completed. Cambridge Histories of Islam, of Iran and of Africa are published or near completion; in progress are Histories of China and of Judaism, while Japan is soon to join the list.

In the early 1970s Cambridge University Press decided the time was ripe to embark on a Cambridge History of Latin America. Since the Second World War and particularly since 1960 research and writing on Latin American history had been developing, and have continued to develop, at an unprecedented rate – in the United States (by American historians in particular, but also by British, European and Latin American historians resident in the United States), in Europe (especially in Britain and France) and increasingly in Latin America itself (where a new generation of young professional historians, many of them trained in the United States, Britain or Europe, had begun to emerge). Perspectives had changed as political, economic and social realities in Latin America – and Latin America's role in the world – had changed. Methodological innovations and new conceptual models drawn from the social sciences (economics, political science, historical demography, sociology, anthropology) as well as from other fields of historical research were increasingly being adopted by historians of Latin America. The Latin American Studies monograph series and the *Journal of Latin American Studies* had already been established by the Press and were beginning to publish the results of this new historical thinking and research.

In 1974 Dr Leslie Bethell, Reader in Hispanic American and Brazilian History at University College London, accepted an invitation to edit *The Cambridge History of Latin America*, and he began work on the project two years later. For the first time a single editor was given responsibility for the planning, co-ordination and editing of an entire *History*.

The Cambridge History of Latin America, to be published in eight volumes, is the first large-scale, authoritative survey of Latin America's unique historical experience during almost five centuries from the first contacts between the native American Indians and Europeans (and the beginnings of the African slave trade) in the late fifteenth and early sixteenth centuries to the present day. (The Press will publish separately a Cambridge History of the Native Peoples of the Americas – North, Middle and South – which will give proper consideration to the evolution of the region's peoples, societies and civilizations, in isolation from the rest of the world, during the several millenia before the arrival of the Europeans, as well as a fuller treatment than will be found here of the history of the indigenous peoples of Latin America under European colonial rule and during the national period to the present day.) Latin America is taken to comprise the predominantly Spanish- and Portuguese-speaking areas of continental America south of the United States – Mexico, Central America and South America – together with the Spanish-speaking Caribbean – Cuba, Puerto Rico, the Dominican Republic – and, by convention, Haiti. (The vast territories in North America lost to the United States by treaty and by war, first by Spain, then by Mexico, during the first half of the nineteenth century are for the most part excluded. Neither the British, French and Dutch Caribbean islands nor the Guianas are included even though Jamaica and Trinidad, for example, have early Hispanic antecedents and are now members of the Organisation of American States.) The aim is to produce a high-level synthesis of existing knowledge which will provide historians of Latin America with a solid base for future research, which students of Latin American history will find useful and which will be of interest to historians of other areas of the world. It is also hoped that the *History* will contribute more generally to a deeper understanding of Latin America through its history in the United States and in Europe and, not least, to a greater awareness of its own history in Latin America. Contributors have been drawn from the United States and Canada, from Britain and Europe, and from Latin America.

For the first time the volumes of a Cambridge History will be published in chronological order: Volumes I and II (Colonial Latin America – with an introductory section on the native American peoples and civilizations on the eve of the European invasion) in 1984; Volume III (from Independence to *c.* 1870) in 1985; Volumes IV and V (*c.* 1870 to 1930) in 1986; and Volumes VI–VIII (1930 to the present) in 1988 or as soon as possible thereafter. Each volume or set of volumes examines a period in the economic, social, political, intellectual and cultural history of Latin America. While recognizing the decisive impact on Latin America of external forces, of developments within what is now called the capitalist world system, and the fundamental importance of its economic, political and cultural ties first with Spain and Portugal, then with Britain, France and, to a lesser extent, Western Europe as a whole, and finally with the United States, the emphasis of the *History* will be upon the evolution of internal structures. Furthermore, the emphasis is clearly on the period since the establishment of all the independent Latin American states except Cuba at the beginning of the nineteenth century, which, compared with the colonial and independence periods, has been relatively neglected by historians of Latin America. The period of Spanish and Portuguese colonial rule from the sixteenth to the eighteenth centuries is the subject of two of the eight volumes. Six are devoted to the nineteenth and twentieth centuries and will consist of a mixture of general, comparative chapters built around major themes in Latin American history and chapters on the individual histories of the twenty independent Latin American countries (plus Puerto Rico), and especially the three major countries – Brazil, Mexico and Argentina. In view of its size, population and distinctive history, Brazil, which has often been neglected in general histories of Latin America, written for the most part by Spanish Americans or Spanish American specialists, will here receive the attention it deserves.

An important feature of the *History* will be the bibliographical essays which accompany each chapter. These will give special emphasis to books and articles published during the past 15–20 years, that is to say, since the publication of Charles C. Griffin (ed.), *Latin America: a guide to the historical literature* (published for the Conference on Latin American History by the University of Texas Press, Austin, Texas, 1971) which was prepared during 1966–9 and included few works published after 1966.

PREFACE TO VOLUMES IV AND V

Volumes I and II of *The Cambridge History of Latin America* published in 1984 were largely devoted to the economic, social, political, intellectual and cultural history of Latin America during the three centuries of Spanish and (in the case of Brazil) Portuguese colonial rule from the European 'discovery', conquest and settlement of the 'New World' in the late fifteenth and early sixteenth centuries to the late eighteenth and early nineteenth centuries, the eve of Latin American independence. Volume III published in 1985 examined the breakdown and overthrow of Spanish and Portuguese colonial rule in Latin America during the first quarter of the nineteenth century and, the main focus of the volume, the economic, social, political and cultural history of the independent Spanish American republics and the independent Empire of Brazil during the half-century from independence to *c.* 1870. With Volumes IV and V *The Cambridge History of Latin America* moves on to the period from *c.* 1870 to 1930.

During the first half-century after independence Latin America experienced, at best, only very modest rates of economic growth and, at least in Spanish America, violent political and ideological conflict and considerable political instability. Besides the war between Mexico and the United States (1846–8) and frequent foreign, especially British, interventions in Latin America, there were also at the end of the period two major wars between Latin American states: the Paraguayan War (1865–70) and the War of the Pacific (1879–83). In contrast, the following half-century, and particularly the period up to the first world war, was for most Latin American countries a 'Golden Age' of predominantly export-led economic growth, material prosperity (at least for the dominant classes and the urban middle classes), ideological consensus and, with some notable exceptions like Mexico during the

Revolution (1910–20), political stability. Moreover, although there was continued foreign intervention in Latin America – mainly US intervention in Mexico, Central America and the Caribbean – throughout the period, there were no major international conflicts in Latin America between the end of the War of the Pacific (1883) and the outbreak of the Chaco War (1932).

Volume IV, the first of these two volumes on the period *c.* 1870 to 1930, consists of twelve general chapters on the economic, social, political, intellectual and cultural history of Latin America as a whole. Two chapters examine the growth of the Latin American economies, the first in the period 1870–1914, the second in the period from the first world war to the eve of the world depression of the 1930s. This growth was largely a result of the greatly accelerated incorporation of the Latin American economies as primary producers into the expanding international economy and significant inflows of foreign capital, particularly from Britain and, in the twentieth century, from the United States. At the same time domestic markets and domestic capital accumulation are not neglected. Latin America's political relations with the major European powers and, above all in Central America and the Caribbean, with the increasingly expansionist United States receive separate treatment. Another chapter analyses the growth of Latin America's population (from 30 million in 1850 to 105 million in 1930), in part the result of mass European immigration especially in Argentina and Brazil. The profound impact of capitalist penetration of the countryside is the subject of two chapters, one concentrating on the traditional highland areas of Mexico, Central America and the Andes, the other on the Spanish Caribbean. The first of these, while claiming that rural economies and societies underwent greater change in the period 1870–1930 than in any previous period except the Conquest, also seeks to show that in many rural areas, especially in the Andes, the forces of change were resisted and pre-capitalist structures survived. Urban society also experienced rapid change in this period, and there are separate chapters on the growth of Latin American cities, especially primary cities like Buenos Aires, Rio de Janeiro and Mexico City, all of which had between one and two million inhabitants by 1930 and rivalled the major cities of Europe and the United States; on the beginnings of industry, especially in Brazil, Argentina, Chile, Colombia and Mexico; and on the emergence of an urban working class as a significant force in many republics and the history of the early Latin American labour movements. Two chapters treat separately the evolution of political and social ideas in Latin America in this period (and in particular the adaptation of liberalism to highly stratified societies with under-developed economies and an authoritarian political tradition, and the influence of positivism on the governing and intellectual elites), and major movements and notable individual achievements in Latin American literature, music and art (as well as the early days of the cinema in Latin America). Finally, the volume concludes with a chapter which examines how the Catholic Church in Latin America adjusted to the decline in its power and privileges in a secular age while retaining the adherence of the vast majority of Latin Americans.

Volume V consists of twenty-one chapters on the economic, social and, above all, political history of the various Latin American countries from *c*. 1870 to 1930. Part One deals in some detail with the history of Mexico in this period. There are chapters on the Porfiriato (the thirty-five-year dictatorship of Porfirio Díaz, 1876–1911), on the Mexican Revolution and on reconstruction under the 'Sonoran dynasty' during the 1920s. Part Two, 'Central America and the Caribbean', has a single chapter on the five republics of Central America and separate chapters on Cuba, Puerto Rico, the Dominican Republic and Haiti. Part Three, 'The River Plate Republics', has four chapters on the economic, social and political evolution of Argentina, which had become in many respects Latin America's most advanced nation by 1930, as well as chapters on Uruguay and Paraguay. Part Four, 'The Andean Republics', has separate chapters on Chile, Bolivia and Peru in the half-century following the War of the Pacific and a single chapter on Colombia, Ecuador and Venezuela. Finally, Part Five is devoted to Brazil. There are chapters on Brazil's coffee-dominated economy in this period, on the political system and the politics of reform during the late Empire (1870–89) and on the social and political structure of the First Republic (1889–1930).

Many of the historians who contributed chapters to these two volumes – twelve of them North American, eight Latin American (three from Brazil, two each from Argentina and Cuba and one from Uruguay), eight British, four continental European and one Puerto Rican – also read and commented on the chapters of their colleagues. I am especially grateful in this respect to Malcolm Deas, Ezequiel Gallo and Colin Lewis. In addition, Christopher Abel, Alan Knight and Rory Miller provided critical assessments of more than one of these chapters. A number of

Latin American historians and historians of Latin America have given valuable advice and encouragement from the very beginning of this project. I would like to take the opportunity here to thank, in particular, John Lynch, Richard Morse and John Womack.

At the Cambridge University Press Elizabeth Wetton was the editor responsible for these volumes of *The Cambridge History of Latin America*. Cynthia Postan was the subeditor of Volume IV, Elizabeth O'Beirne-Ranelagh of Volume V. The index to Volume IV was prepared by Hilda Pearson, the index to Volume V by Ann Hudson. As in the case of the three volumes of the *History* already published Nazneen Razwi at University College London gave invaluable secretarial assistance.

Part One

MEXICO

Revolutionary Mexico

1

MEXICO: RESTORED REPUBLIC AND PORFIRIATO, 1867–1910

The aftermath of war

The Liberals who came to power in 1855, 34 years after Mexico's independence from Spain, had hoped to give Mexico the productivity and stability of its northern neighbour, the United States. Having seen their country lose almost half of its territory to the United States in the recent Mexican–American War (1846–8), they feared that without a measure of both economic growth and political stability the very existence of Mexico as an independent nation–state would be in jeopardy. Their programme envisaged the replacement of what they considered the unsteady pillars of the old order – the church, the army, the regional caciques, the communal villages – with a 'modern foundation'. True to their programme they proceeded first in a series of reform laws and then in the constitution of 1857 to weaken the position of the church. Catholicism ceased to be the official religion of the state. Ecclesiastic courts lost much of their jurisdiction. Marriages could be effected through a civil ceremony. The clergy could now be tried in civil courts. Church lands were put up for sale. The army too was stripped of many of its former prerogatives. Like the church, it lost its judicial privileges. Officers could now be tried in civil courts. For the first time in Mexico's history its head of state and cabinet were, by and large, civilians. In addition many of the once omnipotent caciques, the mainstay of the ousted Conservative regime, who for so long had ruled their local strongholds with virtually complete autonomy, were forced to yield power to new Liberal appointees. With the adoption of the Ley Lerdo in 1856 the Liberals had launched an all out assault not only on the church but also on the communal villages. The new law prohibited ecclesiastical

3

institutions from owning or administering property not directly used for religious purposes and extended the prohibition on corporate property to civil institutions, thus effectively abolishing communal land tenure. Communal land holdings had to be sold. Only individual farmers or private partnerships and companies could henceforth own land.

By declaring that Catholicism was no longer the official religion of Mexico, diminishing the political role of the church and destroying the economic basis of its political power, the Liberals hoped that Mexico, like the United States, would attract European immigrants of all religions. As in the United States, these immigrants would constitute an agrarian middle class which would ensure rapid economic growth, political stability and the development of democratic institutions. At the same time the Liberals expected that the constitutional provisions prohibiting the church and the Indian communities from owning lands would have similar effects. Both institutions were to be replaced by a large class of small landowners who would, some Liberal leaders hoped, like the immigrants become the sinews for modernization, stability and democracy in Mexico. At the very worst, if such development did not come about, many liberals expected that if the land passed from the 'dead hand' of the church into the 'living hand' of capitalist-orientated landowners, a significant economic boom and increasing stability would ensue. These landowners might not be interested in political democracy, but like their counterparts in Argentina, Brazil and Chile they would require political stability as a means of ensuring the success of their newly developed commercial properties. At the same time, the destruction of the old army, dominated by Conservative officers, would put an end to military uprisings and coups. A new army organized by the Liberals would constitute a basically different formation.[1]

When the Liberal president, Benito Juárez, returned to Mexico City in July 1867 after the war against the French, which had followed three years of civil war between the Liberals and the Conservatives, the flush of military triumph could only briefly disguise the extent to which the Liberals had thus far fallen short of many of the goals they had set themselves twelve years earlier. The execution of Maximilian and so the defeat of Napoleon III had indeed removed the threat of European intervention for a long time, and Mexico's survival as an independent nation seemed assured. The church had lost most of its economic and

---

[1] For a detailed discussion of Mexican politics in the period 1855–67, see Bazant, *CHLA* III, ch. 10.

political hold on the country; church-inspired coups were a thing of the past. The old Conservative army, so prone to indiscipline and revolt, had been dissolved for good. Regional government was firmly in Liberal hands. Communal land holdings had been greatly reduced in number. But these developments did not bring the hoped for results. The expropriation of church land did not give rise to a class of small farmers – since the land was auctioned off to the highest bidder, rich local landowners acquired most of it. It thus only added to the economic strength and political cohesiveness of an already dominant class of wealthy hacendados, much to the chagrin of the more radical of Liberals. The new Liberal army was no greater guarantor of stability than the old Conservative one. It consisted of a loose conglomeration of troops – both regular army corps and guerillas – each headed by a different local commander with varying degrees of loyalty to the central government. It was much too large for peace-time needs; yet simply sending the veterans of two wars home without adequate reward for their long service threatened to trigger off new revolts. Despite the new sense of nationalism awakened by the victory against the French and the emergence of Juárez as a genuinely popular national leader, the country was further away from integration than ever before. During the years of war different provinces had come to lead a nearly autonomous existence, deeply isolated in their social, economic, and political life from the rest of Mexico. The parcelling out of communal lands had swelled only slightly the ranks of the middle class. Some of the best lands had been lost to wealthy hacendados. The few peasants who did acquire a plot of their own came to be known among their less fortunate brethren as *los riquitos*. They were evolving into a group very much like the Russian *kulaks* or French *coqs du village*.

These structural problems were compounded by those the civil war and the war against the French had created. Ten years of warfare had left Mexico's economy in chaos. The church wealth on which the Liberals had counted to pay for some of their more ambitious projects had been consumed by the war effort. Mines and fields lay in ruin. The federal tax base had shrunk to vanishing point. During the larger part of Juárez's presidency, as Juárez's last finance minister Francisco Mejía noted in his memoirs, there was literally not a penny in the treasury. The frosty relations with Europe in the aftermath of Maximilian's execution and Juárez's refusal to honour Maximilian's debts did not help matters. The United States, on which Mexico became increasingly dependent as a consequence, could not make up for the loss of European markets and investment capital.

The Mexican state consisted on the one hand of an overdeveloped army, most of whose contingents were only loosely controlled by the central administration, and on the other the enormously weakened remaining branches of the government. After the initial defeat of the Liberals in 1863, most of the bureaucracy had abandoned the Juárez government and joined Maximilian's administration. Even if the bureaucrats had remained loyal to Juárez, they could have done very little for many years as the Liberals' administration only ruled over a small fraction of the country. The state's weakness and the lack of control of the government over the army would have been less severe if its social and political base had been a united and coherent force. Its constituency was the Liberal movement, and the Liberal movement was badly splintered. In name, programme, and terminology Mexico's Liberal party resembled those of Europe, but not in social composition. Only a fraction of its support came from the Mexican bourgeoisie. To begin with, that group was small, consisting chiefly of textile manufacturers and the so-called *agiotistas*, merchants who speculated in loans to the government. The rest of the bourgeoisie was by and large not indigenous but foreign. After Mexico achieved independence, British merchants replaced the formerly dominant Spaniards. By the 1840s and 1850s, the Germans had begun to take over from them. They, in turn, were driven out of many commercial enterprises by French traders, mainly known as Barcelonettes for the town in southern France from which the majority came.

The Liberal movement drew more substantial support from large landowners. Some joined the Liberals because, like the German barons of the fifteenth and sixteenth century, they hoped to succeed to the large land holdings of the church. Others objected to the Conservatives' attempt to impose centralized control over them. Luis Terrazas is typical of this group, except for the fact that he was not born into wealth, but, having started out as a butcher, married into it. Terrazas's grievances against the Conservative regime were manifold. He was contemptuous of its inability to protect his home state of Chihuahua against marauding Indians. He was resentful of its refusal to admit him into its closely knit oligarchy. And he was covetous of the public lands controlled by the central government. Once he became Liberal governor of his native state he utilized his power both to enrich himself by acquiring huge tracts of public lands (and some church properties) and to carry out a popular policy of resisting, with far more energy than his predecessors, the increasingly ferocious attacks on the population of Chihuahua by Apache marauders.

Landowners, like Terrazas, viewed with keen suspicion another group from which the Liberals drew support, the middle class: local merchants, small entrepreneurs, *rancheros*, low-level government employees, and some radical intellectuals. The middle class had come to view the power held by the landowners as a major impediment to its own advancement. They encouraged the central government to tighten the reins on its regional barons by, for instance, exacting a fairer portion of its tax revenues from large estates.

Both wings of the party managed to maintain an uneasy truce and to co-operate in periods of war, but as soon as war subsided profound quarrels and conflicts broke out between them. Nevertheless, landowners and middle class were united in their opposition to the demands of a third group, the 'popular sector'. Its composition, still only incompletely known, was diffuse. It encompassed some peasants and an inchoate proletariat of textile workers, blacksmiths, shop clerks, and the like. Its aims were radical redistribution of property on a large scale. The Liberals had been very reluctant to mobilize this group in the course of the civil war. They remembered well what an uncontrollable force the peasants had become when Father Hidalgo in 1810, and one of the warring factions within the state's oligarchy during the caste wars in Yucatán in the late 1840s, had called on them to join ranks. In the war against the French, however, Juárez had thrown caution to the wind, and issued a general call to arms against the foreign invaders. And again, once organized, the popular movements did not show signs of subsiding quickly.

Juárez's political strategy

In the face of these deep rifts it seems at first surprising that Juárez managed to retain his leadership of the Mexican Liberal movement for more than five years. But in fact it was the divided nature of the Liberal movement that helped Juárez to survive. The two mainsprings of the movement – hacendados and middle classes – alternately attacked him for not being sufficiently responsive to its interests, but neither tried to unseat him because it knew that as long as he remained in power the other side would not prevail. Neither did the popular sector seek to overthrow him. Although acutely discontented with the Ley Lerdo which Juárez continued to implement, they venerated him as one of their own, a once poor Indian who had risen to govern his country and had never ceased proudly to acknowledge his origins.

Shortly after achieving victory over the French and the Conservatives, Juárez reacted to the increasing divisions and impotence of the Liberal movement by attempting to set up a strong centralized state which would have immeasurably increased his independence from his increasingly divided social and political constituency. His prestige then at its peak, he issued a call for new elections and, simultaneously, a referendum on a series of proposed amendments to the constitution. The first added a Senate to the already existing Chamber of Deputies and was intended to divide and dilute the power of Congress. The second gave the president the right to veto any bill subject to the ability of a two-thirds majority in Congress to override it. A third permitted members of his cabinet to answer congressional enquiries in writing rather than in person. A fourth deprived the permanent commission of parliament, a body that continued in session while parliament was in recess, of the right to call for a session of the full Congress at any time. The referendum was not, strictly speaking, over the adoption of these proposals but over the right of Congress to adopt them by simple majority vote rather than having to submit them for special approval by each of the state legislatures. For a brief period, the two main antagonistic wings of the Liberal party united in opposition to Juárez's measures, and as pressure against them mounted, the Mexican president was forced to withdraw the proposed amendments.

To remain in power Juárez now had to resort to greater concessions to the two social groups that had thwarted him. He gave Liberal hacendados virtually unbridled authority over their local strongholds. To win the support of the middle class Juárez expanded the size of the state bureaucracy, one of the favourite sources of employment of the middle class, and directed federal expenditures into areas of particular interest to it, such as improvement of public education, especially in the cities. In 1857 there were 2,424 public primary and secondary schools in Mexico. In 1874, two years after Juárez's death, a government census revealed that their number had increased to 8,103. Perhaps even more important for the middle classes was the fact that Juárez maintained (he probably had little choice in the matter) some democratic institutions. While the government did intervene in elections, these were more honest than they had previously been. Parliament, no longer an impotent body, housed a vocal opposition. The freedom of the press to criticize was nearly complete. Some of the country's best known intellectuals – Manuel de Zamacona, Ignacio Altamirano, Francisco Zarco – became increasingly outspoken in their attacks on the mistakes made by the Juárez government.

One segment of the Liberal middle class whose influence was on the rise in the latter years of the Juárez presidency were those Liberal army officers who continued in active service. There was a certain contradiction in this since both Juárez and the main ideologues of the Liberal party considered militarism one of the principal banes of Mexico. In the constitution of 1857 they had abrogated the judicial privileges of the military, and after the victory over Maximilian large parts of the Mexican army had been demobilized. Nevertheless, as the contradictions within Mexican society mounted and revolts were on the increase, the dependence of the government upon the army grew more and more, and officers were again able to exercise political, social and economic influence in the Mexican countryside.

In order to broaden support for his regime, Juárez also attempted to reach a compromise with some of his old antagonists. The ostensible losers in the ten years of war which had racked Mexico between 1857 and 1867 came off better than they or many contemporaries had expected. This was especially true of the Conservative politicians, landowners and bureaucrats. In 1870, three years after his victory, Juárez issued a broad amnesty for all those who had co-operated with Maximilian. Lands were returned to the landowners and Conservative bureaucrats could once again apply for positions in the government. The church on the whole fared worse than its allies. It never regained the lands and properties it lost and its economic supremacy as Mexico's most important source of credit ceased. It could no longer legally impose taxes on the population. The legal privileges of the clergy, the official supremacy of Catholicism, and the influence of the church in educational matters were never restored to their pre-1857 status. The reform laws continued to be the laws of the land. Nevertheless, in practical terms, the church began to recuperate rapidly from its losses. Contributions from wealthy church members flowed into its coffers and were surreptitiously invested once again in urban property. Juárez made no effort to curtail this renewed accumulation of wealth by the clergy, and the latter gave up its former intransigence towards the Liberals. This attitude may have been inspired by the overwhelming victory of the Liberals after many years of civil war, but it was also the realization of some church leaders that the loss of its lands had actually strengthened its position in the countryside by reducing the potential for conflict between the church and large segments of the rural population. Many peasants now saw the Liberal landowners as their enemy rather than the church. This attitude grew even stronger as church officials became more responsive than in previous years to peasants' complaints and demands.

Juárez had hoped that these conciliatory measures towards Mexico's upper and middle classes as well as towards segments of the army would prevent him from being toppled by a coup and would allow him to pacify the country. The Mexican president's hopes proved to be correct on the first count. Juárez remained in office until he died of natural causes in 1872. His hopes on the second count, however, proved to be illusory. In order to conciliate the country's elite, Juárez had sacrificed the interests of the peasantry. As a result, social unrest in the countryside reached unprecedented proportions during the period of the Restored Republic. The government was too weak to suppress this unrest, and the unrest weakened the Juárez administration even further. This encouraged other forces, ranging from nomadic tribes on the frontier to middle- and upper-class opponents of the regime, to take up arms and challenge the government. As a result the government was even less able to suppress unrest in the countryside. It was a vicious circle.

The causes of peasant unrest ranged from frustrated expectations to a real deterioration in peasant living conditions. The liberal government did nothing to meet the expectations of the peasants or even to protect the peasantry from a further erosion of its economic and social position. The end of the war sent droves of landless and unemployed war veterans into Mexico's countryside, adding to the already overflowing pool of landless and unemployed. The Ley Lerdo had ousted many from the communal lands they had once farmed, then distributed the property, usually unequally, amongst them, if it was not appropriated outright by hacendados or speculators.

The Liberal administration could not have prevented, even had it wanted to, the transfer of church lands from the clergy to large landowners instead of to the peasants. It only controlled a fraction of Mexico during the long years of war against the Conservatives and the French, and its armies needed revenues from the sale of church lands to finance the war. After victory the Liberals could have used both the estates of the defeated Conservatives and the vast and frequently empty public lands to set up a programme of land distribution and to create a class of Mexican farmers. Except for granting some public lands to a limited number of war veterans, however, the Juárez administration never seriously considered implementing such an option. Lands of Conservative hacendados were either returned to their former owners or at best given or sold to Liberal landowners. The Mexican government never attempted to do what the United States government did after the American civil war: diffuse the social tensions brought about by the war with a Homestead Act granting free public lands to settlers. Some of the government lands began to be granted or sold to Mexican hacendados while others were kept in reserve for a vast expected wave of foreign peasant immigrants who never arrived.

Nor did Juárez address another major source of peasant discontent, the unequal burden of taxation. The *alcabala*, internal customs, and the personal contribution – the equivalent of six to twelve days' wages for the typical hacienda labourer – exacted a disproportionately higher toll from the poor than the rich. A hacendado owning land worth 20,000 pesos paid the government the same tax as his employee who had no assets to speak of. The Liberals had originally advocated the elimination of the *alcabala*, not so much because of its disproportionate impact on the poor but because of its interference with free trade. The empty coffers of the treasury kept them from following this through. The hacendados, of course, would not hear of readjusting the tax burden. The only measure finally taken to afford relief to the most hard pressed of taxpayers was to waive the personal contribution for anyone earning less than 26 centavos a day.

Nor did Juárez make more than a feeble effort to relieve the worst excesses of debt peonage and, closely linked to it, the arbitrary power of the hacendado over his peons. In 1868 a Liberal congressman, Julio Zarate, asked that landowners be prohibited from setting up private jails, administering corporal punishment, or visiting the debts of parents on their children. Congress rejected the proposal, claiming that it lacked jurisdiction over the matter and that this was a matter exclusively for the local judiciary. Juárez favoured Zarate's proposal and tried to intervene, but the limited measures which he decreed restricting debt peonage were never implemented.

Peasant uprisings in the Juárez era

During the colonial era armed conflict in the countryside had been of three types, each specific to a certain region. First, there were local rebellions, generally confined to a single village and aimed chiefly at eliminating particular grievances with the colonial administration, rather than seeking to overthrow the colonial system *in toto*. This type of unrest was concentrated in the core regions of the country in central Mexico. Second, there were large-scale uprisings against the colonial system as a whole by groups which had only superficially assimilated Spanish civilization and the Christian religion, and which sought to restore what they considered to be the pre-hispanic social, economic, and religious order. These tended to occur mainly in southern Mexico. Finally, there were the resistance movements of as yet unconquered peoples to Spanish attempts to colonize them. These were confined almost exclusively to the northern frontier.

During the period of the Restored Republic revolts broke out in all three of these regions, but they tended to be more radical in character, larger in scope, longer in duration, and more violent than during the colonial period. One of the most radical eruptions to occur in central Mexico took place in 1868 close to the capital itself. The rebels were denounced as 'rabid socialists' in the Mexico City press, and they seem to have viewed themselves that way. They were strongly influenced by the socialist Plotino Rhodakanati, who saw in Jesus Christ the 'divine socialist of humanity' and 'saviour of the freedom of the world'. He set up a school in Chalco where his theories were propagated by two of his disciples. Their teachings in turn inspired one of their pupils, a peasant named Julio López, to issue a proclamation calling on the peasants of Chalco, Texcoco and other neighbouring towns to rise against local landowners. 'We want socialism', he wrote, 'we want to destroy the present vicious state of exploitation . . . We want land of our own to till in peace.'[2] López's men in fact succeeded in seizing some land around the towns of Chalco and Texcoco and immediately set upon dividing it up amongst themselves. Five months later federal troops routed the rebels: López was arrested and shot.

Socialist influence also manifested itself in states more remote from the capital, like Hidalgo. Two peasants, Francisco Islas and Manuel

---

[2] Quoted in Gaston García Cantu, *El socialismo en México* (Mexico, 1969), 173.

Domínguez, leading a contingent of several thousand men, managed to occupy the town of Tezontepec and the mining centre of Mineral del Monte. Their chief objective was the restoration of land they believed to have been misappropriated by local hacendados. 'Violence is our means of righting the wrongs done us', wrote Francisco Islas in a letter to the newspaper *La Libertad*. 'The government stands behind the hacendados, "society" stands behind them as well, and so do the journalists who are not ashamed to sell their conscience to the highest bidder. What else is there for us to do but fight?'[3] The rebels held out for two months, December 1869 and January 1870. When federal troops finally retook the cities many of them, including Islas and Domínguez themselves, made a getaway into the mountains of Hidalgo, and survived to lead another rebellion against the government several years later.

Peasant movements in southern Mexico continued to be what they had been throughout the colonial period, intensely messianic, intertwining social and religious ideas in one single millenarian vision. The most notable example is a story of a peasant girl, Augustina Gómez Chechep, who lived in the village of Tzarjalhemel among the Chamula Indians. She became the patron of a new religious cult which soon turned into a vehicle of social protest – against white domination. The Chamula uprising (12 June 1869 – 20 October 1870) was eventually quelled by federal troops with the minimum of bloodshed.

The Mayas were more successful. Following the caste wars of 1847–55 they managed to set up an independent state in southern Yucatán and until 1901 resisted numerous attempts by federal troops to re-establish Mexican sovereignty. Moreover, armed with weapons they purchased in neighbouring British Honduras, they frequently ventured out to raid adjacent Mexican territories with relative impunity.

Mexico's northern frontier continued to elude federal control, as it had during the colonial era. The Apache wars, which had gone on unabated since 1831, were reaching a new climax. Pushed further and further west by an onslaught of American settlers, the Indians preyed with increasing frequency on the more vulnerable Mexican frontier. Under the leadership of the legendary Cochise and his successors Victorio and Ju, they all but paralysed frontier life for a time. 'The land cannot be tilled because anyone working it would be murdered by the Apaches. There is no work in the cities because there is scarcity, everything is in decline and no one

---

[3] *Ibid.*, 60, 76.

invests', an editorial in a Sonoran paper stated as late as 1879.[4] Within the span of a few years Cochise's bands caused the death of 15,000 people. The weak and underpaid soldiers sent to fight on the northern frontier were no match for the Apaches.

Only gradually toward the end of Juárez's presidency did Mexico summon the strength to withstand the raiders. The hacendados began to arm and train their peons and to organize them into private militias. The government began to offer generous land grants to anyone willing to defend his property with his life. As a result, existing military colonies were strengthened and new ones were set up. Thus, while the independent peasantry was being decimated in the central and southern regions of the country, it was being strengthened and reinforced in the north. A new alliance between the northern hacendados and the peasants, directed against the Apaches, was developing; in the peasants' eyes, the hacendados acquired legitimacy by organizing the wars against the raiders. In Chihuahua, the leader of the militia who fought the Apache was Joaquín Terrazas, cousin of governor Luis Terrazas who himself helped to organize and finance the Indian wars. In spite of these peasant militias, however, the governments of the Restored Republic proved as incapable of controlling the northern frontier as they were of curbing other types of rebellion.

Organized social protest was only part of the social unrest that characterized the closing years of Juárez's reign. Banditry was rampant. Fugitive peons, dissatisfied peasants, demobilized soldiers scoured the countryside robbing stagecoaches, attacking large estates, and plundering convoys from mines loaded with gold and silver. By the end of 1868 the number of bandits operating on the outskirts of just one city, Guadalajara, in the state of Jalisco, was thought to number around a thousand. Juárez's newly organized police force, the Rurales, made only minimal headway against this most ubiquitous of hazards plaguing the Mexican countryside.

The first Díaz uprising

Juárez's declining popular support was a constant invitation to rivals to unseat him. Some of these men were former conservative *caudillos* whom Juárez had ousted from state government and had replaced with his own

---

[4] Quoted in Luís González y González, 'Los campesinos', in Daniel Cosío Villegas (ed.), *Historia moderna de México: La República Restaurada. Vida social* (Mexico, 1956), 186.

men. Some were former Liberal generals who felt that Juárez had not given them their due. They would issue a proclamation in the local newspaper they controlled, promising 'higher wages', 'juster laws', and a 'more democratic government', assemble a ragtag army of peons working on their haciendas and diverse malcontents, and seize control of a small city or municipality in the vicinity. They rarely got much further before federal troops dispersed them.

There was one exception. Perhaps the most popular figure to emerge from the war against the French was Juárez's erstwhile subordinate, General Porfirio Díaz. Díaz was born in 1830 in the state of Oaxaca, also Juárez's birthplace. He received his schooling in the same Catholic seminary as Juárez. At the age of seventeen, he enlisted in the army to fight the invading American forces. He came too late to see much fighting, but he more than made up for it in the war against the French. He advanced quickly to the position of brigadier general, and in 1862 for the first time gained renown when he was one of the Mexican commanders whose troops inflicted on the French their most humiliating defeat at the first battle of Puebla. Shortly thereafter he was captured by the French but managed to escape. Sometime later he presided over another major military victory at the battle of La Carbonera. He was 37 when the war ended and considered himself Juárez's equal. In 1867 he was a candidate for the presidency against Juárez. He ran again in 1871, and again lost. In 1871, in the Plan of La Noria, named after Díaz's hacienda, he declared that the elections had been fraudulent and called on the people to revolt. Although the plan also contained some vague allusions to the need for social reform it really had only one specific plank: that the presidency should be limited to a single term. To make the programme seem less self-serving than it was, Díaz promised not to run in the next election.

Díaz's call to arms met with some success, provoking an uprising that was more than local in nature. Díaz's brother, Félix, mobilized a formidable strike force in his home state of Oaxaca, consisting of state militia and even some federal troops stationed in the vicinity, and captured the state capital. A number of northern generals, foremost among them the governor of Nuevo León, Gerónimo Treviño, assembled an army of several thousand men and seized large parts of Nuevo León, Durango, Sinaloa, and Zacatecas. Porfirio Díaz himself headed a contingent of one thousand troops with which he aimed to take control of Mexico City. He reached the city's outskirts at Chalco and

Texcoco and reiterated his call for a general uprising, but it was not answered. Juárez sent troops of his own to deal with the rebels and Díaz withdrew precipitously. Meanwhile Félix Díaz's troops in Oaxaca fell into disarray when their leader was murdered by an unknown assassin, and shortly thereafter were routed by federal troops. Treviño's forces did not hold out much longer. Juárez had weathered the most serious uprising he faced since the defeat of Maximilian. But he did not live long to savour it.

The Juárez succession

On 17 July 1872 Juárez suffered a heart attack, and he died the following day. His successor under the constitution was the Chief Justice of the Supreme Court, Sebastián Lerdo de Tejada. Unlike Juárez, Lerdo was not of Indian descent but was Creole; his father was a Spanish merchant. Like Juárez he began his schooling in a Catholic seminary; he went as far in preparing for the priesthood as to take his minor vows. He then turned his back on the priesthood and began to study law. While still a law student he involved himself in Liberal politics and caught the eye of one of the leaders of the Liberal movement, Ignacio Comonfort. Through Comonfort's patronage he was appointed to the Supreme Court when he was only 27 years old. When Comonfort was deposed, Lerdo resigned his seat in the court and became rector of his alma mater, the Colegio de San Ildefonso in Mexico City. Comonfort's successor, Juárez, summoned Lerdo to join his cabinet, first as minister of justice, later as secretary of state. Lerdo became one of the major voices for an independent Mexico during the French invasion. After the war, Lerdo returned to the Supreme Court as its chief justice. In 1871, he challenged Juárez for the presidency, but lost. Unlike Díaz, he did not rebel but resumed his post on the Supreme Court. Although entitled to assume the presidency on Juárez's death by virtue of his position, Lerdo immediately called for new elections which took place in October 1872. This time he won.

The backbone of Juárez's rule during his waning years was the coalition of Liberal intellectuals, whose social liberalism was being replaced more and more by economic liberalism, and the Liberal landowners whose single claim to political or social liberalism – their opposition to the economic and political power of the church – had disappeared once the church lost its preeminence, together with the army, whose influence increased steadily. They now gave their support to Lerdo. In their eyes he seemed to possess the virtues but not the faults of Juárez. Like Juárez in his last years, Lerdo was a conservative on social issues. Unlike Juárez, however, he came from the Creole upper class and lacked his predecessor's occasional bursts of sympathy for the plight of the poorest segments of society.

In many respects Lerdo, implementing similar policies, was far more successful than Juárez had been in his last years. He was able to strengthen the role of the state considerably. In the first days of his presidency the Chamber of Deputies was more responsive to his desires than it had ever been to Juárez's. Moreover, Lerdo was allowed the creation of a Senate thus diluting considerably the power of the Chamber and enhancing correspondingly the pivotal role of the executive.

Lerdo also had, at first, greater success than his predecessor in pacifying the country. The roots of this pacification had been established under Juárez. Lerdo reaped the benefits of his predecessor's recent military victory over Porfirio Díaz. Díaz having been crushed, Lerdo was able to convey an impression of magnanimity by offering an amnesty to Díaz and his men. Díaz was in no position to refuse, however humiliating he found its terms. He was stripped of his military role and permanently exiled to his hacienda, La Noria. Díaz's defeat served to discourage would-be revolutionaries for a time and the first three and a half years of Lerdo's rule were significantly more peaceful than the years of Juárez's presidency.

Lerdo succeeded in extending the power of the federal government to regions that had eluded Juárez's control. He was able to destroy the one regional *caudillo* who had established a kind of peasant republic in Mexico: Manuel Lozada in the territory of Tepic. Lozada, referred to in the Mexican press as the 'Tiger of Arica' (Arica was the mountain range where he frequently had his headquarters), was in some ways characteristic of many *caudillos* who ruled their regions with an iron fist in nineteenth-century Mexico. The term tiger referred to his ferocity in crushing opponents. He was willing to make alliances with anyone who would recognize his power and had thrown his support to both Maximilian and Juárez. For a time he maintained close relationships with the trading house of Barron and Forbes, who in return for supporting Lozada wanted large-scale concessions in Tepic. In other respects, however, Lozada was atypical in comparison with most other *caudillos*.

The basis of his power was the Indian villages to whom he had returned the land that the haciendas had taken from them. Village representatives assumed increasing power within his movement which as a result was increasingly feared and resented by hacendados both in Tepic and in neighbouring states. In return for nominal subordination to his government, Juárez had allowed Lozada widespread control of his region. Lerdo, by contrast, sent federal troops to crush him. In 1873 Lozada was captured and shot, his Indians defeated and many of their lands granted to hacendados.

Mexico's economy developed more rapidly than in previous years, thus increasing Lerdo's prestige. This was due to the greater pacification of the country and to the fact that Lerdo was able to reap the fruits of several economic initiatives taken by his predecessor. In particular, he was able in 1873 to inaugurate Mexico's first important railway line connecting Mexico City to the port town of Veracruz, which greatly hastened Mexico's economic development.

In view of these successes it seems at first surprising that Lerdo was not able to repeat what his predecessor had done: continue in office for more than one term. In 1876 Díaz's attempt to topple Lerdo was far more successful than his previous attempt to topple Juárez. In part this was due to the fact that Lerdo lacked the prestige that the years of leadership during the war against the French had conferred upon Juárez. He was also unsuccessful in maintaining the upper-class consensus in his favour which he enjoyed when he assumed the presidency. Lerdo's standing with these forces had been undercut by a policy of proceeding with far more energy against the church than Juárez had during the years of the Restored Republic. After his victory over church-led forces in Mexico, his expropriation of church properties, and having implemented the reform laws, Juárez had tried to avoid any confrontation with the church and had turned a blind eye on violations by the clergy of some reform laws such as a new accumulation of wealth. Lerdo, by contrast, expropriated church properties, banished foreign-born Jesuits from Mexico and as a symbolic gesture had the reform laws newly incorporated into the constitution.

Lerdo's support among Mexico's upper classes was also undermined by his contradictory policies towards the building of railways. While the Mexican president had enthusiastically supported the construction of the Mexico–Veracruz railway and was just as enthusiastic in advocating an east–west connection between both coasts of Mexico, he was far more reticent about constructing a railway line linking Mexico to the United States. 'Between weakness and strength the desert', he is reported to have said. When pressure mounted on him to accede to the construction of a north–south railway, he tried to get a Mexican company to undertake the bulk of construction. When this company failed to obtain sufficient capital Lerdo finally granted a concession for building the major part of a trunk line to the United States to an American railway promoter, Edward Lee Plumb. As a result of these policies he alienated both the supporters and opponents of the construction of the Mexican–American railway line. Its supporters felt he had waited too long to grant an effective concession for the construction of this line, while its opponents feared that as the result of closer economic and communications links with the United States the latter would control and absorb Mexico. These opponents joined the traditional 'outs' who felt that the fall of an existing administration would give them access to power and government positions. In 1876 they joined Lerdo's strongest opponent, Porfirio Díaz.

THE FIRST DÍAZ ADMINISTRATION, 1876–80

The rising of Tuxtepec

After his forcible retirement to La Noria, Díaz appeared a crushed man, his daily activities ostensibly limited to planting crops and manufacturing chairs. In fact he remained active, soliciting the support of former military cronies for another assault on the presidency. Lerdo's political fortunes having sufficiently soured, Díaz struck in January 1876. At Díaz's request, the military commander of Oaxaca issued a proclamation, the Plan of Tuxtepec, calling for armed revolt against Lerdo and for Díaz's election to the presidency. Like the Plan of La Noria, it embraced the principle of non-re-election. But unlike the Plan of La Noria it extended the principle to the municipal level. The insistence upon municipal democracy was a very popular cause with both the middle and the lower classes of society, as well as with some hacendados whose power was being constantly eroded by the increasing authority of the governors, who were frequently also the state's most important landowners. It had a special appeal for the middle class, who had exercised a large measure of control not only in towns, where they were strongly represented, but even in many villages, which frequently chose as mayors and village administrators people who could read and write and were better off economically than most peasants. The demand for municipal autonomy seemed to have led some members of the peasantry to support Porfirio Díaz, although there is no evidence that he showed any strong interest in gaining their adherence.

At first Díaz's second revolt seemed to peter out even more quickly than his first. Lerdo's troops handily routed Oaxaca's makeshift militia. At Icamole, Lerdo's army defeated troops led by Díaz himself. Lerdo felt he was in a strong enough position to call for new elections, and he was re-elected. But Díaz's dissent was infectious. The new Chief Justice of the Supreme Court, José María Iglesias, constitutionally the next in line for the presidency, charged Lerdo with election fraud and refused to recognize the results. Instead he tried to assume the presidency himself. He gained the support of several governors, senators and deputies who had felt left out by the Lerdo administration. This division within the government infused Díaz's rebellion with new vitality. His troops engaged Lerdo's at Tecoac and inflicted a painful defeat. Under the combined pressure of Iglesias and Díaz, Lerdo resigned and fled the country. Díaz offered to recognize Iglesias as provisional president if he, in turn, would recognize him as the head of the new revolutionary army and promise to hold a new round of elections quickly. Iglesias, overestimating his strength, refused. When Díaz marched against him, Iglesias's troops simply disintegrated. In the spring of 1877, elections were held and Díaz became the new president.

The regime of Porfirio Díaz at first represented much less of a discontinuity with his predecessors than has frequently been assumed. It was a more militarily orientated regime than those of either Juárez or Lerdo, in the sense that a far greater part of the budget was allocated to the military. In order to maintain the loyalty of the army, Díaz placed his own troops as well as those who had fought for Lerdo and Iglesias on the payroll. Nevertheless, Díaz obviously felt that the army was too weak, too divided and too unreliable, to constitute the only or even the main power basis of his regime. He attempted to restore and even strengthen the upper- and middle-class coalition that had constituted the social and political basis of his predecessors' power. With respect to the upper classes, Díaz practised a policy of 'divide and rule'. He removed from power local caciques, loyal to his predecessors, such as Chihuahua governor Luis Terrazas, and put rivals of similar social origins in their place. Nevertheless, as long as they did not resist him, he allowed the men he had so removed to keep their property and to expand their economic influence. For many hacendados, loss of political power was more than offset by Díaz's policy of selling public lands, which gave them great opportunities for enrichment.

At first glance it would seem to have been more difficult for Díaz to gain middle-class support since the economic resources at his disposal had been drastically curtailed by the large amounts of money he had to pour into the reconstituted army. Since at this stage he was incapable of offering large economic rewards to the middle class, Díaz's most important option was to make political concessions. He had the newly elected Congress proclaim the principle of no re-election not only of the president but of the governors as well, which meant that the many 'outs' among the middle classes would have a better chance of gaining power once the terms of office of existing officials had run out. By strengthening municipal autonomy, Díaz gained some support among regional middle classes who had been largely ignored by both Juárez and Lerdo.

Díaz carried out no massive repression, imprisonment, or execution of his enemies. The existing civilian political groups were not banned but continued to exist and to participate in political life. National, regional and local elections continued to be held, and they were no more nor less honest than the ones which his predecessors had organized. The press continued to have a wide margin of freedom. The fact that the opposition to Díaz did not utilize their legal opportunities to combat him in the same way that the opponents of Juárez and Lerdo had done was largely due to the emergence of the first external threat to Mexico's sovereignty since Maximilian's defeat.

For ten years, from 1867 to 1877, Mexico had known a kind of respite from outside intervention which it had rarely experienced before and was rarely to have again. France's fatal experience had killed whatever colonial hopes Europe once nurtured for Mexico. Diplomatic relations with the one-time aggressors, France, Great Britain, and Spain, were not restored but none of these countries was inclined to risk another direct intervention in Mexico. Germany established diplomatic relations, and German merchants assumed some key positions in Mexico's foreign trade, but Germany at this time had no political ambitions in Mexico either.

Relations with the United States had been friendly during the time of the French intervention. Between 1867 and 1877 they began to cool considerably, setting the stage for the confrontations that followed. The sources of conflict were several. As American settlers continued their westward push, Indian tribes and cattle thieves often used the less densely settled and less well defended Mexican border as a sanctuary from which to launch raids into the United States. As a result authorities on both sides of the border were incessantly levelling accusations at each other for not proceeding with sufficient energy against the marauders. There was also the fact that the Mexican government, in order to attract settlers to this dangerous and poverty-stricken region, had established a ten-mile duty-free zone along the American border. Goods sold in the zone were cheaper than those in the adjacent Mexican or American territories. This led to widespread smuggling activities and caused acute discontent among American merchants. Finally, there was Díaz's stated opposition to the generous concessions Lerdo had finally granted American railway promoters. Díaz had publicly given expression to the fears, which he probably did not really share, of Mexican nationalists that the penetration of American railways into Mexico would be but a prelude to the country's wholesale annexation.

In general, during the nineteenth century, both the United States and the European countries recognized 'revolutionary' governments in Latin America once they proved themselves in control and able to stand by their international obligations. In the case of Mexico, the United States abandoned this principle. The Grant administration, in power when Díaz triumphed, refused to recognize Díaz unless he favourably resolved at least some of the controversies between the two countries. Díaz showed himself very amenable. One of his first administrative measures on entering the City of Mexico was to gather together a large number of bankers and merchants in the Mexican capital to raise money for the first instalment on payments which the Lerdo administration had promised to the United States as compensation for damages suffered by Americans in Mexico. The Hayes administration, which succeeded that of Grant, accepted the payment of $300,000, and Díaz took this to imply recognition. He was wrong: Hayes had no intention of recognizing Díaz. Hayes wanted more than such piecemeal concessions, he wanted a piece of Mexico.

One of Hayes's first acts in office was to grant General C. Ord, commander of the military districts along the Mexican border, permission to pursue marauders, Indian raiders, cattle rustlers, and whoever he felt had violated United States law, across the Mexican border without first seeking the Mexican government's consent. Díaz could not brook such a measure without seriously impairing Mexico's sovereignty and opening himself up to charges of having 'sold out' to the Americans. As soon as he was apprised of the Ord instructions, Díaz positioned along the border a large contingent of troops, led by Gerónimo Treviño, and gave orders to resist any American advance into Mexico with every means at their disposal. War between both countries seemed all but inevitable when suddenly both the Americans and the Mexicans began to show extreme circumspection. American troops crossed into Mexico only when they had made relatively sure that Mexican troops were not in the vicinity. Conversely, Mexican troops tried to avoid any meeting with American military units which would have forced them into a conflict. Instead of war there was merely an impasse.

What ultimately defused the crisis was Díaz's persistent wooing of American investors. Díaz sent one of his most capable and trusted advisers, Manuel de Zamacona, to the United States in order to interest American businessmen in Mexican investments. Zamacona enlisted the help of Matías Romero, for many years Juárez's ambassador to the United States, who edited a series of books and pamphlets describing the allegedly boundless opportunities which Mexico offered American investors. At the same time Díaz welcomed to Mexico vocal and influential groups of American promoters, such as Ulysses S. Grant, the former president, granted them valuable railway concessions, and promised them further subsidies. As a result, American investors, only a short time after clamouring vociferously for intervention, became enthusiastic adherents of the Díaz regime and began to pressure the Hayes administration to recognize his government. Moreover, as the prospect of another war, scarcely more than ten years after the last one, became a real possibility, domestic opposition to Hayes's policies mounted. Finally, in 1878 Hayes gave in and recognized Díaz, and in 1880 he withdrew the Ord instruction as well.

Elaboration of the Porfirian strategy

It is not easy to assess what influence Díaz's conflicts with the Americans in 1877 and 1878 had in shaping his regime. They seem to have strongly inspired the three major policies followed by Díaz after 1878, by his temporary successor Manuel González (1880–4) and by Díaz again after 1884. First, Americans as well as other foreign investors and promoters were granted concessions of every kind on extremely generous terms.

Secondly, the Mexican government also attempted to do everything in its power to renew and then to strengthen its links to Europe to balance American influence. Thirdly, political stability was to be maintained at any price. Until about 1900, the application of these policies strengthened the Mexican state. From 1900 to 1910 they laid the basis for one of the most profound social upheavals to take place in twentieth-century Latin America: the Mexican Revolution.

During what remained of his first term in office, internal stability was Díaz's first priority. In order to achieve it, Díaz carried out a complex policy of concessions and repression. During his first term, apart from maintaining many of the political liberties that had existed under Juárez, Díaz made another important political concession: the decision to keep his word and not to run for a second term. This satisfied the 'outs' within both the elite and the middle classes, who now felt that they had a chance of participating in the next administration and thus saw no need to stage the 'traditional' revolution. Where necessary Díaz was of course ready and willing to use brute force to keep dissenters in check. When the governor of Veracruz, Mier y Terán, reported that a number of prominent citizens were plotting against him, Díaz responded with a laconic telegram: *Mátalos en caliente* – kill them in cold blood. He was no less ruthless in dealing with peasants in Hidalgo, Puebla and San Luis Potosí who occupied some neighbouring haciendas thinking that Díaz would support them in their revolutionary endeavour. Díaz in fact opened negotiations with several such groups, and promised to examine their grievances, if they would lay down their arms. Once disarmed, he ordered them shot.

Díaz's domestic policies, which held out the promise of internal stability as well as extremely generous government subsidies, led American promoters to sign contracts for the building of two major railway lines linking the United States to Mexico. Mexico's political elite came to view railway construction as the only means of safeguarding the country's political independence from possible United States military aggression. Díaz clearly hoped that American promoters as well as financiers and politicians would have too much at stake to run the risk of another Mexican–American war, which might finally ruin Mexico. His opponents, however, insisted that massive foreign investments in the long run increased rather than decreased the risks of foreign intervention. If the Mexican government proved incapable of maintaining the type of stability these investors wanted, they would then constitute an extremely powerful lobby in favour of intervention in Mexico.

Díaz also succeeded in the last years of his first term in re-establishing diplomatic relations with France. Such a step was anything but easy, in view of Napoleon's intervention in Mexico. There were strong pressures in Mexico demanding that, in order for relations to be resumed between the two countries, the French should not only give up all claims against Mexico but pay a large indemnity as well. At the same time the Mexican government had repeatedly stated that relations with France could only be re-established if the initiative came from the French. The fall of Napoleon in 1870 and the proclamation of the French Republic had created a new and far more favourable situation. It nevertheless took ten years for both countries officially to exchange ambassadors. This finally happened in 1880 when the French renounced all claims against Mexico and the Mexican government gave up the idea of obtaining reparations from France. By re-establishing relations with France, Díaz sought to create an economic counterweight both to the United States and to other European powers. French capital and French bankers played a decisive role in the establishment of the Mexican National Bank and in later years France became one of the main sources of loans to Mexico.

During and after the Porfirian era, France was to become more than just 'another' European country in the eyes of Mexico's elite. French fashion, culture and architecture were models they sought to imitate. August Comte's positivism strongly influenced the ideology of the regime though it was combined with Herbert Spencer's social Darwinism which soon overshadowed it. Absentee landlords spent part of their time in Paris, and members of the elite sent their children to French schools. Mexico's army was supplied with French artillery, and some of its most distinguished officers studied French military techniques. When Díaz was finally driven from power in 1911, it was to France that he retired.

THE GONZÁLEZ INTERREGNUM, 1880–4

In keeping with his promise, Díaz was not a candidate in the 1880 presidential election; instead, his hand-picked successor, General Manuel González, ran in his place. Many a cynic marvelled at the ingenuity of Díaz's choice. González was widely regarded as the most corrupt and least able of Díaz's protégés. He was likely to be a weak rival should Díaz decide to run for another term in 1884.

González distinguished himself by his corruption, although rumours that he removed all the furniture from the National Palace when he left office turned out to have been exaggerated. González was far less inept than he was frequently made out to be and he appointed an able cabinet of Porfiristas, but he was no Porfirio Díaz. During his term of office, he attempted to implement his predecessors' three basic policies: concessions to foreign and especially US interests, rapprochment with Europe, and maintenance of internal stability at any price. On the whole, however, he was far less able than Díaz had been to prevent profound contradictions from emerging as a result of his efforts to apply all three of these strategies simultaneously.

Seeking to maintain and heighten the interest of foreign investors, especially American railway companies in Mexico, González bolstered the special concessions which Díaz had granted to them with new ones. At González's behest, the Mexican Congress passed a new law to encourage further the transfer of public lands to private hands. The law allowed González to entrust private companies with the task of surveying the public lands and to compensate them with one-third of the land they determined to be 'public'. Not surprisingly the companies rode roughshod over the rights of small landowners, many of whom had farmed these lands for generations but who were unable to produce formal titles. The benefits to both foreign and domestic bidders were several. Much public land could now be acquired that had not been for sale before. Much private land, reclassified as 'public', could now be acquired in one large bid rather than through piecemeal negotiations with a multitude of small plot owners.

An even greater concession to foreign investors was the Mexican government's decision to revoke the old Spanish mining code which had stipulated that a landowner did not also own the minerals beneath his property. This had meant that mining rights had to be acquired separately from surface land so that the state was in possession of a far greater amount of the country's wealth. The new law of 1884 put an end to this principle and proved to be a bonanza both to Mexican landowners and to foreign investors.

But the most powerful of the foreign investment lobbies in Mexico, the American, wanted still more. González's problem was that catering to American demands meant risking a deterioration of his newly restored relations with Europe. In 1882 the United States government proposed to Mexico a special reciprocity arrangement whereby import tariffs on certain goods from each of the two countries would be lifted. The United States hinted that further railway construction in Mexico would be unprofitable and would stop unless such a treaty were signed. González was less than enthusiastic. The treaty not only would fly in the face of the sought-after rapprochment with Europe, but would deprive an already pinched treasury of much-needed tax revenues. Yielding to American pressure, the Mexican Congress in 1883 nevertheless approved the treaty. But several months later it turned around and approved another treaty granting Germany most-favoured-nation status, in effect bestowing the same tariff reductions on Germany and voiding many of the unilateral advantages the United States had gained through its treaty. The United States ambassador protested vehemently. The German minister in Mexico bluntly warned González that not standing by its treaty with Germany would jeopardize Mexico's relations with all of Europe. González narrowly escaped a final showdown: American farmers, fearful of Mexican competition in agricultural goods, pressured the United States Senate into rejecting the treaty.

On other occasions the pursuit of better relations with Europe came into conflict with the need for internal stability. After long and complicated negotiations, González was able to persuade Great Britain to reopen diplomatic relations with Mexico. In return González recognized a debt of £15.4 million to British bondholders contracted by preceding Conservative governments. This agreement was announced in 1884, in the midst of an acute financial crisis. It was denounced in Congress. Rioters took to the streets and peace was reached only after some resounding sabre rattling and several pounds of lead had been fired into densely packed crowds.

The González administration has gone down in history as one of Mexico's most corrupt governments. Its reputation is probably deserved, although in the public eye González's negative image was in part the result of the economic crisis that gripped Mexico in 1884 and a conscious effort on the part of Porfirio Díaz to discredit his successor. As a result of this image, attention has been deflected from the profound transformation that occurred in Mexico between 1880 and 1884. The legal changes that have been outlined above only constitute part of the picture. The first railway line between Mexico and the United States was inaugurated in 1884. US investments in Mexico were increasing at a breathtaking pace. For the first time since Maximilian's defeat Mexico had diplomatic relations with all major European countries. Railway construction and the final defeat of the Apaches, which occurred in the years between 1880 and 1884, opened up vast new expanses of Mexico's northern frontier, much of which had been hitherto inaccessible. Then under Porfirio Díaz, who was elected president again in 1884 and remained president until 1911, Mexico underwent its most profound economic, political and social transformation since the advent of independence in 1821.

THE DÍAZ REGIME, 1884–1900

Between 1877 and 1900 Mexico's population increased from nearly ten million to more than fifteen million. No recent war had checked the increase. A modest improvement in the standard of living had helped it along. The periodic droughts and famines that once penetrated the economic life of many regions ceased to have the devastating impact they once did: now there were railways to bring food to starving villagers and to carry the excess labour force to regions where there was greater demand for it. Medical care by contrast improved only marginally. Although the number of doctors rose from 2,282 in 1895 to 3,021 in 1900, they were concentrated in the cities. Life expectancy in Mexico continued to lag far behind Western Europe and the United States.

The population expansion was quite uneven. Previously sparsely populated frontier states as well as urban areas gained most heavily. Between 1877 and 1910 the population of the border states of Sonora, Chihuahua, Coahuila, Nuevo León and Tamaulipas rose by 227 per cent. Mexico City, Guadalajara, Monterrey and Torreón grew even more markedly. These trends were essentially due to an increase of the native population. In spite of the efforts and hopes of the Díaz administration, immigration continued to be minimal and consisted mainly of upper- and middle-class merchants, investors and technicians. Salaries in industry were far too low to attract European workers except for a few skilled mechanics who were paid very high wages. European farm workers would not accept the low wages paid by Mexican hacendados and as long as the United States was still open to immigration they saw no reason to go south of the border.

Economic development under Díaz

Between 1884 and 1900 Mexico experienced rapid economic growth. The flood of foreign investments – almost $1,200 million worth – helped gross national product to rise at an annual rate of 8 per cent. It was a rate of growth unprecedented in Mexico's history as an independent state. It also produced unprecedented disparities: between agricultural enterprises outfitted with the most modern technology and others where work was often carried out in the most primitive ways; between development of light and heavy industry; between foreign and domestic control of the economy; and between the evolution of different regions.

Economic progress was most pronounced in the export-orientated sectors of the economy. Mining registered the most rapid growth. Until the railways were built mining in Mexico had been confined to precious metals, mainly silver and some gold. Transportation by mule was too expensive for anything else. Virtually non-existent when Díaz first came to power, the railway system comprised 14,000 kilometres of track by the turn of the century, and as a result the extraction of copper, zinc and lead as well as silver became profitable. Silver production rose from 607,037 kilograms in 1877–8 to 1,816,605 kilos in 1900–1 (and 2,305,094 kilos in 1910–11). The production of lead began with 38,860 tons in 1891–2 and rose to 79,011 tons in 1900–1 (and 120,525 tons in 1910–11). The production of copper increased from 6,483 tons in 1891–2 to 28,208 tons in 1900–1 (and 52,116 tons in 1910–11). The cultivation of agricultural cash crops also grew by leaps and bounds. The most spectacular example was henequén (sisal), the production of which rose from 11,383 tons in 1877 to 78,787 tons in 1900 (and to 128,849 tons by 1910). The output of rubber, guayule (a rubber substitute), coffee, and cochineal also increased dramatically. Some export-orientated industry also began to gain a foothold in Mexico. In 1891 the United States passed the McKinley tariff which imposed high customs fees on imported unprocessed ores. Tariffs for processed ores were much lower and as a result the largest United States companies, above all the Guggenheim-controlled American Smelting and Refining Company, set up ore smelters in Mexico.

Economic progress was rapid until the turn of the century for domestically orientated light industry. Textile manufacturing flourished. When the value of silver, on which Mexican currency was based, began to fall in the 1880s, textile imports became too expensive, and the French merchants who had carried on that trade switched to manufacturing textiles in Mexico itself. Huge plants, like that of Río Blanco, sprang up in the regions of Orizaba and Puebla. Light industrial plants for the production of paper, glass, shoes, beer and food processing were also erected. Heavy industry lagged far behind and only emerged after the turn of the century. In 1902 the Compañía Fundidora de Fierro y Acero built a steel plant in Monterrey which by 1910 was turning out 72,000 tons annually.

After 1900 industrial development greatly slowed down. In part this was due to a fall in the living standard after the turn of the century so that the market for industrial goods expanded in a much more limited way than before. Industrial growth was also limited as a result of government policies. The Díaz administration did not go out of its way to lend a helping hand to struggling domestic producers. The New Industries Act of 1881 granted some generous tax exemptions to budding local industries, and accorded some selective tariff protection to certain local industries such as textiles. But it never afforded heavy industries the kind of special protection common in European countries, such as forcing American railway promoters to buy the material they used from Mexican producers. Nor was heavy industry accorded preferential access to credit.

Unlike railways, industry never received subsidies. The Díaz government had no plans for developing particular industries, no programme to stimulate the import of technology, no policies for protecting infant industries. Above all its investments in what could be called human capital were extremely limited. While expenditures for education did increase during the Porfiriato the results were very limited in scope. Between 1895 and 1910 the percentage of the population which could read and write increased from 14.39 to 19.79 per cent. Public vocational education destined to train skilled workers was insignificant. From 1900 to 1907 enrolment in vocational schools increased from 720 to 1,062.

During the Porfiriato, significant discrepancies emerged in the agricultural sector, not so much in the production of goods (both export crops and food staples production increased, though at different rates) as in the level of technical modernization. While a kind of technological revolution took place on plantations producing such cash crops as henequén and sugar, wheat- and corn-producing haciendas were still utilizing old and very traditional techniques. The failure of these landowners to modernize has often been attributed to psychological rather than economic causes. Landowners, it is asserted, had an essentially feudal mentality, valuing land as a status symbol, not an economic resource. They were too preoccupied hobnobbing with the *haute couture* of Paris, visiting the spas of Gstaad (and Garmisch Partenkirchen), and gambling in Monte Carlo to give serious attention to the affairs of their estates. But that does not explain why the people to whom they had entrusted their estates in the meantime would not themselves undertake whatever seemed most likely to return a profit.

Technological advances that resulted in modernizing and cheapening agricultural production in the United States remained unimportant in a country with as cheap a labour supply as Mexico's. In 1911 one of Mexico's leading agricultural experts, Lauro Viadas, compared the cost of an American farmer using modern agricultural implements and a Mexican hacendado working with more primitive technology but employing cheap labour. Production of a similar amount of wheat cost the American farmer 4.95 pesos and the Mexican hacendado 4.50 pesos.

Apart from the disparity between export and domestically orientated production, another significant disparity emerged as a result of Mexico's rapid economic growth: the disparity between foreign and domestic control of the economy. With the exception of agriculture, the most significant branches of the economy were in the hands of foreign capital. Until the end of the nineteenth century, the Díaz government made no effort whatsoever to encourage either Mexican control of some branches of the economy or even to further Mexican participation.

While the Díaz administration was relatively indifferent to Mexican ownership and participation in the new enterprises springing up in the country, the same cannot be said with regard to its attitude towards American versus European control of important segments of the economy. The Díaz government did everything in its power to further European investments without restricting those of the United States. Until the end of the nineteenth century, loans were placed only in Europe and banking concessions were granted exclusively to European bankers. Public works projects, such as port installations in Veracruz or drainage works in the valley of Mexico, were entrusted to British enterprises, above all those owned and controlled by a young but highly experienced British promoter and politician, Sir Weetman Pearson.

On the whole, however, these policies of the Mexican government, while substantially contributing to European economic penetration into Mexico, did not lead to any significant amount of competition or conflict between the Europeans and the United States until the end of the nineteenth century. The United States was still mainly a debtor and not a creditor nation and the largest American banks were still primarily interested in investments within the United States, so that they did not resent European investment in Mexico or the European inroads into the

Mexican financial system. Even in those fields where Europeans (especially the British) and Americans shared similar interests (railways and mines), a kind of division of labour between them had developed, with the British concentrating essentially on central and southern Mexico while American investments tended to be directed above all into the north of the country.

The sharpest and most conflictive rivalry for economic influence in Mexico until the end of the nineteenth century involved not the United States and Britain but two other powers, France and Germany, whose interests in Mexico were on the whole far smaller. The first area of conflict between them was that of Mexico's foreign trade which, until the 1870s, had to a large extent been controlled by German merchants from the Hanseatic cities of Hamburg, Bremen, and Lübeck. By the 1870s French merchants from Barcelonette (the main street of the town is still called Avenue Porfirio Díaz today) displaced their German rivals. This proved to be just the first battle in a long and intense Franco-German struggle in Mexico. A few years later, Franco-German competition emerged at a higher level. In 1888 the Mexican government signed its first important loan agreement with a foreign bank since the fall of Maximilian's government. It negotiated with the German banking house of Bleichroeder, which also handled the personal finances of German Chancellor Bismarck. The Germans not only secured extremely advantageous interest rates, but also forced the Mexican government to sign a secret treaty practically granting the firm a monopoly over the country's external finances. The Mexican government would not have the right to take out any loans without making a prior offer to the house of Bleichroeder. Mexico accepted the onerous German terms, but only six years later, with French help, managed to break Bleichroeder's contract and his hold over Mexican finances.

In yet another field the French won even more significant victories over their German rivals. In all of Latin America, German and French arms manufacturers were vying for the lucrative Latin American arms market. The most important German company in this field was the house of Krupp. While in most of Latin America Krupp was extremely successful, in Mexico, in spite of intense efforts to sell artillery to the country's army, he lost out to his French rivals from Saint Chamond.

Until the end of the nineteenth century, these conflicts were not critical for the Mexican government. It was only in the twentieth century that another type of conflict emerged involving the two major powers interested in Mexico, the United States and Great Britain, which in contrast with the Franco-German rivalry was to have important and lasting consequences for Mexico.

Regional disparities in Mexico's development

Another deep-seated discrepancy that Porfirian development produced was an increasing regional disparity in Mexico between the centre, the south and the north of the country. This disparity was not new. In fact, it went back all the way to the origins of civilization in that region. Long before the European conquest, intensive agriculture, large cities, a highly stratified society, and a complex culture had developed in the central and southern part of present-day Mexico, while the northern region had been inhabited by nomadic hunters and gatherers and some primitive agriculturalists. The coming of the Spaniards brought new differences to these regions. The south-east to a very large degree became marginal in the colonial economy of New Spain, because no mines were found there. The north on the other hand became an essential part of colonial New Spain. It was there that some of the richest mines were discovered after the conquest of Mexico. Unfortunately for the Spaniards, they were not capable of populating this region and constant and relentless attacks by nomadic Indians, above all by the Apaches in the eighteenth century, which continued into the period of Independence, seriously inhibited the economic development of this area. During the Porfirian era, both the north and the south-east of Mexico underwent a tremendous economic boom and both were absorbed into the world market.

Mexico's south-east began to assume traits that were characteristic of much of central America and the Caribbean. The economies of most south-eastern states were geared to one or two export crops with very little agricultural diversification and even less industry. The Peninsula of Yucatán is perhaps the most outstanding example of such a development. Sisal, or henequén as it was called in Mexico, had always been an important crop in Yucatán. As long as it was used mainly for making rope and cordage, its use and thus its market were limited. Demand for henequén rose dramatically when it began to be used by the McCormick reaper in the 1880s and an export boom took place in Yucatán. The haciendas where henequén was produced, as well as the railway system that transported it from Yucatán's interior to the coast, were in the hands of Mexican owners. The buyers and users of the fibre, the largest of which was the American Peabody Company, competed for henequén, but by the end of the century most of these companies had been fused into one large conglomerate: the Chicago-based International Harvester Corporation. It soon came to dominate the market and in co-operation with local merchant firms attempted to manipulate the price of henequén to its advantage.

In contrast to the Yucatán situation, where practically all the estates were Mexican-owned, conditions in other south-eastern states, especially in Chiapas and Tabasco, were somewhat different. Such staples as rubber and to a lesser degree coffee were produced directly by foreign investors. What these states had in common with Yucatán was their one- or two-crop economies and their complete dependence upon world market conditions.

Like the south-eastern periphery, the northern periphery of Mexico also underwent an extremely rapid economic development, and it too was largely orientated towards the world market. Nevertheless, the resemblance between the two regions stops at this point. In contrast to the south-east, the north had a much more diversified economy. It exported a large variety of minerals; copper, tin, and silver as well as commodities such as chick peas, cattle and lumber. A much more important segment of the northern economy, in contrast to that of the south-east, was geared toward production for the domestic market. This was above all the case for new large and highly productive irrigated cotton fields in the Laguna region in the states of Coahuila and Durango. In relation to the rest of the economy, industrial development was more important in the north than in most other parts of Mexico. A steel industry developed in the city of Monterrey and smelters for minerals, both Mexican and American owned, were constructed in the north. On a number of large estates, food-processing industries had sprung up, so that in many respects the northern economy was the most balanced in the country. Foreign investment, however, was far more important and preponderant there than in the south-east. Nevertheless, this was also one of the regions of the country where Mexican capital played an important, though generally subordinate, role in the development of the new industries (except mining) and cash crops during the Porfirian period.

It was in large parts of central Mexico where, in overall terms, the economy underwent the least changes. This was above all the case for the large corn- and wheat-producing estates. This very slow development constituted a stark contrast to a very rapid industrial expansion in the valley of Mexico and its surroundings as well as to new industrial centres in the states of Puebla and Veracruz.

In the eyes of most Porfirian intellectuals, these profound transformations of the economy created the basis for the evolution of Mexico into a modern, independent state on the model of Western Europe or the United States. What really emerged, however, was a country that depended to an unprecedented degree on foreign interests. This dependence took two different but complementary forms. On the one hand, its clearest manifestation was foreign predominance or ownership of important, non-agricultural sectors of the Mexican economy: banking, mining, industry and transportation. On the other hand, Mexico had become a classic example of an underdeveloped country producing raw materials that depended on markets in the industrialized north Atlantic.

The political transformation of Mexico

In the years after 1884 the Díaz regime became the first effective and long-lasting dictatorship to emerge in Mexico since the advent of Independence. During his second term in office Díaz effectively prevented the election of any opponent to the Mexican Congress. By 1888 it had for all practical purposes become a rubber stamp institution. Every candidate had to receive the prior approval of Díaz to be either elected or re-elected. The now subservient Congress approved amendments to the constitution which made it possible for Díaz to 'accede' to the wishes of the population and have himself re-elected in 1888, 1892 (in that year the constitution was changed so as to extend the presidential terms to six years), 1898, 1904 and 1910. Mexico's previously combative opposition press, where criticism of the government was frequently combined with literary brilliance, was largely muzzled and brought under control although opposition at times flared up in small newspapers.

The consolidation of the dictatorship was closely tied to two processes: the achievement of internal stability (the Pax Porfiriana) and the emergence of an effective and powerful Mexican state. These developments in turn were inextricably linked to the economic development of the country.

The 'pacification' of the country was a multi-faceted and complex process which until 1900 was largely (though not entirely) successful and constituted the proudest of achievements for Porfirian ideologists. The conflicts which had constantly erupted in Mexico before the Díaz period had many layers: military coups, *caudillo* uprisings, banditry in the countryside, attacks by nomadic Indians and revolts by peasants and frontier Indian tribes. By the end of the nineteenth century, only two forms of violence were still endemic in Mexico: revolts by frontier Indian groups, and revolts by scattered peasant communities, mainly in the north. All other types of violence had either completely disappeared or had greatly subsided.

This reduction in the level of violence was closely linked to the formation of the Mexican state. And the precondition for the development of the Porfirian state was a constant increase of its revenues. Díaz did not want to use the means by which previous governments had attempted to increase their income (forced loans or higher taxes) since such methods contributed to driving away foreign investors and antagonizing the country's domestic oligarchy. Mexico's revenues under Díaz mainly came from the limited taxes that foreign enterprises paid, the relatively large customs duties levied on goods entering the country, and taxes on precious metals. All of these revenues depended on increasing the level of foreign investments and on improving Mexico's international credit rating which would allow it to secure more loans on better terms. Apart from luring foreign investors into the country, Díaz's main means of increasing revenue was to streamline the financial administration of the country and to modernize it. This process had begun under Juárez but the most effective modernizer proved to be one of the country's most capable financiers, José Yves Limantour, whom Díaz appointed as finance minister in May 1893. By 1896, for the first time in Mexican history, Limantour had balanced the budget. This, in turn, tremendously increased Mexico's credit rating and international loans were not only easier to come by but could now be secured by the Díaz regime at much more advantageous interest rates than ever before.

With such solid financial backing Díaz was in a good position to tighten the reins on the more mutinous and independent-minded groups within the country. One group were the regional caciques who ruled their provinces like feudal fiefdoms. Díaz's first move was to replace many of the most powerful men left over from another era, like Luis Terrazas in Chihuahua, and Ignacio Pesqueira in Sonora, with men loyal to him. There was nothing very novel in this strategy. Virtually all of Díaz's predecessors had done the same when they could. Unfortunately for the government, this had in the past often proved a very temporary remedy. Once firmly in power, the newly installed caciques tended to seek for themselves the same kind of autonomy their predecessors had enjoyed. Moreover, their demoted predecessors usually lingered on in the background, waiting for an opportunity to overthrow the regime that had unseated them. As a result political stability remained precarious and fighting between rival caciques or even conflict between the newly appointed *caudillos* and the federal government were frequent. Under Díaz, the remedy worked much better. The newly constructed railways gave Díaz's army ready access to the provinces and helped to keep potential rebels in check.

Perhaps more important than this was the fact that Díaz encouraged or at least allowed both the caciques in power and those who had been removed from their positions to enrich themselves by acting as intermediaries for foreign investors who wished to settle in these regions or to acquire property there. In this way Díaz gave the members of the local oligarchy, both the 'ins' and the 'outs', a powerful stake in the stability of their region. Any uprising, any local turbulence, might easily frighten potential investors and thus close an important avenue of revenue to the members of the local oligarchy.

There were two other ways in which Díaz attempted to counteract possible uprisings by local strong men. One was to appoint military commanders without any roots in the region they commanded to oversee the local civilian officials. The other was to upgrade the office of *jefe político*, the district administrators, who before the Díaz regime had been officials with limited power. They now commanded the police and auxiliary armed forces in their districts, named district and municipal officials, paved the way for foreign investors and frequently owed their primary loyalty not to the governors to whom they were directly subordinated but to the central government.

Díaz applied a similar tactic of repression combined with co-option and other inducements to a second group which for a long time had opposed a strong central government. This was the traditional middle-class opposition, which operated mainly in the capital city of Mexico. Traditionally, these groups played an important role in the Mexican Congress and edited the most important opposition newspapers. Díaz prevented the election of opponents to the Mexican Congress and continued a policy implemented during the González administration of outlawing all opposition newspapers. The opposition of the middle classes to these repressive measures, however, was muted, because at the same time Díaz was giving thousands of their members new opportunities for economic and social advancement. The number of positions in the state bureaucracy between 1884 and 1900 greatly increased. At the same time, in those states where Díaz had dismissed the local caciques, new positions opened up for ambitious men. The dismissal of local strong men rarely meant their complete elimination in political terms. Luis Terrazas, the strong man of Chihuahua, remained a potent force in local politics and set up a powerful political organization, which Díaz was forced to tolerate and which opposed the existing structure of political power in the state. As a result, a kind of two-party system emerged in Chihuahua and a number of other states at a time when in Mexico City the remnants of democracy were being more and more eroded. This system in turn gave the regional middle classes increased political leverage as both parties competed for their support.

These 'parties' were only regional in nature and far more similar to extended family groups or patron–client coalitions than to the political parties which were developing in Europe during this period. Not only did Díaz never allow real opposition parties to be formed, he was also just as opposed to a government political party. In 1891 some of his principal intellectual and upper-class supporters attempted to cement the Porfirian regime by calling for the formation of a Liberal party based on the 'scientific' principles of positivism. (As a result these men came to be known in Mexico as *científicos*.) The aims of this proposal were at one and the same time to broaden the basis of the regime in order to strengthen it and to impose some kind of restraint upon Díaz himself. At the same time the creation of a party would ensure some kind of orderly succession and prevent what a large part of the Mexican elite most feared: the resurgence of turmoil and conflict in the country were Díaz to die or be incapable of completing his term in office.

Díaz, however, rejected the formation of a political party; he preferred to continue a tactic he had successfully begun to apply after assuming office in 1876, which was to play off different cliques within Mexico's elite against each other. One of these cliques was led by Manuel Romero Rubio, who had been a minister in the government of Lerdo and who later joined Díaz and became his minister of the interior in 1884. Romero Rubio was in many respects the architect of the Porfirian state. He it was who transformed the institution of the *jefe político* and who controlled and manipulated the country's governors. His clique consisted mainly of civilians: financiers, landowners, technocrats, bureaucrats, and so on. After his death in 1895 his most successful and intelligent pupil José Yves Limantour, finance minister from 1893, became the acknowledged leader of this clique. Its main competitor was another clique led by military men. Former president Manuel González was its main spokesman in the first years after Díaz reassumed power, while one of Díaz's closest confidants, Bernardo Reyes, assumed this function in later years. It was composed of military cronies of Díaz, traditional regional strong men and some bureaucrats, and was sharply critical of the increasing power and influence of the *científicos*.

Díaz applied methods of repression combined with inducements similar to those he utilized to pacify regional strong men towards a third force, which throughout the nineteenth century had been a constant threat to any central government in the country: the army. On the one hand, Díaz augmented the military budget (in absolute though not in relative terms) and bought modern arms in Europe, installed many army leaders in important political offices, and allowed them to pad the payroll. He also set up a modern military academy where he attempted to form an elite officers' corps. At the same time, however, Díaz weakened the influence of the army by establishing other para-military forces which were frequently of a better calibre than the army. Much of the internal repression was carried out by auxiliary troops not directly subordinated to the army. One of the most important such forces were the national Rurales, a professional police corps which had existed before Díaz but whose influence and size Díaz greatly reinforced. The soldiers in the army were forcibly inducted into the military and badly paid, so they frequently had only a limited sense of loyalty to their institution. The Rurales, on the other hand, were better paid and better treated. To a lesser degree the same was true of the state Rurales, armed units directly subordinated to the individual state administrations, but with ultimate authority over them retained by the federal government. At the same time, Díaz enlisted into police units some of the most notable bandits, thus turning their energy and talents to his advantage. But it was not Díaz and the central state alone which played a decisive role in putting an end to banditry. Local strong men who had frequently been in league with the outlaws, or at least had turned a blind eye to their depredations as long as their own property was not affected, now discovered that these same bandits might stop the flow of foreign investments into their districts and thus kill the goose that laid the golden egg. Their active help to the government was frequently of decisive importance.

Díaz's policy of repression, conciliation and co-option of all the upper- and middle-class forces which had been the source of uprisings and instability in the early nineteenth century extended to yet another force which for a time had constituted one of the main threats to every liberal government: the Catholic church. Díaz did not pursue Lerdo's anti-clerical policies. While the Díaz government never abolished the legal restrictions which the reform laws placed on the church and did not restore its former properties, in practice a policy reversal was taking place. In many surreptitious ways, which nevertheless were not difficult to detect, the church was accumulating new wealth from investments and from the donations of the faithful. The government made no attempt to restrict this process. It allowed more than twenty-three newspapers which were closely linked to the church to be published, and church-inspired and organized schools multiplied all over Mexico. Díaz's marriage to Carmen Romero Rubio, a devout Catholic who was on the best of terms with the church hierarchy, further underlined the church–state reconciliation, as did the cordial relations of such bishops as Monsignor Gillow of Oaxaca with high administration officials.

In this period the main threat to the church came not from the state but from Protestant missionaries and from dissident movements in the countryside. As American investments and immigration into Mexico increased, so did American missionaries, who were especially active in the northern part of the country. In Chihuahua, Methodist missionaries penetrated even into remote villages and were highly successful in influencing the peasants. As a result many church officials became increasingly nationalistic and increasingly anti-American.

Perhaps an even greater danger to the church were dissident movements among the peasantry. Such movements had always existed but as long as Catholicism was the official religion of the country the church always had the means to repress these movements. Now its possibilities of fighting back were sharply curtailed as 'saints' and 'holy' men and women strongly opposed to the church emerged in different parts of the country. In the state of Sonora thousands of people venerated a young sixteen-year-old girl, Teresita, known as the Saint of Cabora, who healed the sick and was said to perform miracles; in Cohuilimpo, the Indian villagers believed that one of their number whom they called San Juan was a saint. All over central Mexico pre-Columbian idols were hidden and worshipped in caves.

The state only persecuted these cults if they advocated social or political changes. US-based Protestant missionaries were tolerated and at times even supported by Porfirian authorities. Bereft of state aid, the church had to find new ways to counter its religious foes. For priests to preach against idolatry was not enough, since many of these saints and rebels were not just religious but social dissidents as well. The need to pre-empt these social movements and the thirteenth encyclical, Rerum Novarum, of Pope Leo XIII calling for church involvement in social problems led to social activism by segments of the Catholic church. The main proponent of this new trend was the Bishop of Tulancingo. With his help several Catholic congresses to discuss the problems of the peasantry took place during the latter years of the Porfirian era. At a Catholic conference held in 1903 in the city of Tulancingo, Catholic laymen called on hacendados to abolish peonage and to give more instruction and schooling to the peasants. At the same time they appealed to the peasants to accept the God-given order of things and not to rise against their superiors. Church-inspired newspapers frequently pro-tested against expropriations of village lands. The church's new policy was doubtless facilitated by the fact that it had lost its lands and thus was not as involved as it had been in the early nineteenth century in peonage and other forms of peasant servitude.

While the church finally failed to stabilize the situation in the countryside, it was eminently successful in other respects. With Díaz's support it made a political and economic comeback and managed at the same time to increase its support among the peasantry. This support clearly manifested itself during the Revolution when the most radical agrarian revolutionaries (above all the Zapatistas in Morelos) carried out no anti-clerical policies.

On the whole the strengthening of the Porfirian state cost large segments of both the traditional upper and middle classes much of the political power they had hitherto exercised. In return they partook of the fruits of Mexico's rapid economic growth. The same cannot be said of the peasantry which during the Díaz period lost its traditional political rights at the same time that it suffered profound economic losses. It has been frequently stated that Díaz's abolition of existing democratic structures in Mexico scarcely affected the peasants. Most of them were illiterate and could not read the opposition newspapers even when they reached their remote villages, which seldom occurred. They were neither interested in nor did they participate in national elections.

This was probably true, but there was one aspect of democracy in

Mexico which was of decisive importance for a large segment of the peasantry: local autonomy. Most villagers traditionally elected their councils and mayors whose power was not only political but also economic. These officials allocated access to community lands, water and pastures, frequently resolved conflicts within the villages and at times determined who would join the army and who would be exempted from military service. The origins of this village autonomy can frequently be traced back to the pre-Columbian period when the villages in southern and central Mexico enjoyed a large measure of self-sufficiency and political rights. It did not end with the Spanish conquest. Spain allowed many Indian communities to retain lands and communal institutions and granted them a certain measure of autonomy, albeit under the close supervision of state and church officials. Many communities in the northern frontier areas were granted a new and greater degree of freedom from state control as an incentive to settle in this dangerous region and to fight against Indian marauders. On the whole the power and autonomy of village communities tended to increase after Independence. The federal government was far too weak to impinge upon their traditional rights. The only authority powerful enough to seriously challenge village councils and mayors were local and regional caciques. Many of them utilized their new-found power (unlike the colonial state, the weak national state of the nineteenth century could not impose effective restraints upon them) to force their rule upon the villages. Many others, however, were hesitant to attack vested peasant rights. The local caciques were often involved in Mexico's endless civil wars and in critical times they entered into alliances with the villages in order to maintain themselves against rivals or against a hostile federal government. Thus they tended to blend a certain measure of repression and control with attempts to gain the loyalty and support of many of the villages they controlled. This situation changed radically in the last years of the Porfiriato.

The domestication of the northern frontier

During the last quarter of the nineteenth century the Mexican state began to assert its dominion over Mexico's northern frontier: Sonora, Chihuahua, Nuevo León and Durango. The subjugation of the Apaches and the construction of the railways set the stage for a mass immigration from both the United States and the Mexican south. More than 15,000

Americans came to settle there. They were similar in some respects to the Americans who streamed into the rest of Mexico during this period. Like their counterparts in southern and central Mexico many of them were wealthy investors or executives of large corporations. Numerous technicians had been brought in by the American Smelting and Refining Company, owner of most of the mines and smelters of northern Mexico, and similar outfits. Many administrators had been brought in by men like William Randolph Hearst, who needed them to oversee his vast landholdings in the region, and William C. Greene, who needed them to operate his cattle and lumber empire. Numerous other Americans who came into the north, however, belonged to social groups scarcely represented in the rest of Mexico. American railway men occupied all the higher positions not only in the administration, but in the operations division of most Mexican railways, above all in the north, while American miners constituted an important segment of the labour force in mining, especially in one of Mexico's largest mining centres, Cananea in the state of Sonora. In the United States their status would have been no different from that of other workers, but in Mexico they constituted a privileged minority, better paid and better treated than their Mexican counterparts.

The 300,000 or so Mexicans who settled in northern Mexico between 1877 and 1910 bore a somewhat different social character. The mass of migrants were displaced peasants, ruined artisans, or adventurers hoping for better opportunities. Their impact on the region's demographic make-up was enormous: they helped to swell the population of Monterrey from 14,000 in 1877 to 78,528 in 1910 and to transform the obscure village of Torreón, which in the 1870s had numbered a few hundred, into Mexico's most modern and fastest growing city with a population of 23,000 by 1900 and 43,000 by 1910.

The newcomers to the north did not displace the region's elite. The north's great families had indeed relinquished some of their political power in favour of the central government and shared economic power with foreign entrepreneurs, but on the whole they emerged immensely strengthened by the transformations taking place in the border region. The Terrazas–Creel clan in Chihuahua, the Maderos in Coahuila, the steel mill owners of Monterrey constituted the Mexican equivalent of the Rockefellers and Guggenheims in the United States.

In both economic and social terms, the north was one of the most 'modern' regions of Mexico by the turn of the century. Not only was its economy the most diversified in the country, the percentage of rural population was lower than in the rest of Mexico. The literacy rate in the north was the highest in the country. Modern capitalist relations had largely replaced traditional forms of social relations in the countryside. Until the 1890s, peons on large estates had often been paid not in cash but with tokens only redeemable at the estate store. Many peons were bound by debt to the big estates and, even when this was not the case, the insecurity of the countryside, bad communications and Apache raids had made it extremely difficult and dangerous for them to leave their place of residence.

The end of the Apache wars, the newly established communications with the United States, the possibilities many Mexican agricultural workers and especially cowboys had to find work across the border in the United States, and the unwillingness of either the US authorities, American entrepreneurs or, for that matter, Mexican industrial entrepreneurs to return fugitive peons to their haciendas made the system of debt peonage more and more expensive and unprofitable. As a result, Mexican estate owners were forced to find other methods to keep cowboys and agricultural workers on their haciendas. Some of them, such as the cotton producers of the newly irrigated Laguna cotton fields, paid the highest agricultural wages in Mexico. Others granted share-cropping and tenancy arrangements on far more favourable terms than in the rest of the country. While in central Mexico arrangements predominated whereby tenants or sharecroppers received at the most 50 per cent of what they harvested, in the north they usually obtained two-thirds. Many northern cowboys were allowed to have cattle of their own and to graze them on hacienda lands. If they stayed long enough in the same job, they could easily become foremen and earn double what they had obtained before. Some especially progressive landowners such as Francisco Madero in the state of Coahuila set up schools and clinics on their estates, and in times of hunger and bad harvests fed the population of the surrounding villages.

Until the end of the nineteenth century, the economic and social changes produced by the political and economic absorption of the north by both central Mexico and the United States led to substantial improvements for important segments of not only the upper but also the middle and lower classes of society. Nevertheless, the north was also the region that witnessed the most social and political violence during the Porfirian period. In some respects, until the end of the nineteenth century, these conflicts took place between what could be designated as the modern sector of society on the one hand and the 'traditional' elements of northern society on the other. However, the only segment of northern society that completely rejected practically every characteristic of modern industrial society were some of the approximately 50,000 Tarahumara Indians who were concentrated mainly in the state of Chihuahua, many of them in the mountain fastnesses of the Sierra Madre, and who were only marginally involved in the social conflicts which gripped northern Mexico during the Porfiriato and the Revolution of 1910–20.

The Yaqui Indians of Sonora and the former military colonists of Chihuahua, who offered the greatest resistance to Porfirian modernization and who repeatedly staged armed uprisings against the authorities, constituted a traditional sector in the sense that they clung to their established rights and lands. They were not 'traditional' if the term implies opposition to modern technology, industry or production for the market. Under the aegis of Jesuit missionaries during the colonial period, the Yaquis had assimilated sophisticated techniques of intensive agriculture which they successfully applied to the fertile soil of the Yaqui river valley. Many of their products were sold in the markets of the mining regions. At the same time, many Yaqui Indians went to work far away from their native region in mines and haciendas and were considered by their employers to be among their most reliable and expert labourers.

During both the colonial period and the nineteenth century, the former military colonists, who settled mainly in the state of Chihuahua, constituted one of the mainstays of what could best be considered an agrarian middle class. Not only did they own far more land than the average peasant in central or southern Mexico, but they were economically independent. Not only did they have sufficient lands and cattle to subsist on their own, but even if they had wanted to work for neighbouring haciendas the dangerous state of communications during the Apache wars would have made such an option extremely unattractive. Unlike the peasants of southern and central Mexico, whose lands were communally owned until the reform law of 1856 and who thus were not allowed to sell their land, land was a commodity in northern villages that could be freely bought and sold.

The reason that both the Yaqui Indians and many of the former military colonists in the north staged a series of uprisings against the Díaz regime was not that they were opposed to a 'modern' capitalist economy but that they resented the fact that this economy was developing at their expense. The Yaqui Indians staged several bloody uprisings against the Mexican authorities when the latter attempted to confiscate large amounts of their fertile lands for the benefit of the American Richardson Company. For the military colonists in Chihuahua, who in 1891–3 rose in arms against both the state government and the Díaz regime, the land problem was closely intertwined with a tradition of municipal autonomy. The municipal authorities, freely elected by them, had been their main instruments in warding off all kinds of outside attacks both on their lands and on their social and economic status. In 1891 a new law was drafted by the state government which allowed the *jefe políticos* to name the mayors of larger towns. Many of the villages in Chihuahua rose to arms to prevent the authorities from applying the law. These villagers had one thing in common with the Yaquis: an uncommon fighting ability, nurtured through more than one-and-a-half centuries of fighting the Apaches, and the possession of arms. There was one significant difference, however, between the two groups. The Yaquis in Sonora stood alone, isolated by ethnic and social differences from the rest of the population of the state. The military colonists, on the other hand, had powerful though secret allies: some of the largest landowners in the state, former *caudillos* such as Luis Terrazas, attempted to utilize these peasants to exert pressure on the government.

These differences induced the Díaz government to apply very different tactics in the two cases. After years of unsuccessful attempts to convince the Yaquis to accept the loss of most of their lands or to subdue them by increasing intensive military campaigns, the government resorted to new and unprecedented methods of repression. Between 1903 and 1907 it launched a full-scale campaign against the Yaqui Indians and deported a mass of them, whether they resisted the government or not, to the henequén plantations of Yucatán. This tactic not only decimated the Yaquis, it was profitable as well. Colonel Francisco B. Cruz who in the course of three years deported 15,700 Yaquis to Yucatán received 65 pesos per head (man, woman or child) from the hacendados; 10 pesos was paid to him personally and 55 to the war ministry.

The government, however, showed itself far more inclined to carry out a policy of compromise with the rebellious military colonists in Chihuahua, although the compromises were arranged with their elite manipulators rather than with the peasants themselves. As a result of a series of rural uprisings in Chihuahua backed by Terrazas from 1891 to 1893, the latter's rival, Lauro Carrillo, was removed from the governorship of Chihuahua and a man far closer to Terrazas assumed control of the state government. The peasants themselves, except for being granted amnesty, were given far smaller concessions – a slowing down of the land expropriations and the maintenance of some elements of municipal autonomy. In most cases this strategy was successful, but in one case, the most famous of all, it was not. This concerned the small and obscure village of Tomochi in the mountain fastness of western Chihuahua. The Tomochi rebellion of November 1891 was at first no different from that of dozens of other villages in the north. It began as a revolt against the newly installed mayor, a nephew of the district *jefe político*, who grazed his sheep on the villagers' pastures and forced them to work at reduced wages on his own land or on the estates of the finance minister, José Yves Limantour, which were located near the village. When some of Tomochi's inhabitants protested against these exactions the mayor subjected them to the *leva*, the much-feared recruitment into the army. Tomochi's inhabitants protested against these exactions the mayor messianic visions. The leaders of the village, Cruz and Manuel Chávez, were adherents of the cult of the young sixteen-year-old girl, Teresita, the Saint of Cabora. The inhabitants of Tomochi felt that with God on their side they would not have to fear a head-on collision with government troops. After the 80 or so men of the village had twice defeated more than 500 soldiers sent to fight them, a concentrated federal attack by 1,200 troops finally reduced the village to rubble. The leader of the uprising, Cruz Chávez, together with all remaining male inhabitants of Tomochi, were shot. For its part the government had suffered nearly 500 casualties. In all of Chihuahua popular legends soon sprang up about the Tomochi uprising.

In view of the odds on both sides it was a victory that had far more the hallmark of a defeat. The government was forced to carry out a tacit retreat from previous policies by slowing down still further, for a time at least, both the pace of land expropriations and its attacks on village autonomy. As a result, peasant uprisings in Chihuahua began to subside. By the end of the nineteenth century the Díaz government felt that it had the situation in the north well in hand. Except in the Yaqui region, the level of violence subsided and the *caudillos* seemed to have given their unreserved support to the government. Nevertheless, this was only a respite. In the early twentieth century, the conflicts between the modern and the traditional sector flared up once again, this time complicated by new and profound tensions arising within the modern sector itself. Rebellious elements from both groups would in the final account bring down the Díaz regime and overrun all of Mexico in the years between 1910 and 1920.

The expropriation of the peasantry in central and southern Mexico

Even in the Juárez era serious inroads had been made into the lands of the communal villages. But during the Díaz era what had once been mere encroachments turned into a veritable onslaught. When Mexico gained its independence from Spain in the early nineteenth century, it is estimated that approximately 40 per cent of all land suited for agriculture in the central and southern parts of the country belonged to communal villages. When Díaz fell in 1911, only 5 per cent remained in their hands. Over 90 per cent of Mexico's peasants became landless. While there exist no exact yearly statistics on this process, it is generally thought that the wave of expropriations reached a high point under Díaz.

There were more incentives for this kind of expropriation than ever before. As new foreign and domestic markets emerged for the products of Mexican agriculture, the hacendados sought to augment their landholdings in order to maximize output. Some of the most notable cases in which massive increases in market production were coupled with the economic destruction of village communities were caused by the sugar plantations of Morelos and the henequén haciendas of Yucatán.

The emergence of new markets, however, did not constitute the only incentive for land expropriation. Speculation was an equally potent motive. Once a railway was being built, or even if such a line was only in a planning stage, land values along it would soar and speculators of all shapes would pounce upon the land. Acquiring new holdings without having to pay for them was also one way of increasing production without carrying out large-scale investments. For many hacendados this might have been the easiest way to maximize production without any substantial costs.

A more controversial hypothesis is that the hacendados destroyed the villages in order to undermine their economic independence and thus force the inhabitants to work hacienda lands. While this factor did motivate some land expropriation, its importance has been exaggerated.

Only three families of Tarascan Indians of the village of Naranja whose lands had been expropriated from the community by the hacienda of Cantabria worked on that estate. All the others were employed by other haciendas which had no connection with the expropriation. There is strong evidence to indicate that most estates could find sufficient labourers without having to destroy the economic base of surrounding villages. One of the reasons for this increasing availability of labour was the demographic increase of the population of the free villages, which had made it imperative for an increasing number of peasants to find supplementary work on haciendas. There is also some evidence to indicate that when an hacienda expropriated a neighbouring village, the bitterness and resentment this caused among the peasants was so great that most of them worked on other estates rather than the one that had destroyed their community.

Not only were the incentives for expropriating the lands of village communities greater than ever before, but during the Díaz period they found new legal underpinnings. To the Ley Lerdo (see above), which constituted the legal basis for such actions during the Restored Republic, new laws had been added during the administration of Manuel González which allowed private companies to survey public lands, and to keep one-third of what they found for themselves. More important than these new legal underpinnings was the fact that only during the Porfirian era was the Mexican government strong enough to enforce a mass attack on the village communities. The newly built railways gave both the army and the newly strengthened Rurales greater possibilities than ever before of crushing peasant resistance.

There are no exact statistics to establish with any degree of certainty when the process of land expropriation took place and when it reached a high point. Nor is there sufficient explanation for the frequent and at times great disparity in regional developments. Why were so many Indian villages expropriated in Yucatán while in Oaxaca, with perhaps the highest percentage of Indians in Mexico, the villages managed to retain most of their lands and many of their traditional rights? Was this due to the fact that export production was far more important in Yucatán than in Oaxaca? What role did other factors, such as the greater cohesion of communities in Oaxaca, the traditional weakness of the hacienda in that state, the existence of an Indian middle class, and Díaz's personal links to Oaxaca, play? These are questions for which no definite answer exists as yet.

50 *Mexico*

An even more complex problem is who the beneficiaries of these expropriations were. For a long time, too simple a picture of the results of expropriations has been drawn; it was assumed that as a result of Porfirian changes, only two social classes, in the final account, peopled the countryside: an increasingly wealthy group of hacendados and an impoverished group of landless peons.

In reality, however, a growing agrarian middle class, whose existence is not always easy to document, seems to have played an ever-increasing role in the social processes taking place in the countryside. In many villages, groups of wealthy peasants, village usurers and local strong men who were not hacendados profited as much as the latter and at times more from the expropriations of peasant lands. Many of them emerged long before the Porfirian period. The increase of Mexico's population had led to strong differentiations within the villages, and the richer inhabitants became partners of both the landlords and the Porfirian authorities in the expropriation of village lands. Some of them acquired middle-sized properties (*ranchos*), and thus are included in the census data in 1895 and 1900, in which 32,000 '*ranchos*' are counted (not all *ranchos* were independent units as some constituted parts of haciendas). Others, however, invested their wealth in ways which are more difficult to document statistically. Some became wealthy tenants, others rented out cattle to sharecroppers and poorer tenants. The 1900 census names about 400,000 *agricultores*, and while the basis for that category is not well established, it probably embraced most of this agricultural middle class which constituted a substantial segment of the rural population in Mexico's countryside. Their relationships to the villagers were extremely varied. Some of them became usurers, agents of the state or of the hacendados, while others became popular leaders. Many changed in time from one category into the other.

In the village of Anenecuilco in the state of Morelos, the villagers in the late summer of 1909 elected a relatively well-to-do peasant, Emiliano Zapata, to represent them in their attempts to regain the lands which the neighbouring Hacienda del Hospital had taken from them. Hundreds of miles to the north in the frontier village of Cuchillo Parado the villagers also elected a leader, Ezequiel Montes, to help them ward off the attempt of one of Chihuahua's wealthiest hacendados, Muñoz, to seize their land. Both Zapata and Montes enjoyed a higher social status than most other villagers. Zapata came from a well-known family and was relatively well off since he owned land, horses and mules. Ezequiel Montes had no such family credentials. In the 1880s he came to Cuchillo Parado as a landless labourer, bringing with him nothing but his guitar, as a village chronicler disrespectfully wrote. But Montes obviously had more gifts than the ability to sing. He could speak very well, could read and write, knew the surrounding world, and soon gained the confidence of the villagers. In 1903 they elected him to the leadership of the Junta de Vecinos of Cuchillo Parado which was set up to fight Muñoz. Montes was at first far more successful than Zapata. While the Hacienda del Hospital retained the lands it had seized, Muñoz abandoned his attack on Cuchillo Parado.

The two leaders utilized the power and prestige they had acquired by leading their villages' attempts to secure their rights in extremely divergent ways. Zapata led the men of Anenecuilco and finally of all of Morelos into the Mexican Revolution. Montes was appointed mayor of Cuchillo Parado by the state authorities, became the village usurer and was ultimately expelled from the village on the day the Revolution broke out.

It is possible that the rise of this agrarian middle class provides one of the best explanations, though not the only one, for a fact that has puzzled historians for a long time: the relative lack of resistance of peasants in central and southern Mexico to the widespread expropriation of their land. There is little doubt that the weakening of peasant resistance in the 1880s and 1890s as compared to the period between 1876 and 1880 was also linked to the increasing power of the state, the strengthening of the army and its increased mobility with the railways, and the creation of new police units. Repression alone, however, does not offer a sufficient explanation. In addition to the increasing support that the government gained among the emerging middle class, two other phenomena probably contributed to diffusing peasant resistance. One was the dismantling of their main organs of resistance, the village communal administration. With the end of village autonomy, the peasants no longer could count on the traditional organization which had led them in former times in resisting encroachments by landowners or by the state. Another factor, perhaps even more important, was the transformation of the traditional patron–client relationship, which for a long time had dominated life in the Mexican countryside. During the colonial period the patron was the Spanish state, which frequently tried to protect the peasants from the encroachments of landowners in order to prevent the latter from becoming too powerful. Early in the nineteenth century, regional *caudillos*, dependent on peasant support to wage their frequent civil wars with rivals in other regions, had assumed this function. When some hacendados in the state of Guerrero attempted to expropriate lands belonging to free villages, the peasants called on Juan Alvarez, the wealthiest hacendado and most powerful liberal *caudillo* of the region, for redress. Alvarez could and did help. In return thousands of peasants joined his army in 1855 when he overthrew the conservative government of Santa Anna. Alvarez was not unique. Other *caudillos*, such as Conservative Manuel Lozada in Tepic, also heeded calls for help from peasants. Many traditional protectors were absorbed by the Porfirian state and later turned against their former protégés. Having lost their traditional patrons many peasants felt leaderless and abandoned. Porfirio Díaz's personal prestige as well as some limited steps to help a few villages may also have prevented peasant resistance from emerging. There are indications that Díaz at times attempted to assume the traditional mantle of the Spanish colonial state as protector and patron of Indian villages. Repeatedly Díaz wrote to governors and local officials asking them to respect Indians' property rights when the latter could show titles to them, or even to respect *de facto* property rights of Indians. Thus, in 1897 villagers of Tamazunchale asked him for help in preventing expropriation of their land. Díaz sent them to search in the National Archives for the title to their land, and then wrote to the governor of the state of San Luis Potosí:

With reference to the Indians of San Francisco, Matlapa and the rest, there can be no doubt that they are the owners by viceregal grants in long ago times, even though their titles suffer somewhat from defects and irregularities; but even supposing that their titles were irregular or void, they have been considered the owners of the lands which now an outsider is trying to buy because the Indians lack the means to pay for them. The practical result would be an expropriation and the substitution of those villages of Indians by outsiders who would come to inhabit the places they left, but probably after many bloody scenes which the Indians would consider their just vengeance, fanatically convinced with the certain or erroneous consciousness of their rights.[5]

These principles nevertheless conflicted with other more profound tenets of the Porfirian administration: the desire to attract foreign capital and the wish to conciliate the hacendados. Díaz was either unwilling or unable to implement these policies of restraint beyond intervening in a

---

[5] Quoted in Donald Fithian Stevens, 'Agrarian policy and instability in Porfirian Mexico', *The Americas*, 39 (October 1982), 161.

few cases. Until the last years of his regime Díaz took no steps which could have effectively restrained the loss of land or autonomy of the villagers.

In 1910 Díaz took the one measure on a national scale which, had it been taken years before, might have effectively restricted village expropriations. He decreed that no more sales of public lands should take place. By then some of the richest of these lands had already been adjudicated and sold and the measure was of little consequence. It was only in the twentieth century, when for reasons that are described below new patrons were to emerge who called on the peasants to revolt, that they would respond and finally constitute a decisive force in the revolutionary storm that erupted in Mexico after 1910.

The evolution of peonage into slavery or freedom

On many haciendas in central and southern Mexico the status of labourers, generally known as peons, was subject to changes no less drastic than those in the free villages which had been expropriated. As the production of cash crops became more and more profitable, many hacendados began to cut down on tenancy arrangements, preferring instead to employ labourers who tilled the land of the estates for the owners. Tenancy was by no means abolished, but the tenants were more and more pushed on to marginal lands where they were far more subject than ever before to fluctuations of weather. In other cases, sharecropping arrangements even more unfavourable to the peasants replaced existing tenancy conditions. The way the haciendas accomplished this is most clearly illustrated by the evolution of sharecropping patterns on a hacienda near Celaya in the state of Guanajuato. Up to the latter part of the nineteenth century there had been two types of sharecroppers on this hacienda: the *medieros al rajar* and the *medieros al quinto*. The *medieros al rajar* furnished their own agricultural implements and oxen and received 50 per cent of the harvest. The *medieros al quinto* borrowed farm machinery and animals from the hacienda and in return had to pay the usual 50 per cent of their crops, plus one-fifth of the remaining harvest as payment for the use of machinery and animals. This left them with at most 40 per cent of the harvest. By the end of the nineteenth century this hacienda began to cut down on the number of *medieros al rajar* simply by not allowing the sharecroppers to use hacienda grazing lands to tend their cattle. By the beginning of the twentieth century only a few privileged retainers still worked their lands on a half-share basis. All others had become *medieros al quinto*.

A further differentiation took place in the type of labourer that the hacendados employed. In both the southern and northern peripheries of the country, far more sparsely settled than central Mexico, the hacendados frequently faced drastic labour shortages. They reacted to them in very different ways. While in the north peonage tended to disappear, in the southern parts of the country, especially in the henequén plantations of Yucatán, the tobacco-producing Valle Nacional in Oaxaca and the coffee plantations in Chiapas, labourers were bound to the estates by conditions of debt peonage frequently akin to slavery. They were not allowed to leave their estates until their debts had been repaid, and the hacendado made sure by fraud, by overcharging in the company store, and by forcing peasants to accept credits that they frequently did not need that these debts could not be repaid. In Yucatán debt peonage became institutionalized to a far greater degree than in any other part of Mexico. In 1901 an observer reported that:

the legal means to bind *criados* to hacienda consists in an advance payment which in this state means that a worker who leaves can be returned by force by the police to the hacienda. These advance payments are generally made when a young man born on the hacienda reaches the age of 18 or 20 and marries. His master then gives him a hundred to a hundred and fifty, sometimes two hundred pesos, to set up a household and both parties silently agree that this sum as well as other sums which might be advanced at a later date in case of accident or illnesses would never be repaid. They are the price for which the young Yucateco sells his freedom.[6]

In cases where such institutionalization was fragile, brute force was applied.

In 1914 Woodrow Wilson's special representative in Mexico, John Lind, together with the commander of the American fleet in Veracruz, Admiral Fletcher, was invited to visit a Veracruz sugar plantation owned by an American, Sloane Emery, which depended entirely on contract workers. 'They were contract laborers', John Lind later reported:

who were virtually prisoners and had been sent there by the government. Admiral Fletcher and I saw this remarkable situation in the twentieth century of men being scattered through the corn fields in little groups of eight or ten accompanied by a driver, a cacique, an Indian from the coast, a great big burly fellow, with a couple of revolvers strapped to a belt, and a black snake that

6 Karl Kaerger, 'Landwirtschaft und Kolonisation', in *Spanisches Südamerika* (2 vols., Leipzig, 1901–2), II, 637.

would measure eight or ten feet, right after the group that were digging, and then at the farther end of the road a man with a sawed-off shotgun. These men were put out in the morning, were worked under these overseers in that manner, and locked up at night in a large shed to all intents and purposes. Both Admiral Fletcher and I marveled that such conditions could exist, but they did exist.[7]

The isolation of many southern regions, the lack of an industry which would have competed with the estate owners for scarce labourers, the strengthening of both hacienda police forces and the organs of the state made it extremely difficult for the peons to circumvent their owners. These repressive measures were strengthened by a process of divide and rule: rebellious Yaquis from the state of Sonora, vagrants from central Mexico, Chinese and Korean coolies were all brought into the southern regions where the hacendados made use of their antagonisms towards each other and towards the native Maya population of the region to prevent any kind of resistance from emerging. On the whole, the land owners were successful in the economic as well as the social and political fields. Production soared, resistance was extremely limited, and the ensuing stability attracted new capital and investment.

The contradictory tendencies in the countryside – more economic incentives and freedom, versus repression and semi-enslavement – that manifested themselves in the northern and southern peripheries of the country, also appeared in central Mexico. The reason for this was that factors producing labour shortage and others leading to a labour surplus affected central Mexico at the same time, though obviously not always in the same regions. The expropriation of village lands as well as the demographic increase created large segments of unemployed labourers, which in many regions were more than sufficient to meet the needs of the haciendas. In such cases some hacendados discovered the advantages of free over servile labour.

In 1906 Manuel Brassetti, the administrator of the hacienda of Tochatlaco, reported that

on this estate the predominant labour system was based on peons paid by the year (this meant that they received a small advance and purchased all their needs on credit from the *tienda de raya*, settling accounts once a year). They had all contracted large debts with the estate, were lazy, drunk and on the whole bad and rebellious workers; after carefully studying the problem I decided to forgo the 3,000 pesos they owed me and for two years now they are paid by the week

[7] United States Senate Documents, Foreign Relations Committee, Investigation of Mexican Affairs, Report and Hearings 66th Congress, 2nd Session, Senate Document No. 285 (2 vols., Washington, 1920), II, 2326.

. . . When they were in debt they did not work on the Saturday before Holy Week, they became drunk all of Holy Week and it was extremely difficult to get them to work on Easter Tuesday. Since they are paid by the week they work Holy Monday and Tuesday and they are at work on Easter Monday.[8]

According to Manuel Brassetti, the peons were now far happier than before, telling indebted peons on other estates 'you are in bondage, we are free'. In other parts of central Mexico, however, the competition of newly created industries, railway construction, and hacendados in need of more labourers to till their cash crops produced the reverse effect and brought about a shortage of labourers. These real or, at times, perceived shortages led many hacendados to maintain conditions of debt peonage even when they were sometimes economically counterproductive and probably not necessary.

The emergence of a national ruling class

At the other end of the social scale there was also a significant transformation taking place during the Díaz period: the creation of what might be called a national ruling class. Except for the church, which was always national in character, the Mexican economic elite in the early part of the nineteenth century had been essentially local or regional. Some of its members were landowners whose wealth was generally concentrated in one or two states, while those among the elite who lived in Mexico City were essentially merchants and *agiotistas*, speculators whose main income came from granting loans to the government and speculating in government finances. There were few industrialists, none of whom controlled major industries, while most miners and merchants were foreigners.

Some members of the emerging national ruling class of the Porfiriato were regional landowners, but regional landowners who had begun to extend their activities into other branches of the economy and into other regions of the country. The Terrazas–Creel group, probably the wealthiest and most powerful family clan in Porfirian Mexico, is the most notable example. Luis Terrazas was one of the most prominent hacendados in the state of Chihuahua and his son-in-law, Enrique Creel, was a well-to-do landowner and middle-sized financier there. By the turn of the century the two men had combined their activities and

---

[8] Biblioteca del Boletín de La Sociedad Agrícola Mexicana; Segundo Congreso Agrícola de Tulancingo, Mexico, 1906, 144–5.

tremendously expanded their scale of operations. They owned food-processing plants throughout Chihuahua, and controlled Chihuahua's largest bank. They also owned a bank in the newly developed Laguna region of Coahuila. Creel sat on the Board of Directors of two of Mexico City's largest banks, the Banco de Londres y México and Banco Nacional de México. The two men acted as intermediaries for numerous foreign corporations wishing to do business in Mexico, and Creel was chairman of the board of one of the largest and most powerful of these, the Mexican Eagle Oil Company, owned by Sir Weetman Pearson (later Lord Cowdray). Similarly, finance minister José Yves Limantour, the son of a prosperous French merchant, branched out into enterprises in many different states. He acquired large tracts of land in Chihuahua, and, like Creel and Terrazas, sat on the boards of many of the large foreign and Mexican companies doing business in the country.

The wealth of Mexico's new ruling class, other than its land, was above all due to its role as intermediaries for foreign companies. Any large company wishing to do business in Mexico soon learned that retaining these men as lawyers or, better yet, as members of its board of directors was the best way of cutting red tape and surmounting any other kind of economic or political obstacle to their penetration of the Mexican economy. The most powerful, and articulate, segment of this new ruling class was the group of men known as the *científicos*, the group of financiers, technocrats and intellectuals brought together by Manuel Romero Rubio, Díaz's minister of the interior (and his father-in-law) and after the death of Romero Rubio in 1895 led by the finance minister Limantour (see above).

One of the most characteristic traits of the Mexican ruling class was their pro-European orientation. This was very lucidly defined by the German minister in Mexico when he wrote:

In their view, the political future of the country depends entirely on the development of the economy. To realize this, however, the country needs help from abroad, including the United States. Mexico is thus increasingly destined to become an area of activity for capitalist firms from all countries. The cosmopolitans, however, paradoxical as this may sound, see precisely in economic dependency the guarantee of political independence, in so far as they assume that the large European interests that have investments here constitute a counter-weight to American annexationist appetites and that they will pave the way for the complete internationalization and neutralization of Mexico. Behind the scenes, but at the head of the cosmopolitan group, stands the finance minister, Señor Limantour. His allies are *haute finance*, as well as the top-level civil servants with interests in the domestic and foreign companies, senators and deputies, and, finally, the local representatives of European capital invested in Mexico.[9]

These views cannot simply be explained by the fact that the *científicos* represented European interests, while other members of Mexico's oligarchy represented the Americans. The *científicos* in fact were intermediaries for both European and American companies. The reason that they nevertheless preferred the Europeans to the Americans was due precisely to the fact that they had become a national ruling class, whose viewpoints transcended regional limits and assumed national proportions. European support, they felt, was crucial to the maintenance of Mexico's independence. On the other hand, there is little doubt that their intermediary function for European interests was quite different from the role they played with respect to the Americans. Because of their relative weakness in Mexico, the Europeans were far more willing than the Americans to make real concessions to their Mexican intermediaries. It is significant, for instance, that the largest British oil company in Mexico, the Mexican Eagle, took on members of Mexico's elite as partners, though only in a junior capacity. The largest US oil companies in Mexico, Doheny's Mexican Petroleum Company and the Waters Pierce Oil Company, the second of which had links to Standard Oil, never entered into this kind of partnership with members of Mexico's oligarchy.

The European sympathies of Mexico's ruling class were reinforced by an alliance with another group of European origin, which until the late nineteenth century had rarely entered into partnership arrangements with Mexicans. These were the merchants of European origin, essentially French, and to a lesser degree German, who had begun to set up industries in Mexico as imports from Europe became too expensive because of the fall in the price of silver. They requested and obtained substantial capital investment from Mexico's elite, and above all the *científicos*, in their plants.

As a result of these manifold activities, the attitude of the new ruling class seemed schizophrenic to many observers. On some issues they would be completely subservient to foreign interests, while on others they would manifest unexpected surges of nationalism. This national ruling class and the predominant role of the *científicos* within it led to

[9] German Foreign Office papers, Archives of the German Foreign Office in Bonn, Mexico, vol. 17, Wangenheim to Bülow, 7 January 1907.

strong divisions among Mexico's elite. Regional elites frequently opposed their pre-eminence and were supported in their attitude by the one other group which considered itself to be 'national' in character, the army. It was certainly no coincidence that Bernardo Reyes, who led upper-class opposition to the *científicos*, was an army general and one of the most powerful military men in Mexico.

On the whole the changes and transformations that the Díaz regime wrought in Mexico's upper class may have increased the tensions and conflicts among them. Until the turn of the century, however, the Díaz regime succeeded in preventing any of these groups from attempting to further their interests by armed revolt. His regime granted them so many opportunities for accumulating wealth that they simply had too much to lose to wish for an armed uprising.

The emergence of an industrial proletariat

Porfirian modernization greatly increased the size of Mexico's working class, altered its status and its living conditions and profoundly transformed its consciousness. Rapid economic growth led to an increase in the number of industrial workers. Between 1895 and 1900 their number grew from 692,697 to 803,294 (excluding those employed in transportation and the public sector). They were mainly concentrated in the capital and in the states of Mexico, Puebla, Jalisco, Guanajuato and Veracruz and the northern border states.

The conditions under which they lived varied greatly. In the oil region the companies provided housing, built some schools and even established a rudimentary medical service. In return they asked unquestioning obedience. The mayors of the oil company towns were in the pockets of the companies, who also established and controlled the police forces. Unions and strikes were prohibited. In textile factories conditions could be much harsher. In the textile mill of Santa Teresa y Contreras in the capital the workers were not paid in cash but in tokens redeemable only at the company store. Workers complained bitterly that a surcharge of 18 per cent was imposed on all products sold at that store. At the Hercules Textile factory in Querétaro, workers voiced similar complaints, but complained above all about the arbitrary system of punishment established by the company: anyone arriving even a minute later than 5 a.m. when work started could be immediately dismissed. There were no provisions for medical, accident or disability insurance.

Nevertheless until the turn of the century strikes and other protest movements by industrial workers were rare. Not only were living standards rising but, difficult as conditions were, they were still better than those on the haciendas from which so many workers came, or in villages where so many former peasants had lost their lands. In addition the Díaz regime was actively attempting to control industrial workers by encouraging labour organizations like the Congreso Obrero and the Convención Radical which maintained close links with the government. These organizations disseminated propaganda in favour of Díaz and against radical ideologies. They edited two newspapers which preached that 'the respect of a people for the police is the thermometer which marks its civilization'.[10] In 1891 the Congreso Obrero prevented the workers from observing the May Day celebration.

At the same time, these organizations attempted to mediate in some disputes between workers and industrialists and helped to set up mutualist societies. The latter were self-help organizations of workers, exclusively financed by worker contributions which provided minimum benefits in cases of accidents, disability or death.

By the end of the nineteenth century the attitudes of Mexico's emerging working class towards the state as well as towards their employers gradually began to change. One element that greatly shaped and influenced their way of thinking was increasing contact with foreigners. Most factories, especially the large ones, were foreign-owned and even in Mexican-owned enterprises foreigners were frequently taken on as managers. A sense of nationalism gradually developed among Mexican workers which became even stronger when they were confronted with foreign workers in the same enterprises earning several times their own salaries. This was especially the case on the railways where American employees were granted preferential status both in access to jobs and in terms of the salary they earned.

There was yet another way in which Mexican workers came into contact with foreigners. This was through migration to the United States. Thousands of Mexican labourers, especially from northern states, began crossing the border either permanently or for long periods to work in American mines and industries as well as on ranches. The discrimination to which they were frequently subjected provoked strong feelings of nationalism in many of them. In others, however, this

---

[10] David Walker, 'Porfirian labor politics: working class organizations in Mexico City and Porfirio Díaz, 1876–1902', *The Americas* 37 (January 1981), 268, 272.

nationalism was linked to a burgeoning class consciousness as they came into contact with American trade unions, especially with the radical Industrial Workers of the World (IWW).

One of the great differences between the Mexican industrial working class and their counterparts in more developed industrialized countries was the relative weakness of the privileged upper segment of skilled workers. This was on the one hand due to the predominance of extractive and light industries in Mexico which required a lesser number of skilled workers than other industries, but it was also due to the large number of foreigners among the skilled workers.

The taming of the middle class

One of the Porfirio Díaz's greatest successes was his regime's ability to tame Mexico's traditionally rebellious and mutinous middle classes, comprising government bureaucrats, merchants, intellectuals, white-collar employees, artisans and the like. Until the turn of the century this was accomplished with a limited degree of violence and repression.

After returning to office in 1884 Díaz gradually suppressed the rights he had allowed the middle classes to retain during his first term in office. Autonomous political parties all but disappeared, parliamentary elections scarcely existed, and Congress became practically powerless. The press, once the domain of liberal intellectuals, was more and more government controlled. Large segments of the middle classes accepted these restrictions on their power and freedom without manifesting any substantial resistance to the regime. The Porfiriato offered unprecedented opportunities of advancement in economic terms. In many states, where Díaz replaced *caudillos* whom he did not trust by officials loyal to his regime, new opportunities for sharing local and regional power arose for many of the 'outs' among the middle classes.

Many members of Mexico's middle classes were consciously willing to pay a price for Porfirian peace and economic development. Others were simply co-opted by the regime. Those who did not enter government service profited from the general upsurge of the economy. Nevertheless, the number of opponents of the regime gradually began to increase. In contrast to the beneficiaries of the Díaz regime, substantial groups among the middle classes had either not profited or begun to suffer economic losses by the turn of the century.

The greatest losers were muleteers and local transporters who were displaced by the newly constructed railways, and artisans who could not compete with the newly emerging textile industry. The main middle-class opponents of the regime were dissatisfied intellectuals. Some were independent newspapermen such as Filomeno Mata in Mexico City or Silvestre Terrazas in Chihuahua. Even mild criticism of the regime led to newspaper closings and the jailing of dissident editors (Filomeno Mata was jailed 34 times).

Teachers, whose number rose from 12,748 in 1895 to 21,017 in 1910, were especially vocal in their opposition to the regime. While the increase in their number attests to some development of education in Mexico in the Díaz era, a large number of teachers believed that the government was doing far too little to educate the people. The percentage of illiterates scarcely decreased during the Porfiriato in spite of the fact that new schools were built, especially in the large cities. Higher education remained underdeveloped and the relative number of students in the country scarcely increased. The educational politics of the Porfiriato and the underpaid status of many teachers do not constitute the sole explanation for their opposition to the regime, however; the close contact many teachers maintained with the rural population, their strong sense of nationalism and their resentment at the preference given to foreign cultures were no less important.

While the opposition of intellectuals to a dictatorship was an almost natural phenomenon, the same cannot be said of the massive opposition of merchants to the Díaz regime. Merchants do not generally constitute a radical segment of society. Nevertheless in assessing the causes of the Mexican Revolution of 1910, Pablo Martínez del Río, scion of one of the Porfiriato's leading families, attributed the revolutionary upheavals largely to dissatisfied merchants. The roots of this dissatisfaction lay in the fact that in many towns Mexican merchants either had to compete with foreigners or with clients of the oligarchy who secured concessions from foreign companies for running company stores. Small entrepreneurs who attempted to set up factories or small businesses depended on credit from banks which either belonged to foreigners or to members of the oligarchy. All other things being equal these banks gave preferential treatment to well-connected debtors.

THE CRISIS OF THE PORFIRIATO, 1900–10

In spite of the profound social and economic changes that Díaz brought about and the antagonisms that they engendered, the Mexican president was astonishingly successful until the turn of the century in preventing significant forces of opposition to his regime from emerging. Uprisings had been mainly limited to the periphery of the country and they affected either Indian tribes or only a limited number of villages. Industrial labourers, on the whole, tended to be docile and no significant strikes took place. No opposition political groups on a national scale or even on a regional scale emerged. As a result, not only members of Mexico's elite but foreign statesmen as well heaped sycophantic praise on Díaz. In the short span of ten years, from 1900 to 1910, this situation changed dramatically. Regional opposition movements developed. Strikes affecting thousands of workers took place. Three national opposition movements emerged, two of which called for the violent overthrow of the regime.

The Pax Porfiriana had been based on the fact that Díaz had either won over or neutralized groups and classes which had traditionally led revolutionary and armed movements in Mexico: the army, the upper class, and the middle class. Without them, those lower-class rebellions which did break out in spite of the repressive machinery of the Díaz state were easily crushed and never transcended the local level. The profound change in the situation in the first decade of the twentieth century occurred when the Díaz regime proved less and less capable of maintaining this upper- and middle-class consensus. A major split within these two classes took place at a time of increasing lower-class discontent as well as US dissatisfaction with the regime. When members of all these different groups and classes joined forces, the Mexican Revolution broke out and the Díaz regime fell.

There was no single cause for this dramatic turn of events. An economic depression of unprecedented proportions, political changes at both the regional and national level, increasing and more visible government repression, a struggle over the succession of the ageing president, a new surge of nationalism, and Mexico's emergence as a centre of European–American rivalry were all factors which helped to destroy first the Pax Porfiriana and then the regime.

Between 1900 and 1910 the flow of foreign investments into Mexico assumed torrential proportions. It amounted to nearly three billion dollars, three times as much as in the first twenty-four years of Porfirian rule. This new wave of investments led to a sharp rise in prices, which was further accentuated by the decision of the Mexican government to give up silver and adopt the gold standard. The result of these developments was a sharp fall in real wages in many parts of Mexico. This tendency was accentuated when the boom gave way to one of the greatest economic crises that Porfirian Mexico had ever faced. In 1907–8, a cyclical downturn in the United States extended into Mexico, leading to massive lay-offs and reductions in wages. Domestic unemployment was reinforced by the return of thousands of labourers who had migrated to the United States and who had been the first to be dismissed when the recession affected the economy of Mexico's northern neighbour. The economic downturn was compounded by a simultaneously occurring agricultural crisis. Bad harvests, partly due to drought and partly to floods, decimated Mexico's food production and led to sharp price increases at a time when not only real wages but even nominal wages in industry were being reduced.

At this point the full consequences of the Porfirian road to modernization made themselves felt. The Porfirian regime was neither willing nor able to grant relief to important segments of the upper classes, most of the middle classes and the poorest segments of society. It did not provide any tax relief to middle-sized enterprises profoundly affected by the crisis. On the contrary, with full government approval the oligarchy attempted to shift the burden of the crisis not only on to the shoulders of the poorest segments of society but also to the middle classes and to those members of the upper classes who were not closely linked to the *científicos*. During the boom period both foreign entrepreneurs and members of Mexico's new national ruling class were granted significant tax exemptions. When government revenue began to drop sharply as a result of decreased economic activity, the *científicos* attempted to increase taxes paid by Mexico's middle classes. At the same time banks which both foreigners and the oligarchy controlled not only reduced the amount of credit they granted and increased the price of loans, they also began to collect outstanding debts at an accelerating pace.

The government made no attempt to relieve the credit squeeze in any way. While Díaz's administration lowered some tariffs in order to encourage the importation of basic foodstuffs, it did nothing more. The result was ruin or at least great economic difficulties for many of Mexico's middle-class entrepreneurs and a catastrophic reduction in living standards of large segments of the country's population. This policy was partly due to the *laissez-faire* ideology of the Porfirian oligarchy, but even if the Díaz administration had been willing to do more to relieve the effects of the crisis, its capacity to do so was extremely limited. Government revenues at all levels – federal, state, and municipal – accounted for only 8 per cent of the gross national product.[11] This economic crisis, severe as it was, was not the only immediate cause which provoked Mexico's social explosion in the years 1910–20. The internal contradictions that finally produced the Mexican Revolution were deeper and far more complex than the dislocation the crisis of 1907 produced, although this crisis accentuated the already existing contradictions within Mexican society.

One important factor that contributed to the destabilization of the Díaz regime in its last years was the emergence of a strong working-class opposition. Its main manifestations were strikes, unprecedented in their scope and in the official repression they brought forth, and the emergence of a national opposition political party with strong anarcho-syndicalist leanings. The roots of this working-class opposition were multiple. A new generation of workers had emerged who were not former peasants and who did not compare their present situation with even worse conditions on haciendas or villages. An increasing number of workers had at one time or another gone north of the border to work in the United States. There they had been influenced both by the example of higher living standards and union rights and by the anarcho-syndicalist ideology of the IWW. Nationalism played an increasing role in workers' consciousness as they were pitted not only against foreign investors and managers but foreign workers as well.

The most immediate cause of worker dissatisfaction was the sharp decline in living standards between 1900 and 1910. Even in the boom period up to 1907 real wages were eroded by inflation. Between 1907 and 1910 conditions deteriorated drastically, above all in northern Mexico. In Chihuahua the German consul estimated in 1909 that prices of essential foods and products had risen by 80 per cent while nominal wages had fallen by 20 per cent. The result was a catastrophic drop in real wages for those who still had work. For thousands of others who had been laid off in the course of the recession, conditions were obviously even worse. Interestingly enough, however, the most important social movements of Mexican workers which occurred between 1900 and 1910 did not take place during the economic downturn but during the preceding boom. Of the three major labour conflicts that received national attention in those

---

[11] John Coatsworth, 'The state and the external sector in Mexico 1800–1900' (unpublished essay). Estimates of GDP based on Leopoldo Solís, 'La evolución económica de México a partir de la Revolución de 1910', *Demografía y Economía*, 3/1 (1969), 4.

years – a strike in the textile factory of Río Blanco in the state of Veracruz in June 1906; a miners' strike in Cananea in the state of Sonora in January 1907; and a railway workers' movement in Chihuahua in 1908 – purely economic issues were preponderant only in the Río Blanco strike. Even there labour conditions were at least as important. In the other two cases, nationalism was intrinsically linked to the demands that the workers made. The Mexican miners of Cananea resented the fact that American miners brought in from across the border were paid more than double for doing exactly the same work they did. Similar resentments were at the core of a strike staged by Mexican railway men in Chihuahua, who complained that all the best positions in Mexico's railway system were reserved for American workers and employees. In the railway strike a limited compromise was reached, but the other two strikes were suppressed with a ruthless brutality that surpassed anything that had occurred in the early years of the Díaz regime. 'Thank God I can still kill', Díaz is said to have exclaimed, and ordered the ruthless execution of dozens of textile workers in Río Blanco who had called on the Mexican president as arbitrator in their dispute with the company. By this time another blood bath, though of smaller proportions, had taken place in Cananea, where the flames of resentment were fanned by the arrival of hundreds of armed Americans from across the border to put down the miners' movement.

This kind of massive and highly visible repression had constituted the exception rather than the rule during the preceding years of the regime. Díaz preferred to make deals rather than to repress and when he did use repressive means he attempted to keep them as secret as possible. Both the scope and the unprecedented character of the massacres as well as the existence of a labour-orientated national opposition party made Río Blanco and Cananea household words for hundreds of thousands of Mexicans. It led thousands to sympathize with the first and most radical opposition movement on a national scale to emerge during the Porfiriato. This was the Partido Liberal Mexicano (PLM), founded by a number of provincial intellectuals at the beginning of the century. It called for a return to the principles of the radical factions of the liberal movement under Juárez. Increasing repression by the government contributed to a rapid swing to the left, and the party soon assumed anarcho-syndicalist traits and pronouncements. Its most outstanding leaders were two brothers, Enrique and Ricardo Flores Magón, who led their party from exile in St Louis. The newspaper they issued,

Regeneración, was banned in Mexico and had to be brought in illegally from the United States. Nevertheless, it apparently sold over 25,000 copies per issue in Mexico and played a role in inspiring the great strikes which broke out in the country.

The PLM was not only influential among industrial workers but among parts of Mexico's middle classes as well. For them the conflict with the Díaz administration was in part a class conflict and to a very large degree a generational struggle. In the eyes of many of the young, the Díaz regime was a closed dictatorial society subservient to foreign and above all US interests which many of the young felt threatened the integrity and independence of Mexico. Their opportunities for social mobility, they felt, were far smaller than those of the generation of their fathers. The older generation still filled the positions in the federal bureaucracy and Díaz gave no indication that he planned any kind of a turnover. A deeply worried French minister reported to his government in 1900:

in spite of the peace which now reigns in the country there is a real dissatisfaction . . . the basis of this dissatisfaction is a party of the young which under the disguise of adherence to principles hides a lust for power and wishes to take part in the perquisites and privileges of power. Lawyers, judges, engineers, writers and journalists constitute the majority of this party. It pretends to speak in the name of the whole of civilian society and declares that the present military regime should be replaced by a regime of parliamentarianism and free discussion.[12]

The large foreign enterprises that were entering Mexico provided no avenue of escape, no new opportunities for the young educated Mexicans who found no possibility of entering the federal or local bureaucracy. The foreigners preferred to choose middle- and upper-level managers from among their own. Their Mexican employees at higher levels tended to be either friends, family members or clients of their Mexican partners who generally were also members of the oligarchy.

The frustration of the young, educated members of Mexico's middle class did not only have economic roots. Many resented what they considered to be the Porfirian elite's blind acceptance of foreign values and foreign culture. For many, 'dollar diplomacy', the rising emigration of Americans to northern Mexico, and the increasing US investment in that region revived fears of a new US annexation. These fears were

---

[12] French Foreign Ministry Archives, Paris, CC, Mexique, Bd 17, Blondel to Delcassé, 3 December 1900.

strengthened by repeated calls in the American press for the annexation of Mexico.

The PLM was successful in inspiring or strengthening large-scale opposition to the Díaz regime. Its call for a national revolution, however, went unheeded. A series of local revolts did break out, most of them in northern Mexico, under the leadership of returning exiles who brought arms and propaganda with them. They failed not only because they were frequently unco-ordinated, but because the groups that led them were often infiltrated by government agents. A very different kind of opposition ranging all the way from dissident hacendados to militant peasants was to force Porfirio Díaz from power. Its emergence was closely linked to political and social changes which emerged at both the national level and at the regional level in the northern border states of Sonora, Coahuila and Chihuahua and in the central state of Morelos.

At the turn of the century a profound political change took place in Mexico. During the last ten years of his administration, Díaz greatly weakened one of his basic policies, the application of a strategy of divide and rule that had so greatly strengthened his regime in its first years. Until the turn of the century at both the national and regional level Díaz had set up a complex system of checks and balances that prevented any one group or clique from achieving too much power. At the national level Díaz allowed and at times encouraged the growth of cliques rivaling the *científicos*. Their most influential rivals consisted of a loose alliance of northern landowners and businessmen as well as military men whose leader, Bernardo Reyes, was one of Díaz's most powerful generals, and who for many years had been military commander and later governor of Nuevo León and from 1900 to 1904 secretary of war. At the local level traditional *caudillos* who generally held the reins of political and economic power had been replaced by men who owed their ascent to Porfirio Díaz. Some of them were officials sent in from other parts of the country with very few local roots, others were less powerful members of the local elite. They frequently had to compete with their predecessors, and there were constant conflicts between elite cliques and groups. Díaz was the great arbitrator who maintained a precarious balance between them. At the turn of the century it became increasingly clear that Díaz was either less willing or less able to apply this increasingly complex strategy with the same vigour that he had in his first years in office.

At the national level the *científicos* were pressuring Díaz to grant them increasing power, but above all they wanted the Mexican president, who was now over 70 years of age, to indicate very clearly that in case of his death a member of their group would succeed him. The increasing economic power of this group and its success in managing the economy of the country by augmenting Mexico's revenues and enhancing its credit rating abroad certainly played a major role in influencing Díaz. At least as important may have been the fact that the foreign interests who were investing more and more in Mexico wanted some kind of guarantee from the Mexican president that in case of his death the policies he had carried out would continue. In their eyes the best guarantee that Díaz could give them was an indication that the *científicos* with whom they were intimately linked would continue in power. In 1903 Díaz felt that the time had come to make a decisive gesture to reassure both the *científicos* and the foreign investors and financiers. He agreed to Ramón Corral, a member of the *científico* group from the north-western state of Sonora, becoming his vice president and thus indicated that Corral would succeed him should he die during his term of office. Corral was elected vice president in 1904. It was a major victory for the *científicos* that Díaz underlined when he removed their most powerful enemy, Bernardo Reyes, from his post as secretary of war. At the same time the *científicos* set out to undermine both the economic and political power of elite members opposed to them. In Sonora itself the state government, closely linked to Corral, rode roughshod over the opposition of many landowners, including one of the state's wealthiest hacendados, José María Maytorena. In Coahuila, Díaz forced Governor Miguel Cárdenas, who enjoyed the support of large groups of hacendados, to resign and prevented the election of another landowner, Venustiano Carranza, who was backed by most of the state's upper class. Díaz's opposition to important sections of the north-eastern elite as well as the latter's mounting bitterness towards him may have been compounded by their increasing conflicts with foreign interests. The best-known, but by no means unique, conflict of this kind concerned the Madero clan, the wealthiest and most powerful family in the Laguna, if not Coahuila, which had never supported Reyes, although one of its most prominent members, Francisco Madero, had for some years attempted to set up political opposition to the Díaz administration. In contrast to the Torres and Terrazas families, the Maderos had never co-operated harmoniously with the US companies and had become notorious among these companies for their ill-concealed confrontation tactics. At the turn of the twentieth century, Francisco Madero had formed and led a coalition of hacendados in the Laguna region to oppose attempts by the Anglo-American Tlahualilo Company to monopolize the water rights of that irrigation-dependent area. When the Maderos cultivated the rubber substitute, guayule, they had clashed with the Continental Rubber Company. Another conflict developed because prior to 1910 the Maderos owned the only smelting oven in northern Mexico that was independent of the American Smelting and Refining Company.

In Chihuahua the *científico* offensive was not directed against dissident hacendados who scarcely existed but against the peasants and important segments of the middle classes. It was here that the *científicos* scored one of their greatest successes by obtaining full control of the state for one of their most powerful associates, Luis Terrazas and his family clan. In 1903 they effected a reconciliation between the Chihuahuan *caudillo* and Díaz who had fought on opposite sides when Díaz revolted in 1871 and 1876. With Díaz's backing, Terrazas again became governor of his native state in 1903. Chihuahua was now converted into a family undertaking. It was alternately ruled by Luis Terrazas, his son-in-law, Enrique Creel, Luis's son Alberto, and in between by candidates appointed by them. Their power now exceeded the wildest dreams of their predecessors in the pre-Díaz era. Anyone wishing to hold a government post, whether at the local or state level, had to go through the new power brokers. Anyone going to court had to appeal to judges appointed by them. Anyone needing credit had to turn to banks controlled by them. Anyone seeking employment with a foreign company probably had to depend on their mediation. Anyone losing his land to a surveying company or to a hacendado could blame them. The new local oligarchy had not only gained unprecedented power, it also threw off the constraints and obligations its predecessors had borne. It did not respect municipal autonomy, nor did it have to provide protection against the assaults of the Apaches or the federal government. The result was a growing polarization of forces and increasing middle-class bitterness.

The state's free peasants and especially the former military colonists suffered even more as a result of Terrazas' return to power. A new railway line, the Kansas Pacific Railroad, was being built through the mountain region of western Chihuahua where a large part of the former military colonies were located. Land values rose accordingly. Since the government did not need the fighting power of these colonists any more, a full-scale offensive to deprive them of their lands was undertaken by Enrique Creel. A new agrarian law was drafted for the state. It specified that municipal lands could now be sold to the highest bidder. As a result the last holdings of the military colonies began to be expropriated. 'If you do not grant us your protection we will lose our lands for which our ancestors have fought against the barbarians', the inhabitants of one of the state's oldest and most prestigious military colonies, Namiquipa, wrote to Porfirio Díaz.[13] In dozens of the state's villages, such as San Andrés, Cuchillo Parado, and Bocoyna, villagers vainly protested to the central government against the expropriation of their lands. Previous expropriations had impoverished the peasants. Creel's new law threatened their very existence.

The *científico* offensive and the economic crisis of 1907 created an unprecedented and unique situation in the northern triangle of Sonora, Chihuahua and Coahuila. What was unique to this region was that substantial portions from all classes of society ranging from hacendados and the middle classes to industrial workers to the dispossessed former military colonists were united in their opposition to the Díaz regime.

A dissatisfied middle class which resented the fact that it was excluded from political power, that it seemed to garner only the crumbs of Mexico's economic boom, and that foreigners were playing an increasingly important role in the country's economic and social structure existed in most parts of Mexico. Nowhere, however, had it grown as rapidly as in the north, and nowhere had it suffered such losses in so short a span of time. Not only was the northern middle class profoundly affected by the crisis of 1907 which hit the north far more than any other part of Mexico, but as Díaz gave political control of their states to the oligarchy and put an end to the two-party system it also suffered greater political losses.

The same crisis affected the north's industrial working classes to a degree unprecedented in their experience and unparalleled in the rest of Mexico. With the possible exception of Mexico City it was in the north of the country that the greatest number of unemployed workers could be found on the eve of the Revolution. Hacendados who were dissatisfied with some of the policies of the Díaz regime (and especially with the way the *científicos* attempted to shift the burden of the 1907 crisis to other sectors of society) could be found in many parts of Mexico. Most of them were far too afraid of the peasants, from whose expropriation so many of them had benefited, to challenge the Díaz regime. A number of dissident

---

[13] Departamento Agrário, Dirección de Terrenos Nacionales, Diversos, Chihuahua, Exp. 178, Letter of the inhabitants of Namiquipa to President Porfirio Díaz, 20 July 1908.

hacendados in northern Mexico, especially in Sonora and Coahuila, however, entertained no such fears. In Coahuila most of the dissident hacendados were located in the Laguna area. The Laguna had been an unpopulated wasteland before the hacendados reclaimed it. They did not have to confront a mass of peasants whom they had expropriated. The fact that the peons on their estates received the highest wages and enjoyed the greatest freedom found anywhere in the Mexican country- side had created a new kind of paternalistic relation between these landowners and their peons. The hacendados attempted to strengthen this relationship by providing schools and medical care to their workers. Some enlightened landowners, such as Francisco Madero, even extended many of these services to non-resident peons, thus earning their loyalty. In Sonora José María Maytorena protected his Yaqui labourers from deportation by the federal authorities and they regarded him as their patron. The three northern states which had been the main objects of the *científico* offensive constituted the most powerful basis of the opposition movements which emerged in Mexico between 1907 and 1910.

In the state of Morelos the *científico* offensive had equally deep repercussions, but it affected mainly one class of society: the peasantry. The state's governor, Manuel Alarcón, a traditional *caudillo*, not unfriendly to the planters but still considered by a large part of the state's population to have been his own man with whom they could at least deal in times of crisis and who was not a part of the local oligarchy, had died in 1908. He was replaced by Pablo Escandón, who belonged to the landed oligarchy of the state and had close links to the *científicos*. As in Chihuahua power now fell completely into the hands of the local oligarchy. For the state's free villages, Escandón's rule was an unmitigated disaster. As demand for sugar rose, the sugar planters began to expropriate the remaining lands from the hundred or so of free villages which dotted the state of Morelos. The peasants now felt completely abandoned by the Mexican state. Many of them had for a long time considered the central government to be a kind of neutral power to which they could appeal. Now that the myth of a benevolent government in Mexico City, which would act in favour of the peasants if only it knew what really happened, was removed by the appointment of a planter as governor of the state, their readiness to revolt mounted. Like the three northern states of Sonora, Chihuahua and Coahuila, Morelos was to become one of the main centres of the 1910 Revolution.

As a new presidential election approached in 1910 a new struggle for the succession broke out. Dissident members of Mexico's upper and middle classes again sought to limit *científico* influence and to persuade Díaz to choose a non-*científico* as his vice-presidential nominee. Their candidate was Bernardo Reyes and their political organization called itself the Democratic party. Its influence and vigour was greatly increased as the result of a significant tactical error that Díaz committed in 1908. In an interview with an American newspaper correspondent, James Creelman, Díaz seemed to invite candidates to present themselves at the polls. In this interview the Mexican dictator declared that he felt that Mexico was now ripe for democracy, that he would not be a candidate in the next presidential elections and that he welcomed the formation of opposition political groups. It is not clear why Díaz made verbal commitments he did not seriously mean, but their consequences were very definite.

Opponents of the regime felt that Díaz had given his official blessing to an opposition party and that they would suffer no reprisal if they joined such a group. The authorities became disorientated, and for a time allowed such movements a far greater degree of freedom than they had ever enjoyed before. As thousands of people, mainly of middle-class origin, began rallying behind Reyes, Díaz openly told Reyes that he would never accept him as vice-presidential candidate and sent him on a military mission to Europe. Facing the choice of either rebelling or accepting the president's decision, Reyes bowed out of the presidential race.

With the exile of Reyes his upper-class supporters faced an agonizing decision. They had hoped to pressure Díaz and perhaps even remove him from power with the help of a coalition similar to the one that had brought Díaz to power more than 30 years before: an alliance of dissident members of the upper and middle classes with potential rebels within the army. The link to whatever dissidents existed within the army was Reyes. Once he submitted to Díaz this link was broken and the military option ceased to exist. Any serious attempt to pressure Díaz or to overthrow him would have to be based on an entirely different strategy: an alliance with the lower classes of society, including the peasantry. For many of Reyes's supporters, especially in central Mexico, this was an unacceptable option since they feared that once mobilized the peasants would move against them as well and become an uncontrollable force; they therefore withdrew from any active opposition to Díaz.

The dissident hacendados of northern Mexico, especially in Sonora and Coahuila, as we have seen, had no such fears of the peasants. The former Reyes supporters there threw their support behind another national opposition party that was emerging: the Anti-Reelectionist party led by Francisco I. Madero, a wealthy hacendado from Coahuila. Madero became a national figure in 1908 when he published a book on the presidential succession. In it, he characterized Mexico's fundamental problem as that of absolutism and the unlimited power of one man. Only the introduction of parliamentary democracy, a system of free elections, and the independence of the press and of the courts could transform Mexico into a modern, democratic state. The book was very cautiously written. While harshly criticizing the Díaz system, it praised the dictator's personal qualities. It came out, however, against excessive concessions to foreigners and reproached Díaz for being too soft towards the United States. Social questions were scarcely mentioned.

Some post-revolutionary historians, as well as Porfirio Díaz himself, considered Madero a naive dreamer for taking Díaz's promise to hold democratic elections in Mexico seriously. Madero saw himself in a somewhat different light. In an interview he gave in 1911 he said:

At the beginning of the political campaign the majority of our nation's inhabitants believed in the absolute effectiveness of the public vote as a means of fighting against General Díaz. Nevertheless, I understood that General Díaz could only have been toppled by armed force. But in order to carry out the revolution the democratic campaign was indispensable because it would prepare public opinion and justify an armed uprising. We carried out the democratic campaign as if we had no intention of resorting to an armed uprising. We used all legal means and when it became clear that General Díaz would not respect the national will . . . we carried out an armed uprising . . . [Díaz] respected me because since I was not a military man he never believed that I was capable of taking up arms against him. I understood that this was my only defense and without resorting to hypocrisy I succeeded in strengthening this concept in his mind.[14]

When Madero formed his party Díaz did not take it seriously. Moreover, he felt that it might divide and weaken the one opposition group he really feared – Reyes's Democratic party. As a result, in 1908 and part of 1909 Madero was relatively free in his presidential campaign. The philanthropically minded hacendado succeeded in doing what the PLM had conspicuously failed to do. He aroused and mobilized

[14] These remarks were part of an interview that Madero gave to the Hearst Press in 1911. They are quoted in Jerry W. Knudson, 'When did Francisco I. Madero decide on Revolution?', *The Americas*, 30 (April 1974), 532–4.

important sectors of the Mexican peasantry, although his agrarian programme was very diffuse and never called for the kind of land reform that the liberals advocated. When disillusioned supporters of Reyes joined the party, the *anti-reeleccionistas* became the only group in Mexico which embraced members of all classes of society, from wealthy hacendados to lowly peons on large estates. This heterogeneous and unexpected coalition led by a man with no military experience succeeded in overthrowing the Díaz regime in 1910–11.

There are indications, although no absolute proof, that when the Revolution broke out some US corporations (above all, oil interests) actively supported it while the Taft administration showed a degree of 'tolerance' toward Madero's activities which profoundly worried the Díaz government. While US links to the 1910–11 revolutionaries are still the subject of much debate, there is little doubt that relations between the Díaz administration and the US government as well as some American corporations had become more and more strained between 1900 and 1910.

Both the Mexican government and the *científicos* deeply resented the rising tide of US interventionism in Central America and the Caribbean after the Spanish–American War. They were greatly worried by the fact that by the turn of the century, larger and more powerful US corporations were replacing the middle-sized American companies which predominated among US investors in the early years of the Porfiriato. 'The Mexican government has now formally taken a position against the trusts formed with American capital', the Austrian minister to Mexico reported as early as 1902. 'A series of articles appeared in semi-official newspapers pointing to the growing dangers that the intensive activities of the trusts are presenting to the Mexican producers. The latter will soon be slaves of the North American money market.'[15] Díaz refused to heed the calls for more nationalistic policies which emanated above all from Mexico's middle classes, but he did attempt to counteract US influence by encouraging a stronger European presence in Mexico.

These efforts by the Mexican president and the *científicos* elicited strong support in Great Britain. One of the country's most important financiers, Sir Weetman Pearson (Lord Cowdray), who had been active in Mexican public works projects for many years, became the country's most important oil producer in the early twentieth century, challenging

[15] Haus-, Hof- und Staatsarchiv Wien, Politisches Archiv, Mexico Reports, 1902, Auersthal to Goluchowsky, 24 November 1902.

the supremacy which US oilmen had until then exercised in Mexico. The British government showed a strong interest in Mexican oil which was increasingly important to its efforts to have the British navy fuelled by oil instead of coal. For its part the Mexican government went out of its way to help British oil interests by granting them leases on government land and exclusive contracts to supply the government controlled railways (in the process cancelling another contract for oil supplies which a preceding administration had signed with the US-owned Mexican Petroleum Company).

This was the strongest anti-American measure the Mexican government took. But it was not the only one. The US government greatly resented the support Díaz had granted Nicaraguan President Zelaya, whom they were attempting to oust, as well as Mexico's cancellation of a concession for a coaling station which it had previously accorded to the US Navy in Baja California. This cancellation was widely considered in the USA as a Mexican effort to woo Japan. On the whole, the Díaz government's anti-American gestures remained limited in scope and Díaz did his best never to publicize them. As a result, by 1910 his administration was in a paradoxical situation. While the Mexican president's policies were increasingly resented by some US corporations and the Washington administration, Mexico's opposition considered him a satellite of the United States. In the final account, this paradox would contribute greatly to his fall.

The end of the Porfiriato

On 16 September 1910 the Díaz regime seemed to have reached the apex of its power. On that day special ambassadors from all countries in the world participated in lavish ceremonies to commemorate the one hundredth anniversary of the day on which Father Miguel Hidalgo proclaimed the independence of Mexico in the small village of Dolores. Díaz seemed to have resolved most of the difficulties that had plagued him in the two preceding years. Not only had Reyes gone into exile but Francisco Madero, at least in the eyes of the Porfirian authorities, had been eliminated as a serious political force. On 5 June 1910, shortly before the elections, he had been arrested on a charge of sedition. On 21 June the elections took place amid massive charges of fraud by the Anti-Reelectionist party. The government declared that the Díaz–Corral ticket had been re-elected, and that not a single opposition candidate had received sufficient votes to become a member of the new Congress. A few sporadic local uprisings in Valladolid in Yucatán and in Veracruz were put down, and the government was convinced that it was now in full control of the situation. It felt so secure that on 22 July it agreed to release Madero on bail. 'I consider general revolution to be out of the question as does public opinion and the press', the German envoy to Mexico, Karl Bünz, optimistically wrote to his government on 4 December 1910.[16]

On 6 October, Madero had escaped from the city of San Luis Potosí where he had been free on bail awaiting his trial. From San Antonio, Texas, he issued his programme, the Plan of San Luis Potosí. Accusing Díaz of having carried out fraudulent elections, Madero assumed the office of provisional president and called for the people to revolt on 20 November 1910. While the plan was essentially political in character, Madero included a clause in which he promised to return lands unjustly confiscated from village communities to their rightful owners.

The revolt in Madero's native state of Coahuila for which the revolutionary president had hoped did not materialize. An attempt at revolt by Aquiles Serdan, the head of the Anti-Reelectionist party in Puebla, was crushed by the Porfirian authorities. But to the surprise of both Díaz, who was inaugurated on 1 December, and Madero, a popular uprising broke out in the mountains of western Chihuahua. Led by Pascual Orozco and Pancho Villa the revolutionaries soon controlled a large part of the state.

On 14 February 1911 Madero crossed the border from the United States into Mexico and assumed the leadership of the Chihuahuan revolutionaries. In February and March local revolts began to break out all over Mexico. Emiliano Zapata led a peasant uprising in the state of Morelos, while Jesús Agustín Castro, Orestes Pereira and Calixto Contreras revolted in the Laguna region of Coahuila. Smaller revolts broke out in the rest of the country and by April 1911 most of the Mexican countryside was in the hands of revolutionaries. In May the rebels captured their first large city, the border town of Ciudad Juárez. In March the Díaz administration had suffered an enormous blow to its prestige when President Taft mobilized 20,000 men along the US–Mexican border and sent American warships to Mexican ports. While the US government officially stated that the mobilization was intended to

---

[16] GFO Bonn, Mexico 1, vol. 25, Bünz to Bethmann-Hollweg, 4 December 1910.

facilitate enforcement of the neutrality laws, it was not a neutral move. It generated fears in Mexico that the US was prepared to intervene and increased pressure on Díaz, even from his closest supporters, to resign and find a compromise with the revolutionaries. On 21 May 1911 the Treaty of Ciudad Juárez was signed between Madero and the federal government. It provided for the resignation of Díaz and Corral from office by the end of May and their replacement by Francisco León de la Barra, who had not participated in the Revolution, as provisional president. The provisional government was to carry out elections in October 1911. In the meantime, the revolutionary army would be disbanded. Feeling that an imminent victory had been taken away from them, large segments of Madero's supporters strongly objected to the treaty. Madero nevertheless accepted its provisions and in the ensuing months co-operated with the provisional government in attempting to implement it, above all by doing everything in his power to assist in the dissolution of the revolutionary army that had brought about his victory. After some hesitation he even threw his support behind the provisional government's efforts to disarm by force the revolutionaries of the state of Morelos led by Emiliano Zapata. In many parts of the country the revolutionaries did lay down their arms peacefully, convinced that once Madero was elected, the social changes for which so many of them had fought would finally be implemented. On 15 October 1911 Madero was elected president by an overwhelming majority in what was probably the most honest election the country had ever had. He was sworn into office on 6 November 1911, firmly convinced that the Mexican Revolution had ended, its objectives, as he saw them, having been achieved.

2

THE MEXICAN REVOLUTION, 1910–1920

Three theoretical assumptions in liberal sociology long ruled historical study of the Mexican Revolution: mass action is consensual, intentional, and redistributive; collective violence measures structural transformation; and nationalism aggregates interests in a limited division of labour. In plain words, movement of 'the people' is movement by 'the people' for 'the people'; the bloodier the struggle, the deeper the difference between ways of life before and after the struggle; and familiarity breeds solidarity. The most influential scholars of the subject also made two radical suppositions about Mexico in particular. First, the most significant fact in the country in 1910 was the struggle between the upper and lower classes. Second, the conflict was about to explode. And on these premises respectable research and analysis framed a pro-revolutionary story of the rise of the downtrodden: the Revolution began over a political issue, the succession to Porfirio Díaz, but masses of people in all regions quickly involved themselves in a struggle beyond politics for sweeping economic and social reforms. Enormous material destruction throughout the country, the ruination of business, and total defiance of the United States were necessary for the popular struggle to triumph, as it did. And through the struggle the champions of 'the people' became the revolutionary leaders. Economic and social conditions improved in accordance with revolutionary policies, so that the new society took shape within a framework of official revolutionary institutions. The struggle ended in 1917, the year of the revolutionary constitution. The new revolutionary state enjoyed as much legitimacy and strength as its spokesmen said it did.

Hence the professional historical judgement, widely accepted until the 1970s, that the Mexican Revolution had been a 'social' revolution. The movements from 1910 to 1917 were represented as a massive, extremely violent and intensely nationalist uprising, in which 'the people' destroyed the old regime, peasants reclaimed their lands, workers organized unions, and the revolutionary government started the development of the country's wealth for the national welfare, opening a new epoch in Mexican history. In some versions the Mexican Revolution appeared as 'the first social revolution of the twentieth century', for better or worse comparable to the Russian and Chinese Revolutions.

There were problems in this interpretation. From the beginning critics insisted that 'the people' had been used by deceitful leaders for a false cause and dragged into worse conditions. But almost all scholars dismissed such versions as counter-revolutionary propaganda. More troublesome to interpret was a challenge to revolutionary legitimacy by tens of thousands of 'the people' in a Catholic rebellion in the 1920s. The problem that professional historians could not ignore was a sense spreading after 1940 that Mexico was developing along the lines more of the old regime than of the supposed Revolution. Although revolutionary institutions remained formally intact and revolutionary rhetoric continued to flow, peasants and workers benefited less than before, while businesses, above all American companies, multiplied, grew, and made their profits the register of national welfare. If Mexico had had a social revolution in the decade after 1910, what explained the recurrence of old practices in up-to-date patterns 30 years later? Historians who admitted the question gave various answers: the Revolution had died, been betrayed, passed into a new stage. None was convincing. In 1968 the Mexican government bloodily repressed a popular movement for civil rights. The standard interpretation of the Revolution, according to which the people's will had been institutionalized in the government, made historical explanation of the repression impossible. For some young scholars the most tempting explanation was to argue, as the critics always had, that the Revolution had been a trick on 'the people'.

Scholarly debate on the Revolution increased substantially in the 1960s and 1970s. Implicit in the most thoughtful new studies was an impartial mistrust of the old assumptions, a sophisticated use of the old criticisms. 'The people' may move on their own or be moved by others to fight among themselves, and by itself the distinction between autonomous and manipulated movements predicts nothing about differences between their consequences. Bloody struggles may deeply change a society, but not in the ways initially proposed, or they may change it only on the surface. And familiarity often breeds contempt.

Guided by conceptualization more objective than before, new research and analysis have significantly modified the old story and warranted a new interpretation. The struggle that began in 1910 featured not so much the lower versus the upper class as frustrated elements of the upper and middle classes versus favoured elements of the same classes. In this struggle masses of people were involved, but intermittently, differently from region to region, and mostly under middle-class direction, less in economic and social causes than in a bourgeois civil war. In some places destruction was terrible, in others scant and passing or nil. On the whole, business adjusted and continued. Over the long run it increased. From beginning to end foreign activities figured crucially in the Revolution's course, not simple antagonism from the US government, but complicated Euro-American imperialist rivalries, extremely intricate during the first world war. What really happened was a struggle for power, in which different revolutionary factions contended not only against the old regime and foreign concerns, but also, often more so, against each other, over matters as deep as class and as shallow as envy: the victorious faction managed to dominate peasant movements and labour unions for the promotion of selected American and native businesses. Economic and social conditions changed a little according to policy, but largely according to shifts in international markets, the contingencies of war, and the factional and personal interests of temporarily ascendant regional and local leaders, so that relations at all levels were much more complex and fluctuating than official institutions indicated. The state constituted in 1917 was not broadly or deeply popular, and under pressure from the United States and domestic rivals it barely survived until the faction supporting it split, yielding a new faction sufficiently coherent to negotiate its consolidation. Hence several new periodizations, the most plausible running from 1910 to 1920, the year of the last successful factional revolt.

A few old theses are not in dispute. During the Revolution, Mexican society did undergo extraordinary crises and serious changes. Peasant movements and labour unions became important forces. And the constitution represented a new respect for claims to egalitarian and fraternal justice. But from the revisions it now seems clear that basically there was continuity in Mexico between 1910 and 1920. The crises did not go nearly deep enough to break capitalist domination of production. The great issues were issues of state. The most significant development was the improvised organization of new bourgeois forces able to deal with the United States, cope with peasants and workers, and build a new regime and put it into operation. In practice the economic and social reforms were not very different from those accomplished in the same years, without civil war, in Peru, Chile, and Argentina. For all the violence this is the main historical meaning of the Mexican Revolution: capitalist tenacity in the economy and bourgeois reform of the state, which helps to explain the country's stability through the struggles of the 1920s and 1930s and its booming, discordant growth after 1940.

The subject is therefore no longer so much social revolution as political management. And the interpretation here is primarily a political history. It is short on social movements, because however important their emergence, their defeat or subordination mattered more. It is long on the politics that created the new state, because where *fortuna* and *virtú* do their damnedest, only the details reveal the reason for the result.

OCTOBER 1910 – FEBRUARY 1913

The spectre haunting Mexico in 1910 was the spectre of political reform. The country's politics had to change soon, because its central political institution, President Porfirio Díaz, was mortal and 80. And the change would go deep, because after 30 years of vigorous capitalist development and shrewd personal dictatorship, politics meant business. In maze upon maze of graft and collusion between politicians and businessmen, reform meant renegotiation of a myriad of shady deals.

Of the country's several important kinds of conflict, the two most pressing were about business. One was the rivalry between twenty or so big British, American, French, German, Canadian and Mexican banks and companies, for bonds, concessions, and national markets. Treated in the highest and tightest financial and political circles, it remained orderly. The other kind was the conflict between the major firms and hundreds of small Mexican enterprises over local opportunities for profit. These struggles were almost always disturbing, because they threatened established deals. If entrepreneurs big or small pursued a new venture, they risked subverting a local hierarchy of interests and authority; vice versa, subversion could open a new field of transactions. Since the crash of 1907, disappointments in politics and business had so angered some entrepreneurs that they considered a revolution necessary to promote their deals. After the electoral fraud and repression in the summer of 1910, many *anti-reeleccionistas* considered a revolution their duty.

The Porfiriato was a formidable regime to overthrow. Its obvious strengths in a country with a population of 15 million included international respect worth 450 million pesos in loans from European and American bondholders, the treasury running a ten million peso surplus, the Federal Army of 30,000 men, at least another 30,000 men in the Federal Auxiliaries and Irregulars and National Guard, 12,000 miles of railway for troop movements, and 2,500 Rurales. But the entire regime was not in question among the new subversives. For them the removal of the aged dictator and his closest associates would open the country's affairs sufficiently for their purposes.

In October 1910 plans for this revolution matured in San Antonio, Texas. There, having escaped from Mexico, Francisco I. Madero conferred with leading *anti-reeleccionistas* and the most enterprising members of his big, rich family. In early November he published his programme, the Plan de San Luis Potosí. Denouncing the recent presidential, congressional, and judicial elections as fraudulent, he declared himself provisional president, announced a national insurrection on 20 November, and promised 'democratic' elections for a new government. 'Democratic' or not, the prospect of a new government interested financially straitened and politically angry landlords in the northern states, and excited small farmers and merchants throughout the country. A minor clause in the San Luis plan, a promise to review villages' complaints about the loss of their lands, attracted peasants' attention, particularly in Chihuahua and Morelos.[1]

The private Madero strategy for revolution was tidier. Francisco's brother Gustavo – a German diplomat later called him the family's main *Geschäftemacher* – hired a Washington lawyer, Sherburne G. Hopkins, as the movement's legal counsel in the United States. The world's best rigger of Latin American revolutions, in close contact with Standard Oil, Hopkins was to stir up American sympathy for a short uprising of 'the Mexican people'. On 20 November Francisco would lead the capture of a Coahuila border town, Piedras Negras (then called Ciudad Porfirio Díaz), where he would set up a provisional government; and *anti-reeleccionista* agents would raise revolts in Mexico City, Puebla City, and

[1] Isidro and Josefina E. de Fabela (eds.), *Documentos históricos de la revolución mexicana* (27 vols., Mexico, 1960–76), v, 69–76.

Pachuca and in rural districts in Chihuahua and Guerrero. Propaganda would focus on Díaz's connection with the *científicos*, to gratify the Reyistas, the bellwethers of the army. Without much of a fight. Díaz would resign in a couple of months. And the 'democratic' election would go to Francisco Madero.

Parts of this strategy proved successful. Standard Oil negotiated encouragingly with Gustavo Madero. US officials bent neutrality laws for the revolutionaries. And General Reyes, who might have taken the initiative from the Maderos, remained in exile in Europe. But the revolution went haywire.

The government broke the major plots for 20 November. Francisco Madero retreated to Texas, and on 1 December Díaz was reinaugurated. But by January 1911 Maderistas in the Chihuahua mountains had raised some 2,000 guerillas. The Magonista anarchists, resurfacing in Baja California, captured the border town of Mexicali. In February Francisco Madero joined the Maderistas in Chihuahua, where instead of reliable *anti-reeleccionista* agents he found unfamiliar and unruly chiefs, foremost a local haulier, Pascual Orozco, who counted among his lieutenants a notable bandit, Francisco Villa. And the guerillas were not docile peons, but peasants from old military colonies counting on recovery of lost lands.

The army and the Rurales maintained regular order in almost all sizeable towns and along the railways. But on 6 March the United States took crucial action: President Taft ordered the mobilization of US forces on the border. In effect this was an intervention in Mexican politics, and to Mexicans it meant the United States had condemned Díaz. In New York, finance minister Limantour negotiated with Francisco's father, brother Gustavo, and the *anti-reeleccionista* vice-presidential candidate, Francisco Vázquez Gómez. In Mexico, businessmen and politicians hurried to rearrange their deals. Díaz exiled Vice President Ramón Corral to Europe, which opened the possibility of negotiations to replace him.

But revolutionaries multiplied in the northern states. In mid-April Sonora Maderistas occupied the border town of Agua Prieta. South of Mexico City several new bands revolted, most significantly village peasants in Morelos, determined to reclaim from the haciendas the lands their ancestors had farmed. The Maderos then tried to wind down the uprising in new negotiations. But on 10 May, against orders, Pascual Orozco captured Juárez, the most important town on the northern border. New Maderista bands sprang up in every state. Altogether maybe 25,000 revolutionaries were in the field, capturing sizeable towns, threatening state capitals, fighting for office, deals, loot, revenge, and, most alarmingly, land. The national insurrection for which Francisco Madero had called but made no provisions had materialized, with the obvious danger of uncontrollable peasant movements.

The Maderos seized on Orozco's victory to negotiate again. Francisco Madero set up his provisional government in Juárez, and on 21 May signed with Díaz's envoys a treaty ending the hostilities. In effect he repudiated the San Luis plan for a connection with the *científicos*. Under the treaty Díaz resigned on 25 May; he sailed for France a week later. Constitutionally replacing him was his foreign minister, Francisco León de la Barra, until a special election in October. All the Porfirian governors resigned, and several of them and Díaz's closest associates, including Limantour, went into exile too. But replacing Limantour was a banker and businessman whom the *científicos* counted virtually as their own, Francisco's uncle Ernesto Madero. And almost all congressmen, judges, and the federal bureaucracy stayed in place. So did the entire Federal Army and the Rurales, guaranteeing stability. The revolutionary forces were to be disarmed and discharged.

León de la Barra took office, recognized by the US and European governments. With all the regime's formidable resources, he had four months to liquidate the revolution and lubricate the transition to a Madero–*científico* government. Francisco Madero arrived in Mexico City on 7 June, a popular idol, 'the apostle of democracy'. He and his brother Gustavo had four months to transform popularity into votes.

Their campaign suffered no antagonism from the United States, which co-operated with the Federal Army to disperse the anarchists in Baja California. And it suffered no extraordinary difficulties from the economy. The recent fighting had done only slight damage to centres of production and railways. Both the US-owned Mexican Petroleum and Lord Cowdray's Águila Oil had just made major discoveries in the Gulf fields. The Fundidora steel plant in Monterrey was well on its way to a splendid year in output and sales. (For statistics on some important lines of production, see table 1.) And the summer rains were good, promising full harvests in the autumn.

Even so *maderismo* lost political ground. It had no direct support from banks and big companies, which backed the *científicos*. The *científicos* accepted 'the apostle' only to foil Reyes, in case he returned; many of

Table 1. Production in the Mexican economy, selected commodities, 1910–20

(metric tons, except oil in barrels)

Year	Barley	Corn	Cotton	Henequén	Sugar	Wheat	Copper	Gold	Monterrey iron/steel	Oil	Silver
1910	131,700	—	42,776	94,790	159,049	320,785	48,160	41.420	165,373	3,634,080	2,416.669
1911	139,264	—	34,203	116,547	152,551	320,546	56,072	37.120	217,999	12,552,798	2,518.202
1912	120,128	2,062,971	51,222	139,902	146,323	320,849	57,245	32.431	155,247	16,558,215	2,526.715
1913	211,308	—	43,830	145,280	125,922	286,549[a]	52,592	25.810	46,321	25,692,291	1,725.861
1914	232,271	1,961,073	—	169,286	108,262	214,288	26,621	8.635	5	26,235,403	810.647
1915	214,260	—	20,356	162,744	88,480	207,144	206	7.358	8,741	32,910,508	712.599
1916	211,308	—	18,109	201,990	49,210	286,549[a]	28,411	11.748	37,513	40,545,712	925.993
1917	—	—	13,582	127,092	65,396	—	50,946	23.542	49,536	55,292,770	1,306.988
1918	379,525	1,899,625	78,040	140,001	68,894	280,441	70,200	25.313	68,710	63,828,326	1,944.542
1919	—	—	—	113,870	90,546	381,399	52,272	23.586	90,020	87,072,954	2,049.898
1920	—	—	—	160,759	113,183	400,469	49,192	22.864	76,000	157,068,678	2,068.938

Note: [a] Incomplete data

Sources: Institut International d'Agriculture, Service de la statistique générale, *Annuaire international de statistique agricole, 1909 à 1921* (Rome, 1922), tables 7, 13, 19, 33, 56; Enrique Aznar Mendoza, 'Historia de la industria henequenera desde 1919 hasta nuestros días', in *Enciclopedia Yucatanense* (8 vols., Mexico, 1947), III, 779; Frédéric Mauro, 'Le développement économique de Monterrey (1890–1960)', *Caravelle*, 2 (1964), tables 21, 22, 24; Lorenzo Meyer, *México y los Estados Unidos en el conflicto petrolero (1917–1942)* (Mexico, 1968), table 1; and G. A. Roush and Allison Butts (eds.), *The mineral industry, its statistics, technology and trade during 1921* (New York, 1922), 845. The annual average production of corn, 1906–10, was 3,219,624 metric tons. Robert G. Cleland (ed.), *The Mexican year book* (Los Angeles, 1924), 240.

them joined a new and suddenly strong Partido Nacional Católico, which promoted a Madero–León de la Barra slate. General Reyes did return and accepted his presidential candidacy. The Maderistas themselves divided. In Sonora and Coahuila local *anti-reeleccionistas* whom the Maderos trusted, landlords in their own image, emerged in firm control. But in Chihuahua, where the family sponsored *anti-reeleccionista* Abrahám González for governor, it bitterly disappointed revolutionary hero Orozco; he did not rest content as commander of his old force, saved from discharge by conversion into state militia. In Morelos, Francisco Madero infuriated revolutionary leaders by advising them that village claims against haciendas had to await 'study' of 'the agrarian question'. To provoke a scandal favouring Reyes, federal forces under General Victoriano Huerta occupied Morelos. Madero's attempts to mediate failed, and outraged villagers fought back under a chief from a village near Cuautla, Emiliano Zapata. Resentful over the Madero–*científico* coalition, Francisco Vázquez Gómez and his brother Emilio connected with other local chiefs determined to keep their forces in arms as local militia. Gustavo Madero responded by reorganizing the Anti-Reelectionist party into the Partido Progresista Constitucional, which nominated a Yucatán lawyer, José María Pino Suárez, as its vice-presidential candidate. This prompted severe political feuding in half a dozen important states.

On 1 October, in probably the freest election in Mexico's history, Francisco Madero's personal popularity and Gustavo's *progresista* machine carried the day. The Madero–Pino Suárez slate won 53 per cent of the vote; four other slates shared the remainder. On 6 November 1911, recognized by the US and European governments, Madero took office to serve a five-year term. Ernesto Madero remained finance minister.

President Madero stood above all for political freedom. He was no doubt sincere, but in fact he had no choice. He had effective power only over his Cabinet. And in memorable contrast to Díaz's dictatorship a lively public politics did develop, most surprising for its serious political parties. The Partido Progresista and the Partido Católico organized energetically and extensively for the congressional elections in mid 1912.

As long as Madero's government lasted, it enjoyed a growing economy. With rising world mineral prices, mining production increased. The big American Smelting and Refining Company (ASARCO) reported larger smelting profits than ever before; oil production boomed; good rains again in 1912 yielded bigger harvests for domestic

Mexico

Table 2. *Value of Mexican exports and imports, 1910–20*
(dollars)

	Total exports	Exports to US	Total imports	Imports from US
1910	138,006,937	61,092,502	99,864,422	63,858,939
1911	147,462,298	57,311,622	96,823,317	53,454,407
1912	149,119,955	76,767,931	93,438,730	56,079,150
1913	154,392,312	81,735,434	90,610,659	48,052,137
1914	92,285,415	86,280,966	52,391,919	33,215,561
1915	125,199,568	83,551,993	26,331,123[a]	41,066,775
1916	242,688,153	105,065,780	42,214,449[a]	54,270,283
1917	152,872,380	130,370,565	94,915,092[a]	111,124,355
1918	182,199,284	158,643,427	137,666,784	97,788,736
1919	196,264,936	148,926,376	118,139,912[a]	131,455,101
1920	426,178,872	179,331,755	197,706,190[a]	207,858,497

[a] Incomplete data.
Sources: Columns 1 and 3 are derived from Banco Nacional de Comercio Exterior, *México exportador* (Mexico, 1939), 11–12. The first five rows in these columns were recalculated from years ending in 30 June to calendar years. Columns 2 and 4 are from US Department of Commerce, *Statistical abstracts of the United States, 1919* and *1920*, table 283, p. 399, and table 288, p. 407, respectively.

consumption and export. (For statistics on exports and imports, see table 2.)

But better business did not restore the old order. Since political controls had slackened, the economy's growth made the conflict among the big companies worse, rocking the new government hard. The most troublesome conflict was over oil, with Standard and Mexican Petroleum demanding concessions like Águila's, Águila defending its privileges. ASARCO and its American, British, German, French and Mexican rivals and customers lobbied almost as roughly against each other.

Without tight political control economic growth also brought out vigorous organizing among workers. The Mexican Union of Mechanics (UMM, founded in 1900), the Mexican Railway Alliance (AFM, 1907), the Mutualist Society of Dispatchers and Telegraphers (SMDT, 1909), and most powerfully the Union of Conductors, Engineers, Brakemen, and Firemen (UCMGF, 1910) established wide authority in the railway companies. Encouraged by strikes, the new Mexican Mining Union multiplied its branches in the north-east, and the Veracruz and Tampico port workers unionized. Strikes swept the textile mills and urban trades too. Although no textile unions emerged, printers and other tradesmen unionized almost evangelically, some with anarchist leaders.

In addition, Madero faced violent opposition. On 25 November, disgusted with the government's academic attitude towards 'the agrarian question', the Morelos peasant chiefs under Zapata formally denounced Madero, proclaiming in their Plan de Ayala a national campaign to return land from haciendas to villages. This was a deeply disturbing movement, a serious threat of social revolution, at least in the south. Federal troops spent the dry season burning Morelos villages, but could not stop Zapatista guerillas – nor could any other force for the next nine years. In December a very different avenger, General Reyes, revolted in the northeast. From El Paso Emilio Vázquez Gómez urged revolt in Chihuahua.

For a few months the government performed successfully. Most important, it managed Standard's and Mexican Petroleum's contention with Águila so as to preserve Madero's measure of *científico* support. Reyes's revolt fizzled out, ending with Mexico's most prestigious soldier interned in the Mexico City military prison and three anti-Reyista generals promoted to divisional general, the army's highest rank. On Pino Suárez's encouragement, Yucatán set up a Comisión Reguladora del Mercado de Henequén, a valorizing agency that stood against International Harvester and captured the henequén planters' loyalty. In January 1912, a Labour Department opened in the public works ministry. It scarcely interfered with the railway or port unions; they were too powerful. It had no part in resolving a conflict on the National Railways in April, when a strike by American crews brought the entire system to a halt, and the UCMGF replaced them. But it restored order in the mining districts and persuaded Congress to legislate new safety regulations for miners. And it calmed the textile industry by sponsoring grievance committees for workers and conventions for companies to co-ordinate prices and wages.

The government passed a major test in the spring of 1912, a revolt in the state of Chihuahua. On 4 February, after a Vazquista uprising in Juárez, President Taft had ordered US forces to prepare for field service on the border. Although he intended – in a year of US presidential elections – to discourage another Mexican revolution, to Mexicans the order had meant United States condemnation of Madero. Chihuahua's big American mining companies and the Terrazas family whose taxes Governor Abrahám González had raised, quietly connected with the embittered Orozco. On 3 March Orozco and his militia revolted, many of his men again counting on securing land when they won. On 23 March 8,000 Orozquistas destroyed a federal expedition along the railway in southern Chihuahua, where they then posed a threat to Torreón, the strategic point between Juárez and the Bajío. Orozquistas not only dominated Chihuahua but soon operated in Sonora and Coahuila too. Already, however, Taft had corrected his error; on 14 March he had placed an embargo on arms and ammunition shipments from the United States to Mexico, except to the government. On 1 April Madero commissioned General Victoriano Huerta to take a new federal expedition north, where on 23 May Huerta defeated the Orozquistas in southern Chihuahua. Meanwhile Sonora and Coahuila recruited state militia for local defence and duty in the war zone, and the UCMGF, the UMM, and the Mining Union raised volunteer corps. On 7 July Huerta entered Chihuahua City.

But this particular success came dear. It cost so much money that the government could not pay interest on the foreign debt. On 7 June Madero contracted with James Speyer and Company, the *científicos'* favourite New York bank, for a one-year $10 million loan to meet the payments immediately due. But to restore financial respectability he would need a much longer and bigger loan within a year, which Congress would have to authorize. The repression also left Madero with a heavy political debt to the army, which increased its share of the budget from 20 to 25 per cent and doubled in size to 60,000 men, with five more divisional generals, pre-eminent among them Huerta.

During the summer of 1912 foreign conditions for the government's stability began to fail. Crucially, Mexican oil became an issue in the American presidential campaigns. On 3 June, in order to increase revenue to warrant a big loan in the coming year, Madero decreed Mexico's first tax on oil production – 20 centavos a ton, about $0.015 a barrel. American oil companies condemned the tax as 'confiscation'.[2] And they carried much weight both in the Republican party, which on 22 June nominated Taft, and in the Democratic party, which on 2 July nominated Woodrow Wilson. (In August the Progressive party nominated Theodore Roosevelt, the universal jingoist.) The US Senate Foreign Relations Committee named a subcommittee to investigate Taft's policy towards Mexico. Taft sent warships to visit Mexico's Gulf and Pacific coasts, and in September the State Department demanded that the Mexican government secure law and order in its territory or the

---

[2] Lorenzo Meyer, *Mexico and the United States in the oil controversy, 1917–1942* (Austin, Texas, 1977), 31.

United States would 'consider what measures it should adopt to meet the requirements of the situation'.[3]

Meanwhile Gustavo Madero boldly prepared to free the government from dependence on the *cientificos*. He had only a part of the base he needed, for in the congressional elections on 30 June, while his Partido Progresista won a majority in the Chamber of Deputies and a majority of the contestable half of the Senate's seats, the Partido Católico took a large minority in the Chamber and enough seats in the Senate, including one for León de la Barra, to make a majority with the remaining *cientificos* and Reyistas there. But he would not wait for a better chance later. In July Ernesto Madero, the finance minister, started secret negotiations outside *cientifico* banking circles to borrow £20 million (nearly 200 million pesos) in France. If the Maderos succeeded at this financial coup, a purely Maderista government could comfortably hold power until 1916 when Gustavo himself might well be elected president.

The direct road to Maderista ruin opened with the 26th Congress on 14 September. While the government continued secret financial negotiations, Gustavo had his *progresistas* – led by Deputy Luis Cabrera – rant like Jacobins. Styling themselves *renovadores*, they urged a 'renovation' of the country even beyond the San Luis plan's 'democratic' promises, including agrarian reform for the villages.[4] The *católicos* and *cientificos*, led by León de la Barra, made the Senate into a bulwark of opposition. By then *cientifico* exiles in Paris had wind of the government's financial scheme, and they advised their friends in Mexico to subvert it, even in co-operation with the Reyistas.

The first attempt to depose Madero by a military coup failed. In mid October, hurrying to get in before the American elections in November, a group of *cientificos* organized a revolt around General Félix Díaz, Porfirio Díaz's nephew. With US warships waiting offshore, Díaz seized the port of Veracruz and called on the army to take command of the country. Not a single general responded. Within the week the army reoccupied the port, and a court-martial soon locked Díaz into a Veracruz dungeon. But Madero's debt to the military mounted.

On 5 November Wilson won the US presidential election, and his party won both Houses of Congress. High Maderista officials made contact once more with Sherburne Hopkins, who restored friendly

[3] P. Edward Haley, *Revolution and intervention. The diplomacy of Taft and Wilson with Mexico, 1910–1917* (Cambridge, 1970), 48.
[4] Luis Cabrera, *La revolución es la revolución. Documentos* (Guanajuato, 1977), 137–45.

relations with Standard Oil. Mexican politicians deduced that under the Democrats, US pressure on the Madero government would ease. But Taft had four more months in the presidency, until March 1913, and in radical distrust of Wilson and Madero he apparently decided that before he left office a president beholden to the United States and the Republican party should rule Mexico. The US ambassador to Mexico scarcely disguised his new mission. This gave the *católico–científico–* Reyista opposition new courage and a deadline. In December the Mexican government formally requested that Congress authorize the borrowing of £20,000,000 'in Europe'. This gave the opposition a major public issue. On 13 January the bill for the authorization passed the Chamber. But the opposition in the Senate picked it to pieces.

There was trouble too from organized labour. On 26 December, demanding an eight-hour day, the UMM called a strike on the National Railways and snarled up transportation throughout the country. The labour department tried to mediate, in vain. Not until 11 January, thanks to UCMGF intervention, did the UMM accept a ten-hour day and a 10 per cent pay rise. Then, independently, an anarchist centre, the Casa del Obrero, founded in September for unions in Mexico City, encouraged strikes there for shorter hours and higher pay. Anarchist-led unions in Veracruz called a convention of working-class organizations to meet in the port on 1 May and form a national confederation to struggle for the eight-hour day.

The second attempt at a military coup also failed. Better organized than the first, it revolved around General Manuel Mondragón, a *científico* favourite who was supposed to suborn elite units in Mexico City, seize the National Palace, liberate Reyes and Díaz (the latter recently transferred to the capital), instal Reyes as provisional president, and after a decent interval have Díaz elected president. On 9 February Mondragón's units freed Reyes and Díaz. But in the fighting to enter the palace, Reyes was killed. Mondragón, Díaz, and the surviving rebels barely escaped into an armory across town, the Ciudadela. That same day Madero appointed Huerta, who had crushed the Orozquistas, to wipe out the new rebellion. On 11 February Huerta began attacks supposedly against the Ciudadela. The battle, however, soon spread and became more generalized, with artillery daily killing many civilians and destroying much property. Mondragón and Díaz kept demanding Madero's and Pino Suárez's resignation and urging other generals to overthrow the government. Privately the US ambassador and León de la Barra, directing the *católico–*

científico–Reyista alliance, plotted for the same cause. Most assiduously the rebels and conspirators sought to win over Huerta, in vain. Of the army's 100 or so generals, all but the two in the Ciudadela remained loyal. But now Madero depended totally on his generals.

The third attempt succeeded. On 18 February, advised that the now desperate rebels would try to break out of the Ciudadela, Huerta ordered a cease-fire, managed the arrest of the president, vice president, Cabinet members, Gustavo Madero, and the general closest to the Maderos, Felipe Ángeles, and declared himself in charge of the country. Some of the other generals at once recognized his authority. That evening at the US ambassador's invitation Huerta and Díaz met at the embassy and signed a pact: Huerta would become provisional president, appoint a cabinet of *católicos, científicos*, and Reyistas, and – most important to the ambassador – honour Díaz's campaign in 'the coming election' for the regular presidency.[5] That night Gustavo Madero was murdered. On 19 February Francisco Madero and Pino Suárez submitted their resignations, and the *progresista*-dominated Chamber overwhelmingly accepted them. The foreign minister, now provisional president, immediately appointed Huerta as minister of the interior and resigned himself, and Huerta became provisional president. The new Cabinet included León de la Barra as minister of foreign relations, Mondragón as minister of war, and Reyes's son Rodolfo as minister of justice. Almost all the generals who had not yet recognized Huerta's authority now did so; a few retired, none resisted. On 21 February the Supreme Court congratulated the new president. Privately Huerta indicated that he would allow Madero and Pino Suárez to go into exile, but on the night of 22 February, under military guard, the two prisoners were murdered.

FEBRUARY 1913 – AUGUST 1914

The new government lacked support from important quarters. Crucially, it did not satisfy the United States. Since 1910 the rivalry between the United States and Great Britain in Mexico had become more tense, largely because of oil, and to the new administration in Washington the coup looked like a *científico* counter-revolution to favour British interests, namely Águila. The Foreign Office reasoned that when Wilson settled into his presidency, he would recognize Huerta anyway in

[5] Luis Liceaga, *Félix Díaz* (Mexico, 1958), 216.

order to reassert American influence over him. In anticipation Britain, therefore, extended recognition on 31 March 1913, and other European governments soon followed suit. Wilson consequently refused recognition, supposing that he could soon evoke a government more reassuring to Americans. This confusion worried bankers and big businessmen, dubious whether without US blessing the new government could clear the foreign debt payments due in early June.

Besides, extraordinary difficulties soon arose in the economy. Although the oil companies boomed, a decline in the world price of silver during the spring of 1913 increased the flow of precious metals out of the country, depressed the mining industry, and in the northern border states where mining mattered most caused a broad slump in business. Organized labour remained combative. The anarchist unions in Veracruz did not hold their convention for a national confederation, but the Casa del Obrero in Mexico City, in a new organizing drive, staged the country's first public celebration of 1 May. The main railway and port unions together formed the Confederación de Gremios Mexicanos. Representing most of the country's transport workers, the CGM suddenly loomed as a national power.

Moreover the new government soon faced extensive armed resistance. Like the army, Congress, and the Supreme Court, all but a few governors accepted Huerta's authority. But the resurgence of the *científicos* aggravated conflicts, old and new. And revolts against 'usurpation' soon broke out in several states, most dangerously along the nothern border in Sonora, Chihuahua and Coahuila. There, despite the US embargo on arms and ammunition exports to rebels, local leaders mobilized not only the state militias still standing from the campaign against Orozco, but also new recruits from the increasing numbers of unemployed. Sonora's governor had fled into Arizona in late February, but his militia officers had the legislature appoint an acting governor, declare the state's independence from the federal government, and collect federal customs and taxes. A regular state army took shape under the command of a young farmer-politician, Álvaro Obregón. By late March it numbered 8,000 and had isolated the main federal force in Guaymas. In Chihuahua, where Governor González had been murdered in early March, the revolt began disjointedly. But by late March several militia units and many new rebels hoping again to make a claim on land operated together under Francisco Villa. Their revolt encouraged others in Durango and Zacatecas.

In Coahuila, Governor Venustiano Carranza led the resistance. A 53-year-old veteran of Porfirian provincial politics, a landlord related by blood and law to several big north-eastern families (but not to the Maderos), he tried first to rally other governors in defiance of Huerta's coup, but in vain. On 26 March 1913 he had his local subordinates proclaim the Plan de Guadalupe. Denouncing Huerta, Congress, and the Supreme Court for treason, and announcing the organization of the Constitutionalist Army, the Coahuilans named Carranza its First Chief, eventually to assume interim national executive authority and convoke elections for the return to constitutional rule. The Guadalupe plan contained not a word on economic or social reform. And the Constitutionalist Army was small, its highest ranking officer a refugee militia general from Veracruz, Cándido Aguilar, its forces only a few local militia under Carranza's brother Jesús and his cousin Pablo González. But on 1 April Constitutionalist agents hired Hopkins for counsel in Washington. On 18 April envoys from the Sonora and Chihuahua revolutions signed the Guadalupe plan, and on 26 April, to avoid forced domestic loans or dependence on foreign creditors, Carranza authorized the printing of five million paper pesos to pay for the Constitutionalist campaigns.

Elsewhere the main resistance came from the Zapatistas in Morelos. A few chiefs, who had come to regard Madero as the worst enemy, quit the field. But under the Plan de Ayala the others followed Zapata in an independent guerilla war to regain land for their villages. Their very disdain of changes that were only political strengthened their commitment to a national peasant cause and broadened the horizons of their strategy. Zapata found an excellent administrative secretary to manage his headquarters, a one-time engineering student and former accountant, Manuel Palafox. In mid-April 1913 he launched a serious offensive in eastern Morelos. By May the Zapatista movement had the determination and the organization to win at least a regional social revolution.

But the new government survived its debut. As it took shape, it revealed its difference from the previous government as merely factional and personal: its ministers pursued practically the same policies as before on business, labour, and 'the agrarian question'. Most surprisingly and significantly, not Félix Díaz but Huerta emerged as dominant. In March and April 1913 Felicistas organized themselves throughout the country to promote a Díaz–León de la Barra slate in 'the coming election'. But the provisional president raised the army's pay, rigged the appointment of

Mexico

Table 3. *Value of the paper peso in dollars, 1913–16*

Month	1913	1914	1915	1916
January	0.4955	0.3699	0.1431	0.0440
February	0.4873	0.3478	0.1314	0.0407
March	0.4830	0.3138	0.1190	0.0285
April	0.4592	0.3001	0.0923	0.0343
May	0.4702	0.3360	0.0863	0.0229
June	0.4761	0.3313	0.0926	0.0970
July	0.4306	0.3146	0.0739	0.0970
August	0.3936	0.2629	0.0676	0.0380
September	0.3649	0.2108	0.0659	0.0311
October	0.3607	0.2055	0.0714	0.0232
November	0.3580	0.1986	0.0716	0.0099
December	0.3594	0.1870	0.0590	0.0046

Source: Edwin W. Kemmerer, *Inflation and revolution: Mexico's experience of 1912–1917* (Princeton, 1940), 14, 45, 46, 101.

several personally loyal generals as provisional governors, and made peace and a political alliance with Orozco. On 23 April he got a *progresista* majority in the Chamber to set the date for the presidential election six months away on 26 October. Díaz and León de la Barra resigned their candidacies, to embarrass him; some of their underlings plotted to kill him. But unembarrassed and unafraid, Huerta pressed for new negotiations in *científico* circles for the £20 million loan. On 30 May Congress authorized the debt, and on 8 June, just in time to clear the payments due, a consortium led by the Banque de Paris et des Pays-Bas underwrote a ten-year £6 million loan and took six-month options on another £10 million.

The loan could not help the economy. At mid-year ASARCO and other big mining companies reported sharply reduced income; some of them sharply reduced production. Small businesses in the north failed so fast that the state banks pushed their Mexico City clearing house into the red. The rains that summer were poor, leading to higher grain prices and a wider depression. From June to September the peso dropped from $0.48 to $0.36 (for the value of the peso in this period, see table 3).

But politically the new credit amounted to a Huertista coup. Flouting the pact with Díaz, Huerta purged his cabinet of Felicistas, most importantly the war minister Mondragón, who went into exile, followed by León de la Barra. Policies on business, labour and 'the agrarian question' remained the same, but Huerta now had his own men administering them. In mid-July he exiled Díaz as 'special ambassador' to Japan and released Ángeles for exile in France.[6] Britain, approving the changes, announced the appointment of a new minister to Mexico who boasted of his friendship with Lord Cowdray, owner of Águila Oil.

In full control of the army, Huerta increased its share of the budget to 30 per cent and its size to 85,000, reorganized its commands, promoted 50 or so officers to general, appointed several new divisional generals, enlarged the arsenals, and expanded the Rurales to 10,000. Through the summer he threw his forces against the revolutionaries. And under serious federal attacks the Constitutionalist Army fell apart. In Sonora, which remained a Constitutionalist powerhouse, the federals still could not move out of Guaymas. But in the north, reinforced by Orozco and his militia, they regained command over the main towns and railways. In late July they dispelled a Constitutionalist attack on Torreón so thoroughly that Carranza almost lost his First Chieftainship. In the north-east in August they wrecked González's forces and recovered command everywhere but Piedras Negras and Matamoros. In Morelos, where they drove villagers into concentration camps, they scattered the Zapatista guerillas into the surrounding states.

As Huerto grew stronger, the United States went increasingly sour on him. American oil companies and Wilson saw not just a military man but British capital building power in Mexico. In July the United States recalled its ambassador. Thanks to Hopkins, its border officials winked at Constitutionalist smuggling of war material into Sonora and Tamaulipas. In August, before the new British minister had left for Mexico, Wilson sent a special agent to demand that Huerta declare an immediate cease-fire and hold 'an early and free election'.[7] The United States would help to impose the armistice, recognize the new government, and sponsor a new loan. If Huerta refused, the United States would not 'stand inactively by'.[8] Huerta refused. On 27 August Wilson announced his policy of 'watchful waiting' and an embargo without exceptions on shipments of arms and ammunition to Mexico. But Huerta soon placed new orders for arms in Europe and Japan.

By September 1913 Huerta had consolidated his power. He could count not only on the army but also – in a depressed economy – on army-contract suppliers, who had become his fiercely loyal supporters. Playing

[6] *Ibid.*, 302–3.   [7] Haley, *Revolution and intervention*, 98.
[8] Arthur S. Link, *Wilson: the new freedom* (Princeton, 1956), 357–8, 361.

on resentment of the United States, he had developed a programme of military training for civilians that attracted wide subscription by patriotic bureaucrats and clerks. When Congress reconvened, it displayed such disarray among *progresistas, católicos, científicos*, and Reyistas that Huerta took more liberties. He dictated to the Partido Católico its presidential and vice-presidential candidates for the 26 October election, and on 30 September he won from Mexico City banks a three-month loan of 18 million pesos.

The Huertista government then faced three severe tests. The first came from every opposition camp – an attempt to discredit the election of 26 October. During September the Constitutionalist bands in Chihuahua, Durango and Zacatecas had combined under Villa as the Division of the North. On 1 October, in the first major Constitutionalist victory, they captured Torreón and a large military booty. Also during September the Sonora Constitutionalists had welcomed Carranza into their state. There the First Chief took new political positions. He declared that after constitutional restoration 'the social struggle, the class struggle in all its power and grandeur, must begin'.[9] He reordered the Constitutionalist Army, commissioning Álvaro Obregón commander of the North-west Army Corps and Pablo González commander of the North-east. On 17 October he announced the formation of a provisional government, including in his cabinet General Felipe Ángeles, back from France, as undersecretary of war. And on 21 October he affirmed that on the Constitutionalist triumph he would dissolve the Federal Army. On 23 October González's North-east Corps attacked Monterrey. Meanwhile the Zapatistas co-ordinated attacks around Mexico City. And Félix Díaz disembarked in Veracruz to stand in the election.

Huerta reacted shrewdly and boldly. On 10 October, having waited for the new British minister to arrive in Mexico City, he dissolved Congress and convoked elections for the Chamber and Senate coincidentally with the presidential election. The next day the British minister presented his credentials to the provisional president, virtually blessing his latest coup. The Constitutionalist attack on Monterrey failed. On 24 October Huerta decreed the expansion of the army to 150,000. At the polls on 26 October a militarily rigged majority gave Huerta the presidency, his war minister the vice-presidency, and the *católicos* most of Congress, but as Huerta and his war minister were ineligible for elective

[9] Jesús Carranza Castro, *Origen, destino y legado de Carranza* (Mexico, 1977), 199.

office, the executive election was invalid – Huerta remained provisional president. On 27 October Díaz escaped from Veracruz in an American warship.

The second test was another Constitutionalist offensive. From Sonora Obregón co-ordinated with forces in Sinaloa, and on 14 November captured Culiacán. González captured Victoria on 18 November, installed his main Tamaulipas subordinate, Luis Caballero, as provisional governor, and drove on towards Tampico. Villa's Division of the North – now 10,000 men with artillery and trains – pinned down the Chihuahua City garrison, captured Juárez and more military supplies on 15 November, crushed Orozco's militia, compelled the evacuation of the state capital, and occupied it on 7 December. The army reacted competently. In the north-west the federal artillery and gunboats in Guaymas and Mazatlán, targeted on the railways that passed nearby, blocked Obregón from substantial troop or supply movements south. González's drive towards Tampico broke down before federal defences. Throughout the central states federal generals managed a massive conscription, and on 9 December a fresh federal force recaptured Torreón, throwing Villa back into Chihuahua. To consolidate his base there, Villa took a giant step towards economic and social reform, decreeing on 21 December the confiscation without compensation of the vast haciendas in the state, for revenue immediately and allotment to his troops at the war's end. But on 28 December, keenly vexed at Villa for starting 'the social struggle' too soon, Carranza in effect admitted that the government still held the strategic upper hand by authorizing his treasury to issue 15 million more paper pesos to pay for the long campaigns still to come.

The third test was further antagonism from the United States. When Huerta dissolved Congress with the British minister's blessing, President Wilson's opposition became implacable. On 13 October he warned that the United States would not recognize the results of the elections of 26 October. On 1 November he threatened Huerta: resign, or – for the first time – the United States would support the Constitutionalists. On 7 November the State Department announced that Wilson would 'require Huerta's retirement'; the United States would then mediate in the formation of a new provisional government to hold the 'free election' to restore constitutional order.[10] On 12 November a US special agent met

[10] Kenneth J. Grieb, *The United States and Huerta* (Lincoln, 1969), 115–16.

Carranza in Nogales. Under this pressure Great Britain instructed its
minister to abandon Huerta, and the French finance ministry notified the
Mexican government that French banks would not underwrite the £10
million loan.

But the government reacted stubbornly and resourcefully. On 15
November the *católico*-dominated Congress opened. On 15 December it
confirmed Huerta as provisional president and scheduled another
presidential election on 5 July. As a reward Huerta purged the *católico*
leadership but let the church dedicate Mexico to the Sacred Heart of
Jesus and stage grand public ceremonies in honour of Christ the King –
most impressively in Guadalajara – on 11 January 1914. He also tolerated
a new church organization increasingly active in civic affairs, the
Catholic Association of Mexican Youth (ACJM). Compensating for the
failure of credit abroad, he more than tripled the oil tax, got Congress to
authorize a new 100 million peso internal debt, imposed heavy forced
loans on business, decreed a tax on bank deposits, and monetized bank
notes. On 23 December, after another slip in the price of silver triggered a
run on the Banco de Londres, he declared a banking moratorium. On 7
January he lowered reserve requirements from 50 to $33\frac{1}{3}$ per cent, then
suspended interest payments on the national debt until the banks lent the
newly creatable money to the government. American, British, and
French banks protested, but Huerta knew that he could count on private
support from the British minister and Lord Cowdray. And his military
programme for civilians enrolled many new patriots.

In short, by early 1914 the Huertista government had proved itself
the paramount power in Mexico. Although it had lost valuable ground, it
ruled the two-thirds of the country where probably four-fifths of the
population lived. It still controlled all the sea ports. It held hostage the
interests of bishops, businessmen, and bankers. And in the central cities,
because of its anti-Americanism and pro-clericalism, it enjoyed considerable popular allegiance. This moved the United States to boost the
Constitutionalists outright. On 29 January 1914 Wilson advised Great
Britain that he now saw peace in Mexico as coming not from mediation
but from the military victory of the strongest. On 3 February he revoked
the arms embargo, allowing legal exports of war material from the
United States indiscriminately into Mexico. Arms and ammunition
flooded into Sonora, Chihuahua and Tamaulipas. The British minister
was soon recalled to London.

So favoured, on 12 February Carranza authorized the printing of another ten million pesos, and on 3 March dispatched the Constitutionalist marching orders. González's North-east Corps, which by then boasted several notable subordinate chiefs – Luis Caballero, Jesús Carranza, Cesáreo Castro, Francisco Coss, Francisco Murguía, and Antonio I. Villarreal – was to capture Monterrey, Tampico and Saltillo. Obregón's North-west Corps – with Salvador Alvarado, Lucio Blanco, Plutarco Elías Calles, Manuel Diéguez, and Benjamín Hill its principal chiefs – was to conquer the west coast and capture Guadalajara. Villa's Division of the North, which Ángeles joined to command the artillery, was to recapture Torreón for the strategic campaign down the railway towards the centre of the country. Carranza moved his government to Chihuahua to supervise Villa and the drive south.

Huerta again expanded the army, to 200,000 in February and 250,000 in March, with another massive conscription in the central states. He promoted some 250 officers to general, commissioned several new divisional generals, and named Orozco to command a new offensive in the north. He appointed a *católico*-nominated in-law of Limantour's, Eduardo Iturbide, as governor of the Federal District. And on 31 March, having with Lord Cowdray's help exacted from Mexican banks a 45 million peso loan, he announced resumption of payments on the national debt on 15 April.

But the Constitutionalist campaigns developed momentum. On 26 March González had Caballero lay siege to Tampico, and on 8 April, while Jesús Carranza, Coss and Murguía harassed the federal troops elsewhere in the north-east, he, Castro and Villarreal attacked Monterrey. Obregón, having left Calles in command of Sonora and Alvarado besieging Guaymas, took Blanco, Diéguez and Hill to prepare forces in southern Sinaloa and Tepic for movement into Jalisco. On 23 March Villa and Ángeles led 15,000 men against 10,000 federal troops in Torreón, on 2 April took the town and on 14 April destroyed 12,000 federal reinforcements. As Constitutionalist generals conquered new territory, they opened a new and characteristic agency, the Oficina de Bienes Intervenidos, to manage the attachment of private property for military housing and supplies. Meanwhile the Zapatistas had coordinated their guerillas into a regular Army of the South and commenced an offensive in Guerrero. By early April they controlled most of the state and its silver mines.

These advances moved the United States to resume attempts at mediation, this time by force. On 10 April Wilson seized upon an arrest of

American sailors in Tampico to demand that the Mexican government salute the American flag, or face 'the gravest consequences'.[11] Huerta refused. On 14 April Wilson ordered the Atlantic Fleet to Tampico and Veracruz. Four days later the State Department received word that a German ship with arms and ammunition for the Federal Army would dock at Veracruz on 21 April. On 20 April, assured that federal garrisons in the ports would not resist American landings, Wilson decided to occupy Veracruz and Tampico. If Huerta still did not resign, Wilson had plans to run an expedition of marines by rail from Veracruz into Mexico City to overthrow him. The United States could then supervise negotiations between his replacement and the Constitutionalists for a new provisional government, a 'free election', and constitutional restoration. On 21 April 1,200 marines and bluejackets landed in Veracruz.

The intervention failed. The Veracruz garrison resisted, and the Tampico landing never started, because the force had to be diverted to help in Veracruz. By 22 April 6,000 US troops held the port. But instead of resigning, Huerta obtained from Congress dictatorial powers in war, finance, and communications, named railway union leaders to manage the National Railways, mobilized patriotic demonstrations into his programme for militarizing civilians, and urged all rebels to join the federal troops against a Yankee invasion. The *católicos*, the ACJM, and the bishops publicly supported his appeals for national unity against Protestant defilement of the fatherland. On 22 April Carranza denounced the US intervention as a violation of sovereignty. On the advice of private counsel in Washington, to avoid disastrous hostilities along the border, he did not call it an act of war, but he did demand immediate US withdrawal and vowed to fight American intrusions into Constitutionalist territory, including by then the environs of Tampico. Zapata also vowed to fight American forces that moved into his territory. Europeans scoffed at the intervention. South Americans lamented it. Even the American public tended to oppose it.

Accordingly Wilson confined it to Veracruz. On 25 April, to save the shreds of his plan for mediation, he accepted an offer by Argentina, Brazil and Chile to hold a conference to mediate 'between the United States and Mexico'.[12] On 27 April he reimposed a full arms embargo, but it did not stop Constitutionalist border smuggling.

---

[11] Link, *Wilson: the new freedom*, 396.   [12] *Ibid.*, 407.

Huerta accepted the 'ABC' countries' offer of mediation, planning to use it against the Constitutionalists. But deprived of Veracruz customs revenue and military supplies, the government floundered. It could no longer clear the interest on the foreign debt; the peso fell to $0.30 (see table 3). The army pushed conscription and militarization of civilians too far, into the ranks of organized labour, and anarchists in Mexico City resisted. On 27 May the government closed the Casa del Obrero.

Superficially, Constitutionalism gained strength. The First Chief accepted 'ABC' mediation only 'in principle', assuming it would treat only the Tampico incident and the Veracruz intervention, and declared defiantly that his government would continue its war to restore the constitution.[13] But below the surface, because of his displays of independence from the United States, his forces began to divide. Northeastern generals, in whose region the major sources of revenue were American mining and oil companies, welcomed their First Chief's declaration of national authority: it would encourage the companies to pay Constitutionalist taxes. Northern generals, who had their major sources of revenue in expropriated Mexican cattle ranches in Chihuahua and British cotton plantations around Torreón, but had to sell the cattle and cotton to Americans, resented Carranza's defiance of Washington: it might provoke retaliation at El Paso customs. The angriest was Villa, who publicly professed his friendship for the United States.

This division brought out old jealousies. For three months, since Wilson had backed Constitutionalism, the Madero elders in exile in the United States had been manoeuvring to define constitutional restoration narrowly as Maderista restoration. They had considerable allies in Sonora, where the Maderista governor who had fled in 1913 sought to reinstate himself, and in Chihuahua, where the family's old friend Ángeles had much influence with Villa. By May, Villa was convinced that Carranza intended to sabotage him. Constitutionalist chiefs anxious about a Madero revival began pushing Carranza to restrain Villa.

The Constitutionalists continued to move militarily. Already during the Veracruz crisis González, Castro and Villarreal had captured Monterrey, where Villarreal became provisional governor of Nuevo León. On 14 May González, Caballero and Castro took Tampico and began collecting the oil taxes. On 18 May Cándido Aguilar took Tuxpan, where he became provisional governor of Veracruz. On 21 May Villa

[13] *Ibid.*, 408–9.

took Saltillo, delivered it to González, and returned to Torreón. In the west, Obregón, Blanco, Diéguez, and Hill captured Tepic on 16 May and started the campaign toward Guadalajara. Everywhere in Constitution-alist territory more *oficinas de bienes intervenidos* opened, in which some generals discovered irresistible opportunities for private deals. The conquering forces also vented passions for revenge. In rancour against the church – an old northern Liberal anti-clerical anger whetted by the collaboration of the *católicos*, the bishops and the ACJM with Huerta – some generals exercised a particular fury on churches and priests. From Guerrero the independent Zapatista Army of the South recovered all of Morelos but Cuernavaca, and moved strongly into Mexico State and Puebla. In the territory it now controlled villagers were already recovering the land for the sowing season.

But the pressures for division increased. The United States deliber-ately brought them to bear through the ABC Conference, which opened on 20 May 1914 at Niagara Falls, Ontario. In the following weeks the State Department eliminated Huerta's last private British support by recognizing extant British oil and mining concessions. In addition, under American direction the conference did not limit itself to mediating 'between the United States and Mexico' to resolve the Tampico incident and the Veracruz intervention, but kept proposing to mediate between the United States, Huerta and the Constitutionalists to form a new provisional government. A recurrent plan featured Ángeles as president.

Constitutionalism entered a crisis in early June. Carranza moved his government from Chihuahua to Saltillo, ordered that the estates confiscated by Villa be redesignated as merely attached (for eventual return to their owners), stopped Coahuila coal shipments to Villa's railways, and on 11 June had local Zacatecas–Durango forces attack Zacatecas City, to try to build a Central Division to block the Northerners from moving south. On 13 June Villa resigned his command, but on 14 June his generals put him back in charge and against Carranza's orders moved down the railway to attack Zacatecas. On 19 June Carranza dismissed Ángeles from the war ministry. On 23 June the Northerners destroyed a federal force of 12,000 at Zacatecas, delivered the city to local chiefs, and returned to Torreón. On 29 June Carranza appointed González and Obregón as the Constitutionalist Army's first divisional generals, leaving Villa in military limbo.

In this crisis the Constitutionalists held together. On 4 July González had Caballero, Castro and Villarreal meet with Villa's delegates in Torreón to negotiate reunification. The delegates all agreed that Carranza would remain First Chief, and Villa commander of the Division of the North. But they also agreed on radical changes in the Guadalupe plan for reconstituting a regular government. On the triumph of the revolution the Constitutionalist Army would dissolve the Federal Army, take its place, and instate Carranza as provisional president, thereby making him ineligible to stand for regular office. His only function would be to convoke a junta of Constitutionalist chiefs, who would name delegates to a convention. The convention would frame a programme of reforms – to punish the church for its collaboration with Huerta, provide for 'the welfare of the workers', and 'emancipate the peasants economically' – and then oversee the election of a regular government to carry out the reforms.[14] Signed on 8 July, the Pact of Torreón received no approval from Carranza, but no challenge either.

On 13 July the ABC Conference closed with the United States still in Veracruz and committed to recognizing a provisional government negotiated between Huerta and the Constitutionalists. But on 7 July, in the North-west Corps's first major battle, Obregón, Blanco, Diéguez, Hill and a force of 15,000 destroyed a federal force of 12,000 at the railhead west of Guadalajara, and on 8 July occupied the city. There Obregón immediately inflicted shocking anti-clerical punishments on the church.

The day that Guadalajara fell Huerta named Francisco C. Carbajal as foreign minister. Carbajal had represented the Díaz government in the negotiations which led to the Juárez treaty in 1911, and might again preserve the Federal Army and bureaucracy. On 15 July Huerta resigned, and Carbajal became provisional president. On 20 July, aboard a German ship, Huerta sailed from Coatzacoalcos (then called Puerto México) into exile.

Jesús Carranza had already occupied San Luis Potosí, opening the North-east Corps's way straight into the Bajío. Carbajal requested a cease-fire for negotiations. The First Chief refused. On 23 July Wilson warned him that the United States might not recognize his government if it disregarded foreign interests or allowed reprisals against its opponents, and on 31 July he reminded him that without US recognition a

14 Jesús Silva Herzog, *Breve historia de la revolución mexicana* (2 vols., Mexico, 1960), II, 144–60.

Constitutionalist government 'could obtain no loans and must speedily break down'.[15] Carranza replied that the Constitutionalists would offer the same guarantees as always to foreigners and justice according to 'our national interests' to Mexicans.[16]

For the last campaign, to take Mexico City itself, the First Chief revised his strategy. Although the main Constitutionalist force was the Division of the North, by then 30,000 strong, he would not risk letting Villa and Ángeles participate in the final victory. To hold them in Torreón, he had González and Murguía bring 22,000 North-easterners through San Luis Potosí into the Bajío. He ordered Obregón to advance from the west and compel the Federal Army to surrender unconditionally. On 26 July Obregón left Diéguez in Guadalajara as provisional governor of Jalisco and took Blanco, Hill and a force of 18,000 into the Bajío. On 9 August, waiting twenty miles north of Mexico City, he received word that the federal commanders would surrender.

On 12 August Carbajal and most of his Cabinet left for Veracruz and exile. The governor of the Federal District, Iturbide, and Carranza's lately appointed agent in Mexico City, Alfredo Robles Domínguez, assumed responsibility for transitional order in the capital. On 13 August Obregón and Blanco, without González (to his resentment), signed a treaty with representatives of the Federal Army and Navy formally ending the war. The federal troops and Rurales in the capital were evacuated along the railway to Puebla, where Castro and Coss were to manage their disarmament and discharge. Carranza ordered his provisional governors and state commanders to muster out the defeated forces elsewhere. In particular he appointed his brother Jesús to take command of the entire quarter of the country from Oaxaca, where all the federal forces in the west and south were to assemble for discharge, to Yucatán, where there were no local revolutionaries. The most hated federal officers fled into exile, among them Orozco; a few die-hards went into hiding in the Puebla–Oaxaca mountains.

On 15 August Obregón led 6,000 men of the North-west Corps into the capital, posting Blanco with 10,000 more in the southern suburbs to prevent the Zapatistas from entering too. On 20 August Carranza paraded into the city. The next day he established his government in the National Palace and commenced a purge of the bureaucracy. Although

[15] Haley, *Revolution and intervention*, 149–50.
[16] United States Department of State, *Papers relating to the foreign relations of the United States, 1914* (Washington, DC, 1922), 575.

the war had ended, many more *oficinas de bienes intervenidos* opened, old and new offices increasingly serving private interests.

AUGUST 1914 – OCTOBER 1915

The struggle within the Mexican regime to restore its constitutionality had resulted in its destruction – the collapse of all the labyrinthine national, regional and local political and business deals developed over the previous 30 years, the loss of all the powers of international credit, the exhaustion of an overflowing treasury, and the dissolution of the Federal Army and the Rurales. Worse, the ruins remained to encumber the construction of a new regime. The foreign debt had piled up to 675 million pesos, with no prospect of payments on it while the United States held Veracruz; heavy foreign claims for death and destruction of property had also accumulated. The banking system verged on bankruptcy. Against metallic reserves of 90,000 pesos, bank notes and other obligations ran to 340 million pesos, and purely by fiat various Constitutionalist currencies circulated for 60 million pesos more, at an exchange value of only $0.25. Damage to railways and the disruption of mines, mills and factories had aggravated the country's economic depression. Monterrey's Fundidora had almost suspended operations. And as if the war had undone the weather too, for the second summer in a row the rains were poor, which meant either famine or food imports in 1915.

Moreover the victorious forces were at odds over the kind of new regime to construct. Their conflict went deeper than personal rivalry. Because the big revolutionary armies had developed in materially and socially different regions, north-east, north-west, north, and south, each represented a particular array of social forces. Three of the four armies had developed so differently that the struggle to build the new regime would begin as a struggle, however obscured, over the social relations of production. And having developed so separately, the different forces had no party in which to mediate the conflict.

The North-east and North-west Corps were similar. Built around the nuclei of Coahuila and Sonora militia, they had grown into professional armies, the troops fighting for pay, together now 60,000 strong. In reality both consisted of several professional units, belonging to the several generals who had raised them, guaranteed their wages, and (except for Jesús Carranza and a couple of others) obeyed the First Chief and co-operated with each other only for Machiavellian reasons. In both the north-east and the north-west these revolutionary chiefs typically had been enterprising young provincial merchants, farmers, and ranchers around the turn of the century. Frustrated as they matured – some of them Magonistas in 1906, most of them *anti-reeleccionistas* in 1910, almost all of them Maderistas in 1911, all of them municipal or state officials in 1912, and Constitutionalists to save their careers in 1913 – they took the national collapse of old deals as an opportunity to remake them with new partners. In the territories they dominated, thriving inside and outside the *oficinas de bienes intervenidos*, they were reassigning local corners to themselves, their kin, friends, and staffs. And they were asserting their patronage of organized labour. Immediately on the occupation of Mexico City they reformed the National Railways management, threatened the UCMGF and UMM leaderships with punishment for *huertismo*, and cancelled the port unions' contracts; the CGM dissolved. They declared themselves custodians of the already depressed Mining Union and the textile mill committees. On 21 August, on a subsidy from Obregón's headquarters, they re-opened Mexico City's Casa del Obrero. Regarding 'the agrarian question', they saw only the peon and only the symptoms of his plight – his old debts, which they cancelled, and his low wages, which they decreed should increase. Except for a quixotic two or three, they had no interest in redistributing land to peasants.

Pancho Villa's Division of the North was also a professional army, 30,000 regularly paid soldiers, the strongest military body in the country. But formed through a history more complicated than that in the north-east or north-west, it was a more heterogeneous force. Its original units had included militia and contingents of peasants fighting for land. But as the army grew, it had incorporated many new elements, unemployed miners, cowboys, railway trackmen and bandits, who fought for pay, promotion and the main chance. It had the most diverse collection of chiefs. Some had been young sharecropper spokesmen around the turn of the century, humiliated as they matured, often in trouble with the Rurales, Maderistas in 1910, captains of militia against Orozco in 1912, Constitutionalists to save their lives and their men in 1913. Many more had come virtually from nowhere, having distinguished themselves only since 1913, when their nerve, bloodthirstiness and luck had lifted them into high command. In the territory they ruled, they were grabbing everything they could, old and new. The contradictions in the Northern force emerged most clearly in the disposition of the confiscated haciendas. Villa intended to satisfy the peasants who had fought under him to reclaim lost lands, and to grant 'colonies' to the rest of his soldiers.[17] But he could not proceed as long as he might need an army to operate outside his region, because once his men had farms they would not easily go to fight far away. His agency for confiscated properties managed the haciendas like a trust, leasing them to tenants, spending the revenue on military supplies and wages, pensions for Division widows and orphans, and state administration, postponing redistribution of the land until the army could safely disband. But some Division chiefs held large estates which they ran like baronies.

Compounding these complications, Villa had saddled himself with the Maderista politicians resurgent in Sonora and Chihuahua. No more than the North-eastern or North-western generals did these revolutionary leaders have use for projects of allotting land to the troops. Their goal was to have the Division of the North make Ángeles president, so as to pick up the pieces of February 1913 and remake them into a new regime fit for enterprising landlords.

Of all the revolutionary armies, the Zapatista Army of the South was the simplest. It was not professional; its now 15,000 regulars and 10,000 guerillas drew no pay. The Southern Army belonged not to Zapata or to him and all his chiefs, but to the villages that had reared and raised both them and their troops and given the support necessary for a war for land. Rooted, trusted, and trusting in their villages, the Southern chiefs were therefore the most determined of all the revolutionaries to make serious economic and social changes. Neighbourhood heroes at the turn of the century, matured in local struggles to reclaim ancient rights to particular fields, woods, and streams, always in trouble with the police, village leaders by 1910, almost all of them Maderistas in 1911, all Zapatistas by 1912, and Zapatistas since, they had fought longest against the old deals, and now they moved, ignorant of theory but nevertheless compelled, towards the construction of an agrarian anarcho-communism. It helped their cause substantially that with Guerrero's silver they enjoyed the soundest currency in the country. It helped no less that administration of the headquarters remained the charge of Manuel Palafox, who had proved himself an honest, responsible, shrewd, decisive, fearless and

[17] Friedrich Katz, 'Agrarian changes in northern Mexico in the period of Villista rule, 1913–1915', in *Contemporary Mexico: Papers of the IV International Congress of Mexican History* (Los Angeles, 1976), 261, 272.

visionary executor of agrarian reform. In their territory, having shattered the old local monopolies, the Southern chiefs were rearranging trade to furnish local needs. And having expropriated the haciendas, they had Palafox authorizing villages to reoccupy their old lands, administering the rest for army revenue, pensions, and local subsidies, and preparing to grant farms to settlements that had never had them. Another Southern peculiarity was that the headquarters harboured refugee anarchist intellectuals from the Casa del Obrero. The anarchists did not figure in Zapatista decisions on strategy or policy. But they did publicize *zapatismo* as the source of bourgeois civilization.

These conditions alone invited foreign arbitration. Much more importantly, war had just exploded in Europe, which magnified the imperialist responsibilities of the neutral United States. In particular, it confirmed the Monroe Doctrine as a mandate for American hegemony in the western hemisphere. And because it threw world shipping into turmoil, it slowed Mexico's production for export (especially of oil), stunted the country's material capacities for order, and practically dictated American attempts to manage Mexican affairs. Since Carranza had installed himself in the National Palace without US mediation, Wilson refrained from recognizing his government. The United States therefore involved itself directly with Mexico's major social forces. Washington's goals – reconciliation of the remnants of the old regime with at least some champions of the new for a conservative but reputably popular constitutional restoration, an American loan to reform the foreign debt and fund a claims commission, and American financial supervision of Mexico's economic development – tallied well enough with the interests of the twenty or so large foreign and domestic companies. Because of the havoc in Europe, companies that had traded there would have to trade more in American markets now, anyway. But big business had no party or army.

As the best of a bad lot the United States put their money on Villa to build the new regime. Apparently the most pro-American of the Constitutionalist generals, apparently under the renewed Maderista conservative sway, Villa held firm command of the country's strongest fighting machine. If Washington supported him, enough of the Northeastern and North-western generals should flock into his camp to intimidate most of the others into joining him too. A formula for unification was already at hand in the Torreón pact, the convention of

Constitutionalist delegates. By late August 1914 the State Department agent at the Division of the North headquarters had Villa and Obregón negotiating the preparations for the convention. On 1 September, having spied the drift, Hopkins resigned as Carranza's counsel.

So disfavoured, the First Chief became more flexible. On 5 September he called the convention for 1 October in Mexico City. To keep the prospects in his own camp interesting, he decreed the replacement of previously issued Constitutionalist currency by a new issue of 130 million paper pesos. And he manoeuvred to split his opposition. When the Convention opened, its presiding officer was a lawyer who had become one of Carranza's closest advisers, Gustavo Madero's old whip and the 26th Congress's leading *renovador*, Luis Cabrera. There were no Northern to Southern delegates.

The shift toward Villa nevertheless occurred. On 5 October, following Obregón's arguments, the Convention voted to move north to Aguascalientes, in neutral territory, but near Villa's base at Torreón, and to exclude civilians (in particular Cabrera). On 15 October in Aguascalientes it invited Zapata to send delegates, and, once they arrived, approved 'in principle' the Ayala programme for redistributing land to peasants.[18] On 30 October it voted to depose the First Chief, and on 1 November it elected a provisional president, Eulalio Gutiérrez, a San Luis Potosí general. The next day it accepted Villa's occupation of Aguascalientes. On 6 November Gutiérrez was sworn into office. On 10 November, Carranza having refused to retire, the Convention declared him in rebellion, and Gutiérrez appointed Villa commander of the Convention's armies. Already the First Chief had moved his government from Mexico City to Orizaba. By then the value of his peso had fallen to $0.20 (see table 3). Washington judged the trend so satisfactory that on 13 November Wilson ordered the evacuation of the port of Veracruz in ten days' time.

But Carranza had prepared a surprisingly broad resistance. From the first he had the loyalty of Aguilar in Veracruz, González, who headed back north-east, and Jesús Carranza, who had remained in Coatzacoalcos, for the revenue from the Minatitlán oil fields. Once the sudden expansion of Northern control over the Convention alarmed other North-eastern and North-western generals, he had deftly played on

[18] John Womack, Jr, *Zapata and the Mexican Revolution* (New York, 1968), 217–18.

their jealousies. Within a week of the Convention declaring the First Chief in rebellion, almost all the important North-eastern and North-western subordinates – Alvarado, Caballero, Calles, Castro, Coss, Diéguez, Hill, Murguía, Villarreal – declared themselves to be Carrancistas. Obregón too then joined the First Chief in Orizaba. Of all the important subordinates, only Blanco stuck with the Convention. When the United States evacuated Veracruz on 23 November, Aguilar occupied it. On 26 November Carranza established his government in the port, where he had revenue from customs and an outlet for exports to gain dollars to import contraband arms and ammunition.

Not all revolutionaries took one side or another. In many isolated districts local chiefs set themselves up as petty warlords. The most notable, Manuel Peláez, appeared in the northern Veracruz mountains. In November he began selling the oil companies protection for their operations in the nearby lowlands, between Tampico and Tuxpan.

Late in November 1914 Villista and Zapatista forces together occupied Mexico City. In early December Gutiérrez announced his cabinet, including a subordinate of Villa's as undersecretary of war and Manuel Palafox as minister of agriculture. Big businesses in the city received the new government without serious complaint. So did the unions. In almost explicit support, the Mexico Power and Light workers organized the Mexican Electrical Workers' Union (SME), assuring a friendly control of energy not only for the city's factories and trolleys but also for the big mines in Hidalgo and Mexico State.

From Chihuahua into the Bajío, Villista generals recruited thousands of new troops for immediate action. By mid-December their forces had captured Guadalajara and launched offensives against Carrancista garrisons from Sonora to Tamaulipas; and Zapatistas had captured Puebla City. On 4 January in Mexico City Villa incorporated some 1,500 ex-Federal Army officers (including seven divisional generals) for new commands and staff in his expanded armies.

But the Carrancista forces had also gained strength. On 4 December, anticipating a return to the offensive, Carranza decreed the attachment of almost all the country's railways. And wherever Carrancista generals held control, they opened a characteristically Carrancista agency, a local Comisión Reguladora del Comercio, to control the distribution of local supplies and encourage enlistment in their ranks. From Coatzacoalcos, Jesús Carranza crossed the Isthmus of Tehuantepec, sailed up the west coast rallying loyal chiefs as far as Sinaloa, and returned to raise an army in Oaxaca for a southern–western campaign. Diéguez in Jalisco connected with Murguía in Michoacán, where the Villista occupation of Mexico City had accidentally stranded him, and together they harrassed Villista communications through the Bajío. By late December Villarreal held Monterrey, and González held Tampico and its revenue. While the Villistas scoured the depressed north for hard money to import arms and ammunition to maintain their broad offensives, and while the Zapatistas hoarded their silver and redistributed land, the Carrancistas pumped the Gulf's richest companies for taxes and loans to build a new Army of Operations. Under Obregón, with Castro and Coss as his main subordinates, the new corps quickly formed into a skilled and well-supplied force of 12,000. On 15 January 1915 it easily recaptured Puebla, and prepared to move on Mexico City.

Politically too the Carrancistas reorganized. To justify their defiance of the Convention, the generals persuaded the First Chief to publish a programme of reforms. On 12 December 1914 Carranza declared not only that his Constitutionalist movement would continue, but also that in respect for the nation's urgent needs he would issue provisional decrees to guarantee political freedoms, return land to the dispossessed, tax the rich, improve the condition of 'the proletarian classes', purify the courts, re-expel the church from politics, reassert the national interest in natural resources, and facilitate divorce.[19] On 14 December he reformed his Cabinet, with Luis Cabrera as finance minister and other *renovadores* in most of the other ministries. On 6 January he authorized agrarian commissions to hear complaints of dispossession and consider expropriation for grants to landless villages. On 7 January 1915 he ordered oil companies to obtain new licences from his government for all their operations.

The United States upped its bet on Villa. On 8–9 January the US Army chief of staff and the State Department agent in the north met publicly with him in Juárez and El Paso. In the north-east, Ángeles beat Villarreal, taking Monterrey on 10 January. In Oaxaca, for local reasons but with nevertheless important national consequences, a local chief had Jesús Carranza murdered.

To Washington's dismay the Convention collapsed. On 16 January, exposed in correspondence with Carrancistas, provisional president Gutiérrez fled Mexico City for San Luis Potosí and obscurity. His

[19] Fabela and Fabela, *Documentos históricos*, IV, 107–12.

replacement, the Villista Roque González Garza, could preside only over the city's accumulating woes, including food shortages and a typhoid epidemic. Diéguez and Murguía recaptured Guadalajara. And as Obregón's Army of Operations approached Mexico City, the Villista–Zapatista garrison evacuated it, and the Convention retreated into Morelos. On 28 January Obregón occupied the city.

Villa organized his own government in the north, and in mid-February recaptured Guadalajara. His inclination then was to destroy Diéguez and Murguía, to clear his right flank for an attack on Obregón. But Ángeles insisted on heavy reinforcements in Monterrey for a campaign on Tampico. Deferring to him, Villa shifted the bulk of his forces back through Torreón to the north-east. This move alone so demoralized Villarreal that he retired into exile in Texas. And Villa gained a new kind of support in Yucatán, where ex-federal troops revolted in his name.

Meanwhile, as world shipping adjusted to the war in Europe, the oil companies in Mexico resumed booming production for export to the United States. They did not relicence their operations as Carranza had ordered, but Carrancista oil revenue soared. With this and the customs at Veracruz, Carranza sent Alvarado to fight for Yucatán, its Henequén Commission, and more revenue. In Mexico City, in a Jacobin burst of anti-clericalism and anti-mercantilism, Obregón forced loans from the church, levied special taxes on big commercial houses, jailed recalcitrant clergy and merchants, bought the support of the Casa del Obrero, and through it recruited some 5,000 workers to form 'Red Battalions'.

After three months of Carrancista resistance, Wilson tried a more threatening course. On 6 March the United States informed Obregón and Carranza that it would hold them 'personally accountable . . . for suffering caused American lives or property' in Mexico City.[20] For a response Carranza had the benefit of advice from his new legal counsel in the United States, Charles A. Douglas. Another Washington lawyer, long a confidant of the Secretary of State and legal agent in the United States also for the Cuban, Nicaraguan, and Panamanian governments, Douglas was at the time in Veracruz. After consultation with him the First Chief retreated. On 10 March he had Obregón evacuate the famished and fever-ridden capital, which the Zapatistas and the Convention reoccupied. But the Carrancistas gained more valuable ground when on 19 March Alvarado occupied Mérida and the next day Progreso.

---

[20] Haley, *Revolution and intervention*, 155.

By March 1915 the war involved some 160,000 men – 80,000 Carrancistas, 50,000 Villistas, 20,000 Zapatistas, and 10,000 others. The beginning of its end occurred during the next month. In late March Villa launched his campaign toward Tampico. Undistracted, he probably would have crushed the defences mounted there by a newly notable Carrancista subordinate, Jacinto Treviño, González himself having rejoined Carranza in Veracruz. But Diéguez and Murguía threatened Guadalajara again. And Obregón, having left Mexico City, moved with Castro and Hill north into the Bajío, counting on Carrancista chiefs in Hidalgo and Puebla to protect the railway that kept him supplied from Veracruz. On 4 April he fortified the Bajío's key junction, Celaya, with 11,000 men, artillery and machine guns. Villa rushed 12,000 men and artillery to attack the town. The Villistas almost won on 6–7 April, but Obregón's forces held firm. Both sides reinforced, Obregón's to 15,000, with a heavy shipment of ammunition from Veracruz, Villa's to 20,000. The second battle of Celaya began on 13 April. It ended on 15 April with the Villistas retreating north. On 18 April Diéguez and Murguía took Guadalajara.

In Washington in the spring of 1915 the news about German submarines in the North Atlantic shipping lanes buried the news from Celaya. But because the war in Europe had begun to limit American freedom of action abroad, Washington needed political order in Mexico soon. Already it suffered the threat of new trouble: since January Orozco, Felicistas, and Huertistas in the United States had made contact with rebellious Mexican–Americans in South Texas, American Catholic bishops, and Wall Street lawyers, and on 12 April Huerta himself arrived in New York with German funds for a counter-revolution. On 23 April Carranza offered relief: Douglas privately submitted to the State Department a draft of the promises that the First Chief would make if the United States recognized his government, including special protection of foreign lives and property, indemnity for foreign losses, no confiscation to resolve 'the agrarian question', a general amnesty, and respect for religion. In May a high State Department official and the Secretary of Interior promoted a variant counter-revolutionary plan, rigged around Eduardo Iturbide for president; the resulting government, if recognized by the United States, would receive a loan through Speyer of as much as $500 million. But preoccupied then with the *Lusitania* crisis, Wilson decided to press for revolutionary reconciliation. On 2 June he offered support to the 'man or group of men . . . who can . . . ignore, if they cannot unite, the warring factions of the country . . .

and set up a government at Mexico . . . with whom the program of the revolution will be a business and not merely a platform'.[21]

Wilson's offer arrived just as its chances for success sank. During May Villa had reorganized his forces and re-engaged Obregón's – now reinforced by Diéguez and Murguía – in a long, complex battle around León. Recalling Ángeles from the north-east, abandoning Monterrey to local Carrancistas, and cutting the siege of Tampico so thin that it crumbled before Treviño's defences, Villa concentrated 35,000 men against Obregón's 30,000. The decisive combat began on 1 June. By 3 June the Villistas had almost won again; Obregón was wounded, and his replacement, Hill, had only nominal command over Castro, Diéguez and Murguía. But short of ammunition the Villistas broke down tactically, and on 5 June they retreated north again.

On 9 June Villa accepted Wilson's call for reconciliation and proposed immediate discussions with Carranza. But the Carrancistas now had better reasons than ever for continuing to fight. They had some 100,000 men in arms against 40,000 Villistas and 20,000 Zapatistas. Local *oficinas de bienes intervenidos* and *comisiones reguladoras* supported their garrisons. González and Coss were building a new Eastern Army Corps in Puebla to recapture Mexico City. Four more chiefs became divisional generals – Castro, Diéguez, Hill and Murguía. The revenue for an offensive flowed heavily, not only from the oil districts and Veracruz but also from the Henequén Commission, which Alvarado had turned into a regular reservoir of dollars; within a month Alvarado became the seventh divisional general. On 11 June, urging Villistas and Zapatistas to reunify under his authority, Carranza published as his programme of government the promises that he had offered in April to the State Department, and declared his expectation of recognition.

On 18 June Wilson warned Carranza that the United States might soon intervene to save Mexico from herself, but he granted that if Carranza would make 'a genuine effort to unite all parties and groups', then the United States would 'seriously consider' recognizing him.[22] On 21 June Carranza replied that if the United States would remain neutral, 'the Constitutionalist cause will subdue the opposition'.[23] On 27 June the US Department of Justice subdued his main opposition in its jurisdiction, jailing Orozco and Huerta in El Paso. The news must have sharpened the bitterness of Don Porfirio's last days: on 2 July he died in

[21] Arthur S. Link, *Wilson: the struggle for neutrality, 1914–1915* (Princeton, 1960), 476–7.
[22] Haley, *Revolution and intervention*, 164.   [23] Link, *Wilson: the struggle*, 480.

Paris. (Orozco escaped from jail, but was killed by Texas police on 30 August. Huerta, released to house arrest in El Paso, died of cirrhosis of the liver on 13 January 1916.)

Meanwhile, a new opposition for the Carrancistas to subdue had erupted in Oaxaca. On 3 June, under the influence of local conservatives, the state government had declared its independence. But in early July Carranza confidently assigned an old subordinate of his brother's, Jesús A. Castro, to restore Carrancista authority there. More important, *villismo* collapsed as a potential ruling force. Its currency hardly circulated through the north. The practice of special levies decayed into forays of plunder. Many officers and batches of troops deserted; those forces that remained barely held Treviño in Monterrey, and could not stop Obregón, freshly munitioned and reinforced from Veracruz, from moving Cesáreo Castro, Murguía and 20,000 troops north towards Aguascalientes. There 10,000 Villistas mounted resistance. Combat began on 6 July. On 10 July Obregón's forces broke the Villista lines, and the Villistas retreated north yet again. Ángeles left the country to lobby in Washington. Meanwhile González had moved his 10,000-man Eastern Army on Mexico City, from which the Convention fled for the last time on 9 July, and he occupied the capital on 11 July. Local Carrancistas took San Luis Potosí and Murguía took Zacatecas. In a daring stab at recovery a Villista force still in the west bolted across the Bajío and attacked Obregón's supply lines with Veracruz. But on 17 July González evacuated Mexico City to defend the lines. On 2 August having with Coss and his forces repulsed the Villistas, he reoccupied the capital definitively. And Coss became the eighth divisional general.

As *carrancismo* expanded militarily, it became more interesting to big business. Because the Carrancistas now drew regular revenue from exports, they no longer had to levy special taxes; indeed they brought relief from Villa's levies. Their paper pesos increased inflation: from November 1914 to May 1915 the value of the Carrancista peso fell from $0.20 to $0.09 (see table 3). But because the European war and the civil war proscribed productive investment, inflation provided welcome alternatives in commodity speculation. In June the finance ministry made another issue to increase the supply to 215 million pesos, then in July announced that since much of the paper in circulation was counterfeit, it would soon issue a completely new currency of 250 million pesos – in effect soliciting speculation.

Some political connections developed with small businesses. The key

was local military control. Because particular Carrancista chiefs commanded the railways, *oficinas de bienes intervenidos* and *comisiones reguladoras*,
they positively obliged planters, ranchers, manufacturers and merchants
in their districts to accept deals with them – or their kin, friends, and staff.
Given inflation and two years of bad harvests, the highly profitable grain
trade underpinned most of these partnerships. That summer the rains
were poor again, promising another bad harvest, higher profits, and a
consolidation of the new deals.

The Carrancistas also tightened their patronage of organized labour.
Here too the key was local military control. The war itself, frequently
shifting the command over the railways, had already ruptured the
UCMGF and UMM. Now military favours for loyal service and threats
of punishment for *villismo* paralysed them. Under military vigilance
Mining Union locals in the north-east barely survived. Military tolerance
of previous agreements kept the port unions moving freight. Similarly,
with a couple of decrees raising wages, Aguilar kept the Orizaba textile
workers in the mills. And Carrancista subsidies fostered Casas del
Obrero, most of them docile, in 30 or so provincial cities and towns. In
Mexico City, however, where under the Convention unions had grown
freely, González could not maintain control. The electrical workers'
SME had developed its own leadership and strength, and in May it had
won its first strike. On 12 August, despite González, it began another,
which, with help from comrades in Tampico, Pachuca, and the mines of
El Oro in Mexico State, it carried on for eight days and won.

Wilson tried again to mediate among the contending armies. On 11
August in Washington a Pan-American Conference of delegates from the
United States, the 'ABC' countries, Bolivia, Guatemala, and Uruguay
called for 'all prominent civil and military authorities in Mexico' to
arrange another revolutionary convention to devise a provisional
government.[24] The Villista generals and Villa accepted at once, as did the
Zapatistas. But none of the Carrancista generals would discuss the
invitation; all referred the Pan-Americans to the First Chief. On 10
September Carranza formally answered, refusing to discuss anything but
recognition of his government.

On 4 September the Villistas had lost Saltillo, their last foothold in the
north-east. On 19 September they began evacuating Torreón, retreating
to their old base in Chihuahua. On 26 September the last of them left the
town, and on 28 September Murguía occupied it. In the same weeks

---

[24] *Ibid.*, 493.

Carrancista forces moving up from Acapulco drove the Zapatistas back to their old base in Morelos.

Nearly a year of regular warfare among the revolutionaries had ended in Carrancista victory. And on 9 October the Pan-Americans concluded that 'the Carranza party is the only party possessing the essentials for recognition as the de facto government of Mexico . . .'.[25] On 19 October the United States recognized Carranza's government *de facto*, reducing the Villistas and Zapatistas to mere rebels.

OCTOBER 1915 – MAY 1917

In triumph Venustiano Carranza, the First Chief, defined *carrancismo's* new task as 'the reconstruction of the Fatherland'. He meant more than restoring regular railway service and the value of the peso. His country having suffered a history that he now described as 'the disequilibrium of four centuries, three of oppression and one of internal struggles, . . . thirty years of tyranny, . . . the Revolution . . . and a horrible chaos . . ., a barracks coup and an assassination . . .', he meant the deliberate construction of a Mexican state.[26] After three years of civil war he had firmly in mind the form that the state should have. He did not recite theories about it, but he projected it clearly in the policies that he soon undertook – ignoring the Monroe Doctrine, raising taxes on foreign companies, establishing a central bank to manage Mexican finances and promote Mexican business, returning attached estates to the old landlords, institutionalizing the mediation of conflicts among business-men and between business and labour, and crushing disobedient peasants and workers. If these policies succeeded, a centralized state would keep national markets free of privilege, more benefits would go to all Mexicans, and in the consequent prosperity the old dreams of balance and order would come true.

Carrancista 'reconstruction' faced formidable obstacles, the worst being the power behind the Monroe Doctrine. The United States not only recognized Carranza's government on 19 October but also privately detailed its duties, including 'protection of foreign property and prevention of excessive taxation, . . . currency issue based on substantial guarantees', and 'early and equitable settlement' of foreign claims.[27] The

[25] *Ibid.*, 639.   [26] Fabela and Fabela, *Documentos históricos*, IV, 153–6.
[27] Canova to Lansing, 13 October 1915, United States National Archives (USNA), Record Group 59, 812.00/ 16546–1/2; Canova to Lansing, 16 October 1915, USNA 59, 812.00/ 16547–1/2; Lansing, Memorandum to Arredondo, 19 October 1915, USNA 59, 812.00/ 16548–1/2.

domestic obstacles were several. An army of 100,000, which the government could not safely reduce immediately, took heavy doses of revenue. The few big Mexican companies had retrenched, and provincial businessmen, highly suspicious of local Carrancista commanders, conducted their affairs almost in secret. The Mexico City Casa del Obrero, which still had its Red Battalions in arms, had just declared its independence by announcing plans to form a national confederation of unions and affiliate it with 'the International'. Besides, the Villistas, Zapatistas, and exiles were still dangerous threats.

But Carranza had promising powers. At least he enjoyed recognition from the United States, which once more legalized imports of American arms and ammunition for his forces. On 10 November he received recognition from Germany too, and in December from Britain. Moreover he had flowing through his finance ministry the country's main currents of revenue – customs duties from almost all the major ports, mining and oil taxes, and henequén sales. By elaborate counterbalancing he dominated the eight divisional generals in charge of the army. The various offices of attached property he brought under a central Administración de Bienes Intervenidos. For advisers he had Douglas in Washington and several worldly and well-informed associates in Mexico: finance minister Cabrera, no financier but the country's shrewdest political analyst and sharpest polemicist; Alberto J. Pani, an engineer long connected with Mexico City contractors, trusted by Standard Oil, Director General of Constitutionalist railways since 1914, soon to be elected president of the national railways; Ignacio Bonillas, a MIT-trained engineer long connected with Sonora's mining and contracting companies, trusted by Southern Pacific, Constitutionalist minister of communications (railways) since 1913; and not least Fernando González Roa, counsel for Wells Fargo, the National Railways, the Yucatán railways, the Henequén Commission, and the department of agriculture, and senior partner in the law firm handling most foreign claims against Mexico. And he had the *renovadores* to organize support for eventual elections and serve in the regular government to follow.

He also had a sound strategy: discuss with the United States its concerns in Mexico, but delay resolutions until the war in Europe ended, when he could call on the Old World to redress the balance in the New; return estates to landlords who would deal with him; and reassure businessmen by keeping a firm grip on unions. The crucial manoeuvre would be a convention to write a new constitution, which would justify a short-term loan in New York, oblige landlords and businessmen to admit their stakes in the new state, and issue in the Carrancista domination of the regular government.

'Reconstruction' started strongly. At the First Chief's direction Douglas prepared for discussions of claims and a loan. In November and December a new Credit Regulatory Commission inspected the country's twenty-four chartered banks and closed fourteen of them, to prepare for a central bank. Unfortunately the peso fell to $0.04 (see table 3). But in January Cabrera went to Washington to consult with Douglas, then to New York to approach the House of Morgan.

Carrancista dissolution of the Villista threat seemed definitive. On 1 November Villa attacked Agua Prieta, hoping to raise a new war in Sonora and discredit the newly recognized government. But thanks to US permission, the First Chief had reinforcements from Torreón arrive via Eagle Pass, Texas, and Douglas, Arizona, in time to save the town. On 5 November Villa publicly denounced Carranza for having sold Mexico to the United States for recognition, and continued fighting south towards Hermosillo. But Carranza moved Diéguez from Jalisco up to Sonora, driving the Villistas back, and shifted Treviño from Monterrey to join Murguía in a campaign into Chihuahua. On 23 December Treviño occupied Chihuahua City and became the ninth divisional general. On 1 January, back in the Chihuahua mountains, Villa disbanded the remnants of his army into guerillas. On 14 January Carranza declared him an outlaw to be shot on sight.

The First Chief did not deny 'the agrarian question' that Villa and Zapata still represented. On 19 January 1916 he decreed the establishment of a National Agrarian Commission. This was not, however, to redistribute land, but to oversee and circumscribe local decisions on villages' claims. (For statistics on Carranza's land distribution, see table 4.)

Meanwhile the government checked a sudden burst of inflation-provoked challenges from organized labour. On 16 November the UCMGF and shop unions organized a strike on the Mexican Railway. On 30 November Carranza drafted all railway personnel. In November and December textile workers, bakers, typographers and the SME went on strike in Mexico City, as did miners in nearby El Oro, and on 2 January the city's Casa del Obrero and the SME took the lead in forming a new Federación de Sindicatos Obreros del Distrito Federal (FSODF),

Table 4. *Definitive distribution of land to villages under the degree of 6 January 1915 and Article 27 of the constitution of 1917, 1915–20*

Year	Villages	Heads of families	Hectares
1915	0	0	0
1916	1	182	1,246
1917	8	2,615	5,635
1918	57	15,071	68,309
1919	60	14,948	40,276
1920	64	15,566	64,333
TOTAL	190	48,382	179,799

Source: Eyler N. Simpson, *The Ejido. Mexico's way out* (Chapel Hill, 1937), table 17.
Note: The total area of Mexico was 198,720,100 hectares.

which declared a 'class struggle' for 'the socialization of the means of production'.[28] On 13 January Carranza ordered the Casa's Red Battalions mustered out. On 18 January González warned the FSODF that 'the government cannot sanction proletarian tyranny', and on 5 February stopped the Casa's subsidy.[29]

Carranza suffered sharp disappointments. Morgan spurned Cabrera's overture. And after the Mexican government cancelled a Standard Oil subsidiary's concession not registered under the 7 January 1915 oil decree, the oil companies and the State Department accused it of intending to nationalize oil. In February the companies began paying a regular monthly tribute to Manuel Peláez to police their Tampico–Tuxpan fields. And some connected with exiles in the United States, who with private help from inside the State Department rallied around Félix Díaz and secretly shipped him to Veracruz to raise a counter-revolution.

But new circumstances abroad improved the chances for a centralized consolidation. Adjusted to produce for the war in Europe, the American economy had already started to boom in 1915. On its strength, mining and manufacturing in Mexico began to recuperate in early 1916, providing new revenue. And the Carrancista government kept displaying power and competence. On 1 February it announced that González would command a 30,000-man campaign against the Zapatistas in

[28] Luis Araiza, *Historia del movimiento obrero mexicano* (4 vols. in one, Mexico, 1964–5), III, 115.
[29] *Ibid.,* III, 124.

Morelos. On 13 February it announced a commission to draft the new constitution. On 25 February, anticipating Felicista trouble, Carranza promoted Veracruz's Governor Aguilar to divisional general (the tenth). The same day he ordered Cabrera to prepare redemption of the various current pesos by a new issue of 500 million in paper impossible to counterfeit, *infalsificables*. The finance ministry directed governors to relinquish their *oficinas de bienes intervenidos* to its agents. On 5 March, capping an eight-month campaign, Jesús Castro's forces reoccupied Oaxaca City. Such progress favourably impressed the United States, and on 9 March the State Department swore in a regular ambassador to Mexico.

The Carrancista project failed, however, because the Carrancistas underestimated Villa's remaining power and audacity. On 9 March 1916 Villa led 500 guerillas across the border, attacked Columbus, New Mexico, killed seventeen Americans, and withdrew into the Chihuahua mountains. He intended to destroy the United States–Carranza connection, oblige Carranza's generals to overthrow him, and negotiate a new revolutionary coalition with them. This he did not accomplish. But his attack, outraging the American public in a year of US presidential elections, did cause a crisis in US–Mexican relations so serious that its impact altered the shape of 'reconstruction'.

On 15 March 1916 a US Army punitive expedition entered Chihuahua. Wilson had no plans for war with Mexico; his primary concern then was persuading Congress to increase US armed forces to counter Republican cries for a still greater increase for action in the war in Europe. The sinking of the *Sussex* on 24 March left all sober American politicians preoccupied with Europe. The expeditionary force numbered only 6,000 men (later reinforced to 10,000), and had orders only to disperse Villista bands near the border. But the United States took four months, until after the Republican and Democratic nominating conventions, to recover enough calm for deliberations to begin about the retreat of the force.

Through the crisis Carranza managed a masterly diplomacy in the defence of sovereignty and the preservation of peace. From the first he had Douglas's reports on Washington's limited aims. On 13 March, to bind the army into the government, he made Aguilar minister of foreign relations and Obregón minister of war. He let the expedition base itself in Chihuahua without military resistance; not until 12 April, because of a bloody pro-Villa riot in an important Chihuahua market town, did he demand that the expedition withdraw from Mexico. On 28 April negotiations between Wilson's envoys and his own, led by Obregón, began in Juárez. The Americans sought a Carrancista guarantee against another Mexican 'invasion of American territory' and, if Carrancista forces could not police the border, permission for US forces to act for them.[30] For a show of resolution Wilson placed an embargo on arms and ammunition shipments to the Mexican government. Obregón sought the expedition's unqualified and speedy withdrawal. For a show of power and determination to crush rebellion, Carranza had González storm Morelos. The border bandits raided into Texas, and Wilson called up the Texas, New Mexico and Arizona militia. On 11 May the envoys suspended negotiations. On 20 May Wilson won relief in the US Congress: the National Defense Act was passed, which allowed for middling increases in the army and the militia. Meanwhile Carranza had Douglas in Querétaro for consultation, and on 22 May he had Aguilar publish a long note to the State Department explaining that if the United States wanted order in Mexico, it would have to remove its troops from the country and reauthorize arms and ammunition shipments to the government. Aguilar also implied that the Mexican government would pay reparations for border raids.

On 10 June the Republicans nominated a moderate for president. On 12 June, to show Carrancista determination to restore constitutional order, Carranza announced countrywide municipal elections in September. On 16 June the Democrats nominated Woodrow Wilson. Relations between the two countries worsened anyway. Mexican-American rebels raided from Mexico into Texas, and on 18 June Wilson mobilized the entire US militia for service on the border. On 21 June an expeditionary patrol in Chihuahua provoked a skirmish with a Carrancista force and half its men were killed or captured. On 24 June Wilson threatened a major military intervention in Mexico. But Carranza ordered the release of the captured expeditionaries. By the end of the month Wilson had backed off. In early July he and Carranza accepted the renewal of negotiations in a Joint US–Mexico Commission to meet in the United States. But Carranza did not appoint his commissioners for another month, knowing that nothing substantial would happen in negotiations until after the US elections in November. The commissioners he then named were the Carrancistas most likely to make the American connections most advantageous to his government: Luis Cabrera, Alberto Pani, and Ignacio Bonillas.

[30] Arthur S. Link, *Wilson: confusions and crises, 1915–1916* (Princeton, 1960), 290.

But inside the country the First Chief lost much power. The key was the delivery of the war ministry to Obregón, who on 15 March also received Carranza's authorization to order payments directly from the treasury. Extraordinary corruption soon flourished throughout the army. The troop rolls expanded to 125,000. With or without Obregón's approval, generals practically appropriated railways, *oficinas de bienes intervenidos* and *comisiones reguladoras*. Independently, Treviño's command in Chihuahua became a model of graft, and González's campaign in Morelos a showcase of plundering.

Also debilitating was the spectacular failure of the government's monetary policy. On 4 April Carranza instituted the Monetary Commission, a rudimentary central bank, to issue the 500 million *infalsificables* in June. The news fuelled inflation, and as real wages plummeted again, organized labour became intensely combative. Already between 5 and 17 March a convention of delegates representing 100 or so unions in the Federal District and seven states, held by the FSODF and Veracruz anarchists in the port, had founded the Confederación de Trabajadores de la Región Mexicana, for 'class struggle' by 'direct action' for 'socialization of the means of production'.[31] In May the peso fell to $0.02. Defying war ministry regulations, the UCMGF and the main railway-shop unions organized a strike on the Constitutionalist railways for payment on a gold standard. The government repressed the movement, then granted the unions an eight-hour day, the first in any industry in Mexico. Simultaneously the FSODF carried out a general strike in Mexico City for gold-standard payment and at least on paper won its demands. In June the *infalsificable* appeared at $0.10, but currency speculation continued, at the expense of small debtors and workers, and on 31 July the FSODF called another general strike, which closed the city down for several days. The government repressed it, and a court-martial sent the leaders to prison. Strikes also hit mining districts and Tuxpan and Minatitlán oil installations.

In all this disappointment Carranza's only notable domestic success was against Félix Díaz. It took Díaz until July to get together with ex-Federal Army renegades in Veracruz, Oaxaca and Chiapas, and then, because of Jesús Castro's rule in the region, he could not raise an offensive. For such service Castro was made a divisional general, bringing the total to eleven.

As the crisis passed, the Carrancista 'reconstruction' resumed. On 15

31 Rosendo Salazar and José G. Escobedo, *Las pugnas de la gleba, 1907–1922* (2 vols. in one, Mexico, 1923), I, 179.

August the government required foreign companies interested in natural resources to renounce their national rights. On 3 September it staged municipal elections, the first step towards centralized co-ordination of local chiefs. Although the Joint Commission began its sessions on 6 · September and the Americans proposed to postpone discussions of the punitive expedition's withdrawal until Mexico provided 'formal assurance' of protection for foreign lives and property, on 14 September Carranza decreed that mining companies had to resume regular operations or lose title to their property.[32] The same day he announced elections on 22 October for a Constitutional Convention, and the following day he attached all banks and their metallic reserves, around $25 million in gold, to fund a central bank.

But because of the crisis, the substance of 'reconstruction' was regionalized. The crucial conflict in Mexico was now between the government, with a national project but little power, and probably twenty important generals, jealously divided among themselves – a few, mainly Aguilar and Cesáreo Castro, for Carranza; some freewheeling, principally Obregón and González; others in regional strongholds, like Calles in Sonora, Caballero in Tamaulipas, Diéguez in Jalisco, Jesús Castro in Oaxaca, or Alvarado in Yucatán, where he had organized a political machine, the Partido Socialista. Poor rains again that summer tightened the generals' grip on local affairs. And in this disarray the rebels resumed action. On 15–16 September Villa raided Chihuahua City for much military booty. Two weeks later the Zapatistas began raiding into the Federal District.

In October the First Chief and the generals defined their strategies for the new conflict. Carranza's was for the short run, to use his executive office to remove the reasons for his decline before the return to regular government. In his first direct approach to Germany he suggested to Berlin that if it helped to hasten Washington's withdrawal of the punitive expedition, he would provide facilities for U-boats in the Gulf. He waived tariffs on imports of food. And, the *infalsificable* having fallen to $0.03, he ordered payment of taxes and wages on a gold standard. The generals' strategy was, for the long run, not to challenge Carranza directly, but not to let him govern effectively either, and eventually to settle the succession to him among themselves. On 22 October Carranza's and the generals' placemen were elected to the Constitutional

---

[32] Robert F. Smith, *The United States and revolutionary nationalism in Mexico, 1916–1932* (Chicago, 1972), 57.

Convention. The next day González, Obregón and other generals met in Mexico City and formally founded the Partido Liberal Constitucionalista, a covering name for their personal political outfits. The PLC would, they announced, support Carranza for president. It would also provide him with a crippling opposition.

International circumstances in November 1916 fostered Mexico's political decentralization. As the stalemate on the Somme and Wilson's re-election brought the United States and Germany on to a collision course, both Washington and Berlin treated Carranza more cautiously. Neither now favoured a centralized Mexican government, for each expected that the other might eventually win its loyalty. To deny each other a significant ally, both countries encouraged the conflict between Carranza, the generals, and the rebels.

In November the First Chief made another overture to Berlin. He did not break neutrality, but bent it a long way, offering Germany close commercial and military co-operation. But the German foreign ministry rejected the 'suggestion'. Instead the German ambassador bought a surge of pro-Germanism among important generals, and the German secret services manoeuvred to support Villa and to plant saboteurs in Tampico. Once the German government on 9 January sealed its decision to resume unrestricted submarine warfare, foreign minister Zimmermann telegraphed the ambassador new instructions, which arrived on 19 January. The U-boats would go into unrestricted action on 1 February. If as expected the United States then declared war on Germany, the ambassador should propose a German–Mexican alliance to Carranza: 'joint pursuit of the war, joint conclusion of peace. Substantial financial support and an agreement on our part for Mexico to reconquer its former territories in Texas, New Mexico, and Arizona.'[33] But this was a formula for the destruction of the Mexican state.

On 24 November the Joint US–Mexican Commissioners signed a protocol unconditionally requiring the punitive expedition's withdrawal. The prior discussion, however, still implied that US forces could return to Mexico if the Mexican government did not protect foreign lives and property. Paying for the removal of even the implication of an American right to intervene again, Carranza abolished the infamous *infalsificables* (which had fallen to $0.005), decreed a return to gold and silver currency, and postponed for four months the requirement that

---

[33] Friedrich Katz, *The secret war in Mexico: Europe, the United States, and the Mexican Revolution* (Chicago, 1981), 354.

foreign companies renounce their national rights. Then his commissioners reported his refusal of the protocol. On 3 January the US commissioners recommended to Wilson a simple withdrawal, and Wilson ordered the expedition home. But Carranza gained no power. In January he had an envoy in New York ask Morgan for a short-term $10 million loan. Following the State Department's cues, Morgan would not consider the request. On 5 February, the day the last expeditionary troops returned to American soil, the Mexican government asked permission to import embargoed ammunition. The State Department refused to forward the request to Wilson. At the same time the new US military attaché in Mexico City warmly befriended war minister Obregón. Privately American agents began trying to restore contact with Villa, and tribute continued to flow to Peláez.

Meanwhile the generals rode higher and higher. War minister Obregón behaved like the head of an opposition, publicly lambasting the First Chief's *renovador* ministers and associates. The rebels stepped up their campaigns: on 27 November Villa raided Chihuahua City again, for much more military booty; in late December Villistas occupied Torreón for a week, forced a heavy loan, and took more booty. Villa shortly met his match, when Carranza returned Treviño to Monterrey and sent Murguía to Chihuahua. After a defeat by Murguía in early January, Villa drew his troops back into the Sierra Madre, but with the resources for a long guerilla war. In the Tampico–Tuxpan oil fields by mid-January, Peláez had a broad offensive underway. The Zapatistas recovered too. Spending their last silver to buy lots of arms and ammunition in the Carrancista black markets, they opened an offensive across Morelos and into Puebla. By mid-January they had driven González's forces out of their base and were organizing cadres and civilian administration. In early February they had Palafox start organizing local land commissions and a new regular military force.

As if in the eye of a hurricane, the Constitutional Convention opened in Querétaro on 20 November 1916. Most of the 200 or so deputies nominally represented districts in the populous states across central Mexico, from Jalisco to Veracruz, where various generals had had them elected. At least 80 per cent were bourgeois, and 75 per cent of these provincial petty bourgeois. Politically most had had considerable experience: 31 had served in the 26th Congress; probably another 150 had officiated in Maderista state governments, in the Constitutionalist bureaucracy in 1914–15, and on Constitutionalist military staffs.

Ideologically the great majority avowed a simple anti-clerical liberalism. A few of the most bookish professed a liberal reformism they called socialism. One was a serious syndicalist.

On 1 December 1916 the First Chief inaugurated the Convention, presented his draft for the new constitution, and instructed the deputies to terminate their proceedings by 31 January 1917. The only major changes he proposed to the 1857 constitution were to strengthen the presidency, weaken Congress and state governments, and authorize a central bank. In return he recommended a four-year presidential term and no re-election (no vice-presidency either), an independent judiciary, and guarantees for municipal autonomy.

Trusted Carrancistas ran the Convention's executive. But within a week they lost the leadership to a committee run by deputies who often consulted with Obregón and demanded social and economic reforms written into the constitution. On 11 December the committee began reporting revisions of Carranza's draft. The executive complained of a division between loyal 'Carrancista liberals' and upstart 'Obregonista Jacobins'.[34] Its opponents complained of a division between a rightist minority of old, Carrancista civilians and a leftist majority of young, popular soldiers. This was mostly oratory. Once the voting started, the deputies approved article after article with large majorities, some unanimously. Carranza won a stronger presidency and authorization for a central bank. The committee won its social and economic sections: Article 3 outlawed religious education; Article 27 vested in the Mexican nation the ownership of the country's natural resources, specified as Mexican all titles to land and water, and mandated the expropriation of large estates and their subdivision into small farms and communal landholdings; Article 123 limited a day's work to eight hours, guaranteed the right to unionize and to strike, and established compulsory arbitration; Article 130 regulated religious worship and prohibited priests from criticizing either the constitution or the government.

On 31 January 1917 the deputies signed the new constitution, and on 5 February Carranza promulgated it. The new president would enjoy much formal authority. But since he could not effectively impose it, his opposition would have vast scope for protest, denunciation, and agitation.

[34] *Diario de los debates del Congreso Constituyente, 1916–1917* (2 vols., Mexico, 1960), I, 641–82; E. Victor Niemeyer, Jr, *Revolution at Queretaro: the Mexican Constitutional Convention of 1916–1917* (Austin, Texas, 1974), 60–1, 220–2.

Already the international crisis had intensified. Responding to the German announcement on 1 February of its new U-boat policy, Wilson on 3 February had broken diplomatic relations with Berlin. The United States and Germany pulled ever harder against each other's influence in Mexico. American mining and oil companies protested vehemently against the new constitution, especially the 'confiscatory' Article 27.[35] On 8 February Zimmermann, the German foreign minister, advised his ambassador to Mexico to propose 'without delay' the German–Mexican alliance.[36] On 20 February the ambassador made the proposal to foreign minister Aguilar. Meanwhile the German secret services pumped funds to the generals and elaborated networks for sabotage around Tampico. On 1 March Wilson published Zimmermann's initial telegram on German–Mexican alliance, exciting a predictable American uproar. On 3 March the US ambassador to Mexico presented his credentials to Carranza, but shortly afterwards the State Department squashed a New York bank's proposal to lend the *de facto* government $20 million. It also secretly sanctioned ammunition shipments to Peláez. In mid-March German submarines sank three American ships in the North Atlantic. On 6 April the United States declared war on Germany.

Under so much pressure from both directions, Venustiano Carranza and the generals displayed consensus on two crucial questions. First, to avoid another American intervention, they stood together in favour of a foreign policy of neutrality in the war in Europe, a strategy of flirtation with both the United States and Germany. On 12 February Carranza named the pro-American Bonillas as ambassador to Washington, but the next day he publicly emphasized Mexico's neutrality. In the tense weeks following, he postponed the requirement that mining companies return to regular operations, announced that the forthcoming regular government would resume payments on the foreign debt, appointed the pro-American Pani minister of industry and commerce (in charge of oil), and denied to the United States that he even knew of a proposal for a German–Mexican alliance. After the United States declared war, he secretly declined Zimmermann's offer. On 24 April he again postponed the requirement that foreign companies renounce their national rights. But he gave haven to German spies and propagandists; wittingly he kept a Mexican agent for Germany as minister of communications.

---

[35] Haley, *Revolution and intervention*, 245; Smith, *United States and revolutionary nationalism*, 89, 91, 105–6.   [36] Katz, *The secret war*, 363.

Secondly, Carranza and the generals together rigged a constitutional government. On 11 March the army supervised presidential and congressional elections. Of 213,000 votes for president, Carranza won 197,000 (González and Obregón shared the rest). All the congressional seats went to the PLC. On 1 April Carranza authorized provisional governors to hold elections for regular state governments. Almost immediately after the new Congress met on 15 April, the 200 or so deputies divided into 20 unconditional Carrancistas, 80 Obregonistas, and more than 100 'independents'.

On 1 May 1917 the new Mexican state formally appeared. The First Chief was sworn into office in Mexico City as the new president, to serve until 30 November 1920. And the new constitution went into effect. Meanwhile the real 'reconstruction' – the durable reconnection of foreign and domestic business with national and regional politics – continued.

MAY 1917 – OCTOBER 1918

Throughout 1917 the Mexican economy recovered. As the first world war stimulated the American economy, demand for Mexican exports increased. Standard Oil, Mexican Petroleum, and Águila raised oil production faster than ever. Mining companies did well too; their outputs of gold, silver, and copper reached nearly normal levels. Although the rains that summer were poor yet again, rich opportunities reopened in the north-west's irrigated agriculture, where Mexicali's cotton growers, Sonora's chickpea farmers, and Sinaloa's sugar planters became exporting tycoons. In Yucatán the Henequén Commission sharply reduced production, more than doubled the price, and took a record profit. And because of the exports, domestic markets rallied. Monterrey's Fundidora resumed a respectable production. Grain dealers did excellent business with their scant stocks.

The economic recovery offered increases in various kinds of political power: taxes, graft, contracts. But only the taxes flowed to the treasury, and they were not enough to allow Carranza to centralize the other kinds of power. The newly constituted government's revenue ran to 11 million pesos a month, more than previous governments had ever enjoyed. But current expenditures ran to 16.5 million pesos a month, of which 10 million went for the army. The deficit of 5.5 million was paid from the attached bank reserves, which at that rate would not last the year. The government needed a loan maybe just to survive, and certainly to consolidate itself. Otherwise the lion's share of graft and contracts would continue to accrue to whichever generals could command them, consolidating the decentralization of power.

President Carranza set out immediately to gain political and financial control. On 1 May he had war minister Obregón resign, and left his replacement, Jesús Castro, at the rank of undersecretary. On 8 May he asked Congress for legislation to found a central bank. In mid-May a Mexican banker in New York privately sounded Morgan on support. Morgan accommodatingly shunted him to Washington. In late May, at Carranza's invitation, a team of private American consultants arrived in Mexico City to advise the government on fiscal and financial reform. The resort to the United States disturbed Germany, and Zimmermann again secretly proposed an alliance to Carranza. But Carranza put him off.

Carranza continued catering to the old landlords by returning more and more estates to their owners. As one of Cowdray's managers in Mexico reported, 'A tendency to conservatism is observable now that the government is . . . not so dependent on the radical military element. Undoubtedly Carranza is doing his utmost to free himself from the extremists . . . You probably know that they have returned Don José Limantour's properties . . .'[37]

In June finance minister Cabrera announced Mexico's intention to ask American banks for a loan. He then left the ministry to take a seat in the Chamber of Deputies and defend the government's policy. From 12 July to 4 August Pani, the industry and commerce minister, led the country's highly suspicious merchants through a national convention that issued in ringing endorsements of the government and plans for a National Confederation of Chambers of Commerce. On 23 July Congress authorized the government to borrow 250 million pesos abroad, of which 100 million would establish a central bank. Privately Mexican envoys in New York persuaded Morgan to consider a five- or ten-year loan to repay defaults and an eventual refunding of the entire foreign debt. In early August, when the US ambassador reported the oil companies' extreme worries over Article 27, Carranza assured him that the new constitution did not provide for 'confiscation'.[38] Again Zimmermann secretly proposed German–Mexican alliance; again

[37] *Ibid.*, 293.
[38] United States Department of State, *Papers relating to the foreign relations of the United States, 1917* (Washington, DC, 1926), 1072.

Carranza put him off. On 20 August President Wilson announced that the State Department would morally approve American loans to Mexico, and on 31 August recognized Carranza's government *de jure*. On 1 September Carranza sent Cabrera to New York to start formal negotiations for a loan, and called Douglas to Mexico for a month of consultations. Two weeks later US Customs released the Mexican ammunition long embargoed on the border.

But all the palaver and activity yielded not a penny. In New York Cabrera found Morgan unwilling to lend anything unless Washington guaranteed it, and Washington, at war, would not guarantee anything unless Mexico committed itself against Germany. The State Department suggested that Mexico borrow from the US government. Carranza refused. Knowing his need to import specie and corn, the Department then tightened restrictions on American exports of gold, industrial equipment, and food to Mexico. In mid-October Cabrera attacked American oil companies for lobbying against a loan, and on 1 November he ended the New York negotiations.

Meanwhile the generals began to fortify themselves politically for the long run to 1920. Aguilar, now Carranza's son-in-law, left the foreign ministry to become governor of Veracruz. On leave from the army, Obregón made a quick fortune brokering Sonora's chickpea trade, and in mid-September set off on an obvious campaign across the United States, from Los Angeles to Washington, where he obliged Bonillas to introduce him to the Secretary of State. González, who made a fortune brokering Mexico City's grain trade, took charge of the September ammunition shipment to emerge as the country's main military figure. From their official posts in Mexico City, Hill and Treviño cultivated connections in the capital. Calles established his hold on Sonora and Diéguez, elected Jalisco's governor, extended his influence into the surrounding states. Murguía made himself the boss of Chihuahua. Coss was preparing to win the gubernatorial election in Coahuila. Caballero was doing the same in Tamaulipas. And Alvarado elaborated his rule over the entire south-east.

Moreover the economic recovery and the political divisions strengthened labour movements. The UCMGF and the UMM reorganized their old branches as independently as ever. Encouraged by the recent surge of IWW syndicalism in the United States, syndicalist organizers appeared in the mining districts, Torreón, and Tampico. Already in April oil workers in all the Tampico installations had been on strike. In May they had struck again in Minatitlán, in June staged a general strike in Tampico, and in October struck there again. From early September to mid-October textile workers in Puebla and Veracruz shut down several big mills. Most impressively, another labour convention took place in mid-October in Tampico. Delegates representing 29 organizations from the Federal District and 11 states reconstituted the CTRM as the Confederación General Obrera (CGO), declared 'class struggle' by 'direct action' for the 'communization of the means of production', and agreed to base the new CGO strategically in Torreón.[39]

Meanwhile the rebels had at least held their ground. In May Villistas had raided Ojinaga. In July they had raided in southern Chihuahua. Peláez had kept his control in the Tampico–Tuxpan oil fields. The Zapatistas in Morelos had started negotiating to co-operate with other rebel movements. And from June on, after floundering for a year, the Felicistas had been raiding in the Minatitlán oil fields.

With the exhaustion of the British army in Belgium in October and the Bolshevik revolution in Russia in November 1917, the first world war turned strategically into a race to the Western Front between American and German reinforcements. At the same time the terms of American–German conflict in Mexico changed again: whereas the United States, however, continued to oppose a Carrancista concentration of power, Berlin accepted Mexico's neutrality. In November, after his failure in New York, Cabrera went to Washington to request relaxation of the restrictions on American exports to Mexico. Carranza tried to ease agreement by setting up the claims commission that his American consultants had designed. But the State Department stalled so tellingly that Cabrera left Washington in mid-December. And another conspiracy, involving Standard Oil, a high official in the State Department, and the exiles around Iturbide, formed to overthrow the Mexican government. In contrast, German officials in Mexico now offered Carranza a 70 million peso loan to remain neutral for the duration of the war and to favour German trade and investment afterwards. But they could not get Berlin's confirmation.

Without American or German support Carranza had to raise new funds elsewhere, or the government would soon face grave financial difficulty. To pave the way for a domestic loan, he had Pani prepare a national convention of manufacturers. Meanwhile he had González plan an offensive to capture Morelos and its plantations, and he called Diéguez

---

[39] Salazar and Escobedo, *Las pugnas de la gleba*, 1, 245.

from Jalisco and Murguía from Chihuahua for a major campaign to take the Tampico–Tuxpan oil fields. As a long shot he also arranged an approach to Cowdray, for the British collapse in Europe had made Águila acutely vulnerable to American challenges in Mexico.

All but one of these ventures proved disappointing. From 17 to 25 November 1917 the manufacturers met. But unlike the merchants they complained about the new constitution and resoundingly reaffirmed the privacy of their enterprises, which they would defend in a new National Confederation of Chambers of Industry. González's forces secured only the eastern third of Morelos, and the Diéguez–Murguía campaign actually lost ground. Diéguez moved into the oil fields, but Murguía had hardly left Chihuahua when the Villistas raided Ojinaga again, and he had to retreat to his weakened base. Thrashing around the north-east in December, Diéguez ruined the rigging of Coss's election in Coahuila, and provoked Coss to revolt. In Tamaulipas, where Diéguez disrupted Caballero's plans for election in February, a new Felicista band began its own rebellion, and the Pelaecistas strengthened their positions. Only the approach to Cowdray succeeded – a deal in mid-December over the Tehuantepec Railway Company (which Cowdray co-owned with the Mexican government) released $3 million in cash and $4.5 million in stock.

Sharp signs of new trouble soon appeared. On 1 January 1918 the PLC Obregonistas for the first time publicly rebuked the president, for interfering in state elections. On 12 January, because of renewed disturbances along the Texas border, the United States ordered its forces to pursue suspects into Mexico. On 14 January a military plot to overthrow Carranza was discovered, involving garrisons in Mexico City, Veracruz, and other important towns.

Carranza's search for support became increasingly improbable. To counteract the PLC, he encouraged the formation of a new Partido Nacional Cooperatista, starting with a national labour convention in Saltillo, to attract unions away from the CGO. While he went on returning attached properties and encouraged landlords to organize their peons as local militia, he had the National Agrarian Commission for the first time run steadily at least in low gear, in order to interest the villages in his government. Secretly he had Diéguez negotiate with Peláez. And he sent the undersecretary of finance to Washington to try again for relaxation of restrictions on American exports. The last two efforts quickly failed.

Carranza then took a major risk. On 18 February, under Article 27, he decreed a new tax for the oil industry, requiring as a first principle the registration of titles to all oil lands by 20 May, opening unregistered lands to denouncement, and taxing not only the lands but also the rents, royalties, and production on contracts dated before or since the new constitution had become valid. A few days later, as if in reward, Berlin approved a loan, but only five million pesos, and that buried in pesetas in an account in Madrid. The American oil companies not only protested against the tax law. In March they drew International Harvester and some other big companies into an unusually broad coalition to plot the overthrow of Carranza. This time they selected as their candidate to replace him a once notable agent of his, Alfredo Robles Domínguez, who eagerly accepted the duty. Meanwhile another general strike closed down Tampico. Violent American–Mexican confrontation increased along the Texas–Chihuahua border. On 2 April, the State Department charged that the tax law tended to violate vested American rights in Mexico. It warned that the United States might have 'to protect the property of its citizens . . . divested or injuriously affected . . .'.[40] Robles Domínguez started visiting the US Embassy and British Legation almost daily.

Carranza took one of his last chances for help abroad, sending an agent to deal with the Germans in Madrid. At home he barely had room for manoeuvre. The army claimed 65 per cent of the budget. The manufacturers again urged respect for private property, including that of Americans. By mid-April the uproar along the Texas–Chihuahua border sounded like the prologue to war, and Villa raided into southern Chihuahua. In Tamaulipas, having lost the last count in the gubernatorial election, Caballero revolted. Local feuds in Guerrero, Puebla, and Tlaxcala broke into revolts. The undersecretary of war himself had to assume command in Puebla.

Then Carranza's attempt to co-opt labour backfired. On 1 May delegates representing 115 working-class organizations in the Federal District and 16 states convened in Saltillo. Thanks to Carrancista preparations, more than a third of the organizations were docile Coahuila unions. But the Coahuilans lost control to the SME and the Tampico Casa del Obrero. The convention closed on 12 May with the formation of the Confederación Regional Obrera Mexicana (CROM), a shaky but politically independent coalition of trade unionists and syndicalists.

On 20 May Carranza extended the oil tax law's deadline for

[40] Smith, *United States and revolutionary nationalism*, 118.

registration of titles to 31 July, and Pani began discussions with American oil company lawyers about amending the law. The United States relented too, slightly. On 7 June Wilson expressed again the United States's desire for friendly relations with Mexico. Towards the end of the month the State Department decided on 'a most liberal embargo policy'.[41] Licences soon went out for several large shipments of commodities to Mexico, mainly corn.

But by late June the government was running on current revenue. Carranza's representative in Madrid had arranged nothing material with the Germans. The president could no longer have extracted even a prayer of support from Mexico's merchants or manufacturers. He stood no better with the UCMGF, the UMM, or the new CROM. The Villistas still posed a problem for Murguía in Chihuahua. Despite Diéguez's command in Monterrey there were three or four rebellions in Coahuila and Tamaulipas, and the Pelaecistas still patrolled the Tampico–Tuxpan oil fields. The Zapatistas still ruled most of Morelos, although without Palafox (dismissed in the reorientation of strategy towards negotiation). At least a dozen other rebel bands had recovered or sprouted new across the centre of the country. And the Felicistas had multiplied in Puebla, Oaxaca and Veracruz, where they stepped up their operations in the Minatitlán oil fields.

On 15 July 1918 the German army began its attack across the Marne. The drive would not only bring the first world war close to its end, but would also settle the still outstanding political question in Mexico. Congressional elections on 28 July returned a PLC Carrancista majority. And the rains that summer were good, for the first time in five years. But until the German drive had succeeded or failed, Mexican politicians remained in suspense. On 31 July Carranza extended the deadline for application of the oil tax for another two weeks.

Early in August the German failure finally became clear. On 14 August Carranza surrendered the tax law's first principle, cancelling the requirement of registration of titles, and instructed Pani to start negotiations with American oil company lawyers to frame Article 27 into a mutually acceptable organic law. But every politically informed person knew that the president no longer had a chance of regaining power over his rivals. In mid-September Obregón began liquidating his property for cash to enable him to go seriously into politics. Villa, stronger than he

[41] *Ibid.*, 122.

had been in two years, raided again in southern Chihuahua. On 1 October Díaz published his praise of the Allies and called for a union of all 'patriots' to overthrow Carranza.[42] On 20 October his forces began their first major offensive in Veracurz, Puebla and Oaxaca.

NOVEMBER 1918 – JUNE 1920

On 11 November 1918 the first world war ended. The United States, the most powerful victor, enjoyed new freedoms around the world. In particular it enjoyed the freedom of exercising the only foreign pressure in Mexico. Without risking interference from other foreign powers, it could even revoke recognition of Carranza's government, unless, for example, Carranza agreed to negotiate on Article 27 of the constitution. This ended Mexico's chances for centralized government.

Economic conditions after the war confirmed a regionalized 'reconstruction' in Mexico. Although the American boom continued for another two years, American demands for Mexican products varied widely. The demand for precious metals and oil remained high, but the demand for copper dropped quickly and the demand for henequén crashed. The Spanish influenza pandemic, probably the most devastating blow to human life in Mexico in 350 years, also reduced production and trade. Hitting first in the north-east in early October 1918, its awful 'second wave' raged around the country until mid-January. In the army, of 125,000 men on the rolls, 25,270 fell ill with influenza, and 1,862 died. Altogether as many as five million Mexicans may have gone down with Spanish flue. A moderately low estimate of deaths ranges between 2.5 and 3 per cent of the population, around 400,000. And probably half the dead were aged between 20 and 40, so that in only four months 4 per cent of the most able-bodied Mexicans died. Through the economic trends and the pandemic the Gulf fared best, the north-east and north-west next, much better than the north and the west. And the last two regions, whatever their losses, fared better than the centre and the south, and much better than the south-east, which slid into a long depression.

National politics began to move in new directions. From November 1918 the country's most pressing conflicts became part of the struggle scheduled for resolution in the presidential election in July 1920. But although this was no longer a struggle for centralized power, it was much

---

[42] Liceaga, *Félix Díaz*, 489–504.

more than a provincial struggle for central office. It posed questions of historic consequence – whether or not in a deeply contentious Mexican society any provincial group could establish any rule in Mexico City, and if so, what kind of group and what kind of rule. It also posed the dangers of extensive violence again. Since neither Carranza nor any of his rivals had the power to control the succession, and since the PLC was no more than a name for nationally ambitious factions, the struggle would lead not to coalition but to a final test of strength, with each of the strongest factions struggling to impose itself on the others.

There were only two strategic bases for a politics of imposition, the north-west and the north-east. As soon as the war ended, Obregón started organizing his presidential campaign. Well regarded in California and Washington and one of the north-west's richest men, he retained as a civilian his national prestige as Mexico's top military hero. By January 1919 Calles had committed Sonora to him, and Hill in Mexico City built Obregonista support inside and outside the PLC. Meanwhile González started organizing his campaign. Well connected in Texas and the north-east and probably the country's richest general, he held active command in Mexico State, Morelos and Guerrero, and in December recaptured the rest of Morelos for his subordinates, most of them north-easterners, who leased the state's plantations for the 1919 harvest. In the north-east itself several of his kinsmen and old colleagues and subordinates promoted the Gonzalista cause. Treviño in Mexico City did likewise. Neither faction as yet asked organized labour for support – that field was too difficult and divided. The CROM had antagonized the UMM by encroaching on the railway shops, and in November, objecting to a CROM alliance with the American Federation of Labour against the IWW, the FSODF had seceded and founded a syndicalist Gran Cuerpo Central de Trabajadores in Mexico City.

Of the six other important generals, four remained neutral. They were Diéguez in Monterrey; Murguía, who resigned his Chihuahua command and retired to Mexico City; undersecretary of war Castro, who replaced Murguía in Chihuahua; and Alvarado, who left the declining Yucatán to publish a Mexico City newspaper obsessed with the presidential question.

Carranza did not name his candidate. Counting with certainty only on Aguilar and Cesáreo Castro, in Veracruz and Puebla, he had no reason to take so early a choice that would necessarily antagonize either Obregón and his allies or González and his, maybe both camps, and maybe all four neutrals. Thanks to oil and silver production, which steadily increased the government's revenue, he could delay confrontation. On 1 January 1919, he ordered a huge rise in army officers' pay and began a slow, quiet reduction of the troop rolls. On 15 January he publicly condemned presidential campaigns as premature and insisted on their postponement until the end of the year.

Meanwhile he pursued various alliances to strengthen his faction. In mid-November he had sent Pani as minister to France, hopefully to persuade the Paris Peace Conference to annul the Monroe Doctrine, or at least to revive the interest of British and French bankers in Mexico. He bowed to the American oil companies. On 14 November he had extended the exemption from denouncement to the end of the year. On 23 November the agreement that the company lawyers and Pani had drafted to give Article 27 organic form appeared as a president's bill to Congress. Most notably it exempted from its effects lands in which companies had invested for production before 1 May 1917. On 27 December Carranza extended the exemption from denouncement until Congress voted on the bill. (The pro-American trend impressed Cowdray, who three months later sold Águila to Royal Dutch Shell.) Domestically Carranza courted the Catholic hierarchs, proposing reforms of constitutional Articles 3 and 130 to restrain local anti-clerics, and inviting and receiving from Rome a prothonotary apostolic to reorganize the church in Mexico. He continued to return attached property to the landlords – among those favoured in March 1919 was the Terrazas family – and issued a flurry of decrees and circulars protecting their estates. In addition, he prepared local Carrancista candidates for the coming gubernatorial elections, the next in Sonora on 27 April.

Crucially Carranza also tried for an alliance in New York. Since October Morgan had been co-ordinating American, British, and French banks interested in the Mexican debt. In January Carranza's finance undersecretary joined their negotiations. On 23 February Morgan announced the formation of the International Committee of Bankers on Mexico, and a month later, to reassure the ICBM, Carranza allowed Limantour to return from France to visit Mexico. On 29 March his finance undersecretary returned with the Committee's offer: to refund the debt and issue new bonds for 'internal development' on the security of customs revenue under 'international administration'.[43] On 9 April

---

[43] Edgar Turlington, *Mexico and her foreign creditors* (New York, 1930), 275.

Carranza reappointed Cabrera as finance minister, to manage approval of the Article 27 bill and the ICBM offer in a special session of Congress opening on 1 May. He also acted to divide the Gonzalista campaign, dispatching Treviño on a lucrative tour of arms and ammunition plants in Europe.

But for all its promise the Carrancista faction soon suffered rude disappointments. In Paris in April the Council of Four recognized the Monroe Doctrine; Carranza rejected the invitation to Mexico to join the League of Nations. In Chihuahua Villa launched a wide offensive. González gained solid credit with landlords when his forces in Morelos ambushed and killed Zapata on 10 April. In the Sonora gubernatorial election, Carranza's candidate lost, and Calles's won – Adolfo de la Huerta. The special session of Congress would not approve the Article 27 bill or the ICBM offer.

Carranza called Diéguez from the north-east and Cesáreo Castro from Puebla to help Jesús Castro beat Villa down again. In mid-May he threatened force against unregistered new drilling in the oil fields. To divide the Obregonistas he appointed Calles as minister of industry and commerce (with responsibility for oil). To preoccupy González, he expanded his command to include Puebla, Tlaxcala and Oaxaca.

But Carranza's disappointments encouraged his opponents. On 1 June Obregón formally announced his presidential candidacy, and on 27 June he got his first formal endorsement, from Yucatán's Partido Socialista. Undersecretary of war Castro returned from Chihuahua to Mexico City and lent him private support through the war ministry. Despite his new duties, González too became bolder, publicly debating with Obregón how properly to declare a candidacy; and his north-eastern agents organized harder. In Chihuahua, Diéguez had scarcely fought his way into the state's capital when on 15 June Villistas raided Juárez and provoked a 24-hour US intervention. On 8 June the Nuevo León gubernatorial election went to a man whom Carranza had not approved (an old friend of Villarreal's). Carranza suspended the report of the electoral returns, and the state throbbed with agitation – for Obregón and González. In Tampico syndicalists led another general strike. Everywhere in the north-east, because Diéguez's removal had reduced its garrisons, the various rebels resumed frequent raids. On 6 June Murguía became commander in Monterrey, but quickly fell into feuds with local chiefs. On 25 June rebels raided Victoria. In the oil districts Peláez moved near Tampico.

During the summer Carranza made a few gains. Diéguez broke the Villista offensive and established command of Chihuahua. Cesáreo Castro controlled Torreón. González came to believe that he need not formally campaign for the presidency, that after many feints and parries the government and the army would save the succession for him. And a second season of good rains ensured relief from food shortages and imports before the election. But much more importantly the threat against unregistered oil drilling led to another confrontation with the United States. In late June the companies charged that the Mexican government had taken 'overt acts' to confiscate their property.[44] On 22 July the State Department warned Carranza that Washington might revoke recognition of his government. On 8 August the Senate set up a subcommittee chaired by its loudest interventionist, Albert B. Fall, 'to investigate Mexican affairs'.[45] On 19 August, from 60,000 US troops stationed along the border, the second punitive expedition entered Mexico for a week around Ojinaga.

Meanwhile Obregón made gains of his own. On 17 July, thanks to Hill, the PLC formally backed his candidacy. Undersecretary of war Castro planted sympathetic generals in strategic commands in the northern border towns. And Obregonista generals began private negotiations with the CROM's leaders. The Obregonistas wanted the CROM partly to stifle IWW agitation among Sonoran miners, mainly to promote Obregón's campaign elsewhere, not only in Mexico but also in the United States, with the AFL. The CROM's leaders wanted connections with Calles in the ministry of industry and commerce, to recover the organizing authority that they had been losing to the syndicalists. Soon afterward the FSODF left its syndicalist Cuerpo Central and joined the CROM. In the same weeks Governor de la Huerta of Sonora helped the UCMGF organize Sonora's Southern Pacific Railway workers.

On 8 September the Fall committee opened its 'investigation'. On 10–11 September its key witness, the president of the Board of Directors of Mexican Petroleum, testified for eight hours about Carrancista misrule.

Under this domestic and foreign pressure Carranza reached a private decision on his faction's candidate. Judging that connections in Washington mattered more than ever, he chose as his ambassador to the United

<hr>

44 Smith, *United States and revolutionary nationalism*, 154.
45 United States Senate, Committee on Foreign Relations, *Investigation of Mexican affairs: preliminary report and hearings*, 66 Congress, 2nd session (2 vols., Washington, DC, 1920), I, 3.

States Douglas's political pupil, Ignacio Bonillas. In late September Carranza met Diéguez in Coahuila and won his commitment to the choice. On 2 October Bonillas joined them for talks that lasted a week.

Another confrontation with the United States emphasized the importance of Washington connections for Mexican politics. On 19 October the US vice-consul in Puebla disappeared, supposedly kidnapped by Pelaecista rebels. Washington resounded with cries for intervention in Mexico. On 26 October the vice-consul reappeared free, and Washington's cries subsided. On 1 November Carranza announced that now the presidential campaigns could start and that he backed Bonillas.

But in the next six weeks Obregón made his claim on the presidency irrevocable. On 27 October he had started a tour by rail down the west coast. By mid-December he had politicked through Sonora, Sinaloa, Nayarit, Colima, Jalisco, Michoacán, Guanajuato, Mexico State and Hidalgo, and for ten days in Mexico City. On 21 December his allies in CROM announced the formation of the Partido Laborista Mexicano.

González meanwhile reasserted himself. On 5 November he announced that he would soon declare his candidacy. Forces under his command in Puebla then provoked another confrontation with the United States, by arresting the USA vice-consul on 14 November, charging that he had colluded with his kidnappers to give his government a pretext to intervene in Mexican affairs. Washington resounded again with cries for intervention. While Douglas and Bonillas negotiated feverishly in Washington to calm the uproar, González induced Zapatista and Felicista chiefs to accept 'a patriotic amnesty', a truce with him.[46] On 27 November Gonzalistas in Mexico City announced the formation of a Gonzalista party, the Liga Democrática. On 28 November the Secretary of State told Bonillas that unless his government made 'a radical change in its attitude toward the United States', the American people would oblige their government to break relations with it, which would 'almost inevitably mean war'.[47] Back from Europe, Treviño appeared in Monterrey politicking for González. On 3 December Fall introduced a resolution in the Senate asking Wilson to sever diplomatic relations with Carranza's 'pretended government'.[48] On 4 December the vice-consul was released. On 8 December Wilson expressed his opposition to Fall's

---

[46] *El Universal*, 21 November, 30 November, 5 December, 6 December, 16 December, 24 December, 25 December 1919.   [47] Smith, *United States and revolutionary nationalism*, 162.
[48] *Congressional Record*, 66 Congress, 2nd session, LIX, Part 1 (1919–20), 73.

resolution, and the confrontation ended. On 10 December González formally accepted the Liga Democrática's presidential nomination.

Villa too launched a new campaign. On 2 November he had raided Saltillo, throwing the north-east deeper into division and agitation. In mid-December he raided the coal districts, on the road to Piedras Negras. Still feuding with the local chiefs, Murguía failed not only to drive the Villistas out of Coahuila but even to protect the Nuevo León and Tamaulipas railways from the local rebels.

It was clear in Washington and Mexico then that serious violence would erupt before the presidential election. The only question was who would act first – Carranza to crush Obregón, or Obregón to revolt. In either case, once the Carrancistas and Obregonistas joined battle, González could use his forces around the capital for a coup. Neither the Obregonistas nor the Gonzalistas took as menacing the most powerful bodies in favour of a revolt or a coup: American oil companies, the State Department and the US Senate.

In late December Carranza conferred with Aguilar, Diéguez, Murguía and others to prepare the repression. He also prepared Bonillas's campaign. On 13 January 1920, prompted by Douglas and Bonillas, the oil companies requested provisional drilling permits. On 17 January Carranza agreed to grant them. The following day the Partido Nacional Democrático, a group of Carrancista congressmen, governors, and generals, nominated Bonillas for president. In early February the foreign ministry initiated the preliminaries for negotiation of a treaty to establish a mixed claims commission. The reduction of the troop rolls continued.

Obregón expanded his organization in preparation for revolt. While he toured the Bajío and Michoacán again, the Partido Laborista formally pledged him its support. Several important northern politicians indicated their Obregonista sympathies, as did Alvarado. Obregonista agents secretly connected with Villarreal in Texas, the still rebellious Coss in Coahuila, and a major Felicista chief in Veracruz, who agreed to accept an 'amnesty' and await Obregón's instructions for new duty. On 1 February Calles resigned from the ministry of industry and commerce to take full part in the campaign. On 2 February the Obregonistas opened a national convention in Mexico City. On 4 February Obregón himself headed north to tour Aguascalientes and Zacatecas, then east to San Luis Potosí. On 15 February he arrived in Saltillo for two weeks of politicking.

González meanwhile developed his strength in Mexico City. On 31 December, declaring the pacification of the south complete, he took leave from the army. On 13 January, with a speech to the capital's wealthiest gentlemen, he started his formal bidding for allies. His agents multiplied in the north-east.

On 10 February Carranza dismissed Castro as undersecretary of war and appointed his own chief of staff to manage the army, by then 85,000 men. In mid-February Diéguez concluded a month-long inspection of his Chihuahua command. On 27 February, on special presidential orders, he appeared in Sonora for a three-week inspection of the army's forces there, continuing his tour through Sinaloa, Nayarit, Jalisco and Michoacán. The Villistas raided again in southern Chihuahua. Murguía conferred with Carranza in Mexico City and returned to Monterrey publicly opposed to Obregón. In Saltillo Obregón conferred with Calles and on 3 March began a tour of Coahuila, Nuevo León and Tamaulipas. In the Tampico–Tuxpan oil fields the Pelaecistas launched a wide offensive. Altogether these movements alarmed even peons: on 1 February the United States had removed a restriction on immigration from Mexico and by mid-March some 100,000 'vagrant Mexicans' had crossed the border to escape the approaching violence.[49]

In Morelos these movements had a different meaning – an opportunity for the Zapatistas to rise again for their land. In March Obregonista agents made secret contact with the surviving chiefs and won their promises of co-operation in return for promises of respect for their villages.

On 17 March Bonillas arrived in Nuevo Laredo and formally accepted his candidacy. On 21 March he arrived in Mexico City, where his welcoming parade clashed with an Obregonista demonstration. On 25 March Diéguez too arrived in the capital. On 28 March, after almost a year of lying low, Zapatistas resumed their raids in Morelos and the Federal District.

Public events in Washington seemed to favour Carranza. In January the US ambassador to Mexico, in town to help the Fall committee, had resigned. In mid-February Wilson had dismissed the Secretary of State, who had threatened revocation of recognition, and the Senate on 22 March confirmed Wilson's choice to replace him. The following day Wilson nominated a new 'progressive' ambassador to Mexico. But in fact the onslaught of US presidential politics augured ill for Carranza's plans. In March Democrats and Republicans began campaigning in earnest for

[49] J. T. Dickman, General Conditions along the Mexican Border, Weekly Report, No. 362, 20 March 1920, USNA 59, 812.00/ 22844.

their national nominating conventions in June and the elections in November. Both parties would benefit from the violent advent of a new government in Mexico, which would allow them to advocate recognition of it only if it complied with their demands on Article 27 and restored American rights, especially the rights of the oil companies.

On 30 March Carranza sprang the repression, expanding Diéguez's Chihuahua command to include Sonora, Sinaloa, Nayarit, Jalisco and Colima, instructing Diéguez to move heavy reinforcements at once into Sonora, and ordering the arrest of Obregón and the 'amnestied' Felicista chief on a military charge of conspiring to revolt. The attempt quickly failed. In Sonora de la Huerta and Calles denounced Diéguez's appointment, and on 3 April, on the pretext of a UCMGF strike against Southern Pacific, they seized the railways in the state, which blocked traffic along the west coast. Diéguez got to Guadalajara, but no further. On 4 April in Monterrey Obregón met privately with Alvarado, who left immediately for Nogales. Two days later Obregón appeared before a Mexico City court martial and denied the charges against him. On 9 April the Sonora legislature declared Sonoran independence from the federal government. On 10 April Calles took command of all armed forces in the state. On 12 April, under notice to reappear in court the next day, Obregón disappeared from Mexico City, and Hill too fled the city.

Calles sprang the revolt on 15 April, sending a Sonoran force to capture the main railway town in northern Sinaloa. The movement quickly expanded. From Nogales Alvarado raced to Washington and contracted Sherburne Hopkins for counsel to 'the Liberal Constitutionalist Revolution'. The Obregonistas in Sinaloa occupied Culiacán and besieged Mazatlán. The governors of Michoacán and Zacatecas revolted, as did commanders along the railways from Monterrey to Matamoros and Tampico, and in the Tampico–Tuxpan oil fields. Hiding in Morelos, Hill persuaded the Gonzalista commanders there that Obregón and González were secretly co-operating. Obregón himself reappeared in Guerrero, welcomed by the governor and the state commander. On 20 April in Chilpancingo the legislature endorsed Sonora's declaration of independence, Obregón published a Manifesto to the Nation and a Message to the People of the United States announcing his enlistment in Sonora's struggle for 'freedom of suffrage', and the Partido Laborista's executive committee called on Mexico's working class to revolt in the same cause.[50]

[50] Gamoy to State Department, 9 May 1920, USNA 59, 812.00/ 24119.

In response Carranza tried privately for an alliance with González. He proposed that if González halted his campaign for the presidency and offered the government his military services, Bonillas would withdraw his candidacy too, and Carranza and González would negotiate the choice of another civilian candidate. But González wanted more – if Bonillas withdrew his candidacy and Carranza requested González's services, González would halt his campaign and help suppress the revolt, but resume his candidacy 'at an opportune moment'.[51] Carranza refused.

On 22 April the Sonoran Obregonistas published the Plan de Agua Prieta in English.[52] The next day they published it in Spanish. Denouncing Carranza for violations of the constitution, Calles and other local officers and officials named the forces in revolt the Liberal Constitutionalist Army, appointed de la Huerta its interim Supreme Chief, promised that when Liberal Constitutionalists occupied Mexico City the present Congress would elect a provisional president to call general elections, and swore to guarantee 'all legal protection and enforcement of their legal rights to citizens and foreigners, and . . . especially favour the development of industry, trade, and all businesses'.[53] On 26 April the Chihuahua City and Ojinaga commanders revolted in favour of the Agua Prieta plan, and in western Mexico State and Morelos Gonzalista commanders publicly entered discussions with Obregón's agents.

On 27 April Carranza and González negotiated again. González agreed to withdraw his candidacy and help Carranza, if Carranza would replace Bonillas with González's nominee. But on 28 April Carranza refused his nominee and called Murguía to assume command around Mexico City.

In Washington the Republicans took full control of US policy towards Mexico. The Senate would not confirm Wilson's nomination of the new ambassador. The Fall committee shifted into high gear against Carranza: on 29 April it heard Hopkins's testimony that Carranza's government had been 'a ghastly failure', that Obregón would surely overthrow it, and that the new government would establish the right order for business.[54]

González sprang the coup on April 30, when he and Treviño fled the capital, formally denounced Carranza, and, without mentioning the Plan de Agua Prieta, called on the army to fight for 'revolutionary

[51] Hanna to State Department, 30 April 1920, *ibid.*, 812,00/ 23781.
[52] Clodoveo Valenzuela and Amado Chaverri Matamoros, *Sonora y Carranza* (Mexico, 1921), 274–5.
[53] *Ibid.*, 362.   [54] *The New York Times*, 30 April 1920.

principles'.[55] On 3 May the two generals occupied Puebla City and established the headquarters of the Liberal Revolutionary Army, in effect the Gonzalista forces of some 12,000 men in eastern Mexico State, Puebla and Tlaxcala. The coup destroyed the government. On 5 May Carranza postponed the election and, predicting a violent Obregonista–Gonzalista rivalry, called on the army and the people to support him until he could pass the presidency to a regularly elected successor. He ordered Murguía to secure an escape east, and on 7 May he, his Cabinet, Bonillas, the Supreme Court, and many congressmen, officials and their families entrained for Veracruz, where they hoped to reorganize the government under Aguilar's protection.

While the coup succeeded, the revolt expanded again. Villa, Peláez and various Felicista chiefs (although not Díaz himself) indicated their support. On 2 May Obregón, the formerly Gonzalista commanders in Morelos, and Zapatista chiefs – all now Liberal Constitutionalists – occupied Cuernavaca. On 3 May the Juárez commander revolted in favour of the Agua Prieta plan, and on 6 May the Saltillo and Veracruz commanders did likewise. On 7 May Cesáreo Castro surrendered his Torreón command to Liberal Constitutionalists.

As soon as Carranza left Mexico City, the rivalry between the revolt and the coup became explicit. On 7 May Treviño occupied the capital, and González appointed its authorities. The following day the rivalry became official. In Hermosillo, de la Huerta announced the formation of his Cabinet which included Calles as war minister and Alvarado as finance minister. In Mexico City, González also appointed his Cabinet, with himself as war minister. On 9 May, while Liberal Constitutionalists captured Nuevo Laredo, Obregón led 8,000 troops into the capital. The same day, again without mentioning the Plan de Agua Prieta, González asked Congress 'to resolve the present situation'.[56]

The revolt kept spreading. On 10 May Liberal Constitutionalists captured Mazatlán. On 11 May Diéguez's force in Guadalajara mutinied and arrested him, and the governors of Coahuila, Nuevo León, and Tamaulipas fled for the border; on Calles's orders Villarreal moved from El Paso to take command in Monterrey. The next day Coss took Piedras Negras, and the Tampico–Tuxpan Liberal Constitutionalist commander

55 Partido Reconstrucción Nacional, *Recopilación de documentos y de algunas publicaciones de importancia* (Monterrey, 1923), 66–78.
56 L. N. Ruvalcaba (ed.), *Campaña política del C. Alvaro Obregón, candidato a la presidencia de la República, 1920–24* (5 vols., Mexico, 1923), IV, 151.

and Peláez jointly occupied Tampico. Two days later Liberal Constitutionalists took the last border town, Matamoros.

On 12 May Obregón and González conferred at the war ministry. They were in sufficient agreement not to fight each other. González recognized de la Huerta's authority to convene Congress in order to elect the provisional president. But he would not sign the Plan de Agua Prieta or dissolve his Liberal Revolutionary Army until the provisional president took office, and Treviño took command of both Obregonista and Gonzalista forces pursuing Carranza. On 13 May, still in Hermosillo, de la Huerta called Congress into a special session set for 24 May to elect the provisional president. On 15 May González tried another manoeuvre, withdrawing his candidacy for the regular presidential election and so freeing himself for the provisional office.

The news of the rivalry never reached Carranza. Hostile forces of various stripes had blocked his convoy front and rear in Puebla. On 14 May Carranza, some close associates, and guards under Murguía headed on horseback into the northern Puebla mountains, where on 21 May Carranza was killed by local 'amnestied' Pelaecistas. Obregón and González immediately denounced the crime and named a joint commission to investigate it. Treviño removed the captured Carrancistas – Bonillas, Murguía, and a few others – to Mexico City's military prison. On 22 May de la Huerta set the elections for the new Congress for 1 August and the presidency for 5 September.

By then the revolt had overwhelmed the coup. The oil companies, which had withheld payment of taxes during the violence, agreed to pay them to the Liberal Constitutionalists. On 24 May Congress voted for de la Huerta over González by 224 to 28 votes. On 26 May Calles moved into the war ministry. On 30 May de la Huerta arrived in the capital. On 1 June he was sworn into office as provisional president to serve until 30 November. On 2 June, after leading a big military parade through the city, Obregón resigned his command, and a few days later resumed his candidacy for the regular presidential election. On 5 June González resigned his command and went home to Monterrey.

JUNE 1920 – DECEMBER 1920

In the final test the united north-westerners had defeated the divided north-easterners and won responsibility for 'reconstruction'. But because they did not have the strong ties that the north-easterners had with the big national businesses in Mexico City and Monterrey, they did not have the respect and trust required for political establishment. They could not rule as tenured partners legitimately leading associates, but only as conquerors warily dealing with the very forces whose co-operation they needed most for the security of their regime.

Immediately, therefore, their paramount concern was to obtain US recognition as soon as possible. But the Fall committee had just submitted a forbidding report. With the State Department's approval, it recommended that the United States not recognize a government in Mexico without a treaty between the two countries exempting Americans from the application of certain articles of the Mexican constitution, principally Article 27. Under such a treaty, the committee recommended a large American loan to refund Mexico's debt and rehabilitate its railways. If Mexican authorities refused the treaty and applied the constitution to Americans as they did to others, the committee recommended that the United States send forces to Mexico to take charge of all lines of communication from Mexico City to the country's border and sea ports. On 12 June the Republican Convention nominated Harding for president. The party's platform on Mexico, which Fall had drafted, promised recognition when Americans in Mexico enjoyed 'sufficient guarantees' of respect for their lives and property.[57] On 6 July the Democratic Convention nominated Cox, whose party's Mexican platform promised recognition when the United States had 'ample proof' of Mexican respect for American lives and property.[58]

During the summer the north-westerners managed a remarkably orderly provisional government. De la Huerta sent a 'special ambassador' to Washington. On the attraction of rising regular revenue, thanks to the continued oil boom, he had Alvarado announce preparation of a financial programme to refund the foreign debt, then go to New York for private negotiations with Morgan. He admitted twenty-one new divisional generals and 13,000 new troops into the army. He appointed Treviño as minister of industry and commerce, to suffer the oil companies; a CROM leader governor of the Federal District, to check the capital's syndicalists, whom a new Partido Comunista had organized as the Federación Comunista del Proletariado Mexicano; and Villarreal as minister of agriculture, to devise an agrarian reform to pacify the Zapatistas. He kept Diéguez and Murguía in prison, but sent Bonillas

---

[57] *The New York Times*, 11 June 1920.   [58] *Ibid.*, 3 July 1920.

and most of the other Carrancista civilians, along with Aguilar and Cesáreo Castro, into exile. He settled a UCMGF–UMM strike on the Mexican Railway and general strikes in Tampico and Veracruz. And he drew Díaz into formal negotiations to end his rebellion. He even achieved peace with Villa, who on 28 July accepted the government's offer to retire with his men to a ranch in Durango.

Meanwhile Obregón, Hill, and Calles imposed north-western political control on the country. They installed some champions of the revolt as provisional and regular governors, others as state military commanders. And they seized a gaping opportunity to retire González indefinitely. In early July former subordinates of his, angry at the cancellation of their claims to office and deals, tried to revolt in Coahuila and Nuevo León, and failed completely. On 15 July González was arrested. The war ministry court-martialled him on the same charge that Carranza had brought against Obregón. On 20 July, after the court-martial remanded the defendant to a civil court, Calles ordered his release: González prudently retired to exile. On 1 August the congressional elections yielded deputies and senators from the PLC, the Partido Nacional Cooperatista, the Partido Laborista, and a new Partido Nacional Agrarista (ex-Zapatistas), all for Obregón. The only show of enduring opposition arose from the old *católicos*, who assembled the Partido Nacional Republicano to nominate Robles Domínguez for president.

In mid-August de la Huerta had Alvarado launch a public campaign in New York for recognition and a loan. On 26 August Alvarado made 'a deep impression on the . . . financial, business, and professional men' who heard him at the Bankers' Club.[59] In Mexico City the war ministry announced its intention to stamp out entirely the lately organized 'Bolshevists', de la Huerta himself assuring *The New York Times* that 'Mexicans who look to the welfare of their country want foreigners in Mexico for their investments . . .'[60]

The presidential election on 5 September went as planned, an orderly landslide for Obregón. The campaign for recognition intensified. De la Huerta praised Wilson as 'the greatest public man today', accused Harding of 'imperialistic tendencies', deported a few foreign Communists, settled another UCMGF strike, and sent another Douglas pupil as Confidential Agent to replace Alvarado in New York.[61] Obregón declared: 'Our hope . . . is in economy and industry and friendship with

[59] *Ibid.*, 27 August 1920.   [60] *Ibid.*, 28 August, 31 August 1920.
[61] *Ibid.*, 9 September 1920.

our neighbors and foreign capitalists . . . First, we will take care of Mexico's foreign obligations.'[62] The respect Obregón held for American interests so impressed Mexican Petroleum that it leased 800,000 acres of Tamaulipas oil land.) In late September Wilson had a private envoy enter negotiations with Mexico's Confidential Agent for recognition. On 15 October, after consultations with the agent, Wilson's envoy, Obregón and Calles, de la Huerta stated that Mexico would not accept conditions for recognition but would pay 'all that it justly owes in conformity with . . . international law'.[63] On 26 October Mexico's agent formally asked the State Department for recognition, following which the United States and Mexico would exchange protocols recording Mexico's promises of claims and arbitration commissions and no retroaction on Article 27. The same day Mexico's Congress formally declared the victor in the presidential election, Obregón over Robles Domínguez, by 1,132,000 votes to 47,000. On 29 October the Secretary of State indicated that the United States and Mexico would shortly exchange protocols, following which Wilson would recognize the Mexican government.

On 2 November Harding beat Cox badly in the American elections. This ended the chance that the United States would soon recognize any Mexican government upholding the Mexican constitution. Still, the State Department expressed its desire to see Obregón 'auspiciously inaugurated', and the Speyer bank invited clients who held defaulted Mexican bonds to deposit them in anticipation of Mexico's resumption of payments on its foreign debt.[64] On 25 November the State Department proposed that Mexico name commissioners to negotiate a treaty eventually warranting US recognition of Obregón's government. The Justice Department broke pre-inaugural conspiracies among the new exiles on the border.

De la Huerta finished his provisional term in proper order. He ended a Coahuila coal miners' strike by having the government temporarily seize the mines, recall the workers with a pay rise, and transfer profits to the companies. He dispelled a Communist campaign for a national general strike. And on 20 November he staged the first official commemoration of Madero's insurrection ten years earlier, marking the triumph of 'the Mexican Revolution'.[65]

The 'revolution' had been in governance. There was nothing

---

[62] *Ibid.*, 10 September 1920.   [63] *Ibid.*, 16 October 1920.
[64] *Ibid.*, 18 November 1920.
[65] Bernardo J. Gastelum, *La revolución mexicana. Interpretación de su espíritu* (Mexico, 1966), 401.

historically definitive in its principal economic and social results: the same big companies existed as before, plus a few new ones, relying more heavily than ever on American markets and banks; a population reduced by war, emigration, and influenza from 15 million to around 14.7 million; a foreign debt of around 1,000 million pesos, plus more than 300 million pesos in overdue interest; a surplus in revenue amounting to 3 million pesos for the year; an army of almost 100,000 men claiming 62 per cent of the budget; national confederations of merchants and manufacturers; a national confederation of labour at odds with the country's railway unions and the new syndicalist movements; and a still largely landless peasantry still demanding its own lands.

On 1 December 1920, without US, British, or French recognition, Álvaro Obregón was sworn into the presidency. His Cabinet included Hill as minister of war, Calles as minister of the interior, de la Huerta as minister of finance, and Villarreal as minister of agriculture. Obregón also repaid the CROM, leaving its previously appointed leader in charge of the Federal District and granting its secretary-general the directorship of the federal arsenals.

Thus the struggle between the victors of 1914 resulted in a new regime. The central political institution was not a national leader or party but a regional faction, the north-western bourgeoisie, internationally unconsecrated, but indomitably entrenched in the highest levels of the state and ready to manage a flexible, regionalized 'reconstruction' through deals with factions from other classes. The new state itself would therefore serve as the nation's bourgeois party. Its function forecast its programme, a long series of reforms from above, to evade, divide, diminish, and restrain threats to Mexican sovereignty and capitalism from abroad and from below.

3

MEXICO: REVOLUTION AND RECONSTRUCTION IN THE 1920s

The Mexican Revolution was initiated and directed for the most part by the upper and middle classes of the Porfiriato. There were, however, several revolutions within the Revolution. The revolutionary front line was fluid and revolutionary groups were heterogeneous, with very different, even contradictory, objectives. The mass of the people, upon whom the profound changes of the period 1870–1910 had borne heavily, had only a limited sense of what was at stake in the struggle for political power. From 1913 the Sonorans, the north-west faction within the Carrancista or Constitutionalist movement, sought national political power, and in 1920 they finally seized it. The Sonoran hegemony proved complete and long lasting. In effect it was an 'invasion' from the north. The secular habits, the savage pragmatism and the violent struggle for survival of the north-western frontier were totally alien to the Mexican nation at large.[1]

An ex-minister of the period, Luis L. León, has given us a clear picture of how these people of the north-west saw themselves and Mexico, and the programme they wished to impose on the country.[2] He tells us that between 1913 and 1920, the state of Sonora was for the Sonorans their school and their laboratory, both as politicians and as men of business. They described themselves as the Californians of Mexico, who wished to transform their country into another California. Once they took on the gigantic task of controlling national resources of water and land, they were astonished to find that the centre and the south of the country were quite different from their own far north-west. León tells us further that,

* Translated from the French by Mrs Elizabeth Edwards; translation revised by Lady Cynthia Postan and the Editor. The Editor wishes to thank Professor John Womack and Dr Alan Knight for their help in the final preparation of this chapter.

[1] See Hector Aguilar, *La frontera nómada. Sonora y le rev ión mexicana* (Mexico, 1977).
[2] Interviews with Luis L. León by Jean Meyer, Mexico, 1968 and 1973–4.

when they realized what kind of life was led by the peasants of traditional Mexico, they decided that the peasants were not men in the true sense of the term, as they kissed the hands of the great landowners and the priests, did not understand the logic of the marketplace and frittered away what money they had on alcohol and fireworks. The Sonorans had already had a similar experience in their own state with the Yaqui Indians, but this warrior tribe formed only a small minority (it was finally brought under control in 1926), while in the centre-south the majority of the population belonged to a world which the Sonorans did not understand and therefore condemned. Both the violence of the collision between state and church and the peasant insurrection (the Cristero rebellion, 1926–9) which followed were bound up with the profound difference between the men who were administering the state in order to modernize it and those, perhaps two-thirds of the population in 1920, who constituted traditional Mexico.

After a decade of civil war (1910–20) there emerged in Mexico between 1920 and 1930 a new capitalist state. In this respect conflict with foreign oil companies and the church as well as negotiations with organized labour, in particular the CROM (Confederación Regional Obrera Mexicana; Regional Confederation of Mexican Labour), were more significant than the traditional military insurrections of 1923, 1927 and 1929 or the election crises of 1928–9. Innovation was more economic than political, and it was in particular institutional and administrative. It is impossible to separate the main political innovation, the creation of the National Revolutionary party (PNR) in 1929, from the formation of a powerful state.

According to a classic definition, the state is the invitation extended by one group of men to others for the joint accomplishment of a common enterprise. In this case the invitation was not understood by the majority of Mexicans. How could a unified whole be assembled from so many heterogeneous pieces? It was the government which had the unity, that of *imperium* exercised by a small group. The abyss separating the two worlds caused the governors to be impatient and the governed to be resentful. Impatience led to violence, and resentment sometimes to revolt.

The state claimed to take care of all the economic, cultural and political deficiencies in the nation; the federal administration, despite its weakness, provided the country's spinal column. The state, however, although on the offensive, remained structurally weak, for it had to reckon with the strong men of the regions, the caciques or local political bosses, whose co-operation underpinned stability. These included Felipe Carrillo Puerto in Yucatán, Tomás Garrido Canabal, lord of Tabasco from 1920 to 1936, Saturnino Cedillo, *patron* of San Luis Potosí until 1937, Adalberto Tejeda, a power in Veracruz from 1920 to 1935, and many others who, without lasting quite so long, ruled in spite of the centre. Organized labour in the shape of the CROM tried to take over the state, starting with the ministry of industry and commerce headed by the secretary-general of the CROM, but it failed in the face of opposition from the army and other groups.

What emerged was a new form of enlightened despotism, a ruling conviction that the state knew what ought to be done and needed plenary powers to fulfil its mission; Mexicans had to obey. The state rejected the division of society into classes and would preside over the harmonious union of converging interests. The state had to accomplish everything in the name of everyone. It could not allow any criticism, any protest, any power apart from itself. Thus, it had to crush alike the Yaqui Indians, 'illegally' striking railways workers, 'red' workers who rejected the 'good' trade union, the Communist party when it ceased to collaborate (1929), and the Catholic peasants when they resorted to arms. Alongside the violence, and complementing it, the political charade of assemblies and elections concerned no more than a minority. However, the development of the political system and above all the foundation in 1929 of the PNR demonstrated that in a country in the process of modernization, political control has also to be modernized. 'A policy aimed to give to our nationality, once and for all, a firm foundation' was how President Calles defined his policy in 1926,[3] specifying that the construction of the state was a necessary condition for the creation of a nation.

During the presidency of Álvaro Obregón (1920–4) the most important problems were primarily political. These included relations with the United States; the re-establishment of the federal authority over a regionalism fortified by ten years of revolutionary crisis; and the presidential succession of 1924. Under the presidency of Plutarco Elías Calles (1924–8) and during the Maximato (1928–34, during which time Calles as *jefe máximo* continued to exercise real power without himself assuming the presidency), despite the events which surrounded first the

---

[3] Calles, 'The policies of Mexico to-day', *Foreign Affairs*, 1 (October 1926).

re-election and then the assassination of Obregón in 1928, priority was no longer given to political considerations but to economic and social questions, such as the general economic programme, oil, the war of the Cristeros and the impact of the world depression.

In 1920 the words 'revolution' and 'reconstruction' were synonymous. The desire for reconstruction was not a new one, but until 1920 there had been no peace, and without it nothing could be done. After 1920 there was peace of a sort. Interrupted by a military insurrection in December 1923, peace was brutally restored within weeks. From 1920 to 1924 the government had two preoccupations, first, to avoid American intervention and, to that end, to secure the long-desired diplomatic recognition; secondly, to resume payments on the foreign debt in order to regain international credit. These aims imposed prudence and moderation. José Vasconcelos could nevertheless light up the sky with his education policy, as we shall see. In 1924 Vasconcelos went into exile and his ministry was disbanded. Enthusiasm was then transferred to finance, industry and commerce. The year before the United States had recognized the Obregón régime; international credit had been restored and the hour was ripe for the great undertakings which had been planned between 1920 and 1924. Then came economic crisis, first in Mexico itself (1926) and then worldwide, which brought everything to a standstill. The time had come to retreat and to work out the new solutions which would be put into practice during the presidency of Lázaro Cárdenas (1934–40).

THE PRESIDENCY OF OBREGÓN, 1920–4

Álvaro Obregón, the son of a well-to-do Sonoran farmer, hardened by the struggle against nature and the Indian, a veteran of the revolutionary wars, was 40 when he came to power on 1 December 1920. Supported by the army and himself a soldier of genius, the conqueror of Pancho Villa, he was also a remarkable politician capable of allying himself with the labour unions and of rallying the Zapatista agrarian faction to his side. A socialist, a capitalist, a Jacobin, a spiritualist, a nationalist and an americanophile, he was not embarrassed by considerations of doctrine, even though he did preside over the establishment of an ideology – revolutionary nationalism. His main aims were national unity and national reconstruction, and he was to run the country like a big business.

Despite the postwar world depression, which produced a fall in the price of most primary products and an influx of Mexican workers expelled from the United States, the general economic situation in the early 1920s favoured Obregón. At that time Mexico produced a quarter of the world's oil, and oil along with other exports, chiefly mineral, guaranteed the prosperity of the state and the financing of the important social and economic projects characteristic of the period, including the achievements of the ministry of education under José Vasconcelos.

The generals who had determined the course of political life since 1913 were not career soldiers, but victorious revolutionaries, politicians on horseback, readily resorting to arms. Obregón, the prototype of the revolutionary general, understood better than anyone how to make use of the army (although this did not prevent him from having to face, in 1923, a formidable insurrection by his former comrades). The social base of the new system was formed by organized urban labour, which had been linked to the state since the pact of August 1919 concluded between Obregón and the CROM. Fortified by this alliance, the CROM aimed to control the whole labour movement and had in December 1919 organized a political agency, the Partido Laborista Mexicano. The second major pillar of the new regime were the *agraristas*, including the Agrarian Leagues and the Partido Nacional Agrarista of Antonio Díaz Soto y Gama, one of Zapata's secretaries. The common denominator of this triangular system – army, labour unions and *agraristas* – was nationalism. The president controlled it by the complicated ploy of calling on the unions and the rural militias to oppose the army and on the army to break strikes or to deal with the rural militias. The enrichment of the generals, union bosses and politicians, in short of the new governing class, was a feature of the system which also attracted the economic elite of the Porfiriato, without giving them any political power. Neither Obregón nor his successors tolerated the existence of any political party which might call into question the legitimacy of the regime. By force of circumstance, the Roman Catholic church filled the political void and played the part of a substitute opposition, which led, eventually, to the violent confrontation of 1926–9.

Obregón's paramount concern was US recognition. In defence of the interests of the oil companies and American citizens, the US State Department, however, demanded from the Mexican government that it should first take over the debt of the Díaz régime, that it should not apply to the oil companies the provisions of Article 27 of the constitution of

1917 which established the sovereignty of the state over land and subsoil deposits, and that there should be an indemnity for Americans whose interests had been damaged by the Revolution. No Mexican government could agree to such a capitulation. In the absence of sufficient goodwill or of adequate concessions in relation to the debt and the indemnities, Obregón soon gave up the attempt at reconciliation until 1923 when he desperately needed American help to meet a serious political crisis.

Until 1923 the government of Obregón was successful and the future of the Revolution seemed to be assured, despite the deaths of certain revolutionaries, some of them mysterious, like that of Banjamín Hill, the minister of war, who was poisoned, some violent, as in the case of Lucio Blanco, who was abducted in exile in the USA and assassinated. The 'Sonora triangle', Obregón, Adolfo de la Huerta (who had served as provisional president in 1920 and was now minister of finance), and Calles, minister of the interior, remained united; the system functioned well. In 1923 Obregón declared that his successor would be Calles, a man little known nationally and unpopular with many generals, but supported by the CROM and the *agraristas*. The malcontents had the wit to know how to alienate de la Huerta from Obregón and from Calles, in order to make him their candidate, and it was soon clear that the matter had to be settled by force of arms. Obregón, certain of the opposition of many of his comrades in arms, approached the United States to gain their support in the crisis. The Bucareli Street agreements in August 1923 sealed US–Mexican reconciliation at the price of weighty concessions favouring American interests. And it was at this juncture that Pancho Villa was murdered as a precautionary measure. The Revolution had devoured another of its children.

The military rebellion which broke out in December 1923 was of unexpected gravity, for two-thirds of the army were in active sympathy with the movement. Military operations remained frozen throughout December, however, while the fate of the rebellion was being played out in Washington, the issue being whether the State Department would support Obregón or the rebels. To gain the support of the United States, Obregón had to obtain from his Senate ratification of the Bucareli agreements. He obtained it by buying venal senators and terrorizing others with the assassination of their most outspoken member (Senator Field Jurado), as Martin Luis Guzmán related in his novel *La sombra del caudillo* (1929). President Coolidge immediately sent a fleet to blockade the Gulf against the rebels and to deliver the armaments Obregón's troops needed. War broke out on the following day, against rebels who were divided amongst themselves, soldier against civilian, general against general. Obregón took advantage of the situation and in the course of fifteen days and three battles conducted one of his finest campaigns. The rest was no more than a man-hunt: all the rebel leaders, 54 former Obregonistas, lifelong comrades, were shot. This great purge heralded others in 1927 and 1929 and finally brought about the subjugation of an army not yet professionalized which had lost its most important leaders,

The presidential succession crisis of 1923–4, which threw into relief the decisive role the United States still played in Mexican affairs, put an end to what remained of political liberalism in Mexico. Parliamentarians and judges of the Supreme Court were both brought to heel, and Calles won the pre-arranged elections before the eyes of an indifferent nation. Obregón's 'coup' had been successful, and he himself could look forward to returning to power in 1928. But the price had been high. It included the departure of José Vasconcelos from the ministry of education.

During the Obregón administration, Vasconcelos has a virtually free hand with state education. A member of that provincial middle class which had played an important part in the fall of Porfirio Díaz, and a Maderista from the beginning, he had spent long years of exile in the United States until recalled by the triumphant Sonorans in 1920 to take charge of the University of Mexico and, later, of state education.

Vasconcelos was, like all enthusiasts, both admired and detested, a great servant of the state and, though he himself denied it, a great politician. He was also a prodigious writer. According to Mariano Azuela, the story of his life is the best novel about the Mexican revolution. His qualities as a writer, his later flirtation with fascism (for reasons like Ezra Pound's) and his apparent recantation of his revolutionary past have caused his significance as a man of action to be forgotten. He is thought of as a man of letters, while his role as an organizer of an ideological programme upon which Mexican governments continue to depend until the present day is overlooked.

Educated as a lawyer, Vasconcelos was self-taught in cultural matters; he read a great deal (perhaps too much) from Plotinus to Lunacharski and from St Augustine to Tagore. For Mexican intellectuals he suddenly became their 'professor'. While Rector, he paid little attention to the university, though he saw to it that the ministry of education, suppressed by Carranza, was re-established. Then, as a minister, he travelled on horseback into the remotest country districts, debated in Congress, wrote for the newspapers and toured South America, for his brand of populist nationalism burgeoned into a dream of Spanish-American unity, of a 'cosmic race' which was to be born in America from the melting pot of all the ethnic groups.

He laboured to produce the new man, the twentieth-century Mexican, the future citizen of a state which had still not become a nation. This was why President Obregón supported this demonic individual who helped to legitimize his regime in the eyes of history. Obregón provided Vasconcelos with the financial means to do his work; to pay teachers better, build schools, open libraries and publish newspapers and books. Vasconcelos launched a gigantic scheme to implant literacy among children and adults, integrate the Indian into the embryonic nation, validate manual labour, and endow the country with technical training facilities. Even today Mexico has still not exhausted his inheritance.

Consistently with his ambition, Vasconcelos realized that the whole field of education needed attention, vertically and horizontally, from kindergarten to university, from evening classes to agricultural schools. The university interested him least, since it affected relatively few people. His utopian educational ideas could best be described as a form of cultural nationalism. They demanded, in the spirit of a religious crusade, the rapid and large-scale education of all Mexicans, young and old (illiteracy in 1921 was 72 per cent; in 1934 it was still 62 per cent). Teachers were regarded as 'missionaries' and were likened to the Franciscans in the sixteenth century. Books and libraries were essential to the fight, and the 'people's classics' were printed by the million to constitute a basic library in every school and village. Vasconcelos was fortunate in having the support of President Obregón; the budget of the ministry of education was raised from 15 million pesos in 1921 to 35 million in 1923.

Vasconcelos's programme was comprehensive: all the arts had to be mobilized to forge the nation and prevent it from becoming another Texas, another Puerto Rico. The Department of Fine Arts was given the responsibility of stimulating enthusiasm for painting, music and song, while cultural contacts were taken up with the rest of Spanish America. The Mexican school of mural painting emerged from this campaign. Vasconcelos provided painters with the materials to work with, gave them the walls of public buildings to cover and subjects (related to cultural nationalism) to illustrate, with the provocative demand: 'I wish the painting to be done as quickly as possible, over the widest possible area. Let it be a monumental and didactic art, at the opposite extreme from studio painting.' In 1923 the Manifesto of the Union of Workers, Technicians, Painters and Sculptors, signed by David Alfaro Siqueiros, Diego Rivera, José Clemente Orozco, Carlos Merida and others, made this declaration of populist optimism:

The popular art of Mexico is the most important and the healthiest of spiritual manifestations and its native tradition is the best of all traditions . . . We repudiate the so-called studio art and all the art-forms of ultra-intellectual coteries for their aristocratic elements and we extol the manifestations of monumental art as a public amenity. We proclaim that all forms of aesthetic expression which are foreign or contrary to popular feeling are bourgeois and should be eliminated, inasmuch as they contribute to the corruption of the taste of our race, which has already been almost completely corrupted in the towns.[4]

The departure of Vasconcelos in 1924 marked the end of this brief but brilliant phase during which intellectuals and artists had been harnessed to the service of the state under the auspices of the ministry of education. From then on two opposing points of view asserted themselves: on the one hand support for the regime, attended by a culture endowed with a certain social content; on the other, the cultural expression of a refusal to co-operate, accompanied by isolation or foreign exile. Thus, President Calles himself drew a distinction between 'intellectuals of good faith' and others.

Education in Mexico has not infrequently reflected the views of the minister in office: if Vasconcelos is invariably associated with the spiritual approach described above, Moisés Sáenz was the incarnation of the educational policy of Calles, which accorded great importance to rural schools, regarding them as the centre of the community and as a social substitute for the church. The emphasis was laid on instruction of a practical kind, as opposed to academic education. In the words of Sáenz, 'it is as important to rear chickens as to read poetry'.

Sáenz left Mexico at the beginning of the 1930s, after a difference with his successor, Narciso Bassols. He had just spent seven months in the village of Carapan, to observe the practical results of his rural school. His conclusions were published in a book, *México integro*, in which, disillusioned, he declared that the educational policy had been a failure. It

---

[4] José Clemente Orozco, *Autobiografía* (1945; Mexico, 1970), 57–63.

must be conceded that, after Vasconcelos, the share of the national budget allotted to education fell from 15 to 7 per cent and that there was, at least, a comparable decline in enthusiasm. Other educational utopian ideas were to arise during the 1930s, such as the emphasis on sex education and the socialist school; they were to incite considerable polemic, but none of them was to equal the utopia of Vasconcelos in its generosity or its compass.

The intellectuals and artists who had followed Vasconcelos no longer had their appointed place. A number of writers, Jorge Cuesta, José Gorostiza, Salvador Novo, Carlos Pellicer, Bernardo Ortiz de Montellano, Jaime Torres Bodet and Xavier Villaurrutia, together with the composer Carlos Chávez and the painters Agustín Lazo, Manuel Rodríguez Lozano and Rufino Tamayo, whose creative work was highly fashionable in the 1920s, formed a group around the review *Contemporáneos* (1928–31).[5] All, to a greater or lesser degree, bore the mark of Vasconcelos and all were savagely attacked as 'intellectuals of bad faith', 'traitors to the country', *descastados* (untouchables); they were, in fact, fighting the cultural nationalism of Calles, a caricature of that of Vasconcelos, demanding absolute freedom of expression and declaring that Mexico must open its doors to all cultures, particularly from Europe. They devoted a large part of their time to translating, with considerable expertise, the most important writers of the twentieth century. At no time has their influence been stronger than it is today, a fact which may be regarded as a posthumous triumph.

THE PRESIDENCY OF CALLES, 1924–8

The suppression of the de la Huertista rising in 1923–4 demonstrated that when a decision had been taken within the innermost councils of the government, it had to be acepted by the whole 'revolutionary family'; those who refused to submit to the rigours of this principle were crushed. Calles, who became president at the age of 47, was a shadowy figure. The bastard offspring of a powerful Sonoran landowning family, he had been a poor schoolteacher before the outbreak of the Revolution changed his life. He rose through the revolutionary army to become provisional governor of Sonora in 1917 and then minister of the interior under Obregón. Despite his radical reputation and socialist links, Calles was as

[5] Facsimile edition, Fondo de Cultura Económica, Mexico, 1981. See also Martin, *CHLA* IV, ch. 11, 511–12.

determined as Obregón to institute a programme of economic development on capitalist and nationalist lines. The state was to play an
important part and was in no sense opposed to landownership nor to
capital, whether domestic or foreign, provided that it served the national
interests. This form of nationalism led to a rupture not only with the
American oil companies but also with the railway unions as soon as they
opposed the reorganization of the network. Nationalism was the
essential factor in the conflict with the church. Although a nationalist
and a man of iron, Calles was also a realist and knew how to change
course when necessary, as he showed not only when facing the United
States, which he defied right to the edge of the precipice, but no further;
but also in his relations with the church, once the impossibility of
subduing the rebellious Cristeros became clear; and with the CROM, a
faithful ally whom he abandoned to his Obregonista enemies when it
became expedient to do so.

Among Calles's closest political allies were General Joaquín Amaro
and Luis N. Morones, the labour leader. Through Amaro, the minister of
war, Calles embarked upon the difficult task of domesticating the
praetorian guard and turning their officers into a professional officer
class. The attempt was halted by the campaign against the Cristeros
(1926–9) and the resistance of the Obregonista rebels, who were not
finally overcome until March 1929, eight months after Obregón himself
had been assassinated. The CROM, under the leadership of Morones,
minister of commerce, industry and labour, served as a counterbalance to
the army and to General Obregón. Morones, who had formerly played
the Obregonista card, became Calles's right hand and provided the
inspiration for a large part of his socio-economic policy.

Calles, put into the saddle by Obregón, was never strong enough to
shake off the burden of his sponsorship. Ex-president Obregón was
entrenched at the very heart of the political system as the senior and real
chief of the army. Calles was obliged to agree to the constitutional
reforms which made it possible for Obregón to be re-elected to the
presidency for a six-year term in July 1928, contrary to all revolutionary
tradition and at the risk of provoking a rebellion. (A rebellion was in fact
nipped in the bud in October 1927 and this provided an opportunity for
liquidating many of the remaining generals apart from Obregón.) Calles
made use of Morones against Obregón, but had to avoid an open breach.
There is no telling how these subtle manoeuvres would have ended if
Calles had not been relieved of both his powerful colleagues at the same

time. The assassination of Obregón on 17 July 1928, the day after his election, by the Catholic mystic José de León Toral enabled Calles to dismiss Morones, who was suspected by the Obregonistas of being implicated in the assassination.

The politics of the Calles administration were dominated, first, by a serious crisis over oil in the relations between Mexico and the United States; secondly, by the re-election crisis; and, thirdly, by a crisis in church–state relations. Mexico's rupture with the United States and growing domestic political difficulties coincided with a downturn in the economy. Everything and everyone then seemed to conspire against Calles, and this perhaps helps to explain the violence of his reactions against the most defenceless of his adversaries, the Catholic *campesinos*, hitherto mistakenly assumed not to be dangerous.

Conflict with the United States was inevitable from the moment when Calles refused to endorse the agreements negotiated by Obregón. In 1925, having secured the support of the bankers and chambers of commerce in the USA by resumption of payment of interest on the external debt, the Mexican government moved on to the offensive against the oil companies. The petroleum law drafted by Morones in December 1925 disregarded the Bucareli agreements of 1923 and adhered meticulously to the constitution. This could have led to expropriation, which Cárdenas was able to achieve in 1938. When the companies, supported by the American ambassador, Rockwell Sheffield, reacted violently, the attitude of Morones and Calles stiffened. In 1926 Mexico gave material help to the Nicaraguan insurgents against the American marines, and Augusto César Sandino received his general's stars from a Mexican general. Mexico thus appeared as the champion of the struggle against imperialism, and the anti-Mexican lobby in the United States pressed for military intervention, taking advantage of the emotions aroused by the conflict between church and state (see below).

The crisis was resolved in 1927–8, however, by a compromise skilfully negotiated by a new ambassador, Dwight Morrow, thanks to the good offices of the bankers of both countries. (Morrow himself was a partner in the firm of J. P. Morgan.) Without losing face, Calles made the desired concession: the oil law would not be retrospective. Henceforward there was no cloud in the relations between the two countries. As a result neither the Cristero insurgents, nor the conspirators against Obregón's re-election, nor the Obregonista rebels themselves could count on sympathy from the United States.

The dispute with the United States was complicated by the domestic crisis provoked by Obregón. There is no evidence of the existence of a pact between Obregón and Calles providing for them to serve alternate terms as president. From 1924, however, the Obregonistas were working to remove the constitutional barrier to re-election. They needed two years to attain their objective, as well as the personal intervention of Obregón in the congressional elections of 1926. After that, Obregón's intervention in politics became continuous and the struggle with Calles, although never overt, became permanent. Obregón did not agree with either Calles's oil policy or his religious policy. By the end of 1926 all the problems were interacting: constitutional reform and the presidential succession, the beginning of the Cristero war, a major railway strike (see below), insurrection by the Yaqui Indians of Sonora and the threat of American intervention. The general deterioration in Calles's position favoured Obregón. Soon three generals stood as possible candidates for the presidency in succession to Calles and, as in a Shakespearean tragedy, they were all three to die: Arnulfo Gómez and Francisco Serrano in 1927 at the time of the abortive putsch, and Obregón in July 1928, on the very day when, as president-elect, he was to meet Ambassador Morrow to try to put an end to the religious strife.

On church–state relations Calles took an extreme anti-clerical line. The people responded with violence, and the war of the Cristeros, known as the Cristiada, broke out. It was a terrible war of ordinary people rising against the state and its army, containing all the elements of both a revolutionary and of an anti-colonial war, though the government has since been depicted as representing the 'left' and the insurgents the 'counter-revolution'.

The anti-clericalism of the governing faction was a legacy of eighteenth-century rationalism and nineteenth-century liberalism, distorted by a political ignorance of Old Mexico, with its Indian/*mestizo* and Christian population. The constitution of 1917 gave the state the right to control the 'clerical profession', but Carranza and Obregón had been careful not to use it. The anti-clerical lobby, within both the military and the labour movement, re-appeared during the crisis of 1923–4. On the other side, the militants of the Catholic Action movement had been provoked, in February 1925, by the attempt of the CROM to create a schismatic church. The Catholics formed themselves into a fighting organization, the Liga, which returned blow for blow. In the heat of the dispute with the United States, the government, obsessed by the threat of a domestic battle-front, in fact created one – a self-fulfilling prophecy. Legislation was passed in 1926 to make infringements in religious matters criminal offences; the bishops replied with the suspension of church services from 31 July. In August, Calles berated the bishops who had come for an eleventh-hour interview: 'If you are not willing to submit, nothing but recourse to Congress or to arms remains for you.' Congress refused to examine the bishops' petition and a demand for reform signed by a large number of Catholics. There began a lengthy game of chess in which Rome and Washington, Obregón and the state bankers and, finally, Ambassador Morrow intervened. Negotiations dragged on for three years, while a war raged, a war which astonished the church as much as it did the state.

The first disturbances followed the suspension of church services and were spontaneous. Suppression only caused the movement to spread, for the country people (and Mexico was 75 per cent rural) no longer had any other means of protest. The Liga, which had gone underground, was now convinced of the futility of legal action and favoured a solution by force of arms; a general uprising was called for January 1927. In the five states of the west-centre, there was a large-scale insurrection, but the unarmed masses were machine-gunned by the army. Because their aims were fundamentally religious and therefore of permanent validity, the risings were resumed after the soldiers had gone. A state of war ensued which absorbed 45 per cent of the national budget. The severity of the repressive measures, the scorched-earth policy, the realignment of sections of the population, all served to inflame the revolt. The army could not cope with the problem, although it retained control of the towns and railways.

The Cristeros owed their name to the government, after their war-cry of 'Viva Cristo Rey; Long live Christ the King! Long live the Virgin of Guadalupe!' From a total of 20,000 in July 1927, numbers grew to 35,000 by March 1928 and were distributed over thirteen states. The great offensive launched against them by the government in 1928–9 was a failure. In June 1929 the movement was at its height, with 25,000 trained soldiers and 25,000 irregular guerillas. It was at this juncture that the state decided to reach a compromise with the church in order to rescue the rapidly deteriorating situation and, as we shall see, to avoid, in the autumn, the threatened alliance between the Cristeros and José Vasconcelos, a candidate for the presidency of the Republic.

Between 12 and 21 June the institutional conflict was settled in accordance with a plan drafted by Ambassador Morrow. The law of 1926 remained in force, but was not applied; the church resumed its services. When these *arreglos* (settlements) were announced, Mexican stocks rose on Wall Street, the bells rang out and the Cristeros went home. It proved, however, to be only a truce in the conflict between church and state.

THE MAXIMATO

Alvaro Obregón was assassinated on 17 July 1928, the day after his re-election. His 30 generals and his parliamentary bloc should have been able to overthrow Calles, who, with Morones, was suspected of having instigated the crime. Calles, however, knew how to temporize. Taking advantage of his rivals' differences, he entrusted the interim presidency for one year to Emilio Portes Gil, an important politician from Tamaulipas, who was a man of compromise and a follower at the same time of both Obregón and Calles. On 1 September 1928 Calles pronounced his celebrated 'political testament': with it the era of the *caudillos* came to an end and the era of the institutional state opened, beginning immediately with the foundation of the Partido Nacional Revolucionario (PNR), the forebear of the present PRI (Partido Revolucionario Institucional). This masterstroke left the Obregonistas unable to decide between an immediate putsch and an electoral campaign in 1929, as proposed by Calles. They lost several months before finally rebelling in March 1929, by which time it was too late. The praetorians Escobar and Manzo, who had dominated the political scene in July 1928, could not by then muster more than a third of the army to their side. Against them was the United States which provided Calles, by then minister of war, with the material support he needed to crush the revolt in a matter of weeks.

The election of 1929 was no mere formality, for the disappearance of Obregón encouraged those opposed to re-election and all those who were out of office. Faced with an unconvincing official candidate, Pascual Ortiz Rubio, who had been recalled from his ambassadorship in Rio de Janeiro, the still prestigious Vasconcelos tried to assume the mantle of Madero. His triumphal tour took on the glamour of a plebiscite and was so successful that the authorities resorted to all available means against him. The American secret service, whose agents were working for the election of Ortiz Rubio, reported: 'Vasconcelos probably has the largest number of followers, but it seems clear that he will be eliminated. He has the government machine against him, and also the fears of law-abiding and business people who are satisfied with a regime favouring the co-operation of capital and labor, and of the Church.'[6]

The government had been seriously alarmed by a possible combination of Cristero guns in the countryside and the popularity of Vasconcelos in the towns. In January 1929 there had been contact between these two forces. Ambassador Morrow, Portes Gil and Calles hastened to make their peace with the church, and there was then nothing for Vasconcelos to do but to comment: 'the news of the enforced surrender of the Cristeros sends a shiver down my spine. I see Morrow's hand in it. He has in this way deprived us of all grounds for the revolt which the vote-rigging would logically have provoked.'[7] The November elections were quite manifestly fraudulent and the unknown Ortiz Rubio won by a ratio of twenty to one. Vasconcelos escaped abroad, while the terror engulfed his followers.

After masterminding Portes Gil's presidency, Calles understood perfectly how to retain his mastery. He spent six years in the very same role as Obregón had played when he himself had been president, with the same difficulties but more power, for he saw to it that the presidents (three in six years) were reduced to underlings. Without reassuming the presidency himself, he made and unmade others and controlled all the ministries. He was rightly called the *jefe máximo* – hence the name given to this period, the Maximato.

Emilio Portes Gil, the transitional president, turned out in fact to be more difficult to manipulate than had been foreseen, and he adopted a style appropriate to his brief presidency, preferring compromise to repression and discussion to force. He has passed into history as being responsible for three positive decisions: the conclusion of the *arreglos* (settlements) of June 1929, which restored religious peace; the grant of autonomy to the University of Mexico, also in 1929; and the resumption of land distribution (see below), which set him in opposition to Calles. President Ortiz Rubio was dominated by the army, under General Calles, and cruelly derided by public opinion. The generals controlled the

---

[6] National Archives, Washington DC, Military Intelligence Division, 2657-G-605/210, 5 September 1929.   [7] José Vasconcelos, *Obras completas* (4 vols., Mexico, 1957–61), II, 162.

principal ministries and took their orders from the ex-president, without bothering to keep up appearances. Ortiz Rubio, victim of an attempt on his life at the beginning of his presidency and overwhelmed with insults, began to assert himself, timid though he was. General Amaro, for many years minister of war, encouraged him ('Go on, you are the president'). Calles got wind of a possible *coup*, took the initiative, forced Ortiz Rubio to resign on 3 September 1932 and instantly replaced him with General Abelardo Rodríguez, who was elected by acclamation in Congress. Rodríguez, the first millionaire president, who had made his fortune managing customs houses in California, was treated little better than Ortiz Rubio. He also, stimulated by the presidential office, tried to shake off the yoke of his patron, but he could not prevent his ministers from taking their orders from Calles before coming to the council chamber. He did, however, at least serve to the end of his term of office (in 1934).

Both Ortiz Rubio and Abelardo Rodríguez were burdened with an adverse economic situation since, for both national and international reasons, the mining industry was in disarray and agricultural production at its lowest ebb since 1900; moreover, after 1929 the safety-valve of emigration to the United States was no longer available. Even worse, between 1930 and 1934, the United States deported 400,000 Mexicans south across the Rio Grande. The financial collapse provoked by the world economic crisis entailed a 50 per cent devaluation, and the substitution of bank notes for coins of precious metal. But although the coinage disappeared, the public refused to accept notes. It was at this time that popular dissatisfaction with the authorities reached its height.

General Calles, whose political genius had founded the contemporary political system, was obliged to efface himself so that his works would endure. He had sworn, in his 'political testament' speech in 1928, that the time for strong men was past and that he no longer aspired to the presidency. He was not lying, for he never became president again, but it was from a position above the president that he governed the country for a further six years without violating the sacred principle of no re-election. The sole survivor of the heroes of the northern revolution, he reigned as the man of destiny in precarious isolation. A giant with feet of clay, however, his fall came suddenly, without major violence and amid general astonishment, within two years of the election of Lázaro Cárdenas to the presidency in July 1934. Calles had begun to institutionalize the revolution: it was for Cárdenas to complete the process.

ECONOMIC POLICY UNDER CALLES

Álvaro Obregón, like Porfirio Díaz, favoured 'much administration, little politics'; Plutarco Calles could have said 'much economic policy, no politics'. And the first aim of the economic policy of President Calles and his technical experts would seem to have been the liberation of the country from foreign economic domination. The project was part of a proudly nationalist programme of modernization aimed at systematically developing the productive forces of the country, while the structure of the state was being modified through a 'businesslike' re-organization of the federal government.[8] The state was thus transformed into an economic agency, as has been explained by Manuel Gómez Morín, one of the prime activists of this period:[9]

In recent years, the government has been the only source of capital. The old banks have turned to this source in order to re-establish themselves. The Banco de México and the Banco de Crédito Agrícola are its products, and for any enterprise which is planned, there is an inevitable tendency to think in terms of obtaining sufficient capital from the state. The banks, because of their lack of capital or because of the primitive way in which they operate . . . cannot constitute themselves as a direct source of capital . . . The foreign banks, as well as foreign companies, only develop those business activities which interest them, when it is in their interests to develop them, and in whatever ways may suit them, which do not always coincide with the best interests of Mexico. In this way, the state, if it wants to stimulate the economy, sees itself obliged to take the tremendous strain of subsidizing vast business enterprises in critical periods: the exploitation of natural resources remains outside the economic control of Mexico, and a whole range of useful or necessary enterprises are not undertaken, or are undertaken on terms which are far from satisfactory . . . There is not a single Mexican company which could seriously exploit our mineral resources. There is not a single Mexican company which could develop the technical ability to exploit our forestry resources. In short, there are no Mexican companies capable of making use of our natural wealth. With our present banking resources, with current credit procedure, it is impossible to think in terms of developing useful initiatives for the exploitation of our resources. There are no funds with which to start new enterprises or to give impetus to those which

[8] The expression comes from Manuel Gómez Morín, 1922.
[9] Memorandum of Manuel Gómez Morín, cited in Jean Meyer, *Historia de la Revolución mexicana*, XI (Mexico, 1977), 286.

already exist . . . And despite the nationalism which our laws proclaim, we are losing control day by day of our economy and, with it, all hope that we may one day fully control it. If Mexico wishes to create a national economy, its first step must be to seek the necessary instruments to carry out its purpose, that is, to obtain capital which may require the development of that economy. But we must not commit the same mistake as the previous generation. It is not a case of putting Mexico on the market. It is not a case of attracting capital to Mexico indiscriminately. We must obtain capital, but obtain it in accordance with prior planning, obtain it for our own development and not in order to be dispossessed, obtain it, in short, subject to our control and applied to our needs. Instead of foreign companies coming to Mexico to work when, where, and in whatever way may be convenient to them, with no other obligations than to political and administrative laws which, anyway, are always weak, ineffectual and prejudicial, we should try to create our own enterprises upon foundations which are both reasonable and secure, and in accordance with our plans and our purposes, and we should then seek to capitalize them abroad or within our own country. In this way, the capital which we may obtain will be financially subject to the aspirations and policies of Mexico and will be a servant rather than a master of the Mexican economy. To re-establish the confidence of foreign investors in Mexico is a difficult task, but it is not impossible. Its fulfilment requires, naturally, peace and security within the nation, but above all, it requires prudence and technical skills . . . One cannot talk of the domestic capital market, because such a market has never existed . . . But the potential for an internal market exists . . . And it is not absurd to consider that a concerted and intelligent effort could, within a short period of time, encourage new habits and activate local capital totalling between three hundred and five hundred million pesos, which is paralyzed and hidden not so much because of the political and economic situation, but because of the lack of financial methods which might make effective use of it.

It was a programme of classical liberalism – a balanced budget, the restoration of foreign confidence in Mexico's ability to pay its debts and a stable currency. Alberto Pani, minister of finance under Obregón and Calles (1923–7), reduced the salaries of civil servants, abolished departments in every ministry and imposed various other draconian economies. He instituted income tax and mounted other fiscal projects, the effects of which were spread over several generations. The result was that, by 1925, budgetary receipts considerably exceeded expenditure. At the end of 1925 Pani succeeded in renegotiating the foreign debt on better terms. In exchange, the state restored the nationalized railways (Ferrocarriles Mexicanos) to the private sector. With the economy thriving in the early 1920s, thanks mainly to oil exports, interest payments were resumed on the debt. In the same year Pani was able to carry out an ancient project, as ancient as independent Mexico, that of a central bank, the Banco de México, with an initial capital of 50 million pesos. Other banking institutions such as the Comisión Nacional Bancaria were set up, and new financial legislation was passed. In 1926 the Banco de Crédito Agrícola was founded, but plans for banks of Popular Credit, a Bank of Social Security (Banco de Seguridad Social) and a Workers' Bank (Banco Obrero) were frozen by economic recession.

Financial and banking activity was linked with the major public works. In 1925, since there was reasonable hope of obtaining the necessary credits, the Comisión Nacional de Caminos (National Highways Commission) launched a four-year programme to build 10,000 kilometres of roads. At the same time the modern road network was planned. The South Pacific railway, Nogales (Arizona) to Guadalajara, was completed in 1927 with the construction of the Tepic to Guadalajara section.

To open up new lands to modern methods of agriculture, major irrigation works were started. Dams and canals accounted for 6.5 per cent of the national budget between 1925 and 1928. Investment was concentrated in the north and the north-west.

In the mining, oil and electricity sectors, it was not a question of substituting domestic investment for that of foreign companies, but of bringing pressure on the latter to work in the interest of the country. The basic law of December 1925 with its regulating amendment of March 1926 made formal provision for the future recovery of national sovereignty over oil and the development of a petro-chemical industry. However, this initiative provoked such a serious row with the United States that, as we have seen, the Mexican government had to beat a retreat.

The Porfiriato and the first ten years of the Revolution had bequeathed a predominantly capitalist economy unevenly developed between regions: in the lead were the north-west and the north-east, the Federal District and the Gulf. Industry was concentrated in Mexico City and Monterrey and in the corridor linking Puebla with Veracruz, regions which had been relatively little affected by revolutionary violence. The oil boom reached its peak in 1922, after which production steadily declined. In the main centres industrial production had in 1920 just regained the level of 1910. In short, the period from 1910 to 1920 did not witness either the collapse of production or the paralysis of the economy.[10] Production recovered very rapidly but within an economy characterized by geographical and sectoral inequalities, a feature aggravated by the Revolution as well as by the links with the American economy. Despite recession in various sectors, it becomes clear from an overall view that the period from 1920 to 1940 was the second period of expansion (the first having occurred between 1880 and 1910), with a turning-point around 1925 signalling the beginning of a mini-recession, followed by depression. The international situation of Mexico did not change; on the contrary it was marked by greater foreign penetration. Between 1910 and 1929 British and American investment grew. Of the 4,600 million pesos of foreign capital invested in Mexico in 1929, 3,000 million was American and 900 million British. During the world depression, foreign holdings diminished in absolute terms, but the American percentage share increased. External trade continued to develop in the direction of reinforcing ties with the United States. In 1930, as in 1900, foreign trade represented 20 per cent of the gross national product (GNP); but during the period 1900–30 imports from the United States rose from 50 to 70 per cent of total Mexican imports, while exports to the United States were maintained at 70–80 per cent of total exports.

In spite of the postwar world depression, which witnessed a fall in the price of most primary products, the period from 1920 to 1925 was a golden age for Mexico because of its oil and other mineral exports. After a succession of favourable years, however, exports began to fall in 1926–7, and by degrees all, or almost all, sectors of the economy were affected. The Banco de México was obliged to be content with survival, standing impotently by as the recession spread. The public works programme had to be abandoned, and of the 20,000 kilometres of highway projected, fewer than 5,000 were completed. The railways were bankrupt and the state, which had restored them to private ownership, was obliged to take them back under its own control. A financial and banking crisis followed the economic crisis; both the national budget and the balance of payments were in deficit. The government made a desperate effort to honour its international commitments, but in August 1928 it had to resign itself again to suspending interest payments on the foreign debt. The treasury was empty; civil servants and the armed forces were paid in

---

[10] See John Womack Jr, 'The Mexican economy during the revolution, 1910–1920: historiography and analysis', *Marxist Perspectives*, 1/4 (1978), 80–123. Also see Womack, *CHLA*, v, ch. 2.

Table 1. *Mexican exports, 1903–27 (millions of pesos)*

	Gold and silver	Petroleum and derivatives	Other minerals	Remaining exports				Total exports
				Total	Agricultural goods	Livestock products	Manufactures and other goods	
1903–4	103.4	—	29.4	77.5	60.5	10.9	6.1	210.3
1904–5	93.9	—	36.4	78.2	59.1	10.5	8.6	208.5
1905–6	157.1	—	35.6	78.4	62.9	11.7	3.8	271.1
1906–7	123.7	—	36.5	87.8	71.8	11.2	4.8	248.0
1907–8	124.9	—	33.5	84.3	70.2	9.6	4.5	242.7
1908–9	113.1	—	31.2	86.8	67.9	13.9	5.0	231.1
1909–10	119.0	—	37.5	103.5	77.7	20.1	5.7	260.0
1910–11	143.0	—	37.0	113.8	91.3	16.8	5.7	293.8
1911–12	139.5	—	46.7	111.8	83.6	19.9	8.3	298.0
1912–13	130.9	—	58.8	110.7	85.9	19.8	5.0	300.4
1920	134.0	516.8	77.2	127.1	105.4	6.5	15.2	855.1
1921	89.8	576.3	22.9	67.8	60.7	2.3	4.8	756.8
1922	109.9	412.0	46.1	75.6	67.1	4.4	4.1	643.6
1923	116.7	270.2	98.1	83.5	74.3	4.4	4.8	568.5
1924	122.2	293.3	94.8	104.4	96.1	5.0	3.3	614.7
1925	135.7	292.1	119.9	134.8	120.9	9.8	4.1	682.5
1926	137.5	227.6	159.7	167.0	147.6	14.2	5.2	691.8
1927	87.0	133.4	218.7	188.3	161.4	19.4	7.5	627.4

Source: Joseph E. Sterrett and Joseph S. Davis, *The fiscal and economic condition of Mexico.* Report submitted to the International Committee of Bankers on Mexico (1928), 110.

Table 2. *Value of exports, 1909–10 and 1926 (millions of pesos)*

Products	1909–10	1926	Percentage change
Minerals and petroleum	156.5	524.8	+ 336
Agriculture	77.7	147.6	+ 190
Cattle and livestock products	20.1	14.2	− 30
Manufactures and other goods	5.7	5.2	− 8
Total	260.0	691.8	+ 265

Source: Table 1.

arrears, and then only out of funds advanced by the American and British banks.[11] There was a considerable drop in Mexico's gold reserves. In May 1926 the banks had reserves of 110 million pesos, compared with 135 million in 1925. By the end of 1926 the reserves had fallen to 88 million and one year later to 73 million pesos.[12]

The main cause of the financial crisis and the collapse in confidence was a combination of unpropitious circumstances acting on the structure of the Mexican economy. Mexico relied heavily on foreign trade to finance its internal development. When the balance of trade ceased to be positive, in other words when exports ceased to pay for imports – consumer goods for the governing and middle classes, machinery, minerals and metals, vehicles, chemical products, and cereals from the United States following the fall in domestic production of essential foodstuffs (see below) – the whole economy was affected.

The structure of Mexico's foreign trade had not been altered by the Revolution. On the contrary its traditional features became even more entrenched. Mexico was more than ever a country producing and exporting raw materials (see tables 1 and 2). Whereas in 1910 60 per cent of exports had come from minerals and hydrocarbons, by 1926 this figure was 76 per cent. Although agricultural exports had undeniably increased, they were overtaken by the rising exports of oil and minerals. The fall in the figure for cattle reflected the break-up between 1913 and 1920 of the

---

[11] See G. Butler Sherwell, *Mexico's capacity to pay. A general analysis of the present international economic position of Mexico* (Washington, DC, 1929), 70, and J. E. Sterrett and J. S. Davis, *The fiscal and economic condition of Mexico*. Report submitted to the International Committee of Bankers on Mexico (1928), 124. [12] *Estadística Nacional*, January 1928.

Table 3. *Mexico's oil industry, 1911–27*

	Production of crude petroleum (millions of barrels)	Export of crude petroleum and derivatives (millions of barrels)	Unitary value of production (pesos per barrel)	Value of production (millions of pesos)	Taxes on production and sale (millions of pesos)
1911	12.6	0.9	0.20	2.5	—
1912	16.6	7.7	0.25	4.1	0.5
1913	25.7	21.3	0.30	7.7	0.8
1914	26.2	23.4	0.30	7.9	1.2
1915	32.9	24.8	0.40	13.2	2.0
1916	40.5	27.3	0.55	22.3	3.1
1917	55.3	46.0	0.85	47.0	7.1
1918	63.8	51.8	1.40	89.7	11.5
1919	87.1	75.6	1.83	159.0	16.7
1920	157.1	145.5	2.00	314.1	45.5
1921	193.4	172.3	1.89	365.9	62.7
1922	182.3	180.9	1.93	351.7	86.0
1923	149.6	135.6	1.91	285.9	60.5
1924	139.7	129.7	1.95	272.1	54.6
1925	115.5	96.5	2.59	299.3	42.1
1926	90.4	80.7	2.49	225.1	34.8
1927	64.1	48.3	2.46	157.5	19.0

Source: Sterrett and Davis, *The fiscal and economic condition of Mexico*, 197.

system by which livestock was leased to farmers. Even fewer manufactured goods were exported. In 1922 64 per cent of imports came from the United States and by 1926 the figure had risen to 70 per cent. Again, in 1922 up to 80 per cent of all Mexico's exports went to the United States, but in 1926 only 71 per cent went there as a result of zinc being exported to Belgium and Germany.[13] The general tendency thus remained one of heavy dependence on the United States and the mining industry, a combination which gave the Mexican economy a certain fragility. The trend was visible after 1926, and the depression of 1929 confirmed the evidence.

Oil was the first product to cause problems. In 1921 Mexico was second in world production and oil represented 76 per cent of her exports. From 1921 to 1927 production and exports fell by 72 per cent, which included a drop of no less than 42 per cent in one year, 1926–7. There were several reasons, technical, economic and political, for this contraction, which continued to accelerate. Foreign companies had ruthlessly exploited the wells to the full extent of their capacity, sometimes actually destroying them by flooding with salt water.[14] The new borings were less profitable and the companies, angered by Morones's policy towards them, transferred their investments to Venezuela, which by 1927 actually surpassed Mexico in output (see tables 3 and 4).

At the end of 1924 the capital invested in the oil industry was estimated at 800 million pesos, of which 57.5 per cent was American, 26.2 per cent English, 11.4 per cent Dutch and only 3 per cent Mexican. In 1926 certain companies were still making 100 per cent net profit on the sale of crude oil. In 1924 there had been six refineries in Mexico capable of refining 800,000 barrels a day, but in 1927 output had fallen by 40 per cent. By March 1928 only two refineries were operating, and in 1927 almost all the light oil was sent to the refinery instead of being exported. Duties on petroleum, which in 1921 had represented one-third of the national revenue, about 85 million pesos, had fallen by 1927 to one-eighth, about 19 million, and in the same year the companies withdrew their bank deposits, thus bringing about the *de facto* devaluation of the peso.[15]

For a time the export of non-ferrous metals (zinc, copper and lead),

---

[13] *Estadística Nacional*, 15 July 1927, p. 5.
[14] Sterrett and Davis, *The fiscal and economic condition of Mexico*, 200.
[15] Merill Rippy, *Oil and the Mexican Revolution* (Muncie, Indiana, 1972), 166–7; Sterrett and Davis, *The fiscal and economic condition of Mexico*, 200–1.

Mexico

Table 4. *World production of petroleum, 1910–27 (millions of barrels)*

	United States	Mexico	Russia	Persia	Dutch colonies	Venezuela	Colombia
1910	209.6	3.6	70.3	—	11.0	—	—
1911	220.4	12.6	66.2	—	12.2	—	—
1912	222.9	16.6	68.0	—	10.8	—	—
1913	248.4	25.7	62.8	1.9	11.2	—	—
1914	265.8	26.2	67.0	2.9	11.4	—	—
1915	281.1	32.9	68.5	3.6	11.9	—	—
1916	300.8	40.5	65.8	4.5	12.5	—	—
1917	335.3	55.3	63.1	7.1	13.2	0.1	—
1918	355.9	63.8	27.2	8.6	12.8	0.3	—
1919	378.4	87.1	31.8	10.1	15.5	0.4	—
1920	442.9	157.1	25.4	12.2	17.5	0.5	–
1921	472.2	193.4	29.0	16.7	17.0	1.4	—
1922	557.5	182.3	35.7	22.2	17.1	2.2	0.3
1923	732.4	149.6	39.1	25.2	19.9	4.2	0.4
1924	713.9	139.7	45.4	32.4	20.5	9.0	0.4
1925	763.7	115.5	52.4	35.0	21.4	19.7	1.0
1926	770.9	90.4	64.3	35.8	21.2	37.2	6.4
1927	903.8	64.1	72.4	36.8	21.4	64.4	14.6

Source: Sterrett and Davis, *The fiscal and economic condition of Mexico*, 198.

which had increased tenfold between 1921 and 1927, together with agricultural exports, enabled the country to withstand the strain. However, in 1926 exports of silver collapsed as a result of the drop in price on the world market; China and India, the principal purchasers, suspended their dealings. Exports of zinc, lead, copper and agricultural products were not enough by themselves to avert financial difficulties. Capital took flight to the United States, foreign investment declined and the deficit on the balance of payments reached 50 million pesos in 1926.[16]

This was the beginning of the economic crisis of the late 1920s, accompanied by unemployment, bitter strikes and emigration to the United States. At the same time the Cristero war ravaged the countryside and proved a heavy drain on the budget: in 1927 33 centavos out of every peso in the budget was spent on the army. Manuel Gómez Morín and Alberto Pani left office: considerations of politics and war once again prevailed over economic policy. Finally, in 1929 the two sectors not

[16] *Estadística Nacional*, February 1929, pp. 74–6, and Rippy, *Oil and the Mexican Revolution*, 124–5.

previously affected, zinc, lead and copper, and agriculture, were struck by the full force of the world depression. Agricultural exports, which between 1921 and 1927 had risen from 60 to 161 million pesos, dropped to 92 million in 1928 and 52 million in 1930.[17] Output in the mining sector lost half its value between 1929 and 1932.

ORGANIZED LABOUR AND THE STATE UNDER CALLES

One of the essential features of economic policy during the Calles administration was the attempt to reconcile class interests through the mediation of the state. The man identified with this initiative was Luis N. Morones, secretary-general of the principal labour organization, the CROM, who had been a colleague but subsequently became an enemy of Obregón, after the breakdown in their relations in 1923–4. Morones became Calles's right-hand man and was his powerful minister of industry, commerce and labour (1924–8), more powerful, for example, than the minister of the interior (Gobernación). To reconcile capital and labour under the aegis of the state, Morones undertook an enormous legislative and administrative task, in the execution of which he did not hesitate to eliminate 'irresponsible elements' and 'provocateurs' in the labour movement. As an American observer wrote in 1927:

The prime objective of the labor unions, which have secured for this purpose the cooperation of the great employers' organizations, is to create a structure for Mexican industry which will increase the numbers of the working class, provide it with better work and a higher standard of living and, finally, bring about the economic independence of the country.[18]

Morones started from the principle that there was nothing which could not be negotiated if both employers and workers showed 'responsibility' and 'moderation'. In speaking he made regular use of the words 'conciliation', 'co-operation' and 'co-ordination'. Every strike had to be official, agreed to by the union, which had to consult its national executive committee. The minister decided on the legality of the strike, and an illegal strike was doomed to failure. This was advantageous to the employers, who were, theoretically, protected from wildcat strikes on condition that they respected the law, which favoured the workers. In this legislation special attention was paid to problems raised by accidents

---

[17] National Archives, Washington DC, Military Intelligence Division, 2525-G-11/9, 24 May 1932.
[18] W. English Walling, *The Mexican question* (New York, 1927), quoted in Enrique Krauze, *Historia de la revolución mexicana*, x (Mexico, 1977), 25.

and illness; standards of safety were imposed, together with provisions for retirement and minimum wages.

In 1926–7 the reforms of Morones passed an important test with distinction. The textile industry had been in recession for years. Although it was the country's leading industry, it was technologically out of date and paralysed by constant disputes; in 1922 textile strikes represented 71 per cent of the total number of strikes. Morones came to grips with the problem and brought together the representatives of employers and workers in order to resolve the labour problems and to make a start with modernizing the industry. The result of this meeting was a collective contract (*contrato ley*) for the entire textile industry, the adoption of a wage-scale, and the introduction of arbitration at all levels by means of mixed commissions.

Complementing this strategy was a system of protection designed to encourage the creation of national industries, which doubled the fiscal advantages granted to industrialists. A publicity campaign urged Mexicans 'to consume the products of their own country'. Lawyers drafted legislation for nationalizing the electrical industry (*código nacional eléctrico*) and the oil industry, and prepared for the reform of the constitution to enable nationalization of mines, commerce, credit, Communications and the sources of energy. As a result of the economic and political crisis of the late 1920s, however, these measures remained a dead letter for many years.

This policy provoked strife with the oil producers and the State Department, as we have seen, but relations with foreign – chiefly American – bankers and manufacturers were good. Between 1924 and 1928, Ford, Siemens, Colgate, Palmolive, British-American Tobacco and International Match had all established themselves in Mexico. Certainly the degree of industrialization remained modest, for the combination of international and national circumstances was not very favourable; moreover, the majority of managers, technicians and ideologues considered that agriculture and mining products constituted the true riches of the country. From this aspect, Morones was a solitary visionary who heralded the developments of the 1940s. It is too simple to regard Morones as a traitor to the working class, who sold himself to capitalist interests. Morones, like Calles, was one of the great builders of the Mexican state, in which the labour movement played a decisive part.

It is inevitable that any discussion of the workers should concentrate on the CROM. However, the CROM represented only one element within the labour movement, and trade unionism represented only one aspect of the workers' daily life. From 1910 to 1918 the relationship of workers with the state went through successive phases of hostility, indifference, or collaboration; the hopes of the workers fluctuated according to shifts in the relationship. In 1918 Morones, a former electrician, made his famous address at the time of the foundation of the CROM under state patronage; from that point for the next ten years the CROM remained the embodiment of political realism and the sharing of responsibility with the state. In the words of Rosendo Salazar, an old union militant:

The state as an intermediary is the creation of the Mexican Revolution and implies neither the dictatorship of the proletariat nor that of the capitalist state. It excludes all foreign ideology from its sphere and promotes understanding between employers, workers and government. Labour adjusts its demands in accordance with the law and the state gives it protection against abuses by the employers.[19]

The organized labour movement thus became one component in the governmental machine, a situation which led to opportunism and corruption, but also gave much greater influence than the figures would suggest. Workers and artisans, numbering less than 600,000, carried more weight than 4 million peasants; 100,000 union members were instrumental in making the CROM a partner to be respected, because through its Labour party it sent deputies and senators to the Congress and even succeeded in gaining control of the government in several states.

It is difficult to give precise figures, for those which are available are not reliable. The CROM claimed to have 2 million members in 1928, but recognized that the actual membership was much lower and that half of these were peasants. The only reliable figure, that of members who paid dues, amounted to 15,000. In the absence of better information, it may be agreed that the CROM had mustered 100,000 workers, artisans, office workers, small traders and, in theory, 50,000 agricultural labourers. Catholic unions claimed 40,000; 30,000 more may be attributed to the railway workers, who had been weakened by the divisions resulting from the foundation of the CROM; and 20,000 to the CGT (Confederación General del Trabajo). Certainly the Communists, the sworn enemies of the CROM, did not succeed in gaining the confidence of 'the great masses of the workers and of the semi-proletarian peasants'.[20]

The peak of CROM influence was reached between 1924 and 1928

[19] Quoted in Jean Meyer, *La Révolution mexicaine* (Paris, 1973), 102.
[20] See, for example, *Correspondence Internationale*, 25 (20 February 1927), 327.

when its secretary-general Morones was the most important minister in the Cabinet of Calles. It took advantage of the situation in a positive way to improve the position of workers, and in a negative way to fight the other trade unions by all possible means. The religious conflict was exploited in order to eliminate the Catholic unions, and strikes were used to try to break rivals, such as the unions of oil workers, electricians, railway employees and textile workers, who had, all told, more members than the CROM. The CROM demanded that the workers should unite in a single confederation and respect the new laws (which were favourable to them). Strikes of unions not affiliated with the CROM were almost invariably designated as illegal. The economic crisis of 1926 caused strikes to multiply in all sectors, and not infrequently Morones switched from mediation to repression which sometimes caused further strikes.

For ten years the attitude of the CROM was decisive, whether in the promotion or termination of a strike. It launched, supported or revived movements in order to conquer new positions, destroy its enemies or establish a union monopoly. The advances made by the CROM were parallel with those of the government of Calles: when the latter undertook the reorganization of the railways, the CROM seized its opportunity and tried to take the place of the independent unions. In the oil dispute, the CROM went into battle against the companies. All this explains the often bloody character of a struggle which frequently brought workers into conflict with other workers.

The struggle was a bloody one because the independent forces, whether 'red' or 'white', did not lack strength; they were to be found in the textile industry, the railways, certain mines and in the bakeries. When, after Obregón was assassinated in 1928, the CROM suffered a rapid erosion of its power, the independent unions had the chance for revenge: the CROM was stripped of much of its strength, although it retained a considerable capacity for resistance. Between 1928 and 1937 the trade union movement was more deeply divided than ever. It was not until the Cárdenas administration that the CTM (Confederation of Mexican Workers) was founded and gained the dominant position.

All strikes were by nature political and inseparable from inter-party and parliamentary struggles, from conflicts over the presidential succession and from local and national disputes. The railway workers, in particular, had an old tradition of union independence and militancy which went back to the Porfiriato and had been consolidated during the civil war years when they were, by force of circumstances, in the front line. War was above all a matter of the railways. In 1920 the interim president, Adolfo de la Huerta, had facilitated the formation of a Confederation of Railway Workers' Union, then the biggest union in the country. In 1921 it opposed the government of Obregón and had great difficulty in obtaining recognition. When in the same year the Confederation had recourse to a strike, the government defined this decision as *rebelión abierta* (open revolt) and President Obregón sent the army to occupy workshops, stations and trains. The CROM pulled out of the dispute, while de la Huerta, playing the part of overall mediator, strengthened his position with the railway workers. In December 1923, therefore, the de la Huertista rebellion met with some support within the Confederation (as also from other unions, such as certain affiliates of the CGT, which opposed the CROM and the government).

A logical consequence of the defeat of de la Huerta was a purge of railway workers, a purge directed by the CROM, which took the opportunity to try to dominate a sector hitherto closed to it. This manoeuvre, together with the reorganization of the railways which reduced personnel, provoked a series of disputes in 1926 which led to the great railway strike of 1926–7. President Calles reacted in the same way as in 1921, when he was at the ministry of interior: he sent in the troops, one hundred soldiers into each workshop, and backed up Morones, who recognized new unions as so many weapons in the war against the Railway Confederation. In December 1926, when the strike had spread to all regions, the railwaymen did not perhaps fully realize the dangerous position of the government. In fact the dispute with the United States over petroleum and diplomatic issues was at its height and there was some talk of 'sending in the Marines' and of setting the oil wells on fire. In addition, the Yaqui war was raging, and in a matter of days the Cristeros would be in revolt.

The railway strike, which was very bitter, lasted for three months. Soldiers rode on locomotives driven by strike-breakers; it was never known how many trains had been derailed or how many railway workers and saboteurs had been shot. Gradually, during April and May 1927, the agitation lost its momentum and fizzled out in the course of the summer. The victory of government and CROM was a very costly one for workers and railways alike.

Other strikes, even though many and also bitter, paled by comparison with the 1926–7 railway strike. From 1920 to 1926 the textile industry was in a continuous state of unrest, aggravated by disputes between unions. There again the influence of the CROM was overpowering: in order to gain control of the entire national workers' movement, it was obliged, on the strength of its political allegiance, to destroy the unions unwilling to come into line. And each time the opportunity arose, it did so. In the textile sector it engaged in armed combat with the 'reds' and the 'free' unions in the capital city, the state of Mexico, Puebla and Veracruz. After the Textile Convention, there were many fewer strikes because of the agreements drawn up between the employers, the unions and the state. Then came the economic crisis, which weakened the position of the workers, threatened by the piling up of stocks and the slowing down of production.

In all sectors the trend was the same: strikes in 1921, followed by a period of relative quiet; strikes between 1924 and 1926 characterized by divisions within the unions; less numerous but often desperate strikes in subsequent years, under the shadow of economic crisis when factories and mines were closing down. What was the result of so much sound and fury? The hard-won victory of the CROM was to have no future, for in 1928–9 it was removed from governmental power, and it never again became the single organization for the Mexican workers that it would have liked to be.

The 1920s were especially characterized by the reorganization and modernization of existing industries. The process was, however, generally accompanied by a reduction in the numbers of workers, particularly in the mines, on the railways and in the textile industry, a fact which explains the often desperate nature of the workers' resistance. From 1925 onwards the CROM co-operated in the task of modernization and left resistance to its enemies, the 'reds'. Those workers fortunate enough to keep their jobs or to find other employment probably imagined that their lot would improve as a result of the new legislation and of the policy of Morones. Then the slump in Mexico and the world depression brought about the closure of many factories. The CROM and the government tried, without much success, to settle or re-settle unemployed workers in country areas. It was a curious attempt to turn back into peasants workers who had only just emerged from the peasantry in a country which was far from having resolved its own agrarian question. It demonstrates the extent to which Mexico was still, in 1930, a rural country.

AGRARIAN REFORM, AGRICULTURE AND THE PEASANTS

There has probably been some exaggeration of the agrarian contribution to the collapse of the Porfiriato. Similarly in the history of the Revolution the importance of agrarian reform has probably been overestimated. In the course of the civil war decisive legal measures were taken, in an improvised fashion and under pressure of necessity, against large-scale private landownership, as illustrated by the decree of January 1915 and Article 27 of the constitution of 1917. The application of a modified version of the principles embodied in the 1915 decree and Article 27 of the constitution, however, were only put into effect in 1934, and then only in a slow and confused way, with the publication of the Agrarian Code. In accordance with the constitution and the enabling code, land belonged to the nation which, through the state, could recognize it as legitimate private property or expropriate it and concede it either to communities defined by the term *ejido* or to individual smallholders. The concession was inalienable and could not be let, sold or inherited.

Somewhat timidly and halfheartedly, Carranza had already distributed 200,000 hectares before Obregón paid off the Zapatistas and other hard-core guerilla forces, along with his own soldiers, by ratifying the seizures made during the civil war, especially in the Zapatista zone (Morelos and Guerrero). In the course of four years Obregón distributed more than one million hectares, with the political aim of buying peace. President Calles at first followed this initiative, then slowed the process. Like Obregón, he would have preferred to contain agrarian reform within a political framework and to complete it quickly, in order to pass on to modernization and productivity – colonization, irrigation and large-scale capitalist agriculture – which interested him more than distribution.

Because of the Revolution, the colonizing movement begun under the Porfiriato, a pioneering assault on the dry, irrigable lands of Sonora and the tropical forests of Veracruz, Tabasco, Campeche, and so on, had to be halted. It was re-launched by Obregón and Calles with the support of the state (Law on Colonization of 5 April 1926). However, the world depression interfered with this project for massive public works, as we have seen: agricultural exports collapsed; 400,000 Mexicans returned from the United States; and the government was forced to revise economic strategy, thus playing into the hands of the agrarian lobby. Despite Calles's declaration in 1929 that 'Agrarianism such as we have understood and applied it has been a failure',[21] he was obliged to agree to a resumption of the distribution of land. Under Portes Gil in 1929–30, 1,700,000 hectares of land were distributed. During the period from 1915

---

[21] Meyer, *Révolution mexicaine*, 244–5.

to 1933 a total of 7,600,000 hectares was distributed. And in less than two years (1933–4) Abelardo Rodríguez handed out a further 2,500,000 hectares.

The balance sheet of agrarian reform in 1934, on the eve of Cárdenas's great distribution of 18 million hectares, reveals three features. First, the concessions were limited: ten million hectares, perhaps 10 per cent of the cultivated land, had gone to 10 per cent of the peasantry. (*Peones acasillados*, agricultural workers housed on the haciendas, did not benefit from agrarian reform until 1934.) The institutional result was a total of perhaps 4,000 *ejidos*. Secondly, the concessions were concentrated in a small number of districts. And thirdly, these districts were confined to the Old Mexico of the high central plateau and to its southern and south-eastern tropical escarpment (Morelos, Veracruz, Hidalgo). In most cases the central core of the hacienda was respected and the *ejido* plots of land were allocated under separate titles, in small lots of from four to ten hectares. According to local conditions prevailing in each state, the reforms, administered by the authorities, were sometimes executed with vigour, sometimes evaded and sometimes postponed until a later time. Hence there emerged a wide variety of situations and a certain lack of control over the operations, which resulted in corruption and in extortion from the peasants, including those who benefited from the distribution.

Local politics complicated the agrarian problem, because it allowed caciques to control a substantial clientèle and at the same time manipulate landowners. Within the *ejido* the administrative committee arranged and rearranged the distribution of the plots of land to its own advantage, a fact which explains the violence of the struggle for power and the large number of murders perpetrated in the *ejidos*. Paul Friedrich has studied the massacres which lasted for more than 25 years in the region of Naranja (Michoacán), and Luis González has recorded one episode which he describes as 'murderous insanity' at San José de Gracia.[22] The *ejido* of Auchén even acquired the name of the '*ejido* of the widows', since all the men were dead except for one who had become the owner and exploited the whole *ejido*.

Not only did agrarian reform create divisions among the *ejidatarios* themselves, it also divided the peasantry into the 10 per cent who had received a plot of land and those who had received nothing. The tactic of

---

[22] Paul Friedrich, *Agrarian revolt in a Mexican village* (Englewood Cliffs, NJ, 1970); Luis González y González, *Pueblo en vilo; microhistoria de San José de Gracia* (3rd edn, Mexico, 1979), 186, 195.

dividing the peasants into hostile and irreconcilable factions guaranteed that the government controlled the land as well as the electoral loyalty of its owners. From its beginning the agrarian policy had been a weapon brandished alike against the landowners, who were threatened with expropriation, and against the beneficiaries, who were afraid of being ejected from the *ejidos*. Guns were handed out regardless of the risk of non-recovery, as in Veracruz in 1932, to the militias of the *ejidos* called 'social defence forces', so that they could serve as an instrument of repression against the other peasants and as a means of blackmail against the landowners large and small.

The traditional hacendado was hard hit by the threefold ordeal of wars in 1913–17 and 1926–9, economic crisis after 1929 and agrarian reform itself. Henceforth the rural conflict set the landless peasant against his landed neighbour, either traditional small private proprietor or *ejidatario*, and the small proprietor or the *comunero* (member of an Indian community) against the *ejidatario*. The agrarian programme was short-sighted, for mutual antagonisms were endlessly multiplied by the collapse of the established society and by the reform. There were other human elements involved, too – the tenant farmer, the sharecropper, the agricultural labourer, the migrant stockbreeder. Conflicts of class, race and culture raged, and the religious dispute certainly did not help to pacify popular feeling.

Different regional groups representing the provinces against the capital, the periphery against the centre and the north against the south all exploited the peasants, who had helped bring about the fall of Don Porfirio and who in some districts had succeeded by a brief show of force in recovering part of their lands from the great estates. The revolutionaries in power had never had a true agrarian programme; they had had an agricultural programme, which was not the same thing. They never attacked the principle of the hacienda, but were merely in favour of small and medium-sized properties. Between 1915 and 1928 only 10 per cent of the haciendas had been appropriated and, paradoxically, half of these had been small. In fact, the areas invaded by the peasants themselves were of much greater importance. The peasants were granted the temporary satisfaction of seizing and consolidating their power; they were then made use of to dismantle the large private estates in the interests of a capitalist agriculture. The peasants were to be both the instruments and the victims of a Mexican version of the primitive accumulation of capital.

Peasants obtained more than was included in the revolutionary programme, but their success was limited. The politician took the place of the hacendado and the peasant found himself in the same relationship to the government as he had formerly been to his employer, except that the government was to be feared in a different way. 'Nothing has been done to liberate the peasant from the politician', wrote Marjorie Clark in her *Organized labor in Mexico* (1934).

If he wants to escape repression he must take care to belong to whichever is strongest in his region. He is promised land, money, implements if he behaves well; he is threatened with losing the land which he has already received, with seeing his harvests destroyed and his flock slaughtered if he fails to respond to the demands of the group in power. A tyranny equal to that of the *caciques* (bosses) under the régime of Porfirio Díaz has been established.[23]

It is not difficult to see why agrarian reform failed to arouse the enthusiasm of the peasants. The agrarian organizations were dominated by the bureaucracy; they never became genuine peasant bodies. Some peasants, preferring to stay outside them, refused the plots of land to which they were entitled. Such refusals have been attributed to fear, of the great landowner and his 'white guard' or of the priests who opposed the scheme and who sometimes, against the order of the bishops, declared it a mortal sin to accept an ejidal plot of land. Fear certainly played a part, but there was also the peasants' own conception of property and the proper means of acquiring it. All dreamed of becoming landowners, but not by just any method. Luis González has explained that there were only two honourable ways of becoming a landowner – by purchase or by inheritance. Hundreds of thousands of peasants left for the United States in the 1920s, working hard to save eight out of every ten dollars in order one day to buy a plot of land in their native village. A gift always compromises the recipient, and when it was offered by a traditionally mistrusted government, it was difficult to accept. It was definitely unacceptable between 1926 and 1929 when the state and the church were at war. During these terrible years the Cristeros often made the *agraristas* (at least those who had received plots of land) pay dearly, with their blood, for their connection with the state.

Obregón and Calles dreamed of creating a substantial class of dynamic smallholders and owners of medium-sized estates, on the model of the Californian 'farmer'. Such a class already existed in their native north-west – Obregón himself was a perfect representative – and it had

[23] Marjorie Clark, *Organized labor in Mexico* (Chapel Hill, NC, 1934), 161–2.

Table 5. *Agricultural
production per capita
(1900 = 100)*

Regions	1907	1929
Centre	112	69
South	145	98
North	60	318

Source: Clarke Reynolds, *The Mexican
economy: twentieth century structure and
growth* (New Haven, 1970), 105.

benefited from such economic activities of government as agricultural credit, irrigation works and new roads. It seems that while the government parcelled out bits of land on the plateau and in the south-east, it poured money into the north-west. The distribution of land was for the mass of the Mexican Indians and *mestizos* of Old Mexico, but capital investments were for the owners of medium-sized and large estates in other regions. In the northern areas favoured by the Sonorans, there was scarcely an *ejido* to be found in 1934, but there were highways and an irrigation programme representing one-quarter of public investment between 1925 and 1935. In the words of Obregón: 'Fair distribution of land to the proletariat is a first essential of the revolutionary programme, but the foundations of the agricultural life of the country must not be undermined.'[24]

From 1907 to 1929 the output of maize and black beans, the staple foodstuffs of the people, fell by 40 and 31 per cent respectively, while the population increased by 9 per cent. (Although as a result of war, famine, epidemics and emigration Mexico had no more inhabitants in 1920 than it had in 1910, the population grew from under 15 million to 16 million between 1920 and 1930 and to 17 or 18 million – the data are inexact – in 1934.) Conditions in some regions were much graver than the overall figures suggest. The central region, homeland of 45 per cent of the rural population in 1930, witnessed a drop of 31 per cent in its total agricultural production from 1913 to 1929. Table 5 demonstrates the disparities in agricultural production per capita between 1907 and 1929. Total production of maize, which had been 3.5 million tonnes in 1910 and 2.9

---

[24] In Luis González y González, *Los presidentes de México ante la nación* (Mexico, 1966), III, 423.

million tonnes in 1920, had fallen to 2.2 million in 1926 and only 1.5 million in 1929, because of the elimination of the corn-growing haciendas and the proliferation of small, poor producers.[25] Production of beans had grown steadily to over 200,000 tons in 1926, but then declined to under 100,000 tons by 1929.[26] In contrast, the export of foodstuffs expanded throughout the period 1920–7. For example, exports of coffee rose from 10,500 tons (9.3 million pesos) in 1920 to 26,100 tons (28.9 million pesos) in 1927; exports of bananas from 700 tons (0.3 million pesos) to 5,700 tons (8 million pesos); exports of tomatoes from 9,200 tons (0.7 million pesos) to 57,400 tons (19.6 million pesos); and exports of other fresh vegetables from 800 tons (0.2 million pesos) to 14,800 tons (5.5 million pesos).[27]

According to the founder of the Banco Nacional de Crédito Agrícola (1925), Manuel Gómez Morín, and also to President Calles, agrarian credit was to bring the peasantry on to the second stage of agrarian reform: production was to follow distribution. Unfortunately the initial capital was insufficient and the bank was not able to resist the practice of 'preferential loans', that is credit available for important personages, generals or politicians, the new *latifundistas*. In 1926 the major recipient of 'preferential' credit was General Obregón himself. In these circumstances the money did not reach those who really needed it, and it was a miracle that the bank survived until 1930, the year of financial disaster and plunder by the politicians.

The utopia of the Sonorans was an agriculturally prosperous Mexico, based on hard-driving and hard-working farmers served by a sound infrastructure of irrigation, roads, technology and bank loans. There was no serious thought of industrializing the country – Calles had said 'Our heavy industry is agriculture' – but only of giving an industrial finish to agricultural products for export. Mexico was to become a kind of agricultural United States: this principle was essential to the new economic policy, and the involvement first of General Obregón, then of General Calles, in large-scale agricultural undertakings in the north-west of the country is most significant. The northern regions did increase their production and obtained excellent results; their share of the national exports grew, despite all such obstacles as American competition and boycott, inexperience and shortage of credit.

[25] E. N. Simpson, *The ejido. Mexico's way out* (Chapel Hill, NC, 1937), 175, 214.
[26] *Estadística Nacional*, March 1929, p. 95, May 1929, p. 76, and Simpson, *The ejido*, 175, 214.
[27] Sterrett and Davis, *The fiscal and economic condition of Mexico*, 152.

CONCLUSION

In 1920, after ten years of revolution and civil war, a group of men from the Mexican north-west undertook an historic enterprise: nothing less than the transformation of the mosaic which was Mexico into a modern nation-state. During the 1920s Mexico's warring groups were eliminated by fire and sword. Not only was the army brought under control, but the leading revolutionary generals and *caudillos* disappeared, the regional military political bosses were pulled into line, and a kind of centralism triumphed. Saturnino Cedillo, in San Luis Potosí, was in the 1930s the only surviving old-style cacique. At the same time the workers were allowed a corporate existence, the church was put in its place and education given a national character. The problem of power and its orderly transmission in a more or less fragmented society, where parliamentary democracy could not function, was to some extent solved by the creation in 1929 of the PNR. Fifty years later its successor, the PRI, was still in power, providing an example of political stability unique in Latin America.

Under Obregón and Calles, economic as well as political power was once more concentrated in the hands of the president and his ministers and technical advisers. Absolute priority was given to the building of a modern economy, both national and capitalist. The role of the state was paramount: it assumed responsibility for the creation of the financial institutions and for the infrastructure projects which were beyond the means of Mexican private enterprise. There was an identity of interest between the state and the private sector. Indeed in this phase of state building and national capitalist development, there was a basic understanding between the 'revolutionary family', industrialists, bankers and business men, the CROM, capitalist rural interests, and even foreign capitalists. The oil companies, the anarchists and the Communist party were the only groups who refused to co-operate.

The ambitions of the men from Sonora, however, foundered on the twin rocks of economic dependence and economic recession. Mexico's capitalist development was financed in part by foreign investment and, above all, by exports. Since the 1870s the Mexican economy had been successfully integrated into the international economy through its mineral and agricultural exports. The Revolution had not changed the fundamental structure of the Mexican economy. And until 1926 exports financed economic growth. But seven lean years followed, and as the purchasing power of Mexican exports collapsed, the structural weakness of the Mexican economy was laid bare. The limits of that economic nationalism which had been asserted since 1917 had been reached. Obregón, Calles, Gómez Morín, Pani and Morones in the end were unable to perform the nationalist miracle of growth and independence.

Part Two

CENTRAL AMERICA AND THE
CARIBBEAN

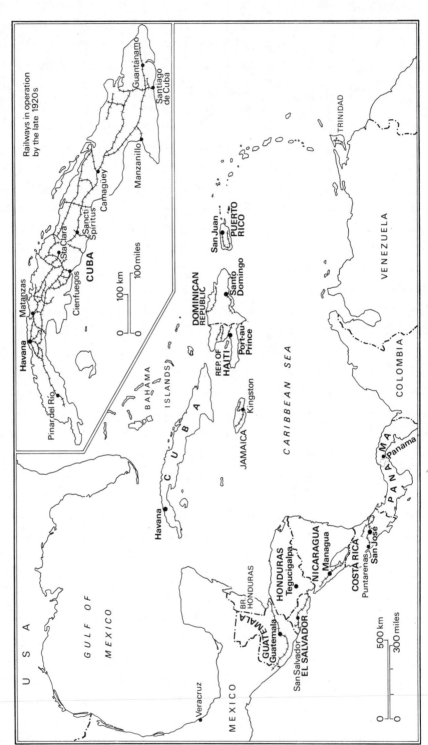

Central America and the Caribbean

Railways in operation
by the late 1920s

CUBA

Havana
Matanzas
Pinar del Río
Sta Clara
Cienfuegos
Sancti
Spíritus
Camagüey
Manzanillo
Santiago
de Cuba
Guantánamo

0   100 km
0   100 miles

U S A

GULF OF
MEXICO

Veracruz

MEXICO

BAHAMA

ISLANDS

C U B A

Havana

JAMAICA

Kingston

BR.
HONDURAS

GUATE
MALA

Guatemala

San Salvador
EL SALVADOR

HONDURAS

Tegucigalpa

NICARAGUA

Managua

COSTA RICA

Puntarenas

San José

PANAMA

Panama

REP. OF
HAITI

Port-au-
Prince

DOMINICAN
REPUBLIC

Santo
Domingo

San Juan

PUERTO
RICO

CARIBBEAN   SEA

TRINIDAD

VENEZUELA

COLOMBIA

0   500 km
0   300 miles

4

CENTRAL AMERICA: THE LIBERAL
ERA, *c*. 1870–1930

The six decades from 1870 to 1930 witnessed the somewhat late full integration of Central America into the capitalist world market through the expansion of its export economies. They also saw the formation of several relatively viable states and, therefore, the strengthening of the division of the United Provinces of Central America established after independence into five republics, even though there were some attempts to restore the lost union. Central American scholars were, and still are inclined to see the history of the isthmus (with the exception of Panama, which only became an independent state in 1903) as a unity. They preserved a somewhat vague, even romantic aspiration that the five *patrias chicas* ('small homelands') should eventually merge again in a *patria grande* (that is to say, a united Central America). Up to a point, there are grounds for such an ambition. In this period, for instance, some of the central features of economic life – for example, the production and export of coffee and bananas – were shared by most Central American countries; as, in politics, they shared the upheavals of Liberal reforms and then the hardships of Liberal dictatorships, as well as a common and very strong dependence on the United States. But much more striking in such a small region are the strong differences which existed between the five Republics. In this chapter we shall frequently be contrasting the evolution of Costa Rica with that of the other countries in the isthmus. Costa Rica, Guatemala and El Salvador, from 1870 to 1930, may be seen as more advanced countries economically and politically than Honduras and, to a lesser degree, Nicaragua. Because of the very divergent previous structures, the expansion of coffee and the spread of banana plantations did not always create the same structures or have the same consequences in all Central American Republics. So although approaching the area as a whole some of its most important historical contrasts will be examined.

197

ECONOMY

Population

Table 1 presents population data for each Central American country and for the region as a whole during the period 1870–1930. As we can see, there was great disparity between the five countries in terms of their populations, rates of population growth and population densities. For example, the so-called 'demographic revolution' was evident in Costa Rica as early as the 1860s, whereas in Guatemala it only began around 1920. El Salvador was already an unusual case, with a population density much higher than was found elsewhere in Latin America.

A common feature of the five countries was the failure of all the endeavours of both Conservative and Liberal governments to foster European or North American rural colonization schemes with the aim of establishing a white peasantry in Central America. A limited number of immigrants did come from Europe and the United States; however, most of them already possessed some capital, and they became influential members of the local upper classes. Towards the end of the nineteenth century, West Indian and Chinese immigrants arrived at the almost deserted Caribbean lowlands of the isthmus, to work in railway construction and later in the banana plantations. But the evolution of the population of Central America is explained more in terms of internal demographic movements than in terms of immigration.

Within Central America, the growth of coffee and banana production provoked considerable internal migration. In Guatemala, for example, coffee production developed in previously sparsely populated regions – the Pacific coast and its immediate hinterland – which were then settled. In the same country, the coffee harvest each year caused a considerable seasonal migration of workers from the Indian communities of the western highlands to the coffee zone and back again. Since the wages paid by the banana plantations were higher than average in Central America, from the beginning these plantations attracted a steady movement of people from the central highlands to the Caribbean lowlands, and from El Salvador and Nicaragua to Honduras and Costa Rica.

Coffee expansion

In Central America natural conditions for the production of high-quality 'mild' coffees are outstanding, notably in the central volcanic highlands.

Table 1. *The population of Central America, c. 1870–c. 1930*

	Population (thousands of inhabitants)	Average annual rate of growth (%)	Density (per square mile)
Guatemala			
1880	1,225	—	29.2
1893	1,365	0.8	32.5
1921	2,005	1.4	47.7
El Salvador			
1878	554	—	68.4
1892	703	1.7	86.8
1899	758	1.1	93.6
1930	1,459	2.1	180.1
Honduras			
1881	307	—	7.1
1895	399	1.9	9.2
1910	553	2.2	12.8
1930	948	2.7	21.9
Nicaragua			
1875	373	—	6.8
1906	505	1.0	9.2
1920	638	1.7	11.6
1930	742	1.5	13.5
Costa Rica			
1864	120	—	6.1
1883	182	2.2	9.3
1892	243	3.3	12.4
1927	489	2.0	24.9
Central America[a]			
1870	2,370	—	14.1
1900	3,533	1.3	21.0
1915	4,915	2.2	29.2
1930	6,019	1.4	35.8

[a] Without Belize.

Sources: Guatemala: Censuses (for 1880, 1893, 1921). El Salvador: Rodolfo Barón Castro, *La población de El Salvador* (Madrid, 1942) (for 1878, 1892, 1899); *Anuario estadístico* (for 1930). Honduras: Héctor Pérez Brignoli, 'Economía y sociedad en Honduras durante el siglo XIX. Las estructuras demográficas', *Estudios Sociales Centroamericanos*, 2/6 (1973), 51–82 (for 1881, 1895, 1910); Nicolás Sánchez Albornoz, *La población de América Latina* (Madrid, 1973) (for 1930). Nicaragua: Alberto Lanuza Matamoros, 'Estructuras socioeconómicas, poder y Estado en Nicaragua (1821–1875)' (San José, 1976, unpublished dissertation) (for 1875); *Censo Nacional de Población* (Managua, 1950) (for 1906, 1920); Albornoz, *La población de América Latina* (for 1930). Costa Rica: Censuses (for 1864, 1883, 1892, 1927). Central America: Woodward, *CHLA* III, ch. 11 (for 1870); Albornoz, *La población de América Latina* (for 1900); Ralph L. Woodward, Jr, *Central America. A Nation Divided* (New York, 1976) (for 1915, 1930).

Most of the countries of this region achieved full integration into the world market through the production and export of coffee. Here the expansion of the coffee economy will be studied in three countries only: Costa Rica, Guatemala and El Salvador. Honduran attempts at coffee production failed, and in Nicaragua, although coffee exports became important after 1870, they did not normally attain as high a percentage of the total value of exports as in the three selected countries, because the new crop competed in the Nicaraguan economy with cattle raising, the traditionally dominant economic activity.

It is perhaps advisable to point out at the outset the sharp contrast between the process of coffee expansion in Costa Rica on the one hand and Guatemala and El Salvador on the other. Because of the absence of strong colonial structures, Costa Rica moved straight into the coffee era a little more than a decade after Independence from Spain, without any significant internal upheavals, and much sooner than the rest of the isthmus. In both Guatemala and El Salvador, by the time of Independence strongly entrenched interest groups had developed. The Liberal reforms demanded by the spread of coffee cultivation were only put into effect following the decline of the world market for dyestuffs, hitherto Central America's main exports, during the 1860s and 1870s, and after a bitter struggle between rival groups. We shall also see that the social structure shaped in Costa Rica by the coffee economy was very peculiar, whereas the rest of the Central American coffee countries shared similar social features.

From the 1830s, coffee became Costa Rica's main cash crop. Its cultivation went through three main periods of growth in three areas of the country. Until the late 1840s it was confined to the central highlands around San José (*Meseta Central*); between 1850 and 1890, following the road to the port of Puntarenas (on the Pacific coast), it spread out towards the heavily forested western edges of the central highlands, in the province of Alajuela; and from 1890, and closely related to the railway developments of the time, it expanded into the Reventazón and Turrialba valleys, to the east of San José. Notwithstanding this expansion, the *Meseta Central* remained by far the most important coffee zone in Costa Rica: in 1890 13,800 (77 per cent) of the 17,940 hectares then planted with coffee bushes were in that region, and in 1935 59 per cent (27,600 of 46,920 hectares) were there.

In Guatemala, cochineal, a product of high value per unit of volume demanding relatively little capital and labour for its production, did not have a strong multiplier effect on the national economy. Guatemala lacked a road network, a modern system of rural credit, and a viable system of labour supply. The Indian communities were left almost free of heavy labour demands for several decades. But from the middle of the nineteenth century, as cochineal became an increasingly weak base for the national economy, the government began to encourage, timidly at first, the production of coffee and other cash crops (sugar, cotton), granting tax exemptions, attempting to spread the necessary technical knowledge and importing machinery. Nevertheless, the Conservatives, who depended on the support of the Indian communities, would not put into effect the necessary reforms without which coffee production could not reach its full potential. Coffee is a product which demands an efficient and cheap transport system (it has a relatively low value per unit of volume), the development of credit institutions (it is necessary to wait several years before any profits are earned by a new coffee-grower), and an abundant supply of land and labour. The Liberal revolution, which introduced the radical reforms needed by coffee interests, was launched in 1871, the same year in which coffee first became Guatemala's main export crop.

The process in El Salvador was quite similar. From around 1850 a sudden drop in indigo exports induced the government to encourage the production of coffee, cocoa, agave and other cash crops. The expansion of coffee cultivation between 1864 and 1880 made it a viable solution for the threatened national economy. Beginning in 1881 – when coffee first became El Salvador's leading crop – considerable reforms were undertaken, changing the country's economic structures in order to favour the interests of the coffee-growers.

In Costa Rica, three processes marked the formation of the territorial basis for coffee expansion: the appropriation of public lands; private land transactions; and the dissolution of communal forms of property. This last process was of little consequence, since the communal lands belonging to Indian communities and to Spanish towns – a form of property abolished from 1841 to 1851 – were not a very important feature of the Costa Rican countryside. At the time of independence Costa Rica had approximately only 60,000 inhabitants. So waste and public lands were plentiful even on the *Meseta Central*, where most of the small population lived. The expansion of coffee production tended to reinforce and extend the fragmented smallholding structure inherited from the colonial period, as the access to public lands remained easy until the 1890s. As for private land transactions, with the development of coffee exports from the 1830s, land prices began to rise rapidly, particularly for lands of the *Meseta Central* suited to coffee groves. From 1800 to 1850, the average price of land in the central valley increased by 1,773 per cent. The degree of land concentration in Costa Rica has been a matter of some dispute. Recent research, however, has shown beyond any doubt that it was not considerable before the 1930s. The causes of this local peculiarity of land tenure in the major coffee zone in Costa Rica – *sui generis* in overall Latin American terms – were mainly the chronic shortage of labour, the excessively high price of land, and the limited financial resources of the principal coffee-growers.

In Guatemala there were also three processes which together form the so-called Liberal agrarian reform, but they are quite different from those in Costa Rica. In the first place, the extensive landed property of the church was seized by the Liberal state in 1873, and later disposed of by sale or even by grants free of charge, sometimes with the specification that the lands so acquired should be planted with coffee or other cash crops. Then a law of 1877 abolished a form of land rent, the *censo enfitéutico*. Most of the lands involved were communal, and as many of the occupants did not have enough money to buy their plots within the decreed six months, the law thus assured their confiscation. These plots, amounting to 74,250 hectares, were seized by the state and sold in public auctions. The third reform was the Liberal decision to sell, on very easy conditions, public lands to the coffee-growers and the producers of other cash crops. Between 1871 and 1883, 397,755 hectares of wastelands were sold. The agrarian reform carried through by the Liberals is one of the factors which explains the development of coffee production in Amatitlán, Suchitepéquez, Sololá and Quezaltenango. As in Mexico, the first Liberal governments wished to foster small and medium-sized holdings and to avoid the formation of very large estates, but in this, even though their agrarian laws were promulgated again in 1888 and 1894, they failed.

In Guatemala most communal lands survived the Liberal reforms. This was not the case in El Salvador. From 1864, when the big expansion of coffee cultivation began, there is some evidence of the usurpation of communal lands. Nevertheless, in 1879 the *ejidos* and communal plots still represented 25 per cent of the total land surface of the small country. Moreover, they were located exactly in the central volcanic highlands where the soil was most favourable to coffee cultivation. President

Zaldívar (1876–85) decided in 1879 to grant full tenure to occupants who planted coffee, cocoa, agave or other cash crops. The communities, Indian or *ladinos* (*mestizos*), yielded to this pressure and tried to produce coffee, but they did not have the necessary techniques and had no capital or access to credit. In 1881, a law abolished the communal land system, and the following year this was extended to the *ejidos*. These lands had to be purchased by their occupants, within a term which was extended several times, but in the event most *comuneros* lost their holdings, which were acquired by the coffee-growers.

Labour was very scarce in Costa Rica throughout the nineteenth century and so wages tended to rise. The causes of this were varied. To begin with, even though demographic growth was not insignificant, the population was still quite small in 1900, and as we have seen there was no large-scale immigration. But undoubtedly the most important factor was the pattern of land tenure. The large number of small proprietors and the peasant smallholding structure, which were inherited from the colonial era and which expanded in the first decades after independence, have already been noted. The fact that he had a small plot of land did not deter the peasant from working as a rural labourer or as a carter as well, but it is nevertheless a fact that the widespread distribution of small landholdings limited the supply of labour. Moreover, from 1899, the lure of the higher wages paid by the United Fruit Company, established in the Atlantic lowlands, provoked internal migrations towards the banana plantations, thus draining labour from the coffee zone. These factors explain why, although personal dependence was not altogether absent, the Costa Rican rural worker was basically an employee, a wage labourer, and not a 'serf'.

In Guatemala, most of the inhabitants were Indians and lived in communities provided with lands. The coffee haciendas were located in sparsely populated zones near the Pacific coast. In 1877, the Liberal government issued the Reglamento de Jornaleros (day-labourers). It allowed the coffee-growers to recruit as labourers, for limited periods, a certain number of Indians from the highland communities, even against the *comuneros'* will. This system was retained throughout the period under consideration, even though some measures were adopted to improve the condition of the coerced rural labourers, for example the establishment of minimum wage levels guaranteed by law from the beginning of the twentieth century.

Though El Salvador had a big population for its small territory, before the Liberal reforms most people lived in communities. The coffee-growers were obliged to seek varied ways of obtaining labour, but the problem vanished after the 1880s as a consequence of the agrarian policy of President Zaldívar. Thousands of peasants were divested of their communal lands and could not obtain new plots. They had to establish themselves on the haciendas as resident workers (*colonos*), or else they lived as squatters for most of the year, working with their families as hired labourers during the coffee harvest. Social unrest was a common feature of the Salvadorean countryside after the reforms, particularly in the western region where the Indian population was greater; the repression of peasant movements was entrusted to the rural guard (*policía montada*) created in 1889.

The beginning of coffee expansion in Costa Rica was financed with small amounts of capital, accumulated during the colonial period and the first decade of independence from cacao and tobacco cultivation, the export of a dyewood (*palo brasil*), and the extraction of precious metals from the mines of Monte del Aguacate, which had been discovered in 1815 and exploited particularly after 1820. When regular exports of coffee to Britain started in 1843, commercial houses in London and Liverpool began to advance credits against future harvests, channelling them through the Costa Rican commercial houses which were established, mostly by the richest coffee-growers, from the 1840s onwards. These commercial houses in turn granted credits to the small producers, who were drawn into economic dependence on the large coffee-producers and on the merchants. This enabled the well-to-do coffee-growers to exercise a high degree of pressure and social control over the small farmers, in order to guarantee them the additional labour needed for the harvesting of their own coffee and even more for working at their large processing plants. In 1857, the government of President Juan Rafael Mora (1849–59) made a contract with the merchant Crisanto Medina to create the Banco Nacional Costarricense, which was to receive deposits, give credit, and issue notes. The bank was inaugurated on 1 January 1858. Its creation seemed to present a dangerous threat to the coffee-producers who practised usury and used it as a form of social control. They thus brought about a *coup d'état* which toppled Mora. The bank ceased operations not only because of this opposition but also due to losses caused by the collapse of a Liverpool firm to which it was connected. From the 1860s onwards, credit-giving establishments multiplied in number, many of them short-lived. The most important were the Banco Anglo-Costarricense, established in 1863, and the Banco de la Unión (1877) which later became the Banco de Costa Rica.

During the long period of Conservative rule in Guatemala before 1871, the structures of credit and finance were very primitive. The rural mortgage was practically unknown, because there was almost no legal security for the money lender. Interest rates could attain 50 per cent, even though the annual legal rate was a mere 6 per cent. The usurers were able to prevent the creation of several banks. With the Liberal revolution there were attempts to create a modern financial system. The church properties, seized in 1873, were used by the government to back the Banco Nacional, established in 1874 as a commercial bank receiving deposits, issuing notes and giving credit. But this bank could not resist the financial panic provoked in 1876 by the war against El Salvador, and disappeared the next year, thus opening the way to the creation of several private commercial banks, all of them authorized to issue notes by the Code of Commerce (1877). This also regulated the mortgage system and established an obligatory public register of landed property and of mortgages. The main banks were the Banco Internacional (1877), Banco Colombiano (1878), Banco de Occidente at Quezaltenango (1881), Banco Americano (1892), Banco Agrícola Hipotecario (1893) and Banco de Guatemala (1894). Nevertheless, credit was still difficult to obtain, and the coffee-growers depended on a personal and commercial credit with high interest rates (12 per cent annually). The banks and other money lenders obtained cheap credit in Europe and then granted loans at high interest rates in Guatemala. By these means, German coffee-producers who kept in contact with the banks of Bremen and Hamburg profited from the long coffee crisis at the end of the nineteenth century, seizing the estates of Guatemalan coffee-growers who owed them money and were unable to pay it back.

The first stages of coffee expansion in El Salvador were financed – at least in part – by mortgaging properties where indigo was produced. Many indigo-growers sold their lands and equipment in order to cultivate coffee. Landowners and city-dwellers (merchants, military, priests, civil servants, etc.) obtained enough credit to initiate the coffee economy. As in Costa Rica, British capital financed future harvests. The first banks appeared after 1880, all of them issuing notes: Banco Occidental, Banco Salvadoreño, Banco Agrícola Comercial. Their credit went to the big landowners, who in turn granted loans to smaller producers. Bank credits especially destined to finance the production of coffee only began around 1920.

Throughout the period under study, the cultivation of coffee remained extensive and quite primitive, except to some extent in El Salvador. On the best lands of the Costa Rican *Meseta Central*, the decline in the average yield per hectare, already evident in 1881, is confirmed by the quantitative data available for the twentieth century. From 1909 to 1956, average yield declined by 52.5 per cent.[1] Production increases were obtained by extending the cultivated area. Central American coffee groves were established as permanent plantation enterprises (unlike in Brazil, where coffee was a frontier or migratory crop), but the use of fertilizers was seriously limited. In the second half of the nineteenth century the custom was established of planting shade trees to protect the coffee bushes from winds and excessive rainfall, and to shield the soil against erosion. Guatemalan cultivation techniques were similar to those used in Costa Rica. But in El Salvador, the sheer scarcity of adequate soils, and sometimes the fact that the coffee groves covered steep hillsides, led to better agricultural techniques, to the extent that the yields in some of the largest coffee farms were the highest in the world.[2]

In contrast to cultivation, processing techniques became increasingly mechanized and technically specialized. Costa Rica led the development of these techniques and taught them to the rest of Central America – and to Columbia. *Beneficio húmedo* (wet processing) began to be used in Costa Rica as early as 1838. The coffee berries were piled in heaps to soften the pulp, and then placed in tanks through which a stream of water passed; there they were continually stirred to free them from the outer pulp. The coffee beans were then spread out upon a platform to dry in the sun, and then the inner husk was removed by water mills. The use of *beneficio* steam machinery imported from England and later from the United States began to spread during the 1850s. Obviously the increasing costliness and technical complexity of the new processing techniques led to the concentration of this stage of production in a few coffee mills. Around 1888 there were only about 256 *beneficios* in Costa Rica, whilst four years earlier there were 7,490 coffee farms.[3] Costa Rica passed on the

---

[1] See Carmen S. de Malavassi and Belén Andrés S., 'El café en la historia de Costa Rica' (unpublished dissertation, San José, 1958), 35–6.

[2] David Browning, *El Salvador. Landscape and society* (Oxford, 1971), 224.

[3] Joaquín Bernardo Calvo, *Apuntamientos geográficos, estadísticos e históricos* (San José, 1887), 47.

knowledge of the processing techniques to Guatemala and El Salvador. In those countries too the processing stage tended to be concentrated in a few large estates or coffee mills. In Guatemala, German coffee-growers used better techniques and so obtained a higher output: in 1913 they owned 10 per cent of the Guatemalan coffee farms, but produced 40 per cent of the processed beans.

In the three countries under study, the growth of coffee cultivation provided the leading impulse towards the modernization of the transport system and decisively influenced the form of the road and railway networks. In Costa Rica, a road capable of taking ox-drawn carts was needed to carry the coffee to the Pacific port of Puntarenas. It was built between 1844 and 1846, financed by a tax levied on coffee exports. The ships carrying the coffee to Europe and the Atlantic coast of the United States took the Cape Horn route, which lengthened the voyage and consequently raised freight charges. The building of the Panama Railway linking the Atlantic and Pacific oceans (1851–5) opened up another possibility, without really solving the problem. In the same period, the Costa Rican government of Juan Rafael Mora signed a contract with the Pacific Mail and Steamship Company, to ensure that their ships called at Puntarenas; this contract was extremely favourable to the Company. Nevertheless, it was still felt necessary to open a road – or a railway – to the Atlantic, and to build a new port on the Caribbean coast. Puerto Limón was established in 1870, but it was not until 1890 that the Atlantic Railway was completed, linking San José to this new outlet. Henceforth Costa Rica enjoyed lower freight charges (due also to the spread of steamships on the Atlantic routes), and direct access to its main markets. The Pacific Railway was also under construction at this time, but was not completed until 1910.

From 1873, the Liberal regime in Guatemala endeavoured to build better and more numerous roads, linking the capital city to Quezaltenango, Huehuetenango, the Pacific ports and later the Atlantic port of Santo Tomás. These projects were financed by the issuing of treasury bonds and the levy of a tax on rural property. Any adult male was forced to work three days each year on the construction and maintenance of roads, or else to pay a certain sum in order to obtain an exemption. The first railway contract which worked was established in 1877–80 with William Nanne: the railway, built with national capital, linked the port of San José with Escuintla (1880) and with the city of Guatemala (1884). A new contract was signed in 1881 for the construction of a railway to the port of Champerico from Retalhuleu to guarantee the transport of coffee produced there; it was completed in 1883. In 1884 a port (later called Puerto Barrios) was established on the Caribbean coast, and a railway leading there was begun with national capital. But its building was interrupted, to be completed only in 1908, after a contract (in 1900) with the Central American Improvement Company Inc. This contract – which marked the beginning of American control over Guatemalan railways – granted the Company the concession for 99 years of the exploitation of Puerto Barrios, lands at both sides of the rails and tax exemptions. In 1912, all the Guatemalan railway network fell under American control through the Guatemala Central Railway Company, which was absorbed by the International Railway of Central America. Between 1881 and 1884, the government of Justo Rufino Barrios signed contracts with ten foreign steamship companies. These contracts included, on behalf of the companies, annual government subsidies, land concessions and tax exemptions.

In El Salvador, the roads needed to ensure coffee transportation were built at the end of the nineteenth century, financed by national and municipal taxes on coffee production and trade. As in Costa Rica and Guatemala, the government attracted foreign steamship companies to Salvadoran ports (Acajutla, La Libertad) through very generous contracts. The railways were built in part with government and national capital (Sonsonate–Acajutla, La Unión–San Miguel). The Salvador Railway Company (which was British) was granted in 1885 a concession to construct a railway linking the main coffee zones to the port of Acajutla. Another railway built later on with American capital connected with the Guatemalan network thus permitting the export of Salvadoran coffee through Puerto Barrios. Deprived of an Atlantic coast, before the construction of the Panama canal El Salvador was more isolated than Costa Rica and Guatemala from the more important world markets for coffee.

The main buyers of Costa Rican coffee during the nineteenth century were Britain, France, Germany and the United States. The commercial and financial links with England only began to weaken after the first world war, as those with the United States became more important. To begin with, Guatemala sold its coffee mainly to Britain. The British remained Guatemala's most important suppliers, but first the United States, then Germany, then during the first world war the United States again, replaced Britain as the principal importers of Guatemalan coffee.

El Salvador, at the beginning of the twentieth century, sold coffee mainly to France, the United States, Germany, Italy and Britain, in that order.

Coffee became the most important export crop first in Costa Rica (during the 1830s and 1840s), then in Guatemala (where it displaced cochineal in 1870) and finally in El Salvador (where it displaced indigo in 1880). Its value as a percentage of total exports reached a maximum at the end of the nineteenth century in Guatemala (92 per cent in 1880) and Costa Rica (91 per cent in 1890). In El Salvador it did not dominate the export trade so thoroughly until the twentieth century, when the Salvadoran economy came to be the most dependent on coffee exports.

It is therefore easy to understand that the crises in the world coffee market – caused by overproduction or occurring as a result of general capitalist crisis – had very serious economic consequences for Central America. The most important of these crises occurred during the period 1897–1907 (as a result of a worldwide overproduction of coffee) and during the 1930s following the crash of 1929; coffee prices did not recover their 1929 level until 1946.

The main effects of the expansion of coffee during this period were similar in Costa Rica, Guatemala and El Salvador. Subsistence agriculture activities were steadily displaced by coffee in certain zones. The development of monoculture not only changed the countryside, it provoked severe crises in the national food supply. Sometimes the food shortage forced governments to pass laws prohibiting the export of grains and cattle and encouraging their importation, setting maximum prices for basic foodstuffs, and so on, but these measures never added up to an effective solution of the problem. In Costa Rica, as the best lands of the central valley were gradually taken over by coffee, the production of maize, beans, sugar-cane (for internal consumption) and cattle for meat and milk supply was relegated to waste lands around the coffee zone. As the sources show abundantly, subsistence crises became frequent and foodstuffs, which had been very cheap at the time of independence, became very costly. In Guatemala, a report from the department of agriculture (a section of the ministry of development) in 1902 declared that the supply of staple products for popular consumption had been adequate and their prices low before the expansion of coffee; but coffee had changed all that, and foodstuffs were now often imported and were expensive. Measures were then adopted to encourage the production of maize, potatoes, beans, rice and wheat, with scarcely any noticeable effect. In the central and most densely populated zone of El Salvador, although later than in Costa Rica and Guatemala, coffee cultivation also ousted maize and other basic foodstuffs, which had began to be produced on less fertile soils, and sometimes on land occupied by squatter peasants during the months separating one coffee harvest from the next.

There can be little doubt that the coffee-growing elite exercised a decisive influence over the social, political and economic life of these countries (particularly Costa Rica). The coffee export tax was the one great source, apart from foreign loans, of finance for important projects such as roads, railways and public buildings. Gradually in Costa Rica, and more precipitously in Guatemala and El Salvador, coffee expansion provoked a thorough reorganization of social and economic structures and was instrumental in the full integration of these countries into the world market, with all the accompanying advantages and disadvantages.

Enclave economies[4]

Banana plantations and gold and silver mines constituted enclave economies in Central America. The plantations, far more important historically than the mining ventures, were at the beginning a kind of projection or consequence of the railway contracts, but they came to be a central feature of the Central American economies on their own account.

Bananas became an object of international trade in 1870, when regular exports from Honduras to New Orleans were established by the New Orleans Bay Island Fruit Company. Rival companies soon appeared. The expansion of the American market then provided a strong incentive for the establishment of banana plantations in Central America from the 1890s.

The first stage in the development of the banana business was marked by strong competition both at the level of production and trade. Bananas were cultivated by independent labourers, with very small investment and good probabilities of profit. The American merchants who shipped the fruit to the United States, while bringing pressure on the Central American producers to keep prices low (as bananas are a very perishable product, the farmers were in a hurry to sell), had to face risks of heavy loss during the voyage and also fierce competition in New Orleans. As a

---

[4] For a definition of enclave economy, see Fernando H. Cardoso and Enzo Faletto, *Dependencia y desarrollo en América Latina* (Mexico, 1973), 48–53. This section follows closely Ciro Cardoso and Héctor Pérez Brignoli, *Centroamérica y la economía occidental (1520–1930)* (San José, 1977), chapter 9.

result specialization began in the export business. Transport in bigger ships provided with refrigeration and the building of adequate storage and loading facilities in some Central American ports demanded large outlays of capital. In addition, the spread of banana cultivation away from the coastline required an adequate transport system to the ports, provided by railway networks.

The consolidation of the big banana companies was a complicated process, involving land concessions by the Central American states, the construction of railways and ports, the introduction of foreign technology and capital, the acumen and skill of certain entrepreneurs, conflicts and mergers between the companies themselves, the confiscation of lands occupied by native independent farmers, and even border conflicts between neighbouring countries.

The United Fruit Company (UFCO), formed in 1899, began its operations in Guatemala by an agreement with the International Railways of Central America, which had received an important concession of waste lands. From 1906, through purchases and new concessions, the banana company expanded its holdings in the Motagua valley. In 1928, using a subsidiary company, the UFCO began to buy lands on the Pacific coast as well, developing its plantations in this region from 1936.

In Honduras, banana production until 1913 was in the hands of native farmers. Several companies, like the Vaccaro brothers, the Hubbard–Zemurray, the steamship line Oterí and the UFCO, shared the shipping and distribution. Around 1913, prices fell and a severe drought affected the plantations, causing a crisis during which some of the companies withdrew. This moment was seized by the powerful UFCO for a large-scale penetration in Honduras. In fact, since 1912 two of its subsidiary companies – the Tela Railroad Company and the Trujillo Railroad Company – had signed substantial railway contracts with the Honduran government, thus obtaining vast land concessions. During the 1920s Honduras produced the majority of UFCO's bananas. The company of the Vaccaro brothers operated in the region of La Ceiba and in the Aguán valley. It was reorganized in 1924 and 1926, becoming the Standard Fruit and Steamship Company. Samuel Zemurray also began his enterprises by buying and selling bananas, but in 1902 he obtained a concession of public lands at the Honduran side of the Motagua river. In 1911, after a crisis which almost ruined him, his enterprise became the Cuyamel Fruit Company. The government of Honduras granted this company new concessions near the Guatemalan frontier, but as the border between the two countries was not clearly delimited, a series of conflicts between Honduras and Guatemala began in 1913; these were in fact merely the effects of the rivalry between the Cuyamel and the UFCO. The conflicts ceased in 1929, when the two companies merged. From 1920, Cuyamel's main plantations were located in the Ulúa valley.

In Nicaragua, banana production was of less importance. The UFCO operated on the Atlantic coast from the 1890s, but exports were quite small. During the 1920s the Cuyamel Fruit Company became established there, and the plantations experienced a certain expansion. Nevertheless, most of these plantations were located on inadequate soils. In 1930, the UFCO sold its properties in Nicaragua, and after that occupied itself exclusively with commercial operations through a subsidiary enterprise, the Cukra Development Company.

In Costa Rica, the beginning of the banana trade was linked to the activities of Minor Keith and the complicated history of the Atlantic Railway. In 1899 the UFCO obtained the use of the concessions granted earlier to Keith. United Fruit managed to manipulate all of the banana business in the country, after ousting two rival enterprises, the American Banana Company and the Atlantic Fruit Steamship Company. In 1927, two new companies on the Pacific coast began to export bananas, but the UFCO soon purchased their plantations and expanded them during the 1930s. In 1930, throughout Central America, the UFCO had overtaken all its rivals: it owned 63 per cent of the 103 million bunches of bananas exported.

The Caribbean coastline of Central America, which saw the first development of banana production, was only sparsely populated. The building of the railways and then the banana plantations generated some migratory currents: from the central highlands to the coast; and from the West Indies and from China to Central America. Honduras also received immigrant workers from El Salvador. And the spread of the banana plantations led to the development of a significant rural proletariat. Although the wages paid by the fruit companies were generally higher than those offered elsewhere in Central America, the position of the plantation workers was prejudiced by several payment practices. For instance, in Honduras it was usual to pay workers in vouchers which were accepted only at the companies' stores, called *comisariatos*; or else to fix their wages in dollars and then to pay them in Honduran currency at an exchange rate below the legal rate. Furthermore, whereas Honduran workers were used to weekly payments, at certain times the companies paid only every 40 days.

The Costa Rican banana exports expanded rapidly after 1880, reaching a maximum of eleven million bunches in 1913, even though starting in 1904 the plantations were plagued by a disease called *mal de Panamá*. After the first world war, exports diminished slowly, to around seven million bunches during the 1920s. The UFCO began at this time to abandon its Atlantic plantations, and to establish itself on the Pacific coast. In the Caribbean zone, banana production was now pursued by Costa Rican farmers, who sold their fruit to the company. In 1927–8 they formed a Costa Rican banana co-operative.

In the 1890s, the Honduran banana exports amounted to around 1.5 million bunches per year. With the penetration of the fruit companies, exports rose sharply: 9.8 million bunches in 1920, 16.3 million in 1925, 29 million in 1929. During the 1920s, Honduras became the world's leading producer of bananas. The *mal de Panamá* appeared in 1926, mainly at the plantations of the Trujillo Railroad Company, provoking the complete abandonment of Puerto Castilla in 1935, which led in turn to the elimination of 125 kilometres of railway in this region.

Exports from Guatemala, which entered the banana market later, amounted to three million bunches in 1913, reaching six million per year during the 1920s and 1930s. In Nicaragua, from 1900 to 1920, banana exports reached a little over 1.5 million bunches per year. They increased to 3 million bunches between 1920 and 1930, but their decline was swift after 1935.

Since 1864, numerous mine concessions had been claimed and granted in Honduras. In the 1870s, mining production began to be encouraged by the government, and to recover from a long period of depression. During the Liberal presidency of Marco Aurelio Soto (1876–83), who in the past had proclaimed agriculture as the cornerstone of Honduran development, the mines were declared to be the mainstay of the national economy. His policy, favourable to mining and foreign interests, was followed by his successors, especially Luis Bográn (1883–91). The concessions to foreign companies were numerous, although only one of them dominated the mining business: the New York and Honduran Rosario Mining Company. This enterprise, between 1921 and 1937, obtained a net profit of 36 per cent and paid dividends which amounted to some $8 million. The main Honduran mineral production was silver, and the most important mining zones were located around the capital, Tegucigalpa. In 1887, minerals represented some 50 per cent of the value of Honduran exports, but with the rise of the banana trade their importance diminished steadily (to only 6 per cent in 1928).

In Nicaragua, gold mining, which guaranteed high profits to some foreign companies, was responsible in 1912 for 23 per cent of the total exports of the country. But as in Honduras, it tended to become less important, especially after 1923. The mines were to be found at Nueva Segovia (San Albino Gold Mining Ltd, Nicaragua Development Syndicate), Chontales, Matagalpa and the Atlantic region.

In Costa Rica, on the other hand, gold and silver mining, located in the north-western region of the country, became more significant after 1920, reaching a peak in 1928. But here, as in Guatemala and El Salvador, mining was not of great importance; it never provided as much as 3 per cent of the country's total exports.

The enclave economies of Central America had little dynamic effect on the national economies as a whole; the economic expansion they generated tended to limit itself to the zones of mines or plantations.

The original concessions granted to the foreign companies were extraordinarily favourable to them. In the case of the banana enterprises, these concessions consisted of lands, the use of other natural resources, tax exemptions, and free import of numerous products (which had a deleterious effect on the development of national industries, as imported goods entered the country free of tax and were sold to the plantation workers at the *comisariatos*). The railway contracts handed the control of all internal transport to the banana companies. The *comisariatos* ousted petty commerce from the plantation zones. The exemptions – above all those of customs duties – generated weak states, with poor financial resources. This was particularly the case in Honduras, where the banana plantations and exports were the core of the national economy. In 1917–18, the exemptions granted to the fruit companies surpassed the total revenue of the Honduran state.

The banana business being highly concentrated, the few possibilities of industrialization it opened up were made good use of by the companies themselves, as a complement to their agricultural activities, which were gradually diversified. Thus in Honduras, the Standard Fruit Company owned from the 1920s sugar mills, liquor manufactures, industrial plants producing vegetable oil, soap and fertilizers from the seeds of cotton, coconut and other products cultivated on its lands or purchased from local farmers.

The most harmful effects of the enclave economy were probably the consequence of frauds and the fact that the conditions under which the concessions were granted by the governments of the small and weak Central American countries remained unfulfilled: clandestine loadings, tax evasion, the building of clandestine railways (in Honduras), the fact that the companies at times failed to construct some of the railway tracts specified in the concessions (which were of national interest, but not of export interest), their practice of varying freight charges on their trains so that the companies were favoured against local producers, and so on.

A different aspect of this question is the foreign companies' absolute lack of respect for the sovereignty of the Central American countries, the sometimes open pressure on local governments, and the intervention in national affairs. United States military intervention on behalf of these enterprises occurred frequently, though generally short-lived: the landing of marines or the arrival of warships in Central American ports might occur any time that the North American properties and citizens felt or declared themselves threatened.

SOCIETY

Social structures

In examining the extent to which economic and political change in the period under discussion affected Central American social structures, it should be noted first that the composition of the upper, dominant groups in society was not significantly changed by the coffee expansion and Liberal reforms. Following the Liberal revolutions, many Conservatives did lose their personal wealth and position through confiscation, or were even forced into exile, while the Liberals used their newly acquired political power to obtain economic advantages (for example, through grants of public and former communal lands). Nevertheless, there is no doubt that the Liberal order allowed a more widely based foundation of power, by including in the new dominant groups many members of the old oligarchies. Even so, this did not avoid fierce struggles within the dominant class. The degree to which former oligarchies were absorbed varied from country to country. It was perhaps minimal in Guatemala and Nicaragua, while in Costa Rica a notable continuity since colonial times has been demonstrated.[5] Important changes were a diminution of the political power and influence of the Catholic church and the professionalization of the national armies; the latter provided one of the few possibilities for social mobility.

The marked presence of foreigners within the dominant social groups deserves some attention. In the coffee business, production was mostly under the control of Central American growers. But in the case of banana plantations, local producers were displaced by North Americans almost everywhere. Foreign economic influence was decisive in trade, transport and finance. Resident foreign merchants – mainly British, German, North American, French and Middle Eastern – became even more numerous during the twentieth century, joining the earlier immigrants who had come as coffee processors and traders. The integration of foreign residents into Central American society was generally incomplete, although in Costa Rica they were often naturalized.

For the general populace, predominantly rural, the great contradiction of Central American liberalism was between the proclamations of equality for all citizens and the actual social situation, which included forced labour (which in Guatemala was even legal). Costa Rica, with its firm structure of smallholdings, was a different sort of country altogether, but in the other Central American countries the surviving Indian communities (mostly in Guatemala) and the rural labourers – either permanently established on the farms (*colonos* or *peones*) or employed as day-labourers (*jornaleros*) – suffered the forced labour system. This reenacted and extended colonial procedures like the *mandamientos* (advance payments creating debts and often tying the peasant to the farm), and the laws against vagrancy. The peasants were cruelly repressed by the landowners and by government troops whenever they tried to organize or to act against their situation. The typical Central American farm had resident labourers who reproduced their labour force partly through a subsistence economy (plots alloted within the farm as part of or a complement to the wage), and day-labourers hired only during harvest time and practising for the remainder of the year a subsistence agriculture as squatters or leaseholders. This system allowed substantial savings in the farmer's expenditure,

5 Samuel Stone, *La dinastía de los conquistadores* (San José, 1975).

and constituted a serious obstacle to the formation of a real capitalist labour market and of a proper rural proletariat.[6]

However, a more typical proletariat did originate from the foreign enclaves, whether mine or plantation. The spread of the banana plantations led to the settlement and economic exploitation of the Caribbean lowlands. The United Fruit Company began the struggle, necessary to make human settlement possible in that region, against yellow fever, malaria and other tropical diseases, and was followed in these efforts by the other fruit companies. As we have seen, migratory currents brought in labour, mainly from the West Indies and from the Central American highlands. The presence of West Indians, not entirely assimilated until the present day, and speaking their own dialects, created a new kind of social and ethnic problem. In Costa Rica, for example, the Chinese and West Indians were not really national citizens for several decades, and they were seriously limited in their freedom to go where they pleased. Before the construction of railways and docks began, and the beginning of the plantation system, what amounted to an ethnic (or 'racial') problem in Central America was the social discrimination suffered by the Indians, mostly in Guatemala – where they formed a clear majority of the population – and in western El Salvador. The rest of El Salvador and the whole of Honduras and Nicaragua were predominantly *mestizo*, and in Costa Rica most of the population (some 80 per cent in 1925) were of European stock.

The heyday of the export economy brought about some urbanization and modernization, which had effects on the social structure of Central American countries. At the end of the nineteenth century, the capital cities began to grow steadily. The varied services needed by the export activities and the strengthened bureaucracy generated by the consolidation of the national states attracted many rural dwellers to the cities. This led to the beginning of an urban middle class, mainly in the capital cities, which was important for the political evolution of the region. On the other hand, the first signs of an urban proletariat appeared also, following the creation of some small factories (textiles, foods and drinks) in San Salvador, Guatemala and San José. Nevertheless, it must be stressed that the artisans still predominated, with full industrialization only occurring in Central America in the 1950s. Urbanization also meant

[6] See Edelberto Torres Rivas, *Interpretación del desarrollo social centroamericano* (San José, 1971), 75–82.

the carrying out of public works such as the paving and lighting of streets, the spread of modern transportation, the construction of large buildings and parks, the proliferation of daily newspapers, some advances in medicine and modest progress in education, even though the latter – except in Costa Rica – remained almost exclusively available to the upper and middle classes. During the first decades of the twentieth century, students arose as a new political force. Needless to say, social conditions being what they were, urbanization also brought about the spread of some very poor districts, including slums.

As we have already noted, Costa Rica had a peculiar economic structure, and the same can be said of its social organization, marked by wider popular participation in education and even in politics, and by a faster development than in the remainder of the isthmus of state assistance to the workers in matters of health, education and labour legislation.

Social struggles

At the beginning of the 1870s, the only social movements which can easily be identified are those which have been called by George Rudé the 'preindustrial crowd': for example, the peasant uprisings in western El Salvador during the 1880s, after the confiscation of communal lands by the Liberal government. The first labour organizations, which appeared at the end of the nineteenth century, were mutual aid societies, clearly following the pattern of the traditional artisan guilds. During the 1920s, in all five countries strong advances in the organization, actions and – though to a lesser extent – the political consciousness of the workers took place. This can be seen in the foundation of the first trade unions and of the Central American Labour Council (1926), which aimed to unify the labour movements throughout Central America and was responsible for the spread of socialist ideas until 1930. The first Communist parties were also founded between 1920 and 1931.

A number of catalysts can be perceived which explain, or help to explain, what happened next to popular movements and organizations. First of all, we have the beginnings of an urban lower and an urban middle class which provided leaders such as Agustín Farabundo Martí (who had rural roots but was educated at a secondary school in San Salvador, where he also began his university studies) or Miguel Mármol (a cobbler). Secondly, despite being actively repressed, the development of a large proletariat at the mines and plantations owned by foreign corporations created an environment favourable to the occurrence of 'modern' strikes, mainly after 1920. The political document which launched the Sandino insurrection was written in 1927 at the Nicaraguan mining centre of San Albino. Finally, there was the clear influence of factors such as the lessening of repression in some Central American countries during the 1920s, the Mexican Revolution, the Russian Revolution and the creation of the Third International.

Nevertheless, the development of trade unions and of popular ideology and struggles was in Central America much slower and less profound than in other Latin American countries such as Mexico, Argentina or Chile. Even the 'modern' strikes at the plantations and mines were, up to 1930, strictly economic and had no political overtones; and the movement led by Augusto Sandino was much more nationalist than socialist. The social effects of the economic depression following the crisis of 1929 permitted, during the 1930s, an accelerating of the pace of the labour movement and organization, gave a big push to the guerilla war in Nicaragua and provided the occasion for the great peasant uprising of 1932 in El Salvador.

Intellectual development

The small cities of these poor countries, where education was restricted to a tiny minority (with Costa Rica a partial exception), could not boast a cultural life comparable to that of their larger Latin American neighbours. However, in this period we have an obviously important exception: Rubén Darío (1867–1916), born in Nicaragua – although living mainly outside Central America – is considered by many to be the greatest of all Hispanic American poets. Under his influence, modernism flourished in Central America, with such names as Alfonso Cortés and José Coronel Urtecho (Nicaragua), José Valdés and Vicente Rosales (El Salvador), Enrique Gómez Carrillo and Máximo Soto Hall (Guatemala), Juan Ramón Molina and Froilán Turcios (Honduras), Rafael Cardona and Julián Marchena (Costa Rica). Apart from modernism, at least two other literary trends deserve mention: Costa Rican *costumbrismo*, which tried to convey the life of the countryside in poetry (Aquileo Echeverría, Joaquín García Monge) or in prose (Manuel González Zeledón); and, also in Costa Rica, the very interesting mystical poetry of Roberto Brenes Mesén.

While some Central American writings are known and read in other Hispanic American countries, it is difficult to find comparable instances in other fields. The Guatemalan composer Jesús Castillo, for example, or the Costa Rican sculptor and painter Max Jiménez are nowadays almost forgotten outside their own countries.

Liberal reforms and Liberal dictatorships

Central American Liberal reforms have distinct similarities when compared from an exclusively institutional point of view. Constitutions, codes, laws regarding the laicization of education and other aspects of social life have a definite resemblance in all five countries, as they were inspired by the same European and North American models. But striking differences are found when the actual meaning and consequences of these reforms are studied (although between the Guatemalan and Salvadoran cases there are close similarities). With regard to the social and political results of Liberal transformations, Costa Rica is the only country where a comparison of laws with reality shows any consistency on points referring to the liberty, equality and rights of the citizens.

The first country to experience a genuine Liberal reform was Guatemala. After a movement which failed (in 1869), a Liberal revolution toppled the Conservative regime of Vicente Cerna in 1871. This revolution was planned on Mexican territory, with the support of the Liberal government of Juárez. Its leaders were Miguel García Granados, president from 1871 to 1873, and Justo Rufino Barrios, president and virtual dictator from 1873 until his death in 1885. The main economic measures of the new Liberal regime have already been mentioned. In the political field, the Liberal constitution of 1879 established a form of government with a strong presidency, centralized and representative, and with a one-house legislative assembly. It also brought about the complete separation between state and church, thus crowning several anti-clerical and secularizing measures taken since 1871. The reality of Liberal political power in Guatemala, however, as in the remainder of the isthmus, was embodied in harsh dictatorships favouring the local oligarchy and export-led economic growth, exercising a repressive vigilance over the working classes and systematically thwarting the constitution. The most important dictator in this period, after Barrios, was Manuel Estrada Cabrera (1898–1920).

In El Salvador, the Liberal reforms were started – after an early failed attempt – by Liberal leaders very much influenced by Guatemala, Santiago González (1871–6) and Rafael Zaldívar (1876–85). Zaldívar was toppled by General Francisco Menéndez (1885–90), under whom the Liberal process was completed by the constitution of 1886. This was the most stable of all Central American Liberal regimes; there were no civil struggles from 1898 to 1931. From 1913 until 1927 the country was governed by the so-called dynasty of the Meléndez–Quiñónez, under three related presidents – Carlos Meléndez (1913–18), Jorge Meléndez (1919–23) and Alfonso Quiñónez Molina (1923–7). As in Guatemala, despite the constitution and other Liberal documents, oligarchic dictatorship is a more apt label for the Salvadoran Liberal regime than representative republic.

In Costa Rica, Liberal measures were undertaken early by mildly Conservative governments such as those of Braulio Carrillo (1835–42) and Juan Rafael Mora (1849–59). The constitution of 1844 was already clearly Liberal. So the *coup d'état* of 1870 led by Tomás Guardia, who became president (1870–82), and the Liberal constitution of 1871 were only a part of a very gradual process of transformation, which saw less dramatic upheavals than those occurring in Guatemala and El Salvador. However, the Liberal state in Costa Rica was, socially as well as politically, less of a grotesque farce than elsewhere in Central America. As early as 1889, the Liberals suffered electoral defeat and accepted it. It is true that in 1917 the constitutional process was interrupted by the dictatorship of Federico Tinoco Granados, but only briefly. The political participation of the popular masses (mainly peasants), and the attitude of most Liberal and Conservative governments, less repressive and more prone to social reforms, gave more stability to the Costa Rican regime. This explains its stronger position with regard to the owners of banana plantations, who in Costa Rica were taxed from 1909 onwards, before the other Central American countries were able to enforce taxation, and who were forced to fulfil their commitments concerning railway construction.

Honduras is a clear case of frustrated Liberal reform. In other words, although the reforms were carried out and the institutional frame of a Liberal state was built, the lack of a strong dominant class at the national level proved it to be, in the long run, a very empty process. During the nineteenth century Honduras had an economy and society consisting of numerous but unimportant local activities which were not really linked to each other within an integrated framework: silver mines (Tegucigalpa), timber (Atlantic coast), cattle raising (Olancho and the southern region), tobacco (Copán), and so on. Local geography made communications difficult, and its effect was reinforced by the destruction and massacre which occurred during the civil wars and 'pacifications' after independence. Between 1876 and the first years of the twentieth century, under the influence of Guatemalan Liberals and of such leaders as Marco Aurelio Soto and Ramón Rosa, a real attempt at Liberal reform was made, with the laicization of state and society, new legal codes, a new tax organization, a railway policy, strong support offered to mines and coffee plantations, and so on. But the lack of a dominant class capable of giving sense to the state and its overall reform policies, and of integrating the country and its local oligarchies, was responsible for the failure of this attempt and for a very unstable and weak government, which was an easy prey to the banana companies. As in the remainder of the isthmus, Honduras suffered dictatorships during this period: those of Marco Aurelio Soto (1876–83), Luis Bográn (1883–91) and Policarpo Bonilla (1893–9).

In Nicaragua a late but quite typical Liberal reform took place under José Santos Zelaya (1893–1909), with such measures as the Agrarian Law of 1902, which established a strong control over the labour force. But Zelaya's nationalism in economic matters (although quite moderate) led many foreign residents to seek the alliance of the Nicaraguan Conservatives, still a force to be reckoned with in spite of the Liberal reforms. The revolt of 1909, which overthrew the Liberal leader and restored Conservative rule, was supported by the United States. Three years later the United States intervened militarily and administered Nicaragua for the next twenty years (see below).

Liberal leaders in Central America shared a positivist ideology. Unlike the old Liberals of the period of independence, even if they did not formally renounce the democratic political ideal, they believed that the national economies of the isthmus had to progress, with the help of strong political and social control, before democracy became feasible. They felt also profound contempt for the Indian and peasant masses, whom they distrusted, and whom they submitted to a harsh repression. It should be clear, however, that the contradiction between strongly Liberal imported institutions and evident social oppression was to be expected. The kind of dependent economic growth experienced in Central American countries had no use for workers with full labour rights and citizenship. On the contrary, it needed firm political and social control and low wages. Costa Rica was an exception, but only a partial one.

The dream of union as a basis for foreign intervention

By the end of the nineteenth century, most Central American states were sufficiently consolidated to make the restoration of their union in a federation difficult. Moreover, such a project had never obtained the support of the dominant classes, and lacked any popular or economic base. It was a dream of middle-class intellectuals and occasionally a tool or a pretext in the hands of ambitious politicians, or even foreign countries such as Mexico and the United States.

Trying to build a new Central American union for his own profit, Justo Rufino Barrios, for example, provoked a war between Guatemala and El Salvador in 1876; he was defeated and killed in Salvadoran territory in 1885. The next unionist project was a consequence of the last British attempt at gunboat diplomacy in Central America in 1894–5. Following a diplomatic incident, British warships blockaded the Nicaraguan port of Corinto, but the intervention of the United States led to a settlement by which Britain recognized Nicaraguan sovereignty over the Mosquito Coast in return for the payment of an indemnity. After that, British withdrawal and American pre-eminence in the isthmus, as in the entire Caribbean, were accepted trends. Seizing the occasion of that last British threat, the Honduran president, Policarpo Bonilla, invited his Central American colleagues to Amapala, where a pact was signed by Honduras, Nicaragua and El Salvador, which were to unite in a Greater Republic of Central America (20 June 1895). The United States seemed at first to accept this measure, but in 1896 the US government did not recognize the ambassador sent to Washington by the new united Republic. In fact the whole project was very fragile, and it was not long before it collapsed, soon after a draft constitution had been written (1898).

At the beginning of the twentieth century, the United States and the Mexican regime of Porfirio Díaz decided to join efforts to intervene in Central American affairs. The United States had already supported the Corinto Convention of 1902, which was signed by all the Central

American republics except Guatemala and which agreed to submit any disputes arising between them to a regional tribunal of arbitrators. When in 1906 Guatemalan revolutionaries tried to overthrow the dictator Manuel Estrada Cabrera with the aid of the Salvadoran government, the result was a war which eventually involved Honduras as well. The United States and Mexico acted together and, with Costa Rica, organized a meeting aboard the North American ship *Marblehead*, where a pact was signed in July 1906, ending the current war and planning a further meeting at San José. But Nicaragua refused to recognize the interference of the United States in Central America, and sent no envoy to the meeting. In San José, the other four countries decided that the presidents of Mexico and the United States would arbitrate the possible aftermaths of the recent war, while a Central American tribunal would settle future problems within the region. The first tribunal, a few months later, failed to settle a complicated affair involving first Nicaragua and Honduras and then Guatemala and El Salvador. Porfirio Díaz and Theodore Roosevelt then convinced the Central American governments to send representatives to a conference in Washington.

The meeting at Washington (1907) decided to promote an important programme of co-operation between the countries of Central America, to establish a Central American Bureau which was to promote reunification, and a Central American Court of Justice to settle future disputes. Soon after this conference, in 1908, the tribunal acted successfully in a question involving Guatemala and El Salvador against Honduras. It functioned until 1917, when it was ended because of its inability to condemn the Bryan–Chamorro Treaty between the United States and Nicaragua. Further attempts at Central American union were made without success in 1921 and 1923.

The question of the inter-oceanic canal: illegitimate birth of Panama and intervention in Nicaragua

Plans for the eventual building of an inter-oceanic canal underwent substantial changes after the Clayton–Bulwer Treaty (1850). Colombia conceded rights in Panama to a French company, the Universal Inter-Oceanic Company, which began construction of the canal in 1882, under the direction of Ferdinand de Lesseps. But the company went bankrupt in 1889 without having completed its work. Its chief engineer, Bunau-Varilla, sold the French concession in Panama to the United States. The

North Americans, however, only became interested in the Panama route after an attempt to build their own canal in Nicaragua failed around 1895, because of extreme difficulties and costliness, and financial problems linked to the world economic depression of the time.

By the time the North Americans resumed their interest in an inter-oceanic canal, new developments had taken place. The second Hay–Pauncefote Treaty with Britain (1901) opened up the possibility of complete control by the United States of a fortified canal. This was of great importance from a strategic point of view, due to growing North American interests both in the Caribbean and in the Pacific ocean. But the Nicaraguan president, Zelaya, was adamant in his decision not to permit foreign control over any part of his country's territory. So negotiations began in 1902 with Colombia over the building by the United States of a canal in Panama, and including the question of North American sovereignty over the canal zone. But in 1903 the Colombian Congress refused to ratify the Hay–Herrán Treaty, because of a military intervention by the United States in Panama without the consent of either Colombia or the local authorities (September 1902). The North Americans then supported the secession of Panama from Colombia, promoting a Panamanian movement led by Dr Manuel Amador. The new country was recognized immediately by the United States, and a treaty was swiftly negotiated (1903) permitting the construction of the canal and establishing North American control, for a century, of a canal zone ten miles wide. The canal opened in 1914, and Panama became the most typical enclave economy of Latin America, utterly dependent on the new inter-oceanic route and the services it demanded. Moreover, it was politically a sort of protectorate of the United States, very much like Cuba.

In the meantime, the possibility of an alternative Nicaraguan inter-oceanic canal was being negotiated by Zelaya with European capitalists. This was contrary to the economic and strategic interests of the United States and, with other factors, led to the rupture of diplomatic relations between the two countries in 1908, and the overthrow of Zelaya in 1909. The United States then seized on the chaotic state of finance in Nicaragua as an opportunity to intervene, landing Marines (1912), confirming a puppet Conservative regime established in 1911, obtaining control over the Nicaraguan customs, railways and National Bank, and creating a National Guard under North American officers. The situation was best encapsulated in the Bryan–Chamorro Treaty (1916), which granted the

United States the perpetual and exclusive right to dig and operate in Nicaragua an inter-oceanic canal, and cemented the *de facto* North American protectorate over this country, even if the provisions which would establish a formal protectorate had to be eliminated from the treaty to secure its ratification by the United States Senate.

The Liberal resistance became a real revolution in 1925–26, with the support of Mexico, when the marines withdrew for the first time. But the Liberal army chief José María Moncada negotiated an agreement with the United States in 1927 in order to win the Nicaraguan presidential election the following year (which he did); his lieutenant, Augusto César Sandino, rejecting this agreement, then became the leader of a national guerilla struggle. He denounced the Bryan–Chamorro treaty and all kinds of United States intervention in Nicaraguan life, and destroyed North American property. For some six years he and his small group, enjoying considerable popular support, successfully challenged not only the National Guard, nurtured and trained by the United States, but US marines as well. Then, with the change in foreign policy brought about by Franklin D. Roosevelt, the marines left the country and Roberto Sacasa was elected. Sandino ceased to fight in January 1933 and approached President Sacasa, only to be treacherously murdered the next year by the National Guard, on the order of its leader Anastasio Somoza García, who already exerted a *de facto* control over the Nicaraguan government.

CONCLUSION

By 1930, the model of economic growth, social control and political organization established by the Central American Liberal oligarchies five or six decades earlier seemed to be exhausted and doomed to failure, assailed by the middle-class and popular movements of the 1920s and having to face the economic crisis of 1929. But as no alternative model to that built during the heyday of the export economy was in sight, the transition to new social, economic and political structures was a very long and difficult process.

The definitive integration of Central America into the world market, which brought about a long period of economic growth, also brought about a dilemma born of the new structures it helped to create, and which is not completely solved even today. The Liberal order, except in Costa Rica, excluded the vast majority of the population, not only from the profits derived from economic growth, but also from any political participation. The peasant masses never completely accepted the new pattern of domination, and the cultural, economic and social abyss between the dominant groups and those they dominated became more profound than ever. Under such conditions, it is difficult to build viable modern nations, or stable political and social structures.

5

CUBA, c. 1860–1934

In the 1860s, Cuba, the richest and most populated of Spain's two remaining American colonies, faced serious economic and political problems. The period of sustained growth, which beginning in the late eighteenth century had transformed the island into the world's foremost sugar producer, had begun to slow down during the previous decade. The production and export of sugar, the colony's staple product, continued to expand, but growing competition from European and American sugar beet and the development of new sugar-cane producing regions posed a threat to the future.

Since the 1840s, conscious of that threat, many alert hacendados (sugar-mill owners) began efforts to modernize (essentially to mechanize) the industry, while doubling their demands for reform of the archaic colonial commercial system. Spain economic weakness, and specifically her lack of sugar refineries and inability to absorb Cuba's sugar production, increasingly revealed Cuba's colonial dilemma: growing economic dependence on markets and technology which her mother country could not provide.

Furthermore, the future of slavery, for centuries an essential element in sugar production, had become bleak. The slave trade to Cuba had been declared illegal by treaties between Spain and Britain in 1817, but the trade managed to continue until 1835, when another treaty between the two nations and stricter vigilance on the part of the Spanish authorities forced it to decline yearly. By 1860 the infamous trade had virtually disappeared.[1] During the 1840s and 1850s, some hacendados had placed

---

[1] By then the number of slaves had declined from a peak of almost half a million (44 per cent of the population) in 1841, to 367,350 (under 30 per cent of a population of 1.4 million) in 1860. Ramón de la Sagra, *Cuba en 1860. Cuadro de sus adelantos en la población, la agricultura, el comercio y las rentas públicas* (Paris, 1863; first published as a Supplement to his twelve-volume *Historia política y natural de la Isla de Cuba*), 9.

their hopes for continued slavery on annexation by the United States, and had even helped to organize armed US expeditions to Cuba, but the victory of the North in the American civil war put an end to that particular brand of annexationist thought. After 1865, the hacendados were fighting a rearguard action, trying to delay abolition and to obtain guarantees of compensation for the loss of their slaves.

Thus by the mid 1860s the majority of the Cuban economic elite concentrated their efforts on obtaining the necessary reforms from Spain to assure them free trade, the *gradual* abolition of slavery with compensation for their losses, and increasing participation in the colonial government. Opposing them, the most intransigent *peninsulares* (Spaniards), who dominated trade and colonial administration, denounced every reform as a step towards independence. One of the arguments most frequently used by the *peninsulares* was that any rebellion against Spain would reproduce in Cuba the fate of Haiti, where in the 1790s a struggle among the whites ended with a devastating and successful rebellion by the blacks.

Convinced that Spain was unwilling or incapable of conceding any reform, a minority of Cubans did in fact favour independence. Some of them, influenced by a nationalistic sentiment seeded at the beginning of the century by philosophers like Félix Varela and poets like José María Heredia, envisaged a free sovereign Cuba, with close economic ties to the United States. Others wanted to end Spanish rule and then, as Texas had done in the 1840s, seek annexation by the United States, a nation which symbolized for them both economic progress and democracy.

During the previous decade opposition to Spain had not only substantially increased, but had spread to all sectors of the population. Burdened by high and unfair taxation (among other things, Cuba was forced to pay for or contribute towards the Spanish expedition to Mexico in 1862, her military campaigns in Africa, the naval war against Peru and Chile in 1866, as well as the salaries of the entire Spanish diplomatic corps in Latin America), governed arbitrarily by a growing swarm of Spanish bureaucrats, discriminated against by *peninsulares* who considered themselves superior to the native population, many Cubans, including the free blacks who constituted 16 per cent of the population, were beginning to express their resentment. The island was becoming divided into two hostile camps: Cubans versus Spaniards. Cubans outnumbered Spaniards 12 to 1 in the western and 23 to 1 in the eastern provinces.

In 1865, the reform movement gained momentum. Political change in

Spain brought the liberals to power and a Junta de Información, formed by members elected in Cuba, Puerto Rico and the Philippines, was to convene in Madrid to discuss constitutional reforms and the slavery question. The Junta, however, was abruptly dismissed in 1867 and its proposals were totally ignored by the Spanish government. In the meantime, an international economic crisis rocked Cuba, forcing a reduction of the *zafra* (sugar harvest). As a result, riding high on the crest of a general and bitter anti-Spanish feeling, the pro-Independence groups decided that their hour had come. 'A España no se le convence, se le vence!' (Spain should be defeated, not convinced!) became their defiant slogan.

In the western regions (the provinces of Pinar del Río, Havana, Matanzas and part of Las Villas), where 80 per cent of the population and 90 per cent of sugar wealth was concentrated, the majority of hacendados were reluctant to risk war with Spain and favoured reforms. In the eastern regions (the provinces of Oriente, Camagüey and the rest of Las Villas), however, with fewer sugar mills and slaves and a more vulnerable economy, hacendados such as Ignacio Agramonte, Francisco Vicente Aguilera, and Carlos Manuel de Céspedes believed in the possibility and necessity of defeating Spain. Moreover, as the construction of roads and railways had been determined by the needs of the sugar industry, the larger and less developed eastern region of the island lacked good communications, a factor which, by hindering the deployment of Spanish troops, emboldened pro-Independence groups. The town of Bayamo, in the rebellious department of Oriente, emerged as the centre of conspiracies. The majority of the clergy were Spaniards, and revolutionary leaders therefore were able to use the secrecy of masonic lodges to organize and co-ordinate their actions.[2]

Recent international developments also encouraged those willing to fight for independence. Spain's lack of success in the Dominican Republic, which she occupied in 1861 and abandoned in 1865, and the failure of Napoleon III in Mexico, resulting in the execution of Emperor Maximilian I, convinced many Cubans that the European powers, and especially declining Spain, could be defeated by determined national

[2] In contrast to what had occurred in the rest of Latin America, during the wars of independence in Cuba the clergy remained almost unanimously loyal to Spain. This was primarily due to the Spanish liberal reforms of 1826–41, which deprived the clergy of most of its resources, and to the Concordat of 1851, which practically transformed the church into an instrument of the Spanish state. After independence, the memory of this anti-Cuban attitude considerably weakened the influence of the Catholic church in Cuba.

resistance. The Dominican episode also had more direct consequences: many militarily experienced Dominicans who came to reside in the eastern part of Cuba were to make an invaluable contribution to the Cuban rebellion.

During the summer of 1868 the conspirators stepped up their activities; refusal to pay taxes spread, propaganda became more belligerent, and emissaries were sent to Havana in a futile effort to persuade reformists to join the rebellion. Contrary to the wishes of more impatient leaders such as Céspedes, the conspirators agreed in July that the rebellion should begin in December.

Several events precipitated the crisis. On 18 September, the growing instability of the Spanish monarchy led to a military rebellion in Spain which ended the rule of Isabel II. Cuban colonial authorities, weary of the results of such political upheaval, adopted a passive, observant attitude. A minor rebellion in the Puerto Rican town of Lares (22 September 1868) was easily crushed by the Spanish forces, but unfounded reports spread throughout Cuba that numerous Puerto Rican groups were ready to continue the struggle. Finally, there were rumours in Oriente that the Spanish authorities were informed of the conspiracy and prepared to take the necessary actions. Convinced that to wait would be disastrous, Céspedes decided to force the issue. On 10 October, without consulting other leaders and with a few followers, he raised the banner of rebellion at his plantation La Demajagua and proclaimed the independence of Cuba.

The colonial government was in no position to react decisively. Poorly informed of incidents in Oriente, and troubled by political turmoil in Spain, Captain General Lersundi paid little attention to news of the uprisings. Despite an initial defeat at the town of Yara, Céspedes had time to increase his heterogeneous band by enlisting discontented Cubans and Dominicans with combat experience. On 18 October he attacked and captured the town of Bayamo, temporarily silencing accusations of personal ambition and confirming himself as leader of the insurrection.

News of Bayamo's fall electrified the island and mobilized the Cuban population. In Oriente and Camagüey several groups followed Céspedes's example and rose in arms. Rebel bands appeared in the central provinces of Las Villas. Even young Havana reformists hastened to join the insurgents. Early in 1869 the colonial government, having dismissed the insurrection as a local incident, was confronted by a rapidly expanding rebellion. Cuba's first war of independence had begun.

Although confined to the eastern region of the island, the war lasted ten years and forced Spain to send over one hundred thousand troops to the 'ever faithful Cuba'. The rebels' courage and tenacity was aided by several basic factors. Peasant support and topographical knowledge gave them superior mobility. Often aware of Spanish troop movements, they could select the best zones for combat or concealment. They became experts in guerilla warfare with the Cuban climate their strongest ally. Unaccustomed to the tropics, many Spanish soldiers became sick with yellow fever and malaria. Fatigue and exhaustion repeatedly disrupted Spanish army operations.

Political conditions in Spain also aided the Cubans. During the war, Spain witnessed the abdication of Isabel II; a military regency; the reign of Amadeo of Savoy (1871–3); the proclamation of a Republic; the restoration of Alfonso XII; and a second Carlist War (1872–6). As a result, the Spanish army in Cuba seldom received adequate attention or supplies. Traditional bureaucratic corruption and political favouritism undermined any serious military effort. Symptomatically, during the first eight years of the war eleven officers held the rank of Captain General in Cuba.

The Cubans had their own share of problems. Divided by petty regionalism, class origins, and different concepts of military strategy, they lacked the discipline and unity essential for victory. In the town of Guaimaro, in Oriente, the Constituent Assembly of 1869 officially proclaimed the Republic, promulgated a liberal constitution, nominally abolished slavery, and approved a motion for annexation by the United States. Unfortunately, it also established a separation of power which was to hamper and ultimately doom the war effort. Authoritarian tendencies, such as those exhibited by Céspedes, frightened delegates under the influence of Camagüeyan leader Ignacio Agramonte, a romantic young lawyer, into creating a legalistic Republic where military commanders could not act without congressional approval. Uninterrupted friction between civil and military authorities followed this decision. Most rebel military leaders were eventually either removed or challenged by an itinerant government (Bayamo was eventually recaptured by the Spaniards) unwilling to yield yet incapable of imposing full authority.

By 1874 many of the elite who had initiated the war – Aguilera, Agramonte, Céspedes – were either dead or in exile. New leaders, humbler in origin but forged in battle, radicalized the struggle. The Dominican Máximo Gómez and the Cuban mulatto Antonio Maceo were foremost among them. The United States' strict neutrality and disregard of Cuban pleas for recognition[3] had by then dispelled all illusions of American support, practically erasing annexationist tendencies among the rebels.

The growing exhaustion of funds supplied by Cuban exiles and the end of Spain's Carlist War, which allowed Madrid to concentrate its efforts on Cuba, convinced Cuban military leaders that their only hope for victory was to invade the island's rich western provinces. The ruin of so many sugar mills would deprive Spain of vital revenues and leave thousands of slaves and peasants free to join the rebels. With a depleted treasury and a seemingly interminable war, Spain would be forced to accept Cuban independence. Early in 1875 Gómez defeated the Spanish forces in Las Villas and was prepared to carry out this plan when another internecine dispute disrupted the project. Returning to Oriente to restore order, he was instead forced to resign his command. The revolutionary momentum began to turn.

By combining military pressure with generous amnesty offers and promises of reform, General Martínez Campos, the new Captain General, further divided the already demoralized rebels. Late in 1877 Cuban President Tomás Estrada Palma was captured. In February 1878 a Cuban commission presented the Spanish government with armistice terms. With the approval of the Spanish authorities, the peace treaty under which the autonomy recently granted to Puerto Rico would be extended to Cuba was signed in the hamlet of Zanjón. (In fact Puerto Rican autonomy was rescinded later in the same year.) Demanding independence and the immediate abolition of slavery, General Antonio Maceo rejected the treaty at Baraguá, and announced his intention of continuing the war. It was a spectacular but a futile gesture: in May the last rebel forces accepted the Zanjón Treaty. Gómez, Maceo and many other Cuban leaders went into exile, and Cuba's first war for independence ended.

The entire conflict, known in Cuba as the Ten Years' War, contributed to the growth and maturity of a national conscience. The vague feeling of collective identity which had emerged in the early nineteenth century became a deep, ardent sentiment. Although racism remained, Spanish

---

[3] President Ulysses S. Grant was inclined to recognize Cuban belligerency, but his Secretary of State, Hamilton Fish, who maintained the traditional US policy of keeping Cuba under the control of a weak power like Spain until the conditions were ripe for annexation, always managed to thwart his intentions. See Philip S. Foner, *A history of Cuba and its relations with the United States* (2 vols., New York, 1962–3), II, 204–20.

warnings that an anti-colonial struggle would trigger off a racial war similar to that of Haiti now carried little weight since blacks had joined whites in the fight against Spain. Memories of Cuban heroes and Cuban victories – and of Spanish brutality (such as the execution of seven university students in 1871) – stirred patriotic emotions which made full reconciliation extremely difficult. On the Spanish side, the war increased the anti-Cuban animosity and distrust felt by the most intransigent *peninsulares*.

The vast destruction of hundreds of sugar mills in the east opened those provinces to expansionist forces in the new modernized sector of the sugar industry. Even in the undamaged western regions the war accelerated a similar process. Many important hacendados began building bigger, more efficient mills, while those who had suffered severe losses or could not afford larger mills were transformed into *colonos* (planters who sold their sugar to the mills), slowing down the trend towards *latifundismo* in the island. Ultimately, the war signalled the decline of the Cuban landed aristocracy, who were decimated and ruined by the long struggle or forced by the Spanish authorities to sell their lands and mills. In many cases American capitalists acquired both at very low prices, marking the beginning of American economic penetration into Cuba.

The three most important developments in the period between the Zanjón peace (1878) and the Second War of Independence which began in 1895 were the rise and decline of the Autonomist party; the United States' displacement of Spain as Cuba's economic metropolis; and the formation and growing influence of José Martí's Cuban Revolutionary party.

In Havana, a few months after the end of the Ten Years' War, prominent members of the old reformist group and many Cubans anxious for reconstruction and prosperity founded a liberal party, the Autonomist party. This powerful national organization's main objective was the achievement of Cuban autonomy by peaceful means. When in 1880 General Calixto García and other rebel leaders attempted an uprising, the party swiftly condemned their action and proclaimed its loyalty to Spain. Simultaneously opposed by pro-Independence groups and by the traditionally intransigent *peninsulares*, the *autonomistas* faced formidable obstacles. Nevertheless, hopes of reform and division among the war veterans gave the *autonomistas* the temporary support of many

Cubans. Despite their organization and brilliant political campaigns, however, their victories were marginal. Ten years after the Treaty of Zanjón, although Spain had finally abolished slavery (1880–6) and extended certain political rights to Cubans, inequality prevailed. In 1890, for example, much to the *autonomistas'* dismay Spain proclaimed universal suffrage, but excluded Cuba. Three years later the Spanish minister Antonio Maura, aware of mounting Cuban irritation, proposed new reforms leading to autonomy for the island. His proposals met with the usual resistance from conservatives in Spain and Havana, and with scepticism from most Cubans. When Maura resigned in 1894 the *autonomistas* had already lost the confidence of the majority and Martí's new Cuban Revolutionary party had succeeded in uniting most groups in favour of independence. A new economic crisis dashed the last hopes of the *autonomistas*. By 1894 a new war for independence loomed on the horizon.

The growing absorption of Cuban exports, notably sugar, by the American market can be demonstrated by a few figures. In 1850 Cuba exported produce worth 7 million pesos to Spain, and 28 million pesos to the USA. By 1860 the figures had risen to 21 million and 40 million pesos respectively. By 1890 Spain imported produce worth 7 million pesos and the United States 61 million pesos. This economic dependence made the island extremely vulnerable to any change in US trade policy. In 1894 when the American government passed the Wilson Tariff on sugar imports, the repercussions in Cuba were disastrous. Exports to the USA fell from 800,000 tons in 1895 to 225,231 tons in 1896. Thus the crisis in the sugar industry, already plagued by a decline in prices and growing international competition, became more acute in 1895, creating a favourable atmosphere for a new rebellion.

The opening of the Second War of Independence centred on José Martí, the man who forged the union of Cuban patriots and founded the Cuban Revolutionary party. Born in Havana on 28 January 1853 of Spanish parents, Martí was a gifted child. Devoted to reading and of a solitary nature he very early on developed a consuming love for Cuba. In 1870 a naive letter criticizing a colleague who enlisted in the Spanish army led the colonial authorities to sentence him to six years of hard labour. Deported to Spain, after a few months in prison he published his first book, *El presidio político en Cuba*, which expressed not only anger, but compassion for the oppressors. In the prologue he wrote what would become the motto of his life: 'Only love creates.' After completing his studies at the University of Zaragoza, Martí travelled throughout Europe, worked as a journalist in Mexico, and taught in Guatemala. He returned to Cuba in 1878 but was forced by the Spanish authorities to leave the island, and he moved to Venezuela. In 1881 he settled in New York where his reputation as a writer enabled him to survive on articles sent to several Latin American journals. Martí's unusually passionate prose and original poetic style increased his reputation in Latin American literary circles. Eventually he concentrated all his energies on the struggle for Cuban independence. His first task, the uniting of bickering Cuban exile groups, was made even more difficult by his lack of a military record. Travelling, lecturing and publishing, he overcame criticism and suspicion, rekindled Cuban enthusiasm, and established a basis for union. In 1892 he created the Cuban Revolutionary party. With his usual fervour, Martí mobilized all available resources for a 'just and necessary war'. His urgency was stimulated by an awareness of growing imperialist trends in the United States.

A man of deep democratic conviction, Martí appealed to Cubans of all races and classes to fight for an economically and politically independent Republic which would guarantee justice and equality not only to all Cubans but even to Spaniards who decided to stay in the island. Fearing that a long war would provoke the rise of military *caudillos*, the destruction of Cuban wealth, and intervention by the USA, Martí planned a struggle which differed from the Ten Years' War. A mass rebellion was to occur simultaneously in every region of the island with sufficient force to guarantee a quick victory. Supported by some rich Cubans and the majority of Cuban tobacco workers in Florida, Martí laboriously gathered as much money as he could and worked feverishly to assemble supplies for the initial blow. In January 1895 military equipment for three expeditions was gathered at the port of Fernandina in Florida. Suddenly, on 14 January, the American authorities confiscated the ships and their matériel.

This disaster drastically altered Martí's project and alerted the Spanish authorities to the magnitude of the conspiracy. To postpone the date for the insurrection would have endangered all those in Cuba committed to the rebellion. After a last desperate effort to obtain new supplies, Martí set the date for the rebellion and departed for the Dominican Republic in order to join Máximo Gómez.

According to plan, on 24 February small groups rose in arms in Oriente, Camagüey, Las Villas, Matanzas, and Havana. In the latter two (smaller) regions, where Spanish military power was concentrated, the rebellion was quickly subdued. Once more the eastern region of the island was to bear the brunt of the struggle. Maceo landed in Oriente on 1 April. On 15 April, after the proclamation in the Dominican Republic of the Manifesto of Montecristi expounding the causes of the war, Martí and Gómez embarked for Oriente. The following month Martí, who in defending the necessity of a civilian government capable of balancing the generals' power had clashed with General Maceo, was killed in a skirmish with the Spanish forces at Dos Ríos.

Martí's death deprived the rebellion of its most distinguished and respected civilian authority. Unrestrained by his presence, Generals Gómez and Maceo proceeded to organize a revolutionary government amenable to their ideas. Both recognized the need for a political organization which could obtain international acceptance and military assistance. But they had not forgotten the disruptive quarrels which had complicated the Ten Years' War. This time no civilian authority would interfere with their military plans. In September 1895, in the town of Jimaguayú, a hastily gathered constituent assembly approved a constitution, article IV of which stated, 'The Government Council shall intervene in the direction of military operations only when in its judgement it shall be absolutely necessary for the achievements of other political ends.'[4] Salvador Cisneros Betancourt, a rich and aristocratic Camagüeyan who had fought in the previous war, was selected as president, and Tomás Estrada Palma, the last president in arms in 1878, was confirmed as delegate and foreign representative of the Republic. Máximo Gómez was named commander-in-chief of the army and Antonio Maceo second in command. Both received sufficient authority to consider themselves almost independent of civilian restraint.

The convention of Jimaguayú symbolized other changes in the character of the war. Few of the delegates belonged to aristocratic families, slavery had disappeared as a divisive issue, annexation was not mentioned and the majority of the delegates were young and inexperienced men. As Enrique Collazo, a distinguished veteran of the Ten Years' War and future historian of this period, put it, 'this revolution was the revolution of the poor and the young'.[5] However, contrary to Martí's vision it was also a war of generals.

---

[4] Leonel Antonio de la Cuesta and Rolando Alum Linera (eds.), *Constituciones Cubanas* (New York, 1974), 127.   [5] Enrique Collazo, *Cuba independiente* (Havana, 1912), 195.

With the revolutionary government legally established, Gómez and Maceo were free to carry out their plan for invading the western regions. Spain's basic strategy was similar to that of the Ten Years' War. Commanded once more by General Martínez Campos, who had defeated the Cubans in the last conflict, Spanish troops built a series of fortified lines (*trochas*) to protect each province and impede rebel movements. This tactic enabled the Cubans to take the offensive. On 22 October 1895, symbolically in Baraguá, Maceo began his march to the west. Gómez awaited him with a small force in Las Villas. A general order had been given to the troops 'to burn and destroy everything that could provide income to the enemy'. By early 1896, having traversed the island in a brilliant campaign, Cuban forces were fighting in the vicinity of Havana with some of Cuba's richest zones wasted behind them.

To confuse the Spaniards and expand their operations, the two generals separated their columns on reaching Havana. Gómez returned to Las Villas while Maceo went on to invade Pinar del Río, the last western province. The invasion was successful, but Spain was not defeated. Martínez Campos was replaced by a tougher general, Valeriano Weyler, who arrived with large reinforcements. In Madrid, the Spanish minister Cánovas del Castillo stated his government's decision: 'Spain will fight to the last man and the last peseta.' The war continued.

With Weyler the struggle reached a new level of intensity. Determined to pacify Cuba at all costs, he took the offensive and rounded up peasants in the military zones into protected camps. Lack of food supplies and inadequate organization transformed this harsh but sound military measure into an inhuman venture which infuriated the rebels and provoked international protests. After nine months of Weyler's war of extermination only two Cuban provinces had been pacified. In December 1896, however, Weyler achieved his most spectacular success. Antonio Maceo, popularly known as the 'Bronze Titan', was killed in a minor battle in Havana province.

Maceo's death, a severe blow for the Cubans, came at a time when a confrontation between General Gómez and the Cuban revolutionary government had reached a critical level. The government tried to assert some measure of authority by attempting to curb Gómez's personal power. The general's reaction bordered on insurrection. The death of the 'Bronze Titan' shook both opponents. His son's heroic death at Maceo's side added a tragic aura to Gómez's reputation. And the declaration by President Grover Cleveland that a civilian Cuban government was a mere 'pretence' made clear the need to compromise.[6] The government left Gómez's power intact, while the general publicly assured Americans that the freely elected government 'in arms' was the supreme authority for all Cuban rebels.[7]

Spanish hopes of victory soared with Maceo's death. Weyler concentrated forty thousand troops in Las Villas, where Gómez had his headquarters, and confidently announced that the province would be pacified in a matter of weeks. With only four thousand men, Gómez fought his best campaign. Eluding the enemy, harassing its columns, attacking by surprise, the old general managed not only to survive but to inflict heavy losses. By May 1897, the Spanish offensive had lost its momentum. In the meantime, in Oriente, profiting from the Spanish army's concentration on Gómez, General Calixto García attacked and captured the towns of Jiguani and Victoria de las Tunas, the latter a strategic crossroads. Two months later Weyler was ordered back to Spain. Cuban successes, the assassination in Spain of Weyler's protector, minister Cánovas del Castillo (by an Italian anarchist who had been in contact with Puerto Rican and Cuban exiles in Europe), and growing American concern about the Cuban situation convinced Madrid that it was time to attempt appeasement. The new moderate minister Praxedes Sagasta promoted General Ramón Blanco to Captain General and sent him to Cuba. Upon reaching Havana, General Blanco proclaimed Cuba's autonomy and named several *autonomistas* as members of the new government.

The Cuban situation had by this time become a major issue in the United States. Convinced that American interests on the island were best protected by Spain, which paid indemnities for damage done to American-owned properties in Cuba, while disdaining the 'Cuban rascals', President Cleveland maintained a 'neutrality' which essentially favoured Spain. However, Congress and particularly the press inveighed against Spanish policies and demanded Cuban recognition. With President William McKinley's inauguration, the anti-Spanish campaign reached emotional proportions. Cubans became innocent victims murdered by butchers like Weyler. At the same time sober, powerful elements added their weight to the campaign. Imbued with Alfred

---

[6] For Cleveland's declaration, followed by one even more explicit by Secretary of State Richard B. Olney, see *Foreign relations of the United States* (Washington, DC, 1897), xxix–xxx.

[7] The compromise was actually a victory for General Gómez. For the text of Gómez's declaration, see Bernabe Boza, *Mi diario de guerra* (Havana, 1906), II, 14–17.

Mahan's ideas of sea power, expansionists such as Theodore Roosevelt welcomed the sight of the American flag in the Caribbean. And some American businessmen, no longer convinced of Spain's capacity to protect their interests in Cuba, increasingly favoured United States intervention.

Under the circumstances, President McKinley displayed remarkable restraint. In his annual message to Congress on 6 December 1897, he refused to recognize Cuban belligerency or independence, and proposed to await the outcome of the newly proclaimed autonomy. The waiting period was brief. The rebels refused to recognize the legitimacy of the new regime, and early in 1898 pro-Spanish elements in Havana launched violent demonstrations against General Blanco and Cuban autonomy. Unduly alarmed, the American consul, Fitzhugh Lee, asked the captain of the battleship *Maine*, on alert in Key West since December, to prepare to sail for Havana. On 24 January, the American government received permission to send the vessel on a 'friendly' visit to Cuba. The following day a silent crowd in Havana harbour witnessed the arrival of the *Maine*. Captain Sigsbee had waited until midday to give the Spaniards ample opportunity to gaze at the symbol of American naval power.

While the *Maine*'s extended visit annoyed the Spanish authorities, a diplomatic incident further strained the situation. A derogatory, private letter written by the Spanish Minister in Washington about President McKinley and Cuban *autonomistas* was intercepted by Cuban revolutionaries and released to the press. Neither the minister's resignation nor Spanish apologies helped to quell the excitement. The press focused on Spanish insincerity toward Cuban reforms and hostility to the United States. The agitation had not yet abated when on 15 February the *Maine* exploded, 260 members of the crew were killed. The Spanish authorities spared no effort to help the survivors and determined that an internal accident had caused the disaster. The United States appointed its own board of enquiry to investigate the issue. But those interested in war found a vindication and a popular slogan, 'Remember the *Maine*, "the hell with Spain"'. On 25 February, acting on his own initiative, Assistant Secretary of State Theodore Roosevelt issued orders placing the navy on full alert.

As the possibilities of war increased, Cuba's future became a debated issue. American opinions ranged from assistance towards full independence to annexation. Open contempt for an inferior race permeated many American views. The US government's position, however, remained unchanged: under no circumstances should a rebel government be recognized. On 9 April, yielding again to American pressure, the Spanish government offered the rebels an unconditional, immediate truce; the offer was rejected. Spain could do no more to avoid war. On 11 April, President McKinley sent Congress a message in which 'in the name of humanity, in the name of civilization, and on behalf of endangered American interests', he asked for powers to intervene forcibly in Cuba. Five days later, after heated debates, Congress approved a Joint Resolution the first article of which declared that 'the Cuban people are, and of right ought to be, free and independent', and the last stated that 'the United States hereby disclaims any disposition or intention to exercise sovereignty, jurisdiction, or control over said island . . . and asserts its determination . . . to leave the government and control of the island to its people'. Four days later the war began. The existence of a Cuban rebel government was totally ignored.

Inadequately informed about the intricacies of Washington politics, Cuban rebels generally welcomed the entry of the United States into the war. Martí, who had dreaded the possibility, and Maceo, who opposed it, were dead. And after three years of bitter fighting the insurgents were ready to co-operate with an ally who had promised independence and guaranteed victory. General Calixto García, who in 1897 had written 'Americans have no reason for interfering in our political affairs, and, on the other hand, we are not fighting to become a yankee factory',[8] was convinced that the United States would respect Cuban sovereignty; and Máximo Gómez, rejecting the Spanish General Blanco's last minute appeal to join forces against 'the common enemy of our race', had answered, 'I only know one race, humanity . . . up till now I have only had cause to admire the United States . . . I do not see the danger of our extermination by the USA to which you refer . . . If that happens, history will judge them . . . it is too late for an understanding between your army and mine.'[9]

The outbreak of war provoked a wave of national enthusiasm in the United States and, surprisingly, in Spain too, where the public had been deceived about the real strength of the United States navy and the deplorable condition of its own. Since 1880, the United States had based

[8] García to Estrada Palma, 31 August 1897, in *Boletín del Archivo Nacional* (Cuba), 26 (January–December 1936), 108–12.
[9] For the full text of the letter, see Amalia Rodríguez Rodríguez, *Algunos documentos políticos de Máximo Gómez* (Havana, 1962), 12–13.

its military strategy on the concept that the country was 'a continental island', geographically shielded from any foreign attack. Accordingly, the navy, 'the aggressive arm of the nation', had received full attention, while the army barely subsisted. As late as 1897, General Schoefield asserted that the army should limit itself 'to act in support of naval operations'. American initial strategy was therefore based on the navy. By defeating the Spanish navy, blockading the island, and supplying the rebels, the USA would force the Spanish army in Cuba to surrender.

Following the policy determined by Washington, the US armed forces were to take no action that could be interpreted as recognition of any Cuban political authority. Rebel forces should be aided and used, but only on a limited scale and strictly for military purposes. The instructions received by Major William R. Schafter before landing his troops in Oriente were typical: 'You can call to your assistance any of the insurgent forces in that vicinity, and make use of such of them as you think are available to assist you, especially as scouts, guides, etc. . . . you are cautioned against putting too much confidence on any persons outside your troops.'[10]

In May, while Washington was beginning to carry out the initial military plan, mobilizing the navy and sending supplies to some Cuban rebels, the Spanish naval squadron under Admiral Cervera managed to enter Santiago de Cuba. Immediately blockaded by Admiral Sampson's fleet, the presence of the squadron nevertheless altered the planned US operations. The landing of troops to attack Santiago de Cuba became necessary. At first, lack of logistic preparation and fear of yellow fever[11] led to the preparation of a 'reconnaissance force' only. But by the end of May, the US government decided to send an expeditionary force capable of defeating the Spanish army in Santiago. That decision reduced the strategic importance of Cuban forces fighting in other areas of the island. Only the army of General Calixto García, which controlled most of Oriente, was considered valuable. Consequently contacts with other Cuban leaders, including commander-in-chief Máximo Gómez, were practically suspended.[12]

---

[10] R. A. Alger [US Secretary of War], *The Spanish-American War* (New York, 1901), 64.
[11] The Americans knew, through impressive figures, the devastation caused in the Spanish army by yellow fever. According to Manuel Muñoz de Lara, *La España del siglo XIX* (Barcelona, 1975), 92, by May 1897 the Spanish army had had 2,129 dead in combat, 8,627 injured, and 53,000 dead or critically ill because of yellow fever. See also Pedro Roig, *La guerra de Martí* (Miami, 1984), 65–6.
[12] It was not until July that General Gómez received a supply expedition from the USA. The condition of the Cuban troops after three years of fighting can be measured by the fact that many soldiers became ill, and some of them died, after devouring American food rations.

Washington's policy of non-recognition was eased by the political weakness of the Cuban revolutionary government. Since the beginning of the war, rebel generals had frustrated all attempts to increase the government's authority. Consequently, the civilian branch of the 'Republic in arms', which Martí had so vigorously defended, had been reduced to a voice without much power. Even at this crucial moment, when the government was desperately struggling to gain official US recognition, the generals failed to support it. Máximo Gómez believed that President McKinley was withholding diplomatic recognition until a true Cuban government was established: 'this government', he wrote, 'is not the result of an Assembly but of the army'.[13] And when, ignoring the Cuban rebel government, American forces established direct relations with General Calixto García, the general acted as if his own government did not exist.

The American expeditionary force attacking Santiago received full support from García's forces. Besides providing scouts and fighting at its side, they kept Spanish garrisons immobilized in the rest of the provinces. By July, despite heroic Spanish resistance, the situation in the city was desperate. Dismissing Admiral Cervera's arguments, Captain General Blanco ordered the fleet to break the blockade. On 3 July 1898, the entire Spanish squadron was annihilated by the overwhelmingly superior American fleet. A few days later, Santiago was occupied by American forces who forbade Cuban rebels to enter the city. Defeated in Manila as well as Santiago, and with Puerto Rico already under American control, Spain sued for peace. While the terms were being discussed in Paris, American troops began to occupy Cuba. On 10 December, with no Cuban representatives, a peace treaty was signed ending Spanish domination of Cuba, Puerto Rico and the Philippines.

The American Military Government in Cuba (1899–1902) faced grave and urgent problems. After three years of war the island was devastated. Population had declined from 1,850,000 in 1894 to 1,689,600 in 1898. Hunger and disease were rampant, and the economy bordered on collapse. Four-fifths of the sugar estates were in ruins; the 1898 *zafra*

---

13 Gómez to Brigadier Méndez Capote in Amalia Rodríguez Rodríguez, *Documentos políticos*, 31. In a strict sense, the general, who knew well how the constituent assembly at Jimaguayú had been formed, was right. But he failed to realize how important it was at this juncture to have a civilian government, backed by the Cuban army, capable of dealing with the USA.

was about two-thirds less than in 1895. About 90 per cent of the island's cattle had been lost, and the tobacco industry had virtually ceased to exist. Communications had broken down. Scattered, poorly equipped, and hungry, the Cuban rebel army nevertheless kept a weary eye on the actions of the American authorities. The possibility of an armed confrontation between former 'allies' became a source of concern for Washington.

The Military Government reacted with efficient energy. Within two years the Cuban army had been peacefully disbanded, public health improved (a cure for yellow fever was finally discovered by Dr Carlos J. Finlay, a Cuban, and Dr Walter Reed) and communications expanded. A new educational system began to emerge. Simultaneously economic recovery began. With less land and capital requirements than sugar, the tobacco industry recuperated rapidly. Held back by low international prices and discriminatory American tariff barriers (sugar imports from Puerto Rico and the Philippines were exempt), Cuba's sugar production rose more slowly. In 1902, despite an influx of American and British capital, the total sugar crop value was $34,850,618, well below the level of 1894.

Favoured by US control over the island – and the weakening of local capital – American capital expanded its penetration in the sugar industry, and began to control railways, public utilities, tobacco and minerals. The immediate result of such growing dominance was the formulation of a powerful Washington lobby seeking better commercial relations with Cuba. As early as 1902, President Roosevelt recommended a reciprocity treaty with Cuba, stating that 'it is eminently for our own interests to control the Cuban market'.

Following the war Cuba's political future seemed clouded. Victory in the 'splendid little war' had encouraged American expansionist tendencies which saw no difference between Cuba, Puerto Rico and the Philippines. Consequently according to many American newspapers Cubans were no longer heroic independence fighters but had become a racially heterogeneous bunch of illiterates unfit to govern themselves. The Teller Amendment (Article 4 of the Joint Resolution) had, however, officially disclaimed any permanent interest in United States occupation and many politicians balked at the idea of openly breaking the agreement. Their uneasiness increased in 1899 when Filipino leader Emilio Aguinaldo, a hero of the fight against Spain, rebelled against

American forces. 'The thought of another Manila at Havana', wrote the Harvard historian Henry Adams, 'sobers even an army contractor.'[14] Cuban nationalism also proved too strong to be easily dismissed. The Cuban army had been disbanded for the minimal cost of three million American dollars, a sum proposed by General García and accepted by General Gómez, but mistrust of American intentions persisted. García died in 1899. Máximo Gómez, the most popular symbol of the Cuban Revolution, refused to go to Havana for the raising of the American flag on Morro's Castle. 'Ours', he wrote, 'is the Cuban flag, the one for which so many tears and blood have been shed . . . we must keep united in order to bring to an end this unjustified military occupation.'[15] The following year municipal elections were held in Cuba. Much to the disappointment of the Americans, nationalistic candidates won almost everywhere. Immediately following the elections, General Alejandro Rodríguez sent a telegram to President McKinley: 'The Cuban National Party, victorious in the election, salutes the worthy representative of the North American nation, and confidently awaits an early execution of the Joint Resolution.'[16]

In the United States anti-imperialist groups joined Democrats in attacking the 'colonialist' policies of the McKinley administration. In May 1900 large-scale embezzlements in the Havana post office were exposed, offering several Democratic senators an opportunity to demand American withdrawal. Under this pressure and with the presidential elections approaching, McKinley decided to establish a government in Cuba. A friendly dependent government seemed preferable to a battle over annexation. On 25 July 1900, General Leonard Wood, the American Military Governor, published a civil order for the provision of elections of delegates to a Cuban constitutional convention.

According to the electoral law established by the American authorities, the right to vote was restricted to males over 21 years of age who had become Cuban citizens under the terms of the peace treaty, and who fulfilled at least one of three alternative requirements: ability to read and write, ownership of property worth US$250 in American gold, or service in the Cuban rebel army. These restrictions, which disfranchised large sectors of the population, did not diminish enthusiasm for an election which heralded Independence. On 5 November 1900, in the Teatro

---

[14] Quoted in David F. Healy, *The United States in Cuba, 1898–1902* (Madison, 1963), 72.
[15] Fernando Freire de Andrade, 18 January 1899, in Amalia Rodríguez Rodríguez, *Documentos políticos*, 48.   [16] Quoted in Healy, *United States in Cuba*, 143.

Martí in Havana, 31 delegates representing six Cuban provinces met to begin the sessions of the Cuban Constitutional Convention. It was the delegates' duty, according to Wood's inaugural address, first to frame a constitution and then to formulate the relations which in their opinion 'ought to exist between Cuba and the United States'.

At the end of January 1901, after the completion of a constitution based on the American model, the delegates began working on the delicate subject of Cuban–American relations. Then General Wood confronted the convention with specific American demands. Among these were the right of the USA to intervene in Cuba and to establish a naval base in Guantánamo. Appalled and incensed, the delegates offered several counter-proposals aimed at saving Cuba's sovereignty. The issue was passionately debated in Cuba. Meanwhile, however, the US Congress approved a resolution introduced by senator Orville H. Platt (henceforth known as the Platt Amendment) which embodied American aspirations and was to be added to the Cuban constitution. The terms of the Amendment, especially Article 3 which gave the United States the right to intervene for 'the maintenance of a government adequate for the protection of life, property and individual liberties', provoked a wave of protests on the island. A delegation sent to Washington received assurances from Secretary of State Elihu Root that 'intervention was not synonymous with intermeddling, or interference with Cuban affairs',[17] but failed to modify American demands. As Manuel Sanguily, one of the most distinguished Cuban orators and patriots, expressed it, the Cuban dilemma was clear: a protected Republic or no Republic at all. On 28 May 1901, by a vote of fifteen to fourteen, the Convention adopted the proposed appendix to the constitution.

Once the constitution was promulgated it was necessary to proceed with presidential elections. When Máximo Gómez, the revered leader of Independence, refused the nomination, two other candidates emerged: General Bartolomé Masó, a prestigious military leader of limited talent, and Tomás Estrada Palma, who had been president of the 'Republic in arms' in the Ten Years' War, and had replaced Martí as the head of the Cuban Revolutionary Junta in exile. The former was the most popular; the latter, having spent most of his life in the United States, was basically unknown in Cuba, but he had the decisive support of Máximo Gómez

---

[17] Elihu Root repeated to the Cubans the official declaration he had sent to General Leonard Wood, Military Governor of Cuba. Root to Wood, 2 April 1901, Elihu Root Papers, Library of Congress, Washington, DC.

(who during the war had had many frictions with Masó), and the backing of General Wood. When Wood appointed five supporters of Estrada Palma to the electoral commission, General Masó withdrew from the race in protest. On 20 May 1902, amid popular jubilation, the duly elected Tomás Estrada Palma was inaugurated as Cuba's first president. That very day American troops began to evacuate the island. Witnessing the raising of the Cuban flag on Havana's Morro Castle, old Máximo Gómez expressed the emotions of many Cubans. 'At last, we have arrived!'

Economic recovery and honesty in public affairs characterized Estrada Palma's term in office (1902–6). A reciprocity treaty signed with the United States in 1903 gave Cuban sugar preferential treatment in the American market, reduced duties on American imports, and encouraged further American investment in the island, thus tying even more tightly Cuba's economy to the US market. Sugar production rose from 283,651 tons in 1900 to 1,183,347 in 1905, while cattle raising, the tobacco industry and several other sectors of the economy continued to recover rapidly from the devastation of the war.

The political situation, however, was less encouraging. Lacking any tradition of self-government or political discipline, with a low level of public education, and impoverished by the war, the Cubans found themselves trapped between growing American control of land and sugar, and Spanish domination of commerce, virtually guaranteed by the peace treaty between the USA and Spain. Politics thus became the principal avenue to economic improvement and one access to national resources. Consequently, political parties quickly became what González Lanuza, a distinguished university professor, called 'co-operatives organized for bureaucratic consumption'. Long-range programmes and loyalty to principles were sacrificed to immediate political gains. The growing, permanent shadow of American dominance and the presence of a numerous and increasing Spanish population (until 1934, thousands of Spanish immigrants poured annually into Cuba), who usually maintained a disdainful attitude toward Cuba's nationalism, were further obstacles to the development of a responsible and mature political system in the island. Old colonial vices, political corruption, local *caudillismo* and disregard for the law reappeared quickly. The manner in which the veterans of the War for Independence 'received' their compensation was distressingly symptomatic. Instead of distributing land, as suggested by some patriotic leaders, Sanguily among them, Congress decided to pay in cash. A foreign loan was obtained, but due to unscrupulous manipulations many soldiers received ridiculously small sums while a few politicians became rich.

Alarmed by these trends, Estrada Palma, an honest, stubborn and reserved man, decided to follow the advice of some of his aides and seek re-election. Apparently Washington favoured his decision,[18] but the president had misjudged the situation. He not only lacked popular sympathy, but he had also alienated many of his initial supporters, including Máximo Gómez, who died in 1905 full of misgivings about the future of the Republic. Estrada Palma's decision moved his two principal opponents, General José Miguel Gómez and Alfredo Zayas, to join forces to form a powerful Liberal party with the two leaders as candidates for president and vice president. Determined to win at any cost, the Moderate party leaders who supported Estrada Palma relied on the government's resources and forces to break the opposition. A series of violent confrontations culminating in the killing of Enrique Villuendas, a popular Liberal figure, persuaded the Liberals to abstain from the presidential campaign. Running alone, Estrada Palma, who probably did not know the extent of the fraud, was re-elected.

After this 'victory', the government did not attempt conciliation. Liberals continued to be harassed and excluded from bureaucratic positions. By the summer of 1906, the opposition was openly preparing for armed insurrection. Since the Republic had no army, the government faced the crisis with a Rural Guard thinly deployed in the interior of the island. When the rebellion broke in August, Estrada Palma, who had complete confidence in the backing of the United States, saw no other alternative than to ask Washington to intervene on his behalf. Deeply involved in the Panama Canal affair, President Theodore Roosevelt, however, wished to avoid any further action which could be interpreted as imperialistic. In an effort to avert intervention he sent two emissaries to Havana to seek a compromise between government and opposition. Regarding such impartiality as a vote of censure on his government, Estrada Palma resigned and made his entire cabinet resign too, leaving the Republic without a government and forcing the United States to take control of the island. Roosevelt immediately proclaimed that the USA had been compelled to intervene in Cuba and that their only purpose was

---

[18] See the favourable report (21 January 1905) of Squiers, US Minister in Havana, in Herminio Portell Vila, *Historia de Cuba en sus relaciones con los Estados Unidos y España* (4 vols., Havana, 1939), IV, 423.

to create the necessary conditions for a peaceful election. 'Our business,' he wrote, 'is to establish peace and order . . . start the new government and then leave the island.'[19]

The man selected to carry on this limited programme was Charles E. Magoon, a lawyer who had been a former governor of the Canal Zone and Minister to Panama. Hard working, conciliatory and 'without a touch of brilliance', Magoon failed to impress the Cubans, but as provisional governor achieved an adequate measure of success. The governor found that the main obstacle to rapid pacification was a group of businessmen, Cuban and foreign, who wanted to perpetuate the occupation by promoting unrest and spreading rumours about anti-American conspiracies. Unimpressed by their threats, Magoon reported that the majority of Cubans wanted to put an end to the intervention. Aware of the need for deeper economic and social reforms, but restrained by his instructions, Magoon inaugurated a programme of public works and attempted to appease bickering political groups by offering jobs and bureaucratic positions (a lesson not lost on the Cubans). He also encouraged the formation of a Conservative party to replace the discredited Moderates and modified the electoral laws to guarantee honest elections. The political reorganization was hindered by the reluctance of the property-owning class to participate in politics, an attitude the governor found irritating and irresponsible. Following Roosevelt's instructions, Magoon also set about organizing a small professional army capable of crushing any insurrection. Arguing that a professional army would soon become an instrument of repression against legitimate opposition, many Cubans – and several American advisers – counselled against the creation of a Cuban army, but it was officially formed in April 1908.

On 1 August 1908, with order fully re-established, municipal and provincial elections were held in which the Conservatives gained a surprising victory over a divided Liberal party. Realizing that defeat was inevitable in the forthcoming presidential elections if they remained disunited, the Liberal leaders José Miguel Gómez and Alfredo Zayas joined together once more on the same presidential ticket as they had in 1905. The Conservatives nominated General Mario G. Menocal and Rafael Montoro, a famous ex-*autonomista* orator. In November, after an orderly campaign tinged with anti-Americanism, the Liberals won

---

[19] Quoted in Allan Reed Millet, *The politics of intervention: the military occupation of Cuba, 1906–1909* (Columbus, Ohio, 1968), 146.

easily. A minor party formed by blacks, the Independent Party of Colour, which became significant later, failed to make any headway. On 28 January 1909, the birthday of José Martí, Magoon officially transferred power to President José Miguel Gómez. American troops stayed a little longer to ensure a peaceful transition, but on 31 March they withdrew from the island. With excessive optimism President Gómez declared, 'Once more Cubans have in their hands the destiny of their nation.'

The second American intervention (1906–9), in spite of its briefness, had a profound impact on Cuban life. Brought about by themselves, it seemed to justify Cuban doubts about their capacity for self-government. It undermined Cuban nationalism and reinforced the 'Plattist mentality' of relinquishing final political decisions to Washington. The submissive attitude of many powerful economic groups, which had annoyed Magoon, increased the gap between the elite who controlled the Cuban economy and the masses. The decline of nationalism and the growth of political cynicism alarmed many Cuban intellectuals who, like Enrique José Varona and Manuel Sanguily, tried to keep alive Martí's ideals.

José Miguel Gómez inherited a Republic with a little more than two million inhabitants (70 per cent white), quite a prosperous economy, and a public debt of $12 million left by Magoon's administration. A congenial, popular man, the president showed respect for democratic institutions, opposed direct American intervention in national affairs and demonstrated, by becoming rich and allowing others to follow his example, how politics could become highly profitable. Nicknamed 'the Shark', he inaugurated an era of public corruption. During his terms cockfighting and the national lottery, previously condemned as 'colonial vices', were re-established, the lottery evolving into an efficient machine of political debasement.

Two issues jeopardized the peace and sovereignty of the Republic in this period. One, the so-called 'Veterans question', was prompted by the permanence of Spanish or pro-Spanish elements in public positions which the veterans of the war for independence considered rightfully belonged to them. The agitation to expel these 'enemies' of Cuba became so threatening that American Secretary of State Philander Knox warned Gómez of the 'grave concern' of the United States. Opposition from many Cuban groups, fear of another American intervention, and some government concessions contributed to calm the veterans. The second issue proved more dangerous. The Independent Party of Colour, founded in 1907 by black extremists who, with valid arguments, accused the Republic of betraying the black population, found its political development blocked by the Morúa Law prepared in 1909 by the Senate's president, Martín Morúa Delgado, a moderate black leader, which banned political parties based on race or religion. Through secret societies of African origin like the Nanigos and in open campaigns, the *independentistas* fought for the abrogation of the law. In May 1912, exasperated by their failure and perhaps encouraged by President Gómez, who could have used a minor crisis as a step towards re-election, the *independentistas* rebelled. Poorly organized and mainly confined to Oriente province, the uprising, nevertheless, provoked a wave of panic in the island. Equally alarmed, the United States government landed Marines in Daiquiri and announced further actions if the Cuban government failed 'to protect the lives or properties of American citizens'. Protesting against such intervention, President Gómez ordered the army to crush the rebellion. By June the leaders of the insurrection were dead and their followers killed or disbanded. The fear and resentment left by the episode hindered black participation in Cuban politics for many years.

With presidential elections approaching, Gómez announced he would not seek re-election. The Conservatives selected General Mario G. Menocal as their candidate once again, with Enrique José Varona, probably the most respected Cuban intellectual of the time, as his running mate. Symptomatically, the slogan for the campaign was 'Honesty, Peace and Work'. Alfredo Zayas became the candidate of a supposedly united Liberal party. But before the elections, the old antagonism between Miguelistas (supporters of President Gómez) and Zayistas surfaced again, splitting the party into two irreconcilable factions. The subsequent alliance of the Miguelistas with the Conservatives doomed Zayas's efforts, and Menocal won five of the six provinces. On 20 May 1913, Gómez stepped down and a Conservative president was sworn in. 'This orderly transmission of authority', President Woodrow Wilson wrote to Menocal, 'is most gratifying and seems to indicate that the Cuban people have successfully undergone one of the severest tests of republican government.'[20]

The new president, a graduate in engineering from Cornell University, had been a distinguished military leader and a successful administrator of Chaparra, the largest sugar mill in Cuba, owned by the powerful

[20] United States Department of State, *Foreign relations of the United States, 1913* (Washington, DC, 1920), 337.

Cuban–American Sugar Company, with whom Menocal had a long and profitable association. Aristocratic and reserved, Menocal affected disdain for politics and displayed a paternalistic conservatism toward 'the working rabble'. He was to serve for two terms.

In his first term (1913–17), he partially fulfilled his electoral promises: official corruption was somehow restrained and, in spite of traditional congressional factionalism, some badly needed legislation was enacted. The Ley de Defensa Económica, which unified the armed forces, regulated the exportation of tobacco and created a Cuban currency, and the Ley de Accidentes del Trabajo (workmen's compensation) are two relevant examples. In 1915 the first labour congress was held in Havana; it demonstrated the emerging strength of the working class, the prevalent influence of anarchism, which had first penetrated the island in the nineteenth century through tobacco workers' organizations, and the tremendous difficulties involved in organizing nationally the sugar workers who constituted, as one of the speakers defined them, a 'rural proletariat'.

With improving economic conditions due to the first world war, and his popularity rising Menocal decided to seek re-election. As usual, the announcement triggered a hostile national reaction. The Liberals formed a united front behind the candidacy of Alfredo Zayas and Colonel Carlos Mendieta. By the summer of 1916 political tension was so charged with violence that a concerned President Wilson issued a warning that 'law and order should be maintained in Cuba at all costs'. Nevertheless increasing possibilities of war with Germany made Washington eager to avoid a crisis in Cuba. Consequently, Menocal, the representative of law and order, received full American support.

On 1 November 1916, noisy but on the whole peaceful elections were held. First reports showed Zayas winning by a large margin, but with the government controlling the information bulletins the number of pro-Menocal votes began to increase. Liberal protests were so intense that an open conflict was averted only when both parties agreed to allow the Supreme Court to decide the issue. After a brief deliberation the Supreme Court declared the Liberals victorious in the provinces of Camagüey and Havana, and the Conservatives in the provinces of Pinar del Río and Matanzas. New elections were to be held in Oriente, where both parties had equal strength, and Las Villas, a traditional Liberal stronghold.

Zayas's chances for electoral victory were thus reasonably high. But the Liberals decided not to wait for new elections. In February 1917, under the leadership of ex-president José Miguel Gómez and accusing the government of persistent repression, Liberals rebelled in several provinces; they rapidly captured Santiago de Cuba, Camagüey and several important towns in the interior. The pattern of 1906 – a rebellion spreading victoriously from the provinces towards Havana – seemed to be repeating itself. Unlike Estrada Palma, however, Menocal was an able military leader, had an army under his command and could count on assistance from the United States. Halted by stiff military resistance in Las Villas, the rebels were further disheartened by the publication of some diplomatic notes from the State Department to William Gonzalez, the American Minister in Cuba, stressing US support for 'legally established governments only'. The notes were accompanied by some display of American military forces at Santiago de Cuba and Guantánamo. The tide turned against the opposition. On 7 March 1917, surrounded by the army, José Miguel Gómez had to surrender in Las Villas. By May the rebellion was finished. For many Cubans, 'las notas de Mr Gonzalez (sic)' became a powerful symbol of American control over their internal political affairs. Menocal promptly paid his debt to Washington by declaring war on Germany immediately after the USA did.

Menocal's second term (1917–21), which began under these inauspicious circumstances, fell well below the level of his first. Corruption became rampant, fraudulent practices occurred in every election, and in spite of economic prosperity the president's popularity consistently declined. To make matters worse during Menocal's last year in power, sugar prices suddenly collapsed, plunging Cuba into her worst economic crisis and adding a new, dramatic dimension to the presidential campaign of 1920. Alfredo Zayas was the candidate of the Partido Popular Cubano, a small ex-Liberal faction, while José Miguel Gómez ran as the Liberal candidate. Zayas's possibilities of victory were quite remote until Menocal decided to back him with all the resources of power. During the elections violence and fraud were so scandalous that another Liberal uprising seemed imminent. Again the USA intervened. On 31 December, President Wilson ordered General Enoch Crowder, who had previous experience in Cuban affairs, to go to Havana as his personal representative. The Cuban government had not been consulted, and Menocal protested over such unilateral action, only to receive the answer that 'it has not been customary nor is it considered necessary for the President of the United States to obtain the prior consent of the President of Cuba to send a special representative to confer with him'.[21] On 6 January 1921, on board the battleship *Minnesota*, Crowder entered Havana.

Before dealing with the economic crisis, Crowder tried to solve the political crisis. Verifying the extent of the electoral fraud, he established new regulations to avoid its repetition and set 15 March as the date for new elections. A few days before that date, claiming lack of guarantees for free and fair elections, the Liberals decided to abstain. Running unopposed Alfredo Zayas was elected president. On 20 May amidst popular discontent and terrible economic conditions Menocal abandoned the presidency. One month later José Miguel Gómez died in New York.

During Menocal's eight years in office, for reasons more related to sugar than politics, Cuba had experienced profound transformations. In 1912 the price of sugar was 1.95 cents per pound, the lowest since the beginning of the century. The first world war and the almost total collapse of European sugar beet production changed the situation and opened a dazzling period of prosperity. After 1914 the price of sugar rose steadily, in 1920 reaching an astonishing 23 cents per pound. But then the price sank to 3.5 per pound. The 'dance of the millions' ended abruptly in bankruptcy and misery.

It is essential to note some of the consequences of this sugar boom. While in the thirteen years before the first world war only 15 sugar mills were constructed in Cuba, from 1914 to 1920 38 mills were built, most of them in the eastern region, converting Camagüey and Oriente into the island's most productive sugar zones. (Their percentage in Cuba's total production rose from 15 per cent in 1902 to 55 per cent in 1922.) As the cane production system used in Cuba was based on extensive planting instead of intensive cultivation, higher profits prompted sugar-mill owners to acquire as much land as possible, weakening *colonos* and transforming *latifundismo* into a formidable economic problem. Furthermore, to keep production costs low, hacendados fought every demand for better wages and resorted to the importation of cheap labour from Haiti and Jamaica, increasing social and racial tensions among peasants and workers. The sugar boom, and the absence of European competition, also intensified American penetration of the Cuban economy (US investments in Cuba rose from $205 million in 1911 to $1,200 million in

---

[21] Quoted in Louis A. Pérez, *Intervention, revolution, and politics in Cuba, 1913–1921* (Pittsburgh, 1978), 127.

1924), increased Cuba's dependence on the USA for its imports as well as sugar exports (51 per cent of Cuba's imports came from the USA in 1914, 83 per cent in 1915) and deepened the trend towards a single-crop economy.

All this explains why the collapse of 1920 had such devastating consequences. Almost all Cuban banks ran out of money, many Cuban-owned sugar mills had to be sold to foreigners, principally Americans, and every sector of the population felt the impact of the economic disaster. The *colono* system, which had been expanding since the end of the nineteenth century, creating what could be termed a rural middle class, suffered a terrible setback. It has been estimated that in the nine years following the crisis of 1921, out of a total of 50,000 *colonos* 18,000 lost their land. And the majority of the survivors became almost totally dependent on the will of the sugar mill owners.[22]

The crisis, however, had its positive results. Many Cubans became aware of their nation's vulnerability to external economic forces, and to the extent of American domination. By 1921, when Zayas assumed the presidency, the economic shock had revitalized Cuban nationalism and engendered a general demand for reforms. Public honesty, legislation to protect Cuban interests, diversification of agriculture, and a firm stand toward the United States became national issues. In 1922, Manuel Sanguily once more raised his voice to condemn the selling of Cuban lands to foreigners;[23] that same year a group of prominent Cubans proposed the creation of a National Bank, and in 1927 the most serious and influential criticism of *latifundismo* in Cuba was published, Ramiro Guerra y Sánchez's *Azúcar y población en las Antillas*. The emergence of a new generation of politicians added a radical, impatient accent to the protesting voices.

Alfredo Zayas, the new president 'elected' in 1921, in the middle of the crisis, was a cultivated, opportunistic lawyer almost totally free of moral scruples. At the moment when 'regeneration' was an increasingly fervent demand, he managed to downgrade Cuban politics to its lowest level. Initially, with the government tottering towards bankruptcy, Zayas had no alternative but to yield to Crowder's pressure for reforms. In June 1922 a new Cabinet, nicknamed the 'honest Cabinet', was formed under Crowder's watchful eye. Reduction of the national budget from $130

22 Alberto Arredondo, *Cuba: tierra indefensa* (Havana, 1945), 333.
23 See his last speeches in *Defensa de Cuba* (Havana, 1948), 146–9. As early as 1909 Sanguily had proposed a law, never approved by Congress, forbidding the selling of Cuban lands to foreigners.

million to $55 million, honest administration of the lottery system, and a serious effort to control public corruption were some of the accomplishments of the cabinet. Crowder's actions, however, provoked strong opposition in Cuba. In June 1922, even the usually pliable Congress adopted a resolution condemning Crowder's interventions in Cuban internal affairs, and reminding him of Elihu Root's original interpretation of the Platt Amendment, which rejected such interference. In 1923 the Zayas government received a loan of $50 million from the House of Morgan and Zayas felt free to exert his authority. Conveniently bowing to the prevalent nationalistic mood, he defied Crowder and dismantled the 'honest Cabinet'. By the middle of the year the old system of graft was back in force. Fortunately for Zayas, Crowder could do nothing to oppose this development. After his promotion to the rank of ambassador he had to follow Washington's new and more cautious policy, based on avoiding direct intervention or even openly pressuring the Cuban government for reforms. As Dwight Morrow, businessman and diplomat, told Crowder, 'good government is no substitute for self-government'.[24] Thus, Crowder was forced to keep a diplomatic silence.

The prevailing mood in Cuba, however, was no longer passive. Since 1922, inflamed by the proclamations of Argentinian students at the University of Córdoba (1918), and influenced by the 'anti-Yankee' feeling of most Latin American intellectuals (for example, José Vasconcelos in Mexico and Manuel Ugarte in Argentina) and the revolutionary events in Mexico, students at Havana University began demanding the forging of a 'new Cuba', free from corruption and Yankee tutelage. Martí's unfulfilled dream of a Republic 'with all and for the benefit of all' became the avowed goal of their efforts. A new and ardent love for Cuba and anguish at her condition appeared in dramas, novels, poems and popular music. Simultaneously young professionals and the leaders of the better organized labour organizations joined in the clamour for reforms. Even *colonos* and hacendados expressed dissatisfaction with prevalent conditions. Significantly, in 1923 a loose alliance of many of these groups formed a 'Veterans and Patriots Association' which published a programme for 'national reconstruction' that included the abrogation of the Platt Amendment, women's suffrage and workers' participation in business enterprises. Almost simultaneously, a

---

[24] Robert F. Smith, *The United States and Cuba: business and diplomacy, 1917–1960* (New Haven, 1960), 100. The author asserts that 'the State Department actually did not make a policy change . . . American business interests were satisfied, so there was no occasion for further action', *ibid.*, 101.

group of young intellectuals published a resounding 'Protest of the Thirteen', condemning not only the Zayas administration's corruption, but the entire Cuban political system. The support they received surprised even the impassive Zayas. 'Times have changed', he confided to senator Wifredo Fernández. But the president did not change.

In 1925, the Cuban Communist party was founded by old Labour organizers like Carlos Baliño, student leaders like Julio Antonio Mella, and several disenchanted ex-anarchists. Its direct influence was minimal, but very soon Marxist concepts, probably not fully studied, appeared in the writings of the new generation. As Joaquín Martínez Sáenz, a lawyer and future revolutionary (he was the main organizer of ABC, an anti-Machado secret organization), expressed it later: 'We were dazzled by the apparent simplicity and clarity of Marxist theories . . . all Cuban problems could be explained through class struggle and yankee imperialism.'[25]

The new political atmosphere gave a special importance to the forthcoming presidential elections. A revitalized Liberal party, with General Gerardo Machado as its candidate, opposed ex-president Menocal, once again the candidate of the Conservatives. The Liberal campaign for 'regeneration' and Machado's 'honesty, roads and schools' generated national enthusiasm. Probably bribed by Machado, Zayas remained neutral, even though his party sided with the Liberals, assuring honest elections. Machado won five of the six provinces. On 20 May 1925 he was sworn in as Cuba's fifth president.

A veteran of the War of Independence with a long but not very distinguished political career, Machado was frank, energetic, and tough. He firmly believed that only a strong hand could save Cuba from corrupt politicians and never hesitated to use harsh methods whenever opposition stood in his way. The first two years of his term fulfilled many Cuban hopes. The government was honest; legislation to protect Cuban products, diversify agriculture and regulate the sugar industry was promulgated, while a vast programme of public works and road construction, including a central highway from Havana to Santiago de Cuba, gave jobs to thousands of Cubans. Lining up behind the president, the traditional political parties followed a policy of *cooperativismo* and thereby transformed Congress into a docile institution. Without real political opposition and amidst collective praise, Machado ruled as no

[25] Letter to the author, dated 18 January 1968. Typically, by 1934, Martínez Sáenz and most of his generation had rejected Marxist ideas and clashed with the Communist party.

other Cuban president had before. Only small groups of students and some labour leaders criticized the government for increasing the public debt through new loans and applying brutal methods when dealing with strikers. The Nationalist Union formed by Colonel Carlos Mendieta and, to a certain extent, the recently founded Communist party (1925) were causes for government concern, but neither of these groups carried very much weight in 1927. The Nationalist Union was only a variation of Cuba's old traditional parties, and the Communists, guided by intellectuals and poets like Rubén Martínez Villena, had little influence among workers.

Propelled by his own political machinery and personal ambition, Machado took a clear step toward dictatorship in 1927. On the pretext of abolishing the right of presidential re-election, a pro-Machado, elected Constitutional Assembly extended presidential terms to six years and invited Machado to accept a new term in power. Then in 1928 Congress passed an Emergency Law prohibiting presidential nominations by any other than the Liberal, Conservative and Popular parties, which had all nominated Machado. After visiting the United States to obtain Washington's approval and playing host to the Sixth International Conference of American States held in Havana, on 1 November 1928 Machado was duly re-elected, unopposed, for a new six-year term.

The glaring unconstitutionality of the whole process and Machado's dictatorial methods aroused the opposition. Menocal came out of retirement to join Mendieta in condemning Machado's actions. Several distinguished political and intellectual figures such as Enrique José Varona strongly protested, and university students, mobilized by a newly formed Student Directory, appealed to the people to fight against a 'fascist' dictatorship. Undaunted, Machado answered with censorship and occasional brutality. In the summer of 1929 he boasted about his popular support and derided the opposition: it consisted of 'a group of corrupt politicians and a bunch of misguided kids'.

The Wall Street crash in October 1929 drastically altered the balance of forces in Cuba. In 1920–1 the slump in sugar prices had created a deep economic crisis in Cuba, but American loans and investments had helped to alleviate the situation. This time it was the American market which collapsed, dragging Cuba into an even worse economic crisis. Sugar production and sugar exports declined sharply. From 1928 to 1932 the price of sugar dropped from 2.18 cents per pound to an all-time low of 0.57 cents per pound. In 1929 tobacco exports amounted to $43,067,000;

in 1933 they only reached $13,861,000. Salaries and wages fell, unemployment soared. And this time there were no palliatives.

The economic crisis eroded Machado's popularity and encouraged the opposition openly to defy the regime. In 1930, after a political meeting in Artemisa had ended in bloodshed, violence increased. By November students had a martyr in Rafael Trejo who was killed in a confrontation with the police, and an admiring national audience. Praise for the gallant youths fighting against tyranny came from all sectors. In the meantime, the traditional politicians who combined forces with Mendieta and Menocal to fight Machado provoked the anger of the younger generation by keeping close contacts with the American Embassy and trying to obtain its open support. They were puzzled by Washington's new policy of caution. The era of direct intervention, the landing of the marines and blunt 'notes' from the State Department was coming to an end. Washington now preferred to veil its intentions behind a cloud of enigmatic words. When in October 1930, Secretary of State Henry L. Stimson was asked if the American government would land forces in Cuba, he summarized a vague answer with this cryptic phrase: 'every case in the future will be judged on its merits and a situation might exist which would distinguish it from the preceding ones'.[26]

Meanwhile, a different kind of political struggle agitated Cuba. In the past, violence had been limited to sporadic clashes among political groups, but now whole sectors of Cuban society, from workers to lawyers, entered the struggle, and the most radical elements of the opposition began to utilise a terrible new weapon: urban terrorism. Terrorism, repression; more terrorism, more repression; the well-known cycles of dictatorship followed their course in Cuba. In August 1931, adopting traditional tactics, Mendieta and Menocal attempted an uprising in the interior of the island, supposedly co-ordinated with some segments of Machado's army. Everything went wrong and the two leaders were easily captured in Río Verde, a zone in Pinar del Río, which gave its name to the episode.

Machado's relief was short lived. The failure of the old leaders allowed the younger generation to move to the forefront and radicalized the struggle. The ABC, a new secret revolutionary organization initially formed by middle-class professionals, published a deep and serious analysis of the causes of the Cuban crisis,[27] and spread fear in government

---

[26] *Foreign relations of the United States, 1930* (Washington, DC), II, 663–5.

[27] The ABC programmes and manifestos can be consulted in *Doctrina del ABC* (Havana, 1942). Some of the most prominent young intellectuals of the period, like Jorge Mañach and Emeterio Santovenia, contributed to the formulation of the programme.

circles with bombs and terrorist attacks. In the background, the continuous decline of Cuban exports increased unemployment and misery. Barely able to pay the army, challenged by an increasing number of enemies, the situation of the government was extremely difficult. Yet Machado was far from defeated. At the beginning of 1933 the political situation in Cuba could be described as one of deadlock: official brutality had not been able to crush the opposition; the opposition had no realistic hope of toppling Machado. Consequently, the election of Franklin D. Roosevelt and his announcement of a 'good neighbour' policy towards Latin America filled Cuba with anxious expectations. Once again Washington's action were to become decisive.

Committed to a policy of non-intervention in Latin American affairs, President Roosevelt decided to send a special envoy to solve the Cuban crisis. In May 1933, Benjamin Sumner Welles, who had previous diplomatic experiences in the Dominican Republic, arrived in Havana as Ambassador Extraordinary. The essence of his mission was to seek a legal solution and avoid a revolution in Cuba which could jeopardize Roosevelt's new policy. Soon after his arrival, Welles offered his mediation to both government and opposition. With the exception of the Student Directory, which branded Sumner Welles as 'another pro-consul of Yankee imperialism', and the Communists (who naturally were not invited), all opposition groups, including ABC, accepted Welles's mediation. Increasingly convinced that Machado had to be removed, Welles began to favour the opposition by insisting on demands which could only weaken the president's power and convince the Cubans that Machado had lost US support.

On 27 July, finally aware of Welles's manoeuvres but still convinced that the ambassador was overstepping his instructions, Machado assured Congress that he would defend Cuba's sovereignty and asked for support against 'foreign intervention'. While the mediation evolved into a frontal confrontation between Welles and Machado, an unexpected event drastically altered the situation. On 4 August a minor strike of bus drivers developed into a general strike which paralysed Havana. Machado reached a compromise with Communist leaders to help him break the strike, but before any action could be taken, the announcement of his resignation by a clandestine radio station sent jubilant crowds to the streets. The inevitable bloody confrontation with the police doomed the government. The following day almost all activities ceased throughout the whole island. On 12 August, after some officers of the army rebelled, Machado bowed to the inevitable, resigned and abandoned the island. Immediately, Carlos M. Céspedes (son of the hero of the Ten Years' War) was sworn in as provisional president of the Republic.

In spite of Welles's support and the participation of ABC, Céspedes's government appeared too hesitant and restrained in a situation of economic crisis and revolutionary tension. On 4 September, taking advantage of the demoralization of the officer corps, the army sergeants rebelled, demanding better living conditions. Immediately the leaders of the Student Directory, who had denounced Céspedes's government as a tool of the Yankee ambassador, joined the rebellion and convinced the sergeants, by now commanded by Fulgencio Batista, to march on the presidential palace and depose Céspedes. As one of the actors wrote, they transformed 'a military uprising into an authentic revolution'.[28]

After an attempt to establish a ruling pentarchy, the students proclaimed Ramón Grau San Martín, a university professor, as president of the Republic. Though lasting only four months, this revolutionary government became the expression of most of the tensions and aspirations which had been growing in Cuba since the 1920s. With young Antonio Guiteras as its most dynamic leader, the government abrogated the Platt Amendment, proclaimed an agrarian reform, encouraged labour unions, gave the vote to women, curbed the power of American companies, and made it obligatory that 50 per cent of workers in all industries were Cubans. But it lacked a political party which could organize mass support, and had to face too many enemies. While the Communists, following the tactics of the Third International, attacked it as 'a lackey of Yankee imperialism', Sumner Welles used all his influence in Washington to convince President Roosevelt not to recognize the revolutionary government because it was too leftist and could not guarantee public order.

The revolutionary government could crush a futile attempt by ex-officers of the army to regain power, and a rebellion of ABC, but it could not restore order or calm the fear of many Cuban sectors (business and labour) about impending economic disaster if the US refused to buy the *zafra*. As the government's radicalism increased, the ranks of its followers dwindled. Internally divided, the Student Directory disbanded, and the sergeants, now colonels, became increasingly alarmed. By December, Batista, who had been in close contact with Sumner Welles,

[28] Enrique Fernández, *La razón del 4 de Septiembre* (Havana, 1950), 40. Six years later, the principal participants in this episode organized the Authentic party, which was to rule Cuba from 1944 to 1952.

was openly conspiring against the government. On 15 January 1934, in spite of Guiteras's desperate efforts to organize para-military units, Batista had mustered enough political backing to demand Grau's resignation. On 17 January, while Grau, Guiteras and many student leaders went into exile, Carlos Mendieta, an honest but very naive politician, was proclaimed president. Five days later, Ambassador Jefferson Caffery, who had substituted Sumner Welles in December, extended to the new government the official diplomatic recognition of the United States. That very year, a treaty between Cuba and the United States abrogated the Platt Amendment.

The turmoil of 1930–4, however, proved to be much more than another episode of political violence in Cuba. The nationalistic, social and political forces unleashed transformed the island and opened a new era. The leaders, parties and ideas which emerged in 1933 dominated and controlled the destinies of Cuba for the next 25 years. The Cuban society which Fidel Castro confronted in 1959, and even Castro's rise to power, cannot be understood without taking into account the profound impact that the frustrated revolution of 1933 had on the history of Cuba.

6

PUERTO RICO, c. 1870–1940

Puerto Rican economy and society developed only slowly during the first three centuries of Spanish colonization. The island, whose precious metal deposits were exhausted by the middle of the sixteenth century, was not very attractive to colonizers. It was used mainly as a military bastion for the defence of Spanish vessels en route from Spain to the Spanish American mainland, and as a port where some of these ships could stock up with fresh water supplies. Apart from Spanish soldiers and officials in San Juan, the island was mainly settled by deserters and runaway slaves who had managed to escape from the plantations on the neighbouring islands, and by some soldiers who, having completed their military service, decided to establish themselves in the country as independent farmers. Local production was fundamentally for family subsistence.

It was not until the end of the eighteenth century that Spain began to concern itself with making Puerto Rico a productive colony rather than one dependent on external financial support. This concern became a vital necessity with the disintegration of the Empire at the beginning of the nineteenth century. A large number of Spanish families from the newly independent mainland colonies, as well as French families from Louisiana and Haiti, began to arrive on the island. The Spanish government gave them land and facilities to start cultivation for export and it did away with some impediments to trade which had been imposed on the island in favour of merchants from Seville and Cadiz.

Given the sparse population of Puerto Rico in the eighteenth century, the scarcest factor of production was labour, and the most readily available resource was land. There are no earlier figures, but as late as 1830, only 5.8 per cent of the land was under cultivation. The proportion of land under cultivation, although increasing considerably, continued to be very small throughout the whole of the nineteenth century; by 1897 it had only reached 14.3 per cent. This was not the result of unequal regional development, as was common in other areas of Latin America. The population of Puerto Rico in the eighteenth and nineteenth centuries was distributed fairly evenly over the island. As British traveller George Flinter remarked in 1834, 'means of extending cultivation are within the reach of all persons, even of the lowest class'.[1] In the early nineteenth century, therefore, practically all the peasants and agricultural labourers, except the slaves, were independent producers.

For the emerging sugar and coffee haciendas of the early nineteenth century, land was also a more readily available factor of production than capital, which was indispensable for the importation of slaves. Internationally, the slave trade was, in any case, facing extinction. Moreover, the revolution in Haiti had generated great fears about the unrestricted expansion of the black population. Although slaves were still imported during the first half of the nineteenth century, the Puerto Rican economy was never predominantly a slave economy and the slave population at its peak (1846) reached only 11.5 per cent of the total population.

Thus the labour problem facing the development of commercial agriculture was how to encourage the settlement of white labourers or drive the existing peasants, who were producing independently for their families' subsistence, to work on the haciendas. This was progressively achieved in the nineteenth century, not through the hire and sale of labour, but through dominion of the land and rights over persons, means associated with the feudal mode of production. The relationship described between land, labour and capital fostered labour regimes based on servile ties: mainly the *agregado* – resident farm labour which is permitted the use of a plot of land for subsistence production with the obligation to devote a certain quota of time to the commercial cultivation of the hacendado; the *medianeo*, or sharecropping – where the direct producer had to divide his produce with the landowner; and the *endeudamiento* – where payment for labour was in kind or *vales* (vouchers) in the hacienda shop and the labourer was placed in a situation of indebtedness and therefore dependency on a particular landowner.

During the nineteenth century, Puerto Rican society experienced, therefore, a very important transformation: from a basically smallholding peasant economy of subsistence production to a predomi-

---

[1] George D. Flinter, *An account of the present state of the island of Puerto Rico* (London, 1834), 17.

nantly seignorial economy of moderate-sized haciendas producing cash crops for export. This was fostered by the mercantilist colonial metropolis, which was interested in the growth of production for the profits it could make through the control of trade. In this way, the metropolitan dominance planted the seeds of its own destruction, as it nurtured the emergence of a resident class with aspirations to power. As production began to be centred on the haciendas, the hacendados, through their control of the production process, also acquired social dominance. And, in Gramsci's terms, their hegemony in civil society fostered the transfer of their hegemonic aspirations to political society. The metropolitan control of the administrative state apparatus was seen by the hacendados not only as the main impediment to their intensification of production of commodities – through the restrictions of the metropolis's control of trade – but also as the main impediment to the comprehensive organization of society in terms of their class conceptions or *weltanschauung*.

Linked to the capitalist world through their export production, 'bourgeois' liberalism provided the ideological tools of the hacendados' self-affirmation vis-à-vis Spanish colonial rule: absolutism was faced with the principle of reason, and the freedom that arises from it; confronted with an authority of 'government by privilege' – oriented towards the defence of Spanish commercial interests – the *criollos* posed the principle of equality before the law. When the hacendados joined the political struggle in 1870 their organization was called the Liberal Reformist party.

Liberalism gave the political organization of the hacendados the character of a broad front; it included other social groups, such as the emerging nuclei of professionals and the artisans, who were in favour of the liberalization of the colonial regime. The Liberal Reformist party (later named Autonomist party) demanded fundamental changes in the colonial regime, and faced with the negative attitude of the metropolis its activities became of an increasingly anti-colonialist nature. A Spanish observer at that time described the party's politics in this manner: 'it makes provincialism [Puerto Rico] a cause above and beyond, and sometimes in detriment to, the national cause [Spain]'.[2]

In this way, Liberal party politics contributed to the upsurge of a Puerto Rican national sentiment which increased as the hacendados

[2] Antonio Alfau y Baralt, *Los partidos antillanos, estudio político* (San Juan, 1886), 11.

attained social dominance, and as the relationships which developed around the hacienda's particular mode of production began to permeate and unify the entire social structure. The broad-front character which liberalism gave to the hacendados' politics strengthened the emerging national sentiment. Politics was viewed as a struggle between Puerto Ricans and *peninsulares*, and Puerto Ricans of different social classes were referred to as members of 'la gran familia puertorriqueña' (the all-embracing Puerto Rican family).

On the other hand, the fact that the hacendados were a seignorial class of an export-orientated agriculture limited the national struggle. With commodity production aimed at exports, the development of a home market had no fundamental importance, unlike the case in the bourgeois struggle in the formation of the European nations. This hindered the development of internal communications and of a united monetary system, which are tremendously important for the integration of an economy and, thus, of a country. This integration was also hampered by the labour regime of the hacendados' commodity production. Servile ties of different kinds bound labourers to particular haciendas, thus rendering impossible the development of a labour market. Local seclusion and insularity stripped all meaning from the national struggle. In 1891, Muñoz Rivera, the most important political leader of the hacendados, stated that 'we have not yet succeeded in moving those masses, in breaking the ice of their indifference and lighting in their hearts the sacred fire of patriotism'.[3]

Political opposition to the Liberal party came from the Conservative party – which later became the Partido Incondicionalmente Español – which represented those groups whose privileged position within the social organization depended upon the colonial regime: the bureaucracy of the colonial administration and, most important, the merchants.[4] The merchants controlled the credit that the hacendados needed for their commercial production, and were also in charge of marketing the produce. They tried to make the most of the situation of dependency in which the hacendados found themselves. This dependency was in itself a source of conflict. The ideological opening of the hacendados to the bourgeois world reinforced their struggle to control the commercial

---

[3] Newspaper article, 'Las causas del mal' (1891), reprinted in his *Campañas políticas* (2 vols., Madrid, 1925), I, 24. Author's translation.
[4] See works by Francisco Mariano Quiñones, *Conflictos económicos* (Mayagüez, Puerto Rico, 1888) and *Historia de los Partidos Reformista y Conservador en Puerto Rico* (Mayagüez, 1889).

aspect of production. On the other hand, the credit relations between hacendados and merchants not only led the hacendados to become interested in trading activities but also involved merchants in production. If the hacendado had a bad harvest, he would have to pay off his credit in land. Thus, a considerable number of merchants were also becoming landowners, and therefore menacing the economic base of the hacendados' incipient social hegemony.

The hacendados' struggle for a dominant position was intimately linked to the control of the administrative state apparatus for the development of an infrastructure for commodity production independent of the merchants (credit facilities, means of communications, and so on) and for the expansion of trade beyond the limits of the existing merchants' control. The hacendados' struggle was not waged, then, against a previously dominant class, where it would have been necessary to present an alternative vision of social life, but against those groups whose social power lay outside the dynamics of social production, in privileges superimposed on the structural dynamics by colonial rule.

The contradictions between ideology – liberalism – and relations of production – seignorial *weltanschauung* – of a socially hegemonic but, because of the colonial condition, economically fragile and politically subordinated class generated towards the end of the century a political style that their own creators named 'possibilist' or 'opportunist'.[5] It set aside ideological issues in favour of a struggle exclusively orientated towards the acquisition of administrative state power.

Within this mercantilist colonial framework, the hacendados could follow two roads. The metropolis had increasingly become dependent upon the use of force through the state administrative apparatus to retain power. One of the alternatives was to meet force with force; in other words, the alternative followed by Cuba – armed insurrection. This required solid support from agricultural labourers and smallholding peasants in a struggle which had for them no meaning because of their position in the seignorial production structure. This alternative also meant breaking away from the principal market for Puerto Rican coffee, now the haciendas' main cash crop, precisely when coffee exports had reached their pinnacle, representing during the 1890s two-thirds of the country's total exports. (In Cuba, sugar was the principal export crop and its main market was the United States.) The Puerto Rican hacendados,

---

5 For example, Muñoz Rivera, *Campañas*, 34. Another clear example of this political style is Juan Arrillaga Roqué, *Memorias de Antaño* (Ponce, Puerto Rico, 1910).

therefore, took a second course, that of using political pressure and bargaining power with a structurally and internationally weak metropolis in order to attain self-government, that is, a local political and administrative autonomy under Spanish rule. In this bargaining and within the emerging 'possibilist' political practice, the hacendados expressed their position in the following terms: 'Neither republicans nor monarchists, but Puerto Ricans!'[6]

An alliance was made with the metropolitan political party which held the greater probability of attaining office in Spain: a right-wing monarchical party. The hacendados agreed to support this party's national politics and the party promised to grant Puerto Rico an autonomist charter as soon as it reached government. This Spanish monarchical party, however, held ideological positions which were contrary to the liberalism that had characterized the previous political stance of the Autonomist party. This alliance was therefore unacceptable to some elements in *la gran familia puertorriqueña* for whom democratic radicalism enjoyed more solid structural bases: that is to say, the professionals and the artisans. As a result the Autonomist party split a year before the United States invasion of 1898.[7]

In November 1897 Spain granted Puerto Rico an autonomist Charter. The only elections held under this Charter, which instituted universal male suffrage for the first time, resulted in an overwhelming victory for the party of the hacendados. It obtained 80.6 per cent of the vote; its splinter group, led by the professional sector, obtained 15.6 per cent and the Unconditionalists, having lost the protection of official patronage, obtained an insignificant percentage of the ballot.

The US invasion in July 1898 thus took place at a time when the social hegemony of the hacendado class was clearly established and precisely when this class had just begun to lay the foundations for its political dominance in its struggle for total hegemony. But its political party had just been divided by its own internal contradictions and since the social sectors that had left the party were enormously important for social

---

[6] Title of a very influential article by Muñoz Rivera in *La Democracia*, 18 July 1896, reprinted in *Campañas*.

[7] See discussions regarding this matter which took place at the Assembly of the Autonomist party and were published in the newspaper *La Correspondencia de Puerto Rico*, 14 February 1897. Pilar Barbosa de Rosario, *La Comisión Autonomista de 1896* (San Juan, 1957) constitutes an excellent analysis of this division from the point of view of the professional sector which the author terms 'idealist'. The general political situation in Spain at that moment can be examined in M. Fernández Almagro, *Historia política de la España contemporánea* (Madrid, 1968), vol. II, ch. 7, vol. III, ch. 1; Bolívar Pagán, *Procerato puertorriqueño del siglo XIX* (San Juan, 1961), 475–6.

communication (professionals and artisans), Puerto Rican society, in spite of the solid hacendado electoral support, thus presented an image of fragmentation and discord.

In addition, the social hegemony of the hacendados rested on a very fragile economic base. Sugar-cane had been Puerto Rico's main cash crop throughout most of the nineteenth century, but it had been going through a serious crisis since the mid 1880s. The upsurge of a highly mechanized beet-sugar industry in Europe limited cane-sugar markets, lowered sugar prices, and forced technical transformations in order to produce raw sugar of comparable quality for refining. But investment in new technology also implied changes in the pattern of land tenure – control over more contiguous land for the agricultural production of the sugar-cane supply required by a larger mill – and changes in the labour market – a floating surplus labour for the *zafra* (harvest) in an economy characterized by shortage of labour. Some sugar hacendados managed to cope with these needed transformations, but, due to the other macro-economic factors, most haciendas collapsed, and, with them, the island's sugar industry.[8]

Coffee agriculture, on the other hand, experienced its golden era precisely in those last two decades of the century. In some regions, this growth was linked to a kind of second colonization, by immigrant entrepreneurs (mostly from Corsica and Mallorca) who displaced earlier settlers: traditional hacendados, middle farmers or independent peasants. Some resentment existed towards these immigrants, not only because of the economic displacement, but also because they often showed stronger emotional ties with their place of origin than with their new society or land.

In 1898 Puerto Rico became a possession of the United States, and the nature of economic power began to undergo a radical change. While in 1895 the sugar industry produced $4,400,000 in exports, 29 per cent of the total value of the country's exports, by 1920 it produced $74,000,000 (that is, sixteen times more), which represented 66 per cent of total exports.[9] In 1895, the North American interests in sugar production were practically non-existent; towards the end of the 1920s almost half of the total production was in the hands of four companies from the new

[8] See Andrés Ramos Mattei, *La hacienda azucarera: su crecimiento y crisis en Puerto Rico (siglo XIX)* (San Juan, 1981).
[9] Victor S. Clark *et al.*, *Porto Rico and its problems* (Washington, DC, 1930), 643.

metropolis. Although of secondary importance, it is interesting to note that in 1895 the value of tobacco exports was 4.4 per cent of the island's total exports; twenty-five years later it had reached 19.3 per cent. And while in 1895 there is no evidence of American interests in the Puerto Rican tobacco industry, by 1920 these interests controlled practically the entire processing and marketing of tobacco.[10]

Puerto Rico and the Philippines did not become American possessions simply as spoils of war, as a result of a military adventure. Though Cuba was undoubtedly more central, both the Philippines and Puerto Rico were clearly within the sphere of American expansionist aims at the time. There is evidence of US strategic-military interests, but economic factors of a more profound character were also present. It has been argued that

except in very specific products the North American nation was conceived from its beginnings as bound to supply itself with the basic necessities of life (that is, within the mythology of self-sufficiency). Sugar was evidently one of the few products which the United States did not produce abundantly. It was necessary, then, to secure territories where sugar was produced or which could be turned into areas of production.[11]

Thus, while towards the end of the nineteenth century 86 per cent of the sugar consumption of the United States was satisfied through imports, in 1932 only 0.4 per cent was imported. The territories acquired directly or indirectly – Hawaii, Puerto Rico, the Philippines and Cuba – contributed 76 per cent of the sugar consumed (see table 1). It was no coincidence that these territories without exception became fundamentally mono-producers of sugar.

Moreover, it should not be forgotten that the Spanish–American War took place at the time of the greatest imperialist territorial expansion the world had known. Africa, for example, which had been less than 10 per cent under outside domination in 1875, was almost completely partitioned by the European nations during the next 35 years. This was the period when the United States, France, and Germany emerged as competitors to Britain in industrial production. The expansion of these economies demanded new markets and began to require also a broader influx of raw materials to be processed. Moreover, given the capitalist nature of these economies, with a tremendous increase in manufacturing,

---

[10] Baily W. and Justine W. Diffie, *Porto Rico: a broken pledge* (New York, 1931), ch. 5. Data on volume of exports in H. S. Perloff, *Puerto Rico's economic future* (Chicago, 1950), 136.

[11] José A. Herrero, *La mitología del azúcar, un ensayo de historia económica de Puerto Rico* (San Juan, 1975), 8.

Table 1. *Sugar contributed to the American market:*
sources of supply

	Average 1897–1901 (%)	1932 (%)
(1) Louisiana (cane)	11.1	2.6
(2) Western USA (beet)	3.2	21.1
(3) Hawaii (cane)	12.0	16.4
(4) Puerto Rico (cane)	2.1	14.7
(5) The Philippines (cane)	0.7	16.6
(6) Cuba (cane)	16.6	28.2
(7) Others	54.3	0.4
Total	100.0	100.0
Subtotal (3 + 4 + 5 + 6)	31.4	75.9

Source: US Tariff Commission Report, no. 73 (Washington, DC, 1934), 159 (quoted by J. A. Herrero, *La mitología del azúcar: un ensayo de historia económica de Puerto Rico* (San Juan, 1975), 9.

there followed accumulations of capital seeking investment. As the surplus of capital increased, interest rates declined and financiers were forced to seek new low-wage labour markets, thus reducing the internal amount of liquid capital accumulated through profitable foreign investment.

The growth of the Puerto Rican sugar industry corresponded perfectly to this pattern of imperialist development. It represented a large investment in land and machinery in a short period of time, yielding profits over a long time-span. Even in the years of the world depression in the late 1920s and early 1930s, these early-twentieth-century investments were producing enormous profits.[12]

Besides being orientated to the consumption needs of the United States, Puerto Rican sugar was also directed to serve as a source of raw material for manufacture in the American economy. This is demonstrated by the fact that no refineries – needed for the final stage in the manufacture of sugar – were allowed on the island (apart from some serving the Puerto Rican internal market exclusively, and at a later date). Puerto Rico became, therefore, an exporter of raw sugar to be processed

[12] A. D. Gayer *et al.*, *The sugar economy of Puerto Rico* (New York, 1938), 155.

by the metropolitan economy, which by 1914 was an important exporter of refined sugar.[13]

The plantation economy, concentrating on a single cash crop for export, reduced the availability of certain commodities which were previously produced locally, thus necessarily raising the level of imports. Towards 1920, the value of imports had increased to more than six times its value at the end of the nineteenth century. The growth in imports was accompanied by the inclusion of Puerto Rico within the United States system of customs and tariffs, which channelled this growing need to import towards North American suppliers. In 1895 imports from the United States represented less than 11 per cent of the island's total imports; fifteen years later, they accounted for 90 per cent of the total. The growth of US trade to Puerto Rico was such that in 1934, during the climax of sugar mono-production, Puerto Rico, with a population of only two million, was America's second largest customer in Latin America and the ninth largest in the world.[14]

The US invasion of 1898 not only represented a change in metropolis but, even more important, a transition in the economic significance of colonial relationships. At the end of the nineteenth century, the Puerto Rican hacendados faced a weak metropolis whose policies were geared towards defending its commercial interests; at the beginning of the twentieth century they found themselves ruled by one of the most powerful capitalist nations, with an expanding economy, and interested in controlling not only trade, but also production in the colony. In this sense, the very nature of social conflicts underwent a radical transformation.

Colonial policy during the first years of occupation was clearly directed towards shattering the hegemony of the hacendados, the owners of the means of production. The offensive national struggle against Spain turned into a defensive struggle against the United States. A class orientated towards change in the nineteenth century was forced, by imperialist capitalism, to defend the traditional agrarian world through which it had developed its (fragile) social hegemony. Evidence for this can be found in literary and other cultural manifestations as well as in political actions. For example, while during the late nineteenth

[13] Data on US Bureau of the Census, *Census of Manufactures 1914* (Washington, DC, 1919), II, 428. The North American interest in raw sugar for processing is confirmed by data presented in US Senate, 59th Congress, 1st Session, Doc. 250, *Production and commercial movement of sugar 1895–1905* (Washington, DC, 1906).
[14] Judd Polk, 'Plight of Puerto Rico', *Political Science Quarterly*, 57/4 (1942), 485.

century the *jíbaro* (countryman) was despised because of his ignorance, his attitude to work, and his primitive or anti-modern customs, during the first decades of the twentieth century this figure was elevated to a national symbol and the 'patriarchal harmony' of the countryside was idealized. Luis Llorens Torres's poetry and its general acclaim is probably the best illustration of this process.[15]

The US invasion of 1898 and the economic policies of the first years of the North American government of the island led to a drastic transformation in the interrelationship between the factors of production. The coffee trade, whose principal market was Europe, was experiencing a severe crisis, and with new tax laws and a restriction of credit as well, many hacendados, middle farmers and independent peasants were forced to sell their farms or part of their landholdings. The economic policy of the first North American governors also had a tremendous impact on the traditional sugar industry. In contrast to coffee, sugar production had been decreasing during the last decade of the nineteenth century, and by the time of the invasion a large proportion of coastal land previously used for sugar-cane was lying idle. New tax laws based on the value of land (instead of the level of production) encouraged local owners to put the land into use in order to pay the established taxes, but the restriction of credit hampered this course of action for most local landowners (of which only a small group had external sources of credit). The properties of many, who were not able to pay the new taxes, were seized by the government and put up for sale by auction. Between 1901 and 1903 more than 600 such cases were authorized.[16]

This situation led to the concentration of a large proportion of productive land in the hands of huge US sugar companies. In 1897 only 2.7 per cent of all cultivated land consisted of farms of over 500 acres (the largest category in the available statistics); in 1910 the figure was 31.4 per cent of which two-thirds consisted of farms of over 1,000 acres whose average size was 2,142 acres.[17] Farms of less than twenty acres represented 33 per cent of all cultivated land in 1897, 12.4 per cent in 1910 and 10.6 per cent in 1920.

Land concentration and the crisis in the coffee industry forced many

---

[15] See Arcadio Díaz Quiñones, 'La isla afortunada: sueños liberadores y utópicos de Luis Llorens Torres', *Sin Nombre*, 6/1 and 2 (1975).

[16] José G. del Valle, *A través de 10 años* (Barcelona, 1907), 116, 198. Also, José de Jesús Tizol, *El malestar económico de Puerto Rico* (San Juan, 1922), 86–8.

[17] US Bureau of the Census, *Thirteenth Census of the US* (Washington, DC, 1913), VII, 989.

former smallholding peasants, and the *agregados* and *medianeros* of the haciendas, now dispossessed of the land which they formerly cultivated for their basic subsistence needs, to seek employment as wage earners in order to buy basic foodstuffs from the market. A wave of migration occurred from coffee-producing areas to areas of growing economic activity, mainly the sugar plantations. From 1899 to 1910 the municipalities primarily given over to sugar cultivation increased their population by 45.4 per cent, while the population of the municipalities which concentrated on the cultivation of coffee decreased by 4.2 per cent.[18] Thus land redistribution and internal migration led to a concentration of large numbers of landless labourers in the sugar-cane areas.

The growth of the commercial cultivation of sugar-cane in Puerto Rico took place at a time of expansion in United States capital exports. This meant that for the North American companies increasingly dominating sugar production, capital was an economic factor of greater abundance than land. Towards the first decade of the twentieth century, the average investment in machinery and buildings by acre of land on farms of more than 500 acres – mainly of company tenure – was almost three times (2.75) the investment made on farms of 100 to 500 acres, associated with hacienda types of tenancy. This abundance of capital generated a tendency towards maximum land utilization, which, combined with the condition of the labour market, brought to an end the *agregado* system which had dominated the organization of production on the hacienda. By the 1920s the average acreage of land used for the cultivation of subsistence crops on the sugar-cane plantations was less than 0.076 per family unit, which was 4.5 times less than in the coffee or tobacco areas.[19]

The relation between the factors of production – land, capital and labour – in the development of commercial production of sugar was completely different from what it had been during the previous century. The productive activity was organized, therefore, on a different basis: on the buying and selling of labour, that is to say, on capitalist relations of production. The possibility of improvement in the worker's material life ceased to be a result of the forces of nature on which he had depended previously for the outcome of his crops; it also ceased to depend on the

---

[18] A. G. Quintero-Rivera, 'El capitalismo y el proletariado rural', *Revista de Ciencias Sociales*, 183–4 (1974), 66–75.

[19] Esteban Bird, *Report on the sugar industry in relation to the social and economic system of Puerto Rico* (Puerto Rico Senate, San Juan, 1942).

paternalistic goodwill of the hacendado. For the sugar corporations the workers formed a homogeneous labour force and individual economic improvement was only possible through an improvement for all: an increase in the daily wages. In this way, the struggle for economic improvements necessarily had to be a collective struggle and, as such, homogeneity came to mean solidarity.

The plantation also broke other elements of the pre-capitalist form of production; it transformed the former isolated and individual productive activity into a collective activity. This generated differences in settlement patterns. In the sugar-cane producing areas the population began to concentrate in the urban centres of the municipalities or in small villages in the countryside. (In the haciendas and in the areas of predominantly small-tenure farms the general rural settlement pattern was one of dispersion: scattered, isolated homes surrounded by land under cultivation.)[20]

The collapse of the old rural world helped to strengthen the emerging solidarity among the proletarianized agricultural labourers. This became manifest in the cultural patterns of daily life, one very illustrative case being the transformation in the co-parenthood (*compadrazgo*) bonds. On the hacienda labourers tended to choose godfathers for their children among the upper social strata, very often the hacendado himself or a member of his family. Among the independent peasants and farmers with small or medium-sized holdings, where production was carried out mostly on a family basis, the co-parenthood bonds were most often between members of the extended family. The plantation did away with both patterns and co-parenthood bonds were then established between friends and fellow workers, all members of the same social class.[21]

The artisans in the urban centres were undergoing a similar process of proletarianization. North American capital was not only invested in sugar but also in tobacco processing, which soon became the island's second export commodity. At the same time, US manufactured exports (with US control of Puerto Rico's commerce) represented a deadly competition for independent craftsmen in several trades (shoemakers, tailors, carpenters, and so on). This, together with the crisis in traditional agriculture, provided the new centres of tobacco processing with a wide

[20] Examples in *The rural land classification program of Puerto Rico* (Evanston, Ill., 1952), 247, 251–3. Also in C. F. Jones and Rafael Picó (eds.), *Symposium on the geography of Puerto Rico* (San Juan, 1955).
[21] See Sidney W. Mintz and Eric Wolf, 'An analysis of ritual co-parenthood in Puerto Rico', *Southwestern Journal of Anthropology*, 64 (1950).

labour market for a wage-based labour regime. From 1899 to 1910 the number of cigar makers increased by 197 per cent. In 1910 74.6 per cent of all cigar makers were employed by centres of more than 100 employees; in 1920, 82 per cent, of which most (78.1 per cent) were employed in factories of over 500 workers.[22]

The artisans, becoming proletarianized cigar makers, brought to the labour struggle a tradition of radicalism and the experience of organization. There is evidence of the existence of artisans' newspapers and ideological pamphlets, of guilds, co-operatives and mutual aid societies, from the 1870s. The first nationwide labour organization was founded in 1898 by these former artisans and they were the leaders in spreading the trade union movement to the countryside. The second decade of the twentieth century was characterized by great strike activity, mainly in the tobacco processing factories and in the sugar-cane plantations, and a tremendous growth of the Free Federation of Workers. After important victories in the economic struggle, in May 1915 proletarianized artisans and plantation workers decided upon the formation of a Socialist party, whose platform was clearly directed towards a radical transformation of society.

The cleavages within *la gran familia puertorriqueña* which had manifested themselves in the split of the Autonomist party in 1897 were immediately reflected in politics after the US occupation. Two political parties were formed: the Federal party represented the hacendados and their interest in maintaining their fragile social hegemony; the Republican party represented at first mainly the professional sector, which although it had constituted the left wing of the *autonomista* movement under Spanish colonial rule offered unconditional support for US rule.

The main aspirations of the professionals were indicated in their struggle to organize society in terms of the importance of the free and independent individual, and the structuring of social relations on the basis of rationality. Vis-à-vis the culture of paternalism and deference which characterized the hacienda social structure, rational social organization epitomized what was 'modern', and individualism was the guarantee for democracy. The establishment of a liberal and modern social system was for the professionals a road to possible future hegemony. To many Puerto Ricans, the US invasion of 1898 symbolized

[22] A. G. Quintero-Rivera, 'Socialist and cigarmaker: artisans' proletarianization in the making of the Puerto Rican working class', *Latin American Perspectives* 10/2–3 (1983), 31.

the arrival of liberalism and modernity. What came to be known as 'Americanization' was their hope for the establishment of a new social order.[23]

With the capitalist transformation of the economic structure during the first decade of United States domination, two distinct groups emerged within the professional sector. The transformation of the seignorial hacienda economy into a capitalist economic structure implied the development of a greater macro-integrated economy, and this created an increased demand for the professional. Capitalist development placed him, on the one hand, in a position of increased importance within the economy, but on the other, transformed his role as an independent producer. Accountants began to flourish, as did corporation lawyers, industrial managers, production engineers, and so on. The resistance of the colonial administration to the development of self-government (because this could enhance the hacendados' dominant position) caused a profound division within the professional sector. Those who had become integrated into the new economy stressed the importance of modernization and, therefore, supported North American domination; but those professionals who had kept their position as independent producers (lawyers, doctors, apothecaries and so on) retained liberalism as their basic ideal. A sizeable group of the latter, who might be called 'Jacobin professionals', abandoned, in 1904, the ranks of the Republican party which their social sector had controlled since 1899, to join the hacendado class in the reunion of *la gran familia puertorriqueña* against the colonial government and for a liberalization of the regime and self-government. Thus the Federal party of the hacendados was transformed in 1904 into the Partido Unión de Puerto Rico (Unionist party).

At the same time as the old landholding national class was losing its defensive battle, new types of proprietors were emerging with the progressive development of the capitalist plantation economy, proprietors who would eventually form a native bourgeois class of an anti-national nature. The plantation economy, concentrating on a single cash crop for export, reduced the availability of certain commodities which were previously produced locally, thus necessarily raising the level of imports. As a result there developed a strong import sector in the economy, dependent on the capitalist plantation system – whose growth

---

[23] For example Dr José C. Barbosa, *Orientando al pueblo* (San Juan, 1939), particularly the essays 'Conversación familiar' and 'Contra americanización'.

fed the need to import – as well as on trade with the United States.

The economic situation which facilitated the development of absentee-owned sugar-cane plantations during the initial years of North American domination also benefited a small group of Puerto Rican landowners who had been able to combine agricultural production with commercial activities (or merchants who had become engaged in production), and who in the organization of their production had begun to move away from the productive relationships typical of the hacienda. This process occurred predominantly in the sugar-cane industry. The incorporation of Puerto Rico into the protected North American market was very favourable for sugar exports. The crisis of the coffee economy in the years immediately following the invasion, which increased the supply of labour for the burgeoning absentee-owned sugar-cane plantations, also provided these Puerto Rican landowners with the necessary manpower for their capitalistic expansion. This increase in the supply of labour together with the greater distancing of these landowners from the hacienda *weltanschauung* explains how they developed their production on basically the same terms as the absentee plantation owners. By the early 1930s, at the pinnacle of sugar production, the combined economic power of this group of Puerto Rican landowners approximately equalled that of the four large absentee-owned companies; in 1934 their sugar mills were producing nearly half the total sugar processed.[24] With the plantation economy threatened by the hacendados through the Unionist party and also by the antagonistic class which the plantation system itself generated – the working class (and its Socialist party) – the class interests of the Puerto Rican mill or plantation owners began to focus on the defence of this economic structure. Internal capitalist competition with the US companies was secondary to the consolidation of the very basis of their position in the organization of production.

Both the mercantile and the sugar-producing bourgeoisie depended upon market relations with the United States, and on the socio-economic formation of plantations, the development of which was stimulated by North American colonial economic policies. The struggle for the establishment of a Puerto Rican nation – and, implicitly, of its own political state – was directed against North American colonial rule, which constituted the backbone of the class interests of these social

[24] Data in Gayer *et al.*, *The sugar economy*, tables 31, 33, 52–4, which have been summarized in A. G. Quintero-Rivera, *Conflictos de clase y política en Puerto Rico* (San Juan, 1976), 66–7.

groups. For this reason, they formed and acted as an anti-national bourgeoisie.

The class structure generated by a capitalist transformation under an imperialist colonial power produced a three-sided conflict. The metropolis and its allied classes controlled government, and tried through state policies to establish the basis for the control of society. The hacendados were menaced from two directions: by the new metropolis and its policies, and by the working class in its struggle against the old paternalistic order. The emerging proletariat engaged in a strong economic struggle against the sugar companies (identified with colonial rule), while its political struggle for a general social transformation was directed also at the representatives of the old order, still dominant in the socio-cultural field.

Once imperialist-dependent capitalism consolidated its overwhelming dominance over the Puerto Rican economy, the contradictions of its structure and development began to appear in a more evident way. These contradictions were manifest in certain economic processes that characterized the years 1925 to 1940. One of these beginning in 1925 was the deterioration of the terms of trade. With a base price index of 100 for 1910–14, the price of Puerto Rican exports in 1937 was 92.5 and the price of its imports, 126. In other words, in order to maintain the same level of imports (in terms of gross product) the Puerto Rican economy had to increase its gross export production by 36.2 per cent. From 1925 to 1934 there were, in fact, great increases in production, which had no effect on commercial income indexes.[25] Trade with the metropolis accounted for over 90 per cent of the island's total imports and exports and the metropolitan absolute control over the colony's mechanism of trade eventually began to affect negatively even those industries whose growth the metropolis had previously encouraged and promoted.

In an open economy, organized around export mono-cultures, the deterioration in the terms of trade has serious effects on the national income. The income generated by the productive sectors of the economy decreased, as did their share of the nation's total income. The income reduction in agriculture, for example, was 32 per cent from 1929 to 1939. The governmental and service sectors experienced a completely artificial

---

[25] Dudley Smith, *Growth of business activity in Puerto Rico and underlying causes* (Washington, DC, 1938), 42.

growth, due mainly to the establishment of direct federal welfare programmes or the so-called 'reconstruction' of the New Deal. In the fiscal year 1939–40, the expenses of the central metropolitan government in Puerto Rico exceeded those of the island's colonial administration, giving evidence of an interesting economic and political process in the 1930s through which New Deal programmes formed a kind of parallel government which responded directly to the metropolitan executive. The governmental participation permitted to the Puerto Rican political organizations was channelled through the colonial administration, and as the official government was shadowed by the 'parallel government' of New Deal programmes, influence or participation in the latter – especially by young liberal Puerto Rican professionals – had a tremendous political impact.[26] In 1936 the New Deal agency PRRA (Puerto Rico Reconstruction Administration) employed nearly 60,000 persons, which was over half the total employment in the sugar industry, and the diversity of its policies was amazing: housing, health, commerce, agricultural co-operatives, community education, and so on.[27] The growth of this 'parallel government' showed that not only at a structural but also at a super-structural level the plantation-centred socio-economic formation of dependent capitalism was in crisis.

Another economic process of this period, through which the contradictions in dependent capitalist development were clearly manifest, centred around employment. Between 1930 and 1940 the population of the country increased by 21.1 per cent, approximately at the rate it had been increasing for the previous century, while total employment increased only by 1.7 per cent, which was much less than in the previous decades when employment had experienced a growth equivalent to the growth of population. The crisis in the production sectors obviously had an impact on employment, but the employment problem in this period goes beyond this, and was rooted in the very development of dependent capitalism.

By the second decade of the century the main industries of capitalist development, sugar-cane and tobacco-processing, had found ways of increasing production without an increase in labour. From 1910 to 1934 sugar production increased more than three times from 347,000 tons to

---

[26] See Thomas G. Matthews, *Puerto Rican politics and the New Deal* (Gainesville, 1960) especially ch. 6.

[27] A. Monteagudo and A. Escamez, *Album de oro de Puerto Rico* (Havana, 1939) and *PRAA según la prensa* (compilation of newspaper clippings bound in three volumes and kept in the Puerto Rican Collection of the General Library of the University of Puerto Rico).

1,114,000, while total agricultural employment in the industry increased only 5 per cent from 87,643 workers to 92,398. This means that while in 1910 25.3 agricultural labourers were needed to produce 100 tons of sugar, in 1934 only 8.3 were used. There are no reliable figures for tobacco-processing in the early 1930s, but between 1910 and 1920 the same process was evident: a 12 per cent increase in production with a 26 per cent reduction in employment.

The stagnation in sugar-cane and tobacco-manufacturing employment brought the proletarianization process to a standstill. It was precisely the transformation in these industries that had provided a material base for the formation of a Puerto Rican proletariat at the beginning of the century, and cigar makers and sugar-cane workers had been the most important sectors in its organizations. The Puerto Rican working class, formed in the initial stage of capitalist development of these industries – when employment was on the increase – was born believing that proletarianization would cover the entire country. As the life patterns of the seignorial world began to disintegrate, workers, through labour education and trade union action, took off the blinkers of deference (and religion) which held them back from the ideological struggle. The victory of socialism, the 1919 programme of the Socialist party suggested, was certain and inevitable.

From the mid 1920s, however, the working class faced a situation in which the seignorial world continued to disintegrate but this did not mean, as it did before, an enlargement of the proletariat. *Agregados* and hacienda labourers were becoming not proletarians but *marginados* (the marginal poor). There was a tremendous growth of underemployment in the service sector, in individual petty trading and in the *chiripeo* (unstable and sporadic jobs). This period also saw the emergence and growth of home-based, domestic industry, characterized by miserable wages and long hours.[28] Neither these workers, nor of course the unemployed, shared the experiences from which the working class had developed the elements of an alternative culture centred on a combative solidarity.

Thus the labour movement was weakened in various ways. The *marginados* were very difficult to organize in the trade union structure of the Free Federation of Workers (FLT). Besides, the increase in the industrial reserve army represented a threat to the trade union struggle. There is evidence of stagnation in gross wages from 1924 onwards, and

[28] See US Department of Labor, *Appendixes supporting report on home needlework industry* (Washington, DC, 1937).

of a proportional reduction in the value of labour in the productive sector. There is also evidence that many strikes were suppressed during this period. But most important of all, the paralysis in the proletarianization process and the growth of *marginados* shattered the faith of the working class in the certainty of its future victory. This led to a coalition of the Socialist party with the pro-American party of the anti-national bourgeoisie in order to participate in government and put through specific measures leading to immediate improvement. In a situation of increasing misery, this (unsuccessful) reformist approach to politics demoralized party militants and in turn led to corruption or apathy. It also generated a tremendous growth of the 'revivalist' Protestant sects.[29]

The contradictory nature of the development of dependent capitalism in Puerto Rico also led to changes within other social classes. By the end of the 1920s, the former quasi-hegemonic class of hacendados had lost the structural basis of its very existence. The absence of a class that could formulate some ideological-cultural project in its struggle for hegemony produced a profound cultural crisis in the country; a crisis which the intellectual generation of the period epitomized as what they termed 'the search for identity'.[30] This crisis was intensified by the crisis in the alternative political ideology of the working class. Also, the dream of Americanization – the new order of democratic modernity – held by the professional sector early in the century disappeared in the economic crisis of the 1930s, vanquished also by the arbitrariness of North American colonial politics of the time.[31]

This ideological identity crisis led to two political movements, each responding to different social classes of the dying world of the hacienda and with nationalism their common denominator. The independent smallholding peasants had traditionally supported the struggles of the hacendado as subordinates in a common culture; they had never, as a class, sought power themselves. Only with the failure of the hacendado's politics and with the threat of monopolistic capitalism did the descendants (in downward mobility) of these peasants, jointly with urban small proprietors, launch themselves independently into politics through a militant nationalism: a desperate struggle in which the participants were determined to do anything, even to destroy themselves, for the

---

[29] See Samuel Silva Gotay, 'La iglesia ante la pobreza: el caso de las iglesias protestantes históricas', *Revista de Administración Pública*, 4/2 (Puerto Rico, 1971).
[30] The best example of which is A. S. Pedreira, *Insularismo* (Madrid, 1934).
[31] Widely illustrated and demonstrated in Roberto H. Todd, *Desfile de gobernadores 1898–1943* (San Juan, 1943). Todd, a professional man, was a founding member of the pro-American party.

conservation of what they considered to be the Puerto Rican way of life.[32]

In spite of being a small group, the Nationalist party was at the centre of most of the important political events of the 1930s since, within the cultural crisis, the party represented a clearly alternative way of life. However, being the last redoubt of the traditional society many of the elements of the alternative they represented were unacceptable to the working class (for example, their defence of Hispanic traditions, their Roman Catholicism, their authoritarian and personalist style of leadership, their deference and sense of respect, and so on). From 1932 the party encouraged preparations for armed struggle. The colonial government, fearing that increased social discontent might bring this about, unleashed the forces of its repressive apparatus against the party, threatening and even destroying civil rights and basic liberties.[33]

The core group of the second type of nationalism came from the second generation of ruined hacendados for whom the professions had provided the most important channel of social re-allocation. The plantation economy, however, did not provide for sufficient growth in this sector and by the 1930s there are numerous references to unemployment among the professional classes, and even to specialized professionals, such as chemists, engineers or economists, taking refuge in government employment.[34] The hacendado class was no longer the main obstacle to development; the obstacles now emerged from the limitations of monopolistic plantation capitalism. The modernizing and Jacobin traditions of the professional sector, which had become separated at the beginning of the century, were thus reunited under a programme of social change through a movement of populist nationalism led by the professional classes. The increasing importance of the public sector in the economy, the participation of these new professionals in the liberal experiments of the New Deal and the illusion of redirecting a dependent economy through government planning, prepared the ground for a new political project through which the descendants of the hacendado class tried to develop the material basis and ideology for a new hegemonic position.

The contradictory development of dependent capitalism culminated

---

[32] For example, Pedro Albizu Compas, *República de Puerto Rico* (Montevideo, 1972), an anthology of 1930–2 documents, 24, 28–30, 69, 77 *et passim*.

[33] ACLU, Commission of Inquiry on the Civil Rights in Puerto Rico, *Report* (n.p., 1937).

[34] See Isabel Picó, *La protesta estudiantil en la década del 30* (San Juan, 1974).

in the stagnation of productive forces, in the proportional reduction of the income generated by the production sectors of the economy, and in a general fall in the standard of living. Plantation capitalism was seen as responsible for working men's misery, the bankruptcy of hacendados, the pauperization of smallholding peasants, unstable employment and growing unemployment, the limitations in the economic participation of the growing professional sector, as well as political corruption and the menace to individual civil liberties. Both the remaining classes of the old seignorial social formation and the classes which developed with its transformation to plantation capitalism had been cast aside since the late 1920s, both at the structural and ideologico-political level. The union of 'the people', with the professionals in the public sector as their natural leaders, emerged as an all-embracing political alternative.

Populism, which was a superstructural response to the development of a certain type of productive base and had a decisive impact upon that base, struck the final blow against the socio-economic formation of plantations and the class politics that their emergence and consolidation had made possible. Furthermore, it opened gateways to the growth of a dependent manufacturing capitalism which in the 1940s and 1950s replaced rural capitalism and transformed Puerto Rican society. Contemporary processes, classes and conflicts were engendered in this transformation.

7

THE DOMINICAN REPUBLIC, *c.* 1870–1930

The proclamation of the independent Dominican Republic on 27 February 1844 crowned the efforts of *La Trinitaria*, a secret society founded for that purpose six years earlier when Santo Domingo, the eastern two-thirds of the island of Hispaniola, was still united with Haiti. It was the second time sovereignty had been proclaimed. The first, so-called 'ephemeral' independence (from Spain), brought about by Núñez de Cáceres in 1821, had only lasted a few months, after which the capital city's keys were handed to the president of Haiti. The new sovereignty lasted long enough – and had a sufficiently appealing legitimation, based as it was on antagonism to neighbouring Haiti – to make 27 February the national holiday on which the birth of the Republic is commemorated. Yet in the period up to 1930 sovereignty was again twice suspended. Before two decades of new-found independence had passed the country had re-annexed itself to Spain, and remained under Spanish control for four years (1861–5); from 1916–24 it was under military occupation by the United States. In the remainder of the period, numerous plans were made to give up sovereignty in exchange for foreign protection. Seen in this light, the country's independence remained, if not ephemeral, at least tenuous. The passage from re-annexation by Spain to occupation by the United States shows the direction in which the external forces, to which the Republic was subjected, changed. From a country still embedded in a European, quasi-colonial network, it had become, by the end of the nineteenth century, a client-state of the United States. It is against the moving background of this pervasive, long-term change that the historical events in the period under discussion should constantly be placed.

What was called independence by the Dominicans was secession to the Haitians. Their doctrine of the unity and indivisibility of the island demanded counter-measures to be taken, and for the next fifteen years numerous invasions into Dominican territory testified to at least this common purpose of successive Haitian governments. Surprisingly, in view of the economic, demographic and military superiority which Haiti enjoyed over her eastern neighbour during much of the nineteenth century, they did not succeed.

Much of the Dominicans' improbable success in defeating the constant waves of invaders may be attributed to Pedro Santana, a cattle rancher from the eastern plains who became the Republic's first *caudillo*-president in 1844 and who was to dominate the politics of the Dominican Republic for the next twenty years. The mode of production of the Dominican Republic's labour-intensive ranches (*hatos*) made for close and often paternalistic ties between the *hatero* and his working men, trained in horse-riding and the use of weapons. Santana was able to build an effective and highly mobile army on the basis of this type of personal following. Juan Pablo Duarte, leader of *La Trinitaria* – and along with Francisco Sánchez and Ramón Mella one of the venerated Founding Fathers of the Republic – saw his urban ideals of a civic democracy promptly clash with the need for forceful military leadership. In the middle of 1844, Duarte once more had to seek the exile from which, only a few months earlier, he had triumphantly returned.

Within a few years of independence and Santana's seizure of power a rival *caudillo* presented himself: Buenaventura Báez, who under Santana had distinguished himself as a military commander in the country's southern areas, where his family and personal following resided, and who became president for the first time in 1849. The contending factions thus created – Santanistas versus Baecistas – were the first real power groupings in the young Republic. Their common traits would character-ize the political movements and 'parties' well into the twentieth century: loosely structured followings with a regional base, grouped around a leader whose title might indicate military experience, but mostly of a non-professional kind. In a society with nearly constant internal warfare, the lines between soldier and civilian were blurred, and it was possible to be a 'general', a landowner and a merchant at the same time. No single one of these activities conferred particular prestige in a country where generals abounded and land was not as yet scarce. The prestige of a *caudillo* derived rather from his capacity to weld personal relationships, on the basis of actual and promised transactions of goods, privileges and loyalties, into a durable and multi-layered network of patronage, of which the leader was both the centre and the apex.

Whatever ideological differences can be discerned between the several politico-military factions without formal organizations or programmes that dominated political life after independence, these had at least some link with the socio-economic structure of the region where they were based. Thus, the fertile central Cibao valley, with a large number of relatively prosperous small and middle-sized tobacco farms, which supported a stable commercial and professional elite in its urban centre Santiago, many of whose sons studied at European universities, tended to sprinkle its political movements with more liberal-democratic notions than did the oligopoly of fine-wood exporters in the north-western region around the port of Monte Cristi, or the eastern group of cattle ranchers. Yet even the powerful Cibao elite, whose export business sustained the country's economy well into the last decades of the nineteenth century, thereby making their region politically powerful, always had to transact with local leaders whose popular appeal was based on a keen Creole insight into political realities and cultural idiosyncrasies. And much the same can be said of the socially much less stable southern coastal regions which from the last quarter of the century when sugar was produced began to challenge the Cibao's supremacy.

The small and thinly spread population – estimated in 1871 at 150,000, in a territory of approximately 50,000 square kilometres – was itself a good reason to doubt the country's capacity to build an adequate civil administration and military apparatus. This doubt was only aggravated by the proximity of the more populous and better organized Republic of Haiti. As a consequence, the external relations of the Dominican Republic were to a great extent governed by the perceived need to seek protection – economically, militarily, politically – from a powerful third country willing to act as a countervailing force against what was seen as Haiti's constant menace.

Even before the proclamation of Independence, a 'Plan Levasseur' – named after the consul of France in Port-au-Prince – had been designed in which France would play the protector's role. Such plans abounded in the second half of the nineteenth century, sometimes concocted by the government in power, sometimes by its – usually exiled – opposition. The most sought-after potential protector-states were France, Spain and the United States. In secret negotiations – which often provoked panicky rumours and deepened political animosity – the Dominicans not only offered all kinds of economic concessions, but often also used as bait the lease or even sale of the north-eastern peninsula of Samaná which with its splendid, strategically located bay had great potential as a naval base and bunker station. Of course, in such negotiations diverse Dominican interests were intertwined. Not only might there be a genuine interest in strengthening the country's economy and defence, but there was also the government of the day's interest to defend itself against internal opposition with the protector-state's support, or conversely, the opposition's aim to seek a strong ally in its struggle against the government; the victors would divide the spoils. These internal political rivalries also made the country's relations to Haiti somewhat more complicated than has been indicated so far. Whereas Dominican governments in power would consistently refer to Haiti's warlike intentions as a reason for foreign protection, conceivably at the same time Dominican exiles might be preparing an invasion from the neighbouring country, abetted by the Haitian authorities; thus, Dominican fear of Haiti and the Dominican government's fear of opposition might coincide. Santana (president 1844–8, 1853–6 and 1858–65) showed a preference for the protection of the United States, otherwise Spain; Báez (president 1849–53, 1856–8, 1868–74 and 1876–8) leaned towards France, or Spain – and later the United States. In 1861, a year in which the civil war made it hard for the United States to intervene, Santana actually persuaded Spain to re-establish political control of the Dominican Republic. However, within two years there began a guerilla struggle against Spanish rule (the War of Restoration), strongly backed by the Cibao and its German-orientated merchants, and independence was restored in 1865.

In retrospect, and compared with the political and economic dependence on the United States which dates from the turn of the century, the predominance of European interests in the Dominican Republic during the late nineteenth century had, perhaps, some advantages. Unlike the United States Europe was far away, and it consisted of a number of rival powers. The Republic's main export crop, tobacco, went mostly to Hamburg; German tobacco buyers and agents were concentrated in Santiago and in the port of Puerto Plata. The London money market provided one of the earliest Dominican foreign loans: in 1869, while Báez was president, the so-called Hartmont loan of £420,000 was arranged; the claims of its bondholders would echo for many years to come. France, too, provided capital; in the 1880s it established a National Bank in Santo Domingo, as well as a telegraph system; it also had shipping interests in the country. In such a configuration, the Dominican governments, however weak on the international scene, had at least a slight chance to play off the remote and competing European powers against each other. They could also threaten the European powers with the growth of United States interests in the Caribbean. Of course, such an unstable balance of power was not deliberately created by the Dominican Republic, but while it was there, the margin for action that it provided was sometimes cleverly exploited. This margin became much smaller once the geographically close United States established its political and economic hegemony, at a time when telegraph, the telephone and steamships were bringing the Dominican Republic ever closer to its northern neighbour. From then on, only rivalries within the US (between economic sectors, political parties or rival government institutions) lent themselves to weak and always delicate Dominican efforts to exploit external forces. No growth in population, in economic resources or in organizational stability during this period could prevent the strengthening and deepening of the Dominican Republic's dependence on the United States.

The period following the Dominican Republic's second independence from Spain in 1865 was one of administrative chaos, revolution and civil war. Santana had died at the end of the Spanish annexation, but his followers regrouped with others against Báez who was president from 1868 to 1874. The main political factions now were called 'reds' (with the Baecistas as their nucleus) and 'blues' (the Cibao opponents of Báez together with the eastern inheritors of the Santana tradition), and they fought each other relentlessly and violently. The six months' government of the idealistic and educated apothecary Ulíses Espaillat in 1876 only served as an ironic counterpoint to all this. In these years Haiti became less active as an invader and more instrumental as a financier and ally of one or other of the contending factions. Similarly, merchants in Curaçao and St Thomas financed the conspiracies and revolutions, as did some merchant-adventurers from the United States.

Towards the end of the 1870s politics began to stabilize. Gregorio Luperón, hero of the War of Restoration, was increasingly recognized as political and military leader of the 'blues'. Born in the northern port of Puerto Plata, of humble social origins, his military talents, self-taught classical education, and his unmistakable talent for leadership and negotiation, enabled him to deal with the partly foreign merchants and the landowners of the Cibao on a basis of mutual understanding. After Báez's last government (1876–8), Luperón's 'blue' party became the most powerful in the country, and attracted several key persons from other regions and from the capital. A party such as this amounted to little more than a network, maintained and manipulated by Luperón through travel and correspondence, but the leader's power – being at the centre of the web – was none the less diminished for that.

Luperón did not aspire to the presidency himself (although he had served as provisional president in 1879–80); he preferred to pick the candidates. Thus he had Monsignor Meriño, the highest prelate of the Republic, govern from 1880–2, and for the next two years (1882–4) the presidency was entrusted to Ulíses Heureaux, a personal protégé of Luperón. Heureaux (or Lilís, as he was popularly known and by which name he is the hero of countless anecdotes and popular tales) was, like Luperón, from Puerto Plata and came from an even poorer background. He received his military training in the War of Restoration, under Luperón. His astuteness, courage and intelligence facilitated his rapid rise, first in military rank, and afterwards in governmental positions in the Cibao area. Once president, Heureaux's challenge to Luperón's political supremacy was only a matter of time. Between 1884 and 1887, two presidents – Billini and Woss y Gil – were appointed more on Heureaux's than on Luperón's instigation, and from then until his death in 1899 Heureaux kept the presidency to himself. Luperón, who sought exile in St Thomas, was kept at a distance. In this way, the political stability wrought by Luperón hardened into a dictatorship. In his cabinets, besides the 'blues' Heureaux increasingly included members from other political factions. Those local 'generals' and their followers who as yet had not chosen Heureaux's side were either persuaded to change their mind with the help of money and appointments, or were ruthlessly eliminated.

The length of Heureaux's dictatorship certainly had much to do with the exceptional political sagacity of this *caudillo*. But the changing economic structure of the country should be taken into account as well. The establishment of modern sugar plantations during these years created a new elite of financiers and agrarian entrepreneurs in the southern coastal areas. This broadened the economic base of the country, and widened the sources of credit for the government, which for the first time could play one powerful regional elite against another. Between 1875 and 1882, some 30 new sugar plantations were founded, mostly on the south-eastern plains which until then had been used for cattle ranching. Among the new sugar planters were quite a few Cubans who had left their country because of the Ten Years' War (1868–78), and who wanted to continue to apply their capital and expertise to a type of modern agriculture which, with the growing United States market so near, seemed to hold much promise. The export of coffee and cacao also increased considerably in the last decades of the century. Between 1888 and 1897, sugar exports doubled from some 400,000 to 800,000 quintales, cacao exports increased from 9,730 to 36,000 quintales and coffee exports from 2,500 to 9,000 quintales. Tobacco exports, on the other hand, stagnated. New ports – San Pedro de Macorís on the south coast, Sánchez on the Samaná Bay – appeared; old ones – Puerto Plata, Santo Domingo – grew (see table 1). The need for labour on the new plantations encouraged seasonal internal migration. Immigrants from Haiti and the neighbouring British islands also came to reinforce the growing sugar proletariat. Increased economic activity attracted more skilled immigrants from the Caribbean and from farther away: Cubans, Puerto Ricans, Sephardic Jews from Curaçao – a small group of whom had already arrived in the 1840s – Italians, Spaniards, and subjects of the Ottoman Empire. By 1898, the population of the Dominican Republic was said to be 458,000. The country's infrastructure improved considerably. Between 1887 and 1909 a number of railways were completed, linking the major exporting towns of the Cibao (Santiago, Moca, La Vega, San Francisco de Macorís) with the ports of Puerto Plata and Sánchez. Bridges and ports were built. Many new towns were founded. The educational system improved under the stimulus of the famed Puerto Rican educator and sociologist Eugenio María de Hostos. Some progress could be noted in the organization of the civil administration. The armed forces underwent the first efforts at professionalization; a small navy was set up. Cultural life also prospered: Pedro F. Bonó (whose noteworthy sociological essays were edited in 1964 by E. Rodríguez Demorizi under the title *Papeles de Bonó*) had published in Paris his *El montero*, one of the earliest Latin American 'realistic' novels. In 1882 Manuel de Jesús Galván's *Enriquillo*, the famous *indianista* novel, appeared. Of the many female poets of the end of the century, Salomé Ureña de Henríquez stands out; her sons Pedro and Max Henríquez Ureña were to acquire international fame as historians of literature. The

Table 1. *Dominican Republic: Customs duties by port (in pesos oro), 1869, 1895, 1896*

	Santo Domingo	Puerto Plata	Sánchez	San Pedro de Macorís	Monte Cristi	Azua	Samaná	Barahona
1869	179,363	396,865	—	—	?	?	?	?
1895	415,996	290,322	210,982	252,103	105,896	32,482	20,185	1,552
1896	503,048	368,687	244,684	221,298	99,182	28,560	28,695	1,908

Source: H. Hoetink, *The Dominican people 1850–1900* (Baltimore, 1983), 65.

poet Fabio Fiallo maintained early contacts with Rubén Darío, J. J. Pérez translated Thomas More, César N. Penson translated works from the Italian and Manuel R. Objío from the French, notably Victor Hugo. In the plastic arts, the paintings and sculptures of Abelardo Rodríguez Urdaneta deserve mention. Finally, regionalism, although not disappearing, could for the first time since independence be made subservient to national policy and to a growing national consciousness.

Before the economic change and economic growth of the 1880s and 1890s, social stratification had been regionally circumscribed. The centres of each region had little contact with each other: a journey overland from Puerto Plata to the capital Santo Domingo had taken some four days, and it had been considered wise to make a will before departure. Every region had some 'important' families, whose names could open doors for their clients. There was hardly any great wealth then: descent, and continuity of residence, were the main determinants of social prestige. A very large portion of the population had been living in virtually a barter economy. All this now changed. The value of land increased, money began to penetrate all social layers; agrarian wage labour became more common. The artisanal differentiation increased, as did the diversity of the service sector of the economy. The regional notables, the *dones*, intermingled more frequently with each other and with the *señores*, the group of assimilated immigrants who had made their fortunes. In this way, a national bourgeoisie was being formed, which towards the end of the century had established exclusive social clubs which were one of the social barriers erected against those who came to belong to the stratum just beneath this top layer: *los de segunda*, those of the second category, who because of skills, education, descent and physical traits, as well as income, were distinguished from 'the people', but were now no longer able to penetrate the national elite. Interestingly, several families, often rather dark skinned, who had risen under Heureaux's patronage and had profited from the long duration of his regime to send their children to the right European universities and have them marry sons and daughters of *señores* and, less frequently, long established families, found a place in this new elite.

The difference in wealth between the two extremes of the social scale increased a great deal in these years. At the same time, between these extremes, many new positions were created, as the division of labour in all sectors of society became more complex. While this process of economic and social expansion was going on, social mobility was considerable and in some cases striking. However, towards the end of the century, when the new stratification had crystallized and stabilized, the social demarcation lines were more clearly drawn and more difficult to cross than had been the case before these changes took place. New residential areas, especially in the capital, began to separate the rich from the poor. More than before, unequivocally negroid features became an obstacle for individual mobility: the new national elite used the pretext of descent as a criterion of selection with greater consistency than had been possible in a time when humble soldiers of fortune, fighting in whatever revolution offered them chances, might become powerful over night, and when fortunes could still be made or lost in a few days of political turmoil. Such chances became rare once Heureaux had imposed his order on society. Even the army, though remaining a channel of mobility for the lower strata, had to pay a social price for its incipient professionalization; as José Martí observed in the early 1890s, Dominican soldiers were predominantly black, whereas there were many mulattos among the officers.

The irony of this process was of course that Heureaux became, in many respects, an anachronism in a society that had been moulded during his regime. The dark-skinned general of popular extraction, thrown up by guerilla war and revolution, now had to hold his own amidst a growing bourgeoisie, a coalition of producers and merchants who, as he well knew, did not accept him socially and whose political loyalty and financial support were, in the last instance, dependent on the peace and order that he would be able to maintain. The honorific title that the nation had bestowed on him was, after all, *El Pacificador*.

Import and export duties had been, since the inception of the Republic, the government's main sources of income. Several arrangements had been devised between merchants and governments to ensure a steady flow of cash. Thus, in the 1870s the system gained acceptance whereby a number of merchants would form a company which would take over the customs administration of a port, in exchange for which control the company would provide the government (that is, the president) with a fixed monthly sum. The leader of the 'blue' party, Luperón, took an active part in the powerful company of Puerto Plata. The president could further borrow money from individual merchants, often in exchange for temporary exoneration from customs duties. Heureaux continued these financing methods. In his financial deals, the distinction between Heureaux as a private person and Heureaux as president was not always easy to make, either in his borrowing or his spending. Of course, such a lack of separation between private and public means prevailed throughout all administrations. In times of financial hardship for the state, the higher officials were supposed to pay the expenses of their office out of their own pockets; on the other hand, it was commonly accepted that such an official should receive commissions in his dealings with private enterprise. Foreign loans were a further source of cash for the governments of the Dominican Republic. Within the Caribbean area, the islands of Curaçao and St Thomas were important financial and trade centres for the independent states. In particular, the long-established Sephardic communities on these islands acted as financiers and brokers: the firm of Jessurun in Curaçao financed much of Buenaventura Báez's political undertakings, and the St Thomas house of Jacobo Pereyra lent considerable sums to the Dominican governments in the last decades of the century. Not only had the Jewish communities on these islands a reliable family network throughout the area, they also had close contacts with the financial centres of Europe and they often served as intermediaries for Dominican governments seeking loans on the European markets. The Hartmont loan (1869) had come about in this manner, as did the loan of £770,000, contracted by Heureaux in 1888 with the Amsterdam bank of Westendorp and Company, which was followed two years later by a further loan of £900,000. In both cases Westendorp arranged the issue of bonds in several European countries. Part of the first Westendorp loan served to settle once and for all the claims of the Hartmont bondholders whose actions, often sustained by diplomacy, had worried a number of Dominican governments. The foreign credit further served to enable Heureaux to lessen his dependence on the local credit companies. The latter realized this, and much of the criticism directed against Heureaux's financial policy came from merchant circles, who feared the loss of the high interest produced by internal loans. The second Westendorp loan was ostensibly made to finance railway building. Heureaux, however, needed money not only to improve the country's infrastructure, but also to perpetuate his own power: countless appointments, 'pensions' and 'assignments' were handed out; many friends had to be paid off; many potential enemies had to be bought.

As part of its contract with the Dominican government, Westendorp was allowed to establish an office in the Dominican Republic, commonly called the *Régie*, which administered all customs; a fixed percentage of the receipts was handed to the government, the rest served for amortization and interest of the loans. Basically, this was the system under which the local credit companies had operated, but now it had become nationwide and under foreign control. The relations between the Dutch director of the *Régie* and President Heureaux became, after some initial frictions, very harmonious indeed. The Dutchman embarked on private commercial ventures of his own, and started to neglect the interests of his superiors and, indirectly, of the bondholders in Europe. Bankrupt, Westendorp transferred its Dominican claims in 1892 to the San Domingo Improvement Company of New York. A year earlier, a commercial treaty with the United States had been signed which exempted a large list of products from import duties in both countries, causing vehement diplomatic protests from several European countries. The loss of European preponderance in Dominican economic and financial matters was now a fact. The independent and simultaneous efforts by Heureaux's minister of finance Eugenio Generoso de Marchena – of Curaçaoan Sephardic origin – to establish a special financial relationship with France were clearly out of tune with the changed circumstances. When de Marchena went so far as to show presidential ambitions, the dictator had him executed.

At the very end of his regime, when he realized how little leeway the new United States connection left him, Heureaux himself made an equally desperate attempt to interest a British consortium in the country's finances. Before this initiative had run its course, Heureaux was killed, on 26 July 1899, in the Cibao town of Moca, by members of the same bourgeoisie of landholders, merchants and financiers which had solidified during his regime, and now wanted to see its growth and status translated into political power.

After some brief transitional governments following the death of Heureaux, Juan Isidro Jiménez was appointed president. Head of an exporting firm of fine woods in the north-western town of Monte Cristi, his estrangement from Heureaux had driven him into exile and even to an attempt at armed invasion. Vice president was Horacio Vázquez, who had been involved in the conspiracy to assassinate Heureaux. Soon the apparently inescapable rivalry between the two highest office-holders made itself felt, leading to the formation of two political factions, the Jimenistas and the Horacistas (also called *bolos* and *colúos*, terms from the ever-popular cockfights). The fanatical and passionate struggle between them would dominate much of the first three decades of the twentieth century. Although continuities with earlier *caudillista* factions are hard to establish, it is perhaps fair to surmise that amongst the followers of Vázquez, a man from the Gibao, many of the former 'blue' party could be counted. A hard core of Lilisistas – admirers of the murdered dictator – persisted for some time, and even got hold of the presidency in 1903 under Woss y Gil, after which they were slowly absorbed by the other movements.

Political life in the Republic in the early years of the twentieth century reached a degree of instability comparable only to the late 1860s and early 1870s. Civil war, revolutions and *coups d'état* were once again all too common occurrences. The semblance of hierarchic organization in civil and military service, created under Heureaux's hard regime, was succeeded by a system in which once again local 'generals' and their following placed themselves at the service of competing political factions. Of these regional *caudillos*, the best known became Desiderio Arias from the Monte Cristi area, who for many years had absolute control over the region (and its customs house); he remained active until the early days of the Trujillo regime when he was killed.

Only the presidency of Ramón Cáceres (1906–11), Vázquez's cousin and one of the murderers of Heureaux, restored some order to the public administration. Some public works were carried out, at least, and the unruly Monte Cristi area was brutally silenced by concentrating the rural population in a few central places, and killing their cattle. When Cáceres was killed, another period of revolutions and brief presidencies began.

Under such circumstances of excessive internal instability, not only was it inconceivable to think of efficient financial administration, it was equally utopian to hope for lasting and effective arrangements with the country's foreign creditors. In 1901, President Jiménez had appeared to be on the verge of reaching a satisfactory understanding with both the San Domingo Improvement Company and the European creditors, when a revolution led by his vice president toppled him. His successor had to allow the United States government itself to represent the interests of the San Domingo Improvement Company from then on. Warships from France, Germany, Holland and Italy appeared on the Dominican coast several times to reinforce the claims of their citizens, some of whom lived in the Dominican Republic, like, for example, the Italo-Dominican Vicini, one of the country's largest sugar planters and traders, who had provided Heureaux with considerable loans.

President Morales Languasco (1904) toyed with a familiar idea: to seek the status of protectorate under the United States flag. US involvement in the internal affairs of the Dominican Republic in fact increased without such a dramatic step actually being taken. In that year, for instance, the United States government appointed a financial agent with the power to intervene in the administration of the customs offices; the receipts, after withholding the creditors' share, should go to such Dominican government as was recognized by the United States. This stipulation, necessary perhaps because of the not infrequent presence of two contending governments on national territory, could easily lend itself to a practice whereby the United States could stop the flow of money to any Dominican government of which it did not approve.

A convention between the two countries, signed in 1907, went a step further. Negotiations with the country's creditors led to a reduction of the foreign debt from a nominal $21 million to $12 million, and of the internal debt from a nominal $2 million to $600,000. The refinancing of the debt was undertaken by the bankers Kuhn, Loeb and Company of New York, who made their loan conditional on the administration of the Dominican customs by the US government and the appointment of the Morton Trust Company of New York as fiscal agent. It was further stipulated in the convention that, except by previous agreement between the two governments, customs duties could not be altered, nor the public debt increased. In practice this meant United States control over all spending departments of the government. When President Cáceres in 1908 established a ministry of public works and wanted to spend $500,000 on several projects, he needed US approval, which was given when Cáceres had a US citizen appointed as the new department's head. Even this direct influence was not sufficient, in the US government's opinion, to ensure that the Republic fulfilled its international obligations. The continuing chaos in those government departments not as yet controlled by North Americans was seen as an obstacle to the implementation of the convention of 1907. Moreover, revolutionaries from time to time occupied ports and customs offices, and incurred debts, which increased the national debt. Direct US intervention, such as the forced resignation of President Victoria in 1912, did not produce the desired results. Nor did the election with the assistance of 'impartial' State Department observers of President Bordas in 1913. In 1914 there was a new development: the appointment by the United States government of a financial expert who would administer and reorganized the entire public finance structure. However, President Juan Isidro Jiménez, although in power thanks to US intervention, refused to meet these and other demands.

On 19 November 1915 the US Minister in the Dominican Republic, William W. Russell, delivered a note from the acting Secretary of State, in which the appointment of a North American 'financial adviser' was again urgently recommended, as was the establishment of a national guard, to be placed under command of United States officers. A rebellion by Desiderio Arias, at the time Jiménez's minister for the armed forces, provided a pretext to send the first US marines to the country to 'assist' President Jiménez, who thereupon resigned. The new president, Francisco Henríquez y Carvajal, refused, however, to heed the urgent recommendations contained in the diplomatic note of 19 November. The United States therefore decided not to recognize his government and cut off that part of the customs receipts to which the Dominican government was entitled. The end of Henríquez's government came when, on 26 November 1916, US navy captain H. S. Knapp officially proclaimed the military occupation of the country. Knapp became the first military governor.

The United States occupation of the Dominican Republic, which lasted eight years (1916–24), had the results and caused the reactions which in the light of the preceding relations between the two countries were predictable. On the one hand, the enforced political stability made it possible to organize the Dominican governmental apparatus effectively. Education, public health, police and public works received efficient attention; Governor Knapp, even though he put United States citizens at the head of most government departments, was careful to make good use of the advice and energy of many capable Dominicans, willing to enter public service under these circumstances. The civil population was effectively disarmed; the army had already been disbanded during President Henríquez's administration – for lack of funds. The horrible violence between civilian factions came to an end. On the other hand, the occupation dealt a severe blow to Dominican self-esteem, and the shocking offence to national dignity left traumatic scars. Further bitterness was caused by acts of tactlessness, aggression and even torture of the civilian population by members of the occupying forces, even though others, especially in the field of public health, were able to win Dominican sympathy.

Table 2. *Dominican Republic: main trading partners,*
1910–16

Year	Percentage of exports and imports				
	USA	Germany	France	UK	Others
Exports					
1910	70.60	19.30	6.67	1.30	2.13
1911	52.34	26.77	9.82	6.94	4.13
1912	58.74	14.32	7.53	10.04	9.37
1913	53.49	19.76	8.48	2.31	15.96
1914	80.96	7.73	2.72	1.76	6.83
1915	79.19	0:04	1.25	0.55	18.97
1916	80.88	—	1.34	0.49	17.29
Imports					
1910	59.75	17.27	3.36	11.44	8.18
1911	59.29	18.22	3.07	11.16	8.26
1912	62.06	19.81	2.74	8.76	6.63
1913	62.22	18.10	2.96	7.88	8.84
1914	66.17	13.79	2.40	8.43	9.21
1915	80.73	1.04	1.02	6.92	10.29
1916	87.13	—	1.30	4.13	7.44

Source: Patrick E. Bryan, 'The transformation of the economy of the
Dominican Republic, 1870–1916' (unpublished PhD thesis, University of London, 1977), 172.

United States involvement in Dominican sugar production had begun
during the first decade of the century. The position of the United States
as the Dominican Republic's main trading partner had been
strengthened considerably in the six years prior to the occupation, not
least because of the collapse of trade with Germany as a result of the first
world war (see table 2). During and after the occupation, US penetration
of the Dominican sugar industry accelerated. Large areas of the southern
coastal region were now in the hands of the South Porto Rico Sugar
Company and other US enterprises, and several legislative measures
were taken to foster US influence, to increase the size of the companies,
and to lower or even cancel export duties on sugar. In the boom harvest
of 1919–20 nineteen *ingenios* produced nearly 200,000 tonnes of sugar.
Without a costly army – and equally expensive revolutions, with an
orderly administration and a relatively prosperous economy, the
country's financial situation improved and the amortization of the
outstanding loans proceeded as a matter of course. On the other hand, the
military government of occupation itself raised the level of the national
debt by contracting several new loans.

In the sugar areas of the south the occupation forces had to contend with armed bands, known as *gavilleros*, which roamed the thinly populated region, plundering indiscriminately, and not afraid of armed encounters. It is hard to judge whether these bands were anything more than the apolitical continuation of a long guerilla tradition, or whether they should be ascribed some nationalist sentiment or even ideology. To clear the area of their activities, the rural population was finally concentrated in a few towns. But by then many country dwellers had already fled spontaneously, selling their plots to eager speculators who would then sell them again to sugar producers, hungry for land. The newly organized Dominican police force was active in the struggle against the *gavilleros*; one of its young officers was the future president and dictator Rafael Trujillo.

Initially, resistance to the occupation from the upper classes was rare. The merchants profited from political stability combined with increased public expenditure, and the intellectuals were for the most part willing to co-operate with the astute and cautious governor Knapp. The entry of the United States into the first world war changed much of this. The US government now paid less attention to Dominican affairs; many of the best-qualified military officers were replaced; Knapp himself was succeeded by the much less tactful governor Snowden. Towards the end of the decade international attention was focused on the plight of the country. In Latin America a publicity and diplomatic campaign was launched; in the United States, labour leader Samuel Gompers showed interest and sympathy. From his exile in Cuba, deposed President Henríquez y Carvajal demanded an orderly restoration of his country's sovereignty and his reinstatement as its president. In 1919 he met with some willingness on the part of the US government to start negotiations on how to end the occupation. The next year, the first Dominican organization to declare itself openly against the country's occupied status, the Unión Nacional Dominicana, made itself known. In 1921, the US Senate ordered an investigation into the alleged atrocities committed against the population of the areas in which the *gavilleros* operated; the resulting report confirmed them. Finally, in 1922, the so-called Hughes–Peynado plan was agreed upon. Alongside the military government, which kept control of security and customs, an 'administrative government' was to be formed. It would prepare for elections, after which the occupation would end. Control of the customs, however, would remain with a US-appointed official until such time as the Republic's debts had been paid. The sugar planter (of Italian descent) Juan Batista Vicini was made provisional president, elections were held and on 18 September 1924 the last US marines left the Dominican Republic.

The presidency now fell into the hands of Horacio Vázquez. His rival Federico Velázquez, who had started his political career as a close collaborator of President Cáceres, but who had since then organized a following of his own, became vice president. In 1924, Vázquez signed a new convention with the United States, which in some respects was an improvement on that of 1907, and which, furthermore, allowed him to contract a foreign loan of $10 million. In the wake of the heated debates engendered by this convention, Velázquez abandoned the vice presidency in 1926. Meanwhile Vázquez's government profited from the benevolence with which the US government treated him, from the new and expanded administrative structure and from the economic prosperity that characterized the mid 1920s. On the other hand, the new army (of which Trujillo in these years became commander) wanted its slice of the budget, as did the president's numerous political allies and friends – and their friends – who had to be satisfied in order to maintain the *caudillo* in power and to preserve stability. As a result corruption became widespread. And finally factionalism raised its head once more. Vázquez's followers demanded that he, who by rather dubious constitutional reasoning had already decided that his presidential term was to be six instead of four years, should present himself for a further term of office. By this time the brief period of relative prosperity had ended and protest against a renewal of the Vázquez administration culminated in a 'civic movement' led by the Santiago politician Rafael Estrella Ureña. Demonstrations, and a march on the capital, plus the decision of Trujillo not to intervene militarily against the opposition movement, determined Vázquez's fate. On 2 March 1930 he resigned after appointing Estrella Ureña minister of the interior and of the police. Estrella Ureña constitutionally succeeded him, and started to prepare for the next general elections.

With Vázquez in exile, the elections of 16 May 1930 would probably have been won by Estrella Ureña and his running mate, Velázquez. It soon became clear, however, that Rafael Leonidas Trujillo Molina, commander of the armed forces, was determined to enter the political race himself as a presidential candidate. He quickly convinced Estrella Ureña to be his future vice president. Their candidacy was supported by a rapidly organized and heterogeneous Confederación de Partidos. Velázquez, suddenly abandoned, succeeded in regaining the support of several leaders of Vázquez's old Partido Nacional but could not hope to win the elections in the face of, on the one hand, an undeniable clamour for change and, on the other, severe intimidation from his opponents and their followers. On 16 August 1930 Trujillo was sworn in as president of the Republic. Just as the 30 or so years of political turmoil which followed the founding of the Republic culminated in the long dictatorship of Ulíses Heureaux, some 30 – often chaotic – years after the violent death of Heureaux the Dominican Republic fell into the hands of a new strong man, this time in charge of a well-trained army. He would maintain his grip on the country until 30 May 1961, the day of his assassination.

The regime of Heureaux had witnessed the transformation of the Dominican Republic from a Europe-orientated producer of tobacco and fine woods to a country in which sugar reigned and the United States dominated. The last-minute efforts of Heureaux to lessen this domination were doomed to fail. In Heureaux's time a feeble beginning was made to professionalize the civil service and the armed forces. The country's infrastructure was considerably expanded to fit its new economic role. In the process, a national bourgeoisie began to form, some of whose members killed the *caudillo*. Foreign debts increased dramatically in this period, and the claims of foreign creditors were closely linked to intervention by foreign states. Trujillo's regime was to witness an incipient industrialization, a further expansion of the export-orientated agrarian sector and concomitant improvements in the country's infrastructure. While economic and geopolitical realities demanded subservience to United States interests, some efforts to lessen this dependence were made. The fact that so many foreign enterprises, from banks to sugar companies, were bought by Trujillo himself tended to decrease somewhat the level of direct foreign control, as did his comparatively austere financial management. Whereas sections of the national bourgeoisie were allowed to increase their wealth during Trujillo's dictatorship, they not only lost all political control, but also had to watch a considerable number of members from lower strata receive economic and political favours from a government that, for all its harshness, could not have stayed in power for so long without an element of populist-nationalism. Small wonder, perhaps, that among those who conspired to kill Trujillo in 1961 were relatives of those who had conspired to kill Heureaux in 1899.

8

HAITI, c. 1870–1930

'Hayti is not a civilized country', observed the provisional president Boisrond Canal in 1902 when discussing with the British Minister in Port-au-Prince a case of police brutality towards a British subject.[1] Canal was speaking as a member of the educated, francophile, mulatto elite, who generally despised the great mass of black citizens whose customs they regarded as barbarous and primitive.

Haiti, which had become the first independent country of Latin America in 1804, was from the outset plagued by deep social and political divisions. While Haitians of all colours saw their defeat of the French colonists as a vindication of the African race, tensions between blacks and mulattos frequently manifested themselves in the new nation. The majority of blacks were descendants of the 450,000 slaves of the colonial period while the mulatto families mostly went back to the small but significant group of *affranchis* or free coloureds. With independence, some of the former slaves had managed to secure small properties, particularly in the north, either as a result of grants or sales of land by the government or by squatting on vacant lands, but the general effect of the early land reforms had been to strengthen the position of the mulattos as the principal landowners of the country.

During the eighteenth century Haiti (Saint Domingue) had been the world's leading producer of sugar, but the fragmentation of the great estates together with the destruction wrought in the revolutionary years led to a dramatic decline in sugar production. Coffee in fact became independent Haiti's main export crop. Efforts had been made by President F. N. Geffrard (1859–67) to increase production of cotton during the US civil war, but with the fall in world prices its cultivation

---

[1] O. Wardrop to the Marquess of Lansdowne, 15 December 1902, Public Record Office, London (PRO), FO 35/177.

ceased to be profitable. Haiti's farmers primarily grew crops for subsistence and for sale at local markets. Although these latter transactions generally used money, the extreme shortage of coins in the late 1870s led to the development of a complicated credit system. Later issues of paper money did little to ease the situation owing to the general lack of confidence in such currency. Most manufactured goods were imported, chiefly from the United States, France and Britain, but by the beginning of the twentieth century Cuban- and Italian-owned shoe factories had been established in the country (with one of the firms producing as many as 1,500 pairs of shoes a week). Also there were companies manufacturing such things as soap and matches. The import–export trade was largely controlled by foreigners, with Germans playing an increasingly significant role. In the early 1880s British steamships were the most frequent callers at Haitian ports, though again German shipping companies were of growing importance. 'As regards commerce, internal trade and industry', observed a US consul in 1884, 'as well as the religious, educational and moral advancement of the country, the influence and advantage of the foreign classes are apparent and undeniable.'[2] Baron de Vastey and other Haitian writers of an earlier period had warned their fellow countrymen of the dangers of economic dependence and had urged a move towards self-sufficiency as a necessary condition of effective political independence. In the period after 1870 Edmond Paul, Louis Joseph Janvier and others urged the development of locally owned industries that would supply home needs and export their products to other states in the region. No major attempts were made, however, to put these ideas into practice.

Haiti in 1870 had a population of about one million. The elite of the country consisted of a small number of families; most of them were mulattos whose strength lay in the capital and in the cities of the south and west. A minority of this elite class were blacks who were particularly strong in the north of Haiti. There was, however, in general a coincidence between colour and class such that the rich tended to be light-skinned and the poor dark; many of the political struggles of the day reflected these social and colour divisions. In the countryside there were some large landowners and also a significant class of middle-sized peasants owning their land and employing small numbers of workers at

[2] J. M. Langston, 'Trade and commerce of Haiti' (20 November 1884) in *Reports from the Consuls of the U.S. on the Commerce, Manufactures etc. of their Consular Districts*, no. 54 (Washington, DC, 1885), 361.

peak seasons. The mass of rural dwellers, though, were poor and worked on tiny plots of land which they owned or where they squatted. They augmented their small incomes by occasional employment on larger estates or by sharecropping. Although if a married man died intestate only his legitimate children would inherit land, most peasants made some provision for their natural children. In any case most of them were not in fact married but *placée*, often with more than one woman at a time. The laws and customs of inheritance frequently led to a subdivision of property; otherwise the property was jointly owned and operated as a single unit. Permission of all the owners was, of course, required in the case of land sales and this sometimes led to complications and lengthy legal wrangles. Men and women in the countryside struggled to feed and clothe their families and to keep their creditors from the door. While the men, clad mostly in blue denim, worked in the fields, women *marchandes* dominated the commerce of the small market towns.

In the towns was to be found a middle class ranging from professional people to small traders and skilled workers; below this was a class of unskilled workers and servants. By the 1880s there existed in the capital a *maison centrale* and a foundry for training apprentices in technical skills. In 1879 manual workers were paid $1.00 to $1.50 per day and the considerable number of immigrant workers, particularly from Jamaica and the Bahamas, suggests that conditions compared favourably with those in the neighbouring islands.[3] The widely held assumption that Haiti of the nineteenth century was 'isolated' needs qualification; Haitians, particularly of the upper and middle classes, travelled abroad for study or as exiles, while foreigners of different classes and from many countries settled in Haiti.

Although Port-au-Prince, with its population in this period of roughly 30,000, was the political and administrative centre of Haiti, the regional capitals and a few other towns enjoyed a sturdy civic life and several of the successful political movements of the time were initiated in the provinces. Many of these towns had their own newspapers and journals and they kept in touch with each other by means of regular boat services; transport by land was often slow and difficult due to the mountainous terrain. Apart from government buildings most of the towns were constructed of wood and were particularly susceptible to fire. Three-quarters of Jérémie was destroyed by fire in 1881, Miragoâne suffered a

---

[3] There were almost 2,000 British West Indian subjects in Haiti in 1875. R. Stuart to Earl Granville, 23 January 1883, PRO, FO 35/118.

similar fate in the following year, while in May 1885 most of Les Cayes was razed to the ground. These fires were frequently started by discontented elements in the population, or occasionally by government supporters, as in October 1883, when President Salomon's men set fire to the business sector of the capital as a warning to the elite not to join the mulatto risings which were taking place in the south. The losses suffered by foreign businessmen in such conflagrations often led to demands for compensation and to threats of foreign intervention. Life in Haiti was also menaced by frequent outbreaks of yellow fever, small pox and malaria, by hurricanes and by occasional earthquakes.

The national government at this time often maintained only a tenuous control over the countryside, large areas of which were dominated by semi-autonomous military leaders supported by peasant irregulars known as *cacos* or *piquets*. General Merisier was one such leader who controlled the mountainous region around the city of Jacmel for many years. His control over his men was enhanced by the fact that he was an *houngan* (Voodoo priest). In 1896 he invaded Jacmel with 40 of his men; the military commandant of the region hid while the invaders indulged in looting and released prisoners from the gaol. After a few hours Merisier withdrew to the mountains, the commandant emerged from hiding and life resumed its normal course. With the political uncertainty resulting from the death of President Hyppolite later in the same year, Merisier took over Jacmel once again and was eventually himself made commandant of the region.

The militaristic style of politics in Haiti goes back to the colonial period when the French governor-general was invariably a military officer. The tradition was strengthened in the revolutionary years when the native leaders were all army officers and it continued into the era of political independence when those generals who had led the revolutionary struggle became heads of state. For the blacks in particular the army provided the only effective channel for rising to political power and consequently the militaristic tradition was constantly under attack from mulatto politicians. Although throughout the nineteenth century and up to 1913 the head of state was invariably an army officer, he always needed the assistance of educated civilians to run the country. Generals have a tendency to lose their nerve when faced by administrative complexities, and there was never lacking a supply of more or less self-seeking bureaucrats to take over such functions. Often these men, mostly from the mulatto elite, would sponsor a black general as presidential candidate, expecting him to act as a façade behind which they would operate; this practice became known as *la politique de doublure* (politics of the understudy).

In the period from the fall of President Silvain Salnave in 1869 until the United States invasion in 1915, political alignments were determined by factors of colour, region and, perhaps most importantly, by personal and family loyalties and antipathies. For most of the period party lines were fairly fluid. Social and economic class factors were not of major significance in determining party affiliations at this time, as the majority of those actively engaged in politics came from the elite. Occasionally, as in the *cacos* and *piquets* risings, the peasants became politically active, but the general effect was limited to removal of an unwanted government; those who had taken part in the rising rarely had any significant influence on the policy of the succeeding regime. In the 1870s, however, under the presidents Nissage Saget (1870–4), Michel Domingue (1874–6) and Boisrond Canal (1876–9) there grew up in Haiti two fairly distinct and coherent political parties, the Liberal party, led by J. P. Boyer Bazelais, and the National party, under Demesvar Delorme. Although mulattos predominated in the leadership of the Liberals, two of its most prominent members, Edmond Paul and Joseph Anténor Firmin, were black. The National party was formed by an alliance of various interests opposed to the traditional mulatto elite and looked to Louis Etienne Lysius Félicité Salomon as its patron; in its membership and leadership it was predominantly black and it contained a significant group of *noiriste* ideologues led by Louis Joseph Janvier. Nevertheless the party had secured support from such prominent mulattos as Frédéric Marcelin and Callisthène Fouchard. In the final months of Canal's regime there was a split in the ranks of the Liberals and this enabled the Nationals to win the elections of 1879 and to recall Salomon from exile to become president of the Republic (1879–88).

Salomon, an educated black Haitian from a wealthy southern family, had been associated with the *noiriste* tendency in Haiti since the revolutionary movements of 1843–7, when he and members of his family had led the *piquets* revolts in the region of La Grande Anse. During his regime the so-called Banque Nationale was founded with French capital and an agricultural law was passed distributing plots of state land to farmers who would grow crops for export. This law also facilitated the further intrusion of foreign-owned companies into Haiti, giving them the rights of nationality which included the possibility of owning land. 'It is thanks to his administration', wrote one of Salomon's most fervent supporters, 'that French capital began to penetrate Haiti.'[4] In 1883 Salomon was faced by the invasion of Miragoâne by a group of Liberals under Boyer Bazelais, and by risings in a number of southern cities. These were successfully put down, though Salomon's concern for his security is partly reflected in his search for United States or French protection for Haiti. It was, however, an alliance of northern blacks that eventually despatched him. The fall of Salomon in 1888 led to a struggle for succession between the French-backed F. D. Légitime and the US-backed Florvil Hyppolite. The latter was ultimately successful and his six-year term of office (1889–96) was marked by relative prosperity and a programme of public works. US demands for the cession of the Môle Saint Nicolas as a naval base were skilfully deflected by the foreign secretary Anténor Firmin. Hyppolite was succeeded by T. A. Simon Sam (1896–1902), whose demise was the signal for a brief civil war between the supporters of Firmin and those of the octogenarian general Nord Alexis who eventually secured the presidency (1902–8). During this struggle occurred the celebrated action of Admiral Hammerton Killick (a *firministe*) who, after having captured a German ship which had been gun-running for Nord, blew himself up with the Haitian flagship rather than submitting to the German gunboat which had been sent to take reprisals. The new president's young mulatto supporters were generally in favour of the country's moving into the United States' sphere of influence and away from the traditional French connection. Nord was succeeded on his death by Antoine Simon (1908–11) who made claims to be a *noiriste* in the National party tradition, but many of those who had initially backed him became disillusioned, particularly after he had signed the McDonald contract (see below), and he was overthrown in 1911.

The degree of political instability in Haiti in the period after 1870 is frequently overstated. During the years 1870–1911 there were nine governments with an average life of four and a half years, which is well above the average length of governments in neighbouring Latin American countries. In the same period the people of the Dominican Republic, for example, suffered under twenty-two governments. However, with the demise of Simon in 1911 began four years of social unrest and acute governmental instability, with six presidents following each

4 L. J. Janvier, *Les Antinationaux* (Paris, 1884), 46.

other in quick succession, culminating in the US invasion of the country and an occupation lasting nineteen years.

The popular religion of the masses in this period, as indeed it is today, was Voodoo. This cult is a development of certain West African religions, into which have been incorporated elements of Christianity. The religion is concerned with the worship of God (*Bon Dieu*) and of the spirits (*loas*); it frequently takes the form of the devotee being possessed, or ridden (*monté*) by a *loa*, like a horse (*chewal*). Sacrifices, particularly of food or drink, are offered to the *loas*. Each temple (*hounfort*) is autonomous and is presided over by a priest (*houngan*) or a priestess (*mambo*). Each of the *loas* has a particular concern. Erzulie Fréda, for example, is the spirit of fertility, Agoué is the spirit of the water, and so on. Just as Haitians would not normally go straight to the president, but to one of his Cabinet ministers, so the worshipper is directly concerned with the appropriate *loa*. In the course of Haitian history many of the *loas* have come to be identified with Christian saints; Erzulie with St Mary, Ogoun with St James the Great, Damballah with St Patrick. The Voodoo religion was a principal means by which the slaves in colonial Saint Domingue had retained their African culture, as well as having provided a means of solidarity and communication for the slaves of different plantations. After the declaration of independence in 1804 the official attitude of Haitian governments, black as well as mulatto, was one of hostility towards the cult and they adopted various means to suppress it. Nevertheless it continued to flourish. Certain governments, such as that of Faustin Soulouque (1847–59) and Silvain Salnave (1867–9) had been noticeably more lenient towards Voodoo and this was a cause of disquiet among the mulatto elite. Attempts had been made by Boyer's government (1818–43) to establish a *concordat* with the Vatican and thus to regularize the situation of the Roman Catholic church in Haiti, but these efforts had been frustrated, partly because of the influence of such anti-clericals as Beaubrun Ardouin and J. B. Inginac. Geffrard's government had, however, signed a *concordat* with Rome in 1860, and from this time onwards the Roman Catholic church played an increasingly significant role in the cultural and political life of Haiti. The church was a crucial instrument for the propagation of the French language and of European culture, and was seen as such by the French government. Religious orders, including the Frères d'Instruction Chrétienne and the Soeurs de St Joseph de Cluny, arrived during the 1860s and opened schools. The governments of Christophe (1806–20) and Pétion (1807–18) had already established a number of *lycées* and primary schools and a few more had been built by succeeding governments; also by the 1870s some Protestant schools existed in Haiti. Nevertheless the Roman Catholic church soon became the most important educational institution in the country. The church tended to be closely associated with the mulatto elite and to reinforce the hegemony of this group. Consequently many members of the black elite were anti-clerical, inclined to Protestantism or freemasonry. President Salomon, for example, was the grand protector of the masonic order and his whole cabinet were freemasons. It should, however, be emphasized that the elite of all shades openly opposed the Voodoo religion, although some of them undoubtedly practised it in secret. The attitude of the established church towards Voodoo has varied from one of vigorous opposition to an almost syncretistic policy of attempting to convince the devotees of the *loas* that these spirits should be thought of as Christian saints.

The anti-clericalism of the black elite politicians, and of the National party which they dominated, was manifested in a number of church–state crises. Salnave had engaged in a running battle with the hierarchy during his two years in office and Salomon's government was suspicious of the power of the church. Thomas Madiou, a mulatto minister in Salomon's cabinet, issued warnings against the Roman Catholic church as a state within the state, while the president himself praised the Protestant churches (in implicit contrast to the Roman Catholics) for their efforts to create a native clergy. The principal Protestant groups at this time included L'Église Orthodoxe Apostolique (Anglican), headed by Bishop Jacques Holly, an American negro who had emigrated to Haiti in the 1860s; this church had ten priests and about a thousand members. The Methodists, whose college in Port-au-Prince had 120 students, were particularly strong in the southern city of Jérémie, where a small Protestant elite emerged in the latter part of the century. Baptists and African Methodist missions were also active in this period. Protestant and masonic anti-clericalism was particularly evident in the activities and pronouncements of the so-called 'ultranationals', led by L. J. Janvier, E. Pinckombe and L. Prost, whose journals, *L'Oeil* and *L'Avant-Garde*, carried virulent attacks on the Roman Catholic hierarchy for its alleged racism, elitism and anti-patriotism.

The Haiti of the period before the US occupation, despite its economic and political problems, manifested a vigorous intellectual life among the small elite of the country. Newspapers and journals abounded in the capital and in the provincial towns. A number of writers emerged as defenders of the black race answering the racist propaganda of European and North American publicists. Haitians of this period took up the themes of earlier writers (including Baron de Vastey, C. S. Milscent and Félix Darfour); among the principal contributors to this debate were Anténor Firmin, Hannibal Price, L. J. Janvier, J. Justin, J. Dévot, J. Auguste, J. N. Léger and Bénito Sylvain.[5] These men proclaimed the equality of the human races and denied any significant differences between them. They saw Haiti as a symbol and as a proof of this equality and in consequence they tended to paint a somewhat rosy picture of their country. Their works, nevertheless, constitute a major contribution to the continuing debate on racial equality.

Many of the poets and novelists at this time tended to adopt European, particularly French, patterns of expression and to dwell upon foreign themes. The writers associated with the literary magazine *La Ronde*, published in the 1890s, reasserted in contrast the need for *une littérature indigène* which had been enunciated by earlier generations. Novelists including Fernand Hibbert, Justin Lhérisson and Frédéric Marcelin and such poets as Etzer Vilaire, Charles Moravia and Georges Sylvain maintained the importance of a specifically Haitian literary tradition distinct from its French parent. Other significant movements among the elite of this period deserve mention. In the first place a group headed by L. J. Marcelin, L. C. Lhérisson and the young Sténio Vincent (a future president, 1930–41), founded in 1892 an École Libre Professionnelle, the purpose of which was to supplement existing agencies, referred to earlier, by training youths of the working class in useful skills and thus to encourage the growth of a middle class which, it was widely believed, would contribute to the political stability of the country. The newspaper *Le Travail*, with its motto 'l'oisiveté mère de tous les vices', propagated the ideas of this group. A further influential movement was the Société de Législation, founded in the same year to discuss the relationship between law and social conditions in Haiti and to recommend legislative reforms when necessary. One of the principal subjects considered by the society was whether the constitutional provision, going back to the first days of independence, which prohibited the foreign ownership of land, should be repealed. The debate on this issue was, however, not restricted to the members of this society. There were those who maintained that

---

[5] These writers are more fully considered in David Nicholls, *From Dessalines to Duvalier: race, colour and national independence in Haiti* (Cambridge, 1979), 126ff.

Haiti could achieve economic development only with an influx of foreign capital and that such an influx would not occur without a change in this law. Some of those opposed to allowing foreign ownership argued that Haiti should rely on her own resources and retain control of her economy even if this meant a slower rate of growth. Others claimed that, while foreign investment was necessary, this could be secured without permitting the foreign ownership of land.[6] However, legislation introduced by Salomon's government in 1883 had, as we have seen, effectively undermined the constitutional provision for certain cases. Divisions on this issue of the foreign ownership of land cut across party affiliations and colour lines.

In the early years of the twentieth century a lively debate took place in Haiti on whether the mentality of the people was essentially Latin or Anglo-Saxon and which of these two cultural traditions should constitute the pattern that the country should follow. The traditional elite was generally francophile. Led by Anténor Firmin, Georges Sylvain and Dantès Bellegarde, this group insisted that Haiti must maintain and strengthen its cultural and political links with France, and they defended classical studies as the basis of national education. The *anglosaxonnistes*, who were strongly represented in the government of Nord Alexis, included F. Marcelin, L. Borno (another future president, 1922–30) and Clément Magloire (editor of *Le Matin*); they favoured a new emphasis upon technical studies and called for closer links with the United States and with Germany. Divisions among Haitians on such questions as education and culture were thus related to an increasing foreign involvement in the internal affairs of the country.

By the turn of the century British influence had decreased. In 1906, for example, there were only six Englishmen in Haiti (though there were still 400–500 British subjects, mostly Jamaicans, Bahamians and Syrio-Lebanese). Much of the commercial sector was controlled by Germans, who outnumbered Americans by two to one; German residents even acted as US vice consuls in a number of cities.[7] In the course of the first decade of the century French involvement in Haiti declined, and control of the Banque Nationale passed out of French hands into those of the

---

6 This matter is dealt with more fully in David Nicholls, *Economic development and political autonomy: the Haitian experience* (Montreal, 1974), 14ff.

7 A. G. Vansittart, 'General report on the Republic of Haiti for the year 1906', PRO, FO 371/266, and J. B. Terres to Assistant Secretary of State, 16 February 1906, in US National Archives (Washington, DC), Department of State, Microfilm T346, roll 10.

National City Bank of New York in 1910–11. US companies became increasingly active in the country, organizing the water supply, mining iron ore and building railways. In 1905 a concession was granted to two Americans to build a railway from Hinche to Gonaïves, and the notorious McDonald contract, signed in 1910, gave rights to an American company to construct a railway and to exploit land each side of the line. Haitian nationalists, including P. F. Frédérique and Rosalvo Bobo, denounced the contract for further undermining the constitutional prohibition on foreign ownership.

The closing years of the nineteenth century saw the arrival of significant numbers of Syrio-Lebanese traders, whose astute business practices enabled them soon to dominate certain sectors of the retail trade, to the detriment of the Haitian *marchandes*. As the first decade of the century progressed these traders also moved into more large-scale commercial operations and their activities aroused widespread hostility; there was even a newspaper called *L'Antisyrien*! Legislation was enacted and reactivated to inhibit these non-nationals, and their requests for protection led to intervention on their behalf by the French, British and United States governments. In addition to intrusions from this cause, rival political groups of Haitians continued to seek foreign support against their enemies, while resident aliens, particularly Germans, played an increasingly active role in fomenting discord and financing revolutions. Also many of the contending parties of the period were linked to interests in the Dominican Republic.

The US invasion and occupation of Haiti on 28 July 1915 is to be explained by a number of interrelated factors. In the first place it must be seen as part of a general US plan for the strategic control of the Caribbean. Throughout the latter part of the nineteenth century there had been efforts by a number of foreign powers to gain a foothold in Haiti, either by establishing a naval base at the Môle St Nicolas, in the north-west of the country, or by securing the island of La Tortue. As we have seen, the US government itself made strenuous efforts to secure the Môle in 1889. With the building of the Panama canal the USA was determined to maintain military control of the region. The establishment of a naval base at Guantánamo Bay in Cuba in 1903 had solved the immediate problem, though Washington was still very much concerned to prevent any other nation securing a base in Haiti. The State Department was worried in particular at the growing German presence in Haiti and feared that in the event of a German victory in Europe the Kaiser would try to establish a Caribbean foothold in the country. Such fears were encouraged by certain business and banking interests in the USA which had assets in Haiti. In addition to the overriding concern for strategic control of the Caribbean, the US government was eager to establish in Haiti a situation favourable to the servicing and repayment of loans and to investment by US companies. To suggest, however, that the invasion and occupation were primarily undertaken in order to safeguard US economic interests would be an error. The actual amount of US investment in the country in 1915 was a mere $4 million. Undoubtedly the US government hoped that this investment level would increase and that American finance would replace European finance, thereby depriving foreign governments of occasions for intervention in the affairs of Haiti; this was the principle behind what is known as 'dollar diplomacy'. 'Relative to the overall thrust of United States imperialism in the Caribbean', Hans Schmidt concludes, in his study of the US occupation, 'Haiti was strategically crucial but economically of little consequence.'[8] In addition to these strategic and economic factors there is also the phenomenon of misguided altruism characteristic of Democratic party foreign policy from Wilson to Carter. The occupation was frequently justified in terms of helping a poor neighbour back onto its feet or (less benevolently) of taking over the running of a country whose natives had proved incapable of governing themselves. (The years immediately preceding the invasion were, as we have seen, years of unusual social unrest and political instability in which, it could be argued, the Haitian elite had finally lost the ability to control popular movements of protest and shown itself unable to govern the country.) Soon after their arrival in Haiti, the Americans took steps to provide a legal façade for the occupation and to find a puppet president. A number of leading Haitian politicians refused the ignominious post, but the president of the Senate, Philippe Sudre Dartiguenave, accepted office and served until 1922. A convention was signed and in 1918 a new constitution imposed.

The policy of the US administration in Haiti was concerned first of all with imposing law and order throughout the country, which it contrived to do with the aid of a *gendarmerie* (later to become the Garde d'Haïti); it

---

[8] Hans Schmidt, *The United States occupation of Haiti, 1915–1934* (New Brunswick, NJ, 1971), 54. Of course, the general concern for strategic control may itself largely be explained in economic terms, but this is a distinct issue.

was manned by Haitians though all the superior officers were Americans. The invasion of 1915 was actually welcomed by many Haitians, particularly by members of the elite, and also by most foreign residents. The general reaction among ordinary Haitians, proud of their 111 years of independence, was, however, one of sullen resentment at this intrusion. Although there was sporadic military resistance in 1915 the real test for the *gendarmerie* came in 1917, when Charlemagne Péralte led a *cacos* army to challenge the invaders. Marine reinforcements were rushed from the USA and battles continued for many months. In 1919 Péralte was killed and the revolt put down.

Haitian resistance continued in the form of a growing nationalist movement; some of those who had at first collaborated with the Americans, including Dantès Bellegarde and Sténio Vincent, joined the opposition. Certain aspects of the occupation had alienated the elite. In the first place the racist attitude of many US officials was hardly disguised. 'These people are niggers in spite of the thin varnish of education and refinement', wrote Colonel Waller, the senior US official in Haiti. 'What the people of Norfolk and Portsmouth would say if they saw me bowing and scraping to these coons I do not know.'[9] Secondly, the emphasis upon technical education at the expense of the classical syllabus of the past was resented by the elite. Large sums were poured not only into the building of roads, the provision of public health facilities and general improvements to the infrastructure, but also into the Service Technique as part of a policy of training doctors, teachers, technicians and agronomists, in the belief that a strong middle class would 'become the backbone of the country and go far to assure stability of government'.[10] Furthermore, the historic constitutional provision forbidding the foreign ownership of land was omitted from the 1918 constitution and a number of US firms took advantage of the situation. Peasants were driven from land which they had worked for generations and resentment was widespread. Even President Dartiguenave began to make life difficult for the US officials, and in 1922 he was replaced by Louis Borno whom the Americans considered more reliable.

Closely related to the growing nationalist demands for US withdrawal were the ethnological and literary movements among Haitian intellectuals. The origins of the ethnological movement go back to the writings of J. C. Dorsainvil in 1907–8. In a number of articles in *Le Matin* and

---

9 Quoted in *ibid.*, 79.
10 *Report of the American High Commissioner in Haiti for 1928* (Washington, DC, 1929), 7.

elsewhere, Dorsainvil asserted that the Haitian people were basically African in their racial composition and cultural heritage, and that this fact had been ignored or suppressed by the elite of the country whose life-style was dominated by European values. As Germans of the early nineteenth century had been led to study their folklore in the wake of the Napoleonic invasion of their country, so Haitians of the occupation period now began to dig into their ethnic past to find a justification and a basis for patriotism. In 1928 Jean Price Mars published his celebrated study of Haitian folklore entitled *Ainsi parla l'oncle*. In it he described in some detail the social customs, folk legends and religious practices of the ordinary people, and criticized his fellow intellectuals for failing to acknowledge and appreciate the African origins of this popular culture. Calling in particular for a more sympathetic approach to the Voodoo religion, he concluded with the plea to his readers to 'despise no longer our ancestral heritage'.[11] This book, together with the writings of Dorsainvil, had a profound effect upon a number of young black intellectuals from the middle class, including Louis Diaquoi, Lorimer Denis and François Duvalier, *noiriste* founders of the Griots group.[12] Reinforcing the impact of the ethnological movement was a new interest in Africa on the part of European anthropologists together with the so-called Harlem revival in the United States associated with the names of Langston Hughes, Countee Cullen and Claude McKay.

The Haitian literary revival of this period was also closely allied to Haitian nationalism. In the mid 1920s three journals began to appear, *La Nouvelle Ronde, La Trouée* and *La Revue Indigène*. The most celebrated writer of this movement was Jacques Roumain, but it also included Carl Brouard, Emile Roumer, Philippe Thoby Marcelin, Normil Sylvain, Richard Salnave, Daniel Heurtelou and Max Hudicourt. These men were mostly the sons of elite mulatto families, but were in revolt against the excessive francophilia of their forebears, and were indignant at the US occupation of their country. Brouard and Roumain were particularly influenced by the ethnological movement; their poems dwelt upon the African roots of the Haitian people and manifest a strong populist tendency. Roumain wrote of 'the slow road to Guinea', referring to the Haitian myth of the sub-Atlantic passage to Africa, along which the soul

---

11 Jean Price Mars, *Ainsi parla l'oncle* (2nd edn, New York, 1954), 236.
12 The group took its name from a traditional African institution: the *griot* is the poet, the story teller, the magician of the tribe who perpetuates tribal customs, beliefs and myths. On the Griots group, see Nicholls, *From Dessalines to Duvalier*, 167–72.

will pass at death. In two well-known poems Brouard contrasts 'Nous', the sophisticated, Europeanized elite, with 'Vous', the mass of the peasants who were the pillars of the edifice.

The literature of the occupation period represents a real shift in Haitian thinking about race. Nineteenth-century writers certainly pointed with pride to the ancient civilizations of Africa, and many of them also defended the Africa of their own day from the charges of ignorant European publicists, but they basically believed that men of all races are equal and fundamentally the same. Furthermore they accepted the European model as the one which Haitians should follow in matters of culture and civilization. Many writers of the occupation period, however, believed that racial differences were significant, and some of them went so far as to root these differences in biological factors.[13] The ideas developing in Haiti at this time are similar to those of the *négritude* movement that began among black students in Paris during the early 1930s, associated with the names of Aimé Césaire (of Martinique), Léopold Sédar Senghor (of Senegal) and Léon Damas (of Guyane).[14]

By the mid 1920s the nationalist movement had united Haitians of different classes and colours in a determination to end the US occupation. President Louis Borno and the group around him found themselves virtually isolated from national life and wholly dependent upon the USA for their positions. Nationalist leaders were frequently imprisoned but the movement continued to grow. In 1929 protests initiated by students spread throughout the country, with strikes and demonstrations in favour of US withdrawal. A state of emergency was declared, and during a march by peasants in the region of Les Cayes, US marines opened fire, killing and wounding several dozen. Worried by these events and by the international publicity they were receiving, President Hoover set up a commission of enquiry under W. Cameron Forbes, a former governor of the Philippines. Hostile demonstrations demanding US withdrawal greeted the commission when it arrived in Haiti. The report of the commission recommended an end to the occupation after a period of rapid Haitianization of the officer corps of the Garde. Borno's reign came to an end in 1930 and after some months under a provisional president, elections were held in which nationalist candidates swept the board. Sténio Vincent, an astute mulatto politician,

[13] See David Nicholls, 'Biology and politics in Haiti', *Race*, 13 (1971), 201–14.
[14] Lilyan Kesteloot, *Les Ecrivains noirs de langue française: naissance d'une littérature* (3rd edn, Brussels, 1965).

was elected president; he was to remain in power throughout the 1930s. In 1934, following the election of a new US president, Franklin D. Roosevelt, and the inauguration of the so-called 'good neighbour' policy, the stars and stripes was lowered to the cheers of ten thousand Haitian spectators. The occupation had achieved its purpose and a continued military presence seemed unwise and costly.

The long-term effects of the US occupation of Haiti (1915–34) were few. Roads and other infrastructural improvements fell into decay. Foreign companies found Haiti less attractive than they had hoped and several of them withdrew from the country. The return of the mulatto elite and the depoliticization of the military also proved short-lived. The lives of the great majority of Haitians who lived and worked in the countryside were generally unaffected. The occupation did, however, hasten the growth of the black middle class and the development of a *négritude* ideology which was incorporated into the *noirisme* inherited from a previous generation, thus paving the way for the rise of François Duvalier. A consequence of the improvement in communications, together with the disarming of the *cacos* and *piquets* groups in the occupation period, was the increase in the power of the capital and the decline of provincial towns, so that from this time onward significant political and cultural movements have generally been centred in Port-au-Prince. This feature of post-occupation Haiti persisted despite the subsequent decay of the road system. Commercial links with the USA continued, though Haiti's economy remained less dependent on foreign trade than that of other Caribbean islands; poverty would seem to be one way of securing relative economic independence! The general structure of the economy was unaffected by the occupation. Coffee remained the principal export, though its percentage of total exports fell owing to a revival in the cotton and sugar industries. Marginal improvements in agricultural techniques were effected partly as a result of the work done by the agricultural school at Damiens and by a number of experimental stations throughout the country. Efforts were made to change the 'indolent and shiftless' life of the peasants; if they were to become citizens of a modern state, declared one US official, 'they must acquire . . . a new set of wants'.[15] In general the rural inhabitants, being of a cautious and conservative disposition, resisted these missionary endeavours. The occupation saw no major growth in manufacturing or in mining. Finally,

---

[15] A. C. Millspaugh, 'Our Haitian problem', *Foreign Affairs*, 7 (1929), 560.

French cultural traditions persisted among the elite throughout the occupation; many nationalists clung tenaciously to the French connection in the face of the new US imperialism in much the same way that Puerto Rican nationalists today look with affection to the language and the culture of an earlier colonialism. The French government did its best to foster this continuing tradition without alienating the Americans. The Roman Catholic clergy were its principal agents, seen by the French minister in Port-au-Prince as 'precious collaborators in our political propaganda'.[16]

The Haiti of 1930 was, then, not vastly different from that of 1870. The population had more than doubled to a total of about 2,400,000. The cities had grown in size, particularly Port-au-Prince, which by 1930 had more than 100,000 inhabitants. Nevertheless well over 90 per cent of the people lived in the countryside as small proprietors, as labourers on land owned by members of their family or as sharecroppers and day-labourers. Many thousands of Haitians emigrated to Cuba and the Dominican Republic either for a period of several years or for the cane-cutting season. Haiti could be called a peasant economy in the general sense that most rural dwellers owned or controlled some land (either individually or jointly), on which they grew crops for local consumption often combined with coffee for export. There was no large rural proletariat as existed in many other Caribbean islands by 1930. The titles to land were often unclear, but efforts made by the authorities during the US occupation to complete a cadastral survey came to nothing. A more intensive cultivation of land and the continual cutting of timber for export and for domestic use led to increasing soil erosion. A deep gulf still separated the predominantly mulatto elite from the rest of the people, though the middle class had significantly strengthened its position. The army, which in the late nineteenth century had been dominated by blacks, was reconstituted and deprived of its political role. High offices of state were mostly held by mulattos of the elite and this led to growing resentment, particularly on the part of the black middle classes. The peak of mulatto supremacy was reached during the presidency of Elie Lescot (1941–6), but since his overthrow in January 1946 Haiti has witnessed political power passing into the hands of black politicians, culminating in the regime of the Duvalier dynasty. The

---

[16] L. Agel au Ministre, 2 June 1921, Archives du Ministère des Affaires Etrangères, Paris, Corr. Pol., Amérique 1918–1940, Haïti 15.

mulatto elite, however, retains much of its economic power and social position. Despite half a century of *négritude*, Haitians, even from the most vocal sections of the black middle class, like their children to marry light-skinned partners. 'Which of them', demanded Sténio Vincent of the *négritude* writers of the 1930s, 'would have dreamed of actually going to some part of the Sudan or the Congo to enter into communion with the souls of our distant Mandingo or Bantu ancestors?'[17] In practice 'civilization' has continued to mean Europe.

[17] S. Vincent, *En posant les jalons* (Port-au-Prince, 1939), I, 153.

Part Three

THE RIVER PLATE REPUBLICS

The River Plate Republics

9

THE GROWTH OF THE ARGENTINE
ECONOMY, *c.* 1870–1914*

A traveller arriving in the Río de la Plata region in the 1870s would have been struck first by the width of the estuary and then, on entering the port of Buenos Aires, by the lowness and simplicity of the buildings. Travelling inland, he would have been stunned by the vast expanses of flat, treeless land, the pampas, stretching away as far as the eye could see, where the overwhelming sense of solitude was only interrupted by the sight of a herd of cattle, or by the sudden appearance of an ostrich or some other example of the local fauna. At that time, the most important commercial activity was carried on in a coastal strip along the estuary of the Río de la Plata and the Paraná, and along the southern course of the river Uruguay in its navigable reaches. The shortage of wood, in addition to the huge distances, was an obstacle to the establishment of permanent settlements inland: prospective settlers were obliged to transport building materials from distant ports or urban areas. Apart from the Paraná, a section of the Uruguay, and the Río Negro, which was in territory still occupied by the Indians, the rivers of Argentina were not navigable, and railways were only just beginning to be built. Moreover, Indians still occupied what was called the 'desert', not far beyond the populated areas of Buenos Aires and Santa Fe provinces, and Indian raids were common. Apart from the provincial capitals, administrative centres which dated from colonial times, there was no extensive network of towns in the interior, and the rural population was sparse. Nevertheless, although there was much to discourage settlement and the putting of land to productive use, the temperate climate was favourable, and conditions, though harsh, were less harsh than in some parts of Europe.

* Translated from the Spanish by Dr David Brookshaw; translation revised by the Editor. The Editor wishes to thank Dr Colin Lewis for his help in the final preparation of this chapter.

During the first half of the nineteenth century, in the area of effective settlement, the north-west and the riverine and coastal corridor which joined it to Buenos Aires, the main economic activity had been cattle ranching which required little labour and capital. Hides and jerked beef were produced for export, and meat for internal consumption. It was not that there was no agriculture, but the high cost of transport limited agricultural activity to the areas near urban centres where the markets were located. The cost of overland transport meant that until the 1870s it was more convenient to import wheat and flour.

Whereas during the colonial period the centre of economic life lay in upper Peru, with the mining camps of Potosí joined to Buenos Aires by a trade route that went through Salta, Tucumán, and Córdoba, the first half of the nineteenth century had witnessed the formation of another economic axis, based initially in the so-called Mesopotamian provinces (Entre Ríos and Corrientes) and later in the province of Buenos Aires, where cattle ranching activities developed, using the river system as an outlet for their products. Later, new circumstances required the expansion of the frontiers in the search for new territories, to the west and south, in Buenos Aires, in Córdoba and Santa Fe, and also in what is now the province of La Pampa.

For it should not be assumed that there were no changes prior to 1870. Leather found a market in the industrialized countries, and there was a significant increase in trade, despite the fluctuations caused, among other things, by blockades and wars. To exports of hides and jerked beef were added fats and tallows by the 1840s. Moreover, sheep rearing had also begun in the 1820s, and exports of unwashed wool became important during the 1840s. In 1822, Argentine exports reached five million silver pesos and stayed at this level until the 1840s, despite considerable annual variations. They then increased, and towards the end of the period reached seven million. Another jump in exports occurred in the period after 1860, when they reached 14 million, and a decade later, in 1870, they had increased still more, to 30 million silver pesos.[1] The increase in the value of Argentina's exports resulted, on the one hand, from the recovery of international prices, which had been declining from the 1820s until the late 1840s, and, on the other hand, from the increasing importance of fats, tallow, and above all wool. Wool represented 10.8 per cent of

---

[1] Francisco Latzina, *El comercio exterior argentino* (Buenos Aires, 1916).

exports in 1837, rose to 12.5 per cent in 1848, and reached 33.7 per cent in 1859.[2]

The expansion of wool production and exports came in response to growing demand from the countries of continental Europe, in particular France, and from the United States. Wool production required a more intensive use of land, labour and capital. In order to provide better care for the sheep, it was necessary to move manpower to the rural areas and thus to improve both transport facilities and internal security. Furthermore the overall growth of the stock of animals, especially sheep – the number of sheep rose from 23 million in 1846 to 70 million in 1884, cattle from 10 million to 23 million – led to an additional demand for new land. Nevertheless, in the 1870s, the country, with a basically pastoral economy, still had vast tracts of land, much of which was not utilized, lying beyond the 'frontier'. Population was sparse, the railway network was rudimentary, port facilities were inadequate and capital was scarce.

FACTORS OF PRODUCTION

Land

Extraordinary economic growth in Argentina between 1870 and 1914, sustained at an annual rate of approximately 5 per cent[3] was, according to many authors, the result of important changes in international trade, changes which brought the New Worlds of America and Oceania into the mainstream of world commerce. It has also been stressed that the decisive factor in the establishment of new trade routes was the reduction in costs of maritime transport. No less important than the increase in world trade and a certain international division of labour was the movement of factors of production, such as capital and labour, between continents which made such changes possible. Nevertheless, this outline, while correct in general terms, does not reflect all the complexity and richness of an historical process which had other less obvious facets. Numerous obstacles and difficulties had to be faced; and various adjustments were needed so that, on the supply side, an adequate

[2] Jonathan C. Brown, *A socio-economic history of Argentina, 1776–1860* (Cambridge, 1979). See also Tulio Halperín Donghi, 'La expansión ganadera en la campaña de Buenos Aires', *Desarrollo Económico*, 3 (April–September 1963). And on Argentina before 1870 in general, see Lynch, *CHLA* III, ch. 15.

[3] Carlos Díaz Alejandro, *Essays on the economic history of the Argentine Republic* (New Haven, 1970), 3.

response might be made to real or potential increases in world demand. Studies of the period have concentrated on aspects related to the growth of demand in the principal centres of consumption of primary products; supply adjustments in the main primary producing economies have still not been studied in depth.

Producers needed to reorganize production so as to increase the output of those commodities (cereals, and later meat in the case of Argentina), where the degree of comparative advantage was greatest. To achieve this, hitherto unused productive resources had to be exploited. In Argentina there was land in abundance, but the vast expanses of territory where Indian tribes still roamed freely had not been settled. In addition, colonization of the land presupposed adequate means of transport in order to take settlers to isolated areas and bring products from those areas to market. How and when did this process come about? Although the complexity of the process defies the construction of a facile chronology, the incorporation of vast tracts of land is the most important starting point.

During the 1870s, it became more and more obvious that the frontier needed to be extended in order to accommodate the growing flocks of sheep and to facilitate the relocation of *criollo* cattle away from prime lands now given over to sheep. The increase in stock led to over-grazing and soil erosion in the land in longest use, which was curious for a new country. At that time, there was no surplus population in search of unoccupied land, at least until the 1870s and 1880s. Rather, there was a need to seek new pastures for an ever larger stock of cattle. However, curiously enough, during the 1870s this expansion in cattle was not due to any significant increase in international demand transmitted by the price mechanism; rather it was due to a different phenomenon. The prices of agricultural exports (hides, wool, etc.) declined after the mid 1870s. This led to a fall in the profitability of livestock raising, which could only be compensated for by an increase in the volume of production, provided that this increase in output could be achieved at lower costs in order to ensure profit. The only way of doing this was through the incorporation of new lands at low or even zero cost, so as to make it possible to increase stocks (capital goods) at minimal additional cost to increase output (wool or hides), thereby increasing earnings. A characteristic of livestock raising is that it produces both consumer goods and capital. The greater availability of grazing land means that more animals may be kept as breeding stock, thus increasing the capital goods. So the incorporation of new lands had the definite effect of increasing the herds and expanding production at minimal cost, thereby compensating for the fall in prices and maintaining the profitability of cattle raising. Thus expansion was not generated by a rise in prices but by the availability of new land and the need to reduce costs in order to maintain the economic viability of stock raising.

It is true that territorial expansion was made possible by an earlier upturn in economic activity, which also made possible the military occupation of the new territories. The fact that the old frontier could be reached more quickly thanks to the railway, and that the Indian campaign of 1879–80 led by General Julio A. Roca could be conducted from a considerable distance thanks to the telegraph, was an important element in the conquest of the desert, but did not mean that the rail network, settlers and arable farming were introduced into the new areas. On the contrary, by 1881 zones that had been settled beyond the Indian frontier of 1876 were almost totally given over to cattle. The proportion of settlers involved in arable agriculture was minimal. It was only later, in areas reached by the railways, that arable farming began to expand and the grain frontier advanced beyond the old cattle frontier. In the early 1880s the railways had not reached the areas which were incorporated after the 'conquest of the desert', and which amounted to 30 million hectares (about 8 million in the province of Buenos Aires, 5 million in Santa Fe, 2 million in Córdoba, and another 14 million in the whole territory of La Pampa).

In contrast, the expansion of agriculture in the late 1880s and 1890s, and especially the production of wheat, first in Santa Fe between 1888 and 1895, then in Buenos Aires after 1895, was directly linked to the growth of the rail network. It grew from 732 kilometres of track in 1870 and 1,313 kilometres in 1880 to 9,254 kilometres in 1890. The tonnage of goods transported increased from 275,000 tons in 1870 and 742,000 tons in 1880 to 5.42 million tons in 1890. In 1884, in the north of the province of Buenos Aires, the area of older settlement, some 7.1 per cent of the land was under cultivation; in the central and southern regions, which included extensive territories incorporated during the 1870s and early 1880s, 1.1 per cent and 0.3 per cent respectively was under cultivation. By 1896, 44.5 per cent of the north was under cultivation, 28.3 per cent of the centre, and 14.6 per cent of the south. And some 83.7 per cent of wheat, and 53.7 per cent of maize produced was transported by rail.[4]

Regional characteristics, but more especially proximity to markets (which was influenced by transport costs), determined the pattern of land use at different times and in different areas during this period. In isolated areas, where there were no navigable rivers and no railways, and where transport costs were therefore high, there was less likelihood of settlement and the development of arable farming. In such areas there was extensive livestock raising on holdings of considerable size worked by the landowners. There was also a system of tenancy and share-cropping, especially in sheep rearing, but it never became as widespread as it did in arable farming in later years. In regions where soil conditions and transport costs allowed, agriculture expanded. Between 1888 and 1895 the area under cultivation increased from 2.5 million to almost 5 million hectares. The most notable expansion occurred in the province of Santa Fe where the actual size of the holdings was smaller, and a great many were owner occupied. At the end of the nineteenth century and during the first two decades of the twentieth, a new wave of agricultural expansion occurred in lands which had already been either totally or partially given over to cattle raising. One of the features of this process is that it did not lead to arable farming replacing cattle raising; rather, the two complemented each other. The result was that on cattle ranches certain areas were set aside for grain production and let out to tenant farmers, whose number thus greatly increased during the period from 1885 to 1914.

The existence of such a large number of tenant farmers has been influential in shaping a common picture of Argentine historiography which has an honourable ancestry among authors of such importance as Miguel Angel Cárcano and Jacinto Oddone, not to mention more recent scholars like Sergio Bagú and James Scobie. Scobie has the following to say on the subject:

Those whose forebears had been able to acquire and keep enormous land grants or who now secured estates enjoyed a gilded existence. Lands whose only worth had been in their herds of wild cattle, lands which could be reached only by

[4] On the connection between railway expansion and the incorporation of new lands, see Colin M. Lewis, 'La consolidación de la frontera argentina a fines de la década del setenta. Los Indios, Roca y los ferrocarriles', in Gustavo Ferrari and Ezequiel Gallo (eds.), *La Argentina del ochenta al centenario* (Buenos Aires, 1980); Roberto Cortés Conde, 'Patrones de asentamiento y explotación agropecuaria en los nuevos territorios argentinos (1890–1910)', in Alvaro Jara (ed.), *Tierras nuevas* (Mexico, 1969).

horseback or oxcart, land occupied largely by hostile Indians underwent a total transformation. British capital had built railroads. Pastoral techniques had been improved and the resources of the pampas were being utilized more thoroughly. Immigrants, newly arrived from European poverty, were available not only for railroad and urban construction but also as sharecroppers, tenant farmers, or peons to raise corn, wheat, flax, and alfalfa, to put up fences, and to tend cattle and sheep. Under such conditions land provided an annual return of from 12 to 15 per cent to the owner and land values often rose 1000 per cent in a decade. Those who already had land, power, or money monopolized the newly developed wealth of the pampas. The man who tilled the soil or cared for the herds eked out a meager existence. If he had left Europe because of poverty and despair, at least he did not starve in Argentina, but few incentives were offered him and, for the most part, title to the land was beyond his grasp.[5]

The opinions of those who have supported this thesis could be summed up as follows: in order to increase earnings from the rent of land the large landowners restricted the supply of land by keeping it off the market; they then left the land they monopolized uncultivated. But in fact the situation was far more complex; the purchase and sale of land was far more fluid than supposed; and the size of estates, as well as the system of tenancy, was linked to other circumstances related to the particular pattern of agricultural and pastoral development in the region. In fact, it happened that whereas towards the end of the century large amounts of land were becoming available as the railways created new links to the markets, there were still not enough farmers prepared to work it. There was therefore no limited resource nor an unsatisfied demand for land. In contrast, during the second decade of the twentieth century, with twenty million hectares under cultivation, new farmers would compete with the old for the best land in a situation where there was no possibility of incorporating new land suitable for agriculture.

The system of tenancy did not hinder access to landownership. In many cases, indeed, it constituted an intermediate step towards it. As a tenant rather than an owner, the farmer's labour yielded better returns because the scale was greater. Moreover, it provided full employment for a family working group who had immigrated precisely because of the availability of land. Finally, there was a fairly active market in medium- and small-sized estates, while transactions in larger properties were fewer. In addition, although land prices rose during the 1880s, they fell

[5] James Scobie, *Revolution on the pampas: a social history of Argentine wheat* (Austin, Texas, 1964), 5.

during the 1890s and the possibilities of acquiring land increased. In his annual report for 1893 the British consul commented:

The prices of lands were exceedingly low in gold in 1891 and 1892; now they are dearer, but are still fairly cheap. The fall in the value of land after the crisis of 1890 was extraordinary . . . The price of the land is soon paid off with good seasons, and the facilities of becoming landowners on a small scale are great. All lands in the Argentine Republic are freehold. The transfer and the registration of properties and the examination of titles is remarkably simple as compared with England.[6]

During the first decade of the twentieth century, the price of land again increased dramatically. This was, however, not a case of speculation, but reflected a significant increase in the profitability of land, especially land given over to livestock due to the shift to meat production and the introduction of British breeds.

Labour supply

The shortage of manpower in Argentina was a persistent problem throughout the nineteenth century and, from the time of the first proposals on the matter by Bernardino Rivadavia in the 1820s, had prompted the idea of pursuing a policy of immigration and colonization which before 1870 met with scant success. Apart from the little interest shown in the subject by landowners, and the complete absence of any interest on the part of political leaders such as Juan Manuel de Rosas, who supposedly did not encourage projects for colonization by foreigners, no consideration was given to the fact that the major difficulty in settling colonists in areas far inland lay in the high cost of transport, which hindered the marketing of products over long distances. From the first years of the Confederation, more successful attempts were made to encourage immigration and colonization. In 1869, the year of the First National Census, Argentina had a population of under 1.8 million inhabitants. By 1895, twenty-five years later, according to the Second National Census the population had grown to almost 4 million, and by the time of the third Census in 1914, it had reached almost 8 million (see table 1). This striking increase could scarcely have been achieved through natural growth alone. It was due in

6 Great Britain, Foreign Office, Report for the year 1893 on the agricultural condition of the Argentine Republic (Annual Series, 1893, Diplomatic and Consular Reports on Trade and Finance, No. 1283), 1893.

Table 1. *Population and rates of growth*

Year	Population	Average annual increase per 1,000 inhabitants
1869	1,736,923[a]	28.5
1895	3,954,911	30.4
1914	7,885,237	34.8

Note: [a]Excluding the indigenous population, and Argentinians abroad or serving in the army in Paraguay.
Sources: **1869**: Argentina, *Primer censo de la República Argentina, 1869* (Buenos Aires, 1872); **1895**: Argentina, *Segundo censo de la República Argentina, 1895*, vol. II (Buenos Aires, 1898); **1914**: Argentina, *Tercer censo nacional, 1914*, vol. II (Buenos Aires, 1916); Zulma L. Recchini de Lattes and Alfredo E. Lattes, *Migraciones en la Argentina* (Buenos Aires, 1969).

large measure to foreign immigration. Between 1870 and 1914 almost 6 million immigrants, mostly Spanish and Italian, arrived in Argentina, although only a little over half of these settled permanently (for annual figures, see table 2). Foreigners represented 12.1 per cent of the total population in 1869, 25.4 per cent in 1895 and 29.9 per cent in 1914. It is important to note not only the effect which immigration had on the absolute size of the population, but also its influence on changes in the birth rate through its effect on the age structure. Between 1869 and 1895 the population as a whole grew at the rate of 30.4 per thousand annually with immigration accounting for 17.2 and natural growth for 13.2. Between 1895 and 1914, the annual growth rate of the population as a whole increased to 34.8 per thousand, immigration accounting for 17.2 and natural growth for 17.6.[7]

The influence of migration on the formation of the labour force was reflected in various ways: first, in its direct contribution to the growth of total population and the increase in the natural growth rate of the population; and secondly in its annual supply of manpower which went straight into the labour market. The vast majority of immigrants were young and male. In 1895, 47.4 per cent of foreigners fell into the 20–40 age range and 23.4 per cent of native-born Argentines. Figures for the

---

[7] Zulma L. Recchini de Lattes and Alfredo E. Lattes, *Migraciones en la Argentina* (Buenos Aires, 1969), 79, 86.

Table 2. *Immigration and emigration, 1870–1914*[a]

Year	Immigrants	Emigrants	Net gain or loss
1870	39,967	—	+ 39,967
1871	20,933	10,686	+ 10,247
1872	37,037	9,153	+ 27,884
1873	76,332	18,236	+ 58,096
1874	68,277	21,340	+ 46,937
1875	42,036	25,578	+ 16,458
1876	30,965	13,487	+ 17,478
1877	36,325	18,350	+ 17,975
1878	42,958	14,860	+ 28,098
1879	55,155	23,696	+ 31,459
1880	41,651	20,377	+ 21,274
1881	47,484	22,374	+ 25,110
1882	51,503	8,720	+ 42,783
1883	63,243	9,510	+ 53,733
1884	77,805	14,444	+ 63,361
1885	108,722	14,585	+ 94,137
1886	93,116	13,907	+ 79,209
1887	120,842	13,630	+ 107,212
1888	155,632	16,842	+ 138,790
1889	260,909	40,649	+ 220,060
1890	110,594	80,219	+ 30,375
1891	52,097	81,932	− 29,835
1892	73,294	43,853	+ 29,441
1893	84,420	48,794	+ 35,626
1894	80,671	41,399	+ 39,272
1895	80,989	36,820	+ 44,169
1896	135,205	45,921	+ 89,284
1897	105,143	57,457	+ 47,686
1898	95,190	53,536	+ 41,654
1899	111,083	62,241	+ 48,842
1900	105,902	55,417	+ 50,485
1901	125,951	80,251	+ 45,700
1902	96,080	79,427	+ 16,653
1903	112,671	74,776	+ 37,895
1904	161,078	66,597	+ 94,481
1905	221,622	82,772	+ 138,850
1906	302,249	103,852	+ 198,397
1907	257,924	138,063	+ 119,861
1908	303,112	127,032	+ 176,080
1909	278,148	137,508	+ 140,640
1910	345,275	136,405	+ 208,870
1911	281,622	172,041	+ 109,581
1912	379,117	172,996	+ 206,121
1913	364,271	191,643	+ 172,628
1914	182,659	221,008	− 38,349

Note: [a]Excluding first-class passengers.
Source: Extracto estadístico de la República Argentina, correspondiente al año 1915 (Buenos Aires, 1916).

Table 3. *Urban and rural population (percentages)*

Year	Total		Foreigners	
	Rural	Urban	Rural	Urban
1869	71	29	52	48
1895	63	37	41	59
1914	47	53	37	63

Source: First, Second and Third National Censuses, 1869, 1895, 1914.

0–20 age range were 21.8 per cent for foreigners, and 60 per cent for native-born.[8] In 1914, there were more foreign than native-born men in the 20–40 age range. This explains why the influence of immigrants in the labour force was greater than their influence in the population as a whole. Among foreigners, there was a ratio of men to women of 1.7 in both 1895 and 1914. In the native population, there were more women, with a man:woman ratio of 0.97 in 1895 and 0.98 in 1914. Immigration also affected regional distribution, as up until 1914 84 per cent of the immigrants settled in the pampa. Finally, foreigners were more prone than natives to settle in the urban areas (see table 3).

There are no studies showing the general levels of employment in Argentina at the end of the nineteenth century. Census figures on jobs, however, for all their imperfections, do provide information on the economically active. In 1869, they amounted to 857,164 out of a potentially active population aged fourteen and over of 1,014,075 (85 per cent). In 1895, the economically active accounted for 1,645,830 out of a potentially active population of 2,451,761 (67 per cent), and in 1914, 3,235,520 out of 5,026,914 (64 per cent).

For 1895 and 1914 respectively, those in regular employment were distributed as follows: 24 and 16 per cent in agriculture or cattle raising, 22 and 26 per cent in industry, and 29 and 33 per cent in service activities. Some 21 and 28 per cent were without fixed occupation – a category which consisted largely of day-labourers (*jornaleros*) and peons, basically a large mass of seasonal workers who were employed in the countryside

[8] Second National Census, 1895, II, xcix.

at harvest time and spent the rest of the year in the city. The most useful indicators for studying changes in employment patterns, not at their absolute level but rather in their variations, are, for urban employment, figures relating to investment in public works and private construction; for employment in the construction of infrastructure, the variations in the extent of the rail network; and for agricultural employment, variations in the area of cultivated land. These sectors, apart from industrial employment where variations were less marked, provided the greatest demand for labour. Annual immigration figures (see above, table 2) measure variations in the supply of labour. Another useful indicator is that of import figures (see below, table 5). Imports in some ways determine variations in industrial activity, public works and railway construction, all of which require imported inputs, but not variations in private construction and cultivated land, which did not require imported goods. It should be stressed that there is a fairly close correlation between variations in imports and net immigration figures.

In the period under consideration, there were sudden changes in the supply of and demand for labour. The increase in imports and in the economic activity that accompanied them produced a sustained increase in the demand for labour. With the crisis of 1890 and the sudden fall in imports, followed by a decline in public works and railway construction, not only did demand for labour fall, but there was also a noticeable reduction in supply, due to a drastic plunge in immigration. A report by the British consul on this subject is revealing:

In 1890 it will be noticed that not only had immigration decreased 60 per cent, as compared with the previous year, but that emigration had increased 107 per cent. The estimated figures for 1891 show that immigration is still decreasing at an alarming rate, and that emigration during the year has, in all probability, exceeded last year's departures. It should be noted that in 1888–89 the immigration direct from abroad alone, not including the arrivals via Monte Video, greatly exceed the 90,000 to 100,000 immigrants estimated by the Chief of the Immigration Department in his report as being the utmost number the country can properly absorb and employ in the course of a year, the number being 130,271 and 218,744 respectively. It is surprising that with a total influx (including via Monte Video) of over 548,000 persons during the last three years there is not even more distress in this country; and the more so as 871,000 immigrants have arrived in the Argentine Republic during the last six years, 1885–90, or 52 per cent, of the total immigration during the past 34 years. The estimated population of this country is 4,000,000 only, so that the number of immigrants landed here in the last six years forms 22 per cent of the total population of the country. Never has such a proportionally large immigration entered a country in so short a period before.[9]

Some of the manpower already in the country moved to the rural sector where the area under cultivation continued to expand during the crisis of the 1890s. This alleviated the problem of unemployment and prevented the crisis from becoming even more serious. Demand for labour increased again when economic activity revived, especially after 1900, and was immediately met by a larger increase in the inflow of immigrants. The labour market which was characterized by excess demand became after 1910, when the rate of growth in cultivated land began to slow down, one of an excess of supply.[10]

It is widely accepted that the notable growth in wealth in Argentina in the period from 1870 to the first world war did not benefit all sectors of the population equally. While the landowners made the greatest gains, the workers did not receive a proportionate share of the growth in the national income. It has even been argued that for various reasons wage levels dropped during most of the period under consideration. For example, Ricardo M. Ortiz maintained that

limited ownership of land . . . [increased] the rate of emigration, encouraged temporary migration, and made it more likely that new arrivals would take up occupations to which they were not accustomed and which in no way corresponded to their objectives. These people came to form an urban proletariat, a social sector which was both large and unstable. This sector consisted of immigrants who sold their labour at a low price, and put up with a life of poverty and extreme privation with their sights set on the time when they could return to their homeland having saved enough to secure their future.[11]

Low and declining wages during the 1880s have generally been attributed, first, to the effects of inflation and, secondly, to surplus labour in the urban sector caused by the lack of opportunities in the rural sector due to a system of landholding which did not favour poor immigrants. James Scobie also maintained that wages were low for most of the period under consideration, especially during the 1890s, although they did begin to climb after 1905. He held that a firm estimate of the fluctuations in wages could be arrived at by converting wages paid in

---

[9] Great Britain, Foreign Office, Consular Reports, Report on emigration to the Argentine Republic and demand of labour, 1891 (Miscellaneous Series, 1892, No. 216).

[10] See Alejandro E. Bunge, *La desocupación en la Argentina, actual crisis del trabajo* (Buenos Aires, 1917).

[11] Ricardo M. Ortiz, *Historia económica de la Argentina, 1850–1930* (2 vols., Buenos Aires, 1955), I, 209.

paper money to day labourers and skilled workers into a common gold unit. Daily wages paid in peso notes in 1871 had a value of 1.20 in gold pesos; in 1880 they were worth 0.75 gold pesos; in 1885, 1.00; in 1890, 0.60; in 1896, between 0.50 and 0.60; in 1901, 0.55 and in 1910, between 1.20 and 1.50.[12] The high cost of living, Scobie added, had an adverse effect on wage levels.

In fact in real terms (that is, in terms of their purchasing power), wages rose until 1886, then fell until the mid 1890s. However, between 1890–5 and the end of the century, there was a significant real increase caused by an increase in money wages which had lagged behind inflation in the later 1880s and early 1890s, but which had then gradually moved ahead as the cost of living fell after 1895. The increase after 1905 was less marked than Scobie believed because of the effect of the rise in food prices during this period. Some authors have confused stability in the exchange rate with stability of prices in this period. In real terms, the increase in wages was minimal between 1900 and 1910 because of the effect of increases in food prices.

Allowing for important fluctuations which occurred over the 30 years, real wages in Argentina increased during this period. Towards the end of the period, a worker could acquire a third more goods and services than his equivalent some three decades previously. The increase would have been greater for those who had actually begun to work 30 years before, due to the effect which their better training, seniority and great experience must have had on their wages. This does not mean to say that workers' lives were easy and that they were not affected by periods of high cost of living, unemployment and poverty, as their own evidence and that of their contemporaries makes clear.[13] And it is true that immigrants wanting to return home faced the problem that wages in gold pesos fell during the period between 1889 and 1895. Foreign consuls warned potential immigrants that they should not confuse wages paid in gold pesos with those paid in paper pesos.[14] Those who remained on a permanent basis, however, were not affected by this particular problem.

[12] James Scobie, *Buenos Aires, plaza to suburb 1870–1910* (New York, 1974), 266.
[13] For further discussion on real wages, see Roberto Cortés Conde, *El progreso argentino 1880–1914* (Buenos Aires, 1979).
[14] See, for example, Great Britain, Foreign Office, Consular Reports, Report on emigration to the Argentine Republic and demand for labour, 1891 (Miscellaneous Series, 1892, No. 216), and consular reports on the years 1892, 1895, and 1899.

Table 4. *British direct and portfolio investments in Argentina, 1865–1913*
(million pounds sterling)

	1865	1875	1885	1895	1905	1913
Total investment	2.7	22.6	46.0	190.9	253.6	479.8
Direct investment	0.5	6.1	19.3	97.0	150.4	258.7
Portfolio investment	2.2	16.5	26.7	93.9	103.2	221.6
Government loans	2.2	16.5	26.7	90.6	101.0	184.6
Corporate securities	—	—	—	3.4	2.2	37.0

Source: Irving Stone, 'British direct and portfolio investment in Latin America before 1914', *Journal of Economic History*, 37 (1977), 706. Uncorrected figures.

Capital

In an economy as primitive as that of Argentina at the beginning of this period, capital was scarce. Native inhabitants owned fixed assets in the form of large tracts of land or urban housing, and moveable assets such as cattle; there were virtually no other outlets for their savings. Financial institutions were few. Yet the need for enormous investments in infrastructure was critical. In a new country of such vast distances as Argentina, with no settled population in the rural areas and with an economy geared towards the export of products to the other side of the Atlantic, cheap overland and maritime transport was absolutely indispensable. Ports and warehouses were equally important. There was considerable activity on the part of private groups both national and foreign, mainly British, with links to international banking, especially in the railway sector. But it was the state which provided the initial impetus. However, since the state was unable to provide all the necessary finance to fund social overhead investment because its revenue, based primarily on import duties, was insufficient, it had to obtain it by means of loans from Europe, mainly Britain. (On British direct and portfolio investment in Argentina in 1865–1913, see table 4.)

It has been said that Argentina lacked the institutions capable of channelling funds into profitable areas of investment. In reality the situation was somewhat different. The sectors of the economy which sought finance always looked to the government to provide money at lower than market interest rates through the public banks. Throughout a large part of the period under consideration, these institutions, in the first instance the Banco de la Provincia de Buenos Aires founded in 1854 and then particularly from the 1880s the Banco Nacional, considerably expanded the supply of money, greatly increasing credit to the private as well as the public sector and reducing their cash reserves to such an extent that they were unable to meet the demands of their depositors – which on two separate occasions, in 1873 and in 1885, albeit under different circumstances, led to a declaration of inconvertibility and in 1890, as we shall see, to their ultimate collapse.

The principal focus of private and foreign banking operations was commerce, particularly overseas trade. This did not mean that the commercial banks had any intrinsic preference for such activities; rather, these were the safest and most profitable areas of operation. It should also be remembered that the rural sector could count on other sources of capital, the best-known of which were the mortgage facilities provided by national and provincial mortgage banks. But credit was also provided by commercial suppliers or their agents, both national and foreign, and grain exporters would offer advances against the harvest. In this way, fencing and agricultural machinery were imported, grazing lands were fenced and millions of hectares sown. In addition, pedigree breeding stock was imported, and the value of livestock and land, one of the main components of national wealth, thereby increased enormously.

It cannot be said that all capital formation originated overseas. We have seen that local capital played no small part in improvements to land and cattle and in urban construction. Table 5 gives an indication of the enormous growth in the capital stock which occurred in Argentina in the period under consideration. Ports, railways, roads, housing, machinery and cattle ranches were all part of a large volume of capital established throughout the three decades from the period of national unification to the eve of the first world war. Both the gold and constant currency series in table 5 yield a rate of growth for the period as a whole of 7.5 per cent, although the crisis of 1890, when the depreciation of the peso against gold was greater than the loss in its domestic purchasing power, led temporarily to a decline in the gold value of the nation's capital stock.

THE PHASES OF GROWTH

The economic history of Argentina from the 1870s to the first world war can be divided into three periods: the first, which began with the end of the 1873–6 crisis and reached its climax with the 1890 crash, was one of

Table 5. *Capital formation: growth of the capital stock, 1857–1914*

Year	Millions of pesos (gold)	Millions of pesos (paper)	Consumer Price[a] Index (1884 = 100)	In paper pesos deflated by Consumer Price Index
1857	368	—	—	—
1884	1.875	1.875	100	1.875
1892	1.407	3.264	159	2.052
1895	2.840	8.577	190	4.514
1914	14.955	33.989	206	16.499

Note: [a] Based on Consumer Price Index (Food Prices) in Roberto Cortés Conde, *El progreso argentino (1880–1914)* (Buenos Aires, 1979).
Sources: **1857, 1884 and 1892:** M. G. and E. T. Mullhall, *Handbook of the River Plate* (reprint, Buenos Aires and London, 1982); **1895:** The Second National Census; **1914:** Study by Alberto Martínez for the Third National Census.

rapid and dynamic growth; the next, which began in 1890 and ended in the second half of the decade, was one of depression; the last, from the late 1890s, was one of great expansion which, except for two short-lived recessions in 1899 and 1907, was sustained until the crisis of 1912.

The factor which determined whether there was expansion or recession in the short or medium term was the balance of payments, which was in turn determined by trade and the movement of capital (for the most part British). Variations in these figures affected money supply, levels of employment and the demand for labour (the latter through the effect which the importation of capital goods had on the level of economic activity). Other variables which had an important effect on the economy, such as the extent of land under cultivation and private construction, fluctuated independently of changes in the external sector.

The period from 1880 to 1890

During the first half of the 1880s, the most significant development was the increase in the number of head of cattle and the output of cattle-based products. Sheep production lagged behind in comparison to the previous decade, but arable farming began to gather momentum and reached considerable heights during the second half of the decade. However, contrary to what is generally thought, expansion in this decade was not fuelled chiefly by the arable and stock-raising export sectors, but by investment in transport, public works, and private building. Thanks to the great inflow of direct and indirect foreign investment, funds were obtained to import capital goods which were transformed into thousands of kilometres of rail track and into important public works. All this kept economic activity at a high pitch, and was the main factor in the expansion which occurred during the period.

Exports grew, but at a slower rate than imports. Moreover, while their volume increased considerably during the 1880s, they were offset by a fall in prices. There was a trade deficit for most of the period (see table 6), but the inflow of capital kept the balance of payments positive. This had an expansionary effect on the money in circulation, thus, like the incorporation of capital goods and the increase in fiscal revenue from rising imports, giving a further boost to economic activity.

1881 saw for the very first time the issue of a single currency for the whole country: the national gold peso (1 gold peso = 25 paper pesos (*corrientes*); 5 gold pesos = £1). Four banks, of which the Banco Nacional and the Banco de la Provincia de Buenos Aires were the most important, were used from 1883 to issue banknotes. With the aid of a foreign loan, the Banco Nacional increased its capital from 8 million to 20 million pesos, whereupon it considerably increased the issue of currency from 42 million in 1883 to 75 million in 1885. In 1885, however, as a result of the heavy demand for gold thanks to a deficit in the balance of payments and a policy of credit expansion, the Banco Nacional, faced with an exhaustion of its reserves, asked the government to suspend the convertibility of its banknotes. The government granted this request and soon extended the suspension to the other banks of issue. Thus Argentina returned to the inconvertible paper currency system. Under the terms of the Guaranteed Banks Law of 1887 banks multiplied in the interior, where the silver standard had up until then been dominant. They were a determining factor in the increase in circulation to 163 million pesos in 1889.

Unlike the United States' system on which it was based, the Argentine arrangement established by the Guaranteed Banks Law of 1887 did not imply government backing for all notes in circulation. The law required banks to buy national bonds in exchange for gold. Each bank would then receive from the government an issue of notes equivalent to their respective purchases of bonds. However, the principle of a national currency backed by gold was breached in two important respects: first, the government in effect exempted the Banco Nacional, the largest bank

Table 6. *Argentina's external trade, 1870–1914 (in millions of gold pesos)*

Year	Imports	Exports	Balance
1870	49.1	30.2	− 18.9
1871	45.6	27.0	− 18.6
1872	61.6	47.3	− 14.3
1873	73.4	47.4	− 26.0
1874	57.8	44.5	− 13.3
1875	57.6	52.0	− 5.6
1876	36.1	48.1	+ 12.0
1877	40.4	44.8	+ 4.3
1878	43.7	37.5	− 6.2
1879	46.4	49.4	+ 3.0
1880	45.5	58.4	+ 12.8
1881	55.7	58.0	+ 2.2
1882	61.2	60.4	− 0.9
1883	80.4	60.2	− 20.2
1884	94.0	68.0	− 26.0
1885	92.2	83.9	− 8.3
1886	95.4	69.8	− 25.6
1887	117.4	84.4	− 33.0
1888	128.4	100.1	− 28.3
1889	164.6	90.1	− 74.4
1890	142.2	100.8	− 41.4
1891	67.2	103.2	+ 36.0
1892	91.5	113.4	+ 22.0
1893	96.2	94.1	− 2.1
1894	92.8	101.7	+ 8.9
1895	95.1	120.1	+ 25.0
1896	112.2	116.8	+ 4.6
1897	98.3	101.2	+ 2.9
1898	107.4	133.8	+ 26.4
1899	116.9	184.9	+ 68.0
1900	113.5	154.6	+ 41.1
1901	113.9	167.7	+ 53.8
1902	103.0	179.5	+ 76.4
1903	131.2	221.0	+ 89.8
1904	187.3	264.2	+ 76.8
1905	205.2	322.8	+117.7
1906	270.0	292.3	+ 22.3
1907	286.0	296.2	+ 10.3
1908	273.0	366.0	+ 93.0
1909	302.8	397.4	+ 94.6
1910	351.8	372.6	+ 21.0
1911	366.8	324.7	− 42.1
1912	384.9	480.4	+ 95.5
1913	421.3	483.5	+ 62.2
1914	271.8	349.2	+ 77.4

Source: Extracto estadístico de la República Argentina correspondiente al año 1915 (Buenos Aires, 1916).

of issue, from the requirement to purchase national bonds; secondly, the government accepted *documentos a oro* (promissory notes in gold) in lieu of gold from other banks, including provincial banks. As a result, although approximately 150 million gold-backed peso notes were issued, actually gold reserves stood at 76 million. The new regulations caused an abrupt increase in issuance – up 95 per cent in three years – which prompted a 41 per cent depreciation in the currency. The sharp increase in prices that followed led to a shortage in money supply and while the public needed more money to finance its transactions, banks were unable to obtain gold with which to buy bonds and hence put new banknotes into circulation. The result was a reversion to a period of gold scarcity, exacerbated by the need to carry on remitting payments abroad. Various attempts were made to salvage the situation: including an unauthorized issue of 35 million pesos, one of the antecedents of the July 1890 revolution which brought down the government of Juárez Celman.[15] The new government of Carlos Pellegrini, however, had no alternative but to issue a further 60 million pesos. In London the Argentine representative, Victorino de la Plaza, attempted to obtain a moratorium from Baring Brothers, the country's principal creditors. In November 1890 the crisis came to a head with the news that Barings would not allow a postponement on payments nor would they continue the quarterly transfer of existing loans.

The enormous external debt incurred in this period – it rose from 100 million pesos in 1885 to 300 million in 1892 – was another determining factor in the crisis. Foreign loans had had far-reaching effects in expanding public spending, imports and money supply to a very high degree. The end of the flow of loans (with the issue of the last tranche of 25 million pesos for sanitation works in 1889) together with the continuing obligation to carry on sending remittances abroad, in payment of existing loans and services, reversed the balance of payments position (which in 1888, for example, had been in surplus by 150 million despite a 28 million trade deficit). In concrete terms, this had a contractual effect and exerted extreme pressure on the gold market.

Government expenditure had risen from 26.9 million pesos in 1880 to 107 million in 1889 and 95 million in 1890 (in gold pesos from 26.9 to 55.8 and 38.1 million). Revenue, on the other hand, though it also increased, did not increase as much, rising from 19.6 million in 1880 to 72.9 million

---

15 See Gallo, *CHLA* v, ch. 10.

in 1889 and 73.1 million in 1890 (in gold pesos from 19.6 to 38.2 and 29.1 million). The deficit had been covered mainly by foreign loans. Between 1890 and 1891, the government found it necessary to make very considerable payments with the treasury coffers empty, declining revenue and rising gold prices as a result of heavy demand in the market, in order to prop up the Banco Nacional whose metallic reserves were exhausted. Barings' refusal to grant a moratorium brought an end to the initial attempts to avert the crisis and an even more difficult period began. In April 1891, the Banco Nacional and the Banco de la Provincia de Buenos Aires were wound up, followed in June by various provincial banks. The government adopted severe fiscal measures, re-establishing export taxes and imposing a 2 per cent tax on bank deposits and taxes on tobacco and alcohol, and so on. In London, Victorino de la Plaza renewed negotiations with the Committee of the Bank of England. After intense deliberations, a Funding Loan of £15 million was granted to consolidate previous loans, and a capital and interest moratorium was declared. On 1 December 1891 the Banco de la Nación re-opened its doors and issued an additional 50 million pesos. In accordance with the agreements made with the creditors, there was to be no further issuance until the end of the century. (In fact the currency in circulation was reduced by several million pesos – from 306 million in 1893 to 295 million in 1898.) In 1893, a new agreement – the Romero Agreement – extended the time allowed for debt payment. Within a strict scheme of monetary discipline, and helped by a notable increase in the quantity and value of agricultural exports, Argentina's financial situation was reversed: the price of gold dropped, the peso revalued and the country managed to comply in advance with its external obligations.

The period from 1890 to 1900

In 1891 at the height of the financial crisis Allois Fliess made the following comments in a report to the minister of finance, Vicente López:

Agriculture and livestock production improved under the most favourable auspices. But what was of the greatest interest to the whole Republic, and filled all social classes with a sense of deep satisfaction, was the excellent wheat harvest . . . Superior in quality and of an extraordinarily high yield in Santa Fe, Entre Ríos, and certain districts of the other provinces, good to normal in practically the whole Republic, commanding fairly high prices in the great consumer centres of Western Europe, partly because of news of poor harvests in North America and Russia . . . Exports were handled with great speed and in the first four months about 220,000 tons had been exported, while all the wheat visible in the great deposits and elevators of Rosario and Buenos Aires had already been sold and was in the hands of the exporters.[16]

The export of wheat, which in 1888 amounted to 179,000 tons, rose to 1,608,000 tons in 1894. Production, which totalled 845,000 tons in 1891, increased to 2,138,000 tons in 1894.[17] In the urban sector, the situation was different. As a result of the decrease in imports, the construction of the rail network, which continued throughout 1890–2 because of work begun in the late eighties, came almost to a halt after 1893. Railway construction virtually stopped for most of the decade and began to recover only towards the end of the period. Nevertheless it expanded from 11,700 km of track in 1891 to 16,700 km in 1900; and goods carried increased from 4.6 million tons in 1891 to 12.6 million in 1901.

Whereas the private building sector which did not depend so much on imported inputs continued to expand despite the crisis, thus alleviating urban unemployment, public works, like to some extent the railway, slumped. Using 1885 as the base year (= 100), the index for private construction rose from 108 in 1891 to 171 in 1900, and for public works fell from 244 in 1891 to 58 in 1900. Industrial production, for which machinery and capital goods had been obtained during the preceding period, was given a boost because it was protected by the exchange rate, which raised the cost of imported articles. However, industrial growth did not stem from protectionist tariffs, but from the reduction in costs and the winning of new markets. It occurred mainly in products using local raw materials (food and drink), and was able to develop as markets widened, thanks to the railways. This was the case with sugar in Tucumán, wine in Mendoza, and the flour mills in Santa Fe and Córdoba.

Exports rose from 103 million gold pesos in 1891 (nominal values) to 154.6 million in 1900, largely because of exports of agricultural produce, especially wheat, while imports rose from 67.2 in 1891 to 113.5 in 1900 (see above, Table 6). In sharp contrast to the 1880s there was a favourable trade balance during almost the whole decade.

From 1893, the government imposed a restrictive policy as regards the money supply. Between 1893 and 1899, as we have seen, money in circulation fell. The ratio of notes and coins in circulation to exports (if

---

[16] Allois E. Fliess, *La producción agrícola-ganadera de la República Argentina en el año 1891* (Buenos Aires, 1892), 10.

[17] See Ministerio de Agricultura, *Estadísticas agrícolas* (Buenos Aires, 1912), and E. Tornquist, *Desarrollo económico en la República Argentina* (Buenos Aires, 1919).

these are taken as a proxy for the growth of economic activity), given that there are no data for gross domestic product, fell from 2.43 in 1890 to 1.59 in 1899, that is to say, a drop of 79 per cent. From 1895, the paper peso went through a process of revaluation. However, this situation had an adverse effect on exporters and agricultural producers who sought to halt the steady appreciation of the peso. This led in 1899 to a monetary reform and a return to the gold standard.

Government expenditure, meanwhile, which had fallen from 55.8 million gold pesos in 1889 to 33.6 million in 1891, remained below 50 million until 1895. Thereafter it began to rise again, reaching 69.6 million in 1900.

The period from 1900 to 1912

There are two central factors in this period. First, the production of cereals, which had been largely confined to Santa Fe where the acreage given over to wheat tripled between 1887 and 1897, spread throughout the province of Buenos Aires, though complementing rather than displacing cattle raising. Secondly, meat became as important as cereals in Argentina's export trade.

Numerous complaints had been made against the conservatism of the cattle producers of Buenos Aires because of the limited growth of cereal production in the province. Large estates, it was said, were an obstacle to farming, which required a system of exploitation based on small producers. But by the 1890s the situation was already beginning to change. Several factors were contributing to a shift towards grain production and mixed farming. The railway made settlement possible in outlying areas of the province, and, following the railway, wheat cultivation spread to the south and west of the province, and also to the north as far as the department of General López in Santa Fe. At the same time new techniques for freezing meat and refrigerated transport across the Atlantic transformed the meat industry. Meat production became more labour-intensive, but it now required the establishment of artificial year-round pastures on which cattle (of improved imported stock) might be fattened. This led to the cultivation of alfalfa, maize and other crops used as fodder being extended into the cattle-producing areas of Buenos Aires province and into areas of Córdoba and La Pampa hitherto given over exclusively to cattle. By the end of the period more of the pampas was given over to alfalfa than to wheat, and more sheep were driven off the pampas to Patagonia. All this was a function of the significant increase in frozen and chilled beef exports (mainly to Britain), which, along with the continued expansion of wheat and maize exports, raised total exports to almost 500 million gold pesos in both 1912 and 1913 (see above, table 6).

To produce prime meat for overseas markets required important measures of domestic adaptation. These included changes in the use of land, in the system of land tenure and in the size of cattle ranches. These changes were further reflected in a sizeable increase in productivity as measured in kilos of meat per hectare, and also in productivity per employee. All this had further consequences: new settlements of population in the rural areas, the creation of towns, and the establishment of transport routes and commercial networks. In cattle-raising areas, tenancy became common where previously the large cattle ranch had predominated. The number of large and small estates decreased, while medium-sized properties increased. This new wave of agricultural and pastoral activity was on a smaller scale than the cattle raising of old, but larger than the agricultural colonies of Santa Fe. A significant increase in the productivity and profitability of land led to the jump in prices after 1905.

The establishment of the rail network had different effects on the formation of markets. In the first place, old regional markets were re-established, but were now linked to the coast, thus forming one national market. Secondly, produce was transported first to the railway centres, which thus became primary markets, and then to the secondary markets on the coast. Produce was transported in waggons to the railheads, which were never more than 18 kilometres from the point of production. At the stations, primary markets were established where the crop was sold and despatched to secondary markets, or else stored when there were no freight cars available. More than 70 per cent of cereal production had to be transported between the months of December and May; hence sheds and rudimentary storehouses were built at many up-country stations. From the primary markets, cereals were transported directly either to the centres of consumption (if destined for domestic use), or to the ports for export. Some 30 per cent of total railway freight was destined for export and about 28 per cent was produce for domestic consumption.[18] Another 34 per cent of rail traffic corresponded to imported goods which were distributed throughout the domestic

[18] Emilio Lahitte, *Informes y estudios de la Dirección de Economía Rural y Estadística*, Ministerio de Agricultura (Buenos Aires, 1916).

market. In 1904, the railways transported almost 12.5 million tons, excluding the 1.4 million tons of stores carried for railway use. Attention should be drawn here not only to the size of the traffic between distant markets, but also to the importance of the transport of locally produced goods for domestic consumption, namely 28 per cent of total rail traffic, and the significance of imports shipped inland for local consumption.

A further characteristic of this trade was that the primary markets had a positive balance in relation to the secondary markets, in terms of the physical volume of goods transported. The secondary markets were concentrated in the coastal areas. According to the volume of goods exported, in 1906 the main markets were the centres of Buenos Aires, Rosario, Paraná and Santa Fe. In 1914, there was an important transfer of secondary markets away from the riverine areas towards the maritime coast. After Rosario and Buenos Aires, Bahía Blanca became the third port for the shipment of exports followed by San Nicolás, La Plata and Santa Fe. While secondary markets were at first established in a number of small ports, the railways gradually led to the concentration of the three main secondary markets at Rosario (on the Central Argentine Railway which transported cereals from Córdoba and Santa Fe), Buenos Aires for west and central Buenos Aires, and Bahía Blanca for southern Buenos Aires and La Pampa. However, of even greater importance was the growth of the primary markets, mainly in the new areas. Between 1885 and 1914 in the older coastal areas of the province of Buenos Aires the number of stations (primary markets) rose from 5 in 1885, to 22 in 1895, to 36 in 1914. In the south and west, the same years saw an increase in stations from 33 to 123. In southern Santa Fe, the number of stations increased from 111 in 1895 to 141 in 1914; in the central area, there was an increase from 68 to 80. In the pampas area of Córdoba, the number of stations rose from 55 in 1895 to 172 in 1914: in the northwestern zone of the province, they rose from 14 to 21. Not only should the vast increase in new markets be noted, but also some important differences. Between 1895 and 1914, growth was much greater in the pampas area of Córdoba than in the province of Santa Fe. This was due to the much earlier development of Santa Fe, which had already reached a significant size in 1895. The difference lies in the fact that more new primary markets appeared in the new areas of Córdoba, which were linked to the general region of the pampas, and not to the traditional northern area, where there was little if any development.

The technological character of arable farming had considerable effects on the economy. The fact that it was more labour intensive led to a more favourable distribution of income. It also led to the settlement of workers in rural areas, the establishment of diverse transport facilities, and the appearance of various activities providing goods and services for the rural population. This resulted in the formation of urban centres in country districts and the formation of a market in the rural sector which had not existed previously. Railways linked inland markets to the urban markets of the coast and thereby ultimately created a national market. When the census of 1914 was carried out, local production was already catering for a high percentage of domestic demand, some 91 per cent of food, 88 per cent of textiles, 80 per cent of construction, 70 per cent of furniture and 33 per cent of metallurgical products.[19] Local demand began to compete with foreign markets for domestically produced foodstuffs.

Growth was thus not only limited to the export sector. Domestic demand increased given the related processes of rural population growth, urbanization and improved means of internal communication. An increase in the number of wage earners and rising real incomes promoted domestic market growth and provided an expanding range of domestic investment opportunities. These were associated with transport and commerce, with construction, with food processing and with textile production.

Some of these activities, such as services and construction, could only be supplied locally. Others, in the first instance, were supplied by imports. However, when transport costs caused the price of imported goods to exceed those produced locally, there was a strong incentive for local production, which was still greater when cheap local raw materials were used. The location of industry was determined by various factors: (1) the site of raw materials (flour, wines, sugar); (2) the existence of a port of exit to overseas markets for frozen meat; (3) the existence of a port for the supply of fuel, raw materials or imported inputs; and (4) the existence of markets with a high density of population and greater capacity for consumption.

Some 30 per cent of all national industrial establishments and investment in manufacturing was concentrated in the Federal capital. Between 1895 and 1913 this preponderance tended to decrease, from 35.1 per cent in 1895 to 21.1 per cent in 1913, as regards the number of

---

[19] Third National Census, 1914, VII, 71.

establishments, and from 36 to 30 per cent as regards capital. Conversely, in the province of Buenos Aires, the number of establishments rose from 23.9 to 30.4 per cent and the amount of industrial capital from 21.6 to 26.3 per cent in the same period. Other provinces in which there was a growth of industry, listed in order of importance of capital invested in manufacturing, were, in 1895, Santa Fe, Tucumán, Entre Ríos and Mendoza, and in 1913 Santa Fe, Mendoza, Tucumán, Córdoba and Entre Ríos. Between 1895 and 1914 the number of industrial establishments increased from 22,204 to 48,779. Capital rose from 327 million pesos to 1,787 million and numbers employed in industry from 175,000 to 410,000.

The most important event during this period was the monetary reform of 1899, which effected the return to the gold standard after several years of continual revaluation of the currency. A strict monetary policy had been applied since 1893; the stock of money remained almost constant for the rest of the decade – in fact it declined slightly – and resulted in the appreciation of the external value of the paper peso during the years immediately prior to the return to gold. Currency appreciation was also facilitated by favourable trade balances, due not only to fewer imports and to the agreements reached for paying off the foreign debt, but also because of the significant increase in exports and the higher prices these fetched. Parity was fixed at 2.2727 paper pesos to each gold peso. This new parity, while taking into account the new purchasing power of Argentine currency and that of other export countries like the United States, nevertheless implied a certain undervaluation of the peso with respect to the dollar.

A Conversion Board was established to regulate the issue of paper money and build up a gold reserve. By 1903, a metallic reserve of 38.7 million gold pesos had been accumulated; this had risen to 55.5 million in 1904, 101.9 million in 1905 and reached 263.2 million in 1913. The issue of notes was then regulated automatically in accordance with the fluctuations in gold reserves, and these in turn were linked to the balance of payments. Because of the excellent results achieved by exports and rising prices there was a substantial increase in the circulation of notes, although not in the same proportion, given that the legal reserve rose from 23.1 per cent in 1903 and 30.9 per cent in 1904 to 72.7 per cent in 1913.

The notes stock, which had declined to 291.3 million pesos in 1899, rose to 380.2 million in 1903, climbing at an annual rate of 8.0 per cent to

823.3 million in 1913. The ratio of currency to exports was 1.72 in 1903 and 1.70 in 1913. In pesos at their 1903 value, the stock of currency rose from 324 million in 1900 to 615 million in 1912. In other words, in twelve years the stock of currency rose, at constant prices, by 90 per cent, at a rate of 5.5 per cent per year.

The boom in exports was reflected in commercial activity and also had repercussions on banking. The Banco de la Nación, founded in 1890, played a leading role and represented 24 per cent of the capital of all banks, 32 per cent of the loans and 37 per cent of the deposits. Foreign banks represented 11 per cent of the capital, 20 per cent of the loans and 20 per cent of the deposits, the remainder corresponding to other independent Argentine banks.[20] The Banco de la Nación established numerous branches in the interior of the country, which enabled credit to reach the most distant rural areas and to play an important role. In 1905, the charter of the Banco de la Nación was reformed. Among other things, this turned it into an exclusively official entity which was authorized to handle rediscounted documents from other banks. The Banco de la Nación, which held 41 per cent of the gold reserves of all banks, sought to lessen the sudden fluctuations in the supply of and demand for gold by withholding it when it was plentiful and selling it when it was in short supply. Other commercial banks soon followed suit.

The process of general expansion was followed by increased government expenditure, which rose from 69.6 million gold pesos in 1900 to 189.6 million in 1914 (158 million paper pesos in 1900 to 419 million in 1914). Revenues, however, did not increase to the same extent, rising from 148 million to 250 million in 1914. Comparing 1900 and 1912 on the basis of the peso at its 1903 level, it can be seen that revenue rose from 162.6 million in 1900 to 258.5 million in 1912 and expenditure increased from 173.6 million in 1900 to 380 million in 1912. This is to say that at constant prices revenue had increased by 59 per cent while expenditure rose by 118 per cent. The public debt, which had grown steadily from 47.5 million gold pesos in 1870 to 88.3 million in 1880, 355.7 million in 1890 and 447.1 million in 1900, rose by a further 28 per cent to 545 million by 1914.

CONCLUSION

The outstanding feature of the period 1880–1912, with the exception of the years 1890–5, was rapid economic growth. All the indicators point to

[20] Angel M. Quintero Ramos, *Historia monetaria y bancaria de Argentina (1500–1949)* (Mexico, 1970).

an average annual growth rate of more than 5 per cent over the three decades, which distinguishes this period from any other in Argentine history. However, it was not just a question of growth. Substantial changes occurred at the same time which modified the face of Argentina and changed the character of its economy.

On the eve of the first world war, Argentina, with a population of almost eight million, had been transformed from a relatively backward country into a modern one. The empty spaces of the pampas had been settled and 24 million hectares were under cultivation, compared to less than half a million 40 years earlier. A vast network of towns had been formed in the rural areas, and an extensive railway network had been constructed which had 34 thousand kilometres of track in 1914, which had permitted the movement of population towards the interior of the country and the development of a market of factors of production and goods at national level. In addition, ports had been constructed to facilitate the entry and exit of goods and people, and considerable impetus had been given to urban construction.

This growth which changed Argentina was based on the exploitation of staples: agricultural and cattle products which found an outlet in international markets. However, it was not limited to this. Because agriculture and meat production were more labour intensive, they had more linkages, especially backward linkages. On the one hand, transport, housing and clothes were required for the population of the new rural agricultural areas and the urban centres which grew up nearby, apart from the ports. These centres were the primary and secondary markets for agricultural production. Demand for these goods led to the appearance of domestic industries in residential construction, food and drink, and textile production, the location and comparative advantages of which depended on the proximity of markets, lower transport costs and, in the case of food, the lower cost of local raw material.

The more intensive use of labour also permitted a better distribution of income and an increase in demand. Equally, it provided an added incentive for investments in other activities within the domestic market.

Although the influence of the foreign sector was considerable, the situation was not such that other sectors remained undeveloped, especially in the domestic market. Indeed, these other sectors even found facilities, in a period of large surpluses, to import capital goods. On the other hand, exports became reasonably diversified and adjusted quite quickly to fluctuations in prices. During the period under consideration, a great effort was made to encourage capital formation.

Without any doubt, the crucial factor in the growth of the Argentine economy in this period was the existence of foreign demand, which was made possible by the reduction in ocean freight charges. However, apart from the demand for foodstuffs, the period witnessed greater fluidity in the international money market, made possible by the greater frequency and speed of communications. It should be added that during the long cycle of recession which began in the 1870s and continued until the end of the century, prices and interest rates fell in the most developed countries, which meant that capital began to seek larger profits outside the domestic markets. On the other hand, it should be pointed out that during a period of railway fever, there was a strong tendency to produce and export capital goods such as railway equipment.

As for the population, the same factors which affected the commercial and money markets made possible the displacement, on a massive scale, of labour across the Atlantic. The fall in freight costs, insurance, and especially the decrease in agricultural prices resulting from the supplies of American cereals, were all responsible for the displacement of Europe's rural population to America. Rural labour was used with greater efficiency in new, fertile lands. This led to better income and higher wages. Although not the main focus of this chapter, the legal and political aspect should be mentioned. The effective exercise of civil liberty and the legal security promised by the constitution, and which was put into practice with the final organization of the state – that is to say, with the organization of the supreme court of Justice and the Federal courts in the provinces – were important prerequisites for guaranteeing the free movements of labour and capital.

All these factors relate to the question of demand. There is also, however, the question of supply. As we have said, around the 1870s meat and grain were not being produced in great quantity for the domestic market, so that, when foreign demand transmitted by means of price mechanisms grew, meat and grain production could not be increased and geared to the export market. Domestic production was tiny in comparison to what was later to be exported, but, basically, there were no incentives for any increase in demand, given that prices were at a low as a result of the heavy demand for American cereals in Europe during the 1870s and 1880s. Argentina needed to make different adjustments in order to incorporate unused resources, such as land, and to obtain other resources such as capital and labour, and in this way reduce its production costs in order to compete in the world markets. This is precisely what it did when it began to make productive use of a vast area of fertile land, organizing agricultural production on a large scale in order to make it more competitive, and at the same time reducing transport and labour costs. Finally, Argentine exports arrived on the European markets when they could compete in terms of price and quality with produce from other new countries.

To put all this into effect in such a vast new country, investment in public goods such as ports and transport facilities was required over and above individual effort. This investment had to be provided within a short period, and on a hitherto unknown scale. However, basically, most of the effort came from the private sector which opened up new land, introduced improvements and agricultural machinery, created pastures, brought in breeding stock and improved the cattle markets, while at the same time carrying out urban construction and developing industries. It was changes taking place on the supply side which enabled Argentina to achieve high rates of economic growth, to compete in foreign markets and, eventually, to become one of the world's leading exporters of foodstuffs on the eve of the first world war.

10

ARGENTINA: SOCIETY AND POLITICS, 1880–1916*

At the end of the 1870s, few Argentines would have imagined that they were on the verge of a prodigious process of social transformation. Little had happened in the 1870s to make anyone expect that the dreams of progress of the politicians active during the 'National Organization' period (1852–62) would be realized. On the contrary, during the presidencies of Domingo F. Sarmiento (1868–74) and Nicolás Avellaneda (1874–80) economic and social progress, though significant, had been slow and laborious. Of the factors which subsequently contributed to Argentina's rapid economic growth, some had not yet appeared and others were only beginning to emerge. Livestock was still of poor quality; the country imported wheat; only a small part of Argentine territory was covered by the transport network; banking services were still in the rudimentary state; and the influx of capital and immigrants was small. Even this hesitant progress had been interrupted by the severe economic crisis of 1874–7. It is not surprising, therefore, that some people had begun to doubt that the progress of the country could be based on the fertility of the pampas, as had always been imagined. Among clear indications of this incipient attitude were the various studies at the time directed towards determining the location of mineral resources, and the 'protectionist' ideology that emerged in the parliamentary debates of 1876.

The first national census of 1869 had provided clear evidence of widespread backwardness in Argentina. That vast area had a population of under 1.8 million, a density of 0.43 inhabitants per square kilometre. Poverty was reflected in the low quality of housing: 78.6 per cent of Argentines lived in miserable *ranchos* of mud and straw. Furthermore,

---

* Translated from the Spanish by Dr Richard Southern; translation revised by Mr Jeremy Butterfield and the author.

77.9 per cent of those over six years of age were unable to read or write. A large part of the territory was totally uninhabited, and what were later to become the fertile pastures of a large part of the provinces of Buenos Aires, Santa Fe and Córdoba were hardly exploited at all. The 'desert', that obsession of the Argentines, seemed untamable, not only on account of the distances that were economically impossible to bridge, but also because of the indomitable armed resistance of the Indian tribes that inhabited the area. Until well into the 1870s, Indian raids were a continuous nightmare for rural authorities and producers.

President Avellaneda was right to point out that 'the frontier question is the most important of all . . . it is the beginning and the end . . . to get rid of the Indians and the frontier means . . . populating the desert'.[1] It was during his tenure as president that the military campaign led by General Julio A. Roca in 1879 put an end to the long-standing problem. Until then, Indian incursions had occurred repeatedly. In 1872, for example, the Indians reached Cañada de Gómez, only a few minutes' journey from Rosario, the second most important city in the country. In 1875 and 1876 a series of invasions carried out by a confederation of Indian tribes led by their most battle-hardened chieftains devastated important districts, including Azul, Olavarría and Tres Arroyos, in Buenos Aires province. Colonel Manuel Pardo recalled these incursions as follows: 'The settlements burned, as though fire from Heaven had descended on them, the fields were shorn of their crops . . . along the trail of the invaded ranches . . . and meanwhile we heard the echoes . . . of men having their throats cut and women and children being carried off into captivity . . .'[2]

Nor was violence confined to the Indian frontier. Although 1870 marked the end of the long war with Paraguay, it did not mark the end of armed confrontation between different regions within the country. During the 1870s, two major rebellions led by López Jordan, the political leader of Entre Ríos, posed a serious threat to internal peace. And in 1880, as we shall see, the most formidable of all the provincial forces, the militias of Buenos Aires province led by Governor Tejedor, rose in arms against the national authorities. It is not possible to give a detailed description here of the many small-scale insurrections of various kinds which took place in the provinces during these years. Particularly noteworthy, however, was a rising led by General Mitre, a former

---

[1] Nicolás Avellaneda, in his prologue to Alvaro Barros, *Indios, fronteras y seguridad interior* (first published 1872–6; Buenos Aires, 1975), 137.
[2] Quoted in J. C. Walther, *La conquista del desierto* (Buenos Aires, 1973), 384.

president of the Republic and leader of the Nationalist party, in 1874 to prevent the president-elect Avellaneda from taking office.

The years before and after 1874 were marked by bitter disputes between the two Buenos Aires-based parties – the Nationalists and the Autonomists led by Dr Adolfo Alsina – which at that time dominated politics in Argentina. In 1877, President Avellaneda tried to solve the institutional crisis by means of the so-called policy of *conciliación*. Many presidential elections of 1880 the Argentine were again divided into Avellaneda (who formed the National party) accepted this invitation, and some of their leaders took part in the national government. This peace, however, lasted only a short time, and on the occasion of the presidential elections of 1880 the Argentines were again divided into two irreconcilable factions: the supporters of General Roca and the supporters of Governor Tejedor of Buenos Aires. So much greater was the economic strength of the province of Buenos Aires that the representative of Baring Brothers, for example, prophesied a decisive victory for Governor Tejedor.

In the event Roca emerged triumphant. First, he was able to count on the support of most of the officers of the National Army. Secondly, the recently formed League of Governors guaranteed him the support of almost all the provinces. Furthermore, although public opinion in Buenos Aires mostly supported Tejedor, Roca succeeded in acquiring powerful allies in important sectors of the political and economic life of the province, including many Buenos Aires Autonomists and a few supporters of General Mitre. The great confrontation of 1880 was military as well as political, and it was no mere skirmish: about 20,000 men took part and approximately 2,500 were killed or wounded. The heaviest fighting was in the surroundings of the city of Buenos Aires, where many of the inhabitants fought on the losing side. It is in the scale and cohesiveness of the political and military coalition formed in the last years of the 1870s that the key to Roca's final success is to be found. At the same time, displaying great political intuition, Roca had put himself at the head of a growing body of opinion in favour of the strengthening of the central government as the only solution to Argentina's political problems. Even old liberals like Domingo Sarmiento began to emphasize the importance of order and peace: 'The synthesis of the modern republican is less sublime [than *"fraternity, equality* and *liberty"*]; . . . it is *peace, tranquillity* and *liberty*.'[3]

---

[3] Domingo F. Sarmiento, *Obras completas* (Buenos Aires, 1953), xxxix, 68.

'It is as though we were a people recently born to national life, for you have to legislate about everything that constitutes the attributes, resources and power of the nation.'[4] With these words, President Roca (1880–6) inaugurated the parliamentary session of 1881. The following years witnessed the approval of a series of laws that overwhelmingly transferred power to the central government. The city of Buenos Aires was federalized, which partially weakened the dominant position enjoyed by the province of Buenos Aires. The National Army was put on a sound footing, and the provincial militias were disbanded. For the first time a common unit of currency for the whole country was adopted. Primary education and the Civil Register (which until then had been in the hands of the Catholic church) were made subject to the jurisdiction of the national authorities. A series of laws reorganized the judiciary, the municipalities and other spheres of public administration.

Many supporters of Roca in the interior had believed that the defeat of Buenos Aires would strengthen their respective provinces. The consequences of Roca's victory, however, seemed to confirm the most gloomy predictions of those who had been defeated. Leandro N. Alem, the future leader of the Radical opposition party, was not very far from the truth when he asserted in 1880 that the future would see the creation of a central government so strong that it would absorb 'all the strength of the peoples and cities of the Republic'.[5] The legislation passed in the 1880s consolidated the authority of the central government and placed the reins of power firmly in the hands of the head of the National Executive. In a sense the presidentialism which followed was merely the consequence of putting into practice the ideas originally proclaimed by the framers of the constitution of 1853. Scarcity of resources, insuperable geographical barriers and strong local political traditions had prevented these ideas being implemented before 1880.

From 1880 Argentina enjoyed several decades of relative political unity and stability. This coincided with, itself facilitated and was underpinned by exceptional economic growth at an average rate of 5 per cent per annum up to the first world war, and beyond.[6] This in turn resulted in, and was to some extent a consequence of, fundamental

---

[4] For the message of Roca, see H. Mabragaña, *Los Mensajes. Historia del desenvolvimiento de la nación Argentina, redactada cronológicamente por sus gobernantes, 1810–1910* (6 vols., Buenos Aires, 1910), IV, 1.

[5] Quoted by H. Rivarola and C. García Belsunce, 'Presidencia de Roca', in R. Levillier (ed.), *Historia Argentina* (Buenos Aires, 1968), IV, 2489.

[6] See Cortés Conde, *CHLA* v, ch. 9.

changes in the demographic and social structure of the country. The pampas in particular were thoroughly transformed, as Walter Larden, who lived and worked on a farm in southern Santa Fe until 1888, discovered. When he returned in 1908, he found everything changed: 'Alas, for the change. Prosperity had come, and romance had gone for ever.'[7]

SOCIETY, 1880–1914

Argentina had 1,736,490 inhabitants in 1869, 3,956,060 in 1895, and 7,885,237 in 1914. The principal cause of this marked increase in population was the massive influx of immigrants. Between 1871 and 1914, 5,917,259 people entered the country; of these, 2,722,384 returned to their countries of origin and 3,194,875 settled in Argentina. The great majority of these immigrants came from Italy and Spain, but there were sizeable contingents from Central Europe, France, Germany, Great Britain and the Ottoman Empire. A very large number of those who settled did so in the provinces of the littoral (the federal capital and the provinces of Buenos Aires, Santa Fe, Córdoba and Entre Ríos), thus consolidating and strengthening a trend that had its origins in the last decades of the eighteenth century. At the same time internal migration, although smaller in quantity than migration from overseas, was by no means insignificant. Between 1869 and 1914 the littoral provinces increased their share of the total population from 48 to 72 per cent. Population growth in the individual provinces in this period ranged from a spectacular 909 per cent in Santa Fe to 216.8 per cent in Entre Ríos. There were also considerable increases in the new territories (especially La Pampa and the Chaco) which had been only sparsely inhabited in 1869. Except for Mendoza and Tucumán, whose populations grew by 324.5 and 205.6 per cent respectively, figures for the remaining provinces are much lower than those recorded for the littoral. In these other provinces, the demographic increase for the period between the censuses of 1869 and 1914 ranged from 118.2 per cent in San Luis to a mere 25.4 per cent in Catamarca.

The ratio of urban to rural population was also substantially modified. The percentage of inhabitants living in urban areas rose from 29 per cent in 1869 to 53 per cent in 1914. The increase recorded in the city of Buenos

---

[7] Walter Larden, *Argentine plains and Andean glaciers* (London, 1911), 49.

Aires was simply phenomenal: the population shot from 181,838 in 1869 to 1,575,814 in 1914. The population of the city of Rosario, in the province of Santa Fe, rose from 23,139 in 1869 to 224,592 in 1914. In the city of Córdoba, too, where growth was encouraged by the development of cereal-growing in the southern departments of the province, there was a significant increase, from 28,523 inhabitants in 1869 to 121,982 in 1914. The cities of Mendoza and Tucumán also expanded rapidly, as a consequence of the development of vineyards in the former and of the sugar industry in the latter. Mendoza grew from 8,124 inhabitants in 1869 to 58,790 in 1914, and Tucumán from 17,438 inhabitants to 92,824 during the same period. Other examples of this rapid increase in the urban population can be found in the districts which today constitute Greater Buenos Aires, but which had not at that stage been incorporated into the Federal Capital. Avellaneda, for example, which had only 5,645 inhabitants in 1869, grew to 139,527 in 1914, while La Plata, which had not even existed in 1869, had 137,413 inhabitants. Other urban centres in the province of Buenos Aires also showed great increases; for example, the southern port of Bahía Blanca grew from 1,057 inhabitants in 1869 to 62,191 in 1914.

In addition to the rapid growth of the cities, there was also a considerable growth in the number of small townships in the littoral. This was one of the factors which, together with the expansion of the railway network, helped to lessen the traditional isolation of the rural areas. The emergence of these centres of population was caused by the changes that occurred in the economic structure of the region. At first, the expansion of sheep raising led not only to a significant reduction in the scale of livestock raising, but also to an increased division of labour within this sector. Both these developments encouraged a greater settlement of people in the region and a notable diversification of the social and occupational structure. As a consequence of this process, which took place from around 1860 to around 1880, the first rural settlements of any importance appeared, especially in the provinces of Buenos Aires and Entre Ríos. Much more marked, however, was the impact in the period after 1880 of the expansion of cereal growing. This process originated in the centre and south of the province of Santa Fe, and spread to the south of Córdoba and the north-west of Buenos Aires province. The expansion of cereal growing led to a significant increase in the number of rural settlements of between 2,000 and 10,000 inhabitants in the pampas from a mere 20 in 1869 to 221 in 1914.

The massive influx of immigrants in this period upset Argentina's demographic and regional equilibrium. At the same time, there were significant changes in the social and occupational structure of the country. Between the censuses of 1869 and 1895, the expansion of the agricultural sector and of tertiary activities coincided with a market reduction in employment in the traditional craft industries and the obsolete transport system. Between the censuses of 1895 and 1914, the mechanization of agriculture caused a comparative reduction in the level of employment in the primary sector, the level of employment in the newly established industries of the littoral increased and the tertiary sector continued to grow; there was a notable expansion in the building industry, especially in the big cities of the littoral. The part played by immigrants in the occupational structure was all-important, and perhaps without parallel elsewhere in the world. In 1914, no fewer than 62.1 per cent of those employed in commerce, 44.3 per cent of those in industry, and 38.9 per cent of those in the agricultural and stock-raising sector were foreign-born. The figures were lower in the case of the public administration and the educational sector, where the proportions were 17.6 and 14 per cent respectively. There was a significant increase in all these proportions in the three areas where the influx of foreign immigrants had been greatest. In the city of Buenos Aires, immigrants employed in commerce and industry made up 72.5 and 68.8 per cent of the respective totals. In Buenos Aires province, the proportion of foreigners employed in the rural sector was 55.1 per cent, while in Santa Fe it was as high as 60.9 per cent. These figures do not include the children of immigrants who, according to existing legislation, were considered to be Argentine. If they are included, then the number of people of recent immigrant origin in the total economically active population is even greater. In cities like Buenos Aires and Rosario, and in cereal-growing areas such as Santa Fe, third generation Argentinians did not account for more than 20 per cent of the total population.

At the entrepreneurial level this phenomenon is even more striking. The majority of the proprietors of commercial establishments (68.4 per cent) and of factories (68.7 per cent), and a significant proportion of the owners of agricultural and stock-raising undertakings (31.9 per cent) had been born outside Argentina. In the three areas of the littoral already mentioned, the proportions were as follows: 78.3 per cent of the commercial entrepreneurs, 73.4 per cent of the industrialists and 56.9 per cent of the rural proprietors. Within the rural sector, there were appreciable differences between agriculturists and stock-raisers. In the first category, the proportion of foreigners in the country as a whole was 40.7 per cent, reaching 62.4 per cent in the province of Buenos Aires and Santa Fe. Of the stock-raisers, the foreigners constituted 22.2 per cent in the country as a whole, and 49.1 per cent in Buenos Aires and Santa Fe.

The disparity between the rural and urban sectors reflected the fact that commerce and industry were concentrated in the region (the littoral) where the great majority of immigrants had settled. In contrast, rural enterprises were distributed evenly throughout the country, and therefore covered regions where immigration had had a very marginal impact. As to the differences between agriculture and stock raising, two factors are worth mentioning. Firstly, stock raising had been the activity undergoing the greatest development even before the beginning of mass European immigration, whereas the expansion of agriculture coincided with the arrival of immigrants on a large scale. Secondly, given the scale of stock-raising enterprises, capital requirements were much higher than those needed to start agricultural activities.

All these figures point to a very marked process of upward mobility, which reached its greatest extent in the urban areas and the cereal-growing region. However, it was also significant in the stock-raising region where the figures would be even more startling if the offspring of immigrants were taken into consideration. The changes in people's relative social positions affected all strata of local society with equal intensity. At certain times and in certain places, this process was so violent that it bewildered even the most perceptive observers. In 1888, the manager of the Rosario branch of the Bank of London and the River Plate reported to London that 'The rapid progress of this province is making it difficult to keep you at all well posted as to the responsibilities of our clients, for it often happens that one year suffices to change a man's position so much for the better that we can no longer bind him to former limits.'[8]

One consequence of this rapid process of social mobility was the great expansion of the middle sectors of society. Estimates based on the census data are not very precise, but it may be roughly calculated that these groups grew from 12–15 per cent of the economically active population in 1869 to around 35–40 per cent in 1914. In the urban areas this expansion was linked to the growth of the tertiary sector and, to a lesser degree, to

[8] Rosario Manager to Buenos Aires (19 June 1888), Bank of London and South America Archives, University College London library.

industrial development. The growth of the administrative apparatus and the educational system was also important. In the rural areas, in contrast, the growth recorded for the middle sectors was closely related to the spread of cereal cultivation. The smaller size of agricultural undertakings made possible the expansion of a stratum of middling and small-scale proprietors who had existed only in limited numbers during the period when stock raising had predominated. At the same time, the greater complexity of cereal-growing undertakings led to the rise of a range of connected activities (commerce, industry and transport), which emerged in the settlements and towns established during those years. There thus arose a very extensive intermediate sector in the rural areas, and this became one of the distinctive characteristics of River Plate society as compared with the subcontinent as a whole.

Not everybody in the intermediate groups, of course, was in the same situation, as is demonstrated by the case of the tenant-farmers. Until the very end of the century it was comparatively easy for tenants to acquire the ownership of the properties which they worked.[9] Thereafter, a change in the scale of agricultural enterprises, the introduction of modern labour-saving machinery and an increase in the price of land due to the exhaustion of new frontier areas made such acquisition increasingly difficult. This phenomenon (which also occurred in countries such as Australia and the United States) led to a marked increase in the comparative numbers of tenants, who around 1914 constituted 60 per cent of all farmers.

The situation of the Argentine immigrant who became a tenant farmer was substantially different from that of his European counterpart. Working a plot of between 200 and 400 hectares, he was himself an employer of labour, especially at harvest time. However, even though he was in a much better position than was normal in his country of origin, he was not as favourably placed as those who had acquired ownership of land in Argentina. This difference was due to the insecurity of tenure, which was reflected in a standard of living (housing, for example) definitely inferior to that enjoyed by the owner-farmers.

Of the immigrants who settled permanently, not all reached highly placed or even intermediate positions in society. Many continued to carry on the same activities as they had when they arrived. The emerging industry of the littoral area employed, for the most part, labour of foreign

---

[9] On this point, cf. Cortés Conde, *CHLA* v, ch. 9 and Rock, *CHLA* v, ch. 11.

origin. In the city of Buenos Aires, for instance, 72 per cent of the workers and employees were immigrants. The living conditions of the urban working class varied according to circumstances. The wages received were, of course, very much higher than in the immigrants' native countries. During certain periods, Argentina experienced the curious phenomenon of foreign immigration of a seasonal character. The famous *golondrinas* ('swallows') immigrated from Italy for the three months of the harvest season: 'in search of perpetual harvest wages, like swallows in search of perpetual summer'.[10]

Within the country, conditions in general tended to improve markedly during the period from 1870 to 1914. In spite of the great increase in the number of inhabitants, there was a substantial reduction in illiteracy, which fell from 77.9 per cent in 1869 to 35 per cent in 1914. There was also a marked improvement in public health, and there were no longer epidemics of yellow fever and cholera in the big cities. In addition, progress was made in housing. Whereas, as we have seen, 79 per cent of the population lived in mud and straw *ranchos* in 1869, this figure had fallen to 50 per cent in 1895. For 1914 there are no data, but all the evidence indicates a continuation of the trend observable between the censuses of 1869 and 1895. The massive influx of immigrants did, however, lead to serious problems in housing. In the last twenty years of the period, especially in the big cities, there was an increase in the number of persons per dwelling, and this gave rise to a series of problems to which the literature of the period amply testifies. Progress in the sphere of labour legislation was hesitant and slow. Nevertheless, laws were passed about days of rest on Sundays and national holidays; there were regulations governing the labour of women and children, and also legislation on industrial accidents. During this period there was also a continuous reduction in the length of the working day, and by the first world war the eight-hour day was becoming the norm in the majority of urban enterprises.

Conditions in the littoral differed from those in the rest of the country. Although there was progress almost everywhere, the disparities between regions continued to be very significant. These disparities were due to various factors, many of which had obtained before the beginning of the period under discussion. The displacement of the centre of economic activity from Upper Peru to the Río de la Plata, which had begun in the

[10] 'Correspondence respecting emigration to the Argentine Republic', in *Parliamentary Papers. Commercial Reports*, vol. LXXVI (London, 1889).

late colonial period, led to the comparative stagnation of those regional economies that did not adapt themselves adequately to new conditions. This happened in the case of Santiago del Estero and most of the old provinces of the north-west. Although with less intensity, a similar process took place in the region of Cuyo, which was closely linked to the Chilean economy. Even in the littoral itself, the province of Corrientes, bordering on Paraguay, suffered a relative decline during the period 1870–1914.

Disparities can also be detected between regions which did experience rapid growth during this period. In Tucumán, for example, which became an area of seasonal migration from the neighbouring provinces, such as Santiago del Estero and Catamarca, and whose growth was based on the rapid development of the sugar industry, social conditions remained markedly inferior to those in the areas where cereal cultivation predominated. Indeed, among the provinces of the interior only Mendoza enjoyed living standards approximately similar to those common in the littoral.

Levels of education in the different provinces serve to illustrate the problem of regional disparity. In 1914, the national illiteracy rate was 35.2 per cent. In the littoral, however, it was only 26.9 per cent, whereas it rose to 57.6 per cent in the rest of the country. These differences become even more striking if one compares extremes, for instance the city of Buenos Aires (22.2 per cent) and the province of Jujuy (64.9 per cent). The 1914 census provides no data regarding the different types of housing, but the 1895 census figures, though indicating in comparison with 1869 a demonstrable recovery in absolute terms, still do not show significant changes in the relative positions of the provinces. The proportion of sub-standard dwellings (*ranchos*), which was around 50 per cent in the country as a whole, was only 35 per cent in the littoral, but rose as high as 78 per cent in the rest of the country.

Economic progress of this nature naturally produced its victims, to be found generally among the inhabitants of the areas of less rapid development. The most striking case is the people whose trades were severely affected by the modernization of the economy. These included the individual weavers of the interior, whose craft activities could not withstand the competition from imported products, and people employed in internal transport, who were swiftly displaced by the extremely rapid expansion of the railway network. In other cases, the impact of this expansion did not lead to a fall in incomes, but it did affect living

conditions in the regions concerned. The reorganization and modernization of stock-raising undertakings had a profound effect on the
established rhythm of labour and style of life. The disappearance of the
Indian frontier, the increasing commercialization of all stock-raising
products and the striking development of the fencing of pastures all
began to establish less erratic rhythms of labour and to limit the great
mobility that had characterized life in the stock-raising areas. In spite of
its picturesque and romantic distortions, contemporary literature
reflected some of these features in its nostalgic evocation of the past life
of the *gauchos* of the Río de la Plata region.

The different social sectors into which the population was divided
gradually became organized. As early as 1854, the Buenos Aires
Commercial Exchange had been founded, and during the period after
1870 several minor chambers of commerce were established, both in the
capital and in the principal cities of the rest of the country. In 1866, the
influential Argentine Rural Society had been founded; its members were
the stock raisers of the province of Buenos Aires. It became firmly
established, however, only after 1880, when similar organizations were
founded in other provinces. The Argentine Industrial Union, formed by
manufacturers from all over the country, was established in 1886. This
was also the period of the earliest workers' organizations, which grew to
very significant dimensions in Buenos Aires, Rosario and the chief
railway centres. Until the end of the nineteenth century the progress of
trade unionism was slow and erratic, but it expanded very rapidly during
the first decade of the twentieth century. In 1901 the FOA (Argentine
Workers' Federation) was established, but this soon yielded place to the
FORA (Argentine Regional Workers' Federation). In 1905 the FORA,
at its Fifth Congress, came under anarchist control. Even though
anarchist influence waned after 1910, FORA remained under anarchist
control until its Ninth Congress in 1915, when syndicalists gained control
of most of the labour movement. In 1907 the UGT (General Workers'
Union) had been founded; this was a minority organization consisting of
trade unions with socialist tendencies. The labour movement of that
period had two principal centres: first, the big ports, at that time true
emporia of labour, in which the most varied activities and occupations
were closely interconnected. Later, the network of transport and related
industries which grew up around the principal railway centres became
the second centre.

The massive influx of immigrants, their assimilation into society, the rise and decline of social groups and the speed of the process of social change naturally led to a series of conflicts and tensions. During the 1870s there were clashes between native Argentines and foreigners, and some of these, like the Tandil massacres in 1871, involved bloodshed. The areas most affected were the rural districts of Santa Fe and Buenos Aires, while the capital and Rosario also witnessed conflicts of a similar nature. Between 1890 and 1895 there were similar clashes, for which once again the agricultural colonies of Santa Fe province were the principal scene. In Buenos Aires city, the crisis of 1890 produced 'chauvinist' reactions which were not of a serious character. Thereafter, this sort of conflict declined, though they recurred occasionally during periods of strikes and terrorist activities, which some people attributed to the action of foreign agitators.

Of much greater importance were various conflicts between different sectors of the population. In Argentina, confrontations between agriculturalists and industrialists, or between national and foreign undertakings, were rare and of little importance. However, there were conflicts between employers and workers, and sometimes between trade unions and the national authorities. Between 1907 and 1916, a period for which we have reliable data, there were 1,290 strikes in the city of Buenos Aires. Of these, five were general strikes.

The sectors most affected by labour stoppages were the lumber industry, clothes manufacturing, building, foodstuffs, metallurgy and textiles. Over half the strikes were aimed at winning increases in wages or reductions in working hours. As might be supposed in this formative period for the trade unions, many of the strikes (35 per cent) had as their objective the consolidation of union organizations. Nearly 40 per cent of the strikes obtained total or partial satisfaction of the workers' demands; most of them, however, were in the end disadvantageous to the strikers.

The above figures are somewhat distorted owing to the occurrence of general strikes of a political nature which were always unsuccessful. The theory of the general strike, which was in vogue in certain European countries, was restricted to a few districts in the country. On most occasions, such strikes did not even affect all the factories situated in the big cities: they were usually confined to the dock areas of Buenos Aires and Rosario and the principal railway centres. One demand always made by the participants in these general strikes was the repeal of the so-called Residence Law of 1902, which enabled the Executive Power to deport foreigners whom it considered dangerous to internal security.

In the rural areas, labour unrest on the same scale as in the big cities did not occur. The most serious conflict took place in 1912. Based on southern Santa Fe province, with ramifications in Córdoba and Buenos Aires, it affected the tenant-farmers of the prosperous maize-growing region, who at that time were facing low prices and high rents. For two months, the tenant-farmers refused to harvest the crop, and did so only when some of their demands had been met by the proprietors. It was after this curious episode, which was a mixture of strike and lock-out, that the Argentine Agrarian Federation was founded by the tenant-farmers of the cereal-growing region. During this period, in contrast, the peons of the stock-raising areas and workers in the north only established organizations very erratically.

Massive immigration had a profound impact on the style of life prevailing in the Río de la Plata littoral. Nevertheless, despite tensions and conflicts, the process of assimilation was, generally speaking, both rapid and peaceful. The residential quarters of Buenos Aires and the agricultural colonies of Santa Fe, to cite two examples, soon developed into real cosmopolitan centres where people of different nationalities were blended together. All aspects of daily life, from eating habits to language, were affected by this rapid assimilation of the immigrants into local society.

Various factors contributed to the rapidity with which the process of assimilation took place. First, in many regions, as has been observed above, the immigrants never constituted an ethnic minority, being sometimes more numerous than the local inhabitants. Furthermore, the majority of immigrants came from countries such as Italy and Spain, which had similar cultural, linguistic and religious characteristics. Moreover, civil legislation and everyday practice were extremely liberal towards the new arrivals, to such an extent that some people complained that the native born suffered discrimination. Of fundamental importance was the part played by the primary educational system (in accordance with Law No. 1,420), which created state schools without ethnic or religious discrimination, and gave education a markedly integrative character. Finally, participation in many shared activities accelerated the process of integration. Around 1914, for example, Buenos Aires had 214 mutual-aid societies, with 255,000 members. The majority (51.4 per cent) of the members belonged to mixed-national societies, consisting of people of different origins. Second in importance were the societies whose members were immigrants of the same nationality; and at the bottom of the list were a small minority of societies formed by native Argentines.

Local usages and customs were transformed not only by immigration but also by the sudden prosperity resulting from the long economic boom. We have already observed how the introduction of cereals modified the physical and social character of the areas concerned. To a lesser extent, there were similar transformations in the stock-raising area. The long barbed-wire fences, the fields planted with alfalfa and the high-quality stock contrasted with the rustic character of the old cattle ranch. Those austere and simple farmhouses which had impressed W. H. Hudson and other foreign travellers with their poverty were replaced by more elaborate, and at times luxurious, rural residences such as those that astonished the French traveller Jules Huret around 1910.

In the big cities the transformation was even more noticeable. Buenos Aires was, like all the metropolises of the time, a city of contrasts: 'Buenos Aires has its Picadilly and its Whitechapel, which here is called "the rubbish-heaps . . ." it has its "palaces", but it also has its "tenements".' These were the contrasts between the northern and the southern part of the city, contrasts continuously denounced in the political speeches of the socialists of Buenos Aires.[11] The south and the north represented the city's two extremes, and these areas in particular made an impression on those who visited them. The most important phenomenon, however, was less spectacular: it consisted of the new districts formed by one-storey houses of a lower middle-class character which sprang up on innumerable plots on the unused land. However, even in 1914, some empty spaces were still visible, standing as a symbol of the closeness of the pampas to the very heart of the city.

Indeed, almost everything in the city was new. Little remained of the austere and provincial Buenos Aires of former times. The city was unrecognizable to anyone who had visited it in 1880. Increasing affluence was soon displayed in the refinement and opulence of public buildings. The big administrative buildings, the extensive parks with their costly monuments, the new avenues, the trams and the underground railway, all bore witness to this sudden collective enrichment. European customs and fashions were transplanted to the Río de la Plata region with an unusual speed, not only because they were brought by the immigrants, but also because there was an increase in the number of

[11] J. Huret, *En Argentine: de Buenos Ayres au Gran Chaco* (Paris, 1914), 30. For the Socialist view, see, for example, the pamphlet by Mario Bravo *La ciudad libre* (Buenos Aires, 1917).

Argentines crossing the Atlantic in both directions. Buenos Aires was changing as quickly as the composition of its population was transformed. In each of the twenty districts that made up the city, at least 43 per cent of the population was foreign-born. In the five most central districts, which were the most populous and active and where commercial establishments, theatres, cafés and administrative buildings were concentrated, the proportion of foreigners fluctuated between 54 and 62 per cent. 'Where is Spanish blood, one wonders. What is an Argentine?' the Frenchman Jules Huret asked in astonishment.[12]

But as well as traffic in people, goods and customs there was, of course, traffic in ideas. Buenos Aires at the turn of the century was receptive to all the scientific, literary and political currents of thought that were in vogue. This receptiveness was fomented by the rapid expansion of secondary and university education, and the creation of innumerable scientific and literary societies. In Buenos Aires, around 1914, hundreds of periodical publications were in circulation, many of them in foreign languages (Italian, English, French, German, Russian, Greek, Danish and Arabic), and several of them became vehicles for some of the new ideas that were entering the country.

Liberalism continued to be the predominant creed among the groups that directed cultural, social, economic and political life. In some groups, this liberalism reflected a certain tension between the optimism characteristic of the period and further intensified by the spectacular material progress of the country, and a certain scepticism caused by the memory of a recent past characterized by instability, conflict and violence. This scepticism was accentuated by the suspicion that the combination of a vast geographical area and the Latin race was not the best foundation for a solidly based stability. Such attitudes found expression in the anxiety to overcome the South American syndrome, as it was known, and in the belief that this would only be possible if the reins of power continued firmly in the hands of those who had governed the country since 1880. Also frequently found was that curious combination of admiration for certain European countries and an ardent patriotism that was created by the feeling of being the founders of a new Republic. This attitude was clearly demonstrated in foreign policy. Thus, for instance, at the First Pan-American Congress (1889) the Argentine delegation proudly and successfully challenged the attempt by

---

[12] Huret, *En Argentine*, 40.

the United States to set up a continent-wide customs union. During the negotiations with European creditors in the wake of the financial crisis of 1890, the foreign minister took an equally firm line. No less consistent was the policy on defence, which aimed at tilting in Argentina's favour the balance of power with Chile and with Brazil. In the last analysis, Argentine politicians did not attempt to hide the pride they felt at guiding the destiny of the country which, by the beginning of the twentieth century, had become the most powerful and prosperous in South America.

This brand of liberalism existed alongside another variant, popular in intellectual and political circles, and of a more decidedly optimistic and universalist character. This strand of liberalism was strongly influenced by Darwin, Spencer, Lombroso, and so on, and by nearly all the positivist and evolutionary theories then in vogue. These tendencies were to be reflected in official publications overflowing with statistics that proudly demonstrated the constant progress of the country. They were to be found also in some unexpected places, like the new and sophisticated Zoological Gardens whose construction was influenced by the ideas contained in Darwin's *Origin of Species.*

Such ideas, or the various combinations of them, did not suffer any serious challenge in the period before the first world war. During the discussion of the secularizing laws passed in the 1880s, the Catholic opponents of these laws proclaimed the same political and economic liberalism that underlay the ideas of the legislators who supported the government's proposals. Perhaps this is one of the reasons why the religious factor was only very sporadically a cause of political dissension in Argentina. Nor did the political opposition put forward ideas openly at variance with those prevailing among the ruling groups; not, at least, in the economic and social sphere, nor in that of existing institutions. In the case of the principal opposition force, the Radical Civic Union, criticism of the regime took on a strong moralistic overtone in reaction to what was considered to be a society excessively cosmopolitan and too obsessed with material welfare. The anti-positivist and nationalist reaction which began to emerge after 1900 can be seen in the speeches and documents emanating from the Radical Civic Union.

As we have seen, until about 1910–15 the labour movement was dominated by the anarchists. The Argentine anarchists, however, were significantly different from their European counterparts. Although both groups utterly rejected participation in parliamentary and electoral processes, and the intervention of the state in negotiations between employers and unions, in Argentina the prevailing doctrine was a kind of anarcho-syndicalism *avant la lettre* which concentrated its activities almost exclusively on the trade union. On the basis of the union the anarchists organized a series of co-operative, recreational and cultural activities which gave them a certain popularity in the working-class districts of Buenos Aires and Rosario. Nevertheless, in spite of their Bakuninist rhetoric, the Argentine anarchists were much more moderate than their European counterparts, and their more radical factions (including terrorists) found little acceptance in the Argentine milieu.

Much the same was true in the case of the socialists, who were moderate even in comparison with the contemporary currents of reformist thought that appeared in Europe. The Argentine socialists soon replaced a series of Marxist premises with ideas derived from the liberal and positivist tradition. At the same time, the political models which they most admired were the British and Australian labour movements, Belgian co-operativism and French radical-socialist tradition. Consequently, it is not surprising that when he visited Buenos Aires, the Italian socialist Enrico Ferri should have characterized his Argentine *confrères* as members of a 'Socialist party of the moon'.[13] Like the anarchists, the socialists did not question the basic foundations of the Argentine economy: they were supporters of free trade and ardent defenders of a strictly orthodox monetary policy. On both subjects, they were, in fact, much more emphatic than the politicians supporting the government. Alfredo Palacios, the first Socialist member of parliament to be elected in the Americas (1904), summed up exactly his party's economic ideology in rejecting the protectionist arguments put forward by the legislators who supported the government: 'While eternally protected industries enjoy the benefits of restrictive legislation, our true national wealth, namely stock raising and agriculture, is neglected.'[14]

The profound economic changes which occurred after 1870 had a pronounced influence on Argentine society, and, among other things, led to new social conflicts. However, these conflicts were in their turn conditioned by increasing well-being, the high rate of social mobility, and the success of an economic process that produced more beneficiaries

---

[13] Juan B. Justo, 'El Profesor Ferri y el Partido Socialista Argentino', *Socialismo* (Buenos Aires, 1920), 129ff.

[14] Quoted in O. Cornblit, 'Sindicatos obreros y asociaciones empresarias', in G. Ferrari and E. Gallo (eds.), *La Argentina del ochenta al centenario* (Buenos Aires, 1980), 595–626.

than victims. Argentina in 1914 bore little resemblance to the rest of Latin America, and, despite the Europeanization of many customs and ideas, it was also different from the Old World. It was in some ways similar to the new societies that had emerged on the plains of Australia and North America. But as we shall now see, the social situation was not mirrored in political and institutional life.

POLITICS BETWEEN 1880 AND 1912

The triumph of General Roca in the struggle of 1880 was followed by the formation of the National Autonomist party (PAN), the earliest nationwide political organization in Argentina. In addition, the National Army acquired a monopoly of force and became, with occasional exceptions, the firm support of the national authorities. In comparison with earlier periods, the new political stability was based on the universally recognized supremacy of the National Executive and a corresponding decline in the power of provincial leaders and *caudillos*. The central government maintained its control over the provinces by means of a graduated system of rewards and punishments, designed to achieve a delicate equilibrium between the need to obtain the support of the governing authorities and the desire to avoid the repetition of seditious acts. The provincial governors had a significant, though subordinate, role in the official coalition (PAN), and were rewarded with positions of prestige on a national scale. The sanctions were no less efficient. They consisted of federal intervention, which the Executive could decree even during periods of parliamentary recess (which could last as long as seven months). This was a powerful instrument for dealing with movements of disaffection. The role of federal intervention was defined thus by Osvaldo Magnasco, one of the most prominent politicians of the official party:

Federal interventions in this country, gentlemen, have invariably been decided on with one of these ends in view: to suppress a certain influence or to re-establish it, to set up a local government capable of guaranteeing the domestic position of the Executive, or to overturn a local government opposed to the central government.[15]

The constitution had facilitated presidential supremacy through such mechanisms as federal intervention. However, it had also placed

[15] Quoted in J. Irazusta, *El tránsito del siglo XIX al XX* (Buenos Aires, 1975), 169.

obstacles in its path: above all, the principle that forbade presidential re-election (a significant difference from, for example, the Mexico of Porfirio Díaz), and the control exercised over the executive by the judiciary and the Congress. The judiciary, especially, managed to maintain a degree of independence from the central powers. Further-more, the liberal principles of the constitution made possible the development of an extremely influential press which kept a close watch over the actions of the national authorities. This press, at least until the beginning of the twentieth century, had more importance in the formation of public opinion than did electoral activities. Ramón Cárcano was not far from the truth when he pointed out to Roca's successor Juárez Celman (1886–1890) that 'a newspaper for a man in public life is like a knife for a quarrelsome *gaucho*; he should always have it at hand'.[16] The turn-out at elections made matters easier: it was low in comparison to subsequent periods, though not so low when compared with that common in other countries of the world during these years. In normal circumstances votes were cast by between 10 and 15 per cent of the population eligible to vote (male Argentines of over 18 years of age; there were no literacy requirements). At times of great political enthusiasm (the years 1890–5, for example), turn-out might rise as high as 20 or 25 per cent of those entitled to vote. Moreover, the poll was much higher in the rural than in the urban areas.

If voting amongst those eligible was low, it was even lower as a percentage of the total male population of voting age. This was due to the enormous number of foreigners resident in the country, the great majority of whom had not acquired citizenship. The reasons for not doing so are unclear. In the first place, the foreigners had not immigrated with this objective in mind, and Argentine legislation did not establish discrimination of any kind with regard to their carrying on their activities in society. Moreover, if they did not become naturalized they could still count on the support of the consuls of their respective countries, some of whom, such as the Italian consuls, were extremely active in keeping the immigrants faithful to their countries of origin. Secondly, citizenship papers were not needed for petitioning and pressuring the authorities, since this could be done through employers' and workers' organizations. Besides, the anarchists and syndicalists attached no importance to the acquisition of citizenship papers. Finally,

---

[16] Quoted by T. Duncan, 'La prensa política en la Argentina: Sud-América. 1885–1892', in G. Ferrari and E. Gallo (eds.), *La Argentina del ochenta al centenario*, 761–84.

the opposition parties, with the exception of the socialists, showed little interest in recruiting foreigners into their ranks.

At that time, political indifference was the characteristic attitude of the majority of the population. Voting was not obligatory (as it was after 1912); on the contrary, from his inclusion in the electoral register until polling day, the citizen had to show interest and diligence in order to be able to vote. Furthermore, the elections were more than once characterized by fraudulent practices of various types, which were quite common at the time. Fraud did not, of course, take place systematically, because the apathy of the population made that unnecessary. It was, however, employed whenever the opposition overcame that apathy and threatened the stability of the governing authorities. There were various kinds of fraud, ranging from the most inoffensive tricks and the purchase of votes to the open use of physical violence. For this to be effective, however, those who indulged in it (sometimes the opposition) had to be able to count on the solid support of their political clientele and to have a proper organization.

This political organization had to supply men to fill the many varied appointments on the national, provincial and municipal administration, and it had to supply members of parliament and journalists to reply to the attacks of the opposition. However, it also had to win some popular support in order to be prepared for elections and even armed revolts, which remained an important feature of Argentine politics. For it was not only regular military forces which took part in armed revolts. On many occasions sizeable contingents of civilians also joined in. Until 1881 the provincial militias were the chief source of civilian involvement in revolts, especially in rural areas. These militias, which were generally led by political *caudillos* with military experience, were the main support of the provincial governments. Some of them, like the Santafesinos in 1880, even played an important part in national politics.

After the disbandment of the militias (1881), armed uprising with significant civilian involvement continued to occur. The revolution of 1890, which failed to overthrow the political system but which led to the fall of Juárez Celman, was organizationally a classic military-civilian uprising led by a political faction. Civilian involvement, however, was on a far smaller scale than in the bloody events of 1880. Nevertheless, during the provincial revolts of 1893 in Santa Fe, Buenos Aires, Corrientes, San Luis and Tucumán, large groups of civilians joined the combatants. In Santa Fe, many hundreds of immigrant farmers took up

arms in defence of the revolutionaries. The number of people involved in
these revolts was similar to the number of voters in the 1894 elections for
the Santa Fe and Buenos Aires districts.

As a consequence of this violence, recruitment in politics had to be
carried out with an eye to the possibility that recruits would be involved
in fighting at great risk to their lives. It was for this reason that strong
bonds of loyalty had to be formed between the leaders and their
followers. Those responsible for cementing these bonds were not the
national leaders, but the *caudillos* (bosses) of the rural districts or the
urban areas. Such people held a key position in the political mechanism,
because they were the real link between the regime and its clientele. The
loyalty of this clientele was not freely bestowed, but was based on a
complex system of reciprocal favours. The political boss provided a
series of services which ranged from the solution of communal problems
to the less altruistic activity of protecting criminal acts. Between these
two extremes, there were small personal favours, among which
obtaining jobs was paramount.

The *caudillos* were men of the most varied origins (small landowners or
merchants, overseers of ranches and, more usually, ex-officers of the
disbanded provincial militias) and, even though at times they held minor
political appointments (as justices of the peace, deputies, etc.), they were
usually content to exercise extra-official influence and power in their
region. They were praised and vilified, and these two extremes represent,
in a way, real facets of an extremely complex reality. Thus it could be
asserted that 'to these *caudillos* the government . . . gives everything and
permits anything – the police, the municipality, the post-office . . . cattle
rustling, roulette, in short all kinds of assistance for their friends and
persecution to their enemies'. On the other hand, the *caudillo* could be
defined as 'the man who is useful to his neighbours and always ready to
be of service'.[17] What is quite evident is that they possessed a great degree
of independence, and that it was necessary to enter into intensive
negotiations in order to obtain their support. In the words of one of the
most influential *caudillos* of the province of Buenos Aires, on the occasion
of the compilation of the list of candidates for the provincial elections of
1894:

What we conventionally refer to as the Provincial Union [the name of the PAN
in Buenos Aires province] is composed of two parts: there is a decorative part,

---

[17] Francisco Seguí, quoted in D. Peck, 'Argentine politics and the Province of Mendoza, 1890–
1916' (unpublished D.Phil. thesis, Oxford, 1977), 36, and Mariano de Vedia, quoted in *ibid.*, 32.

made up of certain absentee landowners who reside in the city of Buenos Aires whose importance is more social and metropolitan than rural, and another part, the real militant electorate, made up of us, who are those who . . . have struggled in the province . . . We respect the decorative value of the other part, but we shall do so only if the real interests of the countryside, that is to say of the real provincial party, are taken into account . . .'[18]

Above this complex and extensive network of local bosses there were the provincial and national directorates of the official party, which was an equally complex and variable group of political leaders. These men were governors, ministers, legislators, and so on, and from their ranks emerged both the president of the Republic and the leader of the PAN, who were often one and the same person. From 1880 to 1916 this ruling group controlled national politics and, with very few exceptions, ruled the destinies of the Argentine provinces. The political opposition and certain more or less neutral observers accused it of being a monolithic and closed oligarchy which used any means to maintain its predominant position; a description which was, up to a point, correct, especially as regards the well-known political exclusiveness which the ruling group displayed. This picture, however, risks being somewhat stereotyped. Among other things, it takes no account of the fact that the ruling group that emerged in 1880 was, to a certain extent, the product of a significant change within the political leadership of Argentina. Carlos Melo, one of the first historians to observe this phenomenon, described it as follows:

At the same time, the conquest of the desert and the distribution of land . . . had increased the numbers of landowners by the addition of rough characters of humble extraction, and no less obscure soldiers rewarded for their military services . . . Both the new urban middle-class group and the new landowners were resisted by the patrician nuclei of old Argentine society, which explains why the former, in their aversion to the latter, gave their support to the president [Roca].[19]

The description of the new type of politician given by Melo is exaggerated, and expresses too rigid a dichotomy. However, it is a good description of a marked tendency and, at the same time, accurately reflects the way the ruling group was seen by its political opponents. This perception, which was quite clear in such places as Buenos Aires, Córdoba and Tucumán, was characteristic of the 1880s, and persisted until at least the middle of the following decade. It was a political phenomenon which reflected what was happening in the social sphere.

---

[18] *La Prensa* (Buenos Aires), 20 December 1893.
[19] C. R. Melo, *La campaña presidencial de 1885–6* (Córdoba, 1949), 22.

The political homogeneity of this ruling group should not be exaggerated. It was made up of people who represented regional interests which were often at variance. The history of the regime was marked by numerous internecine conflicts which had some influence on its final collapse. The periods of stability coincided with epochs of strong personal leadership, especially during the presidencies of Roca (1880–6, 1898–1904). On the other hand, instability predominated when the absence of strong leadership opened the field for all those opposed interests.

During this period, the term 'oligarchy' was used in its classic political sense. The PAN certainly counted among its members many who were prominent in social and economic life. However, many members of the elite were active in the opposition parties and were at times excluded from public life in consequence. Furthermore, the majority of the most prominent figures of the business world displayed a notorious indifference to politics, possibly because the contending groups did not differ very much in their conception of economic organization. One episode provides a good illustration of this phenomenon, because it is the only example of an explicit connection being established between the official faction and an important group of stock raisers in Buenos Aires province. During the election for provincial governor in 1894, the Provincial Union (the official party) was nicknamed the 'cattle party' on account of the well-known involvement in it of the Buenos Aires stock raisers. The Radical newspaper *El Argentino* predicted that the official candidate was going to have the following characteristics:

he will have to be somewhat *high life* (sic). He must above all have connections with the Jockey Club, because this appears to be an indispensable condition for a person who is to govern . . . This gentleman will have the advantage of being . . . a landowner, merchant, politician and financier . . .[20]

Those of the 'cattle party' did not spurn their nickname. Some members, such as Miguel Cané, adopted it with complacent pride: 'Yes, gentlemen, we are "cattle" and "sheep" because we are striving for the enrichment of every district of the province. As "cattle" and "sheep" we demand freedom for men, security for the cattle herds, and improvements in wool production . . .' At the same time, the official press would describe the opposition Radical party as 'pigs', clearly alluding to the support it received from the Agrarian League. However, the political

[20] *El Argentino* (Buenos Aires), 9 November 1893.

rhetoric of the period conceals the fact that the opposition parties (Radicals and *cívicos*) also numbered prominent Buenos Aires stock raisers among their members. The Agrarian League itself was made up of rural proprietors who were far from occupying the humble economic status suggested by the nickname 'pigs'. Finally, on this occasion the opposition was able to count on considerable support in other important financial and commercial circles, both national and foreign.[21]

The pre-eminence of personal rule also led to divisions within the ranks of the official party. Juárez Celman, for example, attempted to depose Roca from the leadership of the PAN and undermine the position held by Roca and his supporters both in the PAN and in the provinces. From 1889 onwards, the supporters of Juárez Celman also launched a bold political offensive against the Federal Capital, chief stronghold of the opposition. Their plan failed, however, because the financial crisis of 1890 created conditions favourable to the military revolt of the opposition. Yet it was not the opposition that benefited from the revolt, but rather Roca, who regained the position he had lost in the PAN, and Vice President Carlos Pellegrini, who became president (1890–2). The forces that supported Juárez Celman were not entirely defeated, and promptly regrouped into the Modernist party, thereby obliging Roca and Pellegrini to seek the support of Bartolomé Mitre, who had led the moderate wing of the revolutionaries and who expected to succeed to the presidency in 1892. In the event a weak compromise candidate, Luis Sáenz Peña, became president (1892–4). His period in office was characterized by unstable coalition cabinets and further armed insurrections organized by the Radicals. The resignation of Sáenz Peña because of ill health, his replacement by the pro-Roca Vice President José Evaristo Uriburu (1894–8) and the defeat of the armed revolts made possible a new consolidation of the power of Roca, which culminated in his election to the presidency for the second time (1898–1904). In 1901, however, Carlos Pellegrini, a national senator at the time, broke with Roca over the handling of the negotiations on the foreign debt. Roca found himself obliged to form a new coalition which in 1904 elected as president Manuel Quintana (1904–6), a former sympathizer of Mitre, and as vice president a Modernist, José Figueroa Alcorta. When Quintana

---

[21] Cané's speech in *La Tribuna* (Buenos Aires), 11 January 1894. The majority of the business community was in fact somewhat indifferent to political developments. For the attitudes of those who did participate in politics, see Ezequiel Gallo, 'Un quinquenio difícil. Las presidencias de Carlos Pellegrini y Luis Sáenz Peña (1890–95)', in Ferrari and Gallo (eds.), *La Argentina del ochenta al centenario*, 215–44.

died in 1906, he was replaced by Figueroa Alcorta (1906–10) who, with the support of the dissident elements in the official party and a few members of the opposition, destroyed the political coalition (especially in the interior) on the basis of which Roca had enjoyed twenty-five years of political predominance.

Roca fell by the very instrument on which he had based his predominance: the enormous power of the presidential office. This power was derived from two sources: a strongly personalist historical legacy, and a national constitution which had granted very extensive powers to the National Executive. To all this was added the fear of chaos and anarchy which had been the legacy of the difficult decades before 1880. Roca clearly described the tremendous tension existing between stability and order on the one hand and political freedom on the other. He was aware of the countless defects which plagued Argentine democracy, but he believed they were rooted in the age-old habits of the people. The cure for political ills, therefore, had to be slow, gradual and firmly based on consolidated and stable national institutions. In 1903, in one of his last presidential addresses, he pointed out clearly what progress had been made and what further steps had to be taken to crown the achievement of the country's institutional organization:

> In our brief and eventful existence as a nation we have travelled . . . through civil wars, tyranny and disorder, an enormous distance, and today we can look to the future without the uncertainties and anxieties of earlier times . . . Without doubt there remain for us . . . many conquests to be made over ourselves, who have such a propensity to set ourselves lofty ideals and to demand of the government, political parties and constitutional practice the last word in political wisdom which supposes a degree of perfection . . . which has still not been attained even by peoples with a centuries-old history. More than on written laws, a republican form of government is founded on public habits and customs.[22]

Thus, Roca did not believe that a perfect representative democracy could be achieved in haste. Towards the end of his life he once again emphasized his old obsessions and strongly defended the guiding principles of his political thought:

> to defend . . . two essential things, which are always in danger: the principle of authority and of national union against the forces, latent but always menacing, of rebellion, anarchy and dissolution. For one must not harbour illusions regarding the solidity of our organization, or of national unity . . . Anarchy is

---

[22] H. Mabragaña, *Los Mensajes*, IV, 66–7.

not a plant that disappears in half a century or a century, in ill-united societies such as ours.[23]

The opposition

Between 1880 and 1914 a variety of groups and parties made up the ranks of the opposition. Some had only an ephemeral life, like the Catholic groups during the 1880s, while others were confined exclusively to a particular province. Of the provincially based parties only two, the Socialists in the federal capital and the Southern League (later called the Progressive Democratic party) in Santa Fe, achieved any influence nationally. The traditional opposition to the PAN came from the forces defeated in 1880, especially the followers of General Bartolomé Mitre. These groups adopted various names (nationalists, liberals, *cívicos*, republicans) and survived until the end of the period. In 1890 the Civic Union was formed. This soon split into two factions, the National Civic Union (UCN) led by Mitre and the Radical Civic Union (UCR) led by Leandro Alem. Although the Radicals suffered from various cases of internal dissension, usually as a result of the attempts of some members to form coalitions with the official party or with the followers of Mitre, they soon became the principal opposition party. After the suicide of Alem in 1896, his nephew Hipólito Yrigoyen became the most prominent figure in the UCR and maintained that position until his death in 1933.

The opposition had no more activists than the government party. On the contrary, the PAN was better organized and had a political clientele, especially in the rural areas, which could be more easily mobilized. It was only during a few periods of political agitation that the opposition was able to mobilize its supporters. During the 1890–4 period, with comparatively honest elections, the numbers of voters rose significantly, and the opposition achieved partial victories in the most developed parts of the country (the capital, Buenos Aires province and the cereal-growing districts of Santa Fe). However, even in these districts the principal political forces were well-matched and enjoyed strikingly homogeneous social support. Only after the passing of the Sáenz Peña Law in 1912 (see below) would differences arise between the electoral strength of the official and opposition parties.

Nor were there significant differences between the leaders of the

[23] Quoted in J. de Vedia, *Como los vi yo* (Buenos Aires, 1922), 6off.

official and opposition parties, as we have seen. There were, of course, no differences with the UCN, an old and traditional Buenos Aires party. The UCR, in its early stages, had been formed by people who were prominent members of the traditional parties. It is true, however, that it had made possible the return to politics of individuals who, for one reason or another, had been excluded from public life. By 1912 this picture had changed somewhat, but the differences were still minor in character. Some time later, Federico Pinedo remarked on these differences, pointing out that:

it cannot be said that between one party and another, *especially up to 1916*, there was any marked difference, because the men of the different parties had the same conception of collective life and similar conceptions as regards economic organization, but there was, and this has perhaps become accentuated, a certain social basis – of category, if not of class – for political antagonism.[24]

The opposition, with a few exceptions, did not put forward programmes very different from those of the official party, and there were few differences as regards economic and social matters. In fact, with the exception of the Socialists in the labour field, the reforms proposed during this period came from the ranks of the PAN. In certain fields (such as tariff and monetary policy), it was also the official party that advanced the most heterodox proposals. The opposition always tried to focus the debate on political and constitutional issues and was more or less uninterested in any other topic. The Radicals themselves were conscious of the fact that the name of the party was perhaps too 'extreme' in view of the modest nature of some of its demands.

The opposition parties demanded honest elections, criticized the concentration of power and often launched bitter attacks against an administration which it considered to be excessively materialistic and, at times, corrupt. But they did not put forward any specific proposal in this field. The two proposals for electoral reform (those of 1904 and 1912) came from the official party. Instead, the opposition demanded that the constitution be implemented to the letter, and their declarations had a strong moralistic content. This is the impression given by both the moving protests of Sarmiento during the 1880s (until his death in 1888) against the 'arrogance' of power and the indifference of the citizenry ('this is a tolerated monarchy'),[25] and the fiery speeches of Alem from 1888 until his death in 1896 denouncing the concentration of power and

[24] Federico Pinedo, *En tiempos de la República* (Buenos Aires, 1946), I, 25.
[25] *Epistolario Sarmiento-Posse* (Buenos Aires, 1946), II, 419.

protesting at the limitation of provincial autonomy and political rights. A similar and even stronger impression is provoked by the abstruse writings of Hipólito Yrigoyen, with his clear-cut division of the world into an evil 'Regime' and a good 'Cause' (the UCR). The same could be said of the more cautious and prudent exhortations of Bartolomé Mitre, demanding a return to more austere practices of republican government. Even the moderate Socialist, Juan B. Justo, the founder of the party in 1894 and its leader until his death in 1928, followed a similar line with his ironical references to, what he derisively called 'Creole politics'.

The opposition was not, of course, entirely free of the defects (fraud, the influence of political bosses, etc.) which it criticized in the official party. Nor was personalism absent from their ranks. Such personalities as Mitre, Alem, Yrigoyen and even Justo played in the opposition parties a role very similar to that of Roca, Pellegrini or Roque Sáenz Peña in the official party. What the opposition challenged, basically, was a style of political life implacably oriented towards their exclusion. It is true that the vices of Argentine politics were also to be found in other countries at the time. However, even where this was the case, as in Spain, opposing forces were able to alternate in power. In Argentina this did not happen, except on the few occasions when divisions within the official faction obliged it to form coalitions, albeit unstable and ephemeral ones, with the more moderate elements of the opposition.

This style of politics affected the forms of action adopted by the opposition. There was a marked contrast between the virulence of its rhetoric and the moderation of its proposals and its programme. The Radicals eventually made 'Intransigence', their stubborn refusal to take part in any kind of agreement or political coalition, into a religious dogma. Furthermore, the opposition sometimes had recourse to armed insurrection as the only means of getting into power. For this purpose, it could count on the support of a few sectors within the armed forces which had not forgotten their old habits. The most serious incident was the Civic Union's revolt of July 1890 which as we have seen forced the resignation of Juárez Celman. Later, in 1892–3, there was a series of provincial uprisings, as a result of which the Radicals came to power for a short time in some provincial administrations. In 1905 the Radicals, now under Yrigoyen, attempted another insurrection, but when this failed they began to concentrate rather more on broadening their political base among the growing urban and rural middle class. Meanwhile, the revolutionary outlook of the Radicals and their almost mechanical propensity to indulge in armed insurrections were exploited with great skill by the governing groups, to demonstrate that there would be a future of chaos and anarchy if the Radicals ever got into power.

THE END OF THE REGIME, 1912–16

In 1916 the principal opposition party, the Radical Civic Union, came to power after winning the presidential elections of that year. This Radical victory was made possible by the electoral law proposed by President Roque Sáenz Peña (1910–14) and passed by parliament in 1912, which established universal, secret and compulsory suffrage for all male citizens over the age of eighteen. Furthermore, the electoral register and the control of elections were entrusted to the army instead of provincial police forces which had been too susceptible to pressures exercised by the government of the day. The so-called Sáenz Peña Law was a consequence of the infighting within the PAN and the final victory of the anti-Roca forces which since 1891 had been pressing for a change in electoral practices. It was also a Conservative response to the threat to stability posed by the conspiratorial activities of the Radical party and, to a lesser extent, by the growth of the Socialist party and the anarchist-led strikes. In the parliamentary debates on the Law in 1911 the official party was confident and certain of an electoral victory in 1916 and thus the legitimation of its dominance. And the elections did indeed show that the party was still an important electoral force. However, it was the leader of the UCR, Hipólito Yrigoyen, who was in the event elected president. What had gone wrong?

In the first place, the official party entered the electoral contest of 1916 in a weakened and divided condition following the confrontation between Roca and Pellegrini during Roca's second administration (1898–1904) and the anti-Roca presidency of Figueroa Alcorta (1906–10). The liberal sectors put forward the candidature of Lisandro de la Torre, the leader of a party which had originally belonged to the opposition, the Progressive Democratic party. This candidature was resisted by the strong Conservative provincial bosses, led by the most powerful, Marcelino Ugarte, who was governor of Buenos Aires province. The result was that the official party entered the contest of 1916 divided and with two candidates, which greatly diminished its chances of victory. The political coalition that had governed the country for 35 years was made up of extremely heterogeneous provincial forces, with marked centrifugal tendencies. Only the presence of strong personalities, especially that of Roca, had maintained the unity of this coalition. Roca died in 1914, and by 1916 so had his principal adversaries within the official parties, Pellegrini (in 1906) and Sáenz Peña (in August 1914). The latter was replaced in the presidency by Victorino de la Plaza (1914–16), who was an experienced politician but who lacked qualities needed for the arduous and complex task of uniting the party in 1916. In the second place, the beginning of the electoral cycle of 1912–16 coincided with the first downturn in the economy for almost twenty years. Thirdly, the Sáenz Peña Law led to an unprecedented political mobilization throughout the country. Voting increased threefold or fourfold in the parliamentary elections of 1912, 1913, and 1914, and rose still further in the presidential elections of 1916. Between 1912 and 1914 the Radicals obtained a number of governorships, and on two occasions (1913 and 1914) the Socialists won in the Federal Capital. What the opposition had been unable to achieve in a quarter of a century, the law achieved in the space of a few years.

The Radicals, united behind a strong candidate, quickly took advantage of the new situation. Radical committees were set up throughout the country, and groups of different origin joined this political force which appeared to have a chance of success. These committees were organized on fairly modern lines in the big cities and in some cereal-growing districts. In the rest of the country, their organization was a replica of the system of political bosses and personal favours which had characterized the Autonomist regime.

The Radicals triumphed in the most prosperous parts of the country. In the Pampa littoral, they won in the Federal Capital, Santa Fe, Córdoba and Entre Ríos. In this region the Radical votes were concentrated in the cities and in rural areas where cereal growing was most important. Although they did not achieve a majority, they also mustered significant support in the stock-raising areas. In the cities their votes came principally from the middle-class districts, although they also obtained support in the working-class districts and, to a lesser degree, in some upper-class residential areas. In the interior of the country, the Radicals won in the most developed provinces (Mendoza and Tucumán), and except for Santiago del Estero they were defeated in the areas which had developed least rapidly since 1888. The Radical electorate was, therefore, based on the intermediate sectors (both urban and rural) of the most advanced parts of the country, but there was a significant measure of support in all regions and among all social classes. These results were a reflection of the moderation, flexibility, and disinclination to make clear-cut definitions about ideology or political programmes that character-ized the leadership of the party.

The official parties found their greatest electoral support in the provinces of the interior and the stock-raising areas of the littoral. In the latter region, it was only in Buenos Aires province that the traditional conservative electoral organization was able to compete successfully with the Radicals. The populist nature of some of its *caudillos* enabled them to win even in some important cities such as Avellaneda. The most obvious of the political weaknesses of the conservatives was their poor electoral showing in the most advanced areas of the country, that is to say the city of Buenos Aires and the province of Santa Fe. Paradoxically, the official parties suffered their most crushing defeats in those areas which had benefited most from the economic boom that began in 1880.

The official parties and the Radicals together obtained over 85 per cent of the votes. The Socialists came a poor third, their votes being confined in practice to the city of Buenos Aires and some surrounding districts, where, however, they had to face strong competition from the Radicals. The moderate character of the Socialists enabled them to offset part of their losses in working-class votes with significant, though minority, support in the middle-class districts. In the rest of the country, the Socialists won a few votes in some cities, especially in those where there were important railway centres. In certain big cities, like Rosario and Bahía Blanca, some workers voted for the Radicals possibly at the instigation of trade-union leaders of syndicalist or anarchist persuasion. The Socialists polled very few votes in the rural areas, even where, as in Tucumán, there was an important sugar industry.

Thirty-six years of Autonomist rule produced a relatively stable political and legal system, thus providing one of the prerequisites for a rapid and sustained process of economic and social growth. In the end, however, it was the Radical opposition and its leader Hipólito Yrigoyen who profited from the momentous changes undergone by Argentine society since 1880. For the followers of Roca and Pellegrini, all that was left was the consolation of having presided over a political transition both peaceful and honourable.

The electoral reform of 1912 was followed by a period of almost two decades during which for the first time constitutional rule and political stability were combined with free and honest elections. Argentina's political ills were, however, only partially the result of its electoral legislation. They were rather the consequence of long-standing institutional habits and traditions that left little space for compromise and the sharing of political power. Yrigoyen was as staunch a believer in the power of the presidency and strong central government as Roca had been. He made even greater use than his predecessors had of the most powerful political weapon at his disposal (federal intervention). Thus the long-standing political traditions of exclusivist government and seditious opposition were not broken and the seeds for future instability were left untouched. In 1930 at a time of intense economic and political crisis the opposition, as in 1874, 1880, 1893 and 1905, chose to associate itself with a military coup rather than to abide by the rules of the democratic game. This time the coup was successful, and not only Argentina's experiment with democracy but almost 70 years of constitutional government came to an abrupt end.

11

ARGENTINA IN 1914: THE PAMPAS, THE INTERIOR, BUENOS AIRES

On the eve of the outbreak of the first world war Argentina had enjoyed since 1880, apart from a quinquennium of depression in the early 1890s, almost 35 years of remarkable economic growth. The main impulse had been exogenous: foreign labour, foreign capital, and favourable foreign markets for its exports. In 1914 around one-third of Argentina's population of almost eight million, which the third national census showed had increased more than fourfold since the first census in 1869, was foreign-born; at least another quarter was composed of the descendants of immigrants from the past two generations. According to later estimates by the United Nations' Economic Commission for Latin America (ECLA), in 1914 foreign investments (around 60 per cent of them British), both public and private, accounted for half the country's capital stock, equal to two and a half years of the value of gross domestic production. Since 1900 foreign investment had risen at an annual rate of 11.41 per cent. British investors possessed around 80 per cent of the Argentine railway system, large tracts of its land, most of its tramways and urban utility companies, and some of its meat-packing plants and industries. ECLA again estimated that the annual rate of growth in the rural sector, already 7 per cent between 1895 and 1908, had risen to 9 per cent between 1908 and 1914. In the great compendium it issued on the Republic's affairs in 1911,[1] Lloyd's Bank of London pointed out that whereas until around 1903 the value of foreign trade in Argentina and Brazil was broadly equal, by 1909 Argentina's had grown by half as much again above its leading rival in the subcontinent. On the eve of the first world war per capita foreign trade in Argentina was almost six times the average in the rest of Latin America. It had attained a magnitude greater

---

[1] Reginald Lloyd (ed.), *Twentieth century impressions of Argentina* (London, 1911).

than Canada's and was already a quarter of that of the United States. The country had catapulted itself among the ranks of the world's leading cereal and meat exporters. It was the largest exporter of maize and linseed. It was second in wool, and third in live cattle and horses. If it ranked only sixth as a producer of wheat, it was still the third, and in some years the second, largest exporter. Despite the competition from cattle for the land, the expansion of wheat production after 1900 was faster than in Canada.

Apart from entrepôts like Holland and Belgium, no country in the world imported more goods per head of population than Argentina. Per capita incomes compared with Germany and the Low Countries, and were higher than Spain, Italy, Sweden and Switzerland. Buenos Aires, the federal capital, with its million and a half inhabitants, was proclaimed the 'Paris of South America'. Having grown at an average rate of 6.5 per cent since 1869, it was now, after New York, the second most populous city of the Atlantic seaboard. It was by far the largest city in Latin America, having for the time being left Rio de Janeiro, Mexico City, Santiago and the rest trailing far behind.

The euphoria of the years before the first world war was sometimes tempered by a sense that Argentina still had an enormous distance to traverse. Among the many European sophisticates who now visited the country, and eagerly debated its accomplishments, there was general agreement that the age of infancy was past; not so that of adolescence. Maturity beckoned in the shape of still greater ministrations of capital and labour. To have infused the Republic with a new population; to have constructed there one of the largest railway systems in the world; to have fenced in the pampas and brought 50 million acres under the plough; to have endowed Buenos Aires and Rosario with the most advanced port facilities; to have introduced into these and other cities from Bahía Blanca to Salta tramways, gas, water and electricity plants; these were undoubtedly considerable achievements. Yet it still left the country far short of fulfilling the destiny which General Roca and his successors had constantly invoked since 1880. This generation had looked to Argentina not merely as a leader in Latin America but as the antipodean counterweight to the United States. It dreamt of a Republic of 100 million people or more, imbued throughout with the same pulsating tempo as its eastern core.[2] Yet in 1914 a population of less than eight

2 Cf. Carlos Pellegrini in Alberto B. Martínez and Maurice Lewandowski, *The Argentine in the twentieth century* (London, 1911), xv.

million inhabited a land mass equal to the whole of continental Europe between the Baltic, the Mediterranean and the Danube estuary. And the hand of change was for the most part visible only in the capital and its immediate pampas hinterland. Beyond this 500-mile radius most of the interior remained in a state of moribund backwardness.

The ambitions of the past generation were predicated upon the indefinite continuation of the present. But objectively there were already many grounds for doubting whether they would ever be realized. Already in 1913 a new depression had brought to an end the inflow of immigrants and foreign capital. These were signs of changing conditions in the outside world. In part they also suggested that Argentina was reaching saturation point in its capacity to absorb resources from abroad. For some time past the best land in Argentina had already been brought into production. Much of what remained would offer far more meagre returns to investors and pioneers alike. The old interior seemed no more likely now to follow the pampas into exporting than ever in its history. The most to be hoped for here was that growth on the pampas would continue to amplify the domestic market and in this way slowly awaken the regions beyond.

In 1914 there was as yet no alternative to the primary export economy. Despite the recent growth of manufacturing – by 1913 local industry provided one-third of Argentina's processed food products, one-eighth of its metals and one-sixth of its textiles[3] – there was as yet no conclusive evidence that the country had an imminent future as a fully fledged industrial power. Local manufacturing was heavily dependent upon the growth of domestic demand and incomes from the export sector and the inflow of foreign investments. At this point, despite the wide adoption of steam power, most industries were simple handicrafts employing little capital or machinery. Locally manufactured foodstuffs, for which raw materials were cheap and abundant, were of high quality. It now made little sense to import beers and table wines, or flour and Italian pastries. But these industries were again an outgrowth of the rural export sectors rather than completely convincing indicators of a new economy in formation. The metals and textile industries were much less firm. Local metallurgical plants used imported raw materials, and were thus highly dependent upon low ocean freights. The new textile industry in Buenos Aires also used a high proportion of imported raw material. Most of it

---

[3] Jorge Schvarzer, 'Algunos rasgos del desarrollo industrial de Buenos Aires', mimeo, CISEA (Buenos Aires, 1979).

still functioned on a mercantile 'putting-out' basis among female seamstresses. At this point the textile industry in Argentina was notably less developed than in Brazil. In 1911 Argentina had 9,000 spindles and 1,200 looms against an estimated one million spindles and 35,000 looms in Brazil.

In 1914 Argentina had few embryos of integrated heavy or capital goods industries. Its relatively scant reserves of coal and iron ore lay in far-flung and then inaccessible regions, mostly in the far south-west. To begin developing these would require an enormous new outlay of capital. Little of it would be forthcoming from abroad, at least not until the state or domestic investors took a lead, as they had done with the railways a half century before. Apart from sugar, wines and flour, recent mild and tentative experiments with tariff protection suggested that the country had no easy in-built capacity to lessen its dependence on imports. Limited markets narrowed the scope for the adoption of advanced technology and economies of scale among industrial producers. The home market was rich but still relatively small, while foreign markets were dominated by the industrial giants of the world. It was difficult to envisage here the linkages between industry and agriculture which prevailed in the United States. Nor did Argentine society have much in common with Germany, Japan or early-nineteenth-century Britain. The high standards of living of its new middle class were constructed upon an easy and painless inflow of foreign imports. They would not easily stomach high cost and for a time necessarily experimental national products. There was a real question at this point whether Argentina had the reserves of labour to sustain any major deepening and diversification of its industrial sector. In the pampas region there were some conditions, analogous perhaps to the classical agrarian revolution, expelling population from the land and the towns. The recent growth of manufacturing was in some degree an expression of this. However, this source of labour was limited, and there was none other like it either elsewhere in Argentina or in its contiguous states. The growth of the urban labour force thus largely depended on the country's attractiveness to emigrants from Europe. But if the attempt to industrialize were to lead to the compression of real wages, as it had done almost everywhere except the United States, Argentina was fast likely to become not an importer but a net exporter of labour. Lastly, it seemed quite beyond the bounds of possibility that the political structure could be remoulded to accommodate change of this magnitude. If at this point opinions were sometimes sharply divided on how much formal participation the system should admit, almost all sectors of the population were at one in their preferences for the present liberal institutions. To them was attributed the country's recent transformation. To abandon them would invite a return to the barren early nineteenth century.

In 1914 Argentina's immediate future thus seemed unlikely to be much of a departure from the immediate past. Yet now that easy expansion on an open land frontier was over, export earnings, and through them in large part the economy's capacity to remain prosperous, would be determined increasingly by world prices and conditions of demand in the meat, cereals and wool importing countries of Western Europe; Argentina could no longer respond to depression, as in the 1870s and the early 1890s, by simply increasing production on virgin land. A period of more modest growth than before thus loomed on the horizon.

THE PAMPAS

In 1914 Argentina was a country of startling regional contrasts. In the aftermath of the recent surge of growth, and with the exception of its drier periphery (like parts of Córdoba and the territory of La Pampa), or the less easily accessible areas (like Entre Ríos), the pampas region (Buenos Aires province, southern Santa Fe, eastern Córdoba, Entre Ríos, and the territory of La Pampa) was now markedly more advanced than the rest of the country. It was covered by a dense network of railways. Its landed estates were clearly demarcated by barbed wire, its landscape dotted with small towns, windmills, scattered homesteads and water troughs. According to the economist and statistician Alejandro E. Bunge, writing immediately after the first world war, this part of the country, including the city of Buenos Aires, had more than 90 per cent of Argentina's automobiles and telephones. Here were also no less than 42 per cent of the railways in the whole of Latin America. The Argentine pampas was the source of half the subcontinent's foreign trade, and the same area absorbed around three-quarters of the educational spending throughout Latin America.[4]

In the past two generations townships had sprouted in great abundance throughout the pampas, most of all along the railway lines.

---

[4] Alejandro E. Bunge, *La economía argentina* (4 vols. Buenos Aires, 1928–30), I, 104–23.

Some were originally the tiny hamlets, or the mere *pulperías*, from the days of Rosas or Mitre. Others, beyond the old frontier, were the result of planned colonization ventures by land or railway companies. Their chief functions were as rail-heads or local markets. They were also centres of small credit and banking operations or petty crafts and trades, many of them discharging these roles as landlocked miniatures of Buenos Aires. Many had grown at roughly the same rate as the population as a whole, at least doubling in size since 1890. They all had large congregations of immigrants in their midst. Many gave the appearance of being thriving civic centres. If most lacked the resources to construct paved roads or modern sewage and power facilities, they established their own newspapers, schools, hospitals and libraries. In 1914 most of the pampas towns were still of recent creation, and as yet none was conspicuously large. Azul, with a population of 40,000 in 1914, was the fourth largest township in the province of Buenos Aires after Avellaneda (an industrial suburb of the Federal Capital), La Plata (the provincial capital), and Bahía Blanca (the leading port of the southern pampas). In this province, an area the size of France and comparably endowed in resources, there were as yet only ten townships with populations in excess of 12,000. Its 50 or so other noteworthy urban centres were scarcely more than villages and subsisted, despite their rail links with the Río de la Plata estuary, as scattered and isolated oases among the farms and *estancias*.

In these and other respects the pampas apparently resembled frontier societies elsewhere at an early parallel stage of development. Yet there were some differences, and these threatened to undermine the capacity of the towns to continue growing from the rudimentary centres they were into the large cities their early pioneer inhabitants expected at least some would eventually become. Successive booms had failed to attract a large permanent and propertied population outside the towns in the country-side itself. In many areas the rural populace amounted to no more than a very thin sprinkling of agricultural tenants, cattle peons or shepherds and seasonal labourers. Where the beef herds were pre-eminent, there were no more than one or two persons per square kilometre. Wheat farming would on average sustain three or four. The highest population densities of the pampas were generally associated with maize cultivation, where there were up to fifteen persons per square kilometre. From 1900 farm machines were adopted on a fairly wide scale on the pampas, and by 1914 they amounted to almost a quarter of the capital stock in the rural sector. Nevertheless farming remained heavily dependent on manual labour. In harvest periods the population of the pampas as a whole would increase by around 300,000. In areas like Santa Fe or Córdoba, relatively close to the populated centres of the interior, the harvesters were often seasonal migrants from Santiago del Estero, Catamarca or San Juan. Many who flowed into the province of Buenos Aires before the first world war, and before the large-scale mechanization of agriculture in the 1920s, however, were short-term immigrants from Europe who usually returned there after the harvest. These 'swallows' (*golondrinas*) were a new embodiment of the rootlessness which had characterized pampas society since the beginnings of Spanish colonization; in them a quality formerly exemplified by the old *gauchos* was reborn. To an extent which seemed anomalous in this rich agrarian society, many farms and towns alike harboured a floating, semi-employed population. These conditions boded ill for the new towns of the pampas. A denser, wealthier and more widely rooted rural middle class, as opposed to these proletarian transients, would have promoted a broader market for local urban services, affording them greater opportunities for growth and diversification.

At root this was a commentary on the land tenure system and the survival of large estates into the twentieth century. In Argentina the estates had appeared in a sequence of waves after independence, following the opening of the frontier against the Indians and the distribution of the land by the state. After 1850 sheep-farming, economic depression and later agriculture had helped prune down many of them. Nevertheless this trend had been mitigated and many times negated by the enormous appreciation in land values from around 1860 onwards. Each successive boom made the possession of land, in as large portions as possible, an iron-clad guarantee of personal security and latterly great wealth. Yet the same inflation, combined with a poorly developed and frequently inequitable land mortgage credit system like the paper *cédulas* of the late 1880s, which usually enabled only those already with land to buy more, had recurrently diminished the range of potential buyers. Its chief casualties were many immigrant farmers with modest or meagre capital resources. Although by 1914 foreigners were in a great majority among the owners of industrial firms, they made up only a third of landowners.

Throughout the nineteenth century there was a body of opinion in Argentina hostile to large estates. It favoured their abolition and the adoption of homestead policies like those in the United States. Belgrano,

Rivadavia, Alberdi, Sarmiento and Avellaneda were each in varied ways representatives of this tradition. They had foreseen the state organizing colonization schemes on a large scale and granting land titles to farmer immigrants, but did not have the power and backing to realize this objective. This was not a country where Lincoln's ideal of rewarding the dispossessed with 'forty acres and a mule' had ever enjoyed a realistic chance of fulfilment. Nor was it entirely akin to Canada, Australia, or New Zealand, where the presence of a colonial state beyond the grasp of local vested interests had lent weight and authority to the pretensions of the small farmer interest. Since 1810 Argentina had been dominated by a shifting *mélange* of Creole landowners, merchants, and bevies of financiers and speculators. From the early 1820s into the 1880s they had pursued land policies which both favoured concentration and conferred upon themselves the greatest benefits from the opening up of the frontier. During the generation immediately before 1914 such monopolistic manipulation was less frequent than before. However, in the interval, the interplay of market forces had failed to dispel entirely the incubus of the past. According to the data in the 1914 census, elaborated by Carlos Díaz Alejandro, smaller farms in the pampas (i.e. between 500 and 1,000 hectares) accounted for only 23.5 per cent of the total land area. Farms of 1,000 hectares and more occupied 61 per cent. The largest 584 holdings in the pampas occupied almost one-fifth of the total area.[5] Landholding was less concentrated in the pampas than in most other parts of the country, but much more so than in frontier regions elsewhere. The mean size of landholdings in Argentina was 890 acres. In New South Wales it was 175 acres, in the United States 130 (and by comparison only 62 in England and Wales).

In many parts of English-speaking America and Australasia cattle and sheep had eventually surrendered a large part of the land to small-scale agriculture, bringing substantial change in land tenure and a higher density of land settlement. As late as 1900 there were still some who expected Argentina to follow a similar course, believing that here too temperate agriculture would eventually fulfil its propensity to construct a firm family-based society of independent yeoman farmers. There was some scattered evidence of this occurring during the 1890s. But in 1900 first British and later American-owned meat-packing plants began to appear. Encouraged by the demand for beef, and aided by the lending

5 Carlos F. Díaz Alejandro, *Essays on the economic history of the Argentine Republic* (New Haven, 1970), 152–62.

policies of the Buenos Aires banks, the landed classes reverted to cattle ranching, investing heavily in imported stock. Land sales which before had aided subdivision largely halted. Cattle encouraged a more extensive land use, and gave a renewed boost to the larger estates. Cattle were also an opportunity to employ less labour at a time when rural wage costs were tending to increase. In the early 1890s a high gold premium had created a wide disparity between wages paid in depreciating pesos and earnings from exports paid in gold. At the time the main effect of this was to boost agriculture. But since then the peso had appreciated strongly, bringing an increase in the relative price of agricultural labour. Yet the resurgence of cattle had no immediate impact upon output in the arable sector, which continued to climb. It first took the land from sheep. Sheep farming was driven out of the pampas and into Patagonia, the sheep population of the province of Buenos Aires declining from around 56 million in 1895 to only 18 million in 1915. However, there was now a much closer juxtaposition and intermingling between pasturing and arable farming on the large estates. The wide adoption of rotational practices, in which cereals or linseed were alternated with alfalfa and cattle, was a sign that arable farming had lost its earlier leading role in the rural economy and become subordinate to cattle ranching.

Most arable farming on the pampas was conducted under a tenancy or sharecropping system. In 1916 only 31 per cent of cereal farms were cultivated by their owners. In many cases the farmers themselves – many of them Italians – were willing accomplices in this arrangement, since it relieved them of onerous investment costs to develop their holdings. Nor was the status of tenant or sharecropper any necessary barrier to prosperity. But by and large the institutions of tenancy along with the recurrent inclemencies of nature – droughts, floods or locust inundations – prevented agriculture ever becoming a straightforward passport to prosperity. Years of exceptionally favourable prices would be closely followed by increases in land rentals or freight rates. Changes in the banking system in the aftermath of the Baring crisis in 1890 did little to facilitate the provision of adequate credit to the farmers, either for land purchases or to finance production. Many became chronically indebted to the landowners, to countryside storekeepers, or the great cereal export houses in Buenos Aires like Bunge y Born, Weil Brothers and Dreyfus and Co. These great oligopsonies also had the whip hand when it came to settling the prices paid to producers. Until the rural strike of 1912, the Grito de Alcorta, many tenants were bereft of even the protection of a written contract and were heavily dependent on the paternalistic goodwill of landowners. The adoption of rotational farming brought a sharp decline in the willingness of tenant farmers to make even minimal improvements on their holdings. One result of this was that the rough-hewn cottages and homesteads which were relatively commonplace before 1900, afterwards under rotational farming gave way to notably lesser quality dwellings, often no more than transient shacks. These were the results of 'sowing the land with *gringos*' (*sembrar con gringos*).

The end product of this was a rural society *sui generis*. Outside the shrinking traditional cattle *estancias*, few of its members resembled the archetypal prostrate tied peasantries of the rest of Latin America, groaning under the weight of time-worn seigneurial obligations. Many were genuine pioneers with the same acquisitive and energetic mentality as their peers elsewhere. Yet amidst all this was the legacy of the early nineteenth century, visible in the survival of many large estates, in an often uneven distribution of wealth and income, and in a relatively large floating population. In most of the pampas the family farm was much less prevalent than in English-language frontier communities elsewhere. During the past two generations the pampas had been laid open to the full force of capitalism. Many farms and *estancias* alike operated as highly efficient enterprises. On the other hand, the land tenure system, especially as it was now developing with cattle at the forefront, imposed limits on the capacity of the land to absorb and maintain population.

THE INTERIOR

If for some life on the pampas had its shortcomings, the opportunities it bestowed were usually infinitely greater than in the rest of the country outside Buenos Aires. One exception was the easily irrigated Río Negro valley. After its colonization by local and foreign land companies, among them a subsidiary of the Buenos Aires Great Southern Railway, this began to develop into a prosperous and middle-class fruit growing area, remitting its products to the city of Buenos Aires. There also seemed a promise of things to come in the territory of Chubut: in 1907, during an attempt to tap supplies of artesian water, rich oil deposits were discovered in the area known from this time forward as Comodoro Rivadavia. It was followed by further discoveries in Neuquén, to the south-west of Río Negro, at Plaza Huincul. But beyond these enclaves and the constantly struggling Welsh agricultural communities also in

Chubut, the vast Patagonian region in the south was underdeveloped. As yet it had evolved little beyond the naturalists' paradise encountered by Charles Darwin during the voyage of the *Beagle* some 80 years before. The great arid and windswept plateau contained nothing but vast sheep ranches, many of them the size of European principalities. In part such mammoth land concentrations illustrated that on average the pastures of Patagonia had only one-tenth of the sheep-carrying capacity of the province of Buenos Aires. It was also due to the manner in which the lands conquered by General Roca in the campaign of 1879 had been squandered by the national government. In 1885 no less than eleven million acres had been distributed among 541 officers and soldiers from the conquering expedition. The arrival of sheep soon afterwards brought only the barest stirrings of activity to the region; after 1900 the Argentine wool trade began to stagnate as it lost its earlier position as leader in the export trade. In 1914 the human population of Patagonia, about a third of the country's territorial area, was a mere 80,000, or 1 per cent of the total, much of it in the Río Negro region. Argentine-born settlers were relatively few. They were mainly simple shepherds, expelled from the province of Buenos Aires along with their flocks following the revival of cattle breeding, token military and naval personnel in garrisons along the Atlantic coast, and a demoralized sprinkling of government officials. Many Patagonian landowners were British, as were many of the farmers of the Río Negro valley. The area also had a marked Chilean influence. Land hunger across the *cordillera* had forced substantial numbers of peasants to retrace the paths of the Araucanian warriors and resettle in Argentine Patagonia. In Bolivia and Peru 30 years earlier a similar emigration of Chileans had led to war and the annexation of land by Chile. Chileans were thus regarded with some suspicion by the Argentine authorities. From time to time Patagonia, especially the Magellan Straits region, was the theatre of boundary disputes between the two countries.

At the other end of the country the north-east was an area of greater topographical and economic variety than Patagonia, but scarcely more developed. The great days of Entre Ríos had ceased after the death of its great *caudillo* Justo José de Urquiza and the suppression of the López Jordán rebellion in the 1870s. Entre Ríos now had railway connections with the Paraná river ports. However, outside some fairly small, often Jewish, agricultural colonies, it remained a peripheral cattle region, employing unimproved Creole herds to produce hides or jerked and salted beef. Most of Corrientes further north had a similar aspect, though here there was some Guaraní peasant agriculture like that across the border in Paraguay. In 1914 some 10,000 hectares of Corrientes was devoted to tobacco cultivation, mainly by peasant smallholders, though trade in tobacco with Buenos Aires was still negligible. There were more marked signs of progress in Misiones, which before had remained almost empty for more than a hundred years after the expulsion of the Jesuits in 1767. Like the Río Negro valley, Misiones had begun to attract capital and labour in the late nineteenth and early twentieth centuries. European colonists, particularly Germans and Poles, were moving into the region, cultivating forest clearings as others like them did across the border in Brazil. Similarly, the eastern Chaco region, particularly around the city of Resistencia, was becoming a small centre of cotton production.

Although during this period domestic sources provided only one-fifth of total national consumption, the main cash crop of the north-east was yerba maté. The contrast between farming on the pampas and conditions on the yerba maté plantations could not have been more striking. In this isolated corner of the Republic, it seemed, one immediately stepped back into the eighteenth century. Yerba maté production had arisen in Argentina for the most part in quite recent years, mainly in Misiones along with parts of Corrientes and the eastern fringes of the Chaco, in face of strong competition from suppliers in Paraguay and Brazil. Producers across the border relied on semi-forced labour. The Argentinians, large and small producers alike, were therefore obliged to copy these same practices. Monthly pay rates for seasonal labourers, known as *mensús*, were often under a third of those for unskilled workers employed the year round in Buenos Aires. The lot of the small permanent labour force was virtual imprisonment on the plantations. They were often held in tutelage by overseers and suffocated by debts to company stores, under outward conditions which most observers found indistinguishable from slavery.

Another industry of the north-east, in the northern reaches of Santiago del Estero, Santa Fe, parts of Corrientes and the Chaco, was the extraction of quebracho hardwood. Throughout this period the quebracho forests were decimated with reckless energy, mainly by British consortia. Only token attempts were made to replace the forest cover. Vast tracts became desolate, dust- or brush-covered wastelands. The timber of the north-western forests was largely employed for railway sleepers, and that of the east for its tannin content, which was shipped in bulk to Europe for the treatment of leather. During the first world war quebracho was also widely employed as a coal substitute on the railways. At that time the industry won some ill-repute on account of its labour practices. However, in normal times a free wage system sufficed to attract labour from among the Guaraní in Corrientes, some of the Chaco Indians, or from among workers from Santiago del Estero, who would often alternate between the quebracho industry and wheat harvesting in Santa Fe or Córdoba.

Outside the Mesopotamian plains of Corrientes and Entre Ríos the region most resembling them in character lay due west from Buenos Aires in Cuyo, especially the province of Mendoza. In the past generation this had become a flourishing area in which both production and population were increasing at a notably faster rate than in the rest of the interior. At the heart of the economy of Cuyo was viticulture. With the tariff protection they were given in the 1880s local wines established a firm position in the Buenos Aires market. Between 1895 and 1910 the area devoted to vines throughout Cuyo quintupled to 120,000 hectares. By 1914 annual wine production was approaching four million litres, and Argentina's production of wine exceeded Chile's, and was double California's. Vines were spreading quickly beyond Mendoza into San Juan, and into small pockets of Catamarca and La Rioja. The wine industry of this period had been largely created by immigrants, by French and Italians with the capital and expertise to organize it along efficient lines; almost alone of the regions outside the pampas Mendoza continued to attract a large number of Europeans. In Mendoza, however, the spread of viticulture was accompanied by a greater subdivision of the land than had occurred in the pampas. Small properties largely replaced the ancient cattle haciendas engaged in trading across the Andes with Chile. Prosperity on the land was reflected in an air of well-being and expansion in the city of Mendoza. By 1914 the city had a population of 59,000. This was four times that of the medium-sized provincial capitals of the interior, such as Santiago del Estero or Salta, and ten times that of the poorest, La Rioja and Catamarca. Both Mendoza and San Juan were becoming provinces of great political vitality. Behind this lay the changes in land tenure accompanying the transition from cattle to vines, land-grabbing among rival coteries of speculators, intense struggles for water rights, and disputes over the terms of credit, as the Buenos Aires banks established a financial stranglehold over the industry. Although the land tenure pattern in

Mendoza favoured smallholders, there was a fairly high degree of concentration in wine processing. Bickering over the prices paid to the cultivators by the *bodegas* which processed the grapes became another source of endemic conflict. By 1914 both these provinces had become centres of a flourishing local populism, which had undertones of neo-federalist hostility towards Buenos Aires.

The second growth centre of the old interior was Tucumán. Grasping the opportunities provided by its naturally moist climate, the coming of the railways in 1876 and the generous tariff privileges bestowed upon it by the national government, Tucumán had launched full tilt into sugar-cane production. By the early years of the twentieth century there were still some traditional activities, such as tanning, to be found here, but they were now vastly overshadowed by sugar plantations, which occupied four-fifths of the cultivated land area of the province. The most vital stage in the growth of sugar in Tucumán was between 1890 and 1895. During this period the earlier benefits of tariff protection were greatly enhanced by the discouraging effect of a high gold premium upon imports. At this point output increased tenfold. Growth was afterwards followed by overproduction in 1896 and a five-year crisis in which many small refineries were forced into liquidation. Between 1900 and 1914 output once more grew threefold, while imported sugar became an increasingly minimal proportion of total consumption. Between 1897 and 1903 government bounties made possible small exports of sugar cane from Tucumán, though this brief phase ended abruptly with agreements in Europe to cease admitting sugar subsidized in this fashion. Sugar in Tucumán advanced at roughly the same rate as vines in Mendoza, and by 1914 occupied a comparable land area. Later in the 1920s the cane-fields moved northwards into Salta and Jujuy. Before this northward dispersion, climatic variations in Tucumán frequently produced large annual oscillations in output. Domestic sugar distributors became adept at manipulating supplies to enhance their returns while minimizing recourse to imports. This was one of several reasons why the sugar industry gained ill-repute among consumers in Buenos Aires.

Like many similar semi-tropical agricultural activities of Latin America, the sugar industry was a diverse mix of modern, highly capitalistic elements and others which evoked a pre-capitalist past. With the exception of quebracho, fruit and sheep farming, and in their different way wines, sugar was the only activity of any substance outside the pampas to attract foreign capital. Many of the sugar refineries, or *ingenios*, were organized as joint-stock ventures with foreign shareholders, and employed imported, usually British, machinery. Cane production in Tucumán was again conducted mainly by smallholders. However, these were *mestizo minifundistas*, quite different from the vine growers of Mendoza. Eighty per cent of the Tucumán farmers operated on seven or eight hectares, and the rest often on less. Meanwhile the *ingenios* had long been under the control of what seemed an impenetrable oligarchy, able to dictate prices to producers and consumers alike, and allegedly possessing extraordinary wealth by virtue of its protected status in the national market.

Labour relations in the Tucumán sugar industry had features similar to those in the yerba maté region in the north-east. In the 1880s and the 1890s there were attempts to create a labour force of European immigrants. But horror stories of conditions in Tucumán percolated through to Buenos Aires, and this source of labour speedily evaporated. Immigrants were then replaced by primitive Indians dredged up from the forays of labour contractors in the Chaco, and by *mestizo* peasants from the south in Catamarca, La Rioja and Santiago del Estero. They were often inveigled into debt and then herded together by rail and cart into Tucumán. For the duration of the harvest these ingenuous and resourceless persons were encamped on the land often under the most extreme and deplorable conditions.

Many in Buenos Aires and abroad regarded the sugar industry as the very symbol of plantation-capitalist infamy. Even Lloyd's Bank, which sought to throw the happiest gloss on the Republic's affairs, called the industry a 'big, bad blot' on the country.

While the wealthy landowners and the big employers, the latter mostly of overseas nationality, are reaping increasingly rich rewards, those who perform toilsomely the actual labour that gives that reward are allowed to pass their lives in conditions that do not conform to the lowest standards of existence. The country that permits wholesale servile conditions among the bulk of its people must inevitably suffer from lack of that virility necessary for its continued progress along an upward path.[6]

By comparison with Mendoza or Tucumán, the rest of the interior languished in stagnation and backwardness. Railways constructed and operated by the national government, which now linked all the

[6] Lloyd, *Twentieth century impressions*, 346.

provincial capitals with Buenos Aires, failed to induce the changes which occurred elsewhere. Beyond the immediate radius served by the railways, goods were still transported by ox-carts or mules. In 1914 the age-old dream that parts of the region close to the *cordillera* would develop as mining centres was still unfulfilled. Many areas remained almost unchanged from the days of the Viceroyalty of the Río de la Plata in the late eighteenth century. Traditional haciendas held sway, sometimes co-existing with *minifundios*, the two together reproducing the classic social polarities of Andean America. Peasant communities were still subject to seigneurial levies. Peasant industries suffered from the incessant competition of imports and their own technological backwardness. With the exception of small sprinklings of petty merchants, many of them Levantines, the area had little new population. Its cities were still small, their crumbling and downtrodden aspect mirroring the indigence of their surroundings. Here provincial administrations and education required almost constant subsidies from Buenos Aires. Amidst all this were periodic outbreaks of political unrest. Local coups were common among feuding factions of landowners, each struggling to monopolize the paltry provincial budgets. Yet in other ways politics had changed during the past two generations. Violent revolt against Buenos Aires, so frequent before 1870 among the old Federalists, had now been completely suppressed. Along with this had also disappeared the peasant or *gaucho* insurrections from the days of 'El Chacho' Peñaloza, or Felipe Varela. There now appeared little political conflict rooted in social or regional antagonisms. Much of society appeared to drift along in contentedly ignorant, parochial equilibrium.

The bulk of the population of the interior was wracked by bronchial pneumonia, tuberculosis and a variety of gastric ailments. The infant mortality rate was double and often treble that of Buenos Aires. Illiteracy rates approached 50 per cent. The interior was also relatively empty, less so than Patagonia, but more so than the pampas. In 1910 it was estimated that only one per cent of the total land area was under cultivation. In the most backward parts, La Rioja and Catamarca, the distribution of a precious water supply from the small streams and rivers flowing down from the mountains was conducted according to the same time-worn rites of the eighteenth century. At the end of the nineteenth century there was a temporary revival in the old cattle and mule trades into Chile and Bolivia. In the Chilean case this was assisted by the growth of mining and the development of the nitrate fields on the Pacific coast. In Bolivia's it accompanied the resurgence of the Salta route to the Río de la Plata following the loss of Bolivia's access to the Pacific in the war with Chile in the early 1880s. For a time this revived the fortunes of the *llaneros* of La Rioja and Catamarca, and Salta's importance as a trade centre. Yet by 1914 this trade had either almost disappeared or shifted in the direction of Mendoza and Tucumán. Though they were thus falling under the orbit of the new centres of growth, the lesser provinces lingered on in a state of unspecialized semi-autarky. Santiago del Estero, whose growing population made it the chief source of internal migrants at the time, had as mixed an agricultural and pastoral economy in 1914 as it had 150 years before. Flood farming along the Río Dulce enabled the production of sugar, wine, cotton and tobacco; mules were still being bred for export to Bolivia. However, this was all very small in scale, faster development being constrained now as in centuries past by the high saline content of the soil. Until the advent of sugar on an important scale in the 1920s and 1930s, Jujuy in the far north-west had only minimal contacts with the markets to the south. Trade was largely confined to the surviving indigenous communities, which exchanged alpaca and llama wool for Bolivian salt and coca across a still scarcely acknowledged frontier. In some areas there had been retrogression. The old silver mines of La Rioja in the west were almost all closed, and sometimes even their whereabouts forgotten, in the aftermath of the fall in world silver prices at the end of the nineteenth century. Forces of tradition were everywhere stronger than those of change. Even the city of Córdoba, which had attracted substantial numbers of European immigrants, whose eastern and southern hinterlands were now part of the pampas economy and which boasted a substantial boot and shoe industry, obstinately refused to cross the threshold into the twentieth century. The city and its surrounding province was still governed by an unchanging oligarchy of local families. Social and political life centred around the university, an institution hidebound by conservatism, scholasticism and clericalism.

BUENOS AIRES

On the outbreak of the first world war nowhere in the provinces, not even other bustling commercial centres like Rosario and Bahía Blanca, could emulate Buenos Aires. In many aspects the city was still, as Sarmiento had depicted it, a lonely outpost of advanced European civilization on the outer limit of the vast, underpopulated, or backward regions to its rear. It was also a great vortex into which flowed much of the wealth of the new export economy. Buenos Aires lorded over its great hinterland first by means of its strategic position at the interstices of international trade. It dominated the fan-shaped railway system stretching out from the estuary of the Río de la Plata across the pampas and into the interior. Although towards 1900 it lost ground to Rosario and Bahía Blanca as an exporter, and was thereafter more important in the meat trade than in cereals, it upheld its traditional lucrative monopoly over the distribution of imports. More so than in any previous period in its history, it was the emporium of banking and finance. It also benefited from the survival of the large estates on the pampas; wealth that might otherwise have remained in the agrarian economy was in part transposed into the great stucco palaces which landowners, bankers and merchants had begun constructing from the early 1880s onwards. This city was also the hub of government, state spending and state employment. After the act of federalization in 1880 its earlier share of the revenues from trade may have slightly dwindled, but the total resources it gathered multiplied with the growth of trade, to be shared among its elites and its phalanxes of functionaries, construction workers and manufacturers. Buenos Aires had by this time been endowed with modern docking facilities for almost 30 years. Incoming visitors were no longer obliged to disembark into skiffs in order to reach the shore. Its great railway stations in Plaza Constitución or Retiro were near-replicas of those in London or Liverpool. With its networks of tramways and underground railway, its modern sewage, water, gas and electricity facilities, its solid and imposing central office blocks, its capacious avenues lined with jacarandas and sometimes paved in Swedish granite, it had become as well-endowed a city as almost any in the world at that time. In 1914 three-quarters of the children of Buenos Aires were attending primary school. Although tuberculosis was still estimated to kill around 20 per cent of the population, the epidemics of yellow fever or cholera which had decimated the population in the 1870s were the last of their kind.

In 1914 not all the territory designated as part of the Federal Capital in 1880 had been built upon. Agriculture and grazing were still to be found within its confines. But new construction, mostly single-storey, flat-roofed dwellings all laid out in the undeviating grid fashion created by the Spaniards, had advanced rapidly with the coming of the immigrants. The tramways had acted on land values in the city as the railways had outside. Between 1904 and 1912 property values had appreciated up to tenfold. The city was now divided into clearly demarcated residential zones, which corresponded to its principal class groupings. On the north side towards the estuary of the Río de la Plata were the homes of the well-to-do or *gente bien*. These stretched from the mansions of Barrio Norte and Palermo towards the city centre through Belgrano to the suburban weekend *quintas* of Vicente López, Olivos and San Isidro across into the province of Buenos Aires. In the centre and the west of the city were many middle-class neighbourhoods which reached as far as Flores. The south was the working-class and industrial zone. Here amidst the modest dwellings of Nueva Pompeya, Barracas, Avellaneda and parts of the Boca were already forerunners of the *villas miserias* of the 1940s and after. These shanty houses were often constructed of rough boarding, discarded packing cases, and simple galvanized zinc roofing. They were stifling cauldrons of heat in summer, and ice boxes in the chill and damp Río de la Plata winter. Many were periodically washed away in the fetid flood waters of the Riachuelo, the small river which divided the capital from the province on this southern side. In this period the more customary dwellings of the poor, housing around 150,000 persons, were the *conventillos* close to the city centre. A half century earlier the oldest of these two-storey, rectangular constructions, whose interiors contained large Spanish-style patios, had been residences of the well-to-do. After the epidemics of the 1870s and the first arrivals of immigrants the rich moved elsewhere. Their homes became tenements. Later others like them were built to house the immigrants. Where 50 years before the *conventillos* had housed a single extended family and its domestic servants, in the early years of the twentieth century they were occupied by as much as a score of families, eking out within a congested, insanitary and turbulent existence. There were often three, four or more persons to each dingy room; between 25 and 30 would share washing facilities and lavatories. Nevertheless, it was probably no worse than the alternatives: Milan, Genoa, Naples, Barcelona, Brooklyn, Philadelphia or Chicago.

One feature which distinguished Buenos Aires from many cities in the United States in this period was that the immigrants, with some exceptions like the growing Jewish community, from the start mixed very easily. The different national groupings created a great profusion of clubs, schools, hospitals and mutual aid societies. Yet few sought to perpetuate their national origins in separate ghetto neighbourhoods, this being due no doubt to the close linguistic affinities between Spaniards and Italians. Another difference between Buenos Aires and comparable cities elsewhere was that until the onset of the trade and financial depression of 1913 permanent unemployment was unusually low. Immigrants dissatisfied with their lot in the city needed merely to spend a summer harvesting in the fields to raise the necessary sum to return to Europe. Even so this left the city with its penniless indigents, especially women and children. From time to time newspapers would publish dramatic *exposés* of what they called the 'begging industry' in which would surface alleged practices such as the hiring of diseased or handicapped children for seeking alms.[7] The city was also crime-ridden, though not unduly so by the standards which prevailed elsewhere. There was no organized Italian Mafia in Buenos Aires. During these years, however, it won great notoriety on account of its white slave traffic. Beginning around 1903 large numbers of the unprotected pauper maidens of Genoa, Barcelona, Amsterdam or Warsaw were kidnapped and sold into a life of prostitution in Argentina. In 1913 there were 300 registered brothels in Buenos Aires, compulsory registration being the only gesture made by the authorities to control the spread of vice and those living from it. These were conditions which reflected the presence of large numbers of unmarried male immigrants among the city's population.

In the generation before 1914 all sectors of the social structure of Buenos Aires had at least doubled in size. Along with this came increasing complexity and diversity. At the apex of society was an elite composed of the great landowners and other large property owners, bankers, and those who controlled the main flow of foreign investment and trade. By 1914 this group had changed substantially by comparison with 50 years before. It no longer embraced only a few score Creole families, most typically descended directly from the Spanish Bourbon merchants of the late eighteenth century. It had become a larger and highly heterodox body with accretions from all the countries in southern and western Europe. On the one side there still remained the ubiquitous Anchorenas, or the Guerricos, the Campos, or the Casares, survivors from four or five generations past. But on the other were many more *parvenu* creations. Among those of more recent Italian background were men like Antonio Devoto, who gave his name to Villa Devoto, soon to become a noted middle-class neighbourhood in the western zone of the Federal Capital. In a manner now typical of the elite as a whole, Devoto

---

[7] See, for example, the *Revista Popular*, March 1919.

had a multiple stake in land, banking, trade, public works contracts and manufacturing. Among his holdings of land in 1910 were 80,000 hectares and seven *estancias* in the province of Buenos Aires, 26,000 in Santa Fe on two *estancias*, another 75,000 in Cordoba among four, and 30,000 on one *estancia* in the more remote La Pampa territory. He also possessed extensive urban properties in central Buenos Aires, and he was the founder and president of the Banco de Italia y Río de la Plata. Others, like Luis Zuberbühler, a second generation Swiss-Argentinian, had comparable fortunes distributed among cattle *estancias*, land colonization companies, forestry and manufacturing. Similarly by 1914 Nicolás Mihanovich, who had arrived a penniless immigrant from Dalmatia about 50 years earlier, had a near monopoly on the coastal steamships plying between Buenos Aires and Asunción along the Paraná river or southwards to the Atlantic settlements of Patagonia.[8] Family appurtenances of the elite were scattered throughout professions like law, the military and public administration. Its members were separated in some degree by rival political affiliations and by clan-like family networks. But usually overshadowing these were the bonds formed by residential propinquity, and a sense of common class affiliation fostered by associations like the Rural Society or the Jockey Club. Much of the upper class lived with an ostentation which rivalled its counterparts in London or New York. Its mansions evoked Paris in architecture and magnificence. Their interiors often contained the most regal imported furnishings and *objets d'art*. Behind them lay great ornate patio gardens. During recent years members of the elite had become avid consumers of the most luxurious American or European limousines.

Observers of this leading sector of Argentine society generally acknowledged that it differed from its counterparts in Latin America in exemplifying a genuine sense of national identity. Georges Clemenceau had remarked, 'The real Argentine seems to me convinced that there is a magic elixir of youth which springs from his soil and makes of him a new man, descendant of none, but ancestor of endless generations to come.'[9] Others found the fierce national pride they encountered reminiscent of Manifest Destiny in the United States. Yet sometimes too what passed as nationalism was regarded as more akin to mere nativism, typical of a highly privileged group confronted by swelling tides of immigrants.

[8] Jorge Federico Sábato, 'Notas sobre la formación de la clase dominante en la Argentina moderna', mimeo, CISEA (Buenos Aires, 1979), 92–6.
[9] Quoted in Lloyd, *Twentieth century impressions*, 337.

While there were some who gave the elite credit for its success in promoting *haute culture*, most notably grand opera, more prurient observers criticized its apparent obsession with horse-racing and other games of chance as typical of a class whose fortunes were built largely on speculation in land. The more negative observers also found strong evocations of old Spain in the freedoms enjoyed by many men against the enforced seclusion of home and family. Women who were also members of the elite were sometimes active outside the home, especially in Catholic charity ventures. There was also a small feminist movement in Buenos Aires. Yet at a time when the suffragette campaign in Britain and the United States was reaching its climax, the accomplishments of most women here seemed unimpressive.

A second major social group in Buenos Aires was the middle class, which by this time had become by far the largest of its kind throughout Latin America. This was another indicator of the country's growing wealth. It also attested to the strong centralizing forces within it, which thrust into the narrow confines of the city a group which might otherwise have developed more widely outside. The middle class had a largely uniform immigrant background. Otherwise it was divided into two broad strata, each with a quite different status in society at large. Of the two the lower was composed of a growing number of petty industrial producers, shopkeepers and traders. According to the census of 1914 around four-fifths of this group in Buenos Aires was made up of foreigners. Its size – perhaps 15,000 to 20,000 strong – was another of the remarkable novelties of the past generation. Scattered throughout the city were multitudes of bakers, tailors, shoe and sandal makers, small brewers, chocolate, soap or cigarette manufacturers, printers, carpenters, blacksmiths and matchmakers along with a roughly equal number of street-corner shopkeepers (*almaceneros*). Most of the manufacturers among this group operated from workshops rather than factories. Outside the meat-packing plants, the flour mills, or a small number of textile and metallurgical firms, each unit usually had a work force no more than half a dozen strong, employing hand-tools rather than machinery, and often marketing its products in the immediate neighbourhood. This situation was not unlike that in many of the capital cities of Europe from London or Dublin to Constantinople. But in Argentina there was no domestic centre of heavy industry elsewhere to balance out light manufacturing. However fast local manufacturing grew after 1890, imports at least kept pace. It was therefore Manchester, Birmingham or

Lyons, and latterly Bremen, Essen and Detroit which serviced a major proportion of Argentina's industrial consumption needs. The manufacturers of Buenos Aires were as yet scarcely more than appendages to an economy still ruled by cereals and meat. The export sector, the commodities it embraced, the wealth which grew from it, closely influenced the development of domestic manufacturing; its access to raw materials and labour, and the growth of purchasing power in the markets it served. In 1914 the manufacturers occupied a relatively low standing in the community at large. They were weak and highly fragmented, and as yet commanded little political voice.

The upper segment of the middle class was entrenched among service and vocational occupations in the professions, in public administration or in white-collar positions in the private sector such as transportation. It differed from the manufacturers and shopkeepers in that its members were by this time mainly native-born. On the other hand many were no more than first generation Argentinians, and typically the upwardly mobile children of the manufacturing and commercial classes. In 'the introduction to the city census of 1910 it was mentioned that between 1905 and 1909 employment in manufacturing had increased from 127,000 to 218,000, or 71 per cent. However, the growth of service occupations from doctors, teachers, public officials to simple tinkers was from 57,000 to an estimated 150,000, or 163 per cent.[10] The middle-class component of this large and rapidly expanding tertiary sector owed much to the recent growth of the bureaucracy, both national and municipal. Expenditures of the national government, for example, were 160 million paper pesos in 1900. By 1910 they had climbed to 400 million. This was an increase in per capita terms from 30 to 58 pesos; a whole new stratum of government employees was its most visible result. By 1914 many members of this sector of the middle class, and those who aspired to join it, were deeply involved in the issue of higher education, since secondary school diplomas and university degrees were the normal prerequisites for admission into the professions and government. Unlike the manufacturers and traders, they had thus become a focus of political activism. In their strong support for the continuing expansion of both the bureaucracy and higher education, they found themselves repeatedly at variance with the elites. But otherwise these two sectors of society had much in common. Both were strongly conservative in economic policy.

---

[10] *Recensement général de la ville de Buenos Aires* (Buenos Aires, 1910), liii.

The middle class had little interest in domestic industrial development, preferring that consumption needs be satisfied cheaply and effortlessly through imports. Whenever its members could do so, they became avid buyers of land alongside the elites, though almost never farmers. In spite of their reputation for political radicalism, their interests and orientations thus indicated no promise of major change in, for example, the conditions which weakened the tenants on the land, or pushed the newly arrived immigrants into the urban *conventillos*.

In 1914 three-quarters of the Buenos Aires working class were immigrants and an overwhelming proportion of the rest were their children. The census of 1914 suggests that the working class made up perhaps two-thirds of the city's employed population, around 405,000 of a total male labour force of 626,000. Workers were employed in large numbers in commerce and the railways. There were other substantial congregations in public services, the tramways, the gas companies and so forth, or more humbly in sewage works and in refuse collection. Still more were employed in manufacturing, either in larger concerns like the meat-packing plants or in the small workshops to be found throughout the city. The structure of the working class was also influenced by the growth of service occupations. Perhaps as many as 20 per cent were employed in domestic service, among whom only about half at this time were women. A further fifth of the employed working-class population consisted of women and children. Among the large unskilled element within the working class immediately before 1914 a substantial portion drifted to and fro across the Atlantic, or alternated work in the city with seasonal harvest tasks outside. In past years, however, the working class too had become increasingly stratified. There were many highly skilled groups in the crafts, in construction, metallurgy or transportation. Some of the upper echelons exhibited the traits of an aristocracy of labour: a conspicuous moderation in political attitudes, a concern with wage relativities, or membership of a skill-based union brotherhood.

In 1914 Buenos Aires lagged conspicuously behind many of the cities of Western Europe, and for that matter its neighbour Montevideo across the Río de la Plata, in social legislation for the working class. There was no minimum wage law, eight- or ten-hour act, pensions or retirement provision. Nor were the state's shortcomings in this respect effectively remedied by co-operative and mutual aid societies or by the trades unions. But any dissatisfaction on this score was often overshadowed by others. In Buenos Aires the main bane of almost every worker's existence was housing. Many of the *conventillos*, as we have seen, were quite deplorable. In 1914 four-fifths of working-class families lived in one room. Otherwise conditions for the workers as a whole mirrored the broader features of the national economy. Imports, in this case mainly clothing, were often costly, partly on account of government tariffs which taxed some of the essentials of working-class consumption. On the other hand this was normally offset by the cheapness of most common foodstuffs and the availability of a nutritious diet. Generally real incomes among workers in Buenos Aires compared well with most Western European cities. The growth of a working-class culture in these years – the tango bars, the boxing and soccer clubs, the trades unions, and many other associations – suggests that a good proportion of the population had the income surplus and the leisure time for a quite rich and variegated existence. Even so there was much evidence of conditions which ranged from unsatisfactory to wretched. Among the large foreign employers of labour, the meat-packing plants were notorious for low wages and oppressive working conditions. Some of the worst abuses were perpetrated by small employers, most of them immigrants themselves. Wages in the city's small stores were at best paltry, and eighteen-hour shifts commonplace.

In 1914 Argentina had thus evolved into an extremely mixed and diverse society. Across the regions many highly advanced or sophisticated structures co-existed with others of immutable backwardness. Immediately before the first world war there were still high expectations that the imbalances would steadily recede as the present wave of growth continued. On this supposition the most pressing issue was political: the country required new institutions to arbitrate between new class and regional interests. To do this it was ready to jettison the oligarchic system of rule and launch itself on a quest for representative democracy. A preparedness for reform was due in some part to social tensions after 1900; at the same time it was also an expression of confidence in the country's ability to maintain its earlier momentum. Events were to show that this assumption was in part ill-founded. In 1914 there remained some areas of the country with an apparently promising future. The development of cotton in the north-east and oil in the south, for example, suggested means both to reduce the import bill and give further impetus to domestic manufacturing. On the other hand the pampas was nearing the peak of its development. In 1914 Argentina's potential for growth and in some respects its freedom of manoeuvre were diminishing. Instead of the earlier smooth upward curve of growth, the period which followed brought an alternating sequence of booms and slumps, more slowly rising consumption, and sometimes highly volatile short-term changes in income distribution among the different social sectors. Against this background came the attempt at democratic reform.

12

ARGENTINA FROM THE FIRST WORLD
WAR TO THE REVOLUTION OF 1930

The decade and a half from the outbreak of the first world war to the
onset of the world depression witnessed overall a continuation of
Argentina's prewar economic prosperity based on the growth of its
export sector. In 1929 Argentina was still the world's largest exporter of
chilled beef, maize, linseed and oats, and the third largest exporter of
wheat and flour. Comparing annual averages for 1910–14 with 1925–9,
exports of wheat increased from 2.1 million tons to 4.2 million, maize
from 3.1 to 3.5 million, and linseed from 680,000 to 1.6 million. Exports
of chilled beef, which averaged only 25,000 tons between 1910 and 1914,
increased to more than 400,000 between 1925 and 1929. Exports as a
whole, which were valued on average at 4,480 million paper pesos at
1950 prices in 1910–14, increased to 7,914 million between 1925 and
1929. Per capita income in Argentina still compared favourably with
most of Western Europe. Standards of living had risen, while illiteracy
rates had again fallen. A substantial part of the population basked in
prosperity and well-being. By 1930 there were 435,000 automobiles
throughout Argentina, a substantially larger number than in many
Western European countries, and a sevenfold increase from eight years
before. Assisted once more by immigration, population rose by almost 4
million between 1914 and 1930, from 7.9 million to 11.6 million. In one
sector, domestic oil, there was spectacular growth. In 1913 Argentina
produced less than 21,000 cubic metres of fuel oil. By 1929 output had
risen to 1.4 million.

On the other hand, growth was less rapid and less smooth than in the
period before the first world war. During the whole 40-year period
before 1910–14 gross domestic product at factor cost increased at an

annual average of 6.3 per cent. Between 1910–14 and 1925–30 the rate fell to 3.5 per cent. Quantum exports grew at a rate of more than 5 per cent before 1914, and only 3.9 per cent after. The rate of growth of the land area sown to crops also fell from 8.3 per cent to 1.3 per cent. There was virtually no expansion in land use in the pampas: the increase was nil in Santa Fe, and minimal in Córdoba, Entre Ríos, and the province of Buenos Aires. Throughout this period population in the pampas continued to grow but at a notably lesser rate than before the war. Between 1895 and 1914 the growth of the rural population was around 1 million, but only 270,000 between 1914 and 1930. In the earlier period the annual rate of increase was 50,000, and in the later period only 22,500. There was also a pronounced fall in the rate at which new townships were founded. Advances in agriculture were less an expression of a growing rural population than of mechanization. Argentina was now a large market for imported farm machinery. Machines which amounted to 24 per cent of the capital stock in the rural sector in 1914 grew to around 40 per cent by 1929. By that year there were an estimated 32,000 combine harvesters, 16,000 tractors and 10,000 threshing machines in Argentina. To some extent increases in agricultural output during the 1920s were also due to substitutions in land use. A near doubling in the production of cereals and linseed between 1922 and 1929 was partly the result of a reduction in the cattle population by 5 million during these years, and the consequent decline in land acreages devoted to cattle and alfalfa fodder. The cattle stock was an estimated 37 million in 1922, but only 32.2 million in 1930. During the same period the land area devoted to alfalfa shrank from 7 to 5 million hectares. With mechanization there was also a decline in the acreage devoted to pasturing horses. On the other hand, the land area devoted to cereals rose from 11 to 19 million hectares. In 1921–2 cereals and linseed represented only 56.5 per cent of the cultivated area in the pampas, but by 1929–30 this had risen to 73.5 per cent.

After 1913 there was little new foreign investment for railway construction. Between that time and 1927 only 1,200 kilometres of new track were added, mostly branch lines or government-built lines in the interior. Between 1865–9 and 1910–14, the railways grew at an annual average of 15.4 per cent. Between 1910–14 and 1925–9 the increase fell to 1.4 per cent. British investment in Argentina ended completely during the war and the immediate postwar period, recovering to only a comparative trickle during the later 1920s. Overall the influx of foreign capital was only about a fifth of the prewar period, while the ratio of foreign over domestic capital diminished from 48 to 34 per cent between 1913 and 1927. Likewise immigration virtually ceased for a decade after 1913. And between 1921 and 1930 the net balance of migrants was only 856,000 compared with 1.1 million between 1901 and 1910. Population grew by an average of only 2.8 per cent in the immediate postwar period compared with 4.3 per cent in the period immediately before the war.[1]

Whereas between 1895 and 1913 there was steady upward growth, the period from 1913 began with depression (1913–17) which was followed by recovery and renewed boom (1918–21); then came another recession (1921–4) followed once more by expansion which continued to 1929.[2] The recessions had many of the features of those in the mid 1870s and early 1890s. They resulted from contractions in Argentina's export markets and a decline in its commodity export prices. From this came balance of payments crises, corrected eventually by falling imports, but at the cost of falling government revenues. The depression of 1913, as in 1873 and 1890, was exacerbated by a cessation of foreign investment. In 1914 the gold standard and peso convertibility schemes established in 1899 were abandoned. (They were restored afterwards for only a brief two-year period between 1927 and 1929.) The depressions of 1913 and 1921 both brought unemployment in the cities and the countryside alike, a fall in urban and rural land values, a spate of bankruptcies and severe credit squeezes. On the other hand during this period Argentina managed to avoid overseas debt crises like that in 1890. In 1913 around three-quarters of foreign investment was private, and the government was largely exempt from its earlier obligation to afford gold-based guaranteed minimum profits.

The depression of 1913 began when the Bank of England raised interest rates to correct a balance of payments deficit in Britain and to check financial uncertainty caused by wars in the Balkans. There was now a net outflow of capital from Argentina through interest and amortization repayments. The crisis deepened with a downward plunge in world cereal and meat prices, and with the failure of the 1913–14 harvest. Some months later, as matters appeared to be on the mend, the outbreak of war in Europe and the withdrawal of shipping from the high seas brought foreign trade almost to a complete standstill, obliging the

[1] Most of these figures appear in Carlos F. Díaz Alejandro, *Essays in the economic history of the Argentine Republic* (New Haven, 1970), chapter 1.
[2] The cycles are best followed in Guido Di Tella and Manuel Zymelman, *Las etapas del desarrollo económico argentino* (Buenos Aires, 1967), 295–420.

de la Plaza government to impose a financial moratorium throughout August 1914. The next year brought some improvement in exports. But by this time as Britain and France shifted to munitions production and an Allied blockade was imposed against Germany, there were growing shortages of imports, only partly remedied by supplies from the United States.

Depression persisted until the end of 1917. From then on export prices rapidly advanced under the stimulus of wartime demand. This was especially true of frozen and canned meat, enormous quantities of which were consumed by the Allied troops on the Western Front. Export earnings, around 400 million gold pesos in 1913–14, had almost tripled by 1919–20 to 1,100 million. Even so the rise of export prices was much less than that of imports: an acute world shortage of manufactured goods weighted the terms of trade heavily against the primary producers. The volume of Argentina's imports fell from an estimated 10 million tons in 1913, most of which was coal, to only 2.6 million in 1918. Yet their cost, inflated by the fourfold rise in shipping rates during the war, more than doubled from around 400 million gold pesos in 1913–14 to almost 850 million in 1919–20. As a neutral country throughout Argentina escaped the physical destruction of the war, including the depredations of submarines in the Río de la Plata. But it could not isolate itself from the highly disruptive economic effects of the war.

Until 1918 there was an uncharacteristically high rate of unemployment in Buenos Aires. In similar situations in the past it had been possible to 'export' unemployment by an outflow of former immigrants. Although after 1913 emigrants consistently exceeded new arrivals for the first time since 1890, the steep rise in shipping rates and the shortage of shipping impeded the operation of the normal escape mechanism, bottling up some of the unemployment in Argentina itself. In 1914 it was estimated that between 16 and 20 per cent of the labour force in Buenos Aires was unemployed. Despite emigration unemployment did not disappear entirely until 1918. The first three years of the war thus brought falling wages, a longer working day and extremely unpropitious conditions for trades unions. There were no strikes of any significance between the last year of prewar prosperity in 1912 and the end of 1916. The war further affected the public sector. After 1913 as imports fell, the De la Plaza government faced diminishing tariff revenues, its principal source of revenue. It was also obliged to employ a larger proportion of revenues in servicing the foreign debt. As had occurred in the mid 1870s and in the early 1890s, the depression thus compelled vigorous efforts to reduce current government spending. De la Plaza suspended public works schemes, and carefully trimmed the government's expenses in day-to-day administration. This fed unemployment. It also contributed to a heavy crop of business failures. Policies of the central government were matched by the provinces and the municipalities. All were obliged to cling rigidly to retrenchment and austerity.

The picture changed somewhat during the upward phase of the cycle between 1917 and 1921. At this point, which saw the steepest increases in export prices, the landed and commercial interests enjoyed an unprecedented bonanza. In 1918 it was reported that some of the meat-packing plants were earning a near 50 per cent return on capital invested. However, there was little immediate relief for other sectors of the population. In place of unemployment came rapidly rising inflation and a heavy redistribution of income against the middle and especially the lower classes. Except for rents, which emigration during the war helped keep fairly stable, inflation bit deeply into all the major components of popular consumption. The price of foodstuffs increased by 50 per cent between 1914 and 1918. The price of simple clothing goods, most of them normally imported, tripled. Domestic textile manufacturing, using mainly wool, afforded scant relief. It helped to reduce unemployment, though perhaps more among women than men, but failed to check rising prices. For many working-class families in Buenos Aires, between the plunge into depression in 1913 and the Armistice in November 1918, real wage levels as much as halved.[3] Falling unemployment and falling standards of living proved an explosive combination. Labour's earlier quiescence abruptly ceased. Between 1917 and 1921 trade unions in Argentina flourished on a scale unknown before and unrepeated until the mid 1940s; strikes, earlier so conspicuously absent, mounted in number, intensity and eventually in violence.

Meanwhile throughout the war imports and therefore revenues continued to fall. Pending changes in the taxation system to reduce the dependence on revenue from import duties, the government could alleviate its need to economize only by contracting new debts. This it managed to do to some degree by acquiring some short-term loans from banks in New York and floating bonds internally. Between 1914 and 1918, as new debts were contracted, the public floating debt almost

---

[3] *Ibid.*, 317. For details of the wartime inflation, see Alejandro E. Bunge, *Los problemas económicos del presente* (1919; Buenos Aires, 1979).

tripled from 256 million paper pesos to 711 million. However, total expenditure in 1918 at 421 million was roughly the same as in 1914, and not far above the figure of 375 million for 1916, the lowest throughout the period. This again changed dramatically after the Armistice when imports began to flow once more. From this point onwards public spending underwent a rapid increase. In 1922 it reached 614 million paper pesos, almost 50 per cent higher than in 1918.[4]

The postwar depression which began in 1921 led once more to unemployment, the collapse of the trade union movement, a decline in imports and another shrinkage in state revenues. In 1920 imports were valued at 2,120 million paper pesos, and only 1,570 million in 1922. Because of an increase in tariffs in 1920 revenues fell during the same period by only 20 million, from 481 to 461 million. However, since public expenditure climbed from 503 to 614 million, the government's floating debt also increased markedly from 682 to 893 million. Otherwise the chief effect of the postwar depression was upon the cattle sector, as the earlier great boom ended. After this came the shift back to arable farming.

During the late 1920s much of the real growth in the rural sector occurred beyond the pampas region. In the north-west Salta and Jujuy developed as sugar producers alongside Tucumán. In 1920 Salta and Jujuy contributed less than 16 per cent of national sugar output. By 1930 their share had risen to almost 26 per cent. The more northerly sugar region differed from Tucumán in that production was mainly conducted on large estates. From the 1920s, and into the following decade, it became common for the *ingenio*-owners of Tucumán to buy up estates northwards. Some they employed for cane production. Others they acquired apparently with an eye to capturing their peasant labour force for work on the plantations.[5] There was further growth of fruit production in the Río Negro valley, cotton, rice, peanuts and cassava in the Chaco, and fruits and yerba maté in Misiones. Domestic raw cotton output increased from an annual average of 6,000 tons between 1920 and 1924 to 35,000 tons in 1930–4. The increase in yerba maté was from 12,000 to 46,000 tons. Río Negro, Chaco and Misiones each grew quickly with an infusion of new European immigrants and the spread of small farming. These were each national territories administered from Buenos

---

[4] Figures on public accounts in David Rock, *Politics in Argentina, 1890–1930. The rise and fall of Radicalism* (Cambridge, 1975), 224.

[5] See Ian Rutledge, 'Plantations and peasants in northern Argentina: the sugar cane industry of Salta and Jujuy, 1930–43', in David Rock (ed.), *Argentina in the twentieth century* (London, 1975), 88–113.

Aires, and in this period the central government played a positive role in colonization. As a result by 1930 capitalist small-farming was established on a significantly wider scale than before the war. On the other hand all these regions were heavily dependent on cheap contract peasant labour. Large numbers of Chileans were brought on to the farms of Río Negro and Neuquén, and Paraguayans, *chaqueños* and *correntinos* to those of the north-east.[6]

After 1913 domestic industry grew overall at roughly the same rate as the economy at large, though increasing at a much faster rate after the war than during the war years. Taking the year 1950 as base 100, the index of industrial production was 20.3 in 1914 and 22.1 in 1918. However, by 1929 it reached 45.6. During the war the annual rate of increase in the index was 0.36, and after the war 2.10.[7] During the 1920s industry also diversified in some measure in fields such as consumer durables, chemicals, electricity and particularly metals. In the late 1920s the metallurgical industry surged forward. Between 1926 and 1929 the output index grew from 29 to 43 (1950 = 100).[8] Even so most of the total increase in manufacturing was again in light and traditional industries, continuing the pattern of the pre-1914 years. The textile industry meanwhile largely stagnated. The growth of manufacturing also failed to affect Argentina's high import coefficient, which remained roughly the same as in 1914, at around 25 per cent.

Of the much smaller volume of foreign investment which entered Argentina in the 1920s in comparison with the prewar period, the major source was now the United States. During this period American investment was almost double British. By 1930 it amounted to around one-third of British investment, having risen from an estimated 40 million gold pesos in 1913 to 611 million in 1929. Where before Americans had been interested almost solely in the meat business, they now became active as lenders to government, as exporters and as investors in local industry. Twenty-three subsidiaries of American industrial firms were established in Argentina between 1924 and 1933; other American goods were manufactured locally under licence. On the surface this suggested a growing maturity in the economy, and its ability to diversify beyond agrarian exports and to generate new sources of employment. Yet in the 1920s industry again grew without changing the

---

[6] For farming in the interior, see Jaime Fuchs, *Argentina: su desarrollo capitalista* (Buenos Aires, 1965), 217–24; also Ricardo M. Ortiz, *Historia económica de la Argentina, 1850–1930* (2 vols., Buenos Aires, 1955), II, 131–48.
[7] Di Tella and Zymelman, *Las etapas del desarrollo*, 309, 393.   [8] *Ibid.*, 391.

basic economic structure very much. Oil apart, relatively few backward linkages flowed from it. The machinery, still much of the fuel, the raw materials and technology of the American companies or domestic firms using American patents were largely imported. The overall result was thus to impose binding additions to the import bill, leaving manufacturing and urban employment as dependent as before on foreign earnings from exports.

Meanwhile the growth of imports from the United States led to strain in Argentina's relations with Great Britain. The value of imports from the United States was 43 million gold pesos in 1914. Afterwards this figure climbed to 169 million in 1918, and reached 310 million in 1920. The trend then continued throughout the 1920s. By 1929 American exports to Argentina were valued at 516 million gold pesos. During the war the Americans gained mostly at the expense of Germany, but then afterwards at the expense of the British, who in the 1920s found themselves under serious challenge in a market they had largely dominated for the past hundred years. The British share of the Argentine market fell from 30 per cent in 1911–13 to only 19 per cent by 1929–30, while the American share increased from 15 to 24 per cent. Although the British increased their exports of coal and railway materials to Argentina, they could not compete against the Americans in the goods for which demand was rising most rapidly: automobiles and capital goods for agriculture and industry. Such changes in the import trade were not followed by a parallel shift in exports: Argentina failed to acquire stable, growing markets in the United States. Despite a temporary increase during the war years, exports to the United States, which were 6.3 per cent of the total in 1911–13, remained at only 9.3 per cent in 1928–30. In the late 1920s, 85 per cent of Argentina's exports were still exported to Western Europe. Indeed the trend with exports was almost the direct inverse of imports. Although Argentina was now buying relatively much less from Britain, its exports to Britain grew from 26.1 per cent in 1911–13 to 32.5 per cent in 1928–30: the country was diversifying its sources of imports, but narrowing its markets for exports.

WAR AND POSTWAR POLITICS

Yrigoyen, 1916–22

Politically the years between 1916 and 1930 witnessed the first and also the most prolonged of Argentina's many abortive experiments with representative democracy. Along with neighbouring Uruguay, Argentina was the leader among the nations of Latin America in seeking to develop the political system and institutions most characteristic of advanced Western societies in the early twentieth century. In 1912 the old ruling class, prompted by its progressive wing led by Roque Sáenz Peña, who was president from 1910 to 1914, had reformed the political system largely in an effort to legitimize and stabilize its own authority. Since the emergence of the Unión Cívica Radical in the early 1890s, confidence in the durability of rule by oligarchy had been gradually undermined. After the failure of the 1905 insurrection the Radicals had begun to broaden their power base, attracting a large following among the burgeoning urban and rural middle classes. Operating semi-clandestinely they continued threatening to overthrow the existing order by force unless their demands for 'democracy' and the 'restoration of the constitution' were met. A second focus of disaffection was the Buenos Aires working class. After 1900 there was a string of sometimes violent general strikes led by militant anarchists. By the time of Sáenz Peña's election in 1910, many suspected anarchists had been gaoled or deported and the movement apparently broken. However, most of the conditions which had produced urban unrest remained unchanged. Manhood suffrage, the representation of minorities in Congress and an end to electoral fraud were offered by Sáenz Peña in his 1912 electoral reform law as a response to this dual threat to stability. In his view political order was essential for continuing economic expansion:

If our self-aggrandizement has begun, it is because we have been able to demonstrate the overriding power of the national government, inspiring a sense of security, peace and confidence. I shall not support oppression, but I condemn revolutions . . . I do not believe we can consolidate our present position, except by perfecting ourselves in a climate of order.[9]

Referring to the Radicals Ramón Cárcano, one of Sáenz Peña's supporters in Congress, declared:

For twenty years there has existed in the country an organized popular, dynamic party, which has had as its banner the liberty of the suffrage and openly supported revolution as the only way to fulfil its ideals . . . For a generation government and nation alike have been constantly having either to suppress rebellion or fearing that rebellion was imminent . . . A change in the electoral system . . . is to adopt at this critical hour the only policy the country is united

---

[9] Roque Sáenz Peña, *Discursos del Dr. Roque Sáenz Peña al asumir la presidencia de la nación* (Buenos Aires, 1910), 40.

on: the policy of disarmament, to eliminate abstention from the elections and rebellion; to incorporate each active political force into the electoral process.[10]

Beyond satisfying the Radicals the aim was to give moderate working-class associations, especially the Socialist party (founded in 1894), an opportunity to displace the anarchists. One conservative member of the National Senate in 1912, Benito Villanueva, suggested the need to 'open up an escape valve and allow two or three socialists into Congress, especially at this time of working class unrest when legislation on strikes is about to be discussed'.[11] Lastly, Sáenz Peña and his group also hoped to prod the oligarchic factions into creating a strong, united conservative party able to gather a large popular following. In 1912 there seemed every prospect that these objectives could be fulfilled. At the end of his term in 1916 Sáenz Peña would thus hand over to a progressive conservative like himself strengthened by having won the presidency openly and fairly at the polls. This would weaken the Radicals, also undercutting their main pretext for revolution. If it failed to domesticate the workers, it would strengthen the hand of government in the event of renewed conflict.

After 1912 events pursued a largely different course from the one anticipated. While the Socialist party built up a large electoral following in the city of Buenos Aires, it failed to capture control over working-class trade unions. Although anarchism continued to decline, a new syndical-ist movement appeared in its place and in 1915 took over the main union federation, the Federación Obrera Regional Argentina. Meanwhile the Radical party underwent spectacular growth in all parts of the country. The conservatives, however, stagnated. Their efforts at self-democratization were only partially successful: unlike their chief rivals, they failed to create a united national movement. After 1912 they were split among the supporters of the governor of the province of Buenos Aires, Marcelino Ugarte, and the leader of the Progressive Democratic party based in Santa Fe, Lisandro de la Torre. In some measure this disunity was a symptom of economic depression; after 1912 falling land prices, credit restraints, and declining export earnings increasingly demoralized the conservative camp. Sáenz Peña did nothing to arrest the process of fragmentation and decay, and by the time he succumbed to cancer in August 1914 matters had been let slide too long to be easily remedied. Sáenz Peña's successor as president, the septuagenarian financier,

---

[10] *Diario de Sesiones*, Cámara de Deputados (1911), II, 160.   [11] *Ibid.*, Senadores (1911), II, 338.

Victorino de la Plaza, was soon caught up in the economic repercussions of the war; he had little opportunity for political manoeuvring. The unexpected result of the 1916 elections was thus a victory for the Radical party and its leader Hipólito Yrigoyen, though by the barest of margins.

Yrigoyen's election to the presidency in the first national elections under universal manhood suffrage in 1916 was widely recognized as portending a new era in the country's political development. The new ruling party embraced large segments of the population which before had enjoyed little real representation. They could be expected to push for innovations. But despite their defeat and their mistrust of Yrigoyen the conservatives were not unduly alarmed. In accepting electoral politics the Radicals appeared to have abandoned the idea of revolution. Yrigoyen had given no hint of a commitment to major change. Despite its substantial middle-class support, his party embraced a good portion of members of the elite. The recent election had done little beyond change the president. The conservatives themselves dominated Congress through their overwhelming majority in the Senate. They were firmly in control of many of the provinces. Their influence was similarly undiminished in other leading institutions: the army, the church, the Rural Society and elsewhere. They had created popular democracy by concession; what they had given they could also take away. Having won his position as much by courtesy of the old ruling class as by his own efforts, Yrigoyen enjoyed a highly conditional mandate: he was to uphold the status quo while reducing the level of popular unrest.

Hipólito Yrigoyen's first six-year term (1916–22) was far from the smooth transition to representative democracy the conservatives had hoped for. It was closely influenced by the wartime inflation which altered the distribution of income among the major social classes, and by the cycles of depression and prosperity which embraced the whole period between 1916 and 1922. Inflation, as we have seen, underlay a protracted outbreak of unrest among the working class of Buenos Aires and in parts of the country outside. Its main episodes were a general strike in Buenos Aires in January 1919 and a spate of rural labour agitation in Patagonia between 1920 and 1922. The economic cycles brought fluctuations in the influx of imports and therefore government revenues. Revenues in turn had a crucial bearing on the government's ability to enhance its popular support and to reduce the influence of the conservative opposition. They bore closely on its relations with the enfranchised upper tiers of the middle class, many of whose members were employed in public administration. Until 1919 the Radical government cultivated the middle class mainly by supporting change and expansion in university education. Afterwards it came to rely increasingly on patronage links. In the longer term Yrigoyen was pushed by a variety of forces into narrowing his political base which came to consist largely of the middle class. From this came class fissures in Argentine politics which had a close bearing on his overthrow in 1930.

At the beginning there was a strong air of continuity between the new Radical administration and its conservative predecessors. Yrigoyen carefully cultivated support from conservative bodies like the church, and his Cabinet was made up of members of the traditional elites. Most were affiliates of the Rural Society, the main guardian of the stock-raising interest. There was also continuity in international affairs, as Yrigoyen reaffirmed neutrality in the war. During his first months in office the new president persistently irritated conservative opinion by secretive political manoeuvres, and by a cavalier attitude to protocol, such as ignoring the accepted practice of being present at the opening of Congress. Yet for the most part on broad policy issues he behaved in a safe and conventional fashion.

The new government's legislative proposals, submitted to Congress in late 1916, were measures under public discussion for some time and were regarded as mild in content. The government requested funds for new colonization schemes on state lands, an emergency fund to assist farmers caught by a recent drought, a new state bank to provide better credit arrangements for agriculture, and the acquisition of shipping to attack the problem of high wartime freights. In 1918 it further proposed the introduction of an income tax. Yrigoyen's error in 1916 was to demand from Congress the large sum of 100 million paper pesos to execute these various measures. Conservatives immediately drew the conclusion that the funds would be employed for partisan purposes. Pleading the need for economy Congress gave them short shrift and rejected them. It was not so much that Congress was opposed to the measures themselves; it was unwilling to grant the executive financial independence – Yrigoyen would be less troublesome if the resources at his disposal were held to the minimum. Disputes of this kind over the sanctioning and disposal of public funds continued throughout his presidency, and were a chief source of the growing rift between the government and the conservative opposition. There were several years in which Congress failed to vote the annual budget, to which the government replied by carrying out expenditures by simple Cabinet resolutions. After 1919 this became Yrigoyen's chief method of increasing state spending. Constant wrangling between the Executive and Congress over financial matters was among the chief reasons for a somewhat barren legislative record before 1922. Yrigoyen's main achievement was the eventual creation of an agricultural mortgage bank in 1920 under Law No. 10,676. Under this legislation farmers were accorded more liberal credit terms for land purchases. The law assisted colonization efforts at the outer limits of the pampas and in the national territories.[12]

The president could only prevail over Congress by changing its composition and winning a majority. To do this he was obliged to control the provinces and supplant the conservative governors and their party machines. Like Roca, Pellegrini, and Figueroa Alcorta before him, Yrigoyen turned to federal intervention. Interventions in the provinces, and related election issues, were the source of some of the fiercest controversies during his first three years in office. The most serious came in early 1917 when Yrigoyen, ignoring Congress's claim that legislation was necessary in such matters, decreed intervention in the province of Buenos Aires against Marcelino Ugarte. Altogether during the six years of his government there were an unprecedented twenty federal interventions, fifteen of them by decree. However, most came after 1918, when the power struggle between Radicals and conservatives entered its more intense phase. Most were also employed in the backward interior provinces, where control over the executive and its store of patronage, jobs and credits, was the key to political dominance. Thanks largely to federal intervention, by 1918 the Radicals won a majority in the National Chamber of Deputies. What they failed to do was achieve control over the Senate, whose members enjoyed a long nine-year tenure, renewable by thirds triennially.[13]

Before 1919 the Radical government sought to strengthen its links with the middle classes by supporting the university reform movement, *La Reforma*, which began in Córdoba in 1918 as the climax to growing agitation for changes in higher education. At this time there were three universities in Argentina: Córdoba (founded in 1617 by the Jesuits), Buenos Aires (1821) and La Plata (1890). Attendance at these institutions

---

[12] See Roberto Etchepareborda, *Yrigoyen y el Congreso* (Buenos Aires, 1956); for agrarian legislation, see Ortiz, *Historia económica*, I, 57.

[13] See Rodolfo Moreno, *Intervenciones federales en las provincias* (Buenos Aires, 1924).

had grown from around 3,000 in 1900 to 14,000 in 1918. For a decade or more before 1918 there were rising tensions in Córdoba between the incumbent and unchanging clerical order and the new middle classes of immigrant background whose numbers were growing steadily in the student body. During the war years long-standing demands for improvements in the university's teaching, and the streamlining of its curricula, were radicalized by events outside the country – especially the revolutions in Russia and Mexico. The reform movement began in Córdoba with a succession of militant strikes and an outpouring of manifestos, organized by a new students' union, the Federación Universitaria Argentina. Demands were made for student representation in university government, the reform of examination practices and an end to nepotism in the appointment of the professorial staff. For much of 1918 the University of Córdoba and the city beyond were consumed in turmoil. In the following year the student strikes spread to Buenos Aires and La Plata.

The Radical government gave the students sustained support. In 1918 Yrigoyen sent to Córdoba personal delegates who were known to favour the reform movement. They implemented many of the changes the students deemed necessary, and sought to link the vague democratic ideals of radicalism and the diffuse body of doctrine emanating from the reform movement. Later the government carried out similar reforms in the University of Buenos Aires. Finally all three universities were given new charters supposedly guaranteeing their autonomy, but in fact bringing them more directly under the control of the central government. When in 1919 and 1921 new universities were created in Santa Fe and Tucumán, the same regime was implanted there. The Radical government's support for the university reform was long regarded as among its more positive and lasting achievements. Here Yrigoyen managed to challenge an area of privilege, and associate himself with democratization, without being circumvented by conservative opposition.

His much less fruitful contact with the Buenos Aires working class and the trade unions stemmed from the keen rivalries between Radicals and Socialists for a popular majority in the capital. The competition between the two parties began during the first elections held in the city under the Sáenz Peña Law in 1912, and persisted throughout the period under 1930. In 1912 the Socialists were already gaining upwards of 30,000 votes in the city. This number later doubled and then trebled as they established a stable position among the electorate. The Socialist party, however, was controlled by middle-class intellectuals and while its main voting strength lay among workers, it also attracted many white-collar groups and small businessmen. Its programme placed little emphasis on the socialization of property; it was mostly concerned with the protection of urban consumer interests. The party's main weakness, which stemmed in large part from the moderate stances it took, was its lack of backing from the trade unions. Before 1910 it was constantly out-manoeuvred by the anarchists, and afterwards by the syndicalists, who in 1915, as we have seen, took over the principal labour federation in Buenos Aires, the FORA. The chief aim of the Radicals was to exploit this fissure between the party and the union and swing voting union members over in their favour.

Competition for the working-class vote, already a leading issue in the presidential election in Buenos Aires in 1916, continued unabated when Yrigoyen assumed power. The Radical offensive began at the end of 1916 on the outbreak of a strike in the port of Buenos Aires. The strike was organized by a group known as the Federación Obrera Marítima (Maritime Workers' Federation), an association led by syndicalists. The syndicalists were a somewhat different species from their anarchist predecessors. For the most part they were not immigrants but native-born. They paid only lip service to the goal of class revolution, and were interested almost exclusively in wage questions. Yrigoyen saw in the maritime strike the opportunity to better his reputation among the working class, and to weaken the Socialists. When it began, the authorities responded with actions which suggested sympathy for the men's cause. They paraded their avoidance of police measures to quell it, as had been the usual practice up until that time. Instead several union leaders were brought before members of the government and urged to accept their arbitration. When a ruling was eventually forthcoming the strikers obtained a settlement which met most of their grievances.

Government intervention in this strike and others swiftly escalated into a major political issue. For a time it won the Radicals a measure of popularity among the trade unions and the voting working class which helped it to electoral victory against the Socialists. In the congressional elections of 1916 in the city of Buenos Aires, the Radicals gained 59,061 votes or 47.1 per cent of the total; in 1918 their vote increased to 74,180, 51.7 per cent of the total. But these electoral successes were at the cost of vehement conservative opposition, which moved quickly beyond

Congress and the press to encompass the major special interest associations led by the Rural Society. In 1917 and 1918 the strikes spread beyond Buenos Aires to the British railway companies. Here, largely due to the high cost of imported coal during the war, working conditions had deteriorated and wages had fallen. When the government again appeared to take the side of the men, opposition spread to British business interests, which branded the government as pro-German. Primed into action by leading British companies, the employers established a strike-breaking body, the National Labour Association, which pledged itself to all-out war against trade union 'agitators'.

For several months afterwards the labour front remained fairly tranquil. Then in early January 1919, working-class discontent suddenly revived with even greater intensity. This episode, known subsequently as La Semana Trágica, stemmed from a strike of metallurgical workers which began in early December 1918. The metallurgical industry had suffered perhaps more than any other during the war. It was entirely dependent upon imported raw materials at a time when prices had reached astronomical levels as a result of high shipping rates and world shortages due to arms manufacture. As the price of raw materials climbed, wages had fallen. By the end of the war the metallurgical workers were in a desperate position. The strike was a battle for survival. Violence immediately ensued, and the police were obliged to intervene. When the strikers killed a member of the city police force, the latter organized a retaliatory ambush. Two days later five persons were killed in an affray between the two sides.

At this the city erupted. Ignoring pleas for moderation from the syndicalists, the workers struck *en masse*, joining a great procession through the city in homage to the victims of the police attack. More outbreaks of violence followed. The affair ballooned at a speed which paralysed the government. As it hesitated, the army intervened. Led by General Luis F. Dellepiane, a former chief of police in Buenos Aires, military detachments, equipped with artillery and machine guns, appeared to quell the outbreak. Dellepiane accomplished his task with little difficulty. The strikers were quickly scattered. Soon all that remained of the movement were sporadic bread riots as food shortages enveloped the city.

While this was done Yrigoyen for the most part sat silently in the background. He was aware of a dangerous wave of opposition in military and naval circles. It sprang not only from his labour policies, but from his juggling with army promotions to favour Radical sympathizers and from his use of the army during recent federal interventions. By January 1919 there were some among the armed forces ready to overthrow him. In this climate the Radical government fell captive to a conservative reaction bent on exacting revenge for the recent disorders. In the strike's aftermath civilian vigilante gangs sprang up in large numbers. After perfunctory drilling and rifle practice from the army they were set loose on the streets. But soon their activities centred upon the city's Russian-Jewish community. Its members became prime targets in the belief that the general strike was the prelude to a Bolshevik revolution, part of an alleged world conspiracy directed from Soviet Russia for the overthrow of capitalism. In Argentina, as in other parts of the Americas and Western Europe infected by similar fears, this suspicion was groundless. Nevertheless the reaction it provoked claimed the lives of up to two hundred victims. Xenophobia together with anti-labour, anti-communist and anti-semitic sentiments were employed by the conservatives to overcome the isolation and disunity which had cost them the election of 1916. They had conjured up a large popular movement, which included many Radicals, and the support of the army made it a parallel and potentially competing focus of authority against the government. As the violence finally subsided, the vigilante groups organized themselves into an association styling itself the Liga Patriótica Argentina (Argentine Patriotic League).

In March 1919 a vital senatorial election was held in the Federal Capital. This the Radicals managed to win, but by a margin of only 3,000 votes out of a total of 99,000 cast. In scarcely a year their share of the vote had dropped from more than 51 per cent to less than 40 per cent. The conservatives, however, represented by the Progressive Democratic party, increased their vote from 9,030 to more than 36,000. This expressed a strong swing away from the Radicals among the middle classes in Buenos Aires. It was both a vote of censure against the government for the recent strikes and a strong gesture of support towards the conservatives.

In late 1920 there was another major spate of unrest – this time in Patagonia. Beginning in the towns it mushroomed outwards among the great sheep ranches. To enforce the strike in the more outlying areas its adherents organized themselves into armed bands. Skirmishes with the ranchers promoted anxious petitions to Buenos Aires for assistance. Alleging that the strike was a cover for Chilean annexationist plots in the region, the Patriotic League demanded action. Once more Yrigoyen was unable to resist. A military expedition was raised to suppress the strike. In a long campaign throughout 1921 and 1922, punctuated by a flood of reports of army brutalities, the strike was broken.[14]

This saga of labour unrest repeatedly revealed the fragility of Yrigoyen's authority. In a bid to reconstruct his support, he turned to populism and patronage. After mid 1919 as imports and revenues recovered, state spending began its steep upward ascent. The stream of federal interventions in the provinces became a torrent. By opening up the bureaucracy to his followers, and rewarding them in the provinces, Yrigoyen rapidly recovered his personal popularity. In late 1919 an attempt to impeach the president from the Senate was filibustered into oblivion by the Radicals, while the strike in Patagonia became in part a means to divert the attentions of the army and the Patriotic League away from politics in Buenos Aires. In the congressional elections of early 1920 the Radicals again beat back the challenge of the Socialists and the Progressive Democrats, the latter's share of the vote declining substantially. After this the conservative electoral challenge rapidly dwindled. (In 1922, as in 1916, they entered the presidential election campaign divided: the Progressive Democrats mustered only 5.8 per cent of the vote, and a new conservative group formed to contest the presidential election, the National Concentration, obtained another 12.2 per cent.) In the country at large by 1922 the Radicals had a political organization which gave them the edge over all their opponents combined. But Yrigoyen's liberal use of federal intervention, and his heavy spending policies as revenues began to decline again during the postwar depression, brought renewed heavy conservative criticism. In rewarding his middle-class clientele, Yrigoyen also provoked frictions with the patrician wing of his own party. Conservatives and Radical dissidents alike bitterly attacked the president's 'personalist' leadership, accusing him of fomenting financial chaos and of promoting corrupt and incompetent party hacks to key positions in government. There were predictions of breakdown unless the slide into 'demagogy' were halted. In 1916 the conservative interests accepted Yrigoyen in the belief that he

[14] The story of Patagonia has been told in dramatic and fascinating detail by Osvaldo Bayer, *Los vengadores de la Patagonia trágica* (2 vols., Buenos Aires, 1972).

would protect continuity and stability. In most areas there was undoubtedly continuity: the reform achievements of the Radicals were insignificant. On the other hand in 1922 stability seemed as distant as at any time during the past 30 years.

Alvear, 1922–8

To the great relief of his opponents, in 1922 Yrigoyen's term came to an end. His successor, elected by a large majority of the provinces and by a plurality of the popular vote against conservative and Socialist opposition, was Marcelo T. de Alvear, a member of one of the country's oldest and wealthiest families. The new president assumed power at the height of the postwar depression. The economic cycle again overshadowed some of the chief issues he faced: the crisis in the beef industry, tariff reform and the public debt. The first of these was chiefly significant as an illustration of the power now wielded by the meat-packing plants in Argentine politics. The second showed that nineteenth-century attitudes towards the tariff and industrial protection still largely prevailed in the 1920s. Meanwhile, Alvear's handling of the public debt issue closely influenced politics throughout the 1920s. It underlay the division of the Radical party in 1924, Alvear's growing weakness as president, and Yrigoyen's resurgence as a popular leader in readiness for the presidential elections of 1928.

The appearance of American and British meat-packing plants after 1900, and growing exports of high-quality chilled beef, induced major changes in cattle ranching in Argentina. In many parts of the pampas, particularly the province of Buenos Aires, there was heavy investment in improved stock, especially shorthorns. At the same time specialization developed among the ranchers between breeders and fatteners. During the war, however, these trends abruptly ceased. The chilled beef trade was suspended, while exports of frozen and canned beef rapidly increased; the shift towards a lesser quality meat made it no longer essential to use a high-grade stock, nor to fatten it on special pasture before slaughter. Between 1914 and 1921 all ranchers, regardless of the quality of their stock, serviced the frozen and canned meat business, and benefited in roughly equal measure from the boom. Several new meat-packing plants were created in Zárate, Concordia and La Plata. Prosperity reached beyond the province of Buenos Aires into less central cattle regions such as Entre Ríos and Corrientes, where the herds were mostly traditional Creole breeds. At the same time urban interests from Buenos Aires and Rosario, equipped with lavish bank credits, were drawn into ranching on a large scale. Between 1914 and 1921 the cattle stock in Argentina increased by around 50 per cent, from 26 to 37 million.

The boom ended in 1921 when the British government ceased stockpiling supplies from Argentina, abolished meat control and began to liquidate its accumulated holdings. In Argentina there were fewer than half the cattle slaughtered for export in 1921 as there were in 1918. Prices also halved. Production of frozen and canned beef declined precipitously and all but disappeared. Afterwards what little trade remained was again, after this seven-year lapse, dominated by chilled beef. For a time all sectors of the cattle economy, from humble alfalfa farmers to the great meat-packing plants like Armour and Swift, suffered from the depression. But because of the vertical organization of the industry, the losses it occasioned were not distributed evenly. Some could protect their margins in some degree by forcing down the prices they paid to the sectors below which serviced them. This power and freedom of manoeuvre belonged most of all to the meat-packing plants. Cattle ranchers with shorthorn stock could also avoid the full impact of the depression by reverting to the chilled beef trade, while the specialist fatteners could follow the lead of the meat-packing plants and cut the prices they paid to breeders. Besides the breeders the main victims of the depression were the cattle owners of Entre Ríos and Corrientes, who had made the mistake of over-investing in Creole stock, and the gamut of wartime speculators, equally overloaded with useless herds, and now facing crippling outstanding mortgage obligations.

At the height of the crisis a segment from among the cattle breeders won control over the Rural Society. This prestigious institution was employed to bring pressure on the government to intervene against the meat-packing plants. They were accused of operating a buying pool to safeguard their own profits. To counter this monopsony the Rural Society proposed the creation of a locally owned packing plant paying higher prices than the American and British buyers. Other measures were conceived to assist ranchers overstocked with Creole cattle. They recommended a minimum price for cattle by the criterion of weight rather than pedigree, and secondly to exclude the foreign meat-packers from supplying the domestic market, thereby reserving it for those with inferior stock. In 1923, with support from the government, legislation was passed by Congress which incorporated most of these proposals, but the attempt at regulation failed in a spectacular fashion. The packers replied by imposing an embargo on all cattle purchases, an action which quickly reduced the ranchers to confusion and division. Soon afterwards the government shelved the entire scheme and no further action was taken. The breeders were obliged to ride out the depression without government assistance.

Alvear's proposals to Congress in 1923 for changes in the national tariff have sometimes been depicted as a strong shift towards protectionism to encourage domestic manufacturing. This was certainly the president's declared aim in the preamble to the measure. He suggested reducing duties on imported raw materials required by the metallurgical industry, and secondly extending the protection afforded sugar and wines in the 1880s to cotton, yerba maté and temperate fruits. However, the impact of this on manufacturing overall was slight. In so far as this part of the measure was protectionist it was largely a continuation of late-nineteenth-century policies. Its chief significance was for agricultural areas like the Chaco and Río Negro which the government was attempting to colonize. Beyond this Alvear also recommended a uniform 80 per cent increase in the tariff valuations of imports. Here the change was not in duties themselves, but in the assessed customs values of imports. Upon these a variable schedule of duties was applied. The increase in the valuations, which Congress trimmed to 60 per cent, was in addition to one of 20 per cent carried out under Yrigoyen in 1920. An 80 per cent increase spread over three years seemed large, but in fact barely compensated for the inflation in import prices during the war. It was, as we have seen, a change in the tariff valuations, not for the most part in the duties themselves; the latter afforded the real opportunity to guide the development of the domestic economy. All this achieved was roughly a return to 1914 eight years after the original valuations had been made. Because of inflation the valuations, which were originally around 25 per cent of real values in 1906, had fallen to an average of only 9.4 per cent in 1921. The tariff reform of 1923 was thus protectionist to only a very limited degree. Its main objectives were different: to increase government revenues while at the same time reducing imports during the postwar recession, to assist colonization schemes, and to guard against a repetition of the events of 1920 which brought a spate of dumping by foreign manufacturers. Among these goals the increase of revenues was the most important. Alvear's message to Congress in 1923 described the present tariff valuations as a 'flagrant injustice', and the cause of 'an unsatisfactory decline in national revenues'.

Perceptions of the tariff issue and domestic industry in the early 1920s were strongly coloured by events during the past decade. Between 1913 and 1920, first with the depression and then with the war, local industry had enjoyed unprecedented, if also quite involuntary, protection. Yet in the eyes of the postwar generation all that appeared to have been achieved was uncontrollable inflation, unjustifiably high returns to pools of profiteering businessmen at the expense of consumers, and a crop of strikes which had been on the point of provoking a workers' revolution. Against this it was essential to return to the stability of the prewar period. Views towards national industry were largely the same as they had been for most of the nineteenth century. Protection was only justifiable for national products which would quickly become price competitive with imports, for the most part agricultural goods; the rest were 'artificial': to foster them through protection would induce chronic inefficiencies in the economy. If they helped employment and reduced the need for imports, they would also inflate prices and depress overall consumption. The tariff reform of 1923 probably had little impact on industry during the 1920s, which grew mainly with the arrival of new immigrants and the beginnings of American investment. If industry overall enjoyed any significantly greater protection in the 1920s than before 1914, this was probably due as much as anything else to the hidden surcharge on imports resulting from the depreciation of the peso between 1921 and 1926.

As a complement to his changes in the tariff, Alvear also tackled the issue of government spending and the public debt. In 1923 his minister of finance, Rafael Herrera Vegas, prophesied 'national ruin' with 'the payment of 1000 million of floating debt and 604 million of budget expenditure'.[15] Both he and Alvear determined to halt the slide, which had been taking place since 1919, towards what they acknowledged was financial anarchy. However, fiscal austerity was extremely unpopular among the rank and file members of the Radical party. For them, high state spending was not only a matter of career opportunities and social mobility but a means of escape from the depression. To control state spending it was essential to clear Yrigoyen's appointments from the

---

[15] Quoted in Rock, *Politics in Argentina*, 225.

administration, many of which were made immediately before the presidential elections in 1922. Regardless of the dangers and its likely effect on his relations with Yrigoyen, Alvear committed himself to this task. He abandoned his predecessor's disputed practice of authorizing expenditures by simple Cabinet resolutions, and restored full congressional supervision over financial affairs. Between late 1922 and 1924 there was a spate of campaigns against administrative corruption, and a long succession of purges and dismissals. By 1925 a semblance of greater order prevailed. With its tariff changes and recovery from the depression, the government's revenue position greatly improved. Although overall Alvear failed to arrest the upward trend in public spending, he eventually matched revenues with expenditures, and managed to slow down the growth of the floating debt.

But this cost him dearly with his party. Under the impact of the purges and swingeing spending cuts Alvear's control over the party swiftly collapsed. In the middle of 1924 the Radicals divided into two irreconcilable bands. One, the majority in Congress and in the constituency committees, renounced Alvear and reasserted their allegiance towards Yrigoyen. They now styled themselves Yrigoyenistas. The rump became the 'Antipersonalist' Radicals, adopting this title to express their opposition to Yrigoyen. The latter group was composed mainly of the party's conservative and patrician wing, and many provincial Radicals alienated from Yrigoyen on account of his use of federal interventions against them after 1919. After 1924 came an embittered struggle between the two factions for supremacy. Politics, not policies, now dominated the Alvear administration. The Yrigoyenista majority in the Chamber of Deputies torpedoed his legislative programme. At first the president aligned himself with the Antipersonalists, but in 1925 in an effort to reunify the party he broke with them, refusing to accept their demand for a federal intervention against the Yrigoyenistas in the province of Buenos Aires. In July 1925 Vicente Gallo, the Antipersonalist minister of the interior, resigned. Without Alvear's support the Antipersonalist challenge quickly flagged. It was soon just another conservative faction, little more than a coalition of provincial groupings dominated by its branch in Santa Fe.

Alvear's reluctance to embrace the Antipersonalists and to use the powers of the president to favour them left the way open for Yrigoyen. After 1924 his followers rapidly reconstructed their party organization. By the time of the interim congressional elections in 1926 Yrigoyenista party committees were flourishing in the cities and the countryside alike, attracting enthusiastic support from a wide variety of popular groups. During this period Yrigoyen's followers revealed themselves as peerless practitioners in the arts of popular mobilization. They deluged the country with propaganda through the press and also the radio. They sought support indiscriminately, making no effort to build a party of compatible interest groups. Helped by the return of prosperity in the mid 1920s, they cultivated expectations throughout the voting population of a return to the spoils bonanza of 1919–22, intimating that all sectors of the population would share in its fruits. At the same time they sought to glorify their leader's person, dwelling upon his virtues as a popular leader, while magnifying and inflating his past achievements. By 1928 Hipólito Yrigoyen enjoyed a popularity unknown in Argentina's past history. He was poised for a triumphal return to the presidency.

Nevertheless, as the election approached, Yrigoyen still had many powerful enemies. Their animosities towards him increased as he again became a contender for power. His position was weak in some of the provinces where Antipersonalists and conservatives were in control. Here memories lingered of the flood of interventions during his past administration, which were remembered as violent and arbitrary usurpations of provincial rights. Opposition against him of this type was no longer confined to provincial landowning oligarchies. In Mendoza and San Juan, under the leadership of the Lencinas and Cantoni families, the opposition had democratized itself to become localist replicas of Yrigoyen's own popular movement. There was still bitter antagonism towards him among the conservatives who had fanned the flames of chauvinism, anti-semitism and anti-communism between 1919 and 1921. Opposition was again undisguisably manifest in the army. Once more rumours of a military *coup d'état* were in the air. Towards the end of Alvear's term reports surfaced of an army plot to prevent his return to power, orchestrated by the minister of war, General Agustín P. Justo.

Among these different groups Yrigoyen was repeatedly denounced for the irresponsible and what seemed patently demagogic manner in which he was manoeuvring his present popular following. His main supporters, the job-hunting middle classes, were regarded by conservative groups as irredeemably corrupt. Yrigoyen now seemed an altogether more dangerous proposition than in 1916. Following the party split of 1924 there were no longer the earlier checks against him which the more conservative wing of radicalism had always in some degree exercised. He was suspected of plotting a popular dictatorship. By this time an interminable succession of election defeats had left the conservative opposition with little remaining confidence in the Sáenz Peña reform. It had failed to produce the type of government they wanted. If some conservatives, Justo for example, would have been content with government by the Antipersonalists, others had recently undergone a further marked shift to the right. They were admirers of Mussolini's Italy and Primo de Rivera's Spain, and advocates of military dictatorship. But with Yrigoyen nearing the zenith of his popularity, there was little that could be done. An attempt to forestall his return to power ran the risk of provoking civil war. At this juncture there was no guarantee that the conservatives would emerge from it the victors. The conservatives had to wait.

Oil and international relations

During the election campaign of 1928 the Yrigoyenistas emerged with an issue which proved crucial in carrying their leader back into the presidency: a state monopoly over oil. This nationalist campaign also focused against American oil interests, particularly against Standard Oil of New Jersey. Here it became bound up in the wider question of relations between Argentina and the United States.

The oil campaign of the late 1920s began some twenty years after the discovery of the rich Patagonian oil fields at Comodoro Rivadavia in 1907, and other smaller ones in Neuquén, Mendoza and Salta. The peculiarities of the history of oil in Argentina were the state's leading part in the industry from its very beginnings, and the early strong determination to prevent oil resources falling into the hands of alien interests. In 1910 legislation was passed establishing a state reserve over a 5,000 hectare area in Comodoro Rivadavia, from which all private claims were for a time excluded. Soon afterwards the state itself commenced drilling operations in Comodoro Rivadavia. Private interests were initially confined to the smaller oil fields in Neuquén and the provinces. Sáenz Peña was a strong supporter of efforts to develop national oil, largely because strikes in Britain immediately before the war appeared to threaten imports of coal. On the other hand, before the war there was little conflict between this small state enterprise and foreign oil companies. At this point the latter showed little interest in developing production in Argentina, and had a stake in the country only as importers. In these early years the industry's progress, with the state sector acting as leader, proved somewhat disappointing. Hopes of reduced imports, which came mainly from Texas and Mexico, were not fulfilled. Before 1914 local production was barely 7 per cent of total consumption. Congress was unwilling to grant sufficient funds. Other difficulties common to ventures of this kind outside industrial countries were encountered in obtaining skilled personnel and equipment. During the war there was an embargo on the export of drilling and refining equipment from the United States. Although attempts to increase domestic production won growing support during the war from the navy and the army to satisfy defence needs, progress did little to alleviate the crisis caused by declining imports of British coal. Furthermore, of the still small total output of crude oil, only a fraction could be refined.

The fuel crisis during the war eroded some of the more extreme prejudices against foreign capital. The sentiment grew that it was a necessary evil to ensure more rapid development. This opinion appeared to be shared by the first Radical government. Between 1916 and 1922 Yrigoyen was perhaps less nationalistic on the oil question than his immediate predecessors. He registered no opposition against the presence of a private sector, most of it in foreign hands. Under his government private companies increased their share of total production from a diminutive 3 per cent to 20 per cent. He used Comodoro Rivadavia as a source of political patronage. Any efforts at reform he made here, as in so many other cases, fell foul of a hostile Congress. His most significant step was the establishment in 1922, shortly before his departure from office, of a supervisory and managerial board for state oil, the Dirección General de los Yacimientos Petrolíferos Fiscales (YPF). Under Alvear, when more favourable conditions for the importation of equipment appeared, the industry began to revive. He appointed a vigorous and committed military administrator to lead YPF, General Enrique Mosconi, at the same time granting them both a good deal of autonomy. Under Mosconi many of the state industry's early difficulties were resolved. In 1925 a large refinery was opened at La Plata. YPF also established its own retailing network, producing and distributing petrol and paraffin. In the immediate postwar period oil in Argentina at last began to attract keen interest among the major companies from abroad. In these years the growth of the YPF was overshadowed by that of the private sector, which by 1928 had increased its share of production to almost 38 per cent. Yet the growth of production was unable to keep pace with domestic demand. Despite a tripling in the total output of crude oil between 1922 and 1928, imports of coal also increased by one-third, and imported oil almost doubled. In 1928 domestic oil fields still supplied less than half of total domestic fuel consumption.

By the late 1920s, long before the Yrigoyenista campaign, there was thus a tradition of state involvement in the oil industry. It was grounded upon nationalist sentiments, which frequently crossed party political lines. Equally, Argentina was the first country outside Soviet Russia to form a vertically integrated state-owned petroleum industry. However, commitment to this had not been carried to the point of excluding private or foreign shares in the industry. In the interests of increasing output and ensuring efficiency, the policy of each government was to permit the growth of the state and private sectors alike. Intervention mainly took the form of protecting the state sector's share of the market and preventing the regular export of oil. After the war this permitted several foreign companies to construct sizeable operations in the country which eventually became the source of the lion's share of production. By 1928 private companies provided one-third of the output from Comodoro Rivadavia, two-thirds of that from Plaza Huincul in Neuquén, and the whole of that in the smaller fields in Salta and Mendoza.

Among the private companies Standard Oil was by this time the most prominent. It now had interests in almost every sphere of the industry. It was still, as before the war, the leading importer of oil, and controlled the main channels of internal distribution. It had substantial interests in refining, and despite YPF by far the largest share in sales of paraffin and automobile fuels. But its activities which now drew most attention were its drilling operations in the province of Salta. Standard Oil established itself here by carefully wooing the provincial authorities, which controlled subsoil rights in the province as the national government did in the national territories of the south. During the 1920s Salta was still under an oligarchy of landowners, the most powerful of them now in sugar. Until recent years the province had been heavily stricken with poverty. With the terms it offered, Standard Oil had little difficulty in amassing a vast area to which it held exclusive exploration and drilling rights. The oil fields in Salta were acquired with the aim of linking up with an overlapping field the company possessed in Bolivia. It intended to lay out a transnational sphere of influence in this corner of South

America. The position it commanded in Buenos Aires would give it the outlet for the exports it intended to develop from Bolivia, and, if it could do so, from Salta itself.

During the 1920s, confronted by a now embittered and highly publicized conflict for supremacy between the private oil interests and YPF, public opinion in Buenos Aires retreated into its prewar hostility towards foreign capital. In typically zealous and ebullient fashion the Yrigoyenistas plunged into a campaign to win political dividends from the prevailing popular mood. In July 1927 they issued a pledge to bring all the nation's oil fields under state control, and to extend this monopoly to refining, subproducts and distribution. They laid the issue before the electorate with characteristic panache, unceasingly cultivating popular aspirations for undisputed local control over national assets and latent resentments against foreign business. Oil nationalization was depicted as the sovereign remedy for the nation's ills. Grandiose promises were delivered that the revenues from oil, once under national control, would permit the cancellation of the foreign debt, and render all future borrowing superfluous. Domestic manufacturers would be endowed with a limitless source of cheap power, which would permit a miraculous and painless transition to an industrial society. A state oil monopoly would make possible the elimination of all other forms of taxation, finally relieving the popular sectors of the irksome duties on imports which inflated the cost of living.

Nationalization soon commanded enormous popularity among the middle classes: once geared to the oil flow, state revenues would no longer be subject to the unpredictable ebb and flow of foreign trade; afterwards there could be virtually no limits to the expansion of the public sector and the bureaucracy. The issue also blended in closely with Yrigoyen's wider struggle against the Antipersonalists and the conservatives: the situation in Salta was portrayed by his followers as the black alliance of Oligarchy and Imperialism, which a state monopoly would shatter. If Yrigoyen could vest control over oil in the hands of the national government, and take it away from the provinces, he would destroy one of the major props of the opposition. With the oil royalties in their own hands, the Yrigoyenistas felt confident of perpetual supremacy.

The nationalist component of this campaign was directed against Standard Oil alone. It largely ignored British oil consortia, such as Royal Dutch Shell. The latter's manoeuvrings were conducted with less fanfare, and had so far attained less success than Standard Oil's. But behind the scenes they were scarcely less ambitious in scope. In recent years control over Argentine oil had become as much a British as an American objective. Standard Oil, however, was the target because of its ill-advised local affiliations with the Salta oligarchy, because of its international ill-repute – and quite simply because it was an American company. Here the oil issue impinged closely on the wider field of international relations, and also upon relations between Yrigoyen and the conservative power groups.

Moreover, anti-Americanism emanated not from the middle classes, nor from the Radical party, but from the landed and exporting interests of the pampas and from the conservatives. Its origin lay principally in long-standing disputes over trade. Although since around the turn of the century, first with Texas oil and afterwards with automobiles and many capital goods, the Americans had built up a large share in the Argentine market, Argentina had failed to develop reciprocal exports to the United States. At the behest of the American farm lobby, Republican administrations in the United States continually kept most of its goods out. Argentina protested vigorously, frequently, but unavailingly against American policy. By 1914, despite the coming of the Chicago meat-packers, Argentina had still failed to establish a market in the United States for its beef exports. The Americans were prepared to accept only its second-rank goods, such as hides and linseed. During the first world war Argentina's exports to the United States increased tenfold in value. However, soon afterwards in 1922 the Frodney-McCumber Tariff restored and in some measure extended the earlier policy of exclusion.

In the 1920s, in face of its still weak position in the American market, Argentina relied heavily on its exports to Britain. But the longer-term stability of this connection was threatened by the growing shift in Argentina's imports from Britain to the United States. By the late 1920s Argentina's trade surplus with Britain roughly matched its deficit with the United States. In Britain, however, there was now a growing campaign in favour of imperial preference. If this were adopted in the effort to reduce Britain's trade imbalances, it would give British dominion producers – Canada, Australia, New Zealand and South Africa – the share in the British market previously accorded to Argentina.

These issues bore closely on the question of Argentine oil and relations with Standard Oil of New Jersey. In 1926 the Coolidge administration in the United States imposed an absolute ban on imports of dressed beef from the Río de la Plata region. It was done ostensibly as a protection against foot-and-mouth disease. But the measure provoked an infuriated response in Buenos Aires as another act of discriminatory protection. Instantly the search began for means of retaliation: Standard Oil stood conveniently at hand. On Yrigoyen's part the campaign against Standard Oil was an act of considerable political astuteness. It enabled him to ride with the popular tide, but also to pose as a champion of wider national interests and the pampas landowning elite. On the other hand in approaching the oil question it was essential to avoid giving any offence to the British, who might seize on this as the pretext to commence commercial reprisals themselves. It was thus Standard Oil alone which bore the brunt of the campaign against foreign capital. Having eliminated Standard Oil, Yrigoyen evidently intended giving the British the role of the main importers of oil and the equipment required by YPF. This would help reduce the trade surplus with Britain, and improve Argentina's bargaining position in face of imperial preference.

THE MILITARY COUP OF 1930

In 1928 Yrigoyen regained the presidency with around 60 per cent of the popular vote, almost 840,000 against the combined opposition's 537,000. As he reassumed office in October the adulation he received recalled the honours bestowed upon the emperors of Rome. Yet this moment, the acme of a public career which now spanned more than half a century, proved his last personal triumph. Less than two years afterwards, in September 1930, his reputation in ruins, he was ignominiously ejected by a military *coup d'état*.

Hipólito Yrigoyen returned to the presidency at the advanced age of 76. He was suspected in some quarters of senility, and two years later this emerged among the pretexts for overthrowing him. The truth was that in 1928 he reappeared with a much more carefully defined strategy and purpose than twelve years earlier in 1916. He was aware that whatever his apparent popular support, the survival of his government rested upon his ability to keep at bay the conservative and military opposition. The oil question had still to be resolved; his return to office amounted to little more than an auspicious beginning in the battle for its control. His supporters had submitted legislation in favour of nationalization to Congress in 1927. The measure had passed through the popularly elected

Chamber of Deputies where the Yrigoyenistas had a majority. But it was then simply ignored in the Senate, where the voices of the interior provinces led by Salta and Yrigoyen's other opponents remained dominant. Here the president had the same problem which had bedevilled his previous administration. To push the legislation through he required a majority in the Senate. To win senatorial elections he needed to control the provincial legislatures; national senators were elected by them and not by popular vote. This meant more federal interventions to clear out the incumbent regimes, but at the risk of exacerbating the resurgent federalism in the interior. At this time elections to the Senate were pending in Mendoza and San Juan. These were the centres of *lencinismo* and *cantonismo* where, as in Salta, opposition to the administration was particularly virulent and entrenched. The new government thus gave much of its immediate attention to politics in the Cuyo provinces. Here it was quickly embroiled in an embittered and often violent struggle for supremacy. The issue was resolved in two climactic episodes. At the end of 1929 the leader of the Mendoza opposition, Carlos Wáshington Lencinas, was assassinated by Yrigoyenistas. The year after, following an acrimonious and almost interminable debate, the president's supporters successfully impugned the election of Federico Cantoni and one of his personal supporters as senators for San Juan. Thus in mid 1930 the Yrigoyenistas were close to final victory. They had quashed the most extreme opposition in the interior. They also stood on the brink of a clear majority in the Senate. Their intention was to resubmit the oil legislation when Congress reconvened in 1931.

During 1929 and for a time into 1930 Yrigoyen was also successful in keeping at bay his conservative opponents in Buenos Aires, adroitly cultivating their sympathies on the matter of trade relations with Britain and the United States. In 1927, soon after the United States had banned imports of Argentine beef, and while the political confrontation with Standard Oil was at its height, the Rural Society led a campaign to promote favourable treatment for imported British goods. Its slogan, 'Buy from those who buy us', was quickly adopted by the new administration. When Herbert Hoover, as president-elect, visited Buenos Aires in late 1928 on a trade promotion tour of the Latin American republics, he met with a hostile reception and was virtually insulted by Yrigoyen himself. However, the following year a British trade mission received a quite different welcome. To its leader, Lord

D'Abernon, Yrigoyen intimated his wish to offer a 'moral gesture' to Britain in acknowledgment of the 'close historical ties' between the two countries. Without seeking an undertaking for compensatory increases in Argentina's exports to Britain, he promised numerous concessions to British firms and British goods in the Argentine market. Among them was an undertaking to acquire all future supplies for the state railways in Britain, by-passing the normal practice of seeking international tenders.

Several aspects of Yrigoyen's second administration thus suggest a carefully calculated and sophisticated strategy slowly undergoing realization and enjoying considerable success. The president was managing to steer a viable middle course between the aspirations of his popular followers on the oil question and the concern of the elites on international trade. This was done at the expense of the Americans and the provinces. Had the government been able to continue in these directions, it would have had very little to fear from the army. In 1929 there were few signs of the confusion, incompetence or paralysis which gripped it in the year which followed, and for which it was most remembered. What transformed these first relative successes into failure, whence matters slid swiftly towards collapse and catastrophe, was the great depression in the wake of the Wall Street crash. It struck in Argentina at the end of 1929, after two years of slowly falling commodity prices and diminishing gold reserves. As the downturn accelerated, Yrigoyen's government responded with orthodox anticyclical measures of the type employed by the conservatives in 1913–14. It abandoned peso convertibility and it sought new loans in Britain and the United States to avoid difficulties with the foreign debt. These were reasonable if uninspiring responses. They expressed the initial expectation in government and banking circles that the crisis would be short lived. The rapid erosion of the government's authority began when it was obliged to curb state spending. Here Yrigoyen finally paid the price for his break with the elites, his tilt towards the popular sectors, and the methods he had countenanced since 1924 to attract their support.

On Yrigoyen's return to power his supporters had immediately launched themselves on a campaign to take over the bureaucracy. By mid 1929 all departments of the administration had become virtual employment agencies serving the political ends of the government. The regime was soon saturated in petty corruption. State spending immediately assumed an upward course. In 1928 there was a 10 per cent fall in revenues against the previous year, but spending increased by 22 per cent. In 1929 the gap increased still further. In this year revenues improved by 9 per cent, but spending accelerated by a further 12 per cent. In 1930, as revenues again declined to around the 1928 level, spending was running at around 23 per cent higher than that year.[16] At length the government was obliged to contemplate economies. By the time the coup came in September there were signs that the upward climb in spending was beginning to level off. However, retrenchment and austerity came precisely at the moment when, with growing unemployment and falling incomes, the demand for relief was increasing. In 1930 Yrigoyen fell into a trap similar to that he had set for Alvear in 1922. Depression swiftly unhinged the government's party and popular backing. Yrigoyen's followers were demoralized, and they soon began to defect in growing numbers.

In the congressional elections of March 1930 the Yrigoyenistas' share of the vote shrank by 25 per cent by comparison with 1928, from 840,000 to a little over 620,000. In the city of Buenos Aires the Yrigoyenistas lost an election for the first time since the party split of 1924. Here they were defeated by the Independent Socialist party, a newly formed offshoot from the old Socialist party now aligned with the conservatives. In the months which followed disillusionment with the government became inflamed opposition. Events in the Cuyo provinces, often ignored before, were now a matter of daily, intense debate. The press conducted long and detailed exposés of administrative corruption. The students, who after *La Reforma* were among Yrigoyen's most vocal supporters, plunged into demonstrations against him. Rival factions of Yrigoyenistas and a right-wing organization known as the Republican League fought openly for control of the streets. The Cabinet disintegrated into warring factions. Reports of the president's senility were bruited with growing insistence.

At last Yrigoyen's most inveterate opponents, many of them nursing grievances against him for more than a decade, had the opportunity to gather the force to overthrow him. The leader of the military coup, General José F. Uriburu, behind whom was General Justo, had long been prominent in denouncing Yrigoyen's intrigues among the army promotion lists. He had been a chief opponent of Yrigoyen's labour policies in the postwar years. During the 1920s he had imbibed fascist and corporatist doctrines. He was contemptuous of the Sáenz Peña Law.

[16] Detailed figures in Carl E. Solberg, *Oil and nationalism in Argentina* (Stanford, 1979), 149.

He was also a member of the Salta oligarchy which had pursued the deal with Standard Oil. The uprising of September 1930 elicited active support from only a minority in the army. But this was enough to achieve its purpose. As Yrigoyen resigned, a vicious struggle for the succession among members of the Cabinet laid bare the total bankruptcy of his administration. Few of Yrigoyen's supporters came to his assistance. Some joined the mobs which ransacked and burned his home in Buenos Aires.

The coup of 1930 was an entirely domestic affair. If Standard Oil had an obvious interest in securing Yrigoyen's downfall, there is no evidence it did so. The coup was greeted in Washington with some sense of expectancy and with a hope for better relations with Argentina, yet subsequent developments during the 1930s left them unrealized. Any possible American influence on events in 1930 was negated by the presence of the British. They were among Yrigoyen's last supporters, reluctant to rejoice in his downfall. It seemed that their hopes of trade concessions would perish with him. After his fall, Hipólito Yrigoyen was banished to the island of Martín García in the estuary of the Río de la Plata where he spent much of what remained of his life. (He died in 1933.) In this now frail, sometimes morally fallible, though never completely ill-intentioned figure, representative democracy in Argentina had lived and died. With his departure, politics in Argentina assumed new directions. The middle classes were cheated of their expectations of perpetual supremacy. The conservatives returned to power under the protection of the military, and remained in power for more than a decade, until the military coup of 1943 and the rise of Perón.

13

THE FORMATION OF MODERN URUGUAY, *c.* 1870–1930*

During the decade of the 1860s Uruguay was a nation of no more than 300,000 inhabitants, of whom more than a quarter lived in the principal port, Montevideo, which was also the political capital. The proportion of foreigners was amongst the highest of any Latin American nation. According to the 1860 census one in three inhabitants (and one in two in Montevideo) was foreign: mainly Italian, Spanish, Brazilian, French, Argentinian or British (probably in that order). Uruguay's one railway line, inaugurated in 1869, was only 20 kilometres long. The nation's transport system in fact consisted of little more than primitive tracks; luckily the society's principal product, cattle, had the virtue of being mobile. For the transport of people, carts were used in the east and centre of the country, whereas in the west the use of sailboats and steamships on the Uruguay river gave this region much better communication with the capital. In spite of the small size of the country – about 180,000 square kilometres – travel in the interior was slow, especially in winter when the swollen rivers and streams blocked land routes. At such times central government, landowners and traders alike seemed more to be living in a medieval backwater rather than in a nation of the modern world, in the second half of the century of the steam engine.

The economy was based on the extensive exploitation of native (*criollo*) cattle. Their heavy hides were shipped to Europe, while part of their thin flesh, after salting and drying in the *saladeros* (meat-salting establishments) to become *tasajo* (jerked beef), was consumed by the slave populations of Cuba and Brazil. For this reason, as in the colonial period,

* Translated from the Spanish by Dr Richard Southern; translation revised by Dr Henry Finch. The Editor wishes to thank Dr Finch for his help in the final preparation of this chapter.

the value of an animal was determined by the weight of its hide rather than its yield of meat. The slaughter of these cattle was not yet a capital offence, and the free provision of food from this source on the *estancias* was by no means economically irrational. Two typical aspects of the political and social life of the period, the endemic civil wars and the paternalism of the *caudillo*-landowner towards the rural poor, are in part explained by these characteristics of the economy.

The importance of trade to this raw material and food-producing country was somewhat unusual. The location of the port of Montevideo on the Río de la Plata, and its natural advantages over Buenos Aires and the ports of Rio Grande do Sul, made it a commercial centre of the first importance. It developed as a major distribution point for European merchandise destined for the Argentine provinces of Entre Ríos, Corrientes and Santa Fe, for Rio Grande do Sul, and even for Paraguay.

Wealthy merchants engaged in both export and import trades, as well as the large landowners, constituted the backbone of the Uruguayan upper classes. In 1857 they had founded the first nationally owned bank, the Banco Comercial. The middle classes, extremely weak in the interior, grew rather more strongly in Montevideo on the basis of commerce and the beginnings of manufacturing activity. The *saladero* industry had created a small urban working class, but the bulk of the lower orders consisted of those who were dependent on the livestock owners and who, as peons and casual workers, lived in dispersed settlements on the vast estates. In the north there was still a hidden slave labour force, imported by wealthy Brazilian landowners from Rio Grande do Sul.

Such a society and such an economy, however, did not generate inequalities and social tensions. On the contrary, in some respects Uruguay stood out within a Latin America characterized in the nineteenth century by sharply differentiated social classes. In the interior, food supply was not yet the monopoly of those who owned cattle and land, and therefore to be a wage-earner was to some extent a matter of choice rather than necessity. The economic distance between individuals was recent in origin and not magnified by racial differences as in Mexico, Peru or Brazil, and therefore might be relatively easily changed. Moreover, as a new country populated by immigrants, upward social mobility in Uruguay was not difficult. In 1847 a member of the social elite complained bitterly, and with good reason, that in Uruguay 'everyone with a white face thinks he has equal rights'.

Civil strife was endemic. From Independence (in 1826) to 1870 many a president faced rebellions and was obliged to leave office before his legal term of four years was concluded. The struggles between *blancos* (or Nationalists) and *colorados*, the two traditional parties, were fuelled by a variety of factors. Central government was unable to impose its authority on a society of cattlemen. Not only did rival centres of power – the rural *caudillos* – emerge, but the use of violence and weapons was an integral part of livestock production. Hence, the economy did not punish chaos but rather, because the ownership of land was still in dispute, conflict was promoted. Moreover the lack of a clearly defined sense of nation, coupled with the ambitions of the dominant classes in Uruguay's powerful neighbours, Brazil and Argentina, encouraged uprisings against central government in Montevideo by those who did not wish to see it strong.

However, already in the 1860s most of these characteristics of the country had begun to change. And by 1870 traditional Uruguay, described by the Brazilian entrepreneur, the barão de Mauá, as 'politically, economically and financially a corpse', was in the process of breaking up. The merchants, mainly foreign in origin, had increased their influence as a result of prosperity achieved during the Triple Alliance War with Paraguay (1865–70). They now demanded a guarantee for the maintenance of their wealth and prominence: strong government and internal peace. The landowners no longer restricted themselves to *criollo* cattle; sheep production had grown during the 1860s. Even the struggle for land was about to end, because a group of very large landowners had emerged, a class which did not require the support of the *caudillo* system for confirmation of its rights. Rebellions which had previously caused the destruction of cattle, a commodity of little value, now did damage to relatively well-equipped *estancias* with pedigree breeding rams. These establishments needed to introduce wire fencing, but were unable to do so while political violence threatened. To kill a steer when the market for *tasajo* was depressed was of comparatively little importance. To kill a sheep which annually yielded a fleece attracting a good price in a keen world market was a crime. Wool production, moreover, helped to strengthen the position of a rural middle class since less land of lower quality was required for sheep. Thus an additional element made for social and political stability in what had previously been such a turbulent society.

The modernization of Montevideo, now with nearly 100,000 inhabitants, had begun. The British traveller, Thomas Hutchinson, who in

1861 noted the 'Moorish architecture of its flat-roofed houses', would have found it difficult to imagine the feverish expansion of the following years. Although the Cerro (the hill overlooking the harbour) and the cathedral – the two mountains of the New Troy described by Alexandre Dumas – still dominated a distant view of the pale city ringed by small farms and *saladeros*, the opening up of new streets and the construction of two-storey buildings indicated the rapid growth of the city. It had expanded beyond its old colonial walls and was now developing along the main street, 18 de Julio, towards the humble dwellings of the eastern suburbs, and the luxurious residences of the wealthy on the banks of the Miguelete stream.

The process of foreign investment, mainly by Britain, had also begun. Loans to the state, land purchases by companies with directorates in London, the installation of Liebig's Extract of Meat Company at Fray Bentos (1863): these were the precursors of what was to develop after 1870, when the British brought railways and water and gas companies. The minimum condition of such investment was of course the maintenance of order.

Finally, the country was integrated more and more closely into the world economy through the growing ease and cheapness with which men and commodities could be transported to and from Europe. Improvements in sailing ships, but above all the triumph of steam power on ocean routes, brought Uruguay into close touch with the needs, the capital, the immigrants, the culture and the fashions of the other side of the Atlantic. Montevideo's contacts with London, Marseilles and Le Havre began to be dependable and regular. The import and export trades became established and their volume increased, while freight rates fell. The umbilical cord which joined the nation with Europe could not now be broken; time would only strengthen it.

MODERNIZATION AND THE WORLD MARKET, 1870–1904

In 1865, on the eve of the war with Paraguay, a *blanco* government was overthrown by *colorado* forces led by Venancio Flores and aided by both Argentina and Brazil. In 1870, at the end of the Paraguayan War, the rebellion of the *caudillo* Timoteo Aparicio, a *blanco*, led to the 'War of the Lances', an attempt to secure at least a share of the power monopolized throughout the war by the *colorados*. The violent conflict lasted two years, and huge losses were sustained, especially by the large landowners.

When a negotiated peace was arranged in April 1872, a new political group separated itself from the traditional parties and condemned them for their role in the political chaos. This group – the *principistas* – consisted of young intellectuals, sons of the oldest but no longer the wealthiest families in Uruguay. Committed to an extreme doctrinaire liberalism, the *principistas* were ardent defenders of a legal order based on European ideas and models in which distrust of the state and a wholehearted belief in the rights of the individual were fundamental. Such principles, and the *principistas'* total commitment to the constitution, did not fit in with the aspiration of the upper classes to secure strong government. The traditional factions of the parties triumphed in the elections of 1872, but this did not prevent the entry of the *principista* leaders to the legislature, which was to be under their influence until 1875. Moreover, José Ellauri, a descendant of the aristocracy of the colonial period, was elected president at the beginning of 1873 following an electoral agreement and, lacking strong party support, his government was neutral and weak. The legislature undertook in 1873 a programme of administrative, judicial and electoral reforms which were basically directed towards strengthening individual rights in opposition to the power of the state. Representatives of economic interests – landowners and merchants – promptly rejected this institutional arrangement, seeing it as a legal framework which could only postpone the achievement of an economic order which would make their investments safer and more profitable. The losses being suffered in the livestock sector, for example, were evident. And although a bank had been established in 1857, credit facilities failed to meet even the most basic needs of producers. Short-term commercial loans and speculation in property values or public debt issues restricted the availability of credit to Montevideo, and thus denied such facilities to the rural economy in the interior. This distortion, prejudicial to the interests of the livestock economy, was particularly marked during the unstable years from 1868 to 1875. Moreover, it was during this period that the wire fencing of pasture and the investment required by the first signs of technical progress in the sector increased its credit requirements. To the discontent of this group was added a more widespread feeling of dissatisfaction when, in 1874, the first symptoms of financial crisis became apparent. Isolated from public opinion, since they had no support outside their own circle, deprived of economic resources, and insufficiently supported by an indecisive executive, the *principistas* were removed from power by a group of army officers intent on ending the *impasse* created by the crisis and the fruitless efforts of the government to overcome it.

With the imposition of military rule in 1876 and the removal of the *principistas*, the dictatorship of Colonel Lorenzo Latorre met the essential requirements of the propertied classes. Latorre carried out the policy that traders, rural producers and foreign investors all needed during a period of favourable trends in export markets. The influence of rural *caudillos* was temporarily nullified by strong centralized government. This regime permitted the extension of the capitalist order to the rural economy, applying a rough and ready justice. Under it, criminals were equated with the rural unemployed, a population marginalized by the fencing of pastures and the new status of the *estancia* as business enterprise. To enable it to function as such, especially during a period of rapid modernization, the landowner's rights to property were consolidated. Internal stability was confirmed through the strengthening of the army (and therefore of the power of the state) by improved weaponry. Central authority was now equipped with sophisticated armaments of the nineteenth century – the repeating rifle and Krupp artillery – and in this way government slowly but inexorably secured a monopoly of physical force over the inhabitants of the country. For this achievement the large landowners composing the Rural Association (founded in 1871) never ceased to give thanks.

Following the unexpected resignation of Latorre in 1880, General Máximo Santos governed the country until 1886. Santos strengthened the structure of the *colorados*, of which he was now head. In addition, the party began to receive the open support of the army, a new and significant factor. Thereafter, and for almost a century, the armed forces and the *colorados* maintained a tacit alliance. This political pact, with all the advantages and safeguards which it offered to the armed forces, neutralized any possible aspirations on their part to a more direct form of political participation; along with other factors, this helped to ensure subsequent political stability, and in the long run effectively guaranteed the institutional order. The evolution of militarism in Uruguay, its rapid decline after 1886 and submission (or perhaps consent) to civil authority have to be seen in these terms.

Santos was not the mere executive arm of the economic oligarchies but was also – and this was new to Uruguay – the representative of a military order which possessed an embryonic officer caste. This group displayed its ambition and cultivated a showy life style, surrounded by a modest court of relatives and hangers-on who rose rapidly on the social scale. It was a time of parades and ceremonies, but also of shady business deals and concessions that undermined the prestige of the system established by Latorre. For the military it was their *belle époque*, a time of euphoria.

The emergence of an opposition front composed of the 'legalist' factions of the *blancos* and *colorados* produced an authoritarian response from Santos which led him down a cul-de-sac of escalating repression. An abortive popular rising was followed by an attack on his life; finally an attempt at conciliation brought an end to his rule. The Santos years witnessed the disintegration of formal militarism. The accusations of nepotism and venality made by the opposition against the government were exaggerated but not unfounded. The initial tacit consent of the rural upper class to a regime which would give stability, now that its modernization project was almost complete, changed to open disillusion once the faults in the system began to outweigh its limited advantages. In November 1886 Santos left for Europe and was succeeded by one of his followers, General Tajes, an inoffensive figure under whom militarism was finally eliminated. Even in favourable conditions its leaders had demonstrated an inability to maintain a rigid authoritarian model. Although under Latorre a modernizing dictatorship had benefited the propertied classes, under Santos militarism was unable to survive the prosperity which it had decisively helped to create.

Militarism succeeded in consolidating not only an internal peace which temporarily eliminated the anarchy of the *caudillos*, but also an external dependence based, as many enthusiastic diplomatic reports reveal, on closer ties with the imperialist powers. This development implied not only a growth of production but also changes in its composition. While the export of hides increased by 30 per cent during 1876–86, wool exports grew by 40 per cent. Indeed in 1884 the value of wool exceeded that of cattle products for the first time. The pastures were rapidly being fenced – 60 per cent of *estancias* invested in wire during the five years after 1877 – and the surplus labour force was abandoned by the capitalist-landowner who now replaced the *caudillo-landowner*, especially in the west and south of the country. Export markets diversified. To the traditional buyers of cattle products (Great Britain, United States, Brazil and Cuba) were added the purchasers of fine merino wools: France, Belgium and Germany.

The British presence in Uruguay grew, encouraged by strong government but also by guarantees of minimum rates of return on its investments. The growth was particularly marked in public debt issues and public services. *The Economist* reckoned the volume of British investment in government bonds in 1884 at £3.5 million, with a further £3 million in enterprises. Amongst the latter, the rapid increase in the railway network was especially marked, growing from 474 kilometres in 1882 to 1,571 kilometres in 1892.

This period of comparative prosperity was accompanied by a rapid growth of population in the final quarter of the century, largely as a result of immigration. According to the earliest figures, in 1873 Uruguay had 450,000 inhabitants, of whom 103,000 were foreigners. After 1875, when as many as 24,000 immigrants landed in a single year, the financial crisis and collapse of institutional government ushered in a decade of very limited immigration to Uruguay, while vast numbers were drawn to Argentina and southern Brazil. Not until after 1882 did a new wave of immigrants arrive. They were predominantly Italians, and had a decisive effect on the growth of Montevideo. Comparing the censuses of 1884 and 1889, it is clear that while the Italian population was growing rapidly, the number from Spain was stationary while the French had almost disappeared. During 1887-9, when immigration reached its highest level in the nineteenth century, net immigration probably exceeded 45,000, reflecting the demand for labour generated by the period of economic growth preceding the crisis of 1890.

Although stability and prosperity were in some measure the products of strong government, old problems concerning the economy, society and political system soon reappeared, and were joined by new ones. The restoration of civilian rule was the work of the *colorados*, who benefited from what remained of Santos's government after the political bases of military power had been dismantled. The transition was effected by the new minister of government, Julio Herrera y Obes (who had been a major figure amongst the *principistas* ousted in 1875). From this office to the presidency (in 1890) was only a short step for a skilful politician who channelled the accumulated resentments against Santos to his favour. The electoral machine developed at the ministry of government during the administration of General Tajes enabled Herrera y Obes to establish a power base closely linked to the oligarchy, which in turn proclaimed his infallibility and the weight of his opinion against that of the majority of the *colorados*. His enlightened despotism proclaimed the need, with a frankness bordering on cynicism, of a 'guiding influence' in the choice of candidates, and this aroused great antagonism within both parties.

It soon became clear that the return to civilian rule was in fact the instrument of a new oppression – that of presidential power – legitimized by a façade of democracy. With the influence of the *caudillos* in abeyance and the army back in barracks, the government had considerable power for its exercise of political coercion. The technical instruments – railway, telegraph and modern armament – had been further improved since the time of Latorre. At the political level, the interior was tightly controlled through the authority of the political *jefes*, who were directly dependent on the orders of the executive. Such devices consolidated the authority of the president, but at the same time it was dissipated by the growing distance between that office and the country at large and the new social forces within it. The popular mass of the *colorados*, organized by José Batlle y Ordóñez, began to seek a party organization more in keeping with the interests of the new sectors of society, those arising from both external and internal migration. For its part the Partido Blanco decided in 1893 to abstain from the electoral process, and it prepared once more for armed struggle. The merchant class, bankers, businessmen, and the majority of rural producers all showed in various ways their dissatisfaction with Herrera y Obes. In addition, the onset of economic crisis in 1890 increased the opposition of the capitalist class to a president who was increasingly less representative of their interests, and who confined himself to defending the last privileges of an impoverished and anachronistic aristocracy.

The crisis of 1890 had complex origins. Following the fall of Santos, the favourable international situation stimulated an influx of Argentine capital which, in the hands of more adventurous financiers attracted by the advantages of the Uruguayan market, served to increase the availability of credit. In this context, the foundation in 1887 of the Banco Nacional by foreign capitalists with the nominal participation of the government contributed to a surge in prices which produced a boom and resulting crash. However, the crisis of 1890 cannot be explained merely as a result of domestic speculative activity, but must be seen also in terms of more fundamental factors. The collapse of the Banco Nacional in 1891, and the refusal of the market to accept its banknotes, implied as in 1875 a defeat for the government. It implied also a triumph for those – traders and foreign investors – whose interests were linked to gold, and who wanted no other monetary base than the gold which they already held. The victory of this financial oligarchy secured for it a monopoly in the supply of credit for the next five years, a monopoly built on the ruins of the crisis which restored conditions of usury to loans to the rural sector, as in times long past. The establishment of the Banco de la República in 1896 ended the monopoly, but this success by its opponents – landowners, small traders, the impoverished aristocracy and the popular masses – was partial. It only succeeded in making credit formally available to those groups who until then had been almost completely excluded from its benefits. It was an important step, but the tradition of a convertible gold-based currency, to which the new official institution was committed, remained intact.

The foundation of the Banco de la República represented a major intervention by the state in the economy. In the same year, the Electric Light Company was transferred to the city administration of Montevideo by its owners who were in debt to the state, and in 1901 the construction of the port of Montevideo was begun. These three economic initiatives by the state marked, as the work of José Pedro Barrán and Benjamín Nahum has shown, the abandonment by the political elite of primitive liberalism and paved the way for the dominant ideology of the post-1904 period, *batllismo*. It should be noted, however, that at this stage the state was either meeting the requirements of particular sectors of domestic or foreign capital, or simply making good its shortcomings. There was no confrontation with capital, as would occur later during the presidencies of José Batlle y Ordóñez.

The presidential election for the successor to Herrera y Obes, at the beginning of 1894, demonstrated both the growing strength of opposition and the stubborn efforts of government supporters to hold on to power. It took 40 votes and 21 days of fruitless sessions in parliament to reach agreement. When a candidate, Juan Idiarte Borda, finally emerged from this process, the country began to move closer to civil war. Political minorities were left without representation. An agreement of 1872 which had in effect sanctioned the co-participation of the *blancos* in government, giving it control of four of the thirteen departments in the interior, was being undermined. This was the result not just of the usual mechanisms of duress and deception, but also of an increase in the number of departments to nineteen and the reduction since 1893 in the number to be controlled by the *blancos* to three. Combined with this was the growing dissatisfaction of the dominant classes with the government, so that it only needed a spark, a pretext even, to set off armed conflict. A defiant display of military force by the *caudillo* Aparicio Saravia on the eve of legislative elections late in 1896 was the prelude to a rebellion the following year.

The rebellion was a protest by the *blancos* at their exclusion from power, but it is important to bear in mind the social background to the revolt. Since the 1870s and the accelerated modernization of the traditional *estancias*, technical change had left the rural working class defenceless. Wire fencing, mechanization and improved transport resulted in growing unemployment, in addition to which the crisis of 1890 dealt the livestock sector a severe blow. In 1891, in the livestock-producing departments, the labour–land ratio was one peon per thousand hectares. Unemployment, vagrancy, pauperization, exodus from the rural areas, falling real wages, hunger and beggary all reduced the rural labourers to conditions of misery. The presence of the rural poor in Saravia's army was one response to this situation. Military recruitment by the government also absorbed a considerable part of the unemployed rural labour force. In all about 15,000 men were mobilized, one-third of them by the *blanco* rebels.

The intransigence of the government and the inconclusive nature of the war itself proved damaging for the landowning class. The loss of horses and livestock, appropriated during the military campaign either by rebels or by government forces, added to problems associated with an acute shortage of labour for sheep-shearing or the agricultural harvest. The Montevideo press echoed the protests of the propertied classes, and the resulting campaign in favour of concluding a peace was directed against President Borda himself, a stubborn opponent of any peace formula. The assassination of Borda in August 1897 removed this impediment. The war was ended with the La Cruz agreement the following month, by which a balance was achieved between the two political parties in a *de facto* division of the government of the country. The new co-participation agreement gave six of the nineteen departments to the *blancos*, and in doing so called into question once more the political unity of the country and the sovereignty of the executive power of the state.

Not until the death of Aparicio Saravia in 1904, following renewed demands by the *blancos* and the resumption of civil war, was the authority of central government decisively established and a modern state structure consolidated. This final civil conflict of 1904 – bloody, immensely destructive, extending through nine long months, and occurring at a time when wars between the political parties were regarded as a thing of the past – captured the attention of both contemporaries and historians. In effect the struggle was between two Uruguays. The one, mainly *blanco*, demanded electoral freedom and a complete political democracy, but also had the support of the traditional Uruguay of *criollo* cattle, the *saladero*, and the paternalism of the *caudillo* landowners (some of whom still survived) towards their peons. The other, principally *colorado*, defended the principle of a unified government, but also represented the new Uruguay of sheep, improved cattle bred for the meat-freezing plant (*frigorífico*) and the British market, and the landowner as capitalist businessman. For Batlle, elected to the presidency in 1903, the war of 1904 was final proof that extensive livestock production and its corollary, the unproductive *latifundios* on which the *blanco caudillos* had their last refuge, had to be eliminated and a reform of land-ownership implemented. The intention could never be realized, however, in part because of the enormous opposition it would have aroused within both Uruguays.

By the end of the nineteenth century, the incorporation of Uruguay into the world economy on the basis of its rural sector exports was complete. The price paid for this degree of integration and prosperity was economic instability. Wool, the most important single export item after 1884, was adversely affected by declining stocks and falling world prices during 1890–1. Tinned meat and meat extract fluctuated severely in European markets; Liebig's extract of meat experienced rising prices up to 1890, but a sharp decline thereafter, while tinned meat encountered declining markets after 1886 and production therefore fell. Other traditional livestock products such as hides also lost importance. Exports of *tasajo* had dropped sharply in 1875 but then experienced sustained growth until the end of the century; nonetheless there were considerable fluctuations in the price that *tasajo* could command, and the cattle economy suffered conditions of overproduction in this period. From the 1870s onward, therefore, the economy of Uruguay was increasingly subject to fluctuations in the exports of its primary products. Such dependence implied a high degree of vulnerability to external economic changes, which had marked and contradictory effects on the stability of the country.

REFORMISM AND THE EXPORT ECONOMY, 1904–18

From the time of his first election in 1903 until his death in 1929, José Batlle y Ordóñez dominated the political life of Uruguay. Twice president (1903–7 and 1911–15), his command of the country was due in large part to his ability to give expression both to its urge to modernize and to the new social forces which were emerging in what was no longer a society dominated by the elite. Son of a president and grandson of a merchant who had belonged to the colonial aristocracy, journalist and founder of the newspaper *El Día* in 1886, Batlle had worked since 1890 for the normalization of institutions and for economic independence for Uruguay from the claims of European capital. In addition he adopted the early demands of the middle and working classes (especially of Montevideo) against the autocratic labour regimes both of national employers and of foreign investors in Uruguay.

Batlle was elected to his first presidency in 1903 by the old *colorado* oligarchy. The military victory of his government over Saravia in 1904 enabled Batlle to consolidate his position as party leader and at the same time ensured the political and administrative unity of the country. The installation of a government of one party, rather than the shared government of the co-participation agreements, was in line with Batlle's personal convictions as well as with the requirements of his programme. He needed the support of large majorities, hence the electoral reforms of 1904 which further strengthened the representation of the ruling Partido Colorado. Judged by the degree of participation, however, the targets were far from being met; scarcely 5 per cent of the total population of one million exercised the right to vote. To change this situation Batlle proposed to do away with the old oligarchic structure of the party by achieving a more direct representation of the electorate from all levels. The district political club was the best instrument for this, and it brought to the constituencies of the interior as well as to those of the city the day-to-day practice of an active internal democracy. Party assemblies also brought the people into closer contact with public life, where previously issues had been discussed in closed circles. Both institutions were used to give effect to the ideal of a broadened political participation, within the framework of one-party government elected by the people.

In spite of the persistent dissatisfaction of the *blancos*, the pacification of the country was a fact after 1904. It is symbolic that that year also saw the installation of the first *frigorífico* in Montevideo. Financial stability and increasing levels of exportable production enabled Batlle to embark on a wide-ranging programme of reforms in line with the changes occurring in Uruguayan society. Immigration still had an impact on the demographic structure. According to the 1908 census, 17 per cent of the total population – 181,000 persons – had not been born in Uruguay. Half of this foreign population lived in Montevideo, which accounted for about one-third of the total population of just over a million. But the significance of this population inflow was not merely quantitative. Particularly in the urban areas, immigrants were associated with the rise of a strong middle class to which access was relatively easy; and they contributed an ideological foundation to the urban proletariat, especially in the early stages of trade union development.

Batlle's reforms considerably broadened the base for the modernization of the country. The state was strengthened through an increase in the number of ministries and the creation of the High Court of Justice in 1907. At the same time the influence of the church was diminished by the progressive limitation of its prerogatives, and by the passage of liberal divorce laws in 1907 and 1913 – the latter making divorce available at the will of the wife and without statement of cause. The benefits of education were extended through the creation of departmental secondary schools in 1912 and free access to secondary and higher education in 1916. In labour matters, the state took the role of conciliator between classes, intervening on behalf of the weakest wage-earners either through protective legislation or with effective guarantees of trade union rights. The most outrageous piece of such legislation (in the eyes of the employers) was the approval in 1915 of the eight-hour working day for all urban workers.

In addition to these social welfare measures, the state also undertook the promotion of a pattern of economic development with a strong nationalist emphasis. The introduction of a co-ordinated protectionist policy in 1912 gave a stimulus to the expansion of manufacturing industry. Batlle also tried to limit the extent of foreign (especially British) penetration in the economy. Foreign capital took the form of loans to the Uruguayan government and direct investments. In both, the position of Britain was dominant. By 1910 loans placed in London totalled £26.5 million, and constituted one of the highest per capita foreign debts in Latin America. Thereafter the proportion of British debt declined as loans were placed with New York banks. In the public utility sector, British investment in railways, trams, telephones, water and gas grew rapidly during 1905–13. Batlle regarded the presence of these companies, and the concessions under which they operated, with great misgiving. Their excessively high tariffs and deficient services were widely acknowledged, and the government sought to enlist the support of US investment (before 1914 largely restricted to the *frigorífico* industry) to challenge their position, but with little success. However, certain state enterprises were established to ensure or challenge control of certain sectors of the economy traditionally dominated by European capital, such as insurance, railways, telephones and the distillation of alcohol. The state also moved into the financial sector, nationalizing completely the capital of the Banco de la República in 1911 to create a state bank, and bringing the Mortgage Bank into state ownership the following year.

These reforms undertaken by Batlle were based fundamentally on a particular conception of the role of the state as a political catalyst designed to give effect to changes made necessary by the dynamics of Uruguayan society. This conception led Batlle to emphasize the dangers implicit in the powers traditionally held by the president. In his view, the increasing complexity of the state entailed the delegation to one office (and one man) of extraordinary powers, the abuse of which had constituted the political history of Uruguay during much of the nineteenth century. Basing his argument on these risks, and on the need to ensure continuity in government policy, Batlle proposed in 1913 a reform of the constitution. In essence, his proposal envisaged the replacement of the presidential executive by a collegiate executive composed of nine members of the majority party. Two were to be appointed by the General Assembly for a period of six years; the other seven would be elected by popular vote with one seat changing annually. This was an audacious proposal. On the one hand it challenged an inter-party consensus that had lasted almost a century. On the other it revealed an attempt to perpetuate the role of the Partido Colorado in power, since it would have to lose five successive elections to be ousted from control of the new executive.

The Partido Blanco, still suffering from the setbacks caused by the end of co-participation in 1904, penalized by subsequent electoral legislation which reduced the representation of minorities in parliament, and led by a directorate mostly drawn from the conservative classes, was a predictable and determined opponent of the proposed new system of government. Clearly the causes of its opposition were not only political but also had to do with the character of Batlle's social reforms. Thus an opposition front emerged which allied the directorate of the *blancos* with an important conservative group, the *riveristas*, who had split off from the *colorados* in March 1913. They, like all the other groups who subsequently broke with the Batllistas, sought to establish their identity in terms of the traditions of the old Partido Colorado, and accused the Batllistas with their 'socialist' sympathies of betrayal of those traditions. Within both party groups, the narrow class interest that united the large landowners with the bankers, merchants and foreign investors caused them to register distrust and subsequently alarm at the activities of the *colorado* government, and this became a polemical issue which divided the country into two irreconcilable camps. The social classes which proudly proclaimed themselves 'conservative' began to identify themselves irrespective of party with the defence of a threatened social order. The debate on the collegiate constitution was not merely a disagreement about the presidential system, but in fact implied support of or opposition to the entire reform programme since 1903.

The elections for the Constitutional Assembly which was to study the proposal, in July 1916, gave a clear victory to its opponents. Batlle's successor as president, Feliciano Viera, presumably influenced by this result, announced that the programme of social reform would be discontinued. Coming from the same party as Batlle, whose ideas he had previously accepted without reservation, Viera's attitude opened a dangerous rift within the ranks of Batlle's followers. The associations of employers communicated to the president their satisfaction at this shift to conservatism. The dispute with Viera, added to the one with Manini Rios at the head of the *riveristas*, revealed the multi-class character of the *colorados*.

Shortly afterwards, the parliamentary elections of 1917 were a second and decisive test of the collegiate proposal, and this time its supporters were victorious. The way was thus opened for the new constitution, which came into force in March 1919. The composition of the executive – the ostensible cause of the long controversy – reflected two unresolved views. The constitution established a two-headed executive power, in which the authority of the president of the Republic was shared with a nine-member National Council of Administration. The former retained certain traditional powers in internal security, foreign affairs and as head of the armed forces, which Batlle had hoped to take away. The latter, restricted to the administrative functions of the state, revealed the weaknesses of an institution that lacked effective support of its own, and was therefore entirely subordinate to the power of the president.

During the period 1904–18, the nature of the economy was determined by parallel processes of modernization and dependence. The consolidation of the state and the complexity of its functions transformed it into an effective agent of economic development, but this made the contradictions of 'outward-directed development' more evident. The continued expansion of agricultural exports demonstrated the dependence of the basic productive sectors (overwhelmingly that of livestock) on overseas consumer markets. The new *frigorífico* industry produced one of the most characteristic changes of the period, the gradual displacement of *tasajo* by frozen beef as the principal meat export. But the most important single export continued to be wool, accounting for 40 per cent of exports during 1906–10, compared with 25 per cent for hides and 16 per cent for meat and extracts. The expansion of the rural sector continued throughout the first decade of the century and most of the second, apart from the brief interruption caused by the financial crisis of 1913. The first world war accelerated the abandonment of *tasajo*, as European demand grew strongly for wool and frozen and processed meat.

The development of transport and communications underwent a decisive phase during the prewar decade. The port of Montevideo, under construction since the beginning of the decade, was opened in 1909. With the arrival of the motor car in 1904 and the electrification of the tramways in 1907, the city of Montevideo expanded to incorporate more distant suburbs. Railways crossed the country from north to south, the network reflecting the requirements of an export-orientated development which also fitted in with British commercial interests. From 1,964 kilometres in 1902, the length of track reached 2,668 kilometres in 1919.

In the manufacturing sector, a growing number of establishments in textiles, household chemicals, tobacco and beverages, metalworking, paper, and so on was matched by the growth of industrial employment, from 30,000 in 1889 to 41,000 in 1908 and 50,000 in 1920. More significant than these quantitative estimates of the size of the labour force, however, is the nature of its demands. Almost invariably they involved improved living standards (higher wages, shorter hours), and strikes became frequent from the beginning of the century when Montevideo became a refuge for 'agitators' expelled from Argentina. This was the beginning of a working-class tradition in which a number of institutions played key roles: the Socialist Workers' Centre, founded in 1896, the International Centre for Social Studies (1898), and the Karl Marx Centre (1904). But above all, the organization of the working class, and perhaps also the particular nature of its struggles, was attributable to the undisguised support given it by Batlle.

The first world war brought prosperity to the Uruguayan economy as a result of the high level of demand in Europe for agricultural products. At the same time domestic industry grew substantially on the basis of home demand. The census of 1920 recorded no fewer than 3,704 establishments engaged in manufacturing and 401 industrial enterprises. But the end of the war also ended this period of prosperity and it was succeeded by a period of economic difficulty. Between 1919 and 1922 exports declined sharply, largely because of adverse trends in the demand for meat. Instability in the European market resulted in a period of sharp fluctuations. Meanwhile, North American capital began a vigorous offensive in the Río de la Plata region, stimulated both by the prosperity of the US economy in the 1920s as well as by the obsolescence of British industry and the declining competitiveness of its products on world markets. After the war both the US government and private sector made more systematic efforts to secure an economic supremacy in the region. Regular shipping services were established or consolidated and direct cable services from New York began. At the same time US news agencies began to supply the Uruguayan press.

The trade of the United States with Uruguay was not based on reciprocity. All of Uruguay's exportable primary products had to compete against similar production in the US. The only products actually to be exported to the US, wool and hides, were subject to considerable instability in that market, and depended largely on favourable changes in US protectionist legislation. Uruguay's imports from the US, on the other hand, grew to such an extent that by 1916 the United Kingdom had ceased to be the principal source of imported goods. The US maintained its supremacy after the crisis of 1920–2 until the depression. The US supplied oil and motor vehicles as well as a variety of agricultural machinery and equipment, but it was really in the export of new manufactures, particularly the range of household electrical appliances, that US producers succeeded in breaking the traditional commercial hegemony of Britain. In addition, the sale of vehicles and the various ancillary investments in the production of tyres and cement, as well as the assembly of vehicles, undermined a principal bastion of British influence in the region, the railway. During the 1920s the inflow of capital kept pace with the growth of sales to Uruguay; as vehicle sales increased, so Wall Street provided financial assistance for the construction or improvement of roads, or for ambitious programmes of public works. In 1923, when there were over 10,000 vehicles in the country, nearly 300 kilometres of roads existed. By 1929, a further 550 kilometres had been built.

Nevertheless the British presence was still decisive. Although during the first world war British investment in Uruguay had virtually ceased, and such additions as there were during the 1920s did not reverse a downward trend, at the end of the 1920s the volume of British capital still exceeded £41 million. As in the nineteenth century, government loans and railways continued to be the main sectors of accumulated British capital. Loans amounted to approximately £20 million, even though no new loan had been placed in London since 1919; in spite of its generally higher interest rates, New York now attracted this business. Among direct investments (accounting for a further £20 million in total) were the public utilities and a meat-freezing plant. The railway system, owned by the Central Uruguay Railway and other smaller British companies, was entering a stage of decline. Afflicted by a shortage of capital which became worse after the war, with ancient rolling stock, high fares and freight rates, and a lack of new development, the railways justified their reputation as an expensive and obsolete form of transport. Competition from road vehicles came in the context of a road development policy promoted by the government and supported (as we have seen) by US capital.

The position of Britain in Uruguay's foreign trade at the end of the decade was ambiguous. It was still the most important market for meat, but it was no longer capable of sustaining its traditional hegemony. As in the rest of Latin America, the failure of British exports to grow significantly in the years of prosperity before the crisis of 1929 was clear evidence that their competitiveness was considerably weakened. British manufactures and trades continued to offer the same commodities as they had sold half a century earlier, at prices and credit terms which were easily improved on by the more enterprising and imaginative salesmen from the United States.

Immigration, which had virtually ceased during the first world war, resumed in the 1920s. Between 1919 and 1930 almost 200,000 immigrants entered the country, though probably three-quarters of that number re-emigrated to Brazil or Argentina during the course of the decade. The new arrivals were composed of a wide variety of nationalities, a consequence of the political dislocations and economic hardship in postwar Europe. Apart from the traditional influx of Spaniards and Italians, there were also Poles, Rumanians, Balts, Serbs and Croatians, Germans and Austro-Hungarians, Syrians and Armenians, all of whom contributed to a process of cultural and religious diversification. Jews came in significant numbers; achieving rapid economic advance through skill and industry, they formed a tightly knit community. The occupational distribution of the new arrivals was dictated by the pattern of demand for labour. The *frigorífico* industry, engineering workshops and textile factories, but above all the distributive trades, absorbed this new labour and the small volume of savings they brought with them. Invariably they settled by preference in Montevideo, and had an important influence on the process of urbanization. In 1930 Montevideo had 655,000 inhabitants, almost 35 per cent of the total population of the country. In that year Julio Martínez Lamas published a major treatise, *Riqueza y pobreza del Uruguay*, whose central theme was that the capital functioned as a suction-pump to the detriment of rural Uruguay.

Within the meat industry, two long-term interconnected trends were drawing to a close: the growth of the *frigorífico* industry and the increased importance of chilled as opposed to frozen meat, and the final decline of the *saladeros* which by now accounted for only 5 per cent of cattle slaughter. The integration of the *frigoríficos* with the world meat market after the war had as its counterpart the virtual disappearance of the trade in *tasajo* dating from colonial times, and the generalized adoption of improved cattle breeds producing meat of the quality now demanded. The *frigorífico* industry, however, was dominated by foreign (mostly US) capital, which owned the main plants and controlled cattle purchases at Tablada. The policy of agreed prices, and the successive pool agreements by which they divided up the Uruguayan market, gave these inter-national companies an effective monopoly which was intolerable particularly for medium and small cattle producers. This was the context in which proposals for state participation in the sector were voiced, resulting in the creation of the Frigorífico Nacional in 1928. However, the results of its early operations were unsatisfactory, and the problems which led to its creation were left unresolved.

The five years preceding the 1929 crisis were marked by another export boom, as world trade recovered. Livestock products still accounted for 95 per cent of exports, and wool and chilled beef were the leading commodities. High export values and a restricted rate of growth of demand for imports allowed the peso to appreciate during the 1920s, and gave an impression of relative stability which was regarded favourably by investors. Nonetheless the balance of payments did contain some disturbing items, notably the level of foreign debt which revealed the vulnerability of the apparent prosperity; in 1929 Uruguay remitted abroad some £3.7 million in debt service payments. The first symptoms of the crisis reached the country during 1929 with adverse trade balances, the export of gold, and the depreciation of the peso. These setbacks emphasized the limitations of an economic structure based on the rural sector, in view of its pronounced dependence on an unstable international market.

The truce which the two traditional parties had tacitly agreed upon when the collegiate constitution of 1919 was accepted rested on a series of complex political agreements. For the *blancos*, this framework offered the advantage of preventing the return of Batlle as president. It also implied (as it did equally for the *colorados*) the acceptance of an inter-party agreement as an unavoidable condition of government. For fifteen years a succession of such understandings ensured a fragile institutional stability. The presidency was held by three figures from different factions of the *colorados*: Baltasar Brum (1919–23), an orthodox Batllista and architect of the new system of inter-American diplomacy; José Serrato (1923–7), an engineer and entrepreneur, and a *colorado* but without close links with any of the major groups; and Juan Campisteguy (1927–31), a lawyer and a prominent member of the dissident *riverista* faction.

This system of co-participation implicit in the 1919 constitution tended to aggravate the internal splits in both political movements. Amongst the *blancos*, and despite conflicting trends, the figure of Luis Alberto de Herrera, who was closely identified with the most conservative rural sectors, rose to prominence. In the Partido Colorado, a series of schisms from 1913 onwards threatened to cause its disintegration, but this was always prevented by the powerful and unquestionable influence of Batlle. His death, at the end of 1929, gave rise to a period of uncertainty. The power vacuum created by his loss proved to be a severe test in the following years of the stability of the institutions whose installation he had inspired and which subsequently depended no less decisively on the weight of his authority. The lack of a leader of his stature – in part attributable to Batlle's own reluctance to groom a successor – and the inevitable struggle over his political legacy, heightened still further the tensions among the *colorados*. The presidential elections of 1930, won by Gabriel Terra, revealed the extent to which the co-existence of conflicting tendencies amongst the Batllistas had depended on the qualities of Batlle himself.

Nonetheless, in the final years of Batllista dominance there was a further wave of reformist measures. The intervention of the state in the cattle market through the creation of the Frigorífico Nacional, with the support of the landowning class, has been mentioned already. In 1931, in a major addition to the state's directly productive activities, the Administración Nacional de Combustibles, Alcohol y Portland (ANCAP) was created. The new organization was to manufacture alcohol and cement; in addition it had a monopoly in the exploitation of those oil deposits which it was hoped to find, and the more significant monopoly of the import and refining of crude oil, powers which brought it into conflict with Standard Oil and Shell. The 'socialist curse', as foreign investors and domestic capitalists saw it, was further intensified at the end of the 1920s with minimum wage proposals for trade and industry, and a pension scheme for company employees to be financed in part by the employer.

It was in this context, in which domestic political tensions were further enhanced by the internal repercussions of the world economic crisis, that the coup of 1933 was prepared. The coup brought to an end that political *modus vivendi*, based on pragmatic deals and opportunistic agreements between antagonistic social and political groupings, for which the economic prosperity of the pre-1929 years had been so necessary.

14

PARAGUAY FROM THE WAR OF THE TRIPLE ALLIANCE TO THE CHACO WAR, 1870–1932

On New Year's Day 1869 foreign troops occupied Asunción, the capital of Paraguay. The almost deserted city was given over to pillage as the soldiers – mainly Brazilians, with a few Argentine and Uruguayan contingents – searched for booty and women. The Allies had been at war with Paraguay for over four years, and now, at last, the exhausted little nation's defences had finally collapsed. Even so, the war was not yet over. Paraguay's president, Marshal Francisco Solano López, continued to fight from makeshift headquarters deep in the forests to the north, his dwindling army maintained only by the conscription of young boys aged between ten and fourteen. Not until 1 March 1870 was he finally cornered at Cerro Corá, near the Brazilian border, and killed.

In the meantime the Allies had set up a puppet government in Asunción. A triumvirate, appointed from anti-López elements, declared the Marshal to be an outlaw and confiscated all his property. The new government also promised to hold elections during the coming year for a constitutional convention which would form the basis for the establishment of a democratic state, after more than half a century of dictatorship under, successively, Dr José Gaspar Rodríguez de Francia (1814–40), who after independence had largely sealed the country off from the outside world; Carlos Antonio López (1840–62), who had ended Paraguay's isolation and begun a process of economic and military modernization; and Francisco Solano López (1862–70), whose dreams of a South American empire had together with the territorial ambitions of Paraguay's neighbours, Argentina and Brazil, led to the disastrous war. At the start of the war Paraguay had a population of somewhat over half a million, but fighting, hunger, and disease had reduced it by more than 50 per cent. Out of an estimated 221,000 survivors the war had spared only 28,000 males, mostly either the very young or the very old. The country was completely in ruins. Towns and farms were abandoned; most property had been destroyed, either by the plundering Allies or by López's scorched-earth tactics. Thousands of people were wandering homeless, dying along the roads from starvation and exhaustion. The treasury was empty, and the Allies showed little interest in providing financial help.

Considering the enormous tasks they faced, the triumvirs – Cirilo Rivarola, José Díaz de Bedoya, and Carlos Loizaga – did remarkably well. They set up emergency work camps for homeless families, formed a militia to suppress looting and banditry, instituted new tax and judicial systems, began a public works programme to provide jobs, and put invalids and orphans under the state's care. The task of administration was made more difficult by the need to get the Allies' approval of all policies. The Allies seldom agreed, for once López was dead the Argentines and Brazilians reverted to their old rivalry. To some extent that gave the Paraguayans more room to manoeuvre, but at the same time it subjected them to cross-pressures. Argentine influence was exerted through the Paraguayan Legion, a band of former exiles who had been living in Buenos Aires at the outbreak of the war and who had joined the Argentine army to fight López. Their leaders were Benigno Ferreira, who headed the triumvirate's newly created militia, Facundo Machaín, and José Segundo Decoud, who was to be the principal author of the 1870 constitution. The Brazilians, the largest occupation force, backed Cirilo A. Rivarola, one of the triumvirs. Rivarola had little education or political talent, but he was useful because he was neither pro-Legion nor pro-López. A former sergeant in the Paraguayan army, he had been arrested and tortured during the war as a result of one of the Marshal's frequent paranoid rages. Thus he could claim to have fought for his country like a good patriot, but without regrets for the old regime. Finally, there was a third faction which might be called Lopista, for it consisted of all those who still revered the fallen dictator. It was headed by Cándido Bareiro, López's commercial agent in Europe. Prevented from returning to Paraguay during the war by the Allied blockade, Bareiro now proceeded to regroup the dispirited Lopistas. His chief recruit was General Bernardino Caballero, who had recently returned from a prisoner-of-war camp. General Caballero was the greatest living hero to nationalistic Paraguayans, for he had fought by the Marshal's side to the last, having fallen into the enemy's hands only at Cerro Corá.

Elections to the constitutional convention were held in July 1870. The Legionnaires won a majority of the seats after a bitter contest marred by much invective and occasional street brawls. When the convention met in August their first move was to dissolve the triumvirate and name Facundo Machaín as provisional president of the Republic. The Brazilian army, however, saw this as a thinly veiled coup and on the following day its troops surrounded the convention. Machaín was forced to resign and Rivarola was made president in his place. Thereafter the convention stuck to the task of writing a constitution. The result was a document reflecting the liberal ideas of the anti-Lopistas. The old regime had rested upon a state-controlled economy; therefore, the new state must encourage private property and free trade. Since López had been an absolute despot the constitution must provide for a democratic republic, based on a separation of the legislative, executive and judicial powers. Reflecting the influence of the United States constitution, each branch of the Paraguayan government would have checks on the powers of the other branches.

The executive branch, as outlined in the 1870 constitution, was headed by a president who was chosen by an electoral college for a four-year term. To prevent his becoming a dictator he was prohibited from serving a second term until eight years had elapsed. A vice president was elected at the same time. The president was also assisted by a five-man cabinet composed of ministers of foreign relations; justice, worship, and public instruction; the treasury; the interior; and war. The legislative branch consisted of a bicameral Congress of 13 senators and 20 deputies. Elections were held every two years to renew half of the Chamber of Deputies and one-third of the Senate. As an additional safeguard against dictatorship Congress was to appoint a Permanent Committee whenever it went into recess in order to keep a watch on the president's acts. The judiciary was headed by a three-man Superior Tribunal. Immediately below it were appeals courts for civil and criminal cases. The constitution provided for a strongly centralized government in which local affairs were handled by political chiefs (*jefes políticos*) appointed by the minister of interior. Although municipalities could elect their own local councils they had little power to decide any but the most petty issues.

This democratic constitution had no chance in a society like Paraguay's, where most people were desperately poor and uneducated. Furthermore, the country's condition at the end of the war called for a strong state to guide the process of rebuilding. Nor were the Allies willing to see a truly free government operating in Paraguay. Even those who wrote the constitution had little patience for the sort of bargaining and compromising that democracy requires. Government was one of the few existing opportunities for a citizen to get rich, and so there was a ferocious struggle to control it. In that kind of atmosphere it was every man for himself. Former friends became enemies, and everyone sought the backing of the occupation armies to further his ambitions.

A central figure in all this postwar intrigue was Juan Bautista Gill, Rivarola's treasury minister. A brilliant but ruthless politician, he soon convinced the Brazilians that he was more capable of governing the country to their liking than the uncouth and inept incumbent. With their support he edged Rivarola out of office and put in Vice President Salvador Jovellanos. Before he could oust Jovellanos and seize the presidency for himself, however, Gill was suddenly arrested and sent out of the country by General Benigno Ferreira, who still commanded the militia. Ferreira was now the dominant figure, although Jovellanos continued to occupy the presidency, and this represented a rise in Argentine influence. It was short-lived, however, for in 1874 a nationalist revolt led by General Caballero sent Ferreira into exile. Once again the Brazilians intervened. Instead of the Lopistas taking power, Gill was brought back to Paraguay in a Brazilian warship and was eventually installed in the presidential palace.

By 1876 both the Argentines and the Brazilians had decided that the costs of occupying Paraguay were running too high. As the price of their signing a peace treaty the Argentines had demanded major territorial concessions from Paraguay which, if accepted, would have given them most of the area west of the Paraguay river known as the Chaco. Now, however, they agreed to international arbitration, and when the final award favoured Paraguay they accepted it and withdrew. The Brazilians, having already negotiated a treaty by which Paraguay surrendered its claims to certain territories in the north and east, saw no further reason to stay. Their troops, too, were removed from Paraguay.

The Gill regime was unable to survive for long without the Brazilians to protect it. Gill was assassinated on 12 April 1877 while walking from his home to the palace. His murderers were a group of men who belonged to no definite party, but who might best be labelled as maverick Lopistas. Although they opposed Gill as a Brazilian puppet they had also quarrelled with Bareiro and Caballero. Their plans now were to co-ordinate the killing of Gill with a revolt by ex-president Rivarola. Unfortunately for them, Gill's death did not bring about the disorder they had counted on. Instead, Vice President Higinio Uriarte took over as provisional president with the support of General Caballero and his friend, General Patricio Escobar, the war minister. Escobar called out the army and, on 17 April, completely routed the rebels. Several of their leaders fell prisoner and were taken back to Asunción in chains.

The next step was for Uriarte to schedule elections for 1878. The Lopistas, having control of the government, had the best chance of electing their leader, Bareiro, to the presidency. The Legionnaires were not only at a disadvantage, but their ranks were split by a personal feud between Facundo Machaín and José Segundo Decoud. In fact, as a result of the quarrel Decoud abandoned his old party and threw his support behind Bareiro. Nevertheless, Machaín was viewed as a dangerous foe by the Lopistas. He had been the principal negotiator of the advantageous peace treaty with Argentina and had gained great popularity thereby. Now he was stirring up public opinion by undertaking the defence of Gill's assassins and publicizing the cruel treatment they were receiving in prison. After all, Gill had been a contemptible figure and little was needed to present his murderers as patriots. With that sort of public forum, Machaín would be a formidable opponent.

Bareiro, Caballero, and Escobar would take no chances of being blocked from power. Accordingly, they accused Machaín of being in touch with Rivarola, who was still at large, and of plotting to overthrow the government. Although utterly false, these trumped-up charges gave the government a pretext to arrest Machaín. Thus on 15 October he joined his clients in prison. This was not enough, however, for even in his cell Machaín continued to be the object of increasing public sympathy. Consequently, Uriarte's police staged a jail-break during the night of 28–9 October, which provided them with an excuse to rush the building and slaughter the defenceless prisoners, including Machaín.

No one dared now to oppose the Lopistas, despite the public revulsion that followed this heinous act. Bareiro was duly installed as president. There was one more man to eliminate, however, before he could fully consolidate his hold on the office. Ex-president Rivarola was still trying to raise a revolt in the mountains to the east. One of Bareiro's first acts, therefore, was to offer him an amnesty. Rivarola was taken in by the ploy and returned to Asunción in December 1878. Within a week he was murdered, stabbed to death one night on a downtown street before horrified onlookers who feared to come to his aid. The Lopistas were now completely in charge, but Bareiro was not to enjoy the fruits of power for long. He was taken ill suddenly on 4 September 1880 and died within a few hours. Immediately the army took over, brushed aside the civilian vice president, and installed General Caballero in the position of power.

THE *COLORADO* PERIOD, 1880–1904

General Caballero's coup brought about an era of political stability lasting nearly a quarter of a century. With the army firmly behind him, he was able to control the government, either directly as president or indirectly from the barracks. After serving out the remainder of Bareiro's term he had himself elected for another four years. Then, in conformity with the constitution, he stepped down in 1886 – but only after guaranteeing that his close friend, General Patricio Escobar, would succeed him.

Orderly government made it possible to attend to Paraguay's serious economic problems. Very little had been done so far to rebuild the country since the war and, moreover, the Jovellanos administration had saddled the treasury with heavy debts. Two large loans, totalling some £2 million, had been negotiated in 1871 and 1872 with the British banking house of Baring Brothers. Much of that money was stolen outright by Jovellanos and his clique, and the rest had been squandered. By 1880 the unpaid interest mounting on the loan brought Paraguay's total debt to over £3 million. Since the treasury was empty, emergency measures were needed to restore the government's credit. This meant the sale of state properties, since those were the only assets it had. They were considerable assets, however, for under the old regime almost all of Paraguay's land, and most of its industry, was state-owned.

The land sale laws of 1883 and 1885 led to a wholesale alienation of the public domain. Prime quality tracts went for 1,200 pesos a square league, while marginal lands sold for as little as 100 pesos. Small buyers were discouraged, however, by the requirement that they purchase at least half a square league. Even at such bargain prices the Paraguayan peasantry, ruined by war and political chaos, could not afford to acquire the farms they once had leased so cheaply from the state. Now they were degraded to the level of peons, forced to give their labour and produce to large private landlords. On the other hand, Caballero and his clique became rich, for they could secure loans from the state bank to purchase the best properties. Having acquired those titles, they could then either choose to run their own large estates or sell the land at huge profits to foreign speculators.

The transfer of most of Paraguay's land from public to private ownership did not result in economic progress, as classical liberal theory would suppose. It gave rise to *latifundios*: great landed estates, often owned by absentee landlords. In many respects these resembled feudal fiefdoms, for their powerful owners, whether wealthy foreigners or influential politicians, brooked little interference from the state. They paid no taxes and administered their own form of justice to the hapless peons who, sunk in debt and tied to the land, resembled medieval serfs more than the citizenry of a republic. As time went on and new land sales were held the existing *latifundios* expanded. By the end of the century some 79 owners accounted for almost half of Paraguay's land; and by 1930 a mere nineteen proprietors, most of them large foreign companies, owned more than half of the national territory. Argentine investors such as the Casado, Sastre, and Pinasco families bought huge estates in the Chaco and along the northern reaches of the Paraguay river. Their interests extended to cattle raising and timber. Other large tracts of land passed into British, French, and American hands. La Industrial, a British firm, controlled much of the trade in yerba maté – Paraguayan tea – which it grew on large plantations in the south. An American company, International Products, owned vast ranches and a meat-packing plant; it was the leading exporter of hides and salted meat. American interests also controlled the production of quebracho extract, a tannin produced from the 'axe-breaker' tree, a common Paraguayan hardwood.

Many educated Paraguayans resented Caballero's giveaway policies, of course, as well as the electoral fraud and official corruption that went with them. By 1887 an opposition movement had formed which called itself the Centro Democrático. The Centro consisted of old Legionnaires who still hated Caballero for his Lopista origins, ex-Lopistas who had broken with him, and a new generation of young idealistic reformers seeking honest government, free enterprise, and civilian control over the military. In response to the Centro's challenge Caballero began to organize his own supporters more efficiently. A month after the Centro was launched he announced the creation of an official party, the National Republic Association.

Caballero's party, like the Centro Democrático, was based on a confused mixture of interests: old Lopistas now mingled with ex-Legionnaires like José Segundo Decoud who had joined the regime either out of opportunism or as the result of quarrels with erstwhile allies. Since the National Republican Association adopted red as the colour of its party banner, its members were nicknamed *colorados*. Meanwhile, the Centro Democrático, which changed its name to the Liberal party in 1894, made blue the colour of opposition. There was little else to distinguish the two groups. Although the *colorados* waved the bloody shirt and claimed to be the political heirs of López, the government's policies followed the same laissez-faire principles that the Liberals professed. Even so, battles between the two parties were often bitter and bloody, for personal and family loyalties were involved in choosing sides. Thus Paraguayans literally wore their politics on their sleeves, flaunting their partisan colours on their ponchos and blouses. Nor were such commitments limited to the educated elites. In a country where patronage and protection were necessary for the humble to survive, political involvement reached down even to the peasants – who were sometimes mobilized as voters, and sometimes as cannon fodder, in the country's political struggles.

By 1890 there were signs that General Caballero was losing his grip on the political system. Although he engineered the election of Juan G. González to the presidency, he was unable to prevent a drift toward *rapprochement* with the Liberals. President González himself was an example of the new mood among many *colorados*. Although one of the founders of the National Republican Association, he originally had been a Legionnaire, as indeed many other *colorados* had been. Consequently, he had many friends among the Liberals, which made him sympathetic to finding some compromise that would allow them to participate in the government. With his urging the Liberals had been offered the vice presidency. Some of them were inclined to accept the offer, but in the end the more intransigent Liberals had prevailed and the country remained polarized.

Meanwhile, the army tended to look askance at González, who was, after all, a civilian. That presented a problem, for all Paraguayan governments needed the army's support to survive. Although it was not very large – only around 2,500 men out of a population of nearly 600,000 – the army's weapons and organization made it a decisive factor in politics. Its importance to the government can be seen from the fact that its maintenance constituted the largest item in the annual budget: about one-fifth of all expenditures. The president had Caballero's blessing, however, so no rebellion against him seemed feasible. That remained true until a Liberal revolt in October 1891 changed the situation. The Liberals' attack had been unexpected, and it nearly toppled González. Only quick, decisive action by the war minister, General Juan B. Egusquiza, saved the regime. After a bloody battle the Liberal uprising was crushed. Egusquiza came out of it as the *colorados'* new military hero.

Like González, Egusquiza was a former Legionnaire who had gone over to Caballero's side. He shared the president's moderate views. Considering his political credentials and his high military position he was, and considered himself to be, the *colorados'* obvious choice for president in 1894. President González believed in civilian rule, however, and favoured José Segundo Decoud as his successor. In order to forestall Egusquiza, who was already campaigning as though he were the candidate, González announced publicly that Decoud was his choice for the party's nomination. Egusquiza was caught by surprise, for he had resigned from the war ministry shortly before, in accordance with the constitution which forbade officeholders from campaigning. Nevertheless, he had many supporters in the army who now rallied to his call for revolt, and González was ousted in June 1893. His vice president, Marcos Morínigo, headed a caretaker government until Egusquiza was elected.

Once in power Egusquiza tried to form a middle-of-the-road government from moderate elements of both parties. The Caballero *colorados* denounced him as a traitor, of course, and the intransigent Radical wing of the Liberal party, led by young intellectuals like Cecilio Báez and Manuel Gondra, refused to accept office in any but a purely Liberal government. On the other hand, the Civic Liberals (*cívicos*), led by the old warhorse, General Benigno Ferreira, agreed to collaborate. With their support, together with that of his own *colorado* followers, Egusquiza was able to give Paraguay four years of stable government and economic progress (1894–8). By the end of his term there were signs that Paraguay was recovering at last from the war and its turbulent aftermath. A census taken in 1899 showed that the population stood at around 635,000, as compared to only 231,000 in 1872. This was due partly to natural increase and partly to a steady influx of immigrants, as well as to the return of expatriates who had fled the country during its worst days of anarchy. Immigrants and expatriates were encouraged by the revival of trade and production. When the *colorados* first came to power in 1880 Paraguay's trade had slumped to only half of what it had been before the war; since then both exports and imports had increased, in real terms, by about 250 per cent. One of the country's most important resources, its cattle herds, had been rebuilt completely. From only 15,000 head in 1870 cattle stocks were now estimated at around 2.6 million. Moreover, the quality of the herds had been improved by the government's encouragement of importing superior breeds. Finally, as another indicator of how far Paraguay had recovered, important strides had been made in education with the building of new primary and secondary schools, and the establishment of a Colegio Nacional.

Like his predecessors, however, Egusquiza eventually faced a succession crisis, for the constitution prevented him from serving two consecutive terms. Rather than back another military officer, who might become a rival, he picked a moderate *colorado* civilian, Emilio Aceval, to head the party's ticket. He also urged the Liberals to run a candidate of their own, which would have given Paraguay its first contested presidential election. Unfortunately, the Liberals were so divided that both factions declined to enter the race rather than face certain defeat. Consequently, Aceval took office without a clear popular mandate. Also, as a civilian he was much less in control of the army than Egusquiza had been. General Caballero now had his opportunity to reassert his leadership. He still had friends among the officers and he found little difficulty in fanning the military's traditional contempt for civilian politicians. In January 1902, the Caballeristas were back in power, following a coup by Colonel Juan Antonio Ezcurra, the war minister. With that, however, Egusquistas, *cívicos* and Radicals joined forces. They also secured help from Argentina, which considered Caballero to be too pro-Brazilian. In 1904, with General Ferreira at their head, the revolutionaries launched an invasion of Paraguay. Fighting went on for four months before the government forces finally gave in, discouraged by desertions of key military commanders and by relentless diplomatic pressure from Argentina. In December 1904, Ezcurra signed a truce and handed power over to the Liberals.

LIBERALISM AND ANARCHY, 1904–23

Having defeated their common enemy, the Radical and Civic Liberals resumed their old quarrel. Cecilio Báez, the Radicals' leader, was arrogant, uncompromising, and aloof; for him, liberalism was a civilizing force, imported from Europe, whose mission was to raise Paraguay out of barbarism. General Ferreira, the *cívico* chief, was a cynical pragmatist for whom politics was the art of manipulating force and diplomacy by adjusting the mixture to the occasion. Although Báez was allowed to assume office as provisional president, Ferreira kept command of the armed forces. From that position he was able to force his own nomination for president on the Liberal party ballot in 1906 and was elected unopposed. The *colorados,* having no faith in the Liberals' professed commitment to honest elections, refused to run any candidates.

Indeed, the *colorados* adopted an official policy of abstentionism. From the time they fell from power in 1904 until 1927 they refused to participate in any elections. Thus they had no representation in Congress or in local government. A disgruntled and disloyal opposition, their aim was to encourage fragmentation among the Liberals and then use the opportunity to grab power. The Civic Liberals, for their part, were not loath to seek *colorado* support in order to offset the strength of the larger Radical faction. Meanwhile, the Radicals turned to the army to oust Ferreira, whom they refused to tolerate in power.

The key to the situation was Colonel Albino Jara, the army's commander-in-chief, who was now being courted by all factions. Although nominally a Liberal, he was, in fact, a simple opportunist who sought power for himself. Obviously Ferreira was his chief stumbling block to the presidency, so Jara lent himself willingly to the Radicals' intrigues. In 1908 he suddenly called the troops out in a revolt that caught Ferreira by surprise, toppled him, sent him into exile, and put a definitive end to his long political career. Then he added to his popularity, and allayed suspicions that he was planning to claim power for himself, by installing a civilian Radical, Emiliano González Navarro, in office as provisional president.

Elections were held in 1910. This time both the *colorados* and the *cívicos* abstained, so the Radicals were able to elect their candidate, Manuel Gondra, without opposition. Gondra, like Cecilio Báez, was a writer and intellectual who had given up scholarship for politics. He had taken over as Radical leader when Báez suddenly retired from party life. Báez, although in the prime of his career, had correctly gauged his talents as lying more in the academic world than in practical politics. For example, he had lost considerable popularity among his party cohorts when, in his frustration at the continuing chaos, he lashed out publicly at the 'cretinism' of Paraguayans. With that the embarrassed Radical Liberals began to think of him as a liability and his influence within the party plummeted. Unrepentant, Báez withdrew to become the rector of the Colegio Nacional, a post he filled with distinction for many years. Meanwhile, Gondra, who had been his disciple and close colleague, had taken his place at the head of the Radicals. It is open to question, however, whether he was any more astute than Báez as a political leader. He shared many of the latter's intellectual and personal qualities, and his two presidencies (1910–11, 1920–2) both ended early with his removal from office. Maybe Gondra was just unlucky, but it is undeniable that he tended to polarize controversy and that he was consistently unable to retain power.

Gondra's first administration had lasted only two months when Colonel Jara suddenly rose up and drove him from office. The coup touched off one of the worst periods of anarchy in Paraguay's history. Having seized power in January 1911, Jara was faced with a serious Radical revolt in March. This was led by Adolfo Riquelme, one of Gondra's ministers who had been a strong advocate of civilian control of the military. After bitter fighting Jara managed to defeat the rebels and take several prisoners, including Riquelme. But then he made the mistake of executing the Radical leaders as a warning to others. Until then he had won popularity by posing as a responsible moderate, arbitrating between intransigent Liberal factions. Now it was clear that he intended to be a tyrant – and a bloody one at that. Moreover, Jara's position was weak in that he had no civilian support. As a Liberal, he was an enemy in *colorado* eyes; and as one who had betrayed both the *cívicos* and the Radicals he was anathema to all Liberals. Even the army could not provide him with a secure base, for the officers were usually connected by family or friends to one or another of the civilian political factions. Consequently, it was only a matter of time before Jara was overthrown. In July there was a second uprising, this time headed by a coalition of *cívicos* and *colorados*, and it succeeded in putting Jara out of power.

The new government was headed by Liberato M. Rojas, a *cívico* who continued to enjoy *colorado* backing. Meanwhile, the Radicals had been regrouping just over the Argentine border. Finally, in November, they invaded. This time their leader was a dashing *caudillo* named Eduardo Schaerer. He had prepared the invasion carefully and his forces were well-equipped, for he had secured a loan of 250,000 gold pesos from a Portuguese moneylender named Manoel Rodrigues, on the promise to repay it with interest from the Paraguayan treasury if the revolution succeeded. Fortunately for Rodrígues, Schaerer did indeed succeed. By

February, 1912, the revolutionaries had made so much progress advancing on the capital that Liberato Rojas resigned the presidency and fled. The *colorados*, led by Pedro Peña, fought on alone, but in March the Radicals finally entered Asunción in triumph. Before the Radicals could consolidate their victory, however, they were challenged once more by Colonel Jara, who raised a revolt in August. This time Jara failed and was killed in the fighting. With that, the Radicals had defeated the remainder of their opposition and Paraguay was restored at last – albeit only briefly – to a semblance of order. Schaerer was elected president by the grateful Radicals, and Rodrigues, whose loan had carried an usurious rate of interest, was repaid in the amount of 2,219,247 pesos.

Schaerer was a very different sort of politician from Báez or Gondra, for he was a practical, 'self-made' man with little patience for intellectuals or theorizing. Unlike his predecessors, he was not committed to the doctrine of laissez-faire; rather, he set about to cure Paraguay's endemic instability by modernizing the government administration and using the state's powers to encourage economic growth. In the former area he took the first steps toward replacing the spoils system with a civil service based on merit, and he also tried to raise the qualifications for judges. To promote economic expansion he set up a Department of Development and an Office of Foreign Exchange, and increased the lending power of the Agricultural Bank. This reflected the fact that Paraguay was still a predominantly agricultural nation and that most of its products were destined for local consumption. Simple industries existed to produce yerba maté, quebracho extract and meat by-products for export. In addition, some timber, tobacco, cotton and citrus fruit was sold abroad. Most of the country's agriculture, however, consisted of growing corn, rice, sugar-cane and manioc for the domestic market. The same was true of the few rude, small-scale industries in existence, which involved such activities as brick- and tile-making, sawmilling, cigar-making, and cloth-weaving. Nevertheless, Schaerer was determined to promote economic development by encouraging foreign trade and investment. The country's railway line was extended southwards to the river port of Encarnación, where it joined the Argentine system. Meanwhile, Asunción's port facilities were modernized to meet the demands of increased river traffic. Foreign capital was sought for the creation of banks, whose lending was intended to stimulate local production. French interests established the Banco de la República, which performed the functions of an official bank, issuing currency, holding government deposits, and handling the state's foreign financial affairs, in addition to acting as an ordinary savings and mortgage bank. In purely commercial banking matters the British-owned Banco Mercantil and the Spanish-owned Banco de España y América were paramount.

Schaerer's administration benefited from the outbreak of the first world war, for in 1914 there was a sudden rise in demand for Paraguay's foodstuffs, especially meat. In order to respond to such demand Schaerer ordered the construction of several new packing plants. The expansion of exports brought a period of unprecedented prosperity which added to Schaerer's popularity. Meanwhile, he wisely ploughed the government's increased revenues, derived from import and export duties, into more internal improvements. Things did not always flow smoothly, however. In 1915 the *cívicos* made a serious bid for power in a coup which forced Schaerer to abandon the capital. Nevertheless, after a few days he was able to crush the revolt and restore order. When he finally stepped down at the end of his term in 1916 he became the first civilian president since the old regime to complete his period in office.

Since the *colorados* continued to abstain from elections, and the *cívicos* were proscribed, the Radicals were able to elect Manuel Franco to the presidency unopposed. Franco represented a compromise between the Schaererista and Gondrista wings of the party. Schaerer, forbidden by the constitution to succeed himself, had vetoed the candidacy of Gondra, whom he personally despised. There was little in common between Schaerer, the bustling, hard-driving 'upstart', and the scholarly, aristocratic Gondra, so it is hardly surprising that the two leaders hated one another. Each had a large personal following as well as a distinctive approach to government. Unfortunately, their personal quarrel was to have tragic consequences for Paraguay.

President Franco proved to be a competent and popular administrator. His style was much different from Schaerer's, however. He had little interest in economic reform and ran the government in an austere fashion more in keeping with the laissez-faire wing of the party. Budgets were carefully balanced and the state's functions were limited chiefly to maintaining order. Nevertheless, Franco did institute two important political reforms: the secret ballot and the civil register of voters. His moderation and fairness even induced the *colorados* to consider abandoning their non-participationist position and co-operate in the process of democratization. On balance, Franco was one of the most popular presidents Paraguay ever had. His approach fitted the mood of the times, which was optimistic about the inevitability of 'Progress' of which there was evidence all around: in the steady growth of population to around 800,000, in the doubling of Paraguay's foreign trade between 1900 and 1919, and in the transformation of Asunción from a humble town of 38,000 at the turn of the century to a prosperous city of 90,000 by the end of the first world war.

Indeed, there is a *belle époque* character to Paraguayan society at this time. As party conflict died down there was little to disturb the social order: no disruptive religious, racial or linguistic cleavages. Paraguay was solidly Catholic; its people were a homogeneous mixture of Spanish and Guaraní Indian, and the blending of those two cultures was reflected in the almost universal bilingualism which served to make Paraguayans feel like an unique people. Social strata existed, of course, but the lines were not rigidly drawn. The old upper class that traced its lineage to colonial times had been impoverished by war and revolution; moreover, even the most aristocratic Paraguayan had Indian blood in his veins. In addition to the old upper class, which devoted itself chiefly to law, politics or agriculture, there was a new, bustling commercial elite drawn mainly from Italian, Spanish, German, French and British immigrants. These new arrivals were quickly accepted into local society and within a generation had been completely integrated. Below those two principal groups was the great mass of peasants. Their daily lives were scarcely touched by any modernizing attempts, whose influences were confined almost entirely to the capital. Finally, there was a small but growing number of town labourers. It was among these that the first signs of real discontent with the established order made their appearance. The port, maritime and transport workers were the first to attempt the forming of unions and the calling of strikes to improve their wages and conditions. Not for another decade, however, would they be strong enough to make any real impression. In the meantime, the country was inclined to dismiss the labourers' complaints scornfully as the work of anarchists, whose malevolence could hardly be allowed to disturb the peace.

This complacent mood came to a sudden halt in 1919. First, the paternalistic Franco died unexpectedly, thus removing the very symbol of 'good times'. Secondly, and truly fatal to the system he had represented, the end of the war in Europe burst the bubble of Paraguay's prosperity. Vice President José P. Montero, who took over the government after Franco's death, was faced with a collapsing economy as export orders were cut drastically and unsold goods lay rotting on the docks. Panic spread, and with it, recrimination. The end of prosperity also signalled the end of the political era of 'good feelings'.

The Radical party convention in 1920 was, as expected, divided over whether to nominate Gondra or Schaerer as its presidential candidate. Gondra, who had spent the last three years in a sort of honourable exile as ambassador to the United States, now returned to claim his right to the presidency, of which he had been deprived earlier by Colonel Jara. His long years of service made him the Liberal party's 'grand old man'. Schaerer had his enthusiastic followers too, but in the end he was forced to recognize that Gondra was backed by most of the convention. A bargain was struck by which Schaerer would be compensated by being made president of the Liberal party.

This compromise was not to last more than a few months. With his customary zeal for efficiency and organization, Schaerer tried to transform the Liberal party from a loose agglomeration of local notables into a well-disciplined machine, with a hierarchy of command and tight control from the centre. Obviously he intended to dominate the party and secure his nomination for president the next time around. The Gondristas were alarmed, and to hinder Schaerer's plans the minister of interior, José P. Guggiari, fomented a rebellion against him among the party's youth organization. Schaerer retaliated by attacking the government from the columns of a daily newspaper he owned, *La Tribuna*. Attack and counter-attack escalated with such viciousness that finally Schaerer and his supporters moved into open revolt. On 29 October 1921 they took over the Asunción police barracks and threatened the government with bloody rebellion unless Guggiari was dismissed from his post. Faced with this challenge to his legal authority, Gondra called on the army to arrest the Schaereristas. When he learned that the army was reluctant to do so, he resigned.

Gondra's resignation threw the political situation into chaos. Schaerer had not intended to overthrow Gondra, but only to bring him to terms. Now he was accused of fomenting the very sort of anarchy he had once helped to suppress. Forced into seeking a compromise, the two factions agreed on Eusebio Ayala as provisional president. Ayala was a writer and diplomat whose factional loyalties were unclear, since he had spent so much of his time in recent years travelling in Europe. He took over on the understanding that elections would soon be held. To make sure that they would, a bill was rushed through Congress and sent to him to sign.

At this juncture, however, the *colorados* decided to fish in troubled waters. Their leader, Manuel Domínguez, had been trying to find an army officer to lead a coup against the Liberals. The obvious choice was Colonel Adolfo Chirife, the commander-in-chief. Chirife had refused to go along with the idea, but nevertheless he continued to have friendly dealings with Domínguez. Now the *colorados* announced that they would support Chirife's candidacy as a non-partisan president who would be 'above politics'. The idea appealed to the Schaereristas too, for ever since Gondra's sacrifice it was much less likely that Schaerer would get his party's nomination.

The Gondrista Radicals exploded when they heard of the scheme. From the floor of Congress they excoriated Schaerer as a traitor and even accused Colonel Chirife of having plotted against Gondra, knowing that by refusing to back the president against Schaerer he was clearing a path to the palace for himself. With that, Chirife turned his back on the Liberals and agreed to be a candidate of a *colorado*–Schaererista coalition. Perceiving that the elections would probably result in Chirife's triumph, the Radicals demanded a postponement. President Ayala had not yet signed the bill fixing the date for elections, and he showed his true Gondrista colours by vetoing it. He would remain in office, he said, to finish Gondra's term. Thus there would be no elections until 1924. Ayala's decision plunged the country into civil war.

In May 1922, Colonel Chirife raised the banner of revolt, having secured the support of a majority of his fellow officers. Ayala hastily reversed his decision to postpone the elections in order to keep the peace, but it was too late. The rebels marched on Asunción and on 9 June there was fighting in the streets. Somehow, miraculously, the government's forces, consisting only of an engineering battalion and the cadets from the Military School, held the city. Even so, thirteen months of bitter fighting lay ahead in which battles would be fought all over the Republic. Both sides changed leaders during the war. Chirife died and was replaced as rebel commander by Colonel Pedro Mendoza. On the government side, Eusebio Ayala resigned to be replaced by Eligio Ayala (no relation), who had been Gondra's finance minister. Gathering around him a group of brilliant young junior officers, some of whom – like José Félix Estigarribia and Arturo Bray – were to become the outstanding military leaders of the next generation, Ayala prosecuted the war more vigorously. Little by little the tide of battle began to turn. Although Colonel Mendoza executed a skilful manoeuvre that nearly captured the capital in July 1923, the government's forces held firm once again and the attackers were forced to give up their siege. With the failure of this second offensive the revolution was exhausted. Schaerer and his followers fled into exile and peace was finally restored. Eligio Ayala, the provisional president, was elected to serve a full term the following year.

THE SOCIAL QUESTION, DIPLOMACY, AND THE APPROACH OF
WAR, 1923–32

Eligio Ayala, who governed Paraguay from 1923 to 1928, gave Paraguay one of her most progressive administrations. In some respects he was a typical Gondrista of the best sort: absolutely honest and extremely parsimonious with the public's money. He put down corruption and favouritism with a heavy hand, and managed the nation's finances so carefully that when he left office there was a budget surplus. Also, like Báez and Gondra, he was an austere and solitary intellectual – solitary, indeed, almost to the point of misanthropy. During the morning hours the doors to the presidential office were always closed as Ayala sat at his desk, alone, writing down his thoughts: notes which his friends collected after his death and published under the title *Migraciones* ('Migrations'). Ayala had travelled extensively in his youth, and his journeys around Europe stimulated his thoughts about his country's problems.

Paraguay's main problems at that time were its continuing poverty, and its vulnerability to a growing foreign threat. Ayala believed that the first problem could be overcome only by a combination of political peace and reform of the land tenure system. To gain peace, he decreed a new electoral law that ensured minority representation in Congress, and followed this up with a guarantee of free elections to the *colorados*. The effect was to split the *colorados* into abstentionists and participationists, with the latter agreeing to test the government's sincerity by entering the 1927 legislative elections. Ayala was as good as his word, with the result that the *colorados* not only took their seats in Congress but decided to enter a candidate in the 1928 presidential elections. It was to be the first time in Paraguay's history that a real contest was held for the presidency.

The agrarian question was dealt with by the 1926 Land Law. According to census estimates, fewer than 6 per cent of those who tilled the land in this agrarian country were owners of farms. Thus, the law aimed at the creation of a large class of yeoman farmers, who would possess family-sized farms of between 6 and 60 hectares (about 15–150 acres). This was to be done either by colonizing peasants on state lands, or by expropriating private *latifundios*, in which case the owners would be compensated at the original price of their purchase. In most cases, the former route was actually taken between 1926 and 1931. About 572,000 acres were distributed to some 17,697 families, who received their titles after working their farms for four years and paying the state back in modest instalments. In order to prevent speculation, or the excessive subdivision of holdings, the law placed restrictions on subletting, reselling or mortgaging the farms; and it forbade the inheritance of parcels of less than fifteen acres. At the same time, reflecting the government's classical liberal outlook, the law prohibited any collective or co-operative farming of these lands.

The foreign threat facing Paraguay came from Bolivia. Both countries claimed the Chaco, the vast wasteland between the Andean *altiplano* and the Paraguay river. During the previous century Bolivia had lost to Chile her territory on the Pacific ocean, and was now looking for an alternative outlet to the sea. Control of the Chaco would give her access to the Paraguay river, which flows southward into the Paraná–La Plata river system, and thence to the Atlantic. An additional incentive arose from the fact that oil had been discovered in the Chaco, on a strip of territory under Bolivia's control. It was reasonable to suppose, therefore, that the entire region harboured fantastic wealth.

While Paraguay was distracted by her internal troubles Bolivia had begun to encroach deeper and deeper into the Chaco by extending a line of forts eastward toward the Paraguay river. It was a stop and go process. Occasionally the Paraguayan government would protest and, unwilling to risk a war, the Bolivians would then agree to a diplomatic conference to settle the conflicting claims by drawing a boundary line, as in the treaties of 1907 and 1913. Since the Paraguayans were equally unprepared for war the resulting boundaries tended to accept the status quo, which meant the recognition of Bolivia's right to territory under her control but with the promise that she would penetrate no further. Before long, however, the Bolivian advance would begin again, but Liberal governments in Asunción usually preferred to overlook the violations, since their depleted treasuries would not bear the cost of mobilization. Then, with the discovery of oil in the 1920s, the Bolivians' advance was accelerated. Oil revenues, paid by the Standard Oil Company for drilling and pumping rights, allowed them to make much more elaborate preparations for war. German officers were brought in to train the army and modern weapons, including tanks, were purchased.

By the time José P. Guggiari, another Gondrista, succeeded Ayala to the presidency of Paraguay in 1928 the situation in the Chaco had become explosive. The Bolivian advance had reached the upper waters of the Paraguay river, where a fort, appropriately named Fortín Vanguardia, was built. All this time the Paraguayan army had been forced to stand by helplessly as the Liberal government vacillated; but finally, on 5 December 1928, a fiery young major named Rafael Franco lost his patience and led his men to attack and destroy Vanguardia. Outraged, the Bolivians retaliated by seizing two Paraguayan forts. Both sides now mobilized for war, but when the Paraguayan recruits reported for duty there were no uniforms, weapons, food, ammunition or medical supplies. Paraguay was completely unprepared to fight. The government had made no plans for the country's defence, having gambled heavily on its ability to persuade the Bolivians to be reasonable. Now that its bluff was called the Guggiari administration was forced to back down and sign a humiliating treaty which, among other things, required Paraguay to rebuild Vanguardia.

War was averted for the time being, but the Liberals never recovered from this blow to the nation's pride. Although Guggiari tried to pacify the opposition by including Schaereristas, *colorados*, and members of a new nationalist organization, the Liga Nacional Independiente, on the National Defence Council, his government was swamped by a rising tide of criticism. Arms hurriedly purchased from Spain turned out to be so antiquated and dangerous to use that they were popularly dubbed *mataparaguayos* ('Paraguayan-killers'). Major Franco, now a national hero, was a constant thorn in Guggiari's side. When he was finally caught in a plot against the government and dismissed from the army, Guggiari's opponents accused him of persecuting patriots. The opposition groups used the National Defence Council as a forum from which to attack the government's war plans.

Emotions reached a peak on 23 October 1931, when a group of student demonstrators were machine-gunned in front of the presidential palace by the soldiers defending it. The students, encouraged by leading opposition figures, had taken over the streets and stoned Guggiari's home in protest over the government's inaction in the face of a recent clash in the Chaco in which a Paraguayan soldier had been killed. Whether the guards lost their nerve in front of the mob, or whether – as the government insisted – one of the students had fired first, the shooting left eleven people dead and scores more wounded. It was the nadir of the

Liberal party rule. Public opinion was so outraged that Guggiari resigned temporarily while Congress held an investigation of the incident. Although he was finally exonerated and resumed office a few months later, the '23 de octubre' was to have far-reaching consequences, for it alienated an entire generation of the country's intellectual elite. Eventually it was to culminate, in 1936, in a revolution that would drive the Liberals from power.

In the meantime, the Liberals were also harried by the serious economic depression that broke upon the world in 1929. Because so large a part of Paraguay's population consisted of self-sufficient peasants, the depression's effects were limited. In Asunción, however, prices declined between 1928 and 1932, which suggests some contraction in the local market. Overseas trade also fell. Exports dropped from a total value of 15.9 million gold pesos to 13.9 million, chiefly because Argentina cut back its purchases. Paraguay was able to maintain a trade surplus only by cutting its imports from 14.3 to 6.5 million pesos. This kind of belt-tightening may have been unavoidable, and even necessary for preparing the country for war, but it may also have contributed to the discontent that infected the urban population during the Guggiari years.

With the opposition once more sullen and withdrawn, the 1932 elections reverted to the traditional pattern of a plebiscite for the official candidate. The Liberals' favourite was ex-president Eusebio Ayala, who was an unfortunate choice for several reasons. He was tainted by the partisan machinations that led to the civil war of 1922–3; both Schaereristas and *colorados* remembered him as the president who tried to remain in power by using his veto to postpone the elections. Nationalist opinion had reason to hold him in contempt too, for he had been Paraguay's diplomatic representative at the signing of the 1913 boundary treaty with Bolivia. During his visit to the Chaco at that time he had noted the enemy's military positions as being far beyond the lines agreed to in 1907, but had preferred to ignore them as the price for peace. In fact, he had even agreed to the insertion of a phrase in the treaty stating that neither country had modified its positions since 1907, although he knew this to be untrue. It was a mistake that was to haunt him later.

In any event, nothing could have preserved the peace in 1932. The Bolivians were in the mood for war, believing their military superiority to be overwhelming. In July they seized the Paraguayan fort Carlos Antonio López at Pitiantuta. No Paraguayan government could have given in to such a provocation at this stage and survived. Once again the reserves were called up – and this time, prepared or not, they marched to the Chaco to fight. The war, the bloodiest in Latin American history, lasted until June 1935, by which time Bolivia had been surprisingly defeated and Paraguay had won control of almost all the disputed territory.

Part Four

THE ANDEAN REPUBLICS

The Andean Republics

15

CHILE FROM THE WAR OF THE PACIFIC TO THE WORLD DEPRESSION, 1880–1930

As Chile entered the 1870s the Republic could look back on 40 years of virtually uninterrupted constitutional stability – unique in Spanish America – and the evolution of a functioning multi-party system in politics. She could also look back on the growth of a modest but promising economy, based on the export of primary products from land and mine. Her population had doubled since Independence, from one to two million by 1875; her foreign trade, dominated from 1830 to 1870 by copper exports, had grown apace, providing adequate revenue for successive governments to initiate transport improvements, notably railways, develop educational programmes, provide urban amenities – and preserve law and order. In foreign affairs, Chile had not only maintained her independence but in the 1830s had also prevented the combined attempt of Peru and Bolivia to assert hegemony on the Pacific coast of South America.

The country's capacity to attain these objectives undoubtedly owed a good deal to the constitutional system created by Diego Portales (1793–1837), backed by a remarkably homogeneous landed aristocracy and based upon the authoritarian, centralizing constitution of 1833. That constitution, coldly realistic, recognized what Chile was rather than what it might aspire to be: it appreciated what Portales called 'the weight of the night', the sheer traditionalism of three hundred years of colonial control, during which the basic lineaments of society had been drawn, and accepted that independence from Spain was indeed a fundamental political act, but had virtually no economic or social content. For the society of Chile was essentially rural: a white aristocracy of land ruled the national life in all its branches while an illiterate peasantry, largely *mestizo*, obeyed. The great estates, virtually separate fiefdoms where the writ of the hacendado ignored the laws of the land, were still, as they had been for three hundred years, the basic social and economic characteristic of the new Republic.

This highly stratified society had evolved a political system much more sophisticated than that of her neighbours. All revolutions polarize opinions, and Chile was no exception. Politically, the Independence period produced conservatives and liberals, the former accepting separation from Spain but anxious to conserve the social *status quo*, the latter seeing in that upheaval the opportunity to extend freedom – from the church in intellectual and educational matters, and from arbitrary authority in politics. The conservatives triumphed in the 1830s but the liberal current still ran strong: from 1830 to 1880 it succeeded in modifying, though by no means destroying, the authoritarian structure of government through limited constitutional reform. And it began to assault the practices as well as the form of governmental authority, chief of which was the interference of the executive power, the president, in elections to the legislative, the Congress, thus generally assuring a pliant majority for its plans. Under the system, men and groups of different views formed embryonic parties which contested elections and, as Chile avoided both the excesses of *caudillismo* and the intervention of the military in the political process, by 1870 a political and constitutional system recognizable as functioning and viable by European or North American standards had evolved, giving Chile the accolade of being 'the England of South America'.

Chile also advanced economically, with exports of agricultural produce (notably wheat) and mining products (chiefly copper) expanding as the century proceeded. From the 1860s, the demands for improvements to the infrastructure, especially railways, forced government to turn increasingly to foreign borrowing as a supplement to trade revenues, but here too, through sound management and probity, Chile acquired an unparalleled reputation for promptly paying her debts, most unusual then in Latin America. By 1870, indeed, political maturity, financial responsibility and orderly evolution were internationally regarded as Chile's distinctive hallmarks in a somewhat disorderly continent. Only Brazil could compete with Chile in international esteem.

The 1870s, however, were a decade of disillusion. The onset of the world depression in international trade hit Chile hard as a primary producer, and internal political squabbling among the different parties threatened her vaunted tradition of governmental continuity. The mild-mannered president Aníbal Pinto (1876–81) sought accommodation with the political opposition rather than using his extensive powers under the constitution, only to find, in the midst of severe economic depression and much social distress, that conciliation was interpreted as weakness. His government, reeling from the effects of the world economic crisis, had been obliged in 1878 to take the currency off the gold standard and adopt a regime of inconvertible paper, a harsh shock to Chilean pride and to international opinion. For those who believed that the authoritarian constitution of 1833 and the presidential system were failing, the moment of confrontation seemed to have arrived.

Outside events then intervened. Since Independence Chile and her northern neighbours, Bolivia and Peru, had disputed the line of Chile's northern boundary in the Atacama desert, but the issue did not become acute until the resources of that barren land – chiefly guano and nitrates – became commercially exploitable, and foreign capital and entrepreneurship moved in to exploit them. A succession of treaties between the separate states regulated their relations, but in 1878 the unilateral abrogation by Bolivia of a treaty with Chile relating to foreign interests in Bolivian Antofagasta precipitated a diplomatic crisis. Peru, linked with Bolivia in a treaty of defensive and offensive alliance, desperately sought to avoid conflict; Chile, knowing of the treaty, sought to put pressure on both her neighbours and, when the Bolivian authorities refused to yield, declared war. The War of the Pacific (1879–83) ensued, at a time when Chile was quite unprepared for it both politically and economically. As it happened, however, her lack of preparation, economic weakness and political uncertainty – not to mention the deplorable state of her armed forces – looked like meticulous planning when compared with her adversaries, and the strong sense of nationalism – non-existent in Peru and Bolivia – was to prove a decisive asset. After an uncertain start, Chilean land and naval forces decisively defeated those of Bolivia and Peru, as they had in the 1830s, and from a country hovering on the brink of political disintegration and economic collapse in 1879, Chile emerged from the war in 1883 with her prospects transformed. Resisting strong Pan-American pressure for magnanimous treatment of defeated foes, Chile secured from the peace an extension of national territory no less than a third of the country's original extent and, in the nitrate regions of the Atacama – Peruvian Tarapacá and Bolivian Antofagasta – mineral wealth which would account for roughly half of ordinary government revenue for the next 40 years.

By the Treaty of Ancón (October 1883), concluded by Chile with a

Peruvian government which Chilean forces had helped to install, Peru ceded to Chile unconditionally and in perpetuity her province of Tarapacá. She also accepted Chilean possession of her provinces of Tacna and Arica for a decade, after which a plebiscite would determine their final ownership, the winner paying the loser ten million Chilean silver pesos. Other terms dealt with Peru's debtors, whose sorry investments had been partly mortgaged by Tarapacá's mineral deposits. A separate truce with Bolivia – the final peace treaty came only twenty years later – secured for Chile Bolivia's sole littoral territory of Antofagasta, with nitrate deposits only second in importance to those of Tarapacá.

The war itself had also given considerable impetus to Chilean industrialization in the provision of matériel, and to both agriculture and transport facilities through the necessity to provision from central Chile the army in the desert and the forces subsequently occupying Peru. This galvanization of the Chilean economy from its state of torpor in 1879 was to be sustained in the 1880s by the dynamic growth of the new nitrate industry. Chile's future seemed assured, and perhaps the most significant impact of her success in war was to enhance an already high reputation, imbuing her leaders with a sense of national self-confidence, in contrast to their feelings of almost universal pessimism a few short years before. No two Chilean statesmen of the nineteenth century better embodied this combination of national aspiration and patriotic pride than the two incumbents of the presidency during the 1880s, Domingo Santa María (1881–6) and José Manuel Balmaceda (1886–91). Both were profoundly liberal by conviction; both were no less autocratic in temperament, and possession of the presidency accentuated this trait: they were, in effect, to preside over the paradox of Chile's greatest material progress the century was to see, combined with the political and constitutional collapse of the system created after Independence by Diego Portales.

THE PRESIDENCY OF SANTA MARÍA, 1881–6

Domingo Santa María assumed the presidency of Chile on 18 September 1881, when the tide of war had already turned decisively in Chile's favour. Like most of his predecessors, he had been hand-picked by the previous president, and like them had been elected with massive intervention by government in the polls. Despite the war political passions ran high, inevitably so when the Congressional opposition, and notably the clerical Conservative party, was well aware of its impotence to ensure a free election. The preceding months had been marked by what the British Minister called 'many violent and indecorous scenes' in the legislature.[1] Nevertheless, Santa María had a clear field. But the manner of his election and the policies he was to unfold, particularly in religious affairs, were to embitter even further political life.

The incoming administration had inherited a religious situation of some delicacy. The death in 1878 of the ultramontane Rafael Valentín Valdivieso, Archbishop of Santiago for some 30 years, had re-opened with the Vatican the vexed question of the *patronato*, the government's claim as successor to the Spanish crown since independence to the right of nomination to high ecclesiastical office. With the death of Valdivieso, so long a thorn in Liberal flesh, President Pinto's government had named a man of more moderate temper, Francisco de Paula Taforo, but the Holy See had refused to accept the appointment. Santa María now sought to grasp this nettle and invited to Santiago an apostolic delegate, Celestino del Frate. But the mission was a total failure: del Frate advised the Pope to reject Taforo's nomination, and Santa María sent him his passports. The question of the *patronato* remained unresolved but, for Santa María, del Frate's mission provided the pretext for a direct confrontation with the church, and legislation was introduced to assault its still substantial prerogatives at three critical junctures of human life – birth, marriage and death.

In his presidential state of the nation message in 1883, having intervened decisively in the Congressional elections of 1882 to guarantee a majority for anti-clerical legislation, Santa María announced his programme – to remove from ecclesiastical jurisdiction the registry of births and deaths and transfer them to the state; to institute civil matrimony; to ensure liberty of conscience; and to permit the dead of whatever religious persuasion to be buried in cemeteries hitherto restricted to Catholics and controlled by the Catholic church. To José Manuel Balmaceda, minister of the interior, who had been educated in a seminary and originally destined for the priesthood, fell the difficult task of piloting these controversial measures into law. For although the government could count on its majority in Congress, it had to face the power of the church outside, and that power was still formidable. 'There is no doubt', wrote the correspondent of *The Times* in 1880, 'that the

---

[1] Pakenham to the Earl of Granville, Santiago, 6 July 1881. No. 38. Diplomatic. London, Public Record Office, Foreign Office archives, Chile (FO 16), vol. 213.

cowled or tonsured man is still the "lord of all" in this country; and with the women under his control, he may well afford to set the sneers of sceptic men and the enactments of the civil law at defiance.'[2]

It was a prophetic observation. The liberal laws were, indeed, forced through Congress, though in the teeth of acrimonious Catholic opposition, but outside Congress the effects were dramatic: for example, the vicar capitular of Santiago not only condemned the law on cemeteries but also refused to apply it, and in retaliation the government closed Catholic burial grounds and prohibited interments within churches, a long-standing but clearly unhygienic practice. Some lugubrious scenes resulted, such as clandestine burials of devout Catholics in defiance of government orders, the picketing of cemeteries by armed soldiers, the concealment of terminal illnesses and the subsequent smuggling of corpses out of houses in all kinds of coffins and by all means of conveyance.[3]

But the law was the law. Despite fierce Catholic resistance the legislation, once on the statute-book, was increasingly applied. The religious laws of the Santa María administration marked a decisive diminution of the power and influence of the church: they also marked the apogee of Chilean liberalism in the nineteenth century, and earned for Balmaceda the implacable hatred of the Conservative party. Much more than this, however, a paradox occurred which only time would reveal: with the passage of the laws the cement of anti-clericalism which had bound together many different men and groups of broadly liberal persuasion began to crumble, and there was no other ideological bond between them. The Radicals and the National party, not themselves benefiting from Santa María's electoral interventions, were nevertheless prepared to support his anti-clerical policies in Congress since they shared his passionate conviction that the powers of the church should be reduced. But that objective achieved, their natural objections to electoral intervention came to the surface. As for the president, with the new nitrate income he now had better opportunities to pursue ambitious programmes but far more political difficulties in doing so, and it would not suffice, in a country whose elite was as politically conscious as that of Chile, for the president simply to use his patronage to build up a personalist following. Santa María had succeeded Aníbal Pinto who, it was generally agreed, was not in the Portalian tradition. But both Santa

[2] *The Times*, 27 August 1880.
[3] Abdón Cifuentes, *Memorias* (2 vols., Santiago, 1936), I, 182–5.

María and Balmaceda were men of exceptionally strong will, absolutely determined to maintain presidential prerogatives according to the written constitution, and both saw the presidency as the dynamic motor of the whole machine. The very change in style from Pinto to Santa María, which Balmaceda was to underline when he came to power in 1886, seemed to the opposition parties not only a change of personality but also one of power, for where Pinto had yielded, Santa María and Balmaceda would fight. Thus the opposition came to confuse a well-founded theory of the limitations of presidential power with mere objections to its exercise by the strong men who wielded it. Furthermore, into an already complex constitutional and political equation there had been injected the unprecedented, unknown quantity of nitrate wealth, and the thorny question of how government should spend it.

THE NITRATE INDUSTRY AFTER THE WAR OF THE PACIFIC

With the end of the War of the Pacific and the accession to Chile of the nitrate regions of the north, the government was faced with a fundamental question of how to re-constitute the ownership of the industry and tap for Chile's benefit this unique natural resource. It was a complex question, first, because the tide of war sweeping across the nitrate regions had dislocated operations in an industry which, already in the late 1870s, had been plagued by uncertainty. That uncertainty had been created by the Peruvian government's abortive attempt in 1875 to assume a form of state control whereby the nitrate grounds and *oficinas* (refineries), hitherto in private hands, national and foreign, were placed under government ownership through the issue of interest-bearing bonds, made payable to bearer and redeemable eventually by the Peruvian government when it could raise sufficient funds. These bonds were, in effect, the title-deeds in 1879 to the then privately owned nitrate fields and factories (excluding hitherto unexploited fields which had not yet been alienated), easily transferable to third parties. But Peru's international credit had long been exhausted, and no loan to redeem the bonds was ever forthcoming. In consequence, their face value began to fluctuate, and when war came and Chilean successes made a Chilean victory most likely the price of bonds plummeted. That Chile would exact large territorial concessions from Peru and Bolivia was obvious to all involved, but no one knew what line her government would adopt towards nitrate interests in general and foreign interests in particular.

More than this, however, a large number of Peru's unsatisfied creditors abroad had long claimed that Peruvian government loans had been mortgaged on her nitrate province of Tarapacá, and had already sought the diplomatic support of their governments to underline the claim. If Chile, then, acquired Peruvian territory, would Chile also assume the debts allegedly secured on it? And if not, what price the future of an industry bedevilled by such imponderables? In such circumstances, many bondholders panicked and unloaded their holdings at ridiculously low prices to bolder speculators who were prepared to take risks against uncertainty. Pre-eminent among these was an English engineer, John Thomas North, who was already engaged in a number of enterprises in Peruvian Tarapacá, where he had lived and worked for over twenty years.

Already in 1880, the Chilean government had begun to debate the question, setting up a deliberative and advisory commission which was followed by another in 1881. Their reports, eschewing the Peruvian model of state intervention in nitrates, recommended the return of the industry to private hands and, to secure the stake of the Chilean government, export taxes on nitrate shipments. Since the nitrate certificates issued by the Peruvian government were the only legal titles to private ownership, those who then held them were in effect recognized as the legitimate claimants to the nitrate properties; thus it was that John Thomas North, 'the Nitrate King', and other non-Chileans secured a large share of the industry at comparatively small cost, realizing huge profits not only on the real value of the properties but also by their subsequent sale to joint stock companies which they floated on the London Stock Exchange in the 1880s.

Thus British interests, which in 1875 had held a minority position in the nitrate industry, came by 1890 to control 70 per cent (by value). The British takeover has been the subject of controversy ever since, largely because it was held that the Chilean government of the day lost a golden opportunity to acquire the industry for the state and thus permitted the major source of government income for the next 40 years to be subject to foreign control. Some historians, indeed, have gone much further than this, asserting that there was collusion between Chilean decision makers and the more efficient and more rapacious foreigners with their greater reserves of capital and higher technology, to whom they abandoned Chilean nitrate interests.[4] Recent research, however, has strongly

[4] Notably, Hernán Ramírez Necochea, *Balmaceda y la contrarrevolución de 1891* (2nd edn., Santiago, 1969).

modified such views. While there is no doubt of the free-enterprise philosophy of Chilean leaders of the day, it is now clear that other considerations of Chile's national interests predominated in their decisions. First, in returning the nitrate industry to private hands, the Chilean government effectively split foreign interests, and made it impossible for their governments to intervene without appearing to favour one set of nationals against another. Thus, whereas the nitrate entrepreneurs were delighted, the Peruvian bondholders were dismayed, and it took the latter twenty years to reach a satisfactory settlement. Secondly, by returning the responsibility for production, shipment, marketing and sale to private interests, while imposing taxes on the export of nitrate, the Chilean government acquired an immediate and major source of revenue without involving itself in such matters. Finally, on the subject of the antebellum Chilean stake in Peruvian Tarapacá, it is now clear that this had already been totally undermined by Peruvian policy in the 1870s, and that while Chilean interests may well have held a more substantial holding than British in 1875, it was more between 1875 and 1879 rather than in the 1880s that this holding was drastically reduced.

For the Chilean government nitrate revenues were a bonanza, and the rapid expansion of the industry and trade in the 1880s provided it with an income which enabled it both to pursue ambitious programmes of public expenditure and also to avoid the need to modernize the internal system of taxation, a path which, had it wished to pursue it, would have brought government into confrontation with the vested interests which dominated Chile's political, economic and social life. As it was, from a contribution of 5.52 per cent of ordinary government revenue in 1880, export taxes on nitrate and iodine (a by-product) rose to 33.77 per cent in 1885 and to 52.06 per cent in 1890.[5] But such windfall wealth was a mixed blessing. The international nitrate market was highly unstable owing to the primary use of the product as a fertilizer and thus subject to the vagaries of climate and agriculture, often of sudden impact and unpredictable behaviour. Overproduction of nitrate, saturating the world market, meant falling prices for producers and distributors alike. Consequently, they looked to restore the balance between supply and demand, and the usual device was a producers' combination to limit output on a quata system until that occurred; moreover, by the late 1880s the majority of those producers and traders were foreigners, less

[5] R. Hernández Cornejo, *El salitre* (Valparaiso, 1930), 177.

sensitive to Chile's national needs than to the interests of their stockholders and their own fortunes. For the Chilean government, increasingly dependent on nitrate revenues as a major proportion of its budget, the unpredictability of the market meant uncertainty of income and planning alike, and producers' combinations the surest way to reduce revenue at a stroke. The fact that control of the industry seemed in the 1880s to be passing increasingly into fewer, and dubious, hands was also worrying. North and his partners, for example, purchased the bonds of the Pampa Lagunas *oficina* during the War of the Pacific for £110,000 and provided a further £140,000 for installations, later floating two London companies at a total capitalization of £2,122,000 to exploit the property. The comparable expansion of his enterprises – and his ambitions – in Tarapacá in the 1880s excited not only the admiration of often misguided investors in London but also the apprehension of native Chileans, not least those whose policies were predicated on a sure and steady income from nitrates. The conflict inherent in this situation came to a head in the presidency of Balmaceda, precisely at the moment when internal Chilean issues, political and constitutional, which had been long in gestation, came to a head to create a national crisis as severe as any in the Republic's history.

THE PRESIDENCY OF BALMACEDA, 1886–91

Though few Chilean presidents can have assumed office under more auspicious circumstances than José Manuel Balmaceda, the political environment of his accession was one of acrimony and conflict. To the out-going president, Santa María, he was the natural successor, and the full weight of the governmental machine was thrown behind his election as the official Liberal candidate, not only to the disgust of the clerical conservative opposition – to whom Balmaceda's name was anathema – but also to the chagrin of some broadly liberal groups for whom, by now, the practice of electoral intervention had become odious. Though such groups recognized Balmaceda's outstanding record as a public servant – member of Congress since 1870, minister to Argentina in the critical year of 1879, foreign minister in 1881, and minister of the interior from 1882 to 1885 – and admired his powers of oratory and persuasion, they objected to the system which would put him in power, and joined moderate conservatives and a small group of opposition Radicals to support a former minister, José F. Vergara. These liberals, the *sueltos* or 'free-lance' party, led by a well-known intellectual, historian and educationalist, Miguel Luís Amunátegui, provided the first evidence that the formerly united Liberal party, the party of government, was now losing its cohesion. But the juggernaut of electoral intervention rolled on unimpeded; Vergara withdrew his candidacy before the final votes were counted, and Balmaceda assumed office on 18 September 1886.

In the five years since Balmaceda first entered government Chile had changed considerably. Not only had the northern frontier been pushed forward some 600 miles by the War of the Pacific, but the process of bringing under more effective central control the still-independent Indian lands south of the river Bío-Bío and the even more remote territory of Magallanes had also begun to gather momentum. Military force and colonization had been the twin arms of successive Chilean governments in this process in the 30 years since the 1850s, but the movement was intermittent and halting, for between the Bío-Bío and the river Toltén further south lay Araucania, inhabited by the fiercely independent Mapuche Indians whose sporadic revolts and more frequent depredations inhibited the progress of settlement. The last general rising of the Mapuche took place in 1880–2: its suppression, largely by Chilean forces transferred from the victorious desert campaigns in the north, was the final nail in the coffin of Indian independence, stubbornly maintained since the beginnings of the Spanish conquest. The building of forts at Temuco and Villarica in 1881 and 1883 respectively in the heart of Indian territory was the physical expression of that fact, and the establishment in 1882 of a General Colonization Agency in Europe to recruit immigrants to southern Chile was, in effect, the deliberate resumption of policies initiated three decades before, but not since then effectively pursued. In 1883 the first German colonists arrived in Talcahuano, to be followed in succeeding years by an influx of European immigrants to Chile averaging over 1,000 a year throughout the 1880s.

Similarly, in Magallanes and Tierra del Fuego, the decade 1875–85 was a period of considerable geographical exploration followed by economic exploitation, particularly in sheep-farming. When in 1876 the governor of the territory, Diego Dublé Almeida, visited the Falkland Islands and brought back sheep (although failing to persuade islanders to accompany them), thus laying the foundations of the region's major activity, Magallanes and Tierra del Fuego ceased to be merely remote appendages of the Chilean Republic, claimed largely for their strategic significance, but became regions of distinctive character and economic importance. Again, European immigration played a decisive part. Though numbers were small – the total population of southern Chile in 1885 was little over 2,000 – quality was more important than quantity alone, and English and Scottish sheep farmers in particular played a major role.

As for the chief prize of the War of the Pacific, the nitrate regions, Balmaceda became president precisely when the nitrate industry was entering its most dynamic phase of expansion. Between 1884 and 1886, at a time when the world market was saturated, the first producers' combination to restrict output had been set up, but this had collapsed, and rising world demand again saw the *oficinas* of Tarapacá in full activity. At the same time, John Thomas North and his associates were launching a large number of new companies on the London Stock Exchange. Tarapacá and to a lesser extent Antofagasta began to boom: ports such as Iquique and Pisagua experienced a growth not only in exports of nitrate but also in imports of foodstuffs, machinery and equipment to sustain the highly artificial mining communities in the Atacama desert, dependent for almost every commodity on the outside world. The short-lived postwar boom in nitrates had already drawn into the regional economy a sizeable migrating population – labourers from central Chile, Bolivia and Peru, engineers and mechanics from Europe, notably Great Britain, and traders, bankers and businessmen; the population of Antofagasta rose from 5,384 in 1875 to 21,213 ten years later, that of Tarapacá as a whole from 38,255 to 45,086 in the same period, and Iquique, the chief nitrate port of Tarapacá, saw an increase from about 9,200 to almost 16,000.

The regional manifestations of economic change in Chile during the 1880s were part of a national process of growth and development which also had social and cultural implications. Its principal motors were the linked factors of population growth and increasing urbanization. Between 1875 and 1885, the total population of Chile increased from 2,075,971 to 2,497,797, but much more striking was the structure of the population. Whereas in 1875 the rural population was almost double the urban – 1,350,426 to 725,545 – by 1885 the proportions had changed dramatically: rural population had increased slowly to 1,456,032, but urban population had risen by one quarter to 1,041,765.[6] The most

---

[6] Population figures in Latin America are notoriously unreliable. Those for Chile, however, are more reliable than most, owing to the existence of a competent, if not entirely perfect, National Statistical Office from 1843, and the work of Markos J. Mamalakis, 'Historical statistics of Chile', (4 vols., Yale University, mimeo), later published in four volumes (Westport, Conn., 1978–83). The figures cited here are from vol. II of the mimeographed version, Table IIAlfl.

striking increases of urban over rural population occurred precisely in the nitrate regions, where population was concentrated more and more in ports of shipment and importation, the nitrate *oficinas* being scattered throughout Antofagasta and Tarapacá, and in those provinces where incipient industrialization had proceeded furthest – Santiago, Valparaíso and Concepción. In Santiago province, while the urban population rose in 1875–85 from about 186,000 to 228,000, the rural population fell strikingly, from 180,000 to 102,000.

The migration of sizeable numbers of rural labourers, who were not attached to specific plots of land as *inquilinos* were, for example, had long been a characteristic feature of Chilean history, not least because of the country's peculiar shape: migrants moved north and south with the seasons of the agricultural year and the production cycle of crops. But, from mid-century, population was increasingly drawn out of the countryside into urban environments and occupations with the development of northern mining, the extraction of coal around Arauco, Coronel and Lebú, the building of railways, and the development of the larger towns with their food and drink processing factories, tanneries, furniture stores, textiles and other basic consumer industries. The years spanning the War of the Pacific saw an accentuation of this movement as industrialization spread, and before the war itself many believed that Chile ought to industrialize more rather than be totally dependent in her export trade on primary products of the land and the mine. Attempts in the 1870s to organize manufacturers as pressure groups, however, came to little. But in 1883, significantly after the spurt in industrialization which the War of the Pacific stimulated, the Sociedad de Fomento Fabril (SFF) was founded, with government encouragement and subventions precisely for this purpose. The SFF has been described by a historian of Chilean industrialization as 'in part pressure group, regulator of internal industrial conflicts, technical service organization and social club'; it represented 'the institutionalization of Chile's industrial sector into a cohesive nucleus that was large enough to effectively maintain industrial objectives before public opinion and to serve as a direct link with the government'.[7] Nothing symbolized better than the SFF the process of change in the Chilean economy which, however slow and imperceptible at first, gathered momentum, entailing in the process social diversification and the emergence of new political forces. But, while the Chile

[7] Henry Kirsch, *Industrial development in a traditional society: the conflict of entrepreneurship and modernization in Chile* (Gainesville, 1977), 42.

which Balmaceda inherited was indeed a Chile in transition, the crisis which was shortly to shake the old constitutional order to its foundations came not from outside the traditional power structure but from within.

Balmaceda assumed office intending to reconcile the diverse liberal groups and, at the same time, to placate the conservatives. Among his first acts was the resumption of relations with the Holy See and the appointment of an agreed candidate as Archbishop of Santiago: Mariano Casanova, a distinguished theologian and a personal friend of the president. It was Casanova who was to take the lead in the establishment in 1888 of the Catholic University of Chile, the country's first private university. Balmaceda's first ministry, composed of representatives of the Liberal and National parties, was a conciliatory one, and Balmaceda quickly gave proof of his aim to avoid the bitter political struggles of the past: municipal elections in Santiago towards the close of 1886 were entirely free of governmental interference, and the defeat of government candidates was offset by the gain of goodwill which resulted from its neutrality.

Such olive branches to calm the political scene were intended to create broad support for Balmaceda's basic internal policy, in fact a continuation of Santa María's programme but one which, with massive revenue flowing in from nitrate duties, could now be greatly enlarged. There was to be heavy public spending on major construction projects such as railways and docks, and in social investment, particularly education, colonization and municipal buildings. Additional expenditure was also allocated to the strengthening of Chile's military capabilities, both defensive and offensive, through port fortifications, new ships of the line, and adequate barracks and military schools – understandable proposals from a Chilean statesman who had been so long at the centre of the conduct of foreign policy, and now, as president and commander-in-chief of the armed forces, was responsible for national security.

Balmaceda's was an ambitious programme, and it was pursued energetically. A new ministry of industry and public works was created in 1887, and within a year was assigned more than one-fifth of the national budget, while the ministry of education took one-seventh. By 1890, in budgetary estimates for an expenditure of $67,069,808, over $21,000,000 was allocated to the ministry of public works and some $6,628,000 to education. Government intentions which these figures represented were translated into action: from a school enrolment of some 79,000 in 1886, the number rose to 150,000 by 1890; railway construction was pushed ahead, assisted in the south by the bridging of the Bío-Bío, Chile's widest river; the great dry dock at Talcahuano was completed and a canal was built along Santiago's own river, the Mapocho. Foreign immigration was encouraged with government assistance: between 1886 and 1890 almost 24,000 Europeans settled in Chile, not only as farmers on the forest frontier but also as skilled artisans in the growing cities. New hospitals, prisons, government offices and town halls were erected.

Such a programme had many implications, however. First, it was predicated on continuing high government income from nitrate exports, and these could not be guaranteed with an unstable world market. Secondly, it created in the hands of government an immense tool of patronage in the shape of governmental posts and the award of contracts, as well as labour forces dependent on them. Thirdly, while it satisfied some, it also disappointed many, whose aspirations, personal or public, had been aroused by the programme itself. A new town hall or school in one community might be an object of pride for its citizens, but it would be one of envy for less favoured neighbours. And there were wider issues surrounding that key question of politics and government: the allocation of resources. Since Chile's adoption of paper money in the crisis of 1878, a growing body of opinion regarded the return to a metallic currency standard as the major national economic objective, though this was still a minority view among politicians, many of whom as wealthy landowners benefited appreciably from the regime of inconvertible paper. To the *oreros*, however, increasingly apprehensive about the quantity of paper in circulation, the liberal rights of emission under loose banking laws, fluctuating exchange rates and high public expenditure, the new nitrate wealth represented quite literally a golden opportunity to retire paper money and return to what they regarded as financial respectability, and the postponement of reform a national disaster. For Balmaceda, however, his programme was paramount, and he so identified himself with what he saw as the national interest that opposition to any part of it came to appear as factious and selfish, if not unpatriotic.

The honeymoon period in national politics which followed Balmaceda's accession lasted little more than a year. By 1888 the various liberal groups which formed the government were already competing with one another for office. In March the former policy of conciliation collapsed. Under pressure from his strongest supporters, the Liberales de Gobierno, Balmaceda allowed intervention in the Congressional elections and, inevitably triumphant, it was they, and they alone, who came to occupy ministerial posts. The National party – small in numbers but strong in talent, and controlling a large part of the Chilean press – were particularly incensed: henceforth, their loyalty to the strong executive, a characteristic feature of the party since the days of Manuel Montt (president from 1851 to 1861), could no longer be taken for granted. As for Balmaceda, increasingly obsessed with his own programme, the problem of allocating favours grew commensurately with the growth of revenue. The public works programme enhanced the value of technocrats and administrators, but people naturally talented in this direction were not necessarily to be found amongst the traditional oligarchy. Hence there came into being 'new men', such as José Miguel Valdés Carrera, minister of industry and public works, or Hermógenes Pérez de Arce, superintendent of railways, technocrats to their fingertips, who believed strongly in what they were doing and in the work their chief had given them. It was not difficult in such circumstances for an opposition already convinced of Balmaceda's obsessive egotism to believe that the president of the republic was building a personal following which would blindly follow his every whim.

Opposition suspicions of Balmaceda's intentions hardened in 1889, when speculation was already rife about likely successors to the presidency in 1891. Among his intimates, Enrique Salvador Sanfuentes, a wealthy hacendado but not prominent politically, was widely tipped as Balmaceda's candidate, since he had risen to favour quite rapidly in 1888, becoming minister of hacienda in April and minister of public works in October. In March 1889, as the key minister in Balmaceda's Cabinet – since he was responsible for the central part of the president's programme – Sanfuentes accompanied Balmaceda to the nitrate regions, the first visit by a Chilean head of state to those recently incorporated parts of the Republic. Balmaceda's well-publicized tour of the northern provinces was for a variety of motives. Apart from its propaganda value for a president politically harassed in Santiago and seeking provincial support, there was a basic economic reason why a visit to the nitrate regions was then opportune. By 1889, the activities of John Thomas North in Tarapacá had grown apace; apart from his nitrate companies, his new Bank of Tarapacá and London, his control of Iquique's water supply through the Tarapacá Waterworks Company, his Nitrates Provisions Supply Company and, above all, his Nitrate Railways Company, owning the line which linked most important *oficinas* to the ports, all betokened an attempt at monopoly which in the eyes of many represented a threat to all other interests in the province, and not least those of the government, whose revenues now turned so precariously on nitrate taxes.

In one respect confrontation had already arrived. In 1886, Santa María's government had cancelled the privileges of the Nitrate Railways Company on the grounds of non-fulfilment of contract, and Balmaceda had inherited a complex legal question as the Company challenged the government in the courts, alleging constitutional impropriety in the annulment of its privileges. Moreover, its lawyers included a number of prominent Chilean politicians opposed to Balmaceda, notably Julio Zegers, North's chief lawyer in Chile and hitherto a life-long liberal associate of Balmaceda's, but by 1889 leader of a liberal group, the *convencionalistas*, whose primary purpose was to eliminate personalism in the choice of future presidents by having an agreed candidate selected at a convention of all liberal groups. Zegers's position as North's lawyer coupled with his political stance, however, led Balmaceda and his coadjutors to see him as a traitor to the national interest which they felt they represented.

Balmaceda's speeches on his northern tour were well-tailored to local pride and expectations but he also took the opportunity to make major pronouncements on the nitrate industry, particularly at Iquique, the capital of Tarapacá. Here he referred to the dangers of a foreign monopoly of the industry, suggested that his government would look more closely at the possibility of encouraging greater Chilean participation in it, and generally persuaded a number of commentators that he intended to pursue a more nationalistic line with regard to foreign interests. Yet he also went out of his way to reassure existing interests that Chile needed their capital and enterprise. It was, in fact, a speech which could mean all things to all men but, with a new nitrate combination possibly in the offing, it was a shrewd tactic to induce hesitancy among the predominantly foreign producers, the chief of whom, John Thomas North, was himself paying a visit to Chile at that time. On Balmaceda's return south the two men met on three separate occasions, but nothing dramatic emerged from the encounters. The Chilean government pursued its attack on North's railway monopoly in Tarapacá, skilfully exploiting other British interests which were equally opposed to it, but it did little to undermine the predominant foreign interest in the nitrate industry as a whole.

It is possible that political preoccupations, which grew in intensity in

1889 and 1890, caused Balmaceda to shelve any plans he might have had: it is equally possible, and on the existing evidence far more likely, that such plans were limited in scope and vague in intention, and Balmaceda's posthumous reputation as an economic nationalist was greatly exaggerated. His primary concern with regard to nitrates had nothing to do with foreign predominance but everything to do with monopolistic control, a danger he thought North represented. That apprehension was shared by other foreign (notably British) producers. At the same time, with falling prices of nitrate in an over-stocked world market, *all* producers, foreign and Chilean alike, had little option in 1890 but to form a common front to restore equilibrium, and hence profitability, through a combination to restrict output and equalize supply and demand. Here Balmaceda had no allies in the nitrate industry and little power to affect events.

As it was, however, the political/constitutional crisis predominated. Balmaceda's return from the north in March 1889 was followed immediately by a cabinet crisis, arising from the resignation of Sanfuentes as a gesture to refute the notion that he was Balmaceda's choice for president in 1891, and the delay in choosing a successor from the various liberal groups. Within less than two months, an adverse vote in the Senate overthrew the ministry, and Balmaceda had to try again. This time he approached the National party but could not accept their terms. Balmaceda's reaction was to form a ministry of those noted for antipathy to the Nationals, who moved into clear opposition. Thus Balmaceda lost his automatic majority in the Senate and his majority in the Chamber of Deputies fell to ten. A further crisis in October made matters worse: Balmaceda apparently agreed not to influence the forthcoming presidential election in return for opposition support in Congress, and appointed a 'neutral' ministry, but within a month that ministry also resigned since, it said, it could not trust the president.

Whilst the parties jostled for ministerial office in 1889, crucial constitutional issues had crystallized, and the opposition increasingly took its stand on them. Whereas, when Balmaceda assumed office, the one significant professed aim of opposition was freedom of elections, by 1890 that had been enlarged to include the independence of the parties from the president and the subordination of the executive to the legislature. The latter demand was best expressed in a constitutional system, like true parliamentary government, where no ministry or cabinet survives without majority support in Congress or Parliament. In Chile, under the constitution of 1833, and despite subsequent modifications reducing the powers of the executive, ministers were only accountable to the president, who made and unmade them himself. On this issue, the constitution was unequivocal. On the other hand, no president, however persuasive or preponderant, could ignore the fact that to Congress was entrusted by that same constitution the right to accept or reject essential legislation, and particularly approval of the budget and the size of the armed forces: these legislative powers were the principal leverage which Congress had over unco-operative presidents, though they had been weakened (in fact but not in law) by executive interference in elections and the establishment thereby of pliant legislatures. Now, however, the progressive alienation of former supporters by Balmaceda's character and policies had effectively nullified that strength, unless the president were prepared to confront Congressional opinion, insist that ministers were accountable to him and to him alone, and demonstrate that the insistence by Congress on its rights could be blunted by buying off or forcing out, by whatever means, what Balmaceda regarded as factious opposition.

Balmaceda seemed prepared to do this. In his next ministry, he appointed as minister of industry and public works José Miguel Valdés Carrera, the best-known protagonist of the claims of Sanfuentes, the alleged 'official' candidate for the presidency in 1891. It was this act which led Julio Zegers and the *convencionalistas* to withdraw their support from government, thus finally depriving Balmaceda of his majority in Congress. Balmaceda then closed Congress and chose a new ministry, including Valdés Carrera, and the first six months of 1890 were marked by opposition attacks on Balmaceda, through the press they controlled and at public meetings, and by government reactions, including the founding of two new newspapers to put its case. Quite contrary to precedent, Balmaceda called no extraordinary session of Congress in this period, and the battle there could not be resumed until the ordinary session was convoked on 1 June, as the constitution insisted. Congress opened with a dignified speech from Balmaceda, proposing constitutional reforms, but opposition motions of censure on the new ministry were carried by large majorities in both Houses. This was followed on 12 June by a motion from Julio Zegers in the Chamber of Deputies to postpone all discussion of the law authorizing the collection of taxes until the president appointed a ministry enjoying the confidence of Congress, a motion which also secured large support. Since Balmaceda stood firm on his prerogatives, and Congress was adamant about its rights, complete impasse obtained, and no business beyond recrimination was transacted. To one foreign observer, indeed, the president was 'losing his hold on the country' and, he thought, 'it is doubtful how far His Excellency could command the services of the troops against Congress'.[8] The troops, however, were shortly to be employed elsewhere.

With government apparently paralysed at the centre, dramatic events took place at the periphery of Chilean territory. Early in July, the longshoremen of Iquique in Tarapacá went on strike, demanding among other things payment in national currency rather than in *fichas*, the employing companies' wage tokens which could only be exchanged in company stores. They were joined by mule-cart drivers, casual labourers and, soon, by nitrate workers themselves, and indiscriminate looting of warehouses and shops began. Despite immediate calls from the harassed employers for government assistance to put down the disturbances, Balmaceda took no action beyond urging employers to come to terms with the strikers. The stony refusal of the employers even to discuss terms turned some miners into saboteurs, and machinery was wrecked at a number of *oficinas*, that of San Donato – owned by prominent partners of John Thomas North – being totally destroyed. At this juncture the government intervened: troops were sent north to engage in bloody battles with the strikers, and wholesale repression of their unions took place. But the strike wave had spread throughout the nitrate provinces and it was almost a month before order was finally restored. It cost Balmaceda dear. His initial inactivity enraged property owners and alarmed the oligarchy, while his final decision to send in troops completely alienated the miners who, in less than a year, were themselves to be troops in the battles against him. Yet the strikes of 1890, the first major social conflict in Chilean history, were also a portent. They had their origins in harsh working and living conditions on the nitrate *pampa* and in the exploitation of labour, unrepresented in the political system of Chile. It is true that, in the late 1880s, new but still insignificant political forces emerged in Santiago, primarily the Democratic party formed in 1887 as an offshoot of the Radicals, and composed of politicians such as Malaquías Concha who believed that more attention should be paid to working-class interests. But it was in the north, in the nitrate deserts, that the real origins of working-class militancy were found, where future

[8] Kennedy, the British Minister, to Salisbury, Santiago, 21 June 1890, no. 47, Diplomatic. FO 16/259.

labour conflicts had their sharpest expression, and where, in time, pioneer organizers emerged to fashion genuine political movements to represent working-class demands.

Though the origins of the labour unrest of mid 1890 were inherent in local conditions, the disturbances were not unrelated to the general political situation and the tension growing throughout Chile as the constitutional crisis remained unresolved. Throughout the winter of 1890 neither president nor Congress would yield: Balmaceda refused to change the ministry to meet Congressional wishes, and Congress continued to refuse to discuss presidential bills, while promoting a number of its own. Personal attacks on both sides appeared in the press; a public meeting of some 8,000 in Santiago in July called on the president to give way, but Balmaceda replied that he would fight to the bitter end. On 24 July, Zegers called in Congress for the impeachment of the ministry and a declaration of Balmaceda's unfitness to continue in office, as a result of which Balmaceda, according to his strict constitutional right, declared Congress closed. Further mediation between government and opposition proved fruitless; from then to the end of the year, the situation deteriorated. Congress not only refused to pass essential legislation, notably the estimates for 1891 and the law governing the size of the armed forces, but also spent its time discussing and censuring the crimes and follies – as it saw them – of the Balmaceda administration. For his part, Balmaceda, by now persuaded that accommodation was impossible, had begun to purge the army of elements whose loyalty might be suspect. The crucial date was 1 January 1891, the deadline in the constitution for the passage of the bills governing the budget and the armed forces. If they were not passed by that date, Balmaceda would have to act unconstitutionally or yield to Congressional demands for a ministry it could trust. The majority in Congress now had little doubt that Balmaceda would fight, and set up a *junta* to resist him, seeking the support of senior officers in the army and navy towards the end of December. While the idol of the army, General Manuel Baquedano, declined to give his support, the navy chief, Admiral Jorge Montt, agreed to support Congress. On 1 January 1891, when Balmaceda declared in a justificatory manifesto the essential laws to be still in force, he set in motion the wheels of Congressional revolt. A week later in defiance of Balmaceda's orders almost the entire Chilean fleet, with a large number of congressmen on board, left Valparaíso for the north of

Chile, to begin a civil war which would last eight months, take over 10,000 lives, and destroy in the process the Portalian system of authoritarian, presidential government.

The war itself was a very strange affair. Assisted by previous purges and immediate wage increases for the army, Balmaceda largely retained its loyalty. The fleet, however, supported Congress and, in February, seized the northern nitrate province of Tarapacá, setting up a rival government at Iquique. Since Balmaceda lacked the means to transport troops north and tackle the congressional forces there, and since Congress lacked an army to attack Balmaceda in central Chile, both sides were obliged to stand off from critical combat until one had secured decisive superiority in arms. The Atacama desert lay between them. In effect, the war was transferred abroad as both sides sought in America and Europe the armaments each required – Balmaceda warships, Congress ground munitions – diplomatic support and the sympathy of international opinion. In all three, the Congressionalists proved more successful. Meanwhile, however, though largely passive, the combatants were not idle in Chile itself. In the north, the Congressionalists recruited and trained an army from the nitrate workers; a crucial factor was the presence of a Prussian military adviser, Emil Körner, recruited by Balmaceda's government in 1886 to modernize and professionalize Chile's army; he quarrelled with the president over service priorities and threw his considerable expertise behind Congressional efforts to create an army. Balmaceda's government, controlling the central valley, was faced with a sullen populace and sporadic sabotage, and did not hesitate to use repressive measures, alienating in the process a good part of neutral opinion in the constitutional conflict. Balmaceda was in a difficult position: deprived of nitrate revenues which, from February 1891, flowed into Congressional coffers; lacking the means to prosecute the war and, indeed, apply a blockade of Congressional ports except on paper by decrees which foreign governments refused to accept; and progressively losing the propaganda war abroad, he could only wait hopefully for the arrival at Valparaíso of two ironclads, then being built in France, and trust that his agents could frustrate Congressional efforts to secure weapons for its new army. That race he lost: at the end of August, the Congressional fleet, loaded with well-drilled, well-armed men, landed near Valparaíso, and in the bloody battles of Concón and Placilla overwhelmed the Balmacedist army, equipped with antiquated weapons and quite inadequately led. The triumph of Congress was complete. Balmaceda took refuge in the Argentine Embassy in Santiago, to write his reflections on the tragedy which had overwhelmed him, to take farewell of his family and friends in a number of poignant letters and, on 19 September, almost exactly five years after his assumption of the presidency, to take his own life with a pistol shot to the head. His adherents, high and low, suffered for their association with exile, loss of property, exclusion from public office and, in some few cases, death. The civil war, like the political struggle which preceded it, had been long and bitter, and its results were to have far-reaching effects on subsequent Chilean history.

One controversy surrounding it concerns the significance of the role played by foreign nitrate interests in the genesis and development of the prewar crisis and in the eventual triumph of the revolution against Balmaceda. According to one view, Balmaceda had a concrete national policy for the nitrate industry, entailing less foreign interest and indeed control, as part of his general programme of enlarging the role of the state in the national economy. It is argued, however, that the threat to foreign interests, personified by North, was paralleled by a threat to the dominant internal oligarchy through the growth of the power of the state, and so both combined to overthrow Balmaceda. Circumstantially, there seems a strong *prima facie* case for this view, and a number of contemporary observers shared it. More recent research, however, has strongly modified and even completely undermined this interpretation. First, it reveals that Balmaceda had nothing like the clearly constructed policy on state intervention in the economy – including nitrates – ascribed to him; secondly, it demonstrates that the principal agents used by Balmaceda to challenge North's attempts at monopoly control were other foreign interests, with which the president was prepared to deal; and, thirdly, it shows that the nitrate policy pursued by Balmaceda's successors, far from being favourable to foreign interests as was previously argued, was in fact much more positively against them than that of the martyr-president. These revisionist views have also restored – for the time being at least, and until fresh evidence is available – more traditional interpretations of the struggle between Balmaceda and his Congress as primarily constitutional and political, rather than economic, with the personal factor also playing a major part. Events succeeding the civil war of 1891 in the internal history of Chile indirectly support the primacy of politics as the determinants of action, as Balmaceda himself testified.

THE 'PARLIAMENTARY REPUBLIC', 1891-1920

In the 'political testament' which Balmaceda wrote shortly before he committed suicide, he prophesied that:

although parliamentary government now exists in Chile. . . there will be neither electoral liberty, nor clearly defined parties, nor peace among the circles of Congress. Victory and the submission of the vanquished will produce a temporary calm; but soon the old divisions will be re-born, with the same bitter situations and moral difficulties for the Chief of State . . . The parliamentary regimen has triumphed on the battle-field, but this victory will not endure . . .[9]

He was to be proved right, though partly for the wrong reasons.

The Congressional victory in 1891 marked a significant divide in Chilean political and constitutional history. Having rebelled in order to assert the predominance of the legislative power over the executive, the triumphant but heterogeneous parties in Congress now controlled Chile. Whereas previously the strong powers of the president and, above all, his capacity to intervene in elections to secure a pliant Congress had, to some extent at least, acted as a barrier to factionalism, those restraints were now removed completely, though the process of dismantling them had begun long before. Temporary unity had been forged in Congress through a common object of aversion – Balmaceda and the system of which he was the last representative – but, that removed, unity went with it, as Balmaceda had foreseen. The legislature now not only predominated over the executive; it controlled it, for the latter lacked the ultimate weapon it must possess in a parliamentary system when faced with obstruction or defeat in the legislature, namely the power to dissolve it and to seek, through new elections, a fresh mandate. A bogus form of parliamentary government was thus imposed on Chile, and personal factors played their part in this transformation. Admiral Jorge Montt had personified the revolution in uniform as commander-in-chief of a rebellious and ultimately successful naval and military force. Not a politician, he was the perfect compromise candidate of the victorious parties for the presidency from 1891 to 1896: conciliatory, mild-mannered, not forceful, and very conscious of the principles of anti-authoritarianism for which the revolution had been fought.

His intention [he told the British Minister] was to allow the Ministers great independence of action in their several Departments of State; to abstain from

---

[9] Translated from J. Bañados Espinosa, *Balmaceda, su gobierno y la revolución de 1891* (2 vols., Paris, 1894), II, 653-4.

interference with the legislative bodies, and to confine the Intendentes and Governors of provinces to their administrative duties, forbidding interference in political matters and especially on elections.[10]

This respect for a parliamentary system eliminated the need to rewrite the existing constitution, and Montt's acceptance of the president's new role – very far removed from the conceptions of most of his predecessors – meant that modifications in practice became far more significant than changes in form. Chief among these was the elimination of direct government interference in elections, the major aim of opposition to Balmaceda: the surrender of that executive weapon after 1891 meant that presidents henceforth had to rely on alliances and coalitions in a multi-party Congress. Thus, automatic majorities for government initiatives no longer existed, and government was the prey of shifting allegiances and temporary alliances. Indecisive rule and hesitant compromise were the inevitable results.

Two other factors compounded this situation. First was a new law of Communal Autonomy approved by Congress in 1892. Long championed by conservatives in particular, and notably by M. J. Irrarázaval, seduced by the example of Switzerland, and also by some liberal groups, who saw in wider powers for local authorities a further barrier to executive influence, this measure sought to free municipalities from central control. But the effective use of more local autonomy depended on adequate financial resources, and for these the legislature did not provide. Hence, central control was replaced by the equally dubious power of the locally powerful, and government agents in elections gave way to the power of the local purse as hacendados and other men of means substituted bribery and corruption for central interference, so that by the end of the century seats in Congress had come to be quoted at a fixed price.

Secondly, and a total paradox, were the character and policies of Balmaceda's heirs, those politicians who had supported him during his life and sought to vindicate his views when he was dead. The persecution of Balmacedists, rigorous while it lasted in 1891 and 1892, abated with the passage of a selective amnesty in 1893, to be followed in 1894 by a more comprehensive measure. Thus by 1894 the prominent supporters of Balmaceda such as Enrique Sanfuentes and Julio Bañados Espinosa had fully returned to public life. The *convivencia chilena*, in this period the

---

[10] Kennedy to Salisbury, Santiago, 7 November 1891. No. 121. Diplomatic. FO 16/266.

social solidarity of the Chilean upper class, had clearly reasserted itself, and the Balmacedists, or Liberal Democrats as they called themselves, returned to politics as if it were business as usual. But not quite: the Balmacedists were, after all, the legatees of Balmaceda's political testament, which had forecast factional politics in the absence of a firm executive. Their task was to make the martyr's words come true. Thus, in order to expose the weakness of a febrile executive, they, more than others, combined with other groups for purely factional advantage, and left them for the same reason: their role in making the parliamentary republic unworkable was a salient feature of the period.

The political panorama at the end of Montt's presidency in 1896 was a mosaic: at one extreme stood the clerical Conservatives, led by the patriarchal Manuel José Irrarázaval, still the party of the church and determined to defend its remaining prerogatives, notably in Catholic education; at the other, the Radical party, distinguished above all by its virulent anti-clericalism and determination to make the state the universal provider of education, but schizophrenic in its attitude to class, undetermined as to whether it was exclusively the mouthpiece of the middle and professional classes or whether it should embrace the lower orders as well. Between these two genuinely ideological groupings lay the amorphous mass of liberals – the Liberal party which had broken with Balmaceda over electoral intervention but now had no ideology to bind it together beyond vague beliefs in electoral liberty, freedom of the press and of association, broad anti-clericalism and the supremacy of the Legislature over the Executive; the National party, increasingly minuscule, and distinguished chiefly by its adherence to impersonal government and, paradoxically, by its loyalty to the tradition and name of the family of Montt; and, finally, the Balmacedists or Liberal Democrats, with a common veneration for the defunct president and a loose attachment to what they believed he had stood for, but united primarily as a disruptive force, determined to extract from the new system the maximum advantage as a large minority party with the power to prevent any other grouping from governing effectively. Chile's multi-party system, antedating the revolution of 1891, but exacerbated by it, was thus distinguished by lack of ideological cohesion making for a genuine party system on the one hand, and by social solidarity across party lines on the other. Opportunism was the creed of most, and only the Conservatives and Radicals had a distinctive ideology, revolving around clerical issues, apart from the still tiny Democratic party, which, alone, actively sought artisan as well as middle-class support. That party, however, only appeared in the Chamber of Deputies in 1894 and in the Senate in 1912, so paramount was the control of the traditional oligarchy and so narrowly restricted the franchise. Chile's political and constitutional form allowed the oligarchy to play a political game, in which different groups jostled for power and influence against a national background of economic and social change which went unreflected in political representation. The 30 years between 1890 and 1920 were thus characterized by increasing social tension as economic changes increased the working class and the urban population, and pressures for social reform – in housing, education, health and working conditions – could not be expressed through political channels. The alternative outlet – sporadic violent protest – was generally met with repression, and the undoubted merits of Chile's parliamentary system, a civilized method of conducting political business on strictly constitutional lines for the small minority which took part in it, were found increasingly incongruent for a national society in a state of rapid transition.

Between 1895 and 1920, Chile's population increased from some 2,688,000 to 3,715,000; in the same period, the growth of urban and rural population more or less kept pace with one another, at around 500,000 each nationally. But the larger cities – Santiago, Valparaíso and Concepción – grew disproportionately faster than the rural population of their respective provinces. Thus Santiago's population increased from some 300,000 to 547,000, while the rural population of the province only rose from 116,000 to 139,000; the corresponding figures for Valparaíso show an urban increase from 173,000 to 266,000, and a rural rise from 48,000 to only 55,000, while those of Concepción are no less striking, with a rise in urban population from 95,000 to 142,000, and in rural, from 94,000 to 105,000.

The growth of the major cities reflected, in part, a national development in which nitrate income acted as a motor to the whole economy. Long before nitrate revenues made their impact, Chile was well on the way to becoming an integrated national economic unit as, from the mid nineteenth century, improvements in communications, and not least railways, knit the country together, enabling the government's writ to run in regions (such as the Norte Chico and the southern forest zone) hitherto largely peripheral to central government concerns. The expansion of wheat cultivation in the south, of viticulture in the central valley, of industrial enterprises in low-technology consumer goods such as textiles, ceramics and building materials – all well under way by the War of the Pacific – reflected that fact, and a degree of industrial concentration had already occurred. These processes, however, were much accelerated by the rise of nitrates in the national economy. The consumer demands of the northern *oficinas* and ports galvanized other parts of the structure, and the ripple effect of nitrate's growth on southern agriculture, for example, was noteworthy: 'Beans, maize, lentils, peas, dried fruit & c.', wrote the British Consul-General in 1887, 'are seldom exported; the Chilean producer finding for these, as for his flour and barley, a better market in the northern desert region . . . In the same way, the large and increasing wine and beer production of the south finds a market in the north . . .'[11] Moreover, the growth of government revenue derived from nitrate also had its impact. Despite cyclical falls in government income caused by the erratic nature of the nitrate trade, the overall trend of rising income from nitrate export taxes between 1891 and 1920 enabled successive governments to push ahead with infrastructural projects which employed sizeable labour forces and created consumer demands, as well as enlarging a government bureaucracy based on Santiago which itself expanded rapidly. Railways are a classic example. By 1893, the great strategic central line built by the government had reached Temuco, 690 kilometres away to the south, and by 1913 Puerto Montt, a further 400 kilometres, while to the north, by 1914 the central line reached Pintados at the southern end of the province of Tarapacá, linking there with the privately owned nitrate railways system. Also in 1914 the Arica–La Paz (Bolivia) line, 438 kilometres long, built by Chile in part-fulfilment of her treaty with Bolivia of 1904, was opened to traffic, to join the existing British-owned line from Antofagasta to La Paz. The Transandine line linking Santiago with Buenos Aires, which was under construction from the 1880s and a major feat of highland engineering, was also open by 1910, while the growth of transverse feeder lines from the central trunk along the length of Chile's heartland – many of them privately owned – proceeded apace in these years. By 1914, Chile possessed 8,638 kilometres of railways, 5,584 kilometres (over 60 per cent) of which were state-owned, compared with less than 50 per cent of the entire national network only seven years before.

The employment such construction created, and the rising permanent

[11] Newman to Salisbury, Valparaiso, August 1887. Report on the Trade and Commerce of Chile for the Year 1886 (London, 1888), *Parliamentary Papers*, C, 3.

railway labour force whose absolute number is difficult to quantify, were probably considerable, and they were a factor in rural migration. So was increasing industrialization. The parliamentary period saw a sizeable expansion of Chilean industry in terms of both the growth of establishments and their variety, and of the labour force to operate them. The food and drink processing industry, cement works, ceramics, sugar refining, clothing; leather products, wood and paper, chemicals, foundries, machine-shops and metalworking establishments all expanded considerably in the period, and largely in private hands. Much of the technology was imported; many of the entrepreneurs were foreign-born, and a good deal of capital came from outside Chile. Nevertheless, by 1914 Chile possessed an increasingly important manufacturing industry, catering primarily for national needs but with some of the larger firms holding export markets in neighbouring countries.

Government stimulation of economic activity in the parliamentary period was not, of course, fuelled entirely by revenues from taxes on nitrate exports, nor income derived from imposts on imports and exports in general, nor from taxation. A sizeable proportion of necessary funds came from foreign loans. Between 1885 and 1914, indeed, over £50 million was borrowed abroad, of which more than 60 per cent was spent on public works, including railways. But Chile's possession of nitrates, coupled with her distinguished reputation as a prompt payer of debts – even during 1891 that record was maintained – gave her high standing in international finance, and loans were easy enough to float on reasonable terms. The modernization of her major cities – Santiago and Valparaíso particularly – through the growth of transport facilities, improved lighting, sanitary improvements and impressive public buildings, owed much to this source. So did educational improvement. For, despite the instability of cabinets, government and administration went on, providing a continuing stimulus to the expansion of public services, of which education was one. Educational development is reflected in growing literacy: in 1885, it was estimated that 28.9 per cent of Chile's population was literate, but by 1910 the proportion was over 50 per cent, though heavily concentrated in the growing cities.

The parliamentary period in Chilean history, 1891 to 1920, was thus a paradox. It was a period of rapid social and economic change, but one of political impasse. It saw considerable urban improvement combined with rural stagnation, so far as the lives of its peasantry were concerned. Socially and occupationally, it was an era of transformation; while the traditional oligarchy, drawing to itself by the social magnet of acceptability 'new men' in banking, commerce, industry and the professions, and from all parts of the Republic, continued its dominance of public life, new groups had emerged – managers, bureaucrats and teachers – and new classes of urban workers, nitrate miners, the lower ranks of the public service, and the petty functionaries of all kinds of enterprises. Moreover, while the economy developed and some social services improved, others did not. The rapid expansion of the cities was marked by a disparity of housing between the urban opulence of the rich and the squalid slum settlements of the poor. A North American visitor to Santiago in 1900 wrote, 'I have been in Santiago houses which have upwards of fifty rooms, and which are furnished as expensively as some of the palaces of Europe',[12] but the *conventillos* in the working-class suburbs presented a different picture. These were one or two storey buildings, housing whole families in a single room; 'beds were often used around the clock, warmed during the day by night shift workers, then left for those returning in the evenings'. But if the cheek-by-jowl contrasts of housing in the great cities between rich and poor was great, that between urban and rural environments was even greater. 'The homes of the rotos [workers] are little better than our pig-pens', wrote our North American visitor of peasant houses in the central valley.[13] Health disparities were even greater: while the Santiago aristocrat might consult physicians in Paris or London for persistent ailments, the poor of Chile died. The overall infant mortality rate (deaths per 1,000 of live births) between 1890 and 1915 was 293,[14] but it fell disproportionately on the poor. And in education, while the overall advance was not insignificant, again the urban areas profited, the rural not at all.

It was these immense differences which created the social question in Chile during the parliamentary period, and which eventually raised the question of the capacity of the constitutional and political mechanism to cope with it. The nitrate riots of 1890 had been a portent of things to come. The first two decades of the twentieth century saw a worsening of social conflict, deriving from particular causes but occasioned by a general situation. Affecting all classes, but the poor more than most, was the steady depreciation of the Chilean peso and the incidence of inflation.

[12] Frank G. Carpenter, *South America, social, industrial and political* (New York, 1900), 218.
[13] *Ibid.*, 239.
[14] Markos J. Mamalakis, *Historical statistics of Chile*, vol. II, *Demography and labor force* (Westport, Conn., 1980), 40. This figure has been calculated from Professor Mamalakis's basic data.

The average annual increase in the cost of living was 5 per cent between 1890 and 1900, 8 per cent between 1900 and 1910, and 6 per cent between 1910 and 1920, modest rates by today's standards, but exacerbated in their effects in the Chile of the period by the impact of inconvertibility of paper money, which enabled producers and exporters to make their profits in international currencies whose values fluctuated little, while paying their labourers in paper which continually depreciated in real value. Price stability in Chile had been elusive since 1878, and was destined to remain so for another hundred years. An attempt to restore it between 1895 and 1898 when Chile temporarily returned to the gold standard failed, largely because the circumstances for conversion were most unpropitious – 1895–8 was the trough of the downturn in world commodity prices which had begun in the 1870s, and also a war scare arose with Argentina which caused the government to divert expenditure to emergency arms purchases. The defeat in 1898 of the *oreros* confirmed the monetary system as one of inconvertible paper, the internal value of which consistently fell. Not surprisingly, therefore, the workers reacted.

In 1903, the port workers of Valparaíso went on strike for higher wages and shorter hours; blacklegging led to riots, and when troops sent from Santiago restored order it was at the cost of 32 killed and 84 wounded. In 1905, when the imposition of import duties on cattle from Argentina in the interests of domestic breeders drove prices up, disturbances in Santiago went on for a week until suppressed at the cost of 60 dead and 300 wounded. This *semana roja* ('red week') was followed in 1906 by a serious strike in Antofagasta, when the British-owned nitrate and railway company refused an increase in wages and an extended midday meal break, and a year later a massive strike was bloodily suppressed at the nitrate port of Iquique, the dead being counted in hundreds. The violent expression of social protest had its counterparts in organizational resistance to labour exploitation and intellectual questioning of 'the system'.

The key figure in the growth of the organized labour movement was Luis Emilio Recabarren (1876–1924), born into a modest family in Valparaíso and a printer by trade. An early and prominent member of the Democratic party, which he joined in 1894, he found his true vocation in 1903 when invited to found and operate a newspaper for the workers' mutual benefit association (*mancomunal*) of the northern nitrate port of Tocopilla. *El Trabajo* was only the first of many workers' organs he was to create and edit. He was elected deputy for Antofagasta in 1906, but Congress refused to let him take his seat. After a period of exile in Argentina and Europe – where unproven statements say he met Lenin – he returned to Chile in 1908, broke with the Democratic party in 1911 and founded the Partido Obrero Socialista in 1912. The POS, which by 1915 had a number of branches in the nitrate north, Santiago and Punta Arenas, was held together by Recabarren's personality and energy. From his nitrate base in Tarapacá, this by now national figure created party newspapers, often of ephemeral existence but of permanent impact, and thereby recruited a small but dedicated band of followers and an imperceptibly growing force for radical social change in Chile. In 1915, the POS held its first national Congress and began to elaborate its institutional structure and to radicalize the existing trade union organizations.

Those organizations had diverse origins and a chequered history. As the Chilean working class grew, and notably the non-agrarian sector, they were faced with a lack of understanding of their living and working conditions by either those who employed them or those who, in theory at least, represented them in Congress. Lacking a true constitutional or political channel to express their grievances, workers in particular localities and specific occupations began to form a variety of self-help organizations from the late nineteenth century. Indeed, the first embryonic unions in Chile had appeared by 1870: mutualist societies among urban artisans, co-operative bodies set up to provide elementary social security for their members and some educational opportunity through self-help classes and publications, but emphasizing co-operation, not confrontation, with employers and government. For these reasons, their lack of interest in changing the social order dramatically, seeking instead a respectable place in it, was quite acceptable to governments and to the Catholic church which, following the papal encyclical *De Rerum Novarum* of 1891 (the first *ex-cathedra* pronouncement to touch seriously on social and economic questions), had patronized a philanthropic approach to the lower orders in Chile. Radically different in outlook and purpose were the so-called 'resistance societies', formed under the influence of anarchist and socialist ideas imported – sometimes by migrant workers and union leaders – from Argentina. Generally industry-based, their immediate objectives were practical, related to working conditions, and their members were united in working together, as port workers, for example, transport operatives, printers, and so on. They were forerunners of later forms of Chilean trade unionism, not least in their political outlook, but their importance declined as anarchism lost its appeal with the passage of time. Finally, and most importantly, there were the 'brotherhoods' or *mancomunales*, most strikingly emergent in the nitrate north where the mining population was ever increasing until 1914, due essentially to internal migration from the south. Socially, the *mancomunales* were highly homogeneous and, though the nitrate population was scattered – each *oficina* was virtually an independent state – there was high mobility of labour as miners moved in search of better conditions from place to place. Hence their organizations were territorial rather than occupational by nature and their concerns were living and working conditions, as well as social improvements such as education. But the *mancomunales* were distinguished above all by their class nature, and it was the *mancomunales* which, though always repressed, mounted the series of increasingly large and more serious strikes in the nitrate regions during the parliamentary period.

Yet the first proper unions arose among crafts and trades in the major cities under anarchist influence in the first decade of the twentieth century. Such were the Carpenters' and Shoemakers' Federations and, most significant of all, the Railway Workers who, a year after a wage cut by the State Railways in 1908, founded their first federation. Though essentially a mutualist body in origin, this organization named itself in 1911 the Grand Workers' Federation of Chile, and in 1917, now named the Chilean Workers' Federation (Federación Obrera Chilena, FOCH), it opened its ranks to all workers. It attracted considerable support, particularly in the north and south of Chile, less so in Santiago and Valparaíso where anarchist influence was still strong. As time went by, as social tensions increased and economic circumstances deteriorated, particularly in the period immediately after the first world war, so the FOCH became more militant. Indeed, the incidence of strikes in Chile and the number of workers involved increased dramatically in those years, rising from 16 strikes involving some 18,000 workers in 1916, to 105 strikes involving 50,000 workers in 1920.[15]

In these developments, Recabarren played a leading role, though he sought to keep his POS and the FOCH as distinct, though co-ordinated, entities. In 1919, FOCH was re-organized: thereafter, its grass-roots expression was the union which affiliated all workers in a particular area,

[15] Brian Loveman, *Chile: the legacy of Hispanic capitalism* (New York, 1979), 227.

irrespective of their jobs, and its expressed aims – like those of the POS – included the abolition of the capitalist system. The progressive radicalization of the FOCH, the impact of the Russian Revolution of 1917 and the growth of an international Communist movement deepened the division in Chilean labour between those, like the Democratic party, who, having played no small part in the organization of the working class, sought to operate within the existing political system, and those, like Recabarren, who had come by the 1920s to reject it. In 1921, the split came: the FOCH decided to affiliate itself to the Moscow-led Red International of Labour Unions and, a year later, the POS became the Chilean Communist party, but both lost members in consequence. It has been estimated that the membership of FOCH alone fell by 50 per cent, from some 60,000 to 30,000 between 1921 and 1922. By then, the parliamentary republic had reached a point of crisis.

Throughout the period of the parliamentary republic political parties and personalities, apart from the Democratic party (which never obtained the support of more than a small minority of what was, in any event, a very limited electorate), jockeyed for power, usually brief in a system of politics characterized by shifting alliances and coalitions. Indeed, for much of the period, opposing groupings were usually referred to as the Alliance and the Coalition, the distinguishing feature being the presence of the Radical party in the former and the Conservative party in the latter. Both were strong minority parties, with deep roots in antagonistic ideologies on questions of state and church, and they provided the only ideological cohesion – not always all that strong – within the two bodies. The rest – Liberals, Liberal Democrats, Nationals, and so on – oscillated in their support of different presidential candidates and their subsequent support of their ministries. The aristocratic game they played, a kind of political 'musical chairs', was obsessive as a way of conducting national business, but not even the most conservative politician was unaware that Chile was changing and that the growth of extra-Congressional forces was gathering momentum. Responses, however, varied. Throughout the period, a number of intellectuals as well as novelists like Luis Orrego Luco and Baldomero Lillo critically dissected the ills affecting the Republic, and in particular the 'social question', that widening division between rich and poor which the political system was apparently unable to resist. Essayists, such as Alejandro Venegas writing as J. Valdés Canje, and Francisco Encina in *Nuestra inferioridad económica* (1912), attacked the country's inability to develop a useful and wider educational system and to establish a truly national economy rather than one subject to the vagaries of international commodity markets or foreign entrepreneurs. While some progress was made in the field of labour and social welfare legislation – a law for workers' housing in 1906, obligatory Sunday rest for workers in 1907, laws for insurance against industrial accidents in 1917 – these were mere palliatives, so rapidly had the working class grown and so limited had been the attempt to tackle fundamental social questions. And rural labour still remained unorganized, depressed, with deplorably low living standards.

Chile's rulers in the period had some achievements to their credit. They presided over a growing economy; they had vastly improved the amenities in major cities and, not least, they had kept the country at peace. War scares over boundary disputes in the south with Argentina had erupted frequently in the 1890s, and arms races had resulted, to the detriment of both countries. But common sense prevailed: in 1902, under British arbitration, Chile and Argentina resolved their conflicting territorial claims in the far south, and signed a general treaty of arbitration for future possible disputes. Two years later a definitive treaty of peace with Bolivia ended the uncertain armistice of the War of the Pacific. No progress was made, however, on the resolution of the Tacna–Arica dispute with Peru, a legacy of that same war, despite frequent attempts to resuscitate the provisions of the Treaty of Ancón to settle it. Chile continued to control both territories and, according to persistent and bitter Peruvian complaint, to harass Peruvian residents, import Chilean settlers and thus swing the balance of the population in Chile's favour for such time as a plebiscite might be held. (At the same time, Chilean governments did put a good deal of money into Tacna and Arica, not least in education.) Yet this issue remained a war of words, protracted and bitter though it was throughout the period.

Where the parliamentary leaders stand condemned is in their apparent inability not so much to recognize a society in transition, for most were aware of changes taking place, but to reform their institutions so as to cater for them. Stronger governments in the period – and notably that of Pedro Montt (1906–10) – presided over rapid infrastructural progress, such as extensive railway building; Montt had also to cope with a devastating earthquake in 1906 which all but destroyed Valparaíso, and an economic crisis in 1907–8, fuelled by stock exchange speculation of the most irresponsible kind, yet the leadership he gave the Republic in his short period in office (he died prematurely) was largely stultified by the system he had to operate, resulting in nine ministries in four years, an average life of four months and twenty-one days. His successor, Ramón Barros Luco, aged 75 when he assumed the presidency, had fifteen ministries in five years, four of which lasted less than three weeks. Between 1891 and 1915, no fewer than 60 ministries were formed, with an average life of a little over four months. Ministerial rotation was, of course, highly democratic in form, and strictly parliamentary in practice, as the many parties jostled for power and position. Chile experienced in these years neither dictatorial government nor military intervention in politics, and these were part of a valuable historical tradition which the parliamentary period underlined. But the price was stultification of ministerial initiative, lack of long-term planning and, above all, a certain discontinuity of government business which led presidents to concentrate on immediate and necessary objectives, such as the passage of the budget or the acquisition of arms, but obliged them to neglect more lengthy measures such as social reform. It is not surprising that the strains in the social fabric of Chile were acute by the end of the period. More remarkable, perhaps, was their containment by the system to that date, despite fierce, sporadic and generally bloody confrontations of workers with the forces at the disposal of government. In this respect, continuity of administration contrasted strongly with instability of politics and government, but it was a national asset which was also eroded. As civil servants and officers in the armed forces themselves began to suffer from deteriorating social and economic conditions, their obedience to a system of government long recognized as effete could no longer be taken for granted.

ALESSANDRI, MILITARY INTERVENTION AND IBÁÑEZ

The 'social question' came to a head during and after the first world war. Though never a belligerent, Chile was an immediate casualty of that conflict, so closely integrated was her export economy in a world trading system now dramatically disrupted. Britain and Germany were Chile's two leading trading partners – indeed the former had been so for most of her independent existence; now the two major maritime powers were at war, and their ships were required elsewhere. Within two months of the outbreak, Chilean nitrate exports had fallen by more than half, and the population of the nitrate region fell dramatically as *oficinas* closed and workers returned south. Since nitrates were the motor of the Chilean economy, the dramatic fall in production – of 134 *oficinas* working in July 1914, only 43 remained active by January 1915 – had a negative effect on almost the entire structure. Yet the crisis, though severe, was also short lived. In 1915, nitrate quickly recovered, first because its use in explosives became of great importance to Britain and her allies, and secondly because the closure, through blockade, of traditional major markets such as Germany and Belgium led to neutrals, notably the United States, increasingly a supplier of munitions to the Western allies, taking larger supplies. This was a portent: one major effect of the war was to enable the United States to become Chile's chief trading partner, as Germany was largely eliminated and British interests – particularly in Chile's import trade – were inevitably curtailed. This process was accentuated after the United States entered the war in 1917, and the boom in Chilean export commodities fuelled a resurgence of general economic activity and industrial expansion, part of which – textiles, for example – grew to compensate for the lack of imports from such traditional suppliers as Britain. But, like the depression which preceded it, the boom was comparatively short-lived. The postwar depression was world-wide, but exacerbated in Chile's case by other factors: the fall in demand of nitrate as hostilities ceased, the fact that large stocks had been accumulated in consuming countries, and the impetus in Germany during the war, when natural nitrate could not be obtained, given to synthetic production. That cloud, then no bigger than a man's hand, would grow inexorably as the process spread to other countries, and would eventually destroy the market in natural nitrate. By the beginning of 1919, a large number of *oficinas* had again ceased working, with much of the labour force, as in the past, migrating south in search of work. In a deepening economic crisis, labour agitation grew markedly in 1918 and 1919 with strikes, massive demonstrations (one in Santiago in November was reported to involve 50,000 workers) and inevitably, given the near-panic reaction of the upper classes, confrontations with the police. These were often bloody affairs: in February 1919 a strike in Puerto Natales in Magallanes of virtually all workers involved in sheep-processing industries was viciously put down at a cost of 15 dead, 4 of them soldiers, and 28 seriously injured. In September, the FOCH, whose provincial branch in Magallanes had called the strike at Puerto Natales, staged a general strike in Santiago, while for part of the year the nitrate provinces of Antofagasta and Tarapacá were under virtual martial law, labour leaders being forcibly sent south.

Such was the background of the rise to national prominence of one of the more significant and controversial figures in modern Chilean history, Arturo Alessandri Palma, twice president of the Republic (1920–5, 1932–8). Of nineteenth-century immigrant Italian stock, Alessandri, born in 1868 on a farm in the agricultural province of Linares, had opposed Balmaceda when a student in 1891, had entered Congress in 1897, and had his first, short, ministerial experience a year later. A typical product of the parliamentary period, Alessandri, a Liberal, had spent almost twenty years in Congress before events in 1915 thrust him to the forefront of national life. Adopted as Liberal candidate for a Senate seat for the nitrate province of Tarapacá in elections that year, Alessandri conducted a demagogic campaign in which the passions of his supporters – many of them working class – and of his opponents spilled over into violence, culminating in March in the assassination of a police inspector. Alessandri's candidature was a direct challenge to traditional political bosses who had run the province as though it were a private fief, and he secured 70 per cent of the very limited vote in an election characterized by much corruption on both sides. More significantly for the future, he aroused national attention through his energy and eloquence, and for his vitriolic attacks on the opposition side of an establishment to which, of course, he had himself belonged for two decades. But the 'lion of Tarapacá', as he was called thereafter, had also established himself as a possible future presidential candidate.

The Congressional elections of March 1915 resulted in a majority in the Senate for the Alianza Liberal – Liberals, Radicals and Democrats – and in the Deputies for the Coalición – Conservatives, Liberal Democrats or Balmacedists, and Nationals. Presidential elections followed in June. Juan Luis Sanfuentes, younger brother of Enrique Salvador Sanfuentes whose alleged candidature as the president's nominee in 1890 had been a fundamental factor in the latter's fall, stood for the Coalición; Javier Angel Figueroa Larraín for the Alianza. Sanfuentes won narrowly, partly through his own personality but no less through his command of ready money. Supported by an unstable coalition of heterogeneous parties and opposed in the Senate by an equally fractious alliance, Sanfuentes could only deploy his not inconsiderable talents for political manoeuvre to resolve the impasse of presidential impotence, a time-wasting task and, as it turned out, a fruitless one. The next Congressional elections, in March 1918, gave the Alianza a bigger majority in the Senate and command of the lower chamber as well. But, within the Alianza itself, which did not so much represent as reflect ill-defined aspirations of the middle and working classes, a deep division existed between those such as Alessandri, who had sensed a new national mood, and those whose political horizons were still limited by the narrower struggle for power and patronage within the existing system, from which, of course, they benefited.

The Sanfuentes administration did at least maintain Chilean neutrality during the first world war, despite considerable pressure from the United States after 1917, and there is no doubt that this was in the national interest. But it created complications. Both Peru and Bolivia, where *revanchist* sentiment against Chile was very strong, had followed Washington's advice and broken relations with the Central European powers, largely in the hope of securing support for their respectives cases against Chile after the war. But little came of this: though the war of words, especially over Tacna and Arica, became more vituperative until in 1918 both Chile and Peru withdrew their respective consuls from the other's territory, actual war scares never became reality. The issue remained on ice, though it proved useful to certain Chilean political interests in 1920.

By that time, national attention – in a period of acute postwar economic depression – was increasingly focused on the presidential elections of 1920. Alessandri, having headed the ministry for a mere six months in 1918 only to see his reform programme rejected, had now clearly emerged as the candidate of those forces in the Alianza Liberal believing in change, and he had been working hard to secure that position. Within the alliance, the Radical party was achieving predominance: it had now declared its official condemnation of both the ruling oligarchy and of the capitalist system, but its rise was resented by the Liberal politicians, many of whom, no less alarmed by Alessandri's emergence, withdrew their support. These dissidents joined the Liberal Democrats and the National party, and proclaimed Luis Barros Borgoño as their candidate, Alessandri's official nomination by the other grouping following in April 1920. The Conservatives, recognizing in Alessandri the major threat to their interests and having no suitable candidate of their own, threw in their lot with the lesser evil and supported Barros Borgoño.

The campaign was marked by great personal energy and scathing

denunciation of the oligarchy by Alessandri, coupled with promises of a
sweeping programme of reform: 'I wish', he said, on his nomination, 'to
be a menace to all reactionary spirits, to those who resist all just and
necessary reform, for they are the propagandists of confusion and
disturbance.'[16] The result was very close. On 25 June, amid unprecedented scenes of public clamour, it was announced that in the electoral
college (elections were then indirect on the model of the United States)
Alessandri had obtained 179 votes to his opponent's 174. Both sides
challenged the result: finally a full Congress passed the issue to a Tribunal
of Honour, which on 30 September declared Alessandri elected, by 177
votes to 176. Congress ratified the result by a vote of 87 to 29 early in
October, and Alessandri assumed the presidency on 23 December 1920.

In the period between the election and Alessandri's finally assuming
the presidency, a peculiar incident had occurred. At a time of great
national uncertainty over the election, and with labour agitation
reaching a peak in the nitrate regions, the government, through its
minister of war, Ladislao Errázuriz, suddenly mobilized the armed
forces, alleging that Peruvian and Bolivian troops were massing on the
northern frontier for an invasion of Chile. This was complete fabrication,
yet throughout July and August a large Chilean army, posted to the
north, waited in vain in the desert region for action. While it did so, many
of its members were made acutely aware of their lack of material and
provisions; of harsh and unhygienic living conditions; of divided
commands and inadequate direction. True or not, the notion grew that
the army was being used for purely political ends, and Alessandri himself
– who in 1919 had had contacts with restive army personnel desirous of
reform – did not discourage that view. What became known as 'the war
of Don Ladislao' reinforced those opinions strongly critical of Chilean
politics and government which had been growing among service officers
for some time. As early as 1907, a military league (Liga Militar) had been
set up as a secret organization of army officers, discontented with the
parliamentary system's inefficiencies and notably those which affected
service effectiveness. Five years later, a similar body for the navy was set
up, equally clandestine, but no less concerned about professional
shortcomings and the system which permitted them. Though these
bodies never really surfaced and were, in effect, disbanded, what they
represented persisted in the minds of certain service personnel, who

---

[16] *El Presidente Alessandri y su gobierno* (Santiago, 1926), 32. No author or compiler is indicated.

increasingly saw in their own underpaid, ill-provisioned and, so far as promotion was concerned, rigidly hierarchical and immobile chains of command, nothing more than a mirror image of the Republic itself.

Alessandri's presidential programme in 1920 was an elaboration of his ministerial programme of 1918. His first minister of the interior, Pedro Aguirre Cerda (who became president in 1938) was in charge of a programme of social reform and economic measures designed to alleviate the worst effects of the worldwide depression now engulfing Chile. Though Congressional obstruction was soon apparent, the parliamentary battle was overshadowed early in 1921 by a tragic event in the nitrate regions. At the *oficina* of San Gregorio, closed at the end of January by the depression in the nitrate market, a dispute between workers and the police erupted into violence in which 41 died and 80 were injured, of whom 32 subsequently died from their injuries. To conservative opinion, Alessandri bore much of the responsibility for inflaming the masses during his campaign; for the opposite camp, he was equally responsible as head of state, ultimately in charge of law and order. In Santiago, Congressional obstruction of his programme persisted, and the opposition retained control of the Senate in the elections of March 1921, although the Chamber of Deputies fell to the Alianza, the Radicals alone gaining a third of the seats. For the next four years, little was achieved, against a background of mounting economic distress and social unrest.

In 1920 the first national census for 25 years showed that the national population had risen by a million, from 2,695,000 to 3,730,000. Santiago had doubled its population and now had half a million inhabitants. Other cities, although their growth was less dramatic, still grew at a rate quite incommensurate with the capacity of the regional economies to absorb the additional numbers in productive employment. Sixteen cabinets in rapid succession had attempted to govern over a period of four years, during which time the value of the peso had fallen by half and government revenue had slumped. By 1924, the treasury was so exhausted that civil service and armed forces' pay was six months in arrears, as one subsequently important military figure recalled many years later:

We had no certainty of getting bread, meat or vegetables for the troops, nor fodder for the horses. One day, the regiment's accountant informed me that our meat purveyor had not provided supplies because six months had passed since he was last paid . . . We could only dig into our own pockets . . . and managed to raise 100 pesos. Can you imagine that? . . . with 100 pesos to buy meat, we had to feed a regiment of 250.[17]

Public demonstrations in the face of distress increased, and a large number of protest organizations sprang up, mostly in support of Alessandri and in opposition to the obstructionism of the Senate, where the National Union, as the former Coalición was now called, had a majority.

Amid talk of civil war, Alessandri and the opposition looked for compromise, and late in January 1924 reached a short-term accord. In return for Alessandri's promise not to use executive pressure in the Congressional elections due in March, the opposition agreed to a number of procedural changes in Congressional business to speed things up. They also agreed – and the decision was fraught with unexpected consequences – to support a proposal to pay members of Congress a salary, contrary to previous practice. But as in 1890, neither side trusted the other. Alessandri, therefore, decided not only on massive intervention in the Congressional election, but also on the use of the army in that process. 'There is', he said shortly before the election, 'a majority in the Senate which . . . has sought to frustrate the movement which I represent and which, at this moment, is embodied in me . . . I have taken it upon myself to purify the parliamentary benches.'[18] Shortly afterwards, instructions about the election were telegraphed to provincial government officials, and the army was used to 'maintain order', a euphemism to cover its often blatant harassment of the opposition. But the latter was by no means inert, and intimidation and bribery were used freely by both sides. In the event, given the greater power of the governmental machine, the Liberal Alliance underlined its majority in the Deputies and won control of the Senate. It was, however, a pyrrhic victory for Alessandri. For what followed was months of sterile debate in Congress on unimportant issues, in which his own fractious following showed itself no more responsible on national issues than the opposition. The one accord they reached was on the bill for Congressional salaries, which passed from the Deputies to the Senate in June. By that time, however, the impatience of the armed forces had reached its limit, though the expression of their exasperation was by no means uniform.

In the higher echelons of the army, a conspiracy was hatched with

[17] Retired General Bartolomé Blanche, as interviewed by Wilfredo Mayorga, *Ercilla*, 7 July 1965, p. 5.   [18] Alberto Cabrero, *Chile y los chilenos* (Santiago, 1926), 258.

Unionist politicians to overthrow Alessandri through an organization called TEA (Tenacity, Enthusiasm and Abnegation), in which General Luis Altamirano, Inspector-General of the army, was involved. Lower down, a number of middle-ranking officers had been meeting at the Santiago Military Club to discuss their professional grievances and the national situation: prominent among them were Major Marmaduke Grove Vallejo and Major Carlos Ibáñez del Campo. As it happened, it was this group which pre-empted the plans of TEA by direct action, though of a moderate kind, early in September.

As the Congressional salaries bill was being debated in the Senate on 2 September, some 50 junior army officers in the public gallery punctuated the debate with loud applause for those who opposed it, and they repeated this action a day later. When the minister of war, a civilian, asked Captain Luis Pinochet for a list of those present, the latter declared that he was no clerk, but the officers agreed to leave the building if Minister Mora would meet them later, and so they departed, their sabres rattling as they left. 'The rattling of the sabres', as this episode was called, began a process of consultation between government and army which resulted in a request from Alessandri for a list of projects they thought essential, for presentation to Congress: if Congress refused them, the president declared, he would close it down and, with the army, 'make a new Chile'. The list was drawn up by Ibáñez, now emerging as the leader of the junior officers, and his aide, Lieutenant Alejandro Lazo, approved by their colleagues, and presented to Alessandri on 5 September. It was a considerable list of demands: veto of the Congressional salary bill; action on the budget (the subject of interminable wrangling in Congress); legislation on the income tax; new laws on promotion, salaries and pensions for the services; stabilization of the erratic peso; immediate payment of back salaries to all government employees; a labour code and other social laws; and, in addition to the dismissal of three ministers specifically named, the future exclusion of the armed forces from the supervision of elections. Prior to its presentation, Ibáñez had persuaded his colleagues to set up a *junta* as their executive body (the Junta Militar y Naval), and it was this body which met the president. It was not a smooth meeting, Alessandri rejecting the demand for the dismissal of ministers as insubordination, but saying that he would do his best on other matters. Lazo declared: 'we have not come to request, but to demand', and only conciliatory words from the senior officer present persuaded Alessandri not to terminate the meeting. Aguirre Cerda, as chief minister, was sent for and the list re-read; his attempts to discuss it were brusquely interrupted, and the meeting ended with the resignation of war minister Mora – one of the *junta*'s demands – and the latter's agreement to communicate through General Altamirano of the high command.

There is no doubt that Alessandri believed he could use the officers for his own purposes; it is equally clear that, whatever sympathies they had with him about Congressional behaviour, they did not trust him, and that they were determined to play not just an active role in the regeneration of Chile but the predominant one. That same afternoon, the cabinet resigned and Alessandri appointed General Altamirano as minister of the interior: Altamirano designated another General, Juan Pablo Bennet, as minister of war and Admiral Francisco Neff as finance minister, thus giving the services strong control of the administration. While some members of the *junta* distrusted Altamirano, an alliance of convenience between the military wings was formed. On 8 September, a day after Alessandri's veto of the salary bill, Congress passed all the *junta*-sponsored legislation in one afternoon, but the *junta* insisted on remaining intact until totally assured that its objectives had really been attained. Alessandri then played his last card: he proffered his resignation as president, but this the *junta* refused, suggesting instead six months' leave of absence abroad which was also approved by Altamirano. Later that same night Alessandri and his family sought refuge in the embassy of the United States, and two days later departed for Argentina, quietly and with no reaction from the people who, four years before, had clamorously installed him in the presidential palace.

Congress was then closed; the civilian members of the ministry resigned, and a governmental *junta* of Altamirano, Bennet and Neff assumed power, with the avowed intention of handing it back to civilians as soon as possible. The other *junta*, however, had other ideas: it rejected above all the notion of restored civilian rule without, first, major constitutional reform to prevent a repetition of what had led to intervention in the first place. And, unlike the new military government, whose representatives were high-ranking officers of considerable social status, the junior officers led by Ibáñez and Grove were acutely aware of Chile's social tensions and they sought social and economic, as well as political, change. The next three months saw a widening of the difference between the two wings of the military movement, against a background of widespread support for the intervention itself. The rift widened progressively from October 1924 to January 1925, as it became increasingly apparent to the *junta militar* that the government was hand-in-glove with right-wing politicians, and quite uninterested in major reforms.

Finally, in January 1925 the critical point arrived. Many prominent *junta* officers were transferred in their commands to areas where they would have little power, and were replaced by men sympathetic to the government. On 16 January, Ladislao Errázuriz, the archetypal conservative to the *junta*'s way of thinking, announced his candidature for the presidency with government support. On 23 January, after careful preparation Grove and Ibáñez sprang a coup, seized the presidential palace, forced the resignation of its incumbent, and installed a new provisional *junta*, headed by the inspector-general of the army. Four days later, he was replaced by a respected civilian, Emilio Bello Codecido, son-in-law of Balmaceda, whose assumption of office was part of the price negotiated with the navy high command, at first ill-disposed towards the coup. A general and an admiral joined Bello Codecido in the ruling *junta*, but its ministry consisted largely of Alessandri supporters, reformists to a man. A telegram to Alessandri in Rome invited his return to resume his presidency, and in March return he did to scenes of massive acclaim.

Throughout these turbulent days and, indeed, since the initial military intervention of September 1924, the key role in the activities of the *junta militar* had been played by Carlos Ibáñez, and it was he who was eventually to emerge as the major force in Chilean government for the next seven years, and, like Alessandri himself, to remain a dominant figure in national life almost until his death in 1960. Despite his long public career, his tenure of the presidency twice (1927–31, and 1952–8), his controversial governments, and the vast volume of literature which has been written about him, Carlos Ibáñez del Campo remains a most enigmatic figure in Chilean history. Nothing in his previous career suggested the role he was to play from 1924. Born in 1877, like Alessandri in the province of Linares, he entered the Military School in Santiago in 1896. He was known to fellow-students as a taciturn, methodical, hardworking cadet, but one who had few intimates. In 1900, after graduation and promotion to first lieutenant, he went with a Chilean military training mission to El Salvador, married a native of the country and, above all, distinguished himself in a conflict with Guatemalan forces in 1906. Thereafter his career was that of a Chilean military man of the middle rank. A consummate horseman, he became commandant of the Santiago Cavalry School in 1921, and was holding that post when the political crisis of 1924 occurred. By then his experience as a soldier had been varied and wide, but it had been a professional career, and he had shown no political ambition. From 1924, however, in circumstances which, in his view, called for patriotism, discipline, order and a clear sense of direction, Ibáñez found his true vocation on the national stage. His characteristics in 1927 were admirably summarized by the British Minister:

He is a man of few words, very reserved, and a keeper of his own counsels; he is poor. . . his house is a model of Spartan simplicity; he is one of the very few men in public life in Chile against whom I have never heard a charge of corruption or venality. I believe that he himself is inspired merely with his desire to serve his country to the best of his ability and his lights . . .[19]

His time, however, had not quite yet arrived.

During his involuntary exile, Alessandri had not been idle. He had spent much time thinking about the constitutional system in Chile. On his triumphant return, with six months to serve before his presidential term expired, he set about the task of its reform in a political climate which the interim government of Bello Codecido had done much to improve. The idea of a constituent assembly to thrash out a new constitution foundered, though Alessandri set up a very large Consultative Commission to deliberate the matter in April. The effective work was done, however, in a subcommittee under his own aegis, which drafted the new constitution to be submitted to a national plebiscite. Yet contrary to all appearances in Santiago, the country was not calm. In May and June, discontent in the nitrate regions erupted in violence, and Alessandri called on the army to quell it. After bloody confrontation the miners surrendered but a massacre took place at the *oficina* of La Coruña, and over 600 lost their lives. The new constitution was submitted to plebiscite on 30 August. It offered voters, who numbered a mere 302,000 out of a total population of more than three million, a choice of total approval, total rejection, or acceptance if it were amended to allow parliamentary government to continue. Only 134,000 voted, of whom 127,000 marked their papers for total acceptance; the Conservatives abstained because they objected to the separation of church and state in the new constitution; the Radicals – the largest and most significant

[19] Hohler to Chamberlain, Santiago, 25 January 1928. Annual Report on Chile for 1927. FO/A 1630/9.

political party – did the same, since they wished the old parliamentary system to continue.

The constitution of 1925 restored strong presidential government to Chile. It provided for direct presidential elections instead of the former indirect system, it allowed the incumbent to serve six years instead of five, although he was not immediately re-eligible, and it created a permanent qualifying tribunal to oversee elections. It separated church and state, with the Archbishop of Santiago, Crescente Errázuriz, acting as a moderating influence on extreme Catholics who opposed it. It limited the delaying powers of Congress on money bills, and included a whole series of important social provisions, including one giving the state the power to limit property ownership if the common good required it. It reversed the practices of the parliamentary period by making ministers accountable to the president rather than Congress, and they could not be members of Congress themselves. Yet it also contained provisions which, as time revealed, weakened its major intentions. Thus, by separating the dates of presidential, Congressional and municipal elections, it subjected the political system to permanent electioneering which thus became the main preoccupation of government to the detriment of business. It allowed for the final selection of the president by an overall majority vote in Congress should no candidate gain a plurality at the polls and, in a multi-party system where this was always likely to occur, this implied bargaining and compromise to validate the popularly successful candidate's election, another weakening factor for a possibly strong executive. Yet it was a reaction – in form at least – to the indecisive years 1891–1925, and it marked the definite expansion of state intervention in national economic affairs. But it still had to be applied.

Alessandri himself had little chance to use his new instrument, for the president was preoccupied in his last months with his minister of war, Carlos Ibáñez. The latter looked with apprehension on the return of civilian rule, and Alessandri, who on his return had surrounded himself with his old sycophantic supporters, made no secret of his animosity towards Ibáñez, the incarnation of the military intervention of 1924. He had been obliged to keep the powerful Ibáñez at the war ministry, but he hoped to ensure that presidential elections late in 1925 would lead to the elimination of the military from politics. Ibáñez, however, had other ideas. Increasingly convinced – and with some reason – that the oligarchy and the politicians had learned little from recent events, he now put himself forward for the presidency, but refused – as precedent demanded – to resign from the war ministry, his lever of power. Fearful of the consequences of a head-on clash, Alessandri resigned in October, handing over power *ad interim* to his opponent of 1920, Luis Barros Borgoño. But at this point, for reasons still obscure, Ibáñez wavered, and agreed to withdraw his candidacy if *all* the political parties could agree on a sole candidate, and this they did, choosing an elderly, amiable but not particularly astute public figure, Emiliano Figueroa Larraín. Only one other candidate stood, a former army doctor and minister of health in the government which preceded Alessandri's return, José Santos Salas, who, with a campaign starting from scratch, without political party backing and without funds, secured 80,000 votes to Figueroa's 184,000. Santos Salas represented the lower classes in that election: he did not win but his candidacy was a sign that the old political parties did not go unchallenged.

For a year and a half, the unhappy Figueroa struggled with a recalcitrant Congress, where the parties reverted to their old political games, and also with his minister of war, Ibáñez, who quietly, efficiently and ruthlessly built up his personal position to the point where in February 1927 he secured the resignation of the minister of the interior and his own appointment to the post. Two months later, President Figueroa resigned; the immediate cause was the demand of Ibáñez for the dismissal of Figueroa's brother as head of the Supreme Court, part of a general clean up he had initiated of the public services which had resulted in widespread arrest and exile. When Figueroa went, Ibáñez took over as president until elections could be held. At the same time, he declared his intention of standing himself, and he had widespread support. Only the now-struggling Communist party – for that body too had suffered from Ibáñez who was a staunch anti-communist – put up a competing candidate, Elías Lafferte, then in exile on the Pacific island of Más Afuera. At the election in May, Lafferte got 4,000 votes; Ibáñez, 127,000 of the 137,000 cast. Thus, elected constitutionally if not exactly properly, Ibáñez assumed the presidency of Chile, with the mission he had been refining since 1924, that of regenerating the Republic in his way.

Ibáñez gave Chile four years of autocratic – some would say repressive – efficient, honest and prosperous government. His ministers were not appointed with any regard to the parties in Congress but were chosen as individuals of technical competence and administrative ability. Indeed, his deliberate intention was to ignore Congress except in so far as it was necessary, under the new constitution, to collaborate in the passage of legislation. And he would brook no opposition there: as the British Minister reported in 1928, Congress had

received Cromwellian treatment at the hands of the President, who has made it clear that the flowers of oratory which grew so luxuriantly in its atmosphere are not to his liking; that they, the two Chambers, are there to give an air of constitutionality to the measures of his government, and that though a little constructive criticism will be accepted, obstruction or opposition . . . will not be tolerated.[20]

Nor was it: left-wing agitators (as Ibáñez saw communists and socialists), professional politicians (whom in the mass he profoundly despised), aristocratic leaders of society – all who opposed his government were treated alike, and faced imprisonment or exile for persistent and troublesome opposition. He restricted freedoms to which Chileans had grown accustomed, such as that of the press which, though not rigorously censored, was certainly watched. He effectively curtailed the privileges of Congress which had degenerated into licence under the previous system; he sought to bring trade unions under central control, and he was tough on their leaders. But such curtailment of rights previously enjoyed, and no less often abused, Ibáñez justified on the grounds of national necessity, as he embarked on an ambitious administrative, economic and social programme.

Credit institutions were set up to encourage both agriculture and industry, and a large programme of public works was inaugurated. A whole stream of educational reforms was initiated – the educational budget doubled between 1925 and 1930 – and they included specific provisions for the growth of technical education, the lack of which had been so lamented by social critics of the parliamentary era. The 'social legislation' of 1924–5 was codified and elaborated; the modern police force of Chile, the *carabineros*, was created through re-organization and better training facilities, and the armed services were professionalized further and well equipped. Many of these reforms had their unattractive side: the new labour laws, for example, were highly paternalistic, but they did recognize for the first time workers' rights to organize, to bargain for improvements with employers, and also, though in a limited way, to strike. There seems little doubt that, with employment rising and the visible signs of economic recovery all around in new works – ports, roads, schools, docks, irrigation projects in the countryside, impressive

[20] *Ibid.*

public buildings in the cities – the Ibáñez era brought the Chilean population as a whole a higher standard of living than ever before, and it is a moot point how many were tacitly prepared to pay the price of losing some freedoms for that result. The politicians, of course, were not: throughout his presidency Ibáñez was plagued by plots and rumours of plots, inspired and often organized by former friends who had now become enemies. But as long as the economy continued to grow, as long as the mass of the people remained content, and as long as the armed forces remained loyal and the political dissidents under control, all would be well.

For three years all did go well. Indices of output volume by sectors – gross domestic product, agricultural production, mining, industrial output and construction – for the period 1914–30 reached their highest peak in 1927–30.[21] Construction advanced spectacularly, as did mining, the latter because of the recovery of nitrates from the depression of the mid 1920s and the rapid growth of large-scale copper mining, exemplified by Chuquicamata in the north and El Teniente in the central valley. Chilean exports, by value in pounds sterling, rose from about £22 million in 1926 to over £34 million in 1929; imports from almost £18 million to £24 million, thus giving Chile a highly favourable balance of trade. At the same time, there was a massive growth in foreign investment: though Ibáñez enacted protective legislation for certain nascent industries, his attitude towards foreign capital for major projects, as in copper mining and public works, was one of liberality, and foreign (notably North American) money poured into Chile during his presidency. United States investment in Chile rose from only $5 million in 1900 to $625 million by 1929, much of it made during the Ibáñez years. Indeed, the predominant position of US interests in large-scale copper mining really derive from this period. The Ibáñez government also contracted large loans abroad to finance the public works programme, and had, in these euphoric years, little difficulty in doing so. Yet budget surpluses were the rule, despite heavy outlays on the new credit institutions, partly because Ibáñez's minister of the treasury for much of the time, Pablo Ramírez, reformed the internal tax structure, producing almost 33 per cent of state revenue from internal taxes in 1929, compared with 24 per cent in 1927.

Ibáñez also had another major achievement to his credit – the

[21] Gabriel Palma, 'Chile, 1914–35: de economía exportadora a sustitutiva de importaciones', *Nueva Historia*, 7 (1982).

definitive solution of the vexatious and long-standing boundary dispute with Peru over the territories of Tacna and Arica. Alessandri had himself, as president, re-opened the issue with Peru, and in 1922 both countries had agreed to submit the question to the arbitration of President Harding of the United States, though what question was to be submitted was not clear. When the parties met in Washington it was only after much tergiversation and legal wrangling that terms were agreed, but in 1925 President Coolidge, Harding's successor, handed down his award: it ordered the plebiscite to be held, and thus broadly upheld the Chilean position, while giving Peru definitive title to a small portion of still-disputed territory, not clearly in Tacna. A commission was established to oversee the plebiscite, and detailed arrangements made to hold it. The political turbulence in Chile in 1925 and further legal wrangles, charges of violence and violence itself punctuated the history of the North American commission until June 1926, when, complete impasse having been reached, it returned home. Before this, however, the United States government had offered both Chile and Peru its good offices as mediator to try to reach an accord by direct negotiations which both sides accepted, though not until July 1928 did the two countries actually resume diplomatic relations, broken off long before. It was Ibáñez who grasped the nettle and, ironically, it was Emiliano Figueroa who went to Peru as ambassador with his proposals in 1928. After much detailed negotiation, but now in an atmosphere of ever-growing cordiality, agreement was reached in 1929; Tacna was returned to Peru; Chile retained Arica. Peru was also to receive US$6 million in compensation for the definitive cession of Arica, and other clauses regulated future border relations and commercial traffic across them. It was a major diplomatic and international initiative, but it did not please all Chileans, and it gave Ibáñez's enemies further ammunition to accuse him not only of internal repression but also of betraying the country.

If economic well-being was the main pillar of Ibáñez's efficient but tough government, the erosion that set in with the advent of the Wall Street crash of 1929 was to undermine it and bring it down. So dependent was Chile in the late 1920s on its primary commodity exports, nitrates and copper, and on foreign loans and investment continuing to fuel public works and development in general, that the dramatic interruption of both exports of commodities and imports of capital, beginning in late 1929 but reaching the peak of its impact in 1930–2, made Chile a primary victim of the world depression which then set in. In 1929, Chilean exports were valued at 2,293 million gold pesos, imports at 1,617 million; she had a favourable balance of trade valued at 676 million gold pesos. By 1930, exports had fallen to 1,326 million gold pesos, and imports to 1,400 million, leaving a deficit of 74 million. By 1932, exports had fallen to 282 million gold pesos by value, and imports to 214 million in the depths of the world depression – Chile's foreign trade, in fact, suffered more than that of any other country in the world. Investment stopped, and by 1932, Chile had to suspend payments on its foreign debt for the first time in over a hundred years.

The social consequences of the dramatic economic downturn appeared first in mining. At the end of December 1929, 91,000 men had been employed in the industry; two years later only 31,000 were in work and, as in previous similar situations, the ripple effects of falling demand for minerals appeared in other sectors of the economy, not least agriculture as markets for foodstuffs declined. As 1930 proceeded, the Santiago newspapers were full of reports of growing unemployment, the abrupt cessation of public works, ministerial studies of economies in administration, cuts in the salaries of government servants, and similar indications of a deepening crisis.

Retrenchment was the government's only possible response, but government revenue fell faster than its capacity to cut expenditure. And, since the economic benefits brought to Chile by the Ibáñez regime were the main justification for acceptance of its political limitations, the disappearance of those gains revived political criticism and censure. The government became increasingly unpopular: press attacks on its handling of the crisis increased and demonstrations began. Ibáñez, struggling against a situation he could not have foreseen, reacted by attempting to silence the critics, and the authoritarian nature of the government was underlined in stricter control of the press, more imprisonments of opposition leaders and physical suppression of demonstrations. By the early months of 1931 the situation had become critical and the central structure of power was beginning to break up.

On 9 July 1931 the finance minister resigned 'for reasons of health', and the whole Cabinet followed, to give Ibáñez a free hand, but it took several days to form a new ministry. The new minister of the interior was Juan Estéban Montero, a Liberal, who, with the finance minister, frankly admitted recent errors, political and economic. Encouraged by such openness, opposition groups took heart: on 19 July, for example, at a meeting of the National Association of Catholic Students, one participant attacked military involvement in government and praised the new ministry. His hopes were premature, as two days later, unable to get its way with Ibáñez, the Cabinet resigned, and another was appointed whose members were closer to the president's way of thinking. Massive street demonstrations began to form in the late afternoon, and grew more boisterous as night came. Amid scenes of mounting tension, the civilian members of the new ministry then resigned, but the next one, formed on 23 July, was faced with street demonstrations in which large numbers were injured and which culminated on 25 July with large-scale violence in different quarters. The medical profession then declared a strike, as did the lawyers, banks closed at midday and commercial activity stopped. The news was then released that the previous day a young medical student, Jaime Pinto Riesco, reading a newspaper with a group of friends, had been shot in cold blood by a policeman who had tried to snatch the paper from him. It was this incident which acted as the final catalyst of resistance to the government: a large number of professional associations (*gremios*) – lawyers, doctors, engineers, dentists, teachers and bank employees – all demanded the restoration of full public liberties, and while public agitation mounted a teacher was also killed by the police. By 26 July it was only too clear that Santiago was on the brink of chaos and, bowing to the inevitable, Ibáñez resigned. The news was met with wild scenes of rejoicing and public demonstrations. As a leading Santiago daily newspaper expressed it: 'What overthrew the dictatorship was not a revolution, but quite the opposite. It was the irresistible force of public opinion which sought to put an end to a revolutionary situation and return to constitutional and legal normality.'[22] The writer might have been less sanguine had he been able to foresee that in the eighteen months after the fall of Ibáñez, Chile would experience no fewer than nine governments in office, ranging from moderate conservative to avowedly socialist, two general strikes, a mutiny in the fleet, and several coups, as the country plunged deeper into economic depression. All that lay in the future as Ibáñez, isolated now more by circumstances than by temperament, went into exile in Argentina. But, like Arturo Alessandri's in 1925, his eclipse in 1931 was temporary. Both would cast long shadows across future Chilean history.

[22] *El Diario Ilustrado*, 24 August 1931.

16

BOLIVIA FROM THE WAR OF THE PACIFIC TO THE CHACO WAR, 1880–1932

The year 1880 marked a major turning point in Bolivian history. The most dramatic event was the total defeat of Bolivia's army at the hands of the Chilean invaders and the loss of its entire coastal territory in the War of the Pacific. Less dramatic but equally important was the establishment of a new government to replace the previous *caudillo* regime. Though the replacement of governments by military coups had not been an uncommon feature of political life in the Republic during the half century since its creation, the new regime did in fact mark a fundamental change in national political development. It represented the first viable republican government of a civilian oligarchic nature. Though the loss of its direct access to the sea remained the most intransigent of Bolivia's international problems from 1880 to the present day, the establishment of a modern political party system and a civilian-dominated government led to political, economic and eventually even social and cultural changes which profoundly shaped Bolivia's historical evolution.

The fundamental stabilization and maturation of Bolivian politics after 1880 was not the result of the war with Chile, but rather derived from basic changes within the Bolivian economy that had begun at least 30 years previously. Whereas Bolivia had been a major mineral exporter throughout the period of colonial Spanish domination, it emerged in the republican period as a minor exporter of silver and other minerals. The collapse of the imperial economy in the 1790s, the regional agricultural disasters of 1804 and 1805, the devastation of the civil wars and international conflicts of the independence period (1809–25), the break-up of the imperial customs union, and finally the collapse of the *mita* system of forced labour after 1825 all contributed to the decline of the silver mining industry. In the 1840s production was only half that of the

1790s. By 1846 it was estimated that there were some 10,000 abandoned mines in the Republic, two-thirds of which still contained silver but were flooded and incapable of producing without the introduction of capital and machines on a major scale. There were, in fact, only 282 active mine owners and their mines in the Republic in 1846 and they employed only some 9,000 miners, most of whom were part-time specialists who worked in agriculture as well.

Apart from mining, woollen textiles for home or local consumption and food processing were the predominant national industries. In the years after independence the republican government attempted to develop the cotton textile industry. But despite sporadic prohibitions and continually heavy tariffs against cheap English cottons, the textile industry of Cochabamba producing *tocuyo* (coarse cotton cloth) never regained its eighteenth-century importance. Whereas in the colonial period it was estimated that the *tocuyo* industry of Cochabamba had several hundred *obrajes* (workshops) producing cloth, these numbered just one hundred by 1846. The cheap cotton textile needs of the Bolivians were now filled by British cloths which dominated the market.

Bolivia thus remained an overwhelmingly rural society. Almost 90 per cent of the 1.4 million population lived outside the cities and hamlets and produced over two-thirds of the national product. Within rural society, the balance between haciendas and free Indian communities remained much as it had been in the late colonial period. In 1846 there were over 5,000 haciendas valued at 20 million pesos, and some 4,000 free communities valued at only 6 million pesos. The majority of the work force, however, lived in the free communities. According to the 1846 census 5,135 heads of families were hacendados and 138,104 heads of households lived in the *comunidades*. Over 620,000 Indians lived on the communities and they made up a total of 51 per cent of the total rural population. The hacienda population of *yanaconas* (or landless labourers) probably numbered between 375,000 and 400,000, and the other 200,000 persons of the rural population were probably freeholders in the southern regions or landless migrating workers who rented lands from either the communities or the haciendas.

While the haciendas obviously constituted the more commercially valuable properties, they nevertheless were in a relative state of stagnation and posed no serious threat to the densely populated regions where the free communities predominated, except in two exceptional areas: the Yungas and the Cochabamba valley. The former was the major

Table 1. *Population of Bolivia for the principal departments
and capital cities, 1846, 1900, 1950*

Department Capital	1846	1900	1950
La Paz	412,867	426,930	948,446
La Paz	42,849	52,697	321,073
Cochabamba	279,048	326,163	490,475
Cochabamba	30,396	21,881	80,795
Oruro	95,324	86,081	210,260
Oruro	5,687	13,575	62,975
Potosí	243,269	325,615	534,399
Potosí	16,711	20,910	45,758
Chuquisaca	156,041	196,434	282,980
Sucre	19,235	20,907	40,128
Santa Cruz	78,581	171,592	286,145
Santa Cruz	6,005	15,874	42,746
Tarija	63,800	67,887	126,752
Tarija	5,129	6,980	16,869
Beni	48,406	25,680	119,770
Trinidad	3,194	2,556	10,759
Total	1,378,896	1,633,610	3,019,031

Sources: **1846:** José M. Dalence, *Bosquejo estadístico de Bolivia* (Chuquisaca, 1851). **1900:** República de Bolivia, Oficina Nacional de Inmigración, Estadística y Propaganda Geográfica, *Censo general de población, 10 de setiembre de 1900* (2 vols., La Paz, 1902–4). **1950:** República de Bolivia, Dirección General de Estadística y Census, *Censo demográfico, 1950* (La Paz, 1955).

source of coca production. The latter had seemingly recovered from the economic shock of the late colonial crisis and was now the principal national producer of the two basic grains, wheat and corn.

Within the free communities there was, however, continuing change and much internal stratification. The elimination of the *mita* obligation had clearly favoured the *originarios*, or original members of the communities with the greatest access to lands. Their numbers seems to have grown or at least stabilized and they were estimated in the 1840s to represent 35 per cent of all heads of households in the free communities. The *agregados* with land (or later arrivals with lesser landholdings in the communities) represented 42 per cent of households and a new and important group of *foresteros* without any land now accounted for 23 per cent of all Indian families. Evidently, the slow growth of population was beginning to create a landless class of Indians in the free communities themselves.

The stagnation of the mining industry and the failure of national manufactures to meet local demands meant that for the first quarter century of its existence – from 1825 until well into the 1850s – Bolivia was in the unusual position of being in a constant deficit in its balance of trade, which could only be met by the illegal exportation of silver and by a very active contraband trade. Government deficits were a constant phenomenon as expenditures, especially of a military nature, far outstripped the resources of the state treasury. By mid-century, Bolivia was if anything in worse condition than it had been at the beginning of its republican life, and it appeared that things would only deteriorate further. However, in the decades after 1850, paradoxically coinciding with the most chaotic political turmoil and violence, the export sector of the Bolivian economy – the mining sector – achieved steady growth, first in the traditional *altiplano*, and later in new areas on the Pacific littoral.

The cause of this growth still remains to be fully determined. To begin with, it is evident that a series of events external to Bolivia played a decisive role in awakening the mining giant. The increasing productivity and declining costs of the steam engine in Europe and North America in the first half of the nineteenth century meant that the steam engine of the 1850s and 1860s was a far cheaper and more readily available and reliable item than it was in the 1820s. Thus the costs of opening up a flooded mine were considerably reduced. Moreover, the growth of Peruvian and Chilean mining in this period provided a general regional background of capital and technical expertise which could be readily exported to the incipient Bolivian industry. Finally, the decline of international mercury prices reduced a major traditional cost item for silver extraction.

These were the favourable general international conditions for the expansion of the mining industry in the Bolivian *altiplano* in the third quarter of the nineteenth century. The capital, however, was at first Bolivian, and the key question remains: where did this capital come from, given the relative stagnation of the Bolivian economy during the quarter of a century after independence? From an analysis of the early mining companies in Potosí and Oruro, it is evident that a disproportionate share of the capital stock came from the merchant and landed aristocracy of the grain-producing Cochabamba valley. It would thus appear that the steady but unspectacular growth of the national population, despite some rather severe cholera epidemics in the 1850s, created an expanding internal market for agricultural production, especially for corn and wheat. From this, the Cochabamba elite was able to extract surplus capital. Also Cochabamba seems to have had a class of incipient entrepreneurs who were more than willing to undertake the risks of heavy capital investments in the traditionally quite unpredictable mining industry.

Starting in the 1830s, it became popular to establish national joint stock companies to mine silver, the most important of which was the Huanchaca Mining Company founded in 1832 to work the Porco mines in the province of Potosí. After heavy investments and many difficulties the company was purchased by the merchant Aniceto Arce in 1852, who was finally able to realize a profit from its production. It was also in the mid 1850s that the Aramayo family bought out the bankrupt Real Socavón Mining Company of Potosí. Finally in 1855 the merchant Gregorio Pacheco took over the Guadalupe mines from one of his debtors in the Chicas district of Potosí province. Thus within a few years the three major silver mining dynasties were implanted in the mining districts of Potosí. With new infusions of capital and leadership, the reorganized companies began to prosper. By the 1860s the three leaders were well into rationalizing their operations and undertaking long-term structural changes in the industry through the introduction of modern machinery, pumping operations and long-term shaft reconstructions. In the 1870s when the silver mines of Caracoles on the Pacific littoral also came into full operation, foreign capital began to arrive in ever increasing amounts. By the second half of the decade the Bolivian silver mining industry can be said to have reached international levels of capitalization and technological development and efficiency. By the late 1870s Bolivia was once again one of the world's leading producers of refined silver, and a thriving and vital export industry had revitalized both the internal economy and Bolivia's international trade.

The development of a modern sector created new demands not only for labour but also for foodstuffs. A new dynamism entered the area of commercial agriculture and the opening up of the new railway links created new markets for hitherto marginal areas. As a result the hacienda system, which like mining had been stagnating for almost half a century, was able to recover and expand. At the same time, the decline in the

Table 2. *Silver production in Bolivia, 1780–1909 (output in marks of silver)*

	Average annual production	Maximum year output	Minimum year output
1590–99[a]	803,272	887,448	723,591
1740–49[b]	92,119[c]	111,947	81,081
1780–89	387,170	416,676	335,848
1790–99	385,283	404,025	369,371
1800–09	297,472	371,416	194,347
1810–19	208,032	338,034	67,347
1820–29	156,110	177,727	132,433
1830–39	188,319	288,154	169,035
1840–49	191,923	256,064	142,029
1850–59	201,482	224,313	189,573
1860–69	344,435[c]	391,304	312,174
1870–79	955,629[c]	1,150,770	391,304
1880–89	1,111,568[c]	1,660,804	597,686
1890–99	1,655,762	2,630,907	1,202,927
1900–09	799,791	1,288,452	385,522

Notes: [a] Maximum output decade in the colonial period.
[b] Minimum output decade in the colonial period.
[c] Estimated production figures. All production figures after 1859 have been converted from kilograms to marks at the conversion rate of 230 grams = 1 mark.
Sources: **Pre-1780:** see the more complete table in Herbert S. Klein, *Bolivia, the evolution of a multi-ethnic society* (New York, 1982), appendix table 2; **1755–1859:** Ernesto Rück, *Guía general de Bolivia, primer año* (Sucre, 1865), 170–1; **1860–75:** Adolf Soetbeer, *Edelmetall-production und Werthverbaltniss zwischen Gold und Silber* (Gotha, 1879); **1876–91:** *The mining industry, its statistics, technology and trade*, vol. 1 (1892), 207; **1892–3:** *ibid.*, vol. 11 (1893), 333; **1894:** *ibid.*, vol. vii (1898), 203; **1895–1904:** República de Bolivia, Oficina Nacional de Inmigración, Estadística y Propaganda Geográfica, *Geografía de la república de Bolivia* (La Paz, 1905), 354–5; **1905–9:** Walter Gómez, *La minería en el desarrollo económico de Bolivia* (La Paz, 1978), 218–20.

importance of the Indian head tax, at one time the major source of government revenues, meant that the national government no longer had a vested interest in protecting the free communities in their lands. The land titles of the free communities were challenged during the administration of Mariano Melgarejo in the 1860s, but Indians resisted and the communities effectively retained control over their lands. But by the 1870s the whites and *cholos* (*mestizos*) were increasing their pressure and the growth of new markets provided the economic incentive for the landed elite to undertake a full-scale attack. The attacks were justified on the classic nineteenth-century liberal grounds that the communities were an anachronistic system of land tenure and a barrier to social integration. The dominant landed class forced upon the communities in the 1880s a system of direct land purchase in which the titles to the land were held by individuals and not the corporate group. The creation of a free Indian 'peasantry' holding *de jure* title gave the hacendados the power to break up the *de facto* control of the communities by purchasing a few small parcels and thus destroying the cohesion of the community. The rest was simple, with fraud and force being as comon as simple purchase, and soon there was a major expansion of haciendas throughout the highlands and the adjacent sub-puna valleys.

Thus the period from 1880 to 1930 saw Bolivia's second great epoch of hacienda construction. Still holding half the lands and about half the rural population in 1880, the Indian communities held in 1930 less than a third of both. The power of the free communities was definitely broken and only the marginality of the lands they still retained and the stagnation of the national economy after the 1930s prevented their complete liquidation.

The progressive decline of the community meant not only the loss of land title, but of social cohesion as well. While many of the haciendas re-created the political and social organization of the free communities, the hacienda *ayllus* or governments, were often powerless to protect their members from expulsion from the estates. Moreover, the need for labourers on the estates was less than the requirements had been for the former free communities. The result was an increased breakdown of Indian social norms, migration to the cities and the expansion of the *cholo* (or *mestizo*) population, rural and urban. The only thing preventing a total destruction of Indian culture was the continued growth of the Indian peasant population throughout the nineteenth century. Though a series of epidemics at mid-century had slowed that growth, the disappearance of such communicable diseases as cholera by the last quarter of the century allowed for the continued strong rates of growth. In addition, in the absence of public education in the countryside prior to the 1930s, the mass of the rural population remained not only illiterate, but largely ignorant of even the national language. Quechua remained the predominant language, with Aymara second.

Bolivia remained predominantly a rural and Indian peasant nation well into the twentieth century, despite the growth of a modern export sector, the dramatic expansion of the commercial agricultural network and the hacienda system, and even the growth of modern urban centres. In 1900 at least three-quarters of the population remained rural and indigenous peoples still accounted for a little over 50 per cent of the total population of 1.6 million (see table 1 above). Spanish remained a minority language in the Republic, though the only one used in national economic and political life.

The civilian governments which were established in Bolivia after 1880 were constructed on the base of a small percentage of the national population. To all intents and purposes they were representative only of the Spanish speakers, at most only a quarter of the national population. And given the literacy requirements for voting, as well as the financial restrictions for holding office, the Bolivian regime was in every sense of the word a limited participation political system. The electorate numbered only 30,000 to 40,000 persons in the period up to 1900. The elite were concerned to keep the Indian masses out of politics as well as denying them access to arms or any other effective means of protest. The army, especially after its professionalization and modernization, became an indispensable tool to maintain Indian submissiveness, and was constantly called upon to suppress the periodic Indian uprisings. The elite divided into political parties and even resorted to arms to overthrow governments. But such acts of conflict and violence were quite circumscribed and largely urban and intra-class affairs. Appeals from the elite to non-elite and non-Spanish speaking groups were extremely rare and the political life for the period 1880–1932 was largely carried out within strictly defined rules. Only once, in 1899, would Indian peasants be allowed to participate even temporarily in a national political conflict, and this intervention ended in total suppression of the Indian *kurakas* (chieftains). For the Indian rural masses, political expression was confined to traditional village elders or temporary leaders of revolts who led them in 'caste wars'. These were uprisings confined to small communities and were exclusively defensive in nature, either protesting against increasing exploitation in general or attacks on land rights in particular. Until well into the twentieth century, national politics were the exclusive concern of only 10 to 20 per cent of the population.

Intellectual life, which had stagnated since independence, revived after 1880 under the combined impact of relatively stable civilian government, increased national wealth, the professionalization of the occupations, and the establishment of modern curriculums in the schools. Individual writers now found kindred groups, and individuals of elite families had ample opportunity to live abroad, and participate in the latest Latin American or European movements. Thus the Bolivian poet Ricardo Jaimes Freyre joined Rubén Darío in Buenos Aires and was a powerful voice in the modernist movement which swept through Spanish American and Spanish letters. Writers like Gabriel René Moreno, Bolivia's leading historian, found employment in the libraries and archives of Chile, and novelists and essayists like Alcides Arguedas, living in Paris, became known throughout the Americas. Bolivians came to term the writers who came of age in this period as the 'generation of the 1880s'. It was the first really coherent generation to appear in the literary life of the Republic and provided an important base upon which all later cultural developments were built. The period from 1880 to 1920 was in many ways a golden age for national literature.

In the sciences, however, the traditional structures of the national universities prevented any serious advance. Although the Bolivian mining industry was as technologically advanced as any in the world by the 1880s, all its machinery and its engineers were imported from the best schools in Europe and North America. Few native engineers were produced and no significant discoveries, even in metallurgy, occurred in Bolivia. The problem in what Bolivians called the 'exact sciences' was the total lack of an infrastructure. Low budgets and part-time teachers prevented the development of scientific laboratories or systematic research. Whereas novelists, poets, essayists, historians, even social scientists could develop out of the traditional professions of law, theology and medicine, this was not possible in the sciences or technology. While Bolivians trained and working abroad did participate in the development of modern science in the advanced countries, until the present day Bolivia has remained an importer of science and technology.

In the plastic arts, economic stagnation and the concurrent decline of the Catholic church in the first decades of the nineteenth century had served to bring to an end the great age of creative artistic activity of the colonial period. Sucre's elimination of tithes and confiscation of church incomes and properties had brought the building of churches to a halt. With the church and wealthy pious citizens no longer available for patronage, the demand for paintings and carvings also declined. The nineteenth-century church also became less tolerant of folk catholicism, more timid in its acceptance of native *cholo* and Indian art styles and archly conservative in its overall artistic taste. Thus when church revenues again became significant after 1880 and major construction was resumed, the clerics and the white elite rejected Bolivia's rich colonial artistic heritage and slavishly adopted the most reactionary of European models. The result of these factors was the stagnation of Bolivian plastic arts until well into the twentieth century, and the elimination of the Indian and *cholo* masses from significant participation in the cultural life of the nation.

The growth of the export sector, especially the silver mining industry in the second half of the nineteenth century, and especially during the two decades after 1880 (see table 2 above for silver production, 1880–99), made the Bolivian economy increasingly vulnerable to international economic forces. Both the importers of manufactured goods who paid for their purchases with hard currency earned from mineral exports, and the government which had become totally dependent on taxes on international trade, were now intimately involved with the fortunes of the export sector, which in turn became ever more vulnerable to fluctuations in international demand the more successful it became. Thus the government, the mine owners and the national elite were subject to international constraints creating problems of stability over which they had little control.

Bolivia was a classic example of an open economy. Since the bulk of internal purchasing power came from the leading mining sector, it was extremely vulnerable to changes in prices of its primary exports. Moreover, even in the mining sector, until late in the twentieth century, it was an economy dominated by one metal – silver until 1900, and then tin. Thus world price changes had a direct and immediate impact on the local economy. Powerful regional elites could be eliminated overnight by abrupt changes in international prices with a consequent disruption of the very foundations of the governing elite. Bolivians learned to live with this uncertainty and tried to respond as quickly as possible to new price incentives. But the limitations of natural resources guaranteed that their response also had its limits and that long-term economic progress was not inevitable for the nation as a whole. It was this uncertainty which explains much of the behaviour of the mine owners who were the predominant political leaders in the post-1880 period.

Having initially organized themselves politically to break the government monopoly over foreign sales and forced local purchases, the new mining elite soon began to operate as a more coherent pressure group to obtain governments more responsive to their needs. With their mines coming into full production just as a long-term secular decline in silver prices was beginning on the world market, the new elite was constantly forced to lower costs and raise productivity. This involved the increasing use of machinery, of electricity and, above all, the modernization of transportation, the most expensive element in the mining process. While the mechanization of the mines and their electrification would be the exclusive concern of the Bolivian mine owners, the transport problems were beyond even their capital resources. Government subsidies and international finance were imperative. Thus the miners wanted stable civilian government whose fiscal resources could be devoted to massive railway construction.

Political parties were created in Bolivia out of the divisions and debates over the War of the Pacific. For the Bolivian mine owners the outbreak of the war in 1879 was a terrible shock. They saw it as a fatal break with their new sources of capital in Chile as well as a serious disruption to international trade. They blamed the preceding military regimes for the war and, grouping themselves around two key figures, Mariano Baptista, a lawyer for the mine companies, and Aniceto Arce, the nation's largest single mine owner, formed a powerful pro-Chilean peace party. Eventually the party threw its weight behind the enlightened General Narcisco Campero who had helped overthrow the Daza military regime in December 1879, and who then directed the diminished Bolivian war effort. The Bolivian mine owners sought a rapid end to the conflict with Chile and indemnification for all lost territories to be used exclusively for railway construction. Meanwhile, the anti-Chilean and anti-peace group gathered their forces behind the popular Colonel Eliodoro Camacho, the leader of the anti-Daza revolt and a leading liberal theoretician. Thus the Conservative and Liberal parties emerged by the end of the war. They were supposedly ideologically opposed. But the Conservatives, who modelled themselves on other similar Latin American parties, were, for example, only modestly pro-clerical. And although the Liberal party was vigorously anti-clerical, the Bolivian church, which had been nationalized by Bolivia's first republican government, was too weak to be the cause of serious conflict. Both parties in fact concentrated their energies on the problems of political and economic modernization.

General Campero completed his legal term in office, and presided over completely free elections in 1884. The eventual winner, after the necessity of a congressional second count, was the maverick mine owner, Gregorio Pacheco, Bolivia's second leading silver producer. With Mariano Baptista as his vice president, Pacheco initiated the era known as the 'Conservative Oligarchy', which lasted from 1884 to 1899. During this period the two parties fully defined themselves, while successive governments concentrated on achieving a settlement with Chile and promoting major railway construction.

Although Pacheco promised to remain neutral in the elections of 1888, in fact the Conservative regime threw its support behind Aniceto Arce. As a result, the election of 1888 became a violent affair with the embittered Liberals finally abstaining altogether. Thus there was a return to the use of violence in politics in the late 1880s. This resort to violence was made inevitable by the refusal of all governments, Conservative and, later, Liberal, to relinquish the presidency to the opposition party. Once in office and close to the only major source of income apart from mining and the haciendas, politicians refused to give up the spoils in office. Voting in all elections was open and readily controlled by central government appointees in all the local districts, and victories in both presidential and congressional elections were easily contrived. The governing party guaranteed its majority in Congress, but did permit a substantial representation there of the opposition parties, to provide an easily supportable escape valve which did not seriously threaten its own control over office. The position of president, however, had to be secured at all costs. Throughout both Conservative and Liberal eras, therefore, political violence was endemic. But it should be stressed that this violence was usually restricted to civilians, to the urban environment, and involved little bloodshed. Violence also seemed to be confined to periods following elections when a defeated opposition party, and most of the voters, felt that the government had violated their rights. The tradition of *golpes* (*coups d'état*) remained a permanent part of the political landscape, but they did not necessarily represent either the breakdown of civilian rule or the instability of political life. While later commentators on Bolivia were to count the number of revolts and assume total disruption, the period from 1880 to 1936 was in fact one of remarkable continuity and stability despite the periodic resort to limited violence.

The presidency of Aniceto Arce (1888–92) was notable for the initiation of the vital railway link from the Chilean port of Antofagasta to the city of La Paz, thus giving Bolivia access to the sea by rail for the first time in its history, and the beginnings of a modern road network. Arce, in what proved to be the most productive of the Conservative regimes, was also instrumental in professionalizing and controlling the army. Another fraudulent election in 1892 brought Mariano Baptista, the ideologue of the Conservative party, to the presidency. Like his predecessors, Baptista (1892–6) concentrated on railway construction. He also signed a preliminary peace treaty with Chile and began the development of Bolivia's natural rubber resources in the Acre territories. In his turn Baptista handed over the presidency to the last of the Conservative oligarchs, the mine owner Sergio Fernández Alonso (1896–99). By this time, however, the power of the Conservative regime, which was firmly entrenched in southern silver mining areas and the city of Sucre, was being progressively eroded by the collapse of silver prices on the world market. In contrast the Liberals found their strength progressively increasing, associated as they were with the rising urban professional classes of La Paz and with non-silver mining groups, above all the new tin miners, who aimed to displace the Conservative oligarchy.

The rise of tin production as the primary industry of Bolivia after 1900 had its origins in developments during the Conservative era. The great age of the modern silver mining industry had seen Bolivia obtaining the latest in mining technology, including the use of power tools and electricity. At the same time, the silver magnates and their Conservative regimes had made modern communications their primary task; in particular, a vital rail network connecting the mining regions to the Pacific coast had been constructed.

When silver collapsed on the international market, technology and communications existed which could be transferred to other metals. In this case a fortuitous expansion in the world demand for tin (for canning and a hundred other new industrial uses), coinciding with the exhaustion of the traditional European tin mines, allowed Bolivia to capitalize on its resources and to respond quickly and effectively. Tin had been an important by-product of silver mining from the earliest times. But the costs of shipping it in bulk to European smelters had always been prohibitive, primarily because of Bolivia's geographic isolation and primitive communications. The availability of cheap railway transportation meant that it suddenly became profitable, for the first time, for Bolivia to export tin. Equally, the fact that tin was to be found in exactly

Table 3. *Tin production in Bolivia, 1900–39 (output in metric tons)*

	Average annual production	Maximum year output	Minimum year output
1900–09	14,909	21,342	9,739
1910–19	24,710	29,100	21,324
1920–29	33,216	47,191[a]	19,086
1930–39	25,864	38,723	14,957[b]

Notes: [a] 1929   [b] 1933.
Source: Walter Gómez, *La minería en el desarrollo económico de Bolivia* (La Paz, 1978), 218–20.

the same mining areas as silver, and often in the very same mines, meant that there was relatively little economic or social dislocation in the shift from silver to tin.

For the traditional silver elite the transition was less easy to accomplish. First of all, the growth of tin mining took on a boom-like quality as production rose from quite minimal levels to massive exports in a period of less than ten years. Although the general mining zones remained the same, there was a subtle but important shift of emphasis northwards, with the mines in northern Potosí and southern Oruro having the dominant role in production. Finally, the shift was so sudden and the capital invested in fixed assets so heavy, that many silver miners found it difficult to change over to tin. The result was that a plethora of foreign companies entered the market, and a new group of Bolivian entrepreneurs emerged for the first time on the national scene.

All these changes caused a major rupture in the national political scene. The old Conservative elite, entrenched in Potosí and its supporting town of Sucre, found itself incapable of containing the growth of the opposition Liberals. At the same time the enormous expansion of La Paz, which now became the key servicing centre for the new tin mining industry, accentuated its dominance in national economic and social life even further. This led to a combined Liberal and regionalist revolt in 1899, in which the largely Liberal elite of La Paz called for local autonomy and the overthrow of Conservative rule.

The revolt of 1899 was in fact a rather costly and extensive military operation, which proved so difficult to win that the Liberals went beyond the traditional rules and encouraged the Indian peasant masses to participate. The result was the temporary intervention of some Indian groups in national political life for the first time since the early years of the Republic. But once victory was achieved by the Liberals, not only was federalism forgotten as La Paz became the *de facto* capital of the nation, but the Indian troops were disarmed and their leaders executed.

The new century thus saw the establishment of a new government and the creation of a new mining industry. The Liberal regime differed from the Conservative regime in few fundamental aspects. Both were committed to massive government subsidization of transport, heavy support for the mining industry and the development and modernization of its urban centres. Both regimes actively sought the destruction of the Indian communities and the expansion of the hacienda system. Finally, both proved to be indifferent to the question of the church, which caused so much conflict in most other Latin American states.

During the Liberal era, the old patterns of political participation persisted. While congressional elections remained relatively free, elections for the presidency were controlled, with a corresponding resort to limited violence as the only means for 'out' politicians to reach the executive office. An open press and civil liberties (for whites and *cholos*) were maintained. But a new type of political leadership now emerged. Reflecting the complexities of the new mining era, the tin miners were far too involved in their own affairs to participate directly in national life. At the same time, the systematic support given to education and professionalization by the Conservatives had created a class of lawyers and *letrados* sufficiently numerous and experienced to run the affairs of the government. Thus was born what later political analysts would call the *rosca*, a government of professional politicians operating primarily in the interests of the leading tin barons of the nation. The economic power groups were now no longer required to intervene directly in the political process to obtain their own ends. The tin miners were able to concentrate fully on the intense and competitive struggle for domination in the Bolivian tin mines.

There were no restrictions on foreign investments in the tin mines and from the beginning of the tin boom Bolivia was open to all types of entrepreneurs and engineers from abroad. European, North American and even Chilean capital competed with local Bolivian capitalists for control of the tin mine sector, and hundreds of companies were established, many of them often working the same local mountain of tin. It is therefore perhaps surprising that after three decades of intense competition Bolivians emerged by the 1920s as the dominant group in the industry.

Of the three major leaders, the most powerful was unquestionably Simón I. Patiño. Born in the Cochabamba valley in 1860, Patiño appears to have come from an artisan and part *cholo* background. He received a local secondary education and then apprenticed himself to various mining and mine equipment importing firms in the 1880s and early 1890s when the silver industry still predominated. In 1894 he purchased his first share in a tin mine in Oruro, in the canton of Uncía on the border of the province of Potosí. By 1897 Patiño had acquired by purchase full control of the mine, and in 1900 he struck one of the richest tin veins ever found in Bolivia. By 1905 his La Salvadora mine had become the single largest tin mine in Bolivia, and Patiño had a full complement of foreign technicians and the latest in refining equipment. From this initial investment, Patiño rapidly expanded his holdings both vertically and horizontally. In 1910 he bought out his neighbour, the British-owned Uncía Mining Company, and in 1924 completed his domination of the two mining centres of Uncía and Llallagua by buying the Chilean Llallagua Company. He now controlled about 50 per cent of national production, with a labour force of over 10,000 workers.

Meanwhile Patiño turned his attention to the vertical integration of his mining operations, and, in a move rare in Latin American capitalist circles, moved to control his European refiners. After joining forces with his North American consumers, he eventually took over in 1916 the world's largest smelter of Bolivian tin, Williams, Harvey and Company of Liverpool. By the early 1920s, Patiño lived permanently abroad and could by then be more accurately described as a European capitalist, given his vast non-Bolivian holdings. Nevertheless, he remained Bolivia's dominant miner, its chief private banker and its most powerful capitalist until his death in 1943.

Of the two other leading tin miners who emerged to divide evenly the other half of total production, one was also Bolivian, belonging to the old silver mining family of the Aramayos, and the other, Mauricio Hochschild, was a European Jew. Both the Aramayo and Hochschild companies had heavy inputs of European capital, but both were – unlike the Patiño firms – largely run from Bolivia itself. While Hochschild had some investments in Chile, his primary residence virtually to the end of his career was in Bolivia, and this was also his principal area of investment. For the Aramayo family too Bolivia was the primary area of activity. Thus by the 1930s, the big three miners who dominated tin production, and a good proportion of the lead, zinc, wolfram and other local mines as well, were based primarily in Bolivia or, like the Patiño companies, wholly owned by Bolivian nationals. Given the totally open nature of the Bolivian mining industry to all foreign entrepreneurs since the middle of the nineteenth century, such national control was truly remarkable.

The withdrawal of Patiño and the other new tin magnates from direct involvement in national affairs left Bolivian politics in the hands of an elite of rising urban upper middle-class professionals and representatives of the provincial landed elite (men of modest landholdings and relatively few peasants, but with solid social backgrounds). Almost all these men had legal training, and while committed to a liberal conception of parliamentary government and constitutional law, believed strongly in the caste system and rule by the white oligarchy.

The social structure of Bolivia remained surprisingly stable, despite all the recent and very rapid changes. Only 13 per cent of the population were listed as 'white' in the census of 1900. Equally, while the census suggested a major growth in urban population since 1846, this was based on the rather generous definition of urban as any community over 200 persons. Using the more realistic definition of towns over 20,000 population, however, little significant change had occurred. From 1846 to 1900, the percentage of the population living in such towns had increased from 6 per cent to only 7 per cent. Even La Paz, the largest urban centre, had only grown to some 55,000 persons in 1900, or just 12,000 more than half a century before. Though new mines had created several new towns in southern Oruro and northern Potosí, the booming mining industry in 1900, with its 13,000 workers, still absorbed only 1 per cent of the economically active population.

Thus despite the growth of a new export sector, the expansion of a new elite, both white and *cholo*, and the massive breakdown of Indian landownership in the rural areas, Bolivia remained surprisingly traditional in its social makeup. The Liberals therefore felt little compulsion to concern themselves with the serious class and caste problems which divided this multi-ethnic society.

The first Liberal president was José Manuel Pando (1899–1904), the great leader of the party in its years of opposition. Once in office, the Liberals virtually adopted all the policies of the Conservatives and, for example, totally rejected federalism. Pando's administration, however, is best known for its abandonment of traditional international positions, and the loss of national territory. The first of two major international disasters was the Acre dispute. In the heart of the Amazonian rubber boom area, the Acre territories adjoined the Brazilian border and were largely populated by Brazilian migrants. When the last Conservative regime succeeded in establishing a customs house on the Acre river at Puerto Alonso and collected an enormous sum on the rubber being shipped through to Brazil, the local tappers revolted. The Liberal government sent in troops to the distant eastern lowlands to crush the revolt, but covert Brazilian support gave the rebels enough strength to stand firm. The result was total defeat for Bolivian arms and the annexation of the Acre territory to Brazil, for the sum of £2.5 million, in the Treaty of Petrópolis in 1903.

The Liberal government had made a stand on the Acre territory – and lost. It was much less aggressive on the Chilean front. Here it went well beyond the most extreme concessions ever proposed by its Conservative predecessors in an attempt to obtain funds and terminate a long-standing and politically sensitive issue which it felt was distracting national resources. Reversing their previous irredentist stand, which demanded an unqualified return of the territory seized during the War of the Pacific, the Liberals signed a formal peace treaty with Chile in 1904. Bolivia agreed to cede all its lands seized along the littoral, and gave up its demands for a Pacific port. In turn Chile agreed to construct a railway from Arica to La Paz, provide a formal indemnification of £300,000, guarantee internal Bolivian railway construction loans, and give up its special most-favoured nation arrangements on trade with Bolivia. While the treaty formally resolved the Pacific littoral question, the issue has in fact remained the major unresolved question of Andean international relations to the present day. At the time the Acre and Chilean accords gave the Liberals relative peace on the international front and extensive financial support to continue the railway construction programme.

The second president of the Liberal era was Ismael Montes (1904–9). A lawyer by training, Montes represented the new breed of middle-class urban politicians. A forceful personality with a shrewd instinct for politics, he was able effectively to prevent the rise of an opposition party of 'outs' until after the first world war. In this effort he was aided by the beginning of the boom in the economy brought about by the rising exportation of tin (see table 4). This provided the funds for the expansion

Bolivia

Table 4. *Bolivia's foreign trade, 1895–1930 (in current thousands of bolivianos)*

Year	Exports	Relative value of minerals (%)	Imports	Difference
1895	20,914	n.a.	13,897	7,017
1896	22,047	n.a.	12,952	9,095
1897	21,990	n.a.	12,457	9,533
1898	27,457	n.a.	11,897	15,559
1899	27,366	n.a.	12,840	14,526
1900	35,658	(67)	13,344	22,314
1901	37,578	(72)	16,953	20,625
1902	28,042	(79)	14,143	13,898
1903	25,162	n.a.	16,253	8,909
1904	31,465	n.a.	21,137	10,328
1905	42,061	n.a.	27,870	14,191
1906	55,155	n.a.	35,810	19,344
1907	50,332	n.a.	37,898	12,434
1908	43,786	(89)	40,808	2,978
1909	63,764	(64)	36,940	26,825
1910	77,622	(72)	48,802	28,820
1911	82,631	(76)	58,371	24,260
1912	90,123	(81)	49,509	40,614
1913	93,722	(82)	54,763	38,959
1914	65,801	(85)	39,761	26,040
1915	95,210	(86)	22,575	72,636
1916	101,485	(81)	31,098	70,387
1917	157,748	(87)	33,481	124,267
1918	182,613	(91)	34,970	147,643
1919	144,252	(88)	61,997	82,254
1920	156,019	(91)	65,340	90,679
1921	66,920	(91)	70,853	−3,934
1922	94,770	(94)	49,967	44,802
1923	107,694	(94)	62,915	44,779
1924	115,191	(95)	62,863	52,328
1925	109,286	(90)	68,665	40,621
1926	122,681	(92)	70,831	51,850
1927	127,084	(92)	96,105	30,979
1928	116,073	(93)	64,391	51,683
1929	140,007	(94)	71,417	68,590
1930	100,306	(93)	52,442	47,864

Sources: Gomez, *La minería*, 191–2, 208–9; and República de Bolivia, Oficina Nacional de Inmigración, Estadística y Propaganda Geográfica, *Sinopsis estadística y geográfica de la república de Bolivia* (3 vols., La Paz, 1903–4), II, 294, 300.

of the state bureaucracy, which in turn he used to buy out all potential opposition.

Moreover, the national elite was also effectively won over to the new Liberal era by a massive commitment to public works. With a positive and sizeable balance-of-trade surplus, Montes was able to secure private international bank funding for governmental loans. In 1906 came a huge US private bank loan which enabled Bolivia to complete its international rail connections with spurs to the major interior cities of Cochabamba and Sucre as well as the international links to the mining centres of Potosí and Oruro. A new railway was constructed to Guaqui on Lake Titicaca, thus linking up with the Peruvian rail network. Major urban construction, sanitation and lighting projects, and generally a high pitch of economic activity took place until the crisis of 1913–14 on the eve of the first world war.

Montes was able to dominate the selection of his successor, Eliodoro Villazón, and then to secure his own formal re-election in 1913. But the second Montes administration (1913–17) was not the unqualified triumph the first had been. Liberal attempts to establish a national bank had created bitter opposition from key elements of the elite. Next the sudden prewar crisis in international trade caused mineral exports to decline by a third between 1913 and 1914 (see table 4). At the same time adverse weather conditions caused a severe agricultural crisis. With government revenues declining, Montes suddenly found himself with an intransigent opposition within the party which he could not buy off. Moreover, having been in power so long, he was unwilling to use tact or subtlety to calm it. The result was the almost inevitable splintering of the Liberal party into two separate groups. The new party which emerged was given the name Republican and was formally established in 1914.

Both Montes and the founder of the new party, Daniel Salamanca, recognized that the new political party was a carbon copy of the Liberals. It drew its strength from the same classes; it unquestioningly supported all demands of the mining establishment; and it was as racist and oligarchic as its opponents. Montes called the Republicans liberal 'apostates', and Salamanca claimed that his party's aim was only to guarantee free elections and restrictions on presidential power. The final result of the return to the two-party system was a recurrence of closed and fraudulent presidential elections and the ultimate resort to violence and coups by the opposition.

The recovery of Bolivia's exports during the first world war (see table 4) enabled Montes to carry through his banking and financial reforms with little Republican opposition, and even to win popular support among the 80,000 or so voters in the Republic in congressional and presidential elections. In 1917 he passed his government on to a more moderate successor, José Gutiérrez Guerra, who proved unable to keep the Republicans under control. With strong support from disgruntled elements in the business community, the Republicans made considerable headway and when Gutiérrez Guerra attempted to control the elections of 1920, the Republican party rose in a successful revolt and ended Liberal rule.

The advent of Republican rule, which lasted until 1934, brought a subtle but important shift in the political system that had evolved since the end of the War of the Pacific. From simple two-party systems, national politics began to evolve towards a multi-party system. At the same time the cultural norms inherited from nineteenth-century liberal ideology and supported by a strong element of racism would slowly begin to change. Finally, the extraordinarily open nature of the national economy would mean that Bolivia was one of the first nations in the world to feel the full effects of the world depression which followed the Wall Street crash of 1929.

The economic growth which had been the hallmark of both Conservative and Liberal periods had initially affected only certain elite groups. By the second decade of the twentieth century, this growth was beginning to have important effects on the *cholo* and Indian sectors. The expansion of the haciendas led to increasing land conflict with the community Indians which in turn led to a series of major revolts in the 1920s. Of even more immediate importance for the elite was the organization of the first modern labour unions in Bolivia. Though organizational activities went back to the nineteenth century, Bolivia was several decades behind its neighbours in labour agitation and organization. It was not until 1912 that the first May Day celebration was held, and it was not until 1916 and 1917 that even local urban labour confederations were established. There were no important national strikes until 1920.

In the 1920s the elite became aware of the existence of alternative demands and of potentially threatening groups outside the elite political arena. As political life became more complex in the Republican era, minor parties emerged which for the first time seriously discussed the problems and potentials of class conflict. The 1920s also witnessed the first stirrings of European Marxist thought as it filtered into Bolivia through Argentinian, Chilean and Peruvian writers.

Almost immediately after seizing power, the Republican party divided into two opposing branches, one led by the urban middle-class intellectual, Bautista Saavedra, and the other by the Cochabamba hacendado and politician, Daniel Salamanca. It was Saavedra and his followers who were able to seize the initiative and take control of the government and the party in 1921. Salamanca and his forces established a new 'Genuine Republican' party and proceeded to agitate actively against the new regime.

The political violence and social conflict in the 1920s was more intense than anything experienced in the previous decades. Hardly was Saavedra installed in office when a massive Indian uprising in Jesús de Machaca in the Lake Titicaca district led to the killing of hundreds of Indians and dozens of local whites and *cholos*. Saavedra unhesitatingly used full force to suppress the revolt and attacked the community governments (*ayllus*) as reactionary institutions that had to be forcibly suppressed. Thus he took a classic nineteenth-century liberal position on the Indian question.

But Saavedra proved more open in his views on organized labour. He began to view it as an important area of potential support, as his own bases in the upper and middle classes were eroded by Genuine Republican and Liberal opposition. He initiated the first modern labour and social legislation in Bolivian history, and expressed a willingness to support limited strike activity and unionization drives – the first time a national president had done so. But faced by increasing strike activities, including serious agitation in the mines and the first general strike which occurred in 1922, Saavedra quickly found himself withdrawing his tentative support. In fact, troops were used in a bloody suppression of miners at Uncía in 1923, one of the first of many such mining massacres.

The 1920s was a period when other members of the elite began slowly to adopt non-traditional positions. In 1920 the first local socialist parties were established. By late 1921 a national Socialist party was founded which, though a small group of intellectuals with minimal labour support, nevertheless began to discuss such basic issues as Indian servitude (*pongueaje*), the legal recognition of the Indian community governments, and the rights of labour and of women. While these ideas were new and revolutionary in the Bolivian context, they were already part of the well-established and more radical Marxist political tradition of all Bolivia's neighbours, including Peru. The famous splintering of the Latin American Marxian socialist parties and the rise of the communist movements in South America in the 1920s, for example, found no echo in Bolivia. Bolivia did not produce even a moderate Marxist party until the end of the 1920s, and its Communist party was established only in the 1950s.

Much of this early labour agitation was associated with the short but very intense depression of the early 1920s which resulted in a severe though temporary drop in mine production and mineral exports (see table 4). Once production resumed by late 1922, labour agitation began to subside. Moreover, Saavedra found that the nascent organized labour movement, though finally establishing its first national federations and producing its first general strike, was too weak a support for his regime. The lower middle classes, finding themselves favoured for the first time by mild social legislation, supported Saavedra. But given his strong personality, it was inevitable that the Liberals and Genuine Republicans would join forces to oppose his regime, and he found it more and more difficult to govern. In his search for popular support he turned towards foreign private capital markets for funds to promote major development projects. He negotiated a US$33 million private banking loan in New York to finance railway construction, public works and a national bank. These were the classic concerns of Liberals and Conservatives before him. But debt servicing for Bolivia was already high and the terms of the loan, which included direct US control over Bolivian taxation services, were totally unacceptable to most Bolivians. There was little question, in fact, that Bolivian negotiators had been corrupted and that despite its excellent credit rating the nation had been forced to pay very high interest rates. The opposition to the so-called 'Nicolaus' loan was immediate and intense.

To add to his problems, Saavedra in the arbitrary manner of Montes also tried to resolve the great debate surrounding the petroleum concessions in the Bolivian eastern lowlands region. In 1920 the Republicans had opened up the reserve areas to foreigners after Bolivian entrepreneurs proved incapable of developing productive wells. In 1920 and 1921, North American entrepreneurs secured concessions, but these smaller companies were fronts for the Standard Oil Company of New Jersey, which in 1921 was permitted by the government to purchase these concessions, add new ones and establish the Standard Oil Company of Bolivia. Given all the special treatment accorded to Standard Oil, and the intense opposition of the elite to Saavedra, it was inevitable that there would be an outcry.

To all the usual issues of corruption, favouritism and presidential domination, Salamanca and his more conservative followers added a totally new theme: economic nationalism. Opposition to exploitation of natural resources by foreign companies started in Bolivia virtually as soon as the first concession was granted in petroleum. While no outcry was ever raised over mining, and Guggenheim and other North American companies actively participated in the economy, petroleum became a special issue and the attack against Standard Oil became part of the rhetoric of both the traditional right and the nascent left movements in Bolivia.

By the end of his term, Saavedra was desperately attempting to appease all factions. On the one hand he helped the mine owners crush the Uncía strike in June of 1923, with indiscriminate killing of workers and their families. On the other hand he carried out a major overhaul of the mining tax structure in late 1923 and succeeded in doubling the government's taxes on tin production. In a rage, Patiño early in 1924 removed his mining company headquarters from Bolivia to the United States and incorporated Patiño Mines and Enterprises in Delaware. He also lent the government £600,000 for railway construction, in return for a guarantee that taxes would not be raised further for five years.

Despite every attempt to control his successor and even prorogue his term, Saavedra was forced late in 1925 to turn his regime over to his own party candidate Hernando Siles, whom he opposed. The following period saw a further splintering of the traditional parties. Faced by Saavedra's control of the Republican party, Siles created his own Nationalist party grouping. He supported the University Reform movement, and in 1928 radical students established the first FUB (National Federation of University Students of Bolivia). Both the socialists and the FUB, though still small groupings of intellectuals, were now suggesting radical transformations of society, with both calling for agrarian reform and the end to 'feudalism'. They urged nationalization of Bolivia's natural resources and changes in the definition of private property, and gave strong support to the nascent labour movement.

At the same time as the political scene was evolving into a more complex arena of conflicting class ideologies, the Bolivian economy began to deteriorate to an alarming degree. In the period 1926–9, the government faced increased budgetary deficits and growing difficulties in meeting its international debt obligations. This was occurring just as the price of tin on the international market had peaked and had begun its long decline into the catastrophe of the world depression. In an attempt to meet this crisis, whose extent was as yet unknown, the government resorted to both traditional and some fairly radical measures. In 1927 and 1928, with the backing of specially created taxes, new US private bank loans were secured. In 1928 the government adopted the reforms proposed by the US Kemerer mission and finally established a government-controlled Central Bank to oversee all aspects of the national money supply. Towards the end of 1928, a temporary flare-up on the disputed Chaco border with Paraguay, which presaged even more bitter conflicts to come, forced Siles to call up the reserves and order reprisals. He did not want a full-scale war to develop, however, and early in 1929 he negotiated an Act of Conciliation with Paraguay.

Politically, Siles had already shown himself to be too much in the traditional mould to permit the free play of democratic forces. The border incident with Paraguay gave him the excuse to declare a formal state of seige and use it to control his internal enemies. This in turn had the effect of galvanizing the Liberals, the Genuine Republicans and the Saavedrista Republicans into a temporary united front.

Meanwhile, the deterioration in international tin prices was making itself felt. In 1929 Bolivia reached its all-time record output of 47,000 tons of tin exported, but at a price which was below that of the early years of the decade. Whereas tin was quoted at $917 a ton in 1927, it had dropped to $794 a ton in 1929 and would eventually bottom out at $385 a ton in 1932. As tin prices declined, so too did government revenues which were primarily taken from tin export taxes. By 1929, 37 per cent of the government budget was going for foreign debt servicing, and another 20 per cent for military expenditure, leaving little for bare government necessities, let alone for public works or welfare.

Justifying his actions, like his predecessors, on the existence of a national crisis, Siles tried to continue in office beyond his presidential term. In mid 1930 he announced plans to have parliament elect him for a new term. He then handed the government over to a military *junta* to oversee his formal re-election. But opposition to this move was universal. For the first time in national politics university students made their power felt by conducting major riots against the government. In response, the army rose in rebellion, and the *junta* was forced to flee. (In the midst of the disorders there was even an invasion of Marxist radicals at the southern frontier town of Villazón. They attempted to lead a worker–peasant uprising, an action which found some echo in the urban labour movement.)

In the following months, an all-party agreement allowed Daniel Salamanca to run unopposed in the presidential elections of January 1931. Salamanca, who took office in March, was however a politician even less attuned to the new developments on the student and labour fronts than either Saavedra or Siles. He was a rural landowner from Cochabamba, a famous parliamentary orator and otherwise an extremely intemperate and unbending nineteenth-century style liberal. His only immediate programmes were honest government and free elections, and even these meaningless slogans he violated as rapidly as his predecessors.

It is clear that by 1930–1 the oligarchic republican government based on limited participation which had been established by the Conservatives in the 1880s and continued by the Liberals after 1900 was beginning to come apart. The world depression struck the open Bolivian economy with unparalleled severity. Tin prices dropped dramatically, production fell and government revenues declined precipitously. At the same time debt servicing arrangements virtually destroyed the government's ability either to generate new unmortgaged taxes or to find funds for even the most minimal necessities. The subtle but by now clearly important shift in political ideology of the governing classes also began to be felt. The university student reform had brought radical Marxist thought into the homes of the white elite for the first time in national politics. The labour movements began to attract national attention with ever more severe strike activity, leading to military intervention in the mines and open warfare. The only popular class which remained relatively quiescent in this agitated period was the Indian peasantry, which had been unusually restive during the previous decade; massive uprisings, one at Jesús de Machaca in 1921 and one at Chayanta in Potosí in 1927 had been suppressed with much bloodshed.

In many ways the depression gave a reprieve to the Salamanca government. Massive lay-offs of workers forced many miners back into the countryside and into subsistence farming, while the depression wiped out most of the gains of the weakly organized labour movement. Indian peasants grew even more passive as the great age of hacienda expansion drew to a close with the end of heavy capital investments in rural landholdings. On the other hand, the university youth would not quietly disappear, and the depression created a greater political awareness which Salamanca was incapable of responding to, except with repression. By the standards of the other countries of South America, Bolivian radicalism remained weak and relatively unsophisticated and a good generation or two behind developments in bordering countries. But the consistent refusal of Salamanca and his followers, unlike the Republicans of the 1920s, to offer a hearing to these ideas meant that the marginal radical and reformist groups found themselves forced into an even more violent confrontation with the traditional political system. These groups were nevertheless still only a small sector of the elite society, and might never have become the threat they did had not Bolivia undergone the greatest military disaster of its history under the leadership of Daniel Salamanca. The Chaco War was to provide the crucial disruptive force by which the traditional system of the 1880–1932 period would finally be destroyed.

The origins of the prewar crisis went back to the decline in tin prices which began in 1927. By 1929 the stocks of unsold tin were also rising, which depressed prices even further. At this time Bolivia, with three other tin producing regions (Nigeria, Malaya and Indonesia), provided close to 80 per cent of world production. Of the four, Bolivia had the lowest-grade ore and the highest transportation costs, and was therefore the highest-cost tin producer. It thus felt the shock waves first and also found it impossible to force the other major producers to cut production voluntarily, since at negative prices for Bolivians the others could still obtain some profit margins. In July 1929 at the urging of Patiño, a voluntary Tin Producers Association was formed by the private companies working in the four major centres of production. They agreed to production cut-backs, which all three major Bolivian companies eagerly carried out in late 1929 and early 1930. But the non-Bolivian companies did not follow suit and by mid 1930 the voluntary scheme was considered a failure.

With free market conditions intolerable and voluntary restrictions impossible to achieve, the producers decided in late 1930 to take the drastic measure of demanding government participation in the production control scheme. This was a major and abrupt change from the private mine owners' former belligerent stand against any kind of governmental intervention in private enterprise. For the first time, the

Bolivian government was assigned the right not only to tax the industry but to control production quotas, and this would lead in the following decades to control over foreign sales. Clearly this was an act of desperation by which the main producers hoped to retain direct control over governmental decisions which affected them. But equally, it made possible the first really powerful intervention of the government in mining affairs. Although there would be rough agreements over quotas, the much reduced production schedules for all the firms meant that any one of them could easily and quickly increase production if their market quotas were changed by governmental decree. This suddenly introduced a special tension into the relationship between the big three mine owners, and brought their competitive conflicts into the very corridors of government. The big miners began to pay considerably more direct attention to the local political scene than they had for some time, and they began to support differing factions in the elite itself.

Since there were only three major governments involved – Bolivia, the Netherlands and Great Britain – it turned out that a forced quota production system could be successfully carried out, and in early 1931 the International Tin Control Scheme was initiated. On 1 March 1931, just a few days before the inauguration of the new Salamanca government, the quotas went into effect and Bolivian production was drastically reduced, creating a massive internal economic crisis for the Republic. Although the scheme of restricting production eventually reduced the world's unsold stock of tin and finally stabilized the price, it was not until 1933 that Bolivian production slowly began to return to even moderate levels.

All these international changes and the resulting shock to the local economy were closely followed by the Bolivian elite. The interim government (June 1930 – March 1931) had experimented with public works schemes and fully supported all Patiño's production plans. It also cut budget outlays to the barest minimum. Serious attention was paid as well to the various national recovery projects being tried out elsewhere in the world. Of all the groups engaging in this debate about the national economy, the Liberals offered the most concrete proposals. Although their approach was an orthodox one, they suggested serious government intervention. But Salamanca seemed oblivious to the whole issue. Constantly asked what his economic ideas were, he replied evasively about the need for honest government. Such vacuous ideas might have been acceptable in times of growth with a stable social order, but were meaningless in the current context. The result was that his Genuine

Republicans suffered total defeat in the congressional elections of January 1931 and the new Congress fell to the Liberals, who had an absolute majority of votes. The rigid Salamanca suddenly found himself faced by a hostile Congress completely outside his control, with an economy he little understood, and a society in severe malaise for which he could provide no solutions.

Almost immediately upon taking office, Salamanca proceeded to alienate most of the major groups in the society. While the previous government had essentially continued the policies of the Saavedra and Siles periods of moderate reform and a strong interest in welfare as a result of the economic crisis, the Salamanca regime was a return to the more rigid orthodoxies of the past. Salamanca also alienated the traditional elite parties by making his government a partisan one, despite the all-party support which had brought it to power.

His first Cabinet in office, despite the domination by the Liberals in Congress and the calls for a government of conciliation to deal with the economic crisis, consisted only of Genuine Republicans. Next he announced to a rather startled public that the primary problem facing the country was not the economic crisis, but radicalism and communism. While radical and communist groups had finally established themselves in national life during the 1920s, they were still essentially a fringe minority, even among the university youth and organized labour movements. This obsession with the 'red' threat was something entirely new on the part of a traditional politician. Moreover, Salamanca radically shifted government policy from a moderate neutral stand on labour to one of open hostility. A national strike by the legal Telegraph Workers' Union was not only opposed by Salamanca, but the union was dissolved, and a sympathetic general strike of the La Paz labour federation was also forcibly suppressed and its leaders jailed. Next the government announced that government employees would be paid in promissory notes as a result of the budget deficit, and in late July 1931 Salamanca announced that Bolivia was defaulting on its external debt.

As the internal economic and political scene became ever tenser, Salamanca began to give much more of his attention to the Chaco border question. Indeed he elaborated the most ambitious and expensive scheme for military penetration of the Chaco ever envisioned by a Bolivian president. It represented a major shift in national policy from a largely defensive to a largely offensive position. On 1 July 1931, Salamanca used a typical border incident to break diplomatic relations with Paraguay. Then, in his presidential address in August, he announced that as a consequence of the continued decline in government revenues virtually all government services had been cut, but went on to announce that the military budgets would be expanded. At the same time a policy of total suppression of union or strike activity among the organized working classes of the nation was proposed. Thus Salamanca had defined extreme positions at the same time as limiting all his political options.

In June, Salamanca had brought Demetrio Canelas, an Oruro party leader, into the ministry of finance. Canelas broke with the conservative policy of the previous months and pressed Salamanca on the need for more radical economic measures to combat the crisis. His primary proposal was for an inflationary monetary solution which was then being adopted by many countries of the world. He wanted Bolivia to get off the gold standard, adopt inconvertible paper money, and then increase the money supply. The Liberals at first opposed these changes, especially as they controlled the Central Bank as well as Congress. But they were forced to accept them when Great Britain itself announced in September that it was going off the gold standard. Bolivia, as part of the sterling bloc, was forced to do the same, and Canelas got his reforms. But prices immediately started rising and the government position became extremely unpopular. In response, the Liberals put new pressure on the government and, after a series of aggressive parliamentary questions to ministers, forced the Salamanca government to come to terms. Those terms included a formal bi-party pact and an agreement to give the Liberals veto power over all economic decisions.

Frustrated in his initiatives and independence in the economic sphere, Salamanca then attempted to implement his ideas on authoritarian government. Claiming a communist menace which few other traditional party leaders seemed aware of, he proposed at the end of 1931 to enact a law of 'Social Defence'. This was a bill granting extraordinary powers to the president to deal with political opposition of the left and with the labour movement. The reaction to this proposal was intense, and in January 1932 mass demonstrations by labour, the small leftist parties, the students and the Saavedristas finally forced the government to withdraw the projected law from Congress. At the same time, Salamanca once more tried to outrun Liberal opposition on the economic front. Faced by government revenues anticipated to reach half of projected basic expenditures, he proposed to float an international loan. This was rejected by the Liberals, who not only obtained the formal ouster of the hated Canelas from the ministry of finance, but finally in March 1932 forced Salamanca to accept three Liberal-appointed ministers in his cabinet.

Salamanca was now completely dependent upon the Liberals in all basic decisions affecting the economy. He also faced increasing radical opposition which he had created in large measure through his anti-strike and law of 'Social Defence' activity. He thus became ever more embittered about the national political scene. But his impotence in national politics was not matched on the international front, and increasingly in the bitter days of 1932 he turned his energies to the Chaco. This was an issue that he could deal with, confident that the nation would follow him wherever he led them, and secure that the Liberals and the radicals could not impede his field of action.

He systematically built up the army at the expense of every other government service. He also pushed the army into an ever more expansive exploration and settlement programme in the Chaco. So clearly aggressive were Bolivia's intentions that throughout the early months of the year radical groups began calling for an end to the war-like preparations. But on this issue there was a split between the fringe radicals and student groups and the more traditional parties. The Saavedristas, who now called themselves the Republican Socialist party, and who had joined the left against the Social Defence Act, fully supported Salamanca's Chaco adventure, while the Liberals also gave Salamanca undivided support in his build-up of the army.

Thus Salamanca found himself with strong traditional backing which he decided to push to the absolute limit. In May and June a major link-up between two army divisions led to a typical minor clash over an important watering spot in the Chaco. Bolivian troops ousted an already entrenched Paraguayan force. Later claiming that such a Paraguayan fort did not exist, the Bolivian army refused to relinquish the new post and began a major and rapid build-up in the area to oppose the expected counter-attack by the Paraguayans. In the last days of June the counter-offensive occurred and was beaten back by the Bolivians. Up to this point, this incident was no different from dozens of others, and the number of troops involved was quite small and the conflict limited. Standard procedure now called for formal negotiation, but at this point Salamanca decided to break with all precedent and push forward with the attack, and by late July full-scale warfare had begun.

This decision of Salamanca had a great deal to do with his bitter frustration in national politics and his perceptions that the deepening economic crisis would lead to social anarchy. The fact that in May the International Tin Control Scheme adopted the radical procedure of prohibiting all tin production for the months of July and August, and of reducing production thereafter to one-third of 1929 output, meant that the most extreme cut-backs were proposed just on the eve of Salamanca's decisions concerning the Chaco. In response to the two-month closing and the extremely unbalanced trade situation which resulted, the government took complete control over all the gold dealings of its citizens and also forced mine owners to hand over 65 per cent of all their letters of exchange upon foreign currencies to the Central Bank. There is little question that this most extreme shutdown of the national export economy was of crucial importance in the decisions taken by the government in the following weeks.

There is no doubt, from all the documentation which has emerged since the war, that Salamanca and the Bolivian government deliberately escalated a typical border incident into a full-scale war to the surprise of even the Paraguayans. It is also evident that when the final decisions were made it was Salamanca who, against the written advice of his general staff, forced the conflict beyond any peaceful settlement and into what would become Bolivia's most costly war in its republican history.

In popular belief, however, it was almost immediately accepted as truth that the Chaco War was the result of a basic conflict over oil lands between Standard Oil of New Jersey, with its support of Bolivian claims, and Royal Dutch Shell, which was entrenched in Paraguay. There is no doubt that towards the end of this long and bloody conflict, when victorious Paraguayan troops were reaching the limit of the Chaco region and approaching the Andean foothills, oil became an important concern in their war aims. But until late 1935 the war was fought hundreds of miles from the nearest fields. Moreover, it was evident after the war that Standard Oil of New Jersey had illegally sold Bolivian oil to Argentina and then Paraguay, while claiming it could produce nothing for Bolivia from these same fields. The cause of the war rather must be found in the complex political conflict within Bolivia and the strains caused by the world depression on a fragile political system. Its continuation can only be understood in terms of Argentine support for Paraguayan aims. The ability of Argentina to prevent peace moves until the end, along with continued Paraguayan successes, meant that once the war began Bolivia had little ability to stop the onslaught. This is not to diminish the importance of the generalized belief that the Chaco War was an oil conflict. In the postwar period fundamental political and economic decisions, including the confiscation of Standard Oil in 1937 and the creation of a state oil monopoly company, were the direct result of this belief.

The Chaco War in effect destroyed the political system which had been in existence in Bolivia since 1880. The end of the war saw the collapse of both civilian government and the traditional political parties. Ideas which had previously been the coinage of only a small group of radical intellectuals now became the concern of much of the politically aware youth and ex-combatants. So distinctive was this change that Bolivians themselves would refer to the groups which came to maturity in the Chaco War as the 'Chaco generation'. The Indian question, the labour question, the land question, and the economic dependence on private mine owners became the new themes of national debate. These discussions led to the creation of new parties and revolutionary movements in the late 1930s and the 1940s, and finally to the social revolution of 1952.

The Chaco War also marked an important turning point in the economic history of the nation. The world depression and the resulting Chaco conflict marked the end of the expansion and even the capitalization of the mining industry. Thereafter production and productivity began to decline in an industry that saw virtually no change in its structure or patterns of investment until 1952. In the rural area as well, the relative stagnation of the national economy brought an end to the great expansion of the haciendas which had lasted from the 1880s until the late 1920s. By the end of this period landless peons had probably doubled and the number of free community Indians was now considerably less than the number of peasants without land. But this fundamental restructuring of the rural economy ended before the complete destruction of the free communities and provided an endless source of conflict in the post-Chaco period as the haciendas went on the defensive.

All the growth which had occurred as a result of the great tin expansion had little impact in modernizing the society as a whole. It was still estimated that in 1940 over two-thirds of Bolivians were primarily outside the market economy, and even as late as 1950 the number of urban artisans in the national economy equalled the number of factory workers. Though two-thirds of the economically active population were engaged in agriculture, Bolivia was still a net importer of foodstuffs, including traditional highland root crops. Thus while the tin boom did affect the third of the nation which was urban and Spanish speaking, its multiplier effects had little impact on the rural population, except possibly to lower their standard of living as a result of the corresponding expansion of the latifundia system.

Bolivia entered the Chaco War as a highly traditional, underdeveloped and export-dominated economy, and emerged from that conflict with the same characteristics. But from being one of the least mobilized societies in Latin America, in terms of radical ideology and union organization, it had become one more advanced than many of its neighbours. For the war shattered traditional elite assumptions and led to a fundamental rethinking of the nature of Bolivian society. The result was the creation of a revolutionary political movement that embraced some of the most radical ideas to emerge on the continent. The war would also create the climate for the development of one of the most powerful, independent and radical labour movements in the Americas. From these perspectives, the Chaco War, like the War of the Pacific before it, would prove to be one of the major turning points in Bolivian history.

17

THE ORIGINS OF MODERN PERU, 1880–1930

The year 1879 was nothing short of catastrophic for the Peruvian people. It marked the outbreak of the War of the Pacific which would bring untold travail, humiliation and ultimately national defeat. At the same time the widespread destruction engendered by the conflict cleared the path to economic modernization. During the next 50 years Peru, the quintessential 'feudal' Latin American society, would be pulled into the developing world economy, its modes of production reshaped by the special demands of Western industrial capitalism in the age of imperial expansion.

The half century after 1879 may be characterized as the dawn of modern Peru, a time not only of rapid economic modernization but also of social and political change. New elites emerged along the coast and coalesced to form a powerful oligarchy, whose political expression, the Civilist party, had before the close of the century seized control of the state.[1] Under its paternalistic aegis and guided by the doctrines of liberal, laissez-faire positivism, currently in vogue throughout the continent, what Jorge Basadre, the dean of Peruvian historians, has called the 'Aristocratic Republic' (1895–1919) was born. The military was reorganized, professionalized and, at least temporarily, brought under civilian control for the first time since Independence. The machinery of government, although not entirely divorced from the traditional *empleomania* characteristic of the structures and forms of the colonial past, was overhauled, modernized and expanded to conform better with the demands and growing complexities of the modern export economy. It was, in short, a period marked by economic prosperity, political stability

---

[1] On the origins of the Civilist party, which secured the presidency for the first time in 1872, see Bonilla, *CHLA* III, ch. 13.

and relative social peace unmatched in the country's post-colonial history.

But it was also a period of profound change in society out of which would emerge the socio-political configurations of contemporary Peru. With the gradual advance of capitalism, peasants migrated and became proletarians, as industrial enclaves formed not only in the cities but in areas of the countryside as well. There the traditional hacienda and small-scale mining systems gave way increasingly to the modern agro-industrial plantation and mining complex, both of which were equipped with technology and economies of scale to produce efficiently and profitably for expanding foreign markets. Finally from this vortex of socio-economic change came the formation and mobilization of a modern labour movement. Its collective response to the widespread economic dislocations produced in the Peruvian periphery by the first world war shattered a decade of relative social peace and signalled the end of the *civilista* 'Aristocratic Republic'.

In a larger sense, however, it was the world economic crisis of 1929 that finally called into question the efficacy of the export-orientated economy. So elaborately constructed by the *civilistas* and indeed expanded in new directions by their middle-class successors during the *oncenio* (the eleven-year government of Augusto B. Leguía, 1919–30), that economy was shaken to its very foundations by the decline in world commodity prices after 1925 and their collapse in 1929. From that time forward there was a growing realization that export dependency constituted the heart of the country's continuing dilemma of underdevelopment. How to change that economic structure and resolve that dilemma formed the centre of a national debate, inaugurated by the great reformer Víctor Raúl Haya de la Torre and the revolutionary José Carlos Mariátegui. The world crisis also signalled the entry of the Peruvian masses into the political arena on a sustained, long-term basis. Modern, populist political parties, notably APRA (Alianza Popular Revolucionaria Americana founded in 1924 by Haya de la Torre) would henceforth greatly influence and shape the nation's political destiny.

Peru is a country whose geographical and demographic configurations are as problematical as her economy and polity. Indeed, her geography is so tortured and fractured by the Andes and her population so divided by race, class and ethnicity that national integration still remains, a century and a half after Independence, an unfulfilled aspiration.

Geographically the country is divided into three principal regions – coast, sierra and *selva*. A narrow coastal strip constitutes 12 per cent of the national territory. (Today the coast contains around 45 per cent of the population, although that was not always the case. It reflects the enormous flow of migration during the greater part of this century from the backward rural interior to the more modern urbanized coast.) While land is fertile along the coast, a paucity of rainfall, because of the peculiarities of the Humboldt Current, renders most of it desert. In places this desert is watered by a number of rivers which flow out of the Andes east to west, carving out broad, fertile valleys at the point where they empty into the Pacific. The sierra region comprises three Andean ranges that run north to south and present severe problems for transportation and agriculture. The heart of the old Inca empire, the sierra's unique productive capacity never recovered from the dislocations of the Spanish conquest of the sixteenth century. Here the majority of the population, ethnically Indian and *mestizo*, eke out a marginal living on isolated estates (haciendas) and peasant villages (*comunidades*) which produce livestock and/or wheat, maize and potatoes at extremely low yields. Here, too, rich mineral deposits can be found which have tended to draw a substantial portion of the population into urban enclaves. (In this century the sierra's economy has increasingly been opened up and articulated with coastal markets and the world economy.) Finally, the *selva* or jungle looms large in both the national territory, of which it constitutes 60 per cent, and in the imagination of policy makers who historically have envisioned its resources and vast space as a potential panacea for resolving the nation's chronic underdevelopment. (With only 6 per cent of the population and still isolated from the country's major productive centres, the *selva* remains, like national integration itself, a largely unfulfilled dream of the future.)

If the determinism of geography contributes to Peru's problem as well as its promise, certain historical legacies, particularly colonialism, have left a searing mark on the national consciousness while largely shaping the problem of modern underdevelopment. The revolutions for independence in the 1820s brought to an end almost 300 years of Spanish colonial rule. However, aside from a major political change which catapulted the local Creole elites into power, the colonial order remained very much intact. As elsewhere on the continent, it was not in their interests to carry out a social revolution that might threaten their political aspirations. Free trade, which had partly motivated the demand for independence, also proved to be a double-edged sword, widening trading opportunities for some sectors of the merchant and landed classes, but proving detrimental to local manufacturers forced to compete with the influx of foreign goods. The formation of a stable, new nation state, like the achievement of economic independence and prosperity, proved elusive in the immediate post-colonial era. Rampant *caudillismo*, complicated by regionalism and particularism, hindered the consolidation of the new nation. It was not until the spectacular guano boom around the middle of the century, which through higher public revenues laid the basis for a general expansion in the power and influence of the central state, that the hope of national unity could begin to become a realistic possibility. The outbreak of the War of the Pacific in 1879, however, ruptured this move towards national consolidation and threw the country back into a period of fragmentation and anarchy reminiscent of the early days of independence.

THE IMPACT OF WAR: FOREIGN AND DOMESTIC

The War of the Pacific, which involved Chile on one hand, and Peru and Bolivia on the other, had a number of complex causes. They centred on the discovery and subsequent competition for valuable mineral wealth, at first gold and silver but then nitrates, in the desolate and largely uninhabited desert region of Atacama. The problem was complicated by the fact that this region had been poorly defined and demarcated during the colonial period and all three emergent nations on the west coast of South America tried to lay claim to its newly found riches. Such an international tinder box was further fuelled by old political antagonisms and rivalries growing out of a delicate regional balance of power, as well as the interference and intrigues of foreign entrepreneurs and powers. Peru tried desperately but unsuccessfully to avoid a military showdown with its vastly more powerful and better organized rival to the south. However, in the end a secret treaty of alliance with Bolivia could not be renounced, and the country went to war early in 1879.

Drawn into a war for which it was shamelessly ill prepared, Peru experienced its first set-back at sea. The core of its small navy, crucial for the defence of a 3,000 mile Pacific coastline, consisted of two ironclad warships, the *Independencia* and the *Huáscar*. The former was lured aground and lost in the Battle of Iquique at the outset of the war. The *Huáscar*, commanded by the legendary Miguel Grau, succeeded for a time in wreaking havoc on enemy ports and shipping. Nevertheless, in an engagement that virtually sealed Peru's fate in the war, the *Huáscar* was later in the year trapped by the larger and more powerful Chilean squadron off Punta Angamos. In one of the world's first major naval battles between ironclads the outnumbered *Huáscar* was crippled and captured, after almost sinking its Chilean counterpart and carrying the day itself.

Once in control of the sea lanes, Chilean forces invaded Peru's three southernmost provinces, including the nitrate-rich Tarapacá, whose mineral wealth and disputed frontiers formed the focal point of the international conflict. Control of the south coincided with a Chilean blockade of Peru's major ports which shut down the country's principal exports (guano, nitrates and sugar) and effectively crippled the war effort by emptying the national treasury. In the midst of these reverses, president Mariano Ignacio Prado, in an unprecedented act by a national leader, abandoned the country for Europe on the lame excuse of personally raising loans abroad for the war effort.

Militarily and politically bankrupt, Peru nevertheless refused to capitulate, leading the Chileans to undertake a land invasion of the north coast in September 1880. Designed to 'punish' the country into submission, a 3,000-strong Chilean army commanded by General Patrick Lynch plundered the plantation-rich sugar-cane valleys of the region, thereby depriving the country of its only remaining economic resource upon which to continue the war. Still the Peruvians were unwilling to sue for peace, particularly in the face of the severity of Chile's territorial demands. The death knell for the Peruvian cause was sounded early the following year when a Chilean invasion force of 25,000 men captured Lima after a fierce fight. When it finally entered the capital on 17 January, however, the invading army did not find a government with which to negotiate a surrender.

Nicolás de Piérola, who had assumed dictatorial powers upon Prado's departure for Europe and who had organized the ill-fated defence of Lima, had fled to the sierra where he sought to raise a new army to continue the war. (Piérola was a former treasury minister, determined anti-*civilista*, and a controversial figure who would become president again in 1895.) His hopes of organizing a unified resistance, however, faded in the wake of a renewed struggle for power among rival factions and *caudillos*. On one side stood the *civilistas*, a group of progressive hacendados, guano consignees and bankers who had gained power in the early 1870s. Their leader, Francisco García Calderón, moved quickly after Piérola's retreat to the sierra to form a new government in Lima whose aim was to negotiate an immediate peace settlement. On the other side, a loose coalition of military officers with the avowed purpose of continuing the resistance formed first around Piérola, who was then deposed in a power struggle in favour of Andrés Cáceres, the hero of a Peruvian victory at Tarapacá. They regarded the *civilistas'* willingness to negotiate as an act of national betrayal.

While issues of war and peace tended to define the evolving political struggle, it also assumed a more ominous social dimension. Defeat on the battlefield had led to the collapse of the oligarchical state, so pains-takingly constructed in the half century since Independence. More significantly, in the eyes of the people the authority and even legitimacy of the ruling classes, which had led the country down the road to war, was now open to question. This was a serious problem in a society skewed and divided along lines of class, caste and hierarchy. With the productive capacity of the country in ruins and the spectre of famine stalking the land, such a breakdown in authority threatened the historic capacity of the elite to continue to exert its unilateral domination and control over the masses. If left unchecked, it could even lead to a popular upheaval of revolutionary proportions.

In fact, manifestations of social dissolution were already beginning to appear. In Lima mobs attacked the Chinese quarter in an attempted pogrom, something that had become increasingly common during periods of stress ever since large numbers of Chinese coolie labourers (about 100,000 between 1849 and 1874) had been imported into the country to replace black slaves who were emancipated in 1854. The same mobs also drove some of the city's wealthy strata to seek refuge for a time in the British embassy. The most dangerous situation from the point of view of the landed classes, however, existed in the rural coastal regions where plantation workers (Chinese coolies) in some cases embraced the invading armies as 'liberators' or in others turned against their masters in an orgy of killing and looting, as occurred in Cañete. Indeed, fear of a general uprising on the part of these 'dangerous classes' served to push the *civilista* oligarchy to sue for peace, hoping thereby to enlist the invading army in the defence of property and the cause of 'law and order' and thereby avert social chaos.

When the war was carried to the central sierra by a Chilean expeditionary force later in 1881, the national struggle showed further signs of being transformed into a social struggle. The Indian peasantry, long oppressed by their overlords, now perceived that their sacred community lands were threatened by a new 'oppressor'. While they resolutely mobilized to defend their homeland from one enemy, some came to harbour the idea of a more complete emancipation. For them the war became a revolutionary struggle against all whites, whether Chilean invaders or the local landowning elite.

Not surprisingly this sentiment among sectors of the Indian masses greatly influenced the course of the war effort as well as the ensuing struggle for political power among rival factions and *caudillos*. At first willing to assist Cáceres's efforts in forming a local army of resistance, the region's elite later recoiled from the idea in the face of his successful mobilization of large irregular forces of peasant guerillas (known since the time of the wars of independence as *montoneros*). Many landowners, not illogically, feared that such forces might turn against them in a class/caste war once the invaders were repelled. Such popular mobilizations traditionally struck fear into the hearts of the Andean elite whose class hegemony had more than once been threatened in the past by similar movements. In fact, the ghost of Túpac Amaru II, the *mestizo* descendant of the royal house of the Incas who mobilized the Indians of the sierra against the injustices of Spanish rule and was executed in Cuzco by the vice-regal authorities in 1782, still cast a long shadow over the collective mentality of the region's upper class. As a result important sectors of that class abandoned the nationalist resistance and shifted to a collaborationist position, believing that negotiation and accommodation with the enemy better served their personal and class interests.

This changing attitude towards the war on the part of sectors of the sierra elite had a number of important ramifications. First, it gave the aspiring *caudillo* Miguel Iglesias, a hacendado from Cajamarca and former follower of Piérola (whose political fortunes were momentarily in eclipse), the opportunity to broaden his political support as champion of the peace party. In August 1882 he issued a proclamation (Grito de Montán) which, in addition to setting forth his presidential ambitions, declared his willingness to negotiate with the Chileans. This action, although denounced as treasonous by Cáceres, attracted considerable support from disaffected officers and war-weary politicians and hacendados. Iglesias managed to form a new government and in 1883 successfully negotiated a peace treaty with Chile. Under the Treaty of Ancón Peru ceded outright to Chile the southern desert region of

Tarapacá with its important nitrate centre Iquique. It also allowed Chile to occupy and administer the provinces of Tacna and Arica for ten years, after which a plebiscite would be held to determine final ownership.

Reluctantly Cáceres accepted the peace, but not Iglesias's claim to the presidency. Thus, as the foreign war drew to a close with the withdrawal in late 1883 of Chilean forces, it gave way to a civil war between Iglesias and Cáceres. In the central sierra Cáceres's *montoneros* not only attacked government forces, but those members of the elite whom they suspected of having collaborated with the enemy. In some places they also seized hacienda lands (often claimed by adjacent Indian communities) and forced hacendados and their families to flee for their lives.

Similar war-exacerbated social tensions in the northern sierra exploded into one of the largest peasant uprisings since Túpac Amaru II. The Atusparia revolt erupted with a sudden fury in 1885 all along the Callejón de Huaylas in the department of Ancash. Assuming many of the attributes of both class conflict and caste war, the revolt was triggered by a series of ill-conceived and poorly timed tax measures imposed by the Iglesias government. Desperate to fill its empty coffers, the government reimposed the hated tribute or head tax (*contribución personal de Indígenas*) on the war-impoverished Indian peasantry. The tax (two *soles* per week) was combined with a revival of corvée labour, similar to the despised *mita* in colonial times. Atusparia, a respected Indian *curaca* (village chief) who supported Cáceres's faction in the continuing civil war, refused to comply with the new measures and, after escaping arrest, raised a peasant army that seized and held Huarás, the departmental capital, for several weeks. Government troops later recaptured the city and savagely repressed the rebellion.

Such incidents of mass uprising, along with a deepening national mood of postwar frustration and discontent, severely weakened Iglesias's already precarious hold on the government. Devoid of funds and increasingly identified by the adroit Cáceres with the national defeat, Iglesias finally capitulated in December 1885 to Cáceres's guerilla army which was on the verge of capturing Lima. Four months later, Cáceres, running unopposed, was overwhelmingly elected president.

A Herculean task of national reconstruction now confronted the new president. Economically the country was prostrate, as can be discerned from the precipitous decline of the national budget which plunged from a prewar high of 74 million pesos to levels ranging from 1 to 13 million in the decade following peace. All social classes were to a greater or lesser

	1870	1894
Millionaires (*millionarios*)	18	
Wealthy (*ricos*)	11,587	1,725
Comfortably off (*acomodados*)	22,148	2,000
Beggars (*mendigos*)		500,000
Workers (*obreros*)	1,236,000	345,000

extent pauperized. An impressionistic, unsystematic, yet revealing attempt by a contemporary to quantify the dimensions of this human tragedy yielded the figures shown in the table.[2]

In addition to inducing a marked proclivity for violence in the body politic, this postwar impoverishment produced some important changes in the composition of the old ruling groups whose landholdings had formed the basis of power during the prewar guano age. Elements of this landed elite were suddenly bankrupted by the war and entered a period of rapid political and social eclipse. They would be replaced in the coming years by a new, upwardly mobile group of entrepreneurs, particularly along the agriculturally rich central and north coast, whose *mentalité* was more atuned to the new capitalist age. Ultimately they would form the core of a new, bourgeois ruling class which, working in tandem with foreign capital, would become the spearhead of economic recovery in the country.

As the country's protracted postwar political and social crisis finally began to subside after Cáceres established what was to become a decade-long military dictatorship (1886–95), thoughtful Peruvians began to debate not only the future course of reconstruction, but also what had caused the national debacle in the first place. Caught up in the general mood of national frustration, introspection and self-criticism, members of the intelligentsia asked what had gone wrong in a country that only a generation earlier had appeared to be on the threshold of national progress and development. While answers varied, a consensus view emphasized the serious ethnic, cultural, geographical and racial fragmentation that had plagued the country ever since Independence. Somehow ways had to be found to bridge not only the enormous geographical division between the sierra and the coast, but also the yawning gap between the 'feudal world' of the Indian peasantry and the more

---

[2] See Ernesto Yepes del Castillo, *Perú, 1820–1920: un siglo de desarrollo capitalista* (2nd edn, Lima, 1981), 124.

'modern' Creole society. Fundamental was the task of constructing a strong, modern nation-state in case, many argued, the Chilean experience be repeated in the future.

Perhaps the most notable national critic of this period, but one who fell decidedly outside the intellectual mainstream of his class, was Manuel González Prada (1848–1918).[3] Influenced alternately by such diverse philosophical currents as positivism, romanticism, socialism and anarchism, González Prada was less the systematic thinker than gadfly critic of all that was held sacred and holy in Peruvian society. Something of a Latin American Voltaire who felt a deep, personal humiliation in the way Peru had lost the war, he lashed out against the corruption and injustices of the existing order. Indeed his moralistic attacks called into question for the first time the very legitimacy of Peru's ruling class. He relentlessly criticized the leaders of the army, landowners and churchmen – in short the country's rulers – for their inability effectively to organize and direct the nation. In effect, he blamed them for Peru's defeat, accusing them of placing their own personal and class interests above those of the *patria*. Moreover, it was pure folly, he argued, to assume that national integration could become a reality without a social revolution that would finally free the oppressed peasant Indian masses who formed the very core of the incipient Peruvian nation. Until they were delivered from the vice-like, exploitative grip of the landed elites, national unity would never be anything more than a hollow dream. While ostracized and ridiculed by many of his contemporaries, González Prada's strident yet acute social criticism would, nevertheless, profoundly influence future generations and make him in many ways the father of modern Peruvian nationalism.

González Prada's views were regarded as threatening and dangerous by the country's re-emerging *civilista* elite. As a result, he was promptly labelled a wild-eyed extremist, a turn-coat to his class, and summarily isolated on the margins of the debate over reconstruction. That task was left to a new generation of progressive *civilista* intellectuals, many of whom could be found teaching at the venerable San Marcos University. Over the next two decades this group, writing in the major journals and newspapers and moving regularly in and out of high government posts,

---

[3] A representative selection of his works can be found in *Anarquía* (Santiago, 1936). The bulk of his extensive writings were edited and published after his death by his son. The standard biography is still Luis Alberto Sánchez, *Don Manuel* (Lima, 1929). See also Bruno Podestá, *Pensamiento político de González Prada* (Lima, 1975).

would serve as the architects of the postwar reconstruction and modernization of Peru. All were influenced in one way or another by positivism in whose doctrines of science and rationalism, order and progress, they discovered the perfect ideological vehicle upon which to found national rehabilitation. Most were rationalists, materialists and utilitarians in the positivist tradition, mildly anti-clerical, strongly opposed to the 'feudal' Hispanic traditions of the colony and advocates of national 'modernization'. For them modernization was perceived as industrialization, limited representative democracy, technical and scientific education and a mode of thought that was at once non-scholastic and non-idealistic. They did not share José Enrique Rodó's critique, in *Ariel* (Montevideo, 1900), of the rising bourgeois nations of the West, particularly the United States. Rather they admired the United States and wished to emulate its success in achieving material development and political democracy.

Two of positivism's most representative *civilista* exponents were Francisco García Calderón, son of a prominent landed family and former president during the Chilean occupation, and Manuel Vicente Villarán, who came from a distinguished Limeño family of lawyers. Although an expatriate at the relatively early age of 30 and never really an actively functioning member of the *civilista* elite, García Calderón nevertheless best reflected and articulated the emerging ideology of his class and generation. The author of many books on both Western philosophy and Latin American society, his main work on Peru, entitled *Le Pérou Contemporain* (1907), was published, revealingly, in Paris, long the main cultural point of reference for the country's westernized Creole elite. In this work, and a companion volume on Latin America published, also in Paris, several years later,[4] he spoke of the need in Peru for strong leadership from a cultivated, unified and progressive oligarchy, guided if need be by a strong leader, what the Venezuelan Vallenilla Lanz would later call a 'democratic Caesar'.[5] This elite would move to capitalize the economy, centralize and modernize the state and gradually incorporate the Indian peasant masses into the nation by way of a system of universal education. Villarán, a practising lawyer and major ideologue of the Civilist party, complemented this ideology by stressing the need for

[4] *Les démocraties latines de l'Amérique* (Paris, 1912), Eng. trans., *Latin America: its rise and progress* (New York, 1913). See also his *La creación de un continente* (Paris, 1913).
[5] Laureano Vallenilla Lanz, *Cesarismo democrático* (Caracas, 1919).

educational reform. Highly critical of the country's antiquated scholastic traditions in higher education, Villarán urged adoption of a utilitarian university curriculum which would produce more engineers than lawyers and thereby better serve the emerging capitalist commonweal.[6]

ECONOMIC RECOVERY AND REFORMATION OF THE LIBERAL OLIGARCHICAL STATE

The first tangible step towards reconstruction, and one which in the praxis clearly reflected positivist ideology, was the so-called Grace Contract. Cáceres's advisers were all too aware that to rebuild after the war Peru, which had defaulted on its foreign debt in 1876 and which had now lost its two main financial assets, guano and nitrates, had to regain access to Western capital markets. The opportunity to accomplish this end presented itself in 1886 in the form of a proposal by Michael Grace, immigrant founder of the developing west coast commercial trading house of Grace and Company, to cancel the national debt in return for the concession to the country's foreign bondholders of Peru's railway network, which would be modernized and expanded, for a period of 75 years. Such a far-reaching proposal, which raised not only the delicate question of national sovereignty but also questions about the model for Peru's economic development, was bound to stir widespread controversy and debate. Cáceres therefore formed a blue-ribbon commission, composed of prominent *civilistas* (who had formed an alliance with Cáceres's ruling Constitutionalist party), to study the proposal and to make recommendations to the government. The commission wholeheartedly endorsed the plan which it envisioned as a basis for the country's future economic relationship with the Western metropolitan nations. The Grace Contract, it believed, would place the country's finances on a sound footing, thereby serving to revive Peru's international trade and commerce and to attract the necessary investment capital, technology and labour from abroad to stimulate economic recovery, progress and prosperity. Not unaware that this same developmental strategy was already fuelling a profound economic advance further to the south in Argentina and Chile, the Cáceres government

---

[6] For example, *Las profesiones liberales en el Perú* (Lima, 1900). See also *Páginas escogidas*, ed. Jorge Basadre (Lima, 1962) for a representative sampling of Villarán's ideas. Another leading exponent of positivism was Javier Prado. See his *El estado social del Perú durante la dominación española* (Lima, 1941) and *La nueva época y los destinos históricos de los Estados Unidos* (Lima, 1919).

pushed the contract, after some modifications, through a recalcitrant Congress in 1889. The final contract ceded the Peruvian railways for a period of 66 years, together with free navigation of Lake Titicaca and up to three million tons of guano, to a corporation of bondholders (the Peruvian Corporation of London) in return for the cancellation of the entire external debt and an annual payment of £80,000 for 33 years.[7]

While the Grace Contract, reinforced by a robust recovery of silver production ($33 million by 1895), laid the foundations for capitalist reconstruction, political strife precipitated by the presidential succession of 1890 once more threatened internal stability. Against the desires of his *civilista* allies who argued for a return to civilian government under their own candidate, Cáceres imposed a loyal subordinate, Colonel Remigio Morales Bermúdez, as his successor. Without the *civilistas* the new regime, with Cáceres remaining the real source of power behind the scenes, assumed a decidedly military character.

This set the stage for the re-emergence of Piérola, who returned from exile to organize what became known as the 'Revolution of 1895'. Piérola was the son of an aristocratic, but impoverished, ultra-Catholic family from Arequipa in the south who had long harboured presidential ambitions. As a young treasury minister in 1869, he engineered the historic shift in the commercialization of guano away from the national consignees to the foreigner Auguste Dreyfus. For that audacious act he gained the undying hatred of the guano-rich *civilista* oligarchy which succeeded in barring him from power until the war with Chile. Then his impulsive, daring and charismatic personality catapulted him briefly into the presidency during the war, and he played a leading part in the political struggles during the ensuing civil wars.

Behind Piérola's rise to power in the 1890s lay a substantial, if disparate, base of support and political programme. The Democratic party he founded in 1889 was essentially anti-military, pro-church, anti-liberal (though not necessarily anti-capitalist) and ostensibly nationalist. It was supported at the top by a powerful group of wealthy southern landowners, the church hierarchy and elements of the old middle classes who were intensely proud and protective of their Hispanic and Catholic traditions. What gave the party and its leader its growing popular

---

[7] On the Grace Contract, see Rory Miller, 'The making of the Grace Contract: British bondholders and the Peruvian government, 1885–1890', *Journal of Latin American Studies (JLAS)*, 8/1 (1976), 73–100.

following, however, was the monetary crisis of the early 1890s which brought in its wake widespread economic convulsions. A major world producer of silver, Peru's economic recovery was interrupted by the general abandonment of silver and adoption of the gold standard around the world. The steady depreciation of Peru's silver-backed currency caused considerable hardship and suffering among the urban artisans and workers whom Piérola succeeded in mobilizing in his quest for power.

On a typically misty March morning in 1895, Piérola galloped into Lima at the head of several thousand irregular troops. After a bloody two days of street fighting with several thousand casualties on both sides, Piérola forced the surrender of Cáceres and occupied the presidential palace. A few months later, on the eve of national elections, Piérola agreed to form an historic alliance with his old enemies the *civilistas*. Unlike Cáceres, Piérola understood that without the backing of the *civilista* oligarchy, it was impossible to rule. For their part the *civilistas* were ready to put aside their long-standing personal antipathy for Piérola. For one thing, the two parties were not that far apart in their ideas on economic recovery. Here too was the 'man on horseback', the charismatic *caudillo* capable of extending the *pax Andina*, the peace and order so cherished by the *civilista* positivists. Thus the way was cleared for Piérola's election in 1895 which was to mark the beginning of a new era in Peruvian politics. For once in power Piérola was able to govern with a broad consensus rare in the country's history. It enabled him to undertake a number of important reforms, many of which further reinforced Peru's growing export-led economic recovery.

The first civilian to occupy the presidency in a generation, Piérola aimed to restore the legitimacy and prestige of civilian government and to reduce the military's prominence in national political affairs. Given the historical significance of the army over the past century, such a task would not be easy. Ever since independence the Peruvian army had constituted the only relatively unified and coherent institution in an extremely fragmented and disarticulated polity. The army, it has been said, was in effect the state during the nineteenth century.[8] The war with Chile had further swollen the ranks of the armed forces, thereby reinforcing its political weight in national affairs.

Piérola was all too keenly aware of the problem. Rampant military *caudillismo* and *golpismo* had, in his view, disrupted the regular,

[8] Sinesio López J., 'El estado oligárquico en el Perú: un ensayo de interpretación', *Revista Mexicana de Sociología*, 40/3 (1978), 1000.

constitutional processes of government for too long. What was needed was a major reform of the armed forces, not only to place it on a more technically proficient and modern basis, but to depoliticize and subordinate it to the civilian-controlled power of the state.

To accomplish this goal Piérola first sharply reduced the regular army and its share of the national budget, retiring or dismissing large numbers of officers loyal to the defeated Cáceres. He then imported a French mission charged with the complete overhaul and reorganization of the military. A new military academy was built at Chorillos outside Lima to create a better educated and technically competent officer corps. At Chorillos the French proceeded to instil a new professional ethic in its graduates, based upon their own elitist conception of the French armed forces. The primary and sole mission of the military was the sacred ideal of protecting the *patria*. To meddle in political affairs was to be seen by the new generation of officers as not befitting a man in uniform whose loftier, patriotic mission in defence of the fatherland elevated him above such common, sordid concerns as politics. Such efforts to instil a more professional attitude, however, while successful in the short term, were in the long run destined to fail. The historic tendency of the armed forces to intervene in politics as guardians of elite interests against threats from below reasserted itself again in 1914, 1919 and 1929, thereafter becoming once again 'endemic'.

Piérola was more successful in altering the armed forces in other ways, however. Compulsory military service was initiated in 1898 and with it the gradual expansion of the armed forces whose size over the next ten years more than tripled. Furthermore, salaries were increased and merit replaced lineage as the means of qualifying for officer status. This had the effect of opening up avenues of mobility for the new middle classes who in time would take over the military and further contribute to its changing character. Eventually even exceptional elements from the masses might aspire to a career as an officer. The military became, as the twentieth century developed, a principal vehicle of mobility in a society long calcified along class lines.

In his fiscal and economic policy Piérola paradoxically appeared as much a modernizing, *civilista* capitalist as a Catholic, hispanophile traditionalist. He quickly moved to reform the antiquated mechanisms of the state to conform with and better promote economic recovery. The tax system, for example, was completely reorganized. Customs duties on key exports like sugar and cotton were removed while tariffs were gradually raised on imports other than machinery in order to stimulate nascent industries like textiles. At the same time the Indian head tax, the cause of so much abuse and injustice in the past, was finally ended, as was the old Spanish practice of tax farming. A new, private corporation, which was eventually nationalized as a state enterprise, was empowered to improve the efficiency and yield of tax collecting. The banking and monetary system was also overhauled. The gold standard was adopted, which not only favoured the costal exporters (Piérola's *civilista* allies), but also benefited state revenues from expanded exports. To promote economic recovery Piérola created the ministry of development, whose work was aided by the formation of several professional associations, the most important of which were the Sociedad Nacional Agraria (1896), the Sociedad Nacional de Minería (1896) and the Sociedad Nacional de Industrias (1895). In one of its first acts the new ministry undertook to revise the anachronistic laws governing commerce and mining, some of which dated back to the Bourbon reforms of the eighteenth century.

For the mass of the population, however, Piérola apparently did very little. Indeed Peru's leading historian, Jorge Basadre, has suggested that Piérola lost an excellent, possibly the last, opportunity to integrate the popular classes into the framework of the nation's political process. This is partly explained by Piérola's profoundly elitist and aristocratic mentality. Like the lords of colonial Peru, he assumed the paternalistic attitude of the protective father before his children, the people. 'When the people are in danger', he liked to say, 'they come to me.'[9] Any structural change in the traditional condition of the masses or their historic relationship to the ruling classes and the state was clearly beyond Piérola's purview.

It was, however, Piérola who inaugurated the 'Aristocratic Republic' (1895–1919), a period of political stability and economic progress unparalleled in the modern history of the country. The dawn of this new, largely bourgeois age was the result of the export-led economic recovery, particularly from the late 1890s (see figure 1), as the full impact of the Grace Contract and the positivist philosophy of the emerging *civilista* oligarchy began to take effect. In a larger sense, this represented the local response to the capitalist expansion of the metropolitan centres during the second industrial revolution. In search of raw materials to fuel this advance and an outlet for surplus investment capital and finished

[9] Quoted in Jesús Chavarría, 'La desaparición del Perú colonial: 1870–1919', *Aportes*, 23 (January 1972), 132–3.

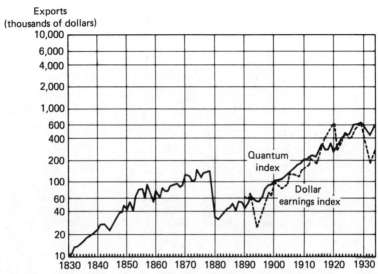

Fig. 1. Peruvian exports, 1830–1930: value and dollar value (1900 = 100). *Source:* Rosemary Thorp and Geoffrey Bertram, *Peru 1890–1977: growth and policy in an open economy* (London, 1978), 5.

manufactured goods, the industrializing countries found the shattered Peruvian economy a particularly attractive and vulnerable field of operation. Since its often antiquated and archaic productive capacity had been largely crippled by war, reconstruction could more easily coincide with both the demands of the metropolis and the capitalist specifications of the new age.

In the period after Independence the British had quickly gained a paramount position in Peru's economy. For the next half century or more, the bulk of Peru's exports, principally guano, nitrates and wool, were sent to Great Britain in exchange for textiles and other manufactures. Economically, at least, England, in effect, replaced Spain as the hegemonic 'colonial' power in Peru. By the twentieth century, however, United States capital began seriously to challenge and erode British economic pre-eminence in Peru. American imports, for example, rose from 7 per cent of the country's total imports in 1892 to almost 30 per cent in 1913, jumped to over 60 per cent during the first world war and finally settled at around 40 per cent in the late 1920s (see figure 2). Direct United States private investment rose from $7 million in 1897 to $23 million in 1908, and jumped to $110 million in 1919 and $140 million in 1924. Moreover, once the Panama canal opened the United States

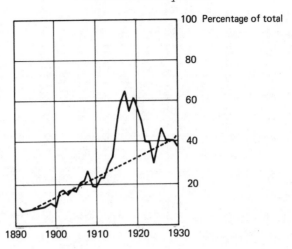

Fig. 2. Percentage of Peruvian imports from the United States, 1891–1930.
Source: William Bollinger, 'The rise of United States influence on the Peruvian economy, 1869–1921' (unpublished MA thesis, University of California, Los Angeles, 1972), 18.

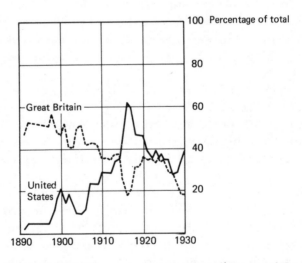

Fig. 3. Percentage of Peruvian exports to the United States and Great Britain, 1891–1930. Peruvian exports to Great Britain rose in absolute terms. The chart reflects their relative decline vis-à-vis Peruvian exports to the United States.
Source: Bollinger, 'The rise of United States influence', 21.

overtook and surpassed Britain as a market for Peruvian exports (see figure 3). During the first quarter of the twentieth century Peru consistently ranked in the top four or five Latin American countries receiving United States investments, behind only Mexico, Cuba and alternately Colombia (1897), Chile (1908, 1914, 1924) and Venezuela (1924). By comparison, as the level of United States investment steadily increased, British capital in Peru declined. In 1880 it stood at $181 million, falling in 1890 to $95 million and then rising to $131 million in 1928 before resuming its definitive slide continuously thereafter.

This shift from British to United States pre-eminence in Peru was also accompanied by a change in the type of capitalist penetration of the country. During the commercial or mercantile phase, British and some American capital had acted primarily as a facilitating, 'inter-mediating' agent between the 'natural', resource-rich Peruvian economy and the international marketplace. In effect it dynamized the Peruvian economy by providing Peruvian producers – planters, ranchers and miners – with the financial and marketing mechanisms both to stimulate production and to market their products. By the end of the century foreign merchant trading houses like Graham Rowe (sugar), Anthony Gibbs (wool), Duncan Fox (cotton), and the Grace Brothers (commodities and shipping) articulated Peru's expanding relationship with the metropolitan market. In the twentieth century, however, United States capital began to penetrate the production stage. This occurred principally in the mining sector, but spilled over into other sectors of the economy (e.g. sugar) in varying degrees as well. During the first three decades of the new century large United States companies began to capture and monopolize areas of production in the export sector formerly controlled exclusively by Peruvian entrepreneurs.

The mining industry, largely because of its capital-intensive and technologically dependent nature, became the classic example of national displacement and foreign takeover. In a state of decadence since Independence, mining, following the railway construction boom of the guano age, had made a vigorous comeback. Spurred by native entrepreneurs, recovery continued after the War of the Pacific and subsequent civil wars with the help of further railway construction by the Peruvian Corporation into the rich copper zones of the central sierra, mainly Casapalca in 1892 and La Oroya in 1893. Peruvian copper production (see figure 4), stimulated by steadily rising prices on the world market after 1895, surged between 1897 and 1903 to 10,000 tons

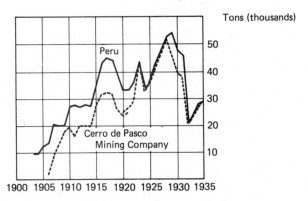

Fig. 4. Peruvian copper production, 1903–35. There is a difference between the Cerro de Pasco figures for 1906–21 and 1920–35: the latter series includes ore purchased from other miners which was then smelted and exported by Cerro as part of its total production. The reason for the dramatic rise in the total percentage of Peru's copper production controlled by Cerro between 1922 and 1923 was the inauguration of the 2,500 ton minimum daily capacity smelter at La Oroya in 1922 which made the furnaces of most other firms obsolete. *Source*: Bollinger, 'The rise of United States influence', 43.

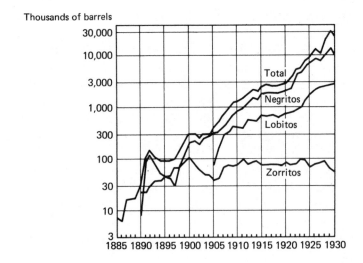

Fig. 5. Peruvian crude oil output, 1885–1930. *Source*: Thorp and Bertram, *Peru 1890–1977*, 97.

per year. As early as 1901, however, aided by a new mining code, a period of intense transfer, reorganization and foreign absorption in the industry culminated in the purchase by a United States syndicate of the vast Cerro de Pasco mines. In the next few years the company built a spur line connecting its deposits with La Oroya and a processing plant at Tinyahuarco. These trends were paralleled by development, beginning in 1896, of the copper deposits at Casapalca by the North Americans Backus and Johnston who, together with Cerro, came to control 92 per cent of Peru's copper production by the first world war.

Two other examples of foreign penetration of the mining sector should be mentioned. Oil fields on the haciendas La Brea and Pariñas in Piura department were developed by the London and Pacific Petroleum Company which was later sold to Standard Oil, to become the International Petroleum Company in 1913. Petroleum production and exports continued to rise thereafter (see figure 5), comprising 10 per cent of total Peruvian exports in 1915 and as much as 30 per cent in 1930.

A more devastating intervention, from the point of view of the native population, occurred in the Amazon region between 1892 and 1910 when a boom in rubber extraction momentarily pushed exports to 30 per cent of the total. Fortunes were amassed overnight by a few at the cost of thousands of deaths from overwork, malnutrition and disease among the Indian labour force which was ruthlessly harnessed to production. The boom collapsed as suddenly as it appeared, however, as the British shifted production to India and Ceylon where cultivation on plantations proved more efficient and profitable.

Foreigners also played a significant role in reorganizing and dynamizing export-orientated coastal agriculture. Sugar plantations had been a feature of coastal agriculture from Lima northwards since the colonial era. However, this region was also dotted with small farming communities, many remnants of earlier pre-Columbian systems, as well as medium-sized, poorly capitalized and rudimentarily operated haciendas, linked haphazardly and often precariously to local markets. A series of economic, technological and political changes around the middle of the nineteenth century, among them the advent of low-cost trans-oceanic steam travel, surplus capital accumulation from the guano boom, the abolition of slavery and the importation of Chinese indentured labour, and disentailment of church lands all served to set in motion a long-term process of 'monoculturalization' for the export of sugar. This process involved a general concentration and monopolization of land at the

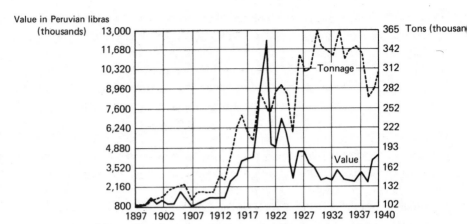

Fig. 6. Peruvian sugar exports, 1897–1940. *Source*: Peter F. Klarén, *Modernization, dislocation and Aprismo: origins of the Peruvian Aprista party, 1870–1932*
(Austin, Texas, 1973), 13.

expense of smaller holdings, crop specialization and mechanization, and
gradual proletarianization of the labour force – in short, the construction
of a modern, large-scale monocultural agricultural sector. While the wars
interrupted this process, it resumed with even greater intensity during
the reconstruction that followed.[10]

Sugar was the main commercial crop involved in this transformation,
its production following the upward trend of prices on the international
commodities markets (see figure 6). However, cotton growing also made
its appearance in coastal commercial agriculture as early as the demand
induced by shortages created by the American civil war. It would not
approach the significance of sugar in the economy, however, until the
turn of the century, particularly from the first world war (see figure 7).
Peruvian growers were quick to respond to price increases on the
international market. Not only did cultivation expand rapidly, but a new,
larger, more resistant fibre, developed by the grower Fermín Tangüis,
dramatically increased yields. Cotton production was concentrated in the
coastal river valleys south of Lima, mainly in the departments of Lima
and Ica. There, although the estates grew moderately in size, sharecropping (called *yanaconaje* on the coast) persisted. The cotton boom of

---

[10] See Peter F. Klarén, 'The social and economic consequences of modernization in the Peruvian
sugar industry, 1870–1930', in Kenneth Duncan and Ian Rutledge (eds.), *Land and labour in Latin
America* (Cambridge, 1977), 229–52.

Production (metric tons)

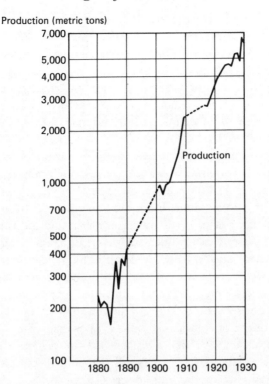

Fig. 7. Peruvian cotton production, 1880–1930. *Source*: Thorp and Bertram, *Peru 1890–1977*, 55.

the twentieth century, however, made such arrangements anachronistic. *Yanaconas* were uprooted and evicted from the cotton estates as economies of scale took hold and a surplus supply of seasonal labour (migrants called *enganchados* from Indian communities in the adjacent sierra) became available. While cotton never reached the level of production, concentration or technological sophistication of sugar, it did provide the financial base for several important oligarchical families, including the Graña, Mujica and Beltrán.

In the sugar industry, which was concentrated in the north, modernization was led after the wars by a group of hard-driving immigrants (the Italian Larcos, Irish Grace and German Gildemeisters), some of whom, as second or third generation 'Peruvians', were in the process of merging socially and politically into the ranks of the country's elite. They were joined by progressive, often foreign-educated nationals such as the Aspíllaga, Chopitea, Pardo and the upstart Leguía, and later de la Piedra, planters who had assimilated abroad the underlying conceptions – a technology of the mind – of modern, scientific, capitalist agriculture. While agrarian production, unlike mining, generally remained in the hands of nationals or nationalizing (second generation) immigrants, however, financing and marketing continued to be controlled by the old foreign trading houses (Grace, Graham Rowe, Gildemeister, etc.).

Foreign immigrants also played a significant role in other sectors of the 'modern' economy. The 1908 census, for example, revealed that nearly 10 per cent of the population of Lima (16,649) was foreign born, with Italians (3,944) comprising about one-quarter of the total. The latter made their imprint in small-scale commerce and industry, with some notable successes that included the ice-cream manufacturer D'Onofrio and the Banco Italiano (later Crédito). Foreign economic power in the capital, however, far outweighed their numbers. According to one 1896 commercial register, foreigners controlled 103 of the 113 merchant importing houses in the city, 161 of the 196 retail stores, 83 of the 94 other stores, 30 of the 43 commercial offices, 74 of the 92 factories and 720 of the 800 taverns (*pulperías*). This fact led the *civilista* Manuel Vicente Villarán to remark that 'we are rapidly becoming a colony of foreigners administered by Peruvian public servants'.[11]

But if Peru's economy and society was increasingly reshaped by foreign entrepreneurs and capital, most members of the emerging *civilista* oligarchy seemed not to object. In part this was due to the mentality of this group which deprecated much that was 'Peruvian' while generally indiscriminately extolling everything that was Western, a world view that was essentially underpinned by racism. It is true that they were displaced from mining and marginalized in important sectors of international commerce and banking, but they retained, for the most part, control of agrarian production in an era of expanding export agriculture. Moreover, an unusual conjuncture of favourable circumstances during the 1890s temporarily activated this group beyond the narrow limits of the export sector and into more diverse import-substituting industries. These factors included steadily rising local demand from wage earners in

---

[11] Quoted in Richard M. Morse, 'The Lima of Joaquín Capelo: a Latin American archetype', *Journal of Contemporary History*, 4/3 (1969), 107. Almost half of this total comprised Chinese (7,693), remnants of the influx of coolies in the mid nineteenth century who had fled the plantations and settled in the coastal cities where they constituted a major force in petty commerce.

the export enclaves, an increasing degree of political stability as the 'Aristocratic Republic' took shape, and a high rate of profit return and capital accumulation from the export sector. Industrial growth was further stimulated by rising tariffs and a rapidly depreciating exchange rate, both of which discouraged the influx of competitive imports from abroad. This has brought two leading revisionist economic historians to modify somewhat the established view of foreign domination which has prevailed in Peruvian historiography in recent years. They argue that there is considerable evidence that 'Peru in the 1890s achieved at least some degree of "autonomous development"', although they acknowledge that its economy was still largely export based and orientated towards metropolitan markets.[12]

While this modest degree of internal economic diversification and industrialization proved short lived, lasting only until the recession of 1907–8, it served to broaden and consolidate the economic and political power of the planter class which was rapidly transforming itself into a new plutocracy. Thus, by the turn of the century, as the urban economy expanded to service the export sector, the names of the most prominent sugar and cotton planters appeared with increasing frequency on the directories of the newly created banks, insurance, textile and utility companies. Already they had established the National Agrarian Society as a powerful semi-official lobby for their interests in the highest echelons of government. It remained only for the state to fall totally under the control of their Civilist party for this new bourgeoisie to assume complete dominance over the country's affairs.

Having backed Piérola in 1895 largely because they lacked a charismatic leader of their own,[13] the *civilistas* used the alliance to secure key government appointments and to position themselves for future elections. In 1899 Piérola stepped down in favour of the planter Eduardo López de Romaña. And in 1903 the *civilistas* broke the alliance and won the presidency outright for their astute strategist and leader Manuel Candamo. Economic power had now been formally joined to political power to form the new, liberal oligarchical state which would stand virtually uninterrupted, if not unchallenged, until 1919.

Nevertheless, it has been argued that this new state was something

---

[12] Rosemary Thorp and Geoffrey Bertram, *Peru 1890–1977: growth and policy in an open economy* (London, 1978), 36.

[13] At one point their party leader Rosas was alleged to have asked his colleagues wistfully: 'Who among us knows how to ride a horse?' Jorge Basadre, *Historia de la República del Perú* (6th edn, Lima, 1968–9), x, 100.

less than a truly national state.[14] For one thing, just as the country was divided on a regional basis, so too its ruling class was regionalized. Local elites in some ways were more cohesive and powerful than any national elite. Big sugar planters like Aspíllaga, Leguía and Pardo (from the north) and Romaña may have emerged at the centre of the oligarchical state, but others, like the miners and the sheep ranchers Fernandini, Olavegoya and Valladares in the central sierra, and the major wool merchants Forga, Gibson and Ricketts, together with their hacendado allies in the south, remained at the margins of this 'national' elite and constituted a regional limit on its exercise of state power.

Moreover, the haciendas themselves comprised another major obstacle to the formation of a truly national oligarchical state. Their boundaries often constituted the limits of central power. In fact, the state's inherent weakness compelled those who governed at the centre to rely on the local lords (*gamonales*) and their allies to keep order and to rule on the local level. Without an effective national police (the Guardia Civil was not created until the 1920s) and with the army still in the process of modernization, the oligarchical state often had little choice but to leave the instruments of violence for the repression and control of the popular classes in the hands of the *gamonales* and their agents. Finally, the foreign controlled mining and sugar enclaves became to some extent 'states within a state', virtually autonomous entities impervious to the authority of the oligarchical state when their respective interests diverged.

With all these limitations the oligarchy was able to achieve its dominance largely because the middle sectors were numerically small and 'dependent' while the popular classes remained heterogeneous, divided and with a limited sense of class identity or solidarity. Race, ethnicity, language (the Indians spoke Quechua and Aymara), geography and the fragmented character of rural society all worked to divide the masses and enable a ruling class to achieve a measure of control over the country. But that control, it should be emphasized, was tenuous and by no means absolute during the period of the 'Aristocratic Republic'.

The composition and internal dynamic of this *civilista* oligarchy has been aptly described by Basadre in the following fashion:

Generally (with some notorious exceptions) this party [sic] was composed of large urban property holders, the great sugar and cotton planters, prosperous businessmen, lawyers with the most famous practices, doctors who had the best clientele and university professors; in short, the most successful people in the

---

[14] Manuel Burga and Alberto Flores Galindo, *Apogeo y crisis de la república aristocrática* (Lima, 1979), 89.

country. The party's directorate was made up of urbane gentlemen, some connected to the countryside, in something like a Creole adaptation of the English country squire. They had an intense club life, resided in houses furnished in the colonial style with rugs and curtains at a time when fresh air was shunned. They dressed in black frock coats and the most fashionable trousers, made by French tailors in the capital, and lived in a happy world, interconnected by marriages within their group.[15]

Within this class an informal group known as the 'Twenty-Four Friends' formed a core elite which met regularly at the exclusive Club Nacional to discuss the management of national affairs. It included two men who occupied the presidency for a total of 24 years (José Pardo and Augusto B. Leguía), at least eight Cabinet ministers, including five treasury ministers, three presidents of the Senate and the publishers of Lima's two major newspapers.[16] Like most Latin American elites they formed a closed, close-knit and cohesive social constellation, bound together by ties of family and kinship. Indeed, Basadre sees them as a closed caste:

Marriages were made among a small number of families, endogamously. Their children's education began in exclusive schools. Playmates continued as schoolmates and as classmates in the universities . . . they greeted each other ceremoniously, they went to Sunday mass together, they dined, drank, and chatted together in the Club Nacional, they occupied the preferred seats at the bullring, race track, and theatres, they also met each other in the Congress, the charity organizations, the university faculties, the Chamber of Commerce, the directors' meetings of the large banks or industrial enterprises, and the parties and discussion groups held in the same drawing rooms, and they saw their names in the social pages of the same newspapers. Families were generally large with an abundance of servants, who were sometimes treated as if they belonged to the same family circle. There were drawing rooms where only those with certain surnames could enter and which were closed to those who had only the power of money; there were families before which one knelt in respect, awe, and adulation. The daughter of one of these once said in Europe, 'In my country I am like a princess.'[17]

EMERGENCE OF THE SOCIAL QUESTION

While the *civilista* oligarchy consolidated its hold on the apparatus of the state, economic and demographic forces began to alter the country's social landscape. The overall population rose from an estimated 2.7

[15] Basadre, *Historia de la República*, XI, 127.
[16] See Dennis Gilbert, *The oligarchy and the old regime in Peru* (Latin American Studies Program Dissertation Series, Cornell University, 1977), 55–6.
[17] Basadre, *Historia de la República*, XVI, 299–300.

million in 1876 to 3.5 million in 1908, and to 4.8 million in 1920. This was 0.9 per cent on an average annual basis, but sharply higher by the end of the century than during and after the wars. Lima's population, also reflecting the impact of the wars, rose only marginally from 100,000 in 1876 to 104,000 in 1891. However, between 1890 and 1930 the city's population tripled, rising to 141,000 in 1908, 224,000 in 1920 and 384,000 in 1932. By contrast the country's other major urban centres, Arequipa, Cuzco and Trujillo, had in 1908 populations of only 35,000, 18,500 and 10,000 respectively. Lima's substantially higher growth rate reflected its rapid development after 1895 as the administrative and financial centre of the expanding export economy. As the economic pace quickened and communications with the interior improved, particularly with the expansion of the railway network, the capital began to attract substantial numbers of migrants. While they came from all classes of the provincial social spectrum, most were from the countryside where they were being pushed off the land by enclosure and demographic pressures (the population of the central sierra, for example, doubled between 1876 and 1940), and pulled towards Lima by the promise of employment opportunities. That promise tended to fade, however, when the modernizing sector was unable to expand fast enough to accommodate all the newcomers, a problem that would intensify as the century developed. As early as 1903 the first urban slum (*barriada*) appeared in the capital – at San Francisco de la Tablada in Lurín. This rural to urban migration is reflected in the percentage of the city's population born outside Lima, which rose from 37 per cent in 1858, to 58.5 per cent in 1908 and to a high of 63.5 per cent in 1920.[18] It is worth noting, however, that despite this trend, the essentially rural and agrarian character of the nation persisted. Lima still contained less than 5 per cent of the national population, as compared to Havana (14 per cent in 1919), Santiago (14 per cent in 1920) and Buenos Aires (19 per cent in 1914).

Internal migration, however, comprised only one part of the demographic equation after 1895. Expanding economic opportunity was accompanied by dramatic improvements in public health. Better sanitation and medical facilities in Lima, and to some extent in the country as a whole, gradually helped to reduce such lethal diseases as malaria, typhoid fever, and smallpox. The mortality rate began to fall after 1895, signalling a shift from the traditional pattern of high mortality

---

[18] Carl Herbold, 'Peru', in Richard Morse (ed.), *The urban development of Latin America 1750–1920* (Stanford, 1971), 109.

and long-term tendency towards population stagnation to a more modern pattern defined by a constant demographic increase. In effect, Peru was beginning to experience the process of 'demographic modernization' which occurred in Europe from the middle of the seventeenth century.

If Lima's population was rapidly growing around this time, so too was its labour force. Historically the working class, such as it was, was clustered not only in the city but also in the nearby port of Callao, the main terminal for the export economy. However, around the turn of the century the growth of manufacturing added a new dimension to this force. It was concentrated mainly in food processing and textile production, the latter receiving an estimated one million pounds sterling in capital investment and supplying a third of local consumption by 1905. Indeed, the number of factories in metropolitan Lima (including Callao) more than tripled between 1890 (69) and 1920 (244), although most were small scale, employing only a handful of workers. The largest concentration was to be found in the big textile factories like El Inca or Vitarte; the latter had some 1,250 workers in 1902 and 3,835 by 1918.

Estimates of the total labouring population of Lima are risky at best. However, according to census figures (which lumped workers and artisans together), it amounted to 9,500 in 1876, 24,000 in 1908 and 44,000 in 1920. Significantly, the proportion of the working class rose from 9.5 per cent of the city's population in 1876 to 16.9 in 1908 and 19.8 in 1920.[19]

With this kind of growth it was not long into the new century before the first stirrings of a nascent labour movement could be discerned. In 1905 the Federation of Bread Workers, 'La Estrella del Perú', one of the earliest to seek authentically proletarian goals, above all, a reduction in working hours, was founded. It may be distinguished from the mutual aid societies, perhaps as many as 62 in the city in 1911, whose purposes, as the name implies, were more associational and fraternal than combative.

The mutual aid societies were the precursors, but it remained for the anarchists to give the labour movement a militantly anti-capitalist tone. Under their aegis the first general strike in the country's history occurred in Lima in 1911. While providing the working class with an ideology to challenge the established order in such newspapers as *La Protesta* (1911–26), anarcho-syndicalists, as elsewhere, seemed to become in time more

---

[19] Peter Blanchard, *The origins of the Peruvian labor movement, 1883–1919* (Pittsburgh, 1982), 8–12.

concerned about promoting their grand design for the abolition of the state, than the tactical problems confronting a growing urban proletariat. By the end of the first world war their influence was already on the wane in the face of competing ideologies such as socialism. Their last great victory, as we shall see, came in the 1919 mobilization for the eight-hour day in Lima. However, their influence continued beyond 1919, particularly in so far as they played a role in the ideological formation of Víctor Raúl Haya de la Torre and José Carlos Mariátegui.

Lima was not the only place where a nascent working class was forming. Along the north coast sizeable proletarian enclaves were emerging in the rural export sector, most notably in the expanding sugar industry and to a lesser degree in auxiliary enterprises such as rice growing. A stable labour supply had historically been a problem for estate owners of the sparsely populated coast, particularly after the abolition of slavery in 1854. The securing of a new source of labour was made possible by state indemnification, financed from guano revenues, which enabled planters to import some 100,000 Chinese indentured servants over the next two decades. But planter exploitation together with Chinese disinclination to remain on the estates after their contracts expired resulted in the termination of this labour source shortly before the outbreak of the War of the Pacific.

With the ending of the wars and the beginning of economic expansion, the planters turned to the sierra for a new supply of labour. Combining pre-capitalist forms of coerced labour with the new demands of capitalist plantation agriculture for wage labour, they resorted to a system of draft labour known as *enganche*. Labour contractors (*enganchadores*), often prosperous local merchants or hacendados, recruited workers (*enganchados*) among the Indian and *mestizo* peasantry, who in return for advance payments were obliged to pay off their debts by working on the coastal plantations. While in some cases subjecting the worker to a form of debt peonage sometimes amounting virtually to enslavement, the arrangement provided a ready source of capital for hard-pressed peasant farmers in a historically underdeveloped region, where not only was peasant access to land blocked by the *latifundista* land tenure system, but the fragile peasant economy was severely depressed by a decade of foreign invasion, civil war and endemic banditry. The cash derived from *enganche* and ensuing wage labour on the coastal plantations, despite its relative hardship and occasional abuses, was viewed as a solution to the problem of peasant survival.

Similarly, further south where cotton plantations were expanding to meet foreign demand, Indian communities in the sierra of Huancavelica were able to survive a long-term crisis through capital remittances from *enganchados* working on cotton estates in Ica. On the other hand, some historians have seen labour out-migration from the central sierra more as a longer-term consequence of capitalism's penetration of the inner structure of the peasant community. A peasant bourgeoisie gradually emerged to monopolize communal land and resources to the detriment of a pauperized stratum of peasants who, cut off from those resources, chose to migrate to the plantations or mines where work was available.[20] One further point should be made here regarding the causes of migration. By the end of the 1920s the population of the sierra was beginning to grow, creating in the process an increasingly acute land shortage, particularly in the peasant communities. This fact did not escape the notice of the labour recruiters from the plantations and mines whose 'harvest' increased accordingly.

Much of this migratory labour flow was seasonal in nature, coinciding with the agricultural cycles in both the sierra and on the coast. Yet growing numbers of *enganchados* were gradually pulled into the incipient capitalist labour market on the coast, either as permanent plantation residents or as transient workers, moving from estate to estate and/or mine or state public works project (irrigation, road building, etc.), wherever they could obtain a better wage. A worker on the Pomalca plantation in Lambayeque, for example, recounted his experiences in that early evolving regional labour market:

I was born in Catacaos (Piura Department) in 1890 . . . My father had a lot of land, but little by little the wealthy landlords of the valley got it away from him. There were many battles over the irrigation water, and the big landowners always won . . . I came to Pomalca in 1913 after working in various haciendas and mines including San Rafael (Casma), Vilca Huaca (Huacho), San Nicolás (Supe) and Cerro de Pasco. . . . In Catacaos the wage rate was sixty *centavos* per day and in Pomalca it was one *sol*; naturally the people came running.[21]

[20] Florencia E. Mallon, *The defense of community in Peru's central highlands: peasant struggle and capitalist transition, 1860–1940* (Princeton, NJ, 1983), chapter 3; Henri Favre, 'The dynamics of Indian peasant society and migration to coastal plantations in Central Peru', in Duncan and Rutledge (eds.), *Land and labour*, 253–68. On the *enganche* system see also Michael J. Gonzales, 'Capitalist agriculture and labour contracting in Northern Peru, 1880–1905', *JLAS*, 12/2 (1980), 291–315, and Peter Blanchard, 'The recruitment of workers in the Peruvian Sierra at the turn of the century: the enganche system', *Inter-American Economic Affairs*, 33 (1979), 63–83.

[21] Douglas Horton, *Haciendas and cooperatives: a study of estate organization, land reform and new reform enterprises in Peru* (Latin American Studies Program Dissertation Series, Cornell University, 1976), 149.

Together with proletarianized *minifundistas* from the small coastal farming communities, whose holdings were absorbed into the expanding plantations, and remnants of the old slave and indentured labour force, these sometime migrants formed part of a new, rural proletariat. By the end of the first world war, the sugar plantations had a work force of almost 30,000, and the cotton plantations a force of over 35,000, a critical mass soon pulled into the nascent labour movement already galvanizing the working class in Lima. Anarcho-syndicalist doctrines, in particular, diffused north from the capital, penetrating the Huacho and Trujillo regions. The result was a widening circle of labour unrest which exploded into violent strikes all along the coast in 1910, 1912, 1916 and 1919.

A similar pattern of peasant migration, proletarianization and labour agitation also developed in the mining enclaves. Mining centres like Cerro de Pasco (copper), Talara (oil) and Quirivilca (copper) drew workers from the nearby sierra where the peasantry was hard pressed after the wars to sustain themselves in their traditional communities. Cerro de Pasco's population, for example, grew from 6,400 in 1876 to 25,500 in 1940, and it alone soon accounted for up to 30 per cent of the total mining proletariat in the entire country. Similarly, the number of workers in the oil industry more than doubled from 9,700 in 1905 to 22,500 in 1920. These mining enterprises produced the notorious 'company towns' whose labour conflicts and special enclave character are legendary in the early history of Latin American capitalism.

Like many of the sugar or cotton workers on the coast, Andean miners retained close, continuing links to their communities, viewing their activities in the enclaves as temporary, indeed secondary, occupations. They migrated to the mines between agricultural seasons in search of extra income, often returning after a few months to resume their agrarian tasks. Even those who chose to remain in the mines for longer periods continued to maintain, through family and kinship, close connections to their villages. As outwardly reflected in their dress, they were both miners and *campesinos*, a sort of 'mixed' or 'transitional' proletariat,[22] quite dissimilar in world view and work objectives from, say, textile workers at Vitarte in Lima.

In the central and southern highlands of Peru, where agrarian structures differed sharply from the north coast, the impact of new

[22] Burga and Flores Galindo, *Apogeo y crisis*, 34–47.

capitalist modes of production was equally varied and profound. The sierra from Cuzco southwards, the core of the old Inca empire, was still heavily influenced and shaped by traditional Indian life and work patterns. The Indian community, for example, had survived the conquest and thereafter persisted, though in a different and changing form, as a pole of resistance to the periodically expanding hacienda system.

As elsewhere along the Andean spine, rural society was dominated by the struggle between the haciendas and the *comunidades* for control of the land, water and labour which constituted the main factors of production. This was a struggle, however, that was gradually being won by the haciendas which early on had laid claim to the most fertile and well-watered land in the intermontane valleys, forcing the *comunidades* into the marginally productive areas that remained, often the rocky, steep and barren slopes of the Andes themselves. The struggle quickened as the nineteenth century drew to a close. Capitalist forms, dynamized by the demand for primary products on the world market, increasingly penetrated the Andean hinterland. In many respects, they followed the path of railway construction, which had begun in a grand manner during the guano age only to be abruptly halted during the crisis decades of the 1870s and 1880s, to be resumed again during reconstruction. The legendary North American entrepreneur Henry Meigg's vision of a central railway was finally completed in 1891. Subsequently branch lines connected Lima with Huancayo in 1908, Cerro de Pasco shortly thereafter and Cuzco and Huancavelica in the 1920s.

In the south, the Mollendo–Arequipa route, completed in 1870, reached Puno in 1908. Its extension further stimulated the wool trade in the southern sierra which had burgeoned because of rising external demand, mainly from Great Britain (see table 1). The trade was organized and articulated by several commercial houses centred on Arequipa, which had been founded around the time of independence by various foreign immigrants such as the Englishmen Gibson, Ricketts and Stafford. Unlike their counterparts in the north, however, these merchant entrepreneurs made no effort to alter or change the pre-capitalist modes of agrarian production in the region. Rather they were content to co-exist with the traditional pastoral structure, trading with the region's hacendados who in turn monopolized the production and appropriation of wool from the peasantry on their estates. In this fashion the modern wool merchandizing sector of the economy actually served

The Andean Republics

Table 1. *Exports of Peruvian wool, 1830–1929*
(metric tons, annual averages)

	Alpaca	Sheep wool	Total
1830–9	342	8	350
1840–9	1,162	64	1,226
1850–9	924	1,006	1,930
1860–9	1,167	1,671	2,838
1870–9	1,582	1,589	3,171
1880–9	1,584	1,040	2,624
1890–9	1,821	1,288	3,109
1900–9	2,492[a]	1,336[a]	3,867
1910–19	3,097[b]	2,700[b]	5,286
1920–9	2,730	1,840	4,570

Notes: [a] Excluding 1901, 1903 and 1907.
[b] 1913–19 only.
The variation in the periods covered by the data explains why for certain years the components do not add up to the total.
Source: Thorp and Bertram, *Peru, 1890–1977*, 64.

to reinforce the 'feudal' character of the region's agrarian system. The wool merchants' profits from exports, in contrast to sugar or cotton, were not large enough to give incentive to the takeover and capitalization of the traditional ranches of the region. Instead they reinvested their profits in local high profit enterprises like mining, construction and textiles which fortified their position as an emerging regional oligarchy.

On the other hand, as wool prices on the world market steadily advanced after 1913, the ranchers themselves moved to intensify production by expanding their pasturelands and flocks, often at the expense of traditional peasant rights. The response from an increasingly dislocated and more intensively exploited peasantry was a series of bloody, though short-lived, uprisings, by one count numbering over 300 between 1901 and 1930.[23] One of the most famous of these revolts erupted in Puno in 1915. It was led by Teodomiro Gutiérrez Cuevas, a former soldier and provincial official, who assumed the Indian name Rumi-Maqui (hand of stone) and tried to revive the lost Indian empire of Tawantinsuyo. Drawing on deeply rooted Andean millenarian senti-

[23] Alberto Flores Galindo, *Arequipa y el Sur Andino, siglos XVIII–XX* (Lima, 1977), 123–5.

ments, Rumi-Maqui raised a ragtag peasant army which attacked several haciendas before being dispersed by the regular army.

Peasant society was similarly disrupted in parts of Ayacucho department by cattle estates whose growth was stimulated during the first quarter of the twentieth century by a growing demand for beef on the rapidly urbanizing coast. In his novel *Yawar fiesta* (1941), José María Arguedas has eloquently recounted the clash, for example, between the *mistis* (a term used by Indians for the white/*mestizo* landowners of the southern Andes), who needed increased grazing land for their herds, and the *comunidades* of Puquio.

Sporadic cases of disruption of peasant society as capitalism advanced also occurred in the 1920s in the central and northern highlands. There the Cerro de Pasco Mining Company, for example, in search of cheap food supplies and a stable labour force, purchased and modernized a number of large haciendas. Aided by the temporary ecological damage caused by its smelting operations, the company acquired close to 30 haciendas, covering 270,000 hectares or 1,057 square miles. Having already dislocated hundreds of small and medium-sized miners in its consolidation of copper mining, the company repeated the process to the detriment of the region's peasants, *colonos* (tenant cultivators on haciendas) and smallholders.

In the process of reorganizing these archaic haciendas for more efficient capitalist production, tenant arrangements, often of long standing, were abruptly terminated, uprooting and dislocating the estates' traditional work force. A similar, though less dramatic, modernization affected highland estates in the north where coastal sugar planting companies like Casa Grande acquired old, often decaying estates in the adjacent sierra in order to secure a stable food and labour supply. *Colonos* were not only uprooted and proletarianized but sometimes transferred to work on the coastal plantation when labour was in short supply.

It seems, however, that only the largest and most powerful capitalist enterprises – for example, Ganadera de Cerro de Pasco, Casa Grande, Pomalca and Fernandini – successfully carried out such estate reorganization plans. Other similarly 'progressive' but less powerful sierra landlords may have wished to follow suit, hoping to evict or otherwise convert their internal work force into wage labourers in order to turn a better profit. More often than not, however, peasants successfully resisted these efforts to force or induce them into relinquishing usufruct of hacienda resources, namely grazing rights and agricultural subsistence plots. These landlords, it seems, lacked the power to enforce their modernization plans.[24]

Capitalism was also affecting highland Indian communities in ways other than by enclosure. As the formation of a commercial economy in the central highlands accelerated, first developed by the region's elites after 1860 and then expanded by the arrival in 1900 of large-scale foreign enterprise in the mining sector, the 'moral economy' of peasant society was gradually but inexorably eroded. Within that society a peasant bourgeoisie emerged, integrating itself into the wider capitalizing network of the regional economy, largely through evolving clientelistic relationships with merchants, miners and progressive hacendados. The result, it has been argued, was a sharpening process of class differentiation, stratification and conflict which, particularly after 1930, left village society severely polarized. On one side stood the emergent peasant bourgeoisie or capitalist small farmer; on the other, an increasingly pauperized, proletarianized stratum of peasants, many of whom chose to out-migrate to the mines, plantations and cities.[25]

Thus, as parts of the sierra were pulled into the international economy towards the end of the century and increasingly thereafter, the social structure, including that of the Indian village, became more complex and differentiated. The privatization of land, commercialization of haciendas, expansion of mining, growth in population, urbanization and the extension of railway and road networks all worked, on the village level, to increase commercial opportunities, intensify pressures on the land and expand the possibilities for wage labour. The result was an accelerating social stratification as traders and market-orientated peasants emerged alongside landless labourers and worker peasants.

While it is clear that parts of Andean rural society were indeed undergoing profound change from the advent of these new economic forces, it is also true that much of that society remained locked into a structure of traditionalism and stagnation that dated back to the seventeenth century. The lynchpin of that structure was the hacienda, whose longevity over the centuries and resistance to change has constituted one of the continuing developmental problems of the twentieth century. Some idea of the hacienda's demographic dimensions

---

[24] See Juan Martínez-Alier, *Haciendas, plantations and collective farms: agrarian class societies – Cuba and Peru* (London, 1977), 67–92. [25] Mallon, *The defense of community*, ch. 3.

at the beginning of the period under review can be gleaned from the 1876 census, which counted 3,867 such units containing 373,355 inhabitants or 24.7 per cent of the rural population. While many haciendas were relatively small or medium sized, comprising between 50 and a few hundred hectares, others occupied enormous, if often under-utilized, areas. In the northern sierra, for example, the hacienda Udima comprised well over 100,000 hectares while the expanding Sociedad Ganadera del Centro in 1930 already embraced some 230,673 hectares.

Despite their size, however, haciendas were generally characterized by low productivity. Even by the twentieth century estates were still more often than not, by modern standards, haphazardly managed (often by absentee landlords), poorly capitalized, with profits consumed rather than reinvested, and only loosely connected to the limited market economy, such as it was. Their work force consisted in the main of Indian *colonos* who, in exchange for a plot of subsistence land (*mañay*), were required to work a certain number of days on estate (*demnse*) land (*faenas*) and/or in the master's household (*pongaje*). While Indians occasionally also worked for wages, they were mostly paid in kind or goods from the hacienda store (*cantina*). Indeed, money was generally a rare commodity in the hacienda world, where barter was the characteristic mode 'of exchange in the market place. In fact, until well into the twentieth century, it was rare to find any system of accounting practised on Andean estates.

Mobility among estate workers was also rare, not only because debt peonage often tied workers to the estate, but also because the relative condition of *colonos*, who enjoyed some measure of security, was better than occasional wage labourers in the often depressed local labour market. So peasant life was largely confined to the estate where periodic religious holidays and festivals brightened an otherwise materially barren, humdrum existence.

Personal relationships in this world were defined by the age-old paternalism that had evolved out of Iberian feudalism and its hybridization in the Andes under the influence of Incaic custom. It was characterized by a certain asymmetrical reciprocity that saw freedom and independence exchanged for the security of a plot of land; obedience, submission and loyalty offered in return for 'protection' and the possibility of acquiring the necessities of life at a subsistence level. A *patron*'s treatment of 'his Indians' could be likened to that of the stern father with his children; if they were 'good', they were rewarded with a certain kindness, even tenderness, but should they 'misbehave', step outside their proscribed roles, challenge the authority of the father, then punishment was meted out to the deviant, often in a violent, even despotic fashion.

Power in this society was, of course, monopolized by the lords. And when benevolent paternalism broke down, as it often did in the context of landlord absenteeism, when subordinates (*mayordomos*) assumed daily management of the estate, little by way of protection could ensure justice for the powerless. The church could exert a certain moral force, but local priests more often than not were on the payroll of the landlords, or at least dependent, as was the church itself, on the largesse of their employer-benefactor. The state, remote and weak, rarely penetrated this world, ceding authority to the lords and their local allies who could and did keep order. If and when it did intervene, as in the case of individual or group rebellion, it collaborated with local power to maintain the established order. At its worst this world was characterized, as González Prada so aptly put it, by the 'tyranny of the justice of the peace, the governor and local priest, that brutalizing trinity that kept the Indian perpetually oppressed'.[26]

THE LIBERAL OLIGARCHY AND THE SOCIAL QUESTION, 1904–19

The social dislocations and tensions that accompanied the diffusion of capitalism along the coast and then its penetration of the sierra became one of the central issues of the times. In the halls of congress and elegant club salons, where the elite gathered to socialize and talk politics, the paramount question was how to deal with the deepening new crisis. Having succeeded in establishing its political hegemony in the country, the *civilista* oligarchy was now increasingly confronted with the longer-term challenge of resolving the social repercussions of the capitalist advance which they had so eagerly embraced. The social crisis threatened seriously to divide the oligarchy and even to erode the legitimacy of the oligarchical state.

The first signs of political discord within the ruling Civilist party, however, were more internal than externally motivated. A generational split within the oligarchy appeared in 1904 over the selection of the

---

[26] Quoted in Julio Cotler, *Clases, estado y nación en el Perú* (Lima, 1977), 123; 'La tiranía del juez de paz, del gobernador y del cura, esa trinidad embrutecedora del indio.'

civilista presidential candidate. The younger, more progressive candidate José Pardo, son of the guano consignee and party founder Manuel Pardo, triumphed over the old guard and became the party nominee. That was tantamount to election, given the party's control of the state and its electoral apparatus, and Pardo assumed office for a four-year term (1904–8).

During Pardo's tenure the social question broke into the political arena. In 1904, that is to say, before the outbreak of serious labour unrest, José Matías Manzanilla, a leading jurist and *civilista* ideologue who had studied the problem from a European perspective, placed before Congress a series of reform measures. The proposed laws dealt with such classic labour/capital issues as mediation and arbitration, worker compensation for job-related accidents, protection of children and women in the work place and the length of the working week. However, the proposals stirred up a hornets' nest of opposition among party conservatives who managed over the next several years to block for the most part their passage in Congress.

Party unity suffered a further blow during the regime of Pardo's successor and protégé, Augusto B. Leguía (1908–12). Leguía, a self-made man who had gained entrance to the oligarchy by virtue of his talent, charm, and business success, soon broke with Pardo and other elements of the party leadership. Highly ambitious and independently minded, Leguía was intent upon charting his own course in office and was soon viewed as a dangerous political maverick by mainstream *civilistas*.

After successfully surviving an attempted Piérolist *putsch* in 1909, Leguía became increasingly embroiled with the party over certain foreign policy and budgetary questions (he departed from the historic laissez-faire policies of the *civilistas* by proposing substantial increases in government spending) as well as over his own arbitrary style of governing. These disagreements came to a head in 1911 when he tried to manage Congressional elections by dissolving the National Election Board (Junta Electoral Nacional). This led a number of *civilistas* to form an anti-Leguía block in Congress (El Bloque) and then, when he succeeded in contriving a legislative majority, to break with the party in order to organize the Independent Civilist party.

Weakened by this deepening split within its own ranks and challenged by increasing urban unrest, *civilista* political control of the country momentarily faltered in 1912. The election to the presidency of Antero

Aspíllaga, the *civilista* candidate, was blocked by a general strike organized by the supporters of the former mayor of Lima and Democrat, Guillermo E. Billinghurst. The contest had to be decided in Congress. There Billinghurst, with strong working-class support in the streets, struck a bargain with Leguía's forces and was elected president.

Something of a political maverick, and an early populist, Billinghurst, although wealthy from family nitrate interests, stood apart from the *civilista* oligarchy. Long a supporter and political protégé of Piérola, he had built up his following among the Lima working class while mayor of the city from 1909. As mayor he had demonstrated a certain paternalistic, if not demagogic, concern for the interests of the new working classes which included efforts to improve their housing, education and general condition. Once in the presidency, Billinghurst tried to expand such progressive policies in an effort to reconcile the growing rift in the country between labour and capital. He formulated a programme that, with certain exceptions, legalized the right of unions to organize and strike while establishing compulsory arbitration panels composed of representatives of both management and labour. Unable to convince a conservative majority in Congress to approve the programme, Billinghurst tried to mobilize the masses directly into the political process by organizing militant worker committees to pressure Congress. A backlash immediately swept through Congress as the outraged oligarchy saw its monopoly of political power suddenly threatened.

Discontent with Billinghurst also manifested itself within the military. In part this was due to the military's perception of a certain 'softness' in the president's attitude towards Chile at a time of delicate negotiations over the thorny question of the future of Tacna and Arica. Billinghurst had also moved to reduce the military share of the budget from 25 to 21 per cent.[27]

Despite widespread popular support, then, the alienation of both the oligarchy and the army proved fatal to the Billinghurst administration. Having earlier worked to depoliticize the military, the *civilistas* now turned around and conspired with it to bring down the government. In 1914 Colonel Oscar R. Benavides led a successful *golpe* against Billinghurst, which cemented the tacit alliance between the army and the

[27] Ernesto Yepes del Castillo, 'El desarrollo Peruano en las primeras décadas del siglo XX', in *Nueva historia general del Perú* (Lima, 1979), 153.

ruling class to maintain the established order. The following year former president José Pardo was re-elected.

The second Pardo administration (1915–19) coincided with the economic dislocations in the Latin American periphery caused by the first world war. At first the war cut the export-dependent Peruvian economy off from its European markets precipitating an immediate depression. Once Peru regained access to its former markets a year or two later, however, exports to the war-ravaged combatants surged. Wartime prosperity, however, brought in its wake some serious economic distortions that intensified existing social tensions. The cost of living in Lima, for example, almost doubled between 1914 and 1918 while wages remained virtually stationary. Part of this inflation was caused by a shift in agricultural production along the coast away from foodstuffs and towards such cash crops as sugar and cotton whose price on the world market soared. A wave of workers' strikes erupted both in Lima and in the export enclaves, where disruptions threatened to cripple the country's major sources of foreign exchange and state revenue as well as damage the interests of some of the most powerful elements in the Civilist party. Pardo responded by finally pushing through Congress some of the labour laws first introduced by Manzanilla over a decade before, including protection of female and child workers, certain mandatory rest days for workers, provision of working-class housing, schools and medical services and prohibition of *enganche*. (These reforms applied only to the modern enclave sectors of the economy, that is to say, to urban, plantation and mine workers. Little or nothing was done for the politically powerless peasant labourers on the haciendas of the sierra.) These palliatives, however, proved ineffective in stemming the mounting unrest in the workplace. Unwilling or unable to go further in the direction of reform, perhaps because the Billinghurst experience had hardened the attitudes of the *civilista* oligarchy, Pardo increasingly fell back upon the time-honoured prescription of state repression. The result was serious class confrontation, especially in Lima, as Pardo's term drew to a close in 1918–19.

A wave of work stoppages culminated early in 1919 in a massive general strike which paralysed the capital. Demanding an eight-hour day and a general lowering of the soaring cost of living, the militant strikers cast a chilling fear through the ranks of the *civilista* political establishment. As the spectre of Bolshevism was raised for the first time in the halls of Congress, the streets of Lima became a bloody battleground between strikers and mounted riot police. What made this situation more politically dangerous and volatile than before was the fact that other sectors of society were adopting a similarly rebellious attitude towards the *ancien régime*. As we have seen, peasant uprisings in the south were intensifying at this time. Perhaps even more ominously, sectors of the middle class not only sympathized with but joined the workers in the streets. Rapid growth in both the state bureaucracy and the private export sector had, as in other Latin American countries, created a new middle class with potentially differing interests, attitudes and aspirations from the entrenched ruling *civilista* oligarchy.

One place where this change in the class structure was readily visible was at the nation's leading university, San Marcos. The number of newly matriculating students, drawn mostly from the provincial and urban middle sectors, nearly doubled between 1907 and 1917. Organized politically as early as 1908, these middle-class students moved thereafter to reform the antiquated curriculum and administrative structures of the university in order to create a new space for their particular needs and aspirations. Just as the Billinghurst interlude had foreshadowed in many ways the coming crisis of the aging *civilista* order, the university reform movement of 1918 symbolized in microcosm the larger societal trends that were undermining that order. Only when the movement was joined in 1919 to the working-class struggle for the eight-hour day, however, would that order come to an abrupt end.

Another indication of ferment and rebellion among sectors of the new middle class and an important ideological contributor to the popular mobilizations of 1919 was the *indigenista* movement. Inspired by the increasing incidence of peasant insurgency over the past decade, some middle-class intellectuals, many of them *mestizo*, began to rediscover the virtues and values of Peru's Indian civilization, both past and present. The main currents of art and literature of the period expressed a strong ethnic and cultural nationalism which served to differentiate the emerging middle sectors from the 'Europeanized' elites. Critical of the economic and political structures created by the *civilistas*, *indigenismo* also had the effect of reinforcing the incipient rebellion of the masses.

In the end the real seeds of the revolt that ended *civilista* rule lay within the body politic of the regime itself which would not modify its essentially anti-democratic and elitist ethos in the face of widespread popular protest. One inherent problem of the regime was its inability to elaborate a national culture, with roots in the popular consciousness, that might have served, at a minimum level, to unify the country and polity and lend legitimacy to the state. To a large extent this failure was due to the foreign rather than national orientation of the dominant class.

Even had the *civilistas* succeeded in formulating and projecting some sort of 'nationalizing' culture, its diffusion among the popular classes would have been problematic at best. Despite an intense debate over the nature of education in society at the turn of the century,[28] between, for example, Alejandro Deustua who defended the elitist, traditional educational system and Manuel Vicente Villarán who sought to democratize and infuse it with a more modern scientific and technical orientation more appropriate in his view to the new capitalist age, the ideological apparatus of the liberal state, unlike its coercive abilities, remained weak and underdeveloped during most of the 'Aristocratic Republic'. As a result public expenditures on education throughout the period were extremely low, resulting in an abnormally high rate of national illiteracy. Furthermore, the content of such scant public education did not work to forge a national culture, but rather served to diffuse the elite's profoundly aristocratic and 'neo-feudal' values among the middle and upper classes, while instilling a sense of resignation and fatalism among the masses.

Such a profoundly elitist educational system was, of course, simply a manifestation of the larger anti-democratic mentality which characterized the *civilista* oligarchy. While it is true, for example, that formal parliamentary democracy, at least in theory, existed during most of the period of *civilista* rule, it was in practice extremely limited. Not only was parliament subordinate to the executive power, but it did not represent the various social strata and regional groupings in society. Thus, the urban middle or working classes were represented to only a limited extent while the peasantry remained totally excluded, unless one accepts the specious argument that their interests were represented by their rural bosses, the big landowners, or *gamonales* as they were called in the Andes. Voting in such a 'democracy' was restricted to about 3 per cent of the total population (104,000 in the 1899 elections, 147,000 in 1915). Yet even with such reduced numbers, electoral politics was customarily 'managed' from above by the dominant party, in this case the *civilistas*, who controlled the electoral apparatus and who resorted to manipulation

[28] See Alejandro Deustua, *La cultura nacional* (Lima, 1937) and Manuel Vicente Villarán, *Páginas escogidas*, ed. Jorge Basadre (Lima, 1962).

through fraudulent procedures and other electoral abuses. In short, electoral fraud was a political constant of the liberal state.

Three figures played key roles in the demise of the old *civilista* regime. Two, Víctor Raúl Haya de la Torre and José Carlos Mariátegui, were drawn from the emerging 'generation of 1919', one as student activist and erstwhile revolutionary and the other as proletarian ideologist. Both were products of the social changes that had gathered momentum since the turn of the century and that were now beginning to alter the political scene. Both also played a leading role in the formation of a new national consciousness. Challenging the ideological and philosophical assumptions of the *civilista* order, much as González Prada had done a generation earlier, they began to formulate what they perceived to be the fundamental problem confronting the nation: its semi-colonial and semi-feudal character. From a theoretical critique of society that in both cases owed much to Karl Marx, they would go on to exert a tremendous influence on the course of national politics for the rest of the century. Yet while emanating from the same social matrix, the two men would differ considerably in the character of their politics, Haya assuming an essentially reformist posture while Mariátegui adopted a revolutionary stance.

Haya de la Torre was born in Trujillo in 1895. His family was upper middle class, with ties to the declining sugar planter aristocracy of the region. As a boy he grew up at a time when capitalism was rapidly transforming and disfiguring the seignorial character of his home town and region. After attending the local university, he, like so many members of his generation and class, left the provinces for the glitter and promise of the capital in order to study law at San Marcos. Soon he was heavily engaged in university politics and in 1919 was one of several leaders who led the students into the streets in support of the workers.

Mariátegui, born a year earlier in 1894, was the product of a broken marriage and grew up, in delicate health, in an economically austere Limeño middle-class environment. Forced by economic circumstance to seek employment at an early age, he became an office boy and then typesetter at the age of fifteen at *La Prensa*, the prestigious and influential Lima daily. Early on his keen, enquiring, largely self-taught mind caught the attention of his employers, and he rapidly moved up in the paper's ranks to become a reporter in 1911. At first he gained a reputation for his witty coverage of the Lima social scene, but, pricked by a developing social concern, he soon became more interested in the political unrest which was then swirling around him in the capital. Gradually radicalized, he left *La Prensa* for a succession of smaller, more progressive newspapers and by the year 1919 was a committed journalist for, and ideologist of, the nascent working-class movement.

THE ONCENIO OF LEGUÍA, 1919–30

The man who would reap the most immediate, direct benefit from the socio-political conjuncture of 1919 was former president Augusto Leguía. Leguía was a proto-typical turn-of-the-century, self-made capitalist whose entrepreneurial genius had left its imprint in a variety of endeavours from sugar exporting, insurance and banking, to railway building and rubber extraction. José Pardo's minister of finance (1904–8), he had become a leader of the progressive wing of the Civilist party and a somewhat embattled president between 1908 and 1912. Ultimately, however, he broke with the *civilistas* and was exiled during Pardo's second term. Sensing that Peru was at an historic crossroads in 1919, Leguía returned to the country in order to try to capitalize politically on the widespread social unrest that was threatening to topple the *civilista* order.

He quickly became the man of the hour. Promising reforms and attacking the *civilistas* with the skill of a seasoned politician, he was wildly acclaimed by those sectors of the middle and working classes suffering from the sharp cyclical swings of the export economy. Elected to the presidency in 1919, he thwarted (with the help of the *gendarmerie*) *civilista* efforts to block his election, dissolved parliament and assumed power. The diminutive new president – he stood barely five feet tall – in only a few short months brought the 25-year period of *civilista* political hegemony to an end. He fashioned a new government, 'La Patria Nueva', which opened with the promise of reform, only to degenerate into an eleven-year dictatorship known as the *oncenio* (1919–30).

During his first three years in power Leguía assumed a 'democratic' reformist posture designed to consolidate his popular base of support. After sweeping the entrenched *civilistas* from office, he moved to diffuse urban working-class tensions by decreeing reforms such as the eight-hour day, compulsory arbitration and a minimum wage. At the same time he dramatically expanded public works, creating new jobs for a working class that was suffering from the postwar collapse of exports. The middle classes, which formed the backbone of the regime and which

Table 2. *The growth of selected middle-sector occupational groups in Lima,*
1920–31

	Number employed		Percentage increase
Occupation	1920	1931	1920–31
Commerce	12,667	25,481	99.01
Public administration	898	5,313	491.65
Legal profession	460	848	84.35
Medical profession	932	2,408	158.37
Engineers and technicians	536	915	74.07
Writers and newspapermen	137	341	153.28
Accountants	492	1,124	128.46
Students	8,643	17,067	97.47

Source: Steve Stein, *Populism in Peru: the emergence of the masses and the politics of social control*
(Madison, 1980), 74. Uncorrected figures.

experienced a phenomenal growth during the *oncenio* (see table 2), also
benefited from Leguía's reforms. For example, the new president paid
careful attention to white-collar grievances in an elaborately detailed
'Ley de Empleado'. Furthermore, his policy of sharply increasing public
sector employment led to a fivefold increase in the number of public
administrators. When Leguía later adopted a more dictatorial posture,
one contemporary opponent, Víctor Andrés Belaúnde, not inappropri-
ately described the regime as 'bureaucratic Caesarism'.

The new president also moved to recognize some of the grievances of
the Indian peasantry, although it is doubtful whether he fully compre-
hended the revolutionary implications of the peasant uprisings that were
continuing to disrupt the southern highlands. In addition to establishing
a commission to investigate the causes of these disturbances, he created a
department for indigenous affairs, established a national Indian holiday
(Día del Indio) and constitutionally recognized, after more than a
century, the legality of Indian communal property in the *comunidades*.
While popular among some peasants (Leguía was extolled in some Indian
circles as the new 'Wiracocha', the supreme God of the Incas), none of
these measures altered in any fundamental way the structure of rural
Andean society. But they did succeed in assuaging Indian discontent in

the south, while solidifying support from sectors of the emerging urban *mestizo* caste who were in the process of rediscovering their Indian roots in the *indignista* movement.

Ultimately, however, to end the social unrest in the country Leguía had to readjust the economy to bring it into line with the realities of the postwar international economy. Leguía's strategy for dealing with the postwar crisis in Peru's export-orientated economy was based on accelerating the growth of the capitalist space in the country by both encouraging foreign capital and considerably expanding the economic role of the state. From business contacts on Wall Street, Leguía was aware that the United States was looking to expand its capital investment and markets in Latin America as a means of combating postwar economic dislocations at home. The new president also understood the long-term implications of the opening of the Panama Canal which inevitably drew the Andean periphery closer to the United States. Large-scale, direct American investment was encouraged in the mining sector whose denationalization was virtually completed during the *oncenio*. And by the end of the 1920s copper (22 per cent of exports) and petroleum (32 per cent) had displaced sugar (16 per cent) and cotton (25 per cent) as Peru's principal exports. (The country's export diversification continued, however, to be a source of economic strength.) During the *oncenio* the Peruvian government, through the banking firm J. W. Seligman and Company, also floated an unprecedented number of bonds on Wall Street. Not since the guano era had Peru so successfully resorted to foreign money markets. Between 1920 and 1928 Peru's foreign debt increased by $105 million.[29] It financed a massive expansion in the country's infrastructure to service the export economy: public works projects aimed at modernizing the country's main cities, especially Lima (sanitation, roads, etc.), extension of the national transportation and communications network, construction of coastal irrigation systems and growth of the state bureaucracy.

While these measures conformed to Leguía's vision of expanding and modernizing the export capacity of the country, the political impact of each expenditure was carefully calculated to enhance the president's power base. Urban modernization not only benefited the middle classes whose voice was now increasingly being heard in the political arena, but also a new group of speculators and builders with close political ties to

[29] Thorp and Bertram, *Peru, 1890–1977*, 115.

the president. Indeed, Leguía favoured the rise of a new plutocracy in the country which to a large extent replaced politically the old *civilista* oligarchy. At the same time, public and official morality sank to an unusually low point, with the level of peculation, graft and fraud comparable to the guano era.

Leguía's reliance on foreign loans to underwrite public spending and his encouragement of foreign capital, while successful in the short run, further distorted the country's chronic export dependency. Domestic tariffs during the decade tended to drift lower, making nascent manufacturing increasingly vulnerable to foreign imports. Moreover, what little capital surplus accumulated from the export sector (sugar, cotton, wool etc.) flowed not into risky import-substituting industrialization, but rather into construction and urban property speculation where quick profits were guaranteed.

Manufacturing, which had shown promise of leading to a more balanced, autonomous development around the turn of the century, continued a long-term decline begun in 1908. This can be readily seen in cotton textile production, the leading domestic industrial sector. Having tripled in the decade 1898–1908, textile production increased by only about 50 per cent in the following decade, after which growth ceased altogether. At the same time foreign firms steadily increased their position in the industry, representing 29 per cent of capacity in 1902, 45 in 1910, 55 in 1918 and over 80 in 1935. Overall the number of new manufacturing enterprises rose only 13 per cent over a fifteen-year span between 1918 and 1933. Most of these were confined to producing materials for the postwar, state-induced construction boom which lasted only until 1926. Even this sector, however, was dominated by a foreign firm, the giant American Foundation Company that was especially favoured by the Leguía regime. By the end of the 1920s the steady decline of industrialization since 1908 'was the most visible indicator of the decline of national capitalism itself'.[30]

Meanwhile, the export sector, particularly cotton, mineral and to some extent sugar production, continued to be economic bright spots during the 1920s. However, sugar soon ran into difficulties (see above, figure 6). Planters miscalculated the trend of international prices and overinvested their wartime profits in new plant and equipment to expand production.

[30] *Ibid.*, 142.

That investment was seriously jeopardized by the vagaries of nature: a major drought was followed by catastrophically heavy rains and flooding midway through the decade. Then the bottom suddenly fell out of the international sugar market beginning in 1925, causing large-scale losses and another wave of concentration and foreign takeover in the industry by 1930.

Foreign loans and deficit spending gave the central state a measure of power during the Leguía era that it had not enjoyed since the guano age. As a result, its force and influence began to reach out and be felt in the interior of the country as never before. The extension of the national transportation/communications network, for example, Leguía's ambitious road-building programme, accomplished with the conscription of Indian peasants (Ley de Conscripción Vial), increased the power of the state at the expense of provincial autonomy. With improved access to remote areas of the hinterland Leguía was able to mount a concerted campaign to root out banditry which was still endemic in certain rural areas and even the environs of Lima. A special Guardia Civil was created for the purpose, although some of Leguía's detractors saw it more as a sort of praetorian guard to be used against his political enemies. This larger police presence in the interior gave the government the ability to bring under greater control those landowners who, with their private armies, had historically monopolized local politics and who at times had even challenged the authority of the central government. A good example of the state's new-found power in the provinces was its liquidation of the rebellion of Eleodoro Benel (1924–7), a powerful hacendado who exercised virtual autonomous control over parts of the department of Cajamarca.

Leguía also adroitly used the state's expanded financial resources to elaborate a system of clientelistic politics which created a new 'official' caste of officeholders and entrepreneurs, at both the national and local level, who were dependent on the state, indeed on Leguía himself, for their very well-being. Moreover, Leguía knew how to acquire and wield the new powers of state in a personalistic, increasingly dictatorial fashion. Early in his regime he moved to emasculate the legislature by so manipulating elections as to fill it with his own supporters and cronies. Soon Congress became little more than a rubber stamp for the president. As early as 1922 Leguía had begun to abandon the populist, reformist policies that had brought him to power. Strikes were increasingly broken by the use of force and the army was mobilized to control the peasant risings in the south. Gradually Leguía narrowed his base of support to the new plutocracy and brutally repressed his opponents.

The only serious challenge to his rule came in 1923 when, in an effort to ensure church support for his 're-election', he proposed to dedicate the country in an elaborate public ceremony to the Sacred Heart of Jesus. Catholicism had always been used by the ruling class as an ideology to legitimize its rule, but now Leguía tried to harness its power for his own personal political gain. Such a cynical and blatantly pro-clerical move, however, aroused widespread opposition which was galvanized against the government by the student leader Haya de la Torre. Street demonstrations turned into riots before Leguía succeeded in repressing the movement and exiling its leaders.

Haya de la Torre had already begun to assume an anti-oligarchical and anti-imperialist position derived from his boyhood experiences with anarcho-syndicalists in Trujillo and later as a leader of the student–worker alliances while at San Marcos University. Once exiled by Leguía, he further developed these positions while a guest of the state in Mexico where he had the opportunity to view not only the effects of the 1910 revolution, but also the impact of North American economic expansion southward into the Caribbean and Central America. It was while in Mexico in 1924 that he founded the Alianza Popular Revolucionaria Americana (APRA), a largely amorphous, populist, anti-imperialist and nationalist political organization which would take root in Peru and elsewhere after 1930. Back again in Mexico in 1928 after his European travels – he visited Germany, the Soviet Union and England where he studied at Oxford – he articulated his still evolving political ideology in a seminal book entitled *El anti-imperialismo y el apra*, first published in Santiago in 1936. (Although written early in 1928 the manuscript remained unpublished for several years because, according to Haya, he lacked the funds and then was too busy with daily political events to revise it.)

In this his most radical book and to a lesser extent in later writings, Haya analysed and attacked, from a largely Marxist yet nationalist perspective, the generally exploitative and disruptive impact of the foreign penetration of Latin America which he saw as the first stage in the transition from feudalism to capitalism. Drawing upon both his Peruvian and Mexican experiences, he described a largely paternalistic, traditional society suddenly overwhelmed and transformed into giant concentrations of monopolistic, foreign, capitalist enterprises. These enterprises, fostered by a greedy and corrupt native ruling class (the *civilistas*) which in effect sold out the real interests of the country, proletarianized the peasantry and sectors of the old middle classes and gained control of the national economy which they manipulated for their own selfish gain. In order to bring this process to a halt, he proposed the creation of a broadly based popular alliance of the 'exploited' classes, peasants, workers and the radicalized sectors of the middle classes (APRA), that would overthrow the imperialists and construct a radical, nationalist, anti-imperialist society (*el estado anti-imperialista*). The working class, he argued, was simply not numerically large enough nor sufficiently politically conscious in Latin America to sustain the anti-imperialist struggle alone. Nor was it necessarily the primary victim of imperialism; wages in the export enclaves were actually higher than in the traditional economy and sections of the middle classes were often even more savagely exploited and abused. He thus became one of the first of a new generation of nationalist Latin American political thinkers to apply and readapt Marxist thought to a non-European, neo-colonial context in which conditions differed sharply from the historical experience of the metropolis. Later, after the overthrow of Leguía in 1930, Haya would apply this analysis with considerable success to Peru where he would organize and lead the populist, but largely petty-bourgeois, Aprista party for the next half a century.

Haya's main rival in organizing the popular forces against the Leguía dictatorship, at least after 1928, was the journalist Mariátegui. He had been exiled by Leguía after the 1919 working-class mobilization and spent the next four years living first in France and then in Italy. There he absorbed the radical thought of Marx, Engels and Lenin along with such revolutionary European socialists as Barbusse, Sorel and Gramsci. Returning to Peru, he collaborated for a time with Haya, who had founded a series of student-run 'popular universities' to instruct, organize and generally raise the level of culture and political conscious-ness of the workers and who organized the 1923 anti-Leguía demonstra-tions. Gradually, however, because of ideological and tactical differences as well as political rivalry, the two men drew apart, until finally they broke definitively in 1928 after an acrimonious exchange of public letters.

Mariátegui, whose major work is entitled *Siete ensayos en interpretación de la realidad Peruana* (1928),[31] adopted a more orthodox Marxist view of Peruvian and Latin American reality. The book was largely an outgrowth of his attempt to stimulate a discourse in progressive intellectual circles on the problematic of revolution in Andean society, from the pages of his remarkable journal *Amauta* (1926–30). In it he formulated a complete historical analysis of society from a Marxist perspective and laid down his formula for revolutionary change in the future. Unlike Haya he viewed capitalism and imperialism in Latin America as wholly destructive forces. (Haya did see some positive aspects to foreign capital investment and later modified his views to the point where he became an advocate of foreign capital in Peru – although with some state controls.) He also believed that capitalism already had evolved to a mature stage. While he saw some virtues in a multi-class alliance, he categorically rejected Haya's notion that the middle rather than the working class should dominate this alliance in the revolutionary struggle. For Mariátegui the middle sectors, even though radicalized, harboured essentially petty-bourgeois values which in the end would compromise the revolution and lead to fascism. Furthermore, while Haya relegated the peasantry to a secondary role in this struggle, Mariátegui believed that it had great revolutionary potential; the miner/ *campesino* at Cerro de Pasco, for example, he saw as embodying a crucial nexus between the urban and rural revolutionary problematic. In the end, Mariátegui believed that Marxism could be welded to such indigenous Andean revolutionary traditions as the *indigenista* movement, Incaic 'socialism', the long history of peasant uprisings (Atusparia, Rumi-Maqui) and the labour movement. Not content simply to theorize, Mariátegui worked diligently until his premature death in 1930 to bring about that revolution by founding the Peruvian Communist party in 1928[32] and the General Confederation of Peruvian Workers in 1929.

Neither Mariátegui nor Haya were able, however, to bring down the Leguía dictatorship. In the wake of the international economic crisis of 1929, the regime fell victim to a military *golpe* which, it should be noted, ended a period of civilian rule (Benavides excepted) dating back to 1895. Peruvian exports plunged on average 59 per cent, imports 63 per cent.

---

[31] Lima, 1928. The work was translated into English as *Seven interpretative essays on Peruvian reality* (Austin, Texas, 1971).

[32] There is some dispute as to whether Mariátegui actually remained a communist, since he diverged from the party line of the Moscow-orientated Communist International for which he was criticized at the first meeting of Latin American Communist Parties in Buenos Aires in 1929.

The national budget plummeted from $50 to $16 million within three years, causing the abrupt termination of public works and the suspension of salary payments to government employees. The prestigious and venerable Bank of Peru and London was even forced to close its doors, resulting in especially intense economic distress in the agricultural sector, particularly in the south where the military *golpe* originated. Unemployment in Lima alone reached an estimated 25 per cent, higher among construction workers and government employees. Workers were even harder hit in the enclave sectors of the economy due to the paralysis of exports. Cerro de Pasco's work force dropped from 12,000 in 1929 to 5,000 in 1932 while wages on the sugar plantations were drastically cut. The stark reality of the economic collapse was perhaps best summarized in 1932 by the minister of finance, who, upon assuming office, 'found the *sol* devalued, service on the public debt suspended, salaries and pensions in arrears, public works paralysed, unemployment growing, the national treasury empty, national confidence diminished and credit almost totally exhausted'.[33]

The Peruvian people turned on Leguía while desperately searching for new political leadership capable of stemming the economic decline. Some would find it in the person of the young *mestizo* army colonel Luis M. Sánchez Cerro, who in August 1930 had raised the Arequipa garrison in revolt and who had overthrown the eleven-year dictatorship of Leguía. Others would look to the charismatic young Haya de la Torre and his fledgling Aprista party, whose ringing slogan – 'sólo el aprismo salvará el Perú' (only *aprismo* will save Peru) – captured the general mood of polarization, desperation and despair. Whomever they chose the popular classes, marginalized during the 'Aristocratic Republic' and again during the *oncenio*, entered with a rush into the mainstream of Peruvian politics, never again to be wholly excluded from the national political process.

A VANISHING LIMA

In 1921 José Gálvez wrote a nostalgic book entitled *Una Lima que se va* (Vanishing Lima). In it he lamented the disappearance of the seignorial life style and many of the old customs characteristic of the city since the colonial days. What Gálvez deplored was, in sociological terms, the rapid

---

[33] Quoted in Aníbal Quijano, *Imperialismo, clases sociales y estado en el Perú, 1890–1930* (Lime, 1978), 114.

'massification' of urban society which had been inspired by Peru's early-twentieth-century encounter with Western capitalism. Peasants, pushed and pulled off the land, were migrating in ever increasing numbers to the cities and agro-industrial enclaves of the new export economy. There economic growth offered the promise, if not always the reality, of steady work and a new life. Crowded into company towns and city slums, this new working class, cut loose from a relatively stable rural order, experienced the disorganizing and disintegrating effects of urban anomie and factory, mine and plantation exploitation. Workers were offered little or no protection from the cyclical oscillations of the international market economy by the *civilista* state, inspired as it was by notions of laissez-faire liberalism and Spencerian social Darwinism. Such conditions ultimately nourished a deepening popular discontent which was first expressed in the rise of the labour movement and then in a more radical political dissent articulated by Haya de la Torre and Mariátegui, one from a largely nationalist-populist, the other from a more orthodox socialist perspective.

The 'Aristocratic Republic' was confronted not only with a dangerous new social question, but at the same time with a new, upwardly mobile urban middle class. Denied political participation by the *civilista* monopoly of power, their economic prosperity threatened by the crisis of the first world war and its aftermath, the urban middle class, reinforced by popular discontent and mobilized by Leguía, ended a generation of *civilista* rule in 1919.

The *oncenio* of Leguía, however, served to deepen the capitalist advance in the country and to reinforce the nation's dependency on the whims of the international marketplace. This was underscored by the onset in 1929 of the world economic crisis and depression which engulfed Peru's export-dependent economy, radicalized the masses and swept Leguía from power. The task of national regeneration was seized by the reform-minded generation of 1919, and both Haya de la Torre and APRA on the one hand and Mariátegui's successors in the Communist party on the other momentarily proceeded to reformulate a more national and revolutionary vision of the future. In the end, however, the oligarchy regrouped behind the popular military *caudillo* Sánchez Cerro. In alliance with the armed forces, it succeeded in repressing the masses and fashioning a period of 'indirect' rule that endured for another generation and mirrored, in a more subtle way, its hegemony during the 'Aristocratic Republic'.

18

COLOMBIA, ECUADOR AND VENEZUELA, c. 1880–1930

The articulate inhabitants of the Republics of Colombia, Ecuador and Venezuela in the half century from 1880 to 1930 – their second half-century of independent existence – usually expressed themselves rather more cautiously on the subject of progress than their contemporaries in more fortunate parts of the world: 'In the political life of all peoples progress is slow', wrote the leaders of the dissident wing of Colombian conservatism in 1896, 'as with the tides – to follow the thought of a well-known English writer [Arthur Hugh Clough] – the waves alternately advance and fall back, but the land conquered is always greater than the land lost; there is a constant advance.' To another Colombian conservative, Miguel Antonio Caro, the advance was never clear to the participants: 'The progress of ideas is mysteriously mixed into human history. The conflict of principles is interwoven with the struggles of parties, and fighting in one band or another, through individual or collective interest, men serve or oppose the cause of civilization, frequently without any aim or consciousness of doing so.'[1]

Armed conflict in this part of the world, endemic in the nineteenth century, persisted into the early years of the twentieth century. The Colombian 'War of the Thousand Days' ended in 1902 with the treaties of Neerlandia and Wisconsin, in which the liberal Generals Rafael Uribe Uribe and Benjamín Herrera respectively admitted defeat in a future banana-growing centre and on board a US warship. Sporadic uprisings in Venezuela persisted for some years after the defeat of the last major armed revolt, the Revolución Libertadora of 1903. The radical liberal guerillas of the province of Esmeraldas, Ecuador, were only finally suppressed as late as 1916.

---

[1] 'Motivos de disidencia', quoted in L. Martínez Delgado, *República de Colombia, 1885–1910* (vol. x of *Historia extensa de Colombia*, 2 vols., Bogotá, 1970), I, 381. Caro in *ibid.*, II, 15.

Some episodes and cycles of the years 1880–1930 – the presumed 'bourgeois revolution' of Eloy Alfaro in Ecuador in 1895, the development of the Venezuelan oil industry, the expansion of Colombian coffee production, the repression of the Guayaquil strike of 1922 and the strike of 1928 in the banana zone of Santa Marta in Colombia – have been studied, but much is only just beginning to be reconsidered, and much remains obscure for reasons that go beyond just the late development of a systematic local historiography. In Colombia the period was one of conservative domination; it has not attracted the sympathy of liberal historians, who see it in terms of a long resistance finally vindicated in 1930, and most Colombian historians who have written on 'the conservative republic' have been liberals, or progressives who, in history as in politics, find it hard to escape the liberal embrace. Conversely, until recently conservatives have dominated Ecuadorean historiography, and have written against liberalism with a virulence that has from time to time won them surprising intellectual, and even political, allies on the socialist left. Venezuelans feel cut off from the nineteenth century by the long dictatorship of Juan Vicente Gómez (1908–35), a figure who still mesmerizes materialists and romantics to the detriment of serious historical study. Besides being partisan, most of the local historical writing has been impatient with political problems as problems of structure or system. There is a gap between the old political historiography of polemic, memoir and anecdote and the new and over-assertive analysis of class and capital. The dimensions of the conflict over the church are also lost between the prolix tangle of the old arguments and the indifference to them of recent decades, which have produced a generation that finds it hard to remember that liberalism was once a sin. The measure of material progress in these years requires sensitivity to the early local scales and circumstances if its impact is to be gauged correctly. This sense of scale is as absent in recent writers anxious to discover new class formations as it was among the boosters of local bourgeois enterprise in the heroic age. There are few reliable foreign observers, and only one of these – Spencer Dixon, British vice consul in Bogotá in 1900 and British Minister there in 1930 – repeated his stay after a substantial number of years. Neither Colombia nor Ecuador attracted many immigrants during this period, and though Venezuela began to attract more in the 1920s the flow was not spectacular. With the exception of the Venezuela–British Guiana boundary affair, the Anglo-German blockade of Venezuela in 1902, and the involvement of the

United States with the secession of Panama from Colombia in 1904, these countries were not the focus of much diplomatic interest. Until the 1920s they received little foreign investment. Yet for all the deficiencies in present knowledge that result from these circumstances, it is still possible to say that in 1930 all three countries were profoundly different from what they had been in 1880.

There are common themes in the history of Colombia, Ecuador and Venezuela between 1880 and 1930, but also great differences. Politically New Granada (Colombia) and Ecuador had diverged as soon as they separated from Gran Colombia. In New Granada the initial civilian rejection of a military dominance, at that time largely Venezuelan, was maintained, and from 1863 until 1885 the 'United States of Colombia' lived under a federal constitution of radical-liberal inspiration. For its part Ecuador had emerged as a nation ruled by the Venezuelan General Juan José Flores, who was president in 1830–4 and 1839–45, and liberal experiences under the civilian Vicente Rocafuerte (1835–9) and such occasional military liberals as General José María Urbina (1851–6) or General Ignacio de Veintemilla in his early phase did not balance the fierce authoritarian and ultramontane years of Gabriel García Moreno, which began in 1857. After García Moreno's assassination in 1875 came nearly a decade dominated by the equivocal figure of Veintemilla, a man who took support where he could get it, and thereafter a series of *progresista* governments, the most notable under General Flores's son Antonio Flores Jijón (1888–92). Flores sought to harmonize the distinct regional interests of the country through sound administration and the avoidance of either the *terrorista* conservatism of García Moreno's successors, or the radical anti-clerical and demagogic liberalism of the heirs of García Moreno's arch-enemy, Juan Montalvo, and of the numerous Colombian adventurers and pamphleteers who sought opportunity or refuge in the south after the Conservative victory in the Colombian civil war of 1885. Thus around 1880, though it would be true to say that neither Republic had achieved any lasting stability, their political difficulties and their likely further evolution were not the same. Colombia's liberal experiments had been more intense – indeed they were the most intense in South America – and were entering a time of crisis. Ecuador's extreme conservatism – again, García Moreno's thorough-going programme has no close parallel elsewhere – had given way to more compromising successors, but to no compromise that went deep: the 'progressives' were a small elite circle, so small that they came to be called *la argolla* (the ring). Signs of a radical-liberal threat to this exclusiveness were already visible in the early 1880s, and Ecuador would not be able to avoid the sort of experiences that her northern neighbour was by then already rejecting.

Colombians and Ecuadoreans at least had in common the persistence of the liberal and conservative currents. In Venezuela, the twenty years that followed the demise of José Antonio Páez's hegemony and the end of the 'conservative republic' in 1846–8 saw the disappearance from the scene of any avowedly conservative current. Under the Monagas family in the 1850s the Republic had gained a reputation for corruption and administrative disorder, worsened by the Federal Wars of 1859–64. The disorder had, however, by 1880 received spectacular correction at the hands of Antonio Guzmán Blanco (1870–87), who used resources and techniques unavailable or inapplicable in the other successor Republics of 'Gran Colombia'. A Colombian visiting Venezuela in 1830 would have been aware that he was in a foreign country. In 1880 such a visitor would have been made much more acutely aware that he was not at home.

COLOMBIA

Colombian liberals were in 1880 aware that the radical constitution of Rionegro (1863), with its exclusion of the church from the official life of the country, its nine 'sovereign' states, its perpetual, confused and necessarily fraudulent elections, its ultimate reliance on the interventions of the Federal Army (the Guardia Colombiana) in the affairs of the states, its vexatious varieties of legislation, anarchic finances and two-year presidential terms, was out of tune with the necessities of the times. It was also, through its own provisions, inconveniently unreformable. When the times became yet more difficult with economic collapse in the mid 1880s, President Rafael Núñez in the midst of civil war simply pronounced it dead, and nominated an 'independent' and conservative constituent assembly to produce a replacement that would guarantee a 'scientific peace'. The constitution of 1886 restored the authority of the central government, reducing the states to departments under governors nominated by the president; *alcaldes* were in their turn to be nominated by the governors. Elections were to be indirect, and a property or literacy qualification was laid down for voters. The Roman Catholic religion was declared the religion of the nation: 'The public powers will protect it and will make sure that it is respected as an essential element of social order.' The church later received further concessions and guarantees in the Concordat of 1887 and the Convention on Mission Territories. The absolute press freedom of the Rionegro constitution era, 1863–85, was replaced first by a spell of *censura previa*, straightforward censorship, and then by enactments that gave the executive powers to deal with subversive publications, and the judges powers over offensive publications. There was an end too to free trade in arms, and the death penalty, abolished by the liberals with such pride, was symbolically restored. President Núñez and his successors also kept in being a larger army, usually around 6,000 strong, and enjoyed certain 'extraordinary faculties'; the presidential term was extended to six years, with the possibility of re-election, though both these provisions were later amended.

This recipe for 'scientific peace' was to prove incomplete, and has undergone successive alterations, but it is the constitution of 1886 in its essentials that still holds in Colombia. And it enjoyed an initial success. Carlos Holguín, who ruled as Núñez's vice president from 1888 to 1892 while the architect of the 'Regeneration' watched the essentials from his semi-retirement in Cartagena, could state at the end of his time in office that 'in the four years that I have governed, no one has heard a shot, not a drop of blood has been spilt, not a tear has been shed. I leave the Republic in peace and I have not contracted debts.' He refused to apply the death penalty, and it virtually fell into disuse. It would seem that in these last years of the nineteenth century, though liberals and dissident conservatives were excluded from participation in government, the former also from elected assemblies, they were only mildly repressed. Carlos Holguín suspended seven periodicals, fining twelve of them and three printers. He used his 'extraordinary faculties' on three occasions, twice to restrict the activities of conservative individuals and once as a family favour for one of the descendants of General Santander. Miguel Antonio Caro, vice president and (on Núñez's death in 1894) president from 1892 to 1898, was more energetic, particularly against some elements in the liberal press: a *cause célèbre* which did the government more harm than good was the closing of the liberal *El Relator* and the exile of its director, the former president (1874–6) Santiago Pérez. But control was rarely exercised in such a direct way, and the picture of the government of the 'Regeneration' painted by radical pamphleteers abroad contrasts with what is revealed by closer inspection: a press by no means uniform, much argument within broad limits, a Congress still fractious, even though it contained only one Liberal, persistent regional dissidence uncowed, a virtual absence of police and an army most of the time not much in evidence. Simple 'republican customs' persisted, and there was nothing outwardly to distinguish those in power from the society of merchants, landowners, lawyers and literati that produced them. It was government by civilian polemicists; Núñez, Caro and Holguín were all argumentative, and would not have conceived of political life without argument in the press or in Congress. Contrast them with Guzmán Blanco or Joaquín Crespo, their contemporaries in Venezuela, and the difference is immediately apparent. Their superficially rarefied disputes are in the clerical and legalistic tradition of Santa Fé de Bogotá, and ability in argument is essential to the most common sort of political career. Excessive argumentativeness might at times be damaging, as in the case of Caro, who could lapse into an irritable dogmatism. The flow of argument was also interrupted by the demands of electoral fraud and civil war.

The ability to make elections was far more important to the circle in power than peace-time forms of repression. The Independent–Conservative alliance of 1885 was soon able to match the hermetic success that in most of the country had been the Liberal prerogative since 1863. The list system was replaced by single-member constituencies, but a combination of official, private and clerical control frustrated any intention there might have been of guaranteeing minority representation. Only two Liberals reached Congress between 1885 and 1904, the Magdalena lawyer Luis A. Robles and the restless Antioqueño aspirant to party leadership, Rafael Uribe Uribe. Electoral advantage was all on the side of the administration parties, the 'Independents' and the Conservatives. The most important electoral agents of this broad coalition were the local officials and the local clergy, who must have delivered many more votes than the enthusiastic 'conservative landowners' of popular mythology; these doubtless existed, but landowners often shirked direct involvement in politics, and, as many of them were liberal, a landowner-controlled electorate would not have produced so uniform a result. The machinery of officialdom and scrutiny had an easier task under the new electoral laws. It was supported by a church that had learnt to trust to its own defence and which became, and remained throughout this period and beyond, a formidable electioneer, proof against everything except conservative division. The army also voted as directed. The Conservative party had in these circumstances no need for a separate organization of its own. It might lose elections in certain cities, but the Republic remained overwhelmingly rural, and most of rural Colombia was conservative.

But electoral systems of too-perfect circularity are a source of weakness. The Liberal party was not silenced, but aggrieved, and the bellicose tendencies within the party were strengthened. Given the right conditions – bad times in the economy, divided government counsels, a little encouragement from abroad, a prospect of supplanting the existing leadership of one's own party even if one were to fail against the government itself – just a few men could start a civil war, and the electoral practices and the exclusiveness of the administrations up to 1899 were a standing pretext for them. The majority of the Liberal party recognized that the radicals' decision to go to war against Núñez in 1885 had been disastrous, and the established leadership was firmly for peace. Liberal ex-president Santiago Pérez persisted in opposing 'new deliriums about machine-guns and rifles, which exist only on paper, which will just sacrifice more patriots and give the Regeneration the theme for more salvations of the country'.[2] It was nonetheless hard for pacific liberals to defend their line if the government refused them all concessions. Habitual reliance on a heavily manipulated system also made Núñez's successors, in particular Miguel Antonio Caro, too careless of opinion in their own party. Caro, faced with criticism of his arbitrary ways from Antioqueño and 'historic' conservatives, groups that did not swallow the 'Regeneration' entire, even began rejecting the epithet conservative for himself, preferring 'Catholic'. Caro ended in 1898 on bad terms with Congress, and as engineer of a disastrous succession designed to exclude the elements in his own party who had lent an ear to his critics or shown signs of compromise. His choice for president in cold Bogotá was the octogenarian invalid from the hot country, Manuel Antonio Sanclemente, who had been a minister in President Mallarino's Cabinet in 1855, and for vice president the hacendado, schoolmaster and litterateur José Manuel Marroquín, a 70-year-old with no political experience besides that which every well-connected Bogotano inevitably acquired for diversion and self-preservation. Theodore Roosevelt in a heated moment was later to refer to this author of rhyming grammatical rules and the local equivalent of *Black Beauty* as 'a well-known South American bandit'.

[2] *Ibid.*, I, 343.

A Liberal revolution in 1895 had been rapidly smothered by the government forces; the country had been relatively prosperous, and the rebellion had not caught on. Temporarily in office before the arrival in the capital of the aged Sanclemente, Marroquín in 1898 offered concessions in electoral, judicial and press matters that might have satisfied Liberals and Conservative dissidents, but these were withdrawn on Sanclemente's taking possession. The Liberals went to war again in August 1899; that is, a small number of Liberal conspirators, with an even smaller number of rifles – perhaps only sixteen – in that month attacked Bucaramanga with a notable lack of success. All the same the subsequent war went on for nearly three years, the 'Thousand Days', and was fought on and off all over the country. Its onset coincided with a fall in the price of coffee, by then Colombia's principal export, and with the resulting depression in all economic activity and weakening of the government's resources. The Liberals received moral and some material support from the Liberal rulers of Venezuela, Ecuador and Nicaragua; they had their successes – they provoked the removal of Sanclemente and his replacement once again by Marroquín – but they were unable to divide their opponents in the field or to match their superior resources in recruits, arms and paper money. They gave up in 1902. It cost tens of thousands of lives – no exact calculation has ever been possible – and an unaccountable loss of property, and it was soon followed by the secession of Panama, with United States encouragement and under United States protection. Both Liberals and Conservatives could share the blame for this, the first for making Panama a theatre of war and the second for their unrealistic dilatoriness in the negotiations for passing the Canal Concession from the French Company to the United States, and for their disregard of Panamanian interests and susceptibilities. Neither party could do anything to oppose the separation, and reactions to it in Colombia varied: impotent shame in a conscious few, indifference in the mass of the population, and conspiratorial envy among a number of separatists in other regions of the country. It is significant that the affair left no lasting anti-American feeling. José Manuel Marroquín finished his term, and was succeeded in 1904 by General Rafael Reyes, veteran of the war of 1885, the merciful victor of the swift little war of 1895, and one of the unreliable candidates that Caro had eliminated from the running in 1898. Reyes had not fought in the war that had just ended; he had spent most of it as Colombian Minister in Paris.

Reyes's presidency-dictatorship, the 'quinquennium' of 1904–9, attempted several political innovations. The most important of these was the representation of minorities, even though it was a representation imposed in Reyes's personal and authoritarian fashion. He named Liberals to two out of the six ministries in his Cabinet, and to the constituent assembly he appointed on suppressing a recalcitrant Congress. General Uribe Uribe served him as a diplomat, and at Reyes's urging sent two of his sons to the Chilean cadet school to prepare them for entry to what was planned to be Colombia's new professional army. (A Chilean military mission was contracted to train it.) Under Reyes the Liberals abandoned their federalism – in 1899 they had still not shed their nominal allegiance to the constitution of Rionegro – and by and large abandoned recourse to civil war. The war saw a shift in the balance of the party leadership: several prominent old 'pacific' leaders had died natural deaths in the course of it, and as usual the battlefields, even of defeat, had made reputations that could be used in peace, chief among them those of generals Benjamín Herrera and Rafael Uribe Uribe. The first was thought the better soldier, and until his death in 1924 his taciturn and solid qualities of leadership had a particular appeal to the important veteran element among Liberals. The son of a sergeant, Herrera had joined the Guardia Colombiana as a volunteer at the age of fifteen, and until the advent of the 'Regeneration' in 1885 he had been a professional soldier, a rarity then in Colombia. No ideologue himself, his practical political sense led him as Liberal leader to encourage the incorporation of workers into the Liberal party, and at the end of his life he was active in the foundation of the free-thinking Universidad Libre. General Uribe Uribe had a less successful military career – he had the disadvantages of coming from Antioquia, a region that was both pacific and conservative, and of being too much of a disciplinarian – but had greater intellectual energy. He had been the sole and effective Liberal voice in Congress in the late 1890s. He carried to Rome his polemic with the Archbishop of Bogotá on whether liberalism was a sin – the future Pope Pius XII declared that it was – and he lectured on socialism. He returned from his diplomatic travels under President Reyes to write on coffee, on improved pasture grasses, and on the banana. He ran his own newspaper, and his correspondence shows him constructing a Liberal network at a level rather below that of the usual notables of the party. In Bogotá he organized a *bloque obrero*, strong in the poor artisan barrio of La Perseverancia. He was not popular among his peers, who found him vain and opportunistic. He and Herrera detested each other. Tensions generated by his individual political courses must have contributed to his assassination in 1914.

General Reyes's aspirations to be the Porfirio Díaz of Colombia had collapsed in 1910 in the face of growing opposition from all quarters, which found an effective issue in his premature attempts to restore good relations with the United States. The slow recovery of the economy had anyhow condemned him to practical frustration: he had plans, but he lacked the financial means to implement them. His mild authoritarianism and occasional vanities had brought him enemies in both parties. Convinced that his support had faded, he without notice abandoned the country while on a tour of the Santa Marta banana zone, whose establishment he had done much to encourage. In the bi-partisan atmosphere of his departure – which also owed something to his tolerance and breadth of vision as well as to his defects – a National Assembly reduced the presidential term to four years, prohibited immediate re-election, provided for annual meetings of Congress, restored direct elections and made some provision for minority representation. It elected president for 1910–14 Carlos E. Restrepo, leader of the Unión Republicana, an ad hoc coalition of some prominent party leaders. The centenary of Independence was thus celebrated amid civic accord, restored liberties and resolute *civilismo*. A *generación del Centenario* has sometimes been seen as attempting to preserve these values.

Under Carlos E. Restrepo's Unión Republicana the political life of the country remained essentially in conservative hands. The restoration of the direct vote also favoured the Conservatives – the Liberals or the dissident conservatives they supported might win in Bogotá and some other towns, but never in the rural electorate as a whole. In 1914 the official machinery, the church, the *caciques* and Conservative *opinión* – that current too had its mystique and its heroes – elected José Vicente Concha president with 300,735 votes against 36,763 for his Republican Liberal opponent. In 1918 they returned Marco Fidel Súarez with 216,595 against his dissident conservative opponent Guillermo Valencia, who with Liberal support gained 166,498 votes, winning in Bogotá and in eleven out of fourteen departmental capitals. In 1922 General Pedro Nel Ospina beat General Herrera by 413,619 votes to 256,213. The Liberals responded to the fraud, violence and clerical participation in the election of 1922 by abstaining in the elections of 1926, which returned Miguel Abadía Méndez unopposed with 370,492 votes. Only in 1930, with the

Conservatives divided, did the Liberals win the presidential elections: Enrique Olaya Herrera received 369,934 votes, Guillermo Valencia, 240,360, and Alfredo Vásquez Cobo, 213,583.

These figures from official sources incorporate much electoral fraud. Under Rafael Núñez's system of 1886, amended in 1910, the suffrage was officially restricted to those who could read or write or who possessed property to a certain value or a certain income – $1,000 and $300 respectively in 1922. It is not difficult to make rough calculations of what the electorate could have been in one region or another, and where fraud prevailed to notice how the number of voters exceeded this possibility, most of all in conservative rural areas. Sometimes this was merely a paper matter, reflecting no real participation or mobilization. But sometimes it was not: it could be the result of the participation of those officially excluded from the franchise that was a characteristic of Colombian elections from the earliest days of the Republic. The figures also include, and the urban share of the Liberal opposition proves this, an undeniable growth in genuine participation. The total electorate was estimated by contemporaries in the early 1920s at somewhat less than 10 per cent of the population. The Liberals, denouncing the way the illiterate and poor peasant Indian departments of Boyacá and Nariño headed the list of Conservative votes, the notorious frauds of the Atlantic coast, the government-controlled votes of the army, the police, the *gendarmeries*, and the drink monopoly, and the blessing of Conservative election-making by priests, both native and foreign, estimated their own real numbers to be at least as high as their opponents'.

These accusations and counter-accusations and the folklore of the system's abuses make it easy to lose sight of the system as a whole. The two traditional currents had roots going back to the earliest years of the Republic. Loyalties were created and confirmed in civil wars, and were bound to persist. Economic change was not of a nature or of an extent to alter them. The Conservatives continued to rely heavily on church support. In the 1920s, particularly under Pedro Nel Ospina, they showed themselves capable of profiting from new economic circumstances, and their popular support was not confined to rural areas: many entrepreneurs were conservatives, and some of these were sincerely and effectively paternalist. The Liberals had abandoned warlike opposition for electoral competition, with ultimate success. They were the only plausible opposition, and their flexibility and the social circumstances of the country effectively prevented the growth of movements of the left:

time and again Colombia's syndicalists, Marxists and anarchists failed to find separate constituencies or to make separate careers, a failure that will be further analysed below. Party organization remained rudimentary, and each current was an alliance of regional groups, always prone to faction, where no one ever had the power to issue anything as formal as a membership card, where the most permanent visible manifestation of the group's existence was probably a local newspaper, where registration campaigns and electioneering had to be brief and cheap. *Giras*, political tours – not entirely unknown in the nineteenth century – became more common in the twentieth: the flamboyant poet-politician Guillermo Valencia made speaking tours by car in the vicinity of the capital, and Jorge Eliécer Gaitán, the Liberal leader assassinated in 1948, made his first political journey to campaign for General Herrera in Boyacá in 1922. By 1930 Alfonso López Pumarejo, the architect of that year's Liberal victory, was campaigning by aeroplane and hydrofoil.

This sort of activity was essential. There was no alternative source of power in Colombian national politics. Of national institutions, the church was both politically mortgaged to the Conservatives, as much directed by them as directing, and itself divided into a string of near-autonomous bishoprics. The Archbishop of Bogotá had little control over other dioceses or over the extensive mission territories and numerous religious orders. The army had changed in the years since the War of a Thousand Days. Many ad hoc generals and colonels still carried their ranks in civilian life, and General Vásquez Cobo, essentially a self-made warrior, was to be given command in the short war against Peru in 1932, although the officer corps was now in most respects professional. But it was small, its prestige was low, and it was conservative. It was quite incapable of independent political action, even of independent conspiracy. Colombia was a lightly governed country, whose revenues before the 1920s had supported only a skeletal administration. What public power there was was in the hands of essentially civilian politicians. Some of these in both parties were of 'oligarchic' extraction, sons of families of old wealth and prestige, but many were not. Colombian fortunes were still modest, and aversion to politics was at least as common an upper-class trait as political ambition. Politics were essentially for politicians, and many of these were from modest origins.

An account that lays some emphasis on a slow mobilization, on evidences of modernity and adaptation, on the *centenario* virtues, often proclaimed and sometimes practised, may be a useful corrective to the usual dismissals of these years as a period of static clientelism. But such an account would be incomplete. Many elements of this imperfect democracy would be familiar to students of the evolutions of other states in Latin America and elsewhere, but the Colombian potential for sectarian violence would not. After the War of a Thousand Days this potential was for a time hidden under General Reyes's even-handed authoritarianism, in the bi-partisan opposition to him and in the Unión Republicana. Thereafter it re-emerged. The 1922 elections were the occasion of sufficient violence to produce concerted and detailed Liberal protest:

Public liberal manifestations carried out in a civilized and pacific fashion were in many places broken up by conservative crowds who attacked them with the tolerance, support, intervention and even authorization of government officials. These attacks in not a few cases were stimulated by the preaching of intransigeant priests from church pulpits. Important cities, among them the capital of the Republic, saw scenes of the most cruel bloodshed, comparable only to savage practices (*el apachismo más salvage*), and the villages and the countryside saw the use of methods of terror which kept them and still keep them in a state of intranquillity that is prejudicial to the regular progress of a well-organized nation.[3]

The government replied that the Liberals exaggerated, that Conservatives were not exclusively to blame, that in a liberal Republic the church had every right to express its opinion and that many so-called political attacks turned out on close examination to have other motives. It did not deny that it had distributed some 3,000 rifles to state governors for the formation of 'civic corps of departmental police'. Nearly half of these went to the notoriously conflictive department of Norte de Santander, and not all of them came back. The Liberals did exaggerate, and historians looking for precedents for the far more intense sectarian violence of the late 1940s and early 1950s have exaggerated too. The electoral violence of 1922 did not leave many dead or injured. The greater danger of a Liberal rising – this is one of the moments where twentieth-century Colombia looked as if it might relapse into the methods of the nineteenth – was averted by prudent leadership. The elections of 1930 were not violent, and the transfer of power to the Liberals, apart from some resistance in the Santanders, was peacefully achieved. But the potential of more widespread violence was there, and later other circumstances and the competing demagogy of Jorge Eliécer Gaitán and of Laureano Gómez would bring it into the open.

Rafael Núñez in 1880 saw the problem of order as first in importance

[3] Anon., *Los partidos políticos en Colombia* (Bogotá, 1922), 22–3.

in Colombia, and there should be no need to justify examining at some length its partial solution in the 50 years to 1930, both in the light of what had passed and what was to come. Political problems have their own autonomy, and no simple relationship with economic change, here as elsewhere. Economic and social changes in this half-century in some ways had less obvious political effect than one might expect from their magnitude. They were accommodated within existing political practices.

In the mid 1880s Colombia's exports of tobacco, quinine bark and coffee fell into a state of prostration. Tobacco had been the leading export since mid-century, and quinine bark, which was gathered, not cultivated, the cause of erratic frontier booms in the regions of Tolima and Santander. These exports were never to recover, and the crisis brought an end to the era of Liberal government with the civil war of 1885. At the time it was not at all clear what economic activity would be found to extricate the Republic from such palpable poverty. Rafael Núñez himself had little faith in agricultural exports, and looked for a revival of mining. New Granada had been a mining colony, not as spectacular as Mexico or Peru, but the leading gold producer in Spanish America and the equal to Brazil in the history of production in the Americas before the 1849 discoveries in California. Though mining in the Pacific coast regions of the Chocó was disrupted by the final emancipation of Colombia's slaves in 1851, production as a whole kept up and averaged between two and three million pesos a year, most of it from Antioquia. Tobacco exports in the best years had exceeded three million pesos, and quinine bark had once exceeded five million, but gold was steadier – a particular advantage for the merchants and entrepreneurs of Antioquia. In the 1870s Colombia's total annual exports have been estimated to fluctuate between ten and fifteen million pesos. In per capita terms they had grown little since the beginning of the century.

The solution was not, however, to come from mining. It was found in coffee, which Colombia had begun to export in the 1850s from the eastern region of Santander, which had itself received the impulse from Venezuela. By the 1880s Colombia was exporting around 100,000 bags a year. That figure rose to near half a million in the early years of the twentieth century, and though the country was as yet producing only a small percentage of the world's coffee, coffee constituted by then almost half the total value of Colombia's exports. By 1930 exports exceeded three million bags, and Colombia had become the world's second producer after Brazil, and the leading producer of mild coffee.

Cultivation had spread from Santander to Cundinamarca and Tolima, and to the west, Antioquia and the areas of Antioqueño colonization in Caldas. Methods of production varied, as farmers adapted already varied local systems to it – sharecropping in Santander, service tenures in Cundinamarca, a mixture of service tenures and smallholdings in the west. Coffee caused and supported migrations, both permanent and seasonal, to the *tierra templada*, the warm slopes of the cordilleras: it offered new opportunities and additional wages. Its processing and commercialization remained predominantly in native hands: foreign capital was present, but the industry both began and remained essentially Colombian. The need to transport coffee brought certain critical extensions to the railways: in 1885 Colombia had only 203 kilometres in use; this had grown to 901 kilometres in 1909, 1,481 kilometres in 1922 and 3,262 kilometres in 1934. In themselves these are not impressive figures, even for what is one of the world's most mountainous countries, and not all these lines served coffee-growing regions. Nevertheless the lines that did were of great importance.

In Antioquia and Caldas coffee sustained, though not always generously, a race of producer-smallholders in symbiosis with the larger *fincas*, the processors and exporters. Into western Cundinamarca and Tolima it attracted as service-tenants (*arrendatarios*) and harvesters the peasantry of the Cundinamarca uplands and Boyacá, some of the poorest in the country. These would not all remain content with their status, and in the late 1920s conflicts on some of the large estates were already visible. But Colombian coffee defies neat social theories. Coffee planting was not the work of any distinct set of bourgeois entrepreneurs; it attracted landowners who had previously engaged in other activities, and merchants who were frequently agriculturalists as well.

Historians' efforts to establish a 'coffee interest' of distinct political orientation have not been successful. It did not take any particular political affiliation to discern what was the most attractive investment available, and government office could offer little in competition. Nor did the establishment of coffee bring an immediate advance in the local bourgeois division of labour, hard to discern as that was throughout the nineteenth century: it was not prudent to put all one's resources into a single enterprise, and investment in coffee could be naturally combined with other lines of business. Through the establishment and maintenance of the estates, through the harvesting and processing and the provision of machinery and sacks – a proportion of both came to be locally made – through transport and other services a high proportion of Colombians came to be more or less directly involved with coffee. Rafael Uribe Uribe, something of a self-appointed representative for coffee in Congress in the late 1890s, estimated that this impressionistic proportion was as high as one in four. As coffee accounted for such a high proportion of Colombia's foreign exchange, as government revenue still depended so much on customs duties, so it can be said that nothing escaped the dominance of coffee. It has been argued that the crop established itself through the artificially low wages that accompanied the introduction of inconvertible paper money in the years after 1885, but this view does not hold up against a close examination. There was growing competition for labour, and wages reacted to it; the tendency is not one of consistent pauperization or proletarianization of labour in coffee. Wages had to be high to attract labour into hard seasonal work in areas that were reputed to be unhealthy and where prices of many commodities were higher than in the regions the workers came from. Given the different seasonal and regional cycles in demand for labour, coffee wages were an additional wage for these migrants. The national market widened and deepened. US Trade Commissioner P. L. Bell summarized this in 1921:

If . . . exports of coffee were taken away the country would lose more than 50% of its foreign buying power and imports would fall off in direct relation to that decrease. Around the coffee crop and coffee prices revolves the economic condition of the entire country, directly affecting even such regions as produce no coffee, because, when coffee-producing sections have sold a large crop at high prices, the resulting proceeds flow into the other non-producing sections in trading for other products such as corn, tobacco, gold, platinum, rubber, chicle, cattle, mules, horses, sheep and goats, hides and skins, cotton, salt etc., and the result is general prosperity. For a good coffee crop sold at high prices means larger investment in real property and increased building activity; it affects municipalities whose tax returns are augmented, and increased expenditures in improvements result immediately. It also means brisk buying in foreign markets of all sorts of merchandise, from the importation of which the Government receives its greatest portion of revenue, in the form of import duties; it therefore directly affects the financial condition of the National Government, which is reflected in that of the various Departments. It also means an influx of capital, which is invested in new industrial plants (such as extensions of old and erection of new cotton mills), in cattle raising, and in the production of more coffee, cotton, sugar etc.[4]

Bell was writing at the beginning of a decade that provided Colombia's first experience of sustained optimism since the early 1870s.

---

[4] P. L. Bell, *Colombia: a commercial and industrial handbook* (Washington, DC, 1921), 166.

Besides coffee, exports of bananas and petroleum were increasing. General Reyes, General Uribe Uribe and the fruit interest of Boston had all been enthusiastic about the banana-producing possibilities of the Santa Marta hinterland on the Caribbean coast. So was General Benjamín Herrera, who owned a property there. The enclave in the long run proved more difficult for the United Fruit Company to manage than its Central American properties. There were too many local landowners and politicians to deal with, the national government was remote and not always co-operative, poor labour relations culminated in, and never recovered from, the strike and massacre of 1928 (see below). The zone was too windy and water was scarce. For all that, production in the 1920s rose to over ten million stems, making Colombia for a short time the world's leading exporter. More than half the banana land was native owned, and though there was constant friction over the prices the Company's export monopoly paid the private growers, some returns remained in Colombia. There was always the hope that the proportion might rise. On the eve of the world crisis bananas represented some 6 per cent of exports.

Even higher hopes were raised by petroleum, which by the late 1920s had come to provide around 20 per cent of the export total. Legend has it that General Virgilio Barco, an early concession-holder, was thrown into the street by a Rockefeller butler when he first tried to negotiate his title in New York. Interest in Colombia grew with the first world war, with uncertainties in Mexico and successes in Venezuela. The 1920s were years of excited exploration, and some success. It was deceptive. Colombia had too many lawyer-politicians, too sensitive a Congress and, worst of all, not enough oil to fulfil these high expectations. Petroleum created few jobs, paid little tax, and the profits mostly went abroad.

Between 1905 and 1929 Colombia's exports multiplied nine times – coffee exports nearly fifteen times. In the same period imports increased eleven times. From 1924 to 1928 exports rose from US$85.5 million to US$130.8 million, imports from US$61.8 million to US$158.9 million. Customs revenues reached an unprecedented level, rising from 19.9 million pesos in 1924 to 41.2 million pesos in 1928. So too did the foreign debt. At the beginning of the century Colombia had been a spectacularly unsatisfactory debtor. Emerging from civil war and hyper-inflation, the Republic had made no proper payment on an already antique foreign debt since 1878. At the derisory figure of 14s 11d per head of population, this was one of the lowest in Latin America, proportionately less than a twentieth of the indebtedness of Argentina or Uruguay. But this was a sign of backwardness, not of prudence. Colombia's fiscal system was a ruin that General Reyes thought the state incapable of repairing: he wished to contract it out entirely to private hands. The currency was the flood of paper produced by the civil war. This disastrous panorama was, however, transformed during the next quarter of a century, and particularly during the 1920s. The Urrutia–Thompson treaty of 1922 brought Colombia an indemnity of US$25 million to compensate for the US-inspired loss of Panama in 1903. The mission of financial advisers led by Dr Edwin Kemmerer, brought in by the government of General Pedro Nel Ospina (1923–6), gave the country's banking and public accounting system an attractive orthodox and up-to-date form, and Colombia began to borrow extensively again abroad, the departments with an abandon that the national government could not control. Dr Kemmerer's countrymen were happy to lend. The long-term national, departmental and municipal foreign debt rose from $27.5 million in 1924 to $203 million in 1928. Whereas the administration of Marco Fidel Suárez (1918–22) spent a little over 13 million pesos on public works, Pedro Nel Ospina's administration during the next four years spent over 55 million, and the last conservative administration of Miguel Abadía Méndez (1926–30), 158 million.

In retrospect this 'dance of the millions', 'prosperity through debt', has been criticized as an episode of national wastefulness, a *despilfarro*. Successive governments are said to have lacked the experience or the power to direct the investment of funds provided by over-eager American lenders. Ignorant provincial appetites had to be satisfied, and few understood the difference between productive and unproductive investment or were troubled by the lack of any coherent national plan. A new type of inflation appeared, and as demand increased and labour was drawn from the old countryside into public works and other new activities the supply of food failed to respond. These criticisms seem unduly harsh, and fail to recapture the spirit of a decade that was the first for a long while to offer even the chance of conscious modernization. By no means all of the investment was misconceived: for example, the transport network was greatly improved. Conservative governments were capable of significant administrative reform: later criticisms of Dr Kemmerer's financial reforms on the grounds of excessive rigidity overlook what he was replacing and combating. Conservatives were also capable of changing their attitudes in the face of new circumstances. The more dramatic and overtly progressive social legislation of the Liberal 1930s has its local precedents in the 1920s. Colombia's leading economist of the time, the learned and eclectic Esteban Jaramillo, served the Conservatives in the 1920s as well as the Liberals in the more difficult years after 1930; the two parties differed in politics, but not on the essentials of political economy. Nevertheless, that regional political forces were still strong, and that they were able through Congress to cut out for provincial ends rising shares of a rising budget, too much of which went on an increased bureaucracy and public works which were perhaps undesirable and certainly unsustainable, remained facts of Colombian political life under the novel economic and fiscal circumstances of the 1920s.

Between 1870 and 1928 the population of Colombia grew from 2,920,000 to 7,212,000. Colombia's four major cities all expanded considerably in the same period. In 1870 Colombia had no city as large as 50,000; Bogotá with 41,000 inhabitants was the largest city, followed by Medellín 30,000, Cali 13,000 and Barranquilla 12,000. Bogotá passed the 100,000 mark around 1905, and by 1928 had 235,000 inhabitants; in the same year Barranquilla had 140,000, while Cali and Medellín had some 120,000 each.

These figures imply a measure of social change, a measure that frequently escaped foreign observers of a country still in 1930 sparsely populated, overwhelmingly rural, three-quarters illiterate, lacking immigrants – the largest immigrant group was the *turco* or Syrio-Lebanese, mostly engaged in petty commerce – remote and unrevolutionary. But the country was significantly different from that described with Germanic completeness by Alfred Hettner and Ernst Rothlisberger in the 1880s. There was a larger urban middle class, something more than the *mestizo* embryo Hettner detected: 'an urban mode of living special to artisans, employees in commerce, owners of little stores and subordinate officials. These in part have left off wearing the *ruana* and straw hat, and imitate the European style of dress of the upper classes, so that for them the collective qualification of *gente de ruana*, to tell the truth, is no longer correct.'[5] He had described a country virtually without industry – 'unless small print-shops and breweries can be called such'; by 1930 Colombia had established a base in textiles, food

5 A. Hettner, *Viajes por los Andes colombianos, 1882–1884* (Bogotá, 1976), 91

processing and other small consumer industries behind protective tariffs. This had not, however, produced much in the way of a mass proletariat. The largest concentrations of labour in Colombia were in the Medellín textile mills, and these were predominantly female. Female too was much of the more scattered labour force in the processing of coffee. Some gold mines employed several hundred workers, as did the Santa Ana silver mine in Tolima, and so did the sugar *ingenios* La Manuelita and Sincerín, but such concentrations of labour were both rare and remote from the centres of power. This is reflected in the early history of Colombian labour organization. It was possible to organize miners, and port, river and railway workers. Some progress could be made with the by no means uniform work force of the banana zone, and with the textile workers, despite their sex and the paternalism of the Medellín employers. Beyond that little could be done with an urban work force that was small and atomized: church-run mutualist organizations were as successful as any other type in these circumstances. Colombia, as the Colombian delegate was firmly told at the congress of Latin American Communist parties in Buenos Aires in 1929, lacked masses.

This problem was compounded by one of consciousness. The best accounts of early agitation in Colombia show recurring frustrations that are particularly Colombian. Efforts to form an autonomous working-class movement had to contend with the powers of absorption of conventional politics, particularly Liberal politics. Generals Uribe Uribe and Herrera did not neglect to appeal to popular elements, to present the Liberal party as the natural vehicle of the workers' cause. Workers saw no contradiction in giving their allegiance for immediate purposes to some socialist organization, while reserving their support in national politics for the Gran Partido Liberal and its heroes, martyrs and veterans. The party was ever open to talent, and it offered at least the opportunity of a wider stage. Its previous history contained episodes and figures of genuine radicalism, and it promised a future. Small wonder that the numbers of socialists, communists, anarchists and other autonomist labour leaders were continually depleted by 'opportunism'.

A second source of frustration derived from the nature of Colombian society, and worked in favour of Conservative governments as well as in favour of the Liberal opposition. The nature of social distances in Colombia did not foster working-class consciousness. Social distances can be made to appear very great, if, say, an *indio boyacense* is compared to a

Bogotá banker, or a black from Valle to a Popayán aristocrat. The distance between Colombian extremes was perhaps modest in comparison with other societies, but in any case the new conflicts were not between such extremes, and they were still conflicts in a society whose scale was intimate. Ignacio Torres Giraldo, an early labour leader writing from his personal experiene, describes how in the strike of the Ferrocarril del Pacífico in 1926 the *gerente*, General Vásquez Cobo, could pay an unescorted visit to strike headquarters in Cali to congratulate the strikers on their discipline, charming them with his gentlemanly manner. General Vásquez Cobo was also a Conservative politician anxious for people's votes. Torres Giraldo, on his way to Moscow, would later pay a return visit to him in the Colombian Legation in Paris. This is not the sort of atmosphere in which the class war flourishes. In part it is that a labour leader of a certain prominence is already a person whose status is far higher than his proclaimed class position, in part it is that there is not yet enough differentiation. There must also have been in Cali the living memory that the black Liberal General David Peña 40-odd years before had made some Conservative matrons sweep the streets. Torres Giraldo has also left an account of the life of María Cano, a Medellín lady whose sympathy for the poor, first inspired by Victor Hugo, led her from good works to election as 'Flor del Trabajo', from that to organizational campaigns among the workers on the Magdalena river and in the Antioqueño mines, and finally to Marxism: a significant early detail is that her family was at first more concerned that she should be properly chaperoned than about what doctrines she was preaching. Diego Monsalve's *Colombia cafetera*, a magnificent folio on the nation's progress compiled in the late 1920s, sets down with pride the number of workers' organizations as a symptom of national modernity, not as a harbinger of conflicts to come. His attitude is at least as defensible as that of those historians of labour who write as if they are chronicling the saints and martyrs of some early church. Nor was the attitude of Conservatives in the 1920s towards the novel *sindicatos* and workers' organizations by any means uniformly alarmist or unenlightened. General Vásquez Cobo was more typical than his rival from Valle, General Ignacio Rengifo, who as minister of government in the late 1920s ran an unsuccessful and much ridiculed campaign for heroic measures against the Red Menace. Such a line was as exotic as the threat it was directed against, and ran counter to Conservative beliefs that their party was more attuned to the essential

Colombian people than the Liberals, that it was Liberals who were usually the exploiters of the nascent proletariat, and that the Conservative tradition of active paternalism derived from the best elements in the colonial tradition, which the party had never abandoned. Such views found echoes, for example in the cauca *indigenista* leader Manuel Quintín Lame, who for all his eccentricities and peculiarities is 'the most formidable Indian leader that this *mestizo* Republic has produced since Independence. 'Dr Quintino', with his knowledge of the civil code and his well-worn copy of *El abogado en casa*, stands clearly within a certain tradition. He found a sympathetic listener in Marco Fidel Suárez, who helped him get access to the National Archives, and in the 1930 elections he supported the Conservatives: 'They had persecuted the Indians in an ordinary fashion while the Liberals had done so in an extraordinary fashion.'[6]

There was not much extraordinary persecution. The Santa Marta banana zone strike and massacre of 1928 was a product of special circumstances: it developed in ways unforeseen by either side, the repression that followed was mild, the government responsible was weakened by it and nothing like it happened again. There were many conflicts in Colombia: conflicts over land, as one would expect in an overwhelmingly rural society with many areas of recent settlement; conflicts that arose from attempts to employ old patterns of rural labour in new circumstances, as in Cundinamarca coffee, or from shifts in demand, as when the opening of the Panama Canal in 1914 provided new opportunities for Cauca cattle. There were even 'modern' conflicts, as were those between native workers and American oil men in Barrancabermeja. But they were not grand conflicts, and they appeared to foreigners (who had no memories of civil war and little interest in elections in Santander) as little islands of discord in a sea of old-fashioned harmony. For them, lack of dramatic progress had its compensations in a general atmosphere of courtesy and security in which native agitators – 'the worst sort of South American politician' – were a minor and irrelevant nuisance, no more. How safe the country was can be recalled from Frank M. Chapman's 1917 account of the life of the American Ornithological Expedition:

From the peon by the wayside to the owners of the haciendas one and all have shown us the most courteous attention. When travelling through remote,

[6] D. Castrillón Arboleda, *El indio Quintín Lame* (Bogotá, 1973), 237.

unsettled regions with a valuable outfit and often considerable sums of money, we have felt as safe (possibly safer!) than when in our own homes. When in camp or at hotels, country inns or posadas, we made no special provision for guarding our equipment and supplies; nevertheless, during the five years of our work we did not suffer the loss of a single item by theft. Indeed, on passing through a certain village where one of our party had previously worked, we were stopped by a native bringing a needle and thread which had been left behind.[7]

ECUADOR

In 1895 Japan, at war with China, bought from Chile a warship, the *Esmeralda*. The Chileans desired to protect their neutrality in this transaction, and arranged through the Ecuadorean consul in New York that the *Esmeralda* should have a fleeting Ecuadorean career before joining the Japanese navy. This 'sale of the flag' involved bribes, and former President José María Caamaño, at that time Governor of Guayas, led a naïve government into thinking that it was a simple diplomatic favour that Ecuador was well advised to perform for an enemy of her sometimes menacing neighbour, Peru. The scandal broke, and there were soon conservative and liberal risings in several parts of the country. On 5 June 1895 a Guayaquil *junta* named the '*benemérito* General Sr. D. Eloy Alfaro' as Jefe Supremo de la República and General-in-Chief of the army in a document proclaimed to carry nearly 16,000 signatures.

Alfaro had not been in Ecuador for ten years, but he possessed a reputation that made him, as the document said, 'the soul of the popular movement which has overthrown the evil oligarchy'. He was the fifth child of a Spanish merchant settled in the hat-making coastal town of Montecristi; his father finally married his Ecuadorean mother when he was 21. By then he had already begun his career in the political and military skirmishes of the coast, in opposition to García Moreno. If one looks for models or parallels to Alfaro's career, the most fitting example is given by Garibaldi, who did indeed in 1851 pass through Guayaquil, when he was already famous for his defence of Rome.

Alfaro was then nine years old. He resembles Garibaldi in courage, elan, the ability to improvise, the common touch, complete disinterestedness, a pre-Marxist republican nobility of character, and in his anti-clericalism. Modern Ecuadorean historiography is so anxious to define the liberal revolution that found in him its essential leader as bourgeois, a

---

[7] F. M. Chapman, *The distribution of bird-life in Colombia* (Bulletin of the American Museum of Natural History, vol. xxxvi, New York, 1917), 9.

movement of coastal merchant and exporting interests against the clerical–latifundist elements of the sierra, that many of these *garibaldino* qualities are forgotten, and the nature of his revolution is distorted, its importance even reduced. Alfaro's father was a merchant, but the first time the young Eloy was left in charge of the business he invested all the disposable capital in a revolution. Later, Eloy himself in exile made a fortune in business in Panama, where he married well too. He spent the fortune on further revolutions, leaving his adored family in straightened circumstances: their letters are fewer than they might be, one son writes, because of the price of stamps. In the intervals between descents on Ecuador he lent his services to the radical-liberal cause in Central America – Alfaro always considered liberalism a universal cause, and by 1895 he certainly had a Latin American reputation himself, derived from his military exploits, spectacular though not always successful, and maintained through his contacts with other liberals and revolutionaries – Joaquín Crespo in Venezuela, the Nicaraguan José Santos Zelaya, the Cubans José Martí and Antonio Maceo, Colombians such as the pamphleteers Vargas Vila and 'El Indio' Uribe; he was the admired friend and ally of the original South American Cicero, his fellow-countryman Juan Montalvo. In short, he was a professional revolutionary. He was no more bourgeois himself than his Colombian counterpart, Rafael Uribe Uribe, was a professional administrator of coffee estates. This did not preclude him from leading what was in its intentions and results a movement that can in part be properly characterized as bourgeois: the Guayaquil merchants and bankers and the cacao planters had not been powerless in previous governments – one might argue that the *argolla* suited many of them better than *alfarismo* – but their dominance appears more secure at the end of the cycle. But the liberal revolution also enjoyed the support of petty-bourgeois groups, such as minor officials and school teachers, and it appealed beyond these to the people.

Alfaro gathered together an army, the nucleus of the liberal army on which he was always heavily reliant, and invaded the sierra. He was careful to point out that he did not regard the struggle as one of region against region, and that there were numerous moderate or honest conservatives in the sierra as much in opposition to the Quito government as he was. There were liberals in the uplands as well, as demonstrations and risings showed. His army had a sense of mission: its half-educated officers and its black and hot-country troops – 'Alfaro o muerte' or 'No pido ni doy cuartel' on their uniforms – were at the very least committed to a revolutionary career open to talent. At first it met with little resistance from government forces 'tired by so much praying, flogging and idleness', and Alfaro entered Quito after a few small battles. More serious resistance came later, and its inspiration came from the church, particularly from Bishop Pedro Schumacher of Portoviejo, an expatriate ultramontane Rhinelander, Bishop Andrade of Riobamba and, at least in liberal opinion, from the foreign regulars. The forces they encouraged could base their operations across the northern border in the Colombian diocese of Pasto, where they received aid and comfort from the conservative Colombian authorities and the Spanish ultramontane Bishop Ezequiel Moreno Díaz. Alfaro held the sierra *manu militari*; despite the observance of the forms of representative democracy, his was a much more thoroughgoing military government than was usual. Alfaro also made the elections, but he could not exclude all his opponents or rivals, and the resulting Congresses were often recalcitrant. He needed a substantial army to stay in power.

The Liberal programme was summarized in a convenient decalogue published in *El Pichincha*, a semi-official Quito radical newspaper:

1. A decree on clerical property (*Decreto de manos muertas*).
2. Suppression of convents.
3. Suppression of monasteries.
4. Obligatory lay education.
5. Freedom of the Indians.
6. Abolition of the concordat.
7. Ecclesiastical secularization.
8. Expulsion of foreign priests.
9. A strong and well-paid army.
10. Railways to the Pacific.

The church in highland Ecuador, powerful under the colony and reinforced (to an extent unwittingly) by García Moreno, was more deeply entrenched and its influence was more unrivalled than anywhere else in Spanish America. The Colombian church had lost its lands and had suffered persecution at the hands of the Liberals, and in comparison with most of the leaders of the church in Ecuador its bishops had learnt prudence. It also had no hope of dominating neo-conservative and Conservative politicians of the calibre of Núñez, Caro or Reyes – to be considered too *beato*, too pious, was not good for a Colombian conservative. The Ecuadorean church had hitherto survived with its lands, *fueros* and influence intact, and no strong secular Conservative party had been left behind by García Moreno, who, Catholic reformer though he was, had been the greatest threat to its autonomy that it had faced so far. Seven out of the ten items on *El Pichincha's* list were direct attacks on church prerogatives.

Alfaro and his successor General Leónidas Plaza, who became president in 1901, worked through the list. Alfaro freed the press from clerical censorship, broke the concordat, expelled Schumacher, Andrade and a quantity of foreigners, and took in hand the secularization of education. A more complete assault on church lands was made under Plaza. While Alfaro earlier had feared rousing even more resistance than he was already meeting, Plaza was able to reach an interesting compromise with sierra landlords and to strengthen his own clientele vis-à-vis his erstwhile leader's at the church's expense. The registration of births, marriages and deaths which had been a clerical monopoly throughout the nineteenth century was nationalized; the state withdrew its support from all forms of ecclesiastical taxation. Civil marriage and divorce were instituted in 1902, and the civil marriage was obligatory. Clerical vows were no longer recognized, and laws were passed against political preaching. The Republic was declared to be no longer officially consecrated to the Sacred Heart, and Roman Catholicism was no longer the religion of state: the 1906 constitution made no mention of the church at all.

Alfaro was not an extreme clerophobe himself; he came from the coast, where the church was weak, and clerophobia developed better in the sierra in long and intimate contact with the enemy. Nor was he as systematic in his arguments as the more rational and in other respects more moderate General Plaza. But both saw that breaking the power of the church was a political necessity, a *sine qua non* if Ecuador was to have coherent national government rather than a series of inherently unstable compromises and alliances. Their motives came from high politics, and can only be accounted bourgeois in the remote sense that the enterprise of coherent national government was somehow essentially bourgeois – a notion that in European history requires a deal of qualification, which can well be applied in Ecuador as well. The extent of clerical control prior to the liberal Revolution has been overshadowed in later accounts by the more *folclórico* details of clerical resistance, and thus the nature of the revolution is misread and its achievements underestimated. The church was less rich than its enemies supposed. The lands it lost were not divided up, but went usually, perhaps at a somewhat higher rent, to new *arrendatarios* (in Quito *arrendatario*, tenant, which elsewhere in the Andes usually refers to a more humble sort of person, is a term that carries social prestige). Secular education took some time before it was as extensive as the old church schools, and it was not always better, particularly in the upper reaches of society. The church, thrown back on its own resources, remained a powerful presence. For all that, a genuine revolution had been carried out.

Alfaro and the American entrepreneur Archer Harman also joined sierra and coast with the Quito–Guayaquil railway, another achievement that has been subsequently rationalized as part of the agenda of the Guayaquil bourgeoisie. It did not seem to be high on their list at the time. The cacao growers, exporters and bankers of the coast were not particularly interested in the mediocre market of the uplands, and were reluctant to foot the bill for the railway. The landowners and manufacturers of the interior often feared competition for their labour and for their products. Congress frequently attacked the contract. Local interests intrigued incessantly about the route even when they were persuaded to support the enterprise. It was more an heroic than a bourgeois affair, and as such it obsessed Alfaro, reinforcing his marked mystical and authoritarian tendencies. Like the San Tomé mine in Joseph Conrad's Costaguana, it was for him the greatest thing in the Republic, and like that mine it even acquired a romantic foreign backer in the shape of a Scottish millionaire, who was rewarded by being made Ecuador's Consul in Perth. The railway organization gave Alfaro critical assistance when he took power for the second time in 1906. When the railway was finished in 1908 Alfaro still could not relinquish power, though he no longer embodied any recognizable cause. His persistent senile meddling culminated in a last failed coup in 1912. He was made prisoner in Guayaquil, a city of wooden houses where the popular mood was so exasperated by now against him that his captors argued that there were no walls thick enough to keep him safe. So he was taken up his own railway, clutching the manuscript of the history he had written of its building, to Quito where the feeling against him was even stronger: people did get killed in the little wars he had started. He and his companions were then murdered in the *panóptico* prison, and their bodies dragged through the streets and burnt in the Ejido park outside the city. 'Qué calvario!', one of them had said on the train. Alfaro remains for many Ecuadoreans an unrivalled symbol of republican will, and for Marxists more of a puzzle than they would care to admit.

Alfaro's death in 1912 left power once again in the more compromising hands of General Plaza, assisted by Archbishop Federico González Suárez, a clerical realist of great prudence and ability, who survived the extremes of both Liberals and Conservatives and who came to exercise great authority. For four years the Plaza administration was faced with a guerilla war in the province of Esmeraldas against the forces of the *alfarista* Colonel Carlos Concha. The new liberalism was not radical, nor did it seek to build any more doubtful railways. More and more it came under the sway of the Guayaquil banks, particularly of the Banco Comercial y Agrícola and its director, Francisco Urbina Jado. The contrast in party reputations between Colombia and Ecuador became a marked one in the years after 1912. Some Colombian Liberals may have been rich – Colombian Conservatives persisted in the 1920s in pointing out that the Liberal party was the party of the most conspicuous rich – but they were not in power. In Ecuador until 1925, although profoundly divided, they were. Alfaro had ended once and for all any prospect of a conservative hegemony. In Ecuador it was the Liberal party that had to carry responsibility for the bad times at the end of the cacao boom. The Liberals repressed the Guayaquil strike of 1922, which was ruthlessly put down by veterans of the Esmeraldas campaign. Their government could not avoid responsibility for the Leyto hacienda massacre in Chimborazo the following year. They were the ones who entered into the excessively onerous and intimate – and inflationary – financial arrangements that kept the government afloat, and which in the case of Ecuador gave Dr Kemmerer the appearance of a liberator. The 1920s in Ecuador were not – as, taken overall, they were in Colombia – years of economic advance. It was the last decade of the predominance of cacao, but a troubled and uneven one. The Conservatives were to some degree better placed to appeal to a popular opposition, and they began to do so in the sierra with an organization called Compactación Obrera. On 9 July 1925 the Liberal government was overthrown by a military conspiracy, the Revolución Juliana of the Liga de los Militares Jóvenes. Short-lived and confused, this only heralded a long period of political fragmentation of which the chief beneficiary was to be a figure who could appeal to both coast and sierra, to politicians of both traditional currents and, from time to time, to the people: José María Velasco Ibarra. His career and his multiple presidencies were to stretch into the 1970s.

General population estimates for Ecuador are hard to find. An official estimate for 1882 was 946,000, a careful guess for 1905 1,150,000; the US

Department of Commerce *Commercial travelers' guide to Latin America* for 1920 says that the total 'is estimated at 1,300,000 to 2,000,000', and inclines towards the lower figure. The population of Ecuador's two major cities both increased steadily throughout the perod. The population of Guayaquil grew from 44,000 in 1890 to 70–75,000 in 1908, and 120,000 in 1930. Quito had only around 50,000 inhabitants when the railway arrived in 1908, but then began to grow more rapidly. By 1930 the city's numbers were roughly equal to Guayaquil's.

Until the 1920s the economic development of Ecuador was in this period less marked by crisis and change than was that of Colombia. Cacao dominated her exports, and these years saw a boom that made her for a time the world's leading producer. The plantations expanded. The system of production was a typical compromise between ideal types: coastal landowners contracted *sembradores*, who would care for a given number of trees until they came into production, receiving both cash advances and the right to grow their own subsistence and cash crops in the meantime. They themselves, their families and other workers would also serve as peons on the producing parts of the plantation. The coast continued to attract labour from the sierra, as it had since at least the eighteenth century. The landowners' advances to their *sembradores* and peons can be made to look like rigorous debt-peonage, but evidence of mobility and competition for labour modifies this picture. So does the literature on the character of the mixed-blood Ecuadorean *costeño*, the *montuvio*, not usually portrayed as deferential. It has been argued that those not employed on cacao were particularly prone to *alfarismo*, but one can hazard that the same attitudes would affect the workers on the plantations.

Cacao plantations were often large enterprises; they were rarely small. Some large landowners were engaged in banking and foreign commerce, but Guayaquil also generated a banking and trading community that was not directly tied to the cacao plantations. Foreign capital was present, but not dominant. Cacao production and commercialization prefigures in some ways the independent banana production on the coast that eventually replaced it, which has not remained subservient to a foreign company. Cacao also produced a small number of millionaires who were able to live in Paris.

World cacao consumption doubled between 1894 and 1903, and again between 1903 and 1912, and again from that year to 1924; that is to say, it increased eight times between 1894 and 1924. In 1894 Ecuador produced 28 per cent of the world's production, more than the 24 per cent produced in the British Empire and twice the quantity of her nearest national rival, Brazil. This proportion declined to 6.5 per cent in 1924, at which date the British colonies in Africa were producing 53.5 per cent. There were clear signs of crisis before the first world war, and the boom came to an end for Ecuador in the 1920s through the combination of British African competition, a world surplus and the arrival and spread of disease.

As elsewhere, in these years one can also see the small beginnings of local import-substituting industrialization, here complicated by the continuity and adaptation of traditional textile production. Despite vicissitudes, this had never disappeared from the sierra. Hat-making also persisted, declining on the coast but surviving better in the Cuenca region, where it held steady until the coming of hatless fashions after the second world war. Better communications, Alfaro's railway among them, produced a certain impact, but no dramatic changes. The conditions of the upland Indian population changed only slowly. In 1916 President Baquerizo Moreno changed the law on imprisonment for debt, a step that was considered to be the legal abolition of *concertaje*, the debt-peonage of the sierra. In 1934 Jorge Icaza published *Huasipungo*, which became the best-known *indigenista* novel of the Andes. The brutish conditions it describes were never general throughout the sierra. The Mexican anthropologist Moises Sáenz, for example, writing in 1933, did not find that population universally oppressed.

VENEZUELA

Antonio Guzmán Blanco, who came to power in Venezuela with the Liberal Revolution of April 1870 and who was to dominate Venezuelan politics until his final unhurried departure for Paris in 1888, was no 'typical *caudillo*' of the Anglo-Saxon imagination. He was born into the aristocracy of Caracas, itself an unusual origin for a Venezuelan politician, the son of the Liberal intriguer, journalist and demagogue Antonio Leocadio Guzmán. When the Monagas era ended in 1858, he held a consular post in the United States. He joined what was to become the nucleus of the 'Federal' command not in the backlands but in Curaçao, and made his way in the hierarchy essentially in staff positions. He was no coward and he could lead troops, but his principal talents were not military. Nor does his seizure of power fit into the pattern so many historians have felt they must impose, that is to say, the domination of

Venezuela by *caudillos* from successive regions. Guzmán represented no region. He constructed an effective coalition from the diverse elements left in play at the end of the Federal Wars. He succeeded because he combined larger political views with ruthlessness and an understanding of what the government's essential resources were and how they could be increased to his advantage. He undoubtedly had a clearer vision of national problems and possibilities than anyone else on the Federal side. He was an able though conspicuously greedy financier, and unafraid of complex foreign and local combinations – he was to be the first Spanish-American multi-millionaire to figure in Parisian society, some years in advance of the *rastacueros* of Argentina. He was a ceaseless and shameless propagandist of his own virtues, as a demagogue his father's son, and as president he orchestrated adulation into a system that made anything previously seen under Páez or the Monagas brothers seem true republican modesty. It is important to stress that it was a system. Guzmán was certainly vain, but he was no fool, and the extravagances were in part a means of control, just as similar extravagances had been in Rosas's Argentina. He placed himself above rivals, just as his public constructions in Caracas placed Caracas above all other Venezuelan cities. Manuel Briceño, a Colombian critic of his government, detected as well a tendency to appeal to the populace over the heads of the educated classes. He also noted a praetorian escort that cleared the streets when the president moved about, an extensive espionage and police system, interference with the mails, imprisonment of opponents, leg-irons in use in the jails, a servile press and violent methods of censorship – all elements more frequently associated with the other lasting dictator of these years, Juan Vicente Gómez.

No previous government had been inspired by such conscious notions of modernization, and it was these that Guzmán and his supporters offered in justification. Guzmán could certainly argue that a country emerging from a decade of Monagas rule, universally recognized as disorderly and corrupt, and five years of civil war (1859–64) followed by the lackadaisical rule of President Falcón, was certainly in need of order. He sought a more dynamic economy for its own sake, for the sake of his government, and for the sake of his private fortune, as he was a frequent monopolist and a universal share-holder in local enterprises. He constructed three hundred kilometres of railway, and his final departure coincided with Venezuela's connection to submarine cable communications. He saw the possibilities of accelerating the country's development by attracting foreign capital on a large scale. He had indeed some success in doing so, though his most grandiose schemes such as the conglomerate partnership he proposed to the Péreire interests in France did not materialize.

Guzmán certainly introduced greater sophistication in government finances, and for a time greater order. He reached a mutually profitable *modus vivendi* with local commercial houses, and his rule provided greater bureaucratic discipline, and a more predictable administrative context; even if it was at a cost, the cost was easily recouped. He was certainly a better administrator than his immediate predecessors or his immediate successors, and his achievements in that sphere and in the codification of Venezuelan law were genuine, even where the first impulse tended to peter out. His educational advances in his first government were remarkable, though here too the performance was not sustained. Guzmán brooked no opposition from the church. Always weaker in Venezuela than in Colombia or in Ecuador, by the time the Pope agreed to terms in 1883 – he was faced with the threat of schism and a Guzmán-inspired Church of Venezuela – it was weaker still. Guzmán reacted to the archbishop's refusal of a triumphal Te Deum in 1870 by expelling him, and went on to establish civil marriage and the civil registry of births and deaths.

Guzmán's coalition maintained the Federal rhetoric – *Dios y Federación* was for long in Venezuela the official phrase for signing off letters – but was centralist in practice, the centralism reinforced by the embryo of a national army and, more important, fiscal subsidy from the national treasury. Guzmán made an example of one dissident, General Matías Salazar, with a formal execution, but his typical methods were more political and conciliatory. His 1881 constitution established the indirect election of the president for a short two-year term, and it is possible that he envisaged a system in which loyal subordinates would take turns in the office under his overall control. The trouble was that subordinates had other ideas. These disloyal inspirations explain the division of Guzmán's ascendancy into three periods in which he exercised power directly: the *Septenio* (1870–7), the *Quinquenio* (1879–84), and the *Aclamación* (1886–7). On two occasions Guzmán found that he had to return from Paris to reassert his authority, the first time by force. He returned to Paris for good in August 1887 at the end of the *Aclamación*, and died there in 1899. Expropriations of his local interests drew aggrieved protests, but the bulk of his fortune – in his own famous phrase 'poco común en América' – was safely out of reach.

His style of government was spectacular. His successors in Venezuela would occasionally imitate it. He had himself awarded the title of *El Ilustre Americano*, and consented that his lieutenant, General Joaquín Crespo, should be called *El Héroe del Deber Cumplido* – the Hero of Duty Performed. Later, General Gómez would become *El Benemérito*. Other such titles appear in the Dominican Republic, in Central America. Europeans and North Americans casually assumed that such bombast was typical of Latin America, and in that way Guzmán did Latin America no service. In fact, such bombast was neither typical – it drew ridicule in Colombia, and protests from Chile – nor was it causal. It was a resort of autocracy in particular circumstances, and reflected the peculiar weakness of the elites of civil society in the Venezuela of Guzmán's time. A similar line of analysis might prosper if applied to other Spanish American cases of dictatorial extravagance. It should also be remembered that in Napoleon III, Kaiser Wilhelm II and in Mussolini, the Old World offered the New some equally immodest examples. A close reader can detect in Manuel Briceño's *Los ilustres* (1884) anticipations of Vallenilla Lanz's remarkable sociological justification of Venezuelan despotism, *Cesarismo democrático* (1929).

Guzmán inherited a country of something less than two million inhabitants, entering on its second cycle of coffee export. It was still overwhelmingly rural, possessing only three cities of any size – Caracas with some 60,000 people, Valencia with 35,000 and Maracaibo with 25,000. It also exported hides and cacao. It had virtually no industry, and even on the level of artisan production achieved less than Colombia or Ecuador. Venezuela was South America's second producer of coffee after Brazil, and in the second half of the last century coffee production shifted from the central highlands to the west, to the Andean states. Coffee engendered there a modest prosperity. It was a small or medium landowner's crop. Much of the labour for the harvest came from Colombia, from as far afield as the upland Colombian department of Boyacá. Most of the coffee, and large quantities of Colombian coffee as well, was exported through Maracaibo, where the German commercial presence was strong – German merchants were much respected for their commercial punctilio, and integrated well into local society; many married Venezuelan girls and established themselves permanently in

Venezuela, a pattern that seems more common among them than among other European or North American merchants. The Andean coffee-producing region, centred on Maracaibo, evolved a society of marked independence and self-confidence, even if one should discount the too-romantic versions of a bourgeois rural Arcadia that coffee, in Venezuela as in Colombia, has subsequently generated. Communications by land between the Andean region and the rest of the country were primitive until the completion by Gómez of the Transandean Highway in 1925.

It is best to admit that we know very little about the economic life of much of Venezuela in these years. Cattle raising remained in many areas the dominant rural activity, but it is still largely unstudied. Much of Venezuela has been depicted, according to the tastes of the author, as the domain of either the *latifundista*, the large landowner, or of the *conuquero*, the shifting small-holder. Some have seen coffee as creating a settled peasantry, which previously did not exist, out of the latter. The argument is plausible, but the studies to sustain it have yet to be carried out. The nature and function of the Venezuelan *latifundio* also awaits exploration. One can hazard a guess that *latifundista* and *conquero* coexisted in many places with little strain, and that in cattle-producing regions life continued on traditional lines. Though vulnerable to civil war, it is hard to conclude that in the nineteenth century this sort of activity was keenly affected by government policy; those concerned would make their customary arrangements with the successive officials who levied the local taxes.

Such humdrum considerations serve to cut Guzmán Blanco down to a smaller size. His ambitions were grand, but Venezuela's insertion in the international economy did not match them. In economic terms, he presided over a country which exported coffee, cacao and hides, which possessed few mines, which could offer few grand contracts, and which had a severely limited domestic market. The economic realities also explain the contrast between local and national historical consciousness: a history of, say, Maracaibo, can include passing observations on the Guzmanato – Guzmán did not favour Maracaibo, which he rightly suspected of harbouring separatist designs – while regarding national policies as at worst a peripheral hindrance to local progress. As in Colombia and Ecuador, without denying the existence and the intermittent and the long-term importance of the nation, local historians frequently ignore national politics with some impunity.

The dominant figure of the decade that followed Guzmán's departure was General Joaquín Crespo (president, 1892–7). He was a *llanero*, a landowner of the cattle plains, and lacked Guzmán's cosmopolitan sophistication and his impulses of self-glorification. He does not therefore stand out among his contemporaries, though he was an effective soldier, capable of inspiring devotion in his followers and respect in his enemies. The late 1890s were also a period of falling coffee prices and this would undoubtedly have dimmed the lustre of any government. Crespo was faced with novel opposition in the campaigns of the *liberal-nacionalista* General José Manuel Hernández, 'El Mocho' Hernández, a quixotic figure who gained extraordinary popularity, and combined armed risings with electoral campaigns influenced by North American examples – it is said that he had watched William Jennings Bryan. 'El Mocho' entered folklore:

> Quién inspira al pueblo fé?
> José!
>
> Quién lucha por serle fiel?
> Manuel!
>
> Por hacer su nombre grande?
> Hernández!
>
> Por eso es que en Venezuela
> de la Guayana a los Andes
> suman vítores doquiera
> a José Manuel Hernández![8]

But governments did not lose elections and Hernández did not win battles. The 1890s, and indeed the succeeding government of Cipriano Castro, were nevertheless a time of continuous political agitation, which conspicuously engaged less privileged persons like teachers, journalists and other such talents looking for careers, and from which the *pueblo* was by no means absent. Crespo considered himself a radical liberal – he aided Alfaro in Ecuador as a combatant in the same cause. The long span of governments such as those of Guzmán and Juan Vicente Gómez has led historians to ignore the interstices between, when authority was much less assured. Figures like Dr Juan Pablo Rojas Paúl (president, 1888–90) and Dr Raimundo Andueza Palacio (president, 1890–2) never looked secure. Nor, for all his greater talent, did Cipriano Castro, who was to seize power in 1899 and to exercise it in his singular fashion until 1908.

As his successor, Joaquín Crespo had chosen General Ignacio

---

[8] Quoted in J. A. de Armas Chitty, '*El Mocho' Hernández. Papeles de su archivo* (Caracas, 1978), 60.

Andrade. He might also have succeeded in sustaining his nominee's authority, but he was killed in the skirmish of 'La Mata Carmelera' when suppressing an early rising against Andrade. Just as Crespo was a lesser figure than Guzmán Blanco, Crespo's successors did not include another of his local prestige and popularity. Into this confused Republic in May 1899 Cipriano Castro led a small invasion ('the sixty') from Colombia, later to be termed the Revolución Restauradora. Castro was an *andino*, a native of the state of Táchira, which borders on Colombia. He had been educated in Colombia, and his politics had the particular tinge of Colombian radicalism – a number of Colombian radicals also sought work or refuge or both in Venezuela as in Ecuador after their fall from power at home in 1885. He had been active in local and national politics in Venezuela, and had been a representative in Congress and governor of his native state. He had spent some years in exile in Colombia while Crespo was in power. Though he was to become internationally famous for his disorderly public and private ways thanks to the Anglo-German-Italian blockade of Venezuela's ports in 1902–3, Castro was also, at his best, a daring and attractive leader. The success of the Revolución Restauradora owed something to luck, but much more to his ability to seize opportunities, his powers of improvisation and his rapid grasp of the national political situation. He was prepared to fight at the right moment, he chose able subordinates, and he won because he was a better politician than his opponents. Once in possession of the Republic (as his best soldier General Gómez put it, 'ya que la república nos pertenece'), he was ruthless in using all possible resources for his personal and political advantage, and his caprices served to show who was the master. Guzmán exalted himself with titles and statues, Castro with scandals, and with defiance of good opinion at home and abroad.

Castro's accession to power has been conventionally taken to be the start of a period of *andino* dominance in Venezuelan politics. Not only was Castro from the Andes, but so was his successor Gómez, and the succeeding presidents prior to 1945, General Eleazer López Contreras and General Isaias Medina Angarita. Marcos Pérez Jiménez, the dictator of the 1950s, was also an *andino*. But Germán Carrera Damas has questioned the usefulness of this characterization of the Castro and Gómez years, pointing out that the essential change comes in the 1920s, when petroleum comes to dominate the economy.[9] The questioning can

---

[9] See, for example, Germán Carrera Damas, 'Proceso a la formación de la burguesía venezolana', in *Tres temas de historia* (2nd edn, Caracas, 1978).

be taken further. Castro's first little army was *andino*, and *andinos* came near to monopolizing the officer corps under Gómez, but outside the army there were plenty of other elements in both regimes. Both Castro and Gómez confirmed the essential *modus vivendi* that had existed between all successful Venezuelan governments and the commercial and business interests of Caracas, Valencia and the ports. Both readily took their profits in such traditional presidential activities as regulating the urbanization of Caracas to their personal advantage and monopolizing its meat supply. With the exception of Gómez's concern for *andino* officers – and Gómez was Castro's principal general – neither the native region nor its inhabitants were particularly favoured. In the campaigns that followed Castro's initial victory Gómez gained a profound knowledge of the country, and he was a good judge of all sorts of men.

Castro survived the Revolución Libertadora of 1903, led by a banker-general who was later on to be one of Gómez's foreign ministers. It had some North American backing. Castro was prepared to grant foreigners concessions and contracts, but incapable of sustaining what Joseph Conrad in *Nostromo* (1904) called 'the conditions of civilized business'. It was his capriciousness, as much as fiscal crisis, that brought about the Anglo-German-Italian blockade of 1902–3. This was not the first such affair – Guzmán Blanco himself had at one time or another broken relations with Holland, Great Britain, France and Colombia, but Guzmán kept bad relations under better control. Castro nonetheless survived the blockade, and was even capable of extracting some local political advantage from it. The blockade also produced declarations of Latin American hostility to debt-collecting expeditions that were important in the formation of regional convictions in international law – the Drago doctrine, named after the Argentine foreign minister who formulated it – and the Roosevelt corollary to the Monroe doctrine: 'persistent wrongdoing' by a Latin American state was to be controlled by United States policing, as the United States could not accept European interventions in the Americas, least of all German naval incursions in the Caribbean.

Five years after the Revolución Libertadora and the blockade Castro was forced to leave for Europe for a surgical operation that could not be performed in Venezuela, and in his absence the government was taken over by his vice president, General Gómez. A United States naval presence stood by off the coast during the transition, and the United States lent discreet assistance to Gómez in preventing Castro attempting to return to the country up until his death in 1924 – his bones finally returned to his birthplace in Capacho in the 1970s. Gómez did not need United States help, but he did offer stability, the 'conditions of civilized business'. He controlled Venezuela until his death in 1935.

He had a natural talent for military organization, and his role in Castro's revolution and its aftermath gave him extensive campaign experience. He was not the first ruler to achieve some partial modernization of the Venezuelan army – Guzmán and Crespo had their better-armed elite forces, or *sagradas* – but increasing revenues gave him greater resources. The armed forces he relied on were a complicated hybrid: he did create a somewhat larger and more professional regular army, but he also maintained networks of veteran civil war officers in the provinces, often on his own lands, who were to organize old-fashioned *levas* of *gente de confianza* in times of emergency. He also maintained the *sagrada* at Maracay, the effective seat of his government. Maracay was the strategic centre of the country, and also a convenient centre of profitable agricultural operations. Living there was Gómez's way of setting himself above everyone. For convenience, he let reliable civilians occupy the presidency. He never gave up command of the army.

His military power was complemented by an extensive espionage system at home and abroad, by the imprisonment of opponents for long terms with leg-irons in the Rotunda jail, by the suppression of all vital public debate: Congress was a servile body of nominees, and there was no opposition press. So much is well known. In Gómez's defence it can be argued that in 1908 he did not take over the cowed Republic of 1935, and that many of those he imprisoned or exiled would have welcomed further civil war, and had they won would not have ruled differently. *Gomecismo* should not be treated as some uniform system for all the years between 1908 and 1934, nor was it immediately consolidated and unchallengeable in 1908. Disarming the country took Gómez many years. He never favoured large garrisons or dispersed arsenals, and petty risings and sallies across the frontier from Colombia continued even in the 1920s. In 1929 General Ramón Delgado Chalbaud, long a prisoner in the Rotunda, mounted a small invasion from Europe in the steamship *Falke*. Delgado was killed soon after landing at Cumaná and the invaders and their allies scattered, but he had at least had an outside chance. If Gómez had died in 1925, not 1935, he would get greater credit for his achievement of order and less criticism for his repression. The victims in exile and the Rotunda were not usually ordinary Venezuelans. Gómez had simple ideas of discipline, and the common touch: he had after all been an Andean farmer and cattleman until his forties, and initially the larger vision had been Castro's, not his.

It can therefore be said that he ran much of the Venezuelan economy with the mentality of a prudent hacendado. As Germán Carrera Damas has insisted, he was not a peasant, but a 'rural bourgeois'.[10] Gómez retained an appetite for land, and acquired vast estates, and through monopolies he made them profitable. Competitors, even the British Lancashire Cattle Company, found access to markets difficult. Gómez was not, however, exclusively interested in land, nor the victim of some 'telluric' obsession. He seized without hesitation the greater possibilities offered by petroleum.

The origins of the Venezuelan petroleum industry go back more than a century, with the foundation in 1878 (in Castro's and Gómez's native state) of the Compañía Petróleo del Táchira. The first concession to a North American was made in 1883, for the exploitation of the asphalt lake of Guanoco. The concession passed to the New York and Bermúdez Company, whose differences with Castro led it to support General Matos in 1903. Castro granted his supporters rights to some six million hectares, establishing the pattern whereby individual Venezuelans received concessions which they then sold to foreign companies. Sometimes foreign companies received concessions directly, as when in 1909–10 Gómez conceded 27 million hectares to the British. The early date of these concessions does not mark the beginning of significant petroleum exports. These can be taken from 1917, when Venezuela exported 21,194 tons. By 1926 Venezuela was exporting nearly four million tons, and petroleum had become the leading export. Production rose to fifteen million tons in 1928. Venezuela was then the world's second producer after the United States, accounting for 8 per cent of total world oil production, and the world's leading exporter.

Venezuela's links to the world economy were thus strengthened to a degree unmatched in Colombia and Ecuador, and in a manner that increased government revenues directly. Gómez spent on roads, and on the army. He founded the Banco Agrícola y Pecuario in 1928, though this initiative was not accompanied by any coherent policy for agricultural development: Venezuelan agriculture, particularly coffee, suffered severely from the maintenance of a high exchange rate in the 1930s.

---

[10] Germán Carrera Damas, 'Cirios para Gómez', in *Jornadas de historia crítica* (Caracas, 1983).

Though the question has been little studied, it is often maintained that the loans from the Banco Agrícola found non-agricultural uses. Oil set off migrations, to the areas of production and to the cities generally, though the numbers directly employed in the industry remained small. Locally, it was the commercial elite that secured the greatest benefits. Finally, the advent of oil and the first world war re-orientated Venezuela's foreign trade decisively towards the United States, which maintained its dominance in the post-war years.

The attempt to strike a balance of Gómez's management of the oil industry has only recently been dispassionately undertaken. Rómulo Betancourt's magnificent *Venezuela – política y petróleo* (1956) – few heads of state have written such a good book – naturally does not set out the case for the defence. Gómez and his entourage profited vastly. Gómez was no selfless patriot – his question 'Is he a friend? – es amigo?' was the Venezuelan equivalent of Franz Joseph's 'Is he a patriot for me?' – but after an unfortunate experience with investments in Germany prior to 1914 he did not invest his wealth abroad. More important, he was a serious student of Venezuela's position in the market, and he employed, particularly in Gumersindo Torres, able men to drive progressively harder bargains with the companies. He was careful to keep a balance between the Americans and Royal Dutch Shell. His record might have ended on a more nationalist note had it not been for the weaker market conditions of the depression. His critics have not always based their attacks on a sound knowledge of the changing market conditions of the time, and they also ignore the unprecedented rapidity with which the Venezuelan oil industry evolved in the 1920s. Faced with powerful and sophisticated interlocutors – the oil companies differed in both these respects from previous foreign entrepreneur-adventurers in Venezuela – Gómez was no simple *vendepatria*. A note of underlying nationalism can be seen in his decision to devote part of the oil revenues to cancelling Venezuela's foreign debt: the last instalment was paid off on 17 December 1930, one hundred years after Bolívar's death. In public finance, Gómez was strictly conservative. What other Latin American government survived the crisis of the world depression?

No other Latin American government so implacably repressed its enemies at home and so vigilantly watched them abroad. At the same time, Gómez employed a number of men of austere and industrious habit who still, despite their compromises, inspire a certain respect:

Gumersindo Torres, Román Cárdenas, Pedro Manuel Arcaya, Eleazer López Contreras, José Gil Fortoul, Laureano Vallenilla Lanz, and Vicencio Pérez Soto all had that quality of *seriedad*, seriousness, that Gómez certainly valued, and which was an essential part of his long ascendancy. Not all Gómez's local appointees were brutal or corrupt: some survived in office well into the next decade after his death. The calibre of his minister of war, General López Contreras, can be seen in the ability with which he handled that finally unpostponable change that came when Gómez died on 17 December 1935.

The population of Venezuela at the end of the Gómez regime was still predominantly rural (77 per cent), and the cities were still small. There were some 3.5 million Venezuelans, but Caracas numbered only 230,000, and neither Maracaibo, Barquisimeto nor Valencia reached 100,000. There had been no massive advances in education or in health. Yet for all his immobility, Gómez left a radically changed country, and one ripe for further change. The oil nexus altered the conditions of government, and Gómez's government had transformed politics. He had made *tabula rasa* of Venezuelan politics, in a fashion achieved by no other ruler of a major Latin American country. No party had been left alive: early in his rule he had rejected even the ritual rhetorical references to the liberal past. After his death traditions of authority persisted – they still persist in Venezuelan political parties – but political life had to be reconstructed anew. It was to find its leaders and its inspiration in the more modern opposition that had emerged, particularly in the student demonstrations of 1928.

Cultural life was not totally asphyxiated, though it is perhaps in its stunting effect there that *gomecismo* exacted the highest price. Individual supporters of the regime – José Gil Fortoul, Laureano Vallenilla – wrote books which are still worth reading. Maracay watched the cultural life of Caracas for signs of subversion, and those who made a name for themselves might receive a summons to make the journey there to be inspected by the general, and their degree of 'friendship' personally assessed, but otherwise Gómez's government was uninterested. This atmosphere permitted some notable private pedagogic achievements – the *liceo* directed by Rómulo Gallegos formed a generation of subsequent political leaders. Gómez liked Gallegos's *Doña Bárbara* (1929): he had it read to him in the open air (not because he was illiterate; he just preferred being read to), and when it grew dark he ordered the reading to continue in the car headlights. He put Gallegos to the test by nominating him as a senator; Gallegos preferred to go into exile.

CONCLUSION

Neither Colombia nor Ecuador attracted more than the fleeting attention of any great power between 1880 and 1930. Panama apart, Colombia was not a strategic country; the Galapagos islands were suspected of holding greater strategic possibilities in this era of coaling stations than mainland Ecuador itself. Venezuela was the subject of Anglo-United States confrontation in 1895 in the matter of the Guiana boundary dispute, and the object of an unusually spectacular European blockade in 1902–3, but it was only in the aftermath of the first world war, with the petroleum consciousness that it gave the great powers, that her resources became a continual preoccupation of Great Britain and the United States. All three Republics were neutral in the war. Though Colombia and Ecuador had short confrontations with Peru on their southern frontiers, and there was some filibustering, none of the three Republics fought an international war in these 50 years. Colombia and Ecuador made some bourgeois progress, at a time when such a notion was still respectable. Venezuela with oil embarked on a course that was, statistically at least, more spectacular. An examination of the evolution of the three countries in this period shows that however similar they may have appeared to be for much of the time to distant observers, politically they enter it as individuals, and emerge from it more individual still. Much of the rationale of this individuality awaits detailed exploration. Regional studies have been made in recent years and are being made that add and will add nuance and sophistication to the picture. There is a slight danger that the predicaments, the trials and tribulations, even the achievements of the national governments risk receiving less than their due attention.

Part Five

BRAZIL

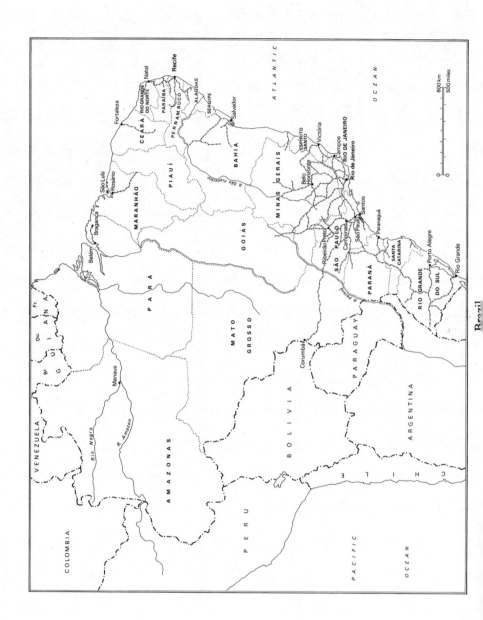

Brazil

19

THE BRAZILIAN ECONOMY, 1870–1930

The 60 years between 1870 and 1930 which comprise the last two decades of the empire and the whole of the First Republic represent the apogee of export orientation in Brazilian economic history. Resources were shifted by government and the private sector to export production, and exports rose from £1.31 to £2.83 per capita from the decade of the 1870s to that of the 1920s, a gain of about 1.6 per cent a year. Much of the social transformation and economic diversification experienced during the period, including European immigration, urbanization, improvements in communications and transportation and a modest level of industrialization, clearly derived from the expansion of exports. This expansion was also the principal attraction of foreign capital. The level of British and United States investments rose from £53 million in 1880 to £385 million by 1929. The world depression of the 1930s brought this era to a close. Exports ceased to exercise a dynamic influence on the economy and autarky and import-substitution had to be increasingly employed thereafter to try to stimulate further growth.

Exports appear to have been the principal stimulus to the onset of per capita economic growth, which seems not to have begun until shortly before 1900. There is no certainty concerning the rate of that growth, since national accounts have only been kept since 1947. An average rate of per capita growth of gross domestic product of almost 2.5 per cent a year has been calculated for the period 1900 to 1929, but downward correction may be necessary. Such a rate surpasses contemporary growth in the industrialized countries. Per capita gross national product at the end of the period 1925–9 may have amounted to US$110, in current dollars.[1]

---

[1] See C. Contador and C. Haddad, 'Produto real, moeda e preços: a experiência brasileira no periodo 1861–1970', *Revista Brasileira de Estatística* (1975); O. Dias Carneiro, 'Past trends in the economic evolution of Brazil, 1920–1965' (mimeo, Cambridge, Mass., 1966), Table 1B.

The centrality of export production during the period 1870–1930 represented in an important sense a continuity with the Brazilian past. From discovery in 1500 to independence in 1822 exports were the principal means by which the Portuguese crown and overseas merchants extracted monopoly profits from the colony; the promotion of exports had therefore been their central concern. They installed and elaborated a cane-sugar raising plantation system at points along the immense coastline, from Maranhão to São Vicente, and especially in Pernambuco and Bahia, employing Amerindian and African slave labour, locally managed by a colonial latifundist landowning class. Sugar remained Brazil's main cash crop throughout the colonial period, although from the late seventeenth century sugar exports fell in value. Towards the end of the eighteenth century, the crown stimulated the diversification of Brazilian plantation production, with some success. Exports of cotton, indigo, rice, cacao and other commodities grew significantly, and sugar revived, partly as a result of the interruptions in colonial trade in the Caribbean between 1776 and 1815. Most of Brazil's other exports were extractive. The coastal forests provided timber and other naval stores. In the interior regions of Minas Gerais, Goiás and Mato Grosso a century-long gold rush began shortly before 1700. Further inland itinerant traders advanced, collecting dyewood, cacao, pelts, feathers, parrots, essences, ipecac, sarsaparilla and the like to sell to exporters. The colony shipped tobacco and other goods to Portuguese African trading stations to pay for slaves and smuggled a variety of European products to the Río de la Plata region in return for the silver of Potosí. Portuguese mercantilist policy sought to provide cheap slave labour to the coastal plantations, limit access to the mining zones, prevent the local manufacture of goods which might profitably be sent from Lisbon, and staunch the leakage of gains into hands other than Portuguese overseas merchants and the crown.

Although population (little more than three million in 1800, including Indians outside Portuguese control, averaging about three persons per ten square kilometres) was concentrated on the coast, an unregulated settlement took place across a vast wilderness. The plantation and mining centres engendered an internal trade in slaves, mules and cattle which extended Portuguese control over a considerable inland area. Even beyond these zones a form of pioneering was practised by settlers, *mestiço* (offspring of Amerindians and Europeans) in technique as well as genes. Their slash-and-burn farming was itinerant, dependent on the wilds for game and fish, occupying the interstices and edges of the colonial economy. They provided the town markets with a few pigs, some tobacco, corn and beans and received in return little more than salt and gunpowder. This subsistence economy, surviving well into the twentieth century, cannot be regarded as the complement of a dual economy, a backward sector awaiting absorption by the modern. Its backwardness resulted from the denial of land titles to the poor and from the retention of revenues within the towns where the royal bureaucrats, overseas merchants, principal planters and mine concessionaires lived. Its continued backwardness was useful to the coastal colony, as a place to exile the non-conforming, as a buffer against attack by tribal peoples and convenient way to achieve their 'civilization', and as a cost-free means of clearing the omnipresent and axe-resistant forest. Pioneer settlement was even a crown project, along Brazil's vague and remote borders with Spanish territories, from Rio Grande do Sul to Mato Grosso.

After 1808, when the Portuguese court, fleeing Napoleon's army, transferred to Rio de Janeiro, Brazil's economic policy was no longer externally determined. Nevertheless colonial structures, and with them the centrality of the export trade (sugar, cotton and now coffee), largely remained intact. Conflicts between the landowning class and the Portuguese overseas merchants soon led to Brazil's political independence. Yet Independence, under a Portuguese prince who proclaimed himself emperor, produced few innovations. The new government was burdened with part of Portugal's London-contracted debt, many of the colonial functionaries were retained in office, the planter class confirmed its monopoly over land rights and its slave properties, and English merchants, privileged by an inequitable commercial treaty that was the price of recognition by Britain, replaced Portuguese export houses in the major ports. The new central government experienced difficulties in establishing its authority within the country. There were rebellions in the peripheral provinces, riots by urban artisans and slave uprisings which were at bottom reactions against the socially and economically disaggregative effects of neocolonialism. Political stability was not achieved until the late 1840s. By then, the debilitating post-Independence commercial treaties had expired, thereby liberating tariff policy. In 1850 a commercial code was written according to the English model, and a land law was passed. The African slave trade was abolished in the same

year under pressure from the British government, embarrassing the
imperial elite, but nevertheless forcing it to think more creatively about
increasing the supply of labour.

The Empire, which survived until 1889, did not pursue with any degree
of consistency or energy economic ends that might be termed developmental. A few national projects were proposed, fewer still – most notably
the census of 1872 and the beginning of a state-operated telegraph
network – were executed. Instead, the interests of regionally dominant
upper classes were supported with a modest level of funding or with
profit guarantees. The landowners of the province of Rio de Janeiro
tended to be the most likely to obtain backing, and they were in fact the
political mainstay of the Empire. As coffee in particular experienced
significant growth rates, export policy came to receive even greater
attention from the central government's bureaucrats. Since the customs
houses represented the nearly exclusive source of their revenues and
certain imports were critical to the government's functioning, they had
reasons of their own to support a policy of export orientation.

The 'business climate' of the Empire, however, was in general mildly
hostile to capitalist entrepreneurship. The most energetic and innovative
businessman of the 1850s and 1860s, Irineu Evangelista de Souza,
though he received the title barão de Mauá, claimed that his career ended
in failure partly because of faltering collaboration or distaste for his
activities within the government. The money supply, apart from brief
intervals, was controlled by a single government bank whose mandate
was to contain rather than to promote private enterprise. Individual
legislative authorization of joint-stock companies was retained until
1882. The emperor's Council of State insisted on the necessity of
scrutinizing incorporations, alleging irresponsible tendencies in
Brazilian businessmen. Government encouragement to business, when
it was offered, normally took the form of exclusive concessions. The
great landowners and merchants, themselves sensitive to the profit
motive, preferred that the economy be steered within channels that
preserved their control of resources and of the government. Their
economy needed to grow only slowly and diversify hardly at all, since the
gains were to accrue to a single, very small class. As one historian has

remarked, 'Class interests were so disparate as to raise serious questions concerning the validity of using the nation as the unit of analysis.'[2]

The Republic, however, set loose the 'spirit of association' and transformed the nature of the economic debate. The provisional government made economic questions its central concern and aggressively promoted economic growth. Would-be capitalists and industrialists, along with certain politically active urban professionals and army officers, angered at the incompetence displayed in the Paraguayan War and by scanty postwar military budgets, promoted an interventionist economic programme. In the last months of the Empire the final abolition of slavery had been decreed and government bonds had been floated to aid planters suffering the uncompensated loss of their slaves. These funds were turned directly over to city creditors, fuelling a sudden boom. The provisional government then authorized the launching of banks of emission, joint stock companies and development schemes in a great speculative wave, dubbed the *encilhamento*, racetrack parlance for the saddling-up. Although numerous initiatives of this ebullient transitional period proved long-lasting, the nationalist coalition lost control by 1894, exhausted by its own excesses, obliged to put down a rebellion of the navy and another in Rio Grande do Sul, and overcome by inflation and the accumulation of foreign debt.

The governments that followed, apparently much less interventionist than those of the nationalists, can be seen to have put constraints on internal development. The first civilian government, for example, cancelled contracts that had been signed with Rio de Janeiro shipyards for the construction of destroyer-class warships. The planter-sponsored government, considering it more prudent to buy its naval vessels from English firms, so as to ensure the retention of British markets and an uninterrupted flow of British capital, let the half-built hulls rust into their ways. Circumstances and contradictions inherent in such policies, however, induced a sizeable number of developmental measures and impelled direct government intervention.[3] The planter's programmes were quite expensive and large in scale. Often it fell to the government to implement them when foreign concessionaires or native entrepreneurs wavered or proved too demanding of official subsidies.

It has often been noted that the planting and exporting interests

---

[2] N. Leff, *Underdevelopment and development in Brazil* (2 vols., London, 1982), I, 7.
[3] See S. Topik, 'The evolution of the economic role of the Brazilian state, 1889–1930', *Journal of Latin American Studies*, 11/2 (1979), 325–42.

desired monetary and fiscal policies that would induce a gradual inflation, thereby shifting real income to them. The overriding concern of civilian governments from 1894 was for their credit-worthiness in the eyes of foreign bankers. This outlook was essential because the same interests which installed these governments were unwilling to accompany their mandate with revenues adequate to cover expenditures. Even more than the Empire, the Republic produced deficits: 32 during its 41 years of existence, and in 13 of them the deficit exceeded 25 per cent of income. These deficits could not be resolved through internal loans. Local bond markets were unorganized, leading the government to the disreputable practice of paying some of its obligations with bonds that were hastily discounted by the recipients. Internal loans, furthermore, could not be applied to foreign debts already contracted and owed in gold. On the other hand, foreign loans were accompanied by conditions that reached into the directing organs of government and commandeered them. The London Rothschilds rescued the finances of the new civilian regime when it granted, in 1898, a funding loan of £10 million, permitting a delay of thirteen years in repayment of principal. But they demanded in return a surcharge on import duties, to be deposited in a reserve account in London, and a gradual retirement from circulation of paper milreis to an amount equivalent to the value of the loan. This deflationary programme remained the centrepiece of government policy, despite severe depressive impact upon production and employment, until 1905.

In spite of foreign loans, federal deficits continued to accumulate. According to the republican constitution, states and municipalities could also contract loans. And so they did: from 1900 to 1912 their foreign debts grew from £5 million to £50 million; the latter was a sum 37 per cent as large as the federal debt. The central government, pressed by its own creditors, disavowed any responsibility for the debts of the local governments. For the planting and exporting interests the deflationary exercise begun in 1898 was extremely painful, since it reduced their earnings in terms of milreis. They therefore achieved a compromise in 1905: the milreis was set at a new, somewhat higher par of 15 pence, but the government would act to prevent it from rising further by opening a Conversion Fund. The Fund would receive gold currencies that were deposited with it at that rate and it would simultaneously enlarge the money supply by issuing paper circulating notes in exchange.

The periodic funding of the Brazilian foreign debt could not be regularly achieved because of the cyclical nature of the export trade, exacerbated by the policies the bankers themselves instigated. Cyclical upswings in the industrial countries increased the demand for Brazil's commodity exports, thereby pushing up their prices. Rising commodity prices attracted an inflow of foreign capital, intensifying the recovery in Brazil and stimulating a disproportionate increase in imports as well as in domestic production. The downswing was equally steep, but more painful, as gold-backed currencies flowed out of the country and the customs houses were piled high with unpaid-for imports, and the foreign debt mounted higher than before. The foreign bankers would be dunned for another loan, but now their coffers were empty or their conditions were too offensive to national sovereignty to be accepted. The only recourse left to the Brazilian government at such a juncture, as in August 1914, was to suspend the rules of the game. It abolished gold conversion and emitted 250 million milreis in paper currency. Monetary orthodoxy, though embraced rhetorically, was only a relative good compared to the government's survival; inflation, though seemingly endemic, was usually undertaken only as a last resort.[4]

The implantation of a national developmentalist economic policy required the creation of a national market, but this was difficult to achieve. Brazil, geographically a subcontinent, was in demographic and economic terms an archipelago. With the important exception of Minas Gerais, the bulk of its population, a little less than ten million in 1870 and seventeen million in 1900, still lived along the extensive coast, clustered around port cities which were in most cases state capitals. Coastwise shipping lines maintained vessels that were over-age and poorly maintained, schedules that were rarely met, and rates that were double or treble those of overseas shippers. The smaller port cities without deepwater channels and dependent on coastal steamers sought funding to deepen their harbours so as to receive ocean-going vessels. These efforts the elites of the larger cities, such as Salvador and Recife, desirous of retaining their role as entrepôts, struggled to quash.

For shorter or longer distances into the hinterlands of the coastal cities stretched networks of rails, roads or trails. These networks were only casually tangential one to the next, and in some cases they were separated by hundreds of kilometres of utter wilderness. The coastal state of Espírito Santo, for example, was linked to adjoining Minas Gerais only

---

[4] See W. Fritsch, 'Aspectos da política econômica no Brasil, 1906–1914', in P. Neuhaus (ed.), *Economia brasileira: uma visão histórica* (Rio de Janeiro, 1980).

by an extremely difficult passage of the Rio Doce. Not until 1905 did construction begin on a railway paralleling the river, and not until the 1930s did it reach Belo Horizonte. Goiás and Minas Gerais were land-locked and isolated states, while Mato Grosso and Acre were accessible only by immense river detours. The cost of transport, it may be imagined, no matter how high external tariffs were set, represented a barrier to inter-regional trade of still more imposing dimension.

To these obstacles were added inter-state and even inter-municipal tariffs. The practice of taxing goods brought from other states and towns began during the Empire. Under the republican constitution, a federalist charter, import tariffs were exclusively levied by the central government, but export duties were granted exclusively to the states. The states which enjoyed large export revenues, principally São Paulo, evidently inspired this clause, which obliged the less fortunate states with no exports to tax to resort to these imposts. Often they were charged indiscriminately on imported goods as well as on goods originating in other states, so that they constituted a kind of tariff surcharge. The federal courts condemned these duties, which had no basis in the constitution, and yet they continued unabated. That this was possible is a clue to the manner in which the interests of the regional upper classes meshed with those who controlled the dominant, exporting states. Though the central government repeatedly intervened militarily in the smaller states to depose one faction or another of these lesser oligarchies, it never attempted to cut off this source of revenue in the interest of creating a national market.

Although nationalist republicans claimed that they desired the creation of such a market, this goal was probably beyond their intentions in another, more profound sense. Access to the factors of production depended in Brazil only to a slight degree upon the workings of a market. Political and social factors largely determined access to credit, entitlement of land, and conditions of employment. This reality came to be attenuated by European immigration and urbanization over the course of the period under study, but it was always the case of the property-owning classes that their rewards derive from their social ranking, that their ability to command resources exceed that to which their position in the market might have entitled them and that they be held immune from competition with persons of lower social status. In these circumstances, youthful ambitions were concentrated upon political goals, a surer path to upward social mobility than entrepreneurship; and risky entrepreneurship, even when successful, was obliged to make its peace with power.

The shift of internal resources to the growth of the export sector may be seen, from the point of view of domestic conditions, as the result of the preferences of the dominant social classes, who considered such a policy optimally profitable, convenient and adaptable to their desire for local autonomy and continued monopoly in the exercise of political power. These policies were nevertheless not without contradictions, arising from circumstances and factors inherent in the policies themselves. The linkages of these dominant classes with their external sources of funding were especially problematic and vulnerable to reactions from within the Brazilian polity. Even so, for most of the period under study the middle classes could be persuaded of their own stake in Brazil's growing incorporation into the world system of trade and finance through the stimulation of exports.

THE GROWTH OF EXPORT DEMAND

By 1870 world trade was entering a new phase, one in which commercial opportunities were to enlarge greatly. During the 1870s cargo-carrying steamships entered into regular service in the South Atlantic, halving the cost of transport, regularizing deliveries and much increasing the range and volume of goods that might be delivered. Industrialization in England had considerably expanded the variety and utility of those goods. In effect Brazil's export-orientation was also entering a new phase. The country was beginning to participate in the industrial revolution by exchanging its agricultural and extractive products for manufactured goods that embodied the new technologies. Undersea cables in the same decade connected Brazil's port cities with Europe, and indirectly with the United States, thereby reducing price and supply uncertainties and much facilitating the transfer of commercial credit. The spread of the industrial system to Germany, the United States and a few other countries intensified competition among manufacturers, thus enhancing the position of suppliers of raw materials and foodstuffs such as Brazil, which experienced improving terms of trade from the 1870s to the outbreak of the first world war.

The growth of exports was critical to Brazilian economic growth, yet for the period as a whole it was rather slow. Most of the increase in the value of Brazil's exports was sandwiched between financial panics and wars and depressions in Europe and the United States. It was also problematic. The number of staple products in world trade was small and geographic factors excluded Brazil from supplying any but a few of them. Prices fluctuated sharply and the threat of widening competition, of exclusion from markets, and the discovery of synthetics clouded prospects for entrepreneurs and policy makers alike. For Brazil, it might be said, the severest disadvantage of the policy of export orientation was the weakness of the stimulus of overseas demand. The difficulty may be observed in a review of the principal articles of trade during this period.

Coffee was by far Brazil's single most successful product in international trade. The plant had been introduced in the eighteenth century, but it achieved a significant place in the export list only in the decade of independence. The coffee bush was highly suitable to the climate and soils of south-eastern Brazil and coffee beans were easy to transport and store. No complex industrial processes were required to prepare them for market. In the 1870s various kinds of mechanical hullers were introduced and commercial roasting techniques were perfected. Late in the 1880s Brazil's Asiatic competitors were ravaged by a blight. With this promising conjuncture, Brazilian planters rapidly expanded their groves. Brazilian coffee was chiefly of low grade. In contrast to Colombia, Jamaica and other growing areas, where it was cultivated by smallholders, Brazil's coffee was unshaded and minimal care was devoted to its tending and harvesting. The resulting cheaper product, however, enjoyed the greater growth in demand from mid-century onwards because of the appearance of a mass market, principally in the United States. There consumption reached 5.5 kilograms per capita by 1921, as caffeine addiction spread among an urbanizing population.

Coffee exports had reached 60,000 tons per annum in the 1830s; by 1871 216,000 tons were shipped. In 1872 the great fertile plateau of São Paulo was opened by the arrival of the railway to Campinas. This state soon ranked first in sales. Stimulated by the inflow of foreign investments in the decade after 1885 and by the cheap money of the Republican provisional government, new planting in São Paulo doubled the Brazilian coffee groves. By 1901 exports reached 888,000 tons. The price of coffee went through three cycles between Independence and 1907, each time ending near US$0.15 per kilogram. The recurring tendency toward low prices discouraged potential competitors. Even though Brazil's market dominance was allowed to erode between 1870 and 1930, in the late 1920s it still possessed 2.1 billion of the world's 3.2 billion coffee bushes. For the period as a whole it supplied more than half the coffee sold in international trade. Unfortunately none of Brazil's other exports enjoyed similar sustained success in world trade, and as a result by 1925–9 coffee provided 75 per cent of foreign earnings. Thus the Brazilian economy was characterized by a very high dependence on the price of a single export product.

Natural rubber, by the late 1880s the second most important article of Brazil's international trade, went from boom to sudden collapse. The industrial applications of rubber multiplied rapidly in the last quarter of the nineteenth century, inducing an extraordinary surge in world demand. Its price, £45 a ton in 1840, rose to £182 in 1870, and to £512 by 1911. Rubber gatherers spread the length and breadth of the Amazon valley, which was the native habitat of several commercially valuable species of latex-bearing trees. Of these the most productive was *Hevea brasiliensis*. In 1870 6,591 tons of natural rubbers were exported; by 1911 shipments amounted to 38,547 tons. During the first decade of the twentieth century rubber provided more than a quarter of Brazil's foreign earnings. Immediately afterward a catastrophic decline in price set in. By the end of the first world war, Brazil had lost nearly all of its export market. *Hevea brasiliensis* had been introduced and acclimatized in Malaya and the Dutch East Indies and there plantations were formed which produced rubber at much lower cost. The Brazilian government projected, but did not execute, an expensive plan to develop the infrastructure of the Amazon region; in the short run it proved impossible to effect a shift to cultivation there. The rubber gathering network gradually came unravelled, and by 1930 exports had slumped to 6,000 tons.

Sugar, the most traditional of plantation crops, and the dynamo of Brazil's colonization, underwent a revival in the world market in the late nineteenth century. New, more efficient processing techniques turned sugar into an article of mass consumption, the cheapest of all carbohydrates, the ever-available caloric supplement to the workers' diet. Brazil participated in this revival through the early 1880s, but then suffered a decline in exports that became precipitous after 1900. Competition from beet sugar, protected in the industrial countries, and from cane sugar in newer producing areas overcame Brazilian planters. Cuba, Puerto Rico and the Philippines acquired preferential access to the United States sugar market after they were absorbed by the United States following the victory over Spain in 1898. Cuba, reduced to a protectorate, witnessed an infusion of US$1,000 million into its sugar sector during the succeeding decade. By then Brazilian cane-sugar exports were stagnant. The value of sugar exports from Pernambuco, the country's most important sugar-growing state, was in 1898 only half what it had been fifteen years before. Brazil's share of the world market, 10 per cent in the 1850s, fell continuously; by the first decade of the twentieth century it was less than 0.5 per cent.

Cotton had also been traditionally an important article of Brazil's overseas trade. At the beginning of the nineteenth century native arboreal long-fibred species supplied 10 per cent of the world market. Although demand for raw cotton increased enormously during the nineteenth century, the spinning mills of England came to be supplied by the United States. During the American Civil war resulting from the attempted secession of the southern states (1861–5) and for a few years afterward, Brazilian cotton was again briefly competitive. In 1870 Brazil exported 42,000 tons. But with the revival of the cotton trade in the United States and increased cultivation in Egypt Brazil lost its British market; by 1880 exports had fallen to half the volume of ten years before.

Brazil had sold cacao since colonial times, most of it gathered from wild stands in the Amazon valley. It was planted on a large scale for the first time in southern Bahia in the 1880s. World demand surged soon afterwards from a little over 100,000 tons to almost 550,000 tons by 1928, stimulated by new forms of consumption. Brazil's participation in this market was, however, modest, supplying little more than a tenth of the world market by the late 1920s. Most of the world's cacao came from Britain's West African colonies. At the beginning of the first world war a few meat packing plants were installed in Rio Grande do Sul and São Paulo. Their early success in overseas sales, however, did not much outlast the period of wartime shortages. Brazil also sold each year a few thousand tons of hides, yerba maté, oil seeds, timber, manganese, pelts and tobacco. None of these added much to export earnings although they were significant stimuli within regional markets of the north-east and south. Brazil, in addition, was a producer of immense quantities of certain other staples such as maize, beans, bananas and manioc meal, but only in unusual circumstances did it manage to sell any of them abroad.

It is remarkable that Brazil, a country of immense territory and varied resources, participated in world trade essentially as a planter of a single crop: coffee. External factors do not entirely explain the narrow range of opportunities exploited nor the erosion of market shares that had been achieved in earlier periods. To a degree the difficulties were beyond remedy. Certain natural disadvantages were present that became more severe or more obvious as world demand developed. For example, the decisive advantage of the Cuban sugar growers was their flatter terrain, more suitable to the needs of the high-capacity grinding mills since it permitted the more rapid delivery of cane to the mill gates and speed of delivery was essential as cane juices quickly evaporate. Rubber cultivation was attempted on a large scale in the Amazon valley only in the 1920s, but then it was discovered that a blight exclusive to the genus *Hevea* destroyed rubber trees when they were planted in close stands. This fungus had not accompanied the rubber seeds that had been transferred to south-east Asia. In other cases the difficulties appear to have been remediable, but the remedies were incompletely applied. The loss of overseas cotton markets occurred even though short-staple cotton had been introduced to Brazilian plantations in the 1860s.

Brazil's overseas trade appears to have been limited to commodities in which overwhelming comparative advantages offset high costs of production and commercialization and high internal taxes. The capital resources necessary to improve methods of production and to organize more efficient marketing arrangements were indeed scarce, but not unavailable. In the absence of private initiatives, the central and state governments seemed willing to provide guarantees and even funding. But these schemes, when they were undertaken, often appear to have been tardy, ill-conceived or incompletely executed. Even in the coffee sector, which generated funds for improvement of productivity on a large scale, a lack of attention to competitiveness was displayed. Instead, the problem of declining market shares was viewed merely as a problem of declining prices. Emphasis therefore was placed almost exclusively upon price maintenance.

The Brazilian government undertook, on an immense scale, to stabilize the price of its principal commodity in world trade. Having greatly enlarged their plantings after 1885, in the late 1890s the Brazilian coffee growers confronted depressed world prices and the effects of the internal deflationary policy that was the condition of the funding loan of 1898. Brazilian delegates at the international coffee conference held in 1902 therefore pressed for a cartel, but they were rebuffed. The state of São Paulo declared a halt to new planting in that same year, later extended through 1912. By 1906 São Paulo had convinced the other principal coffee-producing states of Minas Gerais and Rio de Janeiro to participate in a scheme called 'valorization'. These states were to purchase coffee at a base price of US$0.15 per kilogram and store it against the time when prices might compensate the cost of the operation. Funding was secured from banks in Europe and the United States through the intercession of coffee importers. Thus 660,000 tons were removed from sale within six months. A surcharge was added to new coffee sales, to help defray the warehousing costs, and the federal government was finally persuaded to guarantee the loans. Coffee prices did begin to rise again, and by 1912 they had reached an average US$0.31 per kilogram. By the end of that year all the coffee stored in the United States had been hurriedly sold off in the face of mounting irritation there.

The valorization appears to have lessened the impact in Brazil of the world recession of 1907–8, it may have benefited the planters, and it was certainly profitable for the bankers and intermediaries who made sizeable commissions and increased their presence in the business within Brazil in consequence. The price of coffee might have risen in any case since world demand was still growing. The federal government was, however, won over to the procedure and sponsored a second valorization during the crisis of the first world war. This time 180,000 tons were bought and warehoused, prices climbed sharply, partly because of a severe frost in São Paulo, and the government made a profit. With the postwar slump in commodity prices a third valorization was initiated. By then, however, a levelling-off of world demand had set in and the resumption of new planting in São Paulo overwhelmed the venture. The federal government ended its participation, but São Paulo was hounded by its planters to take on the purchase of coffee single-handed. It declared a 'permanent defence' in 1925, and went on, until the crash of 1929, desperately buying up and storing a series of record harvests. The effect of this policy, which diverted resources from the other sectors of the economy and ignored the issue of productivity, was to encourage foreign competition to expand.

The erosion of market shares and the failure to develop potential markets may, in the case of other export products, also be attributed in part to public policy. The expansionary phase of each export was usually accompanied by parallel efforts on the part of established producers to hamper, through the agency of government, the creation of further producing units. This is easily observable in the coffee business, since coffee spread over state lines and involved inter-state rivalries. Indeed, the enthusiasm of São Paulo planters for republicanism after 1870 may be attributed in large measure to their annoyance at preferences shown by the Empire to the growers of Rio de Janeiro. This rivalry was also displayed by the north-eastern planters of sugar and cotton, who resisted the transfer of these crops to São Paulo, and it is manifest among the merchants who supervised the rubber gathering trade and abhorred the prospect of a domestic rubber plantation regime. Among the victories scored by established planters may be mentioned the extreme retardation of road, rail and port facilities in the interior of the cacao region of southern Bahia.

Heavy rates of taxation of exports reduced Brazil's competitiveness in world markets. Furthermore, to a considerable degree government expenditures were non-developmental. The federal and state governments devoted large sums to the beautification of their respective capitals and to other sumptuous ends, but even apparently developmental projects were often disguises for other purposes. Land colonization schemes whose first step was the purchase of an existing plantation, for example, were really rescue missions for failing planters, and when these estates subdivided the beneficiaries were more likely to be deserving party members who desired to speculate in land than sturdy husbandmen. The government spent much of its revenues, in fact, for the simple purpose of remaining in power. The erosion of competitiveness in world markets was a direct and cumulative outcome. This was politically not an entire disaster. Products which disappeared from the export list, such as sugar and cotton, received protection in the domestic market. Given the size and growth of that market, that was a moderately, even pleasingly, consolatory recompense. For example, Brazil itself consumed, by 1921–3, 77 per cent of its cotton harvests of 115,000 tons.

Brazil was less dependent on a single customer or supplier than most of the other non-industrialized countries of the day. Its coffee and rubber went chiefly to the United States, which levied no duties upon them; indeed, those two products, along with raw silk, were that country's most important tariff-exempt imports. It sought, in return, greater acceptance for its wheat and flour, kerosene, lumber and manufactured goods. Britain, however, was until after the first world war the principal supplier of manufactured goods – and of credit. Germany ranked second. Existing or potential trade complementarities with Africa or the rest of South America were little explored. Brazil's only sizeable exchange with Latin America was its purchase of Argentine wheat, a business in the hands of British intermediaries, in return for yerba maté, for which demand was stagnant. The possibility of tariff union with prosperous Argentina, Uruguay and Chile seems not to have been examined.

The world system of trade and investment upon which Brazil's export orientation was based suffered terrible reverses in the first world war. The war rescued Brazil's rubber, temporarily, from oblivion and provided improved opportunities for the sale of some of its less important exports – sugar, beef, beans, and manganese – to the desperate antagonists, but coffee was not high on the Allies' list of shipping priorities, nor were they much concerned whether the Brazilian economy might collapse for lack of spare parts and fuels. The value in pounds sterling of Brazil's exports fell during the five war years by 16 per cent, in comparison to the booming five previous years, while imports fell by 24 per cent. The cost of shipping climbed sharply, and so did the prices of imports. For example, imported textiles, which cost an average US$0.98 a kilogram in 1913, rose to US$3.46 a kilogram in 1918. Since more than half of Brazil's imports were foodstuffs and raw materials, the impact on the internal economy was severe. Internally prices doubled, buoyed by the emissions of paper currency necessitated by the repatriation of foreign currencies and gold. The federal government was saved at the last moment from default on its foreign loans in October 1914 by a £15 million funding loan raised in London. Rationing was not attempted; ceiling prices were imposed, but only in Rio de Janeiro and even there not effectually. Wages apparently did not keep pace with prices, causing terrible hardship among the urban population and provoking demonstrations and widespread strikes in Rio de Janeiro and São Paulo in 1917.

As a consequence of the Brazilian entrance into the war on the side of the Allies in October 1917, German banks and insurance companies were closed and firms with links to German capital were harassed or put out of business through the application of the British 'Black List'. The Brazilian government acquired, as spoils of war, 40-odd German vessels stranded in the country's ports, thereby doubling its merchant tonnage, but it lost a substantial amount of the value of bank accounts that had been opened in Belgium, with the proceeds of its sales of valorization stocks. More consequential than any of this were the long-term effects of the war, which weakened the economies of all of Brazil's trading partners (except the United States), reducing their capacity to advance credit and import from countries such as Brazil. The faltering British financial centre, critical to Brazilian export orientation, proved especially problematic in the 1920s.

FACTORS OF PRODUCTION

Land

Land, in the sense of dry terrestrial surface, was evidently abundant in Brazil, to the point approaching that of a free good. What rescued it from that category was the ephemeral quality of its soil fertility, at least as farming was practised in Brazil, and the extreme concentration of its land titles. The practice of agriculture in Brazil was limited to forest soils. The more accessible of these were located along the coast to a distance inland of 100 to 400 kilometres. Behind them stretched drier, poorer soils considered fit only for raising cattle. Lands newly cleared of primary forest were prized for spectacular yields. Coffee, it was believed, could only be successful on soils just cleared of virgin forest. Thus coffee planting encouraged a rapid expansion of the frontier in south-eastern Brazil. Coffee bushes were capable of bearing profitably for 40 years, but imprudence in locating the groves often reduced that span. Since most of the coastal strip of forested land derived its rainfall from its ruggedly mountainous topography, its humus quickly eroded.

Speculation in coffee lands introduced a feverish new form of enterprise. Formerly land increased in value as it was cleared and granted legal title; thereafter, as fertility gradually disappeared, so did value. The setting out of coffee seedlings became a business in itself which inflated land prices wondrously. Much of the coffee planting, it might be asserted, was carried out with no thought of growing coffee, but of speculating in mature new groves. The coffee frontier swept forward like a brush fire, obliterating thousands of square kilometres of timber and other forest resources. In the 1920 census, São Paulo's farms, comprising 8 per cent of the area of all Brazil's rural properties, accounted for more than 27 per cent of their value, the equivalent of US$2,600 million in current dollars. None of the gains of speculation reverted to the state. São Paulo, like almost all the other states, did not impose rural land taxes.

Concentration of landownership in Brazil was traditionally extreme. The Portuguese crown had believed that only landed aristocrats would produce for overseas markets, and therefore its grants were enormous, typically 40 square kilometres in extent. Under the Empire this tradition was maintained because the central government was too weak to make effective its law (1850) determining the sale of crown lands at auction. Instead locally powerful elites simply usurped public lands, employing fraud in land offices and evicting in the process smallholding squatters. Only in the southern states of Rio Grande do Sul and Santa Catarina did the Empire effectively promote smallholding. There, following the policy of the Portuguese crown in the peopling of border areas, it settled German and Italian immigrants in official colonies. Their descendants spread within those provinces and formed more colonies, but their influence on the national economy was limited. Nevertheless they presented an economic structure contrasting sharply with the great plantations and ranches.

The Republic granted, in effect, amnesty to the land grabbers, when it bestowed the remaining crown lands upon the states. The state governments then demonstrated the same incapacity to guard the public patrimony as had the Empire. A succession of state laws issued titles to all those whose social prominence had assured the local acquiescence to their private expropriations. During all this time no government had recognized land rights of tribal peoples or had set aside any but the most inconsequential reserves for their use. Although in 1910 the protection of tribal peoples came to be a federal responsibility under a service headed by General Cândido Rondon, the murder of entire tribes, as a preliminary to the private appropriation of state lands, continued to be practised. Landholding, as a consequence of these policies, or lack of them, remained highly concentrated. By 1920 no more than 3 per cent of rural dwellers possessed titles to the rural landholdings included in the census; of this tiny group of landowners, 10 per cent controlled three-quarters of those lands.

Labour

Brazil's population rose from 10.1 million to 30.6 million between 1872 and 1920. Its rate of growth accelerated from 1.85 to 2.15 per cent a year between these dates, and life expectancy rose from 27.4 years in 1872 (when slave life expectancy was about 21.0 years), to about 34.6 years in 1930. The urban population formed a small minority which tended to grow not much faster than the population as a whole. In 1872 persons living in towns of 20,000 or more inhabitants comprised a little less than 8 per cent of the total; by 1920 it was only 13 per cent. Much of this increase may be attributed to the influence of the export trade, since it was precisely those cities most engaged in it which grew the fastest. In 1920 more than half of the urban population resided in Rio de Janeiro and in São Paulo, which since 1870 had risen from tenth to second rank among

Brazilian cities. The labour force grew, between 1872 and 1920, at a rate of about 2 per cent a year. The economically active portion of the population is in fact difficult to calculate because the census of 1920 introduced more stringent definitions of employment, especially of females. Thus between 1872 and 1920 the percentage of females aged ten and over reported as economically active fell from 51 to 14 per cent. Since the ratio of economically active males also fell, from 77 to 75 per cent, it is possible that these lower figures were to some extent a sign of the reduced capacity of the economy to absorb the growing labour force.

Nevertheless, landowners and employers complained unceasingly of a shortage of labour. From 1870 onward the supply of slave labourers, who in 1872 constituted about 20 per cent of persons economically active and 70 per cent of plantation labour, was certainly precarious. From the late sixteenth century until the middle of the nineteenth century more Africans had been transported to Brazil than to any other area of the New World. With the effective suppression of the slave trade after 1850, however, the slave population began to decline. The cause of decline appears principally to have been high mortality, that is, an expropriation rate surpassing subsistence as well as reproduction costs, or simply incompetent and brutal labour management. Manumission and flight also occurred regularly, possibly as escape valves, rather cheaper to tolerate than further application of repressive force. Partly in response to increasing slave resistance, in 1871 a law was passed freeing children born thereafter to slave mothers. Chattel slavery was finished; lifetime slavery was to be gradually extinguished.

Since the free population could not be kept from squatting on unclaimed public lands, where their farming was as productive as that of the large estates, they could not be lured to work for wages that would have yielded a profit to the estate owners. Therefore in regions where unclaimed or unoccupied lands existed, the free population formed mainly a casual labour force, willing only to pay token rents in return for token labour. In zones well removed from the frontier, however, where all the land was already in private title and smallholders were hemmed in by the large estates, sharecropping and various forms of tenancy significantly increased the work force available to the plantations, even before the demise of slavery.

The decline in slave numbers was at first mitigated by an internal traffic which directed them from the stagnant north-east to the coffee-growing states of Rio de Janeiro and São Paulo, and from urban areas to the plantations. By the late 1870s this trade was inadequate, and many of the southern planters, whose earlier experiments in immigrant labour indentures had been failures, became quite despondent, predicting ruin for themselves and the bankruptcy of the central government. It has not been suggested that Brazilian slavery was at any time up to the last year or two before its abolition unprofitable. Indeed several studies have demonstrated the contrary. As long as slavery persisted it was at least as profitable as alternative investments. Nevertheless the General Legislative Assembly voted final abolition of slavery in 1888, in response to political pressure from planters in new zones of production who had no hope of securing a slave work force, the urban middle class, including army officers and civil servants impatient to bring about a more modern society, and ex-slaves and the slaves themselves, who were organizing violent opposition and large-scale abandonment of plantations.

The final transition from slave to free labour proved surprisingly easy, from the point of view of the large landowners. Although many freedmen fled to the cities, most accepted wage and sharecropping contracts on nearby or even the same estates. Pressure upon smallholdings because of population growth (Brazilian law divided inheritances equally among offspring), recurrent droughts in the interior of the north-east, and the continued political impotence of the lower class forced many free men to work on the plantations. In the north-east the effective costs of free labour to the planters were apparently lower than the former costs of maintaining slaves.[5] There was a great deal of migration to new zones of large-scale exploitation for export, such as southern Bahia (cacao) and the western Amazon (rubber). In the Amazon high wages exerted an effective attraction, but control of prices of subsistence goods by the rubber gatherers' outfitters and store keepers offset the expected advantages, and high mortality from disease turned the region into a population sink from which few escaped.

To the coffee region migrated an immense wave of Italian, Spanish and Portuguese workers. Net immigration to Brazil between 1872 and 1930 amounted to some 2.2 million. By 1920 immigrants represented 10 per cent of the male labour force. Much of this migration was subsidized by state and federal governments, thus socializing the planters' costs of labour reproduction. The immigrants were offered yearly contracts which combined money wages for tending and harvesting with the right to plant subsistence crops. Ex-slaves in the

---

[5] See D. Denslow, 'As origens da desigualdade regional no Brasil', *Estudos Económicos* (1973); P. Eisenberg. *The sugar industry in Pernambuco, 1840–1910* (Berkeley, 1974).

coffee regions who continued to work on the plantations were obliged to accept more precarious employments, at wage levels about half those of the Europeans, thereby making a contribution of their own to immigration subsidies. The flux of immigrants was kept as high as possible up to the first world war, and even through the 1920s the state of São Paulo continued to pay part of the costs of passage. This was necessary because the immigrants tended to withdraw to other employments after a few harvests or to re-migrate to their homelands. There was also a clear intent to keep wages low. It has been estimated by one historian that wages in the coffee industry did not rise between 1870 and 1914.[6]

Even though the abolition of slavery placed labour more or less within a market, improved its mobility and monetized to some extent its rewards, the period under study must be considered as transitional from that of a regime based on physical coercion. The social conditions of much of rural Brazil approximated that of servility. Even in the areas of European immigration, the great landowners demanded deference and employed the services of private gunmen to intimidate their workers. Wage earners, according to laws in force as late as 1890, were subject to imprisonment for non-fulfilment of contract. In 1902 Italy, acting upon the reports of its consuls, forbade further subsidization of emigration of its citizens to Brazil. In response the state of São Paulo created arbitration boards to hear complaints. Only in 1916 was equality of contract established in federal law. No other labour rights were effectively enforced before the 1930s.

Public education scarcely contributed to raising the general skill levels. The census of 1872 showed almost 90 per cent of females and 80 per cent of males were illiterate. By 1920 these rates had declined by only ten points each. The governing elite tended to regard the native-born lower classes as largely ineducable; indeed this was a major reason that it collaborated with the planters in schemes for European immigration. Immigrants were generally more literate than the native-born population; in São Paulo only 56 per cent were illiterate compared to 73 per cent of the general population, according to the census of 1920. Had the government spent on primary education the funds it allocated to subsidize immigration, it might have obtained similar economic results and discharged its responsibilities more humanely. Very little schooling

---

[6] Michael Hall, 'The origins of mass immigration in Brazil, 1871–1914' (unpublished PhD dissertation, Columbia University, 1969).

in productive skills was provided for the working class, or even the middle class. By 1920 total enrolment in secondary and technical schools, public and private, was only 62,500. Although early stages of machine production included successful innovations by Brazilians, notably in coffee and yerba maté processing equipment, the organizational and technical skills needed to install manufacturing and commercial enterprises were largely immigrant-supplied.

Capital

There are no estimates of gross capital formation before the 1920s. It has been calculated that it averaged 13.7 per cent of gross national product for that decade, or US$14 a year per capita, in current dollars. According to the same estimate, net capital flow from abroad during the 1920s averaged 8.8 per cent of gross capital formation and net capital stock reached US$260 per capita, in current dollars, by 1929.[7]

The mobilization of domestic capital was not highly institutionalized, at least in the first half of this period. Until well after 1900 most agricultural credit was informal and private: advances from brokers or importers, or loans from private money lenders, many of whom limited their dealings to kinsmen and neighbours. Interest rates began at 12 per cent and often rose to 24 per cent. Agricultural loans, almost up to the time of abolition, required slaves, not land, as collateral. Except for planters of export crops, credit of any kind was rarely available, and it was uncommon even for coffee planters to obtain mortgages.

In 1870 there were only six banks in Rio de Janeiro, two of them English, and there were only nine more in the rest of the country. These banks dealt almost exclusively in deposits and the discounting of short-term commercial paper. The foreign banks confined themselves largely to foreign exchange transactions and expended their best efforts on exchange speculation. The government-controlled Bank of Brazil began in the 1860s to make a few agricultural loans. A few land credit banks were founded after 1875, but they lacked a suitable mortgage law and were not successful. Only after 1900 did government-owned mortgage banks in the state of São Paulo and Minas Gerais provide a limited amount of funding. In 1909 a system of warrants finally became available in São Paulo, an innovation related to the valorization scheme, which

---

[7] Dias Carneiro, 'Past trends', Table 8A.

reduced interest charges to 9 per cent. The value of mortgages registered in land offices throughout Brazil grew tenfold between 1909 and 1929, when they reached the equivalent of US$181 million in current dollars. Much of this may have represented the financing of urban real estate transactions. By 1929 the great majority of these mortgages were at interest rates under 10 per cent, suggesting that the market had become more efficient. Yet the total sum was still quite modest, compared to the value of farm lands revealed in the 1920 census, showing that mortgages were still uncommon.

A low average productivity of investments derived from national savings has been calculated for the 1920s.[8] It seems unlikely that the productivity of capital in earlier decades had been any higher. Domestic enterprises experienced difficulty in growing to a scale that would enable them to apply new techniques and to encompass a national market. Share ownership beyond the limits of the family was almost unknown, except in the organization of banks and railways. Capital was derived from reinvestment of profits, sometimes involving monopolistic pricing, or was pieced together from commercial loans. There was no significant market for industrial bonds or shares. Briefly, during the boom of 1888 to 1893, a few of the banks that were granted the right of emission played the role of financiers to a few large industrial ventures, but these mostly failed. No other banks, not even the Bank of Brazil, undertook such a role thereafter. Thus those forces which had in other countries fused family firms into publicly held corporations were largely absent in Brazil. Occasionally there were formed consortia of two or more families, more or less stable, usually within ethnic groups, and sometimes eventuating in intermarriage. They appeared when newer and more complex technologies had to be installed; for example, in synthetic textiles, paper and cellulose, and chemical industries.

Foreign investment in Latin America increased in cyclical waves, notably 1888 to 1895, 1905 to 1913 and 1924 to 1929. In each of these periods Brazil received a sizeable share of European investments in Latin America, if not one proportionate to its share of Latin America's population. More than half of the foreign capital directed to Brazil financed the central and local governments. It also funded most of the banks, electric, telephone and gas systems, port facilities, railways, steamship lines, and, at the end of the period under study, airlines. Until

[8] *Ibid.*, Tables 27 and 29E.

the first world war this capital was overwhelmingly British. The London Rothschilds were the Empire's exclusive bond-raising agents, the leading exporters and importers were all British, and nearly all the railways were British-owned or financed. The largest British bank, the London and Brazilian, had considerably greater financial resources than the semi-official Bank of Brazil, and even in 1929 foreign banks were still carrying out half of all commercial banking transactions. On the other hand, foreign interests in land, natural resources and productive enterprises were quite limited, unlike the more 'penetrated' economies of Latin America and the then colonial world, and certain sectors – insurance, sugar milling, banking, and railways – began even during this period to be recuperated by Brazilian private capital or public interests. Furthermore, the average rate of return on capital, if the British return is typical, was a moderate 5 per cent. Nevertheless, remissions of interest and profits, which increased gradually during the period under study, represented a considerable charge upon the economy. By 1923 service on the federal and local government debt cost 22 per cent of export revenues.

The activities of British firms up to the first world war may be assessed as generally 'compradorist' in the sense that they concentrated their investments in the export sector. Local entrepreneurs who wanted to build factories to compete with imports were often not funded. There is the spectacular case of a sewing thread mill in Alagoas, bought up by a British firm that dismantled it and heaved the machinery into the São Francisco river. As for British banks, they prospered most when the exchange rates were volatile. They engaged themselves in manoeuvres to destabilize the milreis and resented efforts by the Bank of Brazil to interfere in these dealings. They were reluctant to lend to state-owned companies and even refused on occasion to accept banknotes emitted by the Bank of Brazil. The extreme deflationary measures imposed upon the federal government as the condition of the funding loan of 1898 caused a wave of bankruptcies that wiped out many commercial firms and domestically owned banks, reducing competition with British and other foreign enterprises.

British pre-eminence in the Brazilian economy was, however, subjected to strong challenges after 1900. Their vulnerability arose from their position as financiers and transshippers: since the demand for coffee was largely American and German, American coffee roasters and importers were able to take the place of British middlemen before the first world war, and German export houses, supported by their government's trade offensive, gained strongly in the market for capital goods and took interests in firms which bought their equipment. The 'Black List' revealed the degree to which German trading firms had undercut their competition. In brewing, at one extreme, they controlled the entire domestic output.

AGRICULTURE AND STOCK RAISING

The technological backwardness of Brazilian agriculture was extreme. Slash-and-burn cultivation was mainly extractive, it implied the need for immense forest reserves which supplied many of the farmer's necessities, especially protein and raw materials. Forest lands newly cleared and burned were extraordinarily, if temporarily, fertile. The ashes of the forest provided abundant plant nutrients, often the only fertilizer ever applied. Stumps and logs were left to rot and planting was nearly always carried out uphill and down, encouraging erosion. Some 'cultivated' crops, such as papaya, coconuts, bananas, pineapple and citrus, were often merely allowed to grow wild. When the planted patch was invaded by weeds and pests, it was abandoned, to grow back to secondary woodland or grasses, as it would. When all the woodlands in a given region were exhausted, farmers generally withdrew, and it was turned over to cattle raising. The plough was irrelevant to this regime; indeed in some regions it was entirely lacking. In 1920 less than 14 per cent of farm properties included in the census employed them, and many of these were probably wooden versions. Farm yields were thus nearly entirely a function of the initial fertility of forest soils. Brazil's output of fertilizer was tiny, and in the 1920s 90 per cent of it was exported. Rituals, amulets and prayers were more commonly applied than animal manure, which, according to folk agronomy, 'burned' the land.

Coffee plantations were better managed than the average farm, but even coffee plantations were backward compared to contemporary agricultural knowledge. Available organic fertilizers were only fitfully applied, seed selection was not thought of, bees were not engaged as pollinating agents, and ploughs were improperly utilized. The largest plantations were generally in the hands of managers, since the owners often possessed more than one estate and had multiple interests in the cities. The form of labour contracts discouraged care in cultivating and harvesting and provided excessive advantages to workers in new groves, further stimulating expansion and waste of forest reserves and overplanting. On the sugar plantations of the north-east, where the superior lowland soils were already in use, expansion was carried out in the 1880s by cutting down hillside woodlands. These soils were less appropriate for sugar, required more labour and were subject to erosion. Since the trouble was not taken to remove stumps, the plough could not be employed on the hills. Sugar planters did not apply manure, but left their lands fallow for varying periods. However, the appearance of a fungal disease after 1879 encouraged the introduction of some new cane varieties, some local experimentation in cane breeding, and, briefly, some trials with imported fertilizers. Labour in the canefields remained highly seasonal and intensive, with planting, cultivating, and cutting done by hand. The most significant improvement in cane farming was the introduction in the 1870s of light railways, at first horse-drawn, then steam-powered, to carry the cane to the mills. Modernized steam-powered central sugar mills, heavily subsidized by the government, were installed mainly after the establishment of the Republic. These much improved productivity, and sugar yields about equal to the world average for the period were being achieved by 1910.

There were already two imperial agricultural schools in existence in 1873, and several more schools were founded in a number of the states shortly after the proclamation of the Republic, but they seem to have had little influence on farming practices, except perhaps in São Paulo. Quite a few of the state institutions were in fact practical schools for orphans, and it is not clear whether their graduates ever had the opportunity to apply their learning. During this period only São Paulo had a system of agricultural extension agents.

Food production for the domestic market in this period has been little studied, but it appears to have been a lagging sector. Up to the first world war prices of foodstuffs rose about three times as fast as prices of exports and imports. When coffee planting and rubber gathering surged forward in the 1890s, so did food prices – and food imports. Export growth evidently was based in part on capital resources diverted from the food-supplying sector. The supply of cities was carried out mostly by nearby small farmers, who sold surpluses when they had any. In the vicinity of São Paulo and Rio de Janeiro a few official colonies, opened to native as well as immigrant farm families, were organized to try to increase city food stocks. Cash-cropping small farmers, however, limited to lands abandoned by large-scale planters or to those of poor quality, were starved for credit and preyed on by intermediaries.

Nevertheless production for the domestic market was not stagnant. Although food prices rose steeply, they appear to have risen no faster than wages, in Rio de Janeiro at least, during the period under study, except for the crisis of the first world war. It can be observed, furthermore, that imports of foodstuffs were gradually reduced after 1900: per capita food imports fell from 142 to 34 kilograms between 1903 and 1929. The increasing life expectancy suggests that per capita food consumption was not declining and may have slightly increased. Besides the conversion of former export commodities such as sugar and cotton to the satisfaction of domestic demand, there was some diversification, mostly by smallholders, into wine, oils and fats and dairy products. Wheat, introduced into the diet by the immigrants, proved very difficult to cultivate in Brazil, but potatoes were successfully grown and cultivation of rice was much enlarged. In Rio Grande do Sul rice farming was undertaken on a considerable scale by large landowners for sale to national markets.

Cattle raising occupied vast areas of natural grassland and savanna and areas degraded by farming. Brazilians were much inclined to the consumption of beef. The southernmost state of Rio Grande do Sul, too distant to deliver live animals, industrialized its beef as jerked (pressed and sun-dried) meat. The Brazilian cattle population was somewhat more numerous than the human throughout the period under study. Much of it was crosses of zebu, imported from India in the 1880s and greatly appreciated for its resistance to disease and drought. Cattle raising, as practised in the interior, was extremely economical of labour and capital. Almost never were shelters, fences or watering stations built; animals, after branding, were left to forage and breed as they would. In 1920 the density of cattle on natural range land was about 18 per square kilometre. The only modification of the environment commonly carried out was the burning of fields, to induce the growth of new tender shoots. This had the tendency to promote fire-resistant, unpalatable grasses. Near railheads exotic grasses were planted in formerly forested land, to restore animals driven for long distances, and to fatten them for market.

ENERGY AND TRANSPORTATION

Brazil's coal deposits were low grade and exiguous; in 1929 output from the mines of Santa Catarina amounted to only 360,000 tons. For lack of this resource, wood and charcoal were burned, with further severe consequences for forest reserves, watersheds and topsoil. Per capita domestic use of fuel was estimated at two cubic metres a year. By 1930 Brazil was clearing 330,000 hectares of forest annually for this purpose alone. Since the regrowth of woodlots took about twenty years, this implied the need for a reserve of 66,000 square kilometres, but in fact almost no reserves were maintained. The difficulties in obtaining wood and charcoal limited the activities of railways, smelters and manufacturers. The planting of eucalyptus was resorted to by a few railways, though on an inadequate scale. Imported coal was employed in port terminals and in factories located in port cities, but in the interior wood-stoked boilers were the rule. Some of the early factories also employed hydraulic power, easily installed in a countryside of abundant rains and broken terrain.

Domestic petroleum sources were not discovered in commercial quantity until after the second world war. Imports of petroleum were necessarily restricted, limiting the application of internal combustion engines. Imports of motor vehicles nevertheless increased considerably in the second half of the 1920s. By 1929 more than 160,000 road vehicles were registered and more than 21,000 kilometres of roads had been improved. The first scheduled airline began to operate in 1927, and by 1930 there were four.

Thermal generation of electricity began in the 1880s. Constrained by the need to import coal, it had, however, by 1900 been passed in scale by hydro-generation. Brazil's total electrical capacity passed one megawatt in 1890, ten in 1900, and one hundred by 1908. The construction of large dams and improvement in generation and transmission were carried out in São Paulo and Rio de Janeiro in the 1920s, so that by the end of that decade nearly 780 megawatts were available. Although an impressive rate of growth had been achieved, this was just 22 watts per capita, one-fifteenth that of the United States at the time. Hydroelectric power was as fortuitous a technological advance for southern and south-eastern Brazil as coking coal had been in England two centuries before. It is not possible to imagine the development of industry on the limited base of charcoal, and the cost of importing coal and petroleum would have been as deleterious to industrial growth as it was in Argentina, where industrialization slowed after early rapid gains.

Steam power was early applied to harbour and river craft. By 1873 subsidized coastwise and riverine shipping spread over 36,300 kilometres of routes. Total coastwise shipping rose from a little less than 1 million tons in 1870 to 19 million tons in 1930 (shipping to foreign ports rose during the same period from 2 million to 28 million tons). Steam shipping made possible the extension of the rubber trade to the upper Amazon and its tributaries and improved contact with Mato Grosso via the Río de la Plata. The difficulties of navigation on interior rivers was very great, however. Lack of funds for river and navigation improvement made necessary portages and overnight anchorage. Frieght charges between the upper Xingu river and Belém around 1912, as an extreme example, amounted to nearly ten times those between Belém and New York.

In 1873, there existed only 132 kilometres of canals more than 2 kilometres in length and only 607 kilometres of improved road. Overland transport still depended almost entirely on mule pack trains. By 1889, however, 9,000 kilometres of rails had been built, and by 1930 32,000 kilometres. The railways were entirely a response to the opportunities of the export market, since all of their equipment, except the cross-ties, had to be imported and therefore paid for in foreign currency. Designed to drain the interior of exportable commodities, they did not form a national network. Broad and narrow gauges were employed, even within the same regional network. The largest system was that of São Paulo, where half a dozen lines fanned out towards the coffee-growing areas. A single line then descended the coastal escarpment from São Paulo to the port of Santos. São Paulo was also connected to Rio de Janeiro and to the southern states by way of Sorocaba.

Railways were the principal expense of the central government from the 1860s onward. The largest railway company, the Brazil Central, was government-owned. Private companies, foreign and domestic, sometimes received direct government subsidies to extend their lines; more often there were subsidies in the form of profit guarantees. The states also granted profit guarantees on a more modest scale. The federal government set freight rates, which were kept low, mainly to appease landowners, so that only those lines intensively utilized to ship export crops were able to earn profits. In the late 1890s the expense of covering profit guarantees reached intolerable levels and, since they were owed in gold, they pressed heavily on the balance of payments. The Republican government therefore expropriated many of these lines, leasing most of them out to concessionaires. The installation of railways stimulated agricultural production for the domestic market, as well as serving to bring exports to the docks. Suburban stations on the trunk lines and narrow-gauge suburban lines permitted an augmented flow of foodstuffs and wood for fuel. Rails laid beyond the plantation areas transported live cattle from interior range lands, thereby reducing weight loss suffered in driving, and lumber from the fast-disappearing virgin forests, thereby reducing the waste of hardwoods and cheapening construction costs. Railways were unquestionably a major instrument of Brazil's escape from economic stagnation, yet it must be noted that their stimulus came late and was limited to a few regions.

MANUFACTURING

The development of industry in Brazil may be seen as a process of substitution of handcraft production and of substitution of imports. Of the two, the second is more commonly remarked, since it more visibly affected urban populations and it may be traced in the import lists. But the first was, in the early stages at least, more important. The Brazilian market for non-agricultural goods was supplied in the main by handcrafts. The capacity of the economy to import was, after all, extremely limited, and much of what consumer goods were imported were luxuries for the affluent. Handcrafted goods were produced within the household for its own consumption and for sale or exchange and within artisanal workshops for sale in local markets. Cotton and wool textiles, for example, were widely produced by households before the installation of textile factories. Nearly every household and slave compound included someone who could spin and weave on a hand loom. The scale of domestic handcraft production is suggested by the disproportion in apparent consumption of sewing thread. In 1903 Brazil apparently consumed 1,045 tons of cotton sewing thread, all imported. Yet in the same year 21,900 tons of woven cloth, domestic and imported, were consumed. The ratio of 1:21 is anomalous, considering the modern ratio of about 1:60. It seems likely that at least half of the imported thread was employed in the confection of garments from homespun cloth and of embroidery. Besides this there were many kinds of domestic production – blankets, hammocks, ponchos, covers – that employed no thread. Even in 1966 a survey of rural families in Minas Gerais showed that half of those growing cotton still spun and wove their own cloth.[9]

The transition from handcraft to factory production was not usually abrupt or discontinuous. Handcrafts complemented local factory

[9] Maria de Lourdes Borges Ribeiro, *Inquérito sobre práticas e superstições agrícolas de Minas Gerais* (Rio de Janeiro, 1971), 37–8

production, for example, in the putting-out of cloth in the apparel trades. Much of the food processing industry grew out of domestic workshops which gradually acquired machine techniques. It is often difficult to discover the point at which repair shops began copying whole machines instead of spare parts, and the point at which they put production on a serial basis. Throughout this period many factories employed no steam or electric power at all. According to the census of 1920, the average worker applied just 1.1 horsepower to his job. Furthermore, 10 per cent of the factory work force was employed in firms with no more than four workers.

The German colonists of Rio Grande do Sul demonstrate the progressive incorporation of domestic production within regional and national markets. During the first generation of settlement, the pioneers integrated the material culture of their *mestiço* neighbours with their own. They grew and processed foodstuffs, and artisans among them produced a wide range of consumer and construction goods and agricultural implements. As steamboats were introduced in the 1860s, town merchants began transshipping settlers' products to Rio de Janeiro and other ports. By the 1870s funds from this trade were employed to build consumer goods factories in the major towns. Rural artisans, excluded from town markets, then specialized in a narrower range of processed goods, thereby providing demand for factory-made products.

In São Paulo and Rio de Janeiro, the other important incipient industrial centres, it was the export sector that provided demand and funding for early factories. In São Paulo the brief boom in cotton exports of the late 1860s enabled a few entrepreneurs, mostly planters, to construct small spinning and weaving mills. Eleven were in place by 1884, by which time they provided the only market available to local cotton planters. These mills sold cloth to the plantations for sacking and slave clothing. The planters of western São Paulo were by then willing to buy machine-made cloth for their slaves because slave labour costs were increasing faster than their other expenses.

Abolition created conditions for further development. The self-sufficiency of the slave plantation and its generally depressing effect on wages in the countryside and in towns had stunted demand beyond its gates. The market, in southern and south-eastern Brazil at least, was greatly expanded by the arrival of the immigrant farm workers. Not only were they paid wages and allowed to sell their produce, they aimed at maximizing their incomes, rather than at self-sufficiency. Therefore they purchased many of their necessities. This mass demand was satisfied for the most part by local manufacture. Brazilian labour costs were lower than those embodied in imports. Early manufactures were goods of low value by weight, easy to substitute when raw materials were locally available. Bricks and tiles, beer and beer bottles were early manufacturing successes. The immense cattle and swine herds made local production of soap, candles and leather goods competitive; tinned lard became a modest article of export. By the first world war, according to tax records, imports amounted to less than 5 per cent of the consumption of shoes and boots, less than 15 per cent of hats, and less than 20 per cent of textiles. The cotton textile industry, which boasted 1.3 million spindles by 1919, progressively substituted imports, beginning with coarse unbleached greys and proceeding through fabrics of finer grade.

Capital invested in Brazilian industry, up to 1920, was obtained in the main from importers of immigrant origin and from abroad, largely through émigré entrepreneurs. Planter capital, important in the earliest phase of industrialization in São Paulo, was more closely connected to exporting or the transformation of their own raw materials, and it tended to be gradually replaced by the capital of importers. Some importers turned to manufacturing in order to carry out finishing operations on goods they had imported. Usually dealers in a variety of goods, they were aware of the composition of the import list, of tariffs and domestic taxes and of local demand. They often acted as wholesalers to independent manufacturers and provided them with credit. Nearly all the more important industrialists continued to maintain importing agencies, to assure steady supplies of imported components and to keep abreast of diversifying demand.

In its early phase, Brazilian industry directly favoured the interests of the planters by serving as a market for planter-produced raw materials that lacked favourable export prospects. The planters, however, insisted on high tariffs for imports, such as jute, which competed with Brazilian cotton, and inveighed against the 'artificial' industries that utilized them. They saw to it that tariffs on agricultural implements were kept low. They detested factory jobs which lured away their work force. They often pronounced a phrase later to be repeated sardonically by the enthusiasts of development: 'Brazil is a country essentially agricultural.' Industrialists, on the other hand, did not directly challenge the planters. Instead they associated themselves politically with the plantation interest, partly on the assumption that their prosperity depended on the growth of exports, and partly because they enjoyed the prestige of that association and would have been repelled by the thought of an alliance with the urban middle classes or their own workers.

Despite the political pre-eminence of export-oriented interests, in particular coffee interests, measures favourable to industry were sometimes effectively advanced. High tariffs, as has been mentioned, were largely the inadvertent result of the government's impecunious-ness. Domestic manufacturers also benefited from the planters' prefer-ence for a falling exchange rate, which made imports more expensive. Nevertheless industry enjoyed a certain amount of sympathy in Congress, some of whose members were partisans or survivors of the early Republican provisional government. The industrialists secured laws against government purchases of imports when domestic 'similars' were available, tariff exemptions for machinery, federal loans and interest guarantees for new lines of production, and benevolent interpretations of patent and copyright laws.

The first world war apparently represented an opportunity for Brazilian manufacture, since it reduced the volume of imports of finished goods while elevating their prices and it left the country awash in currency earned from exports and emitted by the government. The failure of wages to accompany the resulting inflation increased the profit rate. Although manufacturing plant could not be much renovated or enlarged because of the interruption of machine imports, factories in some lines of production were stimulated to run extra shifts and increase their output. Nevertheless, imports of raw materials and fuels were more sharply reduced than those of finished goods; scarcity and high costs of inputs, along with higher taxes, narrowed manufacturers' margins. The reported increase in manufactured output may have been exaggerated, since it was based on collections of taxes, which were more thoroughly exacted as import revenues fell. The output of cotton textiles rose from 70 million to 160 million metres between 1914 and 1917. To a considerable degree, however, this production seems to have been warehoused by the manufacturers, who were speculating on further price rises; they were marooned at the end of the war with warehouses full of unsold stock for which they asked government loan guarantees. Even so, the capacity of domestic manufactures to shore up the economy during the crisis increased their acceptance among consumers and earned them credit with the bureaucracy, which appreciated the new source of government revenue.

Until the 1920s industrial output was limited mainly to consumer goods. The census of 1920 counted more than 13,000 manufacturing firms, employing 275,000 workers, less than 3 per cent of the economically active population. (The population census of that year counted 1,264,000 in manufacturing and garment trades – a rough comparison between industrial and artisanal employment perhaps.) Textile factories represented 40 per cent of capital invested in these firms, and food processing, clothing, soap and candles represented another 45 per cent. Within a small intermediate goods sector nearly twice as much was invested in sawmills as in metalworking.

The origins of the iron and steel industry and of metalworking are nevertheless interesting to note, because of their high technical and capital requirements, their tendency to concentrate in cities and their linkages to mining and machine making. Iron smelting had been carried out in Brazil since the seventeenth century, and blast furnaces were built by the crown in the last days of the colony. Over the course of the nineteenth century small iron furnaces continued to operate fitfully in Minas Gerais, their output amounting to a few thousand tons of pig iron. Ironworking and implement making were meanwhile widespread, so that iron and steel imports mainly took the form of inputs to local industry such as wire, sheets, rail, rods and plates. Metalworking was devoted to equipping the export trade, since its own inputs, including skilled workers, were imported and technically advanced. Railway repair yards and shipyards were therefore the largest and best equipped of the metalworking shops.

Large-scale iron and steel manufacture, however, experienced only slight development until the last decade of the period under study. In the 1920s a Belgian firm added steel furnaces and a rolling mill to a newly installed charcoal-fired iron mill in Minas Gerais, and small electrical furnaces in São Paulo and Rio de Janeiro began recycling scrap. In 1910 a British consortium led by an American promoter named Farquhar had obtained rights to mines at Itabira, in Minas Gerais, and sought from the federal government an exclusive concession to export iron ore via the rail line which they planned to rebuild to the port of Vitória. At the same time they promised to construct an integrated mill which was to employ coking coal brought by the same vessels that were to bear off the ore. Negotiations stretched on. There was considerable nationalist opposition to the granting of so large and exclusive a concession, and there was also opposition from the owners of the charcoal and electric mills.

Eventually the world depression diminished world demand for steel, and the consortium abandoned the project. It is likely that they would have delayed as long as possible the delivery of the mill, to which the international iron and steel cartel of the era would have objected. Nevertheless the Farquhar proposal entirely engaged the attention of the government for twenty years and discouraged other potential steel producers. By 1929 Brazil's steel output was only 57,000 tons, 11 per cent of consumption.

THE CRISIS OF EXPORT ORIENTATION

The first world war, as we have seen, caused a sharp decline in the value of Brazil's exports. With the final collapse of the rubber boom at the end of the war Brazil was once more dependent on coffee alone for three-quarters of its foreign exchange earnings. And after a brief postwar commodities boom coffee prices slumped once again. As has been noted, the federal government responded with a third essay at valorization. The third valorization and the 'permanent defence' were perhaps effective in preventing a further fall of the price of coffee in dollars, but the levelling-off of demand and increased overseas competition kept Brazil from realizing an increased volume of sales. Coffee receipts reached 12 per cent of gross national product in 1923 and then began a long decline. Intervention had done little more than secure the income of the planters and encourage new investments in the coffee sector.

In 1924 the federal government, alarmed that the inflationary forces it had set loose were undermining its stability, undertook a policy of deflation. Then late in 1926 it tried again, as it had twenty years before, to adhere to the gold standard through the mechanism of a conversion fund. Again this measure helped to attract foreign capital, which was becoming essential to maintaining the level of imports in the face of rising demand. Brazil had need of a widening range of imports, such as telecommunications and aviation equipment, embodying novel technologies and necessary to improve its competitiveness in world markets. Banks in the United States were ready and eager to advance the funds. Their credits made possible a decline in the trade surplus from 22 to 11 per cent of export receipts between the first and second halves of the decade. The funded debt of Brazil's central and local governments nearly doubled between 1924 and 1930, rising to US$1,295 million. The internal debt grew at an even faster rate, stoked by record deficits in the first half of the 1920s. Oddly, the prewar tariff, eroded by inflation to about half its strength, was not subjected to a general revision. Internal taxation, mainly on transactions, was coming to play a larger role in federal government finances; by the end of the period under study it amounted to about 45 per cent of revenues.

Domestic industry suffered considerably from these vicissitudes. In addition, the prices of manufactured imports were declining while its own competitiveness had been weakened by the wartime interruption in the re-equipping of plant. The share of imports in domestic consumption of cotton textiles rose from 7 per cent in 1921–3 to 17 per cent in 1925–8, and the prices of domestic cotton goods fell by 25 per cent between 1925 and 1927. Cotton textiles represented the worst case, however, since that sector was beset by overproduction, yet even within it those manufacturers who had managed to buy new machinery were achieving profits. Other already established industries reported profits and by the second half of the decade those manufactures included on tax rolls were growing at a rate of about 5 per cent annually. Besides this, the 1920s witnessed considerable diversification of production: pharmaceuticals, chemicals, textile machinery, sugar-milling machinery, automobile parts, weighing devices, truck bodies, gas stoves, and agricultural tools. An indirect measure of the progress of these firms is the apparent consumption of flat steels, which rose from an average 59,000 tons a year in 1901–5 to an average 288,000 tons a year in 1926–30. Many of these new ventures grew out of repair shops which had learned to copy and adapt imported machines and had gone on to contract foreign technicians or to send their own workers abroad to acquire the necessary techniques.

The first world war increased the interest of American firms in the Brazilian market. American banks were established in Rio de Janeiro and São Paulo and scheduled steamships began to operate for the first time between United States ports and Brazil. American investment was more characteristically direct, a phenomenon encouraged by the transformation of business structure in that country after the merger movement. American companies became dominant in petroleum distribution and coffee exporting, where they by-passed the established system of brokers. Electrical and telephone equipment makers established offices to install their products in burgeoning urban power and communications networks. Other American and European multinationals began manufacturing rayon fibre, office machines, photographic papers, phonograph records, light bulbs and automobile tyres, and began assembling automobiles. Some of these ventures can be seen to have been stimulated by protective tariffs, as in the case of nickle plating and pharmaceuticals; others were carried out as the result of invitations by linked investors: the first foreign-owned cement plant was built in the expectation of supplying the Canadian-owned electric company of São Paulo, for example. In many cases, these investments were determined by international cartels, as was the match business by the Swedish trust and cigarettes by the British–American consortium. Many investments that might have been made by multinationals, on the other hand, were aborted by international agreements to which Brazil was not a party and of which it was not even cognizant.

The Brazilian market was not itself free of cartelization. Trade associations that probably engaged in price fixing and quotas existed in the 1920s in metallurgy, shoes, leather, hides, lumber and pharmaceuticals. There were also combinations in restraint of trade at one time or another in flour milling, paper, hats, jute sacking, beer and sugar refining. In most of the other mechanized lines of production firms were so few that they were free to operate oligopolistically within their regional markets. Only cotton textiles lacked price agreements, mainly because efficiency varied so greatly among mills that they lacked a common interest, but even in that industry wage rates were decided by agreement among owners. The government did not exercise sanctions against these practices. A policy of official cartelization was attempted in Rio Grande do Sul from 1928 to 1930 of distributors of jerked beef, wine, lard and lumber. These schemes, forerunners of corporativist planning by the federal government after 1930, were effective in stimulating re-equipment in the lard business, but in the other trades their main effect was to squeeze the margins of the producers.

The collapse of the advanced capitalist countries following the Wall Street crash in October 1929 had a profound impact on Brazilian trade and finances. Coffee, quoted at US$0.50 per kilogram in late 1929, sank to US$0.29 early the next year. The Brazilian government, desperately seeking to salvage its credit, released its entire gold reserve of US$150 million to its foreign bond holders. The state of São Paulo, burdened with 875,000 tons of unsaleable coffee, in 1929 valued at a sum equivalent to 10 per cent of the entire gross national product, cast about for funds to keep the valorization programme going and astonishingly managed to get another £20 million credit. The milreis, however, fell by nearly a quarter in value, money in circulation fell by a sixth and the conversion fund collapsed. The gross national product sank by 14 per cent between 1929 and 1931, the depth of the depression in Brazil, by which point coffee had declined to US$0.17 per kilogram. At the end of 1930, amid business failures, unemployment and social dislocation, the Republic was overthrown.

CONCLUSION

Celso Furtado characterized the 80-year period before 1930 as a transitional phase: the importation of capital, technology and skilled labour was necessary to bring about increased productivity, a monetized market and the beginning of capital accumulation. Viewing 1930 as a watershed, he saw a shift from an external to an internal stimulus to growth, a transformation brought about by the world crisis, but one which he clearly favoured. The more widespread view in Brazil, however, is that export orientation operated contradictorily as an obstacle to growth, that the interests associated with it did not aspire to further development, and that consequently industrialization proceeded in 'surges' only during moments when the international economy was disorganized, by war or depression. Underlying this interpretation is a suspicion that the international capitalist economy was merely imperialist in its workings. Some economic historians have tried to demonstrate that the Brazilian economy, on the contrary, grew and diversified rapidly, as a direct result of its integration into the world economy, that global conditions were at the time favourable to Brazil's development, and that the Brazilian government customarily acted shrewdly and in the national interest. Others, in an attempt at a partial synthesis, have asserted that the alternation of periods of growth and crisis in the world economy was in itself conducive to Brazil's industrialization.

The political and bureaucratic elite which fashioned the policies of export orientation may not have intended to deliver the national economy over to foreign interests, as important as foreign capital was to their strategy, yet they accepted an imported set of policy prescriptions and felt that deviations from them were aberrant, even pathological. Indeed, hidden within the programme of export orientation is an uneasy sense of inferiority that must have been deadly to initiative within the directing cadres and even within the mass of the population. The widespread practice of counterfeiting foreign labels suggests not merely a phase of learning through imitation, but also a contagion of self-doubt and alienation.

Export orientation was a strategy carried out by a bureaucratic elite to promote government stability and economic growth in the interests of a landowning class whose horizons did not extend far beyond short-run speculation. It was not really a national much less a redistributive policy. The gains derived from it were not widely shared. The recent research on the period has not taken up the question of income concentration, but it seems likely that it increased. Economic diversification and the fuller working of the market in towns and cities did make possible social mobility for a small minority in the south and south-east, among whom European immigrants were privileged – a petty bourgeoisie of shopkeepers and artisans, and a smallholding group which sold to city markets. The directing elite did not extend its concerns beyond this stratum. Trade unions they regarded as subversive, workers as indigent dependants, and the unemployed as lazy an potentially criminal. Labour relations in the cities, if practised at all, were considered a form of charity, and it was expected that workers should reciprocate with humility and gratitude. The fate of rural workers who were not under the eye of foreign consuls was not the concern of the federal or state governments. These attitudes clearly did not help to induce higher productivity or to promote development beyond extractive plantation agriculture.

The period under study witnessed the beginning of another form of income concentration: a gap in living standards between the south-eastern region and the rest of the country. By 1920, for example, the ratio of capital per worker in industry was already 59 per cent higher in São Paulo than in the north-east. This phenomenon has been variously explained, but it seems likely that in its inception it was the result of the fuller development in the south-east of markets and productive forces, under the stimulus of the export trade, and of the consequent initiation of a mass market. The federalism of the 1891 constitution, however, and an informal pact that the Republican party of São Paulo arranged with that of Minas Gerais, guaranteed these two states control of the economic policy of the central government. Even the rubber-exporting states of Pará and Amazonas, immense but slightly populated and rivals between themselves, were unable to retain federal revenues collected within their borders, nor to claim the resources of the Acre territory, which instead passed to the federal government. Only once were significant developmental expenditures invested outside the south-east: dam building was undertaken in the north-east as a countermeasure against drought during the presidency of the Epitácio Pessoa (1919–22), the only north-easterner ever to reach that office.

Brazil's participation in the great expansion of world trade and finance after 1870, modest as it was, had the important consequence of initiating economic growth and development. The transformations it worked upon society were, however, uneven, and they were muffled by a dominant class whose developmental goals fell considerably short of the available opportunities. The means of production and the organizational resources amassed during the phase of export orientation constituted nevertheless a valuable resource, to be marshalled in the succeeding crises of the world economy for purposes of development more ambitiously conceived.

20

BRAZIL: THE AGE OF REFORM,
1870–1889

In Brazil, as in many other Latin American countries, the 1870s and 1880s were a period of reform and commitment to change. Intellectuals, professional men, military officers – urban people though often with rural roots – joined associations for the abolition of slavery and organizations for the promotion of mass European immigration, campaigned in favour of federalism and provincial autonomy, argued for the separation of church and state, participated in campaigns for electoral reform, and supported the Republican party. Nor were representatives of the agrarian and mercantile dominant class, known for its conservatism, completely immune to progressive ideas. In the decade before 1870 staunch members of the Conservative party had broken away from their traditional loyalties and joined the Liberal party, while many devoted Liberals left their party to create the Republican party in 1870. Intellectuals also criticized traditional philosophy, condemned romantic literary conventions, and ridiculed the system of education; they cultivated positivist and evolutionist ideas, adopted new forms of expression, and proposed a new system of education more orientated towards science and technology; they repudiated what they perceived as empty liberal rhetoric, criticized the ruling classes, and made 'the people' their subject matter.

By the beginning of the 1890s, reformers could pride themselves on having achieved many of their aims. An electoral reform had been implemented in 1881. Parliament had abolished slavery in 1888. Large numbers of European immigrants had begun to enter the country. And in 1889, a military coup had overthrown the monarchy. The new republican regime adopted a federal system and extended the suffrage. The powers of the church and state were separated. Yet what was perceived as a success by some people seemed a failure to others. Many of those who had struggled to create a new political system soon expressed their disappointment. Rural oligarchies continued to control government, state and federal. And the great majority of the Brazilian population, free poor, ex-slave – and immigrant – continued to be exploited as it always had been. After two decades of reform the country did not seem fundamentally to have changed.

Some historians have attributed the reforms of the late nineteenth century to the influence of foreign ideas on Brazilian society. Abolitionism, social Darwinism, Spencerism, and positivism – they say – all led educated Brazilians to question existing institutions and to concern themselves with changing them. Other historians have seen the reforms as the product of a generational conflict, often described as a conflict between urban and rural groups, or between modern and traditional mores. Young men graduating from professional schools and accustomed to the urban style of living became critical of institutions created by the agrarian elites, from which many of them were descended.[1] The conflict between the rural oligarch (*o patriarca*) and his professional son (*o bacharel*) has even been interpreted in psychoanalytical terms.[2] But the interpretation that has found most favour in recent years relates the reforms to changes in Brazil's economic and social structure during the nineteenth century, and to the emergence of an urban bourgeoisie that allied itself with the most progressive segments of the rural oligarchies in order to fight the traditional elites.

These competing approaches, which have been seen as alternatives, are in fact quite compatible and even complementary. But they are not in themselves sufficient to account for the timing and content of reforms and they raise problems that they cannot solve. There is no doubt, for example, that Brazilian reformers quoted European authors to support their opinions. However, one cannot assume that they had those opinions *because* they had read European authors. In fact, the opposite might be true. It might be more correct to say that their desire to change society in certain ways predisposed them to prefer some European authors to others. Otherwise, how can we explain their preference for Comte over Marx or for Spencer over Fourier? And how can we account for the fact that abolitionist ideas became popular in Brazil only in the

---

[1] See, for example, Gilberto Freyre's classic *Sobrados e mucambos: decadência do patriarcado rural e desenvolvimento urbano* (2nd edn, 3 vols., Rio de Janeiro, 1951).
[2] Luís Martins, *O patriarca e o bacharel* (São Paulo, 1953).

second half of the century although slavery had been condemned in Europe since the Enlightenment?

If we cannot explain the reforms by mere reference to external influences, equally insufficient is the interpretation that opposes urban to rural groups or professional men to landowners, considering one the vanguard of progress and the other the bulwark of tradition. In fact, some of the most eloquent spokesmen for the rural oligarchies and leaders of the Conservative party were lawyers, bureaucrats, and medical doctors – men deeply rooted in the urban environment. And, if in most provinces the Republican party found followers mainly among professional groups, the core of the party in São Paulo was made up of coffee planters.

But even if we can demonstrate that most reformers were from the urban middle classes, we still have to explain why they became alienated from the regime. Similarly, if we can show that most of the militant reformers belonged to the generation born in the second half of the century and were in their thirties or early forties at the time of the proclamation of the Republic, we still have to explain why they, and not the generation before them, launched such a systematic attack against traditional institutions.

In general, we can say that reform in Brazil, as in other Latin American countries, was a response to the new economic and social realities that resulted from capitalist development not only as a world phenomenon but in its specifically Brazilian manifestations. Here, as elsewhere, economic development (urbanization, immigration, improvements in transportation, early manufacturing industry and capital accumulation) provoked social dislocations: the emergence of new social groups and the decline of traditional elites. To the new groups, the institutions created after Brazil's independence from Portugal in 1822 and the political hegemony of traditional landed and commercial oligarchies had become anachronistic obstacles to progress by the 1870s and 1880s.

However, to recognize that economic and social change led to demands for institutional change is not sufficient to explain why the traditional oligarchies were unable to co-opt the new groups or to satisfy their demands. To explain this failure and to understand the purpose and the rhetoric of the reformers, the nature of their demands, and their motives for opposing some institutions rather than others, we ought to look beyond economic change to the prevailing political and cultural institutions they attacked. Before we can explain why the political system created in 1822 became the target of criticism in the 1870s and 1880s, we need to know how the system actually functioned.

During the nineteenth century there were important demographic changes in Brazil. The population grew from 3.8 million in 1822 to a little over 10 million in 1872, and was more than 14 million at the time of the proclamation of the Republic in 1889. Demographic change was greater in some areas than in others, altering the initial distribution of population which had served as the basis for representation. Between 1822 and 1870 the population of the north-east grew at an annual rate of 2 per cent. During the same period, Pará, which benefited from the rubber boom, grew at an annual rate of 3 per cent and São Paulo at 3.5 per cent, mainly as a result of the expansion of coffee plantations. There were also changes in the slave population. Slaves, who constituted more than half of the population in 1822 and 15.8 per cent in 1872, represented a mere 5 per cent in 1888. The slave population diminished in the cities and became concentrated in plantation areas where the economy was expanding. In 1822 almost 70 per cent lived in the sugar-cane areas of the north-east and east. Sixty years later only 35 per cent of the total slave population lived there, while almost 65 per cent were in the coffee provinces of the south.

Immigrants also tended to settle in the south rather than in the north or north-east. Those who arrived between 1872 and 1889 were mainly located in rural areas of São Paulo, Santa Catarina, and Rio Grande do Sul. But many settled in urban centres. Rio de Janeiro had in 1872 a population of 275,000, of which 84,000 were foreign-born. At the same date immigrants represented 12 per cent of the population of Porto Alegre, 11 per cent of Curitiba, and 8 per cent of São Paulo. Their numbers continued to grow. The 1890 census showed that 22 per cent of São Paulo's total population was foreign-born. By that time there were 150,000 foreigners in the country, 70 per cent living in Rio de Janeiro, São Paulo and Minas Gerais, and another 17.6 per cent in Rio Grande do Sul.

A more important phenomenon, however, than either the growth of population or the arrival of immigrants, was capital accumulation due to the extraordinary growth of coffee exports, and to a lesser extent rubber and cacao exports, especially after 1860. Economic growth benefited some provinces more than others, altering their relative economic importance in the national scene. Coffee exports from the centre-south, and from São Paulo above all, increased 341 per cent and coffee prices 91 per cent in the second half of the nineteenth century, while sugar exports from the north-east rose only 33 per cent and sugar prices declined 11 per cent. Despite a steady rise of imports, Brazil had a considerable surplus on its balance of trade after 1861. But profit remittance, mainly to British companies which invested heavily in the most profitable sectors of the economy, interest payments on repeated British loans to finance government expenditure which tended to rise more rapidly than government revenue (in the late decades of the Empire interest payments on the foreign debt consumed on average 40 per cent of the surplus on the balance of trade), and manipulation of the rate of exchange by the British all limited local capital accumulation. Moreover, capital tended to accumulate in the hands of coffee planters and merchants connected with exports and imports. From these groups came part of the capital invested in railways, banks and industries. Only secondarily did capital accumulate in the hands of groups exclusively orientated towards the internal market. And in spite of its expansion the internal market continued to be limited. This peculiar way in which capital accumulation took place in Brazil – as a result not only of its position in the international market, its subordination to foreign markets and foreign capital, but also of decisions made by the Brazilian ruling classes – explains both the nature and the limitations of the changes that occurred in the society during the second half of the century, and to a certain point defines the limits of Brazilian reformism.

One of the consequences of this type of economic growth was that capital accumulation favoured mainly the urban centres and the rural areas related to the import–export sectors of the economy. The city of Rio almost doubled its population between 1872 and 1890. Between 1872 and 1886 the city of São Paulo grew at a rate of 5 per cent a year and from 1886 to 1890 its annual growth was 8 per cent. The population of the city of Salvador went from 129,000 in 1872 to 174,000 in 1890.

Concentration of capital, foreign and local, made it possible to improve urban facilities. Water, sewage, and gas companies, the paving of the streets, and new systems of urban transportation changed life in the big cities. Between 1868 and 1888 streetcars were introduced in Recife, Salvador, Rio de Janeiro, São Luís, São Paulo, and Campinas. In the 1870s a telegraph line linked Brazil to Europe, and in the following years most Brazilian cities were linked to each other. In 1861, 62,233 telegrams were sent. This number increased to 390,277 in 1885–6. In the 1880s, São Paulo, Salvador, Rio de Janeiro and Campinas had telephone services. In 1887 seven lines of streetcars carried a million and a half passengers in São Paulo.

The number of schools also increased in the cities, and illiteracy diminished. But it continued to be high in rural areas. In 1835 the literacy rate in the city of São Paulo was about 5 per cent. It was 42 per cent in 1882. At that time only 29 per cent of the rural population was literate. Journals and newspapers, artistic and cultural associations, inns, theatres, cafés and shops mushroomed, and the big cities acquired a more cosmopolitan atmosphere. In the rich quarters traditional houses built of *taipa* (lath and plaster) were gradually replaced by brick houses of European style. Inside, the heavy rosewood colonial furniture gave place to light English mahogany furniture. Slave quarters gradually disappeared. The free labourers who replaced slaves packed into tenement houses in the centre of the cities or lived in little houses on the outskirts. The streets were no longer the exclusive territory of men, slaves and the lower classes. Upper- and middle-class women were seen with more frequency in the central streets, and men and women were more often together in public places. There were more schools and jobs open to women than before. They could work as teachers, seamstresses, and clerks. In the last decades of the Empire mores were changing but, most important, there were new opportunities for investment, employment, social mobility and political mobilization.

All this, however, happened mainly in the port cities. In the interior only a few towns that functioned as important commercial centres – such as São Paulo, Campinas and Pelotas – developed. Plantation owners brought to the rural areas some progress. They modernized their plantation houses and gardens and promoted cultural and artistic associations in the towns of the backlands. But with those exceptions the contrast between the port cities and the rural areas continued to be striking. Being products more of the expansion of international trade than of the growth of an internal market, Brazilian cities, even more than cities in other parts of the continent, were primarily orientated towards Europe; they played a relatively unimportant role in the transformation of the interior of Brazil.

Railways, for the most part built with foreign capital, began to replace traditional systems of transportation on muleback, oxcarts and barges.

Between 1854 and 1872, 933.3 kilometres of tracks were built; between 1873 and 1889, 8,000 kilometres were added; and at the end of the Empire there were 15,000 kilometres under construction. In some regions railways did create better conditions for the integration of the internal market. However, they were built primarily to facilitate the flow of Brazilian products to the international market and for this reason tended to concentrate in the coffee and sugar areas and were orientated towards the port cities.

The improvement in the means of transportation, the growth of the internal market, capital accumulation, and most of all higher import taxes, which the government was forced to adopt to increase its revenues, all favoured the development of industries. Between 1875 and 1890 the number of factories grew from 175 to more than 600. In 1880 there were 18,100 people registered as industrial workers; ten years later there were about 50,000. Factories producing consumer goods – textiles, beer, cigarettes, soaps, candles, matches, hats – as well as tanneries, foundries, timber mills, and paper and glass factories were concentrated in the urban centres of Minas Gerais, Rio de Janeiro, São Paulo and Rio Grande do Sul, where the availability of labour and capital, an infrastructure of credit and transportation, and the existence of a relatively dependable market created favourable conditions. The Para- guayan War stimulated the manufacture of nautical, optical, and chemical products. By the 1880s the industrialists – although still a small number – felt strong enough to found the Industrial Association in Rio de Janeiro with the purpose of defending their interests. They were among many interest groups that had emerged on the political scene as a consequence of changes occurring in Brazil in the second half of the century. Economic and social change made it increasingly difficult for the political elites to run the nation according to traditional rules, and in the last decades of the century the imperial regime became the target of criticism from many groups in society.

Economic growth generated imbalances between economic and political power. Economic diversification created conflicts of interest between provinces whose economy was mainly orientated to the internal market and provinces mainly orientated to the external market, provinces still dependent on slave labour and provinces where slavery was not an issue any more. Provinces competed for government subsidies and credit. And the pressure to expand the infrastructure made provinces more aware of their dependence on the central government. The situation was complicated by conflicts within each province between planters who modernized their methods of production and those who continued to employ traditional methods. Sugar production underwent a fundamental transformation. In 1857, 66 per cent of the sugar mills in Pernambuco were still moved by animal power, 31 per cent by water, and only 2 per cent by steam. But after 1870 the number of steam mills grew rapidly, reaching 21.5 per cent in 1881. Vacuum pans, centrifugals, and other improvements in the furnaces were introduced. Coffee processing was also improved with the use of driers, hullers, and threshers. All this led to a great increase in productivity. Together with changes in the system of processing there were also changes in the system of labour, with the number of free labourers increasing in some areas while others continued to resort to slaves. Since not all plantation owners had capital enough to modernize their plantations, many had to hold on to traditional practices. They often clashed in the legislature with the representatives of the more productive areas in matters concerning land and labour policies, the routeing of railways, and government subsidies. Some wanted to replace slaves by coolies, others preferred European to Chinese immigrants. Some believed that the government should subsidize immigration and that immigrants should not have access to the land, so they would work on plantations. Others wanted to attract spontaneous immigration by giving them land.

Economic growth and diversification not only generated conflicts within agrarian groups, it created interest groups linked to the railways, industries, banks, insurance, immigration companies, and public utilities. These groups had their own claims, and their interests did not always coincide with the interests of those who controlled the central government. The industrialists, for example, demanded protectionist tariffs and government support, but at the same time they resented political interference and government control. The manifesto issued in 1881 by the newly created Industrial Association accused the government of ignoring the industrialists' efforts and of creating obstacles to their enterprises. It charged the government with favouring coffee planters by adopting a free trade policy that hampered industrial development. The manifesto also criticized the education the ruling classes received in the law schools, which made the leaders of the country men of letters rather than men of science. Finally, it complained about the lack of representation of the 'productive classes' in parliament.[3]

---

[3] '*Manifesto* da Associação Industrial', *Temas*, I (1977), 91–100.

Industrialists had other reasons to be discontented. The frequent crises that struck the capitalist world in the nineteenth century hurt Brazilian businessmen. When banks in London and New York withdrew credit, and prices of export products fell in the international market, bankruptcies followed. In 1857, 1864, and 1873 important enterprises had to be liquidated, causing panic in the financial market and overall discontent, often translated into criticism against government economic policies.

Businessmen and entrepreneurs were not the only groups to resent the political elites, to criticize the ruling classes, and to hope for change. The urban poor suffered with the increase in prices of foodstuffs, and they often saw government policies as responsible for their misfortunes. The growing number of wage labourers in the cities raised new questions and created problems of social control, which an elite habituated to disciplined slaves still did not know how to deal with. The *revolta dos vintens* (penny riot), which caused the fall of a cabinet, was perhaps the most important of the period. It occurred on 1 January 1880 in Rio when the crowd, exasperated by an increase in the price of streetcar tickets, confronted the police, and after three days of rioting was violently repressed.

Artisans and workers who resented competition from foreign products often protested against government policies and demanded protection for national products. Their manifestos sometimes seemed to echo the demands of the industrialists. In 1885, for example, in a letter addressed to the emperor, the Corpo Coletivo União Operária demanded exemption from import taxes on industrial machinery, exemption from property taxes on factories, abolition of privileges and monopolies granted to certain trades, tariffs on foreign manufactures, and credit facilities.[4] But at the same time a rhetoric of class struggle started emerging with more frequency in newspapers addressed to the workers. The number of workers' organizations increased in the last decade of the Empire and the first socialist groups appeared. In the 1880s occasional workers' demonstrations changed the pace of life in the cities.

The new urban masses were not only a source of trouble and concern, they constituted a potential electorate. For the first time politicians addressed themselves to the masses in public places. The first group to do it systematically were the abolitionists. Men like Lopes Trovão (one of the few socialists of the time) left the conference rooms and the salons to talk

---

[4] In Edgard Carone, *Movimento operário no Brasil (1877–1944)* (São Paulo, 1979), 204–10.

Brazil

to the people in the streets. Political mores were changing. An increasing number of women became involved in abolitionist associations. Women's journals multiplied and the first feminist press appeared, demanding access to professional schools for women.

Economic change in the countryside also caused profound social dislocations, which echoed in the political arena. With the expansion of the internal market and improvements in the means of transportation, populations traditionally devoted mainly to subsistence started producing more for the market. This transition was sometimes furthered by the imposition of taxes designed to provide the government with the resources necessary to develop the economic infrastructure. In the backlands, capital accumulation in the hands of merchants and a few artisans and small farmers accentuated social inequality, breaking traditional kinships and forms of accommodation and generating profound social malaise often expressed in popular rebellions.

A good example of this process was the muckers rebellion, which occurred in Rio Grande do Sul between 1868 and 1874. During these years, the traditionally peaceful German communities of São Leopoldo were agitated by a messianic movement that ended in a violent confrontation between the rebels and the local authorities. The rebels, known as muckers, condemned money and trade and rejected the new patterns of social mobility, prestige and class relations based on money. They accused the rich of obscurantism and tried to invert the social patterns by organizing a group ruled by principles of fraternity and equality. Muckers refused to vote and left schools and churches to create their own religion, a religion without a church, valuing direct communication with God. The movement was repressed by the authorities but made the political elites aware of the dangers of a popular rebellion.

About the same time the muckers were causing trouble in the south, the north-east backlands were swept by uprisings known as *quebra quilos* because the rebels protested against the metric system. But there was more to it than just the *quilos*. Poor farmers refused to accept the *quilos*, the draft, and the new taxes imposed by the government. Angry men and women invaded the city halls and notaries, destroyed tax and draft lists, ransacked stores, and terrorized foreign merchants. The government suspected that behind the rebels were the priests who opposed the government because of its protection of the freemasons, condemned by the Pope. But the slogan 'Down with the Masons' shouted by the rioters had more to do with their hostility to the ruling classes than with their loyalty toward the clergy. Both *quebra quilos* and muckers expressed the frustrations caused by increasing social inequalities and exploitation and the disruption of traditional ways of living.

THE POLITICAL SYSTEM OF THE EMPIRE

The political system created at the time of Independence reflected the needs of an elite of landowners and merchants and their clientele. They shared an interest in the maintenance of traditional structures of production based on slave labour and the export of colonial staples to the international market. Most of all, they intended to govern the country without taking any account of the mass of the population, whom they feared and despised. The system was extremely centralized, oligarchical, and unrepresentative. It was not flexible enough to adjust to the changes in the economic and social structure during the second half of the nineteenth century.

Under the constitution of 1824 the chief executive, the emperor, was responsible for the appointment and promotion of personnel in the civil and military bureaucracy. The emperor also implemented the legislation approved by the parliament, and had the final word on the distribution of resources among the different administrative branches. One of the most important responsibilities of the executive was to give or deny permission for the implementation of papal bulls in the country. The emperor also had the power to appoint bishops and to provide ecclesiastical benefices. In addition to his powers as the chief executive, the emperor enjoyed others as a consequence of the Moderating Power, an invention of the French publicist Benjamin Constant that had appealed to those who had drafted the constitution. Among these additional prerogatives he had the freedom to choose and dismiss his prime minister independent of the parliament, to adjourn, prorogue, or dismiss the Chamber of Deputies, and to call for new elections. This meant that if the Chamber denied confidence to a cabinet the emperor could keep the Cabinet and dismiss the Chamber, calling for new elections. He also had the right to appoint the members of the Council of State and to choose each senator from among the three candidates who received the most votes in any senatorial election. It would seem that the constitution had given almost absolute power to the emperor, and in fact this was a common opinion during the First and Second Empires. The constitution, however, had also limited his power by providing that his decisions be submitted first to the Council of State for discussion. One could argue that since the councillors were chosen by the emperor they would tend to agree with him, and even if they happened to disagree they did not have the power to veto his decisions. Yet gratitude was not necessarily a synonym for subservience. The councillors were appointed for life and to a point could be independent of the emperor.

When one looks beyond the words of the constitution to actual practice it becomes evident that, contrary to what his critics said, Pedro II – both by conviction and by temperament – never imposed his will on issues of national importance. In fact, pressured by the councillors, the emperor often acted against his own inclinations. The oligarchies, not the emperor, ruled the country. But the official position the emperor occupied in the political arena focused on him all hopes and resentments. If the leading senatorial candidate was passed over by the emperor in favour of a candidate who was second or third on the list, the unsuccessful candidate expressed his disappointment by attacking the Moderating Power. If the emperor chose a senator from the opposition, he was criticized by the party in power, and if he chose one from the party in power, he was attacked by the opposition. Thus the right to appoint senators and councillors, originally intended to increase his powers, weakened his position in the long run. The same is true of his right to intervene in parliament. Between 1840 and 1889 the emperor dissolved the Chamber eleven times. On eight of these occasions his intervention caused an inversion of the political situation: Liberals were replaced by Conservatives or vice versa. Each time, those forced to step out protested loudly against the abuses of the Moderating Power.

During the 1850s and early 1860s, the period known as the Conciliation, these crises did not have much impact because there was a relative degree of consensus among the elites, with Liberals and Conservatives included in the same Cabinets. But with the growing conflicts of interest resulting from economic and social changes the Conciliation was broken. Liberals and Conservatives competed for power on different platforms, and within each party members representing different and often conflicting interests disagreed on important political issues. As a consequence, not only were Cabinets unstable, but the emperor's intervention became particularly relevant and provoked stronger reactions. The frequent use of the royal prerogative of dissolving the Chamber and calling for elections undermined the prestige of both the emperor and the monarchical system.

The political process was vitiated by electoral fraud, which allowed a Cabinet to manipulate elections in favour of its own party. Since elections did not mean real consultation with the nation, the emperor's interventions were seen as arbitrary and illegitimate gestures intended to force political turnover. Electoral fraud was facilitated by the small size of the electorate. Income qualifications and the system of indirect elections reduced the number of electors to a small percentage of the total population. Only males over 25 (with the exception of military officers and married men over 21) with an annual income of 100 milréis could be voters and only those with an income of 200 milréis could be electors. All women, slaves, and servants (with a few exceptions such as accountants, farm administrators, and chief clerks) were excluded from the electorate. In 1872 the number of electors in the country was approximately 200,000 in a total population of 10,000,000. Such a small electorate could be easily manipulated.

During elections the Cabinets resorted to all sorts of manoeuvres to silence the opposition. They replaced provincial presidents and functionaries loyal to the opposition with others who gave their allegiance to the government. They created parishes where they had friends and abolished them where they had enemies. They harassed rank and file opposition voters, threatening them with conscription, and rewarded those who supported the Cabinet with jobs, promotions, and sinecures. Sometimes they went as far as to mobilize the National Guard to intimidate the opposition by forcing its voters to stay home on election day.

Reforms intended to eliminate electoral fraud and to guarantee representation of the opposition were implemented in 1842, 1855, and 1860, but they all failed. None of those reforms attacked the roots of the problem: the monopoly of land by a minority on which most of the rural population depended, the marginalization of large segments of the population from the productive sectors of the economy, and the lack of institutions that could guarantee the independence of the electors and mediate between them and the government. Most of all, the electoral reforms did not touch the sources of patronage that allowed a minority to control the nation.

This control of the electorate by a minority laid the foundation of a strong oligarchy, which perpetuated itself by blocking from access to power all those who were not willing to accommodate to the rules of patronage. The appointment of councillors of state and senators for life contributed to consolidating this oligarchy. A man who reached the Senate at the age of 40 (the minimum age required by law) could remain there for three or four decades. Some appointed in the middle of the century were still in the Senate when the monarchy was overthrown, almost 40 years later. These, of course, were exceptions. On the average the Senate was renewed every fifteen years. But for members of the Chamber who aspired to a position in the Senate this must have seemed a long time to wait.

Senators constituted a powerful group which monopolized important positions in the government. The permanent members of the Council of State were all recruited in the Senate. And with the exception of one, all cabinet presidents during the Empire were senators. Many senators became presidents of provinces and more than 40 per cent of the senators had titles of nobility.

The men who had created these tenured bodies had hoped that appointment for life – by placing senators and councillors above electoral struggles – would make them immune to political passions. What they had not predicted was that, with time, those bodies would lack the flexibility necessary to respond to changes occurring in society. This explains why abolition of tenure for senators and dissolution of the Council of State or reduction of its jurisdiction were frequent demands in the platforms of the reformers.

Another source of discontent was the lack of balance between economic and political power which became apparent in the final years of the Empire. Originally the number of representatives per province was more or less proportional to the total population (including slaves), and demographic concentration corresponded to economic importance and political power. Economic development and demographic growth broke this correspondence and at the end of the Empire the new economic elites, which were concentrated in a few thriving provinces, felt that their provinces were underrepresented. From the beginning Minas Gerais, the old gold mining area and the most populated of the provinces, had the largest delegation, with twenty representatives. São Paulo had nine, Ceará and Rio de Janeiro eight each. At the end of the Empire Minas continued to have the largest number of representatives and most of the provinces had increased their representation, with the exception of São Paulo, despite the fact that coffee production had made it the richest province in the country. Taking into account provincial resources, São Paulo, Pará, and Rio Grande do Sul were clearly underrepresented at the end of the Empire.

The political preponderance of some provinces was also apparent in the Senate and in the Council of State, where most members were from Rio de Janeiro, Bahia, Minas, and Pernambuco. Moreover, senators did not have to be native to a province or have residence there to represent it. Rio Branco, a native of Bahia, represented Mato Grosso in the Senate. Sales Tôrres Homem, a native of Rio de Janeiro, represented Rio Grande do Sul. Alfredo de Taunay, also from Rio, represented Santa Catarina. Four provinces had a representation in the Senate almost identical to all the other provinces together, and also monopolized Cabinet positions. Between 1847, when the position of president of the Cabinet, or prime minister, was created, and the end of the Empire there were 30 prime ministers; eleven were from Bahia, five from Minas Gerais, five from Pernambuco, four from Rio de Janeiro, two from São Paulo, two from Piauí, and one from Alagoas. From 1840 to 1889 the majority of the cabinet members were from Bahia (57), followed by Rio de Janeiro (47), Minas (35), and Pernambuco (29). These four provinces monopolized the central government, while other provinces that developed in the last decades of the Empire such as São Paulo, Pará, and Rio Grande do Sul had a relatively small representation in the government and grew increasingly dissatisfied with their lack of political power.

Representation was not a serious problem until economic development generated contradictory needs and different regional elites no longer agreed about such things as tariffs, labour and land policies, and government subsidies. The monopoly of power by an oligarchy that did not represent adequately the interests of the most developed areas of the country gave rise to bitter criticism.

The situation would not have become so critical if the provinces had enjoyed more autonomy and if the central government had not exerted so much control over the nation. But the centralization of the political system allowed a small group of politicians, many of whom were appointed for life, to intervene in several different aspects of the nation's life.

The provinces were economically dependent on the central government. Figures for 1868 show that this received 80 per cent of all revenues while the provinces received only 16.7 per cent and the municipalities 2.5 per cent. Provincial presidents were appointed by the central government. When a Liberal replaced a Conservative Cabinet, or vice versa, the new Cabinet immediately replaced all provincial presidents with others more compatible with the new political situation. This practice facilitated relations between the central and the provincial governments but could cause difficulties at the local level. A provincial president often came from outside the province. His term was usually not long enough to allow him to create strong ties, and he moved from one province to another. José Antônio Saraiva, for example, was successively president of the provinces of Piauí, Pernambuco, Alagoas, and São Paulo. João Lins de Sinimbu presided over Alagoas, Sergipe, and Rio Grande do Sul. The provincial presidents had great powers. Many important provincial bureaucrats, the police chiefs, the judges, the head officer of the National Guard, and the army commander depended on him for their appointments. This indirectly gave the central government great control over the provinces. As long as the interests of the politicians who controlled the central government and the regional elites coincided, the system functioned without serious tensions, but when economic and social change generated contradictory or competitive interests between provinces, the situation became strained. The dominant groups in Pará and Pernambuco as well as São Paulo and Rio Grande do Sul complained in the last years of the Empire that the central government did not do enough to satisfy their needs. One answer seemed to be greater provincial autonomy; many thus became sympathetic to federalism.

Another source of conflict in the last decades of the Empire was political interference in the army. The military resented their subordination to provincial presidents and demanded the creation of an independent military hierarchy directly subordinated to the ministry of war. They also resented the fact that promotions to and within the higher echelons of the military depended on the emperor and the Council of State. To those officers who did not have personal links with politicians – and their number was growing in the second half of the nineteenth century – promotion might have seemed an unrealistic dream. The politicians' use of conscription to threaten the opposition during elections was another source of complaint among army officers, as were the draft deferments politicians distributed to their clientele. While army officers were primarily recruited among the upper classes alienation from the system was not a serious problem, but with the democratization of the army, the number who felt victimized by the system in one way or the other increased and the situation became more tense.

After the wars against Argentina in the 1850s and Paraguay in the 1860s, the army became not only more democratic but more cohesive and developed an esprit de corps. Personal conflicts between officers and politicians were then translated into conflicts between the army and civilians. The wars also showed that the Brazilian army was ill-equipped and disorganized. Officers blamed the government for their failures, and when a group of officers decided in the 1870s and 1880s to improve the conditions of the army, they identified political influence as a main obstacle to their goals and became increasingly critical of the political institutions and of the political elites.

Priests committed to the new aggressive line adopted by Pius IX shared some of those feelings. The constitution of 1824 had made Catholicism a state religion, but at the same time the church remained under the control of the state. The government was entitled to intervene in minute details of church life such as the creation or closure of parishes, priests' salaries, and the adoption of textbooks in seminaries. Larger issues, such as the implementation of papal bulls or the recommendation of bishops to the Pope, had been also left to the discretion of the government. During the Empire all those decisions, which intimately affected the life of the church, were made by politicians, and often for political reasons. The church like other institutions was tied to the state and depended on political patronage. Reformist priests devoted to a stricter religious discipline resented the politicians' meddling in affairs of the church. This led to a conflict between church and state in the 1870s.

The central government not only interfered in the army and the church, it also played a major role in the economy. It legislated on import and export tariffs, supervised the distribution of unoccupied lands, formulated labour and immigration policies, and negotiated loans. It controlled banks, railways, and stock companies. No liability company could be created in the country without the permission of the Council of State. The government was not only the regulator but also the protector of national and foreign enterprises, authorizing or prohibiting, providing subsidies, guaranteeing interests, establishing priorities, granting tax exemptions. State patronage, or in other words the patronage of politicians, could determine the success or failure of many initiatives. To a significant degree entrepreneurs were at the mercy of politicians. This system could function without many problems as long as there were relatively few companies, and entrepreneurs either belonged to the elites or could easily find patrons through personal connections. But the system of patronage became more inefficient when business ventures multiplied. Thus it is not surprising that toward the end of the century there was growing condemnation of state intervention in the economy – and, by extension, oligarchical power and the institutions which supported it. In fact, most entrepreneurs, such as barão de Mauá, Brazil's most outstanding railway builder and industrialist of the nineteenth century, could not have survived without government support. Their success depended on tariffs, government contracts, government concessions, government credit and subsidies, and even sometimes on government diplomacy. Capitalism in Brazil developed within the web of patronage and the tension between the patronage system and the free enterprise ideas increasingly asserted by business did not disappear with the Empire.

Those in control of the central government were reluctant to give up the patronage system because it enabled them to dominate the regional elites and to keep a tight control over the army, the church, and economic enterprises. Patronage was their main source of power and political prestige. As a consequence of this practice politicians in Brazil were seen not only as representatives, but as benefactors, their political power depending on their capacity to distribute favours.

For the same reasons the oligarchies were unwilling to create a civil service system, which would have emancipated the bureaucracy from political patronage, as the emperor himself recommended. The creation of a permanent body of bureaucrats, appointed according to criteria of merit and talent, would take away from politicians one of their main sources of favours. The criteria that prevailed in the recruitment of the bureaucracy were personal friendship and party loyalty. Political party turnover always resulted in disruptive bureaucratic turnover. Bureaucrats lost their jobs overnight when their party suffered defeat. Persecution of the political adversary was the norm in the bureaucracy. One politician who was appointed provincial president records in his memoirs that local party leaders expected him to remove elementary school teachers to distant localities to punish their husbands for having supported the opposition.[5] It is easy to imagine the hostility and resentment of those who saw their careers suddenly interrupted by the intervention of powerful political leaders. Men totally dependent on political patronage would come in time to hate a system that made their lives so insecure and would dream of a system that would reward merit and competence.

But patronage, not talent, continued to be the prerequisite of success.

[5] Alfredo d'Escragnolle Taunay, *Memórias* (Rio de Janeiro, 1960), 416.

The free play of the market was not enough to guarantee social mobility. Behind every 'self-made man' there was always a sponsor. The proverb, still valid in Brazil today, that 'one who does not have a godfather dies a pagan' describes well the situation during the Empire. Politicians did not succeed in their careers, functionaries did not occupy public offices, writers did not become famous, generals were not promoted, bishops were not appointed, enterprises were not organized without the help of a patron.

The careers of most politicians of the Empire show that it was not his programme that recommended a candidate to the electorate but his kinship and his associations with powerful figures. The political career of a young man was a family decision. His political options were decided *a priori* by his family. And political struggle was, above all, struggle between factions under the leadership of prestigious families. Whether they came from the landowner elite, like the barão do Cotegipe, who owned a sugar plantation in Bahia, or from a family of professionals like Paulino José Soares de Sousa, the visconde de Uruguai, whose father was a medical doctor and who was himself a lawyer but who married into a family of politicians and landowners in Rio de Janeiro, politicians often represented in the Chamber, the Senate, or the Council of State the interests of plantation owners and merchants to whom they were tied by links of patronage and clientele.

This system of alliances and bargains and the manipulation of the electorate favoured the creation of dynasties of politicians: the Ferreira Franças, the Nabuco de Araújos, the Cavalcanti de Albuquerques, the Soares de Sousas. Fathers promoted their sons, uncles their nephews, and relatives and friends supported one another. Writing about the Cavalcantis, owners of a third of the sugar mills in the province of Pernambuco, Joaquim Nabuco said that they had the influence that a large, rich, and well-established family whose members always occupied prominent positions in government and in the legislature *ought* to have. Politicians like Nabuco, who himself sat in parliament because of family connections, tended to assume that the power of great families like the Cavalcantis derived 'from the nature of things'. Assumptions like this could only produce ambivalence in the minds of those who, like Nabuco, later turned to liberal reform and challenged the traditional oligarchy and the political institutions of the Empire.

This ambivalence would be shared by other people since, as we have seen, the system of patronage was not confined to the furthering of political careers. Bureaucrats, journalists, writers, artists, entrepreneurs, and merchants: everyone had to follow the rules of patronage. Characterizing the situation in the 1860s, the novelist José de Alencar commented: 'Industrial enterprises, commercial associations, banks, public works, financial operations, privileges . . . all these abundant sources of wealth issue from the heights of power. The bureaucracy distributes them to their favourites and denies them to those in disgrace. Everything depends on patronage, even the press, which needs state subsidies to survive.'[6]

The first generation of intellectuals who reached maturity at the time of Independence or immediately after were almost all absorbed by the political system. If the market for their books was limited in a country in which most of the population was illiterate, they could at least survive on patronage and have a career in politics and administration. They became representatives, councillors, senators, ambassadors, public officials. Many received titles of nobility. Domingos Gonçalves de Magalhães, considered the father of romanticism in Brazil, was a member of the Chamber, a diplomat in Europe, a member of the Council of State, and a personal friend of the emperor. He received many decorations and was made barão and visconde de Araguai. Antonio Gonçalves Dias, one of the most outstanding poets of this period, was appointed professor of Latin and History in the famous Colégio Pedro Segundo and later sent to Europe on an official mission. José de Alencar, the most important romantic novelist of the period, was a member of the Chamber, minister of justice, and councillor of state. And just as the politicians organized the nation after Independence according to European constitutional rules, this first generation of Brazilian writers, though intensely nationalist, imported European models and idealized Brazilian reality: a second-generation writer had a character complain, 'They portrayed forests without mosquitos and fevers.'[7] Gradually, however, opportunities for political careers diminished as most positions were filled, and only minor jobs in the bureaucracy or in the court system remained. With a few exceptions writers born in the 1830s, like Bernardo de Guimarães, Casimiro de Abreu, Manuel Alvares de Azevedo – because they died young or because they lacked the opportunities of the earlier generation – neither participated in politics nor had important posts in administra-

---

[6] José de Alencar, *Obras completas* (Rio de Janeiro, 1960), IV, 1097.
[7] Manuel Antônio Alvares de Azevedo, 'Macário', in *Obras completas de Alvares de Azevedo* (8th edn, 2 vols., São Paulo, 1942), II, 66.

tion. They also could not make a living as writers. It is thus not surprising that they felt they had reached a dead end. They postured as bohemians; Byron and Musset were their models. Alienated from the world around them – a world they felt incapable of changing – sunk in their personal torments, they scrutinized their souls endlessly, explored the grotesque, or mocked society.

The growth of the market for books – although modest – and the proliferation of newspapers and journals in the second half of the century opened new opportunities for a literary career. Social criticism and militant reformism offered an alternative to despair and solitude. While Alvares de Azevedo was haunted by personal ghosts, Castro Alves found in the struggle between men and society his source of inspiration and became the poet of the slaves. This third generation of writers condemned the rhetoric, the style and the themes of the previous generations, demanding a more 'objective' view of the world. Realism and naturalism rather than romanticism were their models. Young novelists and poets gave up the parliamentary rhetoric, the conventional prose of the salons, the intrigues of the well-to-do, the idealization of indianism, the lyrical despair of the earlier generations, to focus on the life of 'the people'. In the last years of the Empire and the early years of the First Republic Aluísio de Azevedo described the tribulations of life in a tenement house; Euclides da Cunha, the rebellion in the backlands. Sílvio Romero collected popular tales and songs and condemned 'the history books without science or passion, pages through which great and powerful men parade, but from which the eternal sufferer, the eternal rebel, the eternal hero: the people was absent'.[8] But the contradictions between the old and the new, 'aristocratic' and 'bourgeois' tendencies, remained. To a certain extent these contradictions reflected the position of the intellectual. Even then, when there was a new market for ideas, enough to feed the writers' fantasies of independence, the lives of Brazilian intellectuals continued to depend on patronage.

This dependence, which was, as we have seen, also a fact of life in the world of business, politics, and administration, allowed the ruling classes to control social mobility. Crossing lines of class and colour and harnessing the most talented members of the new emerging classes to the elite, patronage attenuated racial and class conflicts. But patronage had its own contradictions. It secured loyalties but generated resentments. It

[8] Sílvio Romero, *Novos estudos de literatura contemporânea* (Rio de Janeiro, 1898), 7.

could co-opt the enemy but alienate the ally, silence the critic of the system but transform a supporter into an opponent.

Some of the social climbers hardly concealed their ambivalence. Others endured silently the contradictions of their situation. Luís Gama, a mulatto, born of a slave mother and a white father, sold as a slave and later emancipated, became a practising lawyer, a militant abolitionist, and one of the founders of the Republican party in São Paulo. A satirical poet, Gama mocked in his verses a conceited elite that denied its African roots. Yet this did not prevent his becoming one of its members. Even though he was a leader of a political party that advocated the overthrow of the monarchy and an abolitionist in an area controlled by slave owners, Gama died honoured by the elite. His funeral was attended by a crowd ranging from ex-slaves he had helped to emancipate to prominent figures in politics and administration. If Gama expressed his uneasiness in satirical terms, Machado de Assis, another mulatto, hid his behind a veil of subtle irony while conscientiously performing the role attributed to him in the world of whites. As a novelist, he devoted most of his time to the study of whites and their personal anxieties, seldom referring to blacks or to slaves and keeping a reserved attitude towards abolition and politics. Although the experiences of men like Machado de Assis and Gama were quite exceptional they could be seen as evidence of the patronage system's efficiency, and their lives fed the myth of racial democracy and of the paternalism of the Brazilian elites.

Characterizing the alliance of the ruling classes with men of talent, José de Alencar wrote in 1865 that Brazilian elites were constituted of two sorts of people: 'men rich in talent but poor in assets and rich men deprived of enlightenment'. The former, moved by necessity and love of ostentation, sought important positions in administration; the latter offered their support in exchange for consideration and respect.[9]

This alliance of men of talent with men of power explains in part why, in the work of Machado de Assis and other novelists, the ethic of liberalism and the ethic of favour existed side by side. Their novels were written from two contradictory perspectives: on the one hand, from the perspective of a bourgeois ideology, which postulated the autonomy of the individual, the universality of the law, disinterested culture, commitment to thrift and labour; and on the other hand, from the point of view of the ethic of patronage, which stressed the individual's

---

[9] José de Alencar, *Obras completas*, IV, 1080.

dependence, cultivated the exception to the norm, praised leisure and ostentation, validated the 'culture engagé'. The ambivalent ideology resulting from this odd combination expressed the experience not only of the writers but of many other Brazilians. The coexistence of an ethic of patronage with a liberal ethic reproduced at the level of ideology and language the human experience of people living in a society in which capitalism grew within a network of patronage. The ambivalence of this ideology translated the contradictions of the *bourgeois gentilhomme*, who lived in Brazil but had Europe as his point of reference, who used slaves to produce for the international market, who 'had an eye on profit and another on gentility' – a contradiction that existed also in the precarious alliance of black and mulatto intellectuals with the ruling classes, of entrepreneurs with the rural oligarchies, of men of modest origins with the power elite. The ideology expressed contradictions permeating Brazilian society from top to bottom.

When the development of urban markets, the proliferation of schools and cultural institutions, and the growing number of readers opened new opportunities – even if still limited – to entrepreneurs, professional men, writers, artists, and politicians who dreamed of emancipating themselves from the constraints of patronage, these men found in liberalism the arguments they needed to fight the system. But even then their commitment to liberalism was not without ambivalence. They continued to judge patronage from the point of view of liberalism and to judge liberalism from the point of view of patronage.

While in Europe the criticism of liberalism was often made from the perspective of the working classes, in Brazil the lack of an industrial revolution and of a proletariat and the survival of traditional relations of production in many parts of the country made that type of criticism, if not impossible, at least exceptional. As a consequence while in Europe liberalism was on the defensive, it remained in Brazil – in the minds of many – a promise to be fulfilled. It was the hope that the promise *could* be fulfilled that, in the 1870s, was behind the criticism of imperial institutions – a criticism that expressed a naïve belief in the redeeming qualities of progress, science, and reform. However, parallel to this trend towards reform and sometimes within it there continued to run a conservative stream springing from the experience of patronage. The contradictory nature of this process was admirably captured by Machado de Assis's novels, in which both characters and language are constantly shifting between the ethic of patronage and the ethic of liberalism.

Brazilian architecture of this period suggests even more clearly the relations of 'old' and 'new' elements in Brazilian culture. The 'old' and the 'new' were juxtaposed in Brazilian architecture as they were in England but in an inverted way. In England the new technology was often disguised under respectable gothic or renaissance façades. In Brazil, on the contrary, buildings continued to be built according to traditional methods, but the thick walls were covered with paper and mirrors imported from Europe and the façades were decorated with glass windows that came to replace the traditional trellises. The modern was the detail, something to be shown, the genteel exterior that hid coarse structures in art as well as in politics.

If economic development and social change in the last decades of the Empire were not enough to destroy traditional structures, they were enough to generate increasing dissatisfaction – a dissatisfaction increasingly expressed by politicians and intellectuals. In the last decades of the Empire, old politicians who felt marginalized by their party cliques and young men who had to find their way to politics and wanted to replace 'the influence of people by the influence of ideas',[10] as a contemporary put it, found in a programme of reform the lever for a successful career. This was also true for many intellectuals. 'Today, there are two ways of moving upward', said Alencar in the 1860s: 'flattery and criticism, to carp or to beg'.[11] Once the relative unanimity of the elites was broken and new groups challenged the traditional oligarchies, dissent became as instrumental to personal advancement as complicity. To the new generation of politicians and intellectuals, reform offered both a theme and a constituency. When they committed themselves to reform they were not only expressing the interest of social groups from which they descended or with which they identified. They were also moved by their specific needs as politicians and intellectuals who aimed at creating constituencies. Economic and social change provided them with a constituency ready to welcome reformist proposals. And when politicians and intellectuals adopted a reformist rhetoric they helped stir up even more latent discontent and increased the number of those who saw reforms as a panacea for all social problems.

Reformers had their own vocabulary and their own themes. In their rhetoric 'the People' appeared together with other favourite words such as 'progress', 'reason', and 'science'. But in fact, no matter how

---

[10] Quoted in Sérgio Buarque de Holanda (ed.), *História geral da civilização brasileira, II: O Brasil monárquico*, vol. IV, *Declínio e queda do império* (São Paulo, 1971), 307.

[11] José de Alencar, *Obras completas*, IV, 1074.

sympathetic some of them might sound, they lacked any real connections with the people they preferred to protect rather than to represent and to represent rather than to allow them to speak for themselves.

In the eyes of the reformers Europe symbolized progress, and to be progressive meant to recreate the modes of European elites. Living in a country dependent on European markets they looked toward Europe for arguments and models, which not only served as guides but conferred prestige and authority. In spite of the proliferation of cultural institutions, newspapers, and journals and the constant increase in the number able to read, the conditions for the independent production of ideas were still far from ideal. Most of the population continued to be illiterate (78 per cent in 1872). There were few printing houses, and Brazilian writers often had to print their books in Europe. There were few bookshops (in São Paulo, at the end of the century, there were only five), and the internal distribution of books was difficult. It was easier to import books than to produce them locally. All this created obstacles for an internal debate of ideas conducive to the creation of a relatively autonomous culture. 'We are consumers, not producers of ideas', commented Tobias Barreto, a leading intellectual of the 1870s and 1880s.[12]

Reformers imported ideas, but this import continued to be selective, as it always had been. They chose what made sense to them. This explains why the Christian socialism of Lammenais, the utopian socialism of Saint-Simon, Proudhon, or Fourier, and the scientific socialism of Marx and Engels were merely matters of speculation for a few eccentric individuals. Men like Spencer and Comte, who had tried to reconcile order and progress and wanted to regenerate society through a moral revolution, had more appeal to Brazilian intellectuals and politicians than those who put their trust in class struggle or in the proletariat.

Placed between an oligarchy they wanted to combat and the masses they did not trust the reformers of the 1870s and 1880s found their inspiration in positivism. They abandoned Cousin and Jouffroy's eclecticism – which had served the elites of the Regency in the 1830s and the Conciliation of the 1850s and 1860s – to embrace Comte and Spencer. Those authors offered them a doctrine, a method of analysis, a political theory, and most of all the reassuring conviction that mankind was inevitably driven to progress and that change was possible without subverting the social order.

Since the 1830s, a few Brazilians who had studied in Paris had brought

12 Tobias Barreto, *Ensaios de sociologia* (Rio de Janeiro, 1962), 10.

home Comtian ideas, but it was only in the 1860s that those ideas became popular. In Comte, the generation of reformers found support for their programme aiming at reducing the state to a mere custodian of the social order. Comte's respect for civil liberties and his commitment to religious freedom, free association, freedom of speech, and free enterprise could not but appeal to those who resented the centralized political system and the oppressive patronage of the elites. This rather conservative group of reformers found equally appealing Comte's respect for social hierarchy and social inequalities and his conviction that freedom was a right but equality a myth. At a time when women were making their first steps toward higher education, his belief that the family was the basic social unit and that women should be subordinated to their husbands could only attract men raised in a patriarchal society who looked suspiciously at emancipated women. It was also pleasing to them that Comte argued in favour of an elite of technicians and men of science, distinguished by their virtues and knowledge – an elite he saw replacing the 'pedantocracy', the elite of literati, the reformers identified with the Brazilian oligarchies. And nothing could be more attractive to them than Comte's conviction that this new type of intellectual had an important role to play in changing the world. Comte's ideas spoke in particular to doctors, teachers, engineers, entrepreneurs, and students of the Military Academy, who resented the patronage of the traditional elites. Thus, with the exception of a few individuals such as Farias Brito, a follower of Hartman and Schopenhauer, Soriano de Sousa, who found inspiration in neo-thomism, and Tobias Barreto, who devoured everything he could read, especially German literature, most intellectuals of this period became positivists. Even those who, like Sílvio Romero, later moved to different positions had their positivist phase. A few preferred Spencer's evolutionism but the majority followed Littré's version of Comte. The interest in those new ideas grew side by side with the critique of the system and the demands for reform.

THE POLITICS OF REFORM

During the early 1860s a group of leading Conservative politicians, among them Pedro de Araújo Lima (marquês de Olinda), José Tomás Nabuco de Araújo, Zacarias de Góes e Vasconcelos, the marquês de Paranaguá, Sinimbu and Saraiva, convinced of the need to reform the political system, had left their party and joined the Liberal party, creating the Liga Progressista (Progressive League). The League's programme was presented in 1864. It demanded among other things decentralization, electoral reform, reform of the court system, a new Civil Code, and changes in the Commercial Code, especially in the sections concerning stock companies and bankruptcy. With the beginning of the Paraguayan War in 1865, however, the reformist campaign briefly receded. But the pressure for reforms continued to increase within the ranks of the Liberal party, where a more radical faction emerged. The conflict between the radicals and the moderates within the Liberal party led to the fall of the Liberal Cabinet in 1868. The emperor called on the Conservatives, who were to remain in power for the next ten years. The Liberals united themselves and proceeded to attack the government and the emperor. In May 1869 they issued a manifesto (apparently written by senator Nabuco de Araújo) which demanded decentralization, autonomy of the judiciary, creation of a system of education more independent from the state, transformation of the Council of State into an organ exclusively administrative, the abolition of tenure in the Senate, direct elections, creation of a Civil Register, secularization of the cemeteries, religious freedom, the extension of the right to vote to non-Catholics, and the gradual emancipation of slaves. The manifesto ended with a threat: 'Either Reform or Revolution', followed by a conciliatory remark: 'Reform and the country will be saved.'

In spite of its tone the Liberal manifesto did not satisfy the party radicals, and a few months later they issued their own. The new manifesto asked for the abolition of the Moderating Power, the National Guard, the Council of State, and slavery. It demanded elections for provincial presidents and police chiefs, universal suffrage, and direct elections. It also asked the government to restrict itself to administering justice, maintaining order, punishing crimes, and collecting taxes: the functions of a typical liberal state, which would secure freedom of initiative and guarantee civil rights. Everywhere radical clubs were formed. And with the end of the Paraguayan War in March 1870, the opposition intensified its campaign against the government. In December the Republican party was founded in Rio and issued a manifesto published in the first number of the newspaper *A República*. Of the men who signed the manifesto only one was a plantation owner. The others identified themselves as lawyers (fourteen), journalists (ten), medical doctors (nine), merchants (eight), engineers (five), bureaucrats (three), and teachers (two). A few had been militant in the Liberal party and had held important posts in politics and administration. In response to the manifesto several radical clubs declared themselves republicans and several republican clubs appeared. The Republican manifesto did not add much to the others. It made, however, one important suggestion: the creation of a National Convention with powers to change the regime.

In essence all three manifestos of 1868–70 – Liberal, radical and Republican – had the same goals, although they differed in the degree of their radicalism. They intended to curtail government interference in the private sector, to increase provincial autonomy, and to undermine the power of the traditional oligarchies. Their programme of reform appealed to a large spectrum of interests. They spoke to the bureaucrat, the judge, and the teacher tired of the uncertainties of patronage. They spoke to the businessman oppressed by government policies, and to the clergyman and military officer who condemned political interference in their institutions. They spoke to the immigrant who wished to regularize his situation, and to the urban and rural masses burdened by conscription and taxes. They appealed especially to the new young generation of politicians for whom the programme of reforms could win a growing electorate, and to the intellectual who found in reform new sources of inspiration and new constituencies. If the programme seemed to appeal to the emerging urban groups, it also attracted progressive planters and provincial elites dissatisfied with the central government's policies. But most of all the programme was used by the Liberal party politicians to attack the Conservatives between 1868 and 1878 when Liberals were politically ostracized.

The issues raised by the manifestos, however, transcended party boundaries. Among the members of the Liberal party there were some who would not endorse the demands of the most radical. And in the Conservative party there were those who could support a moderate programme of reform. They could win some of the most reluctant members of their party by presenting the reforms as a means of fighting the opposition. This strategy became a necessity when the emperor himself expressed his sympathy for some of the reforms. In the advice he gave to the Regent, Princess Isabel, before his trip to Europe in 1871, the emperor stressed the need to reform the electoral system, the judiciary, the National Guard, and the system of conscription and promotion in the army. He also suggested that immigration be encouraged and slaves gradually emancipated. On one issue he went even further than the Liberals or the Republicans. He suggested the creation of a civil service career that would remove bureaucracy from the manipulation of the political elites. But on other issues he adopted a more conservative line. He opposed the separation of state and church, the extinction of the Moderating Power, the abolition of tenure in the Senate and Council of State, and decentralization. He also disapproved of giving political rights to foreigners. The emperor's support for a moderate programme of reforms only increased their popularity. This explains why a Conservative Cabinet, headed by the barão do Rio Branco (1871–4), launched a series of reforms of which the most important was the emancipation of children born of slave mothers.

The issue of slave emancipation was not new. At the time of Independence a few politicians raised the question without success. Under pressure from the British, the Brazilian government outlawed the trade in 1831, but it continued illegally until 1850, when it was finally repressed. In the late 1840s and early 1850s, coffee planters, concerned with the problem of labour supply, tried to use immigrants on their plantations. The experiment ended in a harsh confrontation between workers and plantation owners. Foreign governments protested against the bad treatment of immigrants and some prohibited immigration to Brazil. After that, only a few stubborn planters continued to use immigrants on their plantations. The overwhelming majority resorted to slaves bought in the cities or in rural areas less dependent on slave labour. As a result, slaves were moved from areas of lower productivity to areas of higher productivity and from urban centres to rural areas. The slave population of the north-east declined while in the coffee areas it increased.

During the 1850s and 1860s several bills proposing gradual emancipation of slaves were presented to the Chamber but they were all rejected. Emancipation found more supporters after the American civil war, when Brazil became one of the few countries still to have slaves. In 1867, the emperor spoke in favour of gradual abolition. Parliament refused to discuss the question. But two years later it approved a law prohibiting slave auctions as well as separation of husband from wife and parents from children under fifteen years old. During the Paraguayan War slaves belonging to the state who served in the army were emancipated (November 1866), and in 1870 senator Nabuco de Araújo succeeded in getting the Senate to approve a budget amendment granting 1,000 contos for slave emancipation. All those measures, although small, were indicative of a growing abolitionist pressure. The inclusion of the issue of emancipation in the Liberal manifesto and the Emperor's approval of gradual emancipation made it impossible for the Conservatives to delay the parliamentary debate. Two Conservative Cabinets resigned before the issue could be brought to discussion. Called by the emperor to form a new Conservative Cabinet, Rio Branco decided in 1871 to present a bill to the Chamber proposing the emancipation of the newborn children of slave mothers. During the debates regional interests prevailed over party loyalties. The opposition came mainly from representatives of the coffee areas. They spoke of bankruptcy, social disorder, political chaos, the dangers of a slave rebellion. Some even argued that the bill was prejudicial to the slaves because it would split families and generate strife among them. And they did not forget to make the classic remarks about the benevolence of the masters and the slaves' good living conditions compared to those of the workers in industrial societies. But the most important argument against the bill was that it hurt the right of property. Some went as far as to say that the bill was a communist invention. The supporters of the bill resorted to a great variety of arguments. They not only condemned the institution on moral terms but also argued that slave labour was less productive than free labour. Some questioned whether the right of property could be applied to people. Far from being based on natural law, slavery, they said, was a 'monstrous violation'. Inside and outside the parliament the question was debated with great excitement. Petitions for and against flooded the parliament, where heated speeches in favour of the bill were applauded enthusiastically from the galleries. Finally, in spite of the sharp opposition, the bill was approved in the Chamber by 65 votes to 45. The law was enacted on 26 September 1871, after having been approved in the Senate by 33 to 7.

The law was a serious blow at the institution of slavery, although its effects would be felt only in the long run. According to the law the newborn children of slave mothers would be free, but the masters had to take care of them until they were eight years old. After that, slave owners could either give the children to the state, in exchange for financial compensation, or use their labour until they were 21.

After the approval of the law of free birth the government turned to other reforms, and in less than four years the Cabinet reformed the court system, the National Guard (1873), the system of conscription (1874), military schools, and pensions. It also approved an increase in military salaries, which had been frozen since the 1850s. The Cabinet also promoted the expansion of railways, doubling the track mileage, established telegraph lines linking Brazil to Europe and the provinces to each other, and subsidized immigration, raising the annual number of immigrants entering the country from 8,000 to 50,000. All those activities were favoured by a period of extraordinary economic prosperity. Soon, however, the 1873 world recession began to affect Brazil, putting an end to this euphoria and provoking the fall of the Cabinet – which had already been weakened by an intervening conflict between church and state.

The conflict had its roots in the policies of Pius IX for strengthening the authority of the Catholic church. The Pope's intolerant opinions in matters of religious discipline and faith and his aggressive religious campaign could only lead to confrontations between church and state, particularly in countries like Brazil where the church was subordinated to the state. The situation became tense after the Pope's encyclicals, *Quanta Cura* and *Syllabus* (1868), condemned many features of modern life, and a Vatican Council proclaimed the dogma of the Pope's infallibility (1870).

The Pope's new aggressive line was followed by many Brazilian priests, especially some young clergymen who had been trained in European seminaries and had returned to Brazil with a renewed sense of religious mission. This militant clergy found intolerable the subordination of the church to the state. They resented the laxity of the traditional clergy who had accommodated themselves to the rules of political patronage. The new priests struggled for more autonomy for the church and more religious discipline.

The issue that triggered the conflict was apparently minor. The Pope had condemned freemasonry and had forbidden Catholics to become masons. The bishop of Olinda, Dom Vital, acting independently, decided to prohibit masons from participating in religious brotherhoods. This could be seen only as an act of insubordination, since the constitution established that papal bulls had no validity without the emperor's approval. The conflict was aggravated by the fact that although the number of masons was small, many important politicians were masons, including the visconde do Rio Branco, the head of the Cabinet. Many priests were also masons. The masonic brotherhoods resisted the bishop's decision and appealed to the government. The bishop, ordered by the government to withdraw his demands, refused. This created a serious impasse. The government had either to bow to the bishop's ultramontane position or punish him for his disobedience. After failing to persuade the Pope to discourage him, the Cabinet decided to punish the bishop, who, after being arrested and tried, was sentenced to jail in 1874. The conflict might have ended there if other members of the clergy had not expressed their solidarity with the bishop. But the incident had widespread repercussions. In the cities and in the backlands there were demonstrations for and against the bishop while the press and parliament debated the issue. The arrest of another bishop, D. Antônio Macedo Costa, who had followed the example of D. Vital, and a second trial and condemnation, further aggravated the situation.

The Conservative Cabinet did not find unanimous support within its own ranks. Important Conservative leaders like Paulino José Soares de Sousa, Antônio Ferreira Viana, and Cândido Mendes condemned the arrests. Liberals were also divided. Many Republicans found themselves in the position of supporting the emperor and condemning the bishops. However, among them were some who used the incident to further the republican cause by arguing in favour of the separation of church and state.

The bishop's arrest caused profound malaise among Catholics and created a serious problem for the Cabinet. A conflict that had started as a small issue about the rights of freemasons had become a confrontation between church and state for which there was no good solution. For the government, the only alternative was to grant amnesty to the two bishops, but for that to happen the Rio Branco Cabinet had to go. In 1874 the Cabinet was replaced and the amnesty came in 1875; simultaneously the Pope ordered the suspension of the bans against the masons. This put an end to the conflict. There were no winners or losers, but the number of those who favoured the separation of the church from the state had increased on both sides, so in the long run the monarchy lost. Many years later, a few months after the proclamation of the Republic, D. Antônio Macedo Costa in a pastoral letter could say triumphantly: 'The throne has disappeared . . . And the altar? The altar still stands.'[13]

Traditional historiography has attributed to this conflict a great role in the fall of the Empire, ignoring the fact that the nation had been divided on the issue. Besides, the position adopted by the Council of State against the bishops represented the opinion of most elite groups. In fact, the Brazilian elites, with notable exceptions, had always cultivated an anti-clerical posture, and there were many who posed as free thinkers. This

---

[13] Joaquim Nabuco, *Um estadista du Império* (Rio de Janeiro, 1975), 830.

was also the attitude of the emperor, who disliked the bishop's ultramontanism. During the crisis even the church had been divided. Many priests had continued to support the rights of royal patronage. For these reasons the role of the so-called *questão religiosa* in the overthrow of the monarchy should not be overestimated.

If the state was harsh with the priests it was more generous with another discontented group, the military. Military complaints against the political system had a history going back to the 1850s. But at that time most of the military were more or less adjusted to the system of patronage. They joined political parties and were courted by politicians. A few famous generals participated in Cabinets. The Paraguayan War had exposed the weaknesses of the Brazilian army and many officers recognized the need to increase the army's efficiency. In 1874, a young officer, Sena Madureira, after travelling in Europe, presented to the minister of war some suggestions for the reorganization of the army. He proposed among other things a new system of recruitment and promotion based on merit and new types of training. His ideas were shared by many young officers. Reform-minded officers founded journals, ran for office, and publicized their complaints in the national press. Many realized that patronage was an obstacle to modernization of the army. In their struggle they developed a new esprit de corps that transcended traditional political party lines. They looked for support among other social groups equally interested in reforming the political system. More and more they came to see the traditional oligarchies as their enemy. Their resentment was expressed by their increasing interest in positivism and republican ideas.

In an attempt to satisfy their demands the government took several measures. It increased their salaries, changed the officers' system of training, making it more specialized, and approved a new conscription law in 1874. The government also altered the system of promotion in 1875, stipulating that war service count double for promotion or retirement. Most of those reforms, however, would never become reality. The recession of 1873 delayed the expected increase in wages for more than ten years. And in 1876 Sena Madureira uncovered schemes used by the elites to avoid conscription of members of their family or clientele. With the passing of time the gap between the oligarchies and the military widened. The appointment of the duque de Caxias, commander of the Brazilian army during the Paraguayan War, as prime minister in 1875, and the presence of two other popular generals (Osório and Pelotas) in the Liberal Cabinets that came after, postponed the crisis for a few years. But the conflict came to a head in the 1880s, with dramatic consequences for the monarchy.

In 1878, the Conservatives were finally ousted from power after ten years of rule. It was the debate over electoral reform that caused the fall of the Cabinet. An electoral reform intended to guarantee the opposition's representation and to curtail government intervention in elections had been approved in 1876. But the reform had been a failure. In the first election only 16 Liberals had been elected instead of the 25 stipulated by the law as the minimum. The Conservatives had won 85 per cent of the seats in the Chamber. The opposition immediately returned to the issue, proposing a system of direct elections.

At the end of ten years, the Liberals could argue that many of the reforms implemented by the Conservatives had been mere palliatives. But the reforms that seemed insufficient to the Liberal opposition were considered too radical by many Conservatives. In 1878 the Conservative party was divided over fundamental questions, just as the Liberals had been in 1868. These divisions reflected the changes occurring in society and the emergence of conflicting groups of interests that expressed themselves in both parties. Under these conditions it became increasingly difficult for any Cabinet to gain the unanimous support of its members in the Chamber. Thus, although some important Conservatives such as Paulino Soares de Sousa, Ferreira Viana, and Francisco Belisário were in favour of electoral reform, the emperor, aware of the split within the Conservatives, called the Liberals to organize the new Cabinet.

After ten years of political ostracism the Liberals were back in power with a programme that did not differ much from the programme of the Conservatives. They proposed to expand the railways and telegraph lines, to implement urban improvements in Rio de Janeiro, to subsidize immigration, to enlarge the elementary school network and to promote electoral reform. The new elections brought into the Chamber a group of young politicians – including Joaquim Nabuco, Rui Barbosa, Afonso Pena, and Rodolfo Dantas – who became important political figures in the last decades of the Empire and during the First Republic.

The debates about electoral reform showed profound rifts within the Liberal party between the moderates and the radicals. This division eventually led to the resignation of the Liberal Cabinet. The immediate cause, however, was the *revolta dos vintens* (penny riot) in Rio in January 1880 (see above). For the first time a popular movement brought down a government. It was the beginning of a new era. And it was not by chance that one of the most controversial issues during the debates over electoral reform was the vote for illiterates. The second question that triggered heated debates was the concession of political rights to non-Catholics, a measure politicians interested in pleasing immigrants were eager to see approved.

Once again, as during the debate about the bill to emancipate children born of slave mothers, or during the confrontation between church and state, there was no party cohesion. There were Conservatives for and against the electoral reform bill, and the same was true of the Liberals. The law which finally emerged was a compromise. It did not grant the suffrage to illiterates, but granted it to non-Catholics, freedmen, and naturalized foreigners. It abolished indirect elections, but it kept the income qualification. It enfranchised all males over 21 who had a net income of 200 milréis and were literate. One of the important innovations was the voter certificate, which eliminated certain kinds of manipulation in the registration process.

The reform had a curious result. By eliminating the two stages characteristic of the system of indirect elections, by fixing at 200 milréis the minimum income required, and by making literacy a prerequisite for voting it actually reduced the number of those who could vote. Before the reform 1,114,066 people were registered as voters and 240,000 as electors. With the institutionalization of direct elections the number of those who could vote went down to 145,296, about 1 per cent of the total population. At the same time political power shifted slightly from rural to urban areas, where literacy rates and income were higher.

The hope of those who had supported the reform seemed to be confirmed in 1881 when 75 Liberals and 47 Conservatives were elected. For the first time the opposition had a significant representation in the Chamber. In the years that followed, however, its positive effects became less clear. In 1884, 67 Liberals, 55 Conservatives, and 3 Republicans were elected. But in the elections that took place in 1885 under a Conservative Cabinet only 22 Liberals were elected out of a total of 125. By then, it had become clear that electoral reform had failed once again to correct electoral fraud. The encouraging results in the first elections after the reform were due to the integrity of the Cabinet that had supported it.

When the Conservatives took power they did not feel the same commitment to the reform and won the elections by an overwhelming majority. Once again, legislation had not attacked the roots of the problem and the vote continued to be controlled by money, prestige, and family connections. And when those failed, violence was still a successful strategy. Yet the politics of opinion continued to make slow progress in the wake of the debates about centralization, abolition of the Senate and the Council of State, immigration, financial policies, and abolition of slavery. Although it was still true that the support of the local leader counted for more than a candidate's platform, the emergence of a new urban constituency and the breaking down of elite consensus created the conditions for a new type of politics. In 1884 the abolitionist leader Joaquim Nabuco went from house to house in Recife competing with João Mariano for the voters' support.

The economic crisis of the 1880s brought new issues to the political debate and accentuated political conflict. The Liberals had inherited a difficult financial situation. The expansion of the railway network and telegraph lines, subsidies given to immigration, and centralized sugar mills and the assistance given to the population of the north-east, devastated by a series of droughts during the 1870s, had represented a tremendous financial burden for the state. Many loans had been made during this period and the foreign debt alone absorbed half of the total state revenues, and amortization of the debt was minimal. Government expenditures were higher than revenues in spite of the growing exports of coffee and rubber. The situation became more difficult in the early 1880s because of the falling prices of Brazilian products in the international market. The Liberal Cabinet that took power in 1881 was forced to postpone the programme of reforms to face a more urgent question: the growing deficit. It had simultaneously to attend to demands for more credit.

As was inevitable, recession brought conflicts of interest to light. Since groups tied to exports – overrepresented in the government – opposed land taxes and taxes on exports, the alternative was to raise taxes on imports. But this hurt importers and consumers. To reduce expenditure – the other alternative available – meant that important projects for the development of the economic infrastructure had to stop. The government was at a dead end. The easy way out in the short run was, as usual, to resort to loans or to issue currency. In either case this would only aggravate the deficit in the long run. Burdened by financial problems and undermined by conflicts between the radical and the conservative factions within the party, Liberal Cabinets lacked stability. Four Liberal Cabinets succeeded each other between 1882 and 1884, unable to assure a majority in the Chamber.

With the exception of electoral reform, most of the Liberal demands of 1869 were still to be met. Every new Cabinet had announced its purpose of guaranteeing the independence of the judiciary, decentralizing administration, giving more autonomy to the provinces, expanding state schools, and balancing the budget. But with the exception of the expansion of the elementary school system they failed to accomplish their programme.

This failure was due in part to the Liberals' reluctance to implement reforms that they had proposed when they were in the opposition but that could now undermine their own power. Once in power, Liberals, with the exception of the most radical, were not willing to go much further than the Conservatives. Martinho Campos, the head of the new Cabinet in 1882, said, correctly, that there was nothing more similar to a Liberal than a Conservative – or even a Republican.[14] They all had a family resemblance. Ideological differences were minor or irrelevant. His opinion was similar to the opinion of one of Machado de Assis's characters, who in an attempt to console a defeated politician tried to convince him that he could change sides. 'You were with them as one is in a ball, where it is not necessary to have the same ideas to dance the same square.'[15]

A careful analysis of the parties' composition revealed that agrarian groups (*fazendeiros*) corresponded to about half of either party while the other half was composed of bureaucrats and professionals, with bureaucrats predominating in the Conservative party and professionals in the Liberal party.[16] The predominance of bureaucrats in the Conservative party is not surprising since Conservatives were in power longer than Liberals and had more chance to control bureaucratic appointments. But considering the instability of the bureaucracy and its recruitment mostly of professionals, the two parties seem to have represented, and received support from basically the same social groups.

---

[14] Arquivo Nacional, *Organizações e programas ministeriais: regime parlamentar do império* (2nd edn, Rio de Janeiro, 1962), 196.   [15] Machado de Assis, *Esaú e Jacó* (São Paulo, 1961), 181.
[16] José Murilo de Carvalho, 'A composição social dos partidos políticos imperiais', *Cadernos DCP* (1974), 15.

The differences between Liberals and Conservatives were essentially rhetorical. Once in power Conservatives could accomplish many of the reforms proposed by the Liberals, and Liberals in power did not go much beyond the limits accepted by most Conservatives. And in both parties there were internal strifes between moderates and radicals, as we have seen. The moderate factions tended to represent the interest of the traditional agrarian elites, the others spoke for the new emerging group of interests. After the fall of the Rio Branco Cabinet this internal division contributed to great political instability. Between 1880 and the fall of the Empire, ten Cabinets were formed and dismissed; the first seven (1880–5) were Liberal. Three times the Chamber was dismissed and the government called for elections. No legislature completed its legal term during this period.

As a result of political instability the emperor was often asked to intervene in the political arena. The constant intervention of the Moderating Power generated resentments and criticisms, which brought about a crisis in the political system. Even the traditional political elites started questioning the regime. Monarchical parties did not spare criticism of the monarchical regime they were supposed to defend. The Moderating Power was the main target of their criticism. The words of an experienced politician, Ferreira Viana, in the Senate on 31 July 1884 expressed the state of mind of many of his colleagues: 'I am tired of acting in this political comedy.'

Soon the politicians were to face a difficult test. Abolitionist pressure brought the question of abolition back to the parliament. The most conservative politicians had hoped that the 1871 law would solve the problem of the abolition of slavery, since it would now gradually come to an end. But as one ardent abolitionist argued, if nothing was done to accelerate the process Brazilians would still own slaves in the third or fourth decade of the twentieth century. This does not seem to have concerned the majority of those who sat in the Chamber of Deputies. Not even when the Liberals returned to power in 1878 did attempts to discuss the problem find support. A bill presented by Nabuco was rejected by 77 votes, with only 16 deputies supporting it. And in the following year, Nabuco, who could not count on the full support of his own party, was not re-elected. Meanwhile, outside parliament the abolitionist campaign gained new allies.

Several factors explain the progress of the abolitionist campaign and the reopening of the question in parliament. Not only were there fewer people dependent on slaves but those who were became increasingly aware of the need to look for alternatives. Planters could expand their coffee plantations only if they had an adequate labour supply, but the slave population fell from 1,566,416 in 1873 to 1,346,097 in 1883, and it continued to decline, to 1,133,228 in 1885 and 723,419 in 1887. The slave population decreased more rapidly in the north-east than in the south, where it tended to concentrate, but even there it declined in relative terms. In São Paulo, slaves represented 28.2 per cent of the total population in 1854 and 8.7 per cent in 1886. And because it could not renew itself, the slave population was ageing. The recognition that sooner or later there would be no more slaves forced the coffee planters to look for alternatives. In a meeting in 1878 a few suggested the use of Chinese immigrants. But the suggestion was not welcomed by most planters, who argued in favour of using either the Brazilian free rural population or Europeans. This was the solution that finally prevailed. In São Paulo the provincial assembly approved many bills subsidizing immigration, and between 1875 and 1885, 42,000 immigrants – predominantly Italians and Portuguese – entered the province. In the next two years another 114,000 arrived. Until the beginning of the 1880s, however, most coffee planters still depended almost exclusively on slaves. In the north-east the population that fled the droughts of the 1870s crowded into the sugar-cane areas, offering cheap labour to the planters.

Changes in the system of processing sugar and coffee and improvements in the means of transportation made it easier for the planters to use free labour. Labour productivity increased and the system of labour could be rationalized. In some circumstances free labour could be even more profitable than slave labour. The process of transition from slavery to free labour was also furthered by the opening of new opportunities for investment. Banks, railways, urban improvements, insurance companies, and manufacturers offered alternatives for capital investment. And even when they did not pay more than the investment on slaves, the planter could protect himself against the uncertainties of agriculture by investing simultaneously in railways, banks and other enterprises. The need to diversify investments became obvious in the beginning of the 1880s, when coffee prices suddenly fell. Free labour could now be more attractive than slave labour because it did not require immobilization of capital. Besides, the price of slaves and the cost of maintaining them had increased in the 1870s to a point where in some areas slave labour cost more than free labour. Nevertheless, although in the late nineteenth century everything seemed to point in the direction of free labour, most planters continued to oppose the abolition of slavery. After all, not only did slaves represent capital already invested but planters were still dependent on slave labour, and were sceptical about the possibilities of replacing slaves with free labourers. Immigrant riots in the main coffee-growing areas had shown that these were men who could not be driven as slaves.

While the planters agonized about the problem of labour, abolitionists made progress, especially among the urban population, and gradually became a political force. In 1884 slavery was in fact abolished in the provinces of Ceará and Amazonas. In São Paulo, a lawyer, Antônio Bento, organized an underground system based on the support of artisans and railway workers, mostly blacks and mulattos, to help runaway slaves. And slaves were fleeing in great numbers from plantations. Slaves had developed a new consciousness, as abolitionism provided them with a new ideology and a strategy. Abolitionists had also changed public opinion and acts of insubordination, which had existed since the beginnings of slavery, had acquired a new meaning. In the past, runaway slaves had been persecuted, but now they encountered increasing support. The urban population who in the past had persecuted runaway slaves now mocked the police. Judges and lawyers enforced with energy the laws that protected slaves and were lenient in the enforcement of repressive laws. The press, both abolitionist and anti-abolitionist – although for different reasons – propagated rumours of slave rebellion: the abolitionist to stress the violence of a system that led men to such despair, the anti-abolitionist to emphasize the need for more repression. Slave owners resorted to all means to fight the abolitionist campaign. They attacked abolitionist speakers, chased abolitionist leaders away from their communities, protested in the press against a government that was unable to control social disorder, and flooded the parliament with petitions. Visiting Rio and São Paulo in 1883 the French engineer Louis Couty had the impression that the country was on the eve of a social revolution.

It was in this atmosphere of excitement on the side of the abolitionists and distress on the side of the planters that Souza Dantas, a Liberal, was called to constitute a new Cabinet in 1884. In the programme he presented to the Chamber he defined his position in regard to slave emancipation: 'Neither to retreat, nor to halt, but not to precipitate . . .

to mark the line that prudence requires and civilization recommends.' He proposed a bill to emancipate, without compensation, slaves who reached the age of 60. The bill provoked a crisis of large proportions leading in the end to the fall of the Liberal Cabinet and its replacement by the Conservatives. Once again the issue transcended party loyalties and the Chamber saw Conservatives and Liberals on both sides. Seventeen Liberals, three from São Paulo, one from Rio, six from Minas and seven from other provinces, voted against the Cabinet. The final record showed 55 votes against the Cabinet and 52 in favour. The opposition to the bill had come predominantly from the coffee areas (of the 41 deputies from those areas, only 7 voted with the Cabinet). The Chamber was dissolved and the Cabinet called for elections.

Never had the country seen a more disputed electoral campaign. Businessmen, bankers, and planters gathered in Clubes de Lavoura e Comércio (Commerce and Agriculture Associations) and accused the abolitionists of being subversive elements threatening the country with economic disorganization and political chaos. 'The abolitionists are like those who in Russia belong to the nihilist party, in Germany are socialists, and in France, communists', remarked one deputy in the Chamber. The abolitionists on their part promoted public meetings and campaigned in the press, arguing that slavery inhibited industrial development and innovation in agricultural methods. It was responsible for the instability of fortunes and the disorganization of the family. It triggered racial hatred, demoralized labour, and helped to keep the free population ignorant and poor. But above all – and this was a decisive argument – it constituted an obstacle to progress.

The election brought to parliament 67 Liberals, 55 Conservatives, and 3 Republicans. Re-elected were 38 deputies who had favoured the bill and 18 who had opposed it. It seemed that the Cabinet had won. But in fact the election had brought in many others who were against the bill, and some, like Nabuco, who had battled for it, had difficulties in being re-elected. At the beginning of the new session a deputy from São Paulo proposed a motion of no confidence in the Cabinet, and the vote ended in a tie. Three weeks later it became clear that the Cabinet could not govern. A new motion of no confidence was voted on, and this time the Cabinet received almost unanimous opposition from the Conservatives (all but three voted against), while nine Liberals voted with the opposition. The emperor called another member of the Liberal party to constitute a new Cabinet in the hope that such a change would secure for the Liberal party the majority in the Chamber. But once again it became clear that the Liberals did not have enough support to rule. Finally, in 1885, the emperor called Cotegipe, a Conservative, to form a new Cabinet. With the Conservatives back in power a bill more moderate than the original was approved and converted into law in September 1885. Under the law of 1885 60-year-old slaves were liberated, but as a form of compensation to their masters they would perform unpaid labour for another three years or until they reached the age of 65.

During the four months of debates there had been a fundamental change in the position of one of the most outspoken Conservative leaders from the coffee areas. Antônio Prado, who had systematically opposed all emancipation legislation, gave his support to the bill. He told the Chamber that indemnification was not necessary if the masters were allowed to keep their slaves until they could replace them with free labourers. Paulistas were aware of the advantages of free labour and were taking steps to solve the problem, he added. This shift in opinion had to do not only with the increasing disorganization of labour, which resulted from slaves' running away from plantations, but also with new prospects for immigration.

While some planters turned to immigrants, others decided that, to keep their slaves from running away, they had to grant them conditional freedom. They emancipated their slaves with the condition that they stay on the plantation for a number of years. In 1887 the number of manumissions rose to 40,000 in São Paulo and the provincial assembly sent a petition to parliament asking for immediate abolition. Planters had come to realize that abolition was the only way to avoid social turmoil. This had become even more clear when the army sent a petition to the princess asking to be relieved of the task of persecuting runaway slaves.

When the legislature reopened in 1888 the new prime minister, João Alfredo Correia de Oliveira, announced his intention to abolish slavery without compensation, and the bill was approved without delay and converted into law on 13 May 1888. Only nine representatives voted against it; eight were from Rio de Janeiro – an area where the coffee plantations were in decline and the planters burdened by mortgages. Contrary to what the Cassandras had predicted, the economy did not suffer from the abolition of slave labour. It recovered quickly from the inevitable disruption of the first years, when several harvests were lost. A few planters whose plantations were already in critical condition faced bankruptcy – not the nation.

Abolition did not fundamentally change labour conditions on the plantation. In the coffee areas immigrants who came to replace slaves often found that life on a plantation was not as idyllic as they had thought and moved to the cities, or left Brazil. But the constant influx of immigrants kept the labour supply which planters needed to expand their plantations. Many ex-slaves stayed on plantations and continued to perform their usual tasks, for which they were paid meagre wages. Others who moved to the cities devoted themselves to minor tasks, remaining at the bottom of the society. Abolitionists seemed to have forgotten the blacks.

As had happened with other reforms promoted during this period – the electoral reform, the reform of conscription, the reform of the National Guard – the results of abolition corresponded neither to the fears of the Conservatives nor to the hopes of the reformers. They were enough, however, to generate frustration among the monarchists, who did not forgive the government for having abolished slavery without compensation. If abolition did not inflate the Republican party membership – as some historians have suggested – it helped to undermine the monarchical system. During the campaign the emperor had been criticized by all factions. For the radical abolitionists, like Silva Jardim, the emperor's sin was not to have intervened more drastically in favour of abolition. For the anti-abolitionists his sin was to have done too much.

Abolition came in 1888 after a tumultuous popular campaign. The year after, the Republic came silently, in the form of a military coup – a conspiracy that united members of the Republican party of São Paulo and Rio with certain army officers.

Since 1870 Republicans had made progress. At the beginning they were a small group. The original nucleus of the Republican party in Rio was about 30 people. The newspaper *A República* had in its first year a circulation of 2,000 copies, but by the end of the year it was already being sold in Rio, Alagoas, Pernambuco, Rio Grande do Sul, São Paulo, and Minas Gerais. The number of issues increased rapidly and two years later it boasted a circulation of 12,000 copies. Republican clubs appeared in several provinces although they were most numerous in Rio de Janeiro, São Paulo, Rio Grande do Sul, and Minas Gerais. In 1889 79 per cent of the newspapers and 89 per cent of the clubs were located in these areas.

Almost everywhere the Republican party had recruited its supporters among the urban population. Students and professionals and a few industrialists formed the bulk of the Republican party in Rio, Minas Gerais, and Rio Grande do Sul. In São Paulo, however, most of the Republicans were plantation owners. Although it has been shown that only 30 per cent of the members of the Republican party were plantation owners, while 55 per cent were professionals and 11 per cent merchants,[17] many plantation owners also had degrees from law, medical or engineering schools and could be listed either as professionals or as plantation owners. Of the 133 delegates who attended the first important Republican meeting in São Paulo in 1873, 76 declared agriculture as their profession. Others identified themselves as businessmen, lawyers, 'capitalists', 'artists', and 'proprietors'. Many had studied at the São Paulo Law School – a centre of abolitionism and republicanism. Some belonged to the second or third generation of plantation owners, others were professionals who had bought plantations or married into plantation owners' families. Manuel Moraes Barros was a lawyer and a plantation owner. Francisco Aguiar de Barros was a public functionary, had an import house, and was also a plantation owner. Muniz de Souza was a deputy in the provincial assembly and a coffee planter. Elías Pacheco Chaves was a coffee planter, an industrialist, a magistrate responsible for orphans, a police chief, and a provincial deputy.

Because of the support it received from men of standing and property, the Republican party in São Paulo became one of the most powerful in the country. As early as 1877 it succeeded in electing three deputies to the provincial assembly. However, two of the Republicans who were elected ran as candidates for the Liberal party – a strategy the Republicans followed many times. Although it was the most important Republican nucleus in the country the Partido Republicano Paulista (PRP) had only 900 registered members in 1880. In 1884, allying themselves with the Conservatives, they succeeded in sending two deputies to the Chamber: Prudente de Morais and Campos Sales, who later, after the proclamation of the Republic, became the first two civilian presidents of Brazil. At the end of the decade there were about 50 Republican clubs in São Paulo. According to estimates for 1889 one-quarter of the electorate in São Paulo was Republican (3,593 Republicans, 6,637 Liberals, 3,957 Conservatives). The party allied several times with the Liberals or the Conservatives – depending on who was in opposition – and adopted a

---

[17] *Ibid.*

very flexible line in fundamental questions such as abolition or the conflict between church and state.

Republicans were also important in Minas Gerais, where many young politicians from traditional Conservative families, like Alvaro Botelho, or from Liberal families, like Afonso Celso, converted to republicanism. Some who had been important politicians in the monarchist parties became Republicans at the last minute. This was true of Antônio Carlos Ribeiro de Andrada, who in 1886 decided to join the Republicans, carrying with him many votes.

In general, however, Republicans received a very small number of votes in Minas and until 1887 the Mineiros had not created an organization that could unite all the clubs in the province. And in Minas as in other provinces many individuals who were Republicans did not qualify as electors. However, here as elsewhere Republican candidates often received the support of their monarchist friends and relatives. Family loyalties were often more important than political convictions. In 1888 when Republicans in Minas ran for a position in the Senate, they received one-third of the votes. It was only then that a Republican party was created in Minas. At this point they already had three deputies in the Chamber of Deputies and several in the provincial assembly. At the eve of the proclamation of the Republic, the Republican party in Minas had become as strong as the other two parties. Some politicians who had been in the Chamber for several years – João Penido, Felício dos Santos, Cesário Alvim – declared themselves Republicans. According to the polls, Republicans received 36 per cent of the votes. Oddly enough, in Rio, where the party had been originally created, the Republicans had less success. Rio was the centre of the monarchist bureaucracy and of big business. There, the Republicans recruited support mainly among the military and professionals. The rural areas were massively monarchist. Over and over again the Republican candidates who ran for elections in Rio were defeated, and Republican newspapers appeared and disappeared. One of the few Republican candidates to be elected for the provincial assembly was José do Patrocínio, a journalist and abolitionist leader, who had received the support of the Abolitionist Confederation. But in spite of its slow progress the party received one-seventh of the votes in the senatorial elections of 1887, and its candidates for the provincial assembly received one-fifth of the votes.

In Rio Grande do Sul the Republican party was organized in 1882. Here as in other provinces, Republicans founded clubs, created newspapers, and ran for election – without much success. In 1886 for the first time they succeeded in placing one candidate, Assis Brasil, in the provincial assembly. Many Republicans in Rio Grande do Sul were foreigners to whom the Republican programme had special appeal. Rio Grande do Sul's economy was mainly orientated to the internal market. The province was the main supplier of meat, jerked beef, leather, and foodstuffs. Immigrants had developed a thriving agriculture based on small properties. The peculiarity of Rio Grande do Sul's economic and social organization made its population particularly sensitive to the issues of decentralization, naturalization, and separation of church and state. This explains why in 1889 the Republicans received more votes than the Conservatives. They did not, however, stop the Liberals, who had always had great support in the province, from winning the elections by a large majority.

The similarity between the Liberal and the Republican programme constituted one of the Republicans' handicaps, not only in Rio Grande do Sul but everywhere. When the Liberals went back into power in 1878, many deserted the Republicans to join the Liberals. Even some of those who had left the Liberal party in 1868 to create the Republican party – Lafayette Rodrigues Pereira, Cristiano Otoni, Salvador de Mendonça – soon returned to their original party, and Lafayette Rodrigues Pereira even accepted the post of prime minister. When the Liberals returned to power in 1878 the only alternative left to the Republican party was to attack their former allies. With that purpose they often supported the Conservatives, who were now in opposition. Between 1878 and 1884 – a period of Liberal hegemony – Republicans did not make much progress. It was only in 1885, when the Conservatives returned to power, that they took on a new life. But while Republicans made advances in the southern provinces, their situation in other parts did not improve much. Only in Pará where the rubber boom had fed an elite that resented centralization did they get more significant support, but even there Republicans constituted only a militant minority. In most of the other provinces there were just a few Republican clubs located in the most important urban centres, gathering a dozen or so idealist professionals.

Because they favoured a federation, the Republicans had initially refused to create a national organization, and clubs kept their autonomy. Republicans from different provinces often disagreed about emancipation, although most believed that the question should be decided by the provinces themselves, rather than be solved by the central government.

In 1884, during the debates over the bill that proposed the emancipation of 60-year-old slaves, Felício dos Santos, a Republican from Minas Gerais, refused to support any bill that did not recognize the right of compensation for the slave owner. But the two other Republicans in the Chamber, who represented São Paulo, Prudente de Morais and Campos Sales, supported the bill. Republicans diverged also about strategy. The great majority followed the opinion of Quintino Bocayuva, the leader of the party in Rio, who adopted a gradualist, legalistic, and democratic line. To enlarge the electoral basis of the party through political propaganda was his programme. Others like Silva Jardim adopted a revolutionary line, cultivating the idea of a popular revolution. There were also those who wanted Republicans to conspire with the military to overthrow the government. Republicans also disagreed about the ideal form of government. The majority defended the principles of sovereignty of the people and favoured a representative form of government; a few dreamed about an authoritarian republican regime like the one suggested by Comte.

Although there were many divergences among Republicans, most seemed to agree with the principles laid down in the constitution they drafted for the state of São Paulo in 1873: provincial autonomy, a bicameral system of government with the executive being an instrument of the legislature, universal suffrage, freedom of conscience, work, the press, and education, separation of the church from the state, abolition of the privileges and titles of nobility, guarantees of private property, and abolition of the system of conscription for the National Guard. Of all those issues the most important was federation. Resentment against centralization had grown so far that in São Paulo it gave rise to a small secessionist group. One of their leaders, Martim Francisco, lamented in the provincial assembly in 1879 the flow of provincial wealth to the imperial coffers, the interference of the central government in provincial affairs, and the inadequate representation of São Paulo in the central government. 'When we want to progress', he remarked bitterly, 'the central web envelops us, our political offices are filled with people alien to our way of life, to our interests, and to our customs.' Years later, after the electoral reform of 1881, he commented that each of São Paulo's nine deputies represented almost double the entire population of Espírito Santo, a province that elected two deputies, and nearly three times the population of Amazonas, which also elected two. He complained that São Paulo contributed 20 million milréis to the national treasury each year, one-sixth of the entire national revenue, but received a mere 3 million – a sum that corresponded to customs duties collected during three months in Santos, the principal port for coffee exports. These facts seemed to Martim Francisco sufficient to justify secession.[18]

His complaints were not unfounded. In 1883 São Paulo had four senators while Minas had ten, Bahia seven, and Pernambuco and Rio de Janeiro six each. While each Paulista senator represented 326,568 inhabitants, a senator from Pernambuco represented 185,138, and the senator from Amazonas represented 80,654. The same striking differences were noticed in the Chamber, where each Paulista deputy represented 145,141, while those from Pernambuco represented 85,448 and those from Amazonas 40,327. In 1889 only 3 out of 69 senators came from São Paulo, the richest province in the country (with a fourth seat vacant). Small provinces like Sergipe, Alagoas, and Paraíba had two while Rio had five, Bahia six, Pernambuco six and Minas Gerais ten. As we have seen, while São Paulo had only nine deputies, Ceará, one of the poorest provinces, had eight, Rio de Janeiro twelve, Pernambuco thirteen, Bahia fourteen and Minas Gerais twenty. It was rare to see a Paulista from the new coffee areas – the most progressive in the country – as a member of the Council of State, which was dominated by Minas Gerais, Bahia, Rio Grande do Sul, and Rio de Janeiro; most of the Paulistas who gained such positions represented plantation owners of the Paraíba valley, where coffee plantations had been in decline since 1870. To aggravate the situation São Paulo often had politicians from other provinces as provincial presidents.

Paulistas from the western parts of the province – the most productive – felt that they did not have a fair representation in the government and they began to see federation as the only adequate form of political organization. This opinion was shared by many people living in other provinces. The Paraenses, for example, also resented the central government, and criticism against centralization had become common in Rio Grande do Sul and Pernambuco. In an agricultural congress that took place in October 1878, the sugar plantation owners of Pernambuco complained bitterly about the government's emission bank which had loaned 25,000 contos to the south-central provinces of Rio de Janeiro, São Paulo, Espírito Santo, and Minas Gerais in the 1870s. To these

---

[18] Tácito de Almeida, *O movimento de 1887* (São Paulo, 1934); Emília Viotti da Costa, *Da monarquia à República. Momentos decisivos* (São Paulo, 1977), 313–16.

provinces, they said, went all the favours. 'While the planter in those provinces, protected by the government, with the advantage of credit, enjoys all comfort and displays an Asiatic luxury . . . the planters of the north are, with few exceptions, obliged to restrict themselves to their subsistence', said one of them.[19] Everywhere, for different reasons, there was an increasing awareness that centralization was a source of favouritism and an obstacle to development and progress. Federalism became the banner of all those who felt constrained by the government and resented the political oligarchies that perpetuated themselves in power through a system of patronage and clientele and through the monopoly of positions in the Senate and the Council of State. In 1885 a proposition signed by 39 Liberal deputies suggested that the electorate decide whether the constitution should be amended to give the country a federalist system. The proposed amendment never became law, and only with the proclamation of the Republic was a federal system adopted.

Federalism became one of the principal goals of the Republicans in their campaign against the monarchical system. From the moment the Conservatives took power in 1885 the Republicans intensified their campaign, trying to enlarge their bases and define new strategies. At a congress held in São Paulo in May 1888, revolutionary strategy was repudiated and the 'evolutionist' strategy was officially sanctioned through the appointment of Quintino Bocayuva as national leader of the party. This event generated a crisis within the party. Silva Jardim published a manifesto on 28 May violently attacking the moderate faction. But his protest had little effect. In the end the pacific faction prevailed. One year later, however, the monarchy was overthrown by a military coup.

By 1887 the leadership of the Republican party had begun to consider the possibility of asking the military for help. Rangel Pestana, a member of the Republican party in São Paulo, suggested to the Permanent Committee of the party that it join together with the military in order to carry out a coup. When he attended the national party congress in Rio he continued to express this point of view, and despite the disapproval of the committee, contacted certain individuals in the military, including Sena Madureira, Serzedelo Carreia, and the visconde de Pelotas. This tactic was favoured by Francisco Glicério, another Republican leader

---

[19] *Trabalhos do Congresso agrícola do Recife. Outubro do 1878. Sociedade Auxiliadora da Agricultura de Pernambuco. Edição facsimilar comemorativa do primeiro centenário 1878–1978* (Fundação Estadual de Planejamento Agrícola de Pernambuco, Recife, 1978), 17, 92, 114, 139, 147, 183.

from São Paulo, who in March 1888 wrote to Bocayuva insisting that he make contacts with the military. Américo Werneck, a leader of the party in Rio de Janeiro, also argued that the triumph of the Republican revolution would come about only through the use of military force. At the same time, the Republican high command in Rio Grande do Sul came out in favour of a militarist solution.

Once they agreed on the importance of obtaining military support, the Republicans started courting the army in several ways. Republican leaders contacted sympathetic officers, and the Republican press gave coverage to conflicts between the army and the government, never missing an opportunity to turn the military against the monarchy, while assuring them of Republican support.

Republicans found great receptivity in the army, where dissatisfaction was rampant. The officers' increasing alienation from the monarchical system coincided with their declining participation in the government. During the nine years of the First Empire (1822–31) twelve military men had seats in the Senate and five in the Council of State. Dom Pedro had appointed four officers to the Senate in the 1840s and two in the 1850s, but in the following 30 years of his reign he appointed only two. Military representation in the Council of State had also decreased. At the time of the proclamation of the Republic there was no military representation in the Council of State. Military representation in the cabinets and in the Chamber had also declined. More importantly, between 1881 and 1889 only civilians had been appointed as ministers of war.

During Cotegipe's Conservative Cabinet (1885–8) there had been several conflicts between military and civilians, conflicts which both Liberals and Republicans had exacerbated in their attempts to undermine the prestige of the Conservatives. Courted by politicians and by the press, the military had acquired an inflated sense of its importance. In 1886 when Cotegipe punished two officers (Cunha Matos and Sena Madureira) who, disregarding the government's prohibitions, had used the press to defend themselves against charges made by government officials, the incident had loud repercussions and many officers expressed solidarity with their colleagues. Marshal Deodoro da Fonseca, disobeying orders from the minister of war, refused to punish Sena Madureira who was under his command. Fonseca resigned from his post in Rio Grande do Sul and moved to Rio where he became the centre of attention. In the Senate, the visconde de Pelotas (Rio Grande do Sul), an experienced politician and a devoted and prestigious officer, warned the government of the imminent risk of a military uprising. The government, however, pursued its policies of disciplining disobedient officers, provoking even more discontent in the army. In 1887 the Military Club, which became the place of gathering of discontented officers, was created. The military became increasingly disillusioned with the political system. Expressing this disillusionment Floriano Peixoto, who later became president of the new Republic, writing to General Neiva in July 1887 commented: 'Our country is in an advanced state of moral corruption and needs a military dictatorship to cleanse it.'[20]

The conflict with the army contributed to the fall of Cotegipe who was replaced by João Alfredo, another Conservative, in March 1888. The new Cabinet, however, which abolished slavery in May, did not last long. And it was in an atmosphere of military unrest and Republican agitation that Ouro Preto, a Liberal, was called in June 1889 to form a Cabinet. Ouro Preto told the emperor that the only way to confront the Republican propaganda was to prove that the monarchical system could satisfy their demands and carry out their promises. In order to achieve this goal, the new minister devised a programme of political, economic and social reforms. But the programme he presented at the congressional session of 11 June was a slightly modified version of the programme presented twenty years earlier by the Liberal party. Ouro Preto proposed the limitation of the senator's term; the reduction of the Council of State to a mere administrative body; election of municipal authorities; nomination of provincial presidents and vice presidents from a list selected by the electors; and universal suffrage. He also suggested that freedom of worship be granted to all, and he proposed that the system of education be reformed to give private initiative more freedom. With regard to economic questions he recommended the reduction of export duties, the enactment of a law facilitating acquisition of land, the development of rapid means of transportation, the amortization of the foreign debt, the achievement of a balanced federal budget and the creation of credit institutions to issue paper currency. He did not include, however, any provision for adopting a federal system, which had been one of the crucial demands of the critics of the monarchy.

When the prime minister presented his proposal to the Chamber, Pedro Luís Soares de Sousa, a deputy from Rio de Janeiro, could not repress an exclamation which certainly expressed the feelings of most of

[20] J. F. Oliveira Vianna, *O ocaso do império* (São Paulo, 1925), 137.

those present: 'It is the beginning of the Republic', he said. Ouro Preto responded, 'No, it is the defeat of the Republic.' He was wrong – a few months later the monarchy was overthrown.

Ouro Preto's programme did not satisfy the radicals and irritated the Conservatives. The Conservatives proposed a motion of no confidence, which was approved by a vote of 79 to 20. A few days later, on 17 June, the Chamber was dissolved and the government called for elections. The situation became increasingly tense. Ouro Preto took measures that offended some important figures in the army. The nomination of Silveira Martins for the presidency of Rio Grande do Sul alienated Marshal Deodoro da Fonseca who had a history of personal conflicts with Martins. And the appointment of Cunha Matos to a post in Mato Grosso also provoked discontent. In late October there were growing rumours that the government might disband or exile insubordinate garrisons to remote areas of the country.

The Republicans took advantage of the irritation among military ranks. On 11 November, a few days before the Chamber was supposed to meet, Rui Barbosa, Benjamin Constant, Aristides Lobo, Bocayuva, Glicério and Colonel Solon met with Marshal Fonseca to convince him to take the initiative of overthrowing the monarchy. The old man still hesitated. He had always been loyal to the emperor and in spite of his irritation at the Cabinet he did not seem willing to support a military coup which would lead to the fall of the monarchy. On 15 November, however, when he left his house to force Ouro Preto to resign he met a stubborn minister decided to resist at all cost. The impasse did not last long. A few hours later a group of Republicans announced to the astonished nation the fall of the monarchy and the installation of the Republic. The royal family was sent into exile. No one rose to defend the monarchy.

The proclamation of the Republic had resulted from the concerted action of three groups: a military faction (representing at the most one-fifth of the army), plantation owners from the west of São Paulo, and members of the urban middle classes. They had been indirectly aided in the attainment of their goal by the declining prestige of the monarchy. Although the 'revolutionaries' were momentarily united by their republican ideal, profound disagreements among them would surface during their first attempts to organize the new regime. In the first years of the Republic, latent contradictions exploded into conflicts which contributed to the instability of the new regime.

CONCLUSION

1889 did not mark a significant break in Brazilian history. The country continued to depend as it always had on the export of agrarian products to the international market and on foreign investments. Power continued in the hands of planters and merchants and their allies. Universal suffrage did not increase the electorate much, since the literacy requirement deprived most of the Brazilian population of the right to vote. The system of patronage remained intact and oligarchical groups continued to control the nation to the exclusion of the masses. Universal suffrage, adoption of a federal system, abolition of tenure for senators, abolition of the Council of State and of the Moderating Power, separation of the church from the state – all those goals the reformers had battled for – did not have after all the miraculous effects they had expected. The main accomplishment of the Republic was to bring to power a new oligarchy of coffee planters and their clients who promoted only those institutional changes that were necessary to satisfy their own needs. For all the other social groups that had hoped that the Republic would represent a break with the past, 15 November was a *journée des dupes*.

21

BRAZIL: THE SOCIAL AND POLITICAL STRUCTURE OF THE FIRST REPUBLIC, 1889–1930*

DEMOGRAPHIC AND SOCIAL CHANGE

At the time of the declaration of the Republic in 1889, Brazil was a country with a low population density, and there were vast areas in the north and the west which were virtually empty or only sparsely populated. Although these generalizations remain true for the entire period of the First Republic (1889–1930), there was nevertheless considerable demographic growth. Between 1890 and 1920 the population almost doubled, increasing from 14.3 million to 27.0 million. This was due to a process of natural growth, combined with mass European immigration in the centre-south. However, the age structure displays a feature characteristic of underdeveloped countries: a very broad base tapering sharply to a narrow peak, the result of high birth rate, coupled with high rates of general and especially infant mortality. The under twenties constituted 51 per cent and 56 per cent of the population in 1890 and 1920 respectively. The forty to fifty age group was almost three times larger than that of the over sixties in 1890, and over three times larger in 1920. The over sixties represented 4.7 per cent and 4 per cent of the population in these years. Estimates for the period between 1920 and 1940 suggest an average life expectancy of only 36–7 years; for the 1900–20 period it was even lower.[1]

In the centre-south where immigration played a major role in population growth and in the development of social stratification, São Paulo was the state which absorbed the majority of the immigrants: 51.9 per cent of the 304,054 immigrants who entered the country between

---

* Translated from the Portuguese by Dr David Brookshaw; translation revised by the Editor.
[1] Aníbal Vilanova Villela and Wilson Suzigan, *Política do govêrno e crescimento da economia brasileira, 1889–1945* (Rio de Janeiro, 1973), 256.

1888 and 1890, 64.9 per cent of the 1,129,315 in the period from 1891 to 1900, and 58.3 per cent of the 1,469,095 in the period from 1901 to 1920. Immigration to the state of São Paulo was the result of government planning, the main objective of which was to supply labour to the coffee sector, the dynamic centre of economic growth in the decades immediately before and after the abolition of slavery (1888). After the failure of experiments with sharecropping the coffee bourgeoisie devised a system of production based on the *colonato*. The landowner would contract a family of *colonos* and pay them an annual salary for tending his coffee plantations. The harvest itself was paid for separately and could apply to any area of agricultural productivity on the estate. There was consequently no necessary link between the coffee plantation tended by a family and the harvesting of its crop. Apart from this, there was a certain amount of part-time work, usually to do with the upkeep of premises and transportation, which was paid on a daily basis and amounted to very little. The colonists were housed and provided with plots of land on which to grow subsistence crops, the excess from which they could sell in the local markets. Occasionally, they were allowed to keep one or two head of cattle, in deep valleys which were susceptible to frost and were therefore not suitable for coffee cultivation. The *colono* system combined a capitalist system of production with a non-capitalist system of renting land. This was particularly so in the case of the type of contractual agreement which was common practice on new coffee plantations, and which in fact was preferred by immigrants. The colonist and his family would plant the coffee and tend the plantation for a period of four to six years, as the coffee bushes usually began to yield a small crop in the fourth year. The *colonos* received practically no monetary payment, but were able to dedicate themselves to the production of food crops, especially corn and beans, between the rows of new coffee bushes. They also usually had a right to the first coffee crop. The production of food crops was not only for consumption by the family but also for sale locally, and indeed there is evidence that the latter was a particularly important factor.

The question of social mobility in rural São Paulo is still controversial. One study of the period between 1871 and 1914 takes the view that opportunities for *colonos* to become smallholders or owners of medium-sized properties were very limited. Access to land required influence, although the price of land was not high, and prospective buyers needed resources which were relatively inaccessible in order to make the land profitable. According to this study, in 1905 a mere 6 per cent at the most of rural landowners were Italian.[2] Another study of a longer period (1886–1934) arrives at a different conclusion, although it does not deny the difficulties and pressures experienced by immigrants. According to this study, a significant proportion of immigrant workers who settled in rural areas were socially mobile, and over the years came to constitute an important sector of small and medium landholders, particularly in western São Paulo, the most dynamic area of the state. This process would have resulted basically from the system of colonization which permitted colonists to save, and which even stimulated some landowners to sell off parts of their estate in order to make new investments elsewhere. The actual frequency of this phenomenon may be debatable but there is no doubt as to its significance. A survey carried out by the Secretariat for Agriculture of the state of São Paulo in 1923, covering the coffee producing municipalities, showed that 37.6 per cent of the rural properties counted belonged to Italians, Spaniards or Portuguese who together represented 87 per cent of the total number of immigrants arriving in São Paulo between 1886 and 1923. Natives of these three countries owned 24.2 per cent of the total number of coffee bushes inspected, with an average of 15,700 productive bushes per estate.[3] Clearly these were small landholders since over half the estates in São Paulo had more than 100,000 bushes and some, more than a million.

Inevitably, the question arises as to why the São Paulo agrarian-mercantile bourgeoisie preferred immigrant, especially Italian, workers to alternative sources of labour. As far as the ex-slaves are concerned, it should be remembered that labour relations had deteriorated during the last years of the slave regime. The growing frequency with which slaves had either fled or revolted presented considerable problems when it came to considering how to transform a slave labour force into wage earners. As immigrant workers arrived on the coffee plantations and problems with the slave population increased, landowners became more and more convinced of the superior quality of immigrant labour. The black population which remained in rural São Paulo after abolition generally speaking followed one of two courses: either it settled in isolated areas where it became involved in subsistence agriculture, or it was relegated on the coffee plantations to the most menial forms of labour not directly

---

[2] Michael M. Hall, 'The origins of mass immigration in Brazil, 1871–1914' (PhD thesis, Columbia University, 1969).
[3] Thomas H. Holloway, *Immigrants on the land. Coffee and society in São Paulo, 1886–1934* (Chapel Hill, NC, 1980).

linked to production. As for the poor free rural workers, they were already primarily engaged in subsistence agriculture and therefore able to maintain a relative degree of independence. To discipline this sector of the population to the labour requirements of the plantation was a problem which landowners preferred to avoid, given the availability of other forms of labour. Finally, various factors explain why immigrant, particularly Italian, workers were preferred over Brazilian labour drawn from other states: the prejudice of landowners against the native Brazilian work force, the existence of powerful interest groups in Italy prepared to provide cheap labour in reasonable quantity, the relatively low cost of international transport compared to inter-regional transport within Brazil, and the opposition of large interest groups to internal labour migration. It should also be stressed that, although in the north-east in particular there was labour to spare, it was not sufficient at the time to cater for the needs of the São Paulo coffee planters, who were interested in the speedy provision of labour on a large scale. Moreover, the rubber boom in the north between 1880 and 1912 absorbed much of the excess labour available in the north-east.

Variations in the level of immigration depended on international conditions, conditions in the country of origin, and above all on the state of the Brazilian coffee economy. The ten years from 1890 to 1900 constitute the period of heaviest immigration both in absolute and relative terms. The prolonged Italian economic crisis which lasted from the mid 1880s to the mid 1890s stimulated emigration, particularly from the north of the country. And while Argentina and the United States experienced a period of recession after 1890, Brazil entered a boom period thanks to coffee, at a time when it urgently needed to substitute its slave labour force and to increase its workforce generally. Immigrants were attracted for the most part by the Brazilian government's programme of assisted passages. Almost 80 per cent of the immigrants who entered the state of São Paulo between 1890 and 1900 had their transport paid in this way. The final years of the decade, on the other hand, witnessed a reversal of this trend. Brazil entered a period of overproduction and crisis in the coffee economy. In 1902 the government embarked on policies designed to limit the creation of new coffee plantations in São Paulo. At the same time, the Italian government, through the Prinetti Decree, prohibited further subsidized immigration to Brazil, in response to the continual complaints made by Italian citizens about living conditions on the plantations in São Paulo. The years 1903 and 1904 saw a negative balance in net immigration to the state of São Paulo. Immigration picked up once more when the Brazilian economy recovered and reached a peak in the years immediately before the first world war. In 1913, 116,640 foreigners entered the country as a whole, a figure equal to the best years of the 1890–1900 decade. However, the war interrupted the flow of immigrants and 1918 saw only 10,772 new arrivals. When immigration increased again during the 1920s it was no longer linked to the fluctuations of the coffee economy. Direct immigration to the large cities rapidly became the norm. In the rural areas of São Paulo and the south of the country, there were by now far more possibilities for small farmers dedicated to the production of food crops.

For the entire period from 1884 to 1933, Italians (1.4 million), Portuguese (1.1 million) and Spaniards (577,000) constituted the three main immigrant groups. As we have seen, the Italians made mainly for the state of São Paulo, and to a lesser extent for the areas of colonization in the south. Between 1884 and 1903, they were by far the largest foreign group to enter the country. From 1903, the number of Italian arrivals decreased considerably, falling to third place in all the subsequent decades. Portuguese immigration was the most stable during the period under consideration, occupying first place during the ten years from 1904 to 1913, and in subsequent periods. The Portuguese generally settled in the cities, where they occupied positions in commerce and in service industries. In 1920, 39.8 per cent of the total number of Portuguese in Brazil resided in Rio de Janeiro, where they constituted the largest foreign group. They were also predominant in the port of Santos, in contrast to their position in São Paulo. The Spaniards were more or less evenly distributed throughout the state of São Paulo. In the port of Santos they formed, after the Portuguese, the second largest foreign group.

After the Italians, Portuguese and Spanish, next in importance were the Germans and Japanese. German immigration was particularly significant in the south and was linked initially to the establishment of small farms. The Germans were not so easily assimilated as the Portuguese, Italians or Spaniards, and as late as the 1930s they formed a distinct cultural community – a factor which was to be a source of anxiety for the Vargas government. As for the Japanese, they began to arrive in Brazil in 1908, under an agreement between the state of São Paulo and Japanese immigration companies, which offered assisted passages and subsidies to immigrants. At first, they were brought in as agricultural workers, but from 1912 the state government began to provide them with land. Up until the mid 1920s Japanese immigration was relatively insignificant. However, in the period between 1924 and 1933, it became the second largest migratory current, totalling some 110,000 people. The Japanese settled mainly in the state of São Paulo where they became small and medium-sized landholders involved in food production.

The north and north-east of the country attracted few immigrants: there was little economic growth (apart from the rubber boom) and no shortage of labour. The ending of the slave system brought, for the most part, a reinforcement of the existing conditions. In the sugar plantation belt, the problem of wage labour was resolved by resorting to a practice which dated from the colonial period, and which involved the establishment of small landholders who were dependent on the large landed proprietor. Placed on small plots of land on which they cultivated subsistence crops, the workers were summoned for labour in the cane plantations whenever required. Labour was usually unremunerated or paid at a scandalously low rate. A similar system of relations was established between small landholders and cattle raisers. Although independent medium-sized estates existed in the north-east, especially in the sugar sector, the dominant system of social relations served to obstruct the formation of a free labour market and the development of a peasant economy.

In the far south, cattle raising on the *latifundia* situated in the south-western part of Rio Grande do Sul, producing jerked beef, which was consumed mainly by the low income groups in the urban centres of the centre-south and north-east, required only a small labour force and did not attract immigrants. Large numbers of Germans and Italians, however, settled in other parts of the state, drawn by the possibility of purchasing land. In the highland zone, they developed the cultivation of wheat and rice, under a combined regime of subsistence and commercial agriculture, most of their produce finding its market in the state of São Paulo. Rio Grande do Sul was therefore unique in that it developed an economy geared to the domestic market, and because it gave rise to a significant nucleus of independent, medium-sized, landed proprietors.

While large numbers of European immigrants were flooding into the centre-south during the last decades of the nineteenth century, there was an important internal migratory movement between the north-east and the north. The effect of this movement on the social structure was, however, relatively limited. From the 1870s, the growth of activities associated with the extraction of rubber in the Amazon basin attracted migrants from the north-east. The periods of drought which devastated the north-east during the 1870s and 1880s were also a major contributing factor in the displacement of the population. According to a rough estimate some 160,000 people were drawn to the Amazon between 1890 and 1900, and throughout the whole period from 1872 to 1920, Ceará, the north-eastern state closest to the Amazon region, presented a negative balance in terms of migration. Nevertheless, around 1912, faced with competition from rubber produced in the British and Dutch colonies in Asia, Brazilian production collapsed, and this had a rapid effect on internal migration. The rubber 'boom' stimulated the growth of some cities and favoured social mobility among certain urban groups. However, the migration of workers did not give rise to any significant social transformation in the region. The labour force, scattered throughout the rain forest area, was subject to extreme exploitation and trapped in various forms of debt bondage which prevented social change.

Internal migration to, and within, the centre-south during the late nineteenth century, and indeed before 1920, was limited. The urban areas and, in particular, the capital of the Republic (the Federal District) were important focal points for migration. And it is worth noting that Minas Gerais consistently presented a negative balance in terms of migration from 1890 onwards, a significant portion of the population making for the agricultural belt of São Paulo and for Rio de Janeiro. The 'spontaneous' displacement of the black population in the years immediately following the abolition of slavery is a subject which has caused some controversy. It seems likely that abolition caused a fairly large number of ex-slaves from the state of São Paulo to return to the north-east from where they had been sold during the years of the internal slave trade. Migration into the capital of the state of São Paulo was not particularly significant. On the other hand, the Federal District would seem to have received a large number of ex-slaves who had abandoned the coffee plantations of the interior of the state of Rio de Janeiro, then in open decline. Between 1890 and 1900, the net total of internal migrants of Brazilian origin entering the capital of the Republic reached a figure of 85,547, while during the same period the state of Rio presented a negative balance in terms of migration of 84,280.

From the early 1920s, the conditions which had limited internal migration in the centre-south during the phase of its economic expansion began to change. Migrants from Minas and the north-east entered the state of São Paulo in growing numbers. In 1928, internal migrants surpassed immigrants, and this was to be the case consistently from 1934. Although the rate of immigration was still considerable during the 1930s, the features of migratory movement would alter definitively, with migrants of Brazilian origin fulfilling a major role in the provision of labour for both the rural areas of the centre-south and industry then in a phase of expansion. This tendency was reinforced on the international level by the world crisis of 1929, and on the national level by measures taken to 'nationalize' the labour force and to establish a quota system for the entry of immigrants.

Many immigrants settled directly in the cities, or were later responsible to a considerable extent for the internal migration from the rural to the urban areas. This migratory current was motivated on the one hand by discontent with labour conditions in rural São Paulo, especially during periods of crisis in the coffee sector, and on the other hand by the opportunities for work in industrial and artisan activities which the cities provided. It was no coincidence that between 1890 and 1900, the decade which saw the greatest influx of foreigners, the state capital of São Paulo grew at a rate of 14 per cent per annum, its population increasing from 64,934 to 239,820 inhabitants. São Paulo became an 'Italian city', in which, by 1893, foreigners constituted 54.6 per cent of the total population. Though foreigners were few in the field of public administration and in the liberal professions, they accounted for 79 per cent of the total work force in the manufacturing industries and 71.6 per cent of those in commerce. In Rio de Janeiro, the federal capital, the immigrant contribution was also significant. In 1890 immigrants already accounted for 39 per cent of the industrial work force and 51 per cent of those involved in commerce.

Throughout the period of the First Republic, Brazil remained a predominantly rural country. In 1920, 69.7 per cent of the working population was involved in agriculture, 13.8 per cent in industry, and 16.5 per cent in the service sector. In the same year, there were 74 cities with more than 20,000 inhabitants, the total urban population constituting 16.6 per cent of the total population (some 4,500,000 people). Broken down by region, cities in 1920 accounted for 15.6 per cent of the population in the north, 10.1 per cent in the north-east, 14.5 per cent in the east, 29.2 per cent in the state of São Paulo, 14.6 per cent in the south, and 2.8 per cent in the centre-west. On the other hand, the largest cities – the state capitals – experienced consistent growth between 1890 and 1920. During the ten-year period from 1890 to 1900, São Paulo, which was beginning its spectacular growth, and Belém, the centre for the export of rubber, grew at a rate of 6.8 per cent per annum, and the overall growth rate of state capitals reached 4.3 per cent. Between 1900 and 1920, the rate of growth of state capitals dropped to 2.7 per cent, although São Paulo continued to grow rapidly (albeit at a lower rate of 4.5 per cent) and other cities like Porto Alegre (Rio Grande do Sul) increased in importance.

From the beginning of the century, the urban network tended consistently towards a process of concentration. Urbanization increased in absolute terms, but the major cities expanded much more rapidly than medium or small urban centres. This tendency would become more acute in the period between 1920 and 1940. In 1920, however, Brazil had only two major cities of more than 500,000 inhabitants: the Federal District with a population of 1,150,000 and São Paulo with 570,000.

POLITICAL AND SOCIAL STRUCTURES

The establishment and consolidation of the Brazilian Empire in the first half of the nineteenth century was the product of a coalition between high-ranking bureaucrats, especially magistrates, sectors of the rural landowning class, mainly in Rio de Janeiro but to a lesser extent in Bahia and Pernambuco, and merchants in the principal cities who were anxious to contain urban social and political agitation. In the conflict over centralization and provincial autonomy, which characterized the early decades of the Empire, there was a clear victory for increasing political and administrative centralization. Supported by the coffee *fazendeiros* of Rio de Janeiro, the bureaucrats, educated within the tradition of Portuguese absolutism, were the main theoreticians and executors of centralization.

Opposition to the centralized regime of the monarchy reappeared in the later decades of the nineteenth century. The social classes which emerged in new areas of economic expansion, particularly the coffee bourgeoisie of São Paulo, began to argue in favour of a federal republic, with a measure of provincial autonomy sufficient for them to be able to levy taxes, formulate their own immigration programme, create their own military force, and contract foreign loans. What united opponents of the monarchy in the Republican party in São Paulo was the struggle for a federal structure, political and administrative decentralization; not, as has sometimes been argued, the issue of the abolition of slavery. After the triumph of the Republic, or more precisely of those regional class interests responsible for the formation of the Republic, the central government lost a considerable degree of power to the provinces, now called states, and their elected presidents.

As the dominant classes in each state became more articulate and those sectors, such as the judiciary, who were not linked to economic activity began to lose their influence in the machinery of state, there occurred a greater convergence between the dominant class and the political and administrative elite. The latter became more attached to their own regions, and as their geographical base shrank, they became more representative. In their turn, the interests of the dominant classes lay entirely within the state political framework as is shown quite clearly in the constitution of political parties which were originally conceived of as state organizations and so remained in their basic characteristic throughout the First Republic. The so-called national parties, such as the Federal Republican party or the Conservative Republican party, never became more than ephemeral attempts to organize a federation of state oligarchies. Even in the late 1920s, the attempt to launch a national Democratic party based on the opposition Democratic parties at state level was no exception to the rule.

Undoubtedly, the emphasis on political regionalization and decentralization served well-defined interests. The new institutional framework created the conditions which enabled the bourgeoisie of São Paulo to gain strength and consolidate its position within the state, and the nation. At the same time regionalism contained the seeds of its own destruction in that neither the state as a whole nor the ruling classes were able to legitimize themselves as representatives of the general interests of the nation.

Presented in simple terms, the political system of the First Republic in Brazil is usually described as being founded on three nuclei of power. At the base of the pyramid were the local potentates, the so-called *coronéis*, who controlled the rural population of a given area. At an intermediate level were the state oligarchies which were constituted to a greater or lesser extent by 'federations of *coronéis*', whose functions differed institutionally from those of the *coronéis* when taken in isolation. At the pinnacle of the power structure was the federal government, which was the product of an alliance between the oligarchies of the most important states, and was therefore the expression of a 'federation of oligarchies'. A feature of the whole system was the low level of political participation by the mass of the population. Furthermore, relations between social classes and groupings were expressed vertically, in accordance with the hierarchy implied by clientalistic relationships, and not horizontally as an expression of opposing class interests. Much attention has been given to the strategic role of the state oligarchies in oiling the wheels of government. While the *coronéis* basically furnished votes, they depended on the influence of the state oligarchies in government for obtaining a whole series of favours, including jobs and investments, which in turn were the basis of their power over the local population. On the other hand, the relationship between the state oligarchies and central government has been interpreted as being one of equality, with much emphasis being laid on the low degree of institutionalization at the national level. The political machinery at the state level determined the choice of the president of the Republic. In turn, the federal government did its utmost to assure the supremacy of the dominant factions at state level by not encouraging political dissidence.

There is no doubt a great deal of truth in this picture, but given the degree of generalization, it inevitably fails to take fully into account all the characteristics of the political system. The relationship between the *coronéis* and the population under their control, as well as that between *coronéis*, the state oligarchy and the federal government, varied considerably from region to region. The socio-economic characteristics of the country were by no means homogeneous. At one extreme was the state of São Paulo, at the other were the states of the north and north-east, not to mention the vast areas of sparse population. While São Paulo was entering a phase of capitalist development characterized by an intense level of immigration, the northern and north-eastern states, where pre-capitalistic relationships predominated, experienced a much lower level of growth, when not actually stagnating or even in recession. Paternalism coupled with violence, above all in relation to the rural population, existed throughout the country as two sides of the same coin, but the use of these two instruments of domination varied in style, frequency and degree of intensity.

Social and political life were dominated throughout the First Republic by clientalistic relationships, even in the major urban centres such as Rio de Janeiro and São Paulo. However, they were particularly strong in rural areas, for it was here that certain ideal conditions ensured the maintenance of social relationships based on the unequal exchange of favours between men situated at opposite ends of the social scale. Productive resources were controlled by a tiny minority; there was an almost total absence of public or private social welfare; and the generally precarious conditions for survival did not allow the dominated classes to pursue any course other than individually to seek the protection of the most powerful elements. Protection, in the form of land, financial assistance or employment, was exchanged for a guarantee of loyalty which, depending on individual cases, meant being prepared to defend the *coronel* physically, or obey his wishes at the ballot box.

A particularly effective instrument of power for the *coronéis* was the family structure known as the *parentela*, which was typical of the north-east. The *parentela* included the extended family, consisting of relatives by marriage, both vertical and collateral, as well as relations by kinship which were the result of ritual, such as godparents, or of adoption. However, not all family members were included in the *parentela* as this was based on loyalty to a patriarch.[4] For this reason, certain individuals linked to one another by blood or marriage were not part of a *parentela* although they were related. It is also worth noting that family norms did not necessarily operate when it came to choosing a new head of a *parentela*. Descendants in the vertical line of a patriarch could be ignored in favour of collateral relatives or relatives by marriage.

Institutionally, the Republic strengthened the power of the *coronéis*, in that the decentralization gave greater power to the *municípios* (counties), which were the smallest political and administrative units in each state. *Municípios* not only gained greater nominal autonomy, but also greater control over revenue. A comparison between the years 1868–9 and 1910 is revealing: in the former, the imperial government received 80.8 per cent of all revenue, the provinces 16.7 per cent and the municipalities 2.5 per cent; in the latter, the central government received 59.9 per cent of the total revenue, the states 21.5 per cent and the municipalities 18.6 per cent. Apart from this, the widening of the suffrage written into the constitution of 1891 strengthened the *coronéis* who, at the local level, gained greater bargaining power.[5] At the same time, however, the strengthening of the power of the states considerably limited the action

---

[4] See Linda Lewin, 'Some historical implications of kinship organization for family-based politics in the Brazilian northeast', *Comparative Studies in Society and History*, 21/2 (April 1979).
[5] Joseph L. Love, 'Political participation in Brazil, 1881–1969', *Luso-Brazilian Review*, 7/2 (1970), 7.

of the *coronéis*, or at least provided a focal point for tension between them and the state oligarchies.

At this point it is important to make some distinctions. In the states of the north and north-east, there were two main political patterns. In certain cases, a powerful family oligarchy would take over the machinery of government, thus minimizing the distinction between local *coronéis* and the state oligarchy. In others, groups representing urban interests, which included many professional politicians, or rural areas linked to the export trade, took power. Their position was, however, fragile and the so-called '*coronéis* of the interior' maintained a considerable degree of autonomy. This occurred throughout a vast region on both sides of the river São Francisco, where whole 'nations of *coronéis*' flourished. With the support of their own private armies, they became real warlords within their area of influence. Moreover, the development of internal trade in states like Bahia, Goiás, Pernambuco, Piauí, and Maranhão encouraged alliances between *coronéis* which crossed state boundaries. As a general rule, *coronéis* preferred to maintain maximum autonomy within their area, and did not object to the fact that the state capitals and coastal zones received a proportionately larger share of state revenue. Furthermore, they reacted against attempts to integrate them into parties or other organizations which might contribute towards the elimination of family feuds and banditry.

In these states, which did not form part of the powerful constellation centred on São Paulo, Minas Gerais and Rio Grande do Sul, the federal government's role was to a far greater extent one of arbitration, in which sometimes it lent its support to the local political oligarchy and sometimes negotiated directly with the *coronéis*. A case in point is the state of Bahia, which was characterized by the autonomy of the *coronéis* in the interior and by the weakness of the parties and of the political institutions of the oligarchy. Military backing from the federal government during the presidency of Marshal Hermes da Fonseca (1910–14) was decisive in the 1912 election for state president, which brought to power J. J. Seabra, a politician whose support came from the urban area of Salvador, the state capital. For several years, Seabra succeeded in controlling the power of the *coronéis* by means of a series of political reforms. Some years later in 1920 during a succeeding administration, the *coronéis* of the interior revolted against the state government, defeated its military forces in various clashes, and threatened to take Salvador itself. The president of the Republic arbitrated in the dispute, through the military commander of Bahia. Arbitration demonstrated the power of the *coronéis*.

The most famous of these, Horácio de Matos, obtained the right to keep his arms and munitions, as well as possession of twelve *municípios* which he held; authorities installed by him were recognized by the federal government. During the 1920s, in the case of Bahia, the traditional pattern by which the governor served as an intermediary between the *coronéis* and the president of the Republic ended once and for all. The latter became an arbitrator in local and regional politics. The *coronéis* of the interior gained greater autonomy vis-à-vis the state government and Bahia became fragmented into a number of states within a state. The result was a brand of federalism far removed from the model set out in the constitution of 1891.

In contrast, in the more developed states, the *coronéis* lacked autonomy, and associated themselves with wider structures such as the dominant political party and the state political machine. Here the dominant element in the whole network of client relationships was the state government, which distributed land, loans and public office. The difference was not without importance. On the surface, the state was merely a *coronel* on a grand scale, which propped up a system of domination similar to that in the north-east. However, the truth was that the relationship between society as a whole and the state was beginning to change. The state was increasingly coming to express class and not merely group interests, and to establish a sphere of autonomy vis-à-vis society. The best example of this process in São Paulo, where a homogeneous dominant class was formed and social differentiation was more intense. The local power of the *coronéis* persisted above all in frontier regions, but to a greater or lesser extent it was subordinate to the state government which controlled most of the resources which the *coronéis* relied on to maintain themselves in power. The state government also had at its disposal considerable military power which practically ensured its superiority when it came to armed conflict. Furthermore, the Paulista Republican party (PRP) had a considerable amount of organizational discipline and cohesion, and was clearly something more than an elaborate network of kinship and client relationships, although these aspects were important. The PRP, it has been argued, represented an intermediate stage between a grouping based on vertical 'client' relationships and a modern political party organized 'horizontally'.[6] Undoubtedly, the relations between state and society remained fundamentally clientalistic. However, given its role as executor of class interests, the state would from time to time take

[6] Joseph L. Love, *São Paulo in the Brazilian Federation, 1889–1937* (Stanford, 1980), 115.

measures whose purpose was the reduction of local power in sensitive areas. In 1906, for example, the president of the state of São Paulo, Jorge Tibiriçá, not only delegated extraordinary powers to the state militia, but instituted a full-time civil police force. Although it is doubtful how independent the police in fact became, it nevertheless represented an attempt to transform the police from their traditional position as an appendage of the big landowners. Similarly, in 1921, the state president Washington Luís stimulated the professionalization of the judiciary, which became less dependent on local power. Among other measures, an entrance examination was established, promotions systematized and salaries increased.

Minas Gerais was a curious case. In terms of its economic structure it bore a certain resemblance to the state of Bahia.[7] However, the two states differed in the degree of their economic development and, above all, in the power of their governmental institutions. In Minas Gerais, the civil service constituted an effective tool for patronage, which was controlled by the party and by the state government. Although it was unequal in its treatment of different regions, the state government was able to offer loans, favours, and public works especially in the field of transport. While the *coronéis* of the interior of Bahia were commercially isolated from the capital up until 1930, in Minas those areas furthest from the urban centres, such as the north of the state, were ever hopeful of obtaining improved means of transport which might integrate them into the markets of the south. Furthermore, from the formation of the Minas Republican party (PRM) in 1897, the *coronéis* were politically subordinate to the state governor and the state political machinery. 'There is no salvation without the PRM' was a well-known slogan among the *coronéis* of Minas during the Old Republic. In Rio Grande do Sul, the figure of the 'bureaucrat *coronel*' was a clear demonstration of the greater power of the state government and of the state Republican party (PRR). If the 'bureaucrat *coronel*' derived his position from his economic power and social prestige in a particular area, he also had to be prepared to take orders from above. The post of *intendente* (county superintendent) which was in theory the domain of the *coronéis* was frequently occupied by people provisionally designated by the state government.[8]

The constitution of 1891 formalized the federal system while at the same time giving expression to the distinction of power between the most

[7] John D. Wirth, *Minas Gerais in the Brazilian Federation, 1889–1937* (Stanford, 1977), 118.
[8] See Joseph L. Love. *Rio Grande do Sul and Brazilian regionalism, 1882–1930* (Stanford, 1971), 79.

powerful and the weakest states. Against the opinion of some military leaders who wanted equal representation for all states, the Chamber of Deputies was established on the basis of proportional representation depending on the number of inhabitants in each state (on the basis of the 1890 census). State autonomy, which benefited the largest units, was guaranteed in the vital matters of distribution of revenue and military power. The levying of certain taxes, the most significant being that of the duty on exports, the second most important source of revenue during the Empire, was taken out of the hands of the central government. This was of considerable benefit to São Paulo which came to outstrip the central government itself in financial terms. The right of states to contract foreign loans enabled São Paulo to finance the expansion of its coffee economy and the improvement of its urban services. The smaller states with low export receipts and in practice lacking the power to impose taxes on the great rural estates tried in vain to obtain a portion of the duty on imports levied by the central government. The individual states had the right to organize their own military forces. Here again, thanks to their resources, the larger states took ample advantage of this right. The state militia of São Paulo in particular was well equipped and its active members were always greater in number than those regiments of the federal army stationed in the state. In 1925 and 1926 the state militia numbered as many as 14,000 men, trained since 1906 by a French military mission. Thus the more powerful states had the financial and military resources to limit interventionist pressures from the federal government.

The election of the president of the Republic reflected the degree of agreement or disagreement between the most powerful states. It is frequently affirmed that the so-called *café com leite* alliance between São Paulo and Minas Gerais effectively controlled the First Republic. This is certainly true to a great extent. However, it is important to bear in mind that there were areas of conflict within the alliance, particularly after 1910 when the entry of a third state on the political scene, Rio Grande do Sul, upset its balance. Ultimately, towards the end of the 1920s, the rupture between the oligarchies of São Paulo and Minas Gerais set off the chain of events which would lead to the Revolution of 1930. Nevertheless, it is true that, generally speaking, power lay with the São Paulo–Minas axis under the Old Republic. In eleven presidential contests, nine of the presidents elected came from these two states, six from São Paulo and three from Minas Gerais. Given the size of its population, the state of Minas was to play an influential role in the Chamber of Deputies, where it held 37 seats, followed by São Paulo and Bahia each with 22. Although it was by no means insignificant, the economy of Minas could not match that of São Paulo. Minas produced foodstuffs mainly derived from cattle raising. In addition, it was a producer of coffee. Fewer opportunities in the economic field encouraged the Minas political elite to expand and to seek posts in central government. During its apogee between 1898 and 1930, the Minas oligarchy was not only influential in the Chamber of Deputies, it was also the grouping which remained for the greatest number of years in charge of key ministries. The direct domination of federal politics by the São Paulo oligarchy which began almost with the birth of the Republic declined from about 1905. However, although this complicated the issue it cannot be said that the interests of São Paulo were no longer predominant at federal level. Given the characteristic features of the federal system, it was vital that São Paulo should control federal politics only in those areas where action at state level was impossible or inadequate: in the area of exchange regulations and financial policies, which guaranteed foreign loans contracted mainly to maintain the value of coffee, and in the matter of immigration laws and the distribution of revenue between the federal and state governments.

Obviously, the political power of each regional unit depended to a great extent on its economic power. However, the degree of cohesion within the state ruling classes and the regional parties was of fundamental importance. This point can be illustrated by a brief analysis of the political structures of São Paulo, Minas Gerais, and Rio Grande do Sul. In 1920 the three states were responsible for more than half of the total value of the country's agricultural and industrial production, excluding the Federal District. In São Paulo, the coffee bourgeoisie lent its political support to the PRP as a result of a long struggle dating from the 1870s in defence of the Republic and above all of federalism. No other party expressed so clearly class interests. Despite the rapid economic growth of São Paulo and the consequent social differentiation, the PRP managed to maintain its position as sole party of the ruling class until 1926, when the Democratic party (PD) was founded. The basic nucleus for economic expansion in the state of São Paulo was the coffee complex, on which all other economic activities as well as the administrative machinery of the state were directly or indirectly dependent. The internal differences within the coffee bourgeoisie between the main producers, bankers and *comissários* were never clearly expressed. In turn, the nascent industrial- ization did not give rise to a class which was radically opposed to the coffee entrepreneurs. Industry developed as an offshoot of the export economy which created a regional market and was responsible for the influx of capital necessary for the purchase of machinery. Industrial investment was often a parallel option to investment in the coffee complex, and adjusted to the conditions of the coffee economy. These circumstances facilitated the amalgamation of the landowner and the industrialist in one person, or at least one family group. Only in 1928 did there emerge in São Paulo a representative organ of the industrial bourgeoisie. Even then, Roberto Simonsen – the first great name among ideologists of industrialization in São Paulo – left no doubt as to the effectiveness of the initiative, when he agreed that the economic structure of Brazil should rest mainly on the cultivation of the soil. The PRP itself was therefore able to represent the limited and subordinate interests of the industrialists of São Paulo, as was seen for example in the struggle in the National Congress to impose tariff barriers for imported textile goods (1928).

In Minas Gerais, the economic activity of the ruling class was divided between coffee, cattle raising and to a lesser extent industry, in geographically distinct sub-regions. Internal political dispute was considerable, especially during the first years of the Republic. Nevertheless, despite frequent disagreements and factional rivalries, the Republican party of Minas (PRM) tended to gather strength and present a united front at the level of federal politics. Minas Gerais did not even witness the emergence of a sizeable opposition party in the 1920s, whereas in São Paulo social differentiation, above all the expansion of the urban middle class, eventually opened the possibility of a horizontal articulation of interests and the founding of the PD. In Minas, the close alliance between the PRM and the state through patronage was always the safest (indeed the only) way by which class interests might be expressed or by which the individual might make progress in the political arena.

In contrast, the unity of the regional ruling class in Rio Grande do Sul was always problematical. Here factional dispute was expressed predominantly through competing parties rather than through rivalries within a single party. It would be wrong, however, to establish a direct causal relation between different economic interests (cattle raising, wheat production, and so on) and this peculiar feature of *gaúcho* politics. From the beginning of the Republic, the Republican party of Rio Grande do Sul (PRR) took power at the regional level, although it had to face opposition from rival parties. Between 1893 and 1895, it was involved in a violent civil war with the Federal party, founded by the old liberals of the Empire and by dissidents from the PRR. In 1923, there was renewed armed conflict between the PRR and the opposition groups of the Liberal alliance. This political division undoubtedly contributed to reducing the influence of Rio Grande do Sul at the federal level, where for a long period it held the balance but was never a serious contender in the struggle for power. It was no coincidence, therefore, that during the presidential campaign of 1929–30 and the ensuing revolution which brought Getúlio Vargas to power, the political forces of the region finally managed to present a united front in the form of the Frente Única Gaúcha.

With regard to the north-eastern states, concerted action on their part could in theory give them a certain weight in federal politics, whether in the choice of president of the Republic, or in the Chamber of Deputies. In the Chamber, Bahia with 22 seats and Pernambuco with 17 constituted a sizeable grouping. For some time, between 1896 and 1911, the state of Pernambuco exercised a degree of influence at the federal level, through its leader Francisco Rosa e Silva. However, he only managed to produce a coalition of north-eastern states sporadically, as in 1906 when he attempted to prevent parliamentary approval of the coffee valorization scheme, which had been drawn up by the states of São Paulo, Minas Gerais and Rio de Janeiro. Indeed, any coalition between the north-eastern states was severely hampered, among other reasons, by problems arising from the characteristics of the federal system with regard to taxation. Given the sparse resources of the region, the various oligarchies competed for favours from the federal government and entered into lengthy disputes among themselves over the right to levy inter-state revenues in the case of goods circulating in more than one state.

A potential destabilizing factor during the First Republic was the failure of the oligarchic political system sufficiently to integrate the armed forces, especially the army. Until the 1880s the army had played only a minor part in national political decision making. The imperial government, although co-opting military figures, was fundamentally civilian and the politicians took pride in pointing out the advantages of the Brazilian system over that of its neighbouring Republics which were invariably subject to military rule. After the suppression of the last of the provincial rebellions in the middle of the nineteenth century, the role of the army was greatly reduced; it was primarily occupied in guarding the frontiers and the military colonies. It was the role of the National Guard to maintain civil order, at least until the beginning of the 1870s.[9] The National Guard mobilized practically the entire free adult male population, under the command of officers who were recruited from among the local landowners. After the Paraguayan War (1865–70) the army became more aware of its potential, and at the same time more conscious of its subordinate role. The bitterness of its struggle in the war also contrasted with the accusations of corruption, favouritism and political gerrymandering levelled at successive cabinets by the press. Gradually, certain officers came to see the army as a civic 'entity' which was independent of social class and of the Empire. They saw the army as an institution willing to make material sacrifices and destined to take power in order to regenerate the nation, for the armed forces embodied in themselves the notion of patriotism. Apart from this global vision, many officers complained of the discrimination suffered by the military, and openly demonstrated their opposition to the general policies of the government. They placed great emphasis on the importance of education, on industrial development, and on the abolition of slavery.

However, the officers were not a homogeneous group. On the one hand, there were those young officers who had attended the Military School at Praia Vermelha in Rio de Janeiro, which was more a centre for the study of mathematics, philosophy and letters than for military sciences. This group came under the influence of Comtean positivism, particularly after the arrival of Benjamin Constant as a teacher at the school in 1872. The Military School in fact was responsible for the training of a group of 'graduates in uniform' who, with a particular view of the world, began to compete with the traditional graduates from the schools of law and medicine. It was from this circle of officers that the concept of the 'soldier citizen' was born, as was criticism against the Empire in favour of modernization and against the slave regime. On the other hand, there were the *tarimbeiros*, a group of older officers, almost all veterans of the Paraguayan War. Many of these had not graduated from the Military School. Less concerned with issues of social reform, this group was nevertheless deeply conscious of the honour of the military

---

[9] This discussion on the armed forces is based on José Murilo de Carvalho, 'As forças armadas na Primeira República: o poder desestabilizador' and Fernando Henrique Cardoso, 'Dos governos militares, a Prudente-Campos Sales', in Boris Fausto (ed.), *História geral da civilização brasileira, III: O Brasil republicano*, vols. i and ii (São Paulo, 1975–7).

community. In the 1880s the two groups united against the imperial government. In the *questão militar* the *tarimbeiros* took the initiative in defending the military against 'insults to its integrity'. However, it was the military graduates who prepared the coup of 15 November 1889 and dragged in the *tarimbeiros*, many of whom, including Marshal Deodoro da Fonseca who proclaimed the Republic, were not in fact republicans.

In spite of these formative differences, which corresponded in part to diverse social origins, it is possible to determine certain common characteristics within the military. Brazilian historians have frequently interpreted the military as being the spokesman of the middle class against the landowning oligarchy. This is, however, a somewhat narrow view. Many army officers were undoubtedly of broadly middle-class origin, but throughout the final decades of the Empire and during the whole of the First Republic, an army career also represented a limited but viable option for the sons of those branches of families within the oligarchy which were in economic decline, especially in the north and north-east. Apart from this it is important to recognize the process of socialization for which the army, as an institution with specific values and relatively independent of society at large, was responsible. Officers were also recruited from what became military families, especially in states like Rio Grande do Sul. The regional background of Brazilian military officers is revealed in the limited data available. Among the 52 officers who were members of the first Congress of the Republic, 24 were from the north-east and 9 from Rio Grande do Sul and the Federal District together, and only one came from São Paulo and Minas Gerais. Of the 30 divisional and brigade commanders in 1895, eight were from Rio Grande do Sul, none from Minas, and one from São Paulo; in 1930 eight were from Rio Grande do Sul, none from either Minas or São Paulo. Significant here was the importance of Rio Grande do Sul where there was a sizeable garrison responsible for the security of the frontier. The almost total absence of military leaders from São Paulo or Minas contributed to the weakening of relations between the army and the two most politically powerful states of the Republic.

Given their origins, army officers frequently gained within the military corporation a distinctive 'status', which was reinforced by the system of endogenous recruitment. It was a 'status' which could not easily be changed for another, and for this reason it was jealously guarded. At the same time, many officers were people of literate urban background, whose profession linked them directly with the centre of power. Given their military tradition, and the family connections many of them had with the oligarchy, the world of politics was not foreign to them. On the other hand, they did not identify themselves with the civilian oligarchies and much less with those of the dominant states. The officers conceived of themselves as protectors of the nation, the creators of an austere but progressive state, free from the political gerrymandering of the *legistas* (the graduates who constituted the political staff of the oligarchies) and the *casacas* (the *nouveaux riches* who accumulated fortunes on the money market). This state would integrate the people – an undifferentiated category inherent in the concept of the nation – and would strengthen national unity. This ideal was very different from the pragmatism of the most powerful oligarchies, such as that of São Paulo, for whom the Republic represented the protection of specific economic interests, the defence of state autonomy and the reinforcement of regional inequalities.

It cannot be said that the army was a persistent destabilizing factor in the oligarchic Republic. Its willingness to act depended on a variety of historical circumstances, and the most active elements changed continually. There was, however, a basic incompatibility between the oligarchies of the most powerful states and the military apparatus, although it was tempered by tactical and defensive alliances. In the end, the fall of the First Republic was due in part to the long-term disaffection, indeed insurrection, of middle-ranking army officers and, ultimately, intervention by the high command of the armed forces.

The political system of the First Republic was characterized by minimal popular participation. The constitution of the Republic (1891) formally expanded the base for political representation. In place of the suffrage based on property and income, as it had been throughout the Empire, the right to vote was extended to all *literate* male Brazilians over the age of 21. The widening of the electorate from the Empire to the Republic brought significant results. A comparison of the last parliamentary elections of the Empire (1886) with the first presidential election in which voters from all states took part (1898) shows an increase of almost 400 per cent in the number of voters. In 1886, 111,700 people voted out of a total population of 13.2 million, representing 0.89 per cent of the population. In 1898, there were 462,000 votes which corresponded to 2.7 per cent of the population of 17.1 million. However, the widening of the franchise does not alter the fact that the number of voters in relation to the total population of the country was extremely low throughout the whole period of the First Republic. In the three competitive elections for the presidency of the Republic (1910, 1922 and 1930), votes counted corresponded respectively to 2.8, 1.9 and 5.7 per cent of the population. Voting was optional; women did not have the vote; and illiterates were excluded in a country where 85.2 per cent of the population was illiterate in 1890 and 75.5 per cent in 1920.[10]

Perhaps more important than the low level of participation in elections was the dependence of the electorate on the local oligarchies. The subordination of the electorate was facilitated by the open vote, and it was therefore not surprising that the urban opposition campaigned for the adoption of the secret ballot throughout the whole period. When it became necessary to break the power of a particular faction or when the normal mechanisms of control ceased to function, it was always possible to resort to fraud, by, for example, including the vote of foreigners or the recently deceased, or falsifying ballot papers (a process which was made all the easier by the absence of an adequately structured state bureaucracy), and, if necessary, force. Obviously, any measures taken to increase the electorate, such as giving the vote to illiterates, would not have altered this situation. Indeed, it might have made it worse, at least initially. In a country with a low level of popular participation and where political citizenship was almost always used as currency for the unequal exchange of favours, the federal Republic, though in theory based on the ideal of democratic representation, was in practice no more than an instrument of the regional oligarchies.

In the rural areas where the mass of the population was dependent on the big landowners, the rural population was differentiated horizontally according to a hierarchy of minor privileges related to the conditions under which they settled and worked the land. Vertically, it was even more fragmented because of the need to maintain relations of loyalty to the big landowners and their kin. Nor did the small and medium-sized landed proprietors, mostly of foreign origin, who established themselves for example in Rio Grande do Sul, constitute an independent class from the political point of view, albeit for different reasons. They were less subject to the domination of the *coronéis*, but more so to that of the state with regard to tax obligations, land concessions and so on. Apart from this, as foreigners or first-generation Brazilians they were less culturally

---

10 Love, 'Political participation in Brazil', 7.

and politically integrated; their basic objectives were primarily related to economic advance. All this explains why the dominant party in Rio Grande do Sul (PRR) managed to maintain proportionately greater control of those *municípios* where landowners of foreign origin predominated than in the rest of the state.[11]

As for the workers on the great coffee plantations of São Paulo, a number of circumstances hindered their social organization. The mass of immigrants entering a strange land were dispersed among isolated estates. This hampered the type of contact which might have led to a consciousness of their common situation and, thus, common action. Within the boundaries of his estate, the landowner held wide powers based on paternalism and coercion. The paternalistic approach was reinforced by certain features of the system of colonization; provision of housing and of strips of land for planting food crops was seen as a concession on the part of the employer rather than payment for services rendered. Coercion was the norm when the landowner held absolute power within his estate or when he dominated state institutions such as the police and the magistrature, and was able to place them at his service.

It would be mistaken, however, to assume that the system of domination in the rural areas produced no reaction among the mass of plantation workers. On the estates in São Paulo, there were constant clashes between landowners and colonists, particularly during the early years of mass immigration. Individual disputes, cases of whole families abandoning plantations, and complaints to consular representatives were common occurrences during the years. There is also evidence of strike threats, especially towards the end of April and beginning of May – the period of the harvest – when the landowners were more vulnerable to pressure. However, there was only one important cycle of strikes during this period. This occurred in 1913 in the area of Ribeirão Preto, near an urban centre, and involved some thousands of colonists from the large estates.

In other areas of the country, the disaffection of the rural population was expressed through movements of a religious type, of which the most important were the Canudos and the Contestado movements. Canudos was an abandoned estate in the north of the state of Bahia, where Antônio Vicente Mendes Maciel – better known as Antônio Conselheiro – and his followers established themselves in 1893. Deep in the *sertão* (backlands) a

---

[11] Love, *Rio Grande do Sul and Brazilian regionalism*, 134.

city grew up with a population which fluctuated between 20 and 30 thousand inhabitants. The people of Canudos defeated a number of military expeditions sent to crush them, in spite of the inequality of strength. Finally, in October 1897, after a struggle lasting many months, Canudos was destroyed. Its defenders, who numbered some 5,000 in the final phase of the war, were either killed in combat or captured and put to death.

The Contestado movement occurred in the south of the country in a frontier area disputed by the states of Paraná and Santa Catarina. It began in 1911 under the leadership of José Maria, who died in the first clashes and was heralded as a saint by the rebels of the Contestado. Unlike Canudos, the movement did not limit itself to one particular centre, but shifted to various points in the region, under pressure from military forces. The rebellion was put down in late 1915, when rebel strongholds were attacked and destroyed by 6,000 soldiers from the army and the police force, assisted by 1,000 civilians who joined in the process of repression.

In considering the principal social movements in the interior of Brazil during the First Republic, Joazeiro, a city in the south of the state of Ceará, which became the centre of activities of the priest Cícero Romão Batista between 1872 and 1924, also deserves mention. There are many common features between events in Joazeiro and the Canudos and Contestado movements. For example, from the point of view of the history of the transformation of the Catholic church in Brazil, particularly in the north-east – a theme which lies outside the scope of this chapter[12] – Canudos and Joazeiro were manifestations of similar developments. On the other hand, when considering social movements as manifestations of rebellion, Joazeiro has little in common with the other two movements. Although Padre Cícero clashed continuously with the ecclesiastical authorities, and at times with factions of the oligarchy, his movement for better or worse fell within the system of domination which prevailed during the First Republic. Put simply, the city of Joazeiro can be seen as an area controlled by a priest-*coronel*, who had a considerable degree of influence within the political oligarchy, particularly after 1909 when Padre Cícero began to involve himself directly in the political struggles.

The Canudos and Contestado movements were attempts to create an

---

[12] For a discussion of the Catholic church in Brazil during this period, see Lynch, *CHLA* iv, ch. 12.

alternative way of life, and were considered sufficiently dangerous for both to be brutally crushed by military forces. This does not mean that they were totally opposed to the power structure of the *coronéis*. Before settling in Canudos, Antônio Conselheiro had been a practising member of the Catholic church, living an ascetic, nomadic life. He summoned the people together in order to build or rebuild churches. He built walls around cemeteries, and he showed concern for the small parish churches of the interior. There is evidence that at this stage he was well looked upon by certain *coronéis*, for whom his disciplined followers built roads and dams. The village of Canudos itself did not depart very much from the traditional pattern of settlement in the interior. There was a certain degree of social and economic differentiation, a considerable degree of trade with the surrounding area, and religious links with the priests of the neighbouring parishes. Canudos was also a source of votes and influence at election time.

The instigators of the Contesdado movement were the followers of a *coronel* who was a member of the opposition and seen as a friend of the poor. Others of varying origins joined this group, among them those who were the victims of the process of modernization in both urban and rural areas: rural workers driven off the land by the construction of a railway and a timber plant, people who had been recruited for railway construction from among the unemployed of large cities and then abandoned at the end of their contract, and criminals who were at large in the region. However, the village settlements which grew up during the Contestado, with their emphasis on equality and fraternity, clashed with established social values, and assumed characteristics which were clearly messianic. This can be seen, among other features, through the way many of the members of the Contestado remained loyal to the monarchy which, it has been argued, represented an eschatological kingdom more than a political institution.[13] The theme of the monarchy, whether because of the form it took or because of the period in which the Contestado movement occurred, was not exploited to any extent by the government. In contrast, the earlier monarchism of Antônio Conselheiro, with its attacks on the Republic, responsible for the introduction of civil marriage and for the taking of cemeteries away from the control of the church, took more concrete forms. As a result it was a mobilizing factor against Canudos in the urban centres, at a time when

---

[13] Duglas Teixeira Monteiro, *Os errantes do Novo Século: um estudo sobre o surto milenarista do Contestado* (São Paulo, 1974).

the possibility of the restoration of the monarchy was seen as a real threat. Canudos, Contestado and Joazeiro were not episodes devoid of significance, nor were they isolated expressions by an ignorant rural population in contrast to the centres of civilization on the coast. In different degrees, these movements can be linked to changes in the Catholic church, to socio-economic changes in their respective areas, and to the political development of the nation itself. Their particular strength as a demonstration of popular religious belief cannot be ignored. Nevertheless, as attempts at independent organization on the part of the rural population, they effectively illustrate the severe limitations of such organization during the period of the First Republic.

Alongside these messianic social movements, social banditry has sometimes been considered as evidence of rebellion on the part of the rural population and of the small urban centres of the interior. We are referring here to the phenomenon of the *cangaço*, warlike bands of armed men which sprang up in the north-east of the country during the second half of the nineteenth century, and whose history spills over into the twentieth century, coming to an end only in the late 1930s. In the beginning the *cangaço* was closely connected to the ties of kinship and limited in its sphere of action to a small area. Gradually, new forms emerged, developing into professional bandit organizations whose sphere of action was much wider. This was the case of the famous group of bandits led by Virgulino Ferreira, known as Lampião. Lampião and his men were active over a long period from 1920 to 1938, and ranged over seven states of the north-east until their final confrontation with the police in which Lampião was killed.

As a general rule *cangaceiros* were white, from families of small landed proprietors or members of the elite who had been on the losing end in disputes over land, trade, or local political power. If this was the general background, some also had specific personal reasons for becoming bandits. Joining the *cangaço* often resulted from a series of events sparked off by the violent death of a close relative. Not having any reason to believe in the powers of the police or the judiciary, the future bandit set about satisfying family honour by his own hand, and ended up by gathering together a group of followers. Significantly, the death of a father in the circumstances described features in the biographies of Lampião and another famous *cangaceiro*, Antônio Silvino, who was active between 1897 and 1914. The bandit armies were recruited from among the poor, of dark skin, who formed the mass of the rural population. For these, banditry meant the possibility of greater individual independence coupled with attractive material incentives.

In the mythology of the poor of the Brazilian north-east, and in the films and songs of the 1960s, the *cangaceiros* are seen as social bandits or even as Brazilian equivalents of Robin Hood. The *cangaceiros* broke with established order by refusing to recognize the authority of the police and judiciary, as well as by the nature of their activities. These included the invasion of estates and the sacking of villages and towns, which were often connected with a desire to damage a particular group or individual within the ruling class. Nor can it be doubted either that many *cangaceiros* gained the co-operation of the poor, whose support was vital for the survival of the armed bands. Antônio Silvino, for example, gained considerable popular prestige by distributing money and part of the booty among the poor. However, it has been shown convincingly that between the *cangaço* and the power structure of the *coronéis*, there was always a relationship of interdependence, in which the *coronéis* represented the dominant sector.[14] For the *cangaceiros* the possibility of breaking the power of the *coronéis* went beyond their convenience and their mentality. The band of armed men counted on the sympathy of the poor, but it depended for its permanent security on the shelter and ammunition which only the powerful could provide. From the point of view of the local elites, the *cangaço* represented an important reserve force, in a situation where political power was segmented and violently contested by rival groups.

The disintegration and ultimate extinction of the *cangaço* resulted from a process by which the intervention of the state, with its growing ability to punish and to patronize, reduced the instability of the local elite, and transformed the *cangaceiros* into mere bandits, whose actions were no longer of any use to their erstwhile protectors. There remained the mythology rooted in the figure of the *cangaceiro*, who is the personification of a supreme physical violence which the poor, under the oppression of their local potentates, cannot hope to emulate.

The framework of social relations which prevailed in the urban centres was undoubtedly different. From the first years of the Republic, the importance of the cities far exceeded their economic significance and electoral weight. It was here that the social groups and classes who

[14] See Linda Lewin, 'The oligarchical limitations of social banditry in Brazil: the case of the "good" thief Antônio Silvino', *Past and Present*, 82 (February 1979).

formed the narrow caucus of public opinion were concentrated. These included representatives of the most enlightened sector of the ruling class, middle-class elements, and, in the case of the Federal District, the military. Also to be found there were the most potentially dangerous sectors: the working class, the low-paid white collar workers, and the urban unemployed and underemployed.

In both Rio de Janeiro and São Paulo, urban *coronéis* flourished, although their sphere of action was more limited than in the rural areas; domination by the oligarchy depended on more than manipulation of the vote. As the seat of the central government, the mayor of the Federal District was nominated by the president of the Republic. In 1928, the PRP managed to amend the constitution of the state of São Paulo to include a clause whereby the president of the state was given the power to choose the mayor of the capital. And the post of mayor of Recife, capital of Pernambuco, also ceased to be an elected post – by a decision of the legislature.

Indiscriminate references to the urban middle class have served to obscure its political role during the First Republic. More than any other, this sector was heterogeneous, divided in terms of income, social mobility, racial origin, and degree of dependence on the regional ruling class. Industrialists and merchants, mostly of immigrant origin, intent on economic and social advance, seem to have played little part in politics. The Brazilian-born middle class, with little economic power, but linked to the ruling class by family ties, was a different case. These were the so-called 'poor relations' of the oligarchy. For them, survival did not generally lie in economic activity, but in the state apparatus, on which they often depended as civil servants. Included in this 'national' middle class were those who moulded public opinion, such as journalists and prestigious figures within the liberal professions. These sectors were generally in conflict with the oligarchies in their struggle to establish a liberal democracy through measures such as the secret ballot and the creation of an electoral commission to curb fraud. However, middle-class participation in the campaigns for liberal democracy varied depending on the sector of the middle class involved, as well as on the influence of specific regional characteristics. Liberal ideology generally attracted the highest strata of the middle class, while the salaried masses of the service sector, such as bank and commercial employees and low-ranking civil servants, seem to have tended towards demands of a similar type to those of the working classes, that is, better salaries or improved housing. Nevertheless, this interpretation runs the risk of being too simplistic if one does not consider inter-class relationships in certain cities. Taking Rio de Janeiro and São Paulo as examples, it is possible to distinguish particular features in their social movements, which can be partially explained by the diversity within the structure of the middle class as well as by the hegemonic role played by the bourgeoisie of São Paulo.

In 1890 in Rio de Janeiro, then the only Brazilian city of any size and also the only one with a diversified social structure, the civil service, liberal professions, and the priesthood accounted for 8.6 per cent of the employed population (compared with 4.6 per cent in São Paulo in 1893). The capital of the Republic would become increasingly a city of services. In 1919, only 38.4 per cent of the economically active population was involved in actual physical production, while 61.6 per cent was involved in the provision of services, 15 per cent of these in domestic services. In Rio de Janeiro the middle class was less dependent on the agrarian bourgeoisie. It comprised the professional and bureaucratic middle class and, more especially, functional groups who were not linked to the coffee bourgeoisie, such as career military officers, students of the Military School at Praia Vermelha, and students in higher education. These sectors attempted to ally themselves to the working class, and provided a multi-class basis to various social movements in Rio de Janeiro such as the Jacobinist movement, which emerged in the last years of the nineteenth century. Jacobinism was rooted in the discontent which prevailed among wide sectors of the population of the capital, who were affected by inflation and bad living conditions, and was permeated with a vaguely patriotic ideology. For these sectors, the tangible cause of their difficulties lay in the fact that commerce was controlled by the Portuguese. In addition, Jacobinism, in attempting to prevent Prudente de Morais from assuming the presidency of the Republic in 1894, was a reaction against the rise to power of the Paulista coffee oligarchy.

In São Paulo, attempts by middle-class sectors to ally themselves with the lower classes were far more tenuous. The large immigrant sector lacked both the conditions and the reasons for presenting itself as a social force. The traditional middle class gravitated towards the coffee bourgeoisie, on which it was economically and culturally dependent. These characteristics, allied to the fact that there were no groups, such as military school students or officers of the armed forces, capable of forming an opposition, meant that social protest in São Paulo was limited to the working class. The liberal Democratic party (PD) was founded in 1926 for the purpose of strengthening 'the purity of republican institutions', and recruited members and voters from among the urban middle class. However, a year after the Revolution of 1930, the PD united with the PRP against the government of Getúlio Vargas.

The working class was concentrated mainly in the Federal District and in the larger cities of the state of São Paulo, particularly the capital. Quantitatively, the structure of industry was based to a large extent on small enterprises, operating with limited capital and technology. On the other hand, the larger units, particularly in the field of textile production, accounted for a considerable proportion of the working population. In 1919, companies with 500 or more workers accounted for 36.4 per cent of the work force in the state of São Paulo, and 35.7 per cent in the Federal District.

It was in the cities that the necessary conditions for the emergence of a labour movement existed. Social relations were less clientalistic and paternalistic; exploitation was more objective; easier contact and communication made possible the birth of a collective consciousness. Despite the fact that their activities were restricted, revolutionary ideologists and organizers established themselves in the urban environment. On the other hand, a number of factors limited the strength of the labour movement, which was never able to exert enough pressure to obtain greater participation in the political field. There was, in general, an abundance of manpower both in São Paulo and in Rio de Janeiro. In São Paulo, in view of its cyclical character, the coffee sector played an important part in the supply of urban labour. While in expansion, coffee encouraged a degree of immigration which exceeded its own needs, and this meant in turn that the surplus joined the urban labour force. At times of crisis in the rural areas, coffee plantation workers were left with no other option but to migrate to the urban centres or return to their countries of origin, as the other sectors of the agricultural export economy were incapable of absorbing them. In the case of Rio de Janeiro, internal migration to the largest urban centre in the country was a significant factor in the growth of the labour force. The size of the work force gave rise to ethnic friction – between Brazilian and foreign immigrants, Portuguese and Italians, and even between Italians from different parts of Italy. At the same time, because industrial expansion was not regular, employment in manufacturing industries was only intermittent, and this meant that improvements in labour conditions were slow. Finally, by emphasizing spontaneous class movements, and by refusing to organize, anarchism could be said to have fed those structural features of the social system which militated against working-class cohesion. Given its ideological perspectives, it also contributed to the failure of the organized working class to adopt a programme of reforms favourable to the broadening of the base of the political system. At the same time, although industry was only of secondary importance to the economy, the leading industrialists were able to exert a considerable degree of influence on the centre of power and could count on the repressive force of the government. The semi-legality of the unions, the violence unleashed on strikers, and the expulsion of foreign labour leaders all contributed to the disunity of the working class.

Strikes had occurred in the urban areas of Brazil since the end of the nineteenth century. However, the phase of major growth in the labour movement within the period under consideration occurred between 1917 and 1920, under the influence of wartime inflation and within the general pattern of labour unrest which followed the end of the first world war. Its high point was the general strike in São Paulo in July 1917, which was joined by 50,000 workers. This period witnessed not only a large number of strikes, but also, in some cases, increased union membership. At the end of 1918, the textile union of Rio de Janeiro, for example, had as many as 20,000 members, no small figure if one considers that a large proportion of the labour force in that particular sector was made up of women and children who did not join the union.

Until the beginning of the 1920s, anarcho-syndicalist ideas predominated among the small groups of organized workers in the city of São Paulo. In Rio de Janeiro, anarcho-syndicalism was less influential. The climate of opinion tended to favour 'apolitical syndicalism', which was geared solely towards improvements in working conditions and wages. This tendency was particularly strong among railway and port workers. The socialists never managed to create more than small partisan sects, which is not surprising in a country where the transformation of society through political participation seemed no more than a utopian dream.

The great strikes of 1917–20 did not bring about any improvement in the conditions of the Brazilian workers in terms of organizational stability. Throughout the 1920s, the labour movement stagnated. Following the failure of the strikes, and in the wake of the Russian Revolution, anarchism went through a period of crisis. A group of former anarchists most closely linked to the workers' struggle, together with a few socialists, founded the Brazilian Communist party (PCB) in 1922. Indeed, one of the characteristics of the PCB was that its main caucus originated in anarcho-syndicalism and not socialism. New concepts were formulated on a wide variety of themes, such as the role of the unions and the party, class alliances, anti-imperialism, and agrarian reform. However, the party did not expand to any great extent during the 1920s, its active membership fluctuating between 73 in 1922 and 1,000 in 1929.

Nevertheless the clear warning given by the strikes of 1917–20, coupled with the steady growth in the size of the working class, produced the first signs within the ruling class of new attitude to the 'social problem', one which was not bent solely on repression. Some social rights were recognized, above all in the service sector, which was a strategically important area for the agricultural export economy. When the labour movement gained new impetus following the 1929 crisis and the 1930 Revolution, attempts to create autonomous working-class organizations would have to compete, on an unequal footing, with government measures aimed at organizing, and controlling, the urban working class.

THE POLITICAL PROCESS

The most sensitive critical features of the oligarchic system of the First Republic lay in the difficulties in adjustment between the different regional oligarchies, in the pressures exerted by the urban middle class for political participation, and in the presence of the armed forces as a destabilizing factor within the state apparatus. In the long term, the domination of the oligarchy was affected by the gradual alteration of the structural basis on which the system of clientalism in social relations rested. This, in turn, was the result of internal migration and urban growth, greater class differentiation and, ultimately, industrial growth. A brief analysis of the political process during the First Republic will show in more concrete terms how the oligarchic system consolidated itself after 1889, and how its crisis developed in the period up to the Revolution of 1930.

The overthrow of the monarchy on 15 November 1889 was the result of a military coup which had been planned by a group of young army officers in Rio de Janeiro. The most well-organized civilian republican group, representing the São Paulo coffee bourgeoisie, had few contacts with the military and doubted the convenience of involving the army in their campaign. The military took power, and provided republican Brazil with its first two presidents, Deodoro da Fonseca (November 1889 – November 1891) and Floriano Peixoto (November 1891 – November 1894). During the first years of the Republic, half of the states were governed by members of the armed forces. On the other hand, the great oligarchies were the dominant social power, and the constitution of 1891, as we have seen, protected the interests of the largest states, especially São Paulo. The armed forces did not act as a homogeneous group in the face of a social class whose party, the PRP, was clearly aware of the interests which it represented, despite a certain amount of dissension. Rivalry within the armed forces occurred between the army and the navy, and between supporters of Deodoro and those of Floriano. While the former symbolized the interests of the *tarimbeiros*, the latter derived support from the graduates of the Military School at Praia Vermelha, the soldier citizens who were active in the Jacobinist movement in Rio de Janeiro. In the end, real or imaginary threats to the consolidation of the Republican regime brought about a *rapprochement* between the coffee bourgeoisie and the military sector. Floriano Peixoto, for example, was supported by wealthy financiers from São Paulo and by its powerful state militia during the Federalist Revolution and the Naval Revolt. While consolidating the Republic, he also, somewhat against his will, opened the way for the new ruling classes of Brazil to enter the political arena. His minister of finance, Rodrigues Alves, represented the political interests of São Paulo, in a strategically planned cabinet. The presidencies of the Chamber and Senate were held by leading figures in the PRP. Hesitation on the part of the military between resentment against the oligarchy and respect for the legality of the republican regime which it had helped to create made it easier for the oligarchy of the principal states, above all São Paulo, to achieve victory. On 15 November 1894, the first civilian president of the Republic assumed power – the Paulista, Prudente de Morais. Opposition was limited to the popular sectors, and to young officers and cadets from the Praia Vermelha School in Rio de Janeiro. Ten years later, in 1904, demonstrations against the government's decision in favour of compulsory vaccination to combat yellow fever again brought together two currents of opposition: popular elements, whose protest was directed largely against the high cost of living and the evacuation of those living in houses condemned as unhygienic, and military officers and cadets from the Military School who, while protesting against vaccination, were also levelling their sights at a higher target, namely that of the 'republic of landowners'. However, the military hierarchy itself gradually withdrew from national politics. The Military Club – which had co-ordinated political activity – was closed between 1896 and 1901.

Now that there was no longer any threat from the military, it remained to institutionalize the oligarchic system. The second civilian president, another Paulista, Campos Sales (1898–1902), set himself this task with three main objectives in mind: to put an end to the hostility which existed between the executive and the legislature, to minimize as much as possible the impact of dissidence within individual states, and to achieve a basic consensus between central and state governments. Thus was born the concept of 'the politics of the governors', a 'doctrine' which was largely lacking in substance, but which was nevertheless sufficient to establish the basis of the oligarchic system. In principle, it sought reciprocal agreement. The central government would support the dominant political groups in the states, while these, in turn, would support the policies of the president of the Republic. In this way, Campos Sales sought to neutralize opposition at the regional level.

To tame Congress, whose function came to be very different from how the constitutional division of powers had envisaged it, among other measures the process by which members were elected to the Chamber of Deputies was modified. On the occasion of elections to the Chamber, candidates accepted as having been elected in their states received a diploma, and the first meetings of the new legislature were thus held with deputies duly bearing their diplomas. However, these diplomas were often challenged, and their validity depended on the decision of a credentials committee, which was chosen by plenary vote from among the members of the new Chamber. The president of the newly elected Chamber played a decisive role in influencing the choice of members of the credentials committee. Until the reform instigated by Campos Sales, the ruling stated that *pro tempore* presidency of the Chamber would fall to the oldest of the diploma-bearing deputies. As a result of the reform, the deputy who had served as president in the previous legislature, always assuming that he had been elected to the new legislature, which was normally the case, continued to serve. Choosing the oldest deputy introduced an element of uncertainty, while the president of the Chamber in the previous legislature was inevitably someone who had supported the president of the Republic. In this way, the executive gained greater control of the candidates who would be officially confirmed as deputies.

The oligarchy of São Paulo and the PRP dominated the political scene at the beginning of the Republic, but could count on the support of Minas Gerais at vital moments, such as the vote on the constitution (1891), and the election of Prudente de Morais (1894). The first three civilian presidents of the Republic were all Paulistas: Prudente de Morais, Campos Sales and Rodrigues Alves (1902–6). Until 1897, when the PRM was founded, the oligarchy of Minas Gerais was divided into various factions (mainly corresponding to sectors of the state economy: coffee, cereals, livestock), a factor which reduced its influence at the federal level. From 1898 when it supported Campos Sales for the presidency and the fiscal and monetary policies which resulted from the agreement signed with Rothschilds for the consolidation of the Brazilian national debt, Minas brought its full weight to bear in federal politics. The fourth civilian president of the Republic, Afonso Pena, who was elected in 1906 and who died in office in 1909, was a Mineiro.

After the scars of civil war had healed, and the PRR had consolidated itself, Rio Grande do Sul began to emerge as a third major star in the oligarchic constellation. At the federal level, the influence of senator Pinheiro Machado illustrated this increasing power. Under his leadership, the *gaúchos* lent their consistent support to Paulista presidents, and to the proposals emanating from São Paulo designed to gain central government approval for foreign loans to support the coffee economy. However, Pinheiro Machado was not exactly a 'client' of São Paulo. Assuming a strategic position in the Senate, he managed to create a new network of alliances. By controlling the Senate credentials committee, and exercising his influence on that of the Chamber, Pinheiro managed to dominate the representatives of the weaker states. This resulted in an alliance between Rio Grande do Sul and some satellite states of the northeast, which to a certain extent would be institutionalized in November 1910 with the founding of the Conservative Republican party (PRC), an attempt to create a national party of the oligarchy. The first opportunity for Rio Grande do Sul to use its influence in a presidential succession came in 1909, when internal dissension within the Minas oligarchy facilitated the candidature of Marshal Hermes da Fonseca to the presidency of the Republic. Hermes was the nephew of Deodoro, and minister of war from 1906 to 1910. Minas and Rio Grande do Sul both rallied to his support. The candidate put forward by São Paulo, with the support of Bahia (which since the Empire had been reduced to a position of secondary importance) was Rui Barbosa, whose political career dated from the Empire, and who was a representative of the tiny enlightened elite of the period. For the first time, the *café com leite* alliance ran into difficulties.

Significantly, the *gaúchos* emerged as a force in federal politics by backing a military candidate. The affinity between the *gaúcho* oligarchy and the army can be attributed to several factors. The importance of the garrison stationed in Rio Grande do Sul (and later in 1919 the creation there of the Third Military Region) seems to have encouraged *gaúchos* of a certain social level to follow a military career. Intermittent fighting in the region also favoured contact between army officers and the political parties. The establishment of links between various officers and the PRR resulted from the Federalist Revolution. Certain ideological features and political peculiarities also contributed to this convergence. Rio Grande do Sul, under Júlio de Castilhos and later the important state leader, Borges de Medeiros, was a region where the influence of positivism was particularly strong, an ideology which also spread through the ranks of the army. Apart from this, the economic and financial policies defended by the *gaúchos* for economic and ideological reasons tended to coincide in many ways with the ideals of the military. Rio Grande do Sul, whose economy was essentially geared to the domestic market, was a centre of opposition to the agrarian export interests, for which the army had little sympathy, and with which it maintained few links. The *gaúchos* defended price stabilization along with conservative fiscal policies, essentially because inflation would cause problems for the jerked beef market in particular. Jerked beef was consumed mainly by the lower classes of the north-east and the Federal District. Any reduction in the purchasing power of these classes resulted in a fall in demand. A conservative financial policy always met with the approval of the military, and not only among the higher ranking personnel. The *tenentista* rebellions of the 1920s were to point to inflation and budgetary imbalance as evils as serious as fraud and regional inequalities.

The candidature of Hermes da Fonseca can be placed in a different context to that of the struggles which followed the proclamation of the Republic. The army was accepted as a political partner in order to end the impasse caused by dissension within the oligarchies. It did not present itself as an autonomous force. It was Rui Barbosa who criticized the intervention of the army into politics during the electoral campaign of 1909–10. He attacked the officer corps and pitted the state militias against the army. Although Rui's political base was essentially the oligarchy of São Paulo, his ideological platform was that of the struggle of the intelligentsia for civil liberties, culture and liberal traditions, against the Brazil which was ignorant, oligarchic and authoritarian. Rui sought to attract the urban vote. He supported democratic principles and the secret ballot. He referred to the need for strong central power, to be achieved by unifying the judiciary, punishing those states which violated the federal constitution, intervening more frequently in the economic and fiscal conflicts within states, controlling the right of individual states to contract foreign loans, and ensuring federal protection of the coffee economy. His programme illustrates that São Paulo was not so much interested in extreme state autonomy as in being the dominant power in a more or less integrated country. The programme of Hermes da Fonseca supported budgetary equilibrium, the impermeability of the constitution, ample state autonomy, and laid particular emphasis on the views and interests of Rio Grande do Sul. It is important to remember, however, that the issue of autonomy was particularly important to the politicians of Rio Grande do Sul, but not in general to the military. The armed forces always supported programmes designed to reinforce the centralization of power. In addition, Hermes deliberately referred to the rights and grievances of workers. And during his administration, he lent his support to the holding of a national workers' congress, in which moderate elements participated under the auspices of the government.

The administration of Hermes da Fonseca (1910–14) witnessed the fragmentation of the decision-making process, which became divided among three sectors: the civilian oligarchies of Minas and, especially, Rio Grande do Sul, the president himself, and a group of army officers, particularly the colonels, who wished to carry out modifications in the control of power within the states. The army officers formed a pressure group around the president, and were largely responsible for the 'salvationist' movement, whose aims were to 'preserve' the purity of republican institutions.

The 'salvationists', anticipating the *tenentes* in the north-east after the Revolution of 1930, intervened in Pernambuco, Alagoas, Bahia and Ceará to bring down oligarchic leaders who, in most cases, counted on the support of the PRC. There were cases of personal ambition behind many such military encroachments, but these reflected more complex issues at play within the army. Entrenched in the central government the 'salvationists' sought to curb the political power of the oligarchies, while at the same time reducing the more blatant aspects of social inequality. They had a relative if transitory success in the north-east, given the weakness of the local elites, but failed in their attempts to name a military candidate for the presidency of Rio Grande do Sul, and to intervene in São Paulo.

The dangerous upheavals which occurred during the Hermes administration served as a warning to the political elites of São Paulo and Minas Gerais, who patched up the *café com leite* alliance in 1914, and elected Wenceslau Brás from Minas Gerais to the presidency (1914–18). Severely damaged by the 'salvationist' movement, the PRC entered a period of crisis, which came to a head in 1915 with the assassination of Pinheiro Machado.

The outbreak of the first world war marked the end of the *belle époque* of the oligarchy. The economic difficulties resulting from the international situation stimulated the emergence of labour agitation between 1917 and 1920, as we have seen. The wave of strikes died down relatively quickly, but other social forces were to threaten the stability of the Old Republic. The pressures of the urban middle class, which sought to widen the base of the oligarchic system, and the attacks of middle-ranking army officers were to alter the political framework. Although these sectors lacked autonomy, they would lend an added dimension to the rifts between and within the regional oligarchies.

In the presidential election of 1919 the growing political participation of the urban population was clearly visible. The election was held in exceptional circumstances because of the death of president-elect Rodrigues Alves (a Paulista, who had been president in 1902–6 and who was re-elected in 1918). It was won by the 'official' compromise candidate, Epitácio Pessoa from Paraíba, the first – and only – north-easterner to serve as president (1919–22) during the First Republic. However, Rui Barbosa, who had been defeated in 1910 and 1914, presented himself as an independent candidate, campaigned on a moderate reformist ticket which included labour legislation, and secured approximately one-third of the votes. He was the outright winner in the Federal District.

The election of 1922 revealed the growing regional tensions within the ruling class; it was the only election in which there was a clear rift between the two major states on the one hand, and a bloc of intermediate states on the other. Moreover the army, prompted by some episodes which involved its honour, intervened on the side of the opposition. The São Paulo–Minas alliance put forward as its candidate during the first months of 1921 the Mineiro politician, Artur Bernardes. Rio Grande do Sul contested his candidature, and denounced the political arrangement as being a way of guaranteeing resources for coffee valorization, at a time when the country was in need of financial stabilization. The politicians of Rio Grande do Sul also feared a possible revision of the constitution which might limit the autonomy of the states, as was, in fact, carried out by Bernardes in 1926. Rio Grande do Sul was joined by Bahia, Pernambuco, and the state of Rio de Janeiro, which ranked fourth, fifth and sixth in terms of electoral importance, and under the banner of the 'Republican Reaction' they put forward Nilo Peçanha as their candidate. Nilo had occupied the presidency for some months after the death in office of Afonso Pena in 1909, and had guaranteed Hermes da Fonseca's subsequent electoral triumph. A man of humble background, he had been a supporter of Floriano Peixoto, and had his political base in the oligarchy of his native state of Rio. The programme of the 'Republican Reaction', which was directly inspired by the politicians of Rio Grande do Sul, concentrated on measures against inflation and in favour of currency convertibility and budgetary stability. The more powerful states were accused of imperialism, and protective measures were requested for all Brazil's export products, not just coffee. Nilo was not opposed to the current policy of coffee valorization, which also benefited the state of Rio de Janeiro, but he was critical of the special treatment given to coffee. This was a theme which was especially dear to the representatives of Rio Grande do Sul. The military's intervention in the succession problem was made all the easier because of its links with the politicians of Rio Grande do Sul and the candidate himself. On the surface, however, it sought to preserve the values and honour of the military establishment, which had been the target for virulent attack through letters published in the Rio newspaper *Correio da Manhã* in October 1921, bearing the false signature of Bernardes.

Bernardes, the 'official' candidate, won the election of March 1922. It only remained for Congress to confirm the result. From the point of view of the regional oligarchies, as soon as one of the candidates was deemed to have won, the defeated parties had to come to an agreement in order to preserve the system. In 1922, the rule was almost broken. Because of the tense situation vis-à-vis the military, consideration was even given to the withdrawal of the president-elect, and the choice of a third candidate. There were also some revolutionary utterances among the army hierarchy. In the event, however, the leader of the Rio Grande oligarchy, Borges de Medeiros, refused to support further opposition. The struggle between the government and the opposition gradually died down. Dissidents within the defeated regional oligarchies and the military hierarchy were gradually neutralized, although the Bernardes administration had repeatedly to resort to declarations of a state of seige.

At another level, the crisis in the oligarchic system was revealed in the breaking of the political monopoly of the PRP in São Paulo, where the Democratic party (PD) was founded in 1926. The creation of the PD resulted from the effects of social differentiation in São Paulo, from the pressures of new generations in favour of a widening of career opportunities and access to the political system, and from ideological disagreements. Among its leading figures were the young sons of coffee planters and of traditional Brazilian families, some industrialists, and above all middle-class professionals, such as lawyers, journalists, and professors from the law faculty. The PD appeared on the political scene as a liberal democratic party. Its aims were to separate republican institutions from republican practice by means of a secret ballot, minority representation, the separation of executive, legislative and judicial powers, and the assumption of electoral supervision by the judiciary. It made vague gestures in the direction of social reforms, while on the economic and financial front its differences with the PRP were superficial. The official newspaper of the PD conveyed a message which was particularly relevant to the aspirations of the traditional urban middle class during the 1920s. Its favourite targets for attack were 'artificial industrialization', which was associated with powerful industrialists of foreign origin, the mass of immigrants controlled by the PRP, and the foreign companies responsible for basic services in the city of São Paulo. Events following the Revolution of 1930 were to show that the PD would not sacrifice its regional interests in order to align with other opposition groups. Nevertheless, during the late 1920s, its activity contributed to the weakening of the political power of the São Paulo oligarchy at the national level.

In the meantime the middle ranks of the army (*tenentes*) had broken with the 'republican order' in a series of *tenentista* rebellions. In July 1922, there was an uprising at the Copacabana fortress in Rio de Janeiro. In

July 1924, the rebels actually got as far as controlling the city of São Paulo for more than two weeks. In October 1924, and in 1926, there were revolts in various cities in Rio Grande do Sul. However, the *tenentista* movement created its great myth through the activities of the Prestes Column, a military force which joined together the revolutionaries from São Paulo and Rio Grande do Sul. Led by Miguel Costa and Luís Carlos Prestes, the future leader of the Brazilian Communist party, the Column undertook a 'long march' through the interior of the country, travelling some 24,000 kilometres between April 1925 and February 1927, when its remnants eventually crossed the border into Bolivia.

The insurrections of the 1920s continued the tradition of rebellion among young army officers, which dated from the beginning of the Republic. There were, however, important differences, which were the result of changes in the military apparatus, in the relationship established over the years between the army and the oligarchic system, and in the political system itself.

The *tenentes* had been educated during a period when both the military and society were going through a process of transition. The officer corps had begun to change with the creation of the Military School at Realengo in 1911, which replaced the old school at Praia Vermelha, closed for good in 1904, after its last revolt. The ideology behind the new school was very different from that of its predecessor. By providing markedly military teaching and discipline, it sought to produce a professional soldier, removed from politics, and directed towards specifically military purposes. Although products of Realengo, the *tenentes* adopted one of the principles of the doctrine of the soldier citizen, namely that of the right of the military to intervene in politics, even against the wishes of the civilian and military authorities. However, the positivist ideologists of Praia Vermelha had tended to lay greater stress on the citizen as opposed to the soldier. In its most extreme form, according to the thinking of Benjamin Constant, positivism held that the 'industrial regime' would ultimately render armies useless; 'the armies hitherto used as tools of destruction [would be] confined to the museum of history'. This corollary to the doctrine of the soldier citizen was unknown to the *tenentes*. Their ideology was not based on the interdependence of the civilian and military worlds, but on the general function of the armed forces as protectors of the people. This military consciousness was helped by the growing organization of the army, and by the concept of the soldier as being a person removed from civilian life. Like the former *tarimbeiros*, the *tenentes* were supremely conscious of the special values of the 'caste' to which they belonged. The initial stimulus to their actions derived in part from the insults directed at the army in the so-called forged letters of October 1921.

At the same time, the *tenentista* movement produced a rift within the military establishment, between middle-ranking officers and their commanders. Despite the fact that they always sought to associate themselves with certain high-ranking personnel, in order to lend some prestige to their rebellions, the rebels never succeeded in attracting the military hierarchy apart from the occasional support of individual figures. Because of this, they became more entrenched in their resolve to cleanse not only society at large, but the very institution to which they belonged. One of the revolutionary leaders, Juarez Távora, for example, openly attacked the minister of war, accusing him of indulging in 'mean and low' (*tacanho e porco*) militarism, which was tailor-made to accord with the whims and weaknesses of President Bernardes.

This division between a section of the officer corps and the army hierarchy can be attributed to various factors. The cohesion of the officer corps as a whole had never been strong in the army, and the situation tended to become more acute as a result of the cautious attitude adopted by high-ranking officers toward the oligarchic system. Within the military framework itself, the system of slow promotion created a large body of men in intermediate positions, whose prospects for achieving higher rank were few. For its part, the hierarchy enjoyed privileges, but was unable to impose complete control of the whole organization. The situation was very different from that prevailing in the navy, which, ever since the days of the Empire, had been considered a stronghold of the aristocracy, where the basic division was between the officer corps and the ratings. It was no coincidence that the main rank and file movement within the armed forces during the First Republic, the Sailors' Revolt of 1910, should have occurred in the navy – in protest against the system of corporal punishment. The navy was relatively immune from *tenentista* influence, the only evidence of rebelliousness being the revolt on the destroyer *São Paulo* in 1924.

With regard to social and political objectives of *tenentismo*, there was an important change of direction with the Revolution of October 1930 and the entry of the *tenentes*, along with other factions, into government. (Prestes had broken with the movement in May, issuing a manifesto in which he proclaimed his adherence to revolutionary socialism.) During the 1920s, however, the *tenentes* were effectively outside the machinery of government, and involved in a struggle against the power structure. They made their presence felt through military action, and their internal differences had not yet been clearly debated. Despite this, however, two tendencies appeared in embryonic form within the movement itself. One of these, formed by Prestes, Siqueira Campos and Miguel Costa, associated the overthrow of the oligarchies with a vaguely popular nationalistic programme. The other, whose most representative figure was Juarez Távora, was not concerned with popular mobilization; it saw military intervention as a means of destroying the oligarchic system, while at the same time curbing 'the excesses of indiscipline among the masses'.

Tenentismo can be seen as a movement which was born at a particularly sensitive point in the state apparatus. It exposed the crisis in the oligarchic system, and offered in its place the prospect of a structure along corporatist lines. The type of political reform advocated by the *tenentes* was based on the need to widen the central government's sphere of action, and included in its ideology elements of anti-liberalism in vogue at the time. This was the essential tone of the movement during the 1920s, preaching as it did a rather naïve brand of social reform, coupled with an equally vague brand of nationalism. Its statements of theory during the 1920s were far more impregnated with 'nationalistic feeling' than with objectives directly attributable to the interests of a social class. The strengthening of the power of the state required uniformity of institutions, the expansion of education, and the consolidation of the government at the national level. Economic issues, including industrialization, were either ignored or given only scant consideration. In so far as their objectives were not clearly defined, while their unselfish idealism was unequivocally stated, the *tenentes* were able to count on the sympathy of those social sectors opposed to the prevailing order, including the working class. On the other hand, as far as the most representative dissident sectors within the oligarchy were concerned, the *tenentes* represented a reserve force which they could manipulate, while avoiding any permanent commitments. Nevertheless the resort to radical methods, namely violence, even though for limited ends, broke with normal political procedures, and created rifts which were only healed as a result of the special circumstances of 1929–30.

By the late 1920s the *tenentes* had been marginalized or were in exile, and the urban middle class was clearly limited in its ability to mobilize itself.

The deepening of the crisis in the oligarchic system was therefore due more to the reappearance of inter-state conflict and problems of adjustment within the oligarchic pact, though now in a new context. In 1926, the Paulista candidate, Washington Luís, assumed the presidency without any problems, and with the support of both Minas Gerais and Rio Grande do Sul. (In order to implement his programme of financial stabilization, which was welcomed by Rio Grande do Sul, Washington Luís nominated to the treasury a *gaúcho* politician who was gaining ascendency within the political oligarchy of his state, Getúlio Vargas.) The difficulty in reaching a unanimous agreement on the presidential succession in 1929 can be blamed on the political initiative of the president himself. During 1928, it had become clear that the dominant political group in São Paulo, encouraged by Washington Luís, did not intend to loosen its grip on the central government. The name of Júlio Prestes – president of the state of São Paulo – emerged as a candidate for the presidency. This broke all the rules of the game. Ever since 1914, the presidency had rotated between São Paulo and Minas, with the exception of 1919, following the death of president-elect Rodrigues Alves. The return of a Mineiro president to power in 1930 would have normally been expected. The intransigence of Washington Luís can be attributed to personal characteristics and to reasons of a more general nature. Taking for granted the inflexibility of the oligarchic system, which made it very difficult for the opposition to achieve any measure of success, the president set about trying to ensure the continuity of his policy of financial stabilization, through the choice of a successor whom he could trust. There was at least one historical precedent in his favour: in 1902, Campos Sales had guaranteed the pursuit of a deflationary financial policy through the (first) election of Rodrigues Alves, which resulted in a Paulista succeeding a Paulista in the presidency. The attitude of Washington Luís should also be seen in the light of a situation in which the São Paulo elite had been gradually losing the most important administrative posts to men from Rio Grande do Sul and Minas Gerais, a tendency which was to increase substantially after 1930.

By imposing the candidature of Júlio Prestes, Washingon believed he could neutralize any serious dissension which might eventually emerge, given that relations between the federal government and Rio Grande do Sul were good. At most, it seemed that Minas Gerais would enter the struggle in isolation, not only without much chance of success, but also without producing any serious repercussions. Sure enough, it was the president of Minas, Antônio Carlos Ribeiro de Andrada, who began to negotiate for an opposition candidate. In order to propel Rio Grande do Sul into a contest which would mean breaking its agreement with the federal government, and losing the advantages which this implied, it was necessary to offer the presidency to that state. In June 1929, after much negotiation, Minas Gerais and Rio Grande do Sul agreed to launch the reticent Getúlio Vargas, now governor of Rio Grande do Sul, as candidate. They obtained the adherence of the tiny north-eastern state of Paraíba, which was to put forward João Pessoa as vice-presidential candidate. The chances of this group achieving victory in the election were slight, for the central government had the support not only of the oligarchy of São Paulo but of seventeen states in all.

The Liberal Alliance was formed as a regional front, which included the vast majority of the political representatives of Rio Grande do Sul and Minas Gerais, and was also joined by the Democratic party of São Paulo. As for Paraíba, in-fighting within the oligarchy caused one fairly influential sector to support the government. It appeared that a new regional rift was emerging, which was of greater importance than any previous rift, but which nevertheless belonged to the traditional pattern of succession disputes typical of the First Republic. The Alliance made great efforts to remain within the limits of the system, to which most of its leaders were committed. Even Vargas openly stated this intention in a letter to Washington Luís in July 1929, and João Neves da Fontoura – leader of Rio Grande do Sul in the Federal Chamber – declared that the opposition was disposed to give its sympathetic consideration to other candidates from São Paulo.

The programme of the Liberal Alliance reflected the aspirations of those regional ruling classes not directly linked to coffee. Its objective was also to gain the sympathy of the middle class – and to some extent the working class. It defended the need to stimulate national output generally, and not just that of coffee. It also opposed the various schemes for coffee valorization in the name of financial orthodoxy, and for this reason it did not disagree on this particular point with the policy of Washington Luís. It proposed certain measures for protecting workers, such as the right to pensions, special regulations regarding the employment of women and children, and the right to paid holidays. (In the major urban centres, where Vargas was obliged to campaign somewhat against his will, he was received enthusiastically – even in São Paulo where the anti-Paulista character of the Liberal Alliance would have been easy to exploit.) As a clear reply to the president who had asserted that the social problem in Brazil was 'a police problem', the opposition platform stated that it could not be ignored, and that it constituted 'one of the problems which would have to be seriously considered by the administrative power'. It laid greatest emphasis on the defence of the rights of the individual, amnesty (in order to gain the sympathy of the *tenentes*), and political reform to guarantee genuinely representative elections. With regard to the theme of industrialization, its programme made the old distinction between natural and artificial industries, namely, those which operated with raw materials available in the country, and those for which materials had to be imported. It condemned the protectionism afforded to the latter, under the allegation that it pushed up the cost of living, while benefiting one or two privileged enterprises. The protection of the rights of the worker was, in turn, set out in terms designed to contrast with the privileges enjoyed by the industrialists. The associations representing most industries in São Paulo supported Júlio Prestes, the official candidate. This attitude can be explained by the firm relations which had been established among the different sectors of the ruling class in São Paulo, and by the fact that the opposition did not present itself as being attractive to the industrial bourgeoisie.

It was in the middle of the electoral campaign, in October 1929, that the world economic crisis began. The opposition leaders began to use the crisis as a new argument with which to demonstrate the ineptitude of the government. The immediate outcome was hardly noticeable. However, the crisis led to disagreement between the coffee sector and the central government. It had come at a time when the problems of overproduction were becoming increasingly serious. The coffee sector requested from Washington Luís financial concessions and a moratorium on its debts. These concessions would be payable through the Bank of Brazil in view of the difficulties which the bank of the state of São Paulo was experiencing. The president, who was particularly anxious to preserve his plan for stability in currency exchange, which would certainly have collapsed if these concessions had been made, refused to attend to the pleas of a sector which he in theory represented. This provoked a wave of discontent in São Paulo. The Congresso dos Fazendeiros, organized not only by supporters of the PD but also by all those rural associations whose leaders in the main supported the PRP, and held at the end of December 1929 and the beginning of January 1930, was a clear manifestation of these grievances. In spite of this, the situation did not reach breaking point. After the Congress, the mobilization of coffee growers decreased and the benefit to the PD in terms of votes was relatively insignificant. The coffee sector, despite its discontent, had no reason to believe that a victory for the Liberal Alliance would result in any greater attention being paid to its interests. Indeed, the regional composition of the opposition and one or two carefully worded pronouncements seemed to indicate the contrary.

The elections of 1 March 1930 were carried out in accordance with the traditions of the Old Republic. Both government and opposition resorted to fraud on a large scale. It is sufficient to remember that Getúlio Vargas obtained 298,677 votes against 982 in his own state. The victory of Júlio Prestes, conceded publicly by Borges de Medeiros, seemed to mark the end of regional division. However, at this point, differences of opinion within the Liberal Alliance began to be voiced. These can be explained in terms of a generation gap rather than ideological disagreement. Alongside the traditional politicians in Minas Gerais and Rio Grande do Sul, there was a group of educated younger Mineiros and *gaúchos* who were busy climbing the political ladder within the shadow of the old oligarchy. In Rio Grande do Sul, men like Vargas himself, Flores da Cunha, Osvaldo Aranha, Lindolfo Collor, João Neves and Maurício Cardoso formed a group known as 'the generation of 1907', which was the year when they had completed their schooling. In Minas Gerais, too, younger political figures emerged, such as Virgílio de Melo Franco and Francisco Campos, both from traditional regional families. Until the late 1920s, these men had not openly denounced the political system of the First Republic. In 1930, however, this sector of the political elite chose to follow the road which until then only the *tenentes* had taken.

Although defeated, the *tenentista* movement was still a force to be reckoned with because of its military experience and its prestige within the army. The conditions were now ripe for a *rapprochement* between younger politicians and rebellious army officers. Even during the electoral campaign, some steps had been taken in this direction. However, the *tenentes* proceeded with the utmost caution. The balance of their relations with the legal opposition was fairly negative. They had been used for the benefit of the opposition without receiving anything in return. Apart from this, the Liberal Alliance contained some of their worst enemies: for example, ex-president Bernardes, who had pursued the Prestes Column and who was seen to synthesize all the vices of the Republic, and João Pessoa, who had been responsible for the prosecution of more than a few military rebels. Among the younger politicians there were several – for example, Osvaldo Aranha – who had played a part in putting down the insurrection in Rio Grande do Sul. In spite of these barriers – and the suspicions were mutual – an agreement was reached. However, significantly, the military leadership of the revolutionary movement was given to a man who represented 'the most responsible sectors of the armed forces', and who had the complete trust of the *gaúcho* leaders. This was Góes Monteiro, then a lieutenant-colonel, who was a native of Alagoas but whose career was closely linked to Rio Grande do Sul. Góes had not been a member of the revolutionary faction during the 1920s. On the contrary, he had fought against the Prestes Column in the north-eastern states.

The conspiracy planned between March and October 1930 went through a series of twists and turns, helped along by an occasional dramatic event, such as the assassination in August of João Pessoa over local political issues. Finally, the rebellion began on 3 October in Rio Grande do Sul, and on the following day in the north-east. In the rebel states the state militias declared their loyalty to the Revolution. The adherence of the army was only immediate in the south, while in Minas Gerais and some north-eastern states there was a degree of resistance. Washington Luís remained in power in Rio de Janeiro. His government's main base of support was São Paulo, where both the state militia and the army prepared to resist troops advancing from the south. The prevailing climate in São Paulo was, however, far from euphoric. The Paulista ruling class, which was in a state of disagreement with its representatives in central government, had not got as far as switching its allegiance to the opposition. However, it had no intention of throwing itself into armed conflict by mobilizing the population under its control. Apart from this, a large sector of the middle class rallied behind the Democratic party which, although it had scarcely participated in the plans for revolution, supported the revolutionaries. These factors contributed to create a climate of expectancy in São Paulo, where an attempt by the central government to call up reservists failed miserably.

Any serious military confrontation in São Paulo was, in the event, avoided by the intervention of the hierarchy of the armed forces in Rio de Janeiro. For the first time, the high commands of the army and the navy united in order to carry out a 'moderating intervention', which deposed Washington Luís on 24 October. The military hierarchy tried to remain in power, and even formed a governing *junta*. On the other hand, pressure from the revolutionary forces advancing from the south, and popular demonstrations in Rio de Janeiro, guaranteed Getúlio Vargas's claim to the presidency. He duly took office on 3 November 1930 as the head of a provisional government. Few could have foreseen that Vargas would remain in power for the next fifteen years.

The Revolution of 1930 was the product of various social groupings whose values and objectives differed widely: dissident regional oligarchies, sectors of the urban middle class, and intermediate ranks in the army. With some exceptions, the urban workers remained outside the movement. The revolutionaries, however, benefited from their sympathy as a result of the prestige of the *tenentes* and the vaguely reformist rhetoric of the Liberal Alliance. (The tiny Communist party had produced its own candidate for the elections and denounced the Alliance as being 'fascist' in character. It is worth remembering, however, that until the eve of the elections at least, the leaders of the party were taking delivery of arms and establishing contact with *tenentista* elements who were plotting in São Paulo.) When considering the 1920s as a whole, the role of the younger generation in voicing political opposition or in revolutionary activity is particularly noteworthy. The PD of São Paulo contrasted clearly with the PRP in the relative youth of its leaders. *Tenentismo* was a movement of junior officers in the army. Within the dissident sectors of the oligarchy, it was the younger elements who adopted revolutionary attitudes. From this viewpoint, the crisis in the oligarchic system can be seen as a consequence of the inability of the system to respond to the demands placed on it, which in return were the result of social differentiation and both upward and downward social mobility.

The demise of the Old Republic in 1930 brought an end to the system of oligarchic rule which had guaranteed the hegemony of the coffee bourgeoisie of São Paulo. However, it did not mark the end of *coronelismo*, particularly in the rural areas. New *coronéis* emerged to replace the old, and the system of patronage remained and adapted slowly to the corporative pact which was gradually elaborated between civil society and the state. The continuation of clientalism, albeit in modified form, was largely due to the fact that the Revolution of 1930 did nothing to change the system of production in the rural areas, although agrarian reform had become relevant to the political debate by this time. Developments after 1930 combined two elements which historically are impossible to separate: the victory of a heterogeneous revolutionary movement and the effects of the world economic crisis. The latter transformed long-standing problems into urgent issues and inevitably speeded up the slow process of change. Given the historical conditions in which the industrial bourgeoisie had been formed, it required a world crisis and the breaking of the hegemony of the São Paulo coffee bourgeoisie for the process of industrialization, for example, to be given renewed impetus. The expansion and centralization of the power of the state was the main feature of institutional change during the years after the Revolution of 1930. It was a move which was dictated by the requirements of the new economic and financial order, but it also corresponded to the interests and concepts of some of those forces, not least the military forces, which had been responsible for the Revolution. The central bureaucracy was expanded and virtually transformed into a new social category with its own interests, apart from carrying out its function as the mouthpiece of the interests of the dominant class. Moreover, the relationship between civil society and the state changed in the sense that the different sectors of the dominant class, the urban middle class and at least one section of the working class now confronted each other and reached agreement largely under the shadow of an increasingly powerful state.

BIBLIOGRAPHICAL ESSAYS

LIST OF ABBREVIATIONS

The following abbreviations have been used for works which occur repeatedly in the bibliographical essays:

AESC	*Annales: Économies, Sociétés, Civilisations*
CHLA	*Cambridge History of Latin America*
HAHR	*Hispanic American Historical Review*
HM	*Historia Mexicana*
JGSWGL	*Jahrbuch für Geschichte von Staat, Wirtschaft und Gesellschaft Lateinamerikas*
JLAS	*Journal of Latin American Studies*
LARR	*Latin American Research Review*

I. MEXICO: RESTORED REPUBLIC AND PORFIRIATO, 1867–1910

In 1958 Daniel Cosío Villegas, one of Mexico's greatest historians whose special field was the history of Mexico from 1867 to 1910, stated that, quite apart from the period of the Restored Republic (1867–76), nearly 2,000 books and pamphlets had been written on the Porfirian period (1876–1910) alone. Yet, with a number of significant exceptions, the most important works on this period of Mexican history have appeared since the 1950s. The secondary literature on the period 1867–1910, and especially on the Porfiriato, is assessed in Daniel Cosío Villegas, 'El Porfiriato: su historiografía o arte histórico', in *Extremos de América* (Mexico, 1949), 113–82; John Womack, Jr, 'Mexican political historiography, 1959–1969', in *Investigaciones contemporáneas sobre historia de México* (Mexico and Austin, Texas, 1971); Enrique Florescano, *El poder y la lucha por el poder en la historiografía mexicana* (Mexico, 1980); and Thomas Benjamin and Marcial Ocasio-Meléndez, 'Organizing the memory of modern Mexico: Porfirian historiography in perspective, 1880s–1980s', *HAHR*, 64/2 (1984), 323–64. The most important, most comprehensive work on the whole period from 1867 to 1910 is the monumental *Historia moderna de México* (Mexico, 1958–72), a huge thirteen-volume collective work edited by Daniel Cosío Villegas. It was written in the 1950s and 1960s under Cosío's direction by a team of historians who collected every available piece of evidence in Mexican, American and European archives, and examined all aspects of life in Mexico, embracing political, economic and social as well as intellectual history.

The Restored Republic has on the whole provoked far less discussion, controversy and literature than the Díaz era that followed it. Most of the controversy on the earlier period has focused on Juárez the man, on the policies of his regime, and on the nature and basis of liberalism. See, for example, Jesús Reyes Heroles, *El liberalismo mexicano* (Mexico, 1957). And see *CHLA* III, bibliographical essay 10. On the question of whether the Juárez regime was basically different from that of Porfirio Díaz, three very different viewpoints have been expressed: Francisco Bulnes, *El verdadero Juárez y la verdad sobre la intervención y el imperio* (Paris, 1904); Cosío Villegas (ed.), *Historia moderna*, vol. 1; and Laurens B. Perry, *Juárez and Díaz, machine politics in Mexico* (DeKalb, 1978). The presidency of Lerdo has produced no such controversies and there are no really sharp differences between the interpretations of Cosío Villegas and Frank A. Knapp, *The life of Sebastián Lerdo de Tejada, 1823–1899* (Austin, 1951).

Four contemporary or near-contemporary works are representative of the wide spectrum of opinion on the Porfiriato: Justo Sierra, *México y su evolución social* (Mexico, 1901), a multi-volume series of essays edited by Porfirio Díaz's best-known intellectual supporter, constitutes a self-portrait and self-justification of the Díaz regime; *El verdadero Díaz y la Revolución* (Mexico, 1920) by Francisco Bulnes, another of the Díaz regime's most influential intellectual supporters and its most critical and intelligent defender in the period during and after the Mexican Revolution; and John Kenneth Turner, *Barbarous Mexico* (2nd edn, 1910; reprint, Austin, Texas, 1969) and Carleton Beals, *Porfirio Díaz, dictator of Mexico* (New York, 1932), two works by Americans which constitute the strongest indictments of the Díaz regime. José C. Valadés, *El porfirismo: historia de un régimen* (3 vols., Mexico, 1941–7) was the first general assessment of the Díaz regime to utilize a large array of hitherto unavailable internal documents of the regime.

One of the most important points of dispute, closely linked to the economic development of Mexico from 1867 to 1910, is the discussion of the origins of Mexico's economic underdevelopment. Was it primarily the result of the laissez-faire economics of the Díaz regime? Or was Mexico's underdevelopment mainly due to the inheritance of the colonial period and to the ceaseless civil wars of the first 50 years after Mexico gained its independence? Was there a real alternative to what developed? What were the effects of foreign investment and penetration? Can Mexico's economy in that period be characterized as feudal, capitalist, dependent? What more general theories (imperialism, dependency, etc.) can be applied to the Mexican case? These are some of the issues that are dealt with in very different ways in Ciro Cardoso (ed.), *México en el siglo XIX. Historia económica y de la estructura social* (Mexico, 1980); John Coatsworth, *Growth against development: the economic impact of railroads in Porfirian Mexico* (DeKalb, 1980; Spanish editions: Mexico, 1976; 2nd edn, Mexico, 1984); Sergio de la Peña, *La formación del capitalismo en México* (Mexico, 1976); and Enrique Semo (ed.), *México bajo la dictadura porfiriana* (Mexico, 1983).

A second problem which has been the centre of controversy and discussion about the Díaz period could broadly be summarized as the agrarian question. This involves a very different set of problems. How important was the expropriation of the lands of free villages and what were the economic and social consequences of this development? What kind of labour conditions existed on Mexico's large haciendas? Was labour predominantly free or was peonage the dominant form of labour on the estates? Were the hacendados mainly feudal landlords thinking above all in terms of power or prestige or were they 'capitalists' seeking to maximize their profits and taking economically rational decisions? The terms of the discussion of the agrarian issue were set by two authors who wrote in the Porfirian period: Andrés Molina Enríquez, *Los grandes problemas nacionales* (Mexico, 1909) and Wistano Luis Orozco, *Legislación y jurisprudencia sobre terrenos baldíos* (2 vols., Mexico, 1895). From 1910 until today practically all writings on the agrarian issue have in one way or the other either confirmed, refuted or in some way dealt with the theories expounded by these two authors. Some of the very different points of view on the agrarian issue are expressed in Friedrich Katz, 'Labour conditions on haciendas in Porfirian Mexico. Some trends and tendencies', *HAHR*, 54/1 (1974), 1–47 and Katz (ed.), *La servidumbre agraria en México en la época porfiriana* (Mexico, 1977); Frank Tannenbaum, *The Mexican agrarian revolution* (Washington, DC, 1929); Arturo Warman,

Venimos a contradecir: Los campesinos de Morelos y el estado nacional (Mexico, 1976), Eng. trans. *We come to object. The peasants of Morelos and the national state* (Baltimore, 1981).

A more recent subject of discussion has been the nature and the real power and effectiveness of the Mexican state which has been examined from differing viewpoints in John H. Coatsworth, 'Los orígenes del autoritarismo moderno en México', *Foro Internacional*, 16 (1975), 205–32, and Juan Felipe Leal, *La burguesía y el estado mexicano* (Mexico, 1972). The discussion about the nature of the state is closely linked to research about the ideology, above all positivism and social Darwinism, of Mexico's leaders during the Restored Republic and the Porfirian era; for example, Arnaldo Córdova, *La ideología de la Revolución Mexicana: la formación del nuevo régimen* (Mexico, 1973); William D. Raat, *El positivismo durante el Porfiriato: 1876–1910* (Mexico, 1975); and Leopoldo Zea, *Positivism in Mexico* (Austin, Texas, 1974).

An important corollary to the analysis of the power of the central state is an examination of the importance and influence of regional and local institutions. This problem has been examined in recent years not only by historians but also by anthropologists. See, for example, Paul Friedrich, *Agrarian revolt in a Mexican village* (Englewood Cliffs, NJ, 1970); Luis González y González, *Pueblo en vilo: microhistoria de San José de Gracia* (Mexico, 1967), Eng. trans. *San José de Gracia: Mexican village in transition* (Austin, Texas, 1974); G. M. Joseph, *Revolution from without: Yucatán, Mexico and the United States, 1880–1924* (Cambridge, 1982); Mark Wasserman, *Capitalists, caciques, and revolution: elite and foreign enterprise in Chihuahua, 1854–1911* (Chapel Hill, 1984); John Womack, *Zapata and the Mexican Revolution* (New York, 1969); Héctor Aguilar Camín, *La frontera nómada: Sonora y la Revolución Mexicana* (Mexico, 1977).

These local studies are inextricably linked to attempts to analyse the different social classes that developed during the Porfirian period at the local, regional and national level. Apart from the peasantry, increasing attention has focused on the working class: see Rodney Anderson, *Outcasts in their own land: Mexican industrial workers, 1906–1911* (DeKalb, 1976); Ciro F. S. Cardoso, Francisco G. Hermosillo and Salvador Hernández, *La clase obrera en la historia de México, de la dictadura porfirista a los tiempos libertarios* (Mexico, 1980); John M. Hart, *Anarchism and the Mexican working class, 1860–1931* (Austin, Texas, 1978); Juan Felipe Leal and José Woldenberg, *La clase obrera en la historia de México: del estado liberal a los inicios de la dictadura porfirista* (Mexico, 1980); and David

Walker, 'Porfirian labor politics: working class organizations in Mexico City and Porfirio Díaz, 1876–1902', *The Americas*, 37 (January 1981), 257–87. On intellectuals, see Jesús Silva Herzog, *El agrarismo mexicano y la reforma agraria* (Mexico, 1964) and James Cockcroft, *Intellectual precursors of the Mexican Revolution, 1900–1913* (Austin, Texas, 1968).

One field that has been the subject of long and varied discussion has been that of the relations of Mexico with other countries during the Porfirian era. For a long time, the only major archives available for this period were the American State Department files, and both Mexican and American historians concentrated on US–Mexican relations to the exclusion of other countries. This situation changed in the 1950s when Daniel Cosío Villegas was able to consult not only American but hitherto inaccessible Mexican records as well. As a result, he wrote a detailed analysis of Mexican–American relations between 1867 and 1910: *The United States versus Porfirio Díaz* (Lincoln, Nebraska, 1963). Unlike the 30-year limit of American archives, most European archives had a 50-year limit; works on the relations between Mexico and the major European powers in the Díaz period came out at a much later date. See Alfred Tischendorf, *Great Britain and Mexico in the era of Porfirio Díaz* (Durham, NC, 1961); Friedrich Katz, *Deutschland, Díaz und die mexikanische Revolution: Die deutsche Politik in Mexiko 1870–1920* (Berlin, 1964).

2. THE MEXICAN REVOLUTION, 1910–1920

Printed sources, bibliography and historiography

The latest, most inclusive and best organized guide to the literature on the Mexican Revolution is W. D. Raat, *The Mexican Revolution. An annotated guide to recent scholarship* (Boston, 1982). Indispensable guides to official documents, pamphlets, newspapers, manifestos, and published correspondence are L. González y González (ed.), *Fuentes de la historia contemporánea de México: libros y folletos* (3 vols., Mexico, 1962–3) and S. R. Ross (ed.), *Fuentes de la historia contemporánea de México: periódicos y revistas* (4 vols., Mexico, 1965–76). The most important body of printed materials is I. Fabela and J. E. de Fabela (eds.), *Documentos históricos de la revolución mexicana* (27 vols. and index, Mexico, 1960–76). Useful reprints from the Mexican press appear in M. González Ramírez (ed.), *Fuentes para la historia de la revolución mexicana* (4 vols., Mexico, 1954–7).

Recent bibliographies and historiographic articles with analysis of the main currents in the literature on the Revolution include: D. M. Bailey, 'Revisionism and the recent historiography of the Mexican Revolution', *HAHR*, 58/1 (1978), 62–79; G. Bringas and D. Mascareño, *La prensa de los obreros mexicanos, 1870–1970. Hemerografía comentada* (Mexico, 1979); C. W. Reynolds, 'The economic historiography of twentieth-century Mexico', in *Investigaciones contemporáneas sobre historia de México. Memorias de la tercera reunión de historiadores mexicanos y norteamericanos* (Mexico and Austin, Texas, 1971), 339–57; J. D. Rutherford, *An annotated bibliography of the novels of the Mexican Revolution* (Troy, 1972); E. Suárez Gaona (ed.), *El movimiento obrero mexicano. Bibliografía* (Mexico, 1978); H. W. Tobler, 'Zur Historiographie der mexikanischen Revolution, 1910–1940', *JGSWGL*, 12 (1975), 286–331; J. Womack, Jr, 'Mexican political historiography, 1959–1969', in *Investigaciones contemporáneas*, 478–92, 'The historiography of Mexican labor', in *El trabajo y los trabajadores en la historia de México. Ponencias y comentarios presentados en la V reunión de historiadores mexicanos y norteamericanos* (Mexico and Tucson, 1979), 739–56, and 'The Mexican economy during the Revolution, 1910–1920: historiography and analysis', *Marxist Perspectives*, 1/4 (1978), 80–123.

General and interpretive

The fullest and still the best chronicle of the Mexican Revolution is J. C. Valadés, *Historia general de la revolución mexicana* (10 vols., Mexico, 1963–7), vols. I–VII.

Notable as old standards which are more or less in defence of the Revolution as a great popular victory are M. S. Alperovich, B. T. Rudenko and N. M. Lavrov, *La revolución mexicana: Cuatro estudios soviéticos* (Mexico, 1960); A. Brenner, *The wind that swept Mexico: the history of the Mexican Revolution* (Austin, Texas, 1971); M. González Ramírez, *La revolución social de México* (3 vols., Mexico, 1960–6); J. Silva Herzog, *Breve historia de la revolución mexicana* (2 vols., Mexico, 1960); F. Tannenbaum, *Peace by revolution: an interpretation of Mexico* (New York, 1933); E. Wolf, *Peasant wars of the twentieth century* (New York, 1969).

Notable as old standards more or less hostile to the Revolution are F. Bulnes, *El verdadero Díaz y la revolución* (Mexico, 1920); E. Gruening, *Mexico and its heritage* (New York, 1928); W. Thompson, *The people of Mexico: who they are and how they live* (New York, 1921); E. D. Trowbridge, *Mexico to-day and to-morrow* (New York, 1919); J. Vera Estañol, *Historia de la revolución mexicana: orígenes y resultados* (Mexico, 1957).

Among the new works, the most suggestive essays are Peter Calvert, 'The Mexican Revolution: theory or fact?' *JLAS*, 1/1 (1969), 51–68; Barry Carr, 'Las peculiaridades del norte mexicano, 1880–1927: ensayo de interpretacion', *HM*, 22/3 (1973), 320–46; François-X. Guerra, 'La révolution mexicaine: d'abord une révolution minière?' *AESC*, 36/5 (1981), 785–814; Jean A. Meyer, 'Periodización e ideología', in *Contemporary Mexico: Papers of the IV International Congress of Mexican History* (Los Angeles and Mexico, 1976), 711–22; Albert L. Michaels and Marvin D. Bernstein, 'The modernization of the old order: organization and periodization of twentieth-century Mexican history', in *Contemporary Mexico*, 687–710; and Enrique Semo, 'Las revoluciones en la historia de México', *Historia y Sociedad*, 2nd ser., 8 (1975), 49–61.

The main revisionist works are J. D. Cockcroft, *Mexico: class formation, capital accumulation, and the state* (New York, 1983); A. Córdova, *La ideología de la revolución mexicana. La formación del nuevo régimen* (Mexico, 1973); A. Gilly, *The Mexican Revolution* (London, 1983); N. M. Lavrov, *La revolución mexicana, 1910–1917* (Mexico, 1978); Jean Meyer, *La révolution mexicaine* (Paris, 1973); R. E. Ruiz, *The great rebellion. Mexico, 1905–1924* (New York, 1980).

Foreign relations, politics and war

The literature about these subjects is most abundant. One outstanding book treats them all three together: Friedrich Katz, *The secret war in Mexico. Europe, the United States, and the Mexican Revolution* (Chicago, 1981). The other notable studies in this category focus on specific or particular questions of state. The most significant such question is foreign relations. The literature on it is almost exclusively about Mexico's relations with the United States. Indispensable as a background is the work of Arthur S. Link, *Wilson: the new freedom* (Princeton, 1956), *Wilson: the struggle for neutrality, 1914–1915* (Princeton, 1960), *Wilson: confusions and crises, 1915–1916* (Princeton, 1960), and *Wilson: campaigns for progressivism and peace, 1916–1917* (Princeton, 1965).

The two most comprehensive treatments, from very different perspectives, are M. S. Alperovich and B. T. Rudenko, *La revolución mexicana de 1910–1917 y la política de los Estados Unidos* (Mexico, 1960) and P. E. Haley, *Revolution and intervention. The diplomacy of Taft and Wilson with Mexico, 1910–1917* (Cambridge, 1970). The view is at least as broad, but the chronological focus is closer, in P. Calvert, *The Mexican Revolution, 1910–1914. The diplomacy of the Anglo-American conflict* (Cambridge, 1968);

M. T. Gilderhus, *Diplomacy and revolution: U.S.–Mexican relations under Wilson and Carranza* (Tucson, 1977); K. J. Grieb, *The United States and Huerta* (Lincoln, 1969); R. F. Smith, *The United States and revolutionary nationalism in Mexico, 1916–1932* (Chicago, 1972); and B. Ulloa, *La revolución intervenida. Relaciones diplomáticas entre México y Estados Unidos, 1910–1914* (Mexico, 1971).

The particular questions that caused the worst problems in Mexican–American relations were oil and Francisco Villa. On oil, see Lorenzo Meyer, *México y los Estados Unidos en el conflicto petrolero (1917–1942)* (Mexico, 1968), translated as *Mexico and the United States in the oil controversy 1917–1942* (Austin, Texas, 1977); Dennis J. O'Brien, 'Petróleo e intervención. Relaciones entre Estados Unidos y México, 1917–1918', *HM*, 27/1 (1977), 103–40; and Emily S. Rosenberg, 'Economic pressure in Anglo-American diplomacy in Mexico, 1917–1918', *Journal of Inter-American Studies and World Affairs*, 17/2 (1975), 123–52. On Villa, see Clarence C. Clendenen, *The United States and Pancho Villa. A study in unconventional diplomacy* (Ithaca, 1981); and Alberto Salinas Carranza, *La expedición punitiva* (2nd edn, Mexico, 1957). Less important but still considerable among Mexico's foreign problems during the Revolution are the topics studied by Larry D. Hill, *Emissaries to a revolution: Woodrow Wilson's executive agents in Mexico* (Baton Rouge, 1973); and W. Dirk Raat, *Revoltosos: Mexico's rebels in the United States, 1903–1923* (College Station, Texas, 1981).

On politics, which in this literature means the struggle to dominate and manage the federal government, the books and articles are most numerous. Particularly interesting are contemporary reports: H. Baerlein, *Mexico. The land of unrest* (2nd edn, Philadelphia, 1914); E. I. Bell, *The political shame of Mexico* (New York, 1914); J. L. De Becker, *De cómo vino Huerta, y cómo se fue. Apuntes para la historia de un régimen militar* (Mexico, 1914); R. Prida, *De la dictadura a la anarquía* (2nd edn, Mexico, 1958). Biased but nevertheless revealing are certain memoirs: A. Breceda, *México revolucionario, 1913–1917* (2 vols., Madrid, 1920 and Mexico, 1914); F. González Garza, *La revolución mexicana. Mi contribución político-literaria* (Mexico, 1936); F. F. Palavicini, *Los diputados* (2nd edn, Mexico, 1976), *Historia de la constitución de 1917* (2 vols., Mexico, 1938), and *Mi vida revolucionaria* (Mexico, 1937); A. J. Pani, *Apuntes autobiográficos* (2 vols., 2nd edn, Mexico, 1950), and *Mi contribución al nuevo régimen, 1910–1933* (Mexico, 1936).

The first professional histories of the initial and middle phases of revolutionary politics remain the best surveys, despite their mistakes, errors, and omissions: C. C. Cumberland, *Mexican Revolution. Genesis under Madero* (Austin, Texas, 1952), and *Mexican Revolution. The constitutionalist years* (Austin, Texas, 1972). The latest surveys of the political history of the period are B. Ulloa, *Historia de la revolución mexicana, período 1914–1917*, vol. IV, *La revolución escindida* (Mexico, 1979), vol. V, *La encrucijada de 1915* (Mexico, 1979), and vol. VI, *La constitución de 1917* (Mexico, 1983).

Political monographs typically have a biographical focus. The standard work on the Maderista government remains Stanley R. Ross, *Francisco I. Madero, apostle of Mexican democracy* (New York, 1955). On Madero's main military lieutenant and nemesis, see Michael C. Meyer, *Mexican rebel, Pascual Orozco and the Mexican Revolution, 1910–1915* (Lincoln, 1967). The most intriguing book about Madero's conservative opposition remains Luis Liceaga, *Félix Díaz* (Mexico, 1958). And the standard work on the general who overthrew Madero and provoked the Constitutionalist movement is Michael C. Meyer, *Huerta, a political portrait* (Lincoln, 1972). Manifestly partisan and faulty but still the most informative treatments of the Villista movement are Federico Cervantes, *Francisco Villa y la revolución* (Mexico, 1960), and *Felipe Ángeles en la revolución* (3rd edn, Mexico, 1964). On Carranza and *carrancismo*, see Álvaro Matute, *Historia de la revolución mexicana, período 1917–1924*, vol. VIII, *La carrera del caudillo* (Mexico, 1980); and Douglas W. Richmond, *Venustiano Carranza's nationalist struggle, 1893–1920* (Lincoln, 1984). Pablo González, Jr, compiled a useful hagiography of his father, *El centinela fiel del constitucionalismo* (Monterrey, 1971). On Carranza's other, more fortunate lieutenant, see Linda Hall, *Álvaro Obregón, power and revolution in Mexico, 1911–1920* (College Station, Texas, 1981).

The first monograph on a collective political exercise is Robert E. Quirk, *The Mexican Revolution, 1914–1915. The Convention of Aguascalientes* (Bloomington, 1960). It is still commendable. But preferable on the same topic is Luis F. Amaya C., *La soberana convención revolucionaria, 1914–1916* (Mexico, 1966). The most accurate account of the *congreso* that delivered the new constitution is E. Victor Niemeyer, Jr, *Revolution at Queretaro. The Mexican Constitutional Convention of 1916–1917* (Austin, Texas, 1974). For an instructive comparison of the two conclaves, see Richard Roman, *Ideología y clase en la revolución mexicana. La convención y el congreso constituyente* (Mexico, 1976).

On the army in politics, the most substantial and interesting study is

Alicia Hernández Chávez, 'Militares y negocios en la revolución
mexicana', *HM*, 35/3 (1985). Another considerable analysis of the
military is Jean A. Meyer, 'Grandes compañías, ejércitos populares y
ejército estatal en la revolución mexicana (1910–1930)', *Anuario de
estudios americanos*, 31 (1974), 1005–30.

On the church, the best guide to the early years is Jean A. Meyer, 'Le
catholicisme social au Mexique jusqu'en 1913', *Revue historique*, 260
(1978), 143–59. For the middle and later years, see, despite its principled
bias, Antonio Rius Facius, *La juventud católica y la revolución mejicana, 1910–
1925* (Mexico, 1963).

The only serious treatment of political ideas is James D. Cockcroft,
Intellectual precursors of the Mexican Revolution, 1900–1913 (Austin, Texas,
1968). The only substantial study of an institution is Marte R. Gómez,
Historia de la Comisión Nacional Agraria (Mexico, 1975). And the only
account of governments' budgetary policies and practices is in James W.
Wilkie, *The Mexican Revolution, federal expenditures and social change since
1910* (Berkeley, Calif., 1967).

Politics in the provinces has provided the material for many
contemporary reports and professional histories. Outstanding is H.
Aguilar Camín, *La frontera nómada. Sonora y la revolución mexicana* (Mexico,
1977). Also useful on Sonora are Francisco Almada, *Historia de la
revolución en el estado de Sonora* (Mexico, 1971), and Clodoveo Valenzuela
and A. Chaverri Matamoros, *Sonora y Carranza* (Mexico, 1921). A lively
and detailed narrative of the Magonista struggle on the California border
during the Maderista insurrection is Lowell L. Blaisdell, *The desert
revolution, Baja California, 1911* (Madison, 1962). The most useful
treatments of Chihuahua are Francisco Almada, *Historia de la revolución en
el estado de Chihuahua* (2 vols., Mexico, 1964–5), and William H. Beezley,
*Insurgent governor, Abraham González and the Mexican Revolution in
Chihuahua* (Lincoln, 1973). The only commendable book on a north-
eastern state is Ildefonso Villarello Vélez, *Historia de la revolución mexicana
en Coahuila* (Mexico, 1970).

Among the studies of politics in other regions of the country, the best
are Romana Falcón, *Revolución y caciquismo: San Luis Potosí, 1910–1938*
(Mexico, 1984); Alicia Hernández Chávez, 'La defensa de los finqueros
en Chiapas, 1914–1920', *HM*, 28/3 (1979), 335–69; Ian Jacobs, *Ranchero
revolt: the Mexican Revolution in Guerrero* (Austin, Texas, 1983); and
Gilbert M. Joseph, *Revolution from without: Yucatán, Mexico and the United
States, 1880–1924* (Cambridge, 1982). See also the essays in David A.

Brading (ed.), *Caudillo and peasant in the Mexican Revolution* (Cambridge, 1980).

On war in Mexico between 1910 and 1920, the most important book is still J. Barragán, *Historia del ejército y de la revolución constitucionalista* (2 vols., Mexico, 1946). Also valuable is Miguel A. Sánchez Lamego, *Historia militar de la revolución constitucionalista* (4 vols., Mexico, 1956–7). On particular Constitutionalist and Carrancista campaigns, see the memoirs of Manuel W. González, *Con Carranza. Episodios de la revolución constitucionalista, 1913–1914* (Monterrey, 1933), and *Contra Villa. Relato de la campaña, 1914–1915* (Mexico, 1935); and Álvaro Obregón, *Ocho mil kilómetros en campaña* (3rd edn, Mexico, 1959). For details on Villista campaigns, see Alberto Calzadíaz Barrera, *Hechos reales de la revolución* (5 vols., Mexico, 1967–8).

Peasant and labour movements

References in the literature to *campesinos* and *obreros* are innumerable. In fact virtually all of the revolutionary, counter-revolutionary, independent, and neutralist movements in Mexico from 1910 to 1920 were of 'country people' and 'workers'. But movements by country people for country people, or by workers for workers, that is peasant or labour movements, were the exception, not the rule.

The surest and most suggestive guide to the agrarian history of these years, since there is still no book on the subject, is F. Katz, 'Peasants in the Mexican Revolution of 1910', in J. Spielberg and S. Whiteford (eds.), *Forging nations. A comparative view of rural ferment and revolt* (Lansing, 1976), 61–85.

Also considerable is Hans W. Tobler, 'Bauernerhebungen und Agrarreform in der mexikanischen Revolution', in Manfred Mols and Hans W. Tobler, *Mexiko, die institutionalisierte Revolution* (Cologne, 1976), 115–70. For indications of how little the distribution of agricultural and ranching property in 1910 changed until the 1920s, see Frank Tannenbaum, *The Mexican agrarian revolution* (Washington, 1929), a classic.

The most interesting monographs on peasant movements have properly had a provincial focus. On the north, see Friedrich Katz, 'Agrarian changes in northern Mexico in the period of Villista rule, 1913–1915', in *Contemporary Mexico*, 259–73. On the midwest, Michoacán, see Paul Friedrich, *Agrarian revolt in a Mexican village* (Englewood Cliffs, NJ, 1970). And on Mexico's mideast, see Raymond

Th. J. Buve, 'Peasant movements, caudillos, and landreform [sic] during the revolution (1910–1917) in Tlaxcala, Mexico', *Boletín de estudios latinoamericanos y del Caribe*, 18 (1975), 112–52, and 'Movilización campesina y reforma agraria en los valles de Nativitas, Tlaxcala (1917–1923)', *El trabajo y los trabajadores*, 533–64. The south, in particular Morelos, was the home of Mexico's most famous, exceptional, and significant peasant movement, that of the Zapatistas. Among several articles and books about their struggle, the best are François Chevalier, 'Un facteur décisif de la révolution agraire au Mexique: Le soulèvement de Zapata, 1911–1919', *AESC*, 16/1 (1961), 66–82; Gildardo Magaña, *Emiliano Zapata y el agrarismo en México* (5 vols., 2nd edn, Mexico, 1951–2); Jesús Sotelo Inclán, *Raíz y razón de Zapata* (2nd edn, Mexico, 1970); and John Womack, Jr, *Zapata and the Mexican Revolution* (New York, 1968). For an important and illustrative comparison, see Ronald Waterbury, 'Non-revolutionary peasants: Oaxaca compared to Morelos in the Mexican Revolution', *Comparative Studies in Society and History*, 17/4 (1975), 410–42.

The first survey of labour movements during the revolutionary years is still useful: V. Lombardo Toledano, *La libertad sindical en México* (2nd edn, Mexico, 1974), as are two other old labour histories: M. R. Clark, *Organized labor in Mexico* (Chapel Hill, 1934), and A. López Aparicio, *El movimiento obrero en México: antecedentes, desarrollo y tendencias* (2nd edn, Mexico, 1952).

An important essay suggesting the lines of a major revision of this history is Marcela de Neymet, 'El movimiento obrero y la revolución mexicana', *Historia y Sociedad*, 1st ser., 9 (1967), 56–73. Two different revisionist labour histories are Barry Carr, *El movimiento obrero y la política en México, 1910–1929* (2 vols., Mexico, 1976), and Ramón E. Ruiz, *Labor and the ambivalent revolutionaries, Mexico, 1911–1923* (Baltimore, 1976). A recent notable survey is Sergio de la Peña, *La clase obrera en la historia de México*, vol. IV, *Trabajadores y sociedad en el siglo XX* (Mexico, 1984).

The particular problems in labour history that have attracted most attention are ideologies and putative or real national federations. On ideologies, see Barry Carr, 'Marxism and anarchism in the formation of the Mexican Communist party, 1910–19', *HAHR*, 63/2 (1983), 277–305; François-X. Guerra, 'De l'Espagne au Mexique: Le milieu anarchiste et la révolution mexicaine (1910–1915)', *Mélanges de la Casa de Velázquez*, 9 (1973), 653–87; and John M. Hart, *Anarchism and the Mexican working class, 1860–1931* (Austin, Texas, 1978). On the famous proto-federation of

1914–15 and its 'red battalions', see Barry Carr, 'The Casa del Obrero Mundial. Constitutionalism and the pact of February, 1915', *El trabajo y los trabajadores*, 603–32; John M. Hart, 'The urban working class and the Mexican Revolution. The case of the Casa del Obrero Mundial', *HAHR*, 58/1 (1978), 1–20; Alicia Hernández Chávez, 'Los Batallones Rojos y Obregón: un pacto inestable', unpublished manuscript, 1979; and Jean A. Meyer, 'Les Ouvriers dans la révolution mexicaine. Les Bataillons rouges', *AESC*, 25/1 (1970), 30–55. On the first serious federation, see Rocío Guadarrama, *Los sindicatos y la política en México: La CROM, 1918–1928* (Mexico, 1981); Pablo González Casanova, *La clase obrera en la historia de México*, vol. VI, *En el primer gobierno constitucional (1917–1920)* (Mexico, 1980); and Harry A. Levenstein, *Labor organizations in the United States and Mexico, a history of their relations* (Westport, Conn., 1971).

There are only two notable books on unions in a particular industry, which, as it happens, was the most strategic of all industries in the country. Neither is so much a study as a memoir: Servando A. Alzati, *Historia de la mexicanización de los Ferrocarriles Nacionales de México* (Mexico, 1946); and Marcelo N. Rodea, *Historia del movimiento obrero ferrocarrilero, 1890–1943* (Mexico, 1944). And there are only two notable treatments of unions in a particular place: S. Lief Adleson, 'La adolescencia del poder: la lucha de los obreros de Tampico para definir los derechos del trabajo, 1910–1920', *Historias*, 2 (October 1982), 85–101; and Francisco Ramírez Plancarte, *La ciudad de México durante la revolución constitucionalista* (2nd edn, Mexico, 1941).

Business, economy, and demography

For a comprehensive and annotated bibliography of most of the old and a large part of the new literature on these subjects, see J. Womack Jr's article in *Marxist Perspectives*, cited above. Though somewhat frustrating, D. G. López Rosado, *Historia y pensamiento económico de México* (6 vols., Mexico, 1968–74) is indispensable.

The history of business in Mexico, in any period, is timid, meagre and obscure. It is possible, however, to draw reasonable inferences and to find significant details in studies done for other purposes. On industries important during the Revolution, see Fred W. Powell, *The railroads of Mexico* (Boston, 1921); Marvin D. Bernstein, *The Mexican mining industry, 1890–1950: a study of the interaction of politics, economics, and technology* (Albany, 1964); Manuel G. Machado, Jr, *The North Mexican cattle industry, 1910–1975: ideology, conflict, and change* (College Station, Texas, 1980); Gonzalo Cámara Zavala, 'Historia de la industria henequenera hasta 1919', *Enciclopedia Yucatanense* (8 vols., Mexico, 1947), III, 657–725; and Enrique Aznar Mendoza, 'Historia de la industria henequenera desde 1919 hasta nuestros días', *Enciclopedia Yucatanense*, III, 727–87. On banking, the most useful treatments are Antonio Manero, *La revolución bancaria en Mexico, 1865–1955* (Mexico, 1957); Walter F. McCaleb, *Present and past banking in Mexico* (New York, 1920), and *The public finances of Mexico* (New York, 1921); and Edgar Turlington, *Mexico and her foreign creditors* (New York, 1930). On companies and entrepreneurs, see Benjamin T. Harrison, 'Chandler Anderson and business interests in Mexico: 1913–1920: when economic interests failed to alter U.S. foreign policy', *Inter-American Economic Affairs*, 33/3 (1979), 3–23; J. C. M. Oglesby, *Gringos from the far north: essays in the history of Canadian–Latin American relations, 1866–1968* (Toronto, 1976); and Julio Riquelme Inda, *Cuatro décadas de vida, 1917–1957* (Mexico, 1957).

The most suggestive books about the structure and operation of the economy during the Revolution remain C. L. Jones, *Mexico and its reconstruction* (New York, 1921), and W. Thompson, *Trading with Mexico* (New York, 1921). Among notable studies in economic history are Donald B. Keesing, 'Structural change early in development: Mexico's changing industrial and occupational structure from 1895 to 1950', *Journal of Economic History*, 29/4 (1969), 716–38; and Edwin W. Kemmerer, *Inflation and revolution: Mexico's experience of 1912–1917* (Princeton, NJ, 1940). See also Frédéric Mauro, 'Le développement économique de Monterrey, 1890–1960', *Caravelle: Cahiers du monde hispanique et luso-brésilien*, 2 (1964), 35–126; and Isidro Vizcaya Canales, *Los orígenes de la industrialización de Monterrey: Una historia económica y social desde la caída del segundo imperio hasta el fin de la revolución, 1867–1920* (Monterrey, 1969).

The most important work on demography is Moisés González Navarro, *Población y sociedad en México (1900–1970)* (2 vols., Mexico, 1974). See also Robert G. Greer, 'The demographic impact of the Mexican Revolution, 1910–1921', unpublished manuscript 1966.

Culture and images

There is a large body of literature on the novel and the mural of the Revolution. But these figments are almost entirely post-revolutionary phenomena. Three novelists actually lived through the Revolution and wrote memorably about it: M. Azuela, *Obras completas* (3 vols., Mexico, 1958–60); M. L. Guzmán, *El águila y la serpiente* (Madrid, 1928), and *Memorias de Pancho Villa* (4 vols., Mexico, 1938–40); and J. Vasconcelos, *Ulíses criollo* (Mexico, 1935), and *La tormenta* (Mexico, 1936).

Another useful contemporary account is John Reed, *Insurgent Mexico* (New York, 1914). See also John D. Rutherford, *Mexican society during the Revolution: a literary approach* (Oxford, 1971), and Merle E. Simmons, *The Mexican corrido as a source of interpretive study of modern Mexico (1870–1950)* (Bloomington, 1957). The images are clearest in the great photographic collection: G. Casasola, *Historia gráfica de la revolución mexicana, 1900–1970* (10 vols., Mexico, 1973), vols. II–V. A highly significant study of the creation and absorption of images is A. de los Reyes, *Cine y sociedad en México, 1896–1930* (Mexico, 1981).

3. MEXICO: REVOLUTION AND RECONSTRUCTION IN THE
1920S

R. Potash, 'The historiography of Mexico since 1821', *HAHR*, 40/3 (1960) remains useful though now out of date. David M. Bailey, 'Revisionism and the recent historiography of the Mexican Revolution', *HAHR*, 58/1 (1978) is an excellent recent survey of the literature on the Revolution. See also Barry Carr, 'Recent regional studies of the Mexican Revolution', *LARR*, 15/1 (1980). The proceedings of the regular meetings of Mexican and US historians are invaluable for their surveys of recent research: from the Oaxtepec meeting in 1969, *Investigaciones contemporáneas sobre historia de México* (Mexico and Austin, Texas, 1971); from Santa Monica (1973), *Contemporary Mexico* (Los Angeles and Mexico, 1976), from Pátzcuaro (1977), *El trabajo y los trabajadores en la historia de México* (Mexico and Tucson, 1979).

Among general works Jorge Vera Estañol, *Historia de la revolución mexicana: orígenes y resultados* (Mexico, 1957) remains useful if a little old-fashioned and dull. José C. Valadés, *Historia general de la revolución mexicana* (5 vols., Mexico, 1976) is much more than a general history: it is full of otherwise inaccessible material and brilliant insights. John W. F. Dulles, *Yesterday in Mexico: a chronicle of the Revolution 1919–36* (Austin, Texas, 1961) is a detailed narrative account of the period. Gustavo Casasola, *Historia gráfica de la revolución mexicana, 1900–1970*, (10 vols., Mexico, 1973) is an important collection of photographs. Recent syntheses include Adolfo Gilly, *La revolución interrumpida* (Mexico, 1972); Arnaldo Córdova, *La ideología de la revolución mexicana* (Mexico, 1973), the best Marxist interpretation; and Jean Meyer, *La Révolution mexicaine* (Paris, 1973).

The old classics by American authors, many of whom had close relations with Mexican leaders, are still indispensable, even though outdated: Charles Hackett, *The Mexican Revolution and the United States* (Boston, 1926); Frank Tannenbaum, *The Mexican agrarian revolution* (Washington, DC, 1929) and *Peace by revolution* (New York, 1933); Wilfrid Hardy Callcott, *Liberalism in Mexico, 1857–1929* (Stanford, 1931); E. N. Simpson, *The ejido, Mexico's way out* (Chapel Hill, NC, 1937); and Ernest Gruening, *Mexico and its heritage* (New York, 1928). Howard Cline, *The United States and Mexico* (Cambridge, Mass., 1953) represents the best of early US scholarship on the Mexican Revolution. See also Charles Cumberland, *Mexico: the struggle for modernity* (New York, 1968).

The best of Mexican revisionism can be found in Luis González y González (ed.), *Historia de la Revolución Mexicana*, (Mexico, 1977). Vols. x and xi on the Calles administration (1924–8) are by Enrique Krauze and Jean Meyer; vols. xii and xiii on the Maximato (1929–34) are by Lorenzo Meyer, Rafael Segovia, Alejandra Lajous and Beatriz Rojas. Peter Smith, *Labyrinths of power: political recruitment in 20th century Mexico* (Princeton, 1978), an important work by an American political scientist, illuminates the whole century and prepares a new theory of the Revolution, as apotheosis of the middle classes.

There are no good biographies of either Obregón or Calles. But on Obregón's early career, see Linda B. Hall, *Álvaro Obregón: power and revolution in Mexico, 1911–20* (College Station, Texas, 1981). Narciso Bassols Batalla, *El pensamiento político de Obregón* (Mexico, 1967) is useful, as are Jorge Prieto Laurens's memoirs, *50 años de política mexicana* (Mexico, 1968) and Alberto J. Pani, *Mi contribución al nuevo régimen 1910–1933* (Mexico, 1936). José Vasconcelos is too important as a public figure and as a writer to be neglected. See his memoirs in *Obras completas* (4 vols., Mexico, 1957–61), and on one particular episode, John Skirrius, *Vasconcelos y la campaña presidencial de 1929* (Mexico, 1978). Francisco Javier Gaxiola, *El Presidente Rodríguez (1932–1934)* (Mexico, 1938) remains the best book on the last administration of the Maximato.

On Mexico's relations with the United States, Robert F. Smith, *The United States and revolutionary nationalism in Mexico 1919–1932* (Chicago, 1972) remains the best study for this period although it is somewhat weak on Mexican events. The Mexican point of view can be found in Luis G. Zorrilla, *Historia de las relaciones entre México y los Estados Unidos de América 1800–1958* (2 vols., Mexico, 1965) and in Lorenzo Meyer, *México y los Estados Unidos en el conflicto petrolero 1917–1942* (Mexico, 1968), Eng. trans. *Mexico and the United States in the oil controversy 1917–42* (Austin, Texas, 1977). George W. Grayson, *The politics of Mexican oil* (Pittsburgh, 1980) is the most recent contribution on this subject.

Regional and local politics have become an important new subject of research. On the political bosses of the south-eastern states see, for example, on Felipe Carrillo Puerto, Francisco Paoli and Enrique Montalvo, *El socialismo olvidado de Yucatán* (Mexico, 1977), and G. M. Joseph, 'The fragile revolution: cacique politics in Yucatán', *LARR*, 15/1 (1980) and *Revolution from without. Yucatán, Mexico and the United States 1880–1924* (Cambridge, 1982); on Garrido Canabal, Carlos Martínez Assad, *El laboratorio de la Revolución* (Mexico, 1979). David Brading (ed.), *Caudillo and peasant in the Mexican Revolution* (Cambridge, 1980) includes case studies on Chihuahua, Guerrero, San Luis Potosí, Michoacán, Veracruz, Tlaxcala and Yucatán.

The standard accounts of the Revolution were distorted by a failure to take seriously the Cristero movement. But see David Bailey, *Viva Cristo Rey. The Cristero rebellion and the Church–State conflict in Mexico* (Austin, Texas, 1974); Jean Meyer, *La Cristiada* (3 vols., Mexico, 1978) and *The Cristero Rebellion. The Mexican people between church and state 1926–1929* (Cambridge, 1976); and, breaking new ground in Mexican local history, Luis González y González, *Pueblo en vilo: microhistoria de San José de Gracia* (Mexico, 1967). Here the 1920s are represented as the true revolutionary years at least in the western and central states, but the revolution was regarded as a murderous apocalypse by the rural population.

Studies of labour in this period are scarce, but see *El trabajo y los tabajadores* mentioned above. Marjorie R. Clark, *Organized labor in Mexico* (Chapel Hill, NC, 1934) remains the best work on the subject after half a century; Alfonso López Aparicio, *El movimiento obrero en México: antecedentes, desarrollo y tendencias* (Mexico, 1952) is a short but classic account. Excellent for the period to 1924 is Barry Carr, *El movimiento obrero y la política en México, 1910–29* (2 vols., Mexico, 1976). See also Ramón E. Ruiz, *Labor and the ambivalent revolutionaries, Mexico 1911–1923* (Baltimore, 1976).

The economic, social and political history of rural Mexico in this period has still for the most part to be written. Paul Taylor, *Arandas, a*

Spanish Mexican peasant community (Berkeley, 1933) was a pioneer work and Nathan L. Whetten, *Rural Mexico* (Chicago, 1948) is excellent. See also Simpson, *The ejido,* and Tannenbaum, *The Mexican agrarian revolution* mentioned above. Marte R. Gómez, *La reforma agraria de México. Su crisis durante el período 1928–1934* (Mexico, 1964) is written by a political actor of the period. Paul Friedrich, *Agrarian revolt in a Mexican village* (Englewood Cliffs, NJ, 1970) is an important study of Michoacán during the 1920s. Important recent publications in this field include: Heather Fowler Salamini, *Agrarian radicalism in Veracruz, 1920–1938* (Lincoln, Nebraska, 1978); Frans J. Schryer, *The rancheros of the Pisaflores. The history of a peasant bourgeoisie in twentieth century Mexico* (Toronto, 1980); and Ann L. Craig, *The first agraristas. An oral history of a Mexican agrarian reform movement* (Berkeley, 1983).

4. CENTRAL AMERICA: THE LIBERAL ERA, *c.* 1870–1930

There is an extensive bibliographical essay in R. L. Woodward Jr, *Central America. A nation divided* (New York, 1976), 278–321.

Three books provide a general view of the period 1870–1930: Mario Rodríguez, *Central America* (Englewood Cliffs, NJ, 1965), which is rather favourable to United States policies in the isthmus; Woodward, *Central America*; and Ciro Cardoso and Héctor Pérez Brignoli, *Centroamérica y la economía occidental (1520–1930)* (San José, 1977). The best general book on an individual Central American state is David Browning, *El Salvador. Landscape and society* (Oxford, 1971).

On the Central American coffee economies, see C. Cardoso, 'Historia económica del café en Centroamérica (siglo XIX): estudio comparativo', *Estudios Sociales Centroamericanos,* 4/10 (1975), 9–55. On the banana plantations, general works are Stacy May and Galo Plaza, *The United Fruit Company in Latin America* (Washington, DC, 1958), which is favourable to the company; Charles Kepner, *Social aspects of the banana industry* (New York, 1936), and Kepner and Jay Soothill, *The banana empire* (New York, 1935), which are far more critical.

By far the best publications on economic history are for Guatemala and Costa Rica. For Guatemala, see Alfredo Guerra Borges, *Geografía económica de Guatemala* (2 vols., Guatemala, 1973); Valentín Solórzano, *Evolución económica de Guatemala* (Guatemala, 1970); Sanford A. Mosk *et al., Economía de Guatemala* (Guatemala, 1958); Mauricio Domínguez T., 'The development of the technological and scientific coffee industry in

Guatemala 1830–1930' (unpublished PhD thesis, University of Tulane, 1970); Julio C. Cambranes, *Aspectos del desarrollo económico y social de Guatemala a la luz de fuentes históricas alemanas 1868–1885* (Instituto de Investigaciones Económicas y Sociales de la Universidad de San Carlos de Guatemala, Guatemala, 1975); Julio C. Cambranes, *El imperialismo alemán en Guatemala. El tratado de comercio de 1887* (Guatemala, 1977); Roberto Quintana, *Apuntes sobre el desarrollo monetario de Guatemala* (Guatemala, 1971). For Costa Rica, see Rodrigo Facio, *Estudio sobre economía costarricense* (2nd.edn, San José, 1972), still useful after more than 30 years; Alain Vieillard-Baron, *La production agricole et la vie rurale au Costa Rica* (Mexico, 1974); C. Cardoso, 'The formation of the coffee estate in nineteenth-century Costa Rica', in Kenneth Duncan and Ian Rutledge (eds.), *Land and labour in Latin America* (Cambridge, 1975), 165–202; Carolyn Hall, *El café y el desarrollo histórico-geográfico de Costa Rica* (San José, 1976) and *Formación de una hacienda cafetalera 1889–1911* (San José, 1978), the best texts available on the coffee economy of Costa Rica; Ana Cecilia Román Trigo, 'El comercio exterior de Costa Rica (1883– 1930)' (unpublished thesis, Universidad de Costa Rica, San José, 1978); Thomas Schoonover, 'Costa Rican trade and navigation ties with the United States, Germany and Europe, 1840 to 1885', *JGSWGL*, 14 (1977) 269–308, which argues for an earlier American pre-eminence in commercial matters than is usually recognized; Carlos Araya Pochet, 'El segundo ciclo minero en Costa Rica (1890–1930)' (Universidad de Costa Rica, San José, 1976, mimeo); Rufino Gil Pacheco, *Ciento cinco años de vida bancaria en Costa Rica* (3rd edn, San José, 1975).

On the economic history of Honduras, see Charles A. Brand, 'The background of capitalistic underdevelopment: Honduras to 1913' (unpublished PhD thesis, University of Pittsburgh, 1972); Vilma Laínez and Victor Meza, 'El enclave bananero en la historia de Honduras', *Estudios Sociales Centroamericanos*, 2/5 (1973), 115–56; Jorge Morales, 'El Ferrocarril Nacional de Honduras: su historia e incidencia sobre el desarrollo económico', *Estudios Sociales Centroamericanos*, 1/2 (1972), 7– 20; Kenneth V. Finney, 'Precious metal mining and the modernization of Honduras. Inquest of "El Dorado"' (unpublished PhD thesis, Tulane University, 1973); *Historia financiera de Honduras* (Tegucigalpa, 1957). On El Salvador, see in particular Browning, *El Salvador*, and David A. Luna, *Manual de historia económica de El Salvador* (San Salvador, 1971); also *Legislación salvadoreña del café, 1846–1955* (San Salvador, 1956). And, on Nicaragua see Pedro Belli, 'Prolegómenos para una historia económica de Nicaragua de 1905 a 1966', *Revista del Pensamiento Centroamericano*, 30/ 146 (1975), 2–30.

The social history of central America has been studied more by anthropologists and sociologists (see Woodward, *Central America*, 313– 14) than by historians. Nevertheless see José L. Vega Carballo, 'El nacimiento de un régimen de burguesía dependiente: el caso de Costa Rica', *Estudios Sociales Centroamericanos*, 2/5 and 6 (1973); James Backer, *La Iglesia y el sindicalismo en Costa Rica* (2nd edn, San José, 1975); Mario Posas, *Las sociedades artesanales y los orígenes del movimiento obrero hondureño* (Tegucigalpa, 1978); Roque Dalton, *Miguel Mármol. Los sucesos de 1932 en El Salvador* (San José, 1972); Thomas F. Anderson, *Matanza* (Lincoln, 1971) and *El Salvador 1932* (San José, 1976). Edelberto Torres Rivas, *Interpretación del desarrollo social centroamericano* (San José, 1971), which is somewhat outdated by recent research on economic and political history, still offers an interesting general interpretation of the history of this period.

On political history, a general overview is offered by Edelberto Torres Rivas, 'Poder nacional y sociedad dependiente: las clases y el estado en Centroamérica', *Estudios Sociales Centroamericanos*, 3/8 (1974), 27–63; Reynaldo Salinas López, 'La unión de Centroamérica, 1895–1922' (unpublished dissertation, Mexico, 1978), discusses US pressures against Central American union.

There are a number of recent works on the Guatemalan Liberal reforms: Jorge M. García L., *La reforma liberal en Guatemala* (Guatemala and San José, 1972); Thomas R. Herrick, *Desarrollo económico y político de Guatemala durante el período de Justo Rufino Barrios (1871–1885)* (San José, 1974); Paul Burgess, *Justo Rufino Barrios* (San José, 1972); Roberto Díaz Castillo, *Legislación económica de Guatemala durante la reforma liberal. Catálogo* (Guatemala and San José, 1973). On Costa Rican political history, Samuel Stone, *La dinastía de los conquistadores* (San José, 1975) is outstanding. See also, José L. Vega C., 'Etapas y procesos de la evolución sociopolítica de Costa Rica', *Estudios Sociales Centroamericanos*, 1/1 (1972), 45–72. About the Honduran Liberal reforms there are two opposing views: Héctor Pérez Brignoli, 'La reforma liberal en Honduras', *Cuaderno de Ciencias Sociales* 1/2 (1973), 2–86, and Guillermo Molina Chocano, *Estado liberal y desarrollo capitalista en Honduras* (Tegucigalpa, 1976).

5. CUBA, *c.* 1860–1934

Among general histories, the *Enciclopedia de Cuba* (12 vols., Madrid, 1975), edited in exile by several Cuban scholars and writers, is an uneven work which contains some valuable essays. Ramiro Guerra y Sánchez *et al.*, *Historia de la nación Cubana* (10 vols., Havana, 1952), is a compilation of essays by different authors which occasionally provides excellent information. Jorge Ibarra, *Historia de Cuba* (Havana, 1968) is a Marxist interpretation. Leví Marrero, *Cuba: economía y sociedad* (9 vols., Madrid, 1976) contains the results of some excellent research but is in desperate need of organization. José Duarte Oropesa, *Historiología Cubana* (4 vols., Miami, 1974) is a good contribution, rendered less valuable by the author's reluctance to display his sources. Hortensia Pichardo, *Documentos para la historia de Cuba* (4 vols., Havana, 1976), selected with some Marxist bias, includes some otherwise inaccessible documents. José Manuel Pérez Cabrera, *Historiografía de Cuba* (Mexico, 1952) is a valuable guide to the literature on Cuba in the nineteenth century. Fernando Portuondo, *Historia de Cuba* (Havana, 1957) was considered the best textbook in Cuba until 1960. Oscar Pino Santos, *Historia de Cuba, aspectos fundamentales* (Havana, 1964) seeks to explain Cuba's economic development or lack of it from a Marxist perspective. Emeterio Santovenia and Raul Shelton, *Cuba y su historia* (4 vols., Miami, 1965) is a clear and reliable work by a Cuban and an American historian. Jaime Suchliki, *Cuba, from Columbus to Castro* (New York, 1974) is a good, unpretentious overview of Cuban history. In spite of a certain tendency to disregard Cuban sources, Hugh Thomas, *Cuba: the pursuit of freedom* (London, 1971) remains the best and most complete history of the island from 1762 to 1968.

On relations with the United States Russell H. Fitzgibbon, *Cuba and the United States, 1900–1935* (Menasha, Wisconsin, 1935) is a well-documented and serious attempt to analyse the different factors which shaped Cuban–American relations while the Platt Amendment was still in force. Herminio Portell Vila, *Historia de Cuba en sus relaciones con los Estados Unidos y España* (4 vols., Havana, 1939) is an important study which goes beyond the scope of its title. Philip S. Foner, *A history of Cuba and its relations with the United States* (2 vols., New York, 1962–3), is an ambitious, well-researched though anti-American work. Lester D. Langley, *The Cuban policy of the United States: a brief history* (New York,

1968) is an excellent survey. In Robert F. Smith, *The United States and Cuba: business and diplomacy, 1917–1960* (New Haven, 1960), published under the impact of the Cuban revolution, the author demonstrates how American economic interests have affected and distorted US–Cuban policy. For a wider study on the same subject, see Dana G. Munro, *Intervention and dollar diplomacy in the Caribbean 1900–1921* (Princeton, 1964).

Ramiro Guerra y Sánchez, *Sugar and society in the Caribbean: an economic history of Cuban agriculture* (New Haven, 1964), originally published in Cuba in 1927, is an indictment of sugar's impact on the island's social and economic conditions; it has had a profound influence on Cuban studies. Leland H. Jenks, *Our Cuban colony* (New York, 1928) is a classic on the impact of American economic imperialism in Cuba. Raymond L. Buell, *Problems of the new Cuba* (New York, 1935) is perhaps the best study on the origins of Cuba's economic problems in the twentieth century. Roland T. Ely, *Cuando reinaba su majestad el azúcar* (Buenos Aires, 1963) is an indispensable work on Cuba's sugar development. H. E. Friedlander, *Historia económica de Cuba* (Havana, 1944) is an interesting but incomplete study of Cuba's economic history, limited essentially to the nineteenth century. Julián Alienes y Urosa, *Características fundamentales de la economía Cubana* (Havana, 1950) is an important contribution to understanding Cuba's economic problems from colonial times to 1940. Lowry Nelson, *Rural Cuba* (Minneapolis, 1950) is a pioneer study on the agrarian situation in Cuba in the first half of the twentieth century. José Alvarez *et al.*, *Study on Cuba* (Miami, 1963) is a serious piece of research, full of reliable data and debatable interpretations. Raul Cepero Bonilla, *Azúcar y abolición* (Havana, 1971) is a study of the economic roots of abolitionist and autonomist movements in the nineteenth century. Julio Le Riverand, *Historia económica de Cuba* (Buenos Aires, 1963) is a cautious Marxist interpretation of Cuba's economic evolution until 1940. Oscar Pino Santos, *El asalto a Cuba por la oligarquía yanki* (Havana, 1973) is interesting, in spite of the vehement title, because it explores the presence and negative influence in Cuba of non-American capitalist groups. For a full discussion of the Cuban sugar industry in the period *c.* 1860–1930, see Moreno Fraginals, *CHLA* IV, ch. 6.

The two classic histories of the Ten Years' War (1868–78) by Cuban historians are Ramiro Guerra y Sánchez, *Guerra de los Diez Años* (Havana, 1950) and Francisco Ponte Domínguez, *Historia de la Guerra de los Diez Años* (Havana, 1972). Among a number of biographies José L. Franco,

Antonio Maceo. Apuntes para una historia de su vida (3 vols., Havana, 1973) and Benigno Souza, *Máximo Gómez, el generalísimo* (Havana, 1953) deserve mention. The political ideas and legislative problems of the Cuban rebels are studied in Enrique Hernández Corujo, *Revoluciones Cubanas: organización civil y política* (Havana, 1929) and *Historia constitucional de Cuba* (Havana, 1960); Ramón Infiesta, *Historia constitucional de Cuba* (Havana, 1942); and Andres Lazcano y Mazón, *Las constituciones de Cuba* (Madrid, 1952). For the texts of the different constitutions, see Leonel Antonio de la Cuesta and Rolando Alum Linera (eds.), *Constituciones Cubanas, 1812–1962* (New York, 1974).

The most recent account of the period between the Ten Years' War and the War of Independence (1895–8) and United States occupation is Louis A. Pérez, *Cuba between empires, 1878–1902* (Pittsburgh, 1984). The *autonomistas* have been studied, with excessive emphasis on the philosophical influences upon them, in Antonio Martínez Bello, *Orígen y meta del autonomismo: exégesis de Montoro* (Havana, 1952); see also Antonio Sánchez de Bustamante y Montoro, *La ideología autonomista* (Havana, 1934) and, an exposition of the party's aims, Rafael Montoro, *Ideario autonomista* (Havana, 1938).

Rafael Pérez Delgado, *1898, el año del desastre* (Madrid, 1976) reaches some sombre conclusions on the condition of the Spanish forces and the behaviour of the Spanish government and press. Mercedez Cervera Rodríguez, *La guerra naval del 98 en su planeamiento y en sus consecuencias* (Madrid, 1977), and José Cervera Pery, *Marina y política en la España del siglo XIX* (Madrid, 1979), are useful modern studies. José Manuel Allende Salazar, *El 98 de los Americanos* (Madrid, 1974) is a serious attempt by a Spanish historian to understand the American side. A general background to Spanish politics is provided by Melchor Fernández Almagro, *Historia política de la España contemporánea* (2 vols., Madrid, 1959) and Pedro Gómez Aparicio, *Historia del periodismo español* (2 vols., Madrid, 1971).

There are four biographies of José Martí in English: Jorge Mañach, *Martí: apostle of freedom* (New York, 1950); Felix Lizaso, *Martí, martyr of Cuban independence* (Albuquerque, NM, 1953); Richard Butler Gray, *José Martí, Cuban patriot* (Gainesville, 1962) and John M. Kirk, *Martí. Mentor of the Cuban nation* (Tampa, 1983). Encumbered by philosophical quotations but useful is Roberto Agramonte, *Martí y su concepción del mundo* (San Juan, Puerto Rico, 1971). Emilio Roig de Leuchsenring, *Martí anti-imperialista* (Havana, 1961) and Philip S. Foner (ed.), *José*

Martí, inside the monster: writings on the United States and American imperialism (New York, 1975), stress Martí's well-known anti-imperialism. From a different perspective, but less scholarly, Rafael Esténger, *Martí frente al comunismo* (Miami, 1966) studies Martí's rejection of Marxism. *Martí: el héroe y su acción revolucionaria* (Mexico, 1966), by the Argentine writer Ezequiel Martinez Estrada, is a more balanced vision of Martí's radicalism. For a short bilingual collection of Martí's ideas, see Carlos Ripoll, *José Martí* (New York, 1980). Martí's writings can be consulted in his *Obras completas* (2 vols., Havana, 1956), or in the 22 volume edition published in Havana in 1973.

Among the older American studies of the Spanish–American war, Walter Millis, *The martial spirit: a study of the war with Spain* (New York, 1931) remains important. Frank Freidel, *The splendid little war* (Boston, 1958) is more important for the illustrations than the analysis. Philip S. Foner, *The Spanish-Cuban-American War and the birth of American imperialism* (2 vols., New York, 1972), while showing the Marxist orientation of the author, has the merit of offering the Cuban side in the conflict. Julius Pratt, *Expansionists of 1898* (Baltimore, 1936) is a classic study on the ideas and economic interests behind the war. See also, more recently, Ernest R. May, *Imperial democracy, The emergence of America as a great power* (New York, 1973) and Charles S. Campbell, *The transformation of American foreign relations, 1865–1900* (New York, 1976).

David F. Healy, *The United States in Cuba, 1898–1902* (Madison, 1963) is the best American study on the subject. Emilio Roig de Leuchsenring, *Historia de la Enmienda Platt* (2 vols., Havana, 1935) is extremely anti-American. A more objective evaluation is provided in Manuel Márquez Sterling, *Proceso histórico de la Enmienda Platt* (Havana, 1941). On the emergence of an ephemeral Socialist party under American occupation, see José Rivero Muñiz, *El primer Partido Socialista Cubano* (Las Vilas, Cuba, 1962); Eduardo J. Tejera, *Diego Vicente Tejera, patriota, poeta y pensador Cubano* (Madrid, 1981) is a biography of the founder of the Socialist party.

General works on the Republic, 1902–33, include Carleton Beals, *The crime of Cuba* (Philadelphia, 1933), written when dictator Machado was in power; the author blames American economic penetration for the Cuban political tragedy. Charles E. Chapman, *History of the Cuban Republic* (New York, 1927) is a historical reflection of the island conditions as seen by an American, at a time when nationalism was at a low ebb and pessimism was rampant in Cuba. Louis A. Pérez, *Army and politics in Cuba, 1898–1958*

(Pittsburgh, 1976) is an interesting account of the rise and fall of the Cuban army, but stronger on the period after 1933. Mario Riera Hernández, *Cuba republicana, 1898–1958* (Miami, 1974) provides a useful chronology and political guide. On Estrada Palma, the first president of the Republic, see Carlos Márquez Sterling, *Don Tomás. Biografía de una época* (Havana, 1953). A valuable defence of the Magoon administration, so severely criticized by the majority of Cuban historians, is provided by David A. Lockmiller, *Magoon in Cuba* (Chapel Hill, NC, 1938). The best study on the period is Allan Reed Millet, *The politics of intervention: the military occupation of Cuba, 1906–1909* (Columbus, Ohio, 1968).

The period from 1908 to 1925, covering the presidencies of José Miguel Gómez, Mario G. Menocal and Alfredo Zayas, has been neglected by Cuban historians. Louis A. Pérez, *Intervention, revolution, and politics in Cuba, 1913–1921* (Pittsburgh, 1978) is an excellent study of the period, demonstrating how Cuban politicians learned to 'manipulate' American diplomacy, but making some sweeping generalizations about Cuban politics. Leon Primelles, *Crónica Cubana, 1915–1918* (Havana, 1955) is a detailed chronology of Menocal's last years in power. José Rivero Muñiz examines the beginning of organized labour under the Republic in *El movimiento laboral Cubano durante el período 1906–1911* (Las Villas, Cuba, 1962). On the rebellion of black groups in 1912, see Serafín Portuondo Linares, *Los independientes de color* (2nd edn, Havana, 1951) and Rafael Fermoselle, *Política y color: la guerrita de 1912* (Montevideo, 1974).

Machado's government and the revolutionary episode of 1933 have attracted considerable scholarly attention. See, for example, Luis E. Aguilar, *Cuba 1933: Prologue to revolution* (Ithaca, NY, 1972); Ana Cairo, *El grupo minorista y su tiempo* (Havana, 1979); Ladislao González Carbajal, *El ala izquierda estudiantil y su época* (Havana, 1974); José A. Tabares del Real, *Guiteras* (Havana, 1973) and *La Revolución del 30: sus dos últimos años* (Havana, 1971); Lionel Soto, *La Revolución del 33* (3 vols., Havana, 1977); Jaime Suchliki, *University students and revolution in Cuba* (Miami 1969); Irwin F. Gellman, *Roosevelt and Batista* (Albuquerque, NM, 1973); and most recently, *Les Annés 30 à Cuba*, (Paris, 1982).

6. PUERTO RICO, *c.* 1870–1940

Useful bibliographical works include Augusto Bird, *Bibliografía puertorriqueña de fuentes para investigaciones sociales 1930–45* (Río Piedras, 1947) and J. Bulnes and E. González-Díaz (eds.), *Bibliografía puertorriqueña de ciencias sociales* (Río Piedras, 1977). The latter classifies, according to subject, books and articles written from 1931 to 1960, many of which deal with or refer to the period before 1930. See also Paquita Vivó (ed.), *The Puerto Ricans: an annotated bibliography* (New York, 1973) which comprises a very limited selection of entries, but contains useful commentaries. A. G. Quintero-Rivera (ed.), *Lucha obrera. Antología de grandes documentos en la historia obrera puertorriqueña* (San Juan, 1971), Eng. trans. *Workers' struggle in Puerto Rico, a documentary history* (New York, 1976), a collection of documents on the labour movement mostly in the period 1870–1940, includes a detailed and annotated bibliography of the labour literature of the period.

Gordon K. Lewis, *Puerto Rico: freedom and power in the Caribbean* (New York, 1963) is an important general survey of the history of Puerto Rico which evaluates the principal studies of the island since the end of Spanish rule (1898). On Puerto Rican intellectual history in the late nineteenth century, see also Gordon K. Lewis, *Main currents in Caribbean thought. The historical evolution of Caribbean society in its ideological aspects 1492–1900* (Baltimore, 1983). Manuel Maldonado-Denis, *Puerto Rico: una interpretación histórica social* (Mexico, 1969), Eng. trans. *Puerto Rico: a socio-historic interpretation* (New York, 1972), includes a good general (but not in-depth) presentation of the political history of Puerto Rico. A. López and J. Petras (eds.), *Puerto Rico and Puerto Ricans* (New York, 1974) is a general reader which includes good articles on the period 1870–1940, both general and monographic. Also important, mainly as polemical interpretative essays, with much new material and ideas are A. G. Quintero-Rivera, *Conflictos de clase y política en Puerto Rico* (San Juan, 1976) and 'Background to the emergence of imperialist capitalism in Puerto Rico', *Caribbean Studies*, 13/3 (1973); A. G. Quintero-Rivera *et al.*, *Puerto Rico: identidad nacional y clases sociales* (San Juan, 1979); and José Luis González, *El país de cuatro pisos* (San Juan, 1980). Reece Bothwell, *Puerto Rico: cien años de lucha política* (San Juan, 1979) is a very useful compilation of political documents.

Laird W. Bergad, 'Agrarian history of Puerto Rico, 1870–1930', *LARR*, 13/3 (1978) is an important article; see also his book, *Coffee and the growth of agrarian capitalism in 19th century Puerto Rico* (Princeton, 1983). Two other studies of a late-nineteenth-century coffee hacienda – Vivian Carro, *Formación de la gran propiedad cafetalera: la hacienda Pietri, 1858–1898*, which constitutes the entire issue of *Anales de Investigación Histórica*, 2/1 (1975), and Carlos Buitrago-Ortiz, *Los orígenes históricos de la sociedad precapitalista en Puerto Rico* (San Juan, 1976) – are worthy of mention. On the Puerto Rican economy and society in the nineteenth century, see also Fernando Picó, *Libertad y servidumbre en el Puerto Rico del siglo XIX* (San Juan, 1979); José Curet, *De la esclavitud a la abolición* (San Juan, 1979); Andrés Ramos Mattei, *Apuntes sobre la transición hacia el sistema de centrales en la industria azucarera. Los libros de cuentas de la hacienda Mercedita 1861–1900* (San Juan, 1975) and *La hacienda azucarera, su crecimiento y crisis en Puerto Rico (siglo XIX)* (San Juan, 1981). On sugar, see also José A. Herrero, *La mitología del azúcar, un ensayo de historia económica de Puerto Rico* (San Juan, 1975) and Moreno Fraginals, *CHLA* IV, ch. 6. The early labour movement is the subject of Gervasio García, *Primeros fermentos de organización obrera en Puerto Rico* (San Juan, 1975) and 'Economie dominée et premiers ferments d'organization ouvriène: Puerto Rico entre le XIX et le XX siècle' (unpublished PhD thesis, University of Paris, 1976). See also Igualdad Iglesias de Pagán, *El obrerismo en Puerto Rico (1896–1905)* (San Juan, 1973). Also important is a series of five articles published in *Revista de Ciencias Sociales*, 18/1–2 and 3–4 (1974); 19/1, 3 (1975) and 20/1–2 (1976), under the general title of 'La clase obrera y el proceso político en Puerto Rico'; Marcia Rivera Quintero's series of articles on 'La incorporación de la mujer al trabajo asalariado' in the newspaper *Claridad*, 10, 17 and 23 June 1977; and Georg Fromm's series on Albizu-Campos (leader of the Nationalist party) and the working class in the 1930s in *Claridad*, 3, 10, 23, 30 June and 6, 13 July, 1977. Five different collections of articles or speeches of Albizu-Campos have also been published: B. Torres (ed.), *Obras escogidas 1923–36* (San Juan, 1975); M. Maldonado-Denis (ed.), *La conciencia nacional puertorriqueña* (Mexico, 1972); Carlos Rama (ed.), *República de Puerto Rico* (Montevideo, 1972); *Independencia económica* (San Juan, 1970); and Villarini and Hernández Cruz (eds.), *Escritos y reseñas políticas, 1930* (San Juan, 1972). A former member of the Nationalist party, Juan Antonio Conetjer, has written several essays on Albizu-Campos: *Albizu Campos y las huelgas en los años 30* (San Juan, 1969); *Albizu Campos* (Montevideo, 1969); and *El líder de la desesperación* (Guaynabo, 1972).

Rosario Natal, *Puerto Rico y la crisis de la guerra hispano-americana (1895–1898)* (San Juan, 1975) is a useful though limited study of the Spanish-American war and its consequences for Puerto Rico. On the PPD, see A. G. Quintero-Rivera, 'Bases sociales de la transformación ideológica del PPD', in Gerardo Navas (ed.), *Cambio y desarrollo en Puerto Rico* (San Juan, 1979). Thomas G. Matthews, *Puerto Rican politics and the*

New Deal (Gainesville, 1960) is a critical interpretation of the first five years of the New Deal. On students and the politics of the 1930s, see Isabel Picó, *La protesta estudiantil en la década del 30* (San Juan, 1974). Aida Negrón de Montilla, *Americanization in Puerto Rico and the public school system* (San Juan, 1970) analyses the papers of the colonial Commissioners of Education during the first three decades of US rule. Finally, on the origins of the Puerto Rican community in the United States, especially New York, Centro de Estudios Puertorriqueños (CUNY), *Labor migration under capitalism* (New York, 1979) is interesting, as are the extraordinary memoirs of a migrant cigarmaker, César Andreu Iglesias (ed.), *Memorias de Bernardo Vega* (San Juan, 1977).

7. THE DOMINICAN REPUBLIC, *c.* 1870–1930

The preservation of historical sources in the Dominican Republic has suffered greatly under the country's historical vicissitudes. Of the important documents that survived, many are in private hands. The former director of the Archivo General de la Nación, Emilio Rodríguez Demorizi, has edited a wide range of source material: *Hostos en Santo Domingo* (2 vols., Ciudad Trujillo, 1939); *Relaciones históricas de Santo Domingo* (3 vols., Ciudad Trujillo, 1942, 1945 and 1957); *Correspondencia del cónsul de Francia en Santo Domingo, 1844–1846*, vol. I (Ciudad Trujillo, 1944); *Documentos para la historia de la República Dominicana* (3 vols., vol. I, Ciudad Trujillo, 1944; vol. II, Santiago, 1949; vol. III, Ciudad Trujillo, 1959); *Correspondencia del cónsul de Francia en Santo Domingo, 1846–1850*, vol. II (Ciudad Trujillo, 1947); *La marina de guerra dominicana 1844–1861* (Ciudad Trujillo, 1958); *Actos y doctrina del gobierno de la Restauración* (Santo Domingo, 1963); *Papeles de Espaillat: Para la historia de las ideas políticas en Santo Domingo* (Santo Domingo, 1963) and *Papeles de Pedro F. Bonó* (Santo Domingo, 1964).

Bibliographies are scarce. Two may be mentioned here: Deborah Hitt and Larman Wilson, *A selected bibliography of the Dominican Republic: a century after the restoration of independence* (Washington, DC, 1968) and Wolf Grabendorff, *Bibliographie zu Politik und Gesellschaft der Dominikanischen Republik: neuere Studien 1961–1971* (Munich, 1973).

Of the general histories, Sumner Welles, *Naboth's Vineyard. The Dominican Republic 1844–1924* (2 vols., New York, 1928), has deservedly been reprinted (New York, 1966) and translated (*La Viña de Naboth*, Santiago, 1939). The author's diplomatic activities in the country made him look favourably upon Horacio Vázquez which shows in the relevant parts of the book, as does his related antipathy towards Heureaux, which he shares, it must be said, with quite a few representatives of traditional Dominican historiography. A more balanced work is Ramón Marrero Aristy, *La República Dominicana: orígen y destino del pueblo cristiano más antiguo de América* (2 vols., Ciudad Trujillo, 1957–8) – in spite of its subtitle. See also Bernardo Pichardo, *Resumen de historia patria* (Barcelona, 1930) and, by the pioneer of Dominican historiography, José Gabriel García, *Compendio de la historia de Santo Domingo* (Santo Domingo, 1896). The financial history of the Republic is dealt with in César A. Herrera, *De Hartmont a Trujillo* (Ciudad Trujillo, 1953). A recent excellent general history is Frank Moya Pons, *Manual de historia dominicana* (Santo Domingo, 1977). Finally, a valuable general reference work is Rufino Martínez, *Diccionario biográfico histórico dominicano, 1821–1930* (Santo Domingo, 1971).

Of importance for an understanding of nineteenth-century Dominican history is *Report of the Commission of Inquiry to Santo Domingo* (Washington, DC, 1871); Samuel Hazard, *Santo Domingo, past and present, with a glance at Hayti* (London, 1873); Padre Fernando Arturo de Meriño, *Elementos de geografía física, política e histórica de la República Dominicana, precedidos de las nociones generales de geografía* (3rd edn, Santo Domingo, 1898); General Gregorio Luperón, *Notas autobiográficas y apuntes históricos* (3 vols., Santiago, 1939); and José Ramón Abad, *La República Dominicana: reseña general geográfico-estadística* (Santo Domingo, 1888; reprinted 1973). There are a number of important contributions on the social and economic structure of the Dominican Republic in the second half of the nineteenth and first half of the twentieth centuries: H. Hoetink, *El pueblo dominicano, 1850–1900: Apuntes para su sociología histórica* (2nd edn, Santiago, 1973), Eng. trans. *The Dominican people, 1850–1900. Notes for a historical sociology* (Baltimore, 1983); Martin D. Clausner, *Rural Santo Domingo. Settled, unsettled and resettled* (Philadelphia, 1973); Patrick E. Bryan, 'The transformation of the economy of the Dominican Republic, 1870–1916' (unpublished PhD thesis, University of London, 1977); and Roberto Cassá, *Modos de producción, clases sociales y luchas políticas: República Dominicana, siglo XX* (Santo Domingo, 1974). On the Dominican sugar industry, see also Moreno Fraginals, *CHLA* iv, ch. 6. A valuable journal of historical studies is *Eme Eme, Estudios dominicanos*, published by the Universidad Católica Madre y Maestra, Santiago. See, for example, Antonio Lluberes, 'La economía del tabaco en el Cibao en la segunda mitad del siglo XIX', *Eme Eme*, 1/4 (1973); Paul Muto, 'La economía de exportación de la República Dominicana: 1900–1930', *Eme Eme*, 3/5 (1974); Frank Moya Pons, 'Datos sobre la economía dominicana durante la Primera República', *Eme Eme*, 4/24 (1976).

The immigration of sugar-cane workers is described by José del Castillo, 'La inmigración de braceros azucareros en la República Dominicana, 1900–1930', *Cuadernos del Centro Dominicano de Investigaciones Antropólogicos* (Universidad Autónoma de Santo Domingo, 1978).

On the US occupation of the Dominican Republic, see Marvin Goldwert, *Dominican Republic: history of American occupation, 1916–1924* (Gainesville, 1962); Antonio de la Rosa, *Las finanzas de Santo Domingo y el control americano* (Santo Domingo, 1969), and, most recently, Bruce J. Calder, *The impact of intervention. The Dominican Republic during the U.S. occupation of 1916–1924* (Austin, Texas, 1984). Also two older works: Max Henríquez Ureña, *Los yanquis en Santo Domingo* (Madrid, 1929) and Melvin Knight, *The Americans in Santo Domingo* (New York, 1928). On the relations between the United States and the Dominican Republic over a longer period, see David C. MacMichael, 'The United States and the Dominican Republic, 1871–1940. A cycle in the Caribbean diplomacy' (unpublished PhD thesis, Eugene, Oregon, 1964). Relations between the Dominican Republic and Haiti get attention in Rayford W. Logan, *Haiti and the Dominican Republic* (New York, 1968). The extensive literature that deals with the heroes and *caudillos* of the Republic generally has more literary than historical pretensions. By far the best in this genre are the vividly written biographical essays by Rufino Martínez, *Hombres Dominicanos* (2 vols., vol. I. Ciudad Trujillo, 1936, vol. II, Santiago, 1943). A more general study of Dominican political leadership is made in Miguel Angel Monclús, *El caudillismo en la República Dominicana* (3rd edn, Santo Domingo, 1962); a valuable contribution to Dominican political history is Julio G. Campillo Pérez, *El grillo y el ruiseñor: Elecciones presidenciales dominicanas, contribución a su estudio* (Santo Domingo, 1966).

On the history of literature, see Joaquín Balaguer, *Historia de la literatura dominicana* (2nd edn, Ciudad Trujillo, 1958); on the history of the plastic arts, see Danilo de los Santos, *La pintura en la sociedad dominicana* (Santiago, 1979).

8. HAITI, *c.* 1870–1930

Max Bissainthe, *Dictionnaire de bibliographie haïtienne* (Washington, DC, 1951) and the appendix published in 1973 by Scarecrow Press together still represent the best bibliography of works on Haiti and by Haitians. Kraus International has published *The complete Haitiana 1900–1980* (New York, 1982) edited by Michel Laguerre. Mention should also be made of Max Manigat, *Haitiana, 1971–1975* (LaSalle, Quebec, 1980) and vol. 39 in the World Bibliographical Series, compiled by Frances Chambers, *Haiti* (Oxford and Santa Barbara, 1983).

James Leyburn's classic, *The Haitian people*, has been issued in paperback (New Haven, 1966), with a new foreword by Sidney Mintz. It remains one of the best introductions to the history and social structure of Haiti, despite its occasional shortcomings. Leyburn failed to recognize the full significance of the urban middle class and of important economic and social distinctions among the rural population. In his discussion of the past he is sometimes the victim of what might be called the 'mulatto legend'. A book by the Polish scholar, Tadeusz Lepkowski, has been translated into Spanish and published in two volumes under the title *Haití* (Havana, 1968–9). The author discusses, among other things, the early history of Haiti, Haitian historiography and the development of agriculture. Robert Rotberg, *Haiti: the politics of squalor* (Boston, 1971) has useful sections on the Haitian economy in this period, but is otherwise undistinguished. Robert Debs Heinl, who was in charge of the US marine mission to Haiti in the early years of the Duvalier regime, has produced a somewhat ethnocentric and anecdotal history of Haiti entitled *Written in blood: the story of the Haitian people* (Boston, 1978). It contains some fascinating illustrations.

Other works which touch on the history of Haiti in this period include Mats Lundahl's impressive work *Peasants and poverty: a study of Haiti* (London, 1979); this book, however, deals only incidentally with the past and relies heavily on secondary sources. Schiller Thébaud, 'L'évolution de la structure agraire d'Haïti de 1804 à nos jours' (unpublished PhD thesis, University of Paris, Faculté de Droit, 1967) contains much useful information. *L'économie haïtienne et sa voie de développement* (Paris, 1967) by Gérard Pierre Charles includes some rather slight historical sections; his writings on Haiti past and present are characterized by a loose and inappropriate use of such terms as 'feudalism' and 'fascism'. In *Economic development and political autonomy: the Haitian experience* (Montreal, 1974), David Nicholls deals with the ideas of Haitian statesmen and intellectuals on economic policies principally in the pre-occupation period. A revised version can be found in David Nicholls, *Haiti in Caribbean context. Ethnicity, economy and revolt* (London, 1985). A good economic history of Haiti has, however, yet to be written.

On the social structure of pre-occupation Haiti, Benoît Joachim's work is important, particularly 'La bourgeoisie d'affaires en Haïti de l'indépendance à l'occupation américaine', *Nouvelle Optique*, 4 (1971) and 'La structure sociale en Haïti et le mouvement d'indépendance au dix-neuvième siècle', *Journal of World History*, 12/3 (1970). Some of the material in these articles has been brought together in Joachim's book, *Les racines de sous-développement en Haïti* (Port-au-Prince, 1979). Alain Turnier, whose work on the relationship between Haiti and the USA is well known, has recently published a fascinating book on a nineteenth-century *cacos* leader, *Avec Mérisier Jeannis: une tranche de vie jacmélienne et nationale* (Port-au-Prince, 1982). Dealing with social movements immediately prior to the US invasion of 1915 is *Les cent jours de Rosalvo Bobo* (Port-au-Prince, 1973), being vol. II of Roger Gaillard's *Les blancs débarquent*; later volumes of this work are referred to below. Georges Corvington has continued his valuable series of volumes, *Port-au-Prince au cours des ans* (Port-au-Prince, 1970–).

Moving from economic and social history to a consideration of intellectual history, G. Martinez's article 'De l'ambiguïté du nationalisme bourgeois en Haïti', *Nouvelle Optique*, 9 (1973) is a good critical discussion – from a Marxist standpoint – of Haitian theorists in the latter half of the nineteenth century. Sections of Claude Moïse's thesis on that remarkable Haitian author and diplomat Joseph Anténor Firmin were published in *Conjonction*, 117 (1971). In chapters 4 and 5 of *From Dessalines to Duvalier: race, colour and national independence in Haiti* (Cambridge, 1979) David Nicholls discusses the role played by ideas of race and colour in the pre-occupation period, and in 'The wisdom of Salomon: myth or reality?', *Journal of Inter-American Studies and World Affairs*, 20 (1978), he considers in more detail the policies of the Salomon government and the claims made on its behalf. Two works on religion, which approach the subject in a historical perspective, are Laënec Hurbon, *Dieu dans le vaudou haïtien* (Paris, 1972) and H. Courlander and R. Bastien, *Religion and politics in Haiti* (Washington, DC, 1966).

In the field of literary history there have been numerous works published in the last twenty years. Raphaël Berrou and Pradel Pompilus have produced a revised and enlarged edition of their *Histoire de la littérature haïtienne* (Port-au-Prince, 1975). It is somewhat uncritical and didactic but is nevertheless a useful manual. On the literature of the pre-occupation period, Roger Gaillard has written a fascinating account of the mulatto Methodist poet from Jérémie, *Etzer Vilaire: témoin de nos malheurs* (Port-au-Prince, 1972). There is a double number of *Conjonction*, 122–3 (1973) dealing with Fernand Hibbert, Justin Lhérisson and Antoine Innocent. Yvette Gindine (Feldman), who contributed to this number, has also written 'Satire and the birth of Haitian fiction, 1901–1905', *Caribbean Quarterly*, 21/3 (1975). Léon François Hoffmann in *Le nègre romantique* (Paris, 1973), more recently in *Le Roman haïtien* (Princeton, 1982), and in a number of articles in *Caribbean Review* and elsewhere has greatly added to our knowledge and appreciation of the Haitian literature of this period.

With respect to the foreign relations of Haiti and the role played by foreign interests in the affairs of the country before 1915, the work of Benoît Joachim is outstanding. His thesis 'Aspects fondamentaux des relations de la France avec Haïti de 1825 à 1874: le néocolonialisme à l'essai' (University of Paris, Faculté des Lettres et Sciences Humaines, 1968) is based principally upon French archival material. In 'Commerce et décolonisation: l'expérience franco-haïtienne au XIXe siècle', *AESC*, 27 (1972), he has published some of the conclusions of his thesis. While Joachim's thesis deals primarily with the period before 1870, Leslie Manigat's long article 'La substitution de la prépondérance américaine à la prépondérance française en Haïti au debut du XXe siècle: la conjoncture de 1910–11', *Revue d'Histoire Moderne et Contemporaine*, 14 (1967), is central. Less controversial and contentious than some of his other writings, this article manifests the same lively and stimulating approach to the Haitian past that we have come to expect from his pen. An English translation has appeared in L. F. Manigat (ed.), *1975 Caribbean yearbook of international relations* (Port of Spain and Leiden, 1976). Rayford Logan, *Haiti and the Dominican Republic* (London, 1968) is a useful volume and especially strong on relations of Haiti with the USA. It does not, however, add a great deal to the excellent work which he has published earlier on this theme.

Moving on to consider the occupation period, Hans Schmidt, *The United States occupation of Haiti, 1915–1934* (New Brunswick, NJ, 1971) is a superb critical study of US policies in Haiti based on a mass of archival material and private papers in addition to printed sources. Cool and academic in tone it nevertheless represents a massive condemnation of US policies. The book, however, deals only incidentally and somewhat inadequately with Haitian reactions to the occupation. Less original and relying heavily on secondary sources is Suzy Castor, *La ocupación norteamericana de Haití y sus consecuencias (1915–1934)* (Mexico, Madrid and Buenos Aires, 1971). Dana Munro has two useful chapters on Haiti in *The United States and the Caribbean Republics, 1921–1933* (Princeton, 1964). In 'Idéologie et mouvements politiques en Haïti, 1915–1946', *AESC*, 30/4 (1975), David Nicholls looks at the role played by race and colour in the period and in chapter 5 of *From Dessalines to Duvalier* he discusses in more detail the intellectual movements of the occupation period.

On the social history of the occupation period, vols. III–VII of Roger Gaillard, *Les blancs débarquent* are essential reading for the years 1915 to 1919. Reference should also be made to Kethly Millet, *Les paysans haïtiens et l'occupation américaine, 1915–1930* (LaSalle, Quebec, 1978).

Dealing particularly with the literature of the occupation period is Ulrich Fleischmann, *Ideologie und Wirklichkeit in der Literatur Hatis* (Berlin, 1969); the main themes of this book have been restated in his *Ecrivain et société en Haïti* (Fonds St Jacques, Martinique, 1975). More accessible to the English reader is J. Michael Dash, *Literature and ideology in Haiti, 1915–1961* (London, 1981). This is an excellent piece of critical work, setting the authors of the period in their social context. Two short monographs on Jacques Stéphen Alexis have appeared in recent years, one by Michael Dash (Toronto, 1975) and the other entitled *Le romancero aux étoiles* by Maximilien Laroche (Paris, 1978). Claude Souffrant deals with Jacques Roumain and J. S. Alexis together with the US poet Langston Hughes in *Une négritude socialiste* (Paris, 1978). Gabriel Coulthard, *Race and colour in Caribbean literature* (London, 1962) remains an excellent introduction to Haitian literature of the occupation period in the setting of wider Caribbean movements.

9. THE GROWTH OF THE ARGENTINE ECONOMY, c. 1870–1914

The best and most complete bibliographical study of the economic history of Argentina in the period 1870–1914 is Tulio Halperín Donghi, 'Argentina', in Roberto Cortés Conde and Stanley J. Stein (eds.), *Latin America: a guide to economic history 1830–1930* (Berkeley and Los Angeles, 1977). Among the general works which appeared after the second world war, Ricardo M. Ortiz, *Historia económica de la Argentina, 1850–1930* (2 vols., Buenos Aires, 1955) was, for many years, the most widely read work on the economic history of Argentina. During the 1960s two works in this field were to have a significant influence: Aldo Ferrer, *La economía argentina: las etapas de su desarrollo y problemas actuales* (Mexico, 1963) which, like Celso Furtado's study of Brazil, examines the structure of the economy from the colonial period to the present and is strongly influenced by the literature on development from ECLA/CEPAL; and Guido Di Tella and Manuel Zymelman, *Las etapas del desarrollo económico argentino* (Buenos Aires, 1967), originally conceived as a thesis under the supervision of W. W. Rostow, which accepts the rapid growth of the period 1880–1914 and seeks to explain why it was not sustained after 1914.

The first chapter of Carlos F. Díaz Alejandro's important work, *Essays on the economic history of the Argentine Republic* (New Haven, 1970), considers the period prior to 1930. Díaz Alejandro moves away from previous interpretations of the period and stresses that Argentina, like Canada and the United States, deserves to be seen within the framework of the staple theory of economic growth (on which see Melville H. Watkins, 'A staple theory of economic growth', *Canadian Journal of Economic and Political Science*, 29/2 (1963)). Vicente Vásquez Presedo, *El caso argentino* (Buenos Aires, 1971), also sees the Argentine case as being unique and different from that of other underdeveloped countries and closer to that of recently settled Anglo-Saxon countries. See also John Fogarty, Ezequiel Gallo and Hector Diéguez, *Argentina y Australia* (Buenos Aires, 1979). The first two chapters of Roberto Cortés Conde, *El progreso argentino 1880–1914* (Buenos Aires, 1979) consider the territorial formation and regional structure of Argentina from the colonial period until the nineteenth century, while the central chapters discuss the development of the land and labour markets during the period 1880–1910. Use is made of new information drawn from business archives, and a number of widely accepted theses are refuted.

Other general works which deserve mention are Roque Gondra, *Historia económica de la República Argentina* (Buenos Aires, 1943), which was an obligatory text in teaching for many years, as was Federico Pinedo, *Siglo y medio de economía argentina* (Mexico, 1961). See also Academia Nacional de la Historia, *Historia argentina contemporánea 1862–1930*, vol. III, *Historia económica* (Buenos Aires, 1965). Among older but nevertheless indispensable works are two studies by Juan Alvarez, *Estudios sobre las guerras civiles argentinas* (Buenos Aires, 1914) and *Temas de historia económica argentina* (Buenos Aires, 1929), as well as Ernesto Tornquist's *The economic development of the Argentine Republic in the last fifty years* (Buenos Aires, 1919) and Michael G. and E. T. Mulhall, *Handbook of the River Plate*, 1863, 1875, 1888, 1892 (reprint, Buenos Aires and London, 1982).

On demographic change, and especially internal and international migration, Zulma L. Recchini de Lattes and Alfredo E. Lattes, *Migraciones en la Argentina* (Buenos Aires, 1969) and *La población de Argentina* (Buenos Aires, 1975) are indispensable. See also *CHLA* v, bibliographical essay 10.

For many years, the most widely accepted work on the rural sector was Horacio C. E. Giberti, *Historia económica de la ganadería argentina* (Buenos Aires, 1954), based principally on the excellent essays of the 1908 Census; it became a classic in its field. Another well-known book is James Scobie, *Revolution on the pampas: a social history of Argentine wheat* (Austin, Texas, 1964). See also Ezequiel Gallo, 'Agricultural colonization and society in Argentina. The province of Santa Fe, 1870–95', unpublished D. Phil thesis, Oxford, 1970; Sp. trans. *La Pampa Gringa* (Buenos Aires, 1983).

Other recent works include Aldo Montoya, *Historia de los saladeros argentinos* (Buenos Aires, 1956); Fernando Enrique Barba, 'El desarrollo agropecuario de la provincia de Buenos Aires (1880–1930)', *Investigaciones y Ensayos*, 17 (July–December 1974), 210–310; Roberto Cortés Conde, 'Patrones de asentamiento y explotación agropecuaria en los nuevos territorios argentinos (1890–1910)' and Ezequiel Gallo, 'Ocupación de tierras y colonización agrícola en Santa Fe', both in Alvaro Jara (ed.), *Tierras nuevas* (Mexico, 1969); Roberto Cortés Conde, 'Tierras, agricultura y ganadería', and Colin Lewis, 'La consolidación de la frontera argentina a fines de la década del setenta. Los indios, Roca y los ferrocarriles', both in Gustavo Ferrari and Ezequiel Gallo (eds.), *La Argentina del ochenta al centenario* (Buenos Aires, 1980); and M. Sáenz Quesada, *Los estancieros* (Buenos Aires, 1980). A number of older works are worthy of special mention because of their permanent value: Miguel Angel Cárcano, *Evolución histórica del régimen de la tierra pública 1810–1916* (Buenos Aires, 1917); Jacinto Oddone, *La burguesía terrateniente argentina* (Buenos Aires, 1967); Mark Jefferson, *Peopling the Argentine pampas* (New York, 1926); Carl C. Taylor, *Rural life in Argentina* (Baton Rouge, 1948); Simon G. Hanson, *Argentine meat and the British market: chapters in the history of the Argentine meat industry* (Stanford, 1938). Estanislao Zeballo, *Descripción amena de la República Argentina* (Buenos Aires, 1888) and the studies carried out by the División de Economía Rural del Ministerio de Agricultura (1900) are indispensable.

On foreign trade and foreign investment, John H. Williams, *Argentine international trade under inconvertible paper money, 1880–1900* (Cambridge, Mass., 1920; repr. New York, 1969), has still not been surpassed; because of its wealth of information on balance of payments, prices, wages, and so on it has, in fact, come to be considered the best economic history of the period. See also Vásquez-Presedo, *El caso argentino*, chapter 2; H. S. Ferns, *Britain and Argentina in the nineteenth century* (Oxford, 1960); A. G. Ford, *The gold standard 1880–1914: Britain and Argentina* (Oxford, 1962) and an older work, Harold E. Peters, *The foreign debt of the Argentine Republic* (Baltimore, 1934). Héctor L. Diegrez, 'Crescimiento e inestabilidad del valor y el volumen físico de las exportaciones argentinas en el período 1864–1963', *Desarrollo Económico* (Buenos Aires) 46/12 (1972), is an article which transcribes information from the important recompilation of statistical evidence on Argentina's foreign trade presented in Roberto Cortés Conde, Tulio Halperín and H. Gorostegui de Torres, *El comercio exterior argentino – exportaciones 1863–1963* (mimeo, Instituto Torcuato Di Tella, Buenos Aires, n.d.) which corrects many previous statistical errors and deficiencies. Also important are D. C. M. Platt, *Finance, trade and politics in British foreign policy 1815–1914* (Oxford, 1971) and *Latin America and British trade, 1806–1914* (London, 1972); A. G. Ford, 'British investment in Argentina and long swings 1880–1914', *Journal of Economic History*, 31/3 (1971), reprinted in Roderick Floud (ed.), *Essays in quantitative economic history* (Oxford, 1974), and 'British investment and Argentine economic development, 1880–1914' in David Rock (ed.), *Argentina in the twentieth century* (London, 1975).

The works of Williams and Ford are mainly studies of the working of the gold standard in Argentina. The work of Williams goes up to the end of the century while that of Ford considers two separate periods, the first from 1880 to 1885 which he classifies as a failure of the system, and the second from 1900 to 1910, which he terms a success. See also Ferns, *Britain and Argentina* and David Joslin, *A century of banking in Latin America* (London, 1963). See also Rafael Olarra Jiménez, *El dinero y las estructuras monetarias* (Buenos Aires, 1967) and his more recent 'Las reformas monetarias 1880–1910', together with Charles Jones, 'Los bancos británicos' in Ferrari and Gallo (eds.), *La Argentino del ochenta al centenario*. Among older works, see Emilio Hansen's classic study, *La moneda argentina* (Buenos Aires, 1916) and José A. Terry, *Cuestiones monetarias* (Buenos Aires, 1899) and *Finanzas* (Buenos Aires, 1918).

The bibliography on transport is, of course, dominated by the railways. The most complete recent work is Eduardo A. Zalduendo, *Libras y rieles*

(Buenos Aires, 1975) which also examines British investment in the railways of Brazil, Canada and India. Also important is Winthrop R. Wright, *British-owned railways in Argentina: their effect on economic nationalism 1854–1948* (Austin, Texas, 1972). See too Colin Lewis, 'Problems of railway development in Argentina 1857–1890', *Inter-American Economic Affairs*, 22/2 (1962) and *British railways in Argentina 1857–1914* (London, 1983); Paul Goodwin, 'The central Argentine railway and the economic development of Argentina 1854–1881', *HAHR*, 57/4 (1977); and the most recent study by Eduardo A. Zalduendo, 'Aspectos económicos del sistema de transporte en la Argentina (1880–1914)', in Ferrari and Gallo (eds.), *La Argentina del ochenta al centenario*. Among older works, which are nevertheless indispensable for various reasons, Raúl Scalabrini Ortiz, *Historia de los ferrocarriles argentinos* (Buenos Aires, 1957), an anti-British view, and A. E. Bunge's well-documented *Ferrocarriles argentinos* (Buenos Aires, 1916) which, as the author points out, is also a contribution to the study of national wealth, deserve mention.

On industry, Adolfo Dorfman's study, published originally as *La evolución industrial argentina* (Buenos Aires, 1942) and later as *Historia de la industria argentina* (Buenos Aires, 1970) remains important. Among more recent works, see Vásquez Presedo, *El caso argentino*, and 'Evolución industrial 1880–1910', in Ferrari and Gallo (eds.), *La Argentina del ochenta al centenario*; Ezequiel Gallo, 'Agrarian expansion and industrial development in Argentina', in Raymond Carr (ed.), *Latin American Affairs. St Antony's Papers, no. 22* (Oxford, 1970); Juan Carlos Chiaramonte, *Nacionalismo y liberalismo económico en Argentina, 1860–1880* (Buenos Aires, 1971); Lucio Geller, 'El crecimiento industrial argentino hasta 1914 y la teoría del bien primario exportado', in Marcos Giménez Zapiola (ed.), *El régimen oligárquico. Materiales para el estudio de la realidad argentina hasta 1930* (Buenos Aires, 1975), 156–200.

10. ARGENTINA: SOCIETY AND POLITICS, 1880–1916

There are a number of general works on the political process in Argentina between 1870 and 1914: Academia Nacional de la Historia, *Historia Argentina contemporánea* (2 vols., Buenos Aires, 1965); Ricardo Levillier (ed.), *Historia Argentina*, vol. IV (Buenos Aires, 1968); E. Gallo and R. Cortés Conde, *La República conservadora* (Buenos Aires, 1972); N. Botana, *El orden conservador. La política argentina entre 1880 y 1916* (Buenos

Aires, 1977); and G. Ferrari and E. Gallo (eds.), *La Argentina del ochenta al centenario* (Buenos Aires, 1980). Still useful are the classic studies by L. H. Sommariva, *Historia de las intervenciones federales en las provincias* (2 vols., Buenos Aires, 1929), José N. Matienzo, *El gobierno representativo federal en la República Argentina* (Madrid, 1917), and Rodolfo Rivarola, *Del régimen federativo al unitario* (Buenos Aires, 1908). Also worth consulting is the documentary compilation by Isidoro Ruiz Moreno (ed.), *La federalización de Buenos Aires* (Buenos Aires, 1980).

Some biographies contain useful information on the period. See, for example, two studies by Agustín Rivero Astengo, *Juárez Celman. Estudio histórico y documental de una época argentina* (Buenos Aires, 1940) and *Pellegrini, 1846–1906* (2 vols., Buenos Aires, 1941); R. Sáenz Hayes, *Miguel Cané y su tiempo, 1851–1905* (Buenos Aires, 1955) and *Ramón J. Cárcano, 1860–1946*; José Arce, *Roca 1843–1914. Su vida y su obra* (Buenos Aires, 1960); A. W. Bunkley, *The life of Sarmiento* (Princeton, NJ, 1952); J. Campobassi, *Mitre y su época* (Buenos Aires, 1980); and D. F. Weinstein, *Juan B. Justo y su época* (Buenos Aires, 1978). Also worth consulting are Leandro Alem, *Mensaje y destino* (8 vols., Buenos Aires, 1955), and Hipólito Yrigoyen, *Pueblo y gobierno* (12 vols., Buenos Aires, 1956). Among the most useful memoirs or autobiographies of active politicians are Paul Groussac, *Los que pasaban* (Buenos Aires, 1919); Ezequiel Ramos Mejía, *Mis memorias* (Buenos Aires, 1936); Ramón J. Cárcano, *Mis primeros ochenta años* (Buenos Aires, 1944); Nicolás Repetto, *Mi paso por la política, de Roca a Irigoyen* (Buenos Aires, 1956); Carlos Ibarguren, *La historia que he vivido* (Buenos Aires, 1955), and Enrique Dickman, *Recuerdos de un militante socialista* (Buenos Aires, 1949).

Very little has been written on the history of ideas. The theme is given summary treatment in José L. Romero, *Las ideas políticas en la Argentina* (Mexico, 1956), Eng. trans. *The history of Argentine political thought* (Stanford, 1963). Extremely valuable is T. Halperín Donghi's recent compilation, *Proyecto y construcción de una nación, 1846–1880* (Caracas, 1979). This work should be read in conjunction with other studies by the same author: 'Un nuevo clima de ideas' in Ferrari and Gallo (eds.), *La Argentina del ochenta al centenario*, and '¿Para qué la inmigración? Ideología y política migratoria y aceleración del proceso modernizador: el caso argentino (1810–1914)', *JGSWGL*, 13 (1976). The following are also worth consulting: H. Biaggini, *¿Cómo fue la generación del ochenta?* (Buenos Aires, 1980); M. Monserrat, 'La mentalidad evolucionista: una ideología del progreso' in Ferrari and Gallo (eds.), *La Argentina del ochenta al* *centenario*; J. C. Chiaramonte, *Nacionalismo y liberalismo económico en la Argentina* (Buenos Aires, 1971), and T. Duncan, 'La prensa política: Sud-América, 1884–1942' in Ferrari and Gallo (eds.), *La Argentina del ochenta al centenario*. An important recent contribution is Natalio Botana, *La tradición republicana. Alberdi, Sarmiento y la ideas políticas de su tiempo* (Buenos Aires, 1984).

There are a few general works on political parties: see Carlos Melo, *Los partidos políticos argentinos* (Córdoba, 1970), Alfredo Galletti, *La política y los partidos* (Buenos Aires, 1961) and Dario Canton, *Elecciones y partidos políticos en la Argentina. Historia, interpretación y balance 1910–1966* (Buenos Aires, 1973). The Radical party has received the most attention from historians. Besides the essays in Alem, *Mensaje y destino* and Irigoyen, *Pueblo y gobierno*, other important works are Gabriel Del Mazo, *El Radicalismo. Ensayo sobre su historia y doctrina* (Buenos Aires, 1957), David Rock, *Politics in Argentina, 1890–1930. The rise and fall of Radicalism* (Cambridge, 1975), and E. Gallo and S. Sigal, 'La formación de los partidos políticos contemporáneos: La Unión Cívica Radical (1890–1916)', *Desarrollo Económico*, 3/1–2 (1963). On the Socialist party, R. J. Walter, *The Socialist party in Argentina 1890–1930* (Austin, Texas, 1977), D. Cuneo, *Juan B. Justo y las luchas sociales en la Argentina* (Buenos Aires, 1963) and J. Oddone, *Historia del socialismo argentino* (Buenos Aires, 1943) are all useful.

Less has been published on the conservative forces in Argentine politics in this period. O. Cornblit, 'La opción conservadora en la política argentina', *Desarrollo Económico*, 56/4 (1975), 599–640, E. Gallo, 'El Roquismo', *Todo es Historia*, 100 (1975) and E. Gallo, 'Un quinquenio difícil. Las presidencias de Carlos Pellegrini y Luis Sáenz Peña (1890–1895)' in Ferrari and Gallo (eds.), *La Argentina del ochenta al centenario*, are worth consulting. Although not devoted specifically to the topic, useful information may be found in J. M. Dulevich, *Caos social y crisis cívica* (Buenos Aires, 1980). Nothing has been written on the different groups which rallied behind the banner of *mitrismo*, and very little on the provincial factions. On the latter, various regional histories contain information: Juan Álvarez, *Ensayo sobre la historia de Santa Fe* (Buenos Aires, 1910); H. F. Gómez, *Los últimos sesenta años de democracia y gobierno en la provincia de Corrientes* (Buenos Aires, 1931); A. Díaz de Molina, *La oligarquía argentina. Su filiación y régimen (1840–1898)* (Buenos Aires, 1973); and Carlos Páez de la Torre, 'Tucumán, vida política y cotidiana, 1904–1913', *Todo es Historia*, 27 (1973). There are also a number of valuable unpublished doctoral theses: Donald Peck, 'Argentine politics and the Province of Mendoza, 1890–1914' (University of Oxford, 1977); A. Liebscher, 'Commercial expansion and political change in Santa Fe Province, 1897–1916' (Indiana University, 1975); and Donna Guy, 'Politics and the sugar industry in Tucumán, Argentina, 1870–1900' (Indiana University, 1973).

The armed rebellions of this period have attracted considerable attention. On the revolution of 1874, there is A. Terzaga, 'La Revolución del 74. Una estrella que sube', *Todo es Historia*, 59 (1974). For the events of 1880, see B. Galíndez, *Historia política Argentina. La Revolución de 1880* (Buenos Aires, 1945); S. Ratto de Sambucetti, *Avellaneda y la nación versus la provincia de Buenos Aires (1873–1880)* (Buenos Aires, 1975); E. M. Sanucci, *La renovación presidencial de 1880* (Buenos Aires, 1959); and N. Botana, '1880. La federalización de Buenos Aires', in G. Ferrari and E. Gallo (eds.), *La Argentina del ochenta al centenario*. Much has been published on the revolution of 1890: J. Balestra, *El Noventa. Una evolución política argentina* (Buenos Aires, 1971); H. Zorraquín Becú, *La Revolución del Noventa. Su sentido político* (Buenos Aires, 1960); L. V. Sommi, *La Revolución del 90* (Buenos Aires, 1957); and a special edition of the *Revista de Historia* (Buenos Aires, 1957) on 'La crisis del 90'. On the provincial revolts of 1893, see R. Etchepareborda, *Tres Revoluciones. 1890–1893–1905* (Buenos Aires, 1968) and E. Gallo, *Farmers in revolt. The Revolution of 1893 in the province of Santa Fe* (London, 1976). Etchepareborda's work also analyses the aborted radical uprising of 1905.

On international relations, see H. J. Ferns, *Britain and Argentina in the nineteenth century* (Oxford, 1962); T. McGann, *Argentina, the United States and the inter-American system. 1880–1914* (Cambridge, Mass., 1967); and G. Ferrari, 'Argentina y sus vecinos' in Ferrari and Gallo (eds.), *La Argentina del ochenta al centenario*. An important subject which has attracted little attention is that of relations with Italy and Spain, the home countries of the vast majority of immigrants.

For the social history of the period, fundamental are the three excellent national censuses of 1869, 1895 and 1914, and the two agricultural censuses (1888 and 1908). There are also two good provincial census reports (Buenos Aires, 1881 and Santa Fe, 1887), and three municipal censuses for the city of Buenos Aires (1887, 1904 and 1909). Much information on the social life of Argentina can be found in descriptions and studies published by foreign writers. The list is a long one, but one could mention by way of example the *Handbooks* by M. G. and E. T.

Mulhall, 1863, 1875, 1883 and 1892 (reprint, Buenos Aires and London, 1982); E. Daireaux, *Vida y costumbres en el Plata* (2 vols., Buenos Aires, 1888); Jules Huret, *En Argentine: de Buenos Ayres au Gran Chaco* (Paris, 1914); A. N. Schüster, *Argentinien: Land, Volk, Wirtschaftsleben und Kolonisation* (2 vols., Munich, 1913); and P. de Giovanni, *Sotto il sole de Maggio. Note e impressione de la Argentina* (Castielo, 1900). Of considerable use is the volume published by Lloyd's, *Twentieth century impressions of Argentina. Its history, people, commerce, industries and resources* (London, 1911).

A topic which has received particular attention from historians is demographic growth, especially in relation to immigration. Useful studies are J. A. Alsina, *La inmigración en el primer siglo de la independencia* (Buenos Aires, 1910), Zulma L. Recchini de Lattes and Alfredo E. Lattes, *La población de Argentina* (Buenos Aires, 1975); N. Sánchez-Albornoz, *La población de América Latina desde los tiempos pre-colombinos al ano 2000* (Madrid, 1973); G. Beyhaut *et al.*, 'Los inmigrantes en el sistema institucional argentino', in Torcuato di Tella *et al.*, *Argentina, sociedad de masas* (Buenos Aires, 1965), and E. Maeder, 'Población e inmigración en la Argentina entre 1880 y 1910', in Ferrari and Gallo (eds.), *La Argentina del ochenta al centenario*. See also Carl Solberg, *Immigration and nationalism in Argentina and Chile 1890–1914* (Austin, Texas, 1970). On European immigration to rural areas see J. C. Korol and H. Sabato, *Cómo fue la inmigración irlandesa en Argentina* (Buenos Aires, 1981) and Ezequiel Gallo, *La pampa gringa* (Buenos Aires, 1983).

On urban growth, see Z. Recchini de Lattes, 'El proceso de urbanización en la Argentina: distribución, crecimiento y algunas características de la población urbana', *Desarrollo Económico*, 48 (1973) and *La población de Buenos Aires* (Buenos Aires, 1971); P. H. Randle, *La ciudad pampeana* (Buenos Aires, 1977); J. Scobie, *Buenos Aires. From plaza to suburb, 1870–1910* (New York, 1971); and Guy Bourde, *Urbanisation et immigration en Amérique Latine, Buenos Aires, XIX et XX siècles* (Paris, 1974).

On the social structure, see G. Germani, *Estructura social de la Argentina* (Buenos Aires, 1954); S. Bagu, *Evolución histórica de la estratificación social en la Argentina* (Buenos Aires, 1961); F. Korn, *Los huéspedes del 20* (Buenos Aires, 1974); and the unpublished PhD thesis by R. Sautu, 'Social stratification and economic development in Argentina (1914–1955)' (University of London, 1968). Also useful are G. Germani, 'La movilidad social en la Argentina' in S. M. Lipset and R. Bendix (eds.), *Movilidad social en la sociedad industrial* (Buenos Aires, 1963); D. Cuneo,

Comportamiento y crisis de la clase empresaria (Buenos Aires, 1967); and O. Cornblit, 'Sindicatos obreros y asociaciones empresarias' in Ferrari and Gallo (eds.), *La Argentina del ochenta al centenario*. For relations between the agrarian and industrial sectors, see E. Gallo, 'Agrarian expansion and industrial development in Argentina, 1880–1930' in R. Carr (ed.), *Latin American Affairs. St Antony's Papers, no. 22* (Oxford, 1970). For the interior provinces see the PhD theses by Donald Peck and Donna Guy mentioned above. Also valuable are E. Gallo, 'The cereal boom and changes in the social and political structure of Santa Fe, Argentina 1870–95' in K. Duncan and I. Routledge (eds.), *Land and labour in Latin America* (Cambridge, 1977) and J. Balan, 'Una cuestión regional en la Argentina: burguesias provinciales y el mercado nacional en el desarrollo exportador', *Desarrollo Económico*, 69 (1978).

On living conditions, the classic studies are A. Bunge, *Riqueza y rentas en la Argentina* (Buenos Aires, 1915) and *Los problemas económicos del presente* (Buenos Aires, 1919), and J. Bialet Masset, *Informe sobre el estado de las clases obreras en el interior de la Argentina* (Buenos Aires, 1904). A more recent work is R. Cortés Conde, *El progreso Argentino* (Buenos Aires, 1980). See also J. Panettieri, *Los trabajadores* (Buenos Aires, 1963). One of the few studies on housing is O. Yujnovsky, 'Políticas de vivienda en la ciudad de Buenos Aires', *Desarrollo Económico* 54 (1974). On education, see J. C. Tedesco, *Educación y sociedad en la Argentina (1880–1900)* (Buenos Aires, 1970) and Francis Korn and L. de la Torre, 'Constituir la Unión Nacional' in Ferrari and Gallo (eds.), *La Argentina del ochenta al centenario*.

On the labour movement the literature is more abundant. Of the studies published by those who participated actively in union organization, the most useful are S. Marotta, *El movimiento sindical argentino* (3 vols., Buenos Aires, 1960), and D. Abad de Santillán, *La FORA. Ideología y trayectoria* (Buenos Aires, 1971). Modern studies include M. Casaretto, *Historia del movimiento obrero argentino* (Buenos Aires, 1947); H. Spalding, *La clase trabajadora Argentina. Documentos para su historia (1890–1912)* (Buenos Aires, 1970); and I. Oved, *El anarquismo en los sindicatos argentinos a comienzos de siglo* (Tel Aviv, 1975).

11. ARGENTINA IN 1914: THE PAMPAS, THE INTERIOR, BUENOS AIRES

A major statistical source for the study of Argentina on the eve of the first world war is Ernesto Tornquist and Co. Ltd, *The economic development of the Argentine Republic in the last fifty years* (Buenos Aires, 1919). For the war period itself students should also consult Tornquist's quarterly publication, *Business Conditions in Argentina* (Buenos Aires, 1913–22). A second compound source of information is the writings of Alejandro E. Bunge. See his *Ferrocarriles argentinos* (Buenos Aires, 1917) and *Los problemas económicos del presente* (1919; Buenos Aires, 1979). Both are encyclopaedic collections of facts and figures. Slightly later came Bunge's *La economía argentina* (4 vols., Buenos Aires, 1928–30), a work containing many of the author's press writings from past years and articles from a major journal he edited, the *Revista de Economía Argentina*. Other important publications are the national census of 1914, *Tercer Censo Nacional* (Buenos Aires, 1915–17), which is far more than a mere population count, and Alberto B. Martínez and Maurice Lewandowski, *The Argentine in the twentieth century* (London, 1911). For population, see also *Recensement général de la ville de Buenos Aires* (Buenos Aires, 1910).

The most outstanding contemporary study of Argentina from abroad in this period is the publication by Lloyd's Bank to celebrate the centennial anniversary of 1910: Reginald Lloyd (ed.), *Twentieth century impressions of Argentina* (London, 1911). Pierre Denis, *The Argentine Republic. Its development and progress*, translated by Joseph McCabe (London, 1922) is a useful geographical survey by a Frenchman, though much inferior to its predecessor from the 1860s by Martin de Moussy. There are insights into manners and customs in W. H. Koebel, *Argentina: past and present* (London, 1914). John Foster Fraser, *The amazing Argentine* (London, 1914) has virtues, though it is often very negative and a little graceless. The view from Spain can be found in Adolfo Posada, *La República Argentina* (Madrid, 1912), and a little later in the many writings of José Ortega y Gasset. Other major works of a similar type are James Bryce, *South America: observations and impressions* (London, 1912); Georges Clemenceau, *South America today: a study of conditions social, political and commercial in Argentina, Uruguay and Brazil* (London, 1911); John A. Hammerton, *The real Argentine: notes and impressions of a year in the Argentine and Uruguay* (New York, 1915); Jules Huret, *En Argentine: de Buenos Ayres au Gran Chaco* (Paris, 1914); Adolf N. Schüster, *Argentinien: Land, Volk, Wirtschaftsleben und Kolonisation* (2 vols., Munich, 1913); Mark C. Jefferson, *Peopling the Argentine pampas* (New York, 1926).

An almost indispensable source for historians of this period is the Argentine press, especially the two great *porteño* dailies, *La Prensa* and *La Nación*. *La Vanguardia* (Socialist) and *La Protesta* (anarchist) are invaluable for social as well as political and purely labour history. Vast numbers of other newspapers await the attentions of researchers. Beyond them are more occasional publications: *Caras y Caretas* (the Argentine *Punch* of these years), the *Revista Popular* and more serious journals such as Rodolfo Rivarola's *Revista Argentina de Ciencias Políticas* or the *Revista de Ciencias Económicas*. Among the major non-Spanish press sources are the *Buenos Aires Herald*, the *Buenos Aires Standard* and *Le Courrier de la Plata* (along with a host of Italian, German, Russian and other counterparts). On economic issues see especially the *Review of the River Plate*. For the considerable secondary literature on the Argentine economy before the first world war, see *CHLA* v, bibliographical essay 9.

The full history of land tenure patterns on the pampas remains to be written. An outstanding contribution is James R. Scobie, *Revolution on the pampas. A social history of Argentine wheat, 1860–1910* (Austin, Texas, 1964). For the literature on the economy and society of the pampas region, see *CHLA* v, bibliographical essays 9 and 10.

Studies of the regions beyond the pampas are more partial and fragmented. See Jorge Balán, 'Urbanización regional y producción agraria en Argentina: un análisis comparativo', *Estudios CEDES*, 2/2 (1979); Marcos Giménez Zapiola, 'El interior argentino y el "desarrollo hacia afuera": el caso de Tucumán', in M. Giménez Zapiola (ed.), *El régimen oligárquico. Materiales para el estudio de la realidad argentina hasta 1930* (Buenos Aires, 1975), 72–115; Donna J. Guy, 'Politics and the sugar industry in Tucumán, Argentina, 1870–1900' (unpublished PhD thesis, Indiana University, 1973) and 'The rural working class in nineteenth century Argentina: forced plantation labor in Tucumán', *LARR*, 13/1 (1979), 135–45; Donald M. Peck, 'Argentine politics and the province of Mendoza, 1890–1914' (unpublished D.Phil. thesis, Oxford, 1977); Juan Carlos Agulla, *Eclipse of an aristocracy. An investigation of the ruling elites of Córdoba*, translated by Betty Crowse (University, Alabama, 1976); Alejandro E. Bunge, *Las indústrias del norte argentino* (Buenos Aires, 1922); Juan Antonio Solari, *Trabajadores del norte argentino* (Buenos Aires, 1937); Osvaldo Bayer, *Los vengadores de la Patagonia trágica* (2 vols., Buenos Aires, 1972); and Carl E. Solberg, *Oil and nationalism in Argentina* (Stanford, 1979) for further comments on conditions in Patagonia. Ian Rutledge, 'The sugar economy of Argentina, 1930–1943' in K. Duncan and I. Rutledge (eds.), *Land and labour in Latin America* (Cambridge, 1976) also contains information on the earlier history of Salta and Jujuy before 1930.

On the history of Buenos Aires in this period the following are useful: James R. Scobie, *Buenos Aires, plaza to suburb 1870–1910* (New York, 1974); Francis Korn, *Buenos Aires. Los huéspedes del '20* (Buenos Aires, 1974); Oscar Yujnovsky, 'Políticas de vivienda en la ciudad de Buenos Aires', *Desarrollo Económico*, 14/54 (1974), 327–71; Hobart A. Spalding, Jr, *La clase obrera argentina. Documentos para su historia, 1890–1916* (Buenos Aires, 1970) and *Organized labor in Latin America. Historical case-studies of workers in dependent societies* (New York, 1977); José Panettieri, *Los trabajadores* (Buenos Aires, 1968); Roberto Cortés Conde, *El progreso argentino: la formación del mercado nacional 1880–1910* (Buenos Aires, 1979), chapter on urban wages; Nicolás J. Labanca, *Recuerdos de la comisaría 3a* (Buenos Aires, 1969), a policeman's memoir. For studies of the elites and the middle classes, see Jorge Federico Sábato, 'Notas sobre la formación de la clase dominante en la Argentina moderna (1880–1914)', mimeo, CISEA (Buenos Aires, 1979); David Rock, *Politics in Argentina, 1890–1930. The rise and fall of Radicalism* (Cambridge, 1975). On Buenos Aires, see also *CHLA* v, bibliographical essay 10.

12. ARGENTINA FROM THE FIRST WORLD WAR TO THE REVOLUTION OF 1930

Many of the books, articles and unpublished theses on Argentina, 1870–1914 in *CHLA* v, bibliography essays 9, 10 and 11 are also relevant for the period from the first world war to the world depression.

The Sáenz Peña Law of 1912 and politics between 1912 and 1916 are discussed in David Rock, *Politics in Argentina, 1890–1930. The rise and fall of Radicalism* (Cambridge, 1975). See also Peter H. Smith, *Argentina and the failure of democracy: conflict among political elites* (Madison, 1974) and Richard J. Walter, *The Socialist party of Argentina, 1890–1930* (Austin, Texas, 1977). Two recent studies by Argentine scholars provide additional information: Natalio Botana, *El orden conservador. La política argentina entre 1880 y 1916* (Buenos Aires, 1977); Oscar Cornblit, 'La opción conservadora en la política argentina', *Desarrollo Económico*, 56/14 (1975), 599–640. For complete electoral data for the period 1912–30, see Dario Cantón, *Materiales para el estudio de la sociología política en la Argentina* (Buenos Aires, 1969).

On the economy between 1914 and 1930 there are several useful traditional sources: Harold J. Peters, *The foreign debt of the Argentine Republic* (Baltimore, 1934); Vernon L. Phelps, *The international economic position of Argentina* (Philadelphia, 1938); Ricardo M. Ortiz, *Historia económica de la Argentina, 1850–1930* (2 vols., Buenos Aires, 1955), especially vol. II. Among several more recent studies the most outstanding are Carlos F. Díaz Alejandro, *Essays in the economic history of the Argentine Republic* (New Haven, 1970) and Guido Di Tella and Manuel Zymelman, *Las etapas del desarrollo económico argentino* (Buenos Aires, 1967). On industrial growth, see Javier Villaneuva, 'El origen de la industrialización argentina', *Desarrollo Económico*, 47/12 (1972), 451–76, and Eduardo F. Jorge, *Industria y concentración económica* (Buenos Aires, 1971).

For international economic relations, see Jorge Fodor and Arturo O'Connell, 'La Argentina y la economía atlántica en la primera mitad del siglo XX', *Desarrollo Económico*, 49/13 (1973); Joseph S. Tulchin, *The aftermath of war. World War I and U.S. policy towards Latin America* (New York, 1971) and 'The Argentine economy during the First World War', *Review of the River Plate* (19 June – 10 July 1970); Pedro Skupch, 'El deterioro y fin de la hegemonía británica sobre la economía argentina 1914–47' in L. Marta Panaca, Ricardo Lesser and Pedro Skupch (eds.), *Estudios sobre los orígenes del peronismo*, vol. II (Buenos Aires, 1973); and Roger Gravil, 'Anglo-US trade rivalry in Argentina and the D'Abernon Mission of 1929', in D. Rock (ed.), *Argentina in the twentieth century* (London, 1975). Also Harold F. Peterson, *Argentina and the United States, 1810–1960* (New York, 1964).

On Yrigoyen's first government, see Rock, *Politics in Argentina*; Peter H. Smith, *Argentina and the failure of democracy*; Peter H. Smith, *Politics and beef in Argentina. Patterns of conflict and change* (New York, 1969) and 'Los radicales argentinos en la defensa de los intereses ganaderos', *Desarrollo Económico*, 25/7 (1967), 795–829; Richard J. Walter, *Student politics in Argentina. The University Reform and its effects, 1918–1964* (New York, 1968), and *The Socialist party of Argentina*; Paul B. Goodwin, *Los ferrocarriles británicos y la U.C.R., 1916–1930* (Buenos Aires, 1974); Osvaldo Bayer, *Los vengadores de la Patagonia trágica* (2 vols., Buenos Aires, 1972). Among more traditional accounts the most useful are Roberto Etchepareborda, *Hipólito Yrigoyen. Pueblo y gobierno* (10 vols., Buenos Aires, 1951); Gabriel Del Mazo, *El radicalismo. Ensayo sobre su historia y doctrina* (Buenos Aires, 1957); and Manuel Gálvez, *Vida de Hipólito Yrigoyen* (Buenos Aires, 1959). On Alvear the field is more limited, but see Rock, *Politics in Argentina*, Smith, *Argentina and the failure of democracy* and Raúl A. Molina, *Presidencia de Marcelo T. de Alvear*

(Buenos Aires, 1965). For the meat issue, see Smith, *Politics and beef*; also Simon G. Hanson, *Argentine meat and the British market. Chapters in the history of the Argentine meat industry* (Stanford, 1938) and Oscar B. Colman, 'Luchas interburguesas en el agro-argentino: la crísis de la carne en el "20"', *Estudios* (Buenos Aires, 1973). The tariff issue has attracted much attention. Of recent literature the best is Díaz Alejandro, *Essays*; Laura Randall, *An economic history of Argentina in the twentieth century* (New York, 1978), 120–6; and Carl E. Solberg, 'Tariffs and politics in Argentina, 1916–1930', *HAHR* 53/2 (1973), 260–84. See also Carl E. Solberg, 'Agrarian unrest and agrarian policy in Argentina, 1912–30', *Journal of Inter-American Studies and World Affairs*, 13 (1971), 15–55. The best study of the conservatives in the 1920s is Marysa Navarro Gerassi, *Los nacionalistas* (Buenos Aires, 1969). On oil, see above all Carl E. Solberg, *Oil and nationalism in Argentina* (Stanford, 1979); also Arturo Frondizi, *Petróleo y política. Contribución al estudio de la historia económica argentina y las relaciones entre el imperialismo y la vida política nacional* (Buenos Aires, 1955), and Marcos Kaplan, 'Política del petróleo en la primera presidencia de Hipólito Yrigoyen, 1916–22', *Desarrollo Económico*, 45/12 (1972), 3–24. The army and the revolution of 1930 are best approached through Robert A. Potash, *The army and politics in Argentina, 1928–1945. Yrigoyen to Peron* (Stanford, 1969) and José Maria Sarobe, *Memorias sobre le revolución del 6 de septiembre de 1930* (Buenos Aires, 1957).

13. THE FORMATION OF MODERN URUGUAY, *c.* 1870–1930

During the period under discussion, there were three national censuses (1852, 1860 and 1908). For official statistics, see *Cuadernos* (Montevideo, 1873–84) and *Anuarios estadísticos* (Montevideo, 1884–); valuable statistical information is gathered together in Juan Rial, *Estadísticas históricas del Uruguay 1850–1930* (Montevideo, 1980). The annual *Mensajes* of the president of the Republic gave an overall picture of the situation in the country, though their origin and motive make it necessary to utilize them with considerable care. See also the *Memorias* of the various ministries, especially those of government, finance and economic development. Diplomatic and consular reports give the point of view of foreign representatives accredited in the country; Juan E. Pivel Devoto has published a substantial part of the correspondence sent to their respective chanceries by the ministers of France, Italy, Spain and Germany. See the *Revista histórica* of the National Historical Museum,

Montevideo, vols. XXXII–XXXIX (1962–8). For the diplomatic and consular documents of the Kingdom of Italy, see also Juan A. Oddone, *Una perspectiva europea del Uruguay* (Montevideo, 1965). A continuous series, albeit with some gaps, of the *Diarios de sesiones* (Chamber of Deputies and Senators, and the General Assembly) was published from 1830. Of the greatest importance are the large circulation newspapers (*El Siglo*, *El Telégrafo Marítimo*, *El Ferrocarril*, *La Democracia*, *El Día*, *El Plata*, *La Mañana*, *El País*); additional sources are the periodical publications of the foreign communities. Of the publications of active economic sectors, the most important are the *Revista de la Asociación Rural* (from 1872) and the *Revista de la Federación Rural* (from 1915), which reflected agrarian interests, and the *Revista Económica Sudamericana* (first and second series, from 1928), representing the industrial sector. Other complementary sources (travellers, memoir-writers and essayists) have been largely analysed in Carlos Real de Azúa, *Viajeros y observadores extranjeros del Uruguay. Juicios e impresiones (1889–1964)* (Montevideo, 1965), *Antología del ensayo uruguayo contemporáneo* (Montevideo, 1964) and 'Prosa del mirar y del vivir', *Capítulo Oriental*, 9 (Montevideo, 1968).

General works include Eduardo Acevedo, *Anales históricos del Uruguay* (2nd edn, Montevideo, 1933–6); Luis C. Benvenuto, *Breve historia del Uruguay* (Montevideo, 1969); Roque Faraone, *El Uruguay en que vivimos (1900–1968)* (Montevideo, 1970); Russell H. Fitzgibbon, *Uruguay. Portrait of a democracy* (New York, 1954); Benjamín Nahum, *La época batllista* (Montevideo, 1975); M. Blanca Paris de Oddone *et al.*, *Cronología comparada de la historia del Uruguay, 1830–1945* (2nd edn, Montevideo, 1968); Francisco R. Pintos, *Batlle y el proceso histórico del Uruguay* (Montevideo, 1938); Alberto Zum Felde, *Proceso histórico del Uruguay y esquema de su sociología* (4th edn, Montevideo, 1963).

On economic growth and development, see José Pedro Barrán and Benjamín Nahum, *Historia rural del Uruguay moderno*, vol. I, *1851–1885*, (Montevideo, 1967), vol. II, *La crisis económica, 1886–1894* (Montevideo, 1971), vol. III, *Recuperación y dependencia, 1895–1904* (Montevideo, 1973), vol. V, *La prosperidad frágil, 1905–1914* (Montevideo, 1977), vol. VI, *La civilización ganadera bajo Batlle, 1905–1914* (Montevideo, 1977), vol. VII, *Agricultura, crédito y transporte bajo Batlle, 1905–1914* (Montevideo, 1978); Luis A. Faroppa, *El desarrollo económico del Uruguay. Tentativa de explicación* (Montevideo, 1965); M. H. J. Finch, *A political economy of Uruguay since 1870* (London, 1981); Simon G. Hanson, *Utopia in Uruguay* (New York, 1938); Instituto de Economía, *El proceso económico del Uruguay*

(Montevideo, 1969); Raúl Jacob, *Breve historia de la industria en el Uruguay* (Montevideo, 1981) and *El Uruguay en la crisis de 1929* (Montevideo, 1977); David Joslin, *A century of banking in Latin America* (London, 1965); Samuel Lichtensztejn, 'Comercio internacional y problemas monetarios', *Nuestra Tierra*, 20 (Montevideo, 1969); Luis Macadar *et al.*, 'Una economía latinoamericana', in *Uruguay hoy* (Buenos Aires, 1971); Julio Martínez Lamas, *Riqueza y pobreza del Uruguay* (Montevideo, 1930); Oscar Mourat, *La crisis comercial en la cuenca del Plata, 1880–1920* (Montevideo, 1973); Juan A. Oddone, *La formación del Uruguay moderno* (Buenos Aires, 1966) and *Economía y sociedad en el Uruguay liberal, 1852–1904* (Montevideo, 1967); Juan Rial, *Uruguay: el país urbano* (Montevideo, 1981) and *Población y desarrollo de un pequeño país: Uruguay, 1830–1930* (Montevideo, 1983); Julio C. Rodríguez, 'Los grandes negocios', in *Enciclopedia uruguaya*, vol. xxviii (Montevideo, 1968); Vivián Trías, *El imperialismo en el Río de la Plata* (Buenos Aires, 1960); Carlos Visca, *Emilio Reus y su época* (Montevideo, 1963); Peter Winn, *El imperio informal británico en el Uruguay en el siglo XIX* (Montevideo, 1975); Israel Wonsewer and Juan Young, *Uruguay en la economía mundial* (Montevideo, 1981); Carlos Zubillaga, *El reto financiero. Deuda externa y desarrollo en Uruguay, 1903–1933* (Montevideo, 1982).

On demographic and social history, see José Pedro Barrán and Benjamín Nahum, *Batlle, los estancieros y el imperio británico*, vol. i, *El Uruguay del novecientos* (Montevideo, 1979), vol. ii, *Un diálogo difícil, 1903–1910* (Montevideo, 1981); see also *Historia rural del Uruguay moderno*, vol. iv, *Historia social de las revoluciones de 1897 y 1904* (Montevideo, 1972); Alfredo Castellanos, *Historia del desarrollo edilicio y urbanístico de Montevideo, 1829–1914* (Montevideo, 1971); Germán D'Elía and Armando Miraldi, *Historia del movimiento obrero en el Uruguay* (Montevideo, 1984); Raúl Jacob, *Las consecuencias sociales del alambramiento entre 1872 y 1880* (Montevideo, 1969); Francisco R. Pintos, *Historia del movimiento obrero en el Uruguay* (Montevideo, 1960); Carlos Real de Azúa, *El patriciado uruguayo* (2nd edn, Montevideo, 1984) and 'La clase dirigente', *Nuestra Tierra*, 34 (Montevideo, 1969); Juan Rial, *La población uruguaya y el crecimiento económico-social entre 1850 y 1930* (Montevideo, 1981); Silvia Rodríguez Villamil and Graciela Sapriza, *La inmigración europea en el Uruguay. Los italianos* (Montevideo, 1982).

For political developments, see José Pedro Barrán and Benjamín Nahum, *Batlle, los estancieros y el imperio británico*, vol. iii, *El nacimiento del batllismo* (Montevideo, 1982), vol. iv, *Las primeras reformas, 1911–1913*

(Montevideo, 1983); José Pedro Barrán, *Batlle, los estancieros y el imperio británico*, vol. v, *La reacción imperial-conservadora, 1911–1913* (Montevideo, 1984); Oscar H. Bruschera, *Los partidos tradicionales y la evolución institucional del Uruguay* (Montevideo, 1962); Gerardo Caetano, *La agonía del reformismo* (Montevideo, 1983); Alfredo Castellanos and Romeo Pérez, *El pluralismo. Examen de la experiencia uruguaya, 1830–1918* (Montevideo, 1981); Göran Lindahl, *Uruguay's new path: a study in politics during the first Colegiado* (Stockholm, 1962); Carlos Manini Ríos, *Anoche me llamó Batlle* (Montevideo, 1970); Juan E. Pivel Devoto, *Historia de los partidos políticos en el Uruguay* (2 vols., Montevideo, 1942), and *La amnistía en la tradición política uruguaya* (Montevideo, 1984); Carlos Real de Azúa, *El impulso y su freno. Tres décadas de batllismo* (Montevideo, 1964), and 'La historia política', in *Enciclopedia uruguaya*, vol. 1 (Montevideo, 1968); Milton Vanger, *José Batlle y Ordóñez of Uruguay: the creator of his times, 1902–1907* (Cambridge, Mass., 1963), and *The model country: José Batlle y Ordóñez of Uruguay 1907–1915* (Cambridge, Mass., 1980); Carlos Zubillaga, *Herrera, la encrucijada nacionalista* (Montevideo, 1976).

Finally, on cultural aspects of the period, see Arturo Ardao, *Espiritualismo y positivismo en el Uruguay* (Mexico, 1950) and *Racionalismo y Liberalismo en el Uruguay* (Montevideo, 1962): Juan A. Oddone and M. Blanca Paris, *Historia de la Universidad de Montevideo. La Universidad Vieja, 1849–1884* (Montevideo, 1963) and *La Universidad uruguaya desde el militarismo a la crisis, 1885–1958* (Montevideo, 1972); Angel Rama, '180 años de literatura' in *Enciclopedia uruguaya*, vol. xi (Montevideo, 1968); Alberto Zum Felde, *Proceso intelectual del Uruguay* (Montevideo, 1967).

14. PARAGUAY FROM THE WAR OF THE TRIPLE ALLIANCE TO THE CHACO WAR, 1870–1932

There are very few scholarly studies dealing with Paraguay between the War of the Triple Alliance (1865–70) and the Chaco War (1932–5). Harris Gaylord Warren, *Paraguay and the Triple Alliance: the postwar decade, 1869–1878* (Austin, Texas, 1978) is a serious study of the early part of this period. However, both the period of General Caballero's dominance of the national political scene and the turbulent years of Liberal rule after 1904 have yet to find their historian. Less scholarly than Warren's monograph but nevertheless valuable, is Teodosio González, *Infortunios del Paraguay* (Buenos Aires, 1931). González was a maverick Liberal senator in the 1920s and his book is a 'muckraking' work that spares neither party in its exposé of Paraguay's intrigues and corruption. It spans the period from the War of the Triple Alliance to González's own time and treats Paraguay's problems topically rather than chronologically. Another valuable work is Carlos R. Centurión's comprehensive *Historia de la cultura paraguaya* (2 vols., Asunción, 1961). It is mainly about literature, but since so much of Paraguay's writing is polemical the reader will gain much information about political questions and alignments. Also recommended is Arturo Bray's *Hombres y épocas del Paraguay* (2 vols., Buenos Aires, 1943 and 1957), which approaches the nation's history through brief biographies of its leading figures.

Some information can be gleaned from general histories. Efraím Cardozo, *Breve historia del Paraguay* (Buenos Aires, 1965), and Julio César Cháves, *Compendio de la historia paraguaya* (Buenos Aires, 1960) are introductory surveys by two of Paraguay's best historians. The former, who died in 1973, was a Liberal; the latter is a *colorado*. Alonso Ibarra, *Cien años de vida política paraguaya, posterior a la epopeya de 1865 al 70* (Asunción, 1973), is a very brief enumeration of the chief events since the start of the War of the Triple Alliance. In English, there are Philip Raine, *Paraguay* (New Brunswick, NJ, 1956), George Pendle, *Paraguay, a riverside nation* (London, 1956), and Harris Gaylord Warren, *Paraguay, an informal history* (Norman, Oklahoma, 1949). All three are useful introductions to Paraguay, but in each case the treatment of the interwar period is the weakest part of the book.

F. Arturo Bordón, *Historia política del Paraguay: era constitucional* (Asunción, 1976), is worth reading in conjunction with Warren's *Paraguay and the Triple Alliance* for its description of the politics of the immediate postwar period. It contains interesting information about the origins of the Paraguayan Legion. A much more serious work is Carlos Pastore, *La lucha por la tierra en el Paraguay* (Montevideo, 1972). Despite Pastore's pro-Liberal partisanship, the book is well-researched and contains valuable information on the land question.

The period after 1904, when the Liberals took power, has received even less attention than the *colorado* era. Most of the writing is concerned with attacking or defending the Liberals' conduct of diplomacy. Some of the better examples of this genre are Policarpo Artaza, *Ayala, Estigarribia, y el Partido Liberal* (Buenos Aires, 1946), which supports the Liberals, and Antonio E. González, *Preparación del Paraguay para la guerra del Chaco* (2 vols., Asunción, 1957), which presents the case against them.

The shooting of students before the presidential palace on 23 October 1931 produced much polemical literature. Efraím Cardozo defended the government in *23 de octubre: una página de historia contemporánea del Paraguay* (Buenos Aires, 1956), and at the same time furnished interesting insights about the *gondrista* and *schaererista* factional struggle in the Liberal party. Probably the best anti-Liberal polemic is Juan Stefanich, *El 23 de octubre de 1931* (Buenos Aires, 1958), which was a direct reply to Cardozo. It also contains a broader indictment of three decades of Liberal party rule. Brief biographical sketches of Paraguayan political and cultural leaders can be found in William Balmont Parker, *Paraguayans of today* (New York, 1920). Finally, no student of this period can fail to be fascinated by the complex personality of Eligio Ayala. His thoughts about his native land were published after his death. *Migraciones* (Santiago de Chile, 1941) is a long essay with many penetrating observations into Paraguayan society by one of Paraguay's most intelligent statesmen.

15. CHILE FROM THE WAR OF THE PACIFIC TO THE WORLD DEPRESSION, 1880–1930

Of general works covering the period, the best to date are, in English, Brian Loveman, *Chile: the legacy of Hispanic capitalism* (New York, 1979) and Fredrick B. Pike, *Chile and the United States, 1880–1962* (Notre Dame, Indiana, 1963) – much more comprehensive than its title suggests, and with an astonishing list of references – and, in Spanish, Leopoldo Castedo, *Resumen de la historia de Chile, 1891–1925* (Santiago, 1982), a brilliantly illustrated book, and the voluminous work by Gonzalo Vial, *Historia de Chile, 1891–1973* (Santiago, vol. I in two parts, 1981; vol. II, 1983), the first three books in an ambitious modern history running to several volumes: those published cover the period 1891 to 1925 in great detail. Diplomatic history is treated by Mario Barros, *Historia diplomática de Chile, 1541–1938* (Barcelona, 1970); constitutional and political history by Julio Heise González, *Historia de Chile. El período parlamentario, 1861–1925* (2 vols., Santiago, 1974, 1974–82); rural affairs by Arnold Bauer, *Chilean rural society, from the Spanish conquest to 1930* (Cambridge, 1975) and the early chapters of Brian Loveman, *Struggle in the countryside: politics and rural labour in Chile, 1919–1973* (Bloomington, 1976); industrial development by Henry Kirsch, *Industrial development in a traditional society: the conflict of entrepreneurship and modernization in Chile* (Gainesville, 1977); labour movements and labour relations by Alan Angell, *Politics and the labour movement in Chile* (London, 1972), Jorge Barría, *El movimiento obrero en Chile* (Santiago, 1971) and the significant 'revisionist' study of Peter De Shazo, *Urban workers and labour unions in Chile, 1902–1927* (Madison, 1983), which seriously challenges the role of Recabarren and the nitrate workers in the formation of class consciousness and left-wing parties. Carmen Cariola and Oswaldo Sunkel, 'Chile' in Roberto Cortés Conde and Stanley J. Stein, *Latin America. A guide to economic history 1830–1930* (Berkeley and Los Angeles, 1977), is an annotated bibliography accompanied by an interpretative essay. Literary history is covered by Raúl Silva Castro, *Historia crítica de la novela chilena, 1843–1956* (Madrid, 1960) and by Castedo, *Resumen de la historia de Chile*.

On the Balmaceda period, see in particular Harold Blakemore, 'The Chilean revolution of 1891 and its historiography', *HAHR*, 45/3 (1965), 393–421, and by the same author, *British nitrates and Chilean politics, 1886–1896: North and Balmeceda* (London, 1974). Of contemporary accounts, J. Bañados Espinosa, *Balmaceda, su gobierno y la revolución de 1891* (2 vols., Paris, 1894) is the best and most detailed, Hernán Ramírez Necochea, *Balmaceda y la contrarrevolución de 1891* (2nd edn, Santiago, 1969) is a suggestive, Marxist interpretation. Much recondite material and contrasting interpretations may be found in Thomas F. O'Brien, *The nitrate industry and Chile's crucial transition, 1870–1891* (New York, 1982) and Michael Monteon, *Chile in the nitrate era: the evolution of economic dependence, 1880–1930* (Madison, 1982).

The parliamentary period has finally begun to command the attention of historians that it deserves; see Castedo, *Resumen de la historia de Chile*, Vial, *Historia de Chile* and Heise González, *Historia de Chile. El período parlamentario*, a spirited defence of its virtues. Paul Reinsch, 'Parliamentary government in Chile', *American Political Science Review*, 3 (1908–9), is not only a brilliant portrait but also an outstanding example of writing 'contemporary history'. Two studies of particular administrations merit citation: Jaime Eyzaguirre, *Chile durante el gobierno de Errázuriz Echaurrén, 1896–1901* (Santiago, 1957), and Germán Riesco, *Presidencia de Riesco, 1901–1906* (Santiago, 1950). Among older works, see also the highly polemical study of Ricardo Donoso, *Alessandri, agitador y demoledor* (2 vols., Mexico, 1952 and 1954), a detailed chronicle of the whole period, including the administration of Ibáñez and the 1930s. Equally fundamental, though less well organized, is the three-volume compilation of the writings of Manuel Rivas Vicuña, a key figure of the epoch, *Historia política y parlamentaria de Chile* (Santiago, 1964), prepared by Guillermo

Feliú Cruz. It is a mine of information, but the historian has to dig for the ore.

As with Balmaceda, there is a massive literature on both Alessandri and Ibáñez, both panegyric and polemical. Apart from Donoso, *Alessandri*, key works on Alessandri are his own *Memorias* (3 vols., Santiago, 1967), Augusto Iglesias, *Alessandri, una etapa de la democracia en América* (Santiago, 1960), and Luis Durand, *Don Arturo* (Santiago, 1952). Ibáñez, who wrote no *Memorias*, is well covered by René Montero, *La verdad sobre Ibáñez* (Santiago, 1953); Victor Contreras Guzmán, *Bitácora de la dictadura* (Santiago, 1942); Ernesto Würth Rojas, *Ibáñez, caudillo enigmático* (Santiago, 1958); Aquíles Vergara Vicuña, *Ibáñez, césar criollo* (Santiago, 1931), a strong critique; and Luis Correa Prieto, *El presidente Ibáñez* (Santiago, 1962), based on personal interviews. The most sustained philippic is Carlos Vicuña, *La tiranía en Chile* (2 vols., Santiago, 1939). The best book on the whole period 1920–31 in English, and the most comprehensive source for further bibliography on military matters, is Frederick Nunn, *Chilean politics, 1920–1931: the honorable mission of the armed forces* (Albuquerque, 1970). Arturo Olavarría, *Chile entre dos Alessandri* (4 vols., Santiago, 1962–5) is full of information from a figure central to Chilean political life for 40 years but, again, the richer veins take some finding. A valuable documentary compilation on the military intervention of 1924–5 is General E. Monreal, *Historia documentada del período revolucionario, 1924–1925* (Santiago, 1926), to which Raúl Aldunate Phillips, *Ruido de Sables* (Santiago, n.d.), with its fascinating reproductions of photographs, provides a valuable pendant.

Economic issues of the 1920s and the 'great crash' are well discussed in Santiago Macchiavello Varas, *Política económica nacional* (2 vols., Santiago, 1931), and the first chapter of P. T. Ellsworth, *Chile, an economy in transition* (New York, 1945), while Albert O. Hirschman, 'Inflation in Chile', in his *Journeys towards progress* (New York, 1963), 159–223, is a brilliant and provocative discussion of that perennial problem in modern Chilean history. But the nearest approach to an economic history is Markos Mamalakis, *The growth and structure of the Chilean economy. From independence to Allende* (New Haven, 1976).

Two other sources for the period, often neglected, should be mentioned – travel accounts and unpublished theses. Most informative and perceptive travel accounts are C. Wiener, *Chili et Chiliens* (Paris, 1888); Eduardo Poirier, *Chile en 1908* (Santiago, 1909), a massive compilation; Frank G. Carpenter, *South America, social, industrial and political* (New York, 1900); Francis J. G. Maitland, *Chile: its land and people* (London, 1914); G. F. Scott Elliott, *Chile* (London, 1907); and Earl Chapin May, *2000 miles through Chile* (New York, 1924). There are a number of excellent theses: J. R. Couyoumdjian, 'Anglo-Chilean economic relations during the first world war and its aftermath, 1914–1920' (PhD, University of London, 1975); Andrew Barnard, 'The Chilean Communist party, 1922–1947' (PhD, University of London, 1977); Peter Conoboy, 'Money and politics in Chile, 1878–1925' (PhD, University of Southampton, 1977), and J. G. Palma, 'Growth and structure of Chilean manufacturing industry from 1830 to 1935' (D.Phil., University of Oxford, 1979).

16. BOLIVIA FROM THE WAR OF THE PACIFIC TO THE CHACO WAR, 1880–1932

General surveys

There are several general histories of Bolivia which cover the period 1880–1932, notably Alcides Arguedas, *Historia general de Bolivia* (La Paz, 1922); Enrique Finot, *Nueva historia de Bolivia* (Buenos Aires, 1946) and Jorge Basadre, *Perú, Chile y Bolivia independiente* (Barcelona, 1948). A more recent and detailed study is Herbert S. Klein, *Parties and political change in Bolivia, 1880–1952* (Cambridge, 1968). Much of the recent research on the social and economic history of the period is summarized in a general history by Klein, *Bolivia, the evolution of a multi-ethnic society* (New York, 1982).

Among more specialized works, Luis Peñaloza, *Historia económica de Bolivia* (2 vols., La Paz, 1953–4), though dated, is still the most complete study available. More schematic but with useful data is Eduardo Arze Cuadros, *La economía de Bolivia, 1492–1979* (La Paz, 1979). A complete survey of organized labour in Bolivian history is provided in Guillermo Lora, *History of the Bolivian labour movement, 1848–1971* (Cambridge, 1977). Intellectual history is dealt with in Guillermo Francovich, *La filosofía en Bolivia* (Sucre, 1945); while historians in particular are well treated in Valentín Abecia Baldivieso, *Historiografía boliviana* (La Paz, 1965). Political thought is studied in Mario Rolan Anaya, *Política y partidos en Bolivia* (La Paz, 1966), which also contains the most complete reproduction of party programmes and platforms. See also Guillermo Lora, *Documentos políticos de Bolivia* (La Paz, 1970). The only serious, though now dated, analysis of the organizational structure of the republican government is N. Andrew N. Cleven, *The political organization of Bolivia* (Washington, DC, 1940). All of Bolivia's constitutions up to the 1950s are contained in the useful compilation and analysis of Ciro Félix Trigo, *Las constituciones en Bolivia* (Madrid, 1958). Among the numerous histories of Bolivia's complex international relations the best is that by Valentín Abecia Baldivieso, *Las relaciones internacionales en la historia de Bolivia* (1 volume to date, La Paz, 1979). Bolivia's close relationship with England is surveyed in Roberto Querejazu Calvo, *Bolivia y los ingleses 1825–1948* (La Paz, 1971).

From different perspectives appear two fine studies of national literature: Enrique Finot, *Historia de la literatura boliviana* (2nd edn, La Paz, 1956), and Fernando Diez de Medina, *Literatura boliviana* (Madrid, 1954). The Bolivian novel is covered in excellent depth by Augusto Guzmán in both his *La novela en Bolivia* (La Paz, 1955) and the work he did for the Pan-American Union, *Diccionario de la literatura latinoamericana. Bolivia* (Washington, DC, 1955). There is as yet no single volume on the plastic arts, though the work of José de Mesa and Teresa Gisbert is fundamental for any appraisal of this area in the national as well as the pre-conquest and colonial periods. A good introduction to Bolivia's architecture is Mesa and Gisbert, *Bolivia: Monumentos históricos y arqueológicos* (Mexico, 1970).

While numerous histories exist of individual religious orders, along with several documentary collections and larger international surveys, the only general history of the Bolivian church is the rapid survey done by Felipe López Menéndez, *Compendio de la historia eclesiástica de Bolivia* (La Paz, 1965). The army is the subject of Julio Díaz A., *Historia del ejército de Bolivia, 1825–1932* (La Paz, 1940). Medicine has been studied in Juan Manuel Balcazar, *Historia de medicina en Bolivia* (La Paz, 1956). But the legal profession has not been adequately treated.

Given the important role of mining and the extraordinary terrain of the country, Bolivia has been the subject of much research by national and foreign scholars in the geological and geographical fields. Much of the very extensive literature is summarized in Jorge Muñoz Reyes, *Geografía de Bolivia* (La Paz, 1977) and in Federico E. Ahlfeld, *Geología de Bolivia* (3rd edn, La Paz, 1972). An interesting attempt made recently to remap the soils and climate of Bolivia using more modern criteria was carried out by the Ministerio de Asuntos Campesinos y Agropecuarios, *Mapa ecológico de Bolivia* (La Paz, 1975). Thomas T. Cochrane, *Potencial agrícola del uso de la tierra de Bolivia* (La Paz, 1973), provides a more traditional but important analysis of the soils of Bolivia. A superficial but still useful study of the distribution of commercial and subsistence plants is Gover Barja Berrios and Armando Cardozo Gonsálvez, *Geografía agrícola de Bolivia* (La Paz, 1971). Still important because of their extensive statistical collections are the government's early twentieth-century surveys. Oficina Nacional de Inmigración Estadística y Propaganda Geográfica, *Sinopsis estadística y geográfica de la república de Bolivia* (2 vols., La Paz, 1903); *Geografía de la república de Bolivia* (La Paz, 1905); and *Diccionario geográfico de la República de Bolivia* (4 vols., La Paz, 1890–1904). An interesting political geography of Bolivia dealing with its famous frontier problems is J. Valerie Fifer, *Bolivia. Land, location and politics since 1825* (Cambridge, 1972). Currently Bolivia also has extensive collections of aerial and satellite photo mapping as well as modern demographic and geographic maps available from the Instituto Militar de Geografía and the Instituto Nacional de Estadística. The satellite maps are discussed and indexed in Lorrain E. Giddings, *Bolivia from space* (Houston, 1977). Finally, the large literature on exploration is described in Manuel Frontaura Argandona, *Descubridores y exploradores de Bolivia* (La Paz, 1971).

The nature of human physiological adaptation to high altitude living has also been the subject of recent scholarly interest and has resulted in a major compilation of the latest findings in Paul T. Baker and M. A. Little (eds.), *Man in the Andes: a multidimensional study of Highland Quechua* (Stroudsberg, Penn., 1976).

The later nineteenth century

The second half of the nineteenth century has until recently received less attention than earlier periods of Bolivian history. The leading political theorist of the period has had all his works published: Mariano Baptista, *Obras completas* (7 vols., La Paz, 1932–4). And an interesting survey of the political upheavals of the period is Nicanor Aranzaes, *Las revoluciones de Bolivia* (La Paz, 1918). The political role of the army has also been studied in James Dunkerley, 'The politics of the Bolivian army: institutional development, 1879–1935' (unpublished D.Phil. thesis, Oxford University, 1979). But few good studies of political life exist for this period and even fewer biographies or administrative studies. There is, however, a superb political novel which captures the era to an extraordinary degree and is one of the best of its genre in Latin America: Armando Chirveches, *La candidatura de Rojas* (La Paz, 1909).

A very good analysis of the revived mining industry is provided in Antonio Mitre, *Los patriarcas de la plata. Estructura socio-económica de la minería boliviana en el siglo xix* (Lima, 1981). Several biographies exist of the leading miners of the period: Ernesto Ruck, *Biografía de Don Avelino Aramayo* (Potosí, 1891); A. Costa du Rels, *Félix Avelino Aramayo y su época, 1846–1929* (Buenos Aires, 1942); Jaime Mendoza, *Gregorio Pacheco* (Santiago de Chile, 1924). But the concern is usually with the non-economic aspects of their lives. Moreover, most of the other sectors of the economy, such as the internal market, regional trade, and public finance are neglected. Nor is there any serious study of the revolution in transportation which occurred in this period or the modernization of the urban centres. That the primary literature exists is evident, for example, in the interesting listing given in Edgar A. Valdés, *Catálogo de folletería de ferrocarriles del repositorio nacional* (La Paz, 1980).

In contrast to the relative neglect of economic history there has been a major renaissance in the social history of this period. This began with an innovative study challenging all the traditional assumptions about the dual social system and political isolation of the Indian carried out by Ramiro Condarco Morales, *Zarate 'El Temible' Wilke. Historia de la rebelión indígena de 1899* (La Paz, 1965). This was followed by three important works which challenged the traditional assumption of hacienda domination in the nineteenth century and of its isolation from the market economy: Sylvia Rivera, 'La expansión del latifundio en el altiplano boliviano: elementos para la caracterización de una oligarquía regional', *Avances*, 2 (1978); Nicolás Sánchez-Albornoz, *Indios y tributos en el Alto Perú* (Lima, 1978); and Erwin P. Greishaber, 'Survival of Indian communities in nineteenth century Bolivia: a regional comparison', *JLAS*, 12/2 (1980). Nor has urban society been totally neglected. Some of Bolivia's urban problems, as well as those of rural society, are discussed in an interesting work by Danièle Demelas, *Nationalisme sans nation? La Bolivie aux xix-xx siècles* (Paris, 1980).

The early twentieth century

The first decades of the twentieth century were ones of intellectual ferment. From the initial stirrings of a critique of racist society in the novels and 'sociology' of Alcides Arguedas, to the more systematic development of an indigenista viewpoint in Franz Tamayo in *La creación de una pedagogia nacional* (La Paz, 1910), writers began to challenge the assumptions of their society. A good survey of this activity is found in Guillermo Francovich, *El pensamiento boliviano en el siglo xx* (Mexico, 1956) and in the studies of literature by Diez de Medina and Finot previously cited.

There has been a general neglect of the Liberal era with the exception of the original and extremely useful study of Juan Albarracín Millán, *El poder minero en la administración liberal* (La Paz, 1972). On the other hand Bolivian intellectuals have been attracted to the political leaders of the 1920s and 1930s, producing the very best such biographies yet written. There exist two outstanding biographies for this period: Benigno Carrasco, *Hernando Siles* (La Paz, 1961) and David Alvestegui, *Salamanca, su gravitación sobre el destino de Bolivia* (3 vols., La Paz, 1957–62). An overall assessment of this period is provided in Klein, *Parties and political change* and in two outstanding surveys: the first volume of Augusto Céspedes's two-volume history of modern Bolivian political history, *El dictador suicida, 40 años de historia de Bolivia* (Santiago de Chile, 1956); and the first three volumes of the five-volume series by Porfirio Díaz Machicado, *Historia de Bolivia. Saavedra, 1920–25* (La Paz, 1954), *Historia de Bolivia. Guzmán, Siles, Blanco Galindo, 1925–31* (La Paz, 1954) and *Historia de Bolivia. Salamanca, la guerra del Chaco, Tejada Sorzano* (La Paz, 1955).

The economic history of this period has also been more fully developed than that of earlier periods. The tin mining industry has finally received an overall economic analysis of some sophistication in the study by Walter Gómez, *La minería en el desarrollo económico de Bolivia, 1900–1970* (La Paz, 1978). Complementing this macro-analysis are detailed studies of the early industry by Pedro Aniceto Blanco, *Monografía de la industria minera en Bolivia* (La Paz, 1910); Herbert S. Klein, 'The creation of the Patiño tin empire', *Inter-American Economic Affairs*, 19/2 (1965); and Donaciano Ibáñez C., *Historia mineral de Bolivia* (Antofagasta, 1943). The political role of the miners is assessed in Albarracín, *El poder minero* and in William Lofstrom, *Attitudes of an industrial pressure group in Latin America: the 'Asociación de Industriales Mineros de Bolivia', 1925–1935* (Ithaca, 1968).

Good overall assessments of the national economy at this time are found in W. L. Schurz, *Bolivia, a commercial and industrial handbook* (Washington, DC, 1921) and Paul Walle, *Bolivia, its people and resources* (New York, 1914). Specific aspects of the economy or national economic policy are reviewed in Charles A. McQueen, *Bolivian public finance* (Washington, DC, 1925) and the excellent study by Margaret A. Marsh, *Bankers in Bolivia. A study in American foreign investment* (New York, 1928). Among the many surveys on banking history, Julio Benavides, *Historia bancaria de Bolivia* (La Paz, 1955), is most useful.

Social changes resulting from the growth of the tin industry, the modernization of the cities and the completion of the hacienda expansion have not been seriously analysed by scholars. Yet there does exist a wealth of data from which to study this problem. Thus in 1900 came the first, and one of the best, national censuses: Oficina Nacional de Inmigración, Estadística y Propaganda Geográfica, *Censo nacional de la población de la república de Bolivia, 1 septiembre de 1900* (2 vols., La Paz, 1902–4). This government office also published numerous geographical studies which were cited above, and from the late 1880s, and with increasing tempo under the very efficient Liberals, almost all the government ministries were publishing annual statistics.

17. THE ORIGINS OF MODERN PERU, 1880–1930

Peruvian historiography for the period 1880–1930 has undergone a virtual revolution during the past two decades. It can be traced back to the middle 1960s, when a number of foreign scholars, many of them anthropologists, arrived in Peru, and at the same time the Instituto de Estudios Peruanos (IEP) was established in Lima by the Peruvian anthropologist, José Matos Mar. The revolution gained momentum with the worldwide interest generated by the so-called Peruvian military revolution of 1968 which inaugurated a perod of intense reform lasting until 1976. Moreover, a decade of relative economic expansion and prosperity during the 1960s, combined with postwar demographic trends, produced a rapid expansion of the country's educational system, particularly at the university level. And a rising middle class, anxious to rediscover its identity and redefine the national experience, created a strong, new demand for knowledge about Peru's history. The result has been an ever increasing production of new and often revisionist works by a new generation of Peruvian scholars that have transformed the traditional landscape of Peruvian historiography.

Any study of the period 1880–1930 must begin with the dozen or more works of Jorge Basadre, the dean of modern Peruvian historians. His seventeen-volume *Historia de la República del Perú* (6th edn, Lima, 1968–9) stands as a towering monument in the field, with five volumes devoted to the period 1880–1930. He also published the most complete, annotated bibliography for the nineteenth and twentieth centuries: *Introducción a las bases documentales para la historia de la República del Perú con algunas reflexiones* (2 vols., Lima, 1971). An equally thorough annotated bibliography, with accompanying analytical essay, for the economic history of the period can be found in Pablo Macera and Shane Hunt, 'Peru', in Roberto Cortés Conde and Stanley J. Stein (eds.), *Latin America: a guide to its economic history, 1830–1930* (Berkeley and Los Angeles, 1977). For further bibliographical reference, see the appropriate sections of Raúl Porras Barrenechea, *Fuentes históricas Peruanas* (Lima, 1963), Carlos Moreyra Paz Soldán, *Bibliografía regional Peruana* (Lima, 1967), and Carl Herbold and Steve Stein, *Guía bibliográfica para la historia social y política del Perú en el siglo XX (1895–1960)* (Lima, 1971). Another useful guide is Alberto Tauro, *Diccionario enciclopédico del Perú* (3 vols., Lima, 1966).

By far the best one-volume history of the period is Manuel Burga and Alberto Flores Galindo, *Apogeo y crisis de la república aristocrática* (Lima, 1979). Comprehensive, interpretative and analytical, this is the work of two of Peru's best young historians. Also useful are Ernesto Yepes del Castillo, *Perú, 1820–1920: un siglo de desarrollo capitalista* (2nd edn, Lima, 1981), 'El desarrollo Peruano en las primeras décadas del siglo XX', in *Nueva historia general del Perú* (Lima, 1979), 137–60, and 'Los inicios de la expansión mercantil capitalista en el Perú (1890–1930)', in Juan Mejia Baca (ed.), *Historia del Perú* (Lima, 1980), VII, 305–403; as well as Aníbal Quijano, *Imperialismo, clases sociales y estado en el Perú, 1890–1930* (Lima, 1978), all from a Marxist perspective. An excellent socio-historical analysis is Julio Cotler, *Clases, estado y nación en el Perú* (Lima, 1977). Also worthy of note are David Scott Palmer, *Peru: the authoritarian legacy* (New York, 1980), David P. Werlich, *Peru: a short history* (Carbondale, Illinois, 1978), Frederick Pike, *A modern history of Peru* (London, 1977), Henry E. Dobyns and Paul Doughty, *Peru: a cultural history* (Oxford, 1976), and Washington Delgado, *Historia de la literatura republicana* (Lima, 1980).

The most comprehensive study of the economic history of the period is Rosemary Thorp and Geoffrey Bertram, *Peru 1890–1977: growth and policy in an open economy* (London, 1978). Shane Hunt has been instrumental in developing a data base for the analysis of patterns of economic growth: for example, see his *Real wages and economic growth in Peru, 1900–1940* (Center for Latin American Development Studies, Boston University, 1977). Pablo Macera has not only analysed the evolution of the export economy but also published valuable data sets from his Centro Peruano de Historia Económica at San Marcos University. See also Baltazar Caravedo M., 'Economía, producción y trabajo (Perú, siglo XX)', in Juan Mejía Baca (ed.), *Historia del Perú*, VIII, 189–361. Others have written from a variety of viewpoints on the problematic of the export economy and foreign economic activity in Peru: for example, Heraclio Bonilla (ed.), *Gran Bretaña y el Perú: 1826–1919. Informes de los Cónsules Británicos* (5 vols., Lima, 1975–7), and 'Emergence of U.S. control of the Peruvian economy, 1850–1930', in Joseph S. Tulchin (ed.), *Hemispheric perspectives on the United States* (Westport, 1978), 325–51; Rory Miller, 'The making of the Grace Contract: British bondholders and the Peruvian government, 1885–1890', *JLAS*, 8/1 (1976), 73–100, 'Railroads and economic development in Central Peru, 1890–1930', in J. Fisher (ed.), *Social and economic change in modern Peru* (Liverpool, 1976), and 'British firms and the Peruvian government, 1885–1930', in D. C. M. Platt (ed.), *Business imperialism 1840–1930: an inquiry based on British experience in Latin America* (Oxford, 1977); and William Bollinger, 'The rise of United States influence in the Peruvian economy, 1869–1921' (unpublished MA thesis, University of California, Los Angeles, 1972). A major data source for the fiscal history of the period is P. E. Dancuart and J. M. Rodríguez (eds.), *Anales de la hacienda pública del Perú* (22 vols., Lima, 1902–8). Peruvian mining in this period has been studied in Alberto Flores Galindo, *Los mineros de la Cerro de Pasco, 1900–1930* (Lima, 1974); Julian Laite, *Industrial development and migrant labour in Latin America* (Austin, Texas, 1981); and Adrian Dewind, 'From peasants to miners: background to strikes in the mines of Peru', *Science and Society*, 39/1 (1975), 44–72. On the onset of the depression, see Rosemary Thorp and Carlos Londoño, 'The effect of the great depression on the economies of Peru and Colombia', in Rosemary Thorp (ed.), *Latin America in the 1930s: the role of the periphery in world crisis* (London, 1984), 81–116.

The study of Andean agrarian society has been given substantial impetus by a group of French scholars, some of them belonging to the *Annales* School: François Chevalier, 'L'Expansion de la grande propriété dans le Haut-Pérou au XXe siècle', *AESC*, 21 (1966), 815–31; C. Collin-Delavaud, *Les Régions côtières du Pérou septentrional* (Lima, 1968); Jean Piel, 'The place of the peasantry in the national life of Peru in the nineteenth century', *Past and Present*, 46 (1970), 108–33; and Henri Favre, 'The dynamics of Indian peasant society and migration to coastal plantations in Central Peru', in Kenneth Duncan and Ian Rutledge (eds.), *Land and labour in Latin America: essays on the development of agrarian capitalism* (Cambridge, 1977), 253–68. On sugar, see Peter F. Klarén, 'The social and economic consequences of modernization in the Peruvian sugar industry, 1870–1930', in Duncan and Rutledge (eds.), *Land and labour*, 229–52, Bill Albert, *An essay on the Peruvian sugar industry, 1880–1920* (Norwich, 1976), and Michael J. Gonzales, *Plantation agriculture and social control in northern Peru, 1875–1933* (Austin, Texas, 1984). On the wool trade, see Alberto Flores Galindo, *Arequipa y el Sur Andino, siglos XVIII–XX* (Lima, 1977), and Manuel Burga and Wilson Reátegui Chávez, *Lanas y capital mercantil en el Sur: la Casa Ricketts, 1895–1935* (Lima, 1981). On peasant movements, see Manuel Burga and Alberto Flores Galindo, 'Feudalismo andino y movimientos sociales (1866–1965)', in Juan Mejía Baca (ed.), *Historia del Perú*, XI, 11–112; Florencia E. Mallon, *The defense of community in Peru's central highlands: peasant struggle and capitalist transition, 1860–1940* (Princeton, NJ, 1983); Rodrigo Montoya, 'Les Luttes paysannes pour la terre au Pérou au XXe siècle' (unpublished PhD thesis, University of Paris, 1977); Wilfredo Kapsoli, *Los movimientos campesinos en Cerro de Pasco, 1880–1963* (Huancayo, 1975); and, finally, Juan Martínez-Alier, *Haciendas, plantations and collective farms: agrarian class societies – Cuba and Peru* (London, 1977). New research is in progress at the Workshop on Rural Society (Taller de Estudios Andinos) at La Molina and the Agrarian Reform Archives (Archivo del Fuero Agrario). Although he has not worked primarily in this period it should be noted that Pablo Macera has inspired numerous younger scholars with his outstanding work on rural society in general and his Seminario de Historia Rural Andina at San Marcos University in particular.

On the social consequences of the War of the Pacific, see Henri Favre, 'Remarques sur la lutte des classes au Pérou pendant la Guerre du Pacifique', in *Littérature et société au Pérou du XIXe siècle à nos jours* (Grenoble, 1975), 54–81; Heraclio Bonilla, 'The War of the Pacific and the national and colonial problem in Peru', *Past and Present*, 81 (1978), 92–118; Nelson Manrique, *Campesinado y nación: las guerillas indígenas en la guerra con Chile* (Lima, 1981); and, most recently, Mallon, *The defense of community*. See also the collection of essays in Wilson Reátegui Chávez et al., *La guerra del Pacífico* (Lima, 1979). On the Indian in Peruvian society during the first half of the twentieth century, see Thomas M. Davies, Jr, *Indian integration in Peru: a half century of experience, 1900–1948* (Lincoln,

Nebraska, 1974). Japanese immigration has been examined in Harvey C. Gardiner, *The Japanese and Peru 1873–1973* (Albuquerque, 1975).

The oligarchical state is the subject of Dennis Gilbert, *The oligarchy and the old regime in Peru* (Latin American Studies Program Dissertation Series, Cornell University, 1977); François Bourricaud *et al.*, *La oligarquía en el Perú* (Lima, 1969); and Sinesio López J., 'El estado oligárquico en el Perú: un ensayo de interpretación', *Revista Mexicana de Sociología*, 40/3 (1978), 991–1007. See also Rory Miller, 'The coastal elite and Peruvian politics, 1895–1919', *JLAS*, 14/1 (1982), 97–120. On the military, see Víctor Villanueva, *Ejército Peruano: del caudillaje anárquico al militarismo reformista* (Lima, 1973).

There is an interesting study of Billinghurst: Peter Blanchard, 'A populist precursor: Guillermo Billinghurst', *JLAS*, 9/2 (1977), 251–73. Two unpublished theses examine the administration of Augusto Leguía: Howard Karno, 'Augusto B. Leguía, the oligarchy and the modernization of Peru, 1870–1930' (University of California, Los Angeles, 1970), and Carl F. Herbold, 'Developments in the Peruvian administrative system 1919–1930: modern and traditional qualities of government under authoritarian regimes' (Yale University, 1973). For the origins of the Aprista party, see Peter F. Klarén, *Modernization, dislocation and Aprismo: origins of the Peruvian Aprista party, 1870–1932* (Austin, Texas, 1973). The history of the labour movement is explored in Denis Sulmont, *El movimiento obrero en el Peru, 1900–1956* (Lima, 1975); Piedad Pareja, *Anarquismo y sindicalismo en el Perú* (Lima, 1978); and Peter Blanchard, *The origins of the Peruvian labor movement, 1883–1919* (Pittsburgh, 1982). See also Steve Stein, *Populism in Peru: the emergence of the masses and the politics of social control* (Madison, 1980).

There is information on the church in Jeffrey L. Klaiber SJ, *Religion and revolution in Peru, 1924–1976* (Notre Dame, Ind., 1977). Diplomatic relations with the United States in the period are considered in Fredrick B. Pike, *The United States and the Andean Republics: Peru, Bolivia and Ecuador*, (Cambridge, Mass., 1977). A major source on intellectual history is Augusto Salazar Bondy, *Historia de las ideas en el Perú contemporáneo* (2 vols., Lima, 1965). See also Jesús Chavarría, 'The intellectuals and the crisis of modern Peruvian nationalism: 1870–1919', *HAHR*, 50/2 (1970), 257–78. Several works consider the ideas of José Carlos Mariátegui: Jesús Chavarría, *José Carlos Mariátegui, 1894–1930, and the rise of modern Peru* (Albuquerque, 1979); Diego Meseguer Illán, *José*

Carlos Mariátegui y su pensamiento revolucionario (Lima, 1974); Harry E. Vanden, *Mariátegui: influencias en su formación ideológica* (Lima, 1975); Robert Paris, *La formazione ideologica di José Carlos Mariátegui* (Turin, 1970); and Guillermo Rouillón, *Bio-bibliografía de José Carlos Mariátegui* (Lima, 1966) and *La creación heróica de José Carlos Mariátegui: la edad de piedra, 1894–1919* (Lima, 1975). Finally, no study of the period could be complete without consulting the writings of, besides Mariátegui himself, Alejandro Deustua, Manuel González Prada, Javier Priado, Francisco García Calderón, Manuel Vicente Villarán, and Víctor Raúl Haya de la Torre.

18. COLOMBIA, ECUADOR AND VENEZUELA, *c.* 1880–1930

Colombia

For Colombia at the beginning of this period there are two travel accounts of exceptional value: E. Rothlisberger, *El Dorado* (1898; Bogotá, 1963) and A. Hettner, *Viajes por los Andes colombianos, 1882–1884* (1888; Bogotá, 1976). There is much useful material in P. J. Eder, *Colombia* (London, 1913) and in R. Gutiérrez, *Monografías* (2 vols., Bogotá, 1920–1). A. Arguedas's diary, *La danza de las sombras* (new edn, Bogotá, 1983), contains a valuable account of society and politics at the end of the 1920s.

Rafael Núñez's journalism is collected in *La reforma política en Colombia* (7 vols., Bogotá, 1946–50). There are various collections of the writings of Miguel Antonio Caro: *Escritos sobre cuestiones económicas* (Bogotá, 1943); his *Obras completas* (8 vols., Bogotá 1918–45) are being completed by the publication of correspondence, most of it scholarly but some of it political, and further writings and speeches in excellent editions from the Instituto Caro y Cuervo. See particularly E. Lemaitre (ed.), *Epistolario de Rafael Núñez con Miguel Antonio Caro* (Bogotá, 1977), particularly valuable as Núñez successfully willed that his own archive should be thrown into the sea. Other printed contemporary texts include C. Holguín, *Cartas políticas* (Bogotá, 1951); R. Uribe Uribe, *Discursos parlamentarios* (Bogotá, 1897); C. E. Restrepo, *Orientación republicana* (2 vols., Bogotá, 1972); and L. Martínez Delgado (ed.), *Revistas políticas publicadas en El Repertorio Colombiano* (2 vols., Bogotá, 1939).

For the politics of the period, see I. Lievano Aguirre, *Núñez* (2nd edn, Bogotá, 1958); E. Rodríguez Piñeres, *Diez años de política liberal* (Bogotá,

1945); H. Delpar, *Red against blue, the Liberal party in Colombian politics, 1863–1899* (University, Alabama, 1981); L. Martínez Delgado, *República de Colombia, 1885–1910* (2 vols., Bogotá, 1970), which is volume x of the *Historia extensa de Colombia*, in course of publication; E. Lemaitre, *Rafael Reyes* (Bogotá, 1967); C. Bergquist, *Coffee and conflict in Colombia, 1886–1910* (Durham, NC, 1978). There is as yet no coherent account of the years 1910–30, but for a compilation of events see J. Villegas and J. Yunis, *Sucesos Colombianos, 1900–1924* (Medellín, 1976). On the labour movement, see M. Urrutia, *The development of the Colombian labor movement* (New Haven, 1969); I. Torres Giraldo, *Los inconformes* (5 vols., Bogotá, 1973) and *María Cano, mujer rebelde* (Bogotá, 1972); for the 1920s P. J. Navarro, *El parlamento en pijama* (Bogotá, 1935); for the church, J. Restrepo Posada, *La iglesia colombiana en dos momentos difíciles de la historia patria* (Bogotá, 1971). An alternative essay on this period is J. O. Melo, 'La república conservadora', in M. Arrubla (ed.), *Colombia hoy* (Bogotá, 1978).

On the Colombian economy, see L. Ospina Vásquez, *Industria y protección en Colombia, 1810–1930* (Medellín, 1955; frequently reprinted); W. P. McGreavey, *An economic history of Colombia, 1845–1930* (Cambridge, 1971), and the criticisms of that work in *Historia económica de Colombia: un debate en marcha* (Bogotá, 1979), published by the Instituto de Estudios Colombianos; J. A. Ocampo, *Colombia y la economía mundial, 1830–1910* (Bogotá, 1984); M. Palacios, *Coffee in Colombia, 1850–1970. An economic, social and political history* (Cambridge, 1980); and M. Arango, *Café e industria, 1850–1930* (Bogotá, 1977). There are two essays on Colombian agrarian history in K. Duncan and I. Rutledge (eds.), *Land and labour in Latin America* (Cambridge, 1977): Malcolm Deas, 'A Colombian coffee estate: Santa Bárbara, Cundinamarca, 1870–1912' and Michael Taussig, 'The evolution of rural wage labour in the Cauca Valley of Colombia, 1700–1970'. On sugar and the Cauca, see P. J. Eder, *El Fundador, Santiago M. Eder* (Bogotá, 1959). M. Urrutia has edited *Ensayos sobre historia económica colombiana* (Bogotá, 1980) and, with M. Arrubla, *Compendio de estadísticas históricas de Colombia* (Bogotá, 1970). For the 1920s, P. L. Bell, *Colombia: a commercial and industrial handbook* (Washington, DC, 1921); D. Monsalve, *Colombia cafetera* (Barcelona, 1927); A. Patiño Rosselli, *La prosperidad a debe y la gran crisis, 1925–1935* (Bogotá, 1981); J. A. Bejarano, *El régimen agrario – de la economía exportadora a la economía industrial* (Bogotá, 1979); H. López, 'La inflación en Colombia en la década de los veintes', *Cuadernos Colombianos*, 5 (Bogotá, 1975); J. Villegas, *Petróleo, oligarquía e imperio* (3rd edn revised, Bogotá, 1975); on bananas, R. Herrera Soto and R. Romero Castañeda, *La zona bananera del Magdalena* (Bogotá, 1979) and J. White, *Historia de una ignominía: la United Fruit Company en Colombia* (Bogotá, 1978); on Antioquia, R. Brew, *El desarrollo económico de Antioquia desde la independencia hasta 1920* (Bogotá, 1977). A useful compendium for this period as for others is A. Pardo Pardo, *Geografía económica y humana de Colombia* (Bogotá, 1972).

　　Civil wars produced many memoirs and polemics. Among the best and more accessible are M. Briceño, *La Revolución (1876–1877)* (Bogotá, 1947); J. H. Palacio, *La guerra de 85* (Bogotá, 1936); M. Grillo, *Emociones de la guerra*, (Bogotá, n.d. (*c.* 1905)); L. Caballero, *Memorias de la guerra de los mil días* (Bogotá, 1939). An attempt at a model for their analysis is contained in Malcolm Deas, 'Poverty, civil war and politics: Ricardo Gaitán Obeso and his Magdalena River campaign in Colombia, 1885', *Nova Americana*, 2 (Turin, 1978).

　　On Panama, see E. Lemaitre, *Panamá y su separación de Colombia* (Bogotá, 1972), and on later relations with the United States, see S. J. Randall, *The diplomacy of modernization: Colombian–American relations, 1920–1940* (Toronto, 1977).

　　An excellent study of its subject is D. Castrillón Arboleda, *El indio Quintín Lame* (Bogotá, 1973). M. Carrizosa de Umaña and R. J. Herrera de la Torre, *75 años de fotografía, 1865–1940* (Bogotá, 1978) is a rare record of Bogotá and Cundinamarca.

Ecuador

R. E. Norris, *Guía bibliográfica para el estudio de la historia Ecuatoriana* (Austin, 1978) provides a guide for Ecuador; there is no Colombian equivalent. The Republic at the beginning of this period is described in F. Hassaurek, *Four years among Spanish Americans* (London, 1868); J. Kolberg, *Nach Ecuador* (Freiburg, 1876); and C. Wiener, *América pintoresca. Descripción de viajes al nuevo continente* (Barcelona, 1884). Three valuable later accounts are E. Festa, *Nel Darien e nell' Ecuador, Diario di viaggio di un naturalista* (Turin, 1909); R. Enock, *Ecuador* (London, 1914); and M. Sáenz, *Sobre el indio ecuatoriano y su incorporación al medio nacional* (Mexico, 1933).

　　Of the older histories, consult O. E. Reyes, *Breve historia general del Ecuador* (3 vols. in 2, Quito, 1967); J. L. R. [J. Le Gouhir y Rodas S. J.], *Historia de la República del Ecuador* (3 vols., Quito, 1920–38); J. L. Mera,

La dictadura y la restauración en la República del Ecuador (Quito, 1932); M. de Veintemilla, *Páginas del Ecuador* (Lima, 1890).

More recently published works are L. Robalino Dávila's *Orígenes del Ecuador de hoy* (10 vols. to date, Puebla and Quito, 1948–) which is uneven and conservative: vol. IV, *García Moreno*, is far better than vols. VII and VIII, which incompletely cover Eloy Alfaro; A Pareja Diezcanseco, *Historia de la República* (2 vols., Quito, 1974). The best introduction to the nineteenth century is E. Ayala, *Lucha política y origen de los partidos en Ecuador* (Quito, 1978). See also H. Malo and E. Ayala (eds.), *Ecuador 1830–1980*, vol. I, *Política y sociedad* (Quito, 1980); G. Drekonja *et al.*, *Ecuador hoy* (Bogotá, 1978); O. Hurtado, *El poder político en el Ecuador* (Quito, 1977); R. Quintero, *El mito del populismo en el Ecuador* (Quito, 1980).

For Eloy Alfaro see also R. Andrade, *Vida y muerte de Eloy Alfaro* (New York, 1916); A. Pareja Diezcanseco, *La hoguera bárbara* (Mexico, 1944); F. Guarderas, *El viejo de Montecristi* (Quito, 1953); and W. Loor, *Eloy Alfaro* (3 vols., Quito, 1947). Selections of Alfaro's writings have been re-published in *Obras escogidas* (2 vols., Quito, 1959), and, with an introduction by Malcolm Deas, *Narraciones históricas* (Quito, 1983). L. A. Martínez, *A la costa* (Quito, 1904) is a vigorous contemporary novel, and M. J. Calle published (under the pseudonym Enrique de Rastignac) some vivid character sketches in *Hombres de la revuelta* (Guayaquil, 1906). The classic essay on coastal character is J. de la Cuadra, *El montuvio ecuatoriano* (Quito, 1937).

Archbishop F. González Suárez, *Memorias íntimas* (Quito, 1944) and L. Dautzemberg, *El Ilmo Sr. Pedro Schumacher* (Quito, 1968) serve as an introduction to church politics; see also E. Ayala (ed.), *Federico González Suárez y la polémica sobre el estado laico* (Quito, 1980). O. E. Reyes, *Vida de Juan Montalvo* (Quito, 1935) is a useful biography, as is also C. de la Torre Reyes, *La espada sin mancha. Biografía del General Julio Andrade* (Quito, 1962). There is no biography of General Leonidas Plaza.

The economy of Ecuador at the turn of the century is still best examined in *El Ecuador. Guía comercial, agrícola e industrial de la república* (Guayaquil, 1909). On cacao and much else, M. Chiriboga, *Jornaleros y gran propietarios en 135 años de exportación cacaotera (1790–1925)* (Quito, 1980) and L. J. Weinman, 'Ecuador and cacao: Domestic responses to the boom–collapse monoexport cycle' (unpublished PhD thesis, University of California, 1970); on the sierra, R. Baraona's CIDA report, *Tenencia de la tierra y desarrollo socio-económico del sector agrícola. Ecuador*

(Washington, DC, 1965) and M. A. Restrepo E., *El rey de la leña* (Buenos Aires, 1958). See also L. A. Carbo, *Historia monetaria y cambiaria del Ecuador desde la época colonial* (Quito, 1953); L. N. Dillon, *La crisis económico-financiera del Ecuador* (Quito, 1927).

J.-P. Deler, *Genèse de l'espace équatorien. Essai sur le territoire et la formation de l'état national* (Paris, 1981) is a useful modern historical geography. The Banco Central del Ecuador, which like its counterparts the Banco de la República in Colombia and the Banco Central in Venezuela has done much to awaken interest in historical study, has published a volume of historic photographs edited by A. Carrión A., *Imágenes de la vida política del Ecuador* (Quito, 1980).

Venezuela

For Venezuela, J. V. Lombardi, Germán Carrera Damas and Roberta Adams, *Venezuelan history: a comprehensive working bibliography* (Boston, 1977) is an indispensable basic bibliography. J. V. Lombardi is also the author of an excellent short history of the Republic, *Venezuela, the search for order, the dream of progress* (New York, 1982). Another useful short history is Judith Ewell, *Venezuela, a century of change* (London, 1984).

The political history of this period receives attention in M. Picón Salas *et al.*, *Venezuela independiente: evolución política y social, 1810–1960* (Caracas, 1962) and its final years in Ramón J. Velásquez *et al.*, *Venezuela moderna. Medio siglo de historia, 1926–1976* (2nd rev. edn, Caracas, 1979). Up to 1890 the relevant volumes of F. González Guinán, *Historia contemporánea de Venezuela* (15 vols., Caracas, 1909–25) are still valuable. Three particularly valuable documentary collections are Pedro Grases and M. Pérez Vila (eds.), *Documentos que hicieron historia* (Caracas, 1962); N. Suárez Figueroa, *Programas políticos venezolanos de la primera mitad del siglo XX* (2 vols., Caracas, 1977); R. J. Velásquez (ed.), *El pensamiento político del siglo XX. Documentos para su estudio* (17 vols. in 16, Caracas, 1983). See also M. V. Magallanes, *Los partidos políticos en la evolución Venezolana* (Caracas, 1973).

On Guzmán Blanco, see Ramón Díaz Sánchez, *Guzmán: elipse de una ambición del poder* (Caracas, 1950; 5th edn, 2 vols. 1968); R. A. Rondón Márquez, *Guzmán Blanco, 'El autócrata civilizador'* (2 vols., Caracas, 1944); R. R. Castellanos, *Guzmán Blanco íntimo* (Caracas, 1969); J. Nava, 'The illustrious American: the development of nationalism in Venezuela under Antonio Guzmán Blanco', *HAHR*, 45/4 (1965); M. B. Floyd, 'Política y economía en tiempos de Guzmán Blanco. Centralización y

Desarrollo, 1870–1888' in M. Izard *et al.*, *Política y economía en Venezuela, 1810–1976* (Caracas, 1976), a volume which contains a number of useful essays on this period. An interesting monograph is A. Lemmo, *La educación en Venezuela en 1870* (Caracas, 1976). For relations with the church, see M. Watters, *A history of the church in Venezuela, 1810–1930* (Chapel Hill, NC, 1930). Among contemporary works the reader might consult Guzmán's own *Documentos para la historia* (Caracas, 1876) and *En defensa de la causa liberal* (Caracas, 1894); M. Briceño, *Los Ilustres. Páginas para la historia de Venezuela* (Bogotá, 1884; 2nd edn, Caracas, 1953) is an able polemic; the author's analysis of Guzmán's system has not yet been entirely superseded. Another contrasting Colombian view is I. Laverde Amaya, *Un viaje a Venezuela* (Bogotá, 1889). In general the literature of travel for Venezuela in these years is poor. It is listed in M. L. Ganzenmuller de Blay, *Contribución a la bibliografía de viajes y exploraciones de Venezuela* (Caracas, 1964).

There is no recent biography of the most prominent of Guzmán's immediate successors, Joaquín Crespo, though M. Landaeta Rosales, *Biografía del Benemérito General Joaquín Crespo* (Caracas, 1895) may be consulted. The 1890s are best approached through R. J. Velásquez, *La caída del liberalismo amarillo: tiempo y drama de Antonio Paredes* (2nd edn, Caracas, 1973); J. A. de Armas Chitty (ed.), '*El Mocho' Hernández. Papeles de su archivo* (Caracas, 1978). The political-military atmosphere of the 1890s, at least for the Andes, is captured with extraordinary freshness in N. Parada's memoirs, *Vísperas y conscienzos de la revolución de Cipriano Castro* (2nd edn, Caracas, 1973) and for the central regions a naive but valuable memoir is A. Martínez Sánchez, *Nuestras contiendas civiles* (Caracas, 1949). V. Lecuna's *La revolución de Queipa* (Caracas, 1954) is a rare autobiographical piece from the great expert on Bolívar; it is evocative and informative.

Cipriano Castro has attracted more attention. See W. J. Sullivan, 'The rise of despotism in Venezuela. Cipriano Castro 1899–1908' (unpublished PhD thesis, University of New Mexico, 1974); Enrique Bernardo Núñez, *El hombre de la levita gris* (Caracas, 1953); M. Picón Salas, *Los días de Cipriano Castro* (Caracas, 1953); I. Andrade, *Por qué triunfó la Revolución Restauradora* (Caracas, 1955); A. Paredes, *Cómo llegó Cipriano Castro al poder* (1906; 2nd edn, Caracas 1954). Castro himself published *Documentos del General Cipriano Castro* (6 vols., Caracas, 1903–8), and E. Pino Iturrieta has edited *Castro, Epistolario presidencial (1899–1908)* (Caracas, 1974). Another close testimony is E. López Contreras, *El*

Presidente Cipriano Castro (2 vols., Caracas, n.d.) with a prologue by M. A. Burelli Rivas. On the blockade, see M. Rodríguez Campos, *Venezuela 1902, la crisis fiscal y el bloqueo* (Caracas, 1977); D. Irwin (ed.), *Documentos británicos relacionados con el bloqueo de las costas Venezolanas* (Caracas, 1982); M. Hood, *Gunboat diplomacy 1895–1905. Great Power pressure in Venezuela* (London, 1975); H. H. Herwig and J. L. Helguera, *Alemania y el bloqueo internacional de Venezuela, 1902–3* (Caracas, 1977). C. Zumeta, *Las potencias y la intervención en Hispanoamérica* (Caracas, 1963) is a sophisticated contemporary Venezuelan comment. The compilation (by W. J. Sullivan) *Cipriano Castro en la caricatura mundial* (Caracas, 1980) is no mere curiosity: it tells more than several conventional monographs. So too do the works of Pío Gil (Pedro María Morantes) which treat the Castro era: *El Cabito* (Caracas, 1951), *Cuatro años de mi cartera* (Caracas, 1975), and the little collection of the ephemera of adulation that he presents in *Los felicitadores* (Caracas, 1952).

The bibliography of the Gómez era is large and uneven in quality. The defence is argued by his minister of the interior, Pedro Manuel Arcaya, in *The Gómez régime in Venezuela and its background* (Baltimore, 1936) and in *Memorias del Doctor Pedro Manuel Arcaya* (Caracas, 1963); this last work has also much that is illuminating on the late nineteenth century. See also Eleazar López Contreras, *Proceso político social, 1928–1936* (Caracas, 1955). For denunciations of Gómez, see José Rafael Pocaterra, *Memorias de un Venezolano de la decadencia* (Caracas, 1937; frequent re-editions); Gustavo Machado and Salvador de la Plaza, *La verdadera situación de Venezuela* (Mexico, 1929); Diego Córdoba, *Los desterrados y Juan Vicente Gómez* (Caracas, 1968). The era is best studied in the documents published in the *Boletín del Archivo Histórico de Miraflores* (Caracas, 1959–), a mine of information on recent history such as no other Latin American country has made available to historians. No recent work on Gómez or on his government as a whole has established itself as definitive. Domingo Alberto Rangel, *Los Andinos en el poder. Balance de una hegemonía, 1899–1945* (Caracas, 1965) has many stimulating intuitions about Castro and Gómez, and has been influential. Rangel's *Gómez, el amo del poder* (Caracas, 1975) adds little new. R. J. Velásquez, *Confidencias imaginarias de Juan Vicente Gómez* (Caracas, 1979) gathers many insights in the form of a fictional monologue. See also L. Cordero Velásquez, *Gómez y las fuerzas vivas* (Caracas, 1971); E. Pacheco, *De Castro a López Contreras* (Caracas 1984). Thomas Rourke (Daniel J. Clinton), *Tyrant of the Andes, the life of Juan Vicente Gómez* (New York, 1937) and J. Lavin, *A halo for Gómez*

(New York, 1954) are still worth consulting. M. Briceño-Iragorry, *Los Riberas* (Caracas, 1957) is a novel about the era, less fanciful than some of the history written under this dictator's strangely potent and lasting spell – analysed in Germán Carrera Damas, *Tres temas de historia* (2nd edn. Caracas, 1978) and *Jornadas de historia crítica* (Caracas, 1983). On the army, Angel Ziemes, *El gomecismo y la formación del ejército nacional* (Caracas, 1979) is original and well-documented. On ideology, see E. Piño Iturrieta, *Positivismo y Gomecismo* (Caracas, 1978). The works of L. Vallenilla Lanz, the most lucid ideologue of the era, are being republished. The first volume of his *Obras completas* (Caracas, 1983) is a welcome re-edition of *Cesarismo democrático* edited by F. Brito Figueroa and N. Harwich Vallenilla.

The economic history of this period has only been studied in patches. There is no satisfactory work on the history of Venezuelan coffee, although A. Ardao, *El café y las ciudades en los Andes venezolanos* (Caracas, 1984) is useful. For Táchira, see A. G. Muñoz, 'The Táchira frontier, 1881–99: regional isolation and national integration in the Venezuelan Andes' (unpublished PhD thesis, Stanford University, 1977). Agriculture in general has received scant attention in this period. Historians seem to have been content to repeat the assertions of S. de la Plaza, *El problema de la tierra* (Mexico, 1938). L. C. Rodríguez, *Gómez, agricultura, petróleo y dependencia* (Caracas, 1983) is largely a study of government policy as reflected in official documents. Much more has been written on petroleum. E. Lieuwen, *Petroleum in Venezuela. A history* (Berkeley, 1954) should be followed by B. S. McBeth, *Juan Vicente Gómez and the oil companies in Venezuela, 1908–35* (Cambridge, 1983), which analyses the dictator's dealings in great detail. Though both authors touch on the impact of petroleum on the rest of the economy, that theme awaits fuller treatment. The general economic evolution of these years may be studied in M. Izard *et al.*, *Política y economía en Venezuela, 1810–1976* (Caracas, 1976); M. Izard, *Series estadísticas para la historia de Venezuela* (Mérida, 1970); R. Veloz, *Economía y finanzas de Venezuela desde 1830 hasta 1944* (Caracas, 1945). M. Landaeta Rosales, *Gran recopilación geográfica, estadística e histórica de Venezuela* (2 vols., Caracas, 1889; 2nd edn, Caracas, 1964) contains a bewildering variety of information on Venezuela at and before that date. For public works, see E. Arcila Farias, *Centenario del Ministerio de Obras Públicas. Influencia de este Ministerio en el desarrollo, 1874–1974* (Caracas, 1974). The world of the German commercial houses and of the Boulton enterprises in the first decades of the century is described in

O. Gerstl's modest and informative *Memorias e historias* (Caracas, 1974). Relations with Great Britain are treated in G. Carl, *First among equals: Great Britain and Venezuela, 1810–1910* (Syracuse, 1980).

19. THE BRAZILIAN ECONOMY, 1870–1930

The historiography of this period may be approached through Nícia Vilela Luz, 'Brazil', in Roberto Cortés Conde and Stanley Stein (eds.), *Latin America: a guide to economic history, 1830–1930* (Berkeley, 1977), which contains several hundred annotated entries of primary and secondary sources, as well as a valuable interpretive article. Important collections of recent scholarship include Colloque Internationale sur l'Histoire Quantitative du Brésil, *L'Histoire quantitative du Brésil de 1800 à 1930* (Paris, 1971); Flávio Rabelo Versiani and J. R. M. de Barros (eds.), *Formação econômica do Brasil; a experiência da industrialização* (São Paulo, 1978); Paulo Neuhaus (ed.), *Economia brasileira: uma visão histórica* (Rio de Janeiro, 1980); Carlos Manuel Pelaez and Mircea Buescu (eds.), *A moderna história econômica* (Rio de Janeiro, 1976); and Werner Baer, *et al.*, *Dimensões do desenvolvimento brasileiro* (Rio de Janeiro, 1978). Among general studies of the Brazilian economy in historical perspective the following deserve mention: Werner Baer, *The Brazilian economy, its growth and development* (Columbus, Ohio, 1979); Mircea Buescu, *História econômica do Brasil, pesquisa e análise* (Rio de Janeiro, 1970); and Carlos Manuel Pelaez, *História econômica do Brasil* (São Paulo, 1979).

The study of Brazilian economic history owes much to three central figures, whose works have been much debated and who represent significant tendencies in policy debates. Roberto Simonsen was an industrialist and political figure whose many essays were designed to show the feasibility of industrialization. Some of these have been collected in *Evolução industrial do Brasil e outros ensaios* (São Paulo, 1973). Caio Prado Júnior, a Marxist historian, wrote mainly on the colonial period, but his *História econômica do Brasil* (São Paulo, 1949) and *História e desenvolvimento* (São Paulo, 1972) deserve mention. Celso Furtado sought specifically to defend a structuralist position in his *A economia brasileira* (Rio de Janeiro, 1954) and in his influential *Formação econômica do Brasil* (Rio de Janeiro, 1959); Eng. trans. *The economic growth of Brazil* (Berkeley, 1963). Two other early studies of importance are J. F. Normano, *Brazil, a study of economic types* (New York, 1935; 1968) and Roy Nash, *The conquest of Brazil* (New York, 1926; 1968).

Until quite recently the economic historiography of Brazil has been institutional, in fact more sociological than economic. Nevertheless a number of monographs which deal in part with economic processes deserve mention. On the plantation system, see Stanley J. Stein, *Vassouras: a Brazilian coffee county* (Cambridge, Mass., 1957); Peter Eisenberg, *The sugar industry in Pernambuco, 1840–1910* (Berkeley, 1974): Jaime Reis, 'From *bangüe* to *usina*', in K. Duncan and I. Rutledge (eds.), *Land and labour in Latin America* (Cambridge, 1977); J. H. Galloway, 'The sugar industry of Pernambuco during the nineteenth century', *Annals of the Association of American Geographers* (1968); Thomas Holloway, *Immigrants on the land: coffee and society in São Paulo, 1886–1934* (Chapel Hill, NC, 1980); Warren Dean, *Rio Claro: a Brazilian plantation system* (Stanford, 1976); and the various essays in II Congresso de História de São Paulo, *O café* (São Paulo, 1975). Richard Graham assesses the impact of Britain on Brazilian development in *Britain and the onset of modernization in Brazil* (Cambridge, 1968). Two excellent regional studies are Pierre Monbeig, *Pionniers et planteurs de São Paulo* (Paris, 1952) and Jean Roche, *A colonização alemã e o Rio Grande do Sul* (2 vols., Porto Alegre, 1969). The regional studies by Joseph Love on Rio Grande do Sul and São Paulo, John Wirth on Minas Gerais and Robert Levine on Pernambuco (see *CHLA* v, bibliographical essay 21) though primarily political, contain useful information on regional economies. Important recent studies of the Amazon region are Roberto Santos, *História econômica da Amazônia 1800–1920* (São Paulo, 1980) and Barbara Weinstein, *The Amazon rubber boom, 1850–1920* (Stanford, 1983).

Economic policy in this period has been much studied. A general institutional approach is Edgard Carone, *A república velha* (São Paulo, 1970). Steven Topik demonstrates government interventionism in 'The evolution of the economic role of the Brazilian state, 1889–1930', *JLAS*, 11/2 (1979), and 'State interventionism in a liberal regime, 1889–1930', *HAHR*, 60/4 (1980). Aníbal Vilanova Villela and Wilson Suzigan, *Política do governo e crescimento da economia brasileira, 1889–1945* (Rio de Janeiro, 1973), Eng. trans. *Government policy and economic growth of Brazil 1889–1945* (Rio de Janeiro, 1977) is an important study that emphasizes the distortions introduced by coffee valorization. Nícia Vilela Luz, *A luta pela industrialização no Brasil* (São Paulo, 1961) analyses pro-developmental debates. See also the collected works of two major figures, Leopoldo Bulhões, *Discursos parlementares* (Brasília, 1979), and Serzedelo Correia, *A problema econômica do Brasil* (Brasília, 1980). Two useful regional studies are Gabriel Bittencourt, *Esforço industrial na república do café: o caso do Espírito Santo, 1889–1930* (Vitória, 1982); and Janice Teodoro da Silva, *Raízes da ideologia do planejamento: Nordeste, 1889–1930* (São Paulo, 1978). Thomas Holloway, *The Brazilian coffee valorization of 1906* (Madison, 1975), and Carlos Manuel Pelaez's essay in *Ensaios sobre café e desenvolvimento econômico* (Rio, 1973), deal with the coffee support scheme. On cartels, see Joan Bak, 'Cartels, cooperatives and corporativism: Getúlio Vargas in Rio Grande do Sul on the eve of Brazil's 1930 revolution', *HAHR*, 63/2 (1983). Government policy in agriculture and railways is discussed by Eulália Lahmeyer Lobo in *História político-administrativa da agricultura brasileira, 1808–1889* (Rio de Janeiro, 1980). An analysis of the impact of tariffs can be found in Maria Teresa R. O. Versiani, 'Proteção tarifária e crescimento industrial nos anos 1906–12: o caso de cerveja', *Pesquisa e Planejamento Econômico*, 12/2 (Rio de Janeiro, 1982). Eulália Lahmeyer Lobo, *História do Rio de Janeiro, do capital comercial ao capital industrial e financeiro* (2 vols., Rio de Janeiro, 1978) is a major study of the economic aspects of urbanization, with important price and wage data. Regional diversity is treated in Antonio Barros de Castro, *Sete ensaios sobre a economia brasileira* (2 vols., Rio de Janeiro, 1971), David Denslow, 'As orígens da desigualdade regional no Brasil', *Estudos Económicos* (1973), and Nathaniel Leff, *Underdevelopment and development in Brazil* (2 vols., London, 1982).

Macroeconomic studies began with O. Dias Carneiro, 'Past trends in the economic evolution of Brazil, 1920–1965' (mimeo, Cambridge, Mass., 1966). Important estimates of national product are to be found in C. Contador and C. Haddad, 'Produto real, moeda e preços: a experiência brasileira no período 1861–1970', *Revista Brasileira de Estatística* (1975), Claudio Haddad, 'Crescimento do produto real brasileiro, 1900/1947', *Revista Brasileira de Economia*, 29 (1975) and, most recently, Leff, *Underdevelopment and development*, which incorporates material from his various essays on this subject: 'Long term Brazilian economic development', *Journal of Economic History* 29/3 (1969); 'Economic retardation in nineteenth century Brazil', *Economic History Review*, 2nd ser., 25 (1972); 'Tropical trade and development in the nineteenth century: the Brazilian experience', *Journal of Political Economy*, 81 (1973). On terms of trade, see R. Gonçalves and A. Coelho, 'Tendências dos termos-de-troca: a tese de Prebisch e a economia brasileira, 1850–1979', *Pesquisa e Planejamento Econômico*, 12/2 (1982). On inflation, see Oscar Onody, *A inflação brasileira, 1820–1958* (Rio de Janeiro, 1960), a pioneering study; Mircea

Buescu, *300 anos de inflação* (Rio de Janeiro, 1973); and Paulo Neuhaus, 'A inflação brasileira em perspectiva histórica', *Revista Brasileira de Economia* 32 (1978). On monetary policy, J. Pandiá Calógeras, *A política monetária do Brasil* (São Paulo, 1960) has been superseded by Paulo Neuhaus, *História monetária do Brasil* (Rio de Janeiro, 1975) and Carlos Manuel Pelaez and Wilson Suzigan, *História monetária do Brasil* (Rio de Janeiro, 1976); the latter is based on monetarist theory.

The profitability of slavery in its final stage is studied in Leff, *Underdevelopment and development*, H. O. Protocarrero, 'Viabilidade económica de escravidão no Brasil, 1880–1888', *Revista Brasileira de Economia*, 27/1 (1973), and Jaime Reis, 'Abolition and the economics of slavery in northeastern Brazil', *Boletín de Estudios Latinoamericanos y del Caribe*, 17 (1974). See also Robert Slenes, 'The demography and economics of Brazilian slavery: 1850–1888' (unpublished PhD thesis, Stanford University, 1975); Pedro Carvalho de Melo, 'Estimativa de longevidade de escravos no Brasil', *Estudos Económicos* (1983) and Kit Taylor, 'The economics of sugar and slavery in northeastern Brazil', *Agricultural History*, 44/3 (1970). A. Martins Filho and R. B. Martins, 'Slavery in a non-export economy: nineteenth-century Minas Gerais revisited', *HAHR* 63/3 (1983) is an interesting recent contribution.

Another aspect of labour supply that has been much analysed is immigration and internal migration. The essential study is T. W. Merrick and D. Graham, *Population and economic development in Brazil, 1808 to the present* (Baltimore, 1979). See also IV Simpósio Nacional dos Professores Universitários de História, *Anais: colonização e migração* (São Paulo, 1969) and Chiara Vangelista, 'Immigrazione, struttura produttiva e mercato de lavoro in Argentina e in Brasile', *Annali della Fundazione Luigi Einaudi* (1975). In addition to his *Immigrants on the land*, Thomas Holloway has contributed essays on this subject in D. Alden and W. Dean (eds.), *Essays in the socioeconomic history of Brazil and Portuguese India* (Gainesville, 1979) and Duncan and Rutledge (eds.), *Land and labour*. See also his 'Condições de mercado de trabalho e organização de trabalho nas plantações na economia cafeeira de São Paulo, 1885–1915', *Estudos Económicos* (1972). Also important is Michael Hall, 'The origins of mass immigration in Brazil 1871–1914' (unpublished PhD thesis, Columbia University, 1969).

On foreign investment during this period, see Leff, *Underdevelopment and development*; Graham, *Britain and the onset of modernization*; Ana Célia Castro, *As empresas estrangeiras no Brasil, 1860–1913* (Rio de Janeiro, 1979); Victor Valla, *A penetração norte-americana na economia brasileira* (Rio de

Janeiro, 1978), and David Joslin, *A century of banking in Latin America* (London, 1963). See also B. R. Magalhães, 'Investimentos ingleses no Brasil e o Banco Londrino e Brasileiro', *Revista Brasileiro de Estudos Políticos*, 49 (1979) and R. Fendt, 'Investimentos ingleses no Brasil, 1870–1913, uma avaliação da política brasileira', *Revista Brasileira de Economia*, 31 (1977). R. Greenhill, 'The Brazilian coffee trade' in D. C. M. Platt (ed.), *Business imperialism 1840–1930* (Oxford, 1978), contests the thesis of neo-imperialism. Emily Rosenberg, 'Anglo-American economic rivalry in Brazil during World War I', *Diplomatic History*, 2 (1978), provides insight into the rise of American influence. Richard Graham, 'A British industry in Brazil: Rio Flour Mills, 1886–1920', *Business History*, 17/1 (1966) examines the largest British manufacturing investment and demonstrates the difficulties of control of overseas firms before the first world war.

The central problem in recent historiography has been that of the development effect of export orientation. Antonio Delfim Netto has argued that the market, up to 1906, permitted Brazil to gain from the trade in coffee: see *O problema do café no Brasil* (São Paulo, 1958). Thereafter, coffee profits were artificially maintained, and the issue has arisen whether the coffee trade or cyclical crises in the trade stimulated further development. Warren Dean, *The industrialization of São Paulo, 1880–1945* (Austin, Texas, 1969); W. Baer and A. Villela, 'Industrial growth and industrialization: revisions in the stages of Brazil's economic development', *Journal of Developing Areas*, 7/1 (1973); and C. M. Pelaez, *História da industrialização brasileira* (Rio de Janeiro, 1972) view export orientation as favouring industrialization, while a contrary view is expressed by Sérgio Silva, *Expansão cafeeira e orígens da indústria no Brasil* (São Paulo, 1976); José de Souza Martins, 'O café e a gênese da industrialização em São Paulo', *Contexto*, 3 (1977); and Wilson Cano, *Raizes da concentração industrial em São Paulo* (São Paulo, 1977). Albert Fishlow's valuable synthesis 'Origins and consequences of import substitution in Brazil' can be found in L. di Marco (ed.), *International economics and development* (New York, 1971). On industrialization, see also Wilson Suzigan, 'Industrialization and economic policy in historical perspective', *Brazilian Economic Studies*, 2 (1976), and F. R. Versiani, 'Industrial investment in an export economy; the Brazilian experience before 1914', *University of London, ILAS Working Papers* 2 (1979), and 'Before the depression: Brazilian industry in the 1920s', in Rosemary Thorp (ed.), *Latin America in the 1930s* (London, 1984).

Other notable studies of industrialization include Armen Mamagonian, 'Notas sobre o processo de industrialização no Brasil', *Boletim do Departamento de Geografía do FFCL de Presidente Prudente*, 2 (1969); Edgard Carone (ed.), *O pensamento industrial no Brasil, 1880–1945* (São Paulo, 1977), a documentary collection, and a historiographical study by E. Salvadori de Decca, 'O tema da industrialização: política e história', *Tudo é História: Cadernos de Pesquisa*, 2 (1978). An important sectoral study is Stanley J. Stein, *The Brazilian cotton manufacture* (Cambridge, Mass., 1957). Alisson Mascarenhas Vaz, 'A indústria textil em Minas Gerais', *Revista de História*, 56/3 (1977) and W. Dean, 'A fábrica São Luiz de Itú: um estudo de arqueologia industrial', *Anais de História*, 8 (1976) concentrate on single firms.

Another recent concern in Brazilian historiography is that of tracing the origin of capital applied in the export sector. Alcir Lenharo, *As tropas da moderação* (São Paulo, 1979) shows the transfer from internal trade into coffee in the early stages of the coffee cycle. Urban food supply is dealt with in Maria Yedda Leite Linhares, *História do abastecimento, uma problemática em questão, 1530–1918* (Brasília, 1979) and M. Y. Leite Linhares and F. C. Teixeira da Silva, *História política do abastecimento* (Brasília, 1979).

20. BRAZIL: THE AGE OF REFORM, 1870–1889

Rubens Borba de Moraes and William Berrien, *Manual de estudos brasileiros* (Rio de Janeiro, 1949), although outdated, is still the most important bibliographical guide. Specifically about the Empire but now also somewhat outdated are Stanley Stein, 'The historiography of Brazil, 1808–1889', *HAHR*, 40/2 (1960), 234–78; George Boehrer, 'Brazilian historical bibliography: some lacunae and suggestions', *Inter-American Review of Bibliography*, 11/2 (1961), 137–49, and 'The Brazilian Republican Revolution, old and new views', *Luso-Brazilian Review*, 3/2 (1966), 43–57. A more recent analysis of the historiography of the last two decades of the Empire is Emília Viotti da Costa, 'Sobre as orígens da República' in *Da monarquia à república: momentos decisivos* (São Paulo, 1977), 243–90.

A variety of interesting data can be found in the travellers' accounts published in the nineteenth century. Particularly informative and containing many useful tables is Santa-Anna Nery, *Le Brésil en 1889* (Paris, 1889). Also relevant for the study of the last decade of the Empire is Louis Couty, *Le Brésil en 1884* (Rio de Janeiro, 1884); C. F. Van Delden

Laerne, *Le Brésil et Java. Rapport sur la culture du café en Amérique, Asie, et Afrique (avec chartes, planches et diagrammes)* (The Hague, 1885); Max Leclerc, *Cartas do Brasil* (São Paulo, 1942) and Alfred Marc, *Le Brésil, excursion à travers de ses 20 provinces* (Paris, 1890).

The years between 1870 and 1889 have been seen as years of crisis for the monarchical institutions. The first versions of the fall of the Empire were written either by monarchists or by republicans. The monarchists overestimated the role of the military in the 1889 coup while the republicans stressed the failure of monarchical institutions and the success of the republican campaign. Written from a republican perspective is José Maria Bello, *História da República, 1889–1954* (4th edn, São Paulo, 1959), Eng. trans. by James L. Taylor, *A history of modern Brazil 1889–1954* (Stanford, 1966); from a monarchist perspective, J. F. Oliveira Vianna, *O ocaso do Império* (São Paulo, 1925) and Heitor Lyra, *História da queda do Império* (2 vols., São Paulo, 1964). During the 1940s and 1950s Marxist historians offered a new interpretation: see, for example, Caio Prado Jr, *Evolução política do Brasil* (São Paulo, 1933) and Nelson Werneck Sodré, *Formação histórica do Brasil* (Rio de Janeiro, 1944). Practically ignored has been the psychoanalytical study of the fall of the Empire by Luís Martins, *O patriarca e o bacharel* (São Paulo, 1953), which relied on Gilberto Freyre's generational model described in *The mansions and the shanties*, trans. by Harriet do Onis (New York, 1963). In the 1960s and 1970s academic historiography made important contributions to the revision of traditional interpretations. The best synthesis of this period appears in a collective work published under the direction of Sérgio Buarque de Holanda, *História geral da civilização brasileira, II: O Brasil monárquico* (5 vols., São Paulo, 1962–72), especially vol. IV, *Declínio e queda do império* and vol. V, *Do império à república*. Although the quality of the essays is uneven and the connections between economic, social, political and ideological changes is often left to the reader, this is the most complete synthesis available. Well informed but somewhat chaotic is João Camillo de Oliveira Torres, *A democracia coroada* (Rio de Janeiro, 1957), a book written from a conservative perspective. For a liberal perspective see Raymondo Faoro, *Os donos do poder, Formação do patronato político brasileiro* (2 vols., São Paulo, 1975). Richard Graham, *Britain and the onset of modernization in Brazil (1850–1914)* (Cambridge, 1968) describes several important changes occurring in Brazilian politics and society during this period and is the best synthesis available in English.

For a long time the history of Brazil was seen as the history of masters and slaves. Historians neglected the population of small farmers, tenants and sharecroppers that constituted the great majority of the population in the nineteenth century. More recently these groups have been the subject of several studies. Some of the most important problems confronting the free population were discussed in Maria Sylvia Carvalho Franco, *Homens livres na ordem escravocrata* (São Paulo, 1969). Particularly interesting is G. I Joffley, 'O quebraquilos, a revolta dos matutos contra os doutores', *Revista de História*, 34 (1978), 69–145. See also Roderick Barman, 'The Brazilian peasantry reexamined. The implications of the Quebra-Quilos revolt (1874–1875)', *HAHR*, 57/3 (1977), 401–25. Armando Souto Maior, *Quebra-Quilos. Lutas sociais no outono do Império* (São Paulo, 1978) considers the *quebra-quilos* as an expression of class tensions and social dislocations in the Brazilian north-east caused by the impact of capitalist development in the backlands. Analogous is Janaina Amado's conclusion in her study on the muckers: *Conflito social no Brasil. A revolta dos Muckers. Rio Grande do Sul (1868–1878)* (São Paulo, 1978). On social banditry, see *CHLA* v, bibliographical essay 21.

Labour history is relatively new in Brazil. For a long time the study of the workers was in the hands of political militants or sociologists more interested in the twentieth-century labour movement. As a consequence the emerging working class of the nineteenth century has received little attention. Edgard Carone, *Movimento operário no Brasil (1877–1944)* (São Paulo, 1979) is a collection of documents. We are still waiting for studies on workers' conditions of living, forms of organization and their participation in the political system. The same lacunae can be found in the study of urban demonstrations and urban riots that multiplied towards the end of the nineteenth century. Sandra Lauderdale Graham, 'The vintem riot and political culture. Rio de Janeiro, 1880', *HAHR* 60/ 2 (1980), 431–50 shows the many possibilities that the study of these urban crowds offer. Another group waiting for a historian are the *capoeiras* – free blacks and mulattos, and perhaps some slaves, who threatened the Rio de Janeiro urban population and who seem to have played an important role in the political life of the last years of the Empire, particularly in the abolitionist campaign. Women also have not received much attention. In a pioneering article, June Hahner has identified several organizations created by middle- and upper-class women in the last decades of the Empire: 'Feminism, women's rights and the suffrage movement in Brazil', *LARR*, 16/1 (1980), 41–64.

The best study of urbanization is Paul Singer, *Desenvolvimento económico e evolução urbana* (São Paulo, 1968). See also Richard Morse, 'Cities and societies in nineteenth century Latin America. The illustrative case of Brazil' in R. Schaedel, J. Hardoy and N. S. Kinzer (eds.), *Urbanization in the Americas from its beginnings to the present* (The Hague, 1978). For a different perspective, see Emília Viotti da Costa, 'Urbanização no Brasil no século XIX' in *Da monarquia à república*, 179–208. On immigration, see *CHLA* v, bibliographical essay 21.

A detailed description of the political institutions can be found in Oliveira Torres, *A democracia coroada*; Buarque de Holanda, *História geral da civilização brasileira, II: O Brasil Monárquico*, iv and v; Faoro, *Os donos do poder*; and Nestor Duarte, *A ordem privada e a organização política nacional* (São Paulo, 1938). Many institutions have been the object of specific studies. The Senate is described in Beatriz Westin Cerqueira Leite, *O Senado nos anos finais do Império, 1870–1889* (Brasília, 1978) which supersedes A. E. Taunay, *O senado do Império* (São Paulo, 1941). For the Chamber, A. E. Taunay, *A Câmara dos Deputados* (São Paulo, 1950) remains valuable. The Council of State is examined in Fernando Machado, *O Conselho de Estado e sua história no Brasil* (São Paulo, 1972).

The best study on political parties and political elites is José Murilo de Carvalho, 'Elite and state building in imperial Brazil' (unpublished PhD thesis, Stanford University, 1974). The first part, revised and expanded, has been published in *A construção da ordem. A elite política imperial* (Rio de Janeiro, 1980). See also his 'A composição social dos partidos políticos Imperiais', *Cadernos do Departmento de Ciencias Políticas da Faculdade de Filosofia e Ciências Humanas da Universidade Federal de Minas Gerais*, 2 (1974), 1–34, and 'Political elites and state building: the case of nineteenth century Brazil', *Comparative Studies in Society and History*, 24/3 (1982). Carvalho revises many traditional notions that have prevailed in the literature. For the study of the imperial elites, see also Olavo Brasil de Lima Jr, and Lucia Maria de Klein, 'Atores políticos do Império', *Dados*, 7 (1970), 62–88, and Ron L. Seckinger and Eul-Soo Pang, 'The mandarins of imperial Brazil', *Comparative Studies in Society and History*, 9/2 (1972). For a study of the political party system from a juridical point Afonso Arinos de Melo Franco, *História e teoria do partido político no direito constitucional Brasileiro* (Rio de Janeiro, 1948) remains valuable.

Although there are no monographic studies of the two main parties there are several studies of the Republican party. Goerge Boehrer, *Da monarquia à república. História do Partido Republicano no Brasil, 1870–1889* (Rio de Janeiro, 1954), is the main source for the study of the party at the national level. For the study of the party in São Paulo, see Emília da Costa Nogueira, 'O movimento republicano em Itu. Os fazendeiros do oeste paulista e os prodromos do movimento republicano', *Revista de História*, 20 (1954), 379–405, and José Maria dos Santos, *Bernardino de Campos e o partido republicano paulista, subsídios para a História da República* (Rio de Janeiro, 1960). The ambiguous position of the Paulista Republican party toward abolition was described by José Maria dos Santos, *Os republicanos paulistas e a abolição* (São Paulo, 1942). Nícia Vilela Luz, 'O papel das classes médias brasileiras no movimento republicano', *Revista de História* 28/57 (1964), 213–28, calls attention to the important role played by the sons of traditional elites who had lost status. Two studies have examined political participation during the last decades of the Empire: Joseph Love, 'Political participation in Brazil, 1881–1969', *Luso-Brazilian Review*, 7/2 (1970), 3–24, and Maria Antonieta de A. G. Parahyba, 'Abertura social e participação política no Brasil, 1870–1920', *Dados* 7 (1970), 89–102.

Much more needs to be investigated before we can begin to understand the sociology of electoral behaviour during the Empire. Meanwhile several studies have been published about the system of patronage. The most complete study is stil Faoro, *Os donos do poder*. It can be supplemented by Simon Schwartzman, 'Regional cleavages and political patriarchalism in Brazil' (unpublished PhD thesis, University of California, Berkeley, 1973). A colourful description of the system of clientele and patronage is found in Maria Isaura Pereira de Queiroz, *O mandonismo local na vida política brasileira* (São Paulo, 1969), reprinted from the original essay published in *Anhembi*, 24–6 (São Paulo, 1956–7). Administration at the local level in one province is examined in Francisco Iglésias, *Política económica do governo provincial Mineiro, 1835–1889* (Rio de Janeiro, 1958).

More research on the formal and informal connections between businessmen and politicians needs to be done. The articles published by Eugene W. Ridings point in the right direction. Particularly interesting are 'Elite conflicts and cooperation in the Brazilian Empire. The case of Bahian businessmen and planters', *Luso-Brazilian Review*, 12/1 (1975), 80–99; 'The merchant elite and the development of Brazil during the Empire', *Journal of Inter-American Studies and World Affairs*, 15 (1973); 'Class sector unity in an export economy. The case of nineteenth century Brazil', *HAHR* 58/3 (1978), 432–50; 'Internal groups and development. The case of Brazil in the nineteenth century', *JLAS*, 9/2 (1977), 225–50.

And we still have much to learn about the political role of economic groups, family links and the importance of patronage in determining party affiliation and party performance. A reading of the biographies of important political figures provides interesting information. Particularly useful are Joaquim Nabuco, *Um estadista do Império: Nabuco de Araújo, sua vida, suas opiniões e sua época* (3 vols, São Paulo, 1936); Luis Viana Filho, *A vida de Rui Barbosa* (São Paulo, 1965); Hermes Vieira, *Ouro Preto, o homem e a época* (São Paulo, 1948); Wanderley Pinho, *Cotegipe e seu tempo* (São Paulo, 1937); Craveiro Costa, *O visconde de Sinimbú, sua vida e sua atuação na política nacional 1840–1889* (São Paulo, 1937); Luis Viana Filho, *A vida de Joaquim Nabuco* (São Paulo, 1944); José Antônio Soares de Souza, *A vida do Visconde de Uruguai, 1807–1866* (São Paulo, 1944); Luis Viana Filho, *A vida do Barão do Rio Branco* (Rio de Janeiro, 1959). The best biography of Pedro II is Heitor Lyra, *História do Imperador Pedro II* (3 vols., São Paulo, 1938–40). In English, see Mary Wilhelmine Williams, *Dom Pedro the Magnanimous* (Chapel Hill, NC, 1937).

A few politicians of the Empire published their memoirs. Particularly interesting are Afonso Celso, *Oito anos de parlamento* (São Paulo, n.d.); Alfredo d'Escragnolle Taunay, *Memórias* (Rio de Janeiro, 1960), *Homens e coisas do império* (São Paulo, 1924), and *Cartas políticas* (Rio de Janeiro, 1889); Albino José Barbosa de Oliveira, *Memórias de um magistrado do império* (São Paulo, 1943); Júlio Belo, *Memórias de um Cavalcanti. Trechos de um livro de assentos de Felix Cavalcanti de Albuquerque e Melo (1821–1901)* (São Paulo, 1940); Visconde de Mauá, *Autobiografia (Exposição aos credores e ao público seguida de o meio circulante no Brasil)* (Rio de Janeiro, 1942). Equally interesting is the correspondence exchanged between political or intellectual figures. Particularly relevant for this period are Raymundo de Menezes (ed.), *Cartas e diário de José de Alencar* (São Paulo, 1967); José Honóro Rodrigues (ed.), *Correspondência de Capistrano de Abreu* (3 vols., Rio de Janeiro, 1954–6); *Correspondência de Machado e Joaquim Nabuco* (São Paulo, 1933); Raymundo de Magalhães (ed.), *D. Pedro II e a Condessa do Barral* (Rio de Janeiro, 1956); José Wanderley de Araújo Pinho (ed.), *Cartas do Imperador D. Pedro II ao Barão de Cotegipe* (São Paulo, 1933); *Correspondência entre D. Pedro II e o Barão do Rio Branco (1889–1891)* (São Paulo, 1957). These last two publications constitute important sources for the study of the emperor's view of the Brazilian system. Even more relevant in this respect is D. Pedro II, *Conselhos à Regente*, introduction and notes by J. C. de Oliveira Torres (Rio de Janeiro, 1958).

The abolition of slavery has attracted the attention of many scholars.

The most complete bibliography available is Robert Conrad, *Brazilian slavery: an annotated research bibliography* (Boston, 1977). Conrad is also the author of the most complete study available in English, *The destruction of Brazilian slavery 1850–1889* (Berkeley, 1971). For a different approach, see Robert Toplin, *The abolition of slavery in Brazil* (New York, 1972) and Richard Graham, 'Causes of the abolition of Negro slavery in Brazil. An interpretive essay', *HAHR*, 46/2 (1966), 123–37. For a more comprehensive study of the process of transition from slavery to free labour including its economic, social, political and ideological aspects, see Emília Viotti da Costa, *Da senzala à colônia* (São Paulo, 1966; 2nd edn, 1982). On the profitability of slavery in its final stage, see *CHLA* v, bibliographical essay 19. In spite of the many studies on abolition we still lack information about the grass roots of abolitionism. Evaristo de Morais, *A campanha abolicionista (1879–1888)* (Rio de Janeiro, 1924) is still useful in this respect. Recently the *caifazes*, an abolitionist organization operating in São Paulo, was examined by Alice Barros Fontes, 'A prática abolicionista em São Paulo. Os caifazes, 1882–1888' (unpublished MA thesis, University of São Paulo, 1976). Paula Beiguelman, *Teoria e ação no pensamento abolicionista* (São Paulo, 1962) called attention to the importance of political mechanisms in the abolition of slavery. Richard Graham in 'Landowners and the overthrow of the Brazilian monarchy', *Luso-Brazilian Review*, 7/2 (1970), 44–56 analyses the impact of abolitionism and abolition on planters. See also Eul-Soo Pang, 'Modernization and slavocracy in nineteenth century Brazil', *Journal of Interdisciplinary History*, 4/4 (1979).

Relations between church and state are examined in George Boehrer, 'The church in the second reign, 1840–1889', in Henry Keith and S. F. Edwards (eds.), *Conflict and continuity in Brazilian society* (Columbia, SC, 1963), 113–40; George Boehrer, 'The church and the overthrow of the Brazilian monarch', *HAHR*, 48/3 (1968), 380–401; and Mary C. Thornton, *The church and freemasonry in Brazil, 1872–75* (Washington, DC, 1948). See also, David Queirós Vieira, 'Protestantism and the religious question in Brazil 1855–1875' (unpublished PhD thesis, American University, Washington DC, 1972); António Carlos Villaca, *A história da questão religiosa no Brasil* (Rio de Janeiro, 1974); Nilo Pereira, *Conflicto entre Igreja e Estado* (Recife, 1976); and António Carlos Villaca, *O pensamento católico no Brasil* (Rio de Janeiro, 1975). For an understanding of the elite's behaviour during the conflict, there is interesting information in Joaquim Nabuco, *Um estadista do Império*.

There are four important essays on the role of the Brazilian military

in the proclamation of the Republic: John Schulz, 'O exército e o
império' in Buarque de Holanda (ed.), *Historia geral da civilização
brasileira*, IV, 235–49; W. S. Dudley, 'Institutional sources of officer
discontent in the Brazilian army, 1870–1889', *HAHR*, 55/1 (1975), 44–
65, and 'Professionalisation and politicisation as motivational factors in
the Brazilian army coup of 15 November 1889', *JLAS*, 8/1 (1976), 101–
25; and June Hahner, 'The Brazilian armed forces and the overthrow of
the monarchy. Another perspective', *The Americas*, 26/2 (1969), 171–82.
For a more theoretical analysis see Frederick Nunn, 'Military professional-
ism and professional militarism in Brazil, 1870–1970. Historical perspectives and political implications', *JLAS*, 4/6 (1972), 29–54. A more
detailed study of the army during the Empire is John Schulz, 'The
Brazilian army in politics 1850–1894' (unpublished PhD thesis,
Princeton, 1973). Nelson Werneck Sodré, *História militar do Brasil* (Rio
de Janeiro, 1968) is also informative. Some biographical studies focusing
on important figures in the army add interesting details: for example,
Raymundo de Magalhães, *Deodoro e a espada contra o império* (Rio de
Janeiro, 1957), a biography of the general who led the coup in November
1889. There is a biographical study of Deodoro in English: Charles Willis
Simmons, *Marshal Deodoro and the fall of Dom Pedro II* (Durham, NC,
1966). The intriguing personality of Benjamin Constant and his role as a
republican and as a positivist is examined by Raymundo Teixeira
Mendes, *Benjamin Constant* (2nd edn, Rio de Janeiro, 1913). The hostility
with which some loyal monarchists evaluated the military and its role in the
overthrow of the Empire is well documented in Visconde de Ouro Preto,
Advento da ditadura militar no Brasil (Paris, 1891) and Eduardo Prado,
Fastos da ditadura militar no Brasil (São Paulo, 1902). This unsympathetic
view was kept alive in the works of historians like Oliveira Vianna, who
did not hide their identification with the monarchy and monarchical
institutions. For an opposite point of view one should consult A.
Ximeno de Villeroy, *Benjamin Constant e a política republicana* (Rio de
Janeiro, 1928). And for a more balanced discussion, see Emília Viotti da
Costa, 'A proclamação da república', in *Da monarquia à república*.

Antônio Cândido de Melo e Souza, *Formação da literatura brasileira*
(2nd edn, 2 vols., São Paulo, 1964) has in an appendix a short biography
of the most important writers of this period. Also useful is José Aderaldo
Castello, *Presença da literatura brasileira. História e antologia* (3 vols., São
Paulo, 1964). For an overview of the history of ideas the best source is
João Cruz Costa, *História das ideias no Brasil* (Rio de Janeiro, 1956), Eng.

trans. by Suzette Macedo, *A history of ideas in Brazil* (Berkeley, 1964). Several books have been published about positivism in Brazil. Most of them associate the middle classes and positivism. Typical is Robert Nachman, 'Positivism, modernization and the Brazilian middle-class', *HAHR*, 57/1 (1977), 1–23. The most reliable source published in Portuguese is Ivan Lins, *História do positivismo no Brasil* (São Paulo, 1964). See also João Camillo de Oliveira Torres, *O positivismo no Brasil* (Petrópolis, 1952). For a critical examination of liberalism, see Maria Stella Martins Bresciani, 'Liberalismo, ideologia e controle social' (2 vols., unpublished PhD thesis, University of São Paulo, 1976).

The problem of cultural dependency and the contradictions generated by the import of European ideas, first discussed by Nelson Werneck Sodré in *Ideologia do colonialismo. Seus reflexos no pensamento brasileiro* (Rio de Janeiro, 1961), became the subject of an important controversy with the publication of Roberto Schwarz's essay 'As ideias fora do lugar' in *Estudos Cebrap*, 3 (1973), 151–61, later reproduced and expanded in his study of Machado de Assis *Ao vencedor as batatas* (São Paulo, 1977). Applying to the study of ideas the 'dependency theory' model, Schwarz noticed a contradiction between the ideology of patronage characteristic of Brazilian society and European liberalism. This contradiction was denied in Maria Sylvia Carvalho Franco, 'As ideias estão no lugar', *Debates* (1976).

Brazilian racial ideology is examined in Thomas Skidmore, *Black into white. Race and nationality in Brazilian thought* (New York, 1974) which includes an extensive bibliography about different aspects of Brazilian society during the Empire and First Republic. For a different interpretation, see Emília Viotti da Costa, 'O mito da democracia racial', in *Da monarquia à república*.

Few studies have been published about cultural institutions. For an overview see Fernando de Azevedo, *Brazilian culture, an introduction to the study of culture in Brazil*, trans. William Rex Crawford (New York, 1950). More specific is Robert Havighurst and Roberto Moreira, *Society and education in Brazil* (Pittsburgh, 1965). The São Paulo law school which was the incubator of most of the professional politicians of the Empire was the subject of two important books: Almeida Nogueira, *A Academia de São Paulo. Tradições e reminiscências* (9 vols., São Paulo, 1906–9) and Spencer Vampre, *Memórias para a história da Academia de São Paulo* (2 vols., São Paulo, 1924). Maria de Lourdes Marioto Haidar examines the secondary school system in her book *O ensino secundário no império brasileiro*

(São Paulo, 1972). Valuable information about the debate over the creation of the university in the nineteenth century can be found in Roque Spencer Maciel de Barros, *A ilustração brasileira e a ideia de universidade* (São Paulo, 1959).

21. BRAZIL: THE SOCIAL AND POLITICAL STRUCTURE OF THE
FIRST REPUBLIC, 1889–1930

The bibliography of Brazilian society and politics during the period from 1889 to 1930 is examined in Thomas E. Skidmore, 'The historiography of Brazil, 1889–1964', *HAHR*, 55/4 (1975), 716–48, and 56/1 (1976), 81–109. An analysis of the modern trends in Brazilian historiography, in which there are references to works written on the period from 1889 to 1930, can be found in José Roberto do Amaral Lapa, *A história em questão* (Petrópolis, 1976).

A general history of the period is Boris Fausto (ed.), *História geral da civilização brasileira, III: Brasil republicano*, vols. I and II (São Paulo, 1977). See also three valuable books by Edgard Carone: *A República Velha: instituições e classes sociais* (São Paulo, 1970), *A República Velha: evolução política* (São Paulo, 1971) and a collection of documents, *A Primeira República, 1889–1930: texto e contexto* (São Paulo, 1969). Among older studies, worthy of particular note are José Maria Bello, *História da República, 1889–1954* (4th edn, São Paulo, 1959), Eng. trans. by James L. Taylor, *A history of modern Brazil, 1889–1954* (Stanford, 1966); and Leôncio Basbaum, *História sincera da República* (4 vols., São Paulo, 1962–68).

Few scholars have attempted a global analysis of the system and the political process of the period. Most noteworthy is Maria do Carmo Campello de Souza, 'O processo político-partidário na Primeira República', in Carlos Guilherme Mota (ed.), *Brasil em perspectiva* (São Paulo, 1968), 181–252. See also Joseph L. Love, 'Political participation in Brazil, 1881–1969', *Luso-Brazilian Review*, 7/2 (1970), 3–24; and Maria Antonieta de A. G. Parahyba, 'Abertura social e participação política no Brasil, 1870–1920', *Dados*, 7 (1970), 89–102. The most important studies on the individual states and their role in national politics are Joseph L. Love, *Rio Grande do Sul and Brazilian regionalism, 1882–1930* (Stanford, 1971) and *São Paulo in the Brazilian Federation, 1889–1937* (Stanford, 1980); John D. Wirth, *Minas Gerais in the Brazilian Federation, 1889–1937* (Stanford, 1977); Robert M. Levine, *Pernambuco in the Brazilian Feder-*

ation, 1889–1937 (Stanford, 1978); and Eul-Soo Pang, *Bahia in the First Brazilian Republic: coronelismo* and *oligarchies, 1889–1934* (Gainesville, 1979). On Minas Gerais, see also Paul Cammack, 'The political economy of the "politics of the states"': Minas Gerais and the Brazilian Federation, 1889–1900', *Bulletin of Latin American Research* 2/1 (1982), 51–65.

June Edith Hahner, *Civilian-military relations in Brazil 1889–1898* (Columbia, SC, 1969) is one of the best studies on the years which followed the proclamation of the Republic up until the time when the oligarchic system was firmly established. An analysis of political changes through government expenditure can be found in Richard Graham, 'Government expenditure and political change in Brazil, 1880–1899: who got what', *Journal of Inter-American Studies and World Affairs*, 19/3 (1977), 339–67. See also Eduardo Kugelmas, 'A Primeira República no período de 1891 a 1909', in Paula Beiguelman (ed.), *Pequenos estudos de ciência política* (2nd edn, São Paulo, 1973). An important biography is Afonso Arinos de Melo Franco, *Rodrigues Alves: apogeu e declínio do presidencialismo* (2 vols., Rio de Janeiro, 1973). Very little has been written on the years following the presidential succession crisis of 1909 or on the political effects of the first world war, apart from texts of an apologetic or superficial type. On the other hand, the crisis of the 1920s and the Revolution of 1930 have been the subject of more serious consideration. A general study on the 1920s is Paulo Sérgio Pinheiro, *Política e trabalho no Brasil* (Rio de Janeiro, 1975). There are several works on the *tenentista* movement. A starting point is Virgínio Santa Rosa, *O sentido do tenentismo* (Rio de Janeiro, 1933). A general analysis can be found in John D. Wirth, 'Tenentismo in the Brazilian Revolution of 1930', *HAHR*, 44/2 (1964), 229–42. With regard to episodes in the *tenentista* movement, see Hélio Silva, *1922: sangue na areia de Copacabana* (Rio de Janeiro, 1964) and *A grande marcha* (Rio de Janeiro, 1965); and Neill Macaulay, *The Prestes column: revolution in Brazil* (New York, 1974). A collection of documents has been published by Edgard Carone, *O tenentismo: acontecimentos – personagens – programas* (São Paulo, 1975). One of the most important contemporary studies on the Revolution of 1930 is Alexandre Barbosa Lima Sobrinho, *A verdade sobre a Revolução de Outubro* (São Paulo, 1933). A historiographical analysis can be found in Boris Fausto, *A Revolução de 1930: Historiografia e história.* See also Celina do Amaral Peixoto Moreira Franco *et al.*, 'O contexto político da Revolução de Trinta', *Dados*, 7 (1970), 118–36; and Boris Fausto, 'A Revolução de 1930', in *Brasil em perspectiva*, 253–84.

Although a great deal has been written on the *tenentista* movement, specific studies on the armed forces are few. Worthy of note is José Murilo de Carvalho, 'As forças armadas na Primeira República: o poder desestabilizador', in Boris Fausto (ed.), *História geral da civilização Brasileira, III: O Brasil republicano*, II, 183–234. In addition to Hahner, *Civilian-military relations*, a valuable analysis which takes in the first years of the Republic is John Schulz, 'The Brazilian army in politics, 1850–1894' (unpublished PhD thesis, Princeton University, 1973). Enlightening data on the socialization process of the military can be found in Nelson Werneck Sodré, *História militar do Brasil* (Rio de Janeiro, 1965). Compulsory military service is the theme of the work by Frank D. McCann, 'The nation in arms: obligatory military service during the Old Republic', in Dauril Alden and Warren Dean (eds.), *Essays concerning the socioeconomic history of Brazil and Portuguese India* (Gainesville, 1977), 211–43. There are one or two useful volumes of memoirs and biographies of military figures. Among these are the books by Estévão Leitão de Carvalho, *Dever militar e política partidária* (São Paulo, 1959) and *Memórias de um soldado legalista* (3 vols., Rio de Janeiro, 1961–); Pantaleão Pessoa, *Reminiscências e imposições de uma vida, 1885–1965* (Rio de Janeiro, 1972); Tristão de Alencar Araripe, *Tasso Fragoso: um pouco da história de nosso exército* (Rio de Janeiro, 1960). Almost nothing has been written on the state militias. One of the few works of quality is Heloísa Fernandes, *Política e segurança. Força Pública do estado de São Paulo; fundamentos histórico-sociais* (São Paulo, 1974).

The classic study on clientalistic relations within the power structure is Victor Nunes Leal, *Coronelismo, enxada e voto: o município e o regime representativo no Brasil* (Rio de Janeiro, 1948), Eng. trans. by June Henfrey, *Coronelismo: the municipality and representative government in Brazil* (Cambridge, 1977). An important analysis of clientalism in the north and north-east of Brazil, particularly in the state of Ceará, can be found in Ralph Della Cava's study on Padre Cícero, *Miracle at Joazeiro* (New York, 1970). With regard to the state of Bahia, see Eul-Soo Pang, *Bahia in the First Brazilian Republic*. The links between kinship, family organization and client relations in a north-eastern state are explored in Linda Lewin, 'Politics and "parentela" in Paraiba: a case study of oligarchy in Brazil's Old Republic, 1889–1930' (unpublished PhD thesis, Columbia University, 1975). See also Maria Isaura Pereira de Queiroz, *O mandonismo local na vida política brasileira* (São Paulo, 1969).

On plantation society and on immigration see *CHLA* v, bibliographical essay 19. Among the social movements in rural areas, the Canudos episode is dealt with in Euclides da Cunha's classic account, *Os sertões* (Rio de Janeiro, 1902), Eng. trans. by Samuel Putnam, *Rebellion in the backlands* (Chicago, 1944). The so-called War of the Contestado is the subject of Maurício Vinhas de Queiroz, *Messianismo e conflito social: a guerra sertaneja do Contestado, 1912–1916* (Rio de Janeiro, 1966) and Duglas Teixeira Monteiro, *Os errantes do Novo Século: um estudo sobre o surto milenarista do Contestado* (São Paulo, 1974). The relationship between messianic movements and national politics has been studied by Ralph Della Cava, 'Brazilian messianism and national institutions: a reappraisal of Canudos and Joaseiro', *HAHR*, 48/3 (1968), 402–20. On the pheno-menon of banditry in Brazil, see Maria Isaura Pereira da Queiroz, *Os cangaceiros* (São Paulo, 1979), Linda Lewin, 'The oligarchical limitations of social banditry in Brazil: the case of the "good" thief Antônio Silvino', *Past and Present*, 82 (1979); Amaury de Souza, 'The cangaço and the politics of violence in northeast Brazil', in Ronald H. Chilcote (ed.), *Protest and resistance in Angola and Brazil: comparative studies* (Berkeley, 1972), 109–31, and Billy Jaynes Chandler, *The bandit king: Lampião of Brazil* (College Station, Texas, 1978).

There are few historical studies devoted to urbanization in this period. The most wide-ranging study is Paul Singer, *Desenvolvimento econômico e evolução urbana; análise da evolução econômica de São Paulo, Blumenau, Porto Alegre e Recife* (São Paulo, 1968). On the city of São Paulo, see Richard M. Morse, *From community to metropolis: a biography of São Paulo, Brazil* (New York, 1974). For the history of Rio de Janeiro, see Eulália Maria Lahmeyer Lobo, *História do Rio de Janeiro. Do capital comercial ao capital industrial e financeiro* (2 vols., Rio de Janeiro, 1978). Michael L. Conniff, 'Rio de Janeiro during the great depression, 1928–1937: social reform and the emergence of populism in Brazil' (unpublished PhD thesis, Stanford University, 1976), although referring more to the post-1930 period, nevertheless contains a good analysis of the politics of the oligarchy of the city during the 1920s.

Studies on the urban social movements have been mainly limited to the working class. Notable exceptions are Décio Saes, *Classe média e política na Primeira República brasileira* (Petrópolis, 1975) and June E. Hahner, 'Jacobinos versus Galegos', *Journal of Inter-American Studies and World Affairs*, 18/2 (1976), 125–54, which deals with the nationalist and multi-class movement in Rio de Janeiro at the end of the nineteenth century. Among studies on the working-class movement and organiza-tion from a predominantly sociological point of view, the most outstanding are Azis Simão, *Sindicato e estado: suas relações na formação do proletariado de São Paulo* (São Paulo, 1966); José Albertino Rodrigues, *Sindicato e desenvolvimento no Brasil* (São Paulo, 1968); Leôncio Martins Rodrigues, *Conflito industrial e sindicalismo no Brasil* (São Paulo, 1966). From the point of view of social history, see Sheldon L. Maram, *Anarquistas, imigrantes e o movimento operário brasileiro, 1890–1920* (Rio de Janeiro, 1979) and Boris Fausto, *Trabalho urbano e conflito social* (São Paulo, 1976). Michael M. Hall, 'Immigration and the early São Paulo working class', *JGSWGL*, 12 (1975) provides a convincing criticism of the theory that the foreign immigrant in São Paulo was predisposed to radical ideology. A detailed description of the anarchist and communist organizations can be found in John W. F. Dulles, *Anarchists and communists in Brazil, 1900–1935* (Austin, Texas, 1973). On the formation of the Brazilian Communist party, see Ronald H. Chilcote, *The Brazilian Communist party: conflict and integration, 1922–1972* (New York, 1974) and Astrogildo Pereira, *Formação do PCB, 1922–1928. Notas e documentos* (Rio de Janeiro, 1962). Documents on the labour movement during the period have been published in Paulo Sérgio Pinheiro and Michael M. Hall, *A classe operária no Brasil, 1889–1930: Documentos*, vol. I, *O movimento operário* (São Paulo, 1979), vol. II, *Condições de vida e de trabalho, relações com os empresários e o estado* (São Paulo, 1981); and in Edgard Carone, *Movimento operário no Brasil, 1877–1944* (São Paulo, 1979).

On relations between blacks and whites in Brazil, see Florestan Fernandes, *A integração do negro à sociedade de classes* (Rio de Janeiro, 1964), translated and abridged under the title *The negro in Brazilian society* (New York, 1969), and Thomas E. Skidmore, *Black into white: race and nationality in Brazilian thought* (New York, 1974). A bibliography on women, including a general history of women, family organization and the feminist movement, was published by the Carlos Chagas Foundation in São Paulo: *Mulher brasileira. Bibliografia anotada* (São Paulo, 1979). See, in addition, June E. Hahner, 'Women and work in Brazil, 1850–1920: a preliminary investigation', in Alden and Dean (eds.), *Essays concerning the socioeconomic history of Brazil and Portuguese India*, 87–117, and 'Feminism, women's rights and the suffrage movement in Brazil, 1850–1932', *LARR*, 15/1 (1980), 65–111; Branca Moreira Alves, *Ideologia e feminismo: a luta da mulher pelo voto no Brasil* (Petrópolis, 1980). For the history of the Catholic church, the most important work is Margaret Patrice Todaro, 'Pastors, prophets and politicians: a study of the Brazilian Catholic church, 1916–1945' (unpublished PhD thesis, Columbia University,

1971). See also Ralph Della Cava, 'Catholicism and society in twentieth-century Brazil', *LARR*, 11/2 (1976), 7–50. The best studies on the role of the intellectuals and education are respectively Sérgio Miceli, *Intelectuais e classe dirigente no Brasil, 1920–1945* (São Paulo, 1979) and Jorge Nagle, *Educação e sociedade na Primeira República* (São Paulo, 1974). An important recent work on the cultural life of Rio de Janeiro during the Old Republic is Nicolau Sevcenko, *Literatura como missão. Tensões sociais e criação cultural na Primeira República* (Rio de Janeiro, 1983). On Brazilian art and architecture, music and literature in this period, see also *CHLA* IV, bibliographical essay 11. Finally, a pioneer work on the violence of the state against the popular classes is Paulo Sérgio Pinheiro, 'Violencia do estado e classes populares', *Dados*, 22 (1979), 5–24.

INDEX